Treasures of the
Confederate Coast:
The "Real Rhett Butler"
& Other Revelations
by
E. Lee Spence
Doctor of Marine Histories

Narwhal Press Inc.
Miami/Charleston

Library of Congress Catalog Card Number: 94-69595

ISBN hardcover: 1-886391-00-9
ISBN paperback: 1-886391-01-7

Classifications suggested by the publisher: American Civil War; archeology, underwater; blockade runners; cruisers, Confederate; diving; Georgia history; *Georgiana* (Confederate Cruiser); *Gone With The Wind*; *H.L. Hunley*, submarine; maritime history; North Carolina history; Rhett Butler (the real); salvage; shipping; shipwrecks; smuggling; South Carolina history; Spence, Edward Lee; Spence's List; submarines, Confederate; submarine *H.L. Hunley*; treasure trove; Trenholm, George Alfred; underwater archeology; wrecks

Front cover cover illustration: Portrait of "The Real Rhett Butler" (George Alfred Trenholm) as he would have appeared in his late thirties, as painted by Judson Arcé de Lignières.
Back cover photos: Diver with skull, courtesy of the Warship *Vasa* Museum, with insert of Dr. E. Lee Spence by Merrily de Lignières.
Title page illustration: Sinking of the Stone Fleet, *Harper's Weekly*, 1/11/1862.

Illustrated & Indexed
Reference Edition

Published by Narwhal Press Inc.
1629 Meeting Street, Charleston, South Carolina, 29405

This book is respectfully dedicated to

Robert R. Nielsen, Sr., and family

Without their assistance, friendship and encouragement,
I would never have taken the time to finish this book.

It is also dedicated to our Lord, who has given me the
ability and opportunity to put all of this together.

Treasures of the Confederate Coast

The U.S. monitor Weehawken was sunk off Morris Island, South Carolina, on December 6, 1863. Contemporary accounts tell of her "terror stricken crew" and the "vain shrieks" of the "men in irons" that went down with her. Engraving from "Frank Leslie's Illustrated Newspaper" of January 2, 1864.

TABLE OF CONTENTS

(Note: This book contains over one hundred photos, maps, and other illustrations. Most are located immediately before or after the above listed sections. Three groups of pictures start with each of the following pages: 181, 259, and 332.)

Treasures of the Confederate Coast

Without the vision and support of the Hack family of Hilton Head Island, South Carolina, these artifacts would never have been recovered. The artifacts are from the Georgiana, which was wrecked in 1863 while attempting to run into Charleston. This photo is by Jo Pinkard, a treasured friend who recorded much of my early work.

AUTHORITIES & ACKNOWLEDGMENTS

I would like to acknowledge and thank the late Howard I. Chapelle, the late William E. Geoghegan, and Mendel L. Peterson, all formerly of the Smithsonian Institution, for their early encouragement of my research on shipwrecks.

The National Endowment for the Humanities, the South Carolina Committee for the Humanities, the Savannah Ships of the Sea Museum, the College of Charleston, and the Nielsen Electronics Institute, all have my appreciation for their financial support.

Persons at the National Archives who provided invaluable help have included Kenneth R. Hall, Larry MacDonald, Teresa F. Matchette, Mike Meier, Rick Peuser, Constance Potter, Bill Sherman, and John K. VanDereedt.

Edwin Bearss, George Fisher, the late Ron Gibbs, and the late Harold Peterson, all then with the United States National Park Service, also helped spur me onward.

The late Harold Edgerton of M.I.T., and the late Edwin Link of Harbor Branch Foundation, the late George Bond of Sea Lab, each loaned me equipment for my searches, and each offered extensive encouragement and fatherly advice.

Archeologists, George Bass, Robert F. Marx, Duncan Mathewson, Ivor Noel-Hüme, Stan South, the late Peter Throckmorton, and Gordon Watts, all helped in developing my appreciation of shipwrecks as an archeological resource.

Historians/archeologists Elizabeth Andrews, Ed Beacham, the late Elias Bull, Priestly Coker, Mal Collet, the late Tom Dickey, Bob Gibson, Harlan Green, Steve Hoffius, Bob Holcombe, Carter Leary, Pat Mellen, Wayne Neighbors, Percy Petit, Paul Reitzer, Wayne Strickland, Jack Thomson, and Mark Wilde-Ramsing each assisted me, and their help continues to be appreciated.

James Dawson and R.C.E. Lander of Lloyd's of London, and D.J. Lyon of the National Maritime Museum in London opened many of their records to me.

Admiral Chris Andreasen, Meg Danley, Chuck Ellis, George Mastrogianis, Mark Friese, Steve Verry, at NOAA, have all aided me in my cartographic searches.

The long roll of divers who have helped me in various ways includes Bill Alge, Jim Batey, John Berg, Clifton Doyle, John Coleman, Jerry Crosby, Bob Densler, Ted Dhooge, Mark Dougherty, Erin Efird, Mel Fisher, Ray Forker, Joe Froelich, the late Mike Freeman, Skipper Keith, Val Gruno, Vic Heyward, Steve Howard, Randy Lathrop, Del Long, Ray Lunsford, Jim Maranville, Pat McCarthy, Mick McCoy, Charles Moore, Hugh Myrick, Bill

Neville, Charles Peery, E. Phillips, the late Ron Renau, Tom & Sally Robinson, Rick Rogers, Kevin Rooney, Drew Ruddy, Hampton Shuping, Steve Swavely, Dan Thomson, Dave Topper, Gene West, Ralph Wilbanks, "Wet Willie", and Jack Williamson.

Books prepared by Anne Edwards, Bruce Berman, Leslie Bright, the late Forrest R. Holdcamper, Dave Horner, Bob Marx, Margaret Mitchell, E.A. Mueller, Ethel Nepveux, Regina Rapier, Don Shomette, William N. Still Jr., the late Frederick Way, and Stephen Wise have been of immense use to me in my work, and some have been referenced frequently in this book.

Special thanks to the Atlantic Marine Insurance Companies of New York who allowed me access to their marine disaster files.

Thanks also go to individuals like Joe Bolchoz, Stan Fulton, the late Beverly Grizzard, Norwood Marlow, the late Hank O'Neal, Bud Parker, Jo Pinkard, Stan Nielsen, Tom O'Rourke, Ned Sloan, Rev. James Storm, Whit Tharin, Buddy Truett, and Roland Young, who have encouraged and/or supported my work in various ways.

Robert R. Nielsen Sr.(and his sons Robert and David) acted as sounding boards in developing many of my theories and provided me with office space and secretarial services.

I have been helped by numerous commercial fisherman, including Walter O'Neal, Jr. and Sr., the entire Magwood family, Joe Porcelli (who also dives), and Wally Shaffer.

I would like to especially thank the family of the late Fred Hack of Hilton Head Island, South Carolina, and the family of the late Mills B. Lane of Savannah, Georgia, for the financial assistance they gave me in some of my early research and explorations. My own family has also been supportive in ways too numerous to list.

The following corporations have assisted me on my various underwater archeological projects: Allis Chalmers; Barringer Research; Bendix; Fisher Research; Gulf Oil; Ingersoll Rand; J.W. Fisher; Klein Associates; McKee Craft; Mercury Motors; Orca Industries; Rolex Watch Co.; Seagram's Classic Wines; Trimble Navigation; White's Electronics; and Zodiac.

Collectively, the help provided by these people, has ranged from moral and financial support to tending my air hoses. Unfortunately, there is no practical way that I can list all of those who deserve recognition and thanks.

Many of the distinguished people listed above have doctorates and other degrees, for simplicity and the fact that I don't know everyone's correct titles, I have not shown degrees. I hope they will understand. For those people who I have inadvertently left out, I still extend my best wishes and thanks.

E. Lee Spence

Authorities & Acknowledgments

The "Real Rhett Butler" & Other Revelations

The Confederate gunboat Nashville at dock in Southampton, England. She was later owned by George A. Trenholm, "the real Rhett Butler," who renamed her the Thomas L. Wragg, and used her as a blockade runner. Resold and reoutfitted as the privateer Rattlesnake, she was destroyed by the U.S. monitor Montauk, on February 2, 1863, in the Ogeechee River, near Fort McAllister, Georgia. Engraving from "Harper's Weekly" of February 15, 1862.

Treasures of the Confederate Coast

This picture of the wrecked blockade runner Celt was taken in 1865. The rocks are part of "Bowman's jetty" which was built in the 1850's to reduce erosion near Fort Moultrie on Sullivan's Island, South Carolina. The wreck of the Stono (ex-U.S.S. Isaac Smith) can be seen to the right of the Celt's paddle wheels. The late Ron Gibbs and I used this photo to locate both wrecks in 1965. Photo courtesy of the U.S. National Archives.

This picture was taken during a low tide in 1965, the remains of the Celt can still be seen, barely protruding from the water and looking much like the nearby rocks. An arrow points out some of the wreckage. Several other Civil War era shipwrecks are located nearby. Photo by L. Spence.

INTRODUCTION

To me the story of the destruction of the Old South is like an extremely romantic but very sad movie, something to be loved and wept over. And cry, I have.

Imagine how you would feel pouring over tens of thousands of pages of government dispatches, tear stained letters, tattered diaries, and contemporary newspapers describing the hopes, successes, loves, suffering, death and destruction experienced by your ancestors. It is impossible not to be emotional. Part of the emotion I feel is based on my family heritage.

Both my parents are from very old Southern families (each with branches going back over fifteen generations), and both had numerous relatives who fought for their homes and beliefs in both the American Revolution and the Civil War. Like their friends and neighbors, my ancestors supported the Confederate Cause and family members fought in virtually every great battle of the Civil War. They served as both officers and enlisted men in the Confederate Army and Navy, and many were wounded, captured, killed in battle, or died of disease while prisoners of war.

My great-great-grandfather, Joseph Speed Jones, was an educated man who loved his native North Carolina and served as a colonel in the local militia and as a captain in the Confederate Army. He fought in thirty-two major battles, including Seven Days Battle, Malvern Hill, Antietam, Fredricksburg, Chancellorsville, Gettysburg, The Wilderness, Spotsylvania Courthouse, Cold Harbor, and Petersburg. He finally surrendered with his cousin, General Robert E. Lee, at Appomattox Courthouse.

His son-in-law, Joseph Temple Spence (who was my great-grandfather) left teaching to serve as a lieutenant. His official request for shoes for his men was eloquent in its simplicity. The justification he gave for the requested shoes plainly stated "my men need them." He was wounded and captured during the horrendous fighting (dramatized in the movie *Glory*) that took place on Morris Island at the entrance to Charleston Harbor. Exchanged for a Federal officer, he immediately returned to duty, but was recaptured and sat out the remainder of the war in a filthy, rat infested, Federal prison where disease claimed thousands of his imprisoned comrades. In bad health from confinement and with virtually no food and no money, he walked the hundreds of miles home to find that Sherman's army had, without any purpose other than revenge and the terrorization of defenseless old men, women and children, burned the Spence family plantation and his ancestral home.

The following year (1866), my grandfather, John Paul Spence, was born in the ruins of the Old South, and grew up during

Reconstruction to become Superintendent of the North Carolina public school system. Like many of his fellow Southerners, he felt Reconstruction did more to destroy the South than the actual war. After his death, Dr. Spence was eulogized as one of the most educated men of his times.

My father, Judson Cauthen Spence, M.A., Ph.D. (Lt. Colonel, United States Regular Army; Colonel, South Carolina Unorganized Militia; and recipient of both the Vietnamese parachutist badge with battle cluster and the Vietnamese "Soldier's Medal of Honor") was born in 1921 and grew up to loyally serve his country as a soldier and as an educator. Now fully retired, he served as a department head and as dean of men for what is now Charleston Southern University. At the time of his retirement, he was a full professor at the Citadel, which was also his undergraduate Alma Mater.

Branches of my father's extended family include Spence, Cauthen, Cheek, Courtney, Bowers, Vandiver, McCoy, Huggins, Bright, Chapelle, Temple, Smith, Speed, Jones, and Lee. His cousin Ernest Vandiver was governor of Georgia when I was a teenager. And his cousin Floyd Spence is currently a United States senator from South Carolina. A more distant cousin Gerry Spence has been called the most successful lawyer in the United States.

During World War II, my father married a beautiful young Southern belle named Mary Virginia Truett. One of her ancestors had put in the first oil well in America. One great-uncle was the famous Southern evangelist George W. Truett. Some of the many branches of her family tree are Truett, Truitt, Coker, Darnell, Drake, Roberts, Riley, Hale, Allen, Melton, Bledsoe, and Marion. Her relative, Francis Marion, had been nicknamed "The Swamp Fox" during the American Revolution. Francis Marion's personal physician, who fought alongside of him in Charleston and Savannah, was Dr. Peter Spence. So even that early both families' fortunes were closely entwined.

My parents live on Sullivan's Island, in a stately home on "Officers Row." Built in the 1890's, the immense house is surrounded with wide verandahs on both the first and second floors. Their yard has the typical Southern charm with magnolias, live oaks, pecans, roses, azaleas, camellias, pomegranates, pears, and grapes.

I was named Edward Lee in honor of several family members, including my great-aunt, Mattie Lee Cauthen McCranie, and my distant relative, General Robert Edward Lee. General Lee's daughter, Anne Carter Lee, died while she and her mother, Mary

Custis Lee, were refugees and were living at the beautiful white columned home of my great-great-great-great-grandfather, William D. Jones. She was just twenty-three and was buried in our family cemetery. Although nearby, General Lee was unable to leave his command to attend her funeral and did not visit her grave until after the war. The Lee's plantation, Arlington, became our country's national cemetery.

My son's name is Matthew Lee Spence. At fourteen he is already tall and handsome. He was named Matthew for his mother's distinguished relative Matthew Fontaine Maury, and Lee for the same reasons I was. Prior to the Civil War, Maury had gained international fame for his brilliance and his mapping weather patterns and ocean currents, and was known as the "Pathfinder of the Seas." But Maury was born a Virginian and, like his more famous cousin Robert E. Lee, he joined the Confederacy. My son is extremely bright, well mannered, sincere and kind, and I believe, like his namesakes Commodore Maury and General Lee, he is destined for great things.

At the time of my birth in 1947, there were still living veterans from both the Union and Confederate armies. The long term effects of the Civil War on the South, especially poverty, a depressed economy, and a nearly ruined educational system, were clearly evident. The rusting remains of wrecked blockade runners still protruded from the shallow waters off public beaches. Cannon balls, musket balls, and uniform buttons of both armies could be picked up from freshly plowed fields that had once been soaked with blood. Some of it, the blood of my ancestors.

As I grew up, I slowly learned about my family and our Southern heritage. My family had lived in the South for almost three hundred years. They settled first in Virginia, then slowly spread out through the Carolinas and Georgia. Many had their homes and livelihoods destroyed during the Civil War, and when the fighting ended many chose to start life over far from the horrors they had suffered. Today, I have "cousins" spread out all over the United States.

I have gone into great detail about my family, not to brag, but to help explain why the historical heritage of the South matters to me, and more importantly why it matters to all true Southerners who lost family and property, in that absolutely terrible war. It explains why we love the song *Dixie*, and why we still stand and respectfully salute the Confederate battle flag.

I came to understand, love, and respect the South. About the time of my childhood, a New South seemed to suddenly spring to life from the economic ruins of the Old South. It was wonderful.

As a child, I talked with people who had actually lived through both the Civil War and Reconstruction. I read the notes and letters pressed in bibles, belonging not just to my family but to those of my friends and acquaintances. One letter joked about "mosquitoes as big as turkey buzzards." Other letters asked about loved family members and spoke of planned marriages.

In the early days of the Civil War, letters, news accounts, and official dispatches described glorious victories, and heroic deeds. They spoke of an expected quick end to the "War." But, as the Civil War drug on, they increasingly mentioned rotted and maggot infested food, starvation, worn out shoes, lice, sickness, insufficient medicines, crushing defeats, amputations performed without anesthesia, death, capture, and imprisonment.

One official dispatch described northern Virginia as reduced to a "dessert wasteland." It went on to say that there wasn't enough food in all of Virginia, the Carolinas, and northern Georgia to feed even 10,000 men. Yet there were hundreds of thousands of soldiers who needed to be clothed and fed.

Even in the capital of the South, rats were being sold as food to a starving populace. The price of bread soared, clothes couldn't be replaced. Many southern soldiers hobbled barefoot into battle, armed with homemade swords, lances and outdated muzzle loading muskets to fight against adequately fed, well clothed, Federal troops, increasingly equipped with repeating rifles.

When the Confederate defenders of Roanoke Island, North Carolina, surrendered, many were armed only with "squirrel rifles, fowling pieces, and carving knives."

Few people realize that, with all of the successes the South had on the field of battle, it was in defense of her ports and the running of the blockade by fast, but unarmed merchant ships, that the South truly shined.

Continued trade with Europe was crucial to the survival of the Confederacy. Without the dramatic actions of the merchant blockade runners, the privateers, and the Confederate Navy, the South could not have fought her valiant duel against the North. It was only after the North completed its stranglehold on the South, by closing off the major Confederate ports of North Carolina, South Carolina, and Georgia, that the Union Army was finally able to crush the Southern Confederacy. With the final closure of

Charleston, and Wilmington to blockade runners, the end was inevitable, and, as expected by both sides, it came swift and hard.

Although much of this book is plain, unadorned facts documented by thousands of reference notes, in parts of it I have attempted to tell of the people who courageously ran the blockade, and/or served aboard the privateers and naval vessels of both sides. In bits and pieces, it recounts their collective fears, dreams, and expectations, in an effort to explain their war at sea. It is a collection of stories colored with both greed and glory. It is peopled with spies, lovers, drunkards, cowards, and heroes. It is an account of people on both sides who risked and/or gave their lives for a cause on the Confederate Coast.

Throughout this volume, a particularly romantic figure keeps appearing. He was tall, brave, and handsome. His business and political philosophies helped shape the War. By the War's end, his companies had managed to ship today's equivalent of many billions of dollars worth of government cotton and war supplies through the Federal blockade, and he had become the richest and most influential man in the South.

It was around this amazing, but relatively unknown shipping and banking magnate, that Margaret Mitchell built her "fictional" blockade runner captain, Rhett Butler, in *Gone With The Wind.* His name was George Alfred Trenholm and his story can be found in Chapter One of this book.

Part of this book is told in the first person, as it is also my story, being an account of my research and discoveries relating to the people, ships, and shipwrecks of the Civil War. I have been awed by the past, and I try to explain how I felt as I came to learn what I now see as important facts. Facts that many historians seem to have ignored for over a hundred years.

One of my early underwater discoveries was that of the location of the tiny *Hunley*, which was the first successful submarine in history. The *Hunley's* story is related in Chapter Two of this book.

In Chapter Three, I write of my research and discoveries relating to the little known steamer *Georgiana*, which I call the "Mystery Ship of the Confederacy." I refer to her as a mystery ship because of her conflicting descriptions in contemporary documents. One report said she was so poorly built that she would shake from stem to stern if a gun were fired from her decks, while another described her as the most powerful Confederate cruiser ever built. Chapter Three attempts to tell the truth about this steamer, which was sunk on her maiden voyage while attempting to run the blockade into Charleston. Additional information relating to the *Georgiana* can be found in Appendices C through E.

Chapter Four is an overview of the data contained in the shipwreck list that follows. Chapter Four also discusses some of the many causes and effects of the Civil War. It tries to pull the pieces together in a way that will enable the reader to more fully understand that each shipwreck was part of a whole. The loss of a single vessel had far reaching effects. For instance, the loss of the blockade running steamer *Stonewall Jackson*, with its cargo of 40,000 pairs of shoes and other military supplies, directly affected an equal number of soldiers soldiers who had needed the shoes, and may have indirectly led to the terrible battle of Gettysburg.

Because the vast majority of blockade running activity took place in the coastal waters of North Carolina, South Carolina, and Georgia, I have always thought of that stretch as the "Confederate Coast," and use that term in the title of this book.

The main body of this work is a listing of ships reported as wrecked in the shallow waters of the Confederate Coast during the Civil War. Those shipwrecks contain treasures with a collective value that is almost beyond comprehension. I have immodestly titled the listing "Spence's List." I call it by my own name because it is part of a larger listing of over 150,000 shipwrecks worldwide that has taken me over thirty years to research and compile. That master list represents what I consider my life's work.

The feelings I experienced while doing my research, and which I try to convey in this book, ranged from laughter and elation, to soul searching pain and tears. I sincerely hope that parts of this book will affect you the same way.

E. Lee Spence
"American by birth,
Southerner by heritage"

My great-great-grandfather, Joseph S. Jones, survived thirty-two major battles, including the battle of the Wilderness, where the forest caught fire and many of the wounded were burned to death. This engraving shows soldiers trying to rescue their comrades from the raging fires.

The song "Bonnie Blue Flag" was written as a Confederate call to arms, while "Dixie" was a hauntingly beautiful pre-war song that was written by a black minstrel in New York, who was homesick for the South where he was born.

George Alfred Trenholm, "The Real Rhett Butler"
as painted by Judson Spence de Lignières

Chapter One: "The Real Rhett Butler"
Page 8

CHAPTER ONE
"The Real Rhett Butler"
(Master Blockade Runner,
George Alfred Trenholm)

George Alfred Trenholm was tall, brave, and handsome. He was a relatively obscure shipping and banking magnate from Charleston, South Carolina, who served as Treasurer of the Confederacy during the last year of the Civil War. Today, few people are aware that he ever lived. Even fewer understand that his sense of daring, his clear thinking, and his business and political philosophies helped shape the course of the Civil War.

Understanding the symbiotic relationship that must exist between business and government during any war, Trenholm saw money to be made in both the tearing down and the building up of a nation. His wealth and power grew even as the South withered and died. By the end of the Civil War, he was undoubtedly the richest and most influential man in the South.

More than any government agency, private company, or individual, Trenholm had helped keep the South's crumbling war machine financed, fed and clothed, but the question lingers whether he did it for grand ideals or for personal gain.

Trenholm acted as the Confederate government's banking and shipping agent, smuggling cotton and gold out of the country to buy up medicines and munitions for the war effort.

But he also speculated heavily in luxuries and merchandise which he sold at outrageous prices. Trenholm threw lavish feasts when the rest of the populace was starving. At a time when rats were being sold in the Richmond market place, he flaunted his wealth by sending guests home with baskets of fine foods and expensive imported wines. Almost to add insult, his servants were dressed better than his guests.

His steamers routinely used part of their valuable cargo space to ship in silk slippers, brocades, and other non-essential items to be sold to the wealthy. Almost everyone seemed to know and accept this. Even though thousands of Southern soldiers were in desperate need of the uniforms and shoes that might have been carried, and even though many of those men marched barefoot to battle in tattered rags, direct criticism of Trenholm was extremely limited. The public knew that many other blockade runners carried only the high profit luxuries, while Trenholm's ships always devoted (for a lucrative fee of course) the largest part of their tonnage capacity to military supplies.

Treasures of the Confederate Coast

Surpassing any other Southern patriot, Trenholm invested over $20,000,000 (which is today's approximate equivalent of $400,000,000) in Confederate bonds enabling the South to keep fighting. He also helped finance privateers and Confederate cruisers, which tied up Yankee vessels that might otherwise have been attacking and capturing his fleet of blockade runners. He put up the huge reward that encouraged the crew of the tiny submarine *H.L. Hunley*. Although successful they did not live to collect it.

At the start of the Civil War, Trenholm secured an option on a fleet of armed ships, which could have been used to blockade the North. But the Confederate government didn't come up with the balance and the ships were never bought. I believe it would have probably brought a quick end to the War, and would have meant victory for the South.

Even before he became Treasurer, Trenholm suggested sound financial policies, which if implemented might have saved Southerners from the crippling inflation that devalued their money and destroyed their credit.

An astute businessman, Trenholm foresaw the effects of a northern blockade and was against the South's early prohibition of the shipment of cotton. The self imposed embargo was meant to pressure England into officially recognizing the Confederate government, but it failed. Instead, it cost the South the opportunity to ship thousands of bales overseas before the blockade made safe and easy shipment impossible.

Trenholm repeatedly proposed policies on international trade, but his suggestions weren't heeded by government officials, who were basically bureaucrats and politicians who didn't seem to comprehend the industrial might of the North.

He helped finance political propaganda favorable to the Confederacy in an effort to win England's sympathy and support.

Trenholm contributed heavily to charities, indiscriminately helping both blacks and whites. He gave money for the relief of crippled soldiers, making no distinction between Southerners and Northerners. He liberally donated to schools, hospitals, churches, and orphanages. His charitable actions were widely reported and he seemed to be the ideal citizen.

But, what were Trenholm's true motives? Was he really a patriot, or was it all an act? A cynic might say that Trenholm's large purchases of government bonds and his charitable contributions were simply the price of doing business. On the surface, he did many fine things, but virtually everything directly or indirectly enhanced his own personal prestige, power and money making

abilities. Having read Trenholm's personal letters, with their extensive moralizing, I prefer to believe his motives were noble.

Using a network of employees and secret agents, Trenholm bribed officials on two continents, socialized with Yankee carpetbaggers, and charmed everyone from "fast" young Southern widows to old preachers, who were continually in his debt for the largess he showed.

Trenholm's companies had been on the verge of bankruptcy at the outbreak of hostilities, but by the end of the Civil War he controlled over sixty first class steamers and his amazingly successful, blockade running ventures had earned today's equivalent of well over one billion dollars in gold, making him both fabulously wealthy and enormously powerful.

There is also evidence to show that he made off with and buried the gold of the Confederate Treasury. Was the money owed to him? I believe it was. Did he dig it up and use it for rebuilding the South? I don't think so.

Trenholm survived the war, but, like many other powerful Southerners, he was imprisoned for "high treason" against the United States. However, the same power that got him into trouble got him out. He used his influence, which even extended into the United States Army to get out of prison.

Although out of prison, only a Federal pardon could restore Trenholm's full rights. Pardons were almost impossible to obtain. Worse still, many Southerners believed that just asking for a pardon was tantamount to conceding that the secession of the Southern States had been illegal. They felt that such a concession would have been an insult to the thousands who had died for the Cause. Many Southerners absolutely refused to apply for a pardon, and had contempt for those who did.

Andrew Johnson, who was then President of the United States, personally granted Trenholm a full pardon and amnesty for all acts he had participated in during the "late rebellion." It was an especially neat trick since Trenholm never officially requested the pardon, nor did he ever admit having done anything wrong.

Instead, others signed letters and requests on his behalf, and he merely signed a letter stating why he felt Southerners should work towards a peaceful future with the Federal government. Unlike many other high ranking Confederates, Trenholm got his full rights back, and he got them without violating Southern sensibilities.

During the post war years, Trenholm fought the Federal government in lengthy lawsuits. The government claimed Trenholm and his partners had illegally converted today's equivalent of billions of dollars in Confederate assets. He disingenuously claimed he was bankrupt, saying he had lost everything in the War. However, his letters from prison and his probated put the lie to that claim.

Trenholm's accusers were right, he was filthy rich and he was keeping it concealed until Federal Reconstruction rule of the South ended. Although everyone realized he was an extremely rich man, Trenholm couldn't expose, use, or admit to the true extent of his wealth until the Carpetbaggers were out of power. Since Trenholm died within two days of ousting of the Reconstruction Governor, he never had a chance to retrieve the missing gold, or withdraw the bank funds, which collectively may have amounted to today's equivalent of several billion dollars.

It was only after researching and discovering the wreck of the blockade running steamer *Georgiana*, that I first realized Trenholm was the historical basis for the dashing Rhett Butler in Margaret Mitchell's award winning Civil War epic, *Gone With The Wind*.

Unfortunately, the importance of that bit of historical insight into the literary world initially escaped me. It was a full twenty years later, that I finally learned through a chance conversation in 1987 with Dr. Robert R. Nielsen Sr., that Mitchell had gone to the grave claiming her novel was pure fiction and saying that there was no real Rhett Butler.

Without trying to, I had discovered a truth that had eluded historians, literary critics, and the general public for over five decades. It was a truth that Margaret Mitchell had unwittingly acknowledged when she wrote *New York Times* book reviewer Donald Adams and said that writers using original sources for background had to use the same sources for their characters. The truth was not only that was Civil War real, so were virtually all of her characters!

Dr. Nielsen is a college president and with his assistance, I quickly began researching Margaret Mitchell and all of her characters in *Gone With The Wind*.

Our quest took us from South Carolina and Georgia, to Washington, New York, New Orleans, and even California.

We examined thousands of pages of material including contemporary newspapers, vessel logs, ship manifests, military dispatches, telegrams, diplomatic correspondence, court records, wills, deeds, and miscellaneous government documents. We even read Trenholm's wife's diary, and his lengthy letters from prison.

The "Real Rhett Butler" & Other Revelations

Trenholm's letters from prison were enigmatic in content, containing lengthy allegories. They seemed to be filled with carefully coded messages. Furthermore, his penmanship appeared purposefully designed to make reading difficult for anyone who was not already familiar with his writing.

I even located Trenholm's "little black book" which contained information on South Carolina's post war, Reconstruction legislators. The book not only recorded their race and political affiliations, but whether they were honest or corrupt. Trenholm described some as carpet-baggers and others as "slippery'" "offensive," "bad," and/or "ignorant." Of Jonathan Baker, a white Radical Republican representative from Edgefield County, Trenholm wrote: "corrupt, Bought $1700." Of Nelson Davis, a black legislator from York County, he recorded "Votes always for money." A few earned praise. Of Horry County's Independent Republican Senator, J.C. Dunn, he wrote "Square & straight forward A1." Trenholm wisely left out any descriptions of his fellow legislators from Charleston.

We visited some of Trenholm's palatial homes, magnificent plantations, and stately commercial buildings. At a few, we swung our metal detectors searching for some of his hidden treasures.

We attended family reunions, and had in depth conversations with descendants of George Trenholm. I met and talked with numerous members of Margaret Mitchell's extended family.

In many cases we were retracing the very steps taken by Mitchell who admitted to Stephen Vincent Benét that she had used diaries and memoirs for background. She later wrote Ruth Tallman that her book's historical background was gleaned from thousands of books, documents, letters, diaries, newspapers and interviews with survivors of the horrors of the War and Reconstruction.

Oddly enough, while Mitchell frequently claimed (and I believe truthfully) that she had been extremely thorough in her research, in an article in the Atlanta Junior League Magazine, she wrote, and I believe falsely, that she never used a history book or a reference work on the Civil War until after her book was sold. I think she was simply worried that she would be unfairly accused of plagiarism.

Together, Nielsen and I were able to identify the historical figures behind virtually every major character in *Gone With The Wind*. In most cases Mitchell had combined several people to come up with one, more compact character, but normally one person made up the essence or core of each character. In our estimation, well over ninety percent of Rhett was based on Trenholm, with the remainder being Trenholm's son, Fred, and Mitchell's first husband, Red Upshaw. Surprisingly, Mitchell actually admitted to Gilbert Goven, who reviewed *Gone With The Wind* for the Chattanooga *Times*, that her characters were composites.

Sometimes little more than the names of characters were changed. Frequently the changes were a variation or an alliteration of the original name. For instance, the real Scarlett's father was Philip Fitzgerald, not Gerald O'Hara. Her mother was Eleanor not Ellen. Eleanor, like Ellen, did bear six children, and one was named Kate, while Scarlett's "real" name in the book was Katie Scarlett. In a letter she wrote on July 11, 1936, Mitchell admitted that nearly all the events in her novel were true, but that in some cases she had combined the events of one person's life with another, and that some of the events didn't actually take place in Atlanta. Despite the fact that Philip and Eleanor Fitzgerald were Mitchell's great grandparents and she drew on many aspects of their lives, Mitchell would later piously claim that she had little use for authors who used their own family for source material.

More importantly, while doing our research, we learned a wealth of new information about Trenholm, gathering enough evidence that, if we ever needed to, we could prove in court that Rhett was indeed based on Trenholm. We also found that Mitchell toned down Trenholm's tremendous wealth and awesome power to make Rhett seem more realistic to a public who only remembered the South's extreme poverty after the war. In a letter to Mrs. Julia Collier Harris, Mitchell related that she had to play down real events to make them more believable.

We concluded that Margaret Mitchell had first kept her characters' true identities secret to protect the privacy and reputations of certain people who were still alive when her book was first published, and to avoid possible lawsuits for libel.

In fact even before the June, 1936, release of her book, Mitchell wrote that she was afraid that Southerners would not like her book even though everything in it was both true and provable.

On July 7, 1936, she complained that while some critics in the North felt Rhett Butler was unrealistic, some Southerners found him so authentic that she might be sued. The next day Mitchell wrote more of her fears of being sued by people who believed Rhett had been modeled after their grandfather.

It has been reported that, prior to publication, Mitchell went through her entire book changing names. Mitchell later stated that she tried to choose Southern names but intentionally avoided using those of people who had lived around Atlanta. She later wrote that she went to great lengths not to embarrass the living or the dead.

The secrecy also aided in protecting the *Gone With The Wind* copyright, which has been described as the most defended copyright in history. It is exactly because of that defense, and the possibility that I might be accused of copyright infringement for using her own words, that I have not been more specific and included direct quotes and references from Mitchell's book and letters in support of my research.

My caution is probably needless, as it is doubtful that the Mitchell estate's lawyers would give me an international forum by taking me to court. I believe a jury would agree that my discovery of the true facts behind her characters places much of Mitchell's story squarely in public domain. I can not believe Mitchell's lawyers would want such a ruling.

Mitchell's grandfather, father, uncle and brother were all lawyers and she was definitely aware of this weakness in her copyright claim. In defense of her own book against a charge of plagiarism made by Susan Lawrence Davis, Mitchell tried to demonstrate that all the historical facts she used in her book were of public record years before Miss Davis' work was published.

Within days after Mitchell's death, her husband had thousands of pages of her research notes, correspondence, and manuscript (including her original drafts and revisions) destroyed. I believe it was a calculated effort to hide the truth, and thus protect the copyright to *Gone With The Wind*, once and for all. Only a few pages were saved as proof of her authorship.

Despite the destruction of her papers and the fifty year cover-up, Dr. Nielsen and I turned up what one editor of *Life* magazine characterized as "overwhelming evidence" that Trenholm was "the real Rhett Butler."

Trenholm and Rhett had brilliant minds and could converse passionately on any subject, especially politics and economics.

Both men had similar beliefs on the lack of preparedness on the part of the South and on the monetary aspects of war, and both expounded on using immigrants to fight the war.

Mitchell was obviously aware that Rhett was a Charleston surname since gossip about Rhett Butler was passed on by Caro Rhett, another GWTW character who was also from Charleston.

In particular, the name Rhett appears to have been taken from Edmund Rhett who was an immediate relative of Trenholm's close friend and political ally, Robert Barnwell Rhett. One of the Rhetts even married a Trenholm.

Treasures of the Confederate Coast

In Mary Boykin Chesnut's book *A Diary from Dixie*, Boykin mentions attending a tea with "the Trenholms" and Edmond Rhett. She wrote "Edmond Rhett has very fine eyes and makes fearful play with them. He sits silent and motionless, with his hands on his knees, his head bent forward, and his eyes fixed upon you. I could think of nothing like it but a setter and a covey of partridges."

Rhett Butler's bold self assurance showed in his eyes as he surveyed Scarlett for the first time. She felt that his direct stare was as insolent as it was lustful.

Since Mrs. Chesnut's book was originally published in 1905, and Mitchell herself said she had read thousands of books and memoirs about the Civil War, there is little question that she read this book and knew about both Trenholm and Edmund Rhett.

Mitchell described Rhett as a tall man, and wrote of his almost too graceful ways and repeatedly mentioned his distinctive smile.

Trenholm's son-in-law described Trenholm as "a tall and very handsome man." Trenholm's pastor, the Reverend Dr. A. Toomer Porter, described Trenholm as "tall and handsome; graceful in his manners" with the "sweetest smile of any man." Another man said Trenholm "was graceful and forceful in debate" while still another eulogized him saying "He was rarely gifted; strikingly handsome in feature, dignified and imposing in presence, with an irresistible charm and grace of manner, of brilliant conversational powers, and possessed of a winning and persuasive eloquence." He was characterized as a self made "merchant prince."

Both men lived extravagantly, dressed in the latest styles, and bought expensive clothes as gifts for others.

Both Trenholm and Rhett had respectable brothers in Charleston. Rhett's brother was a rice planter who's acceptance into society was marked by his participation in Charleston's famed Saint Cecilia Balls. Trenholm's close friends, James L. Pettegrew, Wade Hampton, and R. Barnwell Rhett served as officials in the St. Cecilia Society, and at least one of Trenholm's sons was a rice planter after the war.

Neither man's wealth shielded them from personal tragedy, and both lost daughters that they mourned. The steamer *Georgiana* bore the same name as the child Trenholm lost.

Rhett abused alcohol. Trenholm definitely drank alcohol and there is some evidence that, like many of the very wealthy men of his time, he was addicted to morphine, which was then legal.

Rhett owned four blockade runners at a time when individual ships were commonly set up as separate companies. Rhett's ships made numerous successful trips through the blockade earning him a fortune.

Trenholm's three blockade running companies were the most successful in the South. Together, Trenholm's companies owned or controlled over sixty steamers. Research indicates that, during the course of the war, Trenholm's companies made over $60,000,000 face value in gold. If you figure that gold was officially $20 per ounce in the 1860's versus almost $400 per ounce today, Trenholm's companies made well over one billion dollars in today's money. The buying power would have been even higher. It would be like having one point two billion dollars in gold in economically depressed Russia today.

At the start of the War, both men bought and shipped goods directly out of New York, but were forced to use Liverpool as the main purchase point for supplies when their operations were discovered and shut down. They also used Nassau as a base for the transshipment of their contraband goods.

Both Trenholm and Rhett speculated heavily on cotton. They bought it up at cheap prices and realized great profits on it. Besides shipping munitions and medicines, both profiteered by shipping luxuries like satins, tea, and china through the blockade. Both imported buttons, pins, and thread.

Rhett ran a "combine" that was worth over a million dollars. It not only shipped its own cargoes, the combine bought the cargoes of other boats as soon as they reached the docks and held them for a rise in prices. Trenholm not only headed several companies, collectively worth millions of dollars, his hand was in numerous others.

Remember that although these men were helping the South by bringing in war supplies, they were still profiting from the destruction of their own country. Speculators and profiteers were looked down upon by polite society and were routinely attacked in contemporary gossip, political speeches and newspaper editorials as unpatriotic.

Rhett was always slipping away on some secret venture. Trenholm was not only engaged in the highly secret business of blockade running, the head of the Confederate Secret Service actually operated out of Trenholm's Liverpool offices, and the money to pay the Confederate secret agents in Europe was funneled through Trenholm's companies.

Both were acutely aware that the Confederate government's printing press productions had fueled inflation. Trenholm's becoming Treasurer was partly an effort to help control inflation, which was eroding his fortune just like everyone else's.

By the end of the war, Trenholm was undoubtedly the richest man in the South, and probably in all of America. Although he had invested heavily in the war effort, less than a third of his fabulous earnings had been used to purchase Confederate bonds.

The fictional Rhett's wartime and post wartime wealth exceeded that of any other character mentioned in the book. Obviously, he had not put everything into Confederate paper money or government bonds which had become worthless on the defeat of the South.

Mitchell even wrote that Rhett and Scarlett's mansion was bigger than the Governor's.

Trenholm's servants in Richmond were said to dress better than his guests (a frequent guest was President Jefferson Davis). In Charleston, Trenholm's mansion was so large and beautiful that it surpassed that of the Governor. That magnificent home, Ashley Hall, still stands and now houses a private girl's school, which was once attended by Presidential First Lady Barbara Bush. Over a hundred years later, Ashley Hall's intricately carved, flying spiral staircase remains one of the most beautiful ever built.

At one point Rhett tells Scarlett that he would rather dine on a rat than some of the food in Atlanta. He talks of Richmond as the only place left in the South where good food could be had, and then only for the right price.

Despite the fact that the Confederate capital was under siege and rats were being sold in the city market place to the poorer folk, Trenholm's house in Richmond was known for the extravagant meals.

Both Trenholm and Rhett would have been expected to travel in elegant enclosed carriages, but both fled with their women in open wagons before invading Federal forces. In both cases, when neither a carriage nor an ambulance was available, a mattress had been arranged in the back of an open wagon for the comfort of a person who was too sick to travel sitting up. Mitchell goes into great detail about the poor condition of the wagon and the old nag that pulled it. In the memoirs of Trenholm's friend and pastor, Toomer Porter, we find the following "Next day I succeeded in getting a seat in a wagon, with no springs, the extemporized body being placed directly on the axles. The old, lame mule pulled six of us thirty miles."

Both men joined the Confederacy shortly after the fall of Atlanta. Rhett joined the cavalry and Trenholm accepted a position on President Jefferson Davis' cabinet. Both men's last minute patriotic acts gave them a firm basis to claim to their fellow Southerners that they had indeed been loyal and had risked everything, even their lives, to support "the Cause." Naturally, this would have helped cool some of the ill feelings and jealousies many people would have felt towards them for their speculating and profiteering activities.

The idea of Rhett serving as a non-commissioned officer in the Confederate artillery certainly didn't fit his character as portrayed in the book, but to have had him serve as Treasurer would have made Rhett's real identity too obvious. However, one of Trenholm's sons served as an officer in the Trenholm Light Battery (an artillery unit which was entirely equipped by Trenholm).

When Scarlett needed cash to pay her taxes after the War, Ashley Wilkes told Scarlett that Rhett was the only person who had any money. Aunt Pittypat said Rhett was rich while everyone else was broke. Trenholm's wife wrote in her diary that they had to barter for food with bolts of cloth, because all the Trenholm's had were twenty dollar gold pieces which no one could change.

Like Rhett in *Gone With The Wind*, Trenholm was imprisoned at the end of the war under threat of death. Both refused to admit to Federal officials that they had any of the Confederate Treasury's money, and they both used their connections to obtain pardons without ever having to admit guilt, or actually pay a bribe.

When teary eyed Scarlett, who was wearing a fancy dress she had made from her curtains, visited Rhett in jail she was just hoping to get his gold. Trenholm had a beautiful young lady visit him in jail and he did entrust her with an entire suitcase filled with gold. Both women were young and pretty. Both were recently widowed from Confederate officers and were from good families, and both had "fast" reputations.

The usually "gay and debonair" widow Mrs. Henry King, visited Trenholm often, sitting on the dirty straw at his feet, "softly crying," while he tried to comfort her. A witness later wrote that one would have thought she was the person in jail under a threat of execution instead of the other way around.

On the day Scarlett first met Rhett in *Gone With The Wind*, Scarlett became infuriated with Rhett, and said he was no gentleman. Rhett replied that she was no lady. Their exchange was most certainly based on a meeting between the aforementioned young widow Mrs. Henry King and the famous 19th century English novelist, William Makepeace Thackery.

Treasures of the Confederate Coast

Contemporary accounts state that Thackery, upon being introduced to the young widow during a visit to Charleston, said he had been so looking forward to meeting her because she was "the fastest lady received in society." She replied "I also heard that you were a gentleman - we have both been misinformed." The idea that this was Mitchell's source (for Rhett and Scarlett's rude exchange) is supported by the fact that, only twelve pages earlier, the normally uncritical Melanie Wilkes had mentioned Thackery by name and added her ungracious sentiment that he was not a gentleman. Five pages before that, Mitchell wrote that the word "fast" was the only one that accurately described Scarlett. Quite a coincidence for a book of over 1000 pages.

Incidentally, in her book *Road to Tara: The Life of Margaret Mitchell*, Anne Edwards noted that Scarlett "seemed to owe a lot to Thackery's Becky Sharp." Mitchell claimed to Stephen Vincent Benét that she had "never read Thackery" until 1935.

Scarlett's Aunt Pittypat believed, along with the majority of Atlanta society, that Rhett had hidden millions of dollars belonging to the Confederate treasury.

The natural question would then be - how could a "mere" blockade runner captain have gotten his hands on the Treasury Department gold to have stolen it?

The answer is easy. Trenholm was not a mere blockade runner. By the end of the war, Trenholm was not only the most important figure in blockade running, he was serving as the official Treasurer of the Confederacy.

Even near the end of the war the Confederate Treasury had a large amount of silver and gold on hand. It also had jewels and other treasures placed in the government's care by private citizens. It was Trenholm who actually ordered the treasure placed on a train to ship it out of Richmond in the final days before the fall of the Confederacy, and it was Trenholm who mapped out the route that would be used by the Confederate president (and Trenholm) in their flight from Virginia with that treasure.

Virtually all of the government silver has been accounted for, but the disposition of the government gold and extensive private treasure has never been satisfactorily explained. Its fate remains the subject of much speculation. Naturally many Southerners would have believed that Trenholm, having been Treasurer and the man ultimately in charge of the treasure, simply stole it.

Rhett got out of jail by threatening to expose powerful people in the North who had sold him military supplies with full knowledge that those supplies would be run through the blockade and used against the Federal Army. Trenholm purchased pistols and other weapons of war in New York for exactly the same purpose. So he definitely was in a position to use such leverage, but whether he did so is not known. However, we do know that several American generals signed petitions on his behalf.

After getting out of jail, Rhett went to Scarlett and asked why she hadn't waited to marry him. He told her that he had a half million dollars in a bank in Liverpool, but said he couldn't admit to it or write her a check while he was in jail for fear the authorities would seize his account. He said he was not a thief and came by the money honestly.

Rhett went on to describe exactly the same arrangements that had been authorized between Trenholm's companies and the Confederate government. In fact, it was an exclusive arrangement. Out of all of the thousands of people and numerous companies engaged in blockade running during the Civil War, only Trenholm and his companies actually had the kind of deal outlined by Rhett in that conversation.

Although he freely acknowledged having a fortune from the sale of cotton, he didn't even mention the missing Confederate Treasury Department gold.

A report from Confederate Secretary of State Judah P. Benjamin stated that the government owned cotton had been sold and "the proceeds accruing to the War Departments placed in the hands of Messrs. Fraser, Trenholm & Co." it went on to add "All agents of the War and Navy Departments will be ordered at once to deliver over to Messrs. Fraser, Trenholm & Co. all bonds, cotton certificates in their hands, and will be prohibited from selling or pledging such bonds, certificates, or securities in any manner. Such sale or pledge shall only be made when made at all by Messrs. Fraser, Trenholm & Co. in England."

It is also interesting to note that when Rhett said he had almost half million dollars in his account in Liverpool, it was the same amount that had been "placed to the credit of Fraser, Trenholm in Liverpool" at the start of the War. That amount of gold would be today's equivalent of ten million dollars.

Like Rhett, Trenholm was hauled before numerous boards of inquiry attempting to locate missing Confederate funds. The suit against Trenholm involved "several hundreds of millions of dollars" (which would have been today's equivalent of billions of dollars).

The Federal government eventually confiscated over a hundred separate parcels of real estate from "Trenholm et al." Officially, the court took it for unpaid duties on goods run through the blockade, while also claiming that the real estate had been bought with funds received from the sale of products and ships belonging to the Confederate government. The confiscated properties ranged from gorgeous mansions, commercial warehouses, wharves, much of the Charleston waterfront, stately banks and hotels (including the Planter's Inn which is the present day Dock Street Theater), to entire plantations totaling many thousands of acres. In *Gone With The Wind*, Rhett had expressed his fears to Scarlett about the Yankees confiscating property.

Rhett bought his mother and sister a house on Charleston's famous Battery, but hid the fact that he had paid for it. Although not supported by any deed in the Charleston courthouse, there is both historical and archeological evidence to show that Trenholm's family lived, at least briefly, at 51 East Battery in Charleston after the War.

I personally believe Trenholm, like Rhett, felt morally justified in fighting to hang on to whatever funds he had in his possession. Rhett says in the book that half of the money he had in the bank was his, and he certainly didn't feel he should give the rest to the Federal government. Rhett was aware that people might think he was a thief, but he certainly didn't feel he was one.

The Federal government never located the missing government owned gold or any of the privately owned treasures that had been entrusted to the Confederate Treasury Department (and thus Trenholm) for safe keeping.

Dr. Nielsen and I are convinced that some of it was buried by Trenholm who planned to dig it up once Federal Reconstruction of the South had ended. Unfortunately, Trenholm died within days of the ousting of the Reconstruction governor in South Carolina. A thorough search of the Trenholm properties confiscated by the courts might one day reveal the millions in Confederate government gold that Rhett was believed to have hidden.

James D. Bulloch, who headed the Confederate Secret Service in Europe, actually worked out of Trenholm's Liverpool offices. Mitchell mentions him in her book, saying that Scarlett's husband had contempt for Rhett not returning the Confederate gold, when others like Captain James D. Bulloch (who Mitchell incorrectly titles as admiral) had turned in thousands of dollars to the Federal treasury. For her to have known that Bulloch (who actually operated out of Trenholm's Liverpool offices) had turned in the gold in his charge, she could not have failed to have known that Trenholm had not turned over any of the Confederate funds in his care. Mitchell never mentions Trenholm by name, despite the fact that he was the most important figure in blockade running and the

Treasurer of the Confederacy. The only reason Mitchell didn't mention Trenholm is that much of the book was about him, he was the real Rhett Butler. She had painted his actions and character in a bad light and she didn't want to be criticized or sued for libel by his family.

No one who has read Mitchell's novel or seen the movie would question Rhett's bravery, and apparently Trenholm was equally courageous. Jefferson Davis, president of the Confederate States of America, actually said of Trenholm, "No consideration of personal danger, ever caused him to swerve from the path of duty."

Trenholm was born in 1807, so he would have been fifty-three years old when the South seceded from the Union, while Rhett was just thirty-four. However, since Mitchell says her characters were composites, there is no problem. I believe she combined him with his sons William and Alfred to make a more youthful and thus romantic character.

Rhett told Scarlett that his family always referred to his grandfather as a sea captain, but that he was really a drunken pirate and an embarrassment to his family. However, Rhett's grandfather had accumulated enough money to leave Rhett's father quite wealthy.

Trenholm family legend suggests that Trenholm's father (i.e. his sons' grandfather), whose family had lived in Santo Domingo before that country's revolution was a sea captain who returned to Santo Domingo in 1803 to marry a girl, found her already married, wedded her younger sister, and took his bride to Charleston to live.

Throughout history sea faring people suddenly left without home or country because of political upheaval have turned to piracy as a way to extract revenge or to get together enough quick money to start a new life in another land. Many who fled Santo Domingo did exactly that, but whether Trenholm's father ever resorted to piracy is not known, but rumors to that effect would have been natural.

Mitchell was certainly aware of the revolution in Santo Domingo, as she had Scarlett's mother's family fleeing that island to settle in the South.

Although banking would seem out of character for most sea faring men, both men owned stocks in banks and became bankers after the war, earning respect and friends as they loaned people money. A financial wizard, Trenholm was considered the "master of Southern banking."

Rhett was severely criticized for his socializing with scalawags and carpetbaggers. Although, Trenholm has been politely described as "one of the few respected white men in the state who could get along with the Reconstruction legislators," there is no question that many people resented his working and socializing with them.

Trenholm was a "civic leader - a real joiner." Rhett told Scarlett that he would even join the Ku Klux Klan, if that was what it took to be accepted.

It has been written that Trenholm "understood that wealth acquired through the necessities of a suffering nation, is • • • a trust fund" and there is a great deal of evidence that he used much of his money to help the Confederacy during and after the war.

At one point in *Gone With The Wind*, Rhett reminded Scarlett of her admonishment that it was wrong to keep the Confederate gold, and said he had come to agree with her and that he was using it to put the former Confederates back in control. Scarlett first thought that his new found piety and post war financial support of the Democrats meant that he had changed, but she quickly realized that he was doing it just for appearances.

Despite questions one might naturally have had about their true loyalties and motives, both the fictional Rhett and the real life Trenholm supported the Democrats and openly fought corruption in Reconstruction politics, and both men donated heavily to charity, and thereby reestablished their credibility with the upper crust of post war, polite Southern society.

Trenholm's bequests to schools, orphanages, hospitals and churches were similar to the charitable contributions attributed to Rhett who, in an effort to have his daughter accepted into polite society, contributed to various charities. Unlike the average Southerner, both men attended the Episcopal church. Both donated heavily to church causes, but, hopefully, Trenholm's motives were more sincere than those attributed to Rhett. Having read Trenholm's personal letters with his frequent pious moralizing, I personally believe his motives were noble. However, Dr. Nielsen has read the same materials and has come to the opposite conclusion, seeing him as Machiavellian in nature.

During Reconstruction, Trenholm served on the Board of Directors of the Blue Ridge Railroad, and although work, started before the war, was resumed the company's assets were stolen by corrupt officials. Trenholm blasted the Reconstruction Governor, Sheriff, and Attorney General saying "the entire system is one of self sustaining and self protecting corruption." He accused the men of stealing public money and arranging terms between them in respect to the coveted opportunities of plunder.

Rhett held the Reconstruction officials in contempt and even criticized them to their face when Scarlett invited them into their home, making remarks about their selling spurious bonds for never-to-be-built railroads.

Trenholm's aforementioned "little black book" describes Senator J.C. Hope, of Lexington, South Carolina, as "corrupt," and mentions that he voted for the Blue Ridge Railroad Bill.

George Alfred Trenholm died on December 9, 1876, within days of realizing his goal of removing the Republican "carpet bag governor" from the South Carolina state house. The timing of Trenholm's death may explain why Margaret Mitchell ended her book within pages of the ousting of the Republican governor in Georgia, and why she was unable, or unwilling, to write a sequel.

Suspecting that the star crossed love between Rhett and Scarlett was loosely based on Trenholm's son's ardent, but unsuccessful, multi-continent pursuit of a "tormenting" and "much too pretty" young lady named Ruby Senac, I contacted Ruby's second cousin Regina Rapier to pump her for information. Regina had never met Ruby, but their lives had over lapped and her father had known Ruby quite well.

After getting as much information as I could, and after telling her that I knew that Georgia had a population of over four million of people and that I understood the monumental odds against it, I asked her if she had ever known anyone who had known Mitchell. I was stunned to learn that she was not only Ruby Senac's cousin, but Margaret Mitchell's cousin as well. According to Regina Rapier, her father had even helped Mitchell with her research.

When I subsequently remarked to Regina Rapier that many of the family stories she was telling me were similar to events in *Gone With The Wind*, she said "Well, Margaret took it straight out of the family."

Young Ruby Senac was the daughter of a man who worked directly under Trenholm, and she eventually became the wife of still another man, Henry Hotz, who worked closely with Trenholm. According to family legend, that man was aboard the British yacht *Deerhound*, when it rescued Admiral Raphael Semmes and the crew of the sinking Confederate cruiser *Alabama* off the coast of France. The Charleston *Daily Courier* reported the *Deerhound's* owner as George Trenholm.

Ruby was also the cousin of Confederate Secretary of the Navy Stephen R. Mallory, who served with Trenholm on President Jeff Davis' cabinet. Ruby lived until well after Mitchell had begun her book.

Miss Rapier said that most of the other events in Scarlett's life were based on the life of Mary Ann Fitzgerald who was Mitchell's grandmother and Rapier's aunt. Margaret Mitchell's mother (Maybelle) had been living with Mary Ann Fitzgerald when Margaret was born and Regina Rapier had grown up in Mary Ann Fitzgerald's farm house, which Regina described as "the real Tara." Mary Ann lived to see the book published.

Maybelle Fitzgerald's given name was used for the daughter of one of the grand old dames of Atlanta in the book. The fictional Maybelle Merriwether's boyfriend and eventual husband, René Picard, although of rather diminutive size, was quite daring and had belonged to a Zouave unit and was described as of French heritage from a wealthy and influential family

My research indicates that René Picard was based on a very small, French speaking, Zouave who went by the name of Colonel Zarvona. Zarvona was also from a wealthy and influential family and had a reputation for bravery. He been captured while trying to hi-jack a Federal schooner with the help of the aforementioned Ruby Senac's father.

In the book, the reader first meets Picard while he was collecting donations of money and jewelry, including both Melanie's and Scarlett's wedding rings, at the hospital ball in Atlanta. In real life, Zarvona had been paroled from a northern prison because of his health, but convalesced in Paris, where Ruby Senac and her family were then living. Zarvona undoubtedly participated in the grand balls thrown by Empress Eugenie to help raise money for the beleaguered Confederates.

The incident of the jewelry and wedding rings may have come from the memoirs of Trenholm's close friend and pastor, Dr. A. Toomer Porter. Dr. Porter's school was on the verge of bankruptcy and from his congregation he had collected three hundred and twenty-eight dollars, two or three watches, several diamond rings, breast pins, and "even a wedding ring." The wedding ring and other jewelry was returned to the owners, and Trenholm signed for the balance of the debt, just as Melanie's ring had been purchased and returned by Rhett.

Among Dr. Porter's parishioners was the aforementioned widow Mrs. Henry King who had visited Trenholm in jail, but whether it was her wedding ring, I have been unable to determine. Dr. Porter's memoirs also mention the ladies of his parish cutting up curtains for skirts, just as Scarlett had done prior to visit to Rhett in jail.

The "Real Rhett Butler" & Other Revelations

Although Scarlett and Rhett's daughter in *Gone With The Wind* was nicknamed Bonnie for her eyes which were described as blue as the bonnie blue flag (the first Confederate flag), the book explains that she was actually named Eugenie Victoria after Empress Eugenie, Queen of France, and Empress Victoria, Queen of England. Senac family legend, as related by Regina Rapier, has Ruby and her mother meeting both queens during their trip to Europe. Ruby Senac and her family, along with one of Trenholm's sons, ran through the blockade at Wilmington in a steamer named *Eugenie*, which had also been named for Empress Eugenie. While in Paris, the Senacs, along with Fred Trenholm and the tiny Colonel Zarvona, attended the grand balls thrown by Empress Eugenie.

Upon their safe arrival in Great Britain Ruby Senac's father and Trenholm's son immediately went to meet with Trenholm's partner. The man's elegant new house had a single star carved over the portico of a first floor window. The star represented the "Bonnie Blue Flag that bears a single star!"

Scarlett's first child was a son. He was named for General Wade Hampton, who was said to have been the much admired commanding officer of her late husband. General Hampton was not only a close friend of Trenholm's, Trenholm's son ran Hampton Plantation after the War, and Trenholm helped get General Hampton elected governor of South Carolina.

In *Gone With The Wind*, Scarlett's mother Ellen had wanted to marry her wild cousin, Philippe Robillard, but the family was opposed to it, not so much because he was her cousin but because he was a gambler. Upon Philippe's death in a barroom brawl, Ellen married Gerald O'Hara, winning her family's approval only by threatening to join the convent (run by the Sisters of Lady of Mercy) at Charleston. Based on conversations with Regina Rapier and other information, I have no doubt that portion of Ellen's story was taken from the life of Mitchell's cousin Martha Holliday.

Martha Holliday's family had opposed her marrying her wild cousin "Doc" Holliday who had become a professional gambler. Instead of marrying, Martha eventually became a nun (Sister Melanie) with the Sister's of Mercy in Atlanta. According to one source, after reading the book, Sister Melanie seeing how her name and story had been used "was apoplectic. She was fit to be tied. She was one furious lady of the cloth."

Through Regina Rapier, Nielsen and I secured genealogies of various branches of Mitchell's and Rapier's families (including some of the Fitzgeralds and Hollidays mentioned earlier). Armed with all of the other research we had done, it was easy to spot many of the characters in the book among their family tree. "Old Dr. Fontaine" born in the 1700's and "young Dr. Fontaine" were clearly based on Dr. Michael Fitzgerald, who lived from 1780 to 1864, and his son Dr. Michael Fitzgerald, Jr., who lived from 1811 to 1866.

Despite Mitchell's frequent statements that none of her characters were based on real people, she actually admitted to one correspondent that the little black maid Prissy was modeled after Cammie, a small skittish black girl, who was three years younger than Mitchell and at fifteen years of age served as the Mitchell's house girl. Scarlett's rage against Prissy simply reflected Mitchell's own feelings about Cammie.

After I had released news of my discovery of the real Rhett's true identity, I was invited as an official guest to several of the ceremonies commemorating the fiftieth anniversary of the movie *Gone With The Wind*.

From fellow guest, distinguished Atlanta historian Dr. Franklin M. Garrett, I learned that Trenholm Street in Atlanta is a mere nine blocks from Mitchell Street. Quite a coincidence considering that Atlanta consists of over one thousand four hundred and forty miles of streets and roads, each mile multiplied by many blocks. Both streets were apparently named long before Mitchell was even born, but their proximity may have fascinated Mitchell who, even as a child, loved history and often said that she felt more at home in the stories of the past than in her own century.

In 1939, Dr. Garrett, who was already one of Atlanta's leading historians, believed he had identified some of the Atlanta homes of Mitchell's characters, but the more famous Mitchell quickly stifled his research with her emphatic claim that none of her characters were based on real people. Regardless of Mitchell's protestations, I personally believe Dr. Garrett's instincts as a historian were correct. Had Dr. Garrett not been a true Southern gentleman, I believe he would continued his research, proved his theory, and exposed the facts behind *Gone With The Wind* many years ago. Mitchell and Dr. Garrett became long standing friends.

When Dr. Garrett read a prepublication copy of this chapter he wrote me a letter saying "Margaret Mitchell would never admit that any of her characters in *Gone With The Wind* were based upon real people but I must say that George Trenholm would have been a logical basis for Rhett Butler." He kindly went on to offer "best wishes for the book."

Both of Mitchell's nephews, who were the primary heirs to her estate, attended several of the official fiftieth anniversary functions. After pointing out that I was "in effect calling his aunt a liar," I reminded one nephew that I had "also proved that she was a superb historian." I asked him what he thought of it. His answer was "I like it." I was glad.

Mitchell's other nephew had not only been familiar with Trenholm all along, he told me that all of the checks for the government supplies purchased in England had been written on the Liverpool account of Fraser, Trenholm and Company, and in doing so it became obvious that, like many others in the Mitchell and Trenholm families, he had known the truth all along. George Trenholm was "the real Rhett Butler," and virtually everything else in it was based on real life and real people as well.

In fact, I believe that it was exactly because there was so much more truth than fiction in *Gone With The Wind* that Mitchell once wrote, that she originally expected little demand for her book other than as a reference work.

Other researchers have noted many similarities between certain characters' personalities and those of persons that Mitchell actually knew. I agree with most of their conclusions. However, no published writers made the required leap back in time to find the Civil War people used by Mitchell for the true core of her major characters. In the many books written on Mitchell and *Gone With The Wind*, no one ever suggested that they even suspected George Alfred Trenholm to be "the real Rhett Butler."

For over fifty years, millions of people read, saw and loved *Gone With The Wind*, but never understood its true roots. I too would have missed the truth had it not been for the tiny brass sewing pins (which I now think of as "Scarlett's pins") that I salvaged from the *Georgiana*. Even after realizing Rhett was based on Trenholm, I might never have known that I had made an important discovery and would probably have gone to my grave with the secret of Rhett Butler's true identity, had it not been for my aforementioned chance conversation in 1987 with Dr. Nielsen.

• • •

Chapter One: "The Real Rhett Butler"

Charleston's Dock Street Theater was among the many properties confiscated from George Alfred Trenholm after the Civil War. Photo by L. Spence.

Chapter One: "The Real Rhett Butler"

The "Real Rhett Butler" & Other Revelations

These items were shipped from Liverpool by Fraser, Trenholm, & Co. and were consigned to Fraser & Co. in Charleston. Clockwise, they are a spool for surgical thread, two ivory toothbrushes, handle for a scaple, and a brass match safe. Photo by L. Spence.

Chapter One: "The Real Rhett Butler"
Page 31

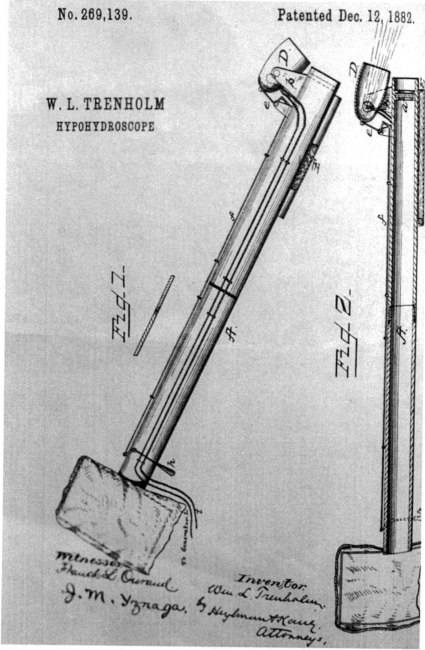

This hypohydroscope was invented in 1882 by William Trenholm. It was to be used to search for things underwater. He may have been inspired by the millions in merchandise, munitions, and gold, which was lost and/or hidden by his father. Diagram courtesy of the United States Library of Congress.

Chapter One:"The Real Rhett Butler"

After the Civil War; George Trenholm was arrested for High Treason and was imprisoned in the City Jail on Magazine Street in Charleston, South Carolina. Photo by L. Spence.

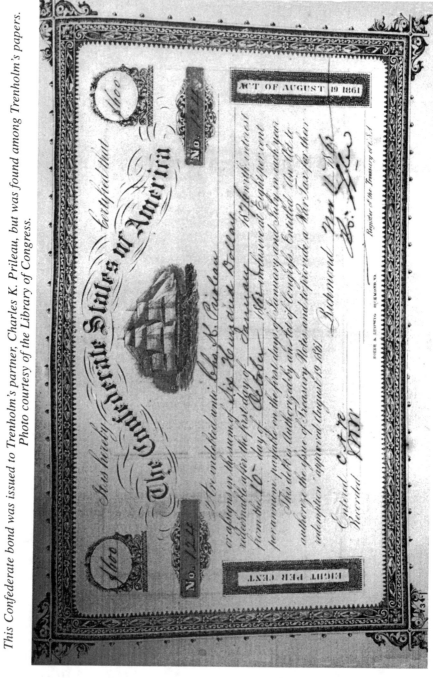

This Confederate bond was issued to Trenholm's partner, Charles K. Prileau, but was found among Trenholm's papers. Photo courtesy of the Library of Congress.

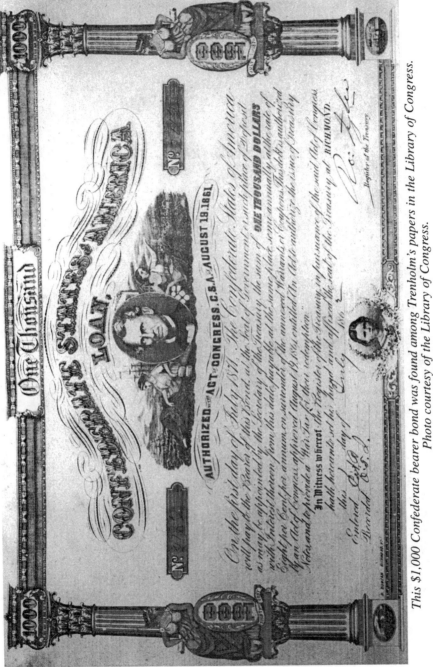

This $1,000 Confederate bearer bond was found among Trenholm's papers in the Library of Congress. Photo courtesy of the Library of Congress.

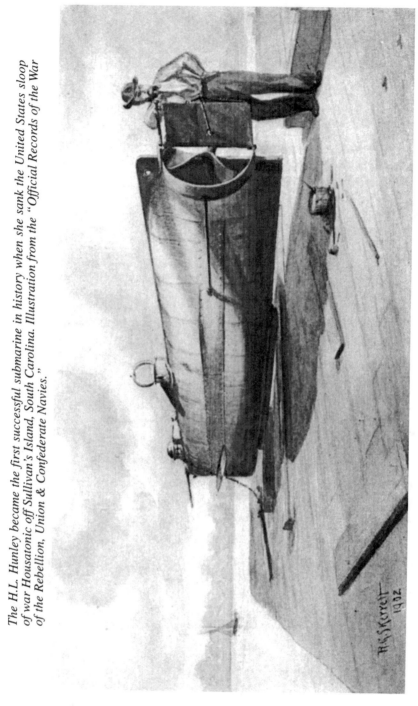

The H.L. Hunley became the first successful submarine in history when she sank the United States sloop of war Housatonic off Sullivan's Island, South Carolina. Illustration from the "Official Records of the War of the Rebellion, Union & Confederate Navies."

CHAPTER TWO
"The First Successful Submarine"
(The story of the *C.S.S. Hunley*)

THE END OF THE SEARCH

I paused over it, puzzled. I peered through the gloom down its length. Scraps of rotting herring from a nearby fish trap drifted by in the steady tidal current.

My mind darted back to the ever present danger of sharks. I shuddered inwardly at the possibility, no the probability, of their deadly presence. I knew that the "World's Record Tiger Shark," was caught in these very waters, and Tiger sharks have been known to be man-eaters.

I lingered over the cylindrical object which formed an unnatural shelf or ledge in the sand. Holding onto the buoy line of the fish trap with one hand, I reached over and broke loose a slender yellow sea whip from its anchorage on the ledge. I carefully rubbed at the spot where it had grown. My fingers, aching from the intensely cold water, showed the tell-tale, almost greasy, black smudge made by over one hundred years old rust.

My gaze swept back to the object, now picking out the raised marks of hand hammered rivets. I carefully observed the contours, I could now see its ends tapering off into the sand. I stared at it, almost not believing it still existed, my mind suddenly plunging back through time.

THE MISSION STARTS

It was just after twilight. The sun had already shined its last light. It was cold, bitterly so. There was no wind and a strange sort of calm hung in the air. The day was February 16, 1864.

I watched as a dozen shivering men somberly pushed and pulled an awkward machine of war through the shallow swirling waters of Breach Inlet near Charleston, South Carolina. Their clothing was the usual Confederate mixture of military and civilian, all of it was worn and thin. Even the patches had been darned.

One man stumbled and fell headlong in the bone chilling waters. I could see but not hear the silent oath he cursed, as he rose to push onwards.

Alongside waded eight men, with their heads lowered as though immersed in thought. Unlike the others, these men were sharply dressed in new uniforms. At least two sported gold braid, marking them as officers.

Treasures of the Confederate Coast

The scene had the air of a funeral procession. The iron fish-boat was the coffin, a floating coffin. The soldiers were the pall bearers, the eight men the living dead, already dressed for eternity.

The eight men were trying to conserve their strength. They would need every bit of their energy to hand crank the primitive submarine to its appointed destination. The tide was already ebbing and they had to hurry to ride with it.

The procession stopped and the crew slowly, carefully, climbed through the two open hatches. As they nodded their silent good-byes to their comrades, I tried to understand what had brought them to this seemingly god forsaken stretch of beach.

THEIR MOTIVES

I wondered whether they had been ordered on this seemingly suicide mission or if they were simply volunteers, each with his own personal reasons and convictions? I wondered if any were simply drawn by the lure of riches that the rich and powerful, shipping magnate George Trenholm had promised them for a successful mission. I doubted the last as there was no joking of wild parties, fast women, and beautiful homes. But maybe they just didn't want to jinx their luck.

THE MAN BEHIND THE REWARD

The men didn't voice any statement or question about Trenholm's motives for posting the reward, which, depending on their target, would have been today's equivalent of a half million or a million dollars. Yet they surely knew, that the sinking of a powerful blockader would have made running the blockade easier for Trenholm's fleet of over sixty swift steamers. They knew that each outward run helped deplete the South's rapidly dwindling resources. They knew that each successful run, in or out, further enriched Trenholm.

They spoke not a single word of criticism against Trenholm, even though Trenholm was personally profiting from the War on a level unequaled by any other person in America. They held back any criticism, if indeed they felt it, because they understood that his ships routinely carried the shot, shell, boots, uniforms, and food so badly needed by the soldiers, unlike many other blockade runners who devoted virtually all of their precious cargo space to unneeded, but even more profitable luxuries.

They had no way of knowing that Margaret Mitchell would later use Trenholm as the historical basis for the dashing Rhett Butler in her Pulitzer Prize winning novel *Gone With The Wind*.

ORDINARY MEN

Unlike Trenholm, these were ordinary men, laborers and mechanics in civilian life. However, there was a sense of almost inordinate pride in their demeanor, and I could feel it spanning the century that separated us.

THE HATCHES CLOSE

The hatches were dogged shut as the last man squeezed into his place along the heavy crankshaft. Sweat beaded the young brows of the men as they felt the first stirrings of claustrophobia within them. The fear welled up, choked at their throats, knotted their stomachs, and finally subsided but never quite went away. The fear remained with these brave men as they steered their torpedo boat towards a thin pinpoint of light shining from the enemy ship on the horizon.

The gears screeched a muted, grinding sort of metallic cry as the men continually forced the crank around. Muscles ached. Sweat from exertion mingled with that of their fear. Someone laughed, a girlish almost hysterical laugh, as he tried to shake away the impending sense of doom that permeated the damp air. Moisture beaded and ran down the already rusting, inside surfaces sides of sub.

She was ballasted to float with her hatch coamings just above the water.

They passed a picket boat. The pickets dressed in heavily soiled, wrinkled Navy blues, bleary-eyed, and not sensing the urgency in the air, failed to notice the low silhouette as the heavily ballasted sub wallowed past in the dark. The clumsy cigar shaped boat plowed forward, waves rolled over her and she would temporarily disappear beneath the sea only to reappear a few yards further along her deadly course.

Peering out the tiny deadlight in the forward hatch, Lieutenant Dixon watched as a graceful porpoise jumped and frolicked near the bow of the tiny submarine. The Lieutenant's thoughts drifted from his duty as he thought of his family, the pleasures they had shared. He thought of their fears for him. He had heard about some of the earlier experiments with this same craft, and some of their disastrous conclusions. He pictured the waters rushing inwards as the trapped men tried to escape through the narrow hatches, to swim upwards to life.

He wondered what had caused the earlier sinkings. He recalled the descriptions of the faces of the crew, contorted in death, reported by the men who had helped pull the bodies from the salvaged vessel. How had their families accepted their deaths, and how had the relatives of the other earlier crews accepted their loss? Did they understand?

What would be his fate this time? Would he succeed? He felt his death, if it should come, all of their deaths, would be easier to accept, if they accomplished their goal.

It wasn't as though he was sure they would die. In fact he doubted that he would have accepted the command if he was sure that he or his men were facing certain death.

The young lieutenant did not think of himself as a martyr, and he clung to a straw of hope, both for success and life. They were nearing their target. They were weary from the hours of back breaking labor.

A MOMENT'S REST

Lieutenant Dixon called out the order to rest, and the men relaxed, hunched over from lack of space, enjoying a moment's reprieve. Water sloshed in the bilges as the devil-boat rolled beneath the waves. The cold damp air, foul with sweat and lack of oxygen, brought nausea. Vomit came up through the mouths and nostrils of some of the men. The candle flickered, the air was running out.

The lieutenant raised the breathing tubes, the air suddenly freshened as a slight wisp of wind whistled down and found its way to the men's faces. Each man sat mumbling his silent prayers, never admitting that he was facing death, but knowing it all the same. None of them felt brave, although all seemed to admire and respect the bravery of the others.

The submarine was barely big enough to accommodate the eight men. It seemed impossible to believe that they were all able to have crammed themselves into its narrow frame. Their ability to rotate the crank shaft at all was due solely to the constant contorting and twisting of their bodies as they turned it over and over.

The rest was good and the men spoke with renewed hope and confidence in the final outcome of their mission. They even began to joke of their coming success.

It was finally starting to seem possible. They would ram the Yankee ship and attach their torpedo to it below the water line. They would back off and detonate the charge. The sloop of war would fill with water and sink like a lead line.

The loss of a heavily armed blockader would demoralize the Union Navy. Hopefully it would panic them into pulling even further off the coast and enable a greater percentage of blockade runners to slip inshore. The blockade runners would carry hundreds of tons of badly needed supplies to the starving Confederacy.

No one voiced their fear of what would happen to their own vessel when the charge exploded. The torpedo, containing ninety pounds of gunpowder, was fastened to the end of a twenty foot spar on the bow of their craft. The barb of the torpedo would pierce deep enough into the hull of the ship to hold it in place as the submarine backed away. Then, from a safe distance, the instrument of destruction would be detonated by pulling a lanyard. But, it was anyone's guess as to whether the distance would be great enough to allow them to survive the concussion.

Sensing that his crew was mentally prepared, Dixon ordered the men to press on, there would be no more stops. As a precaution he reached up, unbolted the hatches, and threw them open. At least his men would have an escape route if their craft sank. With their jaws set in a grim clinch of determination, and their muscles moving with a single minded purpose the crew bent to their duty.

Onward! Forward! Success!

THE ATTACK

As they approached the big ship, Lieutenant Dixon could see that she was swinging at anchor. He could make out the name *Housatonic* emblazoned in large bold letters on her side. Her gun ports were shuttered, but he could see men patrolling her decks.

One of the lookouts halted. The man stared directly at the oncoming sub. He thought it might be a porpoise or a large sea turtle bobbing on the surface. He watched, curiosity born out of boredom growing within him. The lookout had almost decided it was just a log drifting with the current when he realized, it had changed course and was moving diagonally across the flow of water.

Visions of sea monsters leapt out at him. He cringed in fear. Then reason returned. He remembered his duty and cried out the alarm. The iron monster attacked the ship. He raised his musket and fired. He thought he had saved the day as the tiny torpedo boat pulled back from the side of the huge ship.

THE LAST MOMENTS

Within moments there was a thundering roar. The explosion ripped metal, splintered wood and mangled flesh. Sailors, wisely choosing to ignore their pay that they had carefully hidden in their hammocks and sea bags, rushed to abandon ship as the *Housatonic*, mortally wounded, reeled under the death blow and slowly sank to the bottom.

The roar was deafening on the little sub. She shook from stem to stern making her own death rattle as rivets popped and seams opened up.

The *Hunley's* crew struggled towards the open hatches, only to be washed back by the flood of water churned up by the explosion. Their escape route changed to a funnel which siphoned them to their grave.

The submarine rolled and twisted. Giant bubbles of air burst towards the surface. Smaller ones from the men followed as the bitter cold salt water claimed each life. The fish-boat tumbled along the bottom until the last of her buoyancy escaped from her. She came to rest among the sand dollars and sea urchins.

HER PLACE IN HISTORY

Fish and crabs moved in and out of the hulk eating the remains of the life she had once held. Men came out in small boats and dragged around the wrecked warship, searching for the submarine, and failed to find it.

Within days it was almost buried. Only one side remained exposed, the other being buried in a huge drift. She formed a silent ledge on the otherwise flat ocean floor. She spoke to no one of her presence. Her location was lost. The seeds of history had been planted.

She was the first submarine in all of time to actually sink an enemy ship.

RETURN TO REALITY

My mind raced forward a century, I thought of the countless days spent in libraries and archives pouring over musty newspapers and reading through seemingly endless rolls of microfilmed documents. Pages of notes, diagrams, maps, charts, and dreams were recalled.

Now, I had found her. I wanted to stay there forever to savor my find. But adrenaline pumped through my veins. The fear of my surroundings and the exhilarating feeling of discovery would not allow me to wait.

Ignoring safety rules, all else forgotten, I soared to the surface screaming: "The *Hunley*! The *Hunley*! I've found the *Hunley*!"

WHAT IT MEANS

If I am right, and I am fully convinced that I am, the "ledge" that I found was the rusting remains of the first successful submarine. The Confederate submarine *H.L. Hunley* has long been recognized as the greatest technological innovation in naval warfare in over two thousand years. Her discovery would be of major importance. I had felt history come alive as I touched the wreckage.

HOW IT CAME ABOUT

My initial discovery was made in November of 1970. Although I had spent many weeks searching for the wreck with sophisticated electronic equipment, this trip had been to fish for sea bass, not shipwrecks. I was diving from the fishing vessel *Miss Inah*, captained by Joe Porcelli. The actual discovery was serendipity, Porcelli having hung up two fish traps on the bottom,

Chapter Two: "The First Successful Submarine"
Page 42

and I having gone down to retrieve it. It was only by chance that one was caught on the ledge, but it was the research I had done that made me recognize it.

WHAT I DID NEXT

Within days I notified the state archeologist that I thought I had found the *Hunley*. But, not wanting him to make any announcements until I had verified my find, I carefully worded my report in a discouraging manner. I truthfully pointed out that what I found was smaller than what one have expected from the history books, but I left out the details that might have excited him as they did me. I warned him against premature action. With the wording couched in such negative terms, I knew he would not immediately try to take credit for my discovery, and I hoped that he would not try to hinder me from working, as he had done on other sites.

Unfortunately, it only worked part way. The State Archeologist didn't jump my claim, but he still did everything he could to block my work. He wasn't a diver and didn't understand that we were both trying to save history.

In the years that have since slipped by I have been refused permits, and I have been threatened with arrest if I continued my work on the site. To prove to the world that what I found is indeed the tiny sub, I would be risking going to jail.

AFTER THE DISCOVERY

In 1971 I contacted friends in Florida and borrowed a proton magnetometer from friends working with Real Eight Inc. in Satellite Beach, Florida. The magnetometer helped me find wreckage I later positively identified as part of the *Housatonic*.

The wreckage, by calculations I made years later, was off only fifty feet by latitude and eight hundred and fifty-seven feet by longitude from the surveyed position of the wreckage of the *Housatonic* as recorded on a hand drawn chart prepared by the United States government in 1865. The *Housatonic's* wreckage had actually been used as bench mark in the resurveying of the approaches to Charleston Harbor after the war.

Since our method of determining latitude has remained the same and the *Housatonic* was a relatively large vessel an error of fifty feet in latitude is not necessarily an error at all, but just a reading taken on a different piece of her wreckage.

Further checking of the hand drawn chart showed that the northeast corner of Fort Sumter was also shown almost nine hundred feet off in longitude from its position. Fort Sumter hasn't moved. So the difference was an error made during the original survey.

Such an error in longitude is easily explained. The method of determining longitude involves calculating the difference in solar time for a given point and time at Greenwich, England. Eight hundred and fifty-seven feet would be a time keeping error of less than two thirds of a second. In fact, government surveys around the turn of the century later found and corrected the error which was uniform throughout the entire chart.

FEDERAL COURT

On July 7, 1981, I filed papers in Federal Court asking that my title to the "unidentified, wrecked and abandoned vessel or vessels, (believed to be the Steamer *Housatonic* and/or the Submarine *H.L. Hunley*, both sunk in 1864) her tackle, armament, apparel and cargo" be confirmed "against all claimants and all the world," or that I be awarded a "full and liberal salvage award."

The center point of my claim was purposefully offset from the earlier mentioned piece of the *Housatonic's* wreckage for confidentiality purposes, and to insure that my area included other pieces of associated wreckage.

PUBLIC REACTION

Upon the announcement of my filing papers in Federal court for title to the wreckage, some people were surprised that I had let so many years lapse before "announcing" or doing anything about my discovery.

The fact is, I had discussed my findings in a number of newspaper and radio interviews over the intervening years. I had even mentioned the discovery in a book I published in 1976, and discussed it further in a major article I wrote for a special issue of *Argosy* magazine about the same time. Furthermore, I had not sat back and done nothing. I had continued my research to verify my discovery, making additional trips to Washington.

It was on one such trip that I had located the hand drawn chart showing the surveyed position of the *Housatonic*. That trip took place in May of 1981 and the chart was the strongest historical evidence to back up my identification of that wreck to date.

The chart was not housed in the national archives as one might have supposed, so I had not located it on earlier trips even though I had long since suspected its existence.

During the same time period, I had been out to the wreck site numerous times in an effort to pinpoint various pieces of wreckage. In fact, I had located quite a few. On one such trip, my dive tender, Jack Parker of Sullivan's Island, saved my life when I drifted away from the boat and was almost lost in rough seas. Two boats overturned in unrelated accidents in more protected waters that same day, and three people were drowned.

HELP AND HINDRANCE

Mike Douglas and David McGeehee both of Warrington, Florida, had helped me search for the *Hunley* the summer before I actually found her, but the equipment simply wasn't up to the job. Other people that made trips out to the site to help me over the years were Kevin Rooney of Luddington, Michigan; Walter O'Neal junior and senior of Belhaven, North Carolina; Randy Lathrop and Jim Ryan then of Cocoa, Florida; John Christian of Norfolk, Virginia; Bruce Cannon of Mount Pleasant, South Carolina; my father, Dr. Judson C. Spence Sr., and my brother Pat, both of Sullivan's Island. Joe Porcelli and Troy Clanton both of Charleston had been with me on that very first day.

Walter O'Neal Senior provided use of his eighty-five foot shrimp trawler and was slightly injured when we snagged one piece of wreckage and a cable snapped and cut his hand.

I again made my discovery public in my books and magazine articles and with press releases and interviews.

Over the years I made various offers to raise the wreckage and donate it to the Smithsonian or to the Naval Museum at Patriots Point in Charleston. Senators Strom Thurmond and Fritz Hollings lent their support in trying to help get the General Services Administration to issue Sea Research Society (a non-profit organization which I then headed) a license to raise the wreckage.

I also received letters of support from Joseph P. Riley Sr., Mayor Palmer T. Gilliard, and other prominent and distinguished persons from South Carolina. I even received letters from George Wallace then governor of Alabama, who told me of Alabama's plans to make the building where the *Hunley* was built in Mobile, Alabama, into a museum for the then upcoming Bicentennial celebrations. All of this took place in the years between 1970 and 1979.

George Fisher, an underwater archeologist for the National Park Service, although a friend of mine, informed me that if I tried to raise the vessel without a license that the Park Service would take the vessel from me and that I might even face arrest.

Finally, clearances were received from the Navy and the Army Corps of Engineers to conduct the work, and on March 28, 1974, Sea Research Society, a non-profit organization which I then directed, paid the General Services Administration a two hundred and fifty dollars license fee to work the site.

In 1975 the General Services Administration (in response to my inquiries as to why they had not yet issued the actual license) told me that they intended to place the *Hunley* on the National Register of Historic Places and that they had to develop standards by which the work would need to be done, before they could issue the license.

I don't believe that the site ever actually was put on the list, but its very consideration was definitely used it as another reason to delay my return to the site.

The actual license was never issued by the General Services Administration and the fee paid by Sea Research Society was eventually refunded.

FEDERAL ADMIRALTY COURT

In the same year (1975) Mel Fisher filed motions in Federal court claiming title to the wreckage of the *Atocha* off Florida. In 1978 the court ruled against the state of Florida and against the Federal government (both of whom had tried to claim title to the treasure and wreckage discovered by Fisher) and upheld Fisher's claim to ownership of the wreckage.

Encouraged by that ruling, I contacted attorney George Sink in Charleston and began discussing with him the possibility of my filing papers in Federal court to claim title to the wreckage of both the *Hunley* and the *Housatonic*. Attorneys Robert V. DeMarco of Charleston and David P. Horan of Key West were then enlisted to prepare a case to fight for my rights to the wreckage I had discovered. Horan had been Fisher's lawyer, so I felt like I had a winning team.

Although served with copies of the papers I had filed on July 7, 1981, with the Federal District court, the State of South Carolina did not attempt to make any claim against the wreckage which lays just outside of their three nautical mile belt of jurisdiction. It surprised me because I had been told by the State Underwater Archeologist that it was within their jurisdiction and that I would be arrested if I worked the site without their permission.

The Federal government sent lawyers from Washington to argue that the court and the Federal Marshals had no authority on a wreck over three miles from shore.

The Federal judge said that if I could bring the wreck within his jurisdiction he would grant my request to be made custodian of the wreckage until my claim to title was settled.

BACK TO COURT?

It was a "Catch 22" type situation. I was unable to work without being made custodian of the wrecks, and the court wouldn't make me custodian, unless I could bring the wreck into the court's jurisdiction. It seemed to kill my dreams of ever raising the *Hunley*.

But, a 1989 ruling by the Federal Court in Norfolk, Virginia, relative to the wreck of the *Central America* seems to have settled the question as to whether the court has jurisdiction outside of the three mile limit, as that court took jurisdiction even though the wreck was two hundred miles from shore. The court ruled in favor of the original discoverers.

Assuming that no one else finds it first, I will probably once again re-buoy the wreckage and go back to court and, using the court's recent decisions and expanded jurisdiction, and again claim title to all of the wreckage that I have discovered.

125TH ANNIVERSARY

February 17, 1989, was the 125th anniversary of the sinking of the *Housatonic* by the *Hunley*.

The anniversary was officially observed by Civil War, historians, students and scholars that gathered in Mobile, Alabama, the city where the *Hunley* was built.

I was one of three featured speakers at the commemorative dinner ceremonies that were held at the Radisson Admiral Semmes Hotel, in Mobile. Without giving the specific location, I presented the case for my identification of the wreckage. It was well received and most people were in agreement with my conclusions.

The other two speakers were John T. Hunley, of New Orleans, who spoke of his ongoing search for another of Captain Horace Lawson Hunley's tiny submarines, and James E. Kloeppel, author of *Danger Beneath the Waves: A History of the Confederate Submarine H.L. Hunley*, who spoke about the findings of the official court of inquiry held immediately after the sinking. Kloeppel holds to the belief that the *Hunley* survived the actual sinking of the *Housatonic* and was lost while attempting to return to shore. He bases that on report of colored signals lights observed after the sinking. He thinks the lights were from the *Hunley*, I believe they were simply lights or signals between the Federal ships and picket boats attempting to search for and find the *Hunley*.

NATIONAL GEOGRAPHIC

In October of 1989, I sought the help of Mike Freeman, a long time friend who owns American Watersports in Camp Springs, Maryland. I asked Freeman if he wanted to help me with an expedition I was planning. I wanted to return to the wreckage I had tentatively identified as the *Hunley* in hopes of making a positive identification. I also wanted to conduct some additional archeological investigation of the *Housatonic*.

Freeman agreed to contact some of his friends and associates at *National Geographic Magazine* in an effort to get the National Geographic Society to fund the expedition.

Mike told me that Al Chandler of National Geographic was excited about doing the project. Freeman and I later met with officials from National Geographic, and I explained (in detail) my theories and discoveries.

At one meeting, I turned over some of my confidential notes and records (including a photostat of a hand drawn chart, prepared in 1865, which showed a surveyed position for the wreck of the *Housatonic*) giving specific loran coordinates to National Geographic Editor Bill Graves.

We all shook hands and set a date (February 17, 1990) to begin the *"Hunley* Expedition." Our plan was to use a ground penetrating radar pioneered by National Geographic staffer Pete Petrone. However, due to a series of unforeseen circumstances, the start of the expedition was delayed. Had the expedition taken place as scheduled, we would have dedicated it to Al Chandler who died during the early planning of the expedition.

In 1992, after having waited for two more years, I was finally informed that National Geographic Society was no longer interested in pursuing the *Hunley*. My confidential annotated charts were finally returned to me in September of 1994. I am still missing some of my notes.

ONE AUTHOR'S FICTION

A certain author of adventure fiction, has made three trips to Charleston in search of the *Hunley*. I am purposefully not mentioning his name as I wish him no ill will, and certainly don't want to cause him any unnecessary embarrassment. His first *Hunley* expedition started shortly after I filed the aforementioned papers with the Federal court. On his arrival in Charleston, he called me and asked if we could meet. Before his call, I had never heard of him, but I politely agreed to meet.

At that meeting, I learned that an acquaintance, who had called me months before, was actually working for the author as a researcher. Although I had not given the researcher the exact position, I had unwisely explained the proof behind my discoveries. To a competent person, such explanation would be invaluable.

I found this particular novelist to be an interesting and extremely likable fellow, but it was obvious that his adventures were largely on paper. I felt he lacked the knowledge or skills to actually discover a shipwreck on his own. My impression was he was sincerely interested in history, but that he was also after publicity.

The "Real Rhett Butler" & Other Revelations

Since I had already filed papers in Federal court, I went ahead and discussed my discovery of the *Hunley* with him in detail. Realizing that his name and wealth had the ability to impress some people and thus open some doors in the government, I spent quite a few hours negotiating with his lawyer trying to work out a deal whereby we could do a joint venture on the *Hunley*. No agreement was reached between us on the sub.

The novelist was conducting his search under a permit granted to a non-profit company named for a fictional government agency in his novels. I am sure many people believe it is a real agency of the government. It isn't.

Due to insufficient pre-expedition research, his first expedition failed to find either the sub or her victim. However, he did claim to have discovered the blockade runner *Stonewall Jackson*, which I had located and identified many years before. My company's discovery of the *Stonewall Jackson*, the *Norseman*, the *Constance*, the *Georgiana*, and the *Mary Bowers*, had been reported in the Charleston *News & Courier* way back in the summer of 1969.

His claim of discovery of the *Stonewall Jackson*, which is now buried under the dunes of the Isle of Palms, was especially amusing. In the grand style of the great P.T. Barnum, he had the press out in force to observe the discovery.

He had a back-hoe digging a giant hole in the beach. His people were swinging hand held magnetometers over the excavation and were incorrectly explaining to an eager press that their equipment was detecting the wreck. It certainly appeared scientific, but it was a farce. Either it was a public relations stunt or he and his crew were ignorant of the fact that magnetometers are not really metal detectors. Magnetometers simply react to variations in the earth's magnetic field, even an empty hole can be detected. In reality, they had dug a hole, then they had found it. Their discovery was literally "nothing."

The only archeological "evidence" of a shipwreck was a tiny piece of coal, and a small piece of wood which bore no sign of being anything other than driftwood. I personally think it would be extremely difficult to dig an equivalent hole anywhere on the entire Isle of Palms beach and find less evidence of a shipwreck. To claim the discovery of an 874 ton, iron hulled steamer on such flimsy "evidence" is absolutely laughable. In truth, they were digging within a couple hundred feet of the buried steamer, but since I had mentioned the wreck's location to him at our previous meeting, and he had also talked with one of my ex-partners, I am not surprised that he was that close.

Treasures of the Confederate Coast

One other funny thing about that "discovery." When I saw all the commotion on the beach and stopped to ask what was up, I was told that he had discovered the *Norseman*. Not wanting to embarrass the man in front of his admirers, I immediately whispered that was impossible, as that blockade runner is over two miles down the beach, and it is well offshore. Anyway, I understand how he could have made the mistake. I had told him about both ships during the same conversation.

As might have been expected, he also made several other equally extravagent claims, including the statement on television that his divers had "strode the decks" of the United States ironclad steamer *Weehawken*, which he described as "in perfect condition," yet, in reality, was heavily scrapped in the 1870's. One might assume that he was simply trying to gain credibility for a movie which was about to be released. The movie was based on one of his novels, and involved the raising of a very famous shipwreck. I have heard that the movie was quite enjoyable.

I did not get together with him during his second expedition. It is my understanding that, during that expedition, his people finally located the remains of the *Housatonic*. The wreck was exactly where I had reported it. My only surprise was that he didn't find the *Hunley*. Although I could easily be wrong, I suspect that his people, using a proton magnetometer, detected the now buried sub, but due to its size being smaller than might be expected from the history books, failed to recognize it for what it was.

The results of that author's 1994 expedition have yet to be announced, but I know of no reason, other than general bad luck for why they would not have found the tiny sub. I do know that on each expedition, he has had some extremely fine and competent people helping him.

The only reason that I have gone into such detail about this particular author's expeditions, is that many people might are only hearing his side of the story. I know that some will side with him because he is a famous novelist. Others won't stop to examine the facts. Many will incorrectly think I am a claim jumper and a glory hound. His supporters will believe that I am an interloper. I am not. All I ask is that people remember that he makes his living writing fiction (and he is excellent at it), while I make my living researching and uncovering the truth.

FINAL NOTE

Despite the immense frustration resulting from twenty-four years of seemingly endless red tape, outright government interference, and the relatively minor irritation caused by the aforementioned novelist and his entourage (many of whom are extremely fine people), I have not given up on the *Hunley.*

In fact, I recently offered my support to Mark K. Ragan of Bethesda, Maryland, who is attempting to get a historical marker, telling of the *Hunley,* placed at Breach Inlet. Ragan's historical research on the tiny sub actually far surpasses my own, and I have no doubt that he will soon come out with the definitive book on the *Hunley.* Ragan actually built his own experimental sub and tested it in the back waters of Breach Inlet, so he could better understand the experiences of *Hunley's* crew. He has also searched for both wrecks with a magnetometer, but I do not know what he found. With all of that in mind, I both admire and applaud him.

Regardless of who does it, I would very much like to see the historic submarine raised for posterity, and I firmly believe that, like the South, the *Hunley* shall indeed rise again.   • • •

Both hand held metal detectors and boat towed magnetometers were used in my work relative to the Housatonic and Hunley. Photo by Myrna Rowland

Chapter Two: "The First Sucessful Submarine"

Section of a hand drawn 1865 chart which I used to prove that I had indeed found the Housatonic. Although I knew of the chart's existence through my research, it was not in the National Archives, and it took me years to finally locate it.

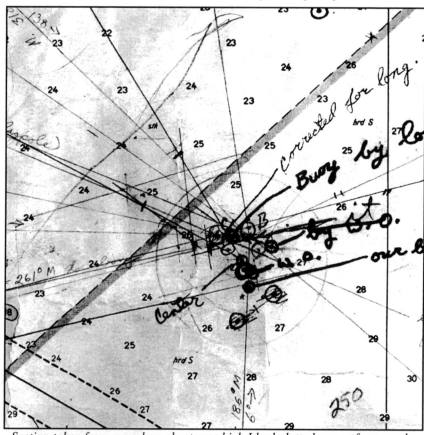

Section taken from a modern chart on which I had plotted some of my work.

Chapter Two: "The First Sucessful Submarine"

The location of the Housatonic is shown off Sullivan's Island, and near the lower edge of this chart.

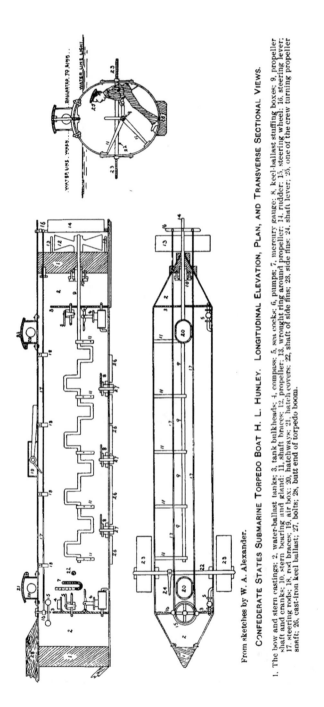

From sketches by W. A. Alexander.

CONFEDERATE STATES SUBMARINE TORPEDO BOAT H. L. HUNLEY. LONGITUDINAL ELEVATION, PLAN, AND TRANSVERSE SECTIONAL VIEWS.

1. The bow and stern castings; 2, water-ballast tanks; 3, tank bulkheads; 4, compass; 5, sea cocks; 6, pumps; 7, mercury gauge; 8, keel-ballast stuffing boxes; 9, propeller shaft and cranks; 10, stern bearing and gland; 11, shaft braces; 12, propeller; 13, wrought ring around propeller; 14, rudder; 15, steering wheel; 16, steering lever; 17, steering rods; 18, rod braces; 19, air box; 20, hatchways; 21, hatch covers; 22, shaft of side fins; 23, side fins; 24, shaft lever; 25, one of the crew turning propeller shaft; 26, cast-iron keel ballast; 27, bolts; 28, butt end of torpedo boom.

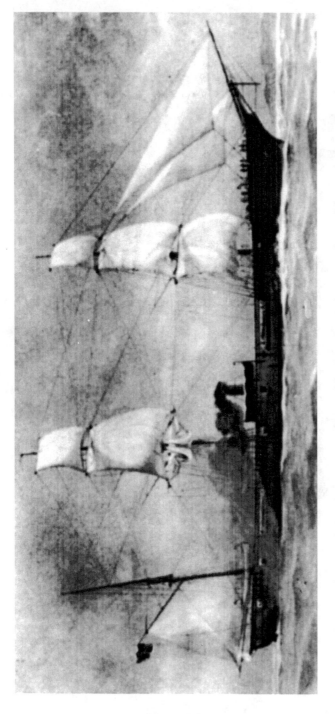

The United States sloop of war Housatonic was the first ship in history to be sunk by an enemy submarine. Illustration from the "Official Records of the War of the Rebellion, Union & Confederate Navies."

This picture was taken of Ron Gibbs and me aboard the fishing vessel Carol El, Captain Wally Shaffer, after my second dive on the Georgiana. Note the stacks of dinner plates and broken jars in front of our feet. Virtually all of the artifacts recovered that day were retrieved from underneath the wreck of the Mary Bowers. Ron (to the viewer's left) is now deceased. He was a very close friend and was then with the National Park Service. 1967 photo by Pat Gibbs.

CHAPTER THREE
"The Mystery Ship of the Confederacy"
(S.S. Georgiana)

THE DISCOVERY

The wind was blowing hard from the east, bringing warm, clear, blue water in from the Gulf Stream. Portuguese man-of-war jellyfish and clumps of Sargasso seaweed floated over the huge waves. The shrimp boat lurched on its anchor line in the shallow water.

I climbed awkwardly over the side and dropped into the trough of a wave. I swam down past the few remaining deck supports into the shattered cargo hold. Encrusted artifacts lay everywhere.

A pile of almost indistinguishable cannon balls lay near two rows of blue edged dinner plates. The plates were heavily encrusted with surface coral and sea worms. I picked up a cylindrical shaped object that was protruding from the sand. I scraped away the thick marine growth. It was a clay beer bottle still corked and sealed. It dated from the 1860's, time of the "Late War of Northern Aggression."

I screamed with joy, my bubbles scattering some of the fish that had clustered around me. I was definitely on the wreck I wanted. I had discovered the resting place of the armed blockade runner *Georgiana*, "mystery ship of the Confederacy." I was 19 years old and the discovery was a dream come true. I had been researching her for seven years and it was definitely a special moment.

THE BEAUTY OF THE WRECK

The sunlight reflected brightly on the sand. Purple sea urchins crawled slowly over the wreckage, which was colorfully decorated with patches of coral, sea whips, sea anemones and sponges. I was in a visual paradise. There was an abundance of sea bass, grouper, sheepshead and flounder.

SPECIAL TREASURE

The treasure I sought was not only gold, but history. The *Georgiana* was the most powerful Confederate cruiser ever built. The *Georgiana's* loss on March 19, 1863, in fourteen feet of water off of the Isle of Palms, South Carolina, was a serious blow to the Confederacy. Built in Great Britain, the steamer had been lost on its maiden voyage with a contraband cargo consisting of hundreds of tons of assorted merchandise, munitions and medicines which, even then, was valued at over a million of dollars.

The cargo was reported to have been owned by John Fraser & Company, a Charleston based blockade running firm, that acted as a conduit for Confederate funds and supplies. The company was headed by a tall handsome Charlestonian, named George Alfred Trenholm. Trenholm was the richest man in the South and through subsequent research, I discovered that Trenholm was the primary historical basis for Margaret Mitchell's "fictional" blockade runner Captain Rhett Butler in *Gone With The Wind.*

THE DAY AFTER THE DISCOVERY

It didn't bother me when I returned the following day and learned that the crystal clear waters had been a once-in-a-decade occurrence for that area.

The wind howled from the north. The now icy waters churned dark and foreboding. Mud swirled around the wreck, boiling to the surface in a brown plume. I bumped or rather was slammed into one piece of wreckage after another. Suddenly I no longer thought that sea urchins were quaint as I felt a dozen sharp spines sink into my hand. I groped blindly. My hand closed around an eel. I jerked my arm back in momentary terror. It was all I could do to conquer my fears.

I slowly reached out again. This time I felt a storage jar. Visions of Cousteau filling amphorae with air and floating them to the surface in the clear waters of the Mediterranean raced through my head. I pushed my regulator into the mouth of the large clay urn, feeling something give as I did it. By purging my regulator I filled the jar and prepared to float to the surface. I would look like a hero returning with his prize. As I closed my lips around the mouthpiece I gagged and vomited, letting the urn make its own unescorted way to the surface. I wasn't a hero. The solid I had hit with my regulator was a large cork. I had unwittingly pushed the cork down into the jar which still contained medicine. Unfortunately, the contents hadn't aged well during the past century. It was extremely foul tasting, and a lesson I wouldn't forget.

The next jar (and there were dozens) had already lost its cork and I pulled it from the sucking mud with a short lived glow of triumph. This one was inhabited by a very large and obnoxious toad-fish which decided that my fingers were the day's chow. A blinding flash of pain had me temporarily convinced that my fingers were gone, but they remained. The toad-fish, like countless of his evil looking brothers, ended up being brutally hacked to death with an archeologist's pick.

The "Real Rhett Butler" & Other Revelations

EARLY AMBITION

My involvement with the *Georgiana* goes back to when I was twelve years old. I was living in France and had just read Captain Cousteau's book *La Monde du Silence* (*The Silent World*) and had decided I wanted to be a diver, or to be more precise, an underwater archeologist. I wanted to find shipwrecks, but first I had to learn about them.

RESEARCHING *GEORGIANA'S* STORY

A friend told me that I ought to look at government records at the American school library. He said I would find what I needed among the red tape that even our ancestors had to face. The librarian showed me a set of books printed by the government in the late 1800's. The books were a verbatim compilation of some of the Civil War records stored by the National Archives. The set had the awesome title of *The Official Records of the Union and Confederate Armies in the War of the Rebellion*. There was a separate series of books for Naval records. The librarian simply called them the "O.R." The entire set contained over 160,000 pages of text, sketches, maps and photos. The books were inadequately indexed with absolutely nothing cataloged under "wrecks" or "shipwrecks," but I eventually managed to locate a tremendous amount of valuable information.

One wreck in particular caught my fancy. It was the wreck of the *Georgiana*. I decided to research and locate her. I didn't worry with the little details, like the fact that the *Georgiana* had sunk over a thousand miles from where we were then living, or that I was only a kid and with no boat and no way to get there. We had family ties to Charleston, and I knew, that when my father finally retired from the Army, our family would return to Charleston. It did not occur to me to worry about whether or not the *Georgiana* had already been found and salvaged. Instead, I plunged head first into my project with the absolute devotion only a youngster can muster. My friends called me a bookworm and regarded me as some sort of a nut as I began to spend my hours reading musty reports and records.

In the "O.R." I found day by day, minute by minute, accounts of virtually every event that had taken place during the war. These books were simply the tip of the iceberg of red tape I had been told about. I copied down every mention of the *Georgiana*. I examined each report for clues. One report mentioned a letter from the United States Consul in Glasgow where the ship was built. I remembered seeing a box of microfilm titled "Consular Dispatches" on one of the other shelves in the library. I relocated it and found a

Treasures of the Confederate Coast

separate roll of film for Glasgow, Scotland. I put it on the microfilm reader and started scanning until I found the year I wanted. I poured over the barely legible handwriting looking for mentions of the *Georgiana*. Instead, I found detailed reports on a ship called the *Louisiana*. The United States Consul at Glasgow had watched her during the entire course of her construction, but had been unable to find anyone who had signed on as a crew member. The Consul was convinced from her name and appearance that the vessel was being built as a Confederate cruiser. Under international law it was illegal for a neutral country like Great Britain to allow a belligerent to construct a warship. But more evidence was needed before the United States government representatives could approach the British authorities and demand they inspect the steamer and stop her from sailing. The American Consul had to find people who would swear that they had been hired to fight as crew aboard the vessel.

There was virtually nothing in the early dispatches about the *Georgiana*. The Consul simply reported rumors about her. The American Consul could not locate the shipyard where she was being constructed. It seemed the *Georgiana* was some sort of a ghost ship. Men were being hired to man her, but no one had actually seen her. One man hired to sail on the "mystery ship" had even been a gunner in the Crimean War.

The Consul pieced the puzzle together a little too late. By the time the Consul realized the *Georgiana* and the *Louisiana* were one and the same, it was too late to organize a successful effort to stop the vessel from sailing. The Consul made a last ditch effort to get the steamer condemned by the Liverpool police, but failed when the detectives sent to inspect her turned out to be Confederate sympathizers. The detectives swore the *Georgiana* was not designed for fighting and said she was so lightly built that "she would shake from stem to stern if a gun were fired from her decks". The report gave the ship's crew a day's grace, as it was Saturday and no other evidence could be gathered until the custom's office opened on Monday morning. The *Georgiana* wisely sailed with the tide on Sunday.

Upon learning this, I immediately wrote the Liverpool Police Department requesting a search of their files for any reports they might still have. Someone at the police department wrote back giving me such data as the middle name and birthplace of the captain, things that even his best friend probably hadn't known when he was alive. It seems "big Brother" was watching even then. My friend had certainly been right about the red tape being helpful. It seemed that the only reports not filed in duplicate were those filed in triplicate, and most of them had survived. I also learned that we get the term red tape from the red cloth ribbon that was used by government officials to tie up bundles of documents. I was finding a wealth of data.

The government records and hangs onto everything. The trick is to know what information to ask for and where to write for it. Fortunately, I found people who knew and were willing to help me.

The registrar of ships at the Customs Office in Glasgow searched his records for me and came up with the *Georgiana's* measurements and a few other choice morsels. "Lloyd's of London" had rated her as A-1 for insurance purposes and had also confirmed certain details as to her size and construction. Contacting the public libraries in Liverpool proved to be another good source. One librarian dug out newspaper accounts describing the *Georgiana* as pierced for fourteen guns with a partial crew of over one hundred and forty men, which if true, would have meant she was almost twice as powerful as the *Alabama*, the most famous commerce destroyer of them all. Every new report brought new answers, new questions and dozens of clues. Various reports stated that the ship's officers wore the gold braid of the Confederate Navy and when she arrived at Liverpool she was flying the "Rebel" flag. The *Georgiana* was said to have been a "very superior steamer", with her top speed described anywhere from 14 to 19 knots. The vessel's long, low, black, lap strake hull was built of iron. The steamer had heavily raked masts and was brig rigged. The *Georgiana's* hull, bowsprit, jib-boom and smokestack were all painted black. The *Georgiana's* clipper bow sported the figurehead bust of a woman. The figurehead, the poop deck and the iron rails around the poop deck were all painted white. The ship's name was blazoned in carved gilt letters on her round stern.

I checked dispatches and customs records from the various ports at which the *Georgiana* stopped to take on coal and supplies. Various reports showed the steamer posing as a privately armed merchant vessel, a British man-of-war, and even as a warship built for the Emperor of China. One thing became clear, the ship and her crew were intent on entering the privateering trade. But first the ship had to run into a port where her crew could take time to properly mount her guns.

THE *GEORGIANA'S* ARMAMENT

Only two guns were mounted on the steamer's decks, and they were not yet fully serviceable. The *Georgiana's* other guns were still sitting in her cargo holds. The only ports where the raider could finish mounting her armament unmolested were in the South. Union spies cabled secret messages advising the South Atlantic Blockading Squadron that the *Georgiana* was on her way to Charleston, South Carolina. Besides her own armament, the steamer may have carried up to five hundred and eighty tons of valuable cargo. The *Georgiana's* contraband cargo was made up of rifles; musket balls; two, state of the art Whitworth breech loading cannon, four Blakely rifled cannon, medicines, liquor, china and other assorted merchandise.

GOLD ON THE *GEORGIANA*

The *Georgiana* also carried ninety thousand dollars in the form of over three hundred and seventy-five pounds of gold coins for payment of her officers and crew, modifications, supplies, etc. The bullion value of the coins would be worth around two million dollars today. The numismatic value could exceed fifteen million dollars.

THE *GEORGIANA'S* DESTRUCTION

Gleaning bits and pieces from the "O.R.", from contemporary Southern and Northern newspapers, and from other sources, I put together the following story of the *Georgiana's* last hours.

Not realizing that her destination and expected time of arrival were already known to the entire blockading squadron, the *Georgiana's* crew left Nassau confident of a safe and successful voyage.

The ship's master was a retired British naval officer by the name of A.B. Davidson (also shown as Dickenson). An experienced captain, Davidson had already taken other ships safely through the thin, but deadly, line of Northern warships. The *Georgiana's* captain hoped that the ship would not even be seen as she ran under the cover of darkness. Arriving off Dewees Inlet, to the north of Charleston Harbor, just before 1:00 a.m., March 19, 1863, Captain Davidson, successfully evaded a schooner and a steamer patrolling near the inlet, then turned the *Georgiana* down the unmarked channel which ran along the present-day Isle of Palms, South Carolina.

The virtually unarmed steamer had already safely traveled over four thousand miles and was only ten miles from the Confederate forts and safety. The *Georgiana* had barely made the turn into the channel when the smoke billowing from her stack was spotted by a lookout aboard the United States armed yacht *America* (namesake of the "*America's* Cup" of sailboat racing fame). The *America* immediately fired at the *Georgiana* with her 24-pounder

Dahlgren boat howitzers, slipped anchor to give chase, and sent up colored signal flares to alert the fleet.

The *Georgiana* had fallen victim to a bureaucratic economy move. The engines were burning cheap bituminous coal rather than the more expensive, almost smokeless, anthracite coal, which Captain Davidson had wanted to carry.

Not giving up, the *Georgiana* steamed onwards, hoping her speed could help her elude the heavily armed, but slower, ships of the South Atlantic Blockading Squadron. The United States steamer *Wissahicken*, flagship of the fleet, came into view and swung alongside of the *Georgiana*. The men aboard the cruiser heard the orders being given aboard the Federal ship. The Confederates could do nothing when they heard the Yankee captain yell which way to trail the big guns and when to fire. Solid shot, ten inches in diameter, passed through one side and out the other, leaving jagged holes in the Rebel steamer's iron hull.

Captain Davidson ordered the steam release valves tied down in an effort to increase boiler pressure and thereby added a couple extra knots of speed. The ship's boiler was dangerously overloaded. It was almost a suicidal effort, but it was hope. The *Georgiana* moved on, increasing her distance from the *Wissahicken*. She was escaping. The *Wissahicken* was now joined by the *Housatonic* (later to become the first ship in history to be sunk by a submarine) and a half dozen other gunboats.

Ahead lay the rest of the fleet of monitors, gunboats and picket boats. Many were already moving in to cut off the *Georgiana's* entrance to the harbor. So far, the Confederate ship had managed to survive a half hour of hell. The *Georgiana's* men, frustrated by the impracticality of trying to stand and fight back, fired a few token rounds, and cursed the laws that had kept the remainder of her guns from already being fully mounted. Speed was the hunted ship's only hope. As the distance slowly widened between the fox and the hounds, the *Wissahicken* fired a lucky shot, striking the *Georgiana* with an exploding shell under her stern. The *Georgiana* was crippled.

The *Georgiana* limped to a stand-still. The crew shut down the steamer's engines and the smoke ceased to belch forth. Someone showed a white light.

Unknown to the Yankees, Captain Davidson was baiting them. The Yankees interpreted the white light as a sign of surrender. The *Wissahicken's* crew cheered and lowered boarding parties to take their prize. The longboats rowed up to the steamer only to be met by a hail of small arms fire as the *Georgiana* suddenly plowed forward at full speed. The *Georgiana's* wily captain had not quenched her fires as it had first appeared. The Confederates had merely diverted the thick smoke into the cargo holds. Davidson had waited until the last possible second and had thrown the *Georgiana's* engines back in gear with a full head of steam. The gunboats could not resume fire for fear of hitting their own men.

Knowing the crippled *Georgiana* had no real way to escape and unwilling to abandon their men in the darkness, the Union ships paused to pick up their boats. Delayed by the ruse, which they considered "the most consummate treachery," the Federal sailors watched as the *Georgiana* disappeared into the darkness. As soon as she was out of sight, Captain Davidson turned and headed the *Georgiana* towards shore. The *Georgiana's* captain realized the crippled steamer could never make the safety of Charleston Harbor, but he hoped he could somehow prevent her and her valuable cargo from falling into Federal hands. The tide was low and the steamer ran aground in 14 feet of water, one mile from the beach and three and a half miles from Breach Inlet.

Captain Davidson immediately had the *Georgiana's* pipes cut to flood her. Then, as an extra precaution, the crew smashed the ship's pumps and doused her engine fires. The ship's boatswain (bo's'n) ordered the crew to lower the *Georgiana's* longboats and abandon ship. The captain, still fearing capture, weighted the ship's logbook and register and threw them overboard along with the secret dispatches he was carrying. Leaving a white light burning from a mast, the crew sadly rowed to shore. A dream had been shattered. It was not recorded whether the *Georgiana's* men were able to save the gold, which may have been hidden beneath heavy cargo.

The Federal ships again caught up with the *Georgiana*. This time the Union sailors held back, waiting to see if the Confederate ship was again playing possum. The Federals didn't suspect that the beautiful ship had already been abandoned, or that she was rapidly filling with water.

The Federal boarding party found a deserted ship, still loaded with hundreds of tons of valuable cargo. The steamer was already filled with water and it was impossible to tow her off. Knowing that they would have to destroy the ship to prevent her recapture, the Federal sailors raced through her grabbing anything they could carry with them.

THE PRIZE

Somehow the sailors managed to locate the ship's liquor. The life of a Federal sailor was hard at its best and the temptation of the liquor was great and some of the sailors quickly guzzled what they could. Setting fire to the iron hulled steamer's wooden decks, the Yankee sailors returned to their ship. Seven of the sailors were immediately confined in irons by their own captain for being drunk and disorderly. The ship burned and blew up for three days. Both sides periodically shelled the wreck to keep the other side away. Besides the liquor, the only items reported as recovered were eight Enfield rifles, nine bayonets, eight battle axes, one patent lead and line, ten pounds of glue, five small jars of preserves, twelve gilt buttons, one table cloth, and nineteen sabers.

THE AFTERMATH

There would be no prize money for the Federal sailors to share, but they had managed to stop the *Georgiana*. The ship was no ordinary blockade runner. The *Georgiana* had been the finest Confederate privateer ever built, but now she would never go sailing in search of unarmed merchantmen. The Rebel steamer would never loot the ships of the United States merchant fleet of their precious cargoes, burn them or sink them. The Union had sunk what they called a pirate, and the entire Federal blockade fleet had reason to celebrate. United States Secretary of Navy, Gideon Welles, wrote to Rear-Admiral Samuel F. Du Pont, Commanding the United States South Atlantic Blockading Squadron, and said "the destruction of the *Georgiana* not only touched their pockets, but their hopes. She was a splendid craft, peculiarly fitted for the business of privateering." The *Georgiana* was a beautiful and very expensive steamer and the South needed her as well as her cargo. The loss of the steamer's cargo meant that ten thousand soldiers would go without new guns, and there was no hope that the South could ever build another ship like her.

No wartime government likes to admit their own losses (probably due to a fear that it might create a defeatist attitude), so the *Georgiana's* loss was barely mentioned in the Confederate papers. The articles didn't mention the *Georgiana's* gold or that she may have been anything other than a merchant ship.

THE *GEORGIANA'S* FIRST VICTIM

The *Georgiana's* story wasn't over. The ghost ship was destined to sink three ships. Unfortunately, for the South, all of them were blockade runners. The *Norseman*, a three masted, iron hulled, screw steamer, running out of Charleston with a load of cotton, plowed into the wreck of the *Georgiana* at high tide. Realizing his ship was sinking, the *Norseman's* captain turned her bow towards shore but she sank before he could run her aground. When the tide went out, the small steamer was in just eight feet of water and must have looked like she was still afloat. The small steamer's captain and crew all made it safely to shore. Part of her deck-load of cotton washed ashore so at some of that was saved. After the war, a rumor surfaced that the *Norseman* (who's tonnage has been variously reported as forty-nine tons, and one hundred and fifty-four tons) had something (I believe gold) hidden beneath her cargo of cotton. Whatever it was, it was never salvaged due to the fine Carolina sand which immediately washed into the wreck.

THE *GEORGIANA'S* SECOND VICTIM

On August 31, 1864, the iron hulled steamer *Mary Bowers* struck the *Georgiana*. It was high tide. The *Mary Bowers* shook. Steel twisted and rivets popped. Thrown to the deck in the crash, Captain Jesse de Horsey, a veteran blockade runner, was unable to reverse the engines. The giant paddle wheels churned the water. The steamer crawled forward. The *Mary Bowers* literally heaved herself up on top of the first wreck. She had struck the *Georgiana* diagonally, crossing through and over the aft end of the forward cargo hold. Abandoned by her crew, the *Mary Bowers* was discovered the following day by the United States frigate *Wabash*. The *Wabash's* men boarded the wrecked blockade runner and took her bell (marked 1864), her binnacle and compasses. Once again the sailors liberated a quantity of liquor (always high on the list of things to be salvaged). The *Mary Bowers* was two hundred and twenty-six feet long and may have been carrying up to six hundred and eighty tons of coal and assorted merchandise. The *Mary Bowers* had been on her third voyage and had left Bermuda only two days earlier. The *Mary Bowers,* probably carried a significant amount of gold to pay her crew, but whether any gold was actually lost was not recorded.

THE *GEORGIANA'S* THIRD VICTIM

Barely five weeks later, the *Georgiana* claimed her third victim. This time it was the *Constance Decimer* sailing from Halifax, Nova Scotia, with a cargo of one hundred and sixty tons of arms and munitions. The *Constance* is believed to have carried a considerable amount of gold coin to pay her crew and for the purchase of a return cargo of cotton. The *Constance* was a long, low, iron hulled, sidewheel steamer with fore and aft smokestacks. The *Constance* was painted a soft gray to blend into the sea fog. It was almost high tide. The *Constance* was built specifically for blockade running and drew only six feet of water. The unfortunate blockade runner must have just missed clearing the rusting stern post of the wrecked cruiser. The blow was partially absorbed as the *Georgiana's* stern section was pushed over on its side. Captain Stewart felt his ship shudder as she brushed over the wreck and

The "Real Rhett Butler" & Other Revelations

incorrectly assumed he had run too close to shore and was hitting a shell bank. Not suspecting his ship had suffered a death blow, Captain Stewart turned the steamer's narrow bow off shore and headed for deeper water. The sea rushed in, alerting the men in the engine room to the pending doom. The crew raced for her boats and rigging. One man failed to make it to safety, the only known death out of all four wrecks. The *Constance* was found by the blockade fleet the next morning. The steamer's decks were underwater and nothing was saved. She had come to rest six hundred and forty yards due south of the wrecks of the *Georgiana* and *Mary Bowers*.

THE PLUNGE INTO OBSCURITY

When the war ended, the wrecks were occasionally visited by salvors (seeking scrap metal) and possibly by fishermen, but the names and locations of the wrecks soon faded into history. As time went on, no one cared, and soon, no one remembered.

The wrecks had become nameless obstructions which were known only by a few captains of fishing trawlers, and they looked at them only as a nuisance that routinely cost them lost nets and down time.

THE RESEARCH PROGRESSES

My notes built up. Over a period of years I accumulated hundreds of pages of data relating to the *Georgiana*. I purchased Coast and Geodetic Survey charts and carefully compared them to an 1865 chart of the same area. I plotted the *Georgiana's* position on the old chart by running an imaginary line along the beach the equivalent of one mile from shore. Then I swung an arc three and one half miles from Breach Inlet. The point where the lines intersected was the point where I figured I would one day find the *Georgiana*. Next, I triangulated the *Georgiana's* location from fixed points which would not have been altered by erosion and the passage of time. Using these points and bearings I transferred the *Georgiana's* position to the modern chart. By my calculations the wreck lay roughly off present day 29th street on the Isle of Palms.

I located a copy of the Army Corps of Engineers report for the year 1872. It mentioned that fourteen shipwrecks had been "removed" from the channels around Charleston since the war. I decided to check further to see if the *Georgiana* was among those cleared. Another Corps of Engineers report gave the names of the ships. The *Georgiana's* name wasn't among them. Later I found a report of a survey made by a diver immediately after the war. It said the wrecks off the Isle of Palms were so badly sanded that their cargoes could not be salvaged (although some salvage was done). Since the wrecks lay outside the normal shipping lanes, there had been no need to remove them. Fearing the wrecks might be permanently buried in deep sands I checked geological survey reports. The reports gave the results of coring samples taken at various points off shore. The samples showed hard packed sand alternating with layers of packed shell. The samples told me that the wrecks would have sunk no further than a few feet into the sand, and at times were probably entirely exposed.

CHARLESTON

When I was a Sophomore in high school my father solved my distance problem by announcing that the family would move to Charleston.

Charleston is a fantastic place with its old forts, houses and sea islands. Crossing the bridges from Charleston to our new home on Sullivan's Island, I easily spotted the remnants of several shipwrecks in the shallow tidal waters. I immediately made contact with some of the local divers who confirmed that they had never located any of the wrecked blockade runners.

AIRBORNE SEARCH

I started renting small airplanes under the pretext of taking private flying lessons. Many hours were spent flying nauseatingly tight circles over the shallow waters off the Isle of Palms. Several times I spotted dark shadows and plumes of billowing silt. Some proved to be schools of fish, others appeared to be obstructions on the otherwise flat ocean floor.

My research convinced me that several of these shadows, were actually the wrecks I sought.

FOUND AT LAST

I then contacted numerous local trawl fishermen, asking each whether he had ever snagged his nets on anything near the shadows and mud plumes I had spotted. Several said they had, but most had no idea whether the obstructions were natural or man made. If they knew a particular hang was a shipwreck, they were still unable to tell me its identity. Walter Shaffer, captain of the fishing trawler *Carol El*, seemed to me to be the most knowledgeable of all of the captains I contacted. Captain Shaffer agreed to help me search for several of the larger hangs. I hoped that one spot in particular would prove not only to be a shipwreck but would actually be the combined wreckage of the *Georgiana* and the *Mary Bowers*. The next weekend we headed out to the area of the most promising shadow.

We began dragging a grappling device trying to snag anything that might be protruding from the bottom. We drug back and forth for about two and a half hours before we hooked into something. I suited up and dove into the water. I was on the *Georgiana* and *Mary Bowers*.

We located the *Constance Decimer* the same day.

A few months later I arranged to put divers down on a shadow I had tentatively identified as the *Norseman*. It was.

THE WRECKS TODAY

Today the *Georgiana* sits on the bottom with her huge boiler only five feet below the surface at low tide.

The *Mary Bowers* came to rest forward of the *Georgiana's* boiler and sits through and across the forward cargo hold of the first wreck.

The shattered privateer is now plumed with a glorious array of sea fans and living corals. Large sections of her hull are still intact and in places the starboard hull protrudes nine or ten feet from the sand.

Under the mud and sand lies even more of the hull of the iron ship. Much of the *Georgiana's* cargo, still in perfect condition, now lies buried, cradled by the silt that hides it.

The *Mary Bowers'* sides have broken out and her cargo has been swept away. Several portholes set in an open position stick up from the sand covering her flattened sides.

The *Mary Bowers* seems poor company for her more majestic companion which she partially covers.

THE THRILL THAT MATTERS

Divers braving the frequent zero visibility salvaged over a million individual artifacts from the *Georgiana*. The recovered artifacts ranged from extremely rare cannons and cannon balls to glass buttons and tiny sewing pins. The *Georgiana's* gold was never located and I believe it still remains on the wreck. Although we found her, we never really worked the *Norseman,* and her treasure might also still be found, but, even finding all of the missing gold wouldn't give me the thrill I felt on that first dive when I realized, I had discovered the *Georgiana*.

Some of the many polychrome, earthenware cups and mugs recovered from the Georgiana. Photo by L. Spence.

Part of the contents of two barrels of medicines salvaged from the Georgiana. Photo by L. Spence.

Lee Spence passes a large storage jar to Steve Howard. The jar contained camphor, which was used in making certain medicines. Photo by Nancy Butler.

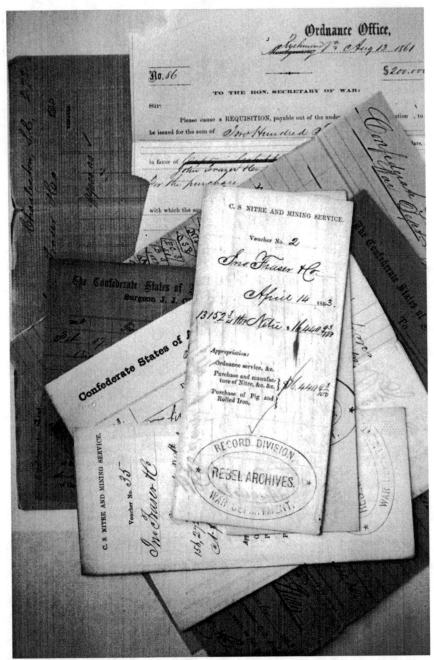

The *Georgiana's* cargo was consigned to *John Fraser & Co.,* which was headed by George Alfred Trenholm. These are are a sampling of the many documents relating to that company's activities. Documents courtesy of the United States National Archives.

Chapter Three: "The Mystery Ship of the Confederacy"

British coat of arms found on the Georgiana/Mary Bowers wreck site. Photo by L. Spence.

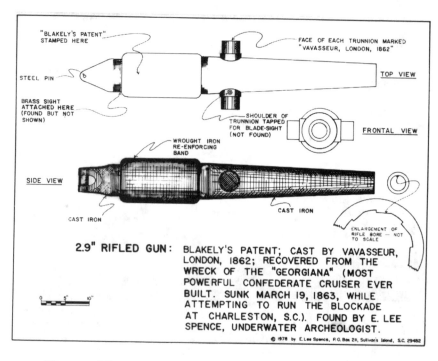

"BLAKELY'S PATENT" STAMPED HERE

FACE OF EACH TRUNNION MARKED "VAVASSEUR, LONDON, 1862"

TOP VIEW

STEEL PIN

BRASS SIGHT ATTACHED HERE (FOUND BUT NOT SHOWN)

SHOULDER OF TRUNNION TAPPED FOR BLADE-SIGHT (NOT FOUND)

FRONTAL VIEW

WROUGHT IRON RE-ENFORCING BAND

SIDE VIEW

CAST IRON

CAST IRON

ENLARGEMENT OF RIFLE BORE — NOT TO SCALE

2.9" RIFLED GUN: BLAKELY'S PATENT; CAST BY VAVASSEUR, LONDON, 1862; RECOVERED FROM THE WRECK OF THE "GEORGIANA" (MOST POWERFUL CONFEDERATE CRUISER EVER BUILT. SUNK MARCH 19, 1863, WHILE ATTEMPTING TO RUN THE BLOCKADE AT CHARLESTON, S.C.). FOUND BY E. LEE SPENCE, UNDERWATER ARCHEOLOGIST.

© 1978 by E.Lee Spence, P.O. Box 211, Sullivan's Island, S.C. 29482

Chapter Three: "The Mystery Ship of the Confederacy"

The "Real Rhett Butler" & Other Revelations

Polychrome earthenware saucer, salvaged from the wreck of the Georgiana. Photo by L. Spence.

This bearing circle was modified for underwater use and was used on the Georgiana wreck site. The pipe slipped over and locked onto one of the many iron base points which had been hammered into the sand around the wreck site by the divers. With the aid of a compass, the circle was zeroed to north. The user then sighted through the tube, and a tape measure was strung from the center post to the object being plotted. A pointer allowed the user to read the degrees directly off the numbered circle. A level was fixed to the top of the sighting tube. Photo by L. Spence.

This scale model of the Mary Bowers was built by Lee Nicholson and is on display at the Confederate Naval Museum at Columbus, Georgia. Photo by L. Spence, courtesy of the Confederate Naval Museum.

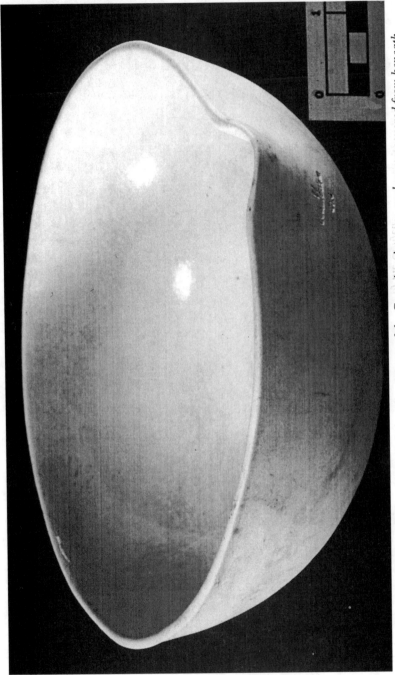

This delicate crucible, made by Wedgwood, was part of the Georgiana's cargo, and was recovered from beneath the wreck of the Mary Bowers. Photo by the South Carolina Institute of Archaeology & Anthropology.

The Federal bombardment of Fort Sumter at the entrance to Charleston Harbor. Engraving courtesy of the United States Library of Congress.

Chapter Three: "The Mystery Ship of the Confederacy"

CHAPTER FOUR
"The War & the Blockade"
(Who, What, When, Where, & Why)

This book covers the years 1861 through 1865. These are the years referred to by many Southerners as "The War Between the States," or as the "the late War of Northern Aggression." Some Federal records refer to those years of fighting as the "War of the Rebellion," but it is more commonly known as the "Civil War."

Following common usage, I call it the Civil War, or simply the War. However, the designation Civil War is actually misleading. It was foisted upon the public by nineteenth century politicians in their effort to justify the United States' attacks against a group of largely agricultural states which had voluntarily and peacefully exercised what they believed was their right to dissolve their union with the more industrialized states of the north.

Passionately believing in and following the principles proclaimed in the 1776 Declaration of Independence and the United States Constitution, the South had formed a new country. That new country was the Confederate States of America. Southerners felt their country had as much right to exist did as the United States of America. I firmly believe the principles of law were on their side.

In any case, the War wasn't fought directly over the question of secession. Proof of that is evidenced by the fact that the War didn't start until over four months after the first states seceded. Also, although none had actually done it, some of the Northern states, such as the State of Maine, had long claimed they had the right to secede from the Union.

Furthermore, the people of the states that actually seceded were truly not fighting among themselves, although there was civil war in some of the border states that had not seceded, and some of that did invade and infect the South.

Relatively few citizens of the states that seceded elected to fight on the side of North, and most of those were already in the United States Army or Navy prior to secession, or had only recently immigrated to the South. Three hundred and twenty-two Southerners, being twenty-five percent of the officers in the United States Navy resigned their commissions to serve in the Confederate Navy. Of those, two hundred and forty-three became line officers.

The rare cases where brothers fought brothers were seized upon by the North to prove their contention that the fighting was a civil war being fought among the general population. However if one looks closely at those cases, they will usually find that at least one of the brothers had been a career officer in the Federal Army or

Navy and had simply retained his commission out of what he saw as his legal duty or obligation.

The war between the armies of the United States and the Confederate States was definitely not a civil war like the one currently being fought in Ireland between the Catholics and Protestants, nor was it a class revolution like the one the peasants and working class of France fought against the nobility of their country.

It was a war between two independent countries (or "States") - the Confederate States of America and the United States of America.

The United State's war against the Confederate States was no more a civil war, than the war in Eastern Europe would have been if the communist government had decided to use force to try to take back Poland or any of the other former communist block countries that seceded from the Union of Soviet Socialist Republics.

In fact, when the Civil War finally started, it was technically over ownership and control of fortifications, arsenals, customs houses, and other properties in the South which had clearly belonged to the Federal government prior to secession.

When the former communist satellites seceded, they took possession of billions of dollars worth of port facilities, factories and buildings which had been built and paid for by the communist central government. This seizure of communist government property was approved by the world at large, but not by the communist government. Soviet Union President Gorbachoff, citing the precedent set by President Abraham Lincoln, threatened to send elite units of the Soviet Army in to "protect" government property in the seceding Soviet states. Fortunately, Gorbachoff was far wiser than Lincoln and didn't carry out his threat.

As a child I was taught by my Southern born parents that the South seceded over "State's Rights" and unequal taxation. Northerners, who were mostly Republicans, believed in relatively weak state governments headed by a strong central government. Southerners, who were primarily Democrats, believed in relatively strong state governments loosely bound together by a central government that answered to the individual states. The South also bristled under heavy export duties levied on cotton by the more populous northern states, who wanted the South's cotton to remain in America to be used by the North's mills.

My parents also told me about slavery in the old South. They didn't try to justify it. Instead, they made it clear they thought it had been terribly wrong. But, they did try to explain it factually. I even met and talked with former slaves and the children of slaves. There was no way I could grow up not understanding the injustices or the reality of slavery.

The importation of slaves, which had been carried on primarily by ships sailing out of New England ports, had been outlawed decades before the War.

Slaves came in all colors and, at one time, were legal even in northern states like New York, and I am not simply speaking of people who were paid "slave wages." I mean real slaves, people who were bought and sold as property.

By far, the majority of slaves were in the South and were black or brown, but some were red, and a few were white (usually having been sold into slavery for some debt or crime). There were even free blacks and Indians that owned other blacks as slaves.

Despite the sympathy evoking television commercials sponsored by one college fund, the first free schools in the South for blacks were started over one hundred years before the Civil War.

Slaves in the South were not routinely abused. Unusually cruel or sadistic masters were thought poorly of by both whites and blacks alike, and were frequently prosecuted under the law. Assault was considered assault, and murder was murder, regardless of the color of the perpetrator's and/or the victim's skin. However, like everywhere else in the world at that time, money was power. If a man got away with assault or murder (of either a free man or a slave), it was typically because of the disparity between the wealth, family and political connections of the perpetrator to his victim and not a direct result of their respective races.

My parents made it clear that they, like most Southerners, were glad that slavery no longer existed, even though the freeing of the slaves had been seen, at the time, as an economic loss to their own ancestors.

Over the years I learned the historical and economic reasons for slavery's continued existence in the Ante-bellum South, even though it had almost entirely died out north of the Mason Dixon Line. With that knowledge I was able to intellectually compare the injustices of slavery, which were many, to the treatment of indentured servants in the North.

The life of indentured servants, who were primarily poor Irish immigrants that had contracted for an average of seven years of labor for their passage to America, was frequently much worse, in a physical sense, than that of slaves. Indentured servants were often harshly beaten and half starved. Some were literally worked to death. If an indentured servant's health was broken through overwork, miserable living conditions, and poor diet, it meant the loss of the balance of seven years work, not the loss of the balance of a lifetime of labor. On the other hand, it was in a plantation owner's best interests to keep his slaves adequately clothed, well fed, healthy and strong.

Despite the paternal, almost protective, attitude most Southern plantation owners had towards their slaves, and despite the fact that indentured servants in the North were free, neither system was right. In fact both were terribly wrong, and it would be hard to say which was worse.

By the time the Civil War started, Charleston and other large southern cities were already teaming with free blacks. Thousands of slaves had already been freed for religious and moral reasons. Thousands more had been freed because many plantation owners no longer wished to be burdened with cradle to grave responsibility for the welfare of their slaves, but still wanted their cheap labor.

Many slaves were freed and allowed to continue living in their old slave quarters, as long as they continued to work for their former masters as share-croppers or tenant farmers.

Other blacks had used their free time (and yes slaves did have free time) to work odd jobs and had purchased their way to freedom.

There were so many free blacks that it was becoming easier for escaped slaves to lose themselves in the crowded cities. There was always someone willing, for money or for moral or religious beliefs, to hide them long enough for them to find safe passage north.

As escape became more common, plantation owners attempted to improve living conditions so the slaves wouldn't want to escape (or worse yet, revolt). As conditions improved and slaves were given even more opportunities to work for themselves, larger numbers were able to buy freedom for themselves and their families.

The freeing of slaves was a cycle that had started and there was no stopping it. The South knew slavery was on its way out. The costs were simply too high. If a slave escaped, the plantation owner's investment was lost.

Wages (paid in cash or in crop shares) for a "free" laborer, white or black, usually amounted to little more than the room and board provided to a slave anyway. It was rapidly becoming cheaper and wiser to free a slave and to hire him back, making use of any new found loyalty to extract even more work from him.

Believe it or not, most Southerners didn't own a single slave, and many free whites in the South were no better off in an economic sense than the slaves. Many pre-war Southerners predicted the economic demise of slavery within a few decades. It was definitely a dying institution and certainly not one that most Southerners would have thought was worth sacrificing body and soul to preserve.

Once the War started, there was actually strong support among the whites in the South to free the slaves so they could fight for the South.

Although, my parents told me repeatedly that the Civil War was not fought over slavery, my school books (published in Chicago, New York, and Boston) said otherwise, and it was not until I was an adult that I truly believed my parents.

I started to become a believer when I learned that Maryland, a southern slave holding state, did not secede and fought on the side of the North. Without Maryland on its side, the North probably would not have won. Washington, nestled between Virginia and Maryland, would have fallen the first week.

Even after secession, the newly elected Republicans in Washington had "sponsored an Amendment to the Constitution guaranteeing the perpetuation of Negro slavery wherever it then existed." It was an effort to pacify the South and restore the Union, "but the Republicans responsible for this movement had mistaken the real issue(s) at stake." Slavery was not the driving force behind secession of the Confederate States and the creation of the Confederacy, and promising to preserve slavery could not satisfy the South.

The question of slavery was no more a factor in the North's actions, than it was in the South's. Less than a week before the firing on Fort Sumter, the *New York Times* was still publishing editorials emphatically stating that the North had no desire to end slavery in the South.

Furthermore, historical records show that once the War started, thousands of free blacks actually fought on the side of the Confederacy, while an even larger number of slaves served in other capacities in the South's war effort. In any case, without the labor provided by the slaves on the plantations, the South could not have continued feeding or clothing its troops for as long as it did. Their contribution to the Confederate cause was not made out of ignorance or intimidation. It was made because blacks saw the assault on the Confederacy as an assault on their own families, homes, and livelihood.

It should also be noted that despite the fact that most Southern country homes and plantations were left defenseless against a slave uprising, there was no general revolt or work stoppage in support of the North. This does not mean that slaves were necessarily happy with the status quo. More probably it means that the slaves realized that, at least in the beginning, such an uprising would not have been welcomed or supported by the North.

The Southern government officially considered (but unfortunately and unwisely rejected) a resolution offering freedom to any slaves that fought for the Confederacy. Had the there been an adequate provision to compensate the slaves owners, the resolution would probably have passed.

Union officers were authorized to enlist "contrabands" (the term commonly used by the military for escaped slaves) for the naval service. However, no matter how competent they might be, they were to be allowed no higher rating than "boys," at a compensation of $10 per month and one ration a day. Although they were no longer called slaves, they were not treated any better.

Later, I learned that Lincoln's Emancipation Proclamation was nothing more than political grand standing. It's words are not quoted like the Gettysburg address and other famous documents because it was a political embarrassment that did not live up to its awesome title. Remember, Lincoln had no legal authority under the Constitution of the United States, which would have allowed him to free the slaves by proclamation alone. Freeing the slaves under the Constitution would have required due process of law and presumably payment of just compensation to their owners. If Lincoln had actually had such authority, and if he had truly cared about the slaves, he would have also proclaimed freedom for all the slaves. But, Lincoln's proclamation specifically excluded the slaves in Maryland, present day West Virginia, and other slave holding areas that had stayed within the Union and fought on the side of the North.

Lincoln's proclamation actually didn't free any slaves at all. It was the Union Army, both before and after the proclamation, that freed the slaves by the thousands. Such freedom was simply a by-product of the War and not the purpose. Lincoln was just trying to politically justify an unconstitutional act (i.e. the seizure of private property without due process of law) that was already taking place.

Saying the fighting was a crusade against slavery may have been outright deceit, but it was politically correct. It immediately reduced England's support of the South. Southern sympathizers in England, who despite their own anti-slavery feelings had supported the South for a myriad of economic and political reasons, suddenly found themselves in the awkward position of appearing to be "pro slavery." The political ramifications of the Emancipation Proclamation hurt the South's chances of winning more than anything the Union Army had tried.

I mentioned in the Introduction, the love Southerners have for the song *Dixie*, and the Confederate battle flag. To most Southerners, neither the song nor the flag represent hate, slavery, or repression of blacks. Instead they remind us of the heroism, sacrifice, dedication and beliefs of our ancestors, and our common love of our beautiful Southland. Remember, the flag of the United States flew over slavery for eight-nine years, and the Confederate flag for fewer than five, yet no one seriously tries to say that the American flag ever stood for slavery. The fact that certain extremist hate groups have unfortunately adopted the Confederate flag as one of their symbols should not be sufficient to turn people against it, for those same groups also routinely carry the United States flag.

The North's total battle casualties (wounded and dead) was roughly 385,000 while the South's battle casualties totaled approximately 320,000. On the surface it appears that the North suffered the greatest. However, the effect on the South was far more devastating and direct, as the North had a population 22,400,000, while the South had a population of only 5,343,000. Virtually all (statistically almost 102%, which was due to the enlistment of old men and children) of the free whites of military age in the South fought for the Confederacy during the War, while less than half (48%) of the North's men of fighting age actually entered service. Furthermore, thousands of the Federal soldiers that died were recent immigrants with little or no family in America to mourn them. Both sides also lost many thousands of soldiers to disease and other causes.

The Federal government spent today's equivalent of over $123,000,000,000 to fight the War, while the South spent $80,000,000,000. But as stated earlier, the South had a far smaller population. The South's economic loss didn't stop with the tax money and donations spent by the Confederate government directly on the War, the South lost many times that amount in burned out and destroyed plantations, homes, bridges, railroads, mills, factories, ships, and other commercial and private property. The non-military losses of the North (with its far larger population) were a very small fraction of those suffered by the South.

The commercial and private costs to the Southern populace conservatively equaled today's monetary equivalent of well over $240,000,000,000. Combined with the military expenditures, it was the equivalent of every man woman and child, black and white, then living in the South, paying over $32,000 for their share of the War. That is approximately sixteen times the per capita national debt during the Eisenhower administration. Knowing that, it should be easy to understand why it took the South more than a century to recover from the disastrous economic effects of the Civil War. Unfortunately, our national debt has again climbed to staggering proportions and now, on a per person basis, equals almost half of that borne by the South to fight the Civil War.

To fight the War, the South had to create, fund and arm both an army and a navy. To finance their military effort the Confederacy collected donations (ranging from gold wedding rings to live chickens), sold bonds, and levied taxes. Many of the taxes were collected in cotton which was subsequently shipped overseas to sell in England. Once the cotton was sold, the Confederate government used the cotton money to purchase uniforms, munitions, and medicines from all over Europe.

President Lincoln realized that the only way he could defeat the Confederacy was to cut off the supplies the South received through it's trade with Europe.

To have randomly captured or sunk unarmed merchant vessels without an "official blockade" would have subjected the Federal government to civil lawsuits (by both American and British citizens) demanding compensation for the "illegal" seizure of vessels and cargo. After officially declaring the blockade, the United States claimed it could "legally" sink any vessel which attempted to enter or leave the blockaded Southern ports without first getting the permission of the Federal fleet.

The only problem was that there had never been a recognized right of a nation to blockade its own ports. International law (in particular the Treaty of Paris of April 16, 1856, which had been ratified by the Confederacy on August 13, 1861) only recognized the right of a belligerent to blockade another nation's ports, not its own.

A lengthy letter from Gideon Welles, Secretary of the United States Navy, warned Lincoln of the ramifications of imposing a blockade on the southern ports. Welles stated that, if the Federal government closed the ports by blockade, the rules and principles of international law would govern. The Confederate States would be considered and treated as a distinct nationality, and their customs collectors, revenue officers, clearances, registers, etc., would be recognized as legitimate. Welles pointed out that the Federal government had been trying to show the Confederacy as an illegal rebellion and warned of the serious consequences of effectively recognizing the Confederate government as legitimate by the declaration of a formal blockade rather than simply closing them by act of civil law and then seizing vessels sailing to or from them as smugglers.

Despite being advised that the declaration of a blockade was de facto recognition that the Confederate States and the United States were indeed two separate countries, Lincoln went ahead with the blockade. Lincoln knew that it was a true war between countries and that it had to be fought that way to win. However, he also knew that he would first lose politically, then lose militarily, if he ever admitted the truth. Politically, Lincoln had to stick to the lie and continue to say it was a rebellion.

The United States government quickly built, leased or purchased a vast number of vessels to participate in the blockade the Southern ports. At times more than two dozen vessels would be stationed off a single port in an attempt to capture or destroy ships trying to violate the blockade.

"Blockade runners" were the South's answer to the Federal blockade. Thousands of merchant vessels were used in that service, and they ran the blockade in grand style.

Blockade runners were of every size, rig, type and description. Many were shallow draft sidewheel steamers. Others were yachts and sailing vessels. But, what they all depended on was their daring, speed, and knowledge of local waters.

By far the majority of blockade running activity took place in and out of the main ports of North Carolina, South Carolina, and Georgia. It is this historically important stretch of coast that I focus on in this book and refer to as the Confederate Coast.

The shallow draft and great speed of the merchant steamers employed in blockade running allowed them to run inside of the relatively slow moving, deeper draft Federal warships used in the blockade.

The coastal waters along parts of the southern east coast are extremely shallow, so a warship drawing eighteen feet of water had to stay a mile or two off shore for its own safety. A blockade runner drawing eight feet of water or less could run within a quarter mile of shore, even at low tide.

Most of the Federal warships plodded along at four to seven knots, while few blockade runners made less than fourteen knots, and many frequently raced along at seventeen knots. Test speeds as high as twenty knots were reported for the fastest runners.

Treasures of the Confederate Coast

Rear-Admiral David D. Porter, U.S.N., wrote "The new class of blockade runners is very fast, and sometimes come in and play around our vessels; they are built entirely for speed."

It is easy to understand how the swifter, shallower draft, blockade runners, using the cover of darkness, out ran the slower moving, deeper draft vessels of the Federal fleet and collectively racked up thousands of successful trips.

The Federal government, realizing the shortcomings of her ships, frequently placed captured blockade runners into service. The captured blockade runners *Bat*, *Peterhoff*, and *Princess Royal* were each put to work "guarding" the Confederate Coast.

The London *Index* reported that just during the period from January 1, 1863, to April, 1864, there were five hundred and ninety attempted trips (by steamers) through the blockade at Wilmington and Charleston, of those, four hundred and ninety-eight were successful. The number of trips made by sailing vessels during the same time period was not mentioned.

Anyone who has seen *Gone With The Wind* has heard of "blockade runners," but few actually understand what they really were, what they actually accomplished, or why they were so important.

As shown in Stephen Wise's excellent reference book, blockade running quickly became the "Lifeline of the Confederacy."

In a relatively short time, blockade running was the only thing allowing the South to continue the War. It was big business. Huge cargo ships, some carrying over a thousand tons of cargo on a single voyage, made frequent runs between the various Southern ports and ports in the Bahamas, Bermuda, Cuba, Mexico, and Canada.

The blockade runners typically brought merchandise, munitions and medicines to the South. The first voyage was said to have paid for the ship. The second voyage made a huge profit, and the third "made you rich beyond your wildest dreams."

Some of the blockade runners were extremely fast, shallow draft steamers built in Great Britain especially for the trade. The London *Times* reported that from the beginning of 1862 through the end of 1864 "no fewer than one hundred and eleven swift steamers were built on the Clyde (River) for the purpose of running the blockade of the Confederate ports." The *Times* went on to say that "the average number of trips made by a blockade-runner does not, however, exceed five, so enormous profits must be realized per voyage to make this peculiar branch of adventure at all remunerative." It failed to mention that at least one large steamer that frequented both Charleston and Wilmington made over forty successful runs through the blockade.

When the fast blockade runner *Advance* was captured off Wilmington, North Carolina, on her 18th run through the blockade, her captain said he would be willing to pay today's equivalent of $2,000,000 in gold for her return. Instead, she was put to work as part of the Federal Blockading Squadron.

Margaret Mitchell patterned her famous *Gone With The Wind* character, Rhett Butler, after Charlestonian George Alfred Trenholm. The handsome and brave Trenholm was the senior partner in the South's two most successful blockade running companies and enjoyed "unlimited credit abroad." Trenholm's companies were involved in over sixty vessels and earned a combined profit of over sixty million dollars (the equivalent of way over a billion of today's dollars) during the War.

One of Trenholm's companies even promised today's equivalent of one million dollars to anyone who sank one of the Union ironclads blockading Charleston.

Although his operations were financially successful, Trenholm lost more ships and cargoes on the Confederate Coast than any other blockade runner. The following is a partial list of blockade runners with a direct Trenholm connection which were lost on the Confederate Coast: *Antonica, Badger, Bendigo, General Beauregard, Elizabeth, Georgiana, Georgiana McCaw, Kate, Lynx, Minho, Phantom, Prince Albert, Raccoon, Rattlesnake, Stonewall Jackson, Stono,* and *Thomas Watson.* Actual ownership was often difficult to trace, as Trenholm, knowing the Federals were watching his companies' activities, tried to keep his "official" involvement to a minimum.

The "notorious" Captain Thomas J. Lockwood, who ran some of Trenholm's ships used to boast that his success lay in "arrangements with (Federal) naval officers" who had been bribed to let him through. When asked what cargo he carried, he once joked "food for the North."

The "fine" blockade runner *General Beauregard* was wrecked on December 11, 1863. The steamer had made sixteen successful trips through the blockade while she was owned by Trenholm, and was trying for her seventeenth when she was lost in fifteen feet of water off Carolina Beach, North Carolina.

The sidewheel steamer *Antonica*, which was once owned by Trenholm, was discovered ashore on Frying Pan Shoals, North Carolina, on December 20, 1863. Her cargo consisted of dry goods, provisions, liquor, etc., most of which was lost. There were no arms or ammunition known to have been aboard.

Trenholm's sidewheel steamer *Bendigo* burned near the entrance to Lockwood's Folly Inlet, North Carolina, on January 3, 1864. She was said to have been a frequent violator of the blockade, regularly running between Nassau and Wilmington.

The *Georgiana McCaw*, a steamer which had just been purchased on behalf of Trenholm, was chased ashore and destroyed at Cape Fear, North Carolina, by the *U.S.S. Victoria* on June 2, 1864, on her first attempt through the blockade.

The 1,000 ton, sidewheel steamer *Agnes E. Fry* was wrecked below Fort Campbell, North Carolina, on December 27, 1864. She was captained by Joseph Fry, a not so distant relative of Margaret Mitchell.

Smuggling must have been in Captain Fry's blood, as he later ran guns to the Cuban rebels. Fry was caught and executed by the Spaniards in 1873.

For more information on George Trenholm, the reader should see Chapter One in this book.

Blockade running vessels usually traveled unarmed and sailed under the British flag. To fight back would have subjected them to imprisonment as prisoners of war at best and as criminals at worst. By sailing unarmed, under a foreign flag, a captured blockade runner's crew could usually get away with claiming that they were neutrals. As such, at least in the early days of the blockade, they were quickly released. Once released they were free to try again. By the end of the War even British citizens were being imprisoned for violating the blockade.

Properly painted blockade runners could disappear like ghosts into the sea mist.

The beautiful twin screw steamer *Hebe* had her hull and smoke funnels camouflaged with a coating of grayish green paint. Unfortunately there was no mist to hide her. She was chased ashore, fired into, and burned in twenty feet of water, while trying to enter Carolina Beach Inlet, North Carolina, with a valuable cargo. Over three hundred and thirty shot and shell were fired into the *Hebe* or at the Confederates who tried to save her. The return fire by the Confederate shore batteries was reported as falling around the Yankees "as thickly as hail."

Both sides destroyed navigational aids they thought would be of use to the other.

A heavily armed "light-ship" was burned by the *U.S.S. Fanny* in September of 1861.

The "Real Rhett Butler" & Other Revelations

The *Frying Pan Shoals Lightship*, which was being converted to an armed battery, was burned by the *U.S.S. Mount Vernon* on December 30, 1861.

The Federals used false light signals, and misplaced buoys in an effort to mislead, capture and/or wreck the blockade runners.

Blockade runners learned to watch for prearranged colored lights that served as ranges to navigate by, and told them when it was safe to enter. Coded signals were precisely exchanged so ships from the Federal fleet couldn't pretend to be blockade runners and slip by the Confederate forts in the darkness.

The steamer *Wild Dayrell* attempting her fifth nighttime run missed her signals and went aground at the mouth of Stump Inlet, North Carolina. Over half of her valuable cargo was destroyed with the vessel. A case of 270,000 percussion caps for muskets was taken from the wreck by the *U.S.S. Florida*.

When the sun rose on the morning of February 5, 1864, the steamer *Dee*, bound from Bermuda with lead and provisions, was discovered ashore and on fire southward of Masonboro Inlet, North Carolina. She had been on her seventh run through the blockade. Less than a week later the steamer *Spunkie* was lost trying to make her ninth trip.

I have personally discovered more than two dozen Civil War wrecks (ranging from ironclads to blockade runners) on the Confederate Coast. However, due to legal restrictions and other practical considerations, I have worked only a few of them. Most of those were off Sullivan's Island and the Isle of Palms, South Carolina. From those few I was able to work, I raised tons of valuable artifacts. I still own over half a million individual artifacts, which I am currently trying to market for well over twenty million dollars. Some of the other wrecks still contain the bulk of their enormous cargoes.

Two of the cannon my team recovered from the *Georgiana* were purchased by the late Fred Hack who donated them to the museum at Fort Jackson in Columbia, South Carolina. Some of the artifacts we recovered are on display at the "Confederate Naval Museum" at Columbus, Georgia. Still more are at the "Ships of the Sea Museum" in Savannah. A sizable portion of the relics we recovered were turned over to the Institute of Archeology and Anthropology at the University of South Carolina for preservation, study, and eventual display.

Dozens of other Civil War era shipwrecks have been found by other divers, especially in the Wilmington, North Carolina area, still others have been found around Savannah, Georgia.

Treasures of the Confederate Coast

Artifacts recovered from the *Modern Greece*, the *Ranger*, *Ella*, and other Civil War wrecks in North Carolina waters, have been preserved by the State and are on display at Fort Fisher Visitor Center/Museum, Kure Beach, North Carolina.

The propeller steamer *Modern Greece* was wrecked on her first run through the blockade. She carried hundreds of tons of gun powder, seven thousand muskets, and many tons of clothing and merchandise. Even back then, her cargo was valued at over a million dollars. The Confederates salvaged "enough liquor to keep most of the Fort Fisher garrison in high spirits for more than a week." A large number of artifacts consisting partly of Whitworth shot and shell, Enfield rifled muskets, lead and tin ingots, spoons, knives, bottles, china, and surgical supplies have been recovered from the wreck by scuba divers. The *Modern Greece* lies in forty feet of water a half mile north of Fort Fisher, and is only two hundred yards off shore.

The North Carolina Underwater Archeology Unit, at Kure Beach, has joined with the Cape Fear Museum, at Wilmington, to provide an underwater archeology educational kit targeted for 8th grade students. Their excellent outreach program fascinates the kids and helps teach them about Cape Fear's underwater heritage.

The Southport Maritime Museum located at Southport, North Carolina, and run by Wayne Strickland, has an excellent display of artifacts recovered from Civil War shipwrecks. Strickland also runs a charter boat that takes divers to a wide range of shipwrecks.

Charles Peery, who is now a medical doctor living in Charleston, located and partially salvaged the sidewheel steamer *Ella*, which was driven ashore on Bald Head Beach, North Carolina, on December 3, 1864. The *Ella* had been bound from Nassau and carried gin, military goods, arms and ammunition, when she was wrecked in six feet of water just over a mile from shore.

The U.S. Army transport *City of New York* was "lashed to pieces by the angry waves" near the entrance to Hatteras Inlet. Her cargo was valued at $200,000 (which would be $4,000,000 in today's dollars) and consisted of fifteen hundred rifles, eight hundred cannon balls, hand grenades, etc. Her cargo would still be worth a fortune today.

The 225' long, blockade running steamer *Stormy Petrel*, with a large cargo of arms and munitions, was driven ashore by the United States gunboats at New Inlet, North Carolina.

The speedy blockade runner *Mary Bowers*, steaming in on high tide, was wrecked one mile off the Isle of Palms, South Carolina, when it ran onto the wreck of the *Georgiana*. The deeper draft cruiser, who's cargo was owned by George Trenholm, had been wrecked over a year earlier when it was chased aground at low tide.

The steamer *Mary Bowers* was a classic blockade runner. She had an iron hull, was two hundred and twenty six feet long, and could carry six hundred and eighty tons of cargo while only drawing six feet of water. The wreck of the *Mary Bowers* still sits on top and across the wreck of the *Georgiana* with less than eight feet of water covering the tops of her boilers at low tide.

The *Georgiana* was reputed to have been the most powerful Confederate cruiser ever built. I discovered her along with the *Mary Bowers* and the *Constance* after talking with numerous commercial fishermen who had snagged nets on some of the wreckage. None of the fishermen had ever suspected the wrecks' true identities. Some had incorrectly assumed the wrecks were barge loads of stone that had been lost during the construction of the Charleston jetties.

Nighttime runs through poorly marked channels were the biggest cause of blockade runners being wrecked.

The blockade running steamer *Stonewall Jackson* was wrecked in less than eight feet of water when she ran aground the night of April 15, 1863, on the Isle of Palms. Accreting sand has now buried the wreck and she lies buried in the first row of dunes near Sixth Street. Although she was partially salvaged, it would have taken almost 900 army supply wagons, each capable of carrying one ton, to have carted off her valuable cargo. The wreck still contains many tons of copper, lead and tin ingots. Part of her cargo consisted of 40,000 army shoes, which were desperately needed by the Confederate soldiers, many of whom were already going barefoot into battle. Boots, shoes, uniforms, and weapons were routinely stripped from the dead to outfit the living.

The Confederate disaster at Gettysburg (July 1-3, 1863) can be attributed in part to the loss of the *Stonewall Jackson's* cargo. The fighting "was brought on unexpectedly when barefooted Confederate soldiers learned that shoes might be had in Gettysburg. The search for shoes discovered Federal outposts, and the battle began." By the time the smoke had cleared, 2,592 Confederates lay dead, 12,709 were wounded, and 5,150 were captured or missing. Among the Confederate dead was "the gallant General Pat Cleburn(e) who ordered an unshod soldier to put on his own boots, while he, in his stocking feet, rode into the fight."

Treasures of the Confederate Coast

The blockade running steamer *Celt*, which was wrecked when it ran aground on Bowman's Jetty near Fort Moultrie on the bend of Sullivan's Island, still sticks out of the water at low tide. The barnacle encrusted remains look just like the scattered rocks of the jetty, so most people miss this wreck even when they are looking for it. I located the *Celt* in 1965 after seeing an 1865 photo of the then more intact wreck in an old book and recognizing the rocks. This wreck, along with several others which I discovered nearby, was later worked by Howard Tower, a very talented amateur underwater archeologist from Jacksonville, Florida.

One of the nearby wrecks is the *Flamingo*. The *Flamingo* was a beautiful steamer with three smokestacks and sidewheels, hardly the stereotype tiny sloop that comes to mind when most people think of blockade runners. That incorrect stereotype was actually invented by Federal propagandists who claimed that the only vessels getting in and out of the Confederate ports were vessels so small and inconsequential that they did not matter. The Federals were lying in an effort to make their blockade appear effective, which was a requirement for it to be legal.

When the blockade running steamer *Presto* ran aground near Fort Moultrie on Sullivan's Island, South Carolina, some of the Confederate soldiers braved the heavy enemy shelling and saved a large amount of liquor. The men later got so drunk it threatened the security of the entire island.

The five hundred ton, twin screw steamer *Vesta* was lost near the South Carolina/North Carolina line when her captain accidentally ran her aground. The accident was attributed to her captain and crew having gotten outrageously drunk, while prematurely celebrating the successful conclusion of their voyage.

The blockade running ship *Thomas Watson* was chased ashore on the northern side of Stono Breakers, one and a half miles off Folly Island, South Carolina. The crew abandoned her leaving their food on the table. The ship's cargo included a cannon and some cannon balls which were thrown overboard by the Yankees who set the vessel afire. The Yankees took a whaling blunderbuss, five harpoons, two bells, and eighteen packages of gold leaf from the wreck.

This book contains information on well over five hundred vessels of various types that were reported as wrecked on the Confederate Coast during the years 1861 through 1865.

These wrecks collectively contain many hundreds of millions of dollars in treasure and artifacts, as well as an incalculable amount of archeological and historical information. If properly worked, they

The "Real Rhett Butler" & Other Revelations

can furnish dozens of museums and thousands of classrooms with display and study material.

I believe billions more was intentionally hidden (much of it by George Trenholm) and, for one reason or another, was never recovered.

Shipwrecks can be a boon to fishermen, salvors, historians, archeologists, and the local tourist industry. These rusting and rapidly disintegrating hulks contain not only the munitions and weapons of war, but also the little domestic items which reveal the habits and idiosyncrasies of the times. Some even contain treasures in the form of gold, silver, and precious jewels.

The discovery of a single virgin wreck, especially if it is a large blockade runner, with literally hundreds of tons of valuable, now antique, merchandise and munitions, could change your life forever. I know, because I have found some.

The crews of blockade runners were well paid for their risks, and they were paid in coin, so almost every blockade runner carried a sizable amount of gold. The valuable metal was also carried for the purchase of supplies and to bribe customs officials in foreign ports.

When the fast sidewheel steamer *Venus* was chased ashore north of Gatlin's Battery, North Carolina, the men of the Federal boarding parties each got sixty to eighty dollars in gold (then worth only twenty dollars an ounce) from the wreck. She also carried a valuable cargo of lead, drugs, dry goods, bacon, and coffee. She was described as one of the finest and fastest vessels engaged in running the blockade.

The *Venus'* presence had been exposed when a "traitor" rang her bell alerting the fleet and allowing them to know where to train their guns in the darkness. I believe some treasure may still be hidden on the wreck.

A "handsome sword, gold mounted" and intended as a gift for General Robert E. Lee, was lost when the blockade runner *Fanny and Jenny* wrecked near Masonboro Inlet. One account said that she "was carrying half a million gold sovereigns" and that the sword's hilt was "studded with jewels."

Over two hundred pounds of Confederate gold was saved from the armed sidewheel steamer *Lynx* when she wrecked near the Half Moon Battery north of Fort Fisher.

The famous Confederate spy, Rose O'Neal Greenhow, was carried to the bottom by one hundred ounces of gold hidden in her clothes when she tried to get ashore from the wreck of the *Condor* after it ran aground on Federal Shoals. The *Condor* had three smoke stacks and was capable of making "tremendous speed."

In July of 1863 over seventeen tons of silver bars were reported to have been captured by the Confederate cruiser *Florida* and transferred to the blockade runner *Robert E. Lee* for the purpose of running it into Wilmington, North Carolina.

When the owner and supercargo of the blockade runner *Diamond* were captured on an inward run, they were described as exhibiting "a reckless demeanor ••• and large amounts of gold."

The fast sidewheel steamer *Arabian* had made three previous successful trips through the blockade and was outbound with a load of cotton, when she was wrecked at New Inlet. So, she probably carried gold received from the sale of her last inbound cargo.

The propeller steamer *Douro* was chased ashore and burned near Wrightsville, North Carolina. She had been previously captured and had been sold in New York, but her new owners had returned her to the dangerous but lucrative trade. She was outbound and may have carried gold hidden under her cargo of cotton.

The Confederate cruiser *Georgiana* not only carried a cargo that cost the Confederates over a million dollars, she carried $90,000 in gold coin when she was lost. Those coins would have weighed a total of 4,500 troy ounces and could be worth over $14,000,000 on the numismatic market today.

Although the *Constance*, which actually wrecked on the *Georgiana*, also carried gold, I can only guess that it was in the neighborhood of half of what the *Georgiana* carried. Unfortunately, when I discovered these two wrecks and had the rights to work them, I was too naive to believe that they really carried gold, and I didn't search for the concealed compartments, which I now know to have been common on blockade runners.

A fortune in gold may be buried under tons of sand and rotting cotton on the wreck of the steamer *Norseman*, which was lost in shallow water off the Isle of Palms after it ran over the wreck of the *Georgiana*. Again, I found the wreck, but again being an ignorant and unbelieving youth, I didn't even spend an hour searching for her gold. (Note: For more on the loss of the *Georgiana*, *Constance*, *Mary Bowers* and *Norseman*, please see Chapter Three and appendices C, D, E, F in this book.)

Although she wasn't sunk, an idea of the riches sometimes carried on outbound blockade runners can be gained from the *Alice*, which carried over 55,000 ounces of gold out of Wilmington in May of 1864. When the steamer *Minnie* was captured earlier the same month 500 ounces of gold were found in a secret drawer. The steamer *Lucy*, bound to Europe with a large amount of bullion, was chased off North Carolina, but got away.

When the blockade runner *Greyhound* was captured off Cape Fear in May of 1864, she proved to be a very valuable prize. Besides carrying a cargo of cotton, tobacco, and turpentine, the beautiful Confederate spy, Belle Boyd, was aboard. As the Federal gunboat approached, a keg containing 1,250 ounces of gold coins was rolled overboard, and Belle burned her secret dispatches. Belle charmed the handsome young prize master and he later helped her escape. The two were afterwards married in England.

Two thousand five hundred ounces of gold in American coinage "and a lot of Confederate bonds" were thrown overboard from the blockade runner *Annie* when she was captured in 36' of water off Cape Fear in October of 1864.

While on the subject of gold. The crew of the *U.S.S. Sabine* was awarded a gold medal by the "Life Saving Benevolent Association of New York" for its role in the rescue of the men of the Federal transport steamer *Governor* when it sank in a hurricane on November 2, 1861.

Even United States warships carried money to pay their men, although most of that would have been in paper. However, even paper can survive on a shipwreck, if it is protected by a layer of mud or sand.

When the *U.S.S. Sumter* was sunk in forty-two feet of water, off Smith Island, North Carolina, it was reported that the "paymasters saved nothing."

The paymaster's safe went down with the *U.S.S. Housatonic* off Sullivan's Island. Many of the survivors lost "quite large sums of money" that they had laid away to send home by the next mail.

The "paymaster's funds" went down with the *U.S.S. Weehawken*, but may be guarded by the ghosts of shackled crew members in the ship's brig who were abandoned to their fate by a "terror stricken crew."

A number of the vessels lost during the War were wrecked by non-belligerent causes and were not true causalities of war. Some were accidentally run aground on sandbars, jetties, or other wrecks (albeit, some of these happened because the blockade runners were forced into nighttime runs and came too close to shore while attempting to avoid enemy ships). Others were sunk in storms. Some steamers caught fire from their own ash, while others were lost when they exploded their boilers through improper use or maintenance. A few vessels simply sank through neglect.

Treasures of the Confederate Coast

Of the wrecks directly attributable to the War, the largest group were burned or scuttled vessels. Scuttling is the intentional sinking of a vessel by opening her sea-cocks or otherwise flooding the vessel.

A sizable number of vessels were scuttled by the Confederates to prevent the Federal forces from entering the rivers and harbors of the Confederate Coast, even more were sunk by the Federal forces to prevent the Confederates from getting in or out. Both sides frequently scuttled and burned grounded, trapped, or captured vessels to prevent their capture or recapture. Relatively few vessels were actually sunk in blazing cannon duels.

Probably ten percent of the well over five hundred vessels reported to have been run aground or otherwise wrecked, between the beginning of 1861 and the end of 1865, never actually sank and were immediately saved. At least another ten percent were completely salvaged, during or after the War. Possibly another twenty percent were partially salvaged, at one time or another, for their armament, rigging, cargoes and/or for the materials with which they were built.

That still leaves over three hundred, virtually untouched, Civil War wrecks in the shallow muddy waters of North Carolina, South Carolina and Georgia. These wrecks are still waiting to be found, studied and/or salvaged. Together, they contain thousands of tons of assorted cargo. The cargo of just one large inbound blockade runner could theoretically amount to tens of millions of dollars on the antiquities market.

We should never forget, these wrecks are also part of our historical and archeological heritage and their salvage should be done in a systematic and scientific manner. All work, whether done as archeology or as commercial salvage, should be properly recorded through photographs, drawings, charts and notes so minimal data will be lost and the wrecks can be studied by others at a later date. Looting is neither salvage nor archeology and should not be condoned by anyone.

The wrecked vessels ranged from ordinary pleasure craft, merchant cargo vessels and fishing boats, to blockade runners, privateers and ironclads. At least four true submarines and five semi-submersible torpedo boats were lost.

The Federal submarine *Alligator* was lost while being towed from Newport News, Virginia, to Charleston, South Carolina, where it was intended to be used to find and explode mines in preparation for an assault on Charleston.

The "Real Rhett Butler" & Other Revelations

The Confederate submarine *H.L. Hunley* was built for the express purpose of attacking and sinking ships of the Federal blockade. The tiny *Hunley* succeeded in sinking the 1240 ton, United States steam sloop of war *Housatonic* in twenty-seven feet of water some three and a half miles off Sullivan's Island, South Carolina. In doing so, the *Hunley* became the first submarine in history to sink a ship. The eight man sub never returned from that first and final mission.

Incidentally, while compiling this volume, I had to wade through vast amounts of misinformation, including one book that claimed the *Housatonic* was the first ship sunk in American waters by a German submarine during the First World War. Believe it or not, that book was published by one state's Division of Archives and History.

In November of 1970, I discovered wreckage which I tentatively identified as the remains of the *Housatonic* and the *Hunley*. But, it was not until 1976 that I located historical evidence, (in the form of sworn eyewitness testimony taken the day after the loss of the *Hunley*), that supported my identification of part of the wreckage as that of the submarine. And, it was not until much later, when I came across original handwritten notebooks and a hand drawn chart prepared in 1865 (after the wreck was surveyed as an obstruction to navigation), that I was able to positively identify the remains of the *Housatonic*.

In late 1989 and early 1990, I shared portions of my confidential files, research, charts and notes on these wrecks with the editors of *National Geographic* magazine in anticipation of doing a joint expedition to the site. A date for the expedition was set, but it was later canceled. (Note: For more on the wrecks of the *Housatonic* and *Hunley* please see Chapter Two of this book.)

A number of semi-submersibles, generically known as "Davids," were also built to attack the Union blockade ships. Each "David" was fitted with an explosive charge or torpedo on a long spar attached to the bow. The idea was to ram the blockade ships, blow a hole in their side and sink them. Although never entirely successful, the threat of these vessels forced the blockade ships to move still further off shore.

Three "Davids" were allowed to sink at their moorings along the old Chisolm's Causeway at Charleston, South Carolina. That area has since been filled in and built over. These three vessels, one of them the original *David* (which was once described as the greatest innovation in naval warfare in over two thousand years), now lie

Treasures of the Confederate Coast

buried under Tradd Street near the United States Coast Guard Station. At least two others were sunk elsewhere around Charleston.

The Confederate States torpedo boat *Squib* was destroyed in the Cape Fear River to prevent her capture at the fall of Wilmington.

Most people know that the first battle between ironclads took place during the Civil War, but most people think that the *Monitor* and the *Merrimack* were the only ironclads built during the War. Actually there were dozens of them.

Quite a few ironclads fought in the waters of the Confederate Coast, and at least sixteen of them were wrecked.

Neither the Federal ironclad *Monitor* nor the Confederate ironclad *Virginia* (ex-*Merrimack*) were sunk in their famous duel off Hampton Roads, Virginia. That battle was the first engagement of ironclads in warfare. The *Monitor* eventually foundered in a storm off Cape Hatteras, while being towed to South Carolina. This wreck and the area immediately around it has been made a National Marine Sanctuary.

Incidentally, the first superintendent of the United States Naval Academy was the commander of the *C.S.S. Virginia* (ex-*Merrimack*), Commodore Franklin Buchanan. His brother was an officer in the United States Navy and served aboard the first vessel to surrender to the *Virginia*.

The Confederate ironclad *Raleigh* was wrecked at the New Inlet Rips on May 7, 1864. The Confederate ironclad *North Carolina* sprang a leak and sank in the Cape Fear River near Fort Caswell in September of 1864. The Confederate ironclad *Arctic* was stripped and sunk in the Cape Fear River as an obstruction on December 24, 1864. The Confederate ironclad *Neuse* almost made it through the War, but was burned and sunk in the Cape Fear in March of 1865, less than a month before General Lee's surrender at Appomattox, Virginia.

The *Neuse's* guns, armor plating, and machinery were salvaged in the 1800's. Her hull, along with approximately 15,000 artifacts, was finally pulled from the water in late 1963, and is now housed at the Caswell/Neuse State Historic Site at Kinston, North Carolina.

Three Federal ironclads (the *Weehawken*; the *Keokuk*; and the *Patapsco*) and four Confederate ironclads (the *Charleston*, the *Palmetto State*, the *Columbia*, and the *Chicora*) were sunk in Charleston Harbor.

Three more Confederate ironclads (the *Georgia*, the *Savannah*, and the *Milledgeville*) were sunk near Savannah.

Interestingly enough, only four of the ironclads on the south east coast were lost as the direct result of enemy action. The ironclad gunboat, *U.S.S. Keokuk*, which was often incorrectly described as a double turreted monitor, sank the day after being hit ninety times while attacking Fort Sumter. The ironclad gunboat, *U.S.S. Patapsco*, which was a true monitor, was sunk by a Confederate mine as it attempted to enter Charleston Harbor. The still uncompleted Confederate ironclad *Jackson* was captured and burned at Columbus, Georgia. The remains of her hull, with her steam engines, shafts and propellers, was raised in 1964, and is currently on display (along with the remains of the Confederate gunboat *Chattahoochee*) at the Confederate Naval Museum, at Columbus.

Another Confederate ironclad, *C.S.S. Albemarle*, was sunk by a Federal torpedo boat at Plymouth, North Carolina.

Most of the wrecked ironclads, from both sides, were raised immediately after the War ended, and a few, including the *Albemarle*, were subsequently repaired and commissioned in the United States Navy. A few (such as the *Keokuk*, *Weehawken*, and *Patapsco*) were partially salvaged for scrap metal in the 1870's.

At least one Confederate ironclad, the *Savannah*, which was scuttled in the Savannah River, remains virtually untouched and intact. The *Savannah* is presently the focus of a government project to either raise the entire vessel or study and preserve it in situ.

The Confederate Privateer *Petrel* was sunk off Charleston by a shell from the United States gunboat *Saint Lawrence*. Five of her men were drowned while the rest were taken prisoner and carried to Philadelphia. Since the government of the United States refused to recognize the legitimacy and sovereignty of the government of the Confederate States and its legal right to commission privateers and organize a navy, the *Petrel's* men were initially refused the rights of prisoners of war. Instead, the unfortunate sailors were treated as pirates.

The North was already in the process of trying another privateer crew as pirates and had stated that they would be hung if they were found guilty. Those men, and the men of the *Petrel*, were spared only after the Confederate government announced that an equal number of Federal prisoners (consisting largely of field grade officers) would be treated in a like manner if the Yankees went ahead with their plans.

The eighty-two ton *Petrel* was armed with only two cannon when she was sunk and she carried no valuable cargo. This wreck probably could be found. Besides having been a privateer, the *Petrel* was an ex-United States revenue cutter and would be an important archeological and historical discovery.

The treatment of privateersmen helps explain why the South kept fighting even after the bloody disaster at Gettysburg and the surrender of major cities like Atlanta, Wilmington, Columbia and Charleston. To surrender without the terms finally agreed to at Appomattox could have meant that tens of thousands of Confederate soldiers would have been placed on trial for treason and executed instead of being correctly treated as prisoners of war.

Fortunately, General Grant was wise enough to simply parole them. He gave the starving Confederates badly needed food and blankets. In fact, Grant even allowed General Lee's men to keep their side arms, and in some cases Grant issued additional weapons and ammunition so they could defend themselves as they made their separate ways home.

The case of each vessel captured by a privateer had to be adjudicated by a Prize Court. In the early days of the War, prize courts could be held in foreign ports, but political pressures soon closed that option. That meant the captured vessels (called prizes), had to be sent into a Confederate port.

Each prize further depleted the crew of the privateer, as each prize had to be sufficiently manned to guard the prisoners and get the vessel safely to port. Most of the captured vessels were of deeper draft than those normally used for blockade running, and many were lost.

As the blockade tightened, privateers found it almost impossible to get their prizes safely into Confederate ports. Privateering, which had held so much promise, quickly came to a halt, not only because the captured Confederates were treated as pirates, but because it was not economically viable.

When the United States steamer *R.B. Forbes*, was wrecked south of Currituck Inlet, North Carolina, she quickly "buried in the sand." The sand would have helped preserve even fragile china, wood and cloth. As a result, her excavation could produce exciting finds.

Even when an historically important wreck is discovered, don't count on government officials looking at the wreck or publicizing it.

In the almost thirty years since I discovered the *Georgiana* off the Isle of Palms, not a single South Carolina official has ever visited the site, even though the vessel is reputed to have been the most powerful Confederate cruiser ever built, and even though the state claimed and took twenty-five percent of everything I found.

The "Real Rhett Butler" & Other Revelations

Despite the fact that a resource not used might as well not exist, North Carolina officials shroud the location of the Confederate steamer *Curlew* and many other wrecks in secrecy. Accessibility is allowed, but only by wading through government red tape that was apparently designed largely to prevent public access to such sites. The *Curlew* was the flagship of North Carolina's famed "Mosquito Fleet," was sunk during the defense of Roanoke Island. Halfway through that fighting, the *Curlew's* commander realized "to his surprise that he had no trousers on."

The American brig *B.T. Martin*, which had been captured by the Confederate privateer *York*, was accidentally run ashore a few miles to the northward of Cape Hatteras. Her cargo consisted of a cylinder boiler, a large iron refinery, cast iron framing, three large iron tanks, stoves, and about forty barrels of potatoes.

The Confederate States privateer *York*, was burnt by her officers and crew four miles south of Bodie's Island light-house, on August 9, 1861, to prevent her capture by the *U.S.S. Union*.

The Confederate steam ferry *Osiris* was set afire and burned by a black man at her wharf on Sullivan's Island. To the Confederates, this act of defiance or bravery was at best arson and at worst treason. Although no actual record of it has been located, the man probably paid for his rash heroism with his life.

The sidewheel steamer *Robert Habersham*, under charter to the Confederate government, had her boiler explode and was blown to pieces at Screven's Ferry on the Savannah River.

Both sides routinely attempted salvage of the wrecks and their cargoes. Sometimes they were successful, other times they were not.

The *U.S.S. Iron Age* was accidentally run aground in ten feet of water at Lockwood's Folly Inlet while attempting to pull the wreck of the *Bendigo* into deeper water. The *Iron Age's* guns on her port side were thrown overboard. She was then burned and blown up by her crew to prevent her capture.

At daylight on January 11, 1864, the English built steamer *Ranger* was observed beached and burning west of Lockwood's Folly Inlet. The Confederates salvaged some muskets and carpenter tools.

Five hundred and twenty-nine Austrian rifled muskets with bayonets; ninety-eight English rifled muskets with long bayonets; one hundred English rifled muskets with regular bayonets; forty English rifled muskets (short); one hundred and ten cavalry sabers; twenty-three boxes of needles, etc. were saved from the wreck of the *Nutfield*.

Treasures of the Confederate Coast

The United States bark *Kingfisher* was wrecked on Combahee Bank on the south end of Otter Island, South Carolina. Her six guns were raised along with all of her shot and shell shortly after she sank.

On the same shoal lies the remains of an unidentified United States Revenue Cutter which was torpedoed by the Confederates, but whether she carried a payroll or any other government money is not known.

Just up the Ashepoo River from those two wrecks lies the remains of the United States armed transport *Boston*, which was lost while carrying men and horses on a foray up the river. The *Boston* was discovered in 1965 by a teen aged diver named Jim Batey. Batey and the late Ron Renau recovered a safe from the wreck. The wreck was later independently discovered and worked by underwater explorer Howard Tower in cooperation with the Institute of Archeology and Anthropology at the University of South Carolina.

Frank and Paul Chance of Richmond Hill, Georgia, salvaged numerous valuable artifacts from the wreck of the Confederate privateer *Rattlesnake* (ex-*Nashville*) in the Ogeechee River. The twelve hundred ton steamer had been blown up near Fort McAllister, Georgia, during an attack by the United States monitor *Montauk*. Although technically amateurs, the quality of their work was well above that of many professional underwater archeologists (including that of the then state underwater archeologist for South Carolina) and they produced an excellent book about the ship and their work.

The steamer *John Randolph*, which was built in 1834 at Savannah and had the distinction of being the first "commercially successful" metal hulled vessel used in the United States, was another casualty of the War. The *John Randolph* was reported wrecked on Sullivan's Island at the fall of Charleston.

The British schooner *Antoinette* was wrecked on the beach halfway down Cumberland Island, Georgia. The schooner's anchors, chains, sails and papers were taken off by the Yankees.

Admiral Dahlgren's flag ship, the *Harvest Moon*, was blown up by a Confederate mine in the middle of Winyah Bay near Georgetown, South Carolina. The vessel's smokestack still sticks out of the water, while the bulk of the shattered, but still largely intact United States gunboat lies buried in the mud and sand.

The United States transport steamer *Thorn* was blown up by a Confederate mine and sunk in just two minutes in the Cape Fear River.

The "Real Rhett Butler" & Other Revelations

The United States gunboat *Otsego* was destroyed by Confederate mines in the Roanoke River. She was thought to have stopped directly on top of a line of the "infernal machines." The United States tug *Bazely* was sunk right alongside the *Otsego* when a mine exploded under her as she tried to pass by. At least four other Union vessels were blown up in the same river.

The United States gunboat *Louisiana* was destroyed by her own people when she was disguised as a blockade runner, loaded with over 200 tons of gun powder and was blown up (using clockwork time fuses) near Fort Fisher in a futile effort to destroy the fort by explosion.

The Federal gunboat *Pickett* was blown up at Washington, North Carolina, on September 6, 1862. Underwater explorer Carter Leary has located this wreck and, at the time of our last discussion, was still attempting to secure support to raise the entire vessel for museum display purposes. His team has recovered a number of interesting artifacts, and the mapping and preservation is being done with the cooperation of the Underwater Division of the North Carolina Department of Cultural Resources.

Carter Leary reports that the 1098 ton steamer *Aphrodite*, with five hundred and ten United States Navy recruits, which wrecked north of Cape Lookout, North Carolina, has been found in about thirty feet of water. No doubt the *Aphrodite* contains a wealth of weapons and accouterments abandoned by the recruits. Divers have already raised some bars of lead and tin.

The United States steamer *Enoch Dean* carrying recently freed slaves to their new homes on the Georgia sea islands was sunk when she hit a snag in a creek near St. Catherine's Sound, Georgia.

A number of blockade runners were wrecked near the inlets north of Winyah Bay, South Carolina. One of them was the beautiful sidewheel steamer *Virginia Dare*. The iron hull of the *Dare* was two hundred and seventeen feet long and only twenty-three feet wide. The *Dare's* steam engine still sticks out of the water, but most of her cargo and fittings were salvaged during the War. Jim Batey and I visited and identified the *Dare* in the 1960's. One of the artifacts Jim found near the wreck was a pewter inkwell, which dated almost a hundred years before the Civil War.

The United States bark *Alice Provost*, with a cargo of seven hundred tons of coal, was wrecked while going into Port Royal Sound, South Carolina.

Many vessels were lost due to age and poor maintenance.

The "frightfully horrible" old United States transport *Quinebaug* was wrecked near Beaufort, North Carolina. Despite the fact that her captain immediately "set her colors half-mast, union down" and aid was quickly rendered by a boat, at least twenty-five lives were lost.

The Confederate steamer *Oconee*, armed with one 32-pounder smooth bore cannon and loaded with three hundred and twenty-five bales of cotton, was swamped and sunk by heavy seas in a violent storm twenty miles south of Tybee Island, Georgia. She had been considered a poor sea risk by the insurers who obviously knew their business.

A shipwreck could bring out both cowardice and heroism, and in any case, even the survivors were shaken by the tragedy.

Over 400 people perished when the United States transport *General Lyon* caught fire during a storm and wrecked on the coast of North Carolina, on March 25, 1865. Her captain, who was described as "crazed with fear," leapt into the first boat launched, but died within seconds as the boat was dashed to pieces. "The frightful shrieks of the women and children, and their piteous supplications for help, were drowned by the roaring of the storm." Despite valiant efforts by the crew, who had remained calm even after the captain's display of cowardice, "many of those below were suffocated. The shrieks and moans of the dying came up to those on the deck, and they could do nothing to save them."

When the Federal steamer *Lavender* was wrecked on Cape Lookout Shoals, her men bravely clung to a small portion of the hull, which was just out of water, for four days and nights without food before they were rescued. Nine men were lost from exposure and drowning, the rest, fourteen in number, were saved at great risk. The wreck went to pieces within two hours after their rescue.

The United States steam gunboat *Dai Ching*, which had originally been built for the emperor of China, was wrecked at the first bend below Tar Bluff on the Combahee River in South Carolina. The *Dai Ching's* loss was attributed in part to cowardice on the part of her pilot.

Quite a few vessels were lost through poor seamanship, or inaccurate charts.

The screw steamer *Emily* was accidentally run ashore above Masonboro Inlet, "through the incapacity of her pilot, who • • • was at once put in the army." There was speculation that something may have been hidden under the salt, but whether or not it was gold or guns was never made clear.

The large screw steamer *Constitution* was lost by stranding at Cape Lookout, on December 26, 1865. Forty lives were lost.

The "Real Rhett Butler" & Other Revelations

Not only people lost lives in wrecks. When the *Star of the Union* was wrecked on Bogue Island, North Carolina, "the beach near her (was) strewed with pressed hay, barrels, and dead horses."

The old sidewheeler *Pocahontas* was wrecked twenty miles north of Cape Hatteras. "By this shipwreck ninety valuable horses were lost; some of them being thrown overboard ten miles from land, and others were left to perish because no one would go down to the lower deck and untie them, that they might swim ashore."

The sidewheel steamer *Tropic* (ex-*C.S.S. Huntress*), which was burned while trying to run the blockade out of Charleston, had been the first vessel to fly the Confederate flag on the high seas.

A group of sixteen old whaling ships, which had been purchased in New England and loaded with stone, were sunk by the Yankees as an obstruction to the shipping channel south east of the lighthouse on Morris Island, South Carolina. The Federal Navy sank a second group of thirteen ships a few weeks later in the shipping channel near Rattlesnake Shoals to the north of Charleston. The sinking of these vessels resulted in an international storm of protest against the North. I located several wrecks from both of these "Stone Fleets" in the mid 1960's.

Fourteen schooners were sunk by the Confederates in the Neuse River, twelve miles below New Berne, as an obstruction. The same was done at Washington, North Carolina. The Pamlico River was "similarly obstructed."

Federal officers purchased twenty-one vessels in August of 1861 for the express purpose of filling them with stone and sinking them as obstructions in the canals and waters of North Carolina.

Not only British and American vessels were casualties of the War. The large French warship *Prony* was lost at Ocracoke, North Carolina, when it ran on top of an earlier wreck. The French, who were Southern sympathizers, spiked or threw overboard her heavy guns along with her cutlasses and all of her small arms to prevent them from falling into the hands of the Yankees.

Bronze cannon are among some of the choicest of the extremely valuable artifacts that can be found from the Civil War.

When the English bark *Sophia* was fired into and chased aground on November 4, 1862, by the *U.S.S. Daylight,* near Masonboro Inlet, her cargo included three bronze field pieces.

Six bronze howitzers were thrown overboard, when the *U.S.S. Columbia* was wrecked off Wrightsville Beach.

Twenty captured bronze cannon were thrown into the river at Columbia, South Carolina, along with a number of iron cannon, tons of shot and shell, over a million musket balls, and thousands of swords, sabers and muskets. A detailed inventory of that material can be found in Appendix B of this book.

Appendix G contains some interesting information relating to the actual enforcement of the blockade.

As previously stated, over five hundred wrecks were reported as wrecked in the shallow waters of the Confederate Coast during the years 1861 through 1865. It is hoped that the reader will realize the diversity and importance of these wrecks, and that he will understand that many of those shipwrecks can still be found. Many are monetarily, historically and archeologically important. I recommend that the reader research them, and then get out and find them, before they are lost forever.

All of the States now claim ownership of at least some of the wrecks within their waters. Unfortunately, many seem to be doing relatively little to discover, publicize, and preserve them. Their claims seem to be in direct conflict with the United States Constitution and various Federal statutes, but they are currently supported by a maze of State and Federal statutes, so watch out. Even without meaning to violate any laws, you might do so, and you could be arrested.

Persons wishing to search for, dive on, or salvage wrecks would be wise to first check with a lawyer.

• • •

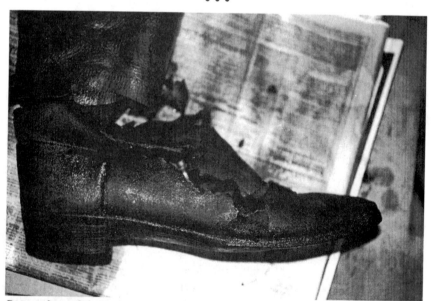

Boot salvaged from the wreck of the Underwriter at Newber, North Carolina. Photo by L. Spence, courtesy of the Underwater Archeology Unit of the North Carolina Department of Cultural Resources.

The Confederates designed and built a wide range of underwater mines (then called "torpedoes"), such as the two pictured above. Some were detonated by contact, others were detonated through the use of galvanic batteries. This photo is of a display at the Fort Fisher Museum & Display Center.

This porthole, held by Underwater Archeologist Mark Wilde-Ramsing, was salvaged from the wreck of the Confederate gunboat Curlew, which was sunk during the defense of Roanoke Island, N.C. Photo by Lee Spence, courtesy of the Underwater Archeology Unit, Fort Fisher Museum and Visitor's Center.

This strange looking tower is the engine of the U.S.S. Oriental, which was wrecked off Pea Island, North Carolina. Photo courtesy of the Underwater Archeology Unit, Fort Fisher Museum and Visitor's Center.

Chapter Four: "The War & the Blockade"

This brass and glass binnacle cover was salvaged from the Modern Greece, which was wrecked at Kure Beach, North Carolina. Binnacles were used to house ships' compasses. Photo by L. Spence, courtesy of the Underwater Archeology Unit, Fort Fisher Museum and Visitor's Center.

Chapter Four: "The War & the Blockade"

This handsome, bronze ship's bell belonged to the blockade runner Stormy Petrel, which was wrecked at New Inlet, North Carolina, on December 7, 1864. Photo by L. Spence, courtesy of the Underwater Archeology Unit, Fort Fisher Museum and Visitor's Center.

Chapter Four: "The War & the Blockade"
Page 111

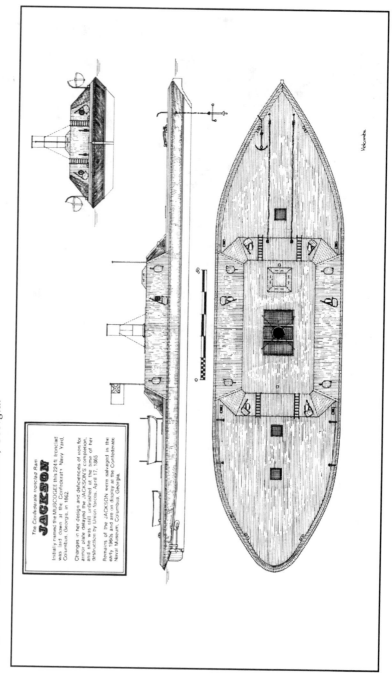

This drawing of the Confederates Stayes ram Jackson (ex-Muscogee) was drawn and provided courtesy of Robert Holcombe. The Jackson was destroyed on April 17, 1865, by the Union forces. Her remains are on display at the Confederate Naval Museum, Columbus, Georgia.

The Confederate Ironclad Ram

JACKSON

Initially named the MUSCOGEE this 224 ft. Ironclad was laid down at the Confederate's Navy Yard, Columbus, Georgia, in 1862.

Changes in her design and deficiencies of iron for armor plate delayed the JACKSON'S completion, and she was still unfinished at the time of her destruction by Union forces, April 17, 1865.

Remains of the JACKSON were salvaged in the early 1960s and are on display at the Confederate Naval Museum, Columbus, Georgia.

Stern section and propellers of the Confederate States ironclad ram Jackson. Photo by L. Spence, courtesy of the Confederate Naval Museum, Columbus, Georgia.

The boilers and steam engines of Civil War steamers usually protrude from the sand and can be easily located with sidescanning sonars like this one. This is the towfish (sensing unit) for a Hydroscan Model 501-T, manufactured by Klein & Associates in Salem, New Hampshire. Photo by Chip Knudsen.

SPENCE'S LIST
Shipwrecks of the Confederate Coast: North Carolina, South Carolina, & Georgia, 1861-1865

Note: Most people consider the Civil War to have begun with the firing on and capture of Fort Sumter, South Carolina, on April 12, 1861, and view the Confederate surrender at Appomattox Courthouse in Virginia on April 9, 1865, as the end of the war. But, in fact, neither the start nor the finish of the war are that easily defined. South Carolina actually seceded on December 10, 1860, a full four months before the action at Fort Sumter, and the Federal blockade of Southern ports officially continued until June 13, 1865. The Confederate Cruiser *Shenandoah*, circumnavigated the world while raiding United States merchant vessels and didn't surrender until November of 1865, when she finally docked at Liverpool, England. So, this list (although limited to the waters of North Carolina, South Carolina, and Georgia) is meant to include all reported shipwrecks from the beginning of 1861 through the end of 1865, regardless of whether they were war casualties, or whether they were later saved or salvaged. Shipwrecks in the latitudes of North Carolina, South Carolina and Georgia waters, but off the Continental Shelf, have not normally been included, unless failure to include them could cause confusion. Most of the following entries refer to single or multiple shipwrecks. A few entries refer to non-shipwreck events which should still be of interest to the reader. An effort has been made to list references chronologically by date of publication, showing the title first, rather than by author. This has been done because the earlier publications were frequently used as sources for later publications, and that information can be more important than who wrote it. Each entry is preceded by a combination of letters and numbers (called an *SL Code*™) for use in indexing and referencing purposes. An explanation of *SL Codes*™ may be found in Appendix A of this book.

1861-1-US-SC/GA-1: The British bark *Hilja*, Captain Henderson, bound from Charleston, South Carolina, to Liverpool, got ashore on the Charleston Bar in January, 1861, but was got off safely and returned to Rebellion Roads in Charleston Harbor. (Note: The *Hilja* was built in Finland in 1853 and was 569 tons.)

References for 1861-1-US-SC/GA-1:
"Charleston Daily Courier," (Charleston, SC), #18763, January 14, 1861, p. 4, c. 7
Lloyd's Register of British and Foreign Shipping, from 1st July, 1860, to the 30th June, 1861, (London, 1860), entry H-351

1861-1-US-SC/GA-2: According to the *Dictionary of American Naval Fighting Ships* five vessels were sunk in the main harbor of Charleston, South Carolina, on January 11, 1861, by the Southerners to block the passage of Federal warships. (Note: This researcher could find no mention of such an act in the Charleston papers, except for an item published in the "Charleston Daily

Courier" of January 21, 1861. The "Courier" was actually quoting the "New York Journal of Commerce" of January 17, 1861. That article mentioned several reports that had been received stating that the ship channel at the entrance to Charleston had been completely blocked by the sinking of two or three vessels. The article reported that the vessels were sunk on January 10, 1861, the day after the *Star of the West* retreated from Charleston Harbor. The ships were said to have been sunk in an effort to block the return of any hostile vessel. The New York paper was further quoted as saying that the reports were either entirely incorrect, or that a part of the channel had been left open to navigation, as Governor Pickens of South Carolina had subsequently sent a telegram to New York inviting New York merchant vessels to use Charleston. It went on to say that several large vessels had entered or left the harbor between the date of the supposed sinking and the publication of the article. The *New York Times* of January 19, 1861, stated "the approach to the main ship channel having been obstructed by the sinking of three or four vessels on the bar, to prevent the entrance of vessels.")

References for 1861-1-US-SC/GA-2:
New York Times, (New York, NY), Volume 10, #2911, January 18, 1861, p. 1, c. 4
"Charleston Daily Courier," (Charleston, SC), #18760, January 10, 1861, p. 1, c. 2
"Charleston Daily Courier," (Charleston, SC), #18769, January 21, 1861, p. 2, c. 4
Dictionary of American Naval Fighting Ships, (Washington, DC), Volume 5, p. 424

1861-1-US-SC/GA-3: On January 19, 1861, the sidewheel steamer *William Jenkins*, Captain Hallett, lying at Carlton's Wharf, near the gas house at Savannah, Georgia, was discovered to be on fire. The steamer was immediately cut loose and moored on the other side of the river. The *William Jenkins* was owned by Jenkins and Deford of Baltimore and was worth about $50,000. The vessel was said to be totally destroyed. She had arrived at Savannah from Boston, via Baltimore on January 18, 1861. The steamer carried an assorted cargo, one third of which was destroyed. The vessel's location was given as "near Lamar's Cotton Press." [Note : The *William Jenkins* had recently been repaired at Wilmington, Delaware, at a cost of $30,000. She had a wood hull and was built by John A. Robb at Baltimore in 1854 (or 1855) of white oak and chestnut with copper and iron fastenings. She had a vertical beam engine manufactured by Murray and Hazzlehurst. It had one fifty-six inch diameter cylinder and a nine foot piston stroke. The steamer had one independent fire pump and good security against fire. The *William Jenkins* was a medium model vessel and was rigged as a topsail schooner. The steamer was surveyed by "American Lloyd's" in January, 1858 and was rated A-1 1/2. She received enrollment #55 at Baltimore on March 23, 1855. That enrollment showed the *William Jenkins* owners as the Merchant and Miners Transportation Company of which Thomas C. Jenkins of Baltimore was president. The vessel measured 1011 83/95 tons, 209' in length (205' on deck), 31'10" in breadth (31' molded), 15'11" in depth (16' depth of hold to spar deck), and 13' draft at load line. The steamer had two decks, two masts, a square stern, no galleries and a plain head. Her water wheels were 26' in diameter and were built of iron. She had a single boiler and one stack. The steamer's coal bunkers were originally reported as of wood, but were later reported as iron. She had four cargo ports in her sides. The *William Jenkins* had no blowers, one smoke pipe, one bilge injection, and bottom valves or cocks to all openings in her bottom. The vessel's frames were twenty-seven inches apart at centers, frames all filled in solid, iron straps, diagonal and double laid. The vessel's hull had a copper bottom.]

References for 1861-1-US-SC/GA-3:
"Permanent Enrollment #55," (Baltimore, Md.), March 23, 1855, National Archives Records Service, Washington, DC, RG 41
"str. *William Jenkins*," (manuscript in bound volume of survey reports for New York, 1851-1859), National Archives Records Service, Washington, DC, RG 92, entry 1432, Volume A, p. 230
New York Marine Register: or American Lloyd's, (New York, New York, 1858/59), pp. 352, 353, #262
"Daily Morning News," (Savannah, GA), January 19, 1861, p. 2, c. 1
"Daily Morning News," (Savannah, GA), January 21, 1861, p. 1, c. 2
"Charleston Daily Courier," (Charleston, SC), #18769, January 21, 1861, p. 1, c. 2
"Charleston Daily Courier," (Charleston, SC), #18770, January 22, 1861, p. 4, c. 7
Encyclopedia of American Shipwrecks, by Bruce D. Berman, (Boston, 1972), p. 151, #2105
Merchant Steam Vessels of the United States 1790-1868, ("Lytle-Holdcamper List"), edited by C. Bradford Mitchell, (Staten Island, New York, 1975), pp. 231, 307

1861-3-US-NC-1: A barrel marked *"John Carver* - ship stores," a "quantity of wood-work with panels like the joiner-work of a deck cabin or forward house" were observed on the edge of the Gulf Stream, north of Cape Hatteras, North Carolina, on March 20, 1861, by the brig *Ianthe*, of Baltimore. (Note: The *John Carver* was a bark.)

Reference for 1861-3-US-NC-1:
New York Times, (New York, NY), Volume 10, #2966, March 25, 1861, p. 8, c. 5, 6

1861-3-US-NC-2: The schooner *Sarah Hibbert*, with cargo, went ashore north of Nags Head, North Carolina, during a gale in March of 1861. (Note: Although she was to be auctioned on April 8, 1861, it isn't clear whether or not she was actually salvaged, or to what extent, as wrecks were often auctioned where they lay, and never salvaged.)

Reference for 1861-3-US-NC-2:
New York Times, (New York, NY), Volume 10, #2971, March 30, 1861, p. 8, c. 6

1861-3-US-SC/GA-1: The ship *Susan G. Owens*, went ashore on Folly Island, South Carolina, but was got off and towed into Charleston on March 22, 1861.

Reference for 1861-3-US-SC/GA-1:
New York Times, (New York, NY), Volume 10, #2966, March 25, 1861, p. 8, c. 6

Treasures of the Confederate Coast

1861-4-US-NC-1: The brig *Black Squall*, bound from Cuba to New York, with a cargo of sugar, was wrecked at Ocracoke Inlet, North Carolina, on April 8, 1861. Two men were drowned.

References for 1861-4-US-NC-1:
New York Times, (New York, NY), Volume 10, #2989, April 20, 1861, p. 8, c. 5
Graveyard of the Atlantic: Shipwrecks of the North Carolina Coast, by David Stick (University of North Carolina Press, Chapel Hill, NC, 1952), p. 247
An Oceanographic Atlas of the Continental Margin, J.G. Newton, O.H. Pilkey and J.O. Blanton, (Duke University Marine Laboratory, Beaufort, NC, 1971), p. 24 entry #305

1861-4-US-NC-2: A schooner "name unknown", crew "supposed to be lost", was reported ashore on Hatteras Shoal, North Carolina, on April 16, 1861. It was thought that she was "the *War Eagle*, from Port-au-Prince for Philadelphia, reported by steamer *Keystone State*." (Note: The dismasted and abandoned brig *War Eagle* was seen by the brig *Costa Rico*, Captain Beels, on April 12, 1861. The *Costa Rico* arrived at New York from Aspinwall, Panama, on April 14, 1861.)

References for 1861-4-US-NC-2:
New York Times, (New York, NY), Volume 10, #2984, April 15, 1861, p. 5, c. 3
New York Times, (New York, NY), Volume 10, #2989, April 20, 1861, p. 8, c. 5

1861-4-US-NC-3: A letter dated at Wilmington, North Carolina, on April 16, 1861, mentioned that the schooner *Alice L. Webb*, said to have been "bound to the South" from New York, with an assorted cargo was wrecked in the vicinity of Ocracoke and Hatteras, North Carolina. (Note: If this report was correct as to the wrecked vessel's identity, it would mean that she was saved and put back into service, as the *Alice L. Webb* was lost off Swansboro, North Carolina, in November of 1863. See also entry 1863-11-US-NC-1.)

Reference for 1861-4-US-NC-3:
New York Times, (New York, NY), Volume 10, #2989, April 20, 1861, p. 8, c. 5

1861-4-US-NC-4: A letter dated at Wilmington, North Carolina, on April 16, 1861, mentioned that the schooner *Stephen Duncan*, bound from Mobile, Alabama, to New York, with cotton, was wrecked in the vicinity of Ocracoke and Hatteras, North Carolina.

Reference for 1861-4-US-NC-4:
New York Times, (New York, NY), Volume 10, #2989, April 20, 1861, p. 8, c. 5

1861-4-US-NC-5: The ship *Witchcraft* was on a northwest course with a northeast wind when she was wrecked within sight of the lights of both Hatteras and Body Island, North Carolina, sometime prior to April 19, 1861. The ship listed off shore when she went aground, thereby exposing her decks to the full force of a heavy sea. She went to pieces in an hour and a half. Fourteen of the thirty-one people aboard were lost. Captain John Hayes, late of the British ship *John Phillips*, which had been sold in Australia, was lost along with his wife and child. Her boats were all stove, and a man named

The "Real Rhett Butler" & Other Revelations

Thomas Bliss later told how he tried to swim for the beach, and succeeded in reaching it only after having drifted two miles southward. A seaman named Moses Smith died of exhaustion, and was buried on the beach. The chief mate, the second mate, the steward and the cook were also lost.

Reference for 1861-4-US-NC-5:
New York Times, (New York, NY), Volume 10, #2988, April 19, 1861, p. 5, c. 2

1861-4-US-SC/GA-1: The schooner *Elite* was reported ashore on Tybee Beach, Georgia, on April 6, 1861. The schooner was got off with the help of a steamer but was blown back on the beach in a high wind. The hull of the *Elite* was sold at auction on April 16, 1861. The schooner was finally got off and towed to Savannah on April 21, 1861.

References for 1861-4-US-SC/GA-1:
"Daily Morning News," (Savannah, GA), April 6, 1861, p. 1, c. 1
"Daily Morning News," (Savannah, GA), April 17, 1861, p. 2, c. 1
"Daily Morning News," (Savannah, GA), April 25, 1861, p. 2, c. 1

1861-4-US-x-1: On April 16, 1861, President Lincoln proclaimed that the "inhabitants of the Southern States" were in a "state of insurrection" and forbade "all commercial intercourse with same." Lincoln further ordered that after fifteen days "all ships and vessels belonging in whole or in part to any citizen or inhabitant of any (of the rebelling states) found at sea or in any port of the United States" be forfeited to the United States. Lincoln also announced that a blockade of the ports within the rebelling states would be put in place, and that any vessels attempting to leave any of said ports were to be "duly warned by the commander of one of the said blockading vessels, who will indorse on her register the fact and date of such warning; and if the same vessel shall again attempt to enter or leave the blockaded port, she will be captured." (Note: See also entry 1861-8-US-x-1.)

References for 1861-4-US-x-1:
New York Times, (New York, NY), Volume 10, #2989, April 20, 1861, p. 1, c. 1
Official Records of the Union and Confederate Navies in the War of the Rebellion, (Washington, DC, 1897), Series 1, Volume 6, pp. 90, 91

1861-5-US-NC-1: The brig *Lydia Francis*, Daniel A. Campbell master, bound from Cuba to New York, with a cargo of sugar, was wrecked at Hatteras Cove, North Carolina, on May 6, 1861. (Note One: This was probably the 262 ton brig *Lydia Frances*, which was built in 1855 at Damariscotta, Maine. That vessel was issued a certificate of registry at New York, New York, on May 14, 1856.) (Note Two: One report refers to the wreck as the *Lydia Martin*, while another shows her as the *Lydia French*. She had been a prize to the *C.S.S. Winslow*.)

References for 1861-5-US-NC-1:

Treasures of the Confederate Coast

Official Records of the Union and Confederate Navies in the War of the Rebellion, (Washington, DC, 1894), Series 1, Volume 1, p. 59
Official Records of the Union and Confederate Navies in the War of the Rebellion, (Washington, DC, 1897), Series 1, Volume 6, p. 78
Confederate Privateers, by William Morrison Robinson, Jr., (Yale University Press, 1928), p. 102
Outer Banks of North Carolina, by David Stick, (UNC Press, Chapel Hill, NC, 1958, p. 118
List of American-Flag Merchant Vessels that Received Certificates of Enrollment or Registry at the Port of New York 1789-1867, compiled by Forest R. Holdcamper, (U.S. National Archives, Washington, DC, 1968), Special List #22, Volume 2, p. 431

1861-6-US-NC-1: The schooner *Lath Rich*, Captain Rankin, of Frankfort, Maine, bound from Matanzas to New York, passed a small vessel sunk, masts gone, sixty miles south of Hatteras, North Carolina, on June 9, 1861.

Reference for 1861-6-US-NC-1:
New York Times, (New York, NY), Volume 10, #3037, June 15, 1861, p. 8, c. 6

1861-6-US-NC-2: The brig *Nathan*, of Mathias, passed quantity of yellow pine timber and some wreck materials off Hatteras, North Carolina, on June 12, 1861.

Reference for 1861-6-US-NC-2:
New York Times, (New York, NY), Volume 10, #3037, June 15, 1861, p. 8, c. 6

1861-6-US-SC/GA-1: A boat placed at the entrance of St. Helena Bar, South Carolina, for the purpose of assisting the British bark *Edward*, by Captain Bonneau, of the schooner *Howell Cobb*, was accidentally run over and destroyed by the steamer *General Clinch*, on June 6, 1861.

Reference for 1861-6-US-SC/GA-1:
New York Times, (New York, NY), Volume 10, #3036, June 14, 1861, p. 5, c. 3, 4

1861-7-US-NC-1: The bark *Linwood*, Henry W. Penny master, thirteen men, bound from Rio de Janeiro to New York, with a cargo of 6,000 bags of coffee, was chased ashore by the *C.S.S. Winslow* and wrecked opposite the village, about six miles north of Hatteras Inlet, North Carolina, on July 16, 1861. She drew fifteen feet of water and was stranded about four hundred feet from the beach. (Note: This was probably the 491 ton bark *Linwood*, built in 1852 at Baltimore, Maryland. That vessel was issued a certificate of registry at New York, New York, on November 26, 1860.)

References for 1861-7-US-NC-1:
Official Records of the Union and Confederate Navies in the War of the Rebellion, (Washington, DC, 1897), Series 1, Volume 6, pp. 67, 78, 79, 80
Confederate Privateers, by William Morrison Robinson, Jr., (Yale University Press, 1928), p. 102
Outer Banks of North Carolina, by David Stick, (UNC Press, Chapel Hill, NC, 1958, pp. 118, 121
List of American-Flag Merchant Vessels that Received Certificates of Enrollment or Registry at the Port of New York 1789-1867, compiled by Forest R. Holdcamper, (U.S. National Archives, Washington, DC, 1968), Special List #22, Volume 2, p. 418

1861-7-US-NC-2: On July 22, 1861, the *U.S.S. Albatross* observed "two ship's hulls under water, with masts standing, on the beach to the northeast of (Hatteras) inlet."

Reference for 1861-7-US-NC-2:
Official Records of the Union and Confederate Navies in the War of the Rebellion, (Washington, DC, 1897), Series 1, Volume 6, p. 688

The "Real Rhett Butler" & Other Revelations

1861-7-US-NC-3: The American brig *B.T. Martin*, of Boston, C.A. French master, bound from Philadelphia to Cardenas, which had been captured by the Confederate privateer *York*, Captain Geoffroy, was accidentally run ashore on July 24, 1861, a few miles to the northward of Cape Hatteras (or "on Nagg's Head"). On July 28, 1861, the wreck and most of her cargo was burned by the *U.S.S. Union*, J.R. Goldsborough commander. Her cargo consisted of one new cylinder boiler, a large iron refinery, cast iron framing, three large iron tanks, stoves, and about forty barrels of potatoes. The brig and her cargo were valued at $60,000. (Note One: One modern source gives her location as at Chicamacomico "20-30 miles N of the Cape.") (Note Two: The *B.T. Martin* was built in 1852 at Bristol, Maine, and was issued a certificate of registry at the port of New York, New York, on December 30, 1858.)

References for 1861-7-US-NC-3:
Official Records of the Union and Confederate Armies in the War of the Rebellion, (Washington, DC, 1882), Series 1, Volume 4, p. 587
Official Records of the Union and Confederate Navies in the War of the Rebellion, (Washington, DC, 1894), Series 1, Volume 1, pp. 59, 60, 818
Official Records of the Union and Confederate Navies in the War of the Rebellion, (Washington, DC, 1897), Series 1, Volume 6, pp. 41, 48
Confederate Privateers, by William Morrison Robinson, Jr., (Yale University Press, 1928), p. 104
Graveyard of the Atlantic: Shipwrecks of the North Carolina Coast, by David Stick (University of North Carolina Press, Chapel Hill, NC, 1952), p. 247
List of American-Flag Merchant Vessels that Received Certificates of Enrollment or Registry at the Port of New York 1789-1867, compiled by Forest R. Holdcamper, (U.S. National Archives, Washington, DC, 1968), Special List #22, Volume 1, p. 69
An Oceanographic Atlas of the Continental Margin, J.G. Newton, O.H. Pilkey and J.O. Blanton, (Duke University Marine Laboratory, Beaufort, NC, 1971), p. 25 chart symbol #607, p. 29 entry #607

1861-7-US-SC/GA-1: A boat with several members of the Phoenix Riflemen on its way from Tybee to the steamer *Ida* capsized on July 17, 1861, drowning Mr. James Graham, a Savannah fruit merchant.

Reference for 1861-7-US-SC/GA-1:
"Daily Morning News," (Savannah, GA), July 19, 1861, p. 1, c. 2

1861-7-US-SC/GA-2: The Confederate States privateer *Petrel*, Captain William Perry, two guns, was sunk off Charleston, South Carolina, by a shell from the United States gunboat *St. Lawrence*, Captain H.Y. Purviance, on July 28, 1861. The *Petrel* fired two or three shots before she was sunk. Five (also shown as two) men were drowned and thirty six captured. The prisoners were carried to Philadelphia aboard the U.S. gunboat *Flag*. A Northern paper reported that "Bills of indictment for piracy" had been found against the *Petrel's* crew. [Note One: The *Petrel* was a schooner of 82 57/95 tons and had once served as the Charleston pilot boat *Eclipse* and as the United States Revenue cutter *William Aiken* (or *Aiken*). She was a fore-and-aft schooner and was considered one of the fastest vessels of her class in the Revenue service. As a revenue cutter, the *William Aiken* was armed with one 12-pounder brass howitzer,

Treasures of the Confederate Coast

working amidships, and a quantity of Maynard rifles. She had been surrendered by Captain Napoleon L. Coste to South Carolina authorities on December 27, 1860, following the passage of the ordinance of secession on the previous day. She was issued a "Letter of Marque and Reprisal" by the Confederate government on July 10, 1861. Thomas Scharf, in his book on the Confederate Navy, described the *Petrel* as "a relic of the Florida War." The *Petrel* was owned by Charlestonians William Whaley, George A. Locke, Q.B. Oakes, Thomas J. Legare, A.J. Salinas, W.M. Martin, Henry Buist, G.W. King, M. Triest, and D. Haas.] (Note Two: Although indicted for piracy, the men of the *Petrel* were never executed as the Confederate government immediately threatened to retaliate by executing an equal number of Union prisoners.) (Note Three: The *Petrel's* position was reported as latitude 32°30' North, longitude 79°09' West, but even if fairly accurate, she was small and would be extremely difficult to locate.)

References for 1861-7-US-SC/GA-2:
New York Times, (New York, NY), Volume 10, #2896, January 1, 1861, p. 8, c. 2
New York Times, (New York, NY), Volume 10, #2902, January 9, 1861, p. 1, c. 3
"Daily Morning News," (Savannah, GA), August 12, 1861, p. 1, c. 1
"Daily Morning News," (Savannah, GA), August 20, 1861, p. 1, c. 4
"Daily Morning News," (Savannah, GA), October 7, 1861, p. 1, c. 5
"Vessel Papers" (manuscript records), United States National Archives, Washington, DC, Record Group 109, file P-50
History of the Confederate States Navy From its Organization to the Surrender of its Last Vessel, by J. Thomas Scharf, (New York, New York, 1887), p. 656
Official Records of the Union and Confederate Navies in the War of the Rebellion, (Washington, DC, 1894), Series 1, Volume 1, pp. 51, 112, 818, 819
Official Records of the Union and Confederate Navies in the War of the Rebellion, (Washington, DC, 1897), Series 1, Volume 6, pp. 52, 61, 63, 65, 69, 74, 94, 95, 219
Official Records of the Union and Confederate Navies in the War of the Rebellion, (Washington, DC, 1901), Series 2, Volume 1, pp. 247, 262, 271, 326, 369, 370
Naval History of the Civil War, by Howard P. Nash, (A.S. Barnes & Co., New York, NY, 1972), p. 297
Shipwrecks of the Civil War: The Encyclopedia of Union and Confederate Naval Losses, by Donald Shomette, (Washington, DC, 1973), pp. 342, 343
Charleston's Maritime Heritage 1670-1865, by P.C. Coker III, (CokerCraft Press, Charleston, SC, 1987), pp. 196, 211
Warships of the Civil War Navies, by Paul H. Silverstone, (Naval Institute Press, Annapolis, MD, 1989), p. 242

1861-8-US-NC-1: The Confederate States privateer *York*, Captain T.L. Skinner (or John Geoffroy), was burnt by her officers and crew four miles south of Bodie's Island light-house, on August 9, 1861, to prevent her capture by the *U.S.S. Union*, J.R. Goldsborough commander. She carried one 18-pounder rifled gun (also shown as one 8-pounder, and as one 6-pounder) mounted on a carriage amidships. Her gun was thrown overboard prior to her being set afire. [Note One: The *York* had been used as the pilot boat (*Florida*) before being fitted out as a privateer at Norfolk. She was just commissioned on July 9, 1861, but had already captured at least to prizes. She was schooner rigged, sixty-eight tons, painted lead color, and had a crew of thirty men. The *York* burned to the water line and "drifted out to sea a mass of flames."] (Note Two: Her position was also given simply as "off Cape Hatteras.")

References for 1861-8-US-NC-1:
Official Records of the Union and Confederate Armies in the War of the Rebellion, (Washington, DC, 1882), Series 1, Volume 4, p. 587
Official Records of the Union and Confederate Navies in the War of the Rebellion, (Washington, DC, 1894), Series 1, Volume 1, pp. 59-61, 818, 819
Official Records of the Union and Confederate Navies in the War of the Rebellion, (Washington, DC, 1897), Series 1, Volume 6, pp. 68, 79, 793, 795
Official Records of the Union and Confederate Navies in the War of the Rebellion, (Washington, DC, 1921), Series 2, Volume 1, pp. 272, 326, 368
Confederate Privateers, by William Morrison Robinson, Jr., (Yale University Press, 1928), pp. 104, 105, 110
Graveyard of the Atlantic: Shipwrecks of the North Carolina Coast, by David Stick (University of North Carolina Press, Chapel Hill, NC, 1952), p. 247

1861-8-US-NC-2: The schooner *Louisa* of Wilmington, two hundred tons burden, bound from the West Indies to Wilmington, North Carolina, (probably with coffee) was chased ashore and totally wrecked "upon a reef near the light-house (probably Smith Island, North Carolina) about 3 miles from the fort," on August 11, 1861, by the *U.S.S. Penguin*, J. W. Livingston commanding. She "keeled over, filled with water - the sea running high - and became a wreck, vessel and cargo, the sea making a complete breach over her."

References for 1861-8-US-NC-2:
Official Records of the Union and Confederate Navies in the War of the Rebellion, (Washington, DC, 1897), Series 1, Volume 6, pp. 85, 86

1861-8-US-NC-3: On August 27, 1861, a number of "large, unwieldy iron surf-boats" intended to carry a company of men each" which were being used to land men two and a half to three miles north of Hatteras Inlet, during the successful Federal assault on that location, "struck the beach" and "were thrown high upon it, there to remain." Two wooden flat-boats landing troops, broke up and went to pieces in the surf. "In this manner three hundred and fifteen troops, including fifty United States Artillery, fifty-five marines, and two navy howitzers were thrown on shore without provisions or supplies of any kind, and much of their ammunition was wetted." One account described the event as follows. The iron-surf boats were "hurled on the beach, the waves sweeping over them, and the men struggling through the water waist-deep to shore. One boat, a cutter from the *Pawnee*, landed safely, and returned for another load of soldiers, but on entering the surf a second time it was swamped, and all on board very narrowly escaped drowning. It was found impossible to get the surf boats out again, and they were swamped and crushed by the surf."

References for 1861-8-US-NC-3:
The History of the Navy during the Rebellion, by Charles B. Boynton, (D. Appelton and Company, New York, NY, 1867), Volume 1, pp. 337, 340
The Navy in the Civil War, (Charles Scribner's Sons, New York, NY, 1905), Volume 2 ("The Atlantic Coast" by Daniel Ammen), p.p. 166, 169
Outer Banks of North Carolina, by David Stick, (UNC Press, Chapel Hill, NC, 1958, pp. 121, 122

Treasures of the Confederate Coast

1861-8-US-NC-4: The small Virginia sloop *Good Egg* was chased ashore about thirty miles up the Rappahannock River near the entrance to Deep Creek on August 29, 1861, by the *U.S.S. Daylight*, but she was immediately got off. It is not known if she was then destroyed or if she was kept as a prize.

References for 1861-8-US-NC-4:
Official Records of the Union and Confederate Navies in the War of the Rebellion, (Washington, DC, 1897), Series 1, Volume 6, pp. 147, 148

1861-8-US-x-1: A lengthy letter from Gideon Welles, Secretary of the United States Navy, to President Abraham Lincoln, dated August 5, 1861, discussed the ramifications of imposing a blockade on the southern ports. Welles stated that, if the Federal government closed the ports by blockade, the rules and principles of international law would govern. The Confederate States would be considered and treated as a distinct nationality, and their customs collectors, revenue officers, clearances, registers, etc., would be recognized as legitimate. Welles pointed out that the Federal government had been trying to show the Confederacy as an illegal rebellion and warned of the serious consequences of effectively recognizing the Confederate government as legitimate by the declaration of a formal blockade rather than simply closing them by act of civil law and then seizing vessels sailing to or from them as smugglers. (Note: See also entry 1861-4-US-x-1.)

References for 1861-8-US-x-1:
Official Records of the Union and Confederate Navies in the War of the Rebellion, (Washington, DC, 1897), Series 1, Volume 6, pp. 53-56

1861-9-US-NC-1: A "light-ship," which had been used as a storeship, and which was run ashore some distance from Fort Ocracoke on Beacon Island, near Ocracoke, North Carolina, was burned by Lieutenant Maxwell of the *U.S.S. Fanny* about September 17, 1861. The light-ship had a quantity of stores aboard when she was burned. Maxwell and his men also destroyed four 8-inch 63-hundredweight guns and fourteen long 32-pounders of 33-hundredweight each which had been at the fort. (Note One: One report stated that she was "inside," which probably meant that she was inside the bar, rather than inside the inlet.) (Note Two: See also entry 1861-11-US-NC-8 for an account of the loss of the French warship *Prony*, which was said to have run aground on this wreck. Also see entry 1861-11-US-NC-10, for an account of the Confederate steamer *Winslow* which was also said to have been lost on this wreck.)

References for 1861-89-US-NC-1:
Official Records of the Union and Confederate Navies in the War of the Rebellion, (Washington, DC, 1897), Series 1, Volume 6, pp. 223-225, 241, 785

The "Real Rhett Butler" & Other Revelations

1861-9-US-NC-2: On September 17, 1861, Lieutenant Eastman, in a launch from the *U.S.S. Pawnee*, proceeded to Portsmouth, North Carolina, where he found three 8-inch navy shell guns lying on the beach and one mounted on a carriage. The guns had already been spiked, and Lieutenant Eastman finished destroying them by breaking off the cascabels and leaving them in the salt water on the beach. Another report stated that four "32-pounders of 27 hundredweight" were destroyed at Portsmouth on the same date, but whether there was confusion over the type of guns, or whether there were a total of eight guns destroyed is not known.

References for 1861-9-US-NC-2:
Official Records of the Union and Confederate Navies in the War of the Rebellion, (Washington, DC, 1897), Series 1, Volume 6, pp. 223-225, 241

1861-9-US-NC-3: Two Federal reports (one from the *U.S.S. Susquehanna* and the other from the *U.S.S. Pawnee*) dated September 20, 1861, stated that fourteen schooners ("prizes and others") had been sunk "entirely across" the Neuse River at a place called Piney Point, some twelve miles below New Berne, North Carolina. Piles had also been placed in the river as an obstruction and the point fortified. One of the reports also stated that the "same has been done at Washington, NC, a fort erected on a point of land guarding the approach up the river, and vessels sunk across." The other report stated that the Pamlico River was "similarly obstructed, and a fort erected on the right bank on a point formed by a bayou or inlet." (Note: See also entry 1862-9-US-NC-2.)

References for 1861-9-US-NC-3:
Official Records of the Union and Confederate Navies in the War of the Rebellion, (Washington, DC, 1897), Series 1, Volume 6, pp. 238-243

1861-9-US-NC-4: An order from Gideon Welles, United States Secretary of the Navy, to Flag-Officer L.M. Goldsborough, stated that Goldsborough was authorized to enlist "contrabands" (the term commonly used by the military for blacks) for the naval service. However, they were to be allowed no higher rating than "boys," at a compensation of $10 per month and one ration a day.

Reference for 1861-9-US-NC-4:
Official Records of the Union and Confederate Navies in the War of the Rebellion, (Washington, DC, 1897), Series 1, Volume 6, p. 252

1861-9-US-NC-5: In a report dated September 28, 1861, Commander S.C. Rowan of the *U.S.S. Pawnee* stated that the prize schooner *Henry Nutt*, Captain Sidney Baker (owner), with a cargo of mahogany, which had been hard aground near the upper bulkhead at Hatteras Inlet, North Carolina, had finally been forced down to the lower bulkhead "where she is now hard aground." Rowan planed to off-load the mahogany to get her off if necessary.

Treasures of the Confederate Coast

(Note One: The *Henry Nutt*, 272 tons, was built at Wilmington, Delaware, in 1852, and was issued a certificate of registry at the port of New York on August 29, 1866.) (Note: The *Henry Nutt* had been a prize to the *C.S.S. Winslow.*) (Note Two: In the sense used above, a bulkhead was a bank of sand separating the deeper waters of the sounds and those within the exterior bar.)

References for 1861-9-US-NC-5:
Official Records of the Union and Confederate Navies in the War of the Rebellion, (Washington, DC, 1897), Series 1, Volume 6, pp. 135, 249, 263, 273
The Navy in the Civil War, (Charles Scribner's Sons, New York, NY, 1905), Volume 2 ("The Atlantic Coast" by Daniel Ammen), p. 164
Confederate Privateers, by William Morrison Robinson, Jr., (Yale University Press, 1928), p. 110
Outer Banks of North Carolina, by David Stick, (UNC Press, Chapel Hill, NC, 1958, p. 118
List of American-Flag Merchant Vessels that Received Certificates of Enrollment or Registry at the Port of New York 1789-1867, compiled by Forest R. Holdcamper, (U.S. National Archives, Washington, DC, 1968), Special List #22, Volume 1, p. 317

1861-9-US-NC-6: The *U.S.S. Pawnee* lost two of its best boats while attempting to free the *U.S.S. Harriet Lane* from a shoal at the mouth of Hatteras Inlet, North Carolina, on September 29, 1861. The *Harriet Lane* finally got off fifty hours later by throwing overboard tons of munitions, guns, and supplies and by kedging. (Note One: A detailed list of the items thrown overboard appears on page 130 of Volume 6 of the *Official Records of the Union and Confederate Navies in the War of the Rebellion.* Some of the more interesting items listed as having been thrown overboard were a "tank" of mercury; two Maynard rifles; four rifled 32-pounders (and their carriages); seventy shot and shell for and 8-inch gun; two hundred and twenty-nine shot and shell for the 32-pounders; five cases of shell, shrapnel and canister for the boat howitzer; and ten pairs of hand and leg irons.) (Note Two: The *Harriet Lane* eventually foundered in the Caribbean Sea on May 13, 1884.)

References for 1861-9-US-NC-6:
Official Records of the Union and Confederate Navies in the War of the Rebellion, (Washington, DC, 1921), Series 2, Volume 1, p. 99
Official Records of the Union and Confederate Navies in the War of the Rebellion, (Washington, DC, 1897), Series 1, Volume 6, pp. 129-131, 135, 136, 186

1861-9-US-NC-7: Commander H.S. Stellwagen had a "stormy passage" and was forced to abandon a vessel filled with stone, while attempting to tow it to Hatteras Inlet, North Carolina, in September of 1861.

Reference for 1861-9-US-NC-7:
Official Records of the Union and Confederate Navies in the War of the Rebellion, (Washington, DC, 1897), Series 1, Volume 6, p. 280

1861-9-US-NC-8: The *U.S.S. Stars and Stripes* met with a "stormy passage" in September of 1861, and lost a schooner (apparently filled with stone), while attempting to tow it to Hatteras Inlet, North Carolina.

Reference for 1861-9-US-NC-8:

The "Real Rhett Butler" & Other Revelations

Official Records of the Union and Confederate Navies in the War of the Rebellion, (Washington, DC, 1897), Series 1, Volume 6, p. 280

1861-9-US-SC/GA-1: The Confederate schooner *Colonel Long*, fourteen tons burden, bound from Miami to Savannah or Charleston, with limes, a barrel of whiskey, a few bags of arrowroot, and a bag of sponges was scuttled at sea, "a little to the southward of Savannah" by the Federal sloop of war *Jamestown* on September 4, 1861. The *Colonel Long* had appeared to have been a "regular fishing smack" when stopped on a previous occasion, but this time had a crew of eight and carried a cargo of limes, part of a barrel of whiskey, a few bags of arrowroot and a bag of sponges, all of which were taken off by the Yankees before she was burned. Her Confederate coasting license and a Confederate flag were found concealed under the ceiling (flooring) of the cabin.

References for 1861-9-US-SC/GA-1:
Official Records of the Union and Confederate Navies in the War of the Rebellion, (Washington, DC, 1897), Series 1, Volume 6, pp. 166-167
Shipwrecks of the Civil War: The Encyclopedia of Union and Confederate Naval Losses, by Donald Shomette, (Washington, DC, 1973), p. 410

1861-10-US-NC-1: On October 7, 1861, the *U.S.S. Albatross'* captain's gig (Lieutenant Neville, and twelve men), and the *U.S.S. Albatross'* first cutter (Master's Mate Harris, and twelve men), capsized in the surf at Bogue Inlet, North Carolina. James R. Hobby, ordinary seaman, and Samuel Nichols, seaman, from the gig were drowned. The remaining men from the gig and the first cutter were rescued by boats from the *U.S.S. Cambridge*. The gig "was stove in and a quantity of arms and a compass were lost."

Reference for 1861-10-US-NC-1:
Official Records of the Union and Confederate Navies in the War of the Rebellion, (Washington, DC, 1897), Series 1, Volume 6, p. 689

1861-10-US-SC/GA-1: The privateer ship *Thomas Watson*, Captain Allen, of Mobile, was chased ashore on the northern side of the Stono Breakers and several miles from Folly Beach, South Carolina, on October 15, 1861. The ship was one and a half to two miles from the beach and her bow was in seven feet of water, while her stern was in nine feet of water. The *Thomas Watson's* crew abandoned her leaving their food sitting warm on the table. An iron 9-pounder (said to be her armament) and some cannon balls were found on the wreck and thrown overboard. The stranded vessel was burned to the water's edge by the Federal gunboat *Vandalia*. Among the items taken from the wreck by the Federals were two bells, a few old nautical instruments, a few old lanterns, a whaling blunderbuss, five harpoons, three compasses, and eighteen packages of gold leaf. [Note One: The *Thomas Watson's* cargo consisted of thirty-two hundred sacks (350 tons) of fine salt, machinery, two printing presses for Evans and Cogswell, blankets, red and gray flannels, and several bales of merchandise for Kerrison and Leiding. She sailed from Liverpool on August 29, 1861, bound for Charleston, with 40 men. She was said to have been loaded by Fraser, Trenholm & Company, and was believed to have also carried "cases of arms."] [Note Two: An American flag, a Dutch flag, a Spanish flag, and an "old secession" (Confederate) flag were found aboard the wreck. Such flags would have been used to conceal the true identity and nationality of a blockade runner.] (Note Three: The *Thomas Watson* was built at Baltimore in 1848 of oak and was copper and iron fastened. The ship was 348 tons and drew fourteen feet of water. The *Thomas Watson* was a full model ship with one deck and a break and a poop cabin. She was issued a certificate of register at the port of New York on November 27, 1856. The ship was metalled in January, 1858, and was rated A-2 for insurance purposes. In 1858 the *Thomas Watson* was owned in New York by G.W. Reynolds. The ship was surveyed in March, 1858. One report described her as having a black hull, bright lower masts, black mastheads, an eagle on her stern, two whaleboats and ship-rigged. Her captain may have altered her mizzenmast to make her resemble a bark prior to her departure from Liverpool.) (Note Four: Fraser, Trenholm and Company was headed by George Alfred Trenholm who was later used as the historical basis for Margaret Mitchell's fictional character Rhett Butler in *Gone With The Wind*.)

References for 1861-10-US-SC/GA-1:
American Lloyd's Registry of American & Foreign Shipping, (New York, New York, 1858), p. 55, #1627
"Daily Morning News," (Savannah, GA), August 27, 1861, p. 1, c. 1
"Charleston Daily Courier," (Charleston, SC), #18987, October 16, 1861, p. 2, c. 2
"Charleston Daily Courier," (Charleston, SC), #18988, October 17, 1861, p. 2, c. 2
Official Records of the Union and Confederate Navies in the War of the Rebellion, (Washington, DC, 1897), Series 1, Volume 6, pp. 213, 214, 323-328
Official Records of the Union and Confederate Navies in the War of the Rebellion, (Washington, DC, 1921), Series 2, Volume 1, p. 268
List of American-Flag Merchant Vessels that Received Certificates of Enrollment or Registry at the Port of New York 1789-1867, compiled by Forest R. Holdcamper, (U.S. National Archives, Washington, DC, 1968), Special List #22, Volume 2, p. 680
Shipwrecks of the Civil War: The Encyclopedia of Union and Confederate Naval Losses, by Donald Shomette, (Washington, DC, 1973), p. 465

1861-10-US-SC/GA-2: The steamer *George W. Coffee*, "well known as the Mount Pleasant (South Carolina) ferry," was sunk at her wharf on October 29, 1861. The cause of the sinking was attributed to "Union sympathizers." The vessel was later raised with the aid of a steam pump, and continued in service until at least June 16, 1864, when she was sold for $41,000 by John S. Riggs. (Note: The "Lytle List" shows a sidewheel steamer *George W. Coffee* as "abandoned or otherwise removed from documentation" in 1850. That steamer was built at Jersey City, New Jersey, in 1848 and her first home port was listed as Charleston, South Carolina. She had been issued a certificate of steam enrollment on May 17, 1848, at the port of New York.)

References for 1861-10-US-SC/GA-2:
"Charleston Daily Courier," (Charleston, SC), #19001, November 1, 1861, p. 1, c. 2
"Charleston Daily Courier," (Charleston, SC), #19003, November 3, 1861, p. 1, c. 2
"Daily Morning News," (Savannah, GA), November 2, 1861, p. 2, c. 3
"Charleston Mercury," (Charleston, SC), Volume 84, #12089, June 16, 1864, p. 2, c. 1, 6 (illustrated advertisement)
"Charleston Mercury," (Charleston, SC), Volume 84, #12090, June 17, 1864, p. 2, c. 1
Private Journal of Henry William Ravenell, edited by A.R. Childs, (Columbia, South Carolina, 1947), p. 94
Merchant Steam Vessels of the United States 1807-1868, ("Lytle List"), by William M. Lytle, (Mystic, CT, 1952), p. 75
List of American-Flag Merchant Vessels that Received Certificates of Enrollment or Registry at the Port of New York 1789-1867, compiled by Forest R. Holdcamper, (U.S. National Archives, Washington, DC, 1968), Special List #22, Volume 1, p. 278

1861-10-US-SC/GA-3: The ferry boat *Osiris* (or *Orsini*), Captain Mansfield, employed by the Confederate Quartermaster's Department in the removal of civilian property from Sullivan's Island, was set on fire by a "Yankee sympathizer" on October 30, 1861, at her wharf on Sullivan's Island, South Carolina. The *Osiris* was entirely destroyed. (Note One: The *Osiris* was valued between $20,000 and $25,000 and had just been repaired at a cost between six and eight thousand dollars. The *Osiris* was a regular ferry between Charleston and Sullivan's Island, and stopping at Castle Pinckney. The ferry boat made two trips a day.) [Note Two: A black man (or boy) "attached to the boat" was arrested in connection with the arson.] [Note Three: The *Osiris* was a sidewheel steamer and was built at New York, New York, in 1838. The vessel measured 183 3/95 tons (or 145 tons), 134'4" in length, 20'4" in breadth, and 7' in depth. She had a wood hull with a billet head, one deck, no galleries, two masts and a square stern. The *Osiris* had been enrolled at Baltimore, Maryland, on May 29, 1855. At the time of the steamer's loss she was owned by the Sullivan's Island Steam Boat Company. The steamer was issued Confederate "Enrollment #16," at Charleston, South Carolina, on July 22, 1861.]

References for 1861-10-US-SC/GA-3:
"Enrollment #105," (Baltimore, Md.), May 29, 1855, National Archives, Record Group 41
"Permanent Enrollment #5," (Charleston, SC), October 22, 1858, National Archives, Record Group 41
"Confederate Enrollment #16," (Charleston, South Carolina, C.S.A.), July 22, 1861, National Archives, Record Group 109, Vessel File O-13-2
"Charleston Daily Courier," (Charleston, SC), #18765, January 16, 1861, p. 2, c. 8, (advertisement)
"Charleston Daily Courier," (Charleston, SC), #19000, October 31, 1861, p. 1, c. 3
"Charleston Daily Courier," (Charleston, SC), #19001, November 1, 1861, p. 1, c. 2
"Daily Morning News," (Savannah, GA), November 2, 1861, p. 2, c. 3
Private Journal of Henry William Ravenell, edited by A.R. Childs, (Columbia, South Carolina, 1947), p. 93
Merchant Steam Vessels of the United States 1807-1868, ("Lytle List"), by William M. Lytle, (Mystic, CT, 1952), p. 165
List of American-Flag Merchant Vessels that Received Certificates of Enrollment or Registry at the Port of New York 1789-1867, compiled by Forest R. Holdcamper, (U.S. National Archives, Washington, DC, 1968), Special List #22, Volume 2, p. 536

1861-10-US-SC/GA-4: The abstracted log of the *U.S.S. Monticello*, for October 30, 1861, states "at 10:15 a.m. discovered a sail ashore at the mouth of Wassaw Inlet," Georgia. (Note: The vessel apparently was a schooner, but nothing in the abstracted log actually says whether the vessel was lost or got off.)

Reference for 1861-10-US-SC/GA-4:
Official Records of the Union and Confederate Navies in the War of the Rebellion, (Washington, DC, 1897), Series 1, Volume 6, p. 695

1861-11-US-NC-1: Two unidentified United States steamers bound to Port Royal, South Carolina, were reported as driven ashore off Hatteras, North Carolina, during the gale of November 1, 1861. (Note: See also entries 1861-11-US-NC-2 through 1861-11-NC-4.)

Reference for 1861-11-US-NC-1:
Official Records of the Union and Confederate Navies in the War of the Rebellion, (Washington, DC, 1897), Series 1, Volume 6, p. 689

1861-11-US-NC-2: The United States steamer *Star of the Union*, commanded by Captain John J. Garvin, was run ashore in a leaky condition on Bogue Island (banks), North Carolina, about twenty miles west of Beaufort, North Carolina, during the gale of November 1, 1861. One report gave her position as sixteen miles from Fort Macon, while another reported her as wrecked at "Rogues Beach," the later obviously just a misspelling of Bogues Beach. Her location was also described as "about eight miles to the eastward of Bogue Inlet." Once aground, she went broadside to the shore and was broken entirely in two. She was afterwards described as "a perfect wreck, her boiler and main shaft under water, and the beach near her strewed with pressed hay, barrels, and dead horses." She was nearly out of the water at low tide. One man was drowned. Eighty of her men made it ashore but were captured by the Confederates. She was one of the transports participating in the Beaufort, South Carolina, invasion expedition and was loaded with sixty-seven horses, hay, provisions, gun carriages, etc. Only fifteen horses reached shore alive. One report stated that she carried quartermaster's and subsistence stores and the baggage wagons and horses of the Connecticut Seventh Regiment. On November 12, 1862, the wrecked steamer and a crowd of people on the beach near it were shelled by both the *U.S.S. Monticello* and the *U.S.S. Gemsbok*. The *Gemsbok* believed that her shells "must have killed and wounded a great many" of the people. (Note One: A report in the Newbern "Progress" stated that the salvaged cargo was expected to be worth $100,000 to the Confederates. Among the items salvaged by the Confederates were two rifled 24-pounders, Sharpes rifles and cartridges, 800 blankets, etc. The Confederates also expected to salvage her engine which was said to be worth $30,000.) (Note Two: Some reports show this vessel as the *Union* or as the *Star of the South*. This was probably the "American steamer *Union*" which was reported in the *New York Times* of December 1, 1861, as stranded on November 9, 1861, while bound from Hampton Roads, Virginia, to Port Royal, South Carolina. See also entry 1861-12-US-NC-2.) (Note Three: The *Star of the Union* was built at Wilmington, Delaware, for Marshal O. Roberts of New York, for inland navigation. Although originally built for just $60,000 and in spite of the fact that her 5/16" iron hull was described as a "mere shell, "the Federal government paid $115,000 for the steamer. She was an iron hulled, sidewheel steamer, and was painted black. She was also described as "of the same style and character as the *Winfield Scott*.) (Note Four: There was a 960 ton steamer called the *Star of the South* which was built at Philadelphia, Pennsylvania, in 1853, but that vessel was a screw steamer and not a side wheel steamer, and the two should not be confused.)

References for 1861-11-US-NC-2:
"Daily Morning News," (Savannah, GA), Volume 12, #265, November 12, 1861, p. 2, c. 3
"Daily Morning News," (Savannah, GA), Volume 12, #269, November 18, 1861, p. 1, c. 1
New York Times, (New York, NY), Volume 11, #3163, November 11, 1861, p. 1, c. 3
New York Times, (New York, NY), Volume 11, #3164, November 12, 1861, p. 1, c. 1, 2, p. 4, c. 1
New York Times, (New York, NY), Volume 11, #3166, November 14, 1861, p. 2, c. 4
New York Times, (New York, NY), Volume 11, #3180, December 1, 1861, p. 5, c. 3 (list of vessels lost in November, and summary for year)
"Vessel Disasters, 1861," (Bound, annotated, clipping file, Atlantic Mutual Insurance Companies of New York), Volume 28, pp. 180, 188, 199, 200
Official Records of the Union and Confederate Armies in the War of the Rebellion, (Washington, DC, 1882), Series 1, Volume 6, pp. 3, 186, 310,
Official Records of the Union and Confederate Armies in the War of the Rebellion, (Washington, DC, 1897), Series 1, Volume 51, Part 2, pp. 369
Official Records of the Union and Confederate Navies in the War of the Rebellion, (Washington, DC, 1897), Series 1, Volume 6, pp. 416, 689, 690, 695
The Navy in the Civil War, (Charles Scribner's Sons, New York, NY, 1905), Volume 2 ("The Atlantic Coast" by Daniel Ammen), p.p. 18, 33
Battles and Leaders of the Civil War, edited by Robert U. Johnson and Clarence C. Buel, Volume 1 of 4 volumes (Century Co., New York, NY, 1884-87, reprinted by Thomas Yoseloff Inc. 1956), p. 676
List of American-Flag Merchant Vessels that Received Certificates of Enrollment or Registry at the Port of New York 1789-1867, compiled by Forest R. Holdcamper, (U.S. National Archives, Washington, DC, 1968), Special List #22, Volume 2, p. 652
Naval History of the Civil War, by Howard P. Nash, (A.S. Barnes & Co., New York, NY, 1972), p. 60
Merchant Steam Vessels of the United States 1790-1868, "The Lytle-Holdcamper List," by William M. Lytle and Forrest R. Holdcamper, revised and edited by C. Bradford Mitchell, (Staten Island, New York, 1975), p. 202

1861-11-US-NC-3: Although the captain of the steamer *Union* expressed the opinion that the steamer *Winfield Scott* was lost, "she having suddenly disappeared" during the gale of November 1, 1861, she actually survived. The *Winfield Scott*, Captain Seldy, which carried five hundred men from the 50th Pennsylvania Regiment, jettisoned its "whole cargo" and two cannon during the storm. This iron hulled quartermaster's steamer was aided by the *U.S.S. Bienville*. (Note: The *Winfield Scott* was finally wrecked in January of 1862 in Pull and Be Dammed Creek at Daufuskie Island, South Carolina. For more information on her actual loss, please see entry 1862-1-US-SC/GA-5 in this book.)

References for 1861-11-US-NC-3:
"Daily Morning News," (Savannah, GA), Volume 12, #269, November 18, 1861, p. 1, c. 2

Treasures of the Confederate Coast

New York Times, (New York, NY), Volume 11, #3164, November 12, 1861, p. 1, c. 1, 2, p. 4, c. 1
New York Times, (New York, NY), Volume 11, #3166, November 14, 1861, p. 2, c. 3
Official Records of the Union and Confederate Armies in the War of the Rebellion, (Washington, DC, 1882), Series 1, Volume 6, pp. 3, 144, 186
Official Records of the Union and Confederate Armies in the War of the Rebellion, (Washington, DC, 1882), Series 1, Volume 6, pp. 3, 186
Official Records of the Union and Confederate Navies in the War of the Rebellion, (Washington, DC, 1897), Series 1, Volume 6, p. 416
The Navy in the Civil War, (Charles Scribner's Sons, New York, NY, 1905), Volume 2 ("The Atlantic Coast" by Daniel Ammen), p.p. 18, 33

1861-11-US-NC-4: The United States steamer *Mayflower*, Captain Phillips, was observed with her colors "union down" and was believed to have been run ashore or sunk on the coast of North Carolina during the gale of November 1, 1861, but she was actually taken in tow by another vessel and saved. The "little" *Mayflower* had been part of an invasion force bound to Port Royal, South Carolina. (Note: This may have been the 262 ton steamer *Mayflower*, which was built at New York, New York in 1845. That vessel was issued a certificate of steam enrollment at that port on July 5, 1845.)

References for 1861-11-US-NC-4:
New York Times, (New York, NY), Volume 11, #3163, November 11, 1861, p. 1, c. 3
New York Times, (New York, NY), Volume 11, #3164, November 12, 1861, p. 1, c. 4
New York Times, (New York, NY), Volume 11, #3166, November 14, 1861, p. 2, c. 2, 3
Official Records of the Union and Confederate Navies in the War of the Rebellion, (Washington, DC, 1897), Series 1, Volume 6, p. 417
List of American-Flag Merchant Vessels that Received Certificates of Enrollment or Registry at the Port of New York 1789-1867, compiled by Forest R. Holdcamper, (U.S. National Archives, Washington, DC, 1968), Special List #22, Volume 2, p. 470
Naval History of the Civil War, by Howard P. Nash, (A.S. Barnes & Co., New York, NY, 1972), p. 60

1861-11-US-NC-5: The gale of November 1, 1861, caused the loss of "a number of the schooners loaded with stone" at Hatteras Inlet, North Carolina. (Note: See also entry 1861-12x-US-NC-1.)

Reference for 1861-11-US-NC-5:
Official Records of the Union and Confederate Navies in the War of the Rebellion, (Washington, DC, 1897), Series 1, Volume 6, p. 412

1861-11-US-NC-6: The new 300 ton, Spanish steamer *Neustra Señora de Regia*, Captain Reynals, after getting ashore in the gale of November 1, 1861, near Ocracoke, North Carolina, was obliged to put into Georgetown, South Carolina, with machinery disabled and the vessel somewhat injured.

Reference for 1861-11-US-NC-6:
"Daily Morning News," (Savannah, GA), Volume 12, #261, November 7, 1861, p. 2 c. 1

1861-11-US-NC-7: The "mammoth ship" *Great Republic* was reported as driven ashore in a "terrific storm near Hatteras" in early November, 1861. (Note: The *Great Republic*, 3356 tons, was built in 1853 at Boston, Massachusetts, and was issued a certificate of registry at the Port of New York on February 21, 1855.)

References for 1861-11-US-NC-7:
"Daily Morning News," (Savannah, GA), Volume 12, #261, November 7, 1861, p. 2 c. 1
"Daily Morning News," (Savannah, GA), Volume 12, #265, November 12, 1861, p. 2, c. 3
"Daily Morning News," (Savannah, GA), Volume 12, #266, November 13, 1861, p. 1, c. 1, 2

The "Real Rhett Butler" & Other Revelations

List of American-Flag Merchant Vessels that Received Certificates of Enrollment or Registry at the Port of New York 1789-1867, compiled by Forest R. Holdcamper, (U.S. National Archives, Washington, DC, 1968), Special List #22, Volume 1, p. 291

1861-11-US-NC-8: The large French corvette *Prony*, (also reported as *Proney, Pomona, Prona,* and *Pronna*), Captain C.H. de Fontanges de Couzan, went ashore inside of the breakers at Ocracoke, North Carolina, on November 5, 1861. She was a sidewheel steamer of 700 (or 800) tons burden, 320 horse power, and was armed with six 30-pounders. Three of her guns were spiked and three were thrown overboard along with her cutlasses and all of her small arms to prevent them from falling into the hands of the Yankees. About 3 p.m. on the 7th she was blown up and thoroughly destroyed by her captain. [Note One: A Confederate report stated that "a hole had been knocked in (the *Prony's*) bottom by the lightboat which the Yankees had sunk and burned in September." Her officers and crew (variously reported as one hundred and one hundred and forty men) were saved by the Confederate steamer *Albemarle*, "after they had been ignored by the Federal vessels." For information on the light-ship, please see entry 1861-9-US-NC-1.] (Note Two: This was probably the wreck identified in the *New York Times* of November 12, 1861, as the French war vessel *Cantilabria* or *Calabria*, as early reports erroneously identified the *Prony* as the *Catinat*. For more on that report see next entry.)

References for 1861-11-US-NC-8:
"Daily Morning News," (Savannah, GA), Volume 12, #264, November 11, 1861, p. 2, c. 1
"Daily Morning News," (Savannah, GA), Volume 12, #266, November 13, 1861, p. 1, c. 1
New York Times, (New York, NY), Volume 11, #3164, November 12, 1861, p. 1, c. 2, p. 4, c. 2
New York Times, (New York, NY), Volume 11, #3165, November 13, 1861, p. 1, c. 2, 3, 4
New York Times, (New York, NY), Volume 11, #3166, November 14, 1861, p. 8, c. 1, 2
New York Times, (New York, NY), Volume 11, #3180, December 1, 1861, p. 5, c. 3 (list of vessels lost in November, and summary for year)
Official Records of the Union and Confederate Navies in the War of the Rebellion, (Washington, DC, 1897), Series 1, Volume 6, pp. 397-405, 418, 742, 785

1861-11-US-NC-9: The *New York Times* of November 12, 1861, reported the French war vessel *Cantilabria* or *Calabria* as run aground near Beaufort, North Carolina, during the storm of November 5, 1861. The same paper gave her position as "off Hatteras." The vessel was described as 2,500 tons and was said to have been blown up by her captain. (Note: See also previous entry.)

References for 1861-11-US-NC-9:
New York Times, (New York, NY), Volume 11, #3164, November 12, 1861, p. 1, c. 1, p. 4, c. 2

1861-11-US-NC-10: The Confederate States sidewheel steamer *Winslow* (a.k.a. *Warren Winslow*, formerly the *Joseph E. Coffee*, a.k.a. *J.E. Coffee*), P. McCarrick master, was wrecked November 7, 1861, on a sunken hull outside of Ocracoke, North Carolina, while attempting to go to the assistance of the French corvette *Prony* which was ashore near there. Her crew escaped. [Note One: The *Winslow* had a wooden hull and was armed with one 32-pounder pivot and one small brass 6-pounder rifle (also shown as armed with one 32-pounder and one 8-pounder). She had been purchased at Norfolk in 1861.] (Note Two: The sunken hull upon which the *Winslow* wrecked was said to have been that of a lightship sunk by the Federal forces in September of 1861. This was probably the light-ship mentioned in entries 1861-9-US-NC-1, and 1861-11-US-NC-8.) (Note Three: The "Lytle-Holdcamper List" shows this steamer as burnt "to avoid capture.") (Note Four: The steam boat *Joseph E. Coffee*, 207 tons, was built in 1846 at New York, New York. She was issued a certificate of enrollment on July 18, 1846.)

References for 1861-11-US-NC-10:
"Daily Morning News," (Savannah, GA), Volume 12, #264, November 11, 1861, p. 2, c. 1
New York Times, (New York, NY), Volume 11, #3165, November 13, 1861, p. 1, c. 3
Official Records of the Union and Confederate Navies in the War of the Rebellion, (Washington, DC, 1894), Series 1, Volume 1, pp. 51, 59, 67
Official Records of the Union and Confederate Navies in the War of the Rebellion, (Washington, DC, 1897), Series 1, Volume 6, pp. 68, 270, 785
Official Records of the Union and Confederate Navies in the War of the Rebellion, (Washington, DC, 1921), Series 2, Volume 1, pp. 272, 273, 312
Confederate Privateers, by William Morrison Robinson, Jr., (Yale University Press, 1928), pp. 102, 103, 107-109, 113-115
Outer Banks of North Carolina, by David Stick, (UNC Press, Chapel Hill, NC, 1958, pp. 117, 118, 120, 125, 128, 129, 131, 142
List of American-Flag Merchant Vessels that Received Certificates of Enrollment or Registry at the Port of New York 1789-1867, compiled by Forest R. Holdcamper, (U.S. National Archives, Washington, DC, 1968), Special List #22, Volume 1, pp. 388, 389 note 1
Merchant Steam Vessels of the United States 1790-1868, "The Lytle-Holdcamper List," by William M. Lytle and Forrest R. Holdcamper, revised and edited by C. Bradford Mitchell, (Staten Island, New York, 1975), pp. 105, 116

1861-11-US-NC-11: On November 14, 1861, Lt. Jeffers of the *U.S.S. Underwriter* sank three schooners filled with stone "athwart the channel in 9 feet water" in Ocracoke Inlet, North Carolina, in an effort to block the channel. The vessels were chained together bow and stern. (Note: See also entry 1861-12x-US-NC-1.)

References for 1861-11-US-NC-11:
Official Records of the Union and Confederate Navies in the War of the Rebellion, (Washington, DC, 1897), Series 1, Volume 6, pp. 428-430

1861-11-US-SC/GA-1: The log of the United States gunboat *Albatross* for November 7, 1861, shows two Federal steamers as reported to have gone ashore off Charleston, South Carolina, during the gale of November 1, 1861. (Note: The two vessels were apparently part of a fleet bound to Port Royal Sound, South Carolina. Please see entries 1861-11-US-SC/GA-2 through 1861-11-US-SC/GA-5 of this book.)

Reference for 1861-11-US-SC/GA-1:
Official Records of the Union and Confederate Navies in the War of the Rebellion, (Washington, DC, 1897), Series 1, Volume 6, p. 689

1861-11-US-SC/GA-2: The Savannah "Daily Morning News" of November 4, 1861, reported that two Federal steam transports, laden with cattle and provisions, were driven ashore a few miles north of Georgetown, South Carolina, during the storm of November 2, 1861. (Note One: This would seem to place the wrecks in the vicinity of North Island or DeBourdieu Island, South Carolina.) (Note Two: See also entries 1861-11-US-SC/GA-1 and 1861-11-US-SC/GA-3 of this book.)

Reference for 1861-11-US-SC/GA-2:
"Daily Morning News," (Savannah, GA), November 4, 1861, p. 2, c. 1

1861-11-US-SC/GA-3: The United States transport steamer *Osceola*, Captain Morrill, went ashore on the Day Breaker, off North Island, near Georgetown, South Carolina, in a severe gale on November 2, 1861. The transport carried potatoes, vegetables and thirty-nine head of cattle, some of which swam to shore. The officers and crew took to their boats and landed on North Island where they were captured by the Confederates. (Note One: The *Osceola* was described as "bilged in two hours," but her machinery was expected to be saved. She was afterwards reported as "being successfully overhauled," but the report may have been in error.) [Note Two: The steamer was owned in New York and had previously been engaged as a cattle boat between Cuba and Honduras. The *Osceola* was part of a Federal fleet of fifty or sixty vessels being sent South to capture a deep water port to be used as a depot. The vessel was built at Brooklyn, New York, in 1848, was schooner rigged with two masts and was copper sheathed. She was fastened with copper and treenails. The *Osceola* was said to be a poor sea risk and to have insufficient security against fire, so she was classed 5-A2 for insurance purposes. The *Osceola's* hull was built of oak, chestnut, etc., with composition fastenings and she had a large cabin on deck. The steamer measured 177 18/95 tons (or 173 tons), 120' along her keel, 117'8" in length, 22' in breadth and 7'4" in depth of hold, and she drew seven feet of water at her load line. The vessel's frame was of white oak and cedar. The steamer had one (also shown as two) iron propeller(s) seven feet in diameter. The *Osceola* had one smokestack and one flued boiler (17' X 6'5") which was mounted on her deck. She had "knees under her spar deck." The steamer's boiler was built in 1858 by Hogg and Delawater of New York. The *Osceola* was fitted "with vertical direct-acting engines, with two cylinders, each 24 inches in diameter and a stroke of piston of two feet; she was also supplied with one tubular boiler and her propeller was seven feet in diameter and made of iron." She was also shown as having had just one engine with one twenty-two inch cylinder with a twenty-six inch stroke. The vessel had a square stern, no galleries, and no figure head. She was owned by P.N. Spoford

Treasures of the Confederate Coast

Esq. of New York.] (Note Three: "Lytle's list" shows the *Osceola* as having been stranded at Savannah, Georgia.) (Note Four: This is probably one of the two vessels mentioned in entry 1861-11-US-SC/GA-2.)

References for 1861-11-US-SC/GA-3:

"Reports of Steamers, Volume B," (bound manuscript), National Archives, Record Group 92, entry 1432, p. 430

"Permanent Enrollment #55," (New York, NY), May 17, 1860, National Archives, Record Group 41

"Permanent Register #18," (New York, NY), August 3, 1860, National Archives, Record Group 41

"Permanent Register #19," (New York, NY), August 3, 1860, National Archives, Record Group 41

"Permanent Register #20," (New York, NY), August 5, 1860, National Archives, Record Group 41

"Daily Morning News," (Savannah, GA), Volume 12, # 258, November 4, 1861, p. 2, c. 1

"Daily Morning News," (Savannah, GA), Volume 12, #261, November 7, 1861, p. 2 c. 1

"Daily Morning News," (Savannah, GA), Volume 12, #265, November 12, 1861, p. 2, c. 3

"Charleston Daily Courier," (Charleston, SC), #19005, November 6, 1861, p. 2, c. 2

New York Times, (New York, NY), Volume 11, #3166, November 14, 1861, p. 2, c. 3, 4

New York Times, (New York, NY), Volume 11, #3167, November 15, 1861, p. 1, c. 4

New York Times, (New York, NY), Volume 11, #3180, December 1, 1861, p. 5, c. 3 (list of vessels lost in November, and summary for year)

"Steam Vessels #1, 1850's," (bound manuscript, Atlantic Mutual Insurance Companies of New York), entry for *Osceola*

"Vessel Disasters, 1861," (bound annotated clipping file, Atlantic Mutual Insurance Companies of New York), Volume 28, pp. 191, 199

Official Records of the Union and Confederate Armies in the War of the Rebellion, (Washington, DC, 1882), Series 1, Volume 6, pp. 3, 186

Official Records of the Union and Confederate Navies in the War of the Rebellion, (Washington, DC, 1901), Series 1, Volume 12, pp. 288, 293

The Navy in the Civil War, (Charles Scribner's Sons, New York, NY, 1905), Volume 2 ("The Atlantic Coast" by Daniel Ammen), pp. 18, 33

Merchant Steam Vessels of the United States 1807-1868, ("Lytle List"), by William M. Lytle, (Mystic, CT, 1952), p. 146

Battles and Leaders of the Civil War, edited by Robert U. Johnson and Clarence C. Buel, Volume 1 of 4 volumes (Century Co., New York, NY, 1884-87, reprinted by Thomas Yoseloff Inc. 1956), p. 676

List of American-Flag Merchant Vessels that Received Certificates of Enrollment or Registry at the Port of New York 1789-1867, compiled by Forest R. Holdcamper, (U.S. National Archives, Washington, DC, 1968), Special List #22, Volume 2, p. 536

Encyclopedia of American Shipwrecks, by Bruce D. Berman, (Boston, 1972), p. 138, #1524

Naval History of the Civil War, by Howard P. Nash, (A.S. Barnes & Co., New York, NY, 1972), p. 60

Merchant Steam Vessels of the United States 1790-1868, ("Lytle-Holdcamper List"), edited by C. Bradford Mitchell, (Staten Island, New York, 1975), pp. 165, 287

1861-11-US-SC/GA-4 or 1861-11-US-NCx-1: The transport steamer *Peerless*, foundered in thirteen fathoms of water in a hurricane on November 2, 1861. The *Ocean Atlas of the Carolina Margin* shows the *Peerless* as wrecked off Hatteras, North Carolina, as does John Mills' *Canadian Coastal and Inland Steam Vessels, 1809-1930*. However, more detailed, and presumably more accurate, contemporary reports show her as lost off Charleston, South Carolina. Those reports state that her crew of twenty-three was saved by the U.S. gunboat *Mohican*. The captain was the last person to leave the sinking ship and "by almost superhuman exertions" he saved his trunk and other property. The remainder of the crew saved only the clothes they wore. (Note One: The 690 ton sidewheel steamer was owned by Captain J.T. Wright of New York City. The *Peerless* had been under charter to the United States Quartermaster's Office and was carrying cattle when she was lost. The Government later paid $100,000 to her owners for the loss. The steamer had formerly plied Lake Ontario between Lewiston and Toronto.) [Note Two: The *Peerless* was built as hull #19, on the Clyde River by Alexander Denny at Dumbarton, Scotland, in 1852. After she was finished she was disassembled and transported in five thousand separate pieces to Montreal, where she was transshipped to the Niagara Dock and Harbour Company on the mouth of the Niagara for final assembly. She was completed in 1852, but was not launched until January 6, 1853. Canadian records show her as built in Ontario, Canada (one report says at Queenston in 1853, another at Toronto in 1855). Her engines, designated #7, were constructed by Tulloch and Denny in Scotland. She was fitted with two direct-acting trunk engines, with cylinders of 57" (also shown as 5'7") in diameter, and had a stroke of piston 5'10" (6'). Her water wheels were of iron and were 24' (26') (incorrectly shown in one report as "twenty-four inches in diameter." She was supplied with tubular boilers in her hold. She had three watertight compartments and her rig consisted of a foresail and jib. Her length on deck was 227'6", her breadth of beam 26', her depth of hold 12' and she drew 6'5" when loaded. (Canadian records show her as 175' in length and 26' in breadth.) She was said to have been framed with wrought iron plate, 7/16 and 3/8 of an inch in thickness, and they were fastened with rivets 3/4" thick. Her rivets were 2 1/4" apart.] (Note Two: Although there originally was a question about it, this is definitely not the iron hulled wreck located in 100' of water off Charleston, South Carolina, at Loran numbers 45314.6/60179.0, as that vessel was a screw steamer.) (Note Three: Due to conflicting data, as to the actual location of the loss, this entry has been assigned duel SL Codes.) (Note Four: The *Peerless* may have been one of the vessels mentioned in entry 1861-11-US-SC/GA-1 of this book.) (Note Five: There is a lithograph at the Public Archives of Canada, Ottawa, entitled "Toronto, C.W. in 1854 taken from the Top of the Jail," which shows the *Peerless*. A rendering of the vessel by Erik Heyl appears in his book *Early American Steamers*.)

References for 1861-11-US-SC/GA-4 or 1861-11-US-NCx-1:

"Vessel Surveys" (bound manuscript insurance surveys, by Haswell), entry for *Peerless*, National Archives, Record Group 92

"Vessel Disasters, 1861," (bound annotated clipping file, Atlantic Mutual Insurance Companies of New York), Volume 28, pp. 191, 200

New York Times, (New York, NY), Volume 11, #3166, November 14, 1861, p. 2, c. 3, 4

New York Times, (New York, NY), Volume 11, #3167, November 15, 1861, p. 1, c. 4

Official Records of the Union and Confederate Armies in the War of the Rebellion, (Washington, DC, 1882), Series 1, Volume 6, pp. 3, 186

Official Records of the Union and Confederate Navies in the War of the Rebellion, (Washington, DC, 1901), Series 1, Volume 12, pp. 257, 258, 260, 288

The Navy in the Civil War, (Charles Scribner's Sons, New York, NY, 1905), Volume 2 ("The Atlantic Coast" by Daniel Ammen), p. 18

Battles and Leaders of the Civil War, edited by Robert U. Johnson and Clarence C. Buel, Volume 1 of 4 volumes (Century Co., New York, NY, 1884-87, reprinted by Thomas Yoseloff Inc. 1956), p. 676

Treasures of the Confederate Coast

Graveyard of the Atlantic: Shipwrecks of the North Carolina Coast, by David Stick (University of North Carolina Press, Chapel Hill, North Carolina, 1952), pp. 51, 247
Early American Steamers, by Erik Heyl, (Buffalo, NY, 1964), Volume 3, pp. 275, 276
An Oceanographic Atlas of the Carolina Continental Margin, by J.G. Newton, (Duke University Marine Laboratory, Beaufort, NC, 1971), p. 28
Naval History of the Civil War, by Howard P. Nash, (A.S. Barnes & Co., New York, NY, 1972), p. 60

Canadian Coastal and Inland Steam Vessels 1809-1930, by John Mills, (Steamship Historical Society of America, Providence, RI, 1979), p. 90, #2178

1861-11-US-SC/GA-5 or **1861-11-US-NCx-2:** The steamer *Governor*, Captain Phillips, under charter by the United States Navy as a troop transport, foundered in thirteen fathoms of water in a hurricane on November 2, 1861. She was carrying a battalion of four hundred "fine marines" under Major John G. Reynolds. Seven of *Governor's* crew were drowned or crushed to death. The remainder of the people were saved by the United States gunboats *Sabine*, Captain Ringgold; *Isaac Smith*; and *Rover*. The crew of the *Sabine* was awarded a gold medal by the "Life Saving Benevolent Association of New York." The *Governor* had a small supply of stores on board. Nearly all of the arms were saved, but the haversacks, knapsacks, canteens and 9000 cartridges of ammunition were lost. (Note One: The "Lytle-Holdcamper Steamship List" shows the United States transport *Governor* as wrecked off Hatteras, North Carolina, and gives the date as November 20, 1861, but the file card notes used in its preparation show the location as off Charleston. The *Ocean Atlas of the Carolina Margin* also lists her as wrecked off Hatteras and gives the date of loss as October 31, 1861. Most contemporary accounts give the date as November 2, 1861, and place the wreck further south. At least one contemporary account states that she foundered off Charleston, South Carolina.) [Note Two: The *Governor* was built by Samuel Sneeden at New York, New York, in 1846 of "white oak, etc. and fastened in an excellent manner." Her hull had been extensively repaired in 1858. She measured 644 81/95 tons, 230'3" in length, 28'3" in breadth, 10'3" in depth, and 7' in draft. She had one deck, no masts, a square stern and a billet head. She had condensing engines and her boiler was mounted on deck. She was issued a certificate of steam enrollment at the port of New York on March 28, 1846. She was owned by Albert Dailey and Company of New York. The *Governor* was described as a staunch vessel built to "run on the sound between New York and Providence, R.I." However, "never in her best days (was she) adapted to a sea voyage."] (Note Three: Due to conflicting data, as to the actual location of this wreck, this entry has been given duel SL Codes.) (Note Four: This may have been one of the vessels mentioned in entry 1861-11-US-SC/GA-1 of this book.) (Note Five: Erik Heyl in his book *Early American Steamers* shows the *Governor* as 235'x28'2"x10'1"; 650 tons; vertical beam engine; cylinder 48" diameter with 11' stroke; and 30' diameter water wheels. Heyl has a drawing of the steamer based on an illustration in "Leslie's Weekly" and a painting at the Mariner's Museum at Newport News, Virginia.") [Note Six: In 1989, Randy Lathrop and I dove on the wreck of an unidentified wooden hulled sidewheel steamer approximately 22.8 miles off Little River Inlet (South Carolina, North Carolina line). The wreck was in 78' of water at Loran-C coordinates 45333.5/59483.5. The wreck had been discovered by Captain Billy Long, a commercial fisherman, who had put divers (Blaine Garren, Randy McCormick and Hampton Shupen) down on the wreck shortly before Lathrop and I were asked to make their dive. Long's divers had tentatively identified the wreck as that of a blockade runner. However, Lathrop and I found New York State Militia and regular United States belt buckles. One buckle appeared to be a pre Civil War type of buckle used by officers of the United States Marines. The numerous buckles, musket parts, sword handles, haversack hooks, knapsack fastenings, canteen necks and other items we observed, appear to be evidence that the wreck was that of a Union transport lost during the first part of the war, and that it may be the *Governor*. At the first Battle of Bull Run, Major Reynolds had commanded a battalion of U.S. Marines, supporting the 14th Regiment of the New York State Militia, which could explain the New York militia buckles we found.] [Note Seven: Some people believe that Captain Long's wreck may actually be that of the *Suwanee*, which was lost on December 4, 1866, while carrying arms and ammunition for the Mexican Republic, or even another vessel. The *Suwanee* (ex-*Pampero*) was a sidewheel, wooden hulled steamer, of 350 tons. She was built in Baltimore, Maryland, in 1850, and was first home ported at Washington, D.C. However, the *Suwanee* is shown in the "Lytle-Holdcamper List" as foundered without loss of life off Cape Romano, Florida.]

References for 1861-11-US-SC/GA-5 or 1861-11-US-NCx-2:
"Vessel Surveys" (bound manuscript insurance surveys, by Haswell), entry for *Governor*, National Archives, Record Group 92
"Temporary Register," #295, (Boston, MA), Oct. 11, 1861, National Archives, Record Group 41
New York Times, (New York, NY), Vol. 11, #3163, November 11, 1861, p. 1, c. 1, 3, 4
New York Times, (New York, NY), Volume 11, #3164, November 12, 1861, p. 1, c. 3
New York Times, (New York, NY), Volume 11, #3165, November 13, 1861, p. 1, c. 3
New York Times, (New York, NY), Volume 11, #3166, November 14, 1861, p. 2, c. 3, 4
New York Times, (New York, NY), Volume 11, #3167, November 15, 1861, p. 1, c. 4, 5
New York Times, (New York, NY), Volume 11, #3180, December 1, 1861, p. 1, c. 3
"Daily Morning News," (Savannah), Nov. 18, 1861, p. 1, c. 1
"Charleston Daily Courier," (Charleston, SC), #19107, Nov. 21, 1861, p. 1, c. 4
"Vessel Disasters, 1861," (bound annotated clipping file, Atlantic Mutual Insurance Companies of New York), Volume 28, pp. 184, 192, 199, 200
Official Records of the Union and Confederate Armies in the War of the Rebellion, (Washington, DC), Series 1, Volume 2, pp. 383, 386, 388, 391, 392

Treasures of the Confederate Coast

Official Records of the Union and Confederate Navies in the War of the Rebellion, (Washington, DC, 1901), Series 1, Volume 12, pp. 223, 232-249
The Navy in the Civil War, (Charles Scribner's Sons, New York, NY, 1905), Volume 2 ("The Atlantic Coast" by Daniel Ammen), p. 17
Graveyard of the Atlantic: Shipwrecks of the North Carolina Coast, by David Stick (University of North Carolina Press, Chapel Hill, North Carolina, 1952), pp. 51, 247
Battles and Leaders of the Civil War, edited by Robert U. Johnson and Clarence C. Buel, Volume 1 of 4 volumes (Century Co., New York, NY, 1884-87, reprinted by Thomas Yoseloff Inc. 1956), pp. 674, 676
Early American Steamers, by Erik Heyl, (Buffalo, New York, 1965), Volume 4, pp. 125, 126
List of American-Flag Merchant Vessels that Received Certificates of Enrollment or Registry at the Port of New York 1789-1867, compiled by Forest R. Holdcamper, (U.S. National Archives, Washington, DC, 1968), Special List #22, Volume 1, p. 288
Encyclopedia of American Shipwrecks, by Bruce D. Berman, Mariners Press, (Boston, MA, 1972), p. 122, #786
Naval History of the Civil War, by Howard P. Nash, (A.S. Barnes & Co., New York, NY, 1972), pp. 58, 59
Manuscript 3x5 file card for steamer *Governor* used in preparation of "Lytle-Holdcamper List," National Archives, Record Group 41
Merchant Steam Vessels of the United States 1790-1868, ("Lytle-Holdcamper List"), by William M. Lytle and Forest R. Holdcamper, revised and edited by C. Bradford Mitchell, (Staten Island, New York, 1975), pp. 87, 167, 206, 265, 288
An Oceanographic Atlas of the Carolina Continental Margin, by J.G. Newton, (Duke University Marine Laboratory, Beaufort, North Carolina, 1971), p. 28
"Wreck Miscellanea," column by E. Lee Spence, in *ShipWrecks*, Volume 1, #2, p. 4

1861-11-US-SC/GA-6: The "Charleston Daily Courier" of November 5, 1861, reported that the Savannah riverboat *Swan* was rumored to have been lost on a trip to the northward of Port Royal, South Carolina. But the *Swan* was subsequently reported as safe at Beaufort, South Carolina.

References for 1861-11-US-SC/GA-6:
"Charleston Daily Courier," (Charleston, SC), #19004, November 5, 1861, p. 1, c. 2
"Charleston Daily Courier," (Charleston, SC), #19007, November 8, 1861, p. 4, c. 3

1861-11-US-SC/GA-7: On November 6, 1861, (during the battle for Port Royal Sound) the Confederate States steamers *Lady Davis* and *Huntress* burned some light boats which they had intended to use to block Skull Creek, South Carolina. The boats apparently had been received too late to be used to block the creek, so they were burned instead.

Reference for 1861-11-US-SC/GA-7:
"Charleston Daily Courier," (Charleston, SC), #19009, November 11, 1861, p. 1, c. 3

1861-11-US-SC/GA-8: Two "large" vessels from the Federal fleet went ashore on Martin's Industry (shoal) on November 6, 1861, during the battle of Port Royal Sound, South Carolina. The two vessels were afterwards lightened and got off.

References for 1861-11-US-SC/GA-8:
"Charleston Daily Courier," (Charleston, SC), #19007, November 8, 1861, p. 4, c. 3
"Charleston Daily Courier," (Charleston, SC), #19009, November 11, 1861, p. 1, c. 3

1861-11-US-SC/GA-9: The "Charleston Daily Courier" of November 7, 1861, reported that a Union vessel had been driven ashore during an engagement between the Federal Fleet of forty-four vessels and the Confederate Fort on Hilton Head Island, South Carolina, on November 6, 1861. The paper went on to state that Commodore Tatnall was at "a convenient distance with his little fleet of three ships pouring heavy fire into her (the Federal vessel's) sides." The

The "Real Rhett Butler" & Other Revelations

"Charleston Daily Courier" of the next day stated that the original report had been incorrect.

References for 1861-11-US-SC/GA-9:
"Charleston Daily Courier," (Charleston, SC), #19006, November 7, 1861, p. 1, c. 1, p. 4, c. 3
"Charleston Daily Courier," (Charleston, SC), #19007, November 8, 1861, p. 4, c. 3

1861-11-US-SC/GA-10: The Federals were reported to have lost one gunboat, which burned, during the Federal attack on Hilton Head Island, South Carolina, on November 6 or 7, 1861. Another account stated that the vessel was scuttled by the Federals after she had already caught fire.

References for 1861-11-US-SC/GA-10:
"Charleston Daily Courier," (Charleston, SC), #19007, November 8, 1861, p. 4, c. 3
"Charleston Daily Courier," (Charleston, SC), #19009, November 11, 1861, p. 1, c. 3
New York Times, (New York, NY), Volume 11, #3165, November 13, 1861, p. 1, c. 1-3

1861-11-US-SC/GA-11: Shortly after the fall of Port Royal, South Carolina, the Confederates obstructed Walls Cut (an inland passage from Port Royal Sound to Savannah) by sinking an unidentified brig and driving three rows of piles. The piles were removed by the Yankees and the hulk was towed to where it wouldn't block the cut.

References for 1861-11-US-SC/GA-11:
"Charleston Mercury," (Charleston, SC), #11384, February 27, 1862, p. 1, c. 5

1861-12-US-NC-1: About the middle of December the Confederates using the steamer *Uncle Ben* towed "four large, heavy wooden cribs, diamond shape, about forty or fifty feet wide and twelve feet deep, which they moored on the shoal and in the channel way close together at the north western end of Zeek's Island (North Carolina), and filling three of them with stone • • • sunk them and completely blocked the channel of New Inlet at that point." The fourth crib was to be sunk nearby.

Reference for 1861-12-US-NC-1:
Official Records of the Union and Confederate Navies in the War of the Rebellion, (Washington, DC, 1897), Series 1, Volume 6, p. 499

1861-12-US-NC-2: On December 18, 1861, a fire was observed by the *U.S.S. Albatross*, while she was operating off the coast of North Carolina. The fire proved to be a burning wreck, identified only as the *Union*. On the following day the *U.S.S. State of Georgia* fired into the wreck with eight guns and the *U.S.S. Albatross* fired into her with two guns. (Note: This was probably the steamer *Star of the Union* which was wrecked on Bogue Island, North Carolina, on November 1, 1861. That wreck is described in entry 1861-11-US-NC-2.)

References for 1861-12-US-NC-2:
Official Records of the Union and Confederate Armies in the War of the Rebellion, (Washington, DC, 1882), Series 1, Volume 6, pp. 3, 186, 310
Official Records of the Union and Confederate Navies in the War of the Rebellion, (Washington, DC, 1897), Series 1, Volume 6, pp. 689, 690

Treasures of the Confederate Coast

1861-12-US-NC-3: The log of the Confederate steamer *Ellis* for December 29, 30 & 31, 1861, mentions the wreck of the steamer *Leonora* which apparently was in the immediate vicinity of Roanoke Island, North Carolina. The wreck was probably quite recent as the *Ellis* was assisting the *C.S.S. Manassas* in the removal of the *Leonora's* boiler and "works."

References for 1861-12-US-NC-3:
Official Records of the Union and Confederate Navies in the War of the Rebellion, (Washington, DC, 1897), Series 1, Volume 6, chart facing p. 555, pp. 786, 787

1861-12-US-NC-4: The *Frying Pan Shoals Lightship* which had been removed from its station and anchored in the Cape Fear River, just above Fort Caswell, North Carolina, was burned by the *U.S.S. Mount Vernon* on December 30, 1861. The vessel was being fitted out as a floating fortress and had just been pierced for eight guns (six broadside and two astern) but the guns had not yet been mounted. She was deserted and riding at anchor within close range of the fort when she was destroyed. (Note: At least two modern sources incorrectly give the date of loss as December 31, 1862.)

References for 1861-12-US-NC-4:
"Daily Morning News," (Savannah, GA), Volume 13, # 7, January 9, 1862, p. 2, c. 2
Official Records of the Union and Confederate Navies in the War of the Rebellion, (Washington, DC, 1897), Series 1, Volume 6, p. 493
The Navy in the Civil War, (Charles Scribner's Sons, New York, NY, 1905), Volume 2 ("The Atlantic Coast" by Daniel Ammen), p. 175
Graveyard of the Atlantic: Shipwrecks of the North Carolina Coast, by David Stick (University of North Carolina Press, Chapel Hill, NC, 1952), pp. 58, 247
An Oceanographic Atlas of the Continental Margin, J.G. Newton, O.H. Pilkey and J.O. Blanton, (Duke University Marine Laboratory, Beaufort, NC, 1971), p. 17 chart symbol #45, p. 20 entry #45

1861-12-US-SC/GA-1: The ship *Lewis*, 4th rate, which had been intended to be used as part of the first Stone Fleet at Charleston, South Carolina, was accidentally run aground on Tybee Island, Georgia, in early December, 1861, and eventually broke up. (Note One: The *Lewis* was built at Portsmouth, New Hampshire, in 1820. She was 101' in length, 26'2" in breadth, 13'1" in depth of hull, and 307 49/95 tons. She had two decks, three masts, a square stern, no galleries, and a billet head. She was purchased on October 28, 1861, at New London, Connecticut, by George D. Morgan and R.H. Chappell for $3,250.) (Note Two: The *Lewis* is incorrectly shown in Bruce Berman's *Encyclopedia of American Shipwrecks* as sunk on December 21, 1861, "4 miles SSE off Fort Sumter and 3 miles ESE of light on Morris Island, Charleston, South Carolina Used by Union forces during Civil War to block harbor.) (Note Three: For additional information on the first Charleston Stone Fleet see entry 1861-12-US-SC/GA-8 in this book.)

References for 1861-12-US-SC/GA-1:
"Permanent Register #9," (New London, CT), October 22, 1861, National Archives, Record Group 41
Official Records of the Union and Confederate Navies in the War of the Rebellion, (Washington, DC, 1901), Series 1, Volume 12, pp. 418, 419

The "Real Rhett Butler" & Other Revelations

Official Records of the Union and Confederate Navies in the War of the Rebellion, (Washington, DC, 1921), Series 2, Volume 1, p. 126
Dictionary of American Naval Fighting Ships, (Washington, DC, 1970), Volume 5, Appendix I, pp. 430, 433
Encyclopedia of American Shipwrecks, by Bruce D. Berman, (Boston, 1972), p. 130, #1159

1861-12-US-SC/GA-2: The ship *Meteor*, which had been intended to be used as part of the first "Stone Fleet" at Charleston, South Carolina, parted her only anchor chain and drifted ashore on the south edge of the channel by Tybee Island, Georgia, December 4, 1861, and eventually bilged and broke up. (Note One: The *Meteor* was built at Newbury, Massachusetts, in 1819. She was 106'5" in length, 26'1.25" in breadth, 13'5/8" in depth of hold, and 325 40/95 tons. She had a square stern, no galleries, and a billet head. The ship had been purchased on November 4, 1861, at Mystic, Connecticut, by George D. Morgan and R.H. Chappell for $4,000.) (Note Two: The *Meteor* is incorrectly shown in Bruce Berman's *Encyclopedia of American Shipwrecks* as sunk on December 21, 1861, "4 miles SSE off Fort Sumter and 3 miles ESE of light on Morris Island, Charleston, South Carolina Used by Union forces during Civil War to block harbor.) (Note Three: For additional information on the first Charleston Stone Fleet see entry 1861-12-US-SC/GA-8 in this book.)

References for 1861-12-US-SC/GA-2:
"Permanent Register #12," (New London, CT), November 1, 1861, National Archives, Record Group 41
Official Records of the Union and Confederate Navies in the War of the Rebellion, (Washington, DC, 1901), Series 1, Volume 12, pp. 418, 419
Official Records of the Union and Confederate Navies in the War of the Rebellion, (Washington, DC, 1921), Series 2, Volume 1, p. 142
Dictionary of American Naval Fighting Ships, (Washington, DC, 1970), Volume 5, Appendix I, pp. 430, 433
Encyclopedia of American Shipwrecks, by Bruce D. Berman, (Boston, 1972), p. 134, #1347

1861-12-US-SC/GA-3: The bark *Phoenix*, which had been intended to be used as part of the first "Stone Fleet" at Charleston, South Carolina, struck the Tybee Bar and was towed ashore at Tybee Island, Georgia, in early December, 1861. The vessel was placed where her hull and load of stone could serve as a breakwater. (Note One: The *Phoenix* was built at Philadelphia, Pennsylvania, in 1811. She had a wooden hull and measured 109'8" in length, 28'8" in breadth, 14'4" in depth of hold, and was 403 84/95 tons. She had a square stern, no galleries, and a woman figurehead. She had been purchased on November 9, 1861, at New London, Connecticut, by George D. Morgan and R.H. Chappell.) (Note Two: The *Phoenix* is incorrectly shown in Bruce Berman's *Encyclopedia of American Shipwrecks* as sunk on December 21, 1861, "4 miles SSE off Fort Sumter and 3 miles ESE of light on Morris Island, Charleston, South Carolina Used by Union forces during Civil War to block harbor.) (Note Three: For additional information on the first

Treasures of the Confederate Coast

Charleston Stone Fleet see entry 1861-12-US-SC/GA-8 in this book.)

References for 1861-12-US-SC/GA-3:

"Permanent Register #13," (New London, CT), November 4, 1861, National Archives, Record Group 41

Official Records of the Union and Confederate Navies in the War of the Rebellion, (Washington, DC, 1901), Series 1, Volume 12, pp. 418, 419

Official Records of the Union and Confederate Navies in the War of the Rebellion, (Washington, DC, 1921), Series 2, Volume 1, p. 177

Dictionary of American Naval Fighting Ships, (Washington, DC, 1970), Volume 5, Appendix I, pp. 430, 433

Encyclopedia of American Shipwrecks, by Bruce D. Berman, (Boston, 1972), p. 140, #1584

1861-12-US-SC/GA-4: The bark *South America*, 606 tons, which had been intended to be used as part of the first "Stone Fleet" at Charleston, South Carolina, but which had arrived at Tybee in a sinking condition, was towed ashore at Tybee Island, Georgia, in early December, 1861. The vessel was placed where her hull and load of stone could serve as an improvised jetty and wharf for the landing of Federal troops. (Note One: The bark had been purchased on November 7, 1861, at New Bedford, Massachusetts, by George D. Morgan and R.H. Chappell for $3,600.) (Note Two: The *South America* is incorrectly shown in Bruce Berman's *Encyclopedia of American Shipwrecks* as sunk on December 21, 1861, "4 miles SSE off Fort Sumter and 3 miles ESE of light on Morris Island, Charleston, South Carolina Used by Union forces during Civil War to block harbor. Berman describes her as a "Packet" and shows her as built in 1832.) (Note Three: For additional information on the first Charleston Stone Fleet see entry 1861-12-US-SC/GA-8 in this book.)

References for 1861-12-US-SC/GA-4:

Official Records of the Union and Confederate Navies in the War of the Rebellion, (Washington, DC, 1901), Series 1, Volume 12, p. 418

Official Records of the Union and Confederate Navies in the War of the Rebellion, (Washington, DC, 1921), Series 2, Volume 1, p. 211

Dictionary of American Naval Fighting Ships, (Washington, DC, 1970), Volume 5, Appendix I, pp. 430, 433

Encyclopedia of American Shipwrecks, by Bruce D. Berman, (Boston, 1972), p. 145, #1829

1861-12-US-SC/GA-5: The bark *Cossack*, 254 tons, which had been intended to be used as part of the first "Stone Fleet" at Charleston, South Carolina, but which had arrived at Tybee in a sinking condition was towed ashore at Tybee Island, Georgia, in early December, 1861. (Note One: She had been purchased at New York by George D. Morgan and R.H. Chappell for $3,200. The *Cossack* was placed where her hull and load of stone could serve as an improvised jetty and wharf for the landing of Federal troops.) (Note Two: The *Cossack* is incorrectly shown in Bruce Berman's *Encyclopedia of American Shipwrecks* as sunk on December 21, 1861, "4 miles SSE off Fort Sumter and 3 miles ESE of light on Morris Island, Charleston, South Carolina Used by Union forces

The "Real Rhett Butler" & Other Revelations

during Civil War to block harbor.) (Note Three: For additional information on the first Charleston Stone Fleet see entry 1861-12-US-SC/GA-8 in this book.)

References for 1861-12-US-SC/GA-5:
Official Records of the Union and Confederate Navies in the War of the Rebellion, (Washington, DC, 1901), Series 1, Volume 12, p. 418
Official Records of the Union and Confederate Navies in the War of the Rebellion, (Washington, DC, 1921), Series 2, Volume 1, p. 67
Dictionary of American Naval Fighting Ships, (Washington, DC, 1970), Volume 5, Appendix I, pp. 430, 433
Encyclopedia of American Shipwrecks, by Bruce D. Berman, (Boston, 1972), p. 114, #426

1861-12-US-SC/GA-6: The bark *Peter Demill*, 300 tons, which had been intended to be used as part of the first "Stone Fleet" at Charleston, South Carolina, but which had arrived at Tybee in a sinking condition was towed ashore at Tybee Island, Georgia, in early December, 1861. The *Peter Demill* was placed where her hull and load of stone could serve as an improvised jetty and wharf for the landing of Federal troops. (Note One: The bark had been purchased on November 7, 1861, at New London, Connecticut, by George D. Morgan and R.H. Chappell for $2,600.) (Note Two: The *Peter Demill* is incorrectly shown in Bruce Berman's excellent book, *Encyclopedia of American Shipwrecks*, as sunk on December 21, 1861, "4 miles SSE off Fort Sumter and 3 miles ESE of light on Morris Island, Charleston, South Carolina Used by Union forces during Civil War to block harbor. Berman shows her as 340 tons.) (Note Three: For additional information on the first Charleston Stone Fleet see entry 1861-12-US-SC/GA-8 in this book.)

References for 1861-12-US-SC/GA-6:
Official Records of the Union and Confederate Navies in the War of the Rebellion, (Washington, DC, 1901), Series 1, Volume 12, p. 418
Official Records of the Union and Confederate Navies in the War of the Rebellion, (Washington, DC, 1921), Series 2, Volume 1, p. 176
Dictionary of American Naval Fighting Ships, (Washington, DC, 1970), Volume 5, Appendix I, pp. 430, 433
Encyclopedia of American Shipwrecks, by Bruce D. Berman, (Boston, 1972), p. 139, #1579

1861-12-US-SC/GA-7: The Savannah "Daily Morning News" of December 20, 1861, reported that "one of the Lincoln gunboats got aground yesterday in Port Royal River, (South Carolina), near one of our batteries on the main. The enemy was fired upon and in attempting to get into a flat, it was sunk, and thirty of them were killed."

Reference for 1861-12-US-SC/GA-7:
"Daily Morning News," (Savannah, GA), #19007, December 20, 1861, p. 2, c. 2

1861-12-US-SC/GA-8: A Confederate officer filed the following report on the sinking of the first "Stone Fleet" (consisting of sixteen vessels filled with granite) off Charleston, South Carolina. "On the afternoon of December 18 (1861) a large increase in the blockading squadron was observed. The majority of the vessels appeared to be old whaling and trading vessels. On the 19th, the weather being bad, not much progress was made in their preparations for sinking. A few of the vessels were stripped. By dawn on the morning of the 20th great activity was observed; fifteen (actually sixteen) vessels were placed in line more or less direct across the main ship channel, about four miles south-southeast of Fort Sumter and three miles east-southeast of the light on Morris Island. By evening all had been stripped, dismasted, and sunk. From the observations made the vessels appeared to have been placed in a single irregular line, with intervals of 100 feet, making a distance of about 3,500 feet in extent from shoal to shoal, and completely occupying the channel. The vessels commenced to settle immediately, and at the end of the week but little was to be seen of any of their hulls. They have now entirely disappeared. Large portions of the wrecks have, from time to time, come ashore." The proceedings were conducted under the immediate direction of Captain H. Davis of the *U.S.S. Wabash*. The vessels were "nearly all condemned whalers - some of them 60 and 70 years of age - the queerest, quaintest specimens of shipbuilding afloat." They included: the bark *Amazon*, 318 tons (which had been purchased at Fairhaven, Massachusetts, on October 30, 1861, for $3,675); the ship *America*, 418 tons (which had been purchased at New Bedford, Massachusetts, on November 8, 1861, for $5,250); the bark *American*, 329 tons (which had been purchased at Edgartown, Massachusetts, on November 1, 1861, for $3,370); the ship *Archer*, 322 tons (which had been purchased at New Bedford, Massachusetts, on October 28, 1861, for $3,360); the ship *Courier*, 381 tons (which had been purchased at New Bedford, Massachusetts, for $5,000); the bark *Fortune*, 292 tons (which had been purchased at New London, Connecticut, on October 28, 1861, for $3,250); the ship *Herald*, 274 tons (which had been purchased at New Bedford, Massachusetts, on October 24, 1861, for $4,000); the ship *Kensington*, 357 tons (which had been purchased at New Bedford, Massachusetts, on October 28, 1861, for $4,000); the bark *Leonidas*, 231 tons (which had been purchased at New Bedford, Massachusetts, on November 27, 1861, for $3,050); the ship *L.C. Richmond*, 341 tons (which had been purchased at Fairhaven, Massachusetts, on October 25, 1861, for $4,000); the ship *Maria Theresa*, 330 tons (which had been purchased at New Bedford, Massachusetts, on October 31, 1861, for $4,000); the ship *Potomac*, 356 tons (which had been purchased at Nantucket, Rhode Island, on November 1, 1861, for $3,500); the ship *Rebecca Sims*, 400 tons (which had been purchased at Fairhaven, Massachusetts, on October 21, 1861, for $4,000); the ship *Robin Hood*, 395 tons (which had been purchased at Mystic, Connecticut, on October 20, 1861, for $4,000); the bark *Tenedos*, 245 tons (which had been purchased at New London, Connecticut, by on October 16, 1861, for $1,650); and the ship *William Lee*, 311 tons (which had been purchased at Newport, Rhode Island, on November 19, 1861, for $4,200). Most were old whaling vessels and had been home ported in the various whaling ports of New England. All of them were purchased for the United States Navy by George D. Morgan and R. H. Chappell, especially to be sunk in an effort to obstruct the entrance to Charleston Harbor. All of the vessels had been "prepared for quick scuttling before leaving the North. Nothing was required but to drive out a plug and the water rushed in with force enough to fill them in an hour." The vessels which were loaded with stone to aid in the blocking of the channel were nick-named the "Stone Fleet" or the "Stone Whalers." Some accounts state that they were placed in a checkerboard pattern approximately two and one half nautical miles south east of the Charleston Light. The arrangement was not intended to obstruct the flow of water, but was meant to form a series of shoals, "around which the tide will whirl and eddy, making an intricate labyrinth which no vessel could navigate." At low water on the following day the Federal boat crews returned to the sunken hulks and cut away their masts and rigging. "It was a singular sight to see the big spars topple over with a crash and a creak as soon as the rigging was severed by a few blows of an axe. It is not often that persons are permitted to destroy valuable property, and feel at the same time that they are doing right. On this occasion, however, such a sentiment could be properly entertained, and from the energy which the jack-tars displayed in using their axes (they apparently) considered the privilege one to be thoroughly enjoyed. Smashing things was a luxury, and the inclination to indulge in it was gratified without stint. After everything that could be saved was taken from the *Robin Hood*, her rigging was cut and frapped or secured to the masts, in order to make an illumination and pyrotechnic display worthy of the successful issue of the expedition. She was fired early in the evening, and her burning afforded a novel and beautiful sight to most of those who witnessed it. The blockading squadron was especially entertained. Their lives are such a dull and tedious round of monotony that a far less magnificent spectacle would have afforded them a topic of conversation for a month." (Note One: A second "Stone Fleet" was sunk off the Isle of Palms, South Carolina on January 25 & 26, 1862, and information on that fleet is contained in entry 1862-1-US-SC/GA-4 of this book.) (Note Two: Bruce Berman's *Encyclopedia of American Shipwrecks* lists the ship *Corea*; the bark *Cossack*; the bark *Frances Henrietta*; the bark *Garland*; the bark *Harvest*; the ship *Lewis*; the ship *Meteor*; the bark *Peter Demill*; the ship *Phoenix*; and the bark *South America*, as having been sunk as part of this fleet, but this is not supported by official documents. For more information on the *Corea* see entry 1861-12x-US-SC/GA-2; on the *Cossack* see entry 1861-12-US-SC/GA-5; on the *Frances Henrietta* see entry 1861-12x-US-SC/GA-3; on the *Garland* see entry 1861-12x-US-SC/GA-4; on the *Harvest* see entry 1861-12x-US-SC/GA-1; on the *Lewis* see entry 1861-12-US-SC/GA-1; on the *Meteor* see entry 1861-12-US-SC/GA-2; on the *Peter Demill* see entry 1861-12-US-SC/GA-6; on the *Phoenix* see entry 1861-12-US-SC/GA-3; and on the *South America* see entry 1861-12-US-SC/GA-4.) (Note Three: A report in the London *Times* of January 10, 1862, gave the name of one of the vessels as the *Richmond*, and incorrectly lists the *Rebecca Sims* as two separate vessels, the *Rebecca* and the *Sims*.) (Note Four: The bow and stern (marked *Courier*, New Bedford) of a vessel washed ashore at St. Mary's in February of 1862.)

References for 1861-12-US-SC/GA-8:

New York Times, (New York, NY), #3173, November 22, 1861, p. 4, c. 5
New York Times, (New York, NY), #3174, November 23, 1861, p. 1, c. 5
New York Times, (New York, NY), #3177, November 27, 1861, p. 4, c. 4, 5
New York Times, (New York, NY), #3180, November 30, 1861, p. 4, c. 5
New York Times, (New York, NY), #3188, December 10, 1861, p. 1, c. 3-6
New York Times, (New York, NY), #3199, December 23, 1861, p. 4, c. 3
New York Times, (New York, NY), #3202, December 26, 1861, p. 1, c. 5, 6; p. 4, c. 6
New York Times, (New York, NY), #3203, December 27, 1861, p. 4, c. 6
New York Times, (New York, NY), #3229, January 28, 1862, p. 5, c. 1
New York Times, (New York, NY), #3233, February 1, 1862, p. 1, c. 6; p. 2, c. 1-3; p. 4, c.3
New York Times, (New York, NY), #3242, February 12, 1862, p. 8, c. 5, 6
New York Times, (New York, NY), #3243, February 13, 1862, p. 1, c. 6; p. 4, c. 4, 5; p. 5, c. 1
"Charleston Daily Courier," (Charleston, SC), #19049, December 30, 1861, p. 4, c. 2, 3
"Charleston Daily Courier," (Charleston, SC), #19061, January 14, 1862, p. 4, c. 2, 3
"Charleston Daily Courier," (Charleston, SC), #19071, January 27, 1862, p. 1, c. 2
"Charleston Mercury," (Charleston, SC), Volume 80, #11377, March 4, 1862, p. 2, c. 1
"Daily Morning News," (Savannah, GA), January 4, 1862, p. 1, c. 2, p. 2, c. 1, 2
"Daily Morning News," (Savannah, GA), January 8, 1862, p. 1, c. 2
"Daily Morning News," (Savannah, GA), January 13, 1862, p. 1, c. 4, p. 2, c. 2
"Times," (London, England), #24138, January 9, 1862, p. 9, c.1
"Times," (London, England), #24139, January 10, 1862, p. 7, c. 5, 6
"Times," (London, England), #24146, January 18, 1862, p. 7, c. 4
"Times," (London, England), #24150, January 23, 1862, p. 10, c. 1
History of the Confederate States Navy From its Organization to the Surrender of its Last Vessel, by J. Thomas Scharf, (New York, New York, 1887), pp. 435,435n, 436, 436n, 662
Official Records of the Union and Confederate Armies in the War of the Rebellion, (Washington, DC, 1882), Series 1, Volume 6, pp. 42, 43
Official Records of the Union and Confederate Navies in the War of the Rebellion, (Washington, DC, 1901), Series 1, Volume 12, pp. 418-424, 445, 467, 474
Official Records of the Union and Confederate Navies in the War of the Rebellion, (Washington, DC, 1921), Series 2, Volume 1, pp. 34, 36, 67, 87, 90, 101, 119, 123, 126, 135, 183, 189, 193, 221, 241
The Navy in the Civil War, (Charles Scribner's Sons, New York, NY, 1903), Volume 1 ("The Blockade and the Cruisers" by James Russell Soley), p. 107
The Navy in the Civil War, (Charles Scribner's Sons, New York, NY, 1905), Volume 2 ("The Atlantic Coast" by Daniel Ammen), pp. 41, 42
Dictionary of American Naval Fighting Ships, (Washington, DC, 1970), Volume 5, Appendix I, pp. 430-434

The "Real Rhett Butler" & Other Revelations

Encyclopedia of American Shipwrecks, by Bruce D. Berman, (Boston, 1972), p. 106, #84, #91; p. 107, #93, #127; p. 114, #422, #426, #427; p. 120, #697, #702; p. 121, #737; p. 123, #843; p. 124, #877; p. 129, #1099, #1120; p. 130, #1149, #1159; p. 132, #1268; p. 134, #1347; p. 139, #1579; p. 140, #1584, #1609; p. 141, #1652; p. 142, #1694; p. 145, #1829
Charleston's Maritime Heritage 1670-1865, by P.C. Coker III, (CokerCraft Press, Charleston, SC, 1987), pp. 218, 219

1861-12-US-SC/GA-9: On December 21, 1861, a large sailing vessel "endeavoring to enter Tybee," Georgia, from the north went ashore on the North Breakers and was afterwards reported in a "bad position." The Savannah "Daily Morning News" of December 23, 1861, reported that "no vessel that ever got on that shoal has ever been saved." The next day the paper said that the vessel was still there and "appears to be settling down." The paper expected the vessel to be a total loss."

References for 1861-12-US-SC/GA-9:
"Daily Morning News," (Savannah, GA), December 23, 1861, p. 1, c. 1
"Charleston Daily Courier," (Charleston, SC), December 25, 1861, p. 4, c. 2

1861-12-US-SC/GA-10: The fine blockade running schooner *Prince of Wales*, of Nassau, Captain W.F. Adair, bound from Nassau to a Confederate Port, was run ashore in an effort to save her crew after she was fired into by a Union gunboat on December 24, 1861. The shot took effect on the hull but did not injure anyone. The schooner's location was given as inside of the breakers at North Inlet and nine miles from the entrance to Georgetown, South Carolina. Captain Adair set the *Prince of Wales* afire to prevent the vessel and its cargo from falling into the hands of the enemy. The schooner carried one thousand sacks of salt, sundries, and oranges. (Note One: One report states that the *Prince of Wales* was burned by the *U.S.S. Gem of the Sea.*) (Note Two: Jim Batey, Ron Renau, and I found the wrecks of three wooden hulled sailing vessels while diving at North Inlet in 1966. We tentatively identified the two newer wrecks as the *Prince of Wales* and the *Liverpool*. The third wreck was smaller and appeared much older. For more information on the *Liverpool*, please entry 1862-4-US-SC/GA-4.)

References for 1861-12-US-SC/GA-10:
"Charleston Daily Courier," (Charleston, SC), #19047, December 27, 1861, p. 2, c. 3
"Vessel Papers" (manuscript records), United States National Archives, Washington, DC, Record Group 109, files P-17, P-80
Official Records of the Union and Confederate Navies in the War of the Rebellion, (Washington, DC, 1901), Series 1, Volume 12, pp. 428-430, 459
Personal knowledge of E. Lee Spence of dive he made with Jim Batey and Ron Renau, circa summer, 1966.
Manifest, contained in miscellaneous documents, microfilmed by E. Lee Spence, at United States National Archives (Washington, DC, 1972), roll 2
History of Georgetown County, South Carolina, by George C. Rogers, (Columbia, South Carolina, 1970), p. 394

1861-12x-US-NC-1: The following vessels were purchased at Baltimore, Maryland, on August 13, 1861, by Captain H.S. Stellwagen of the United States Navy for the express purpose of filling them with stone and sinking them as obstructions in the waters of North Carolina: the schooner *Alvarado*, Captain Harrington, (purchased for $1,200); the *Augustus Holly,* Captain Carlisle; the schooner *Cambria*, Captain White, (purchased for $1,500); the schooner *Delaware Farmer* (purchased for $500, but returned because of a disputed title); the schooner *E.D. Thompson* or *Ed. Thompson* (purchased for $600); the schooner *Ellen Goldsborough*, Captain Stone, (purchased for $1,500); the schooner *Friendship*, Captain Skinner, (purchased for $1,100); the schooner *G.P. Upshur,* Captain Jones, (purchased for $800); the schooner *Hero*, (purchased for $600); the schooner *John Alexander*, Captain Miles (purchased for $2,000); the schooner *Mary and Hetty* (purchased for $1,500, and later reported as at Hatteras Inlet); the schooner *Mary Frances*, (purchased $800); the schooner *Orion*, (purchased for $800); the schooner *Patriot*, (purchased for $600); the schooner *Sarah Bibbey*, (purchased for $800); the schooner *Somerfield* (or *Summerfield*), Captain North, (purchased for $1,500); the schooner *South Wind,* Captain Todd, (purchased for $1,500); the schooner *Southerner*, (purchased for $900 and later reported as at Hatteras Inlet); the schooner *William L. Jones*, (purchased for $600); the schooner *William W. Burns* (purchased for $400); and the schooner *W.L. Bartlett* (purchased for $1,000). Additional vessels (captured as prizes, and deemed as unfit for service) were undoubtedly also used as obstructions. Specific locations mentioned to be obstructed included Hatteras Inlet, Ocracoke Inlet, Loggerhead Inlet and Oregon Inlet. The vessels were to be placed "over the inner bulkheads, not on the outer bars, but at the line of meeting of the waters of the sea and of the sound inside the headlands." Several reports mentioned the impossibility of permanently closing the Inlets and one put it as follows. "It may be that the sinking of a few schooners will obstruct present channels, but no earthly power can stop the rush of these waters to their destination - the ocean. Everywhere the bottom sands are alive and creeping; in a few days, or weeks at most, the current sweeps beneath the sunken hulks, and either engulfs them to a greater depth or quickly and surely washes a channel elsewhere." Two of the vessels were lost in their passage to Hatteras Inlet, and two were later sunk in the harbor (one of those having stores on board). (Note One: The *John Alexander*, the *Ellen Goldsborough*, the *Alvarado*, the *South Wind*, the *Somerfield*, and the *Friendship* were described as the "lightest" of the vessels and it was directed that they be reserved for obstructing canals.) (Note Two: See also entries 1861-11-US-NC-5 and 1861-11-US-NC-11.)

References for 1861-12x-US-NC-1:

The "Real Rhett Butler" & Other Revelations

Official Records of the Union and Confederate Navies in the War of the Rebellion, (Washington, DC, 1897), Series 1, Volume 6, pp. 50, 64, 93, 162, 186, 188, 199, 206, 234, 252, 257, 259, 261, 267, 268, 279, 280, 290, 308-310, 315, 316, 318, 319, 344, 345, 377, 378, 410, 412, 414, 428-430
Official Records of the Union and Confederate Navies in the War of the Rebellion, (Washington, DC, 1921), Series 2, Volume 1, p. 33, 50, 73, 76, 78

1861-12x-US-SC/GA-1: Bruce Berman's *Encyclopedia of American Shipwrecks* lists the bark *Harvest*, 314 tons, as sunk on December 21, 1861, "4 miles SSE off Fort Sumter and 3 miles ESE of the light on Morris Island, Charleston, South Carolina Used by Union forces to block harbor. Part of the Stone Fleet." (Note One: The *Harvest* was purchased for the U.S. Navy on October 21, 1861, at New Bedford, Massachusetts, by George D. Morgan and R.H. Chappell for $4,000.) (Note Two: This vessel has not been listed in entry 1861-12-US-SC/GA-8 because, although official records show that she was purchased to be sunk as part of the Stone Fleet, they do not actually show her as having been used for that purpose.)

References for 1861-12x-US-SC/GA-1:
Official Records of the Union and Confederate Navies in the War of the Rebellion, (Washington, DC, 1901), Series 1, Volume 12, pp. 418, 421
Official Records of the Union and Confederate Navies in the War of the Rebellion, (Washington, DC, 1921), Series 2, Volume 1, p. 99
Encyclopedia of American Shipwrecks, by Bruce D. Berman, (Boston, 1972), p. 123, #843

1861-12x-US-SC/GA-2: The ship *Corea*, 356 tons, is listed in Bruce Berman's *Encyclopedia of American Shipwrecks* as sunk on December 21, 1861, "4 miles SSE off Fort Sumter and 3 miles ESE of the light on Morris Island, Charleston, South Carolina Stone cargo. Used by Union forces to block harbor entrance." (Note One: The *Corea* was purchased for the U.S. Navy at New London, Connecticut, by George D. Morgan and R.H. Chappell for $2,300.) (Note Two: This vessel has not been listed in entry 1861-12-US-SC/GA-8 because official records show that, although purchased to be sunk as part of the Stone Fleet, she was actually transferred for the use of the army and was still afloat as late as January 8, 1862.)

References for 1861-12x-US-SC/GA-2:
Official Records of the Union and Confederate Navies in the War of the Rebellion, (Washington, DC, 1901), Series 1, Volume 12, pp. 418, 474
Official Records of the Union and Confederate Navies in the War of the Rebellion, (Washington, DC, 1921), Series 2, Volume 1, p. 66
Encyclopedia of American Shipwrecks, by Bruce D. Berman, (Boston, 1972), p. 114, #422

1861-12x-US-SC/GA-3: The bark *Frances Henrietta*, 407 tons, is listed in Bruce Berman's *Encyclopedia of American Shipwrecks* as sunk on December 21, 1861, "4 miles SSE off Fort Sumter and 3 miles ESE of the light on Morris Island, Charleston, South Carolina Used by Union forces to block harbor entrance." (Note One: The *Frances Henrietta* was purchased for the U.S. Navy at New Bedford, Massachusetts, on October 19, 1861, by George D. Morgan and R.H. Chappell for $4,000.) (Note Two: This vessel has not been listed in entry 1861-12-US-SC/GA-8 because official records show that, although purchased to be sunk as part of the Stone Fleet, she was transferred for the use of the army and was still afloat as late as January 8, 1862.)

References for 1861-12x-US-SC/GA-3:
Official Records of the Union and Confederate Navies in the War of the Rebellion, (Washington, DC, 1901), Series 1, Volume 12, pp. 418, 474
Official Records of the Union and Confederate Navies in the War of the Rebellion, (Washington, DC, 1921), Series 2, Volume 1, p. 87
Encyclopedia of American Shipwrecks, by Bruce D. Berman, (Boston, 1972), p. 120, #702

1861-12x-US-SC/GA-4: The bark *Garland*, 243 tons, is listed in Bruce Berman's *Encyclopedia of American Shipwrecks* as sunk on December 21, 1861, "4 miles SSE off Fort Sumter and 3 miles ESE of the light on Morris Island, Charleston, South Carolina Used by Union forces to block harbor." (Note One: The *Garland* was purchased for the U.S. Navy at New Bedford, Massachusetts, on October 28, 1861, by George D. Morgan and R.H. Chappell for $3,150. She was 92'5" in length, 24'4" in breadth, and 16'6" in depth. The *Garland* had been built as privateer at Quincy, Massachusetts, in 1815, and had been rebuilt in 1845.) (Note Two: This vessel has not been listed in entry 1861-12-US-SC/GA-8 because official records show that, although purchased to be sunk as part of the Stone Fleet, she was transferred for the use by the U.S. Army Quartermaster's Department as a store ship. She was still afloat as late as January 8, 1862.)

References for 1861-12x-US-SC/GA-4:
Official Records of the Union and Confederate Navies in the War of the Rebellion, (Washington, DC, 1901), Series 1, Volume 12, pp. 418, 445, 467, 474
Official Records of the Union and Confederate Navies in the War of the Rebellion, (Washington, DC, 1921), Series 2, Volume 1, p. 90
Encyclopedia of American Shipwrecks, by Bruce D. Berman, (Boston, 1972), p. 121, #737

1862-1-US-NC-1: Charles Foard's chart of Civil War wrecks in the Wilmington, North Carolina, area shows a wreck near Lockwood Folly Inlet, North Carolina, as the "*Kate II*, 1/4/62." However, a check of contemporary records for that date failed to produce any support for such a wreck. (Note: This could have been the schooner *Kate* which was lost on April 2, 1862, at the inlet. For information on that wreck, please see entry 1862-4-US-NC-1.)

References for 1862-1-US-NC-1:
Official Records of the Union and Confederate Navies in the War of the Rebellion, (Washington, DC, 1898), Series 1, Volume 7, pp. 196, 197, 704, 705
A Chart of Wrecks of Vessels Sunk or Captured Near Wilmington, NC, Circa 1861-65, compiled by Charles H. Foard, (Wilmington, North Carolina, 1962)

1862-1-US-NC-2: Two unidentified vessels were reported as sunk by the Confederates in the channel near Zeek's Island, North Carolina, sometime prior to January 7, 1862. It was also reported that the Confederates were getting ready to sink a third vessel near the same place.

Reference for 1862-1-US-NC-2:

The "Real Rhett Butler" & Other Revelations

Official Records of the Union and Confederate Navies in the War of the Rebellion, (Washington, DC, 1897), Series 1, Volume 6, p. 696

1862-1-US-NC-3: The abstracted log of the Confederate steamer *Ellis* for January 8-17, 1862, describes it's (and other vessel's) efforts in the preparation and sinking of various unidentified vessels at the barricade between Fort Forrest and Roanoke Island, North Carolina. The vessels were first filled with sand and then chained together and sunk in conjunction with a row of pilings extending across Croatan Sound. (Note One: Whenever the rig was given, the vessels were always described as schooners.) (Note Two: One account described the obstructions as "a double row of piles and sunken vessels stretching well across the sound and between the forts on Pork and Wier Points.") [Note Three: "On the mainland, nearly opposite Fort Bartow (Pork Point), was Fort Forrest. This was placed on hulks sunk in the sand." Another account describing Fort Forest states that an old canal boat was sunk in the mud at Redstone Point, on the deck of which was mounted eight guns.]

References for 1862-1-US-NC-3:
Official Records of the Union and Confederate Navies in the War of the Rebellion, (Washington, DC, 1897), Series 1, Volume 6, chart facing p. 555, p. 787
The Navy in the Civil War, (Charles Scribner's Sons, New York, NY, 1905), Volume 2 ("The Atlantic Coast" by Daniel Ammen), pp. 179, 182
Outer Banks of North Carolina, by David Stick, (UNC Press, Chapel Hill, NC, 1958, p. 137

1862-1-US-NC-4: The Savannah "Daily Morning News" of February 1, 1862 stated that General Burnside's official report to Washington said that he had reached Hatteras, North Carolina, "after a foggy and stormy passage, and that most of his smaller vessels were anchored safely in the harbor, before the severest portion of the gale." General Burnside went on to report that the "propeller *City of York*, loaded with powder, rifles and bombs, is wrecked. The gunboat *Zouave*, loaded with seventeen hundred rifles, three hundred boxes of powder, thirty-two boxes of revolvers, grape shot and loaded bombs; the *New Brunswick* with the 4th Maine Regiment; the *Pocahontas* with the Rhode Island battery; the *Eastern Queen*, and between thirty and forty other vessels are missing, and are probably lost." (Note One: The army steamers *New Brunswick* and *Eastern Queen* were part of the fleet later reported as safely anchored in the sound inside of Hatteras Inlet, so General Burnside's fears for those two vessels apparently were unwarranted.) (Note Two: For more on the loss of the *City of York* see entry 1862-1-US-NC-5. For more on the *Zouave* see entry 1862-1-US-NC-7. For more on the *Pocahontas* see entry 1862-1-US-NC-9.) (Note Three: General Burnside cut the hair on his chin, but let his beard grow thickly on the sides, giving rise to the term "sideburns.")

Treasures of the Confederate Coast

References for 1862-1-US-NC-4:
"Daily Morning News," (Savannah, GA), Volume 13, #27, February 1, 1862, p. 1, c. 1
Official Records of the Union and Confederate Navies in the War of the Rebellion, (Washington, DC, 1897), Series 1, Volume 6, pp. 582, 585, 586
Outer Banks of North Carolina, by David Stick, (UNC Press, Chapel Hill, NC, 1958, p. 139
Ship Ashore!: The U.S. Lifesavers of Coastal North Carolina, by Joe A. Mobley, (Division of Archives and History, North Carolina Department of Cultural Resources, Raleigh, NC, 1994), p. 22

1862-1-US-NC-5: The "splendid and commodious" United States transport steamer *City of New York* was "lashed to pieces by the angry waves" on the outer bar, near the entrance to Hatteras Inlet, North Carolina, on January 13 (or 15), 1862. "Those on board were in the greatest of peril. She struck on Monday afternoon, and swung around almost at once so as to lie nearly broadside to the sea among the breakers; the waves making a breach over her decks, and her officers and crew were obliged to cling to her rigging to prevent being swept overboard. Such was the violence of winds and waves that no assistance could be given her. On Tuesday her foremast was cut away, and when it fell it carried her pipes with it, and she became a perfect wreck. Those on board now lashed themselves to bulwarks and rigging to prevent being washed away; and thus without food or aid, in this awful peril, and yet within site of so many friends, they passed another night. On Wednesday they were rescued, but the steamer and cargo were lost. The cargo consisted in part of some four hundred barrels of gunpowder, fifteen hundred rifles, eight hundred shells, Sibley tents, and hand grenades." (Note One: One report listed her as loaded with "powder, rifles and bombs," while another stated she was "laden with supplies and ordnance stores." Still another account described her cargo as worth "two hundred thousand dollars, mostly ordnance stores.") [Note Two: The *City of New York* (also reported as the *New York* or as the *City of York*) had a wood hull. She was a screw steamer of 574 tons and was built at Hoboken, New Jersey, in 1852. She was issued a certificate of steam registry at the port of New York (her first home port) on February 6, 1852.] (Note Three: See also entry 1862-1-US-NC-4.) (Note Three: This wreck should not be confused with the wreck of the ship *York*, which was lost at Bogue Inlet, North Carolina, on January 16, 1862. That wreck is described in entry 1862-1-US-NC-8.)

References for 1862-1-US-NC-5:
"Daily Morning News," (Savannah, GA), Volume 13, #27, February 1, 1862, p. 1, c. 1
The History of the Navy during the Rebellion, by Charles B. Boynton, (D. Appelton and Company, New York, NY, 1867), Volume 1, p. 380
Official Records of the Union and Confederate Armies in the War of the Rebellion, (Washington, DC, 1883), Series 1, Volume 9, p. 355
Official Records of the Union and Confederate Navies in the War of the Rebellion, (Washington, DC, 1897), Series 1, Volume 6, p. 582
Graveyard of the Atlantic: Shipwrecks of the North Carolina Coast, by David Stick (University of North Carolina Press, Chapel Hill, NC, 1952), pp. 51, 247
Battles and Leaders of the Civil War, edited by Robert U. Johnson and Clarence C. Buel, Volume 1 of 4 volumes (Century Co., New York, NY, 1884-87, reprinted by Thomas Yoseloff Inc. 1956), p. 664

The "Real Rhett Butler" & Other Revelations

Outer Banks of North Carolina, by David Stick, (UNC Press, Chapel Hill, NC, 1958, p. 139
List of American-Flag Merchant Vessels that Received Certificates of Enrollment or Registry at the Port of New York 1789-1867, compiled by Forest R. Holdcamper, (U.S. National Archives, Washington, DC, 1968), Special List #22, Volume 1, p. 132
An Oceanographic Atlas of the Carolina Continental Margin, by J.G. Newton, (Duke University Marine Laboratory, Beaufort, NC, 1971), p. 28
Merchant Steam Vessels of the United States 1790-1868, ("Lytle-Holdcamper List"), by William M. Lytle and Forrest R. Holdcamper, revised and edited by C. Bradford Mitchell, (Staten Island, NY, 1975), pp. 37, 250
Ship Ashore!: The U.S. Lifesavers of Coastal North Carolina, by Joe A. Mobley, (Division of Archives and History, North Carolina Department of Cultural Resources, Raleigh, NC, 1994), p. 22

1862-1-US-NC-6: The abstracted log of the *U.S.S. Hetzel* on January 14, 1862, states: "Fresh gale from N.W. At 7:30 a.m. a steamer outside the bulkhead (at Hatteras Inlet, North Carolina) raised ensign, union down. At 8 one of the steamers of General Burnside's expedition ran ashore on the bar. At 8:45 steamer on bar cut away her foremast and at 11 her smokestack went by the board." (Note: It is not clear whether the log is referring to just one, or as many as three separate steamers. The log may well be referring to the wreck of the steamer *City of New York* which is described in entry 1862-1-US-NC-5, and/or the United States gunboat *Zouave* described in entry 1862-1-US-NC-7. Both of those vessels were also mentioned in entry 1862-1-US-NC-4.)

Reference for 1862-1-US-NC-6:
Official Records of the Union and Confederate Navies in the War of the Rebellion, (Washington, DC, 1897), Series 1, Volume 6, p. 694

1862-1-US-NC-7: On January 14, 1862, the United States gunboat *Zouave* (ex-*Marshal Nye*, a.k.a. *Marshal Ney*) was "driven in the shallow water upon her own anchor, staved and sunk," inside the bar at Hatteras Inlet, North Carolina. "During the day wreckers were set to work to recover as many articles as possible." She was armed with one thirty-pounder Parrott gun and two twelve-pounder rifled field pieces. [Note One: Her signal letters were NGFW and she was attached to the First Brigade (Brigadier General J.G. Foster) as part of General Burnside's invasion fleet when she was lost.] (Note Two: The *Zouave* was actually the old screw steamer *Marshall Nye*, 203 tons. She had a wood hull and was built at Hoboken, New Jersey, in 1854. Her first home port was New York, New York, where she was issued a certificate of steam enrollment on June 17, 1854.) (Note Three: She should not be confused with the armed tug *U.S.S. Zouave* which is listed in the official records as having been purchased at New York on December 20, 1861, and as having continued in service until she went out of commission at New York on June 14, 1865. That vessel was reported at Newport News, Virginia, on February 7, 1862.) (Note Four: The gunboat *Zouave* is also mentioned in entry 1862-1-US-NC-4 of this book.)

References for 1862-1-US-NC-7:

Treasures of the Confederate Coast

The History of the Navy during the Rebellion, by Charles B. Boynton, (D. Appelton and Company, New York, NY, 1867), Volume 1, p. 380
Official Records of the Union and Confederate Armies in the War of the Rebellion, (Washington, DC, 1883), Series 1, Volume 9, p. 351
Official Records of the Union and Confederate Navies in the War of the Rebellion, (Washington, DC, 1897), Series 1, Volume 6, pp. 472, 473, 582, 603
Battles and Leaders of the Civil War, edited by Robert U. Johnson and Clarence C. Buel, Volume 1 of 4 volumes (Century Co., New York, NY, 1884-87, reprinted by Thomas Yoseloff Inc. 1956), p. 665
Merchant Steam Vessels of the United States 1790-1868, "The Lytle-Holdcamper List," by William M. Lytle and Forrest R. Holdcamper, revised and edited by C. Bradford Mitchell, (Staten Island, New York, 1975), p. 449
Encyclopedia of American Shipwrecks, by Bruce D. Berman, Mariners Press, (Boston, MA, 1972), p. 133, #1280
Merchant Steam Vessels of the United States 1790-1868, ("Lytle-Holdcamper List"), by William M. Lytle and Forrest R. Holdcamper, revised and edited by C. Bradford Mitchell, (Staten Island, NY, 1975), pp. 137, 279

1862-1-US-NC-8: The British ship *York*, of Dublin, was accidentally run ashore to the east of Bogue Inlet, North Carolina, on January 16, 1862. She was about 800 tons burden, and was reported to have carried "a great many tons of wrought iron." (Note One: She apparently was not trying to run the blockade as she was reportedly bound to the Capes of Delaware. Her cargo was discharged by the Confederates.) (Note Two: The wreck was said to be broadside to the steep beach with her anchor about one hundred and fifty yards from shore. Her position was also reported as "near the mouth of the Cape Fear River." The wreck was burned by the U.S. bark *Gemsbok* on January 16, 1862.) (Note Two: This may have been the vessel reported simply as "The British vessel burnt by the Federals went ashore north of Swansboro, in Onslow County.") (Note Three: This wreck should not be confused with the wreck of the steamer *City of New York*, which was lost at Hatteras Inlet, North Carolina, a few days earlier. That wreck is described in entry 1862-1-US-NC-5.)

References for 1862-1-US-NC-8:
"Daily Morning News," (Savannah, GA), Volume 13, #22, January 27, 1862, p. 2, c. 1
Official Records of the Union and Confederate Armies in the War of the Rebellion, (Washington, DC, 1883), Series 1, Volume 9, p. 422
Official Records of the Union and Confederate Navies in the War of the Rebellion, (Washington, DC, 1897), Series 1, Volume 6, pp. 520, 521, 690
A Chart of Wrecks of Vessels Sunk or Captured Near Wilmington, NC, Circa 1861-65, compiled by Charles H. Foard, (Wilmington, North Carolina, 1962)

1862-1-US-NC-9: The sidewheel steamer *Pocahontas*, 428 tons, which had been chartered by the U.S. Army as a horse transport was stranded and wrecked "with the Rhode Island battery," near Kinnakeet, North Carolina, on January 18, 1862. She was described as "old and unseaworthy" and it was said that her chief officer and engineer had been drunk the entire trip. "She had on board one hundred and thirteen valuable horses. During the gale her boilers first gave way, and they were patched up; then the grates fell down; then the steering-gear was broken; then the smoke-pipe came down; and, finally, she sprang a leak and was run ashore. By this shipwreck ninety (or 94) valuable horses were lost; some of them being thrown overboard ten miles from land, and others were left, as was said, to perish because no one would go down to the lower deck and untie them, that they might swim ashore." Her crew of fifty survived. (Note One: The location of the wreck was also described as twenty miles north of Cape Hatteras.) (Note Two: The *Pocahontas* had a wood hull and was built in 1829 at Baltimore, Maryland, which was also her first home port.) (Note Three: See also entry 1862-1-US-NC-4.)

References for 1862-1-US-NC-9:
"Daily Morning News," (Savannah, GA), Volume 13, #27, February 1, 1862, p. 1, c. 1
The History of the Navy during the Rebellion, by Charles B. Boynton, (D. Appelton and Company, New York, NY, 1867), Volume 1, pp. 379, 380
Official Records of the Union and Confederate Armies in the War of the Rebellion, (Washington, DC, 1883), Series 1, Volume 9, p. 108
Official Records of the Union and Confederate Navies in the War of the Rebellion, (Washington, DC, 1897), Series 1, Volume 6, p. 583
Battles and Leaders of the Civil War, edited by Robert U. Johnson and Clarence C. Buel, Volume 1 of 4 volumes (Century Co., New York, NY, 1884-87, reprinted by Thomas Yoseloff Inc. 1956), p. 665
Outer Banks of North Carolina, by David Stick, (UNC Press, Chapel Hill, NC, 1958, p. 139
Encyclopedia of American Shipwrecks, by Bruce D. Berman, Mariners Press, (Boston, MA, 1972), p. 140, #1603
Merchant Steam Vessels of the United States 1790-1868, ("Lytle-Holdcamper List"), by William M. Lytle and Forrest R. Holdcamper, revised and edited by C. Bradford Mitchell, (Staten Island, NY, 1975), pp. 175, 290
Ship Ashore!: The U.S. Lifesavers of Coastal North Carolina, by Joe A. Mobley, (Division of Archives and History, North Carolina Department of Cultural Resources, Raleigh, NC, 1994), pp. 22-24

1862-1-US-NC-10: Sometime in January, 1862, the United States floating battery *Grapeshot*, which was being towed to North Carolina as part of General Burnside's invasion fleet, "pitched and sheered so much in the heavy sea that she could not be towed, and it was found necessary to rescue her crew before she could go down. The boat which took these off was swamped under the guards of the steamer, and all on board were pitched into the sea, and with the greatest difficulty were saved. The tow-line was then cut, and the *Grapeshot* left to her fate. She went ashore some fourteen miles above Hatteras (Hatteras Inlet, North Carolina), and her cargo of hay and oats served to keep alive some horses which got ashore there from the wreck of the *Pocahontas*." (Note One: She was armed with two twelve-pounder Dahlgren rifled boat guns, and two twelve-pounder mountain howitzers, and was described as a ninety-six foot long barge or canal boat. Besides hay and oats, she carried "other stores." Her signal letters were JSDF.) (Note Two: For more on the wreck of the *Pocahontas*, please see entry 1862-1-US-NC-9.)

References for 1862-1-US-NC-10:
The History of the Navy during the Rebellion, by Charles B. Boynton, (D. Appelton and Company, New York, NY, 1867), Volume 1, p. 379
Official Records of the Union and Confederate Navies in the War of the Rebellion, (Washington, DC, 1897), Series 1, Volume 6, pp. 472, 473
Outer Banks of North Carolina, by David Stick, (UNC Press, Chapel Hill, NC, 1958, p. 139

1862-1-US-NC-11: On January 19, 1862, the Confederate steamer *Ellis* took the schooner *A.C Williams* and sank her at the barricade that ran between Fort Forrest and Roanoke Island, North Carolina. (Note: The barricade was designed to obstruct passage by the Federal fleet through Croatan Sound.)

References for 1862-1-US-NC-11:
Official Records of the Union and Confederate Navies in the War of the Rebellion, (Washington, DC, 1897), Series 1, Volume 6, chart facing p. 555, p. 787

1862-1-US-NC-12: The Confederate steamer *Ellis* took two schooners to the "upper battery" to be filled with sand and then towed one (the schooner *Josephine*) back to the barricade in Croatan Sound that ran between Fort Forrest and Roanoke Island, North Carolina, and sank her on January 20, 1862.

References for 1862-1-US-NC-12:
Official Records of the Union and Confederate Navies in the War of the Rebellion, (Washington, DC, 1897), Series 1, Volume 6, chart facing p. 555, p. 787

1862-1-US-NC-13: On January 21, 1862, the Confederate steamer *Ellis* took a schooner to the "upper battery" to be filled with sand and then went down to the barricade in Croatan Sound than ran between Fort Forrest and Roanoke Island, North Carolina, and chained several vessels together. The same day she returned to the upper battery and took the schooner *Carter* down to the barricade and sank her.

References for 1862-1-US-NC-13:
Official Records of the Union and Confederate Navies in the War of the Rebellion, (Washington, DC, 1897), Series 1, Volume 6, chart facing p. 555, p. 788

1862-1-US-NC-14: The Confederate steamer *Ellis* sank the schooner *Spuell and Moss* on January 25, 1862, at the barricade of scuttled vessels, chain and pilings that ran between Fort Forrest and Roanoke Island, North Carolina.

References for 1862-1-US-NC-14:
Official Records of the Union and Confederate Navies in the War of the Rebellion, (Washington, DC, 1897), Series 1, Volume 6, chart facing p. 555, p. 788

1862-1-US-NC-15: On January 27, 1862, the Confederate steamer *Ellis* sank the schooner *Zenith* at the barricade in Croatan Sound between Fort Forrest and Roanoke Island, North Carolina. (Note: This may have been the 103 ton schooner *Zenith* which was built at Swansboro, North Carolina, in 1834. That vessel was issued a certificate of enrollment at New York, New York, on October 29, 1834.)

References for 1862-1-US-NC-15:
Official Records of the Union and Confederate Navies in the War of the Rebellion, (Washington, DC, 1897), Series 1, Volume 6, chart facing p. 555, p. 788
List of American-Flag Merchant Vessels that Received Certificates of Enrollment or Registry at the Port of New York 1789-1867, compiled by Forest R. Holdcamper, (U.S. National Archives, Washington, DC, 1968), Special List #22, Volume 1, p. 748

The "Real Rhett Butler" & Other Revelations

1862-1-US-NC-16: The records aren't clear but appears that on January 28, 1862, the Confederate steamer *Ellis* sank a schooner by the name of *Rio* at the barricade in Croatan Sound. (Note: The barricade ran between Fort Forrest and Roanoke Island, North Carolina.)

References for 1862-1-US-NC-16:
Official Records of the Union and Confederate Navies in the War of the Rebellion, (Washington, DC, 1897), Series 1, Volume 6, chart facing p. 555, p. 788

1862-1-US-NC-17: On January 29, 1862, the Confederate steamer *Ellis* went up to Weir's Point battery and took the schooner *Triplet* in tow and sank her at the barricade in Croatan Sound between Fort Forrest and Roanoke Island, North Carolina. (Note: Weir's Point was the eastern terminus of the new Croatan Sound Bridge.)

References for 1862-1-US-NC-17:
Official Records of the Union and Confederate Navies in the War of the Rebellion, (Washington, DC, 1897), Series 1, Volume 6, chart facing p. 555, p. 787
Outer Banks of North Carolina, by David Stick, (UNC Press, Chapel Hill, NC, 1958, p. 137

1862-1-US-NC-18: The steam tug *E.H. Herbert*, Captain William Mathe, of Baltimore, Maryland, was lost January 30, 1862, off New Inlet, North Carolina. The crew was saved by the schooner *William H. Mailler*, Captain Seth C. Avery, when the tug was observed with its union down and sinking.

References for 1862-1-US-NC-18:
New York Times, (New York, NY), Volume 11, #3240, February 10, 1862, p. 1, c. 1, 2

1862-1-US-NC-19: The log of the Confederate steamer *Ellis* for January 31, 1862, states that the *Ellis* "took the schooner *Southern Star* in tow and carried her down and put ballast in her" (in preparation of sinking the schooner at the barricade that ran between Fort Forrest and Roanoke Island, North Carolina). The log also reported the steamer *Raleigh* as "employed in sinking schooners at the barricade."

References for 1862-1-US-NC-19:
Official Records of the Union and Confederate Navies in the War of the Rebellion, (Washington, DC, 1897), Series 1, Volume 6, chart facing p. 555, p. 788

1862-1-US-NC-20: Sometime in January of 1862, "a boat from the transport *Ann E. Thompson,* containing twelve persons, was swamped among the breakers (on the bar at Hatteras Inlet, North Carolina), and Colonel (Joseph W.) Allen and Surgeon (Frederick A.) Weller, of the 9th New Jersey, were drowned. The death of these much-esteemed officers cast a gloom on the whole fleet."

References for 1862-2-US-NC-20:
The History of the Navy during the Rebellion, by Charles B. Boynton, (D. Appelton and Company, New York, NY, 1867), Volume 1, p. 380
Battles and Leaders of the Civil War, edited by Robert U. Johnson and Clarence C. Buel, Volume 1 of 4 volumes (Century Co., New York, NY, 1884-87, reprinted by Thomas Yoseloff Inc. 1956), p. 665

1862-1-US-SC/GA-1: The ship *Emerald*, 518 tons, which was to be used as part of the second "Stone Fleet" at Charleston, South

Treasures of the Confederate Coast

Carolina, was accidentally run aground on Tybee Island, Georgia, in early January, 1862, and eventually broke up. (Note One: She had been purchased on November 21, 1861, at a cost of $5,500 at Sag Harbor, New York, by George D. Morgan and R.H. Chappell.) (Note Two: The *Emerald* is incorrectly shown in Bruce Berman's *Encyclopedia of American Shipwrecks* as sunk on January 20, 1862, "On south edge of Rattlesnake Shoal, Maffitt's Channel, Charleston, South Carolina") (Note Three: For more information on the second Charleston Stone Fleet see entry 1862-1-US-SC/GA-4 in this book.)

References for 1862-1-US-SC/GA-1:
Official Records of the Union and Confederate Navies in the War of the Rebellion, (Washington, DC, 1901), Series 1, Volume 12, p. 510
Official Records of the Union and Confederate Navies in the War of the Rebellion, (Washington, DC, 1921), Series 2, Volume 1, p. 78
Dictionary of American Naval Fighting Ships, (Washington, DC, 1970), Volume 5, Appendix I, pp. 432, 433
Encyclopedia of American Shipwrecks, by Bruce D. Berman, (Boston, 1972), p. 117, #577

1862-1-US-SC/GA-2: The bark *Marcia*, 343 tons, which had been intended to be used as part of the second "Stone Fleet" at Charleston, South Carolina, was accidentally run aground and sunk after crossing Port Royal Bar, South Carolina, on January 7, 1862. (Note One: The bark was purchased on December 10, 1861, at Portland, Maine, by G.D. Morgan and R.H. Chappell for $4,200.) (Note Two: The *Marcia* is incorrectly shown in Bruce Berman's *Encyclopedia of American Shipwrecks* as sunk on January 20, 1862, "On south edge of Rattlesnake Shoal, Maffitt's Channel, Charleston, South Carolina" Berman shows her as 356 tons.) (Note Three: For more information on the second Charleston Stone Fleet see entry 1862-1-US-SC/GA-4 in this book.)

References for 1862-1-US-SC/GA-2:
Official Records of the Union and Confederate Navies in the War of the Rebellion, (Washington, DC, 1901), Series 1, Volume 12, p. 511
Official Records of the Union and Confederate Navies in the War of the Rebellion, (Washington, DC, 1921), Series 2, Volume 1, p. 134
Dictionary of American Naval Fighting Ships, (Washington, DC, 1970), Volume 5, Appendix I, pp. 432, 433
Encyclopedia of American Shipwrecks, by Bruce D. Berman, (Boston, 1972), p. 132, #1254

1862-1-US-SC/GA-3: The pilot boat *Chace* got ashore on January 20, 1862, near the Sullivan's Island, South Carolina, breakwater, but later got off.

References for 1862-1-US-SC/GA-3:
"Charleston Daily Courier," (Charleston, SC), #19068, January 22, 1862, p. 2, c. 4
"Charleston Daily Courier," (Charleston, SC), #19069, January 23, 1862, p. 2, c. 4

1862-1-US-SC/GA-4: A Confederate officer filed the following report on the sinking of the second "Stone Fleet" off Charleston, South Carolina. "On January 20 another fleet came to anchor off the port. The vessels were mostly of a smaller class than those of December. They were fourteen in number - barks and brigs. They were stripped and towed northwardly to their positions, which was on the south edge of the shoal known as the Rattle Snake (Rattlesnake Shoals), and opposite the entrance of the Maffitt Channel, with the exception of one vessel, which was placed on the eastern edge of the shoal about two and a half miles east of the other vessels and between the shoal and the Long Island (present day Isle of Palms, South Carolina) beach." Other reports give the date of the actual sinking as January 25 & 26, 1862. The following vessels were sunk: The ship *Bogota*, 300 tons; the bark *Dove*, 151 tons (which had been purchased at New London, Connecticut, for $2,500); the bark *Jubilee*, 233 tons (which had been purchased at Portland, Maine, on November 28, 1861, for $2,000); the ship *Majestic*, 297 tons (which had been purchased at New Bedford, Massachusetts, on December 2, 1861, for $3,150); the bark *Margaret Scott*, 330 tons (which had been purchased at New Bedford, Massachusetts, on November 30, 1861, for $4,000); the ship *Mechanic*, 335 tons (which had been purchased at Newport, Rhode Island, on November 13, 1861, for $4,200); the bark *Messenger*, 216 tons (which had been purchased at Salem, Massachusetts, on November 16, 1861, for $2,250); the ship *New England*, 368 tons (which had been purchased at New London, Connecticut, on November 21, 1861, for $5,000); the ship *Newburyport*, 341 tons (which had been purchased at Gloucester, Massachusetts, on November 30, 1861, for $4,500); the bark *Noble*, 274 tons (which had been purchased at Sag Harbor, New York, on December 2, 1861, for $4,300); the ship *Peri*, 265 tons (which had been purchased at Portland, Maine, on November 29, 1861, for $3,500); the brig *Stephen Young*, 199 tons or 200 tons (which had been purchased at Boston, Massachusetts, on November 27, 1861, for $1,600); and the ship *Timor*, 289 tons (which had been purchased at Sag Harbor, New York, on October 30, 1861, for $2,200). Most of these were old whaling vessels which had been purchased in New England especially to be sunk as obstructions in an effort to block off the entrance to Charleston Harbor. The vessels which were loaded with stone to aid in the blocking of the channel were nick-named the "Stone Fleet" or the "Stone Whalers." This was the second such fleet to be sunk at Charleston. The first having been sunk on December 19 & 20, 1861. The sinking of these two fleets created an international uproar against the United States which was severely criticized for its actions. About fifty whaleboats were saved. Secret orders had also been given to the captains of the vessels to "bring away papers,

Treasures of the Confederate Coast

chronometer, charts, compasses, spyglass" and other portable items. (Note One: Information on the first Charleston Stone Fleet is contained in entry 1861-12-US-SC/GA-8 of this book.) (Note Two: Bruce Berman's *Encyclopedia of American Shipwrecks* lists the bark *Edward*, the ship *Emerald*, the bark *Marcia*, the ship *Montezuma*, and the ship *Valparaiso*, as having been sunk as part of the second Charleston Stone Fleet, but this is not supported by official documents. For more information on the *Edward* see entry 1862-1x-US-SC/GA-2; on the *Emerald* see entry 1862-1-US-SC/GA-1; on the *Marcia* see entry 1862-1-US-SC/GA-2; on the *Montezuma* see entry 1861-1x-US-SC/GA-3, and on the *Valparaiso* see entry 1862-1x-US-SC/GA-4.)

References for 1862-1-US-SC/GA-4:
"Daily Morning News," (Savannah, GA), January 29, 1862, p. 1, c. 6
New York Times, (New York, NY), #3229, January 28, 1862, p. 5, c. 1
History of the Confederate States Navy From its Organization to the Surrender of its Last Vessel, by J. Thomas Scharf, (New York, New York, 1887), pp. 435,435n, 436, 436n, 662
Official Records of the Union and Confederate Armies in the War of the Rebellion, (Washington, DC, 1882), Series 1, Volume 6, pp. 42, 43
Official Records of the Union and Confederate Navies in the War of the Rebellion, (Washington, DC, 1901), Series 1, Volume 12, pp. 418, 423, 424, 426, 510-515
Official Records of the Union and Confederate Navies in the War of the Rebellion, (Washington, DC, 1921), Series 2, Volume 1, pp. 75, 115, 132, 135, 140, 142, 150, 158, 162, 175, 214, 224, 230
The Navy in the Civil War, (Charles Scribner's Sons, New York, NY, 1903), Volume 1 ("The Blockade and the Cruisers" by James Russell Soley), p. 107
Dictionary of American Naval Fighting Ships, (Washington, DC, 1970), Volume 5, Appendix I, pp. 430-436
Encyclopedia of American Shipwrecks, by Bruce D. Berman, (Boston, 1972), p. 115, #493; p. 116, #530; p. 117, #577; p. 128, #1068; p. 132, #1243, #1254, #1259; p. 134, #1334, #1344; p. 135, #1391; p. 136, #1438, #1444; p. 137, #1451; p. 139, #1575; p. 146, #1850; p. 147, #1929; p. 149, #1978
Charleston's Maritime Heritage 1670-1865, by P.C. Coker III, (CokerCraft Press, Charleston, SC, 1987), pp. 218, 219

1862-1-US-SC/GA-5: The United States Army transport steamer *Winfield Scott* was wrecked in Skull Creek near Port Royal Sound, South Carolina, in January, 1862. One report stated that the steamer was lost at "Dawfuskie" (Daufuskie) Island, South Carolina, in February, 1862, and that she was broken in two in "Pull and Be Damned Creek." (Note One: The *Winfield Scott* which had originally cost $60,000 had been sold to the United States Department of the Army for $115,000. The steamer's hull was of 5/16" iron and was described as a "mere shell.") (Note Two: The *Winfield Scott* had been incorrectly reported as lost off North Carolina during the storm of November 1, 1861, but had saved herself by sacrificing the whole of her cargo. For more on that report see entry 1861-11-US-NC-3.) (Note Three: This does not appear to have been the screw steamer *General Winfield Scott*, 1162 tons, which was built in 1861, at Philadelphia, and was transferred to the United States War Department the same year, as that vessel is shown in the "Lytle List" as having a wooden hull.)

References for 1862-1-US-SC/GA-5:

The "Real Rhett Butler" & Other Revelations

"Report of vessels employed by the U.S. in the Department of the Carolinas which have been lost," (manuscript list), National Archives, Record Group 92, entry 1407, Box 123
"Lost," (manuscript list of vessels), National Archives, Record Group 92, entry 1407, Box 123, Section "Vessels Wrecked and Lost"
"Vessel Disasters, 1861," (bound annotated clipping file, Atlantic Mutual Insurance Companies of New York), pp. 188, 189, 200
Official Records of the Union and Confederate Armies in the War of the Rebellion, (Washington, DC, 1882), Series 1, Volume 6, pp. 3, 144, 186
Official Records of the Union and Confederate Navies in the War of the Rebellion, (Washington, DC, 1901), Series 1, Volume 12, pp. 28, 292
Merchant Steam Vessels of the United States 1807-1868, ("Lytle List"), by William M. Lytle, (Mystic, CT, 1952), p. 7
Battles and Leaders of the Civil War, edited by Robert U. Johnson and Clarence C. Buel, Volume 1 of 4 volumes (Century Co., New York, NY, 1884-87, reprinted by Thomas Yoseloff Inc. 1956), p. 676

1862-1x-US-SC/GA-1: An endorsement dated February 14, 1862, by C.H. Davis of the South Atlantic Blockading Squadron on a report concerning the Stone Fleet, stated that the vessel *Jupiter* had been sunk at Charleston, South Carolina. (Note: This report probably referred to the bark *Jubilee*, which was sunk as part of the second Charleston Stone Fleet about January 24, 1862. For more on the *Jubilee* and the second Charleston Stone Fleet see entry 1862-1-US-SC/GA-4.)

References for 1862-1x-US-SC/GA-1:
Official Records of the Union and Confederate Navies in the War of the Rebellion, (Washington, DC, 1901), Series 1, Volume 12, pp. 467, 474, 511
Official Records of the Union and Confederate Navies in the War of the Rebellion, (Washington, DC, 1921), Series 2, Volume 1, p. 115
Encyclopedia of American Shipwrecks, by Bruce D. Berman, (Boston, 1972), p. 128, #1068

1862-1x-US-SC/GA-2: The bark *Edward*, 340 (or 274) tons, is incorrectly listed in Bruce Berman's *Encyclopedia of American Shipwrecks* as sunk on January 20, 1862, "On south edge of Rattlesnake Shoal, Maffitt's Channel, Charleston, South Carolina Sunk by Union forces to block harbor entrance. Second Stone Fleet." (Note One: Although originally purchased as part of the Stone Fleet the *Edward* was actually used as one of two giant pontoons to support a floating machine shop moored in Machine-Shop Creek near Port Royal, South Carolina. The other pontoon was the old whaling ship *India*.) (Note Two: The *Edward* had been purchased for the U.S. Navy at New Bedford, Massachusetts, by George D. Morgan and R.H. Chappell, on November 15, 1861, for $4,000.)

References for 1862-1x-US-SC/GA-2:
Official Records of the Union and Confederate Navies in the War of the Rebellion, (Washington, DC, 1901), Series 1, Volume 12, p. 510
Official Records of the Union and Confederate Navies in the War of the Rebellion, (Washington, DC, 1921), Series 2, Volume 1, p. 77
Encyclopedia of American Shipwrecks, by Bruce D. Berman, (Boston, 1972), p. 116, #530
The South Besieged: Volume Five of The Image of War, 1861-1865, Doubleday & Company Inc., Garden City, NY, 1983, p. 126

1862-1x-US-SC/GA-3: The ship *Montezuma*, 424 tons, is incorrectly listed in Bruce Berman's *Encyclopedia of American Shipwrecks* as sunk on January 20, 1862, "On south edge of Rattlesnake Shoal,

Treasures of the Confederate Coast

Maffitt's Channel, Charleston, South Carolina Sunk by Union forces to block harbor entrance. Second Stone Fleet." (Note One: The *Montezuma* was purchased for the U.S. Navy at New Bedford, Massachusetts, by George D. Morgan and R.H. Chappell, on November 15, 1861, for $4,800.) (Note Two: A report from United States Brigadier-General Gilmore, dated at Tybee Island, Georgia, on April 1, 1862, mentions the "hulk *Montezuma*, anchored in Lazeretto Creek.") (Note Three: For more on the second Charleston Stone Fleet see entry 1862-1-US-SC/GA-4.)

References for 1862-1x-US-SC/GA-3:
Official Records of the Union and Confederate Navies in the War of the Rebellion, (Washington, DC, 1901), Series 1, Volume 12, pp. 510, 701
Official Records of the Union and Confederate Navies in the War of the Rebellion, (Washington, DC, 1921), Series 2, Volume 1, p. 150
Encyclopedia of American Shipwrecks, by Bruce D. Berman, (Boston, 1972), p. 135, #1391

1862-1x-US-SC/GA-4: The ship *Valparaiso*, 402 tons, is incorrectly listed in Bruce Berman's *Encyclopedia of American Shipwrecks* as sunk on January 20, 1862, "On south edge of Rattlesnake Shoal, Maffitt's Channel, Charleston, South Carolina Sunk by Union forces to block harbor entrance. Part of second Stone Fleet." (Note One: The *Valparaiso* was purchased for the U.S. Navy at New Bedford, Massachusetts, by George D. Morgan and R.H. Chappell, on November 22, 1861, for $5,500. Although intended to be used as part of the second Charleston Stone Fleet, the *Valparaiso* was not used as planned. Instead she was sold at public auction on September 2, 1865, at Bay Point, South Carolina, by Rear-Admiral Radford to English and Company for $625.) (Note: For more on the second Charleston Stone Fleet, please see entry 1862-1-US-SC/GA-4.)

References for 1862-1x-US-SC/GA-4:
Official Records of the Union and Confederate Navies in the War of the Rebellion, (Washington, DC, 1901), Series 1, Volume 12, p. 511
Official Records of the Union and Confederate Navies in the War of the Rebellion, (Washington, DC, 1921), Series 2, Volume 1, p. 230
Encyclopedia of American Shipwrecks, by Bruce D. Berman, (Boston, 1972), p. 149, #1978

1862-2-US-NC-1: During the first week of February, 1862, the log of the Confederate steamer *Ellis* shows that vessel and several others as busily engaged in the preparation and positioning of schooners for sinking at the barricade that ran between Fort Forrest and Roanoke Island, North Carolina.

References for 1862-2-US-NC-1:
Official Records of the Union and Confederate Navies in the War of the Rebellion, (Washington, DC, 1897), Series 1, Volume 6, chart facing p. 555, p. 789

1862-2-US-NC-2: On February 6, 1862, the Confederate steamer *Ellis* went to Weir's Point battery on Roanoke Island, North Carolina, to raise a schooner (presumably to move and sink at the barricade across Croatan Sound). (Note: The *Ellis* sank at least two

The "Real Rhett Butler" & Other Revelations

schooners at the barricade on this date. One of the two schooners was referred to in the *Ellis'* log simply as "the white schooner.")

References for 1862-2-US-NC-2:
Official Records of the Union and Confederate Navies in the War of the Rebellion, (Washington, DC, 1897), Series 1, Volume 6, chart facing p. 555, p. 789

1862-2-US-NC-3: Daniel Ammen in his work "The Atlantic Coast" says "in an engagement at Roanoke Island on the 7th (1862), a gunboat on the stocks, and another vessel with lighter frame had been set on fire at the shipyard" by the Confederates. "Competent persons were sent on shore to destroy boilers and machinery and ways."

Reference for 1862-2-US-NC-3:
The Navy in the Civil War, (Charles Scribner's Sons, New York, NY, 1905), Volume 2 ("The Atlantic Coast" by Daniel Ammen), p. 185

1862-2-US-NC-4: The *C.S.S. Curlew*, Lt. Commander Thomas T. Hunter, was struck by a 100-pounder Parrot shell fired from the *U.S.S. Southfield* and sunk in front of Fort Forrest on North Carolina mainland, on February 8, 1862, during the defense of Roanoke Island. The shell went through her "decks and bottom as though they had been made of paper." She was set afire by her own crew and her magazine exploded. Halfway through the fighting, Commander Hunter realized "to his surprise that he had no trousers on." (Note One: Some records show her as armed with two guns, others as armed with four thirty-two pounders. In any case, it was reported that her guns were recovered.) [Note Two: She was variously described as a tug and as a passenger steamer. Another account stated that the *Curlew* was an "iron-hulled side-wheel, river steamboat. The report went on to say she was serving as the flagship of North Carolina's famed "Mosquito Fleet" and that she received a direct hit and was sunk "near Fort Forrest (Manns Harbor)" in Croatan Sound.] [Note Two: The *Curlew* was purchased by the Confederate government at Norfolk, Virginia, in 1861. She was 236(260) tons and was built at Wilmington, Delaware in 1856. She was 150' in length, drew 4'6", and could make 12 knots. Her first home port was Edenton, North Carolina.] (Note Three: One report erroneously gives the wreck's location as "near Fort Fisher.") (Note Four: The *Curlew* assisted in the capture of the *U.S.S. Fanny*, which was the first Federal vessel to be taken intact by the Confederates.) (Note Five: Despite the fact that a resource not used might as well not exist, the State of North Carolina shrouds the location of this wreck in secrecy. Accessibility is allowed, but only by wading through government red tape that was apparently designed largely to prevent public access to the site.)

References for 1862-2-US-NC-4:

Treasures of the Confederate Coast

History of the Confederate States Navy From its Organization to the Surrender of its Last Vessel, by J. Thomas Scharf, (New York, NY, 1887), pp. 389, 394

Official Records of the Union and Confederate Armies in the War of the Rebellion, (Washington, DC, 1883), Series 1, Volume 9, p. 185

Official Records of the Union and Confederate Navies in the War of the Rebellion, (Washington, DC, 1897), Series 1, Volume 6, pp. 590, 594, 595, 635

Official Records of the Union and Confederate Navies in the War of the Rebellion, (Washington, DC, 1921), Series 2, Volume 1, p. 251

Graveyard of the Atlantic: Shipwrecks of the North Carolina Coast, by David Stick (University of North Carolina Press, Chapel Hill, NC, 1952), pp. 52, 247

Battles and Leaders of the Civil War, with a new introduction by Roy F. Nichols, (1956 reprint of 1887 edition by Thomas Yoseloff Inc., New York, NY, 1956), Volume 1, pp. 625, 638, 642, 645

Outer Banks of North Carolina, by David Stick, (UNC Press, Chapel Hill, NC, 1958, p. 143

Dictionary of American Naval Fighting Ships, (Washington, DC, 1963), Volume 2, p. 512

An Oceanographic Atlas of the Continental Margin, J.G. Newton, O.H. Pilkey, & J.O. Blanton, (Duke University Marine Laboratory, Beaufort, NC, 1971), p. 25 chart symbol #693, p. 29 entry #693

Encyclopedia of American Shipwrecks, by Bruce D. Berman, (Boston, 1972), p. 114, #438

Shipwrecks of the Civil War: The Encyclopedia of Union and Confederate Naval Losses, by Donald Shomette, (Washington, DC, 1973), pp. 256, 257

Merchant Steam Vessels of the United States 1790-1868, ("Lytle-Holdcamper List"), by William M. Lytle and Forrest R. Holdcamper, revised and edited by C. Bradford Mitchell, (Staten Island, NY, 1975), p. 49

Civil War Naval Squadrons, by Thomas R. Bullard, (Oak Park, IL, 1988), p. 15

The C.S.S. Curlew: Flagship of North Carolina's 'Mosquito Fleet,' by Glenn R. Williams, published in *ShipWrecks* magazine, Volume 1, #3, pp. 57-62

1862-2-US-NC-5: The Confederate States sidewheel river steamer *Sea Bird* (or *Seabird*) was run into and sunk by the *U.S.S. Commodore Perry* in a battle off Elizabeth City, North Carolina, on February 10, 1862.

She was armed with two rifled guns and had $30,000 in cash on board. (Note One: The *Sea Bird* was described as a "small passenger steamer" and had been made Commander W.F. Lynch's flagship after the loss of the *Curlew*. She was a wooden vessel and had been purchased at Norfolk, Virginia, in 1861. She was 202 tons and was built at Keyport, New Jersey, in 1854. Her first home port was New York, New York. At the time of her loss, she was valued at $30,000. Her boiler and machinery were thoroughly destroyed.) (Note Two: The date of loss was also given as February 7, and the location as in Croatan Sound.) (Note Three: This may have been the 202 ton steam boat *Sea Bird*, which was built at Keyport, New Jersey in 1854. That vessel was issued a certificate of steam enrollment at New York, New York, on August 1, 1854.)

References for 1862-2-US-NC-5:

"Charleston Mercury," (Charleston, SC), Volume 80, #11382, February 25, 1862, p. 1, c. 4

History of the Confederate States Navy From its Organization to the Surrender of its Last Vessel, by J. Thomas Scharf, (New York, NY, 1887), pp. 389-392

Official Records of the Union and Confederate Navies in the War of the Rebellion, (Washington, DC, 1897), Series 1, Volume 6, pp. 596, 608, 622, 635, 646

Official Records of the Union and Confederate Navies in the War of the Rebellion, (Washington, DC, 1921), Series 2, Volume 1, pp. 266, 273, 306

The Navy in the Civil War, (Charles Scribner's Sons, New York, NY, 1905), Volume 2 ("The Atlantic Coast" by Daniel Ammen), p. 184

Graveyard of the Atlantic: Shipwrecks of the North Carolina Coast, by David Stick (University of North Carolina Press, Chapel Hill, NC, 1952), pp. 52, 247

List of American-Flag Merchant Vessels that Received Certificates of Enrollment or Registry at the Port of New York 1789-1867, compiled by Forest R. Holdcamper, (U.S. National Archives, Washington, DC, 1968), Special List #22, Volume 2, p. 633

Naval History of the Civil War, by Howard P. Nash, (A.S. Barnes & Co., New York, NY, 1972), p. 77

Merchant Steam Vessels of the United States 1790-1868, ("Lytle-Holdcamper List"), by William M. Lytle and Forrest R. Holdcamper, revised and edited by C. Bradford Mitchell, (Staten Island, NY, 1975), p. 196

The "Real Rhett Butler" & Other Revelations

1862-2-US-NC-6: On February 10, 1862, the *U.S.S. Whitehead* discovered the Confederate States schooner *Black Warrior* run ashore, abandoned, and on fire off Elizabeth City, North Carolina. The Federals scuttled her after first taking off six muskets, twelve boarding pikes, and books and papers of the "rebel paymaster." (Note One: The *Black Warrior* had been part of a small fleet organized by the Confederates for defense against a fleet of twice its size which carried four times the armament. It was reported that the *Black Warrior* had kept up a brisk fire against the enemy before her captain was forced to run her aground and set her afire.) (Note Two: The *Black Warrior*, Lieutenant Harris, was a large vessel and was armed with two 32-pounders and was loaded with "a large amount of provisions and stores for the Confederate vessels." She was valued at $20,000.)

References for 1862-2-US-NC-6:
History of the Confederate States Navy From its Organization to the Surrender of its Last Vessel, by J. Thomas Scharf, (New York, NY, 1887), pp. 389, 391
Official Records of the Union and Confederate Navies in the War of the Rebellion, (Washington, DC, 1897), Series 1, Volume 6, pp. 616, 617, 623
Official Records of the Union and Confederate Navies in the War of the Rebellion, (Washington, DC, 1921), Series 2, Volume 1, p. 249
The Navy in the Civil War, (Charles Scribner's Sons, New York, NY, 1905), Volume 2 ("The Atlantic Coast" by Daniel Ammen), p. 185
Graveyard of the Atlantic: Shipwrecks of the North Carolina Coast, by David Stick (University of North Carolina Press, Chapel Hill, NC, 1952), pp. 52, 247

1862-2-US-NC-7: On February 10, 1862, the gunboat *Appomattox*, Lieutenant Commander Simms, which was serving as part of a heavily outgunned Confederate fleet in the Pasquotank River during the battle for Elizabeth City, North Carolina, tried to flee up the Dismal Swamp Canal, and finding itself "about two inches too wide to enter" was set on fire by her own crew and blown up. (Note One: One account stated that the *Appomattox* escaped during this action, but that seems to have been an error.) (Note Two: The *Appomattox* was built in 1850 as the sidewheel steamer *Empire*, 120 tons, at Philadelphia, Pennsylvania which was also her first home port. She had a wood hull and was armed with one 32-pounder and one howitzer.)

References for 1862-2-US-NC-7:
History of the Confederate States Navy From its Organization to the Surrender of its Last Vessel, by J. Thomas Scharf, (New York, NY, 1887), pp. 389, 391
Official Records of the Union and Confederate Navies in the War of the Rebellion, (Washington, DC, 1897), Series 1, Volume 6, pp. 595, 596, 788, 789
Graveyard of the Atlantic: Shipwrecks of the North Carolina Coast, by David Stick (University of North Carolina Press, Chapel Hill, NC, 1952), pp. 52, 247
Naval History of the Civil War, by Howard P. Nash, (A.S. Barnes & Co., New York, NY, 1972), p. 77
Merchant Steam Vessels of the United States 1790-1868, ("Lytle-Holdcamper List"), by William M. Lytle and Forrest R. Holdcamper, revised and edited by C. Bradford Mitchell, (Staten Island, NY, 1975), pp. 12, 64

1862-2-US-NC-8: On February 10, 1862, the Confederate gunboat *Forrest*, Lieutenant Commander James L. Hoole (or Hoover), which had been damaged and was on the railway at the shipyard, was set on fire and destroyed during the battle for Elizabeth City, North Carolina. (Note: The *Forrest* had been armed with two guns and was said to have been worth $21,500. One of the guns was a 32-pounder.)

References for 1862-2-US-NC-8:

"Charleston Mercury," (Charleston, SC), Volume 80, #11382, February 25, 1862, p. 1, c. 4, 5
History of the Confederate States Navy From its Organization to the Surrender of its Last Vessel, by J. Thomas Scharf, (New York, NY, 1887), pp. 389-391
Official Records of the Union and Confederate Navies in the War of the Rebellion, (Washington, DC, 1897), Series 1, Volume 6, pp. 590, 594-597, 608, 62, 623, 635, 784-786, 789
Official Records of the Union and Confederate Navies in the War of the Rebellion, (Washington, DC, 1921), Series 2, Volume 1, p. 253
The Navy in the Civil War, (Charles Scribner's Sons, New York, NY, 1905), Volume 2 ("The Atlantic Coast" by Daniel Ammen), p. 185
Graveyard of the Atlantic: Shipwrecks of the North Carolina Coast, by David Stick (University of North Carolina Press, Chapel Hill, NC, 1952), pp. 52, 247
Outer Banks of North Carolina, by David Stick, (UNC Press, Chapel Hill, NC, 1958, p. 143

1862-2-US-NC-9: A steamer, "name unknown, intended for the rebel Navy, on the stocks and nearly completed, was burned during the action off Elizabeth City, North Carolina, February 10, 1862." She was estimated to have been worth $18,800.

Reference for 1862-2-US-NC-9:

Official Records of the Union and Confederate Navies in the War of the Rebellion, (Washington, DC, 1897), Series 1, Volume 6, p. 623

1862-2-US-NC-10: The Confederate States steamer *Fanny*, Captain Taylor, was run aground and set fire by her commander on February 10, 1862, during the battle of Elizabeth City, North Carolina, to prevent her capture. (Note One: She had an iron hull and a single propeller. The former tugboat had been captured from the Federals on October 1, 1861, in Loggerhead Inlet, North Carolina, and was valued at $23,000. The *Fanny's* engine and boiler were thoroughly destroyed.) (Note Two: She is often described as the first armed vessel captured intact during the Civil War. At the time of her capture from the Federals she carried a cargo valued at $150,000 and was described as having the "best armament of all the tugs, one being a Sawyer's rifle gun." Her armament was once reported as including twenty-six cutlasses. She mounted one 8-pounder rifled cannon and one 32-pounder rifled cannon. The 32-pounder was recovered from the wreck by the *U.S.S. Valley City*.)

References for 1862-2-US-NC-10:

"Charleston Mercury," (Charleston, SC), Volume 80, #11380, February 21, 1862, p. 4, c. 4
History of the Confederate States Navy From its Organization to the Surrender of its Last Vessel, by J. Thomas Scharf, (New York, NY, 1887), pp. 379, 380, 389, 392
Official Records of the Union and Confederate Navies in the War of the Rebellion, (Washington, DC, 1897), Series 1, Volume 6, pp. 276-278, 280, 596, 608, 616, 618-620, 622, 623, 646, 738
Official Records of the Union and Confederate Navies in the War of the Rebellion, (Washington, DC, 1898), Series 1, Volume 7, p. 700
Official Records of the Union and Confederate Navies in the War of the Rebellion, (Washington, DC, 1921), Series 2, Volume 1, pp. 252, 273, 285
The Navy in the Civil War, (Charles Scribner's Sons, New York, NY, 1905), Volume 2 ("The Atlantic Coast" by Daniel Ammen), p. 185
Graveyard of the Atlantic: Shipwrecks of the North Carolina Coast, by David Stick (University of North Carolina Press, Chapel Hill, NC, 1952), pp. 52, 247

The "Real Rhett Butler" & Other Revelations

Outer Banks of North Carolina, by David Stick, (UNC Press, Chapel Hill, NC, 1958, pp. 132, 141
Naval History of the Civil War, by Howard P. Nash, (A.S. Barnes & Co., New York, NY, 1972), p. 77

1862-2-US-NC-11: On February 10, 1862, the Federals took possession of and destroyed a Confederate fort mounting four guns and a schooner mounting one gun. This apparently took place near Roanoke Island in Albemarle Sound, North Carolina.

Reference for 1862-2-US-NC-11:
Official Records of the Union and Confederate Navies in the War of the Rebellion, (Washington, DC, 1897), Series 1, Volume 6, p. 590

1862-2-US-NC-12: Eight cannon and one schooner were destroyed by the Federals at Edenton, North Carolina, on February 12, 1862.

Reference for 1862-2-US-NC-12:
The Navy in the Civil War, (Charles Scribner's Sons, New York, NY, 1905), Volume 2 ("The Atlantic Coast" by Daniel Ammen), p. 185

1862-2-US-NC-13: The Confederates sank an unidentified schooner as an obstruction about fifty yards within the mouth of the Albemarle and Chesapeake canal on February 14, 1862. The schooner was supported by piles and logs and formed a complete barrier.

References for 1862-2-US-NC-13:
Official Records of the Union and Confederate Navies in the War of the Rebellion, (Washington, DC, 1897), Series 1, Volume 6, p. 638
The Navy in the Civil War, (Charles Scribner's Sons, New York, NY, 1905), Volume 2 ("The Atlantic Coast" by Daniel Ammen), p. 186

1862-2-US-NC-14: A schooner (name and owners unknown), loaded with furniture, was captured by the *U.S.S. Commodore Perry* during the action off Elizabeth City, North Carolina, on February 10, 1862. (Note: The schooner, valued at $2000, was sunk as obstruction in the outlet of the Albemarle and Chesapeake canal on February 14, 1865, by the *U.S.S. Underwriter.*)

References for 1862-2-US-NC-14:
"Charleston Mercury," (Charleston, SC), Volume 80, #11384, February 27, 1862, p. 1, c. 3
Official Records of the Union and Confederate Navies in the War of the Rebellion, (Washington, DC, 1897), Series 1, Volume 6, pp. 623, 638

1862-2-US-NC-15: A schooner (name and owners unknown) was sunk as obstruction in the outlet of the Albemarle and Chesapeake canal on February 14, 1865, by the *U.S.S. Underwriter.* (Note: The schooner had been captured off Elizabeth City, North Carolina, on February 10, 1862. At the time of her capture she was loaded with forty-five hundred bushels of corn, and valued at $7000.)

References for 1862-2-US-NC-15:
"Charleston Mercury," (Charleston, SC), Volume 80, #11384, February 27, 1862, p. 1, c. 3
Official Records of the Union and Confederate Navies in the War of the Rebellion, (Washington, DC, 1897), Series 1, Volume 6, pp. 623, 638

1862-2-US-NC-16: A fine large dredging machine was scuttled and burned as an obstruction near a row of piles, one half mile inside of the outlet of the Albemarle and Chesapeake canal by the Confederates on February 14, 1862. She sank diagonally across the

Treasures of the Confederate Coast

canal blocking all but six feet on one side and ten feet on the other. The hull was burned to the waterline.

References for 1862-2-US-NC-16:
Official Records of the Union and Confederate Navies in the War of the Rebellion, (Washington, DC, 1897), Series 1, Volume 6, pp. 638, 639
The Navy in the Civil War, (Charles Scribner's Sons, New York, NY, 1905), Volume 2 ("The Atlantic Coast" by Daniel Ammen), p. 186

1862-2-US-NC-17: The United States steamer *I.N. Seymour* (a.k.a.-*Seymour, J.N. Seymour*, and as *Isaac N. Seymour*), Acting Master Francis S. Wells, ran on an anchor (left by the transport steamer *Louisiana*) "in the center and near the entrance of the channel" at Hatteras Inlet, North Carolina, on February 20, 1862, sank in 7'6" (9'6") of water, and was reported as a "total loss." (Note One: At least some of the machinery, ordnance, etc. was saved immediately, and apparently the entire vessel was later raised, as official records show her as still in service throughout the war.) [Note Two: The *I.N. Seymour*, official number 91441, was built in 1860 at Keyport, New Jersey, and received a certificate of registry on July 14, 1860. She was purchased the following month for the U.S. Navy at New York by George D. Morgan from a Mr. Schultz at a cost of $18,000. She was a wooden hulled side-wheel steamer of 133 (140) tons. She was 100' in length, 19'8" in breadth, and 7'6" in depth of hold. Her draft loaded was 6'6" while her draft light was 5'6". She had one single beam engine, with a thirty inch diameter cylinder with a six foot piston stroke. At the time of her sinking, her armament consisted of one thirty-pounder Parrott rifle and one twelve-pounder Parrott rifle. She went out of commission on May 16, 1865, and on June 20, 1865, was ordered to be turned over to the Light House Board at Washington. While with that service she was operated as the *U.S.L.H.B. Tulip*. She was documented as the *Magnolia* on June 7, 1882, and was finally placed under foreign registry in 1888.]

Reference for 1862-2-US-NC-17:
Official Records of the Union and Confederate Navies in the War of the Rebellion, (Washington, DC, 1897), Series 1, Volume 6, pp. 591, 657, 658, 694
Official Records of the Union and Confederate Navies in the War of the Rebellion, (Washington, DC, 1921), Series 2 Volume 1, p. 106
List of American-Flag Merchant Vessels that Received Certificates of Enrollment or Registry at the Port of New York 1789-1867, compiled by Forest R. Holdcamper, (U.S. National Archives, Washington, DC, 1968), Special List #22, Volume 1, p. 335
Merchant Steam Vessels of the United States 1790-1868, ("Lytle-Holdcamper List"), by William M. Lytle and Forrest R. Holdcamper, revised and edited by C. Bradford Mitchell, (Staten Island, NY, 1975), p. 99, note 3

1862-2-US-NC-18: The "Charleston Mercury" of February 24, 1863, reported that a prize schooner taken by the Confederate privateer *Retribution* had been run aground in New Inlet, North Carolina, under the guns of Fort Fisher. The schooner was loaded with fish, salt, etc.

The "Real Rhett Butler" & Other Revelations

1862-2-US-NC-19: The United States steamer *R.B. Forbes*, commanded by Acting Volunteer Lieutenant William Flye, was accidentally run aground four miles south of Currituck Inlet (also reported as ashore at Nag's Head), North Carolina, on February 26, 1862. Her two 32-pounders and all of her shot and shell were immediately thrown overboard in hopes of floating her, but one propeller broke off further disabling her, and she quickly "buried in the sand" to the extent that her men "could walk nearly all around her at low water." Following standard practice, she was torched by her own crew to prevent her from falling into the hands of the Confederates. The steamer's small arms, chronometers, spyglasses, etc. were saved. [Note One: The *R.B. Forbes* was a twin screw steamer of 350 (or 329 tons) tons and had an iron hull. She was built by Otis Tufts in 1845 at Boston, Massachusetts. Her first document was Permanent Enrollment #15, issued at Boston, on February 24, 1846. She was purchased by Captain W.L. Hudson at Boston, Massachusetts, for the United States Navy on September 20, 1861, for $52,500. The total cost of her repairs while in government service was $6,818.74. The *R.B. Forbes* was classed 4th rate and measured 121' in length, 25'6" in breadth and 11'7.5" in depth. The steamer drew a maximum of 12'3" and could make a speed of eleven knots. She had two inclined double cylinder engines with 36" diameter pistons and 36" piston stroke. The steamer had one boiler.] (Note Two: She was armed with one 30-pounder Parrott rifle on her bow and two 32-pounders of 57 hundredweight. Her bow gun had "broken a drift" earlier the same day and had been thrown overboard for safety prior to her grounding.) (Note Three: Some documents incorrectly show the *R.B. Forbes* as having a wood hull.)

References for 1862-2-US-NC-19:
"Record of Metal Vessels Built in the United States," (bound manuscript volume), Volume 1, p. 6, United States National Archives, RG 41
"Charleston Mercury," (Charleston, SC), Volume 80, #11386, March 3, 1862, p. 1, c. 2
"Daily Morning News," (Savannah, GA), Volume 13, #55, March 10, 1862, p. 1, c. 4
Records of General Courts Martial and Courts of Inquiry of the Navy Department, 1799-1867, Court of Inquiry, #3108, March 4, 1862, NARS M-273, roll 99, frames 0001-0035
Official Records of the Union and Confederate Navies in the War of the Rebellion, (Washington, DC, 1897), Series 1, Volume 6, pp. 664, 672, 673
Official Records of the Union and Confederate Navies in the War of the Rebellion, (Washington, DC, 1921), Series 2, Volume 1, p. 188
Graveyard of the Atlantic: Shipwrecks of the North Carolina Coast, by David Stick (University of North Carolina Press, Chapel Hill, NC, 1952), pp. 57, 58, 247
Merchant Steam Vessels of the United States 1790-1868, ("Lytle-Holdcamper List"), by William M. Lytle and Forrest R. Holdcamper, revised and edited by C. Bradford Mitchell, (Staten Island, NY, 1975), p. 179

Treasures of the Confederate Coast

1862-2-US-SC/GA-1: On February 14, 1862, the Federals burned a "very old worthless craft, without a cargo," which had been aground on a shoal in Bull's Bay, South Carolina.

References for 1862-2-US-SC/GA-1:
Official Records of the Union and Confederate Navies in the War of the Rebellion, (Washington, DC, 1901), Series 1, Volume 12, pp. 547, 548

1862-2-US-SC/GA-2: On February 14, 1862, the Federals captured and sank the coasting sloop *Edisto*, with 1600 bushels of rice, in Bull's Bay, South Carolina.

References for 1862-2-US-SC/GA-2:
"Charleston Daily Courier," (Charleston, SC), #19089, January 17, 1862, p. 2, c. 3
"Daily Morning News," (Savannah, GA), #40, February 18, 1862, p. 1, c. 1
"Charleston Mercury," (Charleston, SC), Volume 80, #11377, March 4, 1862, p. 2, c. 1
Official Records of the Union and Confederate Navies in the War of the Rebellion, (Washington, DC, 1901), Series 1, Volume 12, pp. 547-550

1862-2-US-SC/GA-3: On February 14, 1862, the Federals captured and sank the coasting schooner *Wandoo* (probably *Wando*) with eighteen hundred bushels of rice, in Bull's Bay, South Carolina.

References for 1862-2-US-SC/GA-3:
"Charleston Daily Courier," (Charleston, SC), #19089, January 17, 1862, p. 2, c. 3
"Daily Morning News," (Savannah, GA), #40, February 18, 1862, p. 1, c. 1
"Charleston Mercury," (Charleston, SC), Volume 80, #11377, March 4, 1862, p. 2, c. 1
Official Records of the Union and Confederate Navies in the War of the Rebellion, (Washington, DC, 1901), Series 1, Volume 12, pp. 547-550

1862-2-US-SC/GA-4: On February 14, 1862, the Federals captured and sank the coasting schooner *Elizabeth*, with eighteen hundred bushels of rice, in Bull's Bay, South Carolina.

References for 1862-2-US-SC/GA-4:
"Daily Morning News," (Savannah, GA), #40, February 18, 1862, p. 1, c. 1
"Charleston Mercury," (Charleston, SC), Volume 80, #11377, March 4, 1862, p. 2, c. 1
Official Records of the Union and Confederate Navies in the War of the Rebellion, (Washington, DC, 1901), Series 1, Volume 12, pp. 547-550

1862-2-US-SC/GA-5: On February 14, 1862, the Federals captured and burned the coasting schooner *Theodore Stoney*, with twenty-five hundred bushels of rice, in Bull's Bay, South Carolina. The *Theodore Stoney*, Captain Roberts, was described as a fine craft of fifty-four tons.

References for 1862-2-US-SC/GA-5:
"Charleston Daily Courier," (Charleston, SC), #19089, January 17, 1862, p. 2, c. 3
"Daily Morning News," (Savannah, GA), #40, February 18, 1862, p. 1, c. 1
"Charleston Mercury," (Charleston, SC), Volume 80, #11377, March 4, 1862, p. 2, c. 1
Official Records of the Union and Confederate Navies in the War of the Rebellion, (Washington, DC, 1901), Series 1, Volume 12, pp. 547-550

1862-2-US-SC/GA-6: On February 14, 1862, the Federals captured and sunk the coasting schooner *Patriot*, Captain Wood, with 1,800 (or 1,850) bushels of rough rice, in Bull's Bay, South Carolina. (Note: She was afterwards reported safe.)

References for 1862-2-US-SC/GA-6:
"Charleston Daily Courier," (Charleston, SC), #19089, January 17, 1862, p. 2, c. 3
"Charleston Mercury," (Charleston, SC), Volume 80, #11377, March 4, 1862, p. 2, c. 1, p. 4, c. 3

The "Real Rhett Butler" & Other Revelations

1862-2-US-SC/GA-7: A small sail boat manned by Colonel W.P. Shingler and three of his slaves capsized off Battery Point in Charleston Harbor, South Carolina, on February 16, 1862. The three black men and five others who set out from shore in a small boat, were credited with saving Colonel Shingler's life.

Reference for 1862-2-US-SC/GA-7:
"Charleston Daily Courier," (Charleston, SC), #19089, February 17, 1862, p. 1, c. 5

1862-3-US-NC-1: On March 14, 1862, Commander Rowan, U.S.N., described the obstructions in the Neuse River below Newbern, North Carolina, as evidently "prepared with great care." The lower barrier was composed of a series of piling driven securely into the bottom and cut off below the water; added to this was another row of pointed and iron capped piles, inclined to an angle of about forty-five degrees down stream. Near these was a row of thirty torpedoes (mines), containing about two hundred pounds of powder each, and fitted with metal fuses connected with spring percussion locks, with trigger lines attached to the pointed piles. The second barrier was quite as formidable, about one mile above the first, and abreast of Fort Thompson. It consisted of a line of sunken vessels closely massed and of chevaux de frise, leaving a very narrow passage close to the battery."

References for 1862-3-US-NC-1:
The Navy in the Civil War, (Charles Scribner's Sons, New York, NY, 1905), Volume 2 ("The Atlantic Coast" by Daniel Ammen), pp. 192, 193

1862-3-US-NC-2: On March 14, 1862, the *U.S.S. Delaware* opened fire on "steamboats that were attempting to escape up the (Neuse) river, one of them having a schooner in tow. One of the steamers was run on shore and burned."

Reference for 1862-3-US-NC-2:
The Navy in the Civil War, (Charles Scribner's Sons, New York, NY, 1905), Volume 2 ("The Atlantic Coast" by Daniel Ammen), p. 192

1862-3-US-NC-3: At 4:30 on the afternoon of March 23, 1862, the *U.S.S. State of Georgia* observed the bark *Glenn* on fire (presumably just inside the inlet at Beaufort, North Carolina). The bark was still burning at midnight. Earlier reports had stated that the *Glenn* was being converted to privateer. (Note: This may have been the bark *Glen*, 287 tons, which was built at Freeport, Maine, in 1848. That bark was issued a certificate of registry at New York, New York, on September 10, 1851.)

References for 1862-3-US-NC-3:
Official Records of the Union and Confederate Navies in the War of the Rebellion, (Washington, DC, 1898), Series 1, Volume 7, pp. 136, 282, 729
List of American-Flag Merchant Vessels that Received Certificates of Enrollment or Registry at the Port of New York 1789-1867, compiled by Forest R. Holdcamper, (U.S. National Archives, Washington, DC, 1968), Special List #22, Volume 1, p. 283

Treasures of the Confederate Coast

1862-3-US-NC-4: The steamer *Albemarle* was accidentally run on some piles or obstructions and sunk in New Berne Harbor, North Carolina, on March 31, 1862. It was determined that she was "hopelessly damaged." Lieutenant A. Murray, U.S.N., commanding the *U.S.S. Louisiana* gave the order to have set afire and destroyed. All of her stores, provisions, etc. were removed before she was burned. (Note One: The *Albemarle* had been captured by the Federals on March 15, 1862, off New Berne. The Confederates had used her as a cargo ship and a transport. The Federals put her to work in the same area and she was transporting wounded servicemen when she was lost.) (Note Two: This may have been the sidewheel steamer *Albemarle*, 183 tons, built in 1855 at Wheeling, Virginia, which was also her first home port. That vessel had a wood hull and was listed in the "Lytle-Holdcamper List as A62. A62 means that in 1862 she was removed from documentation as a merchant vessel because she had been abandoned, dismantled, exempt from documentation, or "removed for an unknown cause.")

References for 1862-3-US-NC-4:
Official Records of the Union and Confederate Navies in the War of the Rebellion, (Washington, DC, 1898), Series 1, Volume 7, pp. 116, 203, 204, 702, 703, 710
Merchant Steam Vessels of the United States 1790-1868, ("Lytle-Holdcamper List"), by William M. Lytle and Forrest R. Holdcamper, revised and edited by C. Bradford Mitchell, (Staten Island, NY, 1975), pp. xiii, 5

1862-3-US-SC/GA-1: The small Confederate gunboat *Rattlesnake* was driven ashore on a flat near Hog Island Channel, Charleston, South Carolina, in a "blow" on March 3, 1862. The gunboat fell over on her broadsides and filled with water. The vessel was to be lightened and it was thought she would be gotten off immediately. (Note One: This was probably the ex-schooner *Putnam*, 180 tons burden, owned by Robert Hunter of Charleston, which was issued a privateering commission, under the name *Rattlesnake*, to carry 100 to 150 men and to be armed with two long 12-pounder guns.) (Note Two: The same day "a small boat, containing three Negroes was upset off Southern Wharf. They were immediately rescued, however, having sustained no further injury than that caused by fright and a thorough ducking.")

References for 1862-3-US-SC/GA-1:
"Daily Morning News," (Savannah, GA), #53, March 6, 1862, p. 2, c. 2
"Vessel Papers" (manuscript records), United States National Archives, Washington, DC, Record Group 109, file R-5
"Charleston Mercury," (Charleston, SC), Volume 80, #11377, March 4, 1862, p. 2, c. 1

1862-3-US-SC/GA-2: On March 26, 1862, the brig *Empire*, partially loaded with cotton, got on the north breaker of the North Edisto Bar. The *U.S.S. Crusader* tried to kedge her off but the wind and rough seas caused her to bilge that night. (Note: This may have been the brig *Empire*, 197 tons, which was built in 1848 at Scituate, Massachusetts. That brig was issued a certificate of enrollment at the port of New York on May 26, 1859.)

References for 1862-3-US-SC/GA-2:
Official Records of the Union and Confederate Navies in the War of the Rebellion, (Washington, DC, 1901), Series 1, Volume 12, p. 676
List of American-Flag Merchant Vessels that Received Certificates of Enrollment or Registry at the Port of New York 1789-1867, compiled by Forest R. Holdcamper, (U.S. National Archives, Washington, DC, 1968), Special List #22, Volume 1, p. 214

1862-3-US-SC/GA-3: The bodies of M. Dillon and John McGinty were found on March 27, 1862, in Wadmalaw Sound, South Carolina. Their deaths were attributed to the capsizing of their boat. Both of the dead had been employed by the State.

References for 1862-3-US-SC/GA-3:
"Charleston Daily Courier," (Charleston, SC), #19121, March 28, 1862, p. 1, c. 3

1862-3-US-SC/GA-4: On March 28, 1862, two armed boats from the U.S. bark *Restless* destroyed the schooner *George Washington*, Captain Finegan, with 3200 bushels of rice, 50 bushels of corn and 20 bushels of rice meal. The schooner was scuttled in two places and burned in the inland passage near Mill Island, South Carolina.

References for 1862-3-US-SC/GA-4:
"Charleston Daily Courier," (Charleston, SC), #19123, March 31, 1862, p. 2, c. 2
"Daily Morning News," (Savannah, GA), #73, April 1, 1862, p. 1, c. 3
Official Records of the Union and Confederate Navies in the War of the Rebellion, (Washington, DC, 1901), Series 1, Volume 12, pp. 666-668

1862-3-US-SC/GA-5: Contemporary newspaper accounts reported that on March 28, 1862, two armed boats from the U.S. bark *Restless* burned the schooner *Julia Worden* (or *Julia Warden*), Captain Kroeg, in the inland passage between Bull's Bay, South Carolina, and Charleston. (Note: The newspaper reports are in conflict with the "Official Records" which show the *Julia Worden* simply as captured and not as destroyed.)

References for 1862-3-US-SC/GA-5:
"Charleston Daily Courier," (Charleston, SC), #19123, March 31, 1862, p. 2, c. 2
"Daily Morning News," (Savannah, GA), #73, April 1, 1862, p. 1, c. 3
Official Records of the Union and Confederate Navies in the War of the Rebellion, (Washington, DC, 1901), Series 1, Volume 12, pp. 666-668, 681, 682, 719, 793

1862-3-US-SC/GA-6: On March 28, 1862, two armed boats from the U.S. bark *Restless* burned a schooner belonging to Mr. Thompson, in the inland passage between Bull's Bay, South Carolina, and Charleston.

References for 1862-3-US-SC/GA-6:
"Charleston Daily Courier," (Charleston, SC), #19123, March 31, 1862, p. 2, c. 2
"Daily Morning News," (Savannah, GA), #73, April 1, 1862, p. 1, c. 3

1862-3-US-SC/GA-7: On March 28, 1862, two armed boats from the U.S. bark *Restless* burned Mr. Doar's sloop, the *Mary Louisa*, with two thousand and sixty bushels of rice and one hundred bushels of corn, near the lighthouse at Cape Romain, South Carolina.

References for 1862-3-US-SC/GA-7:

Treasures of the Confederate Coast

"Charleston Daily Courier," (Charleston, SC), #19123, March 31, 1862, p. 2, c. 2
"Daily Morning News," (Savannah, GA), #73, April 1, 1862, p. 1, c. 3
Official Records of the Union and Confederate Navies in the War of the Rebellion, (Washington, DC, 1901), Series 1, Volume 12, pp. 666-668

1862-3-US-SC/GA-8: In Admiral S.F. Du Pont's letter of March 29, 1862, to Gen. T.W. (sic) Sherman, Du Pont mentions the proposed sinking of "certain hulks" in the Savannah River.

Reference for 1862-3-US-SC/GA-8:
Official Records of the Union and Confederate Navies in the War of the Rebellion, (Washington, DC, 1901), Series 1, Volume 12, p. 673

1862-4-US-NC-1: The schooner *Kate* (a.k.a. *Leonora*, a.k.a. *Lucy C. Holmes*) of Nassau, New Providence, with a cargo of salt, was accidentally run aground in the surf near Lockwood Folly Inlet, North Carolina, on the morning of April 2, 1862, while attempting to run the blockade. Her crew abandoned her after first setting her afire. Men from the U.S. gunboats, *Mount Vernon, Cambridge* and *Fernandina*, put the fires out and attempted to get her off, but after failing, scuttled her, reignited the fires, and fired shot into her. The gunboats then stood by until her masts fell, and her deck fell in. Her papers, logbook, "a secession flag and a private signal marked *Leonora*" were saved from the wreck. (Note: Charles Foard's chart of Civil War wrecks in the Wilmington, North Carolina, shows two wrecks by the name of *Kate* in the immediate vicinity of Lockwood Folly Inlet. He shows one wreck as the *"Kate II, 1/4/62,"* the other as the *"Kate III, 4/4/63."* For information on the *Kate II*, see entry 1862-1-US-NC-1. For information on the *Kate III*, see entry 1863-4-US-NC-1.)

References for 1862-4-US-NC-1:
Official Records of the Union and Confederate Navies in the War of the Rebellion, (Washington, DC, 1898), Series 1, Volume 7, pp. 196, 197, 704, 705
A Chart of Wrecks of Vessels Sunk or Captured Near Wilmington, NC, Circa 1861-65, compiled by Charles H. Foard, (Wilmington, North Carolina, 1962)
An Oceanographic Atlas of the Continental Margin, J.G. Newton, O.H. Pilkey and J.O. Blanton, (Duke University Marine Laboratory, Beaufort, NC, 1971), p. 17 chart symbol #75, p. 20 entry #75

1862-4-US-NC-2: The *U.S.S. Monticello* received a dispatch from the *U.S.S. Jamestown* on April 26, 1862, bringing news of a "rebel steamer being ashore on the bar at New Inlet (North Carolina), and orders" to get underway with the *U.S.S. Victoria* and proceed around the shoals to New Inlet. Upon arriving, they saw a large side-wheel steamer showing English colors lying in the river below Zeek's Island, and apparently aground. The steamer proved to be the famous blockade runner/privateer *Nashville*. The *Nashville* got off, but was later wrecked in the Seven Mile Bend section of the Ogeechee River near Fort McAllister, Georgia. (Note One: An account of the loss of the *Nashville*, which had been renamed *Rattlesnake*, is described in this book under entry 1863-2-US-

The "Real Rhett Butler" & Other Revelations

SC/GA-7.) (Note Two: Persons interested in learning more about the *Nashville* should read Dave Topper and Frank and Paul Chances excellent book *Tangled Machinery and Charred Relics*.)

References for 1862-4-US-NC-2:
Official Records of the Union and Confederate Navies in the War of the Rebellion, (Washington, DC, 1898), Series 1, Volume 7, p. 718
Tangled Machinery and Charred Relics: The Historical and Archeological Investigation of the C.S.S. "Nashville," by F.N. Chance, P.C. Chance, and D. L. Topper, (Orangeburg, South Carolina, 1985), pp. 72, 105

1862-4-US-NC-3: The *U.S.S. Shawsheen* sank a schooner filled with sand near the entrance to the Albemarle and Chesapeake canal in late April of 1862.

Reference for 1862-4-US-NC-3:
The Navy in the Civil War, (Charles Scribner's Sons, New York, NY, 1905), Volume 2 ("The Atlantic Coast" by Daniel Ammen), p. 194

1862-4-US-SC/GA-1: An unidentified schooner was examined by the *U.S.S. Onward* on the night of April 1, 1862, and allowed to proceed. "Shortly afterwards, having been alarmed by another vessel of the blockading squadron, she was run on shore on Sullivan's Island" and wrecked. (Note: This may have been the schooner mentioned in entry 1862-4-US-SC/GA-2, despite the differences in the descriptions of location.)

Reference for 1862-4-US-SC/GA-1:
Official Records of the Union and Confederate Navies in the War of the Rebellion, (Washington, DC, 1901), Series 1, Volume 12, p. 708

1862-4-US-SC/GA-2: A blockade running schooner (formerly the *Experiment*), from Nassau, New Providence, with a cargo of salt was chased ashore on the beach of Long Island (present day Isle of Palms, South Carolina) on April 2, 1862. Both the vessel and the cargo were originally hoped to be saved, but it was later reported that the schooner was leaking badly and was expected to bilge. Three hundred and fifty sacks of salt, her sails, rigging, etc., were saved. (Note: This may have been the schooner mentioned in entry 1862-4-US-SC/GA-1, despite the differences in the descriptions of location.)

References for 1862-4-US-SC/GA-2:
"Charleston Daily Courier," (Charleston, SC), #19126, April 3, 1862, p. 2, c. 2
"Charleston Daily Courier," (Charleston, SC), #19127, April 4, 1862, p. 2, c. 3
"Daily Morning News," (Savannah, GA), #76, April 4, 1862, p. 1, c. 5

1862-4-US-SC/GA-3: A large brig belonging to the Federals and loaded with cotton, furniture and other loot "stolen" from the plantations and residences on Edisto Island, South Carolina, was reported ashore on Edisto on April 9, 1862.

Reference for 1862-4-US-SC/GA-3:
"Charleston Daily Courier," (Charleston, SC), #19131, April 9, 1862, p. 1, c. 2

1862-4-US-SC/GA-4: Just before sunset on April 10, 1862, the Federal gunboat *Keystone State* spotted the schooner *Liverpool*, of

Treasures of the Confederate Coast

Nassau, ashore on the outside of the point of North Inlet, South Carolina. The schooner had been set on fire and deserted. The *Liverpool* was of 150 to 180 tons burden and was evidently deeply laden. (Note: Jim Batey, Ron Renau, and I found the wrecks of three wooden hulled sailing vessels while diving at North Inlet in 1966. We tentatively identified the two newer wrecks as *Liverpool* and the *Prince of Wales*. The third wreck was smaller and appeared much older. For more information on the *Prince of Wales*, please entry 1861-12-US-SC/GA-10.)

References for 1862-4-US-SC/GA-4:
Official Records of the Union and Confederate Navies in the War of the Rebellion, (Washington, DC, 1901), Series 1, Volume 12, pp. 677, 679
Personal knowledge of E. Lee Spence of dive he made with Jim Batey and Ron Renau, circa summer, 1966.

1862-4-US-SC/GA-5: The schooner *Sir Robert Peel*, with a valuable cargo, was chased by the Federal blockading steamers while approaching the coast near Georgetown, South Carolina, in early April, 1862, and was burned by her own captain to prevent her falling into Federal hands. (Note One: This may have been the schooner *Sir Robert Peel*, W. Gyles master, 88 tons, which was built at Dartmouth in 1846 and was partly fastened with iron bolts. That vessel was 64'6"x17'5"x10'8".) (Note Two: A runaway slave, named Allen Davis, during an interrogation aboard the *U.S.S. James Adger* on April 28, 1862, mentioned a "brig" called the *Sir Robert Peel* as, at that time, being in Charleston.)

References for 1862-4-US-SC/GA-5:
"Charleston Daily Courier," (Charleston, SC), #19136, April 15, 1862, p. 2, c. 2
"Daily Morning Herald," (Savannah, GA), Volume 13, #86, April 16, 1862, p. 1, c. 1
"Vessel Papers" (manuscript records), United States National Archives, Washington, DC, Record Group 109, file S-130
Lloyd's Register of British and Foreign Shipping, from 1st July, 1863, to the 30th June, 1864, (London, 1863), entry S-494
Official Records of the Union and Confederate Navies in the War of the Rebellion, (Washington, DC, 1901), Series 1, Volume 12, p. 786

1862-4-US-SC/GA-6: On April 12, 1862, the schooner *Samuel Adams* was seen under sail and making for the Charleston Bar, with several of the blockading steamers (U.S. steamer *Huron*, U.S. ship *Onward*, etc.) in hot pursuit. When the schooner was off the western end of Long Island (present day Isle of Palms, South Carolina), her captain, realizing that he would be unable to escape, ran her ashore near the beach. It was hoped that most of the cargo could be saved, but the vessel was expected to be lost, as the weather was extremely rough and the enemy shelled the stranded schooner for some time. The *Samuel Adams'* cargo was said to be salt and merchandise (candles, soap, olive oil, rum, etc.). The *U.S.S. Huron* fired twelve shells from her eleven inch gun and eighteen from her 20-pounder Parrot gun.

References for 1862-4-US-SC/GA-6:

The "Real Rhett Butler" & Other Revelations

"Charleston Daily Courier," (Charleston, SC), #19135, April 14, 1862, p. 2, c. 2
"Charleston Daily Courier," (Charleston, SC), #19136, April 15, 1862, p. 2, c. 2
Official Records of the Union and Confederate Navies in the War of the Rebellion, (Washington, DC, 1901), Series 1, Volume 12, pp. 695, 737, 738

1862-4-US-SC/GA-7: On April 25, 1862, an unidentified brig was burned in the Riceborough River to prevent her from falling into the hands of the Federals who had gone up the river in the *U.S.S. Potomska* and the *U.S.S. Wamsutta* to capture her. It was thought that the brig had entered the river by running through Doboy or Sapelo Sound, Georgia.

References for 1862-4-US-SC/GA-7:
The Navy in the Civil War, (Charles Scribner's Sons, New York, NY, 1905), Volume 2 ("The Atlantic Coast" by Daniel Ammen), p. 64

1862-4-US-SC/GA-8: On April 26, 1862, the schooner *Chase*, of Nassau, was chased ashore by the United States steamer *Huron* near the middle of Raccoon Key (described as "the island on which Romain light stands") and set on fire by her own crew to prevent its capture. The heavy surf extinguished the fire and she was boarded the following day by a boat from the U.S. ship *Onward* who attempted to save her (and described her as registered as twenty tons but seeming much larger by American standards). The Federals were planning to burn her if their efforts to get her off proved unsuccessful. (Note: This was probably the schooner described in entry 1862-4-US-SC/GA-9, despite the differences in the descriptions of her location.)

References for 1862-4-US-SC/GA-8:
Official Records of the Union and Confederate Navies in the War of the Rebellion, (Washington, DC, 1901), Series 1, Volume 12, pp. 781, 795

1862-4-US-SC/GA-9: On April 26, 1862, the *U.S.S. Huron* ran an unidentified schooner ashore at Bull's Bay, South Carolina. The Federals attempted to board the schooner with their boats, "but the sea was so high and the wind blowing so strongly from the northeast that the boats could not approach her." "She, however, was thumping heavily on the beach, with the sea breaking over her." (Note: This was probably the schooner *Chase* described more fully in entry 1862-4-US-SC/GA-8, despite the differences in the descriptions of her location.)

Reference for 1862-4-US-SC/GA-9:
Official Records of the Union and Confederate Navies in the War of the Rebellion, (Washington, DC, 1901), Series 1, Volume 12, p. 738

1862-5-US-NC-1: The Federal transport *Oriental* was wrecked "near Bodie Island," North Carolina, on May 8, 1862. No lives were lost. (Note One: The *Oriental* was a screw steamer of 1,202 tons. She was built at Philadelphia, Pennsylvania, in 1861, and had an iron hull. Her first home port was New York, New York, and she was issued a certificate of steam register on September 21, 1861.) (Note Two: To this day, her huge engine towers out of the water off Pea Island.) (Note Three: Artifacts recovered from the *Oriental* may be seen at the Fort Fisher Historic Site, Kure Beach, North Carolina.)

References for 1862-5-US-NC-1:

Official Records of the Union and Confederate Armies in the War of the Rebellion, (Washington, DC, 1898), Series 1, Volume 52, Part 2

List of American-Flag Merchant Vessels that Received Certificates of Enrollment or Registry at the Port of New York 1789-1867, compiled by Forest R. Holdcamper, (U.S. National Archives, Washington, DC, 1968), Special List #22, Volume 2, p. 533

Graveyard of the Atlantic: Shipwrecks of the North Carolina Coast, by David Stick (University of North Carolina Press, Chapel Hill, NC, 1952), p. 247

An Oceanographic Atlas of the Continental Margin, J.G. Newton, O.H. Pilkey and J.O. Blanton, (Duke University Marine Laboratory, Beaufort, NC, 1971), p. 25 chart symbol #654, p. 29 entry #654

Merchant Steam Vessels of the United States 1790-1868, ("Lytle-Holdcamper List"), by William M. Lytle and Forrest R. Holdcamper, revised by C. Bradford Mitchell, (Staten Island, NY, 1975), pp. 164, 287

Artifacts and photographs on display at the Fort Fisher Visitor's Center/Museum, Kure Beach, NC, 1994

1862-5-US-NC-2: The *U.S.S. Hunchback* descending the Chowan River, North Carolina, on May 15, 1862, broke up the ferry at New Landing or Gate's Ferry and "let go the flat" after first destroying it for ferry purposes.

Reference for 1862-5-US-NC-2:

Official Records of the Union and Confederate Navies in the War of the Rebellion, (Washington, DC, 1898), Series 1, Volume 7, p. 710

1862-5-US-NC-3: On May 18, 1862, the *U.S.S. Hunchback* ascended the Meherrin River, North Carolina, about twelve miles and found a deserted battery, an earthwork with five embrasures, and the river obstructed by a sunken schooner (one report says "vessels") with a chain across, trees and logs chained together being above it.

References for 1862-5-US-NC-3:

Official Records of the Union and Confederate Navies in the War of the Rebellion, (Washington, DC, 1898), Series 1, Volume 7, pp. 376, 710

1862-5-US-NC-4: The *U.S.S. Hunchback* ascended the Blackwater River in North Carolina on May 24, 1862, and found three schooners sunk "athwart the stream" as obstructions two or three miles above the river's mouth. The center schooner was immediately moved (but apparently not raised) to clear a channel.

References for 1862-5-US-NC-4:

Official Records of the Union and Confederate Navies in the War of the Rebellion, (Washington, DC, 1898), Series 1, Volume 7, pp. 376, 440, 711, 736

1862-5-US-NC-5: The captain of the *U.S.S. Hunchback* recorded in his log on May 24, 1862, that he had ascended the Black River to within sight of the Nottaway River (the mouth of which is approximately at the North Carolina-Virginia line) and that he could see sunken vessels in it (which had been placed there by the Confederates as obstructions).

Reference for 1862-5-US-NC-5:

Official Records of the Union and Confederate Navies in the War of the Rebellion, (Washington, DC, 1898), Series 1, Volume 7, p. 711

The "Real Rhett Butler" & Other Revelations

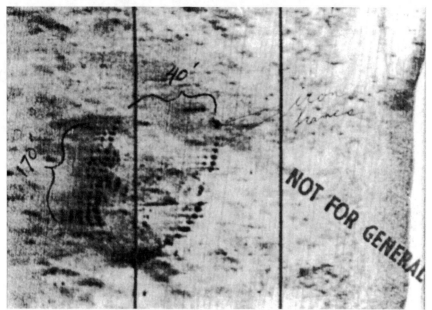

The iron ribs of this shipwreck can be clearly seen in this sidescan sonar printout made by a Klein Hydroscan 501-T. Photo courtesy of Shipwrecks Inc.

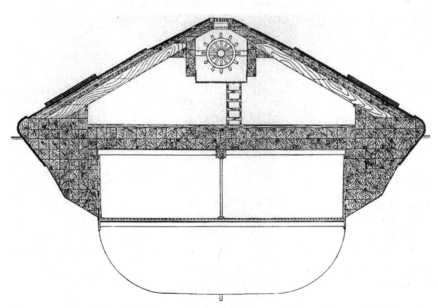

Cross section of the Confederate ironclad Atlanta. Illustration copied from the "Official Records of the War of the Rebellion, Union and Confederate Navies."

Side and top views of the C.S.S. Columbia, which was wrecked near Fort Moultrie, S.C., in January of 1865. Illustration copied from the "Official Records of the War of the Rebellion, Union and Confederate Navies."

No. 14.—Rebel ram *Columbia.*

The "Real Rhett Butler" & Other Revelations

Admiral Dahlgren (center) with the officers of the Federal blockading squadron off Charleston, South Carolina. Photo courtesy of the United States National Archives.

Treasures of the Confederate Coast

The Federal Navy purchased a fleet of old whaling vessels and East Indiamen for the express purposes of loading them with stone and sinking them in the shipping channels leading into Charleston, South Carolina. Illustration from "Harper's Weekly" of December 14, 1861.

American. Robin Hood. Henrietta. Potomac. Fortune. Cora. Maria Theresa. L. C. Richmond.

Archer.   Leonidas.   S. America.   Courier,   Herald.   Timoor.   Kensington.

This engraving shows part of the Federal "Stone Fleet" bound to Charleston, South Carolina, for sinking. Illustration taken from "Harper's Weekly" of December 14, 1861.

Treasures of the Confederate Coast

The sinking of the "Stone Fleet" off Charleston, South Carolina. Engraving from "Frank Leslie's Illustrated Newspaper" of January 11, 1862.

The "Real Rhett Butler" & Other Revelations

The sinking of the "Stone Fleet" off Charleston, South Carolina.
Engraving from "Frank Leslie's Illustrated Newspaper" of January 11, 1862.

Treasures of the Confederate Coast

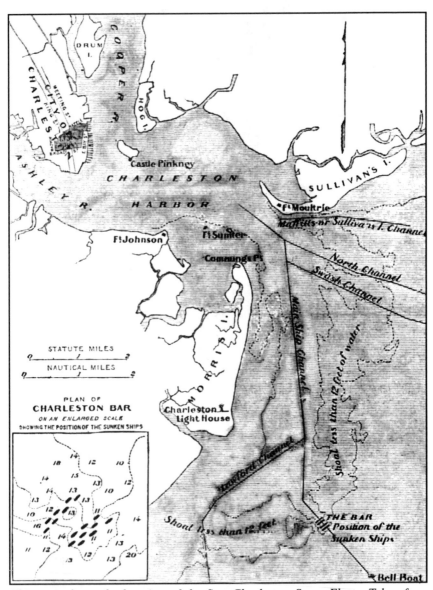

This map shows the location of the first Charleston Stone Fleet. Taken from "Frank Leslie's Illustrated Newspaper" of January 11, 1862.

The "Real Rhett Butler" & Other Revelations

1862-5-US-NC-6: The wrecks of the steamer *Stag* and two schooners (one report says three schooners) were found by the *U.S.S. Hunchback* on May 29, 1862. The vessels had been sunk as obstructions in the Blackwater River about one-fourth mile from the railroad bridge at Franklin, North Carolina. The bridge across the river was destroyed. The wrecks were also described as a short distance below the railroad depot.

References for 1862-5-US-NC-6:
Official Records of the Union and Confederate Navies in the War of the Rebellion, (Washington, DC, 1898), Series 1, Volume 7, pp. 440, 711

1862-5-US-SC/GA-1: The schooner *Sarah*, from Nassau, loaded with an assorted cargo, was run ashore and burned by her crew near the entrance to Bull's Bay, South Carolina, to prevent her capture by the United States gunboat *Onward* on May 1, 1862. The *Sarah's* tonnage was estimated as about one hundred tons. (Note: In the margin next to the entry for the schooner *Sarah*, G. Hore master, 95 tons, in "Lloyd's Register" for 1863/64 is the word "lost," but this may or may not have been the same vessel. That vessel was built at Lyme Bay, England, in 1819.)

References for 1862-5-US-SC/GA-1:
Official Records of the Union and Confederate Navies in the War of the Rebellion, (Washington, DC, 1901), Series 1, Volume 12, pp. 793, 794, 800
Lloyd's Register of British and Foreign Shipping, from 1st July, 1863, to the 30th June, 1864, (London, 1863), entry H-351

1862-5-US-SC/GA-2: About four o'clock on the morning of May 2, 1862, the U.S. Bark *Restless* chased a schooner ashore "towards the southern end" of Bull's Island, South Carolina, which was immediately set on fire and abandoned by the schooner's crew. The Federals, on boarding, extinguished the fire and managed to get her off successfully. The schooner was described as "a good vessel" and carried a cargo of "salt and 100 hundred boxes." [Note: From a log book and from "English colors" found aboard the schooner, she was believed to be the *Flash* (formerly called the *C.K. Lawrence*), of and from Nassau, sailing under an English register. Her crew was captured by the U.S. ship *Onward*. The schooner was towed off and was sent to the port of New York for adjudication.]

References for 1862-5-US-SC/GA-2:
Official Records of the Union and Confederate Navies in the War of the Rebellion, (Washington, DC, 1901), Series 1, Volume 12, pp. 795, 796, 810, 811

1862-5-US-SC/GA-3: The blockade running schooner *Edwin*, bound from Nassau, New Providence, was run ashore by the United States gunboat *Alabama* at a battery near Lighthouse Inlet, Morris Island, South Carolina, on May 8, 1862, while attempting to run into Charleston. The schooner was reported as both bilged and filled with water, but there were still hopes that she could be towed into

Treasures of the Confederate Coast

Lighthouse Inlet and saved. The schooner's cargo was consigned to Mr. C. Mitchell of Charleston and consisted of twenty-five cases brogans, one case of hats, ten bushel barrels of kerosene, two bushel barrels of hams, nine boxes of cheese, five bushel barrels of alcohol, five kegs of ink, fifteen kits mackerel (sic), eighty-three boxes of candles, and eighty sacks of salt. Colonel Hatch and some soldiers from his regiment on Morris Island, waded out to the wreck in waist deep water and removed much of her cargo. Most of the *Edwin's* cargo except for the salt was saved and auctioned. (Note: The vessel was owned by the Importing and Exporting Company of South Carolina. The *Edwin* had previously run a cargo of cotton, turpentine and rice from Charleston to Nassau and was returning to Charleston when she was lost.)

References for 1862-5-US-SC/GA-3:
"Daily Morning News," (Savannah, GA), #107, May 10, 1862, p. 2, c. 2
Official Records of the Union and Confederate Navies in the War of the Rebellion, (Washington, DC, 1901), Series 1, Volume 12, pp. 800, 801
Lifeline of the Confederacy: Blockade Running During the Civil War, by Stephen R. Wise, (University of South Carolina, Columbia, South Carolina, 1983), pp. 125, 126

1862-5-US-SC/GA-4: A flat belonging to Mr. J.I. Middleton, which was taken by the Federals during a foray up the Waccamaw River, South Carolina, on May 21, 1862, was sunk less than half a mile from where they took it. The flat was loaded with plunder when it was accidentally sunk.

Reference for 1862-5-US-SC/GA-4:
"Charleston Daily Courier," (Charleston, SC), #19172, May 29, 1862, p. 2, c. 3

1862-5-US-SC/GA-5: The brig *Joseph* was burned by the Confederates in the Waccamaw River within sight of the Federal gunboats which had run up near Georgetown, South Carolina on May 21 (or 22), 1862.

References for 1862-5-US-SC/GA-5:
Official Records of the Union and Confederate Armies in the War of the Rebellion, (Washington, DC, 1902), Series 1, Volume 14, pp. 512, 513
Official Records of the Union and Confederate Navies in the War of the Rebellion, (Washington, DC, 1901), Series 1, Volume 13, pp. 22, 23
History of Georgetown County, South Carolina, by George C. Rogers, (Columbia, South Carolina, 1970), pp. 399, 400

1862-5-US-SC/GA-6: On May 25, 1862, the sidewheel steamer *Nellie* (or *Nelly*) [ex-*Governor Dudley*, ex-*Cawtawba* (or *Catawba*)], Captain Moore (or Morgan), bound from Nassau, with medicines and merchandise, which had been spotted and fired at by a United States schooner off Dewees Island, was run ashore on the southern end of Long Island (present day Isle of Palms, South Carolina). The *Nellie* was reported to have been shelled, but she was not believed to have been hit. Most of her cargo was saved and the remainder was expected to be saved. It was said that even the damaged goods went for "extravagant prices." The steamer was reported to be badly damaged and leaking. She was described as left dry at low tide. (Note One: Her registered owner was J.A. Enslow. The *Nellie's* owners sold her where she lay to Robert Hunter for $1700. At least part of the steamer's machinery was removed. Her cargo was saved and sold at auction. She was built at New York, New York, in 1838, as the *Governor Dudley* and had been renamed the *Cawtawba* on May 8, 1857. Her first home port was Wilmington, Delaware. She had a wood hull and was 177'x24'x10' with a draft of 6'. The vessel was 408 tons burden. She had one 38" cylinder with a 10' piston stroke.) (Note Two: The *Nellie* was described in contemporary accounts as "an old boat, nearly used up in both her hull and machinery." Her speed was noted as "not over eight or ten knots, with a full head of steam." She had made five previous successful runs through the blockade.) (Note Three: Stephen Wise in his book *Lifeline of the Confederacy* lists her as built at Wilmington, Delaware.)

References for 1862-5-US-SC/GA-6:
"Charleston Daily Courier," (Charleston, SC), #19169, May 26, 1862, p. 2, c. 2
"Charleston Daily Courier," (Charleston, SC), #19170, May 27, 1862, p. 2, c. 2
"Charleston Daily Courier," (Charleston, SC), #19171, May 28, 1862, p. 2, c. 2
"Charleston Daily Courier," (Charleston, SC), #19172, May 29, 1862, p. 2, c. 2
"Charleston Daily Courier," (Charleston, SC), #19173, May 30, 1862, p. 2, c. 3
"Charleston Daily Courier," (Charleston, SC), #19176, June 3, 1862, p. 1, c. 3
"Charleston Daily Courier," (Charleston, SC), #19178, June 5, 1862, p. 2, c. 2
"Daily Morning News," (Savannah, GA), #120, May 27, 1862, p. 2, c. 3
"Daily Morning News," (Savannah, GA), #121, May 28, 1862, p. 1, c. 5
"Daily Morning News," (Savannah, GA), #122, May 29, 1862, p. 2, c. 1
Official Records of the Union and Confederate Navies in the War of the Rebellion, (Washington, DC, 1901), Series 1, Volume 12, pp. 628, 629
Official Records of the Union and Confederate Navies in the War of the Rebellion, (Washington, DC, 1901), Series 1, Volume 13, p. 142
Merchant Steam Vessels of the United States 1790-1868, ("Lytle-Holdcamper List"), edited by C. Bradford Mitchell, (Staten Island, New York, 1975), p. 87
Lifeline of the Confederacy: Blockade Running During the Civil War, by Stephen R. Wise, (University of South Carolina, Columbia, South Carolina, 1983), pp. 124, 138, 598
Charleston's Maritime Heritage 1670-1865, by P.C. Coker III, (CokerCraft Press, Charleston, SC, 1987), p. 302

1862-6-US-NC-1: The blockade running schooner *Sereta*, of Nassau, was chased into Shallote Inlet, North Carolina, by the U.S. gunboat *Penobscot* on June 8, 1862, where she was abandoned by her crew. The schooner was then boarded and burned by the Federals. Her cargo consisted of salt and fruit. Her log book was taken off by the Federals before she was burned.

References for 1862-6-US-NC-1:
Official Records of the Union and Confederate Navies in the War of the Rebellion, (Washington, DC, 1898), Series 1, Volume 7, pp. 465-467
A Chart of Wrecks of Vessels Sunk or Captured Near Wilmington, NC, Circa 1861-65, compiled by Charles H. Foard, (Wilmington, North Carolina, 1962)

1862-6-US-NC-2: The schooner *Scuppernong* was burned in the North River near the bridge at Indiantown, North Carolina, on June 9, 1862. She was laden with oak timber which was to have been

Treasures of the Confederate Coast

used in the construction of a Confederate steamer at Deep Creek, North Carolina.

References for 1862-6-US-NC-2:
Official Records of the Union and Confederate Navies in the War of the Rebellion, (Washington, DC, 1898), Series 1, Volume 7, pp. 487, 701

1862-6-US-NC-3: On June 26, 1862, the schooner *Ellen*, which was chased ashore and set on fire while trying to run in at Bald Head channel, North Carolina, was got off and taken in tow by the *U.S.S. Victoria* but sank within fifteen minutes.

Reference for 1862-6-US-NC-3:
Official Records of the Union and Confederate Navies in the War of the Rebellion, (Washington, DC, 1898), Series 1, Volume 7, p. 720

1862-6-US-NC-4: The schooner *Emily*, of Nassau, loaded entirely with salt, was burned under the guns of Fort Caswell, North Carolina, by the U.S. steamers *Victoria*, *Mount Vernon* and *Mystic* on June 26, 1862. The Federals saved two anchors, a Confederate flag, a chronometer, a clock, some cable and some rigging.

References for 1862-6-US-NC-4:
Official Records of the Union and Confederate Navies in the War of the Rebellion, (Washington, DC, 1898), Series 1, Volume 7, pp. 504, 505
A Chart of Wrecks of Vessels Sunk or Captured Near Wilmington, NC, Circa 1861-65, compiled by Charles H. Foard, (Wilmington, North Carolina, 1962)
An Oceanographic Atlas of the Continental Margin, J.G. Newton, O.H. Pilkey and J.O. Blanton, (Duke University Marine Laboratory, Beaufort, NC, 1971), p. 17 chart symbol #54, p. 20 entry #54

1862-6-US-NC-5: The steamer *Modern Greece* was run ashore 1/2 mile north (also reported as 3/4 mile eastward) of Fort Fisher, North Carolina, on June 27, 1862 by the *U.S.S. Cambridge*. She was making her first run through the blockade and was flying the British flag when she was run ashore. She carried one thousand tons of gun powder, seven thousand Enfield rifles, liquor, clothing, etc. She was chased ashore by the *U.S.S. Stars and Stripes*, Lieutenant R.S. Cook commanding. Her passengers and crew saved all of their private property. The Confederates salvaged "enough liquor to keep most of the Fort Fisher garrison in high spirits for more than a week." They also managed to salvage six Whitworth cannon, five hundred stands of arms, and a large amount of powder and clothing. (Note One: Powder, arms and whiskey were among the items reported as remaining aboard the wreck. Some accounts report her as having had two heavy guns and four brass guns aboard which were not salvaged.) (Note Two: The *Modern Greece* had an iron hull, was screw propelled, and schooner rigged. She was painted a slate color. Her hull was built by Richardson at Stockton-on-Tess, England, in 1859, and had four bulkheads. She was 210'x29'x17' and was owned by Z.C. Pearson and Company.) (Note Three: A large number of artifacts consisting partly of Whitworth shot and shell, Enfield rifled muskets, lead and tin ingots, spoons, knives,

The "Real Rhett Butler" & Other Revelations

bottles, china, and surgical supplies have been recovered by scuba divers. Many of the artifacts have been preserved and are on permanent display at the Visitor's Center/Museum at nearby Fort Fisher. The wreck lies in less than forty feet of water and is just over two hundred yards off shore. Additional artifacts from this wreck are displayed at the Cape Fear Museum in Wilmington and at Southport Maritime Museum in Southport, North Carolina. For more information on the *Modern Greece's* artifacts, please see Leslie Bright's excellent book *The Blockade Runner Modern Greece and Her Cargo*.)

References for 1862-6-US-NC-5:
"Daily Morning News," (Savannah, GA), Volume 13, #148, June 28, 1862, p. 2, c. 1
Lloyd's Register of British and Foreign Shipping, from 1st July, 1861, to the 30th June, 1862, (London, 1861), entry 927
Official Records of the Union and Confederate Armies in the War of the Rebellion, (Washington, DC, 1887), Series 1, Volume 18, pp. 415, 416
Official Records of the Union and Confederate Armies in the War of the Rebellion, (Washington, DC, 1897), Series 1, Volume 51, Part 2, pp. 584, 585
Official Records of the Union and Confederate Armies in the War of the Rebellion, (Washington, DC, 1900), Series 4, Volume 2, p. 52
Official Records of the Union and Confederate Navies in the War of the Rebellion, (Washington, DC, 1898), Series 1, Volume 7, pp. 514-518, 588, 729
Official Records of the Union and Confederate Navies in the War of the Rebellion, (Washington, DC, 1899), Series 1, Volume 8, pp. 88, 89, 118, 119, 152
Graveyard of the Atlantic: Shipwrecks of the North Carolina Coast, by David Stick (University of North Carolina Press, Chapel Hill, NC, 1952), pp. 62, 247
A Chart of Wrecks of Vessels Sunk or Captured Near Wilmington, NC, Circa 1861-65, compiled by Charles H. Foard, (Wilmington, North Carolina, 1962)
Personal knowledge from dive made to the *Modern Greece* by E. Lee Spence and John Miller in 1965
An Oceanographic Atlas of the Continental Margin, J.G. Newton, O.H. Pilkey and J.O. Blanton, (Duke University Marine Laboratory, Beaufort, NC, 1971), p. 17 chart symbol #73, p. 20 entry #73
The Blockade Runner Modern Greece and Her Cargo, by Leslie S. Bright, (Division of Archives and History, North Carolina Dept. of Cultural Resources, Raleigh, NC), 1977
Wreck Diving in North Carolina, University of North Carolina, Sea Grant Publication, #78-13, p.6
Lifeline of the Confederacy: Blockade Running During the Civil War, by Stephen R. Wise, (University Microfilms International, 1983), p. 597
The Blockade Runners, by Dave Horner, (Florida Classics Library, Port Salerno, FL, 1992), Chapter 14, pp. 48, 204, 205

1862-6-US-SC/GA-1: On June 26, 1862, an expedition under the command of Lieutenant F.M. Bunce of the *U.S.S. Monticello* found and burned two schooners, one lying high and dry, the other at the high-water mark, at the town of Little River, All Saints Parish, South Carolina.

References for 1862-6-US-SC/GA-1:
Official Records of the Union and Confederate Navies in the War of the Rebellion, (Washington, DC, 1898), Series 1, Volume 7, pp. 507, 720

1862-7-US-NC-1: An unidentified schooner was burned near Masonboro Inlet, North Carolina, on July 6, 1862. It was believed that the schooner had been run ashore for the sole purpose of unloading her cargo and had afterwards been burned by the Confederates to prevent detection. This may have been the wreck described by the *U.S.S. Monticello* as burned on the same date "on the beach near Deep River Inlet."

References for 1862-7-US-NC-1:

Treasures of the Confederate Coast

Official Records of the Union and Confederate Navies in the War of the Rebellion, (Washington, DC, 1898), Series 1, Volume 7, pp. 547, 720

1862-7-US-NC-2: On July 9, 1862, the *U.S.S. Monticello*, while off New Inlet, North Carolina, observed the wreck of a rebel schooner (presumably at New Inlet) and stood in and opened fire with her 30-pounder rifle and pivot gun. The *Monticello's* fire was returned by the batteries along the beach and one rifle shot from the fort.

Reference for 1862-7-US-NC-2:
Official Records of the Union and Confederate Navies in the War of the Rebellion, (Washington, DC, 1898), Series 1, Volume 7, p. 720

1862-8-US-NC-1: The English sloop *Lizzie* (ex-*Spray*), of Nassau, Captain W.R. Green, was captured off Wilmington, North Carolina, by the *U.S.S. Penobscot* on August 1, 1862. The sloop which was about 41 tons burden, was considered unseaworthy, so her cargo was removed, and she was immediately destroyed by burning. Her cargo consisted of 220 salt in bags, one bale of blankets, 5 boxes of sheet tin, 2 boxes of arrowroot, 2 tierces of soda ash, 2 cases of caustic soda, and 1 case of enameled cloth. (Note One: The sloop had a crew of five including her master. One of the people aboard the sloop was Captain Brown, of Smithville, who appears to have been a Cape Fear pilot. She was previously documented out of New York and Wilmington, North Carolina. This appears to have been the 41 ton sloop *Spray*, which was issued a certificate of enrollment at the Port of New York on November 14, 1840. That vessel was built at Islip, New York, in 1840.) (Note Two: There may have been two vessels called the *Spray*, as Charles Foard's chart of Civil War wrecks sunk near Wilmington, North Carolina, appears to list this vessel twice, once as a steamer, and once as a sloop.)

References for 1862-8-US-NC-1:
Official Records of the Union and Confederate Navies in the War of the Rebellion, (Washington, DC, 1898), Series 1, Volume 7, pp. 612, 613, 659
List of American-Flag Merchant Vessels that Received Certificates of Enrollment or Registry at the Port of New York 1789-1867, compiled by Forest R. Holdcamper, (U.S. National Archives, Washington, DC, 1968), Special List #22, Volume 2, p. 649
A Chart of Wrecks of Vessels Sunk or Captured Near Wilmington, NC, Circa 1861-65, compiled by Charles H. Foard, (Wilmington, North Carolina, 1962)

1862-8-US-NC-2: The United States steamer *Isaac N. Seymour* was bilged and sunk up the Neuse River, North Carolina, on August 24, 1862. (Note One: The Submarine Company had offered to raise her for $6,000, but the offer was declined and she was raised by the U.S. Army and Navy the following month at a far lower cost.) (Note Two: Built at Keyport New Jersey, in 1860, as the *I.N. Seymour*, she had a wood hull and was 133 tons. She was issued a certificate of register on July 14, 1860, at the Port of New York.

The "Real Rhett Butler" & Other Revelations

She was purchased by the United States Navy on October 26, 1861, and was commissioned as the *Isaac N. Seymour*. On June 20, 1865, the steamer was taken into the Lighthouse service as the United States Lighthouse Boat *Tulip*. She was redocumented as the *Magnolia* on June 7, 1882. She was also known as the *J. N. Seymour*, and as the *Seymour*. Her official number was 91441. She was sold foreign in 1888.)

References for 1862-8-US-NC-2:
Official Records of the Union and Confederate Navies in the War of the Rebellion, (Washington, DC, 1898), Series 1, Volume 7, pp. 671, 672
Official Records of the Union and Confederate Navies in the War of the Rebellion, (Washington, DC, 1899), Series 1, Volume 8, pp. 82, 83, 102
List of American-Flag Merchant Vessels that Received Certificates of Enrollment or Registry at the Port of New York 1789-1867, compiled by Forest R. Holdcamper, (U.S. National Archives, Washington, DC, 1968), Special List #22, Volume 1, p. 335
Merchant Steam Vessels of the United States 1790-1868, ("Lytle-Holdcamper List"), edited by C. Bradford Mitchell, (Staten Island, NY, 1975), p. 99

1862-8-US-SC/GA-1: The steamer *Emma* was burned by her crew to prevent her capture after she was run aground near Fort Pulaski, Georgia, while attempting to escape from the Savannah River on August 30, 1862. It was thought that her machinery and her cargo of cotton and turpentine could be saved. (Note: The *Emma* had a wood hull and was built at Charleston, South Carolina, in 1861, and was 460 tons burden. She measured 150'x30'x9'9".)

References for 1862-8-US-SC/GA-1:
Official Records of the Union and Confederate Navies in the War of the Rebellion, (Washington, DC, 1901), Series 1, Volume 13, pp. 278, 282, 508
Lifeline of the Confederacy: Blockade Running During the Civil War, by Stephen R. Wise, (University of South Carolina, Columbia, South Carolina, 1983), p. 558

1862-9-US-NC-1: The Federal gunboat *Pickett* was blown up at Washington, North Carolina, on September 6, 1862. One report stated she was sunk "while attacking." Six men were wounded, and twenty, including Captain Nicoll, were killed. (Note One: The *U.S.S. Picket*, was 295 ton, and was listed alternately as a sidewheel steamer and as a propeller steamer. She was purchased at a cost of $24,850. She had been used by General Burnside as his headquarters ship, in an effort to show he had faith in all of the vessels, and thus lessen criticism of the unseaworthy fleet he had put together to carry his men into the sounds of North Carolina.) (Note Two: Her guns were immediately recovered and it was thought that "the machinery can be saved.") (Note Three: Underwater explorer and historian J. Carter Leary has located this wreck, and is attempting to secure support to raise the entire vessel for museum display purposes. He reports that her iron hull was 98' in length but had been lengthened to 125'. The added construction was of black walnut and covers the entire exterior of her iron hull. Her bottom was sheathed with copper. Recovered artifacts include

Treasures of the Confederate Coast

three artillery short swords, six loaded 3.5" Hotchkiss shells, four bayonets, five Austrian Jager rifles, and even some fired Confederate Minnie balls. The mapping and preservation is being done with the cooperation of the Underwater Division of the North Carolina Department of Cultural Resources.)

References for 1862-9-US-NC-1:
Official Records of the Union and Confederate Armies in the War of the Rebellion, (Washington, DC, 1887), Series 1, Volume 18 pp. 5-7
Official Records of the Union and Confederate Armies in the War of the Rebellion, (Washington, DC, 1900), Series 3, Volume 4, p. 916
Graveyard of the Atlantic: Shipwrecks of the North Carolina Coast, by David Stick (University of North Carolina Press, Chapel Hill, NC, 1952), pp. 53, 247
Battles and Leaders of the Civil War, edited by Robert U. Johnson and Clarence C. Buel, Volume 1 of 4 volumes (Century Co., New York, NY, 1884-87, reprinted by Thomas Yoseloff Inc. 1956), p. 663
An Oceanographic Atlas of the Continental Margin, J.G. Newton, O.H. Pilkey and J.O. Blanton, (Duke University Marine Laboratory, Beaufort, NC, 1971), p. 24 entry #281
Telephone interview of Carter Leary by E. Lee Spence, 1989, and October 22, 1994

1862-9-US-NC-2: On September 22, 1862, H.K. Davenport, Commander of the *U.S.S. Hetzel*, wrote Acting Rear-Admiral S.P. Lee, Commander of the North Atlantic Blockading Squadron, that there were a number of vessels in the Neuse River which had been sunk by the Confederates to block the approach to New Berne, North Carolina. Commander Davenport suggested that the vessels might be raised and sold. He also reported that Captain L.B. Pratt, of the wrecking steamer *Dirigo*, had proposed to raise the vessels for half of their value. (Note: See entry 1861-9-US-NC-3 for information on fourteen schooners sunk in the Neuse River at Piney Point, some twelve miles below New Berne, as they may have been the same wrecks.)

Reference for 1862-9-US-NC-2:
Official Records of the Union and Confederate Navies in the War of the Rebellion, (Washington, DC, 1899), Series 1, Volume 8, p. 83

1862-9-US-NC-3: An unidentified schooner, believed to have been carrying a cargo of salt, was chased ashore at a bluff near Fort Fisher, North Carolina, on September 26, 1862, by the U.S. steamers *Mystic* and *State of Georgia*. The schooner was scuttled and set afire by her own crew. She was thoroughly destroyed.

References for 1862-9-US-NC-3:
Official Records of the Union and Confederate Navies in the War of the Rebellion, (Washington, DC, 1899), Series 1, Volume 8, pp. 92, 93
A Chart of Wrecks of Vessels Sunk or Captured Near Wilmington, NC, Circa 1861-65, compiled by Charles H. Foard, (Wilmington, North Carolina, 1962)
An Oceanographic Atlas of the Continental Margin, J.G. Newton, O.H. Pilkey and J.O. Blanton, (Duke University Marine Laboratory, Beaufort, NC, 1971), p. 17 chart symbol #76, p. 20 entry #76

1862-9-US-NC-4: The brig *Volant* was wrecked at New Inlet, North Carolina, in September of 1862. (Note: This may have been the brig *Volante*, 307 tons, which was built at New York, New York, in 1853. That brig was issued a certificate of register at the port of New York on January 24, 1853.)

References for 1862-9-US-NC-4:

The "Real Rhett Butler" & Other Revelations

Graveyard of the Atlantic: Shipwrecks of the North Carolina Coast, by David Stick (University of North Carolina Press, Chapel Hill, NC, 1952), pp. 52, 247
List of American-Flag Merchant Vessels that Received Certificates of Enrollment or Registry at the Port of New York 1789-1867, compiled by Forest R. Holdcamper, (U.S. National Archives, Washington, DC, 1968), Special List #22, Volume 2, p. 711
An Oceanographic Atlas of the Continental Margin, J.G. Newton, O.H. Pilkey and J.O. Blanton, (Duke University Marine Laboratory, Beaufort, NC, 1971), p. 25 chart symbol #598, p. 29 entry #598

1862-9-US-SC/GA-1: The Savannah "Daily Morning News" of September 15, 1862, reported a "Yankee War vessel" as lost on Hilton Head Island, South Carolina.

Reference for 1862-9-US-SC/GA-1:
"Daily Morning News," (Savannah, GA), September 15, 1862, p. 1, c. 2

1862-10-US-NC-1: An unidentified schooner loaded with salt was driven ashore near Fort Fisher, North Carolina, on October 6, 1862, by the U.S. steamers *Mystic* and *State of Georgia* and was destroyed.

Reference for 1862-10-US-NC-1:
Official Records of the Union and Confederate Navies in the War of the Rebellion, (Washington, DC, 1899), Series 1, Volume 8, p. 120

1862-10-US-NC-2: A large schooner called the *Adelaide*, of Halifax, with about six hundred barrels of spirits of turpentine in the hold and thirty-six bales of cotton and some tobacco on deck, which had been abandoned by the Confederates, was burned inside of New Topsail Inlet, North Carolina, on October 22, 1862, by the U.S. steamer *Ellis*, Lieutenant William B. Cushing commanding. The schooner's papers and flag were taken off before she was burned.

References for 1862-10-US-NC-2:
Official Records of the Union and Confederate Navies in the War of the Rebellion, (Washington, DC, 1899), Series 1, Volume 8, pp. 151, 152
The Navy in the Civil War, (Charles Scribner's Sons, New York, NY, 1905), Volume 2 ("The Atlantic Coast" by Daniel Ammen), p. 184

1862-10-US-SC/GA-1: The British steamer *Minho* was run ashore on a submerged wreck near Bowman's Jetty, by Fort Moultrie on Sullivan's Island, South Carolina, on October 20 (or 29), 1862, by the *U.S.S. Flambeau*. It was the *Minho's* fifth run through the blockade. (Note One: The *Minho's* position was also reported as a quarter mile south of Fort Moultrie and at the entrance to Charleston Harbor.) [Note Two: The hull of the vessel was sold where she lay for $6,000. Part of the *Minho's* cargo was sold at the auction house of R.A. Pringle, on Meeting Street in Charleston, South Carolina, on November 5, 1862. The salvaged portion of the steamer's cargo is known to have included coffee; sugar; matches; candles; spices; sardines; cigars; cigar lighters; three hundred and three cases and barrels of assorted brandies; one hundred and fifty-six cases and barrels of claret, gin, whiskey, assorted wines, sherry; two hundred and twenty-one cases of champagne; twenty-five barrels of bottled ale; twelve barrels of bottled porter; silver plated castors; locks; rat traps; bottles; coffee and tea pots; hammers; spittoons; knives; forks; spoons; needles; stew pans; frying pans; percussion caps; vases; one hundred dozen wine glasses; one hundred and forty dozen tumblers; decanters; medicines (morphine, opium, quinine); stationary; shoes; sundries; dry goods; clothes; eighteen gross cavalry gilt buttons; ten gross cavalry small gilt buttons; eighteen gross eagle gilt buttons; ten gross eagle small gilt buttons, etc. Most of the goods were said to have been undamaged and brought good prices. An invoice dated January 22, 1863, at Charleston, and made out to the owners of the steamer for $11,858.88 is for freight from Bermuda on forty-three cases of rifles and five hundred and eighteen cavalry swords shown as received at the Charleston Arsenal in a damaged condition from the wreck of the *Minho*.] (Note Three: The *Minho* was a three masted, propeller steamer. The steamer had an iron hull, sported the figurehead of a woman, and was square rigged forward. One report stated that she was 1253 tons, while another described her as one of the largest of the blockade runners. She was registered to George Wigg and was owned by Fraser, Trenholm and Company and the Navigation Company. She had been built by Paisley in England in 1854. Stephen Wise in his book *Lifeline of the Confederacy* gives her measurements as 175.3'x22'x13.5', with a draft of 7' forward and 8.5' aft. Wise gives her tonnage as 253 tons register and 399 gross tons.] [Note Four: In 1965 and 1966, with the help of Pat and Ron Gibbs of the United States National Park Service, and Jim Batey and Ron Renau of Palmetto Divers, I located the remains of several wrecks in the vicinity of Drunken Dick Shoals and Bowman's Jetty, one of which we identified as the *Minho*, which had been partially salvaged after the war. I wrote about these wrecks in several articles and books published in the 1970's and early 1980's. Several, including the *Minho*, were worked years later by Howard Tower of Jacksonville, Florida. Tower, although technically an amateur, is rightfully respected as an authority on shipwrecks, and writes extensively about his many ventures. However, after reading several articles where he was represented as the discoverer, I called and asked him what was going on. He told me that he had never read about my earlier work and that he had independently researched and located each wreck. However, in light of the fact that I physically pointed out the locations of the *Celt*, *Stono*, *Flamingo*, and *Minho*, to Tower and his divers, I can only assume that he has forgotten the exact sequence of events. Prior to Tower's diving on any of these wrecks, his boat captain, Ralph Wilbanks, told me that Tower had been criticizing one of my publications (which would mean Tower had to have been familiar with my previous work). Wilbanks said Tower did not believe me when I wrote, that part of the *Celt* actually stuck out of the water at low tide. He said that Tower had been to the site and found no trace of the wrecks. I told Wilbanks that Tower probably saw it, but failed to recognize the protruding wreckage because it now looks more like part of the rock jetty than part of a steamer. Wilbanks accepted my offer to meet them the next time they went to the site and show them where the wrecks were located. When the boat arrived, I waded out, climbed aboard and showed them exactly where to look. Even though it had been years since I had been on the site, my information was definitely accurate, as one diver immediately recovered a brass lantern from alongside the wooden hull of the *Stono*. Tower and his team went on to do an excellent job and they recovered a number of interesting artifacts including the remains of a case of muskets. I mention all of this only to set the record straight, and not to criticize Tower or detract from his work. In any case, I definitely respect Tower for what he accomplished on these wrecks.]

References for 1862-10-US-SC/GA-1:

"Daily Morning News," (Savannah, GA), October 25, 1862, p. 2, c. 1
"Charleston Daily Courier," (Charleston, SC), #19304, November 1, 1862, p. 1, c. 2
"Charleston Daily Courier," (Charleston, SC), #19307, November 5, 1862, p. 3, c. 3, p. 4, c. 2
"Charleston Daily Courier," (Charleston, SC), #19308, November 6, p. 4, c. 4
Times, (London, England), #24403, November 14, 1862, p. 5, c. 6
"Confederate Archives," Chapter 9-25-160-F-195
"Collector's Returns," Charleston, South Carolina, July-December, 1862, #3 (in red)
Official Records of the Union and Confederate Navies in the War of the Rebellion, (Washington, DC, 1901), Series 1, Volume 13, pp. 395-397
Official Records of the Union and Confederate Navies in the War of the Rebellion, (Washington, DC, 1903), Series 1, Volume 16, p. 354
"Vessel Papers" (manuscript records), United States National Archives, Washington, DC, Record Group 109, Microfilm roll 20, M909, file M-16, frames 0752-0773
Shipwrecks of the Civil War: The Encyclopedia of Union and Confederate Naval Losses, by Donald Shomette, (Washington, DC, 1973), pp. 138, 446
Charleston's Maritime Heritage 1670-1865, by P.C. Coker III, (CokerCraft Press, Charleston, SC, 1987), p. 302

1862-10-US-SC/GA-2: The steamer *Scotia*, Captain Libby (or Lebby), bound from Nassau to Charleston, with one hundred and six tons of merchandise, went ashore on Bull's Breakers (South Carolina) on October 24, 1862. The *Scotia's* cargo consisted of sheets, blankets, woolens, etc. for the Confederate Army. Captain Libby believing it would be impossible to get the *Scotia* off, launched a small boat with two passengers. Leaving the crew behind, he abandoned her. When the Federals boarded the wreck and took the crew prisoner they threw the *Scotia's* men in irons as they were drunk and unmanageable. Captain Libby was described by the Federals as "an old offender." The Charleston papers thought that the *Scotia* had gone to pieces, but the steamer had actually been towed off and taken to Port Royal as a prize.

References for 1862-10-US-SC/GA-2:
"Charleston Daily Courier," (Charleston, SC), #19299, October 27, 1862, p. 2, c. 3
"Charleston Daily Courier," (Charleston, SC), #19301, October 29, 1862, p. 2, c. 2
Official Records of the Union and Confederate Navies in the War of the Rebellion, (Washington, DC, 1901), Series 1, Volume 13, pp. 409-415

1862-10-US-SC/GA-3: The British steamer *Anglia*, Captain Newlands, which left Nassau on October 20, 1862, with a valuable general cargo, was kept off the coast so long (in trying to evade the Federal blockade fleet), that her captain, running short of fuel, ran her into the harbor at Bull's Island, South Carolina, on October 26, 1862, where she was afterwards reported as hard aground in front of Jack's Creek, four miles from the Cape Romain lighthouse. The Federals got her off.

References for 1862-10-US-SC/GA-3:
"Charleston Daily Courier," (Charleston, SC), #19299, October 27, 1862, p. 2, c. 3
"Charleston Daily Courier," (Charleston, SC), #19301, October 29, 1862, p. 2, c. 2
Official Records of the Union and Confederate Navies in the War of the Rebellion, (Washington, DC, 1901), Series 1, Volume 13, pp. 410-414

1862-11-US-NC-1: The English bark *Sophia* (or *Sophie*), 375 tons, of Liverpool, James Forbes master, was fired into and chased aground on November 4, 1862, by the *U.S.S. Daylight*. The wrecked bark's position was given as 2 1/2 miles to the westward of Masonboro Inlet. The *Sophia* was then burned to the water's edge by the *U.S.S. Mount Vernon*, Lt. James Trathen commanding. The unfortunate blockade runner was bound from Nassau to Baltimore with a cargo of salt, saltpeter, soda ash, three brass field pieces, gun carriages, trucks, etc. Fifteen men from the *U.S.S. Daylight* were captured by the Confederates when their longboat was lost in the surf near the *Sophia*. One hundred and thirty-five shot and shell were expended by the *U.S.S. Daylight* in the chase and destruction of the unarmed bark. (Note One: This may have been the bark *Sophia*, 347 tons, which was built at Baltimore, Maryland, in 1855. That bark was issued a certificate of registry on July 8, 1862.) (Note Two: See also entry 1862-11-US-NC-2.) (Note Three: A type setting error in the book *The Blockade Runners* shows the date of her loss as June 27, 1862.

References for 1862-11-US-NC-1:
Official Records of the Union and Confederate Navies in the War of the Rebellion, (Washington, DC, 1899), Series 1, Volume 8, pp. 193-199, 207, 226, 242
A Chart of Wrecks of Vessels Sunk or Captured Near Wilmington, NC, Circa 1861-65, compiled by Charles H. Foard, (Wilmington, North Carolina, 1962)
List of American-Flag Merchant Vessels that Received Certificates of Enrollment or Registry at the Port of New York 1789-1867, compiled by Forest R. Holdcamper, (U.S. National Archives, Washington, DC, 1968), Special List #22, Volume 2, p. 645
An Oceanographic Atlas of the Continental Margin, J.G. Newton, O.H. Pilkey and J.O. Blanton, (Duke University Marine Laboratory, Beaufort, NC, 1971), p. 17 chart symbol #86, p. 20 entry #86
The Blockade Runners, by Dave Horner, (Florida Classics Library, Port Salerno, FL, 1992), Chapter 14, p. 206

The "Real Rhett Butler" & Other Revelations

1862-11-US-NC-2: On November 5, 1862, the *U.S.S. Mount Vernon* spotted a bark and a schooner close to land near the wreck of the bark *Sophia*. The captains of the bark and the schooner both ran their vessels ashore at that place. The two vessels were quickly destroyed by the heavy surf setting on the beach. (Note: For more on the *Sophia* see entry 1862-11-US-NC-1.)

References for 1862-11-US-NC-2:
Official Records of the Union and Confederate Navies in the War of the Rebellion, (Washington, DC, 1899), Series 1, Volume 8, pp. 198, 199
A Chart of Wrecks of Vessels Sunk or Captured Near Wilmington, NC, Circa 1861-65, compiled by Charles H. Foard, (Wilmington, North Carolina, 1962)
An Oceanographic Atlas of the Continental Margin, J.G. Newton, O.H. Pilkey and J.O. Blanton, (Duke University Marine Laboratory, Beaufort, NC, 1971), p. 17 chart symbols #85, 86, p. 20 entries #85, 86

1862-11-US-NC-3: On November 17, 1862, the U.S. gunboat *Cambridge* observed the British schooner *J.W. Pindar* near Masonboro Inlet, North Carolina. The gunboat immediately bore down and fired her 30-pounder Parrott rifle into the schooner. The *Cambridge* ran the schooner ashore and sent a boat to burn her. The burning of the schooner, with its cargo of salt, was accomplished, but the *Cambridge's* boat overturned in the surf and eleven of her men were captured by the Confederates.

References for 1862-11-US-NC-3:
Official Records of the Union and Confederate Navies in the War of the Rebellion, (Washington, DC, 1899), Series 1, Volume 8, pp. 214, 215, 226
A Chart of Wrecks of Vessels Sunk or Captured Near Wilmington, NC, Circa 1861-65, compiled by Charles H. Foard, (Wilmington, North Carolina, 1962)
An Oceanographic Atlas of the Continental Margin, J.G. Newton, O.H. Pilkey and J.O. Blanton, (Duke University Marine Laboratory, Beaufort, NC, 1971), p. 17 chart symbol #90, p. 20 entry #90

1862-11-US-NC-4: The English schooner *Anna Maria* (or *Ann Maria*) of Nassau, was bilged and sunk in four fathoms of water off Shallotte Inlet, North Carolina, on November 18, 1862. She had been run aground and captured by the *U.S.S. Monticello*, Lt. Commander D.L. Braine. The schooner was described as about eighty tons and carried salt, lard, flour and sugar. The schooner's compass and a few charts were taken off before she was sunk. (Note: This may have been the ninety-six ton schooner *Ann & Maria* which is shown in "Lloyd's Register" of 1862/63 as having foundered. That vessel was built at Dartmouth in 1820 and was owned by Crews & Company.)

References for 1862-11-US-NC-4:
Lloyd's Register of British and Foreign Shipping, from 1st July, 1862, to the 30th June, 1863, (London, 1862), entry A-677
Official Records of the Union and Confederate Navies in the War of the Rebellion, (Washington, DC, 1899), Series 1, Volume 8, pp. 218-219
A Chart of Wrecks of Vessels Sunk or Captured Near Wilmington, NC, Circa 1861-65, compiled by Charles H. Foard, (Wilmington, North Carolina, 1962)

1862-11-US-NC-5: The English schooner *Ariel*, of Halifax, 80 tons, was run aground and burned off Shallotte Inlet, North Carolina, on November 18, 1862, by the *U.S.S. Monticello*, Lt. Commander

Treasures of the Confederate Coast

D.L. Braine. The schooner was about 80 tons and carried salt, lard, flour and sugar. The schooner's compass and a few small items were taken off for use by the *Monticello*. (Note: The *Ariel* was reported as destroyed to the eastward of the schooner *Anna Maria* which was captured and destroyed the same day. For more information on that wreck, please see previous entry.) (Note Two: Charles Foard's chart of Civil War wrecks near Wilmington, North Carolina, incorrectly shows the date of loss for this vessel as August 11, 1862.)

References for 1862-11-US-NC-5:

Official Records of the Union and Confederate Navies in the War of the Rebellion, (Washington, DC, 1899), Series 1, Volume 8, pp. 218-219

A Chart of Wrecks of Vessels Sunk or Captured Near Wilmington, NC, Circa 1861-65, compiled by Charles H. Foard, (Wilmington, North Carolina, 1962)

1862-11-US-NC-6: A small English bark or brig was chased ashore one mile from Fort Fisher and between the fort and Zeek's Island, North Carolina, on November 17, 1862, by the *U.S.S. Daylight*. The vessel was driven "hard and fast" ashore and was later reported destroyed. The vessel had an English ensign flying and was believed to have been outward bound. This may have been the "unknown brig" shown just over one mile south of New Inlet on Charles Foard's chart of Civil War wrecks around Wilmington, North Carolina. Another source lists an unidentified brig as lost "E. by S of New Inlet" on November 17, 1862. (Note: See also entry on the *Fanny Lewis*.)

References for 1862-11-US-NC-6:

Official Records of the Union and Confederate Navies in the War of the Rebellion, (Washington, DC, 1899), Series 1, Volume 8, pp. 215-217, 226

A Chart of Wrecks of Vessels Sunk or Captured Near Wilmington, NC, Circa 1861-65, compiled by Charles H. Foard, (Wilmington, North Carolina, 1962)

An Oceanographic Atlas of the Continental Margin, J.G. Newton, O.H. Pilkey and J.O. Blanton, (Duke University Marine Laboratory, Beaufort, NC, 1971), p. 17 chart symbol #74, p. 20 entry #74

1862-11-US-NC-7: The Savannah *Daily Morning News*, of November 20, 1862, reported a schooner and the brig *Fanny Lewis*, Captain Gardner, as run ashore at New Inlet, North Carolina, on November 17, 1862. Captain Gardner and eight of the brig's crew were drowned while attempting to reach shore. Her running ashore was attributed in a subsequent account to the efforts of the blocking vessels. She was saved by the Confederates, and on January 28, 1863, the Federals made another unsuccessful effort to destroy her, this time at her anchorage near the Confederate battery on Zeek's Island. [Note One: The brig (or brigantine) *Fanny Lewis* was owned by John Fraser & Co. which was headed by George Alfred Trenholm, who was the "real Rhett Butler."] (Note Two: See also previous entry for unidentified bark or brig chased ashore by the *U.S.S. Daylight*.)

References for 1862-11-US-NC-7:

The "Real Rhett Butler" & Other Revelations

"Daily Morning News," (Savannah, GA), Volume 13, November 20, 1862, p. 2, c. 1
Official Records of the Union and Confederate Navies in the War of the Rebellion, (Washington, DC, 1899), Series 1, Volume 8, pp. 470, 484, 485
George Alfred Trenholm: The Company that went to War, by Ethel Trenholm Seabrook Nepveux, (Charleston, SC, 1973), p. 64

1862-11-US-NC-8: The sidewheel steamer *Kate* was lost when she accidentally ran on the obstructions in the Cape Fear River near Smithfield, North Carolina, on November 18, 1862. Her cargo was saved, but the vessel was a total loss. The loss was reported by refugees who were picked up on November 22, 1862, near Masonboro Inlet by the *U.S.S. Mount Vernon.* (Note One: Charles Foard's chart of shipwrecks of the Cape Fear area shows this wreck as the *Kate I.*) (Note Two: Stephen Wise shows this vessel as built as the *Carolina* at Greenpoint, New York, in 1852, and says her name was changed to *Kate* when she was purchased by John Fraser and Company in December of 1861. He also credits her with fourteen successful runs through the blockade out of fourteen attempts. Wise gives her dimensions as 165' in length, 29'10" in breadth, 10'4" in depth of hold, and 477 tons burden. When I checked the Lytle-Holdcamper List for additional information on the *Carolina,* I found more questions, not answers. Holdcamper does show a wooden hulled, 477 ton sidewheel steamer named the *Carolina* as built at Greenpoint, New York, in 1852, but shows her as captured on May 28, 1862, rather than as sunk on November 18, 1862. Holdcamper makes no mention of the *Carolina* as operating under the name *Kate,* and notes her as named *C.S.S. Gordon* on July 15, 1861, and as renamed *C.S.S. Theodora* in the fall of 1861. Holdcamper goes on to show her as operating as the *Nassau* in the winter of 1861-62. Going back to Stephen Wise's book, I found a separate listing for a vessel called the *Gordon.* That vessel is shown as having made six successful runs in seven attempts. Wise shows the *Gordon* as built as the *Carolina* by Samuel Snedon at Greenpoint, New York, in 1851, and as 177' in length, 27'6" in breadth, 11'2" in depth of hold, and 518 tons burden. The name changes and capture dates given by Wise for the *Gordon* are similar to those Holdcamper gives for the *Carolina,* and they certainly seem to be referring to the same vessel. However, Holdcamper never shows her as the *Kate,* and it seems unlikely that she was captured in late May yet was returned to blockade running in time to be lost in mid-November. In any case, I don't believe the *Kate* was the ex-*Carolina,* built at Greenpoint in 1851/52. Volume One, Series II, of the "Official Records" shows the *Theodora* as the ex-*Gordon,* ex-*Carolina,* as a "side wheel, iron privateer" of 500 tons and 175' in length. The same source shows her as manned by fifty men, and

Treasures of the Confederate Coast

gives her battery on August 16, 1861, as two 62-pounders and two 32-pounders. Volume 8, Series I, of the "Official Records" shows the *Kate* as very fast and as drawing nine feet of water. It also said that when she was chased on a previous run, she had thrown overboard 10,000 stand of arms. Another report in the same volume mentioned "the steamer *Carolina*, or *Kate*, a schooner, and lightboat." A footnote shows her as "also mentioned as the *Catherine* and as the *Carolina*.") (Note Two: The Savannah *Daily Morning News* reported the *Kate* as sunk at the Smithville Wharf at Cape Fear, North Carolina.) (Note Three: John Fraser & Company was headed by George Alfred Trenholm who was later used as the historical basis for Margaret Mitchell's fictional character Rhett Butler in *Gone With The Wind*.)

References for 1862-11-US-NC-8:
"Daily Morning News," (Savannah, GA), Volume 13, November 20, 1862, p. 2, c. 1
Official Records of the Union and Confederate Navies in the War of the Rebellion, (Washington, DC, 1899), Series 1, Volume 8, pp. 80, 82, 86, 88-90, 93, 103, 118-120, 152-156, 196, 260
Official Records of the Union and Confederate Navies in the War of the Rebellion, (Washington, DC, 1921), Series 2, Volume 1, p. 269
A Chart of Wrecks of Vessels Sunk or Captured Near Wilmington, NC, Circa 1861-65, compiled by Charles H. Foard, (Wilmington, North Carolina, 1962)
List of American Flag Merchant Vessels that received Certificates of Enrollment or Registry at the Port of New York 1789-1867, compiled by Forest R. Holdcamper, (U.S. National Archives, Washington, DC, 1968), Special List #22, Volume 1, p. 287
Merchant Steam Vessels of the United States 1790-1868, ("Lytle-Holdcamper List"), edited by C. Bradford Mitchell, (Staten Island, NY, 1975), p. 30 (entry for *Carolina*, and note 3)
George Alfred Trenholm and the Company that Went to War 1861-1865, by Ethel Trenholm Seabrook Nepveux, (Charleston, South Carolina, 1973), pp. 37-40, 57, 58
Lifeline of the Confederacy: Blockade Running During the Civil War, by Stephen R. Wise, (University Microfilms International, 1983), pp. 570, 571, 582

1862-11-US-NC-9: On November 20, 1862, the *U.S.S. Mount Vernon* discovered a water logged, half burned schooner, loaded with rosin, turpentine and shingles, seven miles south and east of Fort Fisher, North Carolina and destroyed it. The schooner had previously been captured by the U.S. gunboat *Chocura* and her captain had openly declared her to be a Confederate vessel. She was being towed to port when she started filling with water and was set on fire and abandoned. (Note: This was probably the unidentified schooner shown by some sources as wrecked that date "7 mi. SE Ft. Caswell.")

References for 1862-11-US-NC-9:
Official Records of the Union and Confederate Navies in the War of the Rebellion, (Washington, DC, 1899), Series 1, Volume 8, pp. 199, 220, 221, 226
A Chart of Wrecks of Vessels Sunk or Captured Near Wilmington, NC, Circa 1861-65, compiled by Charles H. Foard, (Wilmington, North Carolina, 1962)
An Oceanographic Atlas of the Continental Margin, J.G. Newton, O.H. Pilkey and J.O. Blanton, (Duke University Marine Laboratory, Beaufort, NC, 1971), p. 17 chart symbol #58, p. 20 entry #58

1862-11-US-NC-10: A vessel, bound out through the blockade with a load of turpentine, was burned by the Confederates on November 23, 1862. The burning took place about five miles up river from the mouth of the New River, North Carolina, and was done to prevent the vessel from falling into the hands of a U.S. Navy expedition headed by Lt. Cushing.

References for 1862-11-US-NC-10:
Official Records of the Union and Confederate Navies in the War of the Rebellion, (Washington, DC, 1899), Series 1, Volume 8, pp. 230, 231

1862-11-US-NC-11: The *U.S.S. Ellis*, Lt. Cushing commanding, was accidentally run aground five hundred yards from the bluffs on New River, North Carolina, and "1 1/2 miles from the inlet," on November 23, 1862. She was set on fire by her crew in an effort to prevent her from falling into the possession of the Confederate cavalry under Captain Newkirk. The vessel burned and blew up. The *Ellis* had been returning from a successful expedition up the New River when she was destroyed. (Note One: Lt. Cushing managed to save all of his men and even took off the *Ellis'* rifled howitzer. The *Ellis'* "pivot gun, some ammunition, two tons of coal, and a few small arms" were left aboard by the Federals. The Confederates expected to save a great deal from the vessel and reported that she was but little damaged, as she was built of iron.) [Note Two: The *Ellis* was a 4th rate, sidewheel steamer of two guns (one a 32-pounder rifled gun, the other a brass howitzer).] (Note Three: The Confederates had purchased her at Norfolk in 1861 and classed her as a tugboat. She had been captured from the Confederates at the fall of Elizabeth City, North Carolina, and after condemnation, she had been purchased from the New York Prize Court on May 19, 1862, for $18,000. At least one report at the time of her capture from the Confederates had stated that she had been "run into," "run down," and "cutting her through," implying that she had been sunk.)

References for 1862-11-US-NC-11:
"Charleston Mercury," (Charleston, SC), Volume 80, #11382, February 25, 1862, p. 1, c. 4
"Daily Morning News," (Savannah, GA), Volume 13, November 29, 1862, p. 2, c. 1
Official Records of the Union and Confederate Navies in the War of the Rebellion, (Washington, DC, 1897), Series 1, Volume 6, p. 623
Official Records of the Union and Confederate Navies in the War of the Rebellion, (Washington, DC, 1899), Series 1, Volume 8, pp. 230-233
Official Records of the Union and Confederate Navies in the War of the Rebellion, (Washington, DC, 1921), Series 2, Volume 1, pp. 78, 252
The Navy in the Civil War, (Charles Scribner's Sons, New York, NY, 1905), Volume 2 ("The Atlantic Coast" by Daniel Ammen), pp. 194, 195
Graveyard of the Atlantic: Shipwrecks of the North Carolina Coast, by David Stick (University of North Carolina Press, Chapel Hill, NC, 1952), pp. 52, 53, 247
An Oceanographic Atlas of the Continental Margin, J.G. Newton, O.H. Pilkey and J.O. Blanton, (Duke University Marine Laboratory, Beaufort, NC, 1971), p. 20 entry #132, p. 21 chart symbol #132

1862-11-US-SC/GA-1: On November 2, 1862, the U.S. gunboat *Penobscot* chased the English schooner *Pathfinder*, of Nassau, ashore about two miles to the westward of Little River, South Carolina. The schooner was loaded with salt, boots, shoes, olive oil, liquors, cutlery, etc. The *Pathfinder* was set afire and destroyed. (Note: See also entry 1864-12-US-NC-4.)

Treasures of the Confederate Coast

References for 1862-11-US-SC/GA-1:
Official Records of the Union and Confederate Navies in the War of the Rebellion, (Washington, DC, 1899), Series 1, Volume 8, pp. 175, 190

1862-11-US-SC/GA-2: The Confederate steamer *Fire Fly* (or *Firefly*) was burned in the Savannah River near the Gas Works at Savannah, Georgia, on November 5, 1862. The entire upper portion of the boat was consumed. (Note One: The steamer must have been repaired, as this is probably the same vessel which was reported as burned near Savannah on December 21, 1864. See also entry 1864-12-US-SC/GA-9 of this book.)

References for 1862-11-US-SC/GA-2:
"Daily Morning News," (Savannah, GA), November 6, 1862, p. 1, c. 1
Official Records of the Union and Confederate Navies in the War of the Rebellion, (Washington, DC, 1901), Series 1, Volume 16, p. 484

1862-12-US-NC-1: An unidentified schooner was chased ashore off New Inlet, North Carolina, on December 3, 1862, by the U.S. gunboat *Mount Vernon*, which fired twelve 100-pound shells at her. The schooner was reported as "fast filling with water and the sea making a complete breach over her." (Note: The Savannah *Daily Morning News* reported the schooner as bound to Wilmington and said she was ashore on Smith's Island, six miles south of Fort Fisher.)

References for 1862-12-US-NC-1:
"Daily Morning News," (Savannah, GA), Volume 13, December 4, 1862, p. 1, c. 1
"Daily Morning News," (Savannah, GA), Volume 13, December 11, 1862, p. 2, c. 1
Official Records of the Union and Confederate Navies in the War of the Rebellion, (Washington, DC, 1899), Series 1, Volume 8, pp. 254, 255, 261

1862-12-US-NC-2: The U.S. ironclad *Monitor*, Commander J.P. Bankhead, foundered in a storm off Cape Lookout, North Carolina, on December 31, 1862, while being towed from Virginia to South Carolina by the *U.S.S. Rhode Island*. Four of her officers and twelve of her men were lost. [Note One: This famous vessel was best known for its battle against the Confederate ironclad *Virginia* (ex-*U.S.S. Merrimack*) in Hampton Roads, Virginia, on March 9, 1862. That was the first engagement of ironclads in warfare, and it ended with both sides claiming victory. The *Monitor's* distinctive turret earned her the nickname "cheese box on a raft." The Federal Navy quickly saw the advantages of this type of vessel and turned out numerous "monitors" of various sizes and classes.] [Note Two: The original *Monitor* was built by John Ericsson at Green Point, Long Island, New York, for $280,000. She was built of iron and wood with a single revolving gun turret. She was a screw propelled steamer of 776 (987) tons. Her double trunk engine had two cylinders in one casting. Each cylinder was 36" in diameter with a 27" piston stroke. She had two return tube "box" boilers. The steamer measured 172' in length, 41'6" in breadth and 11'4" in depth. Just after being launched her draft was measured as 7'3" forward and 8'1" aft. She was armed with two 11-inch guns in her turret.] [Note Three: On January 30, 1975, the United States Secretary of Commerce designated as a Marine Sanctuary an area of the Atlantic Ocean around and above the submerged wreckage of the *Monitor* pursuant to the authority of the Marine Protection, Research and Sanctuaries Act of 1972 (P.L. 92-532). The *Monitor* Marine Sanctuary "consists of a water column in the Atlantic Ocean one mile in diameter extending from the surface to the seabed the center of which is 35°00'23" north latitude and 75°24'32" west longitude or approximately 16.10 miles south-southeast of Cape Hatteras Light." The water depth at the *Monitor* is between 200' and 220'.] (Note Four: In 1955 Robert F. Marx, then a Marine Corps diver, reported that he had found the wreck of the *Monitor*. He was incorrect, as his wreck was in less than fifty feet of water and he placed the location miles from where its actual resting place. He definitely found something, and he now speculates that it may have been another monitor, although it is more likely that the "turret" was simply a large, upright, can shaped boiler.) (Note Five: In the early 1970's I was a consultant to the Trident Foundation which was the original group to pursue the *Monitor* in the correct location. Trident Foundation, headed by Roland Womack had enlisted my help along with that of expert shipwreck researcher Bob Fleming in Arlington, Virginia. We had determined the *Monitor's* true position of sinking through contemporary records and by back tracking the log of the *Rhode Island*. The primary, or best guess, site that we had calculated through our research, matched up with an unidentified wreck reported by the United States Navy in World War II. All of us were convinced that the "unidentified wreck" was the *Monitor*. We sought the help of Duke University, the United States Naval Academy, and the National Geographic Society. All three institutions, along with several others we had also contacted, eventually got involved. They even used the same research vessel we had suggested. But, somehow or another Trident Foundation got left out of the loop. The expedition was conducted without us. We were absolutely correct on our calculations and identification, but, as far as I know, Womack, who was the driving force behind Trident Foundation, never got any of the credit that he so richly deserved.)

References for 1862-12-US-NC-2:
"Daily Morning News," (Savannah, GA), Volume 14, #4, January 6, 1863, p. 2, c. 1
Official Records of the Union and Confederate Navies in the War of the Rebellion, (Washington, DC, 1899), Series 1, Volume 8, pp. 342, 343, 352-354
Official Records of the Union and Confederate Navies in the War of the Rebellion, (Washington, DC, 1921), Series 2, Volume 1, p. 148
Graveyard of the Atlantic: Shipwrecks of the North Carolina Coast, by David Stick (University of North Carolina Press, Chapel Hill, NC, 1952), pp. 53-57, 247

Treasures of the Confederate Coast

Battles and Leaders of the Civil War, edited by Robert U. Johnson and Clarence C. Buel, Volume 1 of 4 volumes (Century Co., New York, NY, 1884-87, reprinted by Thomas Yoseloff Inc. 1956), p. 729

Always Another Adventure, by Robert F. Marx, (World Publishing, Cleveland and New York, 1967), pp. 52-71

Personal experiences of Edward Lee Spence, researcher and member of the Board of Advisors for the Trident Foundation (*Monitor* Project).

Monitor Marine Sanctuary: An Archaeological and Engineering Assessment: operations Manuel, by Department of Commerce, National Oceanic and Atmospheric Administration, Office of Coastal zone Management, 1979, pages 1, 8, 9 (book located at University of Florida, Library West, government documents #c 55.8:M 33/2)

Ship Ashore!: The U.S. Lifesavers of Coastal North Carolina, by Joe A. Mobley, (Division of Archives and History, North Carolina Department of Cultural Resources, Raleigh, NC, 1994), pp. 24, 25

1862-12-US-NC-3: At least two modern sources incorrectly give the date of loss of the *Frying Pan Shoals Lightship* as December 31, 1862. The *Frying Pan Shoals Lightship* which had been removed from its station and anchored in the Cape Fear River, just above Fort Caswell, North Carolina, was actually burned by the *U.S.S. Mount Vernon* on December 30, 1861. The vessel was being fitted out as a floating fortress and had just been pierced for eight guns (six broadside and two astern) but the guns had not yet been mounted. She was deserted and riding at anchor within close range of the fort when she was destroyed.

References for 1862-12-US-NC-3:

Official Records of the Union and Confederate Navies in the War of the Rebellion, (Washington, DC, 1897), Series 1, Volume 6, p. 493

The Navy in the Civil War, (Charles Scribner's Sons, New York, NY, 1905), Volume 2 ("The Atlantic Coast" by Daniel Ammen), p. 175

Graveyard of the Atlantic: Shipwrecks of the North Carolina Coast, by David Stick (University of North Carolina Press, Chapel Hill, NC, 1952), pp. 58, 247

An Oceanographic Atlas of the Carolina Continental Margin, by J.G. Newton, (Duke University Marine Laboratory, Beaufort, NC, 1971), p. 20

1862-12x-US-SC/GA-1: The brig *Santa Clara*, the ship *Sebasticook*, and the ship *A.B. Thompson*, were sunk by the Confederate forces in the Savannah River in 1862 to obstruct the channel and thereby prevent the Federal fleet from attacking Savannah, Georgia. (Note: See entries 1862-12x-US-SC/GA-2 through 1862-12x-US-SC/GA-4 of this book for specifics on these three vessels.)

References for 1862-12x-US-SC/GA-1:

"Daily Morning News," (Savannah, GA), June 7, 1861, p. 1, c. 2
"Daily Morning News," (Savannah, GA), August 23, 1861, p. 1, c. 2
"Daily Morning News," (Savannah, GA), August 27, 1861, p. 1, c. 1
"Daily Morning News," (Savannah, GA), November 9, 1861, pp. 2, c. 5
"Savannah Morning News," (Savannah, GA), October 20, 1879, p. 3, c. 3
"Savannah Morning News," (Savannah, GA), November 18, 1879, p. 3, c. 4
History of the City Government of Savannah, Georgia, by Thomas Gamble, Jr., (1900), p. 256

1862-12x-US-SC/GA-2: The brig *Santa Clara*, which had been a prize to the Confederate privateer *Jeff Davis*, was sunk as an obstruction in the Savannah River by the Confederates in 1862. [Note One: This may have been the half brig *Santa Clara* which was built of mixed woods with copper and iron fastenings, at Eastport, Maine, in 1853. That *Santa Clara* was a full model brig, with one deck, a half poop and bow ports. That vessel was metalled with zinc in 1856 and, when surveyed in 1857, was classed A-2 for insurance

The "Real Rhett Butler" & Other Revelations

purposes. The half brig *Santa Clara* measured 189 46/95 (or 198) tons and was issued "Permanent Register #106" at Passamaquoddy, Maine, on August 2, 1853. From that *Santa Clara's* various certificates of register and enrollment she appears to have been a frequent trader out of Maine and Maryland.] (Note Two: See also entry 1862-12x-US-SC/GA-1 of this book.)

References for 1862-12x-US-SC/GA-2:
"Record of Registers, Volume 12," (bound manuscript, abstracts), p. 194, National Archives, Record Group 41
"Record of Enrollments, Volume 22," (bound manuscript, abstracts), p. 194, National Archives, Record Group 41
American Lloyd's: Registry of American & Foreign Shipping, (New York, New York, 1858), p. 172, #1647
"Savannah Morning News," (Savannah, GA), October 20, 1879, p. 3, c. 3
"Savannah Morning News," (Savannah, GA), November 18, 1879, p. 3, c. 4
History of the City Government of Savannah, Georgia, by Thomas Gamble, Jr., (1900), p. 256

1862-12x-US-SC/GA-3: The ship *Sebasticook*, which had been owned in Maine and had been seized by the Confederates in June, 1861, was sunk as an obstruction in the Savannah River by the Confederates in 1862. [Note One: The *Sebasticook* was built at Bath, Maine, in 1856. The ship's hull was of mixed woods and she was copper and iron fastened. In 1858 the *Sebasticook's* owner was listed as Jenks and Harding, and her captain as Chase. The *Sebasticook* was a full model ship, with two decks, and half poop. The ship measured 559 76/95 (or 549) tons, and drew eighteen of water. The vessel was classed A-2 for insurance purposes. The *Sebasticook* was issued "Permanent Register #19, at Bath, Maine, on April 19, 1856, and "Permanent Register" #89 at Boston, Massachusetts, on March 30, 1859.] (Note Two: See also entry 1862-12x-US-SC/GA-1 of this book.)

References for 1862-12x-US-SC/GA-3:
"Record of Registers, Volume 13," (bound manuscript, abstracts), p. 154, National Archives, Record Group 41
"Record of Registers, Volume 14," (bound manuscript, abstracts), p. 126, National Archives, Record Group 41
American Lloyd's: Registry of American & Foreign Shipping, (New York, New York, 1858), p. 51, #1488
"Savannah Morning News," (Savannah, GA), October 20, 1879, p. 3, c. 3
"Savannah Morning News," (Savannah, GA), November 18, 1879, p. 3, c. 4
History of the City Government of Savannah, Georgia, by Thomas Gamble, Jr., (1900), p. 256

1862-12x-US-SC/GA-4: The ship *A.B. Thompson*, (ex-Captain Hussey), which had been a prize to the Confederate privateer *Lady Davis* and had arrived at Savannah, Georgia, in August, 1861, was sunk as an obstruction in the Savannah River by the Confederates in 1862. [Note One: The ship had been built at Brunswick, Maine, in 1853. The ship's hull was of oak and hackmatack and was copper and iron fastened. The hull was metalled in April, 1857, and again in December, 1859. The *A.B. Thompson* was a full model ship with two decks and a cabin house. At the time of her capture the ship was owned by D. Hood and Company. The *A.B. Thompson* which was classed A-2 for insurance purposes, measured 980 tons and drew

Treasures of the Confederate Coast

19' of water. The *A.B. Thompson* was issued "Permanent Register #81" at Portland, Maine, on October 18, 1853.] (Note Two: See also entry 1862-12x-US-SC/GA-1 of this book.)

References for 1862-12x-US-SC/GA-4:
"Record of Registers, Volume 12," (bound manuscript, abstracts), p. 210, National Archives, Record Group 41
American Lloyd's: Registry of American & Foreign Shipping, (New York, New York, 1858), p. 1, #7
American Lloyd's: Registry of American & Foreign Shipping, (New York, New York, 1863), p. 3, #1
"Savannah Morning News," (Savannah, GA), October 20, 1879, p. 3, c. 3
"Savannah Morning News," (Savannah, GA), Nov. 18, 1879, p. 3, c. 4
Official Records of the Union and Confederate Navies in the War of the Rebellion, (Washington, DC, 1897), Series 1, Volume 6, pp. 116, 182
History of the City Government of Savannah, Georgia, by Thomas Gamble, Jr., (1900), p. 256

1863-1-US-NC-1: The *U.S.S. Columbia*, Lt. J.P. Couthouy commanding, was run ashore and burned at Masonboro Inlet, North Carolina, on January 14, 1863. She was described as wrecked in eight feet of water, near the breakers and 1/2 mile from the beach. (Note One: The *Columbia's* six 24-pounder smooth bore howitzers were spiked with rat-tailed files and thrown overboard. Her captain, eleven of her officers and twenty-eight men were captured by the Confederates. The Yankees saved nothing from the wreck, except a chronometer, a sextant, and her 30-pounder Parrott rifle. The Parrott rifle was later lost overboard from the U.S. gunboat *Penobscot*. The Confederates lost one lieutenant and nineteen men while attempting to salvage the wrecked gunboat.) (Note Two: The *Columbia* had been purchased on November 4, 1862, from the United States Prize Court at Key West, Florida, by the Navy Department for $66,000. Her hull was made of 1/2" iron and she measured 168' in length, 25' in breadth, and 14' in depth. She was 503 tons and had two engines with 36" diameter cylinders with 30" piston strokes. She had horizontal, tubular boilers.) (Note Three: A Sea Grant publication put out by the University of North Carolina lists a wreck located fifty feet north of the Wrightsville Beach jetty which lies in ten feet of water approximately one hundred yards from shore. The publication states that the wreck has not been positively identified but that it is thought to be the remains of the *U.S.S. Columbia*.)

References for 1863-1-US-NC-1:
Official Records of the Union and Confederate Navies in the War of the Rebellion, (Washington, DC, 1899), Series 1, Volume 8, pp. 422,426, 428, 430-437, 458, 470, 483, 499, 506
Official Records of the Union and Confederate Navies in the War of the Rebellion, (Washington, DC, 1921), Series 2, Volume 1, p. 62
Graveyard of the Atlantic: Shipwrecks of the North Carolina Coast, by David Stick (University of North Carolina Press, Chapel Hill, NC, 1952), p. 247
A Chart of Wrecks of Vessels Sunk or Captured Near Wilmington, NC, Circa 1861-65, compiled by Charles H. Foard, (Wilmington, North Carolina, 1962)
An Oceanographic Atlas of the Continental Margin, J.G. Newton, O.H. Pilkey and J.O. Blanton, (Duke University Marine Laboratory, Beaufort, NC, 1971), p. 17 chart symbol #91, p. 20 entry #91
Wreck Diving in North Carolina, University of North Carolina, Sea Grant Publication, #78-13, p. 7

1863-1-US-NC-2: An unidentified schooner was forced aground at New Topsail Inlet, North Carolina, January 21, 1863.
References for 1863-1-US-NC-2:

The "Real Rhett Butler" & Other Revelations

An *Oceanographic Atlas of the Continental Margin*, J.G. Newton, O.H. Pilkey and J.O. Blanton, (Duke University Marine Laboratory, Beaufort, NC, 1971), p. 20 entry #124, p. 21 chart symbol #124

1863-1-US-SC/GA-1: The schooner *Lotus*, of Boston, Captain Thomas Quinn, with a cargo of sutler's stores, was run ashore on North Island Beach, one and a half miles from the Georgetown, South Carolina, light-house on January 15, 1863. While her cargo was being salvaged by the United States gunboat *Sebago*, it was discovered that the schooner carried a great many casks of liquor "concealed in barrels of potatoes and put up in various ways for smuggling." (Note One: The *Lotus* was not a regular blockade runner as she had "legally" cleared from New York on December 23, 1862, bound for Port Royal, South Carolina, which was in Federal hands. She carried a crew of four men and a boy, and four passengers.) (Note Two: This was probably the 132 ton schooner *Lotus* which was built in 1853 at Ellsworth, Maine. That vessel was issued a certificate of enrollment at New York, New York, on March 4, 1861. She was surveyed in May of 1858 and was listed in *American Lloyd's* for that year as A-2 1/2 for insurance purposes. She was a full model schooner and had one deck and a half poop and drew nine feet of water. She had iron fastenings and was built of mixed wood.)

References for 1863-1-US-SC/GA-1:
New York Marine Register: or American Lloyd's, (New York, New York, 1858), p. 272, #2364
Vessel log of the *U.S.S. Sebago*, January 16, 17, 19-21, 23, & 30, 1863, National Archives, Record Group 24
Official Records of the Union and Confederate Navies in the War of the Rebellion, (Washington, DC, 1901), Series 1, Volume 13, pp. 512, 513, 657
List of American-Flag Merchant Vessels that Received Certificates of Enrollment or Registry at the Port of New York 1789-1867, compiled by Forest R. Holdcamper, (U.S. National Archives, Washington, DC, 1968), Special List #22, Volume 2, p. 424

1863-1-US-SC/GA-2: The blockade running steamer *Tropic* (ex *C.S.S. Huntress*), Captain D. Bremond, was burned (either accidentally, or by her captain to prevent capture) while attempting to run the blockade into Charleston, South Carolina, on January 8 (or 18), 1863. The *Tropic's* officers and crew were rescued (captured) by the United States gunboat *Quaker City*. The steamer was carrying a cargo of turpentine and three hundred and twenty-six bales of cotton when she was lost. (Note One: The *Huntress* is reputed to have been the first vessel to fly a Confederate flag on the high seas, and had taken part in the battle of Port Royal Sound, South Carolina, on November 6 & 7, 1861.) (Note Two: She was a wooden hulled sidewheel steamer and had been built as the *Huntress* in 1838 at New York, New York. The steamer was issued her last permanent enrollment (as a United States vessel) at New York City on June 23, 1860. She had been purchased for $15,000 in New York by Lieutenant William B. Hall for the state of Georgia in

Treasures of the Confederate Coast

March 1861 for use as a state gunboat, but had been turned over to the Confederate Navy in April of 1861. She served as a Confederate transport operating out of Charleston, South Carolina, until October 1862, when she was purchased by A.J. White and Son for use as a blockade runner. The *Tropic* had one deck, a square stern, no galleries, a billet head, and two masts. The steamer was 333 13/95 tons, and measured 172' in length, 23'6" in breadth, and 9'6" in depth of hold. Although built in New York in 1838, the steamer's first home port was New London, Connecticut. She was issued a certificate of steam enrollment on April 5, 1839, at the port of New York. (Note One: "Lytle's List" shows the steamer as "abandoned or otherwise removed from documentation" in 1862.) (Note Three: Some sources show the *Huntress* as measuring 500 tons, 230' in length, and 24'6" in breadth, with a draft of 6'6" and a speed of 16-20 knots. Stephen Wise in his book *Lifeline of the Confederacy* shows her as 225' in length and 24.5' in breadth.)

References for 1863-1-US-SC/GA-2:
"Permanent Enrollment #28, April 16, 1853, (New York, NY), National Archives, Record Group 41
"Permanent Enrollment #132, September 29, 1854, (New York, NY), National Archives, Record Group 41
"Permanent Enrollment #141, October 11, 1854, (New York, NY), National Archives, Record Group 41
"Permanent Enrollment #27, January 16, 1855, (New York, NY), National Archives, Record Group 41
"Permanent Enrollment #70, June 23, 1860, (New York, NY), National Archives, Record Group 41
"Permanent Enrollment #73, June 27, 1860, (New York, NY), National Archives, Record Group 41
"Charleston Daily Courier," (Charleston, SC), #19301, October 29, 1862, p. 1, c. 2, p. 3, c. 4, (advertisement, with description)
"Charleston Daily Courier," (Charleston, SC), #19302, October 30, 1862, p. 1, c. 2
"Charleston Daily Courier," (Charleston, SC), #19386, February 7, 1863, p. 2, c. 2
"Charleston Mercury," (Charleston, SC), Volume 82, #11675, February 7, 1863, p. 2, c. 1
"Charleston Mercury," (Charleston, SC), Volume 82, #11706, March 17, 1863, p. 2, c. 1
"Daily Morning News," (Savannah, GA), Volume 14, #65, March 18, 1863, p. 2, c. 1
"Vessel Papers" (manuscript records), United States National Archives, Washington, DC, Record Group 109, files H-74, T-64
History of the Confederate States Navy From its Organization to the Surrender of its Last Vessel, by J. Thomas Scharf, (New York, New York, 1887), pp. 88, 89, 688n, 792n
Official Records of the Union and Confederate Navies in the War of the Rebellion, (Washington, DC, 1901), Series 1, Volume 13, pp. 516-518
Official Records of the Union and Confederate Navies in the War of the Rebellion, (Washington, DC, 1921), Series 2, Volume 1, pp. 256, 269
Merchant Steam Vessels of the United States 1807-1868, ("Lytle List"), by William M. Lytle, (Mystic, CT, 1952), p. 87
List of American-Flag Merchant Vessels that Received Certificates of Enrollment or Registry at the Port of New York 1789-1867, compiled by Forest R. Holdcamper, (U.S. National Archives, Washington, DC, 1968), Special List #22, Volume 1, p. 334
Shipwrecks of the Civil War: The Encyclopedia of Union and Confederate Naval Losses, by Donald Shomette, (Washington, DC, 1973), pp. 433, 444
Lifeline of the Confederacy: Blockade Running During the Civil War, by Stephen R. Wise, (University of South Carolina, Columbia, SC, 1983), p. 622
Charleston's Maritime Heritage 1670-1865, by P.C. Coker III, (CokerCraft Press, Charleston, SC, 1987), p. 303
Warships of the Civil War Navies, by Paul H. Silverstone, (Naval Institute Press, Annapolis, MD, 1989), p. 240

1863-1-US-SC/GA-3: The reference work *Official Records of the Union and Confederate Navies* quotes a Richmond paper dated February 2, 1863, as stating "Beauregard's ironclads had raised the blockade of Charleston, South Carolina, and sunk two (Federal blockading) vessels, and that the French and Spanish consuls had been taken out to witness the fact." The Confederate vessels involved were the gunboats *Palmetto State* and *Chicora*, which were assisted by three small steamers. At least one account reported the *U.S.S. Mercedita* as sunk in five fathoms of water, but that report was incorrect, as the *Mercedita*, although rammed and badly damaged by the *Palmetto State*, was not sunk. Captain William H. Parker, who was aboard the *C.S.S. Palmetto State* described the ramming as follows: "We crossed the bar and steered directly for the *Mercedita*. They did not see us until we were very near. The lieutenant on deck then hailed us, and ordered us to keep off or he would fire. We did not reply, and he called to us, 'You will be into me!' Just then we rammed him on the starboard quarter and fired the bow gun. The shell from it, according to Captain Stellwagen, who commanded her, went through her diagonally, penetrating the starboard side, through the condenser, through the steam-drum of the port boiler, and exploded against the port side of the ship, blowing a hole in its exit four or five feet square. She did not fire a gun, and in a minute her commander hailed to say he surrendered." The *Mercedita* was later towed to Port Royal, South Carolina, and repaired. During the same engagement, the *C.S.S. Chicora* attacked the *U.S.S. Keystone State*, killing and wounding forty of the Union ship's men. The Federal commander lowered her colors in surrender, but afterwards "treacherously" hoisted them and made her escape.

References for 1863-1-US-SC/GA-3:
"Charleston Mercury," (Charleston, SC), Volume 82, #11670, February 2, 1863, p. 1, c. 2
"Charleston Mercury," (Charleston, SC), Volume 82, #11676, February 9, 1863, p. 2, c. 1
"Charleston Mercury," (Charleston, SC), Volume 82, #11682, February 16, 1863, p. 1, c. 2, 5
"Daily Morning News," (Savannah, GA), #27, February 2, 1863, p. 1, c. 1; p. 2, c. 1
New York Times, (New York, NY), Volume 12, #3550, February 9, 1863, p. 1, c. 1-3, p. 4, c. 1
New York Times, (New York, NY), Volume 12, #3551, February 10, 1863, p. 1, c. 1-6
New York Times, (New York, NY), Volume 12, #3555, February 15, 1863, p. 1, c. 1-3
New York Times, (New York, NY), Volume 12, #3557, February 17, 1863, p. 1, c. 3, 4
Times, (London, England), #24483, February 16, 1863, p. 12, c. 1,2
Confederate Military History, edited by General Clement A. Evans, (Confederate Publishing Co., Atlanta, GA, 1899), Volume 12, pp. 67-71
Official Records of the Union and Confederate Navies in the War of the Rebellion, (Washington, DC, 1899), Series 1, Volume 8, p. 503
Official Records of the Union and Confederate Navies in the War of the Rebellion, (Washington, DC, 1901), Series 1, Volume 13, pp. 579-581, 595, 596, 607, 611, 612, 614-623, 660
Charleston's Maritime Heritage 1670-1865, by P.C. Coker III, (CokerCraft Press, Charleston, SC, 1987), pp. 227-230

1863-1-US-x-1: The sidewheel steamer *Nina*, loaded with a "contraband" cargo, foundered on January 25, 1863, while bound from Nassau to Charleston, South Carolina. (Note One: The *Nina* had made one previous successful trip through the Federal blockade.) [Note Two: The *Nina* was built by Thomas McDowell at Washington Township (now South River), New Jersey, in 1848, and measured 145' in length, 26' in breadth, and 9'6" in depth of

Treasures of the Confederate Coast

hold. She was 205 tons register and 338 tons burden. She had been purchased for $40,000 and was owned by the Importing and Exporting Company of Georgia. The *Nina* had a "crosshead" vertical engine with a 36" cylinder and a 9' piston stroke. Her paddle wheels were approximately 23' in diameter. She received her first steam enrollment at the Port of New York on July 24, 1848, but was home ported at Charleston starting the following year. She received a Confederate enrollment or register in 1861.] (Note Three: This vessel is listed because she could easily be in the waters covered by this book.)

References for 1863-1-US-x-1:
"Daily Morning News," (Savannah, GA), May 4, 1863, p. 2, c. 2
Official Records of the Union and Confederate Navies in the War of the Rebellion, (Washington, DC, 1895), Series 1, Volume 2, p. 60
List of American Flag Merchant Vessels that received Certificates of Enrollment or Registry at the Port of New York 1789-1867, compiled by Forest R. Holdcamper, (U.S. National Archives, Washington, DC, 1968), Special List #22, Volume 2, p. 512
Early American Steamers, by Erik Heyl, (Buffalo, New York, 1969), Volume 6, pp. 231 (with illustration), 232
Merchant Steam Vessels of the United States 1790-1868, ("Lytle-Holdcamper List"), edited by C. Bradford Mitchell, (Staten Island, NY, 1975), p. 34
Lifeline of the Confederacy: Blockade Running During the Civil War, by Stephen R. Wise, (University of South Carolina, Columbia, SC, 1983), pp. 300, 338, 470, 599, 600
Charleston's Maritime Heritage 1670-1865, by P.C. Coker III, (CokerCraft Press, Charleston, SC, 1987), p. 303

1863-2-US-NC-1: The two hundred ton schooner *Industry*, with a cargo of salt, was partially burned and scuttled in three fathoms of water off New Topsail Inlet, North Carolina, on February 2, 1863, by the *U.S.S. Mount Vernon*. (Note: At one point her position was described as one hundred yards from the beach. Her position was also given as five miles to the northward of New Topsail Inlet.)

References for 1863-2-US-NC-1:
Official Records of the Union and Confederate Navies in the War of the Rebellion, (Washington, DC, 1899), Series 1, Volume 8, p. 499
A Chart of Wrecks of Vessels Sunk or Captured Near Wilmington, NC, Circa 1861-65, compiled by Charles H. Foard, (Wilmington, North Carolina, 1962)
An Oceanographic Atlas of the Continental Margin, J.G. Newton, O.H. Pilkey and J.O. Blanton, (Duke University Marine Laboratory, Beaufort, NC, 1971), p. 20 entry #129, p. 21 chart symbol #129

1863-2-US-NC-2: Charles Foard's chart of Civil War wrecks around Wilmington, North Carolina, shows an "unknown" wreck half way between Rich Inlet and New Topsail Inlet, North Carolina, and gives the date of loss as February 2, 1863. (Note: This could have been the prize vessel captured by the *Retribution* which was lost by John Gordon, when he mistook the blockade runner *Giraffe* for a Federal blockader. The report on that loss isn't clear, but it appears to have taken place on the Cape Fear coast in early February, 1863, so it certainly can't be ruled out.)

Reference for 1863-2-US-NC-2:
Official Records of the Union and Confederate Navies in the War of the Rebellion, (Washington, DC, 1899), Series 1, Volume 8, pp. 470, 863, 864
A Chart of Wrecks of Vessels Sunk or Captured Near Wilmington, NC, Circa 1861-65, compiled by Charles H. Foard, (Wilmington, North Carolina, 1962)

The "Real Rhett Butler" & Other Revelations

1863-2-US-SC/GA-1: The river steamer *William H. Starke*, with a cargo of two thousand bushels of corn, and "perhaps other articles," sank in twenty feet of water in the Savannah River on February 3, 1863. (Note One: The *William H. Starke* had been engaged in the trade between Augusta, Shell Bluff, and the Confederate batteries. The wreck was said to be about twenty miles below Augusta, Georgia.) (Note Two: She was five or six years old and was said to have broken in two simply from "wearing out." Her machinery was expected to be saved.)

References for 1863-2-US-SC/GA-1:
"Charleston Mercury," (Charleston, SC), Volume 82, #11674, February 6, 1863, p. 1, c. 2
"Daily Morning News," (Savannah, GA), Volume 14, #31, February 6, 1863, p. 1, c. 1
"Daily Morning News," (Savannah, GA), Volume 14, #32, February 7, 1863, p. 1, c. 2

1863-2-US-SC/GA-2: The screw steamer *Thistle*, Captain L.M. Murray, was reported ashore on Sullivan's Island, South Carolina, in February, 1863. (Note One: Most of the stranded blockade runner's cargo was taken out, and she was sold, as she lay, to Captain John Ferguson "and others" for the sum of $80,000. The steamer was finally gotten off on March 8, 1863, through the "skillful" efforts of Captain Ferguson and was towed to Charleston where she was said to be perfectly sound.) (Note Two: The *Thistle's* iron hull was built by Lawrence Hill and Company, at Port Glasgow, Scotland, in 1859, and she was engined by A. & J. Inglis, Whitehall Foundry. The steamer measured 606 tons burden, 386 gross tons, and 206 registered tons. She was 194'6" in length, 25'2" in breadth, and 12'11" in depth. The *Thistle* was renamed the *Cherokee* and was captured attempting to run out of Charleston on May 17, 1863. The captured blockade runner later served as the United States steamer *Cherokee*.) (Note Three: Stephen Wise's book *Lifeline of the Confederacy* gives her dimensions as 184.5'x25.2'x12.5'.)

References for 1863-2-US-SC/GA-2:
"Charleston Mercury," (Charleston, SC), Volume 82, #11682, February 16, 1863, p. 2, c. 1
"Charleston Mercury," (Charleston, SC), Volume 82, #11684, February 18, 1863, p. 2, c. 1
"Charleston Mercury," (Charleston, SC), Volume 82, #11699, March 9, 1863, p. 2, c. 1
"Daily Morning News," (Savannah, GA), #42, February 19, 1863, p. 1, c. 2
"Daily Morning News," (Savannah, GA), #58, March 10, 1863, p. 1, c. 5
Times, (London, England), #24520, March 31, 1863, p. 12, c. 3
Times, (London, England), #24527, April 8, 1863, p. 12, c. 4
"Vessel Papers" (manuscript records), United States National Archives, Washington, DC, Record Group 109, file T-20
Official Records of the Union and Confederate Navies in the War of the Rebellion, (Washington, DC, 1902), Series 1, Volume 14, pp. 181, 688
Official Records of the Union and Confederate Navies in the War of the Rebellion, (Washington, DC, 1921), Series 2, Volume 1, pp. 55, 56
Merchant Steam Vessels of the United States 1790-1868, ("Lytle-Holdcamper List"), edited by C. Bradford Mitchell, (Staten Island, NY, 1975), p. 34
Lifeline of the Confederacy: Blockade Running During the Civil War, by Stephen R. Wise, (University of South Carolina, Columbia, SC, 1983), p. 621
Charleston's Maritime Heritage 1670-1865, by P.C. Coker III, (CokerCraft Press, Charleston, SC, 1987), pp. 279, 303

Treasures of the Confederate Coast

1863-2-US-SC/GA-3: The Savannah "Daily Morning News" of February 25, 1863, reported a rumor which stated that an iron merchant steamer from Nassau had gone aground several miles above Sullivan's Island during the night of February 23, 1863. That would have placed it off the present day Isle of Palms, South Carolina. The paper said that the rumor "needs confirmation."

References for 1863-2-US-SC/GA-3:
"Daily Morning News," (Savannah, GA), #47, February 25, 1863, p. 1, c. 1

1863-2-US-SC/GA-4: The French government steamer of war *Renaudin* went ashore at Bowman's Jetty on Sullivan's Island, South Carolina, on February 23, 1863, while attempting to enter Charleston Harbor. The *Renaudin* was reported off the next day.

References for 1863-2-US-SC/GA-4:
"Charleston Mercury," (Charleston, SC), Volume 82, #11689, February 24, 1863, p. 2, c. 1
"Charleston Mercury," (Charleston, SC), Volume 82, #11690, February 25, 1863, p. 2, c. 1
"Daily Morning News," (Savannah, GA), #46, February 24, 1863, p. 2, c. 1
"Daily Morning News," (Savannah, GA), #47, February 25, 1863, p. 1, c. 1
Official Records of the Union and Confederate Navies in the War of the Rebellion, (Washington, DC, 1902), Series 1, Volume 14, pp. 736, 737

1863-2-US-SC/GA-5: The "fine" blockade running steamship *Havelock*, Captain L.M. Coxetter, bound to Charleston with an "excellent assortment of goods" got ashore on Drunken Dick Shoals off Sullivan's Island, South Carolina, about February 25, 1863. The Confederate ironclads *Chicora* and *Palmetto State* were immediately sent to protect her and she got off after throwing overboard ten slabs of iron plating and forty or fifty boxes of tin. (Note One: The Savannah "Daily Morning News" of February 25, 1863, reported that a British steamer attempting to run the blockade into Charleston, South Carolina, during the night of February 23 (or 24), 1863, had accidentally run aground on the shoals about one mile from the beach on Sullivan's Island. That report did not identify the steamer by name, but it was undoubtedly the *Havelock*.) (Note Two: On December 11, 1863, the *Havelock's* luck ran out and she was finally chased ashore and destroyed near Fort Fisher, North Carolina. For more on her destruction, see entry 1863-12-US-NC-3.)

References for 1863-2-US-SC/GA-5:
"Charleston Mercury," (Charleston, SC), Volume 82, #11690, February 25, 1863, p. 2, c. 1
"Daily Morning News," (Savannah, GA), #47, February 25, 1863, p. 1, c. 1
"Daily Morning News," (Savannah, GA), #48, February 26, 1863, p. 2, c. 2
"Vessel Papers" (manuscript records), United States National Archives, Washington, DC, Record Group 109, file H-47

1863-2-US-SC/GA-6: The United States monitor *Montauk*, Commander J.L. Worden, struck a Confederate torpedo (mine) in the Great Ogeechee River near Fort McAllister, Georgia, on February 28, 1863, and was immediately beached in the mud and repaired. (Note: The *Montauk*, 750 tons, 200'x46'x11'6", had been built by contract with John Ericsson for $400,000. She was launched at Green Point, New York, on October 9, 1862.)

References for 1863-2-US-SC/GA-6:
New York Times, (New York, NY), Volume 12, #3577, March 12, 1863, p. 8, c. 5
Official Records of the Union and Confederate Navies in the War of the Rebellion, (Washington, DC, 1901), Series 1, Volume 13, pp. 700-705
Official Records of the Union and Confederate Navies in the War of the Rebellion, (Washington, DC, 1921), Series 2, Volume 1, pp. 149, 150
Georgia Historical Markers, by C.P. Scruggs, p. 42

1863-2-US-SC/GA-7: The Confederate privateer *Rattlesnake* (ex-*Thomas L. Wragg*, ex-*Nashville*), which had been accidentally run aground in the Ogeechee River near Fort McAllister, Georgia, was shelled, burned and blown up during an attack by the United States monitor *Montauk* on February 28, 1863. As the Confederate gunboat *Nashville*, the *Rattlesnake* had been the first vessel to fly the Confederate flag in English waters. She had later been sold to private parties, and "for several months the *Nashville*, was loaded with cotton, but, though constantly on the alert," (was bottled up in the Ogeechee by the Yankees, and "never ventured to run out." She finally withdrew up the Ogeechee "and reappeared, after a length of time, thoroughly fitted as a privateer, and presenting a very fine appearance." But, before she could blast her way through the blockade, she ran aground, and, without the ability to maneuver, became a sitting duck for the Federal guns. The *Rattlesnake* was a sidewheel steamer and was built of oak and composition fastened at New York in 1852 (or 1853) by Thomas Collyer. Her engine had one 85" diameter cylinder with an 8' piston stroke and was built by Novelty Iron Works in New York. The steamer measured 1220 30/95 (or 1200) tons, 215'6" in length, 34'6" in breadth, 21'9" in depth of hold, and 12' in draft. The *Rattlesnake* was described as a "substantial good built boat," and as "proverbially fast." The vessel was rigged with two masts and plenty of sails. She had spoon guards. The vessel was coppered and put in good order in September, 1854. The steamer originally had an awning deck and houses mounted in the ordinary way. The hull was repaired with diagonal wood braces on the ceiling (flooring), and caulked and yellow metalled as reported on May 12, 1857. The vessel's wooden hull was patched with copper on December 14, 1858. The vessel's ceiling was opened and found rotten and was well repaired as reported on February 15, 1859. The steamer had a round stern, no galleries, a billet head, two decks and three masts. The steamer had a side lever engine with one cylinder 86" in diameter with an 8' piston stroke. The steamer had an independent fire pump and was considered to have good security against fire. The vessel was rated A-2 for insurance purposes in 1858. The vessel was medium model

Treasures of the Confederate Coast

and schooner rigged. The vessel was taken into the Confederate Navy at the start of the war and made four trips through the blockade as warship. In March of 1862 she was sold to John Fraser and Company, who changed her name to *Thomas L. Wragg* and used her to make four trips through the blockade as a "private merchant" blockade runner. In November of 1862 she was sold to a private stock company, renamed the *Rattlesnake*, and outfitted as a privateer. (Note One: Stephen Wise in his book *Lifeline of the Confederacy* shows the *Nashville* as 216'x34'9"x22' and 1800 tons burden.) (Note Two: On July 21, 1868 it was announced that a contract had been entered into by Captain Thomas Britt and Joseph Cosman in Savannah with the Federal government to raise the wreck, but the operations, if they took place at all, were unsuccessful. The wreck was rediscovered and worked briefly in the late 1950's by John Nasworthy of Savannah, Georgia. Then, in the early 1980's it was extensively worked by Dave Topper of Fairfax, South Carolina, and Frank and Paul Chance of Richmond Hill, Georgia. The trio made detailed drawings of the wreckage and recovered thousands of individual artifacts. The Chances and Topper published an excellent book on their work titled *Tangled Machinery and Charred Relics: The Historical and Archeological Investigation of the C.S.S. Nashville*. Unfortunately, the State of Georgia, who had shown no real interest in the wreck for over a century, suddenly decided it was important and valuable and, furthermore, that it should belong to the State because it was imbedded in State land. In a subsequent legal battle, the State won, and the Court ruled the salvors had to turn over all of the artifacts to the State of Georgia.) (Note Three: John Fraser and Company was headed by George Alfred Trenholm who was later used as the historical basis for Margaret Mitchell's fictional character Rhett Butler in *Gone With The Wind*.)

References for 1863-2-US-SC/GA-7:

"Permanent Enrollment #4," (Charleston, SC), May 18, 1854, National Archives, Record Group 41
"Permanent Enrollment #8," (Charleston, SC), December 23, 1854, National Archives, Record Group 41
"Permanent Enrollment #6," (Charleston, SC), May 8, 1855, National Archives, Record Group 41
"Permanent Register #11," (Charleston, SC), March 20, 1855, National Archives, Record Group 41
New York Marine Register: or American Lloyd's, (New York, New York, 1858/59), pp. 346, 347, #179
Vessel Log of the *U.S.S. Wissahicken*, February 28, 1863, National Archives, Record Group 24
"Charleston Daily Courier," (Charleston, SC), Volume 52, #16618, January 9, 1854, p. 1, c. 2 (description of vessel)
"Charleston Daily Courier," (Charleston, SC), #19406, March 3, 1863, p. 2, c. 1
"Charleston Mercury," (Charleston, SC), Volume 82, #11694, March 2, 1863, p. 1, c. 1
"Charleston Mercury," (Charleston, SC), Volume 82, #11695, March 3, 1863, p. 2, c. 1
"Charleston Mercury," (Charleston, SC), Volume 82, #11706, March 17, 1863, p. 1, c. 3
"Charleston Mercury," (Charleston, SC), Volume 82, #11710, March 21, 1863, p. 1, c. 3
"Daily Morning News," (Savannah, GA), Volume 14, March 2, 1863, p. 1, c. 1
"Daily Morning News," (Savannah, GA), Volume 14, March 17, 1863, p. 2, c. 1
"Daily Morning News," (Savannah, GA), Volume 14, March 21, 1863, p. 1, c. 2
"Daily Morning News," (Savannah, GA), Volume 14, June 14, 1866, p. 2, c. 3
New York Times, (New York, NY), Volume 12, #3577, March 12, 1863, p. 8, c. 5
New York Times, (New York, NY), Volume 14, #4129, December 17, 1864, p. 1, c. 2

The "Real Rhett Butler" & Other Revelations

"Steam Vessels #1, 1850's," (bound manuscript, Atlantic Mutual Insurance Companies of New York), entry for *Nashville*
"Vessel Papers" (manuscript records), United States National Archives, Washington, DC, Record Group 109, file R-5
History of the Confederate States Navy From its Organization to the Surrender of its Last Vessel, by J. Thomas Scharf, (New York, New York, 1887), pp. 637, 638, 795, 796
Official Records of the Union and Confederate Armies in the War of the Rebellion, (Washington, DC, 1885), Series 1, Volume 14, pp. 3, 214, 217, 218, 417
Official Records of the Union and Confederate Navies in the War of the Rebellion, (Washington, DC, 1901), Series 1, Volume 13, pp. 696-710
Official Records of the Union and Confederate Navies in the War of the Rebellion, (Washington, DC, 1921), Series 2, Volume 1, pp. 261, 264
The Navy in the Civil War, (Charles Scribner's Sons, New York, NY, 1903), Volume 1 ("The Blockade and the Cruisers" by James Russell Soley), pp. 215-218
The Navy in the Civil War, (Charles Scribner's Sons, New York, NY, 1905), Volume 2 ("The Atlantic Coast" by Daniel Ammen), p. 86
Merchant Steam Vessels of the United States 1807-1868, ("Lytle List"), by William M. Lytle, (Mystic, CT, 1952), pp. 164, 259
List of American-Flag Merchant Vessels that Received Certificates of Enrollment or Registry at the Port of New York 1789-1867, compiled by Forest R. Holdcamper, (U.S. National Archives, Washington, DC, 1968), Special List #22, Volume 2, p. 499
Shipwrecks of the Civil War: The Encyclopedia of Union and Confederate Naval Losses, by Donald Shomette, (Washington, DC, 1973), pp. 327-328
Georgia Historical Markers, by C.P. Scruggs, pp. 41, 42
Personal interviews with Bill Kensey by E. Lee Spence, Savannah, Georgia, 1976; March 1983
Personal interview with Paul Garrett by E. Lee Spence, Savannah, Georgia, 1976; March, 1983
Personal interview with John Nasworthy by E. Lee Spence, Savannah, Georgia, March, 1983
Personal observation during dives on wreck of the *Nashville* by E. Lee Spence, Ogeechee River, Georgia, February, 1983
Series of personal interviews with Dave Topper, Frank Chance and Paul Chance by E. Lee Spence, Richmond Hill, Georgia, February and March, 1983; January, 1984
Lifeline of the Confederacy: Blockade Running During the Civil War, by Stephen R. Wise, (University of South Carolina, Columbia, SC, 1983), pp. 597
Tangled Machinery and Charred Relics: The Historical and Archeological Investigation of the C.S.S. Nashville, by Franklin N. Chance, Paul C. Chance and David L. Topper, 1985
Charleston's Maritime Heritage 1670-1865, by P.C. Coker III, (CokerCraft Press, Charleston, SC, 1987), pp. 189, 212, 214, 271
Warships of the Civil War Navies, by Paul H. Silverstone, (Naval Institute Press, Annapolis, MD, 1989), p. 213

1863-2x-US-NC-1: A typo on page 300 of the 1983 edition of Stephen Wise's excellent book, *Lifeline of the Confederacy: Blockade Running During the Civil War*, gives the date of loss for the steamer *Nutfield* as February 4, 1863. The correct date of loss was February 4, 1864. See the main entry for the *Nutfield* under that date.

References for 1863-2x-US-NC-1:
Official Records of the Union and Confederate Navies in the War of the Rebellion, (Washington, DC, 1899), Series 1, Volume 9, pp. 459-461, 465, 482
Official Records of the Union and Confederate Navies in the War of the Rebellion, (Washington, DC, 1900), Series 1, Volume 10, p. 504
Graveyard of the Atlantic: Shipwrecks of the North Carolina Coast, by David Stick (University of North Carolina Press, Chapel Hill, NC, 1952), pp. 64, 247
A Chart of Wrecks of Vessels Sunk or Captured Near Wilmington, NC, Circa 1861-65, compiled by Charles H. Foard, (Wilmington, North Carolina, 1962)
Lifeline of the Confederacy: Blockade Running During the Civil War, by Stephen R. Wise, (University Microfilms International, 1983), pp. 300, 368, 601

1863-2x-US-SC/GA-1: Some reports incorrectly list the Federal steamer *Governor Milton*, as lost on February 10, 1863, in the Edisto River, South Carolina. The actual date of loss was July 10, 1863. (Note: For more information on the loss of the *U.S.S. Governor Milton* see entry 1863-7-US-SC/GA-1.)

References for 1863-2x-US-SC/GA-1:
"Charleston Mercury," (Charleston, SC), Volume 83, #11805, July 13, 1863, p. 2, c. 3

Treasures of the Confederate Coast

"Report of vessels employed by the U.S. in the Department of the Carolinas which have been lost," (manuscript list), National Archives, Record Group 92, entry 1407, Box 123
Official Records of the Union and Confederate Armies in the War of the Rebellion, (Washington, DC, 1885), Series 1, Volume 14, pp. 131, 136, 137
Official Records of the Union and Confederate Armies in the War of the Rebellion, (Washington, DC, 1890), Series 1, Volume 28, pp. 194-199
Official Records of the Union and Confederate Navies in the War of the Rebellion, (Washington, DC, 1901), Series 1, Volume 13, pp. 359-361, 364, 366, 371

1863-3-US-NC-1: On March 3, 1863, an unidentified boat lying on the beach at Little River Inlet, North Carolina, was destroyed by Acting Master Drain of the U.S. schooner *Matthew Vassar*.

Reference for 1863-3-US-NC-1:
Official Records of the Union and Confederate Navies in the War of the Rebellion, (Washington, DC, 1899), Series 1, Volume 8, p. 585

1863-3-US-NC-2: The Savannah *Daily Morning News* of March 6, 1863 reported the steamer *Cornubia*, bound from Bermuda to Wilmington, as ashore on the North Carolina coast about fifteen miles south of the Cape Fear bar. Regardless of the report, the *Cornubia* definitely was not lost on that voyage. The *Cornubia* (a.k.a. *Lady Davis*) continued to successfully run the blockade until she was captured on November 7, 1863, after being run ashore eleven miles north of New Inlet, North Carolina, by the United States gunboats *James Adger* and *Niphon*. The papers captured with the steamer "quickly became a Rosetta stone to unlock the management secrets of the Confederate Army-Navy-Treasury blockade running fleet." The *Cornubia* was a sidewheel steamer of 588 92/95 tons burden, 411 gross tons, and 259 registered tons. She was built at Hayle in 1858. She had an iron hull with four bulkheads and measured 190'x24'6"x12'6". The *Cornubia* was taken into service with the United States Navy as the *U.S.S. Cornubia*.

References for 1863-3-US-NC-2:
"Daily Morning News," (Savannah, GA), Volume 14, #55, March 6, 1863, p. 2, c. 2
Lloyd's Register of British and Foreign Shipping, from 1st July, 1863, to the 30th June, 1864, (London, 1863), entry C-829
Official Records of the Union and Confederate Navies in the War of the Rebellion, (Washington, DC, 1899), Series 1, Volume 8, pp. 612, 630, 706
Official Records of the Union and Confederate Navies in the War of the Rebellion, (Washington, DC, 1899), Series 1, Volume 9, pp. 273-277, 279
Official Records of the Union and Confederate Navies in the War of the Rebellion, (Washington, DC, 1900), Series 1, Volume 10, pp. 273-286, 288-291, 832 (note)
George Alfred Trenholm and the Company that Went to War 1861-1865, by Ethel Trenholm Seabrook Nepveux, (Charleston, South Carolina, 1973), pp. 50, 51
Lifeline of the Confederacy: Blockade Running During the Civil War, by Stephen R. Wise, (University Microfilms International, 1983), p. 549

1863-3-US-SC/GA-1: The English blockade running steamer *Wave Queen* (or *Queen of the Wave*), from Nassau, with an assorted cargo (including ammunition and clothing) on English account, was run ashore and burned by the *U.S.S. Conemaugh*, near the mouth of the North Santee River, South Carolina, about March 2, 1863, and was expected to be a total loss. It was her first and only attempt to run the blockade. Her cargo was valued at $250,000. Official Federal dispatches stated three thousand two hundred sheets of tin, twenty ounce bottles of quinine, twenty-three ounce bottles of morphine, fifteen pounds of opium, several bales of calico, two anchors, a complete binnacle, and twelve reams of paper were saved from the wreck. The wrecked steamer was set on fire and was later reported as broken up by the waves. The *Wave Queen* had an iron hull, but by March 8, 1863, the waves had already "broken her in two." She had been described as a "new Clyde built steamer" and as a "magnificent vessel." The wrecked steamer was afterwards blown up by the Federals in an effort to further destroy her. (Note One: Some sources show the date of the loss as early as February 24, and as late as March 24, 1863. Stephen Wise in his book *Lifeline of the Confederacy* shows her as a screw steamer built by Alexander Stephens and Sons at Kelvinghaugh, England, in 1861. Wise shows her as 775 tons burden and as 180'x30'x12.5'.) (Note Two: In 1967, Jim Batey and I located the wreck of a large steamer, with a riveted iron hull, in the breakers on the north side of the entrance to the North Santee River. The wreck was almost entirely buried in a large sand bar. That wreck, which I have tentatively identified as the *Wave Queen*, was located at approximately 33°08'12" North latitude and 79°14' West longitude.)

References for 1863-3-US-SC/GA-1:
"Charleston Mercury," (Charleston, SC), Volume 82, #11697, March 5, 1863, p. 2, c. 1
"Daily Morning News," (Savannah, GA), Volume 14, #55, March 6, 1863, p. 2, c. 2
"Daily Morning News," (Savannah, GA), Volume 14, #103, May 4, 1863, p. 2, c. 2
Times, (London, England), #24520, March 31, 1863, p. 12, c. 2
Times, (London. England), #24576, June 4, 1863, p. 7, c. 5
Official Records of the Union and Confederate Navies in the War of the Rebellion, (Washington, DC, 1901), Series 1, Volume 13, pp. 687-690, 736, 746
History of Georgetown County, South Carolina, by George C. Rogers, (Columbia, South Carolina, 1970), p. 408
Shipwrecks of the Civil War: The Encyclopedia of Union and Confederate Naval Losses, by Donald Shomette, (Washington, DC, 1973), p. 446
Lifeline of the Confederacy: Blockade Running During the Civil War, by Stephen R. Wise, (University of South Carolina, Columbia, SC, 1983), p. 628

1863-3-US-SC/GA-2: The steamer *Georgiana* was lost on the night of March 19, 1863, while attempting to run past the Federal Blockading Squadron and into Charleston, South Carolina. She was sunk in fourteen feet of water off Long Island (present day Isle of Palms) after a desperate chase in which she came so close to the Yankee guns that her crew even heard the orders being given on the enemy vessels. With solid shot passing entirely through her hull, her propeller and rudder damaged, and with no hope for escape, the *Georgiana's* captain ran her aground. Once aground, the *Georgiana's* crew scuttled her and escaped to shore. The Yankees then set her on fire. The partially submerged wreck burned and blew up for three days. Later the United States Secretary of Navy wrote:

Treasures of the Confederate Coast

"the destruction of the *Georgiana* not only touched (the Confederate's) pockets, but their hopes. She was a splendid craft, peculiarly fitted for the business of privateering." (Note One: I discovered the wreck in 1967 with the help of commercial fisherman Walter L. Shaffer. Today the *Georgiana* sits on the bottom with her huge boiler only five feet under the surface. Although the visibility rarely lets anyone see it, she is now plumed with a glorious array of Sea Fans, Sea Whips, and living corals. Large sections of the hull are still intact. In places the starboard side of the shattered blockade runner protrudes over nine feet from the sand. Under the mud and sand lies the remainder of the hull of the ill-fated warship. The ship's deck was white pine and has long since been eaten away. Near the forward cargo hatch I found boxes of pins and buttons, assorted merchandise, munitions and cannons. Much of my work was funded by the Hack family of Hilton Head Island, South Carolina. They donated the two extremely rare Blakely patent cannons I salvaged to the Fort Jackson Museum at Columbia, South Carolina.) [Note Two: The log of the United States steamer *James Adger* for March 19, 1863, recorded a "strange steamer ashore." The steamer later was identified as the *Georgiana*, Captain M.B. Davidson, from Nassau with a cargo of medicines, munitions and merchandise. The Federal steamer sent two boats to ascertain the *Georgiana's* condition. When they returned part of their crews were drunk and seven of them were confined in irons for drunkenness. The Federal sailors also recovered eight Enfield rifles, nine bayonets, eight battle axes, one patent lead and line, ten pounds of glue, five small jars of preserves, twelve gilt buttons, one table cloth, and nineteen sabers. A United States consular dispatch dated at Liverpool on January 6, 1863, had stated. "The steamer *Georgiana*, just arrived at Liverpool from the Clyde. She is new and said to be a very superior steamer. She arrived at this port on the 4th instant (January, 1863). Yesterday while lying here she had the Rebel flag flying at her mast. She has not as yet been entered to load at the customs, but by the advertisement on the slip enclosed is to load and clear for Nassau. 'Brig Rigged steamer *Georgiana* s.s. - Liverpool 580 tons, Capt. Davis - Hull painted black - built of iron - round stern, carvings and name on the same gilt - bust female figurehead - painted white - poop deck, iron railings around same painted white - draws when loaded fifteen feet aft and fourteen feet forward - steams twelve knots.' The *Georgiana* was purchased expressly to run the blockade and was reported as bound to Charleston." Thomas Scharf (who had served in the Confederate

Navy), in his *History of the Confederate Navy*, described the *Georgiana* as the "most powerful" Confederate cruiser. The London *Times* of April 8, 1863, described her as follows: "She is a fine modeled vessel, and said to be very fast. There is not the least doubt of her being intended as a privateer. She had two heavy guns mounted when she arrived. The Governor (of Nassau), at the request of the (United States) Consul, ordered her to be searched (while she was at Cochran's anchorage in Nassau). The report returned that she was an "armed merchantman." Sworn testimony in court stated that her guns were "larger than the guns merchant ships ordinarily carried." The *New York Times* of March 30, 1863, stated that the *Georgiana* had two guns mounted and was "considered more formidable than the *Alabama*." The next day the same paper reported a spy's description of the vessel as "a superior vessel, pierced for either fourteen or twenty guns, and built expressly for the rebel navy." The spy had gone on to report that the *Georgiana* was "altogether a faster, stauncher, and better vessel than either the *Oreto* or *Alabama*." The *New York Times* reported her as 800 tons British measurement and as 150 horsepower. The "Charleston Daily Courier" of March 21, 1863, described the *Georgiana* as 236' in length, 250 horsepower, and drawing just 11'6" of water, and capable of making "from fifteen to seventeen knots." "Lloyd's Register" for 1863/64 gave her measurements as 205'6" in length, 25'2" in breadth, and 14'9" in depth of hold, and her tonnage as 519 gross and 407 net. "Lloyd's Register" also showed her as having three bulkheads.] (Note Three: The *Georgiana* is said to have been carrying $90,000 in gold coin when she was lost. I never found the gold, which would have weighed about 350 pounds, and may have been hidden in a false compartment in her keelson. That much in gold coin could have a 1993 numismatic value in excess of $15,000,000. A passenger named Mr. Habe had tried to return to the *Georgiana* with "Captain Hudson and mate" on March 22, 1863, but was unsuccessful in recovering anything. One wonders if he was going after the gold.) (Note Four: Contemporary accounts published in the *Charleston Daily Courier* reported the *Georgiana's* cargo as consigned to Fraser and Company, a blockade running firm headed by George Alfred Trenholm. It was a direct result of my research on the *Georgiana* that I later proved through research that Trenholm was the historical basis for Margaret Mitchell's *Gone With The Wind* character. The *Georgiana* is believed to have been named for George and Anna Trenholm's infant daughter Georgiana. Georgiana, like Rhett and Scarlett's Bonnie, died as a child. For

Treasures of the Confederate Coast

more on the Butler/Trenholm connection, see Chapter One of this book.) [Note Five: The wreck of the *Georgiana* is situated at latitude 32°46'47" North, longitude 79°45'35" West (Loran-C lines 45498.3, 60454.1). For additional information on my research and discovery of the *Georgiana*, please read Chapter Three of this book.] [Note Six: This is not the wreck off Sullivan's Island (correctly or incorrectly) designated as the *Georgiana*, on the 1865 chart drawn by E. Willenbucher for the "Annual Report of the Secretary of the Navy." That *Georgiana* is shown in Adrian Lonsdale's *Guide to Sunken Ships in American Waters*, as having been wrecked at latitude 32°44.5' North, longitude 79°49.9' West.] (Note Seven: The blockade running steamers *Norseman*, *Mary Bowers*, and *Constance* each ran onto the wreck of the *Georgiana* and were lost. For more information on those losses see entries 1863-5-US-SC/GA-2, 1864-8-US-SC/GA-2 and 1864-10-US-SC/GA-1.)

References for 1863-3-US-SC/GA-2:

"Department and Consular Letters," (Bound press copy of manuscript dated January 6, 1863), Volume 1, pp. 6, 7, National Archives, Record Group 45, entry 152

"Charleston Mercury," (Charleston, SC), Volume 82, #11705, March 16, 1863, p. 2, c. 1

"Charleston Mercury," (Charleston, SC), Volume 82, #11709, March 20, 1863, p. 2, c. 1

"Charleston Mercury," (Charleston, SC), Volume 82, #11711, March 23, 1863, p. 2, c. 1

"Charleston Daily Courier," (Charleston, SC), Volume 61, #19420, March 20, 1863, p. 2, c. 2

"Charleston Daily Courier," (Charleston, SC), Volume 61, #19421, March 21, 1863, p. 2, c. 2

"Charleston Daily Courier," (Charleston, SC), Volume 61, #19422, March 22, 1863, p. 4, c. 6

"Charleston Daily Courier," (Charleston, SC), Volume 61, #19423, March 23, 1863, p. 2, c. 2

"Daily Morning News," (Savannah, GA), #68, March 21, 1863, p. 1, c. 3

"Daily Morning News," (Savannah, GA), #103, May 4, 1863, p. 2, c. 2

"Southern Confederacy Atlanta," (Atlanta, GA), March 24, 1863, p. 3

Vessel log of the *U.S.S. James Adger*, March 19, 21 & 30, 1864, National Archives, Record Group 24

New York Times, (New York, NY), Volume 12, #3592, March 30, 1863, p. 4, c. 1, 2

New York Times, (New York, NY), Volume 12, #3593, March 31, 1863, p. 8, c. 2

New York Times, (New York, NY), Volume 12, #3597, April 5, 1863, p. 8, c. 2

Times, (London, England), #24527, April 8, 1863, p. 12, c. 4

Times, (London. England), #24576, June 4, 1863, p. 7, c. 5

Times, (London, England), #24852, April 21, 1864, p. 14, c. 5

Times, (London. England), #25098, Feb. 2, 1865, p. 10, c. 6, p. 11, c. 1

U.S. Consular Dispatch, (Liverpool, England), #206, January 8, 1864

U.S. Consular Dispatch, (Liverpool, England), #250, March 29, 1864

U.S. Consular Dispatch, (Glasgow, Scotland), #67, February 23, 1864

U.S. Consular Dispatch, (St. Georges, Bermuda), #110, April 20, 1864

U.S. Consular Dispatch, (Halifax, Canada), #91, May 12, 1864

"Diplomatic Instructions," Records of the Department of State, Great Britain, National Archives, 18:50, pp. 407, 446, 447, 483, Index

"Diplomatic Dispatches," Great Britain, General Records of the Department of State, Volume 82, National Archives, Record Group 59, Doc. Film 436, dispatch #301, enclosures 1-10

Dispatches from U.S. Consuls in Glasgow, 1801-1906, Volume 7, roll 7, micro copy #T-207, November 11, 1862, to December 18, 1869, report #86, June 18, 1864

"Vessel Papers" (manuscript records), United States National Archives, Washington, DC, Record Group 109, files G-34, G-35

Lloyd's Register of British and Foreign Shipping, from 1st July, 1863, to the 30th June, 1864, (London, 1863), entry G-158

"General Map of Charleston Harbor, South Carolina, Showing Rebel Defenses and Obstructions," drawn by E. Willenbucher for the Annual Report of the Secretary of the Navy, (U.S. Coast Survey, 1865)

History of the Confederate States Navy From its Organization to the Surrender of its Last Vessel, by J. Thomas Scharf, (New York, New York, 1887), p. 802

Official Records of the Union and Confederate Armies in the War of the Rebellion, (Washington, DC, 1885), Series 1, Volume 14, pp. 3, 232

Official Records of the Union and Confederate Navies in the War of the Rebellion, (Washington, DC, 1895), Series 1, Volume 2, pp. 199, 222

Official Records of the Union and Confederate Navies in the War of the Rebellion, (Washington, DC, 1896), Series 1, Volume 3, pp. 121, 127

The "Real Rhett Butler" & Other Revelations

Official Records of the Union and Confederate Navies in the War of the Rebellion, (Washington, DC, 1899), Series 1, Volume 9, pp. 80, 81, 250
Official Records of the Union and Confederate Navies in the War of the Rebellion, (Washington, DC, 1900), Series 1, Volume 10, pp. 386, 406, 468
Official Records of the Union and Confederate Navies in the War of the Rebellion, (Washington, DC, 1901), Series 1, Volume 13, pp. 754, 769-775
Official Records of the Union and Confederate Navies in the War of the Rebellion, (Washington, DC, 1903), Series 1, Volume 14, pp. 172, 173, 178, 253
Official Records of the Union and Confederate Navies in the War of the Rebellion, (Washington, DC, 1903), Series 1, Volume 15, pp. 658, 659-661, 670
Official Records of the Union and Confederate Navies in the War of the Rebellion, (Washington, DC, 1903), Series 1, Volume 16, pp. 8, 9, 34, 36, 37
Official Records of the Union and Confederate Navies in the War of the Rebellion, (Washington, DC), Series 2, Volume 3, pp. 645, 712-716, 740, 804, 874, 1120
Guide to Sunken Ships in American Waters, by Adrian L. Lonsdale and H.R. Kaplan, (Arlington, VA, 1964), p. 70
"Diver Lee Spence," by Eugene Warner, *Sandlapper* magazine, (Columbia, SC), April, 1970, pp. 40-43
"Salvaging the Cargo of the *Mary Bowers*," by E. Lee Spence, *The Conference on Historic Site Archeology Papers 1969*, (1971), Volume 4, part 1
"A Comment on Diving Operations in South Carolina," *The Conference on Historic Site Archeology Papers 1969*, (1971), Volume 4, part 2
"Underwater Archeology in South Carolina," by E. Lee Spence, *The Conference on Historic Site Archeology Papers 1970*, (1971), Volume 5, Part 1
"Treasure Diver," by Katherine Hatch, in *Treasure World*, (February-March, 1972), pp. 44, 45
A Look at South Carolina's Underwater Heritage, by E. Lee Spence, (Charleston, SC, 1974), pp. 6-9
"Underwater Archeology on the *Georgiana*," ("Salvage of the *Georgiana*"), by E. Lee Spence, presented before the International Conference on Underwater Archeology, (Charleston, SC, 1974)
Spence's Guide to South Carolina, by E. Lee Spence, (Charleston, SC, 1976), pp. 1-5
"Civil War Shipwrecks," by E. Lee Spence, *Argosy* magazine, 1977 treasure hunting annual, pp. 34-38, 90
Wreck Chart, by E. Lee Spence, (Sullivan's Island, SC, 1979)
"Wreck of the *Georgianna* (sic)," by Kevin Rooney, *Skin Diver* magazine, (Los Angeles, CA), March, 1980, pp. 80, 81, 86, 87
Lifeline of the Confederacy: Blockade Running During the Civil War, by Stephen R. Wise, (University of South Carolina, Columbia, SC, 1983), pp. 226, 229-232, 568, 569
Shipwrecks of South Carolina and Georgia, 1520-1865, by E. Lee Spence, (Charleston, SC, 1984), pp. 47-55, 634, 635, 656, 657, 722-736
Charleston's Maritime Heritage 1670-1865, by P.C. Coker III, (CokerCraft Press, Charleston, SC, 1987), pp. 214, 274, 286, 303
Warships of the Civil War Navies, by Paul H. Silverstone, (Naval Institute Press, Annapolis, MD, 1989), p. 212
"*Georgiana*," by E. Lee Spence, *Atlantic Coastal Diver* magazine, (Baltimore, MD, 1979), pp. 21-27
"South Carolina's Underwater Treasures," by E. Lee Spence, *Treasure* magazine, Volume 13, #7, July, 1982, pp. 72-77
"The Rhett Butler Connection," by Dr. E. Lee Spence, *Treasure Diver* magazine, Volume 1, #1, September, 1989, pp. 34-41
The Blockade Runners, by Dave Horner, (Florida Classics Library, Port Salerno, FL, 1992), Chapter 14, pp. 207-209, 223, 225

1863-3x-US-NCx-1 or 1863-3x-US-SC/GAx-1: The "Charleston Mercury" of March 11, 1863, reported that "four submarine contrivances, intended for work in Charleston Harbor, were recently sent from New York in tow of the steamer *Ericsson*. After fourteen days passage the steamer arrived at Port Royal (South Carolina) with only one of the machines, the others having broken loose and gone to the bottom." (Note: This entry has been given two SL Codes and is included because of the possibility that the loss actually took place in the waters covered by this book.)

References for 1863-3x-US-NCx-1 or 1863-3x-US-SC/GAx-1:
"Charleston Mercury," (Charleston, SC), Volume 82, #11701, March 11, 1863, p. 2, c. 1
"Charleston Mercury," (Charleston, SC), Volume 82, #11739, March 27, 1863, p. 1, c. 3, 4

1863-4-US-NC-1: Charles Foard's chart of Civil War wrecks in the Wilmington, North Carolina, shows a wreck near Lockwood Folly Inlet, North Carolina, as the "*Kate III*, 4/4/63." However, a check

Treasures of the Confederate Coast

of contemporary records for that date failed to produce any support for such a wreck. This could have been the schooner *Kate* which was lost on April 2, 1862, at the inlet. (Note: For information on the *Kate*, see entry 1862-4-US-NC-1.)

References for 1863-4-US-NC-1:
Official Records of the Union and Confederate Navies in the War of the Rebellion, (Washington, DC, 1898), Series 1, Volume 7, pp. 196, 197, 704, 705
A Chart of Wrecks of Vessels Sunk or Captured Near Wilmington, NC, Circa 1861-65, compiled by Charles H. Foard, (Wilmington, North Carolina, 1962)

1863-4-US-NC-2: The large United States gunboat (or transport steamer) *Louisiana*, Captain Renshaw, loaded with troops, was sunk in the Tar River (also shown as the Pamlico River) by the Confederates, as it tried to pass the Confederate battery at Hill's Point, seven miles below Little Washington, North Carolina, on April 5, 1863.

References for 1863-4-US-NC-2:
New York Times, (New York, NY), Volume 12, #3603, April 12, 1863, p. 1, c. 2, p. 4, c. 1
New York Times, (New York, NY), Volume 12, #3604, April 13, 1863, p. 4, c. 1
Official Records of the Union and Confederate Armies in the War of the Rebellion, (Washington, DC, 1887), Series 1, Volume 18, pp. 213, 224, 241

1863-4-US-SC/GA-1: The hermaphrodite brig *Georgia's Pride*, Captain Lee Hallman, from Charleston, South Carolina, was run over and sunk, on April 1, 1863, by the gaff-rigged cutter *Blue Draeke*, Captain Richard Franklin, thirteen miles southeast of Little River Inlet, at the South Carolina/North Carolina line. The *Blue Draeke* carried a cargo of two thousand pounds of herring, while the *Georgia's Pride* had a cargo of 1300 bags of salt. Both vessels were lost, however, the *Blue Draeke's* anchors were located and salvaged on November 6, 1863.

References for 1863-4-US-SC/GA-1:
"Charleston Daily Courier," (Charleston, SC), Volume 61, #19422, March 22, 1863, p. 4, c. 2
Vessel Log of the Blue Draeke, (Atlantic Mutual Insurance Companies of New York), final entry, April 1, 1863
"Charleston Mercury," (Charleston, SC), Volume 83, #11914, November 20, 1863, p. 1, c. 1, p. 2, c. 4
Official Records of the Union and Confederate Navies in the War of the Rebellion, (Washington, DC, 1902), Series 1, Volume 14, p. 494

1863-4-US-SC/GA-2: The Confederate transport steamer *Marion*, Captain John Flynn, was accidentally blown up and sunk in thirty feet of water in the Ashley River near the mouth of Wappoo Creek, South Carolina, on April 6, 1863, while laying torpedoes (mines). The steamer's whole bottom was blown out and her machinery destroyed. The *Marion* had a wood hull and was built at Charleston, South Carolina, in 1850, and passed to Confederate hands in 1860 (or 1861). The vessel had two decks, one mast, no galleries, no figure head, and sidewheels. The vessel measured 258 71/95 tons, 132'4" in length, 30' in breadth, and 7'2" in depth of hull. (Note: A typographical error in Donald Shomette's book *Shipwrecks of the*

The "Real Rhett Butler" & Other Revelations

Civil War shows the *Marion* as lost near the mouth of the Ashley River, "NC")

References for 1863-4-US-SC/GA-2:
"Permanent Enrollment #13," (Charleston, SC), August 11, 1853, National Archives, Record Group 41
"Permanent Enrollment #11," (Charleston, SC), October 10, 1855, National Archives, Record Group 41
"Charleston Mercury," (Charleston, SC), Volume 82, #11722, April 7, 1863, p. 2, c. 1
"Charleston Daily Courier," (Charleston, SC), Volume 61, #19434, April 7, 1863, p. 2, c. 2
"Daily Morning News," (Savannah, GA), #82, April 8, 1863, p. 2, c. 2
Official Records of the Union and Confederate Navies in the War of the Rebellion, (Washington, DC, 1903), Series 1, Volume 16, pp. 386, 402, 412
Merchant Steam Vessels of the United States 1807-1868, ("Lytle List"), by William M. Lytle, (Mystic, CT, 1952), p. 121
Shipwrecks of the Civil War: The Encyclopedia of Union and Confederate Naval Losses, by Donald Shomette, (Washington, DC, 1973), pp. 317, 318
Charleston's Maritime Heritage 1670-1865, by P.C. Coker III, (CokerCraft Press, Charleston, SC, 1987), p. 254
Warships of the Civil War Navies, by Paul H. Silverstone, (Naval Institute Press, Annapolis, MD, 1989), p. 241

1863-4-US-SC/GA-3: The sidewheel steamer *Etiwan* (variously spelled as *Etowan*, *Etowah*, *Etwan*, or *Hetiwan*), having exploded a torpedo (mine) under her hull and being in a sinking condition, was forced to run herself aground near Fort Johnson in Charleston Harbor, South Carolina, on April 4 (or 6), 1863. She was got off, but she ran aground near same place on June 7, 1864, and was immediately shelled by the Federal batteries on Morris Island. (Note One: The wreck was removed and repaired after the war. She was used by the United States Quartermaster's Department, and was later renamed and documented as the *Saint Helena*. She was built at Charleston in 1834 and was 132 tons. She had a wooden hull. Her official number was 22339.) (Note Two: The location of the second wreck of the *Etiwan* is shown on the 1865 chart drawn by E. Willenbucher for the "Annual Report of the Secretary of the Navy," and is listed in Adrian Lonsdale's *Guide to Sunken Ships in American Waters*, as having been wrecked at latitude 32°45.3' North, longitude 79°53.1' West.) (Note Three: See also entry 1864-6-US-SC/GA-2 of this book.)

References for 1863-4-US-SC/GA-3:
"Vessel Papers" (manuscript records), United States National Archives, Washington, DC, Record Group 109, file E-26
"General Map of Charleston Harbor, South Carolina, Showing Rebel Defenses and Obstructions," drawn by E. Willenbucher for the Annual Report of the Secretary of the Navy, (U.S. Coast Survey, 1865)
Official Records of the Union and Confederate Navies in the War of the Rebellion, (Washington, DC, 1901), Series 1, Volume 13, p. 823
Official Records of the Union and Confederate Navies in the War of the Rebellion, (Washington, DC, 1903), Series 1, Volume 16, p. 412
Guide to Sunken Ships in American Waters, by Adrian L. Lonsdale and H.R. Kaplan, (Arlington, VA, 1964), p. 70
Shipwrecks of the Civil War: The Encyclopedia of Union and Confederate Naval Losses, by Donald Shomette, (Washington, DC, 1973), pp. 264, 265
Merchant Steam Vessels of the United States 1790-1868, ("Lytle-Holdcamper List"), edited by C. Bradford Mitchell, (Staten Island, NY, 1975), p. 67
Warships of the Civil War Navies, by Paul H. Silverstone, (Naval Institute Press, Annapolis, MD, 1989), p. 239

1863-4-US-SC/GA-4: A torpedo raft (or "Devil") used by the *Weehawken* during the Federal fleet's April 7, 1863, attack on

Treasures of the Confederate Coast

Charleston, South Carolina, broke loose and washed ashore the next day. The raft was later reported as on the "reef between Fort Sumter and Morris Island."

References for 1863-4-US-SC/GA-4:
"Charleston Mercury," (Charleston, SC), Volume 82, #11726, April 11, 1863, p. 1, c. 5
"Charleston Mercury," (Charleston, SC), Volume 82, #11738, April 25, 1863, p. 1, c. 3, 4
"Charleston Daily Courier," (Charleston, SC), Volume 61, #19561, September 3, 1863, p. 1, c. 2
Times, (London, England), #24542, April 25, 1863, p. 12, c. 1
Official Records of the Union and Confederate Navies in the War of the Rebellion, (Washington, DC, 1901), Series 1, Volume 13, p. 800

1863-4-US-SC/GA-5: The United States ironclad steamer *Keokuk*, Commander A.C. Rhind, sank at her moorings in shallow water three and one half miles from Fort Sumter and directly off Fort Shaw and a thousand yards from the beach on Morris Island, South Carolina, on April 8, 1863. The *Keokuk's* loss was attributed to the heavy shelling she received from the Confederates the previous day when the Federal fleet had attacked Fort Sumter with the hope of entering the harbor and capturing Charleston. A total of eight thousand six hundred and twenty rounds were said to have been fired by both sides during the battle. The ironclad had been hit ninety times. The Confederate projectiles had been "polished to the smoothness of a knife blade." Apparently for political reasons, the loss of the *Keokuk* was treated as almost insignificant and the New York papers made it seem like the results of the battle were proof of the superiority of the Federal fleet, despite the fact that the fleet had failed to enter the harbor. The Savannah papers at first incorrectly identified the sunken vessel as the Federal ironclad steamer *Montauk*. The *Keokuk* was a double casemated, twin screw monitor. The double turreted monitor was armed with two 11-inch Dahlgren smooth-bore cannons. The ironclad's casemates had six port holes and did not revolve as did the turrets on conventional monitors. The paymaster's funds were saved, but most of the personal effects were lost. "Many pieces of the *Keokuk's* furniture, with the spy glasses and other effects of her officers, were washed ashore on the Morris Island beach. Most of these articles when found were covered with clotted blood." The Federal vessel's guns were salvaged by the Confederate forces in a daring series of nighttime operations in which Confederate divers unbolted the tops of the turrets and removed the guns. The entire job was done in secrecy within range of the Federal guns while the Federal forces were trying to figure their own way to raise the vessel. The *Keokuk* was reported in late April of 1863, as "fast settling in the quicksands." The ironclad measured 677 tons, 159'6" in length, 36' in breadth, 13'6" in depth of hull. The vessel had nine engines (four main, two blowing, one ballast, and two pumping, with diameters of cylinders measuring respectively 23", 14", 12" and 4", and piston strokes measuring respectively 20", 14", 10", and 6") and twin screws. There is a very detailed and interesting description of the *Keokuk's* unique design in the "Charleston Mercury" of April 10, 1863. The steamer was built at a cost of $228,244.63 under the name *Moodna* and was launched at New York on December 6, 1862. The wreck of the *Keokuk* was extensively scrapped in the 1870's by Professor Maillefert's salvage company, under a government contract. (Note One: The wreck is shown on the 1865 chart drawn by E. Willenbucher for the "Annual Report of the Secretary of the Navy," and is listed in Adrian Lonsdale's *Guide to Sunken Ships in American Waters*, as having been wrecked at latitude 32°41.6' North, longitude 79°51.6' West, that position is fairly close to the actual location.) (Note Two: Jim Batey and I located this wreck during a magnetometer survey in 1971.)

References for 1863-4-US-SC/GA-5:
"Charleston Mercury," (Charleston, SC), Volume 82, #11723, April 8, 1863, p. 1, c. 2
"Charleston Mercury," (Charleston, SC), Volume 82, #11724, April 9, 1863, p. 2, c. 1
"Charleston Mercury," (Charleston, SC), Volume 82, #11725, April 10, 1863, p. 1, c. 2
"Charleston Mercury," (Charleston, SC), Volume 82, #11725 (sic), April 11, 1863, p. 1, c. 3
"Charleston Mercury," (Charleston, SC), Volume 82, #11728, April 14, 1863, p. 1, c. 4, p. 2, c. 1
"Charleston Mercury," (Charleston, SC), Volume 82, #11731, April 17, 1863, p. 1, c. 1, p. 2, c. 1
"Charleston Mercury," (Charleston, SC), Volume 82, #11733, April 20, 1863, p. 1, c. 4, p. 2, c. 1
"Charleston Mercury," (Charleston, SC), Volume 82, #11734, April 21, 1863, p. 1, c. 2, p. 2, c. 1
"Charleston Mercury," (Charleston, SC), Volume 82, #11736, April 23, 1863, p. 2, c. 1
"Charleston Mercury," (Charleston, SC), Volume 82, #11737, April 24, 1863, p. 1, c. 3, 4
"Charleston Mercury," (Charleston, SC), Volume 82, #11747, May 8, 1863, p. 2, c. 1
"Charleston Mercury," (Charleston, SC), Volume 84, #12019, March 23, 1864, p. 1, c. 5
"Daily Morning News," (Savannah, GA), #83, April 9, 1863, p. 1, c. 1; p. 2, c. 1
"Daily Morning News," (Savannah, GA), #94, April 22, 1863, p. 2, c. 1
"Daily Morning News," (Savannah, GA), #98, April 27, 1863, p. 1, c. 2
"Daily Morning News," (Savannah, GA), #107, May 8, 1863, p. 2, c. 3
"Daily Morning News," (Savannah, GA), December 31, 1863, p. 1, c. 1
New York Times, (New York, NY), Vol. 12, #3603, April 12, 1863, p. 1, c. 1, p. 4, c. 1
New York Times, (New York, NY), Vol. 12, #3604, April 13, 1863, p. 1, c. 1, p. 4, c. 1
New York Times, (New York, NY), Volume 12, #3605, April 14, 1863, p. 1, c. 1-6, p. 8, c. 1, 2
New York Times, (New York, NY), Volume 12, #3606, April 15, 1863, p. 8, c. 1-3
New York Times, (New York, NY), Volume 12, #3614, April 24, 1863, p. 8, c. 2, 3
Times, (London. England), #24541, April 24, 1863, p. 9, c. 4
Times, (London. England), #24542, April 25, 1863, p. 12, c. 1, 3, p. 14, c. 1
Times, (London. England), #24543, April 27, 1863, p. 12, c. 1, 2
Times, (London. England), #24544, April 28, 1863, p. 7, c. 5
Times, (London. England), #24549, May 4, 1863, p. 12, c. 2
Times, (London. England), #24573, June 1, 1863, p. 9, c. 4
"General Map of Charleston Harbor, South Carolina, Showing Rebel Defenses and Obstructions," drawn by E. Willenbucher for the Annual Report of the Secretary of the Navy, (U.S. Coast Survey, 1865)
"Salvage Log," B. Maillefert, (in the collection of the South Carolina Historical Society at Charleston, SC), June 19, 21 & 23, 1873; July 12, 14 & 24, 1873; August 27, 1873; September 4, 1873; and August 7, 1874.
Confederate Military History, edited by General Clement A. Evans, (Confederate Publishing Co., Atlanta, GA, 1899), Volume 12, p. 72
Official Records of the Union and Confederate Navies in the War of the Rebellion, (Washington, DC, 1902), Series 1, Volume 14, pp. 6, 24-110
Official Records of the Union and Confederate Navies in the War of the Rebellion, (Washington, DC, 1921), Series 2, Volume 1, p. 120
The Navy in the Civil War, (Charles Scribner's Sons, New York, NY, 1903), Volume 1 ("The Blockade and the Cruisers" by James Russell Soley), p. 250
Guide to Sunken Ships in American Waters, by Adrian L. Lonsdale and H.R. Kaplan, (Arlington, VA, 1964), p. 70
Naval History of the Civil War, by Howard P. Nash, (A.S. Barnes & Co., New York, NY, 1972), p. 194
Shipwrecks of the Civil War: The Encyclopedia of Union and Confederate Naval Losses, by Donald Shomette, (Washington, DC, 1973), p. 81

Treasures of the Confederate Coast

Charleston's Maritime Heritage 1670-1865, by P.C. Coker III, (CokerCraft Press, Charleston, SC, 1987), pp. 236, 238, 242-245, 249

1863-4-US-SC/GA-6: The United States Army steamer *George Washington*, armed with two 24-pounder brass Dahlgren boat howitzers and a 20-pounder James gun, was burnt by the Confederates in the Coosaw River, one mile east of Port Royal Ferry, and five hundred yards from shore, near Chisolm's Island, South Carolina, on April 9, 1863. At least two lives were lost. The steamer was 243 tons and was built at New York, New York, in 1851, and had been under charter from C.H. Campbell to the Federal government for $250 per day. She had a wooden hull and sidewheels. As a transport the vessel could carry about three hundred troops. The steamer had been altered to a gunboat under the orders of General Mitchell. The Confederates and the Federals each raised one of the howitzers. The James gun was apparently left on the wreck. The *George Washington* was issued a certificate of steam register at the port of New York on August 30, 1851.

References for 1863-4-US-SC/GA-6:
"List of Steamers Chartered by the U.S and in the Service of the Quartermaster's Department at Port Royal, South Carolina" (Manuscript lists, dated November 30, 1862, and January 31, 1863), National Archives, Record Group 92, entry 1407, box 123
"Charleston Daily Courier" (Charleston, SC), Volume 61, #19438, April 11, 1863, p. 2, c. 1
"Charleston Daily Courier" (Charleston, SC), Volume 61, #19453, April 29, 1863, p. 2, c. 1
"Charleston Mercury" (Charleston, SC), Volume 82, #11726, April 11, 1863, p. 2, c. 1
"Charleston Mercury" (Charleston, SC), Volume 82, #11734, April 21, 1863, p. 1, c. 2
"Daily Morning News," (Savannah, GA), #87, April 14, 1863, p. 1, c. 2, 3
"Daily Morning News," (Savannah, GA), #88, April 15, 1863, p. 1, c. 1
"Daily Morning News," (Savannah, GA), #89, April 16, 1863, p. 2, c. 2
New York Times, Volume 12, #3606, April 15, 1863, p. 4, c. 1, p. 8, c. 1, 4
Records of General Courts Martial and Courts of Inquiry of the Navy Department, 1799-1867, Court of Inquiry, #3225, May 15, 1863, NARS M-273, roll 2, alphabetical card index 1861-1867
"Report of vessels employed by the U.S. in the Department of the Carolinas which have been lost," (manuscript list), National Archives, Record Group 92, entry 1407, Box 123
Official Records of the Union and Confederate Armies in the War of the Rebellion, (Washington, DC, 1885), Series 1, Volume 14, pp. 3, 280-283, 891
Official Records of the Union and Confederate Armies in the War of the Rebellion, (Washington, DC), Series 1, Volume 53, pp. 4, 5
Official Records of the Union and Confederate Navies in the War of the Rebellion, (Washington, DC, 1902), Series 1, Volume 14, pp. 114-121
List of American-Flag Merchant Vessels that Received Certificates of Enrollment or Registry at the Port of New York 1789-1867, compiled by Forest R. Holdcamper, (U.S. National Archives, Washington, DC, 1968), Special List #22, Volume 2, p. 424
Merchant Steam Vessels of the United States 1790-1868, ("Lytle-Holdcamper List"), edited by C. Bradford Mitchell, (Staten Island, NY, 1975), pp. 84, 264

1863-4-US-SC/GA-7: The Confederate blockade runner *Stonewall Jackson* (formerly the British steamer *Leopard*), Captain W.F. Black, was spotted and fired into by the vessels *Flag* and *Huron* of the Federal blockading squadron while attempting to run into Charleston, South Carolina, on April 12, 1863. She was then run ashore and burned by her crew on what would have been her ninth trip through the blockade. The *Stonewall Jackson*, eight hundred and seventy-two tons, carried several pieces of field artillery, two hundred barrels of saltpeter, forty thousand army shoes, a large assortment of merchandise, and tin, zinc, lead and copper ingots. The steamer was run ashore on Long Island (present day Isle of Palms, South Carolina) about one and a half miles from the Breach Inlet batteries at high tide, and was left almost high and dry with the falling tide. The steamer's machinery and cargo were largely salvaged immediately after the wreck. The *Leopard* was built and engined by Denny and Brothers at Dumbarton, Scotland, in 1858. She had two cylinders of 66"x75" stroke, and sidewheels. The *Leopard's* name, ownership and nationality were changed when she was issued Confederate "Register #4," at Charleston, South Carolina, on February 20, 1863. Like many other blockade runners, the steamer was owned by Fraser, Trenholm and Company. The vessel had one deck, a round stern, a stem head, two masts and sidewheels. The vessel measured 872 (formerly 862) tons, 223'9" in length, 27'1" in breadth, and 14'7" in depth. (Note One: "Lloyd's Register" for 1863/64 lists an iron hulled steamer *Leopard* but shows her as screw propelled. "Lloyd's Register" gives her measurements as 223'x28'16'4" and her tonnage as 734 gross and 499 net. It may or may not have been the same vessel.) (Note Two: Stephen Wise in his book *Lifeline of the Confederacy* gives her tonnage as: 691 gross tons; 824 tons burden; 435 tons register; and 1230 tons displacement. Wise gives her measurements as 22'x27'x14'8" with a draft of 11'. Wise gives the location of the wreck as off Sullivan's Island, South Carolina.) (Note Three: For many years there was a wreck partially exposed at low water near this location, and in 1965 I examined it and tentatively identified it as the *Stonewall Jackson*. That wreck is now entirely buried in the beach near sixth street on the Isle of Palms, South Carolina. A best selling author, who writes adventure novels and dabbles in shipwreck expeditions, claimed to have discovered this wreck in 1980 but his people dug in the wrong area and found only a small piece of worm eaten wood and a tiny bit of coal. I am not mentioning his name because I sincerely like him and would prefer to spare him some embarrassment.) (Note Four: Fraser, Trenholm and Company was headed by George Alfred Trenholm who was later used as the historical basis for Margaret Mitchell's fictional character Rhett Butler in *Gone With The Wind*. Like Rhett's fictional company, Trenholm's company shipped Confederate cotton out of Charleston and war supplies out of Liverpool.)

References for 1863-4-US-SC/GA-7:
Confederate "Register #4," February 20, 1863, (Charleston, SC), National Archives, Record Group 109, Vessel File, S-29-12
"Daily Morning News," (Savannah, GA), Volume 14, #86, April 13, 1863, p. 2, c. 1
"Daily Morning News," (Savannah, GA), Volume 14, #103, May 4, 1863, p. 2, c. 2
"Charleston Daily Courier," (Charleston, SC), Vol. 61, #19439, April 13, 1863, p. 2, c. 2

Treasures of the Confederate Coast

"Charleston Mercury," (Charleston, SC), Volume 82, #11727, April 13, 1863, p. 2, c. 1
Times, (London. England), #24548, May 2, 1863, p. 14, c. 1
Times, (London. England), #24576, June 4, 1863, p. 7, c. 5
Lloyd's Register of British and Foreign Shipping, from 1st July, 1863, to the 30th June, 1864, (London, 1863), entry L-216
"General Map of Charleston Harbor, South Carolina, Showing Rebel Defenses and Obstructions," drawn by E. Willenbucher for the Annual Report of the Secretary of the Navy, (U.S. Coast Survey, 1865)
Official Records of the Union and Confederate Armies in the War of the Rebellion, (Washington, DC, 1885), Series 1, Volume 14, pp. 3, 286
Official Records of the Union and Confederate Navies in the War of the Rebellion, (Washington, DC, 1902), Series 1, Volume 14, pp. 126, 127
Official Records of the Union and Confederate Navies in the War of the Rebellion, (Washington, DC, 1922), Series 2, Volume 3, p. 874
"Vessel Papers" (manuscript records), United States National Archives, Washington, DC, Record Group 109, Microfilm roll 19, file L-15, frames 0419-0428; Microfilm roll 27, M909, file S-29, frames 2195-2245
Lifeline of the Confederacy: Blockade Running During the Civil War, by Stephen R. Wise, (University of South Carolina, Columbia, SC, 1983), pp. 585, 586
Charleston's Maritime Heritage 1670-1865, by P.C. Coker III, (CokerCraft Press, Charleston, SC, 1987), pp. 282, 303
The Blockade Runners, by Dave Horner, (Florida Classics Library, Port Salerno, FL, 1992), Chapter 14, pp. 130, 209-210

1863-4-US-SC/GA-8: The Savannah "Daily Morning News" of April 17, 1863, reported a rumor that a "Yankee gunboat prowling" in the neighborhood of Fort McAllister (on the Ogeechee River in Georgia) had been sunk.

Reference for 1863-4-US-SC/GA-8:
"Daily Morning News," (Savannah, GA), #90, April 17, 1863, p. 2, c. 3

1863-4-US-SC/GA-9: The "Charleston Mercury" of April 27, 1863, reported that the blockade running sloop *Eagle*, Captain Brenon, laden with upland cotton, tobacco, etc., bound from Savannah to Nassau, was spotted while passing Cabbage Island, Georgia. The Yankee signal corps sent up rockets and thereby alerted the blockade fleet. A three masted "Yankee gunboat" chased the *Eagle* ashore two miles inside of Warsaw Sound, Georgia. The *Eagle's* crew took what personal effects they could, scuttled her and set her afire before abandoning her "to prevent her capture by the blockaders." She was owned by Mr. Marcus Cohen of Savannah and Mr. A.M. Cohen of Waresboroh (sic) and, including her cargo, was valued at $5,000.

References for 1863-4-US-SC/GA-9:
"Charleston Mercury" (Charleston, SC), Volume 82, #11739, April 27, 1863, p. 2, c. 1
Times, (London. England), #24556, May 6, 1863, p. 11, c. 5

1863-4-US-SC/GA-10: A schooner identified only as a United States Revenue cutter (or schooner) which had been lying with an armed bark in close proximity to Otter Island, South Carolina, at the mouth of the Combahee and Ashepoo Rivers, was reported as sunk by a Confederate torpedo (mine) set off under the direction of Captain Stephan Elliott, Jr., C.S.A., on April 23, 1863. Four lives were reported to have been lost on the schooner which was entirely sunk. (Note: There was no indication as to whether or not any government money was aboard the vessel.)

References for 1863-4-US-SC/GA-10:
"Charleston Mercury" (Charleston, SC), Volume 82, #11740, April 28, 1863, p. 2, c. 1
"Daily Morning News," (Savannah, GA), #100, April 30, 1863, p. 2, c. 1

1863-4-US-SC/GA-11: The schooners *George Chisolm*, Captain Johnston, and *Antoinette*, along with several others, were reported destroyed by the Federals at Murray's Inlet, South Carolina, on April 27, 1863. "One or more" of the vessels were described as "lately arrived" through the blockade from Havana. Some of the vessels were said to have been loaded with cotton. Their position was described as "high up in the Inlet, out of range of a steamer." (Note One: This report was later discredited as exaggerated, and it was said that only the *Gold Linen* was destroyed. For more of that vessel see entry 1863-4-US-SC/GA-12 of this book.) (Note Two: See entry 1863-12-US-SC/GA-2 of this book for the December 8, 1863, loss of the *Antoinette*.)

References for 1863-4-US-SC/GA-11:
"Charleston Daily Courier," (Charleston, SC), Volume 61, #19454, April 30, 1863, p. 1, c. 2
"Charleston Daily Courier," (Charleston, SC), Volume 61, #19455, May 1, 1863, p. 2, c. 2
"Daily Morning News," (Savannah, GA), #103, May 4, 1863, p. 2, c. 2
Official Records of the Union and Confederate Armies in the War of the Rebellion, (Washington, DC, 1885), Series 1, Volume 14, pp. 3, 286

1863-4-US-SC/GA-12: The large English schooner *Golden Liner* (or *Gold Linen*), of Halifax, just arrived and still loaded with a valuable cargo of flour, brandy, sugar and coffee, was captured and burned by a Federal expedition from the United States steamer *Monticello* and the United States schooner *Matthew Vassar* on April 27, 1863. The destruction was variously described as carried out "at" or "inside of" Murrell's Inlet, South Carolina. One report stated that the Federal force was headed by Acting master L.A. Brown, while another indicated it was headed by Lt. Braine of the *Monticello*. (Note One: David Stick in his book *Graveyard of the Atlantic*, incorrectly shows the *Golden Liner* as lost in the Cape Fear River.) (Note Two: See also entry 1863-4-US-SC/GA-11 of this book.)

References for 1863-4-US-SC/GA-12:
"Charleston Daily Courier," (Charleston, SC), Volume 61, #19455, May 1, 1863, p. 2, c. 2
Official Records of the Union and Confederate Armies in the War of the Rebellion, (Washington, DC, 1885), Series 1, Volume 14, pp. 3, 286
Official Records of the Union and Confederate Navies in the War of the Rebellion, (Washington, DC, 1898), Series 1, Volume 8, pp. 828, 829
Official Records of the Union and Confederate Navies in the War of the Rebellion, (Washington, DC, 1902), Series 1, Volume 14, p. 191
Graveyard of the Atlantic: Shipwrecks of the North Carolina Coast, by David Stick (University of North Carolina Press, Chapel Hill, NC, 1952), p. 247
History of Georgetown County, South Carolina, by George C. Rogers, (Columbia, South Carolina, 1970), p. 408
Shipwrecks of the Civil War: The Encyclopedia of Union and Confederate Naval Losses, by Donald Shomette, (Washington, DC, 1973), pp. 427, 428

1863-4-US-SC/GA-13: On April 28, 1863, a steamer and a schooner from the Federal fleet employed in the blockade of Little River anchored off Magnolia Beach, South Carolina, and landed a party of men, who marched across the beach and burned a summer house belonging to the Oaks Plantation. The Federal forces also burned a schooner loaded with salt which was lying in the creek. The schooner was owned by Messrs. Comins and Edwards of Augusta, Georgia.

Reference for 1863-4-US-SC/GA-13:
"Daily Morning News," (Savannah, GA), #107, May 8, 1863, p. 2, c. 3

1863-4-US-SC/GAx-1: The steamer *Barrosa* (or *Berosa*), Captain W.F. Adair, was abandoned in the Gulf Stream, latitude 29°50' North, longitude 79°50' West, after it started taking on water and all pumping and bailing failed. Captain Adair, Mr. J.W. Elder, one of the owners, Mr. S. Crib, mate, and Messrs. Williamson, Dye and Clear, engineers, with one of the firemen, arrived in Charleston, on April 10, 1863, from the Edisto, by the Savannah Railroad, under an escort from Lt. Col. Miller's Battalion, by whom they were taken in custody on their reaching Governor Aiken's place on Pon Pon (Edisto). The *Barrosa* had sailed from St. Mary's, Georgia, on April 8, 1863. [Note: This entry has been placed under South Carolina/Georgia, because it can also be argued, that even though the stated latitude/longitude of her loss would place her south and east of St. Augustine, that she might actually be in the area covered by this volume. Remember, her people made shore in South Carolina, and an account of their safe arrival at Charleston was published in the Charleston papers less than two days after she had reportedly sailed from St. Mary's, Georgia, which seems odd (but not impossible) if she did indeed wreck off Florida.]

References for 1863-4-US-SC/GAx-1:
"Daily Morning News," (Savannah, GA), Vol. 14, #89, April 16, 1863, p. 2, c. 1
Official Records of the Union and Confederate Navies in the War of the Rebellion, (Washington, DC, 1902), Series 1, Volume 14, pp. 161, 164
Warships of the Civil War Navies, by Paul H. Silverstone, (Naval Institute Press, Annapolis, MD, 1989), p. 239

1863-4-US-x-1: The United States submarine *Alligator* was lost in a storm at sea on April 2, 1863. The *Alligator* had left Newport News, Virginia, under tow of the *U.S.S. Sumter* on April 1, 1863, and was bound to Port Royal, South Carolina, when the vessels got into a storm and the steamer was forced to cut the submarine loose. The submarine had been intended to be used to discover and explode mines in preparation for an assault on Charleston. The assault took place on April 7, 1863, and failed largely due to the Confederate mines. The *Alligator* was designed by the French inventor Brutus de Villeroy and launched by Neafie and Levy, Philadelphia, Pennsylvania, on April 30, 1862, under a subcontract from Martin Thomas. The vessel was completed in June of 1862. She was said to be about 30' long and 6' or 8' in diameter. "It was made of iron, with the upper part pierced for small circular plates of glass, for light, and in it were several water tight compartments." It had originally been fitted with sixteen paddles protruding from the sides to be worked by men inside, but on July 3, 1862, she was ordered to Washington Navy Yard to have her folding oars replaced by a propeller which was powered by a hand crank. It was said to be capable of seven knots. "The *Alligator* was to have been manned by sixteen men, besides one in submarine armor, who was the explorer, and a captain who was to steer the craft. An air pump in the center of the machine, to which were attached two air tubes, attached to floats, was to furnish air to the occupants, the machine being of course air tight. The entrance to it was through a man-hole at one end, which was covered with an iron plate, with leather packing." She was to have been submerged by the flooding of compartments. The *Alligator* was also described as a "semi-submarine boat," 46' (or 47') long and 4'6" in diameter, with a crew of seventeen. (Note: This entry is included because of the possibility that the loss actually took place in the waters covered by this book.)

References for 1863-4-US-x-1:
Official Records of the Union and Confederate Navies in the War of the Rebellion, (Washington, 1899), Series 1, Volume 8, p. 636
Official Records of the Union and Confederate Navies in the War of the Rebellion, (Washington, DC, 1921), Series 2, Volume 1, p. 32
Dictionary of American Naval Fighting Ships, (Washington, DC, 1959), Volume 1, p. 34
Civil War Naval Chronology 1861-1865, compiled by Navy History Division, Navy Department, (Washington, DC, 1971), Volume 3, p. 54, paragraph 26

1863-5-US-NC-1: The schooner *Sea Bird*, with a cargo of coal for the United States Navy, was burned by the Confederates on May 22, 1863, in the river just below Wilkinson's Point, about thirty miles below New Berne, North Carolina. The burning schooner was discovered by the United States army steamer *Allison*. The *Allison* captured two men from men from "Whitford's band of guerrillas," and a schooner that was found near by. The men from the *Allison* went ahead and scuttled the *Sea Bird*.

References for 1863-5-US-NC-1:
Official Records of the Union and Confederate Navies in the War of the Rebellion, (Washington, DC, 1899), Series 1, Volume 9, pp. 38, 39, 51, 124

1863-5-US-SC/GA-1: On May 12, 1863, the United States steamer *Monticello* shelled five schooners while they were aground in Murrell's Inlet, South Carolina, setting one on fire and damaging the others.

References for 1863-5-US-SC/GA-1:
Official Records of the Union and Confederate Armies in the War of the Rebellion, (Washington, DC, 1902), Series 1, Volume 14, pp. 286-287
History of Georgetown County, South Carolina, by George C. Rogers, (Columbia, South Carolina, 1970), p. 408

1863-5-US-SC/GA-2: The small English propeller steamer *Norseman* (also shown as the *Norman* or *Norsman*), Captain Applebee (or Pat

Rooney), bound from Charleston with 250 bales of cotton, was sunk in about twelve feet of water off of Long Island (Isle of Palms, South Carolina), after running upon a submerged wreck ("supposed to be the wreck of the *Georgiana*") at high tide, about 10:00 p.m. on May 19, 1863. She sank in about fifteen minutes. Her deck load of cotton floated ashore and was saved. She had made one previous successful run through the blockade. The *Norseman* was a small vessel of 49 (or 197) tons. The little steamer had three masts, was schooner rigged and drew nine feet of water. (Note One: There is some contemporary evidence that she may have had treasure hidden under her cargo of cotton. If so, it was not recovered due to the shifting sands which quickly filled the wreck.) (Note Two: In 1967, while using a rented plane to search for shipwrecks from the air, I spotted a wreck about one half mile off the beach near 30th street on the Isle of Palms, South Carolina, which I later tentatively identified as being the wreck of the *Norseman*. The wreck was afterwards dived upon by two of my company's employees, Drew Ruddy and Jim Batey, who confirmed that it was the wreck of an iron hulled steamer, but no actual salvage was performed by myself or my company which was called Shipwrecks Inc.) (Note Three: For more on the wreck of the *Georgiana* see entry 1863-3-US-SC/GA-2 in this list and see Chapter Three and Appendix C in this book.)

References for 1863-5-US-SC/GA-2:

"Charleston Daily Courier," (Charleston, SC), Volume 61, #19473, May 22, p. 1, c. 2
"Charleston Mercury," (Charleston, SC), Volume 82, #11752, May 12, 1863, p. 2, c. 1
"Charleston Mercury," (Charleston, SC), Volume 82, #11754, May 14, 1863, p. 2, c. 1
"Charleston Mercury," (Charleston, SC), Volume 82, #11761, May 22, 1863, p. 2, c. 1
Times, (London. England), #24580, June 9, 1863, p. 14, c. 3
"Vessel Papers" (manuscript records), United States National Archives, Washington, DC, Record Group 109, file N-22
Official Records of the Union and Confederate Navies in the War of the Rebellion, (Washington, DC, 1895), Series 1, Volume 2, pp. 199, 222
Official Records of the Union and Confederate Navies in the War of the Rebellion, (Washington, DC, 1899), Series 1, Volume 9, pp. 80, 81, 250
Official Records of the Union and Confederate Navies in the War of the Rebellion, (Washington, DC, 1901), Series 1, Volume 13, pp. 754, 755
Official Records of the Union and Confederate Navies in the War of the Rebellion, (Washington, DC, 1922), Series 2, Volume 3, p. 874
Lifeline of the Confederacy: Blockade Running During the Civil War, by Stephen R. Wise, (University of South Carolina, Columbia, SC, 1983), p. 600
Charleston's Maritime Heritage 1670-1865, by P.C. Coker III, (CokerCraft Press, Charleston, SC, 1987), p. 214

1863-5-US-SC/GA-3: The London *Times* reported that on May 20, 1863, a large steamer was discovered by the *U.S.S. Powhatan*, as it was trying to escape from Charleston, South Carolina, via the North Channel. The steamer turned to try to run back to Charleston, but was cut off by the Federal fleet before she could get back inside the Charleston bar. "The Anglo-rebel was bored through and through (by the heavy Federal cannon fire) and sunk in about eight fathoms of water. Nothing but her topmasts were visible the next morning at daylight. She was a very large steamer, loaded with an immense cargo of cotton and tobacco. Her name was not ascertained, nor the fate of her officers and crew. They were probably drowned, going down with the ship, as she went under very suddenly."

Reference for 1863-5-US-SC/GA-3:
Times, (London. England), #24586, June 16, 1863, p. 10, c. 2

1863-5-US-SC/GA-4: A manuscript list prepared at Charleston, South Carolina, on August 23, 1866, showed the *Thomas F. Secor* (or *T.F. Secor*), chartered by the United States, as having burned at Seabrook's Landing on Hilton Head Island, South Carolina, in May, 1863. The steamer *Thomas F. Secor* had a wood hull and was 210 tons. The vessel was built at New York in 1846 and received a certificate of steam enrollment at that port on June 8, 1846. The *Thomas F. Secor's* first home port was New York, New York.

References for 1863-5-US-SC/GA-4:
"Report of vessels employed by the U.S. in the Department of the Carolinas which have been lost," (manuscript list), National Archives, Record Group 92, entry 1407, Box 123
Merchant Steam Vessels of the United States 1807-1868, ("Lytle List"), by William M. Lytle, (Mystic, CT, 1952), p. 183
List of American-Flag Merchant Vessels that Received Certificates of Enrollment or Registry at the Port of New York 1789-1867, compiled by Forest R. Holdcamper, (U.S. National Archives, Washington, DC, 1968), Special List #22, Volume 2, p. 667

1863-6-US-NC-1: The *U.S.S. Sumter* (or *Sumpter*), 464 tons, was sunk eight and one half miles south south east from the lighthouse on Smith Island, North Carolina, in a collision with the U.S. Army transport steamer *General Meigs* on June 24, 1863. The transport escaped unharmed. No lives were lost on either vessel. The *Sumter* was a 4th rate, screw steamer. She had formerly been named *Atlanta* and had been purchased in 1859 for the Paraguay Expedition. The *Sumter* had a wood hull and was armed with four 32-pounder 27 hundredweight guns and one 20-pounder Parrott rifle. Her position was given as "Smith's Island Light bearing WNW 8 or 9 miles distant." She was lost in seven fathoms of water. The "paymasters saved nothing."

References for 1863-6-US-NC-1:
Records of General Courts Martial and Courts of Inquiry of the Navy Department, 1799-1867, General Court Marshal #3267, June 30, 1863, NARS M-273, roll 2, alphabetical card index 1861-1867
Official Records of the Union and Confederate Navies in the War of the Rebellion, (Washington, DC, 1899), Series 1, Volume 9, pp. 89, 90
Official Records of the Union and Confederate Navies in the War of the Rebellion, (Washington, DC, 1921), Series 2, Volume 1, p. 216

1863-6-US-SC/GA-1: The Federals destroyed the pontoon bridge at Combahee Ferry, South Carolina, on June 2, 1863, and set fire to many dwellings on the river banks.

References for 1863-6-US-SC/GA-1:
"Charleston Mercury," (Charleston, SC), Volume 82, #11771, June 3, 1863, p. 2, c. 1
"Charleston Mercury," (Charleston, SC), Volume 82, #11785, June 19, 1863, p. 1, c. 2, 3
"Charleston Mercury," (Charleston, SC), Volume 82, #11797, July 3, 1863, p. 1, c. 1

Treasures of the Confederate Coast

1863-6-US-SC/GA-2: The Confederate screw steamer *Stono* (ex-United States gunboat *Isaac P. Smith*) was attempting to run the blockade with a load of cotton when she was chased back over the Charleston Bar by the United States gunboat *Wissahicken* and wrecked on Bowman's Jetty near Fort Moultrie on Sullivan's Island, South Carolina, on June 5, 1863. The vessel had been built at Brooklyn, New York, in 1861 by Lawrence and Foulkes, master builders, for John Smith and David Hamilton, of Cocksackie, equal partners. The steamer's first home port was New York, New York. The *Isaac Smith* was sold to the Federal Navy at New York on September 9, 1861. On January 30, 1863, the *Isaac Smith* was captured by the Confederates in the Stono River and renamed. As a United States gunboat the steamer had carried a complement of fifty-six men and was armed with one 30-pounder and eight 8-inch guns. The *Stono* was a screw steamer (Swiftsure propeller, beam engine) with a square stern, round tuck, no galleries, no figure head, one deck and no masts. The vessel measured 453 26/95 tons, 171'6" in length, 31'4" in breadth, 9' in depth of hold, and 9' (7') draft. (Note One: The *Stono's* passengers included Felix Senac and his family as well as Alfred Glover Trenholm. Felix was a Confederate Navy officer who was on his way to Europe where he was to serve a conduit for paying the Confederate secret agents. Alfred and his father, George Alfred Trenholm, were later used by Margaret Mitchell as models for her fictional character Rhett Butler in *Gone With The Wind*.) (Note Two: I located and identified the wreck of the *Stono* in 1965 with the help of Ron A. Gibbs of the United States National Park Service. The wreck was worked in the late 1980's by Howard Tower, a very talented amateur underwater archeologist from Jacksonville, Florida.) (Note Three: The *Official Records of the War of Rebellion* incorrectly shows the *Stono* as "burned by the Confederates at the evacuation of Charleston in 1865.")

References for 1863-6-US-SC/GA-2:

"Permanent Enrollment #24," (New York, NY), April 5, 1861, National Archives, Record Group 41
"Charleston Daily Courier," (Charleston, SC), #19382, February 3, 1863, p. 2, c. 2
"Charleston Daily Courier," (Charleston, SC), #19386, February 7, 1863, p. 1, c. 2
"Charleston Mercury," (Charleston, SC), Volume 82, #11669, January 31, 1863, p. 2, c. 1
"Charleston Mercury," (Charleston, SC), Volume 82, #11670, February 2, 1863, p. 2, c. 1
"Charleston Mercury," (Charleston, SC), Volume 82, #11672, February 4, 1863, p. 1, c. 1
"Charleston Mercury," (Charleston, SC), Volume 82, #11775, June 8, 1863, p. 2, c. 1
"Charleston Mercury," (Charleston, SC), Volume 82, #11776, June 9, 1863, p. 1, c. 1
"Daily Morning News," (Savannah, GA), June 9, 1863, p. 2, c. 2
"Vessel Papers" (manuscript records), United States National Archives, Washington, DC, Record Group 109, files I-7, I-44, S-77
History of the Confederate States Navy From its Organization to the Surrender of its Last Vessel, by J. Thomas Scharf, (New York, New York, 1887), pp. 670, 703n
Official Records of the Union and Confederate Navies in the War of the Rebellion, (Washington, DC, 1902), Series 1, Volume 14, pp. 190, 219, 252, 494
Official Records of the Union and Confederate Navies in the War of the Rebellion, (Washington, DC, 1921), Series 2, Volume 1, pp. 109, 267

The "Real Rhett Butler" & Other Revelations

Merchant Steam Vessels of the United States 1807-1868, ("Lytle List"), by William M. Lytle, (Mystic, CT, 1952), p. 91
Saga of Felix Senac, by Regina Rapier, (Atlanta, Georgia, 1972), p. 109
Shipwrecks of the Civil War: The Encyclopedia of Union and Confederate Naval Losses, by Donald Shomette, (Washington, DC, 1973), pp. 370, 371
Lifeline of the Confederacy: Blockade Running During the Civil War, by Stephen R. Wise, (University of South Carolina, Columbia, SC, 1983), p. 617
Wreck of the Georgiana, Mystery Ship of the Confederacy, by Edward Lee Spence, (prepublication copy, Charleston, South Carolina, 1989), Appendix E
Charleston's Maritime Heritage 1670-1865, by P.C. Coker III, (CokerCraft Press, Charleston, SC, 1987), pp. 223, 303
Warships of the Civil War Navies, by Paul H. Silverstone, (Naval Institute Press, Annapolis, MD, 1989), pp. 92, 238

1863-6-US-SC/GA-3: The bark *Whistling Wind* (or *Windward*), Captain Thomas Butler, bound from Philadelphia to New Orleans, with a cargo of coal, was captured and burned on June 6, 1863, east of Cape Romain, South Carolina, by Lieutenant Charles W. Read, commanding the Confederate steamer *Clarence*. Lt. Read reported the bark as "insured by the Federal government for $14,000. Read took off the vessel's chronometer and papers. Lt. Read recorded in the *Clarence's* log that he captured the bark in latitude 33°39' North, longitude 71°29' West. The *Whistling Wind* was a full model bark and was shown in "American Lloyd's" of 1858 as owned by C.E. Peters. She was rated A-2 for insurance purposes measured 349 tons (or 350), drew twelve feet of water. She was built in 1855 at Bluehill, Maine, of mixed woods and was iron fastened. She had one deck with a deck cabin and had been surveyed in 1858. The *Whistling Wind* was issued a certificate of register at the port of New York on April 18, 1863.

References for 1863-6-US-SC/GA-3:
New York Marine Register: or American Lloyd's, (New York, New York, 1858/59), p. 112, #1469
Official Records of the Union and Confederate Navies in the War of the Rebellion, (Washington, DC, 1895), Series 1, Volume 2, pp. 324, 331, 332, 354, 655
List of American-Flag Merchant Vessels that Received Certificates of Enrollment or Registry at the Port of New York 1789-1867, compiled by Forest R. Holdcamper, (U.S. National Archives, Washington, DC, 1968), Special List #22, Volume 2, p. 725
Shipwrecks of the Civil War: The Encyclopedia of Union and Confederate Naval Losses, by Donald Shomette, (Washington, DC, 1973), p. 221

1863-6-US-SC/GA-4: The sidewheel steamer *Ruby*, Captain Peat, bound from Nassau, went ashore on the breakers of Folly Island, South Carolina, while attempting to run the Federal blockade on June 10, 1863. (Note One: A large portion of the *Ruby's* cargo was thrown overboard and everything possible was done to get her off, but without success. Captain Peat set the steamer on fire and she was abandoned and afterwards blew up. The Federal forces inhumanely fired grape and canister at the crew while they were trying to wade to shore in neck deep water. One man was lost.) (Note Two: The *Ruby*, 400 tons, belonged to a Manchester firm and carried a general cargo with some government property. The steamer's crew was only able to save the mails she was carrying.

Treasures of the Confederate Coast

Portions of the steamer and her cargo were scavenged by the Federal troops from Morris Island.) (Note Three: This was the *Ruby's* tenth try at running the blockade. She had made eight previous successful runs through the blockade and had been turned back once.) (Note Four: Donald Shomette in his book *Shipwrecks of the Civil War* states the possibility that this *Ruby* may have been the 1391 ton steamer built by Jones and Quiggins for the Confederate government. That was definitely not case as the vessel built by Jones and Quiggins was not even completed until early 1865. Stephen Wise in his book *Lifeline of the Confederacy* shows her as built by Henderson and Company at Renfrew, Scotland, in 1854. Wise gives her dimensions as 177.4'x17.1'x8.3'. The 1865 vessel was 261'x33'x9'.) (Note Five: Jim Batey and I found the remains of the *Ruby's* iron hull at the entrance to Lighthouse Inlet in 1966.) (Note Six: The Federals at first reported the wreck as that of the *Havelock*. That steamer was lost near Fort Fisher, North Carolina, on December 11, 1863. For more on the *Havelock's* destruction, please see entry 1863-12-US-NC-3.)

References for 1863-6-US-SC/GA-4:
"Charleston Daily Courier," (Charleston, SC), Volume 61, #19491, June 12, 1863, p. 1, c. 2
"Charleston Mercury," (Charleston, SC), Volume 82, #11779, June 12, 1863, p. 2, c. 1
"Daily Morning News," (Savannah, GA), #129, June 13, 1863, p. 2, c. 3
Vessel log of the *U.S.S. James Adger*, June 11, 1863, National Archives, Record Group 24
"Vessel Papers" (manuscript records), United States National Archives, Washington, DC, Record Group 109, file R-19
Official Records of the Union and Confederate Navies in the War of the Rebellion, (Washington, DC, 1902), Series 1, Volume 14, pp. 252-254, 301, 302
Official Records of the Union and Confederate Navies in the War of the Rebellion, (Washington, DC, 1922), Series 2, Volume 3, p. 874
Shipwrecks of the Civil War: The Encyclopedia of Union and Confederate Naval Losses, by Donald Shomette, (Washington, DC, 1973), pp. 459, 460
Lifeline of the Confederacy: Blockade Running During the Civil War, by Stephen R. Wise, (University of South Carolina, Columbia, SC, 1983), pp. 221, 611
Charleston's Maritime Heritage 1670-1865, by P.C. Coker III, (CokerCraft Press, Charleston, SC, 1987), p. 303
Warships of the Civil War Navies, by Paul H. Silverstone, (Naval Institute Press, Annapolis, MD, 1989), p. 221
The Blockade Runners, by Dave Horner, (Florida Classics Library, Port Salerno, FL, 1992), Chapter 14, pp. 210-211

1863-6-US-SC/GA-5: The Confederate iron clad ram *Atlanta* (ex British steamer *Fingal*), Commander Webb, grounded on a shoal in the Wilmington River off Cabbage Island, Georgia, on June 17, 1863. (Note One: Contemporary Savannah newspaper accounts reported the *Atlanta* as riddled by the heavy shot of the Federal monitors and even stated that she was sunk, wrecked and nearly demolished. This was not the case, as the ram actually suffered relatively little damage, but she was surrendered to the Federals who got her off and towed her to New York for repairs.) (Note Two: The *Atlanta* was an iron casemated ram armed with two 7-inch and two 6.4-inch Brooke rifles. The vessel was 204' long and 41' wide.)

References for 1863-6-US-SC/GA-5:

The "Real Rhett Butler" & Other Revelations

"Charleston Daily Courier," (Charleston, SC), Volume 61, #19652, December 29, 1863, p. 1, c. 5, 6
"Charleston Mercury," (Charleston, SC), Volume 82, #11787, June 22, 1863, p. 2, c. 1
"Daily Morning News," (Savannah, GA), June 18, 1863, p. 1, c. 1, p. 2, c. 2
"Daily Morning News," (Savannah, GA), June 20, 1863, p. 2, c. 2
"Daily Morning News," (Savannah, GA), June 24, 1863, p. 1, c. 1
"Daily Morning News," (Savannah, GA), June 27, 1863, p. 1, c. 1, 2
"Daily Morning News," (Savannah, GA), July 3, 1863, p. 1, c. 1, p. 2, c. 3
"Daily Morning News," (Savannah, GA), September 29, 1863, p. 2, c. 3
Times, (London. England), #24603, July 6, 1863, p. 9, c. 2
Confederate Military History, edited by General Clement A. Evans, (Confederate Publishing Co., Atlanta, GA, 1899), Volume 12, pp. 72, 73
Official Records of the Union and Confederate Navies in the War of the Rebellion, (Washington, DC, 1902), Series 1, Volume 14, pp. 290-292
Official Records of the Union and Confederate Navies in the War of the Rebellion, (Washington, DC, 1921), Series 2, Volume 1, p. 248
Georgia Historical Quarterly, (Savannah, 1934), Volume 18, pp. 162, 163

1863-6x-US-SC/GA-1: The London *Times* of July 6, 1863, reported that several vessels which had "recently" been attempting to run the blockade in South Carolina had been sunk by the broadsides of the Federal cruisers. The "Times" article also said that the officers of the blockading squadron were intending to sink all blockade runners rather than capture them, due to the frauds committed in the prize courts, whereby the captors were deprived of their prize money.

Reference for 1863-6x-US-SC/GA-1:
Times, (London, England), #20603, July 6, 1893, p. 9, c. 2

1863-7-US-NC-1: The blockade running steamer *Kate*, Captain Stubbs, was chased on shore at the south end of Smith's Island, North Carolina, on July 12, 1863, by the *U.S.S. Penobscot*. The *Kate* carried an assorted cargo of merchandise and was burned by the Federals who also fired 9" and 11" shells through her. (Note Two: Early reports stated that two binnacles complete with compasses, one parallel rule, one ratchet brace, two sea water hydrometers and some papers were the only items saved, but the vessel was floated free by the Confederates on July 31, 1863, who had apparently also stripped her of her cargo and everything else that could be removed. The vessel was seized the following day by the Federal gunboats *Mount Vernon*, *James Adger*, *Iroquois* and *Niphon*.) [Note One: Approximately three months old, this *Kate* was built and engined by T.&W. Dudgeon, at London, England in 1863 and was 344 tons burden. Her tonnage is also given as 477 gross and 367 net. She had two engine cylinders of 26" with a 21" stroke, and was listed as 120 h.p. The *Kate* had twin propellers, one on each side of the stern post clear of her rudder post. She was built entirely of iron, round, full bottom, very sharp forward, small shield for figurehead, one funnel, telescope fashion, and two masts, schooner-rigged, and hinged so as to lower down. She had a house which ran nearly her length and went entirely across from side to side. The *Kate* had four bulkheads, a bridge amidships, and was steered by a large wheel, placed well forward; there was also an auxiliary wheel aft. Her dimensions were described as 165' in length, 22.6' (or 22') in breadth, 13'6" (or 13') in depth of hold, drew 5'4" forward and 7'2" aft. This blockade runner was registered to E. James and was owned by Beech and Root and Company. She was making her fourth attempt to run the blockade (the previous three having been successful) and was bound from Nassau to Charleston with a general cargo (liquors, medicines, etc.).] [Note Three: Several modern sources show her name as the *Kate (2nd)* or *Kate II*, but that was probably done just to differentiate her from other vessels named *Kate* which were lost in North Carolina waters during the Civil War.]

References for 1863-7-US-NC-1:
Lloyd's Register of British and Foreign Shipping, from 1st July, 1863, to the 30th June, 1864, (London, 1863), entry K-20
Official Records of the Union and Confederate Navies in the War of the Rebellion, (Washington, DC, 1899), Series 1, Volume 9, pp. 120-123, 142-144, 152, 166, 167, 193, 250, 301, 779, 783
The Navy in the Civil War, (Charles Scribner's Sons, New York, NY, 1903), Volume 1 ("The Blockade and the Cruisers" by James Russell Soley), p. 162
Graveyard of the Atlantic: Shipwrecks of the North Carolina Coast, by David Stick (University of North Carolina Press, Chapel Hill, NC, 1952), p. 247
A Chart of Wrecks of Vessels Sunk or Captured Near Wilmington, NC, Circa 1861-65, compiled by Charles H. Foard, (Wilmington, North Carolina, 1962)
An Oceanographic Atlas of the Carolina Continental Margin, by J.G. Newton, (Duke University Marine Laboratory, Beaufort, NC, 1971), p. 17 chart symbol #41, p. 20 entry #41
Lifeline of the Confederacy: Blockade Running During the Civil War, by Stephen R. Wise, (University Microfilms International, 1983), p. 582

1863-7-US-NC-2: A squad of Yankees under the command of Lieutenant William Banta, Jr. (USA), boarded the steamboat *Colonel Hill* and burned it. (Note: The original report wasn't clear, but the destruction appears to have taken place on July 20, 1863, in the Tar River outside of Tarboro, North Carolina, and by the bridge to Hamilton.)

Reference for 1863-7-US-NC-2:
Official Records of the Union and Confederate Navies in the War of the Rebellion, (Washington, DC, 1889), Series 1, Volume 27, Part 2, p. 973

1863-7-US-NC-3: A squad of Yankees under the command of Captain Emory Cummings, boarded the steamboat *"Governor _____ "* and burned it. (Note: The original report wasn't clear, but the destruction appears to have taken place on July 20, 1863, in the Tar River outside of Tarboro, North Carolina, and by the bridge to Hamilton.)

Reference for 1863-7-US-NC-3:
Official Records of the Union and Confederate Navies in the War of the Rebellion, (Washington, DC, 1889), Series 1, Volume 27, Part 2, p. 973

1863-7-US-NC-4: A report from Bermuda dated July 21, 1863, stated that a half a million dollars in silver bars had been captured by the Confederate privateer *Florida* and transferred to the blockade runner *Robert E. Lee* for the purpose of running it into Wilmington, North Carolina. (Note One: Half a million dollars in silver would have weighed 41,666 troy ounces, which is over seventeen troy tons.) (Note Two: For another mention of the *Robert E. Lee* carrying treasure see entry 1863-11-US-NC-2.)

Reference for 1863-7-US-NC-4:
Times, (London. England), #24636, August 13, 1863, p. 10, c. 1

1863-7-US-SC/GA-1: The small, wood burning, United States Army steamer *Governor Milton*, (ex-*G.W. Bird*), was accidentally run onto "the spiles" (pilings), while retreating down the Edisto River, after a short engagement with the Confederate battery at Wiltown Bluff, South Carolina, on July 10, 1863. Her assistant engineer, Mr. Mills, was killed. The steamer *John Adams* attempted to get her off but failed, and she was set on fire by her own crew to prevent her from falling into the hands of the Confederates. (Note One: The piles had been placed as obstructions by the Confederates, and were located just down river from the bluff. Subsequent Federal reports stated that her guns were burned with the boat, but in reality, the Confederates took two brass rifled 6-pounder field pieces with carriages, etc. from the wreck. The Confederates reported the salvaged guns as "uninjured and in good order.") (Note Two: This steamer had been previously captured by the United States from the Confederates in Florida. That capture was made on October 7, 1862, by a Federal force commanded by Lieutenant George W. Bacon, in a small creek above Hawkinsville while her "engineer and mate, then in charge, were asleep." She was in poor condition when captured and was valued at only $2,000. She was immediately sent to Beaufort, South Carolina, to have her machinery repaired. She was described as "a little tug.") (Note Three: Some reports give the date of loss as February 10, 1863, so this vessel has been briefly mentioned under *SL Code* 1863-2x-US-SC/GA-1.) (Note Four: She was 68 tons and measured 85'x20'x4'8". She was probably the sidewheel steamer *George M. Bird*, 75 tons, which was built at Covington, Florida, in 1858. That vessel was originally home ported at Cedar Keys, Florida, but her certificate of registry or enrollment was abandoned in 1860.)

References for 1863-7-US-SC/GA-1:
"Charleston Mercury," (Charleston, SC), Volume 83, #11805, July 13, 1863, p. 2, c. 3
"Report of vessels employed by the U.S. in the Department of the Carolinas which have been lost," (manuscript list), National Archives, Record Group 92, entry 1407, Box 123
Official Records of the Union and Confederate Armies in the War of the Rebellion, (Washington, DC, 1885), Series 1, Volume 14, pp. 131, 136, 137
Official Records of the Union and Confederate Armies in the War of the Rebellion, (Washington, DC, 1890), Series 1, Volume 28, pp. 194-199
Official Records of the Union and Confederate Navies in the War of the Rebellion, (Washington, DC, 1901), Series 1, Volume 13, pp. 359-361, 364, 366, 371
Merchant Steam Vessels of the United States 1790-1868, ("Lytle-Holdcamper List"), edited by C. Bradford Mitchell, (Staten Island, New York, 1975), p. 84
Warships of the Civil War Navies, by Paul H. Silverstone, (Naval Institute Press, Annapolis, MD, 1989), p. 236

Treasures of the Confederate Coast

1863-7-US-SC/GA-2: The Confederate steam scow *Gabriel Manigault*, was struck and burned by some of the Federal shells, while lying at a partially constructed battery at Vincent's Creek, between Morris Island and James Island, South Carolina, on July 12, 1863.

References for 1863-7-US-SC/GA-2:
"Charleston Mercury," (Charleston, SC), Volume 83, #11806, July 14, 1863, p. 2, c. 1
"Charleston Mercury," (Charleston, SC), Volume 83, #11826, August 6, 1863, p. 2, c. 1
"Charleston Mercury," (Charleston, SC), Volume 83, #11831, August 12, 1863, p. 2, c. 1
Official Records of the Union and Confederate Armies in the War of the Rebellion, (Washington, DC, 1890), Series 1, Volume 28, Part 1, pp. 371, 534, 546, 577, 594
Official Records of the Union and Confederate Navies in the War of the Rebellion, (Washington, DC, 1902), Series 1, Volume 14, p. 719

1863-7-US-SC/GA-3: The sidewheel steamer *Raccoon*, Captain F.M. Harris, bound from Nassau to Charleston, was chased ashore on Drunken Dick Shoals off Sullivan's Island, South Carolina, on July 19, 1863. The *Raccoon* was burned by her captain to prevent her capture. The steamer had been fired at by the United States steamer *Ironsides*, but, until her grounding, she had not been injured. (Note One: This was the *Raccoon's* third attempt through the blockade. The first two had been successful. She was described as "one of the swiftest steamers afloat," and it was rumored that she was intending to fit out as a privateer upon her arrival at Charleston.) (Note Two: A voucher signed by the major commanding the Confederate arsenal at Charleston is made out in the amount of $7999.92 for the freight on ninety-nine coils of lead weighing five tons which apparently had been carried on the *Raccoon* when she was lost.) (Note Three: She was variously reported as owned by Messrs. John Fraser and Company of Charleston and Fraser, Trenholm and Company of Liverpool. Both were blockade running firms controlled by George Alfred Trenholm, the man Margaret Mitchell used as the historical basis for her fictional character Rhett Butler in *Gone With The Wind*.)

References for 1863-7-US-SC/GA-3:
"Charleston Daily Courier," (Charleston, SC), Vol. 61, #19524, July 21, 1863, p. 1, c. 3
"Charleston Mercury," (Charleston, SC), Volume 82, #11779, June 12, 1863, p. 2, c. 1
"Charleston Mercury," (Charleston, SC), Volume 82, #11812, July 21, 1863, p. 2, c. 1
"Daily Morning News," (Savannah, GA), July 21, 1863, p. 1, c. 1
"Daily Morning News," (Savannah, GA), July 22, 1863, p. 2, c. 4
Harper's Weekly, August 29, 1863, p. 556 illustration
"Vessel Papers" (manuscript records), United States National Archives, Washington, DC, Record Group 109, file R-4
Official Records of the Union and Confederate Navies in the War of the Rebellion, (Washington, DC, 1902), Series 1, Volume 14, pp. 235, 236, 367
Lifeline of the Confederacy: Blockade Running During the Civil War, by Stephen R. Wise, (University of South Carolina, Columbia, SC, 1983), p. 607
Wreck of the Georgiana, Mystery Ship of the Confederacy, by Edward Lee Spence, (prepublication copy, Charleston, South Carolina, 1989), Appendix E
Charleston's Maritime Heritage 1670-1865, by P.C. Coker III, (CokerCraft Press, Charleston, SC, 1987), p. 303

1863-8-US-NC-1: The U.S. armed tug *Crocus*, Acting Ensign J.L. Winton commanding, was wrecked on Bodie's Island, North

The "Real Rhett Butler" & Other Revelations

Carolina, on Aug. 17, 1863. Apparently she had mistaken a light on the island for the Hatteras Light and was bearing south when she ran aground. Only a few provisions were saved. No lives were lost. [Note: The *Crocus* was built as the *Solomon Thomas* at Mystic, Connecticut, in 1863, and was issued a certificate of steam enrollment at the port of New York on March 3, 1863. She had been purchased at New York for $23,000. She was classed as a 4th rate and was a screw propelled steamer. She was 122 (or 129) tons burden, 79' in length, 18'6" in breadth, 9'3" in depth and drew 7'6". She had low pressure engines and was armed with two guns.]

References for 1863-8-US-NC-1:

Official Records of the Union and Confederate Navies in the War of the Rebellion, (Washington, DC, 1899), Series 1, Volume 9, pp. 162, 163, 187
Official Records of the Union and Confederate Navies in the War of the Rebellion, (Washington, DC, 1921), Series 2, Volume 1, p. 68
List of American-Flag Merchant Vessels that Received Certificates of Enrollment or Registry at the Port of New York 1789-1867, compiled by Forest R. Holdcamper, (U.S. National Archives, Washington, DC, 1968), Special List #22, Volume 2, p. 644
Merchant Steam Vessels of the United States 1790-1868, ("Lytle-Holdcamper List"), by William M. Lytle and Forrest R. Holdcamper, revised and edited by C. Bradford Mitchell, (Staten Island, NY, 1975), p. 200

1863-8-US-NC-2: The twin screw steamer *Hebe* was chased ashore, fired into, and burned by the *U.S.S. Niphon* and the *U.S.S. Shockokon* (or *Shokoken*), while trying to enter New Inlet, North Carolina, on August 18, 1863. Over three hundred and thirty shot and shell were fired into the *Hebe* or at the Confederates who tried to save her. The return fire by the Confederate shore batteries was reported as falling around the Yankees "as thickly as hail." A number of balls struck the deck and sides of the *Niphon* but none of her men were injured. The *Hebe* carried a cargo of drugs, coffee, clothing and provisions. [Note One: The *Hebe* had an iron hull, with four bulkheads and was built and engined by J.&W. Dudgeon of London, England, in 1863. Her tonnage was shown in "Lloyd's Register" of 1864/65 as 477 gross and 367 net. She was 165' in length, 23' (or 22') in breadth, 13'6" (or 13') in depth of hold, and had a draft of 7'. The *Hebe* was also described as "a beautiful little steamer," "her hull and smoke funnels camouflaged with a coating of grayish green paint." She was also described as "like the *Kate*." She was owned by Collie and Crenshaw and Company (or F. Muir) and had made two successful trips through the blockade prior to her loss.] (Note Two: The position of the wreck was described in contemporary accounts as eight miles north of Fort Fisher, North Carolina, and as "about halfway between Fort Fisher and Masonboro Inlet." She was also described as one to two miles north of Gatlin's battery, which was located four miles north of Fort Fisher. A Sea Grant publication prepared by the University of North

Treasures of the Confederate Coast

Carolina states that the wreck is in twenty feet of water south of Carolina Beach Inlet and North of the Carolina Beach Fishing Pier.)

References for 1863-8-US-NC-2:
"Daily Morning News," (Savannah, GA), Volume 14, #201, August 25, 1863, p. 2, c. 1
Times, (London. England), #24656, September 5, 1863, p. 9, c. 3
Times, (London. England), #24657, September 7, 1863, p. 7, c. 2
Times, (London, England), #24705, November 2, 1863, p. 8, c. 2
Times, (London, England), #24714, November 12, 1863, p. 6, c. 3
Lloyd's Register of British and Foreign Shipping, from 1st July, 1864, to the 30th June, 1865, (London, 1864), entry H-193
Official Records of the Union and Confederate Navies in the War of the Rebellion, (Washington, DC, 1899), Series 1, Volume 9, pp. 165-174
Official Records of the Union and Confederate Navies in the War of the Rebellion, (Washington, DC, 1900), Series 1, Volume 10, pp. 443, 504
The Navy in the Civil War, (Charles Scribner's Sons, New York, NY, 1903), Volume 1 ("The Blockade and the Cruisers" by James Russell Soley), p. 162
Graveyard of the Atlantic: Shipwrecks of the North Carolina Coast, by David Stick (University of North Carolina Press, Chapel Hill, NC, 1952), pp. 63, 247
An Oceanographic Atlas of the Continental Margin, J.G. Newton, O.H. Pilkey and J.O. Blanton, (Duke University Marine Laboratory, Beaufort, NC, 1971), p. 17 chart symbol #88, p. 20 entry #88
Wreck Diving in North Carolina, University of North Carolina, Sea Grant Publication, #78-13, p. 6
Lifeline of the Confederacy: Blockade Running During the Civil War, by Stephen R. Wise, (University Microfilms International, 1983), pp. 276-279, 301, 574
The Blockade Runners, by Dave Horner, (Florida Classics Library, Port Salerno, FL, 1992), Chapter 14, pp. 211-214

1863-8-US-NC-3: The U.S. armed brig *Bainbridge*, Acting Master T.J. Dwyer, foundered in a gale off Cape Hatteras, North Carolina, on August 21, 1863. She normally carried a crew of about forty. The sole survivor was a black man named James White, who was picked up in a boat by the British brig *South Boston* on the following day. (Note: The *Bainbridge* was bound from New York to Port Royal, South Carolina, and was armed with six 32-pounders of 27 hundredweight each and one 12-pounder rifle. She had been purchased by the government in 1842 for $49,790. The *Bainbridge* was brig rigged, built of wood, 259 tons, 100' in length, 25' in breadth, and 11'6" in depth. She drew 10 forward and 13'6" aft. The brig could make a maximum speed of eleven knots. She was to have reported to Rear-Admiral J.A. Dahlgren for duty in the South Atlantic Blockading Squadron.)

References for 1863-8-US-NC-3:
"Daily Morning News," (Savannah, GA), Volume 14, #204, August 29, 1863, p. 2, c. 1
Times, (London. England), #24656, September 5, 1863, pp. 9, c. 1, 3
Official Records of the Union and Confederate Navies in the War of the Rebellion, (Washington, DC, 1902), Series 1, Volume 14, pp. 433, 514
Official Records of the Union and Confederate Navies in the War of the Rebellion, (Washington, DC, 1921), Series 2, Volume 1, p. 42
Graveyard of the Atlantic: Shipwrecks of the North Carolina Coast, by David Stick (University of North Carolina Press, Chapel Hill, NC, 1952), pp. 58, 247

1863-8-US-NC-4: The screw steamer *Georges Creek*, 448 tons, foundered off Cape Hatteras, North Carolina, on August 22, 1863. (Note: The *Georges Creek* was built in 1853 at Philadelphia, Pennsylvania, which was also her first home port. She was issued a certificate of steam enrollment at the port of New York on April 30, 1853.)

References for 1863-8-US-NC-4:

The "Real Rhett Butler" & Other Revelations

Merchant Steam Vessels of the United States 1790-1868, "The Lytle-Holdcamper List," by William M. Lytle and Forrest R. Holdcamper, revised and edited by C. Bradford Mitchell, (Staten Island, New York, 1975), p. 280
Encyclopedia of American Shipwrecks, by Bruce D. Berman, Mariners Press, (Boston, MA, 1972), p. 122, #775
Merchant Steam Vessels of the United States 1790-1868, ("Lytle-Holdcamper List"), by William M. Lytle and Forrest R. Holdcamper, revised and edited by C. Bradford Mitchell, (Staten Island, NY, 1975), pp. 84, 264

1863-8-US-NC-5: The schooner *Alexander Cooper* was burned on August 22, 1863, at a wharf six miles up the sound from New Topsail Inlet, North Carolina, by men from the *U.S.S. Shockokon.* [Note One: The Federals, commanded by Ensign Cony, had "shouldered their dingy and carried it through the thickets across the neck of land, half a mile in width" relaunched it and approached the schooner by surprise. They captured ten men, but had to release seven. (Cony) took those who seemed most intelligent and good-looking, who turned out to be privates." The Federals later learned that among those released were two officers, Captain Adams and Captain Latham.] (Note Two: The schooner's position is listed in one reference work as "near Cape Fear-inside Topsail sound at Sloop Point." David Stick in his book, *Graveyard of the Atlantic,* writes that the wreck took place "Near Cape Fear.") (Note Three: This was the 46 ton schooner *Alexander Cooper*, which was built in Talbot County, Maryland, in 1848. She was issued a certificate of enrollment at New York, New York, on March 29, 1860. The schooner had officially "cleared from New York for Port Royal," South Carolina, which was then in Federal hands, so she may have been a prize that had been taken by the Confederates rather than a blockade runner.)

References for 1863-8-US-NC-5:
Official Records of the Union and Confederate Navies in the War of the Rebellion, (Washington, DC, 1899), Series 1, Volume 9, pp. 176-178
The Navy in the Civil War, (Charles Scribner's Sons, New York, NY, 1905), Volume 2 ("The Atlantic Coast" by Daniel Ammen), pp. 198, 199
Graveyard of the Atlantic: Shipwrecks of the North Carolina Coast, by David Stick (University of North Carolina Press, Chapel Hill, NC, 1952), p. 247
A Chart of Wrecks of Vessels Sunk or Captured Near Wilmington, NC, Circa 1861-65, compiled by Charles H. Foard, (Wilmington, North Carolina, 1962)
List of American-Flag Merchant Vessels that Received Certificates of Enrollment or Registry at the Port of New York 1789-1867, compiled by Forest R. Holdcamper, (U.S. National Archives, Washington, DC, 1968), Special List #22, Volume 1, p. 29
An Oceanographic Atlas of the Continental Margin, J.G. Newton, O.H. Pilkey and J.O. Blanton, (Duke University Marine Laboratory, Beaufort, NC, 1971), p. 20 entry #128, p. 21 chart symbol #128

1863-8-US-SC/GA-1: The sidewheel steamer *Robert Habersham* (or *Haversham*), Captain T.S. Daniels, blew up on August 4, 1863, while anchored at Screven's Ferry on the Carolina side of the Savannah River. The steamer's boiler exploded tearing the boat to pieces and causing her to sink. Eight or ten of the twenty-five persons on board were injured. (Note One: The "Lytle-Holdcamper List" incorrectly shows her as lost with "all hands.") (Note Two:

Treasures of the Confederate Coast

The *Habersham* had been in the freighting business for several years, but was under charter to the Confederate government at the time of her loss. She was owned by Captain Henry J. Dickerson of Savannah, Georgia. The steamer had a wood hull with sidewheels and was built at Savannah in 1860. She was 173 tons.)

References for 1863-8-US-SC/GA-1:

"Enrollment #3," (Savannah, GA), September, 1859, National Archives, Record Group 41
"Enrollment #1," (Savannah, GA), May 22, 1860, National Archives, Record Group 41
"Charleston Mercury," (Charleston, SC), Volume 82, #11826, August 6, 1863, p. 1, c. 4
"Daily Morning News," (Savannah, GA), August 4, 1863, p. 1, c. 1
Official Records of the Union and Confederate Navies in the War of the Rebellion, (Washington, DC, 1902), Series 1, Volume 14, p. 493
Shipwrecks of the Civil War: The Encyclopedia of Union and Confederate Naval Losses, by Donald Shomette, (Washington, DC, 1973), p. 455
Merchant Steam Vessels of the United States 1790-1868, ("Lytle-Holdcamper List"), edited by C. Bradford Mitchell, (Staten Island, NY, 1975), p. 186
Warships of the Civil War Navies, by Paul H. Silverstone, (Naval Institute Press, Annapolis, MD, 1989), p. 241

1863-8-US-SC/GA-2: The steamer *Oconee* (ex-Confederate gunboat *Savannah*, a.k.a. *Old Savannah*, ex-*Everglade*), Captain O.F. Johnson (or Johnston), with 323 (or 325) bales of compressed upland cotton and ninety tons of coal, was swamped and sunk by heavy seas in a violent storm south of St. Catherine's Island, Georgia, on August 19, 1863. (Note One: One report stated that the *Oconee* was sunk twenty miles out of Tybee. A boat with four of her officers and eleven of her men was captured two days after the sinking. Her men were said to have been "in uniform." The remainder of the steamer's crew escaped.) [Note Two: She was armed with one 32-pounder smooth-bore and had participated in the defense of Port Royal Sound in the battle of November 6 & 7, 1861. The cotton was the property of the Confederate government. The vessel had been launched from the yard of Mr. S. Whitlock at Newtown Creek, Williamsburg, New York, on September 26, 1856, and was first named the *Everglade*. The vessel measured 475 (or 400, or 406, or 486) tons, 173' in length, 28'8" in breadth, 8' in depth of hold, and 4'6" (5') in draft. The steamer was a sharp model boat with a deck cabin and had a single deck. The steamer was built for shoal water. The vessel's hull was built of oak and cedar, with copper and iron fastenings, and was double iron strapped. The steamer had two inclined engines with 32" diameter cylinders and 8' piston stroke. The steamer had a large paddle wheel. The vessel's coal bunkers were built of wood. The *Oconee* was considered a poor sea risk and was classed A-2 for insurance purposes. Her one independent fire pump was described as insufficient security against fire.] (Note Three: Stephen Wise in his book *Lifeline of the Confederacy* gives the steamer's dimensions as 169'6"x30'x8'6".)

The "Real Rhett Butler" & Other Revelations

(Note Two: Thomas Scharf in his *History of the Confederate States Navy* describes the *Oconee* as a "small sidewheel steamer.")

References for 1863-8-US-SC/GA-2:
American Lloyd's: Registry of American & Foreign Shipping, (New York, New York, 1858), p. 340, #106
"Charleston Daily Courier," (Charleston, SC), Volume 61, #19554, August 26, 1863, p. 1, c. 2
"Charleston Mercury," (Charleston, SC), Volume 83, #11842, August 26, 1863, p. 1, c. 1
"Daily Morning News," (Savannah, GA), August 24, 1863, p. 1, c. 3
Times, (London. England), #24656, September 5, 1863, p. 9, c. 3
"Steam Vessels #1, 1850's," (bound manuscript, Atlantic Mutual Insurance Companies of New York), entry 392
History of the Confederate States Navy From its Organization to the Surrender of its Last Vessel, by J. Thomas Scharf, (New York, New York, 1887), p. 89
Official Records of the Union and Confederate Navies in the War of the Rebellion, (Washington, DC, 1902), Series 1, Volume 14, pp. 492-494, 694
Official Records of the Union and Confederate Navies in the War of the Rebellion, (Washington, DC, 1921), Series 2, Volume 1, pp. 266, 752
Georgia Historical Quarterly, (1934), Volume 18, pp. 160-162
Merchant Steam Vessels of the United States 1807-1868, ("Lytle List"), by William M. Lytle, (Mystic, CT, 1952), pp. 60, 142
Shipwrecks of the Civil War: The Encyclopedia of Union and Confederate Naval Losses, by Donald Shomette, (Washington, DC, 1973), pp. 363, 364
Merchant Steam Vessels of the United States 1790-1868, ("Lytle-Holdcamper List"), edited by C. Bradford Mitchell, (Staten Island, NY, 1975), p. 68
Lifeline of the Confederacy: Blockade Running During the Civil War, by Stephen R. Wise, (University of South Carolina, Columbia, SC, 1983), p. 613
Warships of the Civil War Navies, by Paul H. Silverstone, (Naval Institute Press, Annapolis, MD, 1989), p. 238

1863-8-US-SC/GA-3: A letter dated August 20, 1863, and published in the "Charleston Mercury" stated that the steamer *New Brunswick* was "stranded" on the Charleston Bar and her cargo was being taken out in lighters.

Reference for 1863-8-US-SC/GA-3:
"Charleston Mercury," (Charleston, SC), Volume 83, #11850, September 4, 1863, p. 1, c. 4

1863-8-US-SC/GA-4: The Confederate submarine *H.L. Hunley* (or *Hunley*, or *American Diver*) was accidentally swamped and sunk by the steamer *Etiwan* in Charleston Harbor, South Carolina, on August 29, 1863, and five of her crew drowned. (Note One: This was the "boat" with C.S.A. lieutenants Payne and Hasker, that was reported in the "Charleston Mercury" as having parted its moorings and sunk while conducting experiments in Charleston Harbor. That account stated that four men from the ironclad *Chicora* and a fifth man from the *Palmetto State* were drowned. A similar report in the "Savannah Daily Morning News" listed Payne and Hasker as lieutenants with the Confederate Navy and listed the dead from the *Chicora* as Frank Doyle, John Kelly, Michael Cane and Nicholas Davis. A letter dated September 26, 1863, was probably talking of this sinking when it mentioned that a six man submarine had recently sunk in Charleston Harbor with the loss of its crew.) (Note Two: The submarine was raised and once again manned. The *Hunley* sank two more times. Once on October 15, 1863, while being tested in the harbor, and again on February 17, 1864, during a successful attack on the United States gunboat *Housatonic*. The

Treasures of the Confederate Coast

unlucky submarine was said to have sunk a total of four times, drowning a total of twenty-five men.) (Note Three: The tiny submarine was designed by Horace L. Hunley of Mobile, Alabama, and was hand cranked.) (Note Four: Many of the Federal reports of the *Hunley* refer to her a *David*, and a contemporary news story that "Rev. Wm. B. Yates, the Seaman's Chaplain" was seeking donations for "the gallant crew of the *David*, all being veteran seamen," shortly after the October 15, 1863, sinking of the *Hunley*, may well indicate that she was also considered a *David* by the Confederates.) (Note Five: For additional information and references on the *Hunley*, please see entries 1863-10-US-SC/GA-1 and 1864-2-US-SC/GA-2, and Chapter One in this book.)

References for 1863-8-US-SC/GA-4:
"Charleston Daily Courier," (Charleston, SC), Volume 61, #19598, October 16, 1863, p. 1, c. 2
"Charleston Daily Courier," (Charleston, SC), Volume 61, #19617, November 7, 1863, p. 1, c. 2
"Charleston Daily Courier," (Charleston, SC), Volume 61, #19618, November 9, 1863, p. 1, c. 2
"Charleston Daily Courier," (Charleston, SC), Volume 61, #19624, November 16, 1863, p. 1, c. 2 (contains Hunley's obituary as published in the Mobile "Advertiser and Register")
"Charleston Daily Courier," (Charleston, SC), Volume 61, #19625, November 17, 1863, p. 1, c. 2
"Charleston Mercury," (Charleston, SC), Volume 83, #11846, August 31 (misdated as August 30), 1863, p. 2, c. 1
"Charleston Mercury," (Charleston, SC), Volume 83, #11878, October 9, 1863, p. 1, c. 4, 5
"Charleston Mercury," (Charleston, SC), Volume 83, #11904, November 9, 1863, p. 2, c. 1
"Daily Morning News," (Savannah, GA), September 1, 1863, p. 2, c. 4
New York Times, (New York, NY), Volume 13, #3878, February 27, 1864, p. 3 (marked supplement), c. 1, 2
History of the Confederate States Navy From its Organization to the Surrender of its Last Vessel, by J. Thomas Scharf, (New York, New York, 1887), pp. 760, 761
Confederate Military History, written by Brig. Gen. Ellison Capers, edited by General Clement A. Evans, (Confederate Publishing Co., Atlanta, Georgia, 1899), Volume 5, p. 297
Official Records of the Union and Confederate Armies in the War of the Rebellion, (Washington, DC, 1890), Series 1, Volume 28, Part 1, pp. 145, 146
Official Records of the Union and Confederate Navies in the War of the Rebellion, (Washington, DC, 1902), Series 1, Volume 14, pp. 229, 231, 238, 327-337, 692, 693
Official Records of the Union and Confederate Navies in the War of the Rebellion, (Washington, DC, 1921), Series 2, Volume 1, p. 256
Shipwrecks of the Civil War: The Encyclopedia of Union and Confederate Naval Losses, by Donald Shomette, (Washington, DC, 1973), p. 256
Charleston's Maritime Heritage 1670-1865, by P.C. Coker III, (CokerCraft Press, Charleston, SC, 1987), p. 264
Warships of the Civil War Navies, by Paul H. Silverstone, (Naval Institute Press, Annapolis, MD, 1989), p. 221

1863-8-US-SC/GA-5: On the night of August 30, 1863, the steam transport and munitions carrier *Sumter*, returning from Morris Island, South Carolina, with six hundred men, who had just been relieved, was fired upon by mistake from Battery Bee on Sullivan's Island, and was sunk. "One shot penetrated the hull, and in about four hours all the men aboard were gotten off. Very soon afterward the steamer went to pieces. The soldiers were said to have been from the 12th or the 23rd regiment of the South Carolina volunteers. They lost "nearly all of their guns, accouterments and ammunition." Several men were killed, and a few were drowned, when they tried to escape by swimming. Estimates of the total dead varied between eight and twenty-five. She was lost on the "east end of fort reef," fifty to seventy yards inside of the Cumming's Point buoy and about

The "Real Rhett Butler" & Other Revelations

eight hundred to a thousand yards from Fort Sumter. Some of the early reports misidentified her as the steamer *Rebel* or as the steamer *Chesterfield*. (Note: Although I do not believe it is, there is some confusion as to whether this was the former steamer *Habana*, which was taken into confederate service as the *Sumter* on June 3, 1861. The *Habana* was a screw steamer of 499 tons and was built by Reaney Neafie in 1859 at Philadelphia. She was first home ported at New Orleans. That vessel had a wood hull, was 170.9"x28.1"x18' and drew 14.5". Her engines were built by Merrick and Sons at Philadelphia. That vessel was sold to Fraser, Trenholm and Company in the summer of 1863 and later became the British blockade runner *Gibraltar*. She was safe at Liverpool when the war ended.)

References for 1863-8-US-SC/GA-5:
"Charleston Daily Courier," (Charleston, SC), Volume 61, #19559, September 1, 1863, p. 1, c. 2
"Charleston Mercury," (Charleston, SC), Volume 83, #11847, September 1, 1863, p. 2, c. 1
"Charleston Mercury," (Charleston, SC), Volume 83, #11848, September 2, 1863, p. 2, c. 1
"Charleston Mercury," (Charleston, SC), Volume 83, #11849, September 3, 1863, p. 2, c. 1, 2
"Daily Morning News," (Savannah, GA), September 1, 1863, p. 2, c. 1
Times, (London, England), #24680, October 3, 1863, p. 9, c. 1
History of the Confederate States Navy From its Organization to the Surrender of its Last Vessel, by J. Thomas Scharf, (New York, New York, 1887), p. 697
Official Records of the Union and Confederate Armies in the War of the Rebellion, (Washington, DC, 1890), Series 1, Volume 28, Part 1, pp. 397, 398, 450, 689-712
Official Records of the Union and Confederate Armies in the War of the Rebellion, (Washington, DC, 1891), Series 1, Volume 35, Part 2, p. 624
Official Records of the Union and Confederate Navies in the War of the Rebellion, (Washington, DC, 1899), Series 1, Volume 9, pp. 229, 230
Official Records of the Union and Confederate Navies in the War of the Rebellion, (Washington, DC, 1902), Series 1, Volume 14, p. 755
Merchant Steam Vessels of the United States 1790-1868, ("Lytle-Holdcamper List"), edited by C. Bradford Mitchell, (Staten Island, NY, 1975), pp. 85, 91, 205
Lifeline of the Confederacy: Blockade Running During the Civil War, by Stephen R. Wise, (University of South Carolina, Columbia, SC, 1983), p. 570
Charleston's Maritime Heritage 1670-1865, by P.C. Coker III, (CokerCraft Press, Charleston, SC, 1987), p. 230
Warships of the Civil War Navies, by Paul H. Silverstone, (Naval Institute Press, Annapolis, MD, 1989), p. 241

1863-9-US-NC-1: The blockade runner *Arabian* was accidentally run ashore near Fort Fisher, at New Inlet, North Carolina, on September 15, 1863, while trying to slip past the Federal ships. She had made three previous successful trips through the blockade and was outbound with a load of cotton. Both the cotton and the vessel were said have been privately owned. (Note One: The grounded steamer was afterwards destroyed in a gale. A diagram showing the wreck's position on the bar off Fort Fisher can be found in Volume 10 of the "Official Records-Navy.") (Note Two: The *Arabian* was 174' in length, 24' in breadth, 18'4" in depth, and was 263 registered tons. She had a wooden hull and her sidewheels were 26' in diameter. The vessel was built by the Niagara Harbor Company, Niagara, Ontario, Canada, 1851, and had a single vertical beam engine with a single cylinder. She was owned by Robert Henry

Treasures of the Confederate Coast

Sawyer and Ramos A. Menendez, and was flying the English flag when she was wrecked.)

References for 1863-9-US-NC-1:
"Charleston Mercury," (Charleston, SC), Volume 83, #11868, September 28, 1863, p. 1, c. 2
Official Records of the Union and Confederate Navies in the War of the Rebellion, (Washington, DC, 1899), Series 1, Volume 9, pp. 211, 214, 216, 248, 785
Official Records of the Union and Confederate Navies in the War of the Rebellion, Series 1, Volume 10, pp. 125 (illustration), 504
Graveyard of the Atlantic: Shipwrecks of the North Carolina Coast, by David Stick (University of North Carolina Press, Chapel Hill, NC, 1952), p. 247
A Chart of Wrecks of Vessels Sunk or Captured Near Wilmington, NC, Circa 1861-65, compiled by Charles H. Foard, (Wilmington, North Carolina, 1962)
An Oceanographic Atlas of the Continental Margin, J.G. Newton, O.H. Pilkey and J.O. Blanton, (Duke University Marine Laboratory, Beaufort, NC, 1971), p. 17 chart symbol #66, p. 20 entry #66
Lifeline of the Confederacy: Blockade Running During the Civil War, by Stephen R. Wise, (University Microfilms International, 1983), pp. 532-533

1863-9-US-NC-2: The handsome blockade running steamer *Phantom*, Captain Porter, bound into Wilmington from Bermuda, with a cargo of arms, medicine, etc., was chased ashore and destroyed on September 23, 1863, by the *U.S.S. Connecticut*, John J. Almy Commander. (Note One: Contemporary reports placed the wreck near Rich Inlet, North Carolina. A Sea Grant publication put out by the University of North Carolina gives the location as in Topsail Inlet, North Carolina. Stephen Wise in his book, *Lifeline of the Confederacy: Blockade Running During the Civil War*, states that she was "destroyed near Topsail Inlet while trying to enter New Inlet.") [Note Two: The *Phantom* was built of steel plate by William C. Miller and Son at Liverpool, England, in 1863. She was a screw steamer and was engined by Fawcett, Preston and Company. Her dimensions were 192.9'x22'x12.4' and she was 322 gross tons and 266 register tons (one report estimated her tonnage as 500 tons). She was reported to have been "encased with steel plates, and her six portholes had steel shutters."] (Note Three: The *Phantom* was said to have been an "18-knot steamer" and was successful in four of her five attempts to run the blockade. She was sold to the Confederate government by Fraser, Trenholm and Company in July of 1863. Fraser, Trenholm and Company was headed by George Alfred Trenholm who was later used as the historical basis for Margaret Mitchell's fictional character Rhett Butler in *Gone With The Wind*.) (Note Four: Like the screw steamer *Georgiana*, some reports stated that the *Phantom* "was probably intended for a pirate," but when she was examined by the British authorities they reported "that she was not adapted for war purposes, the steel plates being thin and the hull fragile.") (Note Five: See also entry 1864-12-US-NC-3.)

References for 1863-9-US-NC-2:
Times, (London, England), #24688, October 13, 1863, p. 8, c. 4
Annual Report of the Secretary of the Navy, 1864-1865, (Volume 6, #1, of Executive Documents, Washington, DC, 1865), p. 728

The "Real Rhett Butler" & Other Revelations

Official Records of the Union and Confederate Armies in the War of the Rebellion, (Washington, DC, 1890), Series 1, Volume 29, Part 2, pp. 763, 764
Official Records of the Union and Confederate Armies in the War of the Rebellion, (Washington, DC, 1891), Series 1, Volume 33, p. 1228
Official Records of the Union and Confederate Navies in the War of the Rebellion, (Washington, DC, 1895), Series 1, Volume 2, pp. 145, 391
Official Records of the Union and Confederate Navies in the War of the Rebellion, (Washington, DC, 1899), Series 1, Volume 9, pp. 214, 216, 217, 221, 222, 228, 230, 248, 250, 277, 341, 774
Official Records of the Union and Confederate Navies in the War of the Rebellion, (Washington, DC, 1900), Series 1, Volume 10, p. 504
Graveyard of the Atlantic: Shipwrecks of the North Carolina Coast, by David Stick (University of North Carolina Press, Chapel Hill, NC, 1952), p. 247
A Chart of Wrecks of Vessels Sunk or Captured Near Wilmington, NC, Circa 1861-65, compiled by Charles H. Foard, (Wilmington, North Carolina, 1962)
An Oceanographic Atlas of the Continental Margin, J.G. Newton, O.H. Pilkey and J.O. Blanton, (Duke University Marine Laboratory, Beaufort, NC, 1971), p. 20 entry #123, p. 21 chart symbol #123
George Alfred Trenholm and the Company that Went to War 1861-1865, by Ethel Trenholm Seabrook Nepveux, (Charleston, South Carolina, 1973), p. 64
Wreck Diving in North Carolina, University of North Carolina, Sea Grant Publication, #78-13, p. 7
Lifeline of the Confederacy: Blockade Running During the Civil War, by Stephen R. Wise, (University Microfilms International, 1983), pp. 281, 282, 300, 604

1863-9-US-NC-3: The blockade runner *Elizabeth* (or *Elisabeth*, formerly *Atlantic*) accidentally got ashore at Lockwood's Folly, North Carolina, and was burned by her own captain on September 24, 1863, to prevent her from being captured by the Federals. Her cargo was principally steel and saltpeter. (Note One: The date of loss was also given as September 26, 1863, and the location as "off Cape Fear, North Carolina." Her location was also described as being twelve miles from Fort Caswell.) (Note Two: The *Elizabeth* was a wooden hulled, sidewheel steamer had been bound from Nassau to Wilmington when she was lost. Her registered owner between February, 1862, and October, 1862, was A.L. Davis of Nashville. In October, 1862, the vessel was sold to John Fraser and Company. Her dimensions were 216'x28'x10' and she was 660 (or 623) tons burden. The *Elizabeth* was a converted Gulf coast steamer and had made seven successful runs through the blockade prior to her loss. She had been built in New York in 1852 and she had a vertical beam engine with a 40" cylinder and a 10' stroke. The *Elizabeth* was issued a certificate of steam registry at New York, New York, on September 11, 1856.) (Note Three: John Fraser & Co. was headed by George Alfred Trenholm who was later used as the historical basis for Margaret Mitchell's fictional character Rhett Butler in *Gone With The Wind*.) (Note Four: For another mention of the wreck of the *Elizabeth*, please see entry 1864-1-US-NC-1.)

References for 1863-9-US-NC-3:
"Charleston Mercury," (Charleston, SC), Volume 83, #11872, October 2, 1863, p. 1, c. 2
"Daily Morning News," (Savannah, GA), Volume 14, #234, October 5, 1863, p. 1, c. 1
Official Records of the Union and Confederate Navies in the War of the Rebellion, (Washington, DC, 1899), Series 1, Volume 9, p. 234
Official Records of the Union and Confederate Navies in the War of the Rebellion, (Washington, DC, 1900), Series 1, Volume 10, p. 504
Graveyard of the Atlantic: Shipwrecks of the North Carolina Coast, by David Stick (University of North Carolina Press, Chapel Hill, NC, 1952), pp. 63, 247
A Chart of Wrecks of Vessels Sunk or Captured Near Wilmington, NC, Circa 1861-65, compiled by Charles H. Foard, (Wilmington, North Carolina, 1962)

Treasures of the Confederate Coast

List of American-Flag Merchant Vessels that Received Certificates of Enrollment or Registry at the Port of New York 1789-1867, compiled by Forest R. Holdcamper, (U.S. National Archives, Washington, DC, 1968), Special List #22, Volume 1, p. 63
George Alfred Trenholm and the Company that Went to War 1861-1865, by Ethel Trenholm Seabrook Nepveux, (Charleston, South Carolina, 1973), p. 40
Merchant Steam Vessels of the United States 1790-1868, "The Lytle-Holdcamper List," by William M. Lytle and Forrest R. Holdcamper, revised and edited by C. Bradford Mitchell, (Staten Island, New York, 1975), p. 15
Lifeline of the Confederacy: Blockade Running During the Civil War, by Stephen R. Wise, (University Microfilms International, 1983), pp. 301, 534

1863-9-US-SC/GA-1: The very fast steamer *Diamond*, Captain Andrew Milne, bound from Nassau, with a cargo of brandy and cigars, was captured off St. Simons Island, Georgia, by the *U.S.S. Stettin*, on September 23, 1863. "Aboard of her were found as passengers Victor Malga, former owner of the blockade runner *Aries*, and Antoine Solcedo, supercargo." These men were believed to own the *Diamond* and were described as exhibiting "a reckless demeanor ••• and large amounts of gold." "A ledger was found, by entries in which it would seem that these men have interests in nearly all the blockade-runners known." A large case of revolvers was said to be concealed somewhere in the steamer. She was making her first attempt through the blockade when she was captured. (Note: The *Diamond* had an iron hull, sidewheels, two stacks, and one mast aft. Her capacity was said to be "190 tons British measurement - about 300 tons American.")

References for 1863-9-US-SC/GA-1:
Times, (London, England), #24698, October 24, 1863, p. 9, c. 4
Lifeline of the Confederacy: Blockade Running During the Civil War, by Stephen R. Wise, (University Microfilms International, 1983), p. 553

1863-10-US-NC-1: The propeller steamer *Douro*, Captain Jenkins, was chased ashore and burned by the *U.S.S. Nansemond* on October 11, 1863. (Note One: The *Douro's* position was given as being "just above the wreck of the steamer *Hebe*" while another report described her as "a perfect wreck just above the *Hell*." The *Hebe's* position was further described in contemporary accounts as eight miles north of Fort Fisher, North Carolina, and as "about halfway between Fort Fisher and Masonboro Inlet." David Stick in his book, *Graveyard of the Atlantic,* gives the location of the *Douro* as at Wrightsville on one page, but describes it as "between Fort Fisher and Masonboro Inlet" on another. Dave Horner in his book *The Blockade Runners* states "the location of the wreck of the *Douro* is near the surf zone above Fort Fisher, just north of the remains of the *Hebe*. The hulk of the blockade runner *Venus* also is close by.") (Note Two: For information on the wreck of the *Hebe* see entry 1863-8-US-NC-2. For information on the *Venus*, please see entry 1863-10-US-NC-3.) [Note Three: The *Douro* was burned to the water's edge and several shot put through her machinery. "All on board escaped, excepting the second and third masters, two of the crew, and a passenger." The *Douro* had previously been described in contemporary reports as being of Liverpool, 185 tons register. She was once captured for running the blockade and had been sold in New York but her new owners had returned her to the dangerous but lucrative trade. The *Douro* made a total of two successful runs through the blockade out of a total of four tries. At the time of her loss she was outbound with a cargo of 500 (or 250) bales of cotton, 279 boxes of tobacco, 21 (or 20) tierces leaf tobacco, and an unspecified quantity of turpentine and rosin, all of which was owned by the Confederate government. The *Douro* had been owned in Wilmington, North Carolina. It appears that the vessel was originally powered as a sidewheel steamer, but this may simply be confusion in the records.]

References for 1863-10-US-NC-1:

Times, (London, England), #24705, November 2, 1863, p. 8, c. 2
Times, (London, England), #24714, November 12, 1863, p. 6, c. 3
Official Records of the Union and Confederate Navies in the War of the Rebellion, (Washington, DC, 1899), Series 1, Volume 8, pp. 592, 593
Official Records of the Union and Confederate Navies in the War of the Rebellion, (Washington, DC, 1899), Series 1, Volume 9, pp. 232-234
Official Records of the Union and Confederate Navies in the War of the Rebellion, (Washington, DC, 1900), Series 1, Volume 10, p. 504
Graveyard of the Atlantic: Shipwrecks of the North Carolina Coast, by David Stick (University of North Carolina Press, Chapel Hill, NC, 1952), pp. 63, 247
A Chart of Wrecks of Vessels Sunk or Captured Near Wilmington, NC, Circa 1861-65, compiled by Charles H. Foard, (Wilmington, North Carolina, 1962)
An Oceanographic Atlas of the Continental Margin, J.G. Newton, O.H. Pilkey and J.O. Blanton, (Duke University Marine Laboratory, Beaufort, NC, 1971), p. 17 chart symbol #89, p. 20 entry #89
Lifeline of the Confederacy: Blockade Running During the Civil War, by Stephen R. Wise, (University Microfilms International, 1983), p. 554
The Blockade Runners, by Dave Horner, (Florida Classics Library, Port Salerno, FL, 1992), Chapter 14, pp. 214

1863-10-US-NC-2: The *U.S.S. Madgie* (or *Madgil*), Acting Master Polleys, foundered in eighteen (also shown as "several") fathoms of water, twelve miles south east of the lightship on Frying Pan Shoals, North Carolina, on October 11, 1863. All of the officers and crew were saved, but everything else was a total loss except her chronometer and a few private effects. The *Madgie* was being towed from Charleston to Hampton Roads by the *U.S.S. Fahkee*, Acting Ensign Webb, when she was lost. [Note One: The *Madgie* had been purchased at New York on October 14 (or 15), 1861, for $13,000. She was a wooden hulled screw steamer, 220 tons (or 218 tons), 122'10" in length, 22'7" in breadth, and 8'5" in depth. Her battery included one 30-pounder Parrott rifle, one 20-pounder Parrott rifle, two 24-pounder broadside howitzers, and one 12-pounder smooth bore. She was built in 1858 at Philadelphia, Pennsylvania, which was also her first home port. Total cost of repairs while she was in government service was $26,924.93.]

References for 1863-10-US-NC-2:

"Charleston Mercury," (Charleston, SC), Volume 83, #11891, October 24, 1863, p. 2, c. 1

Treasures of the Confederate Coast

Official Records of the Union and Confederate Navies in the War of the Rebellion, (Washington, DC, 1899), Series 1, Volume 9, pp. 237, 238
Official Records of the Union and Confederate Navies in the War of the Rebellion, (Washington, DC, 1921), Series 2, Volume 1, p. 131
An Oceanographic Atlas of the Continental Margin, J.G. Newton, O.H. Pilkey and J.O. Blanton, (Duke University Marine Laboratory, Beaufort, NC, 1971), p. 17 chart symbol #61, p. 20 entry #61
Merchant Steam Vessels of the United States 1790-1868, ("Lytle-Holdcamper List"), by William M. Lytle and Forrest R. Holdcamper, revised and edited by C. Bradford Mitchell, (Staten Island, NY, 1975), p. 133

1863-10-US-NC-3: The sidewheel steamer *Venus*, bound from Nassau to Wilmington, with a valuable cargo of lead, drugs, dry goods, bacon, and coffee, was chased ashore between one and two miles north of Gatlin's Battery, North Carolina, on October 21, 1863, by the *U.S.S. Nansemond.* The iron hulled steamer was then destroyed by shelling from the *U.S.S. Iron Age* and the *U.S.S. Niphon.* (Note One: The *Venus* was a fine vessel, and was heavily laden with a valuable cargo of commissary and quartermaster's stores. Her presence had been exposed when a "traitor" rang her bell alerting the fleet and allowing them to know where to train their guns in the darkness. Three men were killed, twenty-eight taken prisoner and twenty-two made their escape. The men of the Federal boat crews that boarded the *Venus* each got sixty to eighty dollars in gold from the wreck.) (Note Two: The *Venus* was described as one of the finest and fastest vessels engaged in running the blockade. One report stated she was 265' in length, measured 1,000 tons. Another gave her measurements as 159'x17.1'x8.7'. She is said to have drawn only eight feet of water.) (Note Three: The *Venus'* position was also described as about five miles above Fort Fisher. She was also reported as within a short distance from the wrecks of the *Hebe* and the *Douro.* One account stated she was lost "at the mouth of the Cape Fear River." David Stick in his book, *Graveyard of the Atlantic,* gives the location of the wreck as "Near Cape Fear." Dave Horner in his book *The Blockade Runners* states "Today the location of the wreck is known, and the vessel's hull can be found fairly intact. Tons of lead remain inside her, as do handsome pieces of crockery bearing the ship's name.") (Note Four: The *Venus* had made six successful runs through the blockade prior to her loss. She was built by J.&G. Thomson at Govan, Scotland, in 1852, and was owned by Crenshaw and Collie and Company.) (Note Five: For more information on the *Hebe*, please see entry 1863-8-US-NC-2. For more information on the *Douro*, please see entry 1863-10-US-NC-1.)

References for 1863-10-US-NC-3:
"Charleston Mercury," (Charleston, SC), Volume 83, #11892, October 26, 1863, p. 2, c. 1
"Charleston Mercury," (Charleston, SC), Volume 83, #11903, November 7, 1863, p. 1, c. 2
"Charleston Mercury," (Charleston, SC), Volume 83, #11928, December 7, 1863, p. 2, c. 1
Times, (London, England), #24712, November 10, 1863, p. 8, c. 6
Times, (London, England), #24714, November 12, 1863, p. 6, c. 3

The "Real Rhett Butler" & Other Revelations

Official Records of the Union and Confederate Navies in the War of the Rebellion, (Washington, DC, 1899), Series 1, Volume 9, pp. 248-251, 277, 785
Official Records of the Union and Confederate Navies in the War of the Rebellion, (Washington, DC, 1900), Series 1, Volume 10, pp. 443, 504
The Navy in the Civil War, (Charles Scribner's Sons, New York, NY, 1903), Volume 1 ("The Blockade and the Cruisers" by James Russell Soley), pp. 162, 163
Graveyard of the Atlantic: Shipwrecks of the North Carolina Coast, by David Stick (University of North Carolina Press, Chapel Hill, NC, 1952), p. 247
A Chart of Wrecks of Vessels Sunk or Captured Near Wilmington, NC, Circa 1861-65, compiled by Charles H. Foard, (Wilmington, North Carolina, 1962)
An Oceanographic Atlas of the Continental Margin, J.G. Newton, O.H. Pilkey and J.O. Blanton, (Duke University Marine Laboratory, Beaufort, NC, 1971), p. 17 chart symbol #68, p. 20 entry #68
Lifeline of the Confederacy: Blockade Running During the Civil War, by Stephen R. Wise, (University Microfilms International, 1983), pp. 276-279, 301, 624
The Blockade Runners, by Dave Horner, (Florida Classics Library, Port Salerno, FL, 1992), Chapter 14, pp. 26, 140, 214-216

1863-10-US-NC-4: A Yankee journal bearing the date October 29, 1863, and quoted in various southern papers, reported that "there was a well-substantiated rumor in Portsmouth" that a steamer carrying the 99th New York Regiment and two full batteries, which "left Fortress Monroe a few days previous" had "gone to Davy Jones' locker," in a terrible gale off Hatteras, North Carolina. The Confederate papers went on to say that the "99th Regiment, was for a long time stationed at Deep Creek, Norfolk County, and stole enough from peaceable citizens in that vicinity to make death to them terrible, indeed under any circumstances." In other words the article was implying that the men of the 99th were doomed to Hell for their thievery. (Note: Although no mention of this loss has been found in the "Official Records," this is supported in part by orders dated October 9, 1863, which direct the commander of the 99th Regiment of New York Volunteers in Virginia to prepare the regiment "to be embarked for New Berne, North Carolina.")

References for 1863-10-US-NC-4:
"Daily Morning News," (Savannah, GA), November 7, 1863, p. 2, c. 1 (had no volume or issue number)
Official Records of the Union and Confederate Armies in the War of the Rebellion, (Washington, DC, 1890), Series 1, Volume 29, Part 2, pp. 276, 277

1863-10-US-SC/GA-1: On October 15, 1863, the Confederate submarine *H.L. Hunley* sank in Charleston Harbor, South Carolina, drowning her designer, Horace L. Hunley, and seven other men. "The boat left the dock at 9:25 a.m. and disappeared at 9:35. As soon as she sank, air bubbles were seen to rise to the surface of the water, and from this fact it is supposed the hole in the top of the boat, by which the men entered, was not properly closed. It was impossible at the time to make any effort to rescue the unfortunate men, as the water was some nine fathoms deep." [Note One: The "Charleston Daily Courier" of October 16, 1863, gave the dead as "Capt. Hunley, Brockbank, Park, Marshall, Beard, Patterson, McHugh, and Sprague." The article simply referred to the *Hunley* as "a small boat (sunk) in Cooper River."] Five of the men who drowned with Horace Hunley were described as mechanics from

Treasures of the Confederate Coast

Mobile, Alabama. On October 18 a "Mr. Smith provided with submarine armour found the sunken submarine boat" and subsequently raised her. Captain Hunley was buried with military honors in Magnolia Cemetery at Charleston, South Carolina. The grave is in a prominent location and is marked with an obelisk. Horace Hunley was just thirty-six years old at the time of his death. Hunley's obituary described him as "possessed of ample fortune, in the prime of manhood." Hunley was said to have had a "presentiment" that he would "perish in the adventure." The *Hunley* sank again on February 17, 1864, during a successful attack on the United States gunboat *Housatonic*. The unlucky submarine was said to have sunk a total of four times, drowning a total of twenty-five men.) (Note Two: Many of the Federal reports relative to the *Hunley* refer to her a *David*, and a contemporary news story that "Rev. Wm. B. Yates, the Seaman's Chaplain" was seeking donations for "the gallant crew of the *David*, all being veteran seamen," shortly after the October 15, 1863, sinking of the *Hunley*, may well indicate that she was also considered a *David* by the Confederates.) (Note Three: After the *Hunley* was raised and reconditioned, she was ordered not to do any more diving. She was reballasted to float with her hatch coamings just above water and was equipped with a spar torpedo containing ninety pounds of gunpowder.) (Note Four: For additional information and references on the *Hunley*, see entries 1863-8-US-SC/GA-4 and 1864-2-US-SC/GA-2 and Chapter One of this book.)

References for 1863-10-US-SC/GA-1:

"Charleston Daily Courier," (Charleston, SC), Volume 61, #19598, October 16, 1863, p. 1, c. 2
"Charleston Daily Courier," (Charleston, SC), Volume 61, #19617, November 7, 1863, p. 1, c. 2
"Charleston Daily Courier," (Charleston, SC), Volume 61, #19618, November 9, 1863, p. 1, c. 2
"Charleston Daily Courier," (Charleston, SC), Volume 61, #19624, November 16, 1863, p. 1, c. 2 (contains Hunley's obituary as published in the Mobile "Advertiser and Register")
"Charleston Daily Courier," (Charleston, SC), Volume 61, #19625, November 17, 1863, p. 1, c. 2
"Charleston Mercury," (Charleston, SC), Volume 83, #11846, August 31 (misdated as August 30), 1863, p. 2, c. 1
"Charleston Mercury," (Charleston, SC), Volume 83, #11878, October 9, 1863, p. 1, c. 4, 5
"Charleston Mercury," (Charleston, SC), Vol. 83, #11904, November 9, 1863, p. 2, c. 1
New York Times, (New York, NY), Volume 13, #3878, February 27, 1864, p. 3 (marked supplement), c. 1, 2
History of the Confederate States Navy From its Organization to the Surrender of its Last Vessel, by J. Thomas Scharf, (New York, New York, 1887), pp. 760, 761
Confederate Military History, written by Brig. Gen. Ellison Capers, edited by General Clement A. Evans, (Confederate Publishing Co., Atlanta, Georgia, 1899), Volume 5, p. 297
Official Records of the Union and Confederate Armies in the War of the Rebellion, (Washington, DC, 1890), Series 1, Volume 28, Part 1, pp. 145, 146
Official Records of the Union and Confederate Navies in the War of the Rebellion, (Washington, DC, 1902), Series 1, Volume 14, pp. 229, 231, 238, 327-337, 692, 693
Official Records of the Union and Confederate Navies in the War of the Rebellion, (Washington, DC, 1921), Series 2, Volume 1, p. 256
Naval History of the Civil War, by Howard P. Nash, (A.S. Barnes & Co., New York, NY, 1972), pp. 210-213
Shipwrecks of the Civil War: The Encyclopedia of Union and Confederate Naval Losses, by Donald Shomette, (Washington, DC, 1973), p. 256
Charleston's Maritime Heritage 1670-1865, by P.C. Coker III, (CokerCraft Press, Charleston, SC, 1987), p. 264
Warships of the Civil War Navies, by Paul H. Silverstone, (Naval Institute Press, Annapolis, MD, 1989), p. 221

The Confederate States privateer Petrel was sunk off Charleston, South Carolina, on July 28, 1861, by the United States gunboat St. Lawrence. The Petrel's men were unjustly indicted for piracy.

Lt. Cushing's torpedo launch on its way to sink the Confederate States ironclad ram Albemarle. Illustration taken from the "Official Records of the War of the Rebellion, Union & Confederate Navies."

The "Real Rhett Butler" & Other Revelations

The Confederate States rironclad ram Albemarle was sunk at Plymouth, North Carolina, in October of 1865. Illustration taken from the "Official Records of the War of the Rebellion, Union & Confederate Navies."

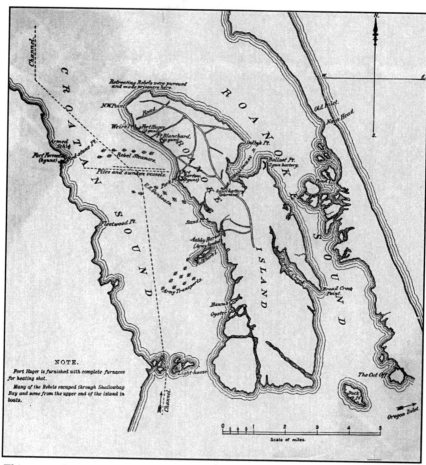

This map shows the position of the Union and Confederate fleets during the February 8, 1862, battle for of Roanoke Island, North Carolina. The maps on this and the next three pages were copied from the "Official Records of the War of the Rebellion, Union & Confederate Navies."

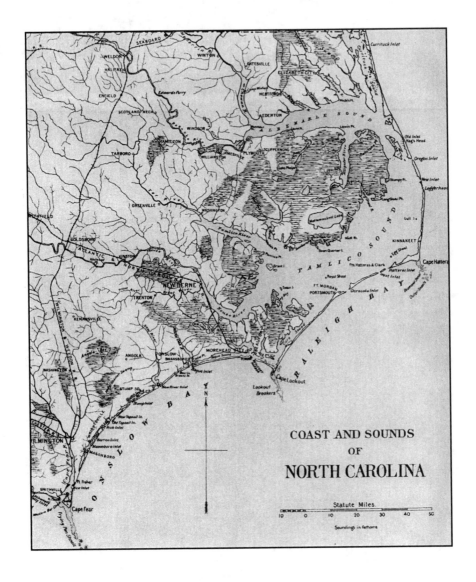

COAST AND SOUNDS
OF
NORTH CAROLINA

Statute Miles.

Soundings in fathoms

Treasures of the Confederate Coast

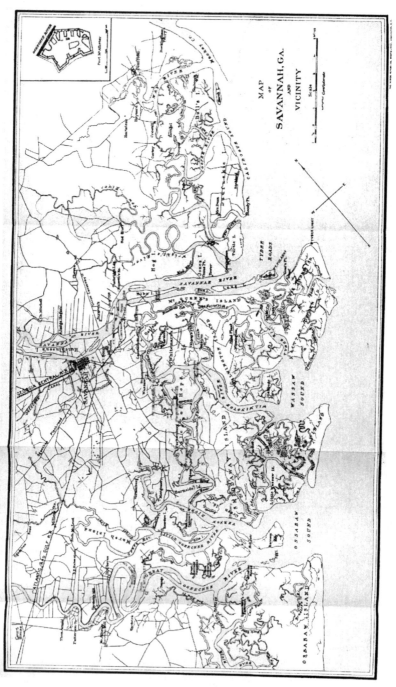

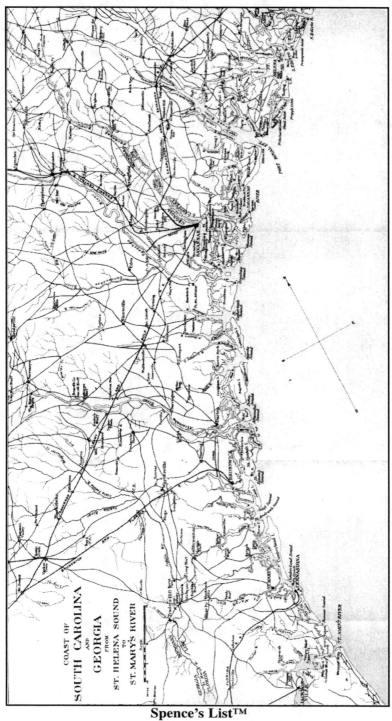

COAST OF
SOUTH CAROLINA
AND
GEORGIA
FROM
ST. HELENA SOUND
TO
ST. MARY'S RIVER

The Martin's Industry lightship was stationed on the shoal by the same name off Port Royal Sound, South Carolina.

The "Real Rhett Butler" & Other Revelations

1863-10-US-SC/GA-2: The blockade running schooner *Rover* was driven ashore at Murrell's Inlet, South Carolina, on October 19, 1863, and was burned by her own crew, after her cargo had already been safely landed on the beach. The Federals landed seventeen men on the nearby beach, ten of whom, including an ensign named Tillson, were captured by Company B of the 21st Georgia Cavalry under Lieutenant Ely Kennedy.

References for 1863-10-US-SC/GA-2:
"Charleston Daily Courier," (Charleston, SC), Volume 61, #19606, October 26, 1863, p. 1, c. 3
"Charleston Mercury," (Charleston, SC), Volume 83, #11892, October 26, 1863, p. 2, c. 1
Official Records of the Union and Confederate Armies in the War of the Rebellion, (Washington, DC, 1890), Series 1, Volume 28, Part 1, pp. 736, 737
History of Georgetown County, South Carolina, by George C. Rogers, (Columbia, South Carolina, 1970), p. 411

1863-10-US-SC/GAx-1 (1863-8-US-MD/VA-1): An item in the Savannah "Daily Morning News" stated that the schooners *Coquette* and *Two Sisters* and the steamers *Satellite* and *Reliance* had been stripped and scuttled at Port Royal on October 23, 1863. (Note One: Although the article didn't state which Port Royal, it certainly appeared to indicate the scuttling of the vessels took place at Port Royal, South Carolina. Other evidence shows that such an assumption is incorrect and the destruction actually took place up the Rappahannock River in Virginia.) (Note Two: Paul Silverstone in his excellent book *Warships of the Confederate Navies* shows the *Satellite* as the ex-*U.S.S. Satellite* which had been boarded and captured by the Confederate Lieutenant John Taylor Wood, with four boats and sixty men, at the mouth of the Rappahannock River, Virginia, on August 23, 1863, as stripped and scuttled on September 2, 1863. Silverstone shows the *Reliance* as the ex-*U.S.S. Reliance* which had been captured in the Rappahannock on August 19/23, 1863, and states that she was operated briefly by the Confederates but was destroyed by them at Port Royal, Virginia, to prevent recapture on August 28, 1863.) [Note Three: The *Satellite* was built at New York, New York, in 1854, and was purchased by George D. Morgan from Hammond, at a cost of $19,000, for government use on July 24, 1861. She was commissioned on September 27, 1861 at the New York Navy Yard for the Potomac Flotilla. She was 217 tons burden, 120'7" in length, 22'9" in breadth and 8'9" in depth. She had sidewheels and a complement of 43 (or 40) men. Classed as a tug, 4th rate, she was armed with one 8-inch gun of 55 hundredweight and one 30-pounder Parrott rifle (or one smooth-bore 32-pounder and one 12-pounder howitzer). Lieutenant Wood cruised the Chesapeake Bay for a day or two taking three prizes. Her guns were removed before she was destroyed.] [Note Four: The tug *Reliance*, official number 21956,

Treasures of the Confederate Coast

was built by B.C. Terry at Keyport, New Jersey, and was launched June 4, 1860. Her first home port was New York, New York. She was acquired by the United States Navy Department from A. Degroot, on May 7, 1861, at a cost of $15,000, and was commissioned on May 13, 1861. She was a wooden hulled, screw steamer of 90 tons burden, with one boiler and two vertical direct acting engines with 17" cylinders. She carried a complement of 17 (or 40) men and was armed with one 24-pounder pivot howitzer and one 12-pounder pivot howitzer (or one 30-pounder Parrott and one 24-pounder howitzer). Her guns were removed before she was destroyed. In 1865 the *Reliance* was raised, sold, and returned to merchant service. She was finally lost on April 26, 1883.]

References for 1863-10-US-SC/GAx-1 (1863-8-US-MD/VA-1):
"Daily Morning News," (Savannah, GA), October 25, 1863, p. 2, c. 4
Confederate Military History, edited by General Clement A. Evans, (Confederate Publishing Co., Atlanta, GA, 1899), Volume 12, pp. 74, 75, 108, 109
Official Records of the Union and Confederate Navies in the War of the Rebellion, (Washington, DC, 1921), Series 2, Volume 1, pp. 190, 202
List of American-Flag Merchant Vessels that Received Certificates of Enrollment or Registry at the Port of New York 1789-1867, compiled by Forest R. Holdcamper, (U.S. National Archives, Washington, DC, 1968), Special List #22, Volume 2, pp. 587, 631
Merchant Steam Vessels of the United States 1790-1868, ("Lytle-Holdcamper List"), edited by C. Bradford Mitchell, (Staten Island, NY, 1975), pp. 182, 195, 293
Warships of the Civil War Navies, by Paul H. Silverstone, (Naval Institute Press, Annapolis, MD, 1989), pp. 97, 98, 120, 242, 243

1863-11-US-NC-1: The "Charleston Mercury" of November 9, 1863, reported that the schooner *Alice L. Webb*, Captain Vanbrunt, of New York, mistook Swansboro for Beaufort, North Carolina, and "beached" on the bar about a half mile from the beach on November 4, 1863. She was bound from New York to Beaufort with provisions and furniture for John Watson (Note One: The schooner's crew surrendered to the Confederate pickets. On November 13, 1863, the stranded schooner was observed by the U.S.S. *Mount Vernon*, discharged, scuttled, and abandoned, lying in three feet of water in the breakers. The *Mount Vernon* fired four shots at her. The Federals believed she had been run ashore intentionally and that her "miscellaneous" cargo belonged to a merchant named Mr. Dibble. John Watson was described as "a Connecticut man" who intended to set up a store in Beaufort.) (Note Two: The *Alice L. Webb* had a wood hull with two masts, she was 111 tons burden. She was built at Stamford, Connecticut, in 1862, and was issued a certificate of enrollment at the port of New York on July 3, 1860.) (Note Three: A schooner believed to be the *Alice L. Webb* had been reported lost off Ocracoke, North Carolina, in April of 1861, for more on that report, please see entry 1861-4-US-NC-3.)

References for 1863-11-US-NC-1:
"Charleston Mercury," (Charleston, SC), Volume 83, #11904, November 9, 1863, p. 2, c. 2

The "Real Rhett Butler" & Other Revelations

Official Records of the Union and Confederate Armies in the War of the Rebellion, (Washington, DC, 1890), Series 1, Volume 29, Part 2, pp. 452, 453

Official Records of the Union and Confederate Navies in the War of the Rebellion, (Washington, DC, 1899), Series 1, Volume 9, p. 780

List of American-Flag Merchant Vessels that Received Certificates of Enrollment or Registry at the Port of New York 1789-1867, compiled by Forest R. Holdcamper, (U.S. National Archives, Washington, DC, 1968), Special List #22, Volume 1, p. 31

1863-11-US-NC-2: The Savannah *Daily Morning News* and the "Charleston Mercury" (both of November 17, 1863), both reported that the Confederate steamer *Robert E. Lee* was destroyed by her officers after being "surrounded by the enemy" while trying to run the blockade off Wilmington, North Carolina, with a load of valuable stores. (Note One: The reports were incorrect. The *Robert E. Lee* was captured, not destroyed. She carried a cargo of one hundred and fifty cases of Austrian rifles, 214 large cases and bales of shoes and blankets, 250 bags of saltpeter, 61 barrels salt provisions, 30 pigs of lead, etc. She was flying the Confederate flag when captured, but burned it before it could be confiscated. She was said to have "treasure (hidden) in her keelson."] (Note Two: For an earlier mention of the *Robert E. Lee* carrying treasure through the blockade, please see entry 1863-7-US-NC-4.)

References for 1863-11-US-NC-2:
"Charleston Daily Courier," (Charleston, SC), Volume 61, #19625, November 17, 1863, p. 1, c. 2
"Charleston Mercury," (Charleston, SC), Volume 83, #11911, November 17, 1863, p. 1, c. 6
"Charleston Mercury," (Charleston, SC), Volume 83, #11913, November 19, 1863, p. 2, c. 1
"Charleston Mercury," (Charleston, SC), Volume 83, #11917, November 24, 1863, p. 2, c. 1
"Daily Morning News," (Savannah, GA), Volume 14, #273, November 17, 1863, p. 2, c. 4
Official Records of the Union and Confederate Navies in the War of the Rebellion, (Washington, DC, 1899), Series 1, Volume 9, pp. 275, 276, 284, 286-291

1863-12-US-NC-1: The "Charleston Mercury" of December 17, 1863, reported that the fast running steamer *Sea Breeze* was run ashore and set afire by her crew near Wilmington, North Carolina, but the fire was put out and she was towed off. (Note: Although the date was not given, this apparently took place in late November or early December of 1863.)

Reference for 1863-12-US-NC-1:
"Charleston Mercury," (Charleston, SC), Volume 83, #11936, December 17, 1863, p. 2, c. 1

1863-12-US-NC-2: The steamer *Ceres* ran aground off Old Inlet, North Carolina, on December 6, 1863, while attempting her first run through the blockade. (Note One: She was set on fire by her crew in an attempt to prevent her from falling into the hands of the enemy. However, she floated with the tide and was captured by the *U.S.S. Violet*. She was later towed north by the *U.S.S. Montgomery*.) (Note Two: The *Ceres* was owned by Crenshaw and Collie and had been built in London, England, in 1863 by J.W. Dudgeon. Her dimensions were 173'x22'10"x12'5". She was 271 registered tons and 479 tons burden. She had an iron hull and twin screws.) (Note Three: She was finally destroyed by fire on October 1, 1869.)

References for 1863-12-US-NC-2:

Official Records of the Union and Confederate Navies in the War of the Rebellion, (Washington, DC, 1899), Series 1, Volume 9, pp. 336-339, 341, 350, 402, 583

Official Records of the Union and Confederate Navies in the War of the Rebellion, (Washington, DC, 1900), Series 1, Volume 10, p. 504

Merchant Steam Vessels of the United States 1790-1868, ("Lytle-Holdcamper List"), by William M. Lytle and Forrest R. Holdcamper, revised and edited by C. Bradford Mitchell, (Staten Island, NY, 1975), pp. 32, 249

Lifeline of the Confederacy: Blockade Running During the Civil War, by Stephen R. Wise, (University Microfilms International, 1983), p. 544

1863-12-US-NC-3: The "fine" blockade running steamer *General Beauregard* (ex-*Havelock*, a.k.a. *Beauregard*) was chased ashore "between Flag Pond Hill and Dick's Bay • • • about a mile south of Gatlin's Battery," North Carolina, on the night of December 11, 1863, by the *U.S.S. Howquah*. [Note One: The *Beauregard* was a sidewheel steamer 223'2" in length, 26'2" in breadth, 14'3" in depth of hold, 339 tons register, 629(?) tons burden, and drew 7'6" (or 10') of water. She was built by H.&G. Thomson in Govan, Scotland, in 1858, and was owned by J. Archibald Wilson and the Chicora Importing and Exporting Company of Charleston.] (Note Two: This steamer had made sixteen successful trips through the blockade and was trying for her seventeenth when she was lost. Her cargo included one thousand pounds of brown sugar, one thousand pounds of coffee, three boxes of candles, fifteen hundred pounds of bacon, and one gross knives and forks consigned to the "Wayside Home." She had once served as a ferry boat between Glasgow and Dublin.) (Note Three: Dave Horner in his book, *The Blockade Runners*, relates an interesting tale of between sixty and seventy thousand dollars worth of gold on the *Beauregard*. That much gold, if in coin, could be worth millions of dollars today. Horner was told about the gold by the great grandson of a man that actually sailed on the *Beauregard*. The *Beauregard's* gold was said to have been consigned "to a British export house in payment for previously contracted supplies." The gold had been in a strong box hidden under the captain's bunk on the starboard side of the steamer. Unfortunately, the account does not match with the facts. The story has the vessel as lost on an outbound trip loaded with cotton rather than an inbound trip loaded with provisions and merchandise. However, even though she was inbound there may indeed have been gold, because gold was shipped both ways through the blockade.) (Note Four: The wreck's location is given in a Sea Grant publication put out by the University of North Carolina as in fifteen feet of water, one hundred yards southeast of Spartenburg Avenue, Carolina Beach, North Carolina.) (Note Five: On an earlier trip,

The "Real Rhett Butler" & Other Revelations

while attempting to run into Charleston, she had run aground on Drunken Dick Shoals and got off only after throwing overboard "some ten slabs of iron plating and forty or fifty boxes of tin." On that voyage her cargo was said to have been consigned to Messrs. John Fraser & Co. John Fraser and Company was headed by George Alfred Trenholm. Trenholm was later used as the historical basis for Margaret Mitchell's fictional character Rhett Butler in *Gone With The Wind*. For more on that accident, please see entry 1863-2-US-SC/GA-5.)

References for 1863-12-US-NC-3:
"Daily Morning News," (Savannah, GA), Volume 14, #48, February 26, 1863, p. 2, c. 2
"Daily Morning News," (Savannah, GA), Volume 14, #297, December 17, 1863, p. 2, c. 2
"Charleston Daily Courier," (Charleston, SC), Volume 61, #19646, December 21, 1863, p. 2, c. 1
"Charleston Mercury," (Charleston, SC), Volume 83, #11942, December 24, 1863, p. 2, c. 1
"Confederate Archives," NARS, Chapter 2,-48-164
Returns of Collector of Customs, Charleston, South Carolina, January to June, 1863, #4
Official Records of the Union and Confederate Navies in the War of the Rebellion, (Washington, DC, 1899), Series 1, Volume 9, pp. 234, 354, 355
Official Records of the Union and Confederate Navies in the War of the Rebellion, (Washington, DC, 1900), Series 1, Volume 10, pp. 443, 504
"Richmond Whig," (Richmond, Virginia), December 16, 1863, p. 2, c. 1
Graveyard of the Atlantic: Shipwrecks of the North Carolina Coast, by David Stick (University of North Carolina Press, Chapel Hill, NC, 1952), p. 247
A Chart of Wrecks of Vessels Sunk or Captured Near Wilmington, NC, Circa 1861-65, compiled by Charles H. Foard, (Wilmington, North Carolina, 1962)
An Oceanographic Atlas of the Continental Margin, J.G. Newton, O.H. Pilkey and J.O. Blanton, (Duke University Marine Laboratory, Beaufort, NC, 1971), p. 17 chart symbol #81, p. 20 entry #81
"Vessel Papers" (manuscript records), United States National Archives, Washington, DC, Record Group 109, M909, roll 15, file H-47, frames 0094-0098
George Alfred Trenholm and the Company that Went to War 1861-1865, by Ethel Trenholm Seabrook Nepveux, (Charleston, South Carolina, 1973), p. 63
Lifeline of the Confederacy: Blockade Running During the Civil War, by Stephen R. Wise, (University Microfilms International, 1983), pp. 287, 301, 574
The Blockade Runners, by Dave Horner, (Florida Classics Library, Port Salerno, FL, 1992), Chapter 14, pp. 161-172

1863-12-US-NC-4: The British schooner *G.O. Bigelow* (or *G.A. Bigelow*), bound from Bermuda to Beaufort, North Carolina, with forty tons of salt (or merchandise), was scuttled and burned at the entrance of Bear Inlet, North Carolina, on December 16, 1863, by the *U.S.S. Mount Vernon*. Her cargo was gotten off before the Yankees found her. (Note: The schooner was described as about ninety tons, twenty years old, and in a very dilapidated condition.)

References for 1863-12-US-NC-4:
"Charleston Daily Courier," (Charleston, SC), Volume 61, #19645, December 19, 1863, p. 1, c. 1
"Charleston Mercury," (Charleston, SC), Volume 83, #11945, December 29, 1863, p. 2, c. 1
Times, (London, England), #24766, January 12, 1864, p. 9, c. 4
Official Records of the Union and Confederate Navies in the War of the Rebellion, (Washington, DC, 1899), Series 1, Volume 9, pp. 341-344, 375, 780

1863-12-US-NC-5: The sidewheel steamer *Antonica*, Captain W.F. Adair, was discovered ashore on Frying Pan Shoals, three miles from the extreme point of Smith's Island, North Carolina on December 20, 1863, by the *U.S.S. Aries*. All forty-two crew, passengers and officers of the *Antonica* were captured. [Note One: Stephen Wise in his book, *Lifeline of the Confederacy: Blockade Running During the Civil War*, stated that the vessel "ran aground

Treasures of the Confederate Coast

while trying to enter Old Inlet Dec. 19, 1863, (and was) destroyed by the *Governor Buckingham* and others." Dave Horner in his book *The Blockade Runners* states "Today the remains of this famous ship are buried in the sand about three and a half miles due south of Cape Fear.] (Note Two: It was incorrectly believed by the "Charleston Mercury" that the vessel was towed off. She was a large steamer capable of carrying twelve hundred bales of cotton and had been well known as the blockade runner *Herald* The steamer had made twenty-four successful runs through the blockade prior to her being lost on her twenty-fifth attempt. Her cargo consisted of dry goods, provisions, liquor, etc., most of which was lost. There were no arms or ammunition known to have been aboard. The steamer was reported as broken across her bottom.) (Note Three: She had been built as the *Herald* by John Reid and Company in England. Her engine was built by J.&G. Thomson of Govan, Scotland, and had two cylinders. The steamer was purchased by Fraser, Trenholm and Company in late 1861 and was sold to the Chicora Importing and Exporting Company of Charleston in November of 1862, at which time her name was changed to *Antonica*. Her register of February 1862 showed her as owned by Charles Taylor.) (Note Four: Fraser, Trenholm and Company was headed by George Alfred Trenholm who was later used as the historical basis for Margaret Mitchell's fictional character Rhett Butler in *Gone With The Wind*.) (Note Five: Captain W.F. Adair had previously been captain of the ill-fated steamer *Barrosa* which he was forced to abandon in the Gulf Stream, latitude 29°50' North, longitude 79°50' West, after it started taking on water and all pumping and bailing failed. The *Barrosa* had sailed from St. Mary's, Georgia, on April 8, 1863.)

References for 1863-12-US-NC-5:
"Daily Morning News," (Savannah, GA), Volume 14, #89, April 16, 1863, p. 2, c. 1
"Charleston Mercury," (Charleston, SC), Volume 83, #11946, December 30, 1863, p. 2, c. 1
Official Records of the Union and Confederate Navies in the War of the Rebellion, (Washington, DC, 1899), Series 1, Volume 9, pp. 80, 234, 250, 341, 362-368, 422, 731 (chart), 775, 781
Graveyard of the Atlantic: Shipwrecks of the North Carolina Coast, by David Stick (University of North Carolina Press, Chapel Hill, NC, 1952), p. 247
A Chart of Wrecks of Vessels Sunk or Captured Near Wilmington, NC, Circa 1861-65, compiled by Charles H. Foard, (Wilmington, North Carolina, 1962)
An Oceanographic Atlas of the Carolina Continental Margin, by J.G. Newton, (Duke University Marine Laboratory, Beaufort, NC, 1971), p. 17 chart symbol #40, p. 20 entry #40
George Alfred Trenholm and the Company that Went to War 1861-1865, by Ethel Trenholm Seabrook Nepveux, (Charleston, South Carolina, 1973), pp. 50-61, 70
Lifeline of the Confederacy: Blockade Running During the Civil War, by Stephen R. Wise, (University Microfilms International, 1983), pp. 287, 288, 301, 575
The Blockade Runners, by Dave Horner, (Florida Classics Library, Port Salerno, FL, 1992), Chapter 14, pp. 19, 130, 140, 168, 216, 217

1863-12-US-NC-6: The screw steamer *Quincy*, foundered off Cape Hatteras, North Carolina, with the loss of sixteen lives, on December 20, 1863. (Note: She had a wood hull, was 396 tons, and

The "Real Rhett Butler" & Other Revelations

was built in 1857 at Buffalo, New York, which was also her first home port. She was issued a certificate of steam enrollment at the port of New York on December 8, 1863.)

References for 1863-12-US-NC-6:
Merchant Steam Vessels of the United States 1790-1868, "The Lytle-Holdcamper List," by William M. Lytle and Forrest R. Holdcamper, revised and edited by C. Bradford Mitchell, (Staten Island, New York, 1975), p. 576
Encyclopedia of American Shipwrecks, by Bruce D. Berman, Mariners Press, (Boston, MA, 1972), p. 141, #1624
Merchant Steam Vessels of the United States 1790-1868, ("Lytle-Holdcamper List"), by William M. Lytle and Forrest R. Holdcamper, revised and edited by C. Bradford Mitchell, (Staten Island, NY, 1975), pp. 179, 291

1863-12-US-NC-7: A schooner identified only as having been lost on December 24, 1863, is shown on a Charles Foard's chart of Civil War shipwrecks of the Wilmington, North Carolina, area. Its location is shown as approximately half way between New Topsail Inlet and New River Inlet.

Reference for 1863-12-US-NC-7:
A Chart of Wrecks of Vessels Sunk or Captured Near Wilmington, NC, Circa 1861-65, compiled by Charles H. Foard, (Wilmington, North Carolina, 1962)

1863-12-US-SC/GA-1: The United States monitor *Weehawken*, Commander Jesse Duncan, was sunk off Morris Island, South Carolina, on December 6, 1863. Four officers and twenty men were drowned. Contemporary accounts tell of the last moments of her "terror stricken crew" and the "vain shrieks" of the firemen manning the pumps, and of "men in irons" that went down with her. (Note One: The loss was attributed to improper stowage of ammunition combined with rough seas. The "paymaster's funds and the papers of the ship (went down) with her.") (Note Two: The *Weehawken* was a "*Passaic* Class" monitor with a single revolving turret. The vessel measured 844 tons, 200' in length, 46' in breath, 12'6" in depth, and 10'6" in draft. The gunboat had two Ericsson vibrating engines, and two Martin boilers. The *Weehawken* was armed with one 15-inch Dahlgren smooth-bore and one 11-inch Dahlgren smooth-bore. She had a complement of seventy-five men. The slow moving gunboat was rated at only five knots. The *Weehawken* was built by contract with Zeno Secor & Company of New York at the yard of Joseph Coldwell at Jersey City, New Jersey, at a total cost of $465,110.73, and was launched on November 5, 1863.) (Note Three: At least one hundred and thirty tons of iron was removed from the wreck of the *Weehawken* by Professor Maillefert's salvage company in 1873.) (Note Four: This wreck is shown on the 1865 chart drawn by E. Willenbucher for the "Annual Report of the Secretary of the Navy," and is listed in Adrian Lonsdale's *Guide to Sunken Ships in American Waters*, as having been wrecked at latitude 32°43.0' North, longitude 79°50.9' West.) (Note Five: Jim

Treasures of the Confederate Coast

Batey and I examined and identified this wreck in 1966 after a commercial fisherman snagged his trawl net on it. A famous author who writes adventure fiction and sponsors underwater archeology expeditions, re-investigated this wreck in the summer of 1981. Besides claiming it as his discovery, the man claimed that the wreck was intact and that his divers walked its deck. He made the claims even though a week before his "discovery," I had furnished him with copies of my extensive notes on 19th century scrapping efforts that had reduced the wreck to a mere scrap pile. I think it is safe to assume he was just over enthusiastic, or that he was hyping the wreck for publicity purposes. Anyway he writes interesting fiction.)

References for 1863-12-US-SC/GA-1:
"Charleston Daily Courier," (Charleston, SC), Volume 61, #19641, December 15, 1863, p. 1, c. 2
"Charleston Daily Courier," (Charleston, SC), Volume 61, #19648, December 23, 1863, p. 1, c. 5, 6
"Charleston Mercury," (Charleston, SC), Volume 83, #11934, December 15, 1863, p. 2, c. 1
"Charleston Mercury," (Charleston, SC), Volume 83, #11938, December 19, 1863, p. 2, c. 1
"Charleston Mercury," (Charleston, SC), Volume 84, #12019, March 23, 1864, p. 1, c. 5
"Daily Morning News," (Savannah, GA), December 22, 1863, p. 1, c. 2
"Daily Morning News," (Savannah, GA), December 31, 1863, p. 2, c. 1
New York Times, (New York, NY), Volume 13, #3813, December 12, 1864, p. 3 (marked supplement), c. 1
New York Times, (New York, NY), Volume 13, #3814, December 14, 1864, p. 5, c. 1
New York Times, (New York, NY), Volume 13, #3816, December 16, 1864, p. 4, c. 2, 3
New York Times, (New York, NY), Volume 13, #3819, December 19, 1864, p. 3 (marked supplement), c. 1
Records of General Courts Martial and Courts of Inquiry of the Navy Department, 1799-1867, Court of Inquiry, #3432, December 10, 1863, NARS M-273, roll 2, alphabetical card index 1861-1867
"Private Journal" by Charles Follen Blake, (bound manuscript, Library of Congress, 70-55848), p. 75
"Vessel Papers" (manuscript records), United States National Archives, Washington, DC, Record Group 109, file M-275
"General Map of Charleston Harbor, South Carolina, Showing Rebel Defenses and Obstructions," drawn by E. Willenbucher for the Annual Report of the Secretary of the Navy, (U.S. Coast Survey, 1865)
"Salvage Log," B. Maillefert, (in the collection of the South Carolina Historical Society at Charleston, SC), July 1 & 16, 1873; August 2, 1873; and September 22, 1873
Official Records of the Union and Confederate Armies in the War of the Rebellion, (Washington, DC, 1890), Series 1, Volume 28, Part 2, pp. 553, 594
Official Records of the Union and Confederate Navies in the War of the Rebellion, (Washington, DC, 1902), Series 1, Volume 15, pp. 161-170, 212
Official Records of the Union and Confederate Navies in the War of the Rebellion, (Washington, DC, 1921), Series 2, Volume 1, p. 238
The Navy in the Civil War, (Charles Scribner's Sons, New York, NY, 1903), Volume 1 ("The Blockade and the Cruisers" by James Russell Soley), p. 249
Guide to Sunken Ships in American Waters, by Adrian L. Lonsdale and H.R. Kaplan, (Arlington, VA, 1964), p. 70
Shipwrecks of the Civil War: The Encyclopedia of Union and Confederate Naval Losses, by Donald Shomette, (Washington, DC, 1973), pp. 161-165
Charleston's Maritime Heritage 1670-1865, by P.C. Coker III, (CokerCraft Press, Charleston, SC, 1987), pp. 238, 240, 248, 255
Warships of the Civil War Navies, by Paul H. Silverstone, (Naval Institute Press, Annapolis, MD, 1989), p. 8

1863-12-US-SC/GA-2: The British schooner *Antoinette*, of Nassau, was run ashore on the beach about "halfway down" Cumberland Island, Georgia, on December 8, 1863. The schooner was a total loss. (Note One: The *Antoinette's* register, crew list, and clearance were captured by the United States bark *Brazilia* which also took off the schooner's anchors, chains, and sails. Nothing else of value was believed to remain on the wreck.) (Note Two: See also entry 1863-4-US-SC/GA-11.)

References for 1863-12-US-SC/GA-2:

The "Real Rhett Butler" & Other Revelations

Report of the Secretary of the Navy, Second Session, 38th Congress, 1864-1865, (Washington, DC, 1865), p. 724
Official Records of the Union and Confederate Navies in the War of the Rebellion, (Washington, DC, 1902), Series 1, Volume 15, pp. 173, 174

1863-12-US-SC/GA-3: The coal bark *Alice Provost*, Captain Nichols, bound from Philadelphia with seven hundred tons of coal, went ashore while going into Port Royal Sound, South Carolina, on December 12, 1863, and was a total wreck. The bark's crew was taken aboard the United States gunboat *Vermont*. (Note: This was probably the bark *Alice Provost* which was built at Westerly, Rhode Island, in 1856. That bark was of medium model, with one deck and a long poop. She was four hundred and ninety-six tons and drew twelve feet of water. She was built of oak and had copper and iron fastenings, and was metalled in August of 1857. At the time of her survey in 1857, she was owned by Sturges, Clearman and Company. She was issued a certificate of register at the port of New York on December 22, 1856.)

References for 1863-12-US-SC/GA-3:
American Lloyd's: Registry of American & Foreign Shipping, (New York, New York, 1858), p. 64, #42
New York Times, (New York, NY), Volume 13, #3819, December 19, 1864, p. 3 (marked supplement), c. 1
Official Records of the Union and Confederate Navies in the War of the Rebellion, (Washington, DC, 1902), Series 1, Volume 15, p. 177
List of American-Flag Merchant Vessels that Received Certificates of Enrollment or Registry at the Port of New York 1789-1867, compiled by Forest R. Holdcamper, (U.S. National Archives, Washington, DC, 1968), Special List #22, Volume 1, p. 31

1863-12-US-SC/GA-4: The *Charleston Daily Courier* of December 31, 1863, quoted a correspondent of the New York *Herald* as saying that the "famous floating battery, which was used by the Rebels against Sumter when Major Anderson held the works, broke adrift in the late gale (December 17, 1863), and smashed through and carried away the obstructions, and now lies ashore near the north end of Folly Island." (Note: The battery had been designed by Lieutenant J.R. Hamilton, C.S.N., and had originally been "constructed of palmetto logs and armored with boiler iron, over which railroad iron was fastened. The roof was bomb-proof and it mounted four heavy guns." Sometime prior to the gale, the plating had been removed to use in the construction of one of the iron clad ships. The "late gale" was probably the storm of December 17, 1863, and rather than Folly Island, the battery may have washed ashore on the northern part of Morris Island, South Carolina, as Morris Island was frequently referred to as Folly Island in contemporary accounts, and that location seems to make more sense.)

References for 1863-12-US-SC/GA-4:
"Charleston Daily Courier," (Charleston, SC), Volume 61, #19654, December 31, 1863, p. 1, c. 1, 2
History of the Confederate States Navy From its Organization to the Surrender of its Last Vessel, by J. Thomas Scharf, (New York, New York, 1887), pp. 657, 658

Treasures of the Confederate Coast

1863-12-US-SC/GA-5: The Federals destroyed a schooner, loaded with turpentine for Nassau, during a raid on Murrell's Inlet, South Carolina, on December 23, 1863.

References for 1863-12-US-SC/GA-5:
Official Records of the Union and Confederate Navies in the War of the Rebellion, (Washington, DC, 1902), Series 1, Volume 15, pp. 154, 155
History of Georgetown County, South Carolina, by George C. Rogers, (Columbia, South Carolina, 1970), p. 412

1863-12-US-SC/GA-6: An item which originally appeared in the *New York Times* gave a rare description of diving operations during the Civil War. The author of the account had witnessed civilian divers scraping the hulls of the Federal monitors off Morris Island, South Carolina, in December, of 1863. The divers were employed by the U.S. Navy under a contract with Messrs. Joseph H. Smith and James B. Phelps. An excerpt from the account follows: "The diver, when clothed in his armor, is weighted with 185 pounds. Besides his armor, he has two leaden pads, fitting to his breast and back. The soles of his shoes are of lead, an inch and a half thick. All this weight is intended to overcome the buoyancy given by the mass of air, forced into the armor and dress, the latter of India rubber, worn by the diver. When below the surface, he can instantly bring himself up by closing momentarily the aperture in the helmet for the escape of the air. His buoyancy is immediately increased, and he pops up like a cork. • • • Besides cleaning the Monitors, the divers perform other important services. They have ransacked the interior of the *Keokuk*, attached buoys to lost anchors, and made under water examinations of the rebel obstructions. Waters (one of the divers) recently examined the sunken *Weehawken*, and met an unusual danger for even his perilous calling. The sea was so violent that he was twice thrown from the deck of the Monitor. Finally, getting of the iron ladder, he climbed to the top of the turret, when a heavy sea cast him inside the turret between the guns. Fearing that his air hose would become entangled, he made his way out with all possible speed, and was forced to give up his investigations until calmer weather offered a more favorable opportunity."

References for 1863-12-US-SC/GA-6:
"Charleston Daily Courier," (Charleston, SC), #19725, March 25, 1863, p. 1, c. 6
"Charleston Mercury," March 23, 1864, Volume 84, #12019, p. 1, c. 5

1863-12x-US-SC/GA-1: The Confederate sidewheel steamer *Talomico*, two guns, twenty men, was accidentally sunk at Savannah, Georgia, in 1863. (Note: The *Talomico* had served as a transport since 1861 and was commanded by First Assistant Engineer James L. Fabian, and piloted by Pierce Gadsen.)

References for 1863-12x-US-SC/GA-1:
Official Records of the Union and Confederate Navies in the War of the Rebellion, (Washington, DC, 1921), Series 2, Volume 1, pp. 268, 273, 307

The "Real Rhett Butler" & Other Revelations

Warships of the Civil War Navies, by Paul H. Silverstone, (Naval Institute Press, Annapolis, MD, 1989), p. 241

1864-1-US-NC-1: The U.S. Flagship *Fahkee*, Rear Admiral S.P. Lee, discovered the sidewheel steamer *Bendigo* (ex-*Milly*) aground and burning one half mile to the westward of the entrance to Lockwood's Folly Inlet, North Carolina, on January 3 (2 or 4), 1864. (Note One: The *Bendigo* had apparently mistaken the wreck of the steamer *Elizabeth* for a blockader and had tried to run between the wreck and land, which caused her to run aground where she was burned by her crew. She was afterwards shelled by the blockade fleet. The present depth around the wreck is said to be six feet.) (Note Two: The *Bendigo* had an iron hull and was 178 tons. She drew 8' forward and 8'6" aft. She was said to have been a frequent violator of the blockade, regularly running between Nassau and Wilmington, North Carolina. Records confirm that she had made at least two successful runs prior to her loss. She was originally registered as owned by M.I. Wilson but was owned by Fraser, Trenholm and Company at the time of her loss.) (Note Two: Fraser, Trenholm and Company was headed by George Alfred Trenholm who was later used as the historical basis for Margaret Mitchell's fictional character Rhett Butler in *Gone With The Wind*.) (Note Three: For more on the wreck of the *Elizabeth*, please see entry 1863-9-US-NC-3.)

References for 1864-1-US-NC-1:
"Charleston Daily Courier," (Charleston, SC), Volume 62, #19667, January 16, 1864, p. 1, c. 4
"Charleston Mercury," (Charleston, SC), Volume 84, #11959, January 15, 1864, p. 2, c. 1
Official Records of the Union and Confederate Armies in the War of the Rebellion, (Washington, DC, 1891), Series 1, Volume 33, p. 1
Official Records of the Union and Confederate Navies in the War of the Rebellion, (Washington, DC, 1899), Series 1, Volume 9, pp. 153, 250, 341, 385-386, 396, 398-401, 409
Official Records of the Union and Confederate Navies in the War of the Rebellion, (Washington, DC, 1900), Series 1, Volume 10, pp. 441, 504
Graveyard of the Atlantic: Shipwrecks of the North Carolina Coast, by David Stick (University of North Carolina Press, Chapel Hill, NC, 1952), pp. 63, 247
A Chart of Wrecks of Vessels Sunk or Captured Near Wilmington, NC, Circa 1861-65, compiled by Charles H. Foard, (Wilmington, North Carolina, 1962)
Wreck Diving in North Carolina, University of North Carolina, Sea Grant Publication, #78-13, p. 5
Lifeline of the Confederacy: Blockade Running During the Civil War, by Stephen R. Wise, (University Microfilms International, 1983), pp. 301, 537, 538

1864-1-US-NC-2: The *U.S.S. Iron Age*, Lt. Commander Stone, was accidentally run aground at Lockwood's Folly Inlet, North Carolina, on January 10, 1864, while attempting to pull the wreck of the *Bendigo* into deeper water. The *Iron Age's* guns on her port side were thrown overboard. She was then burned and blown up by her crew to prevent her capture. (Note One: The *Iron Age* was a wooden hulled, screw steamer of the 4th rate. She was 424 tons, 144' in length, 25' in breadth, and 12'6" in depth. She was built at Kennebunk, Maine, in 1862. Her first home port was Boston, Massachusetts. She was purchased by Commodore J.B.

Treasures of the Confederate Coast

Montgomery for the United States Navy on April 28, 1863, for $60,000. She was commissioned on June 25, 1863. Total cost of repairs while she was in government service was $17,409.71. She was armed with three 30-pounder Dahlgren rifles and six 8-inch Dahlgren smoothbores. Her Parrot rifle was recovered.) (Note Two: Contemporary reports stated that she was in only seven feet of water at high tide. A Sea Grant publication put out by the University of North Carolina gives her present depth at ten feet.) (Note Three: For more on the wreck of the *Bendigo*, please see entry 1864-1-US-NC-1.)

References for 1864-1-US-NC-2:
"Charleston Daily Courier," (Charleston, SC), Volume 62, #19667, January 16, 1864, p. 1, c. 4
"Charleston Mercury," (Charleston, SC), Volume 84, #11959, January 15, 1864, p. 2, c. 1
"Charleston Mercury," (Charleston, SC), Volume 84, #11977, February 5, 1864, p. 1, c. 6
Annual Report of the Secretary of the Navy, 1864-1865, (Volume 6, #1, of Executive Documents, Washington, DC, 1865), p. 724
Official Records of the Union and Confederate Navies in the War of the Rebellion, (Washington, DC, 1899), Series 1, Volume 9, pp. 396-401, 404, 437
Official Records of the Union and Confederate Navies in the War of the Rebellion, (Washington, DC, 1921), Series 2, Volume 1, p. 109
Graveyard of the Atlantic: Shipwrecks of the North Carolina Coast, by David Stick (University of North Carolina Press, Chapel Hill, NC, 1952), pp. 63, 247
A Chart of Wrecks of Vessels Sunk or Captured Near Wilmington, NC, Circa 1861-65, compiled by Charles H. Foard, (Wilmington, North Carolina, 1962)
Merchant Steam Vessels of the United States 1790-1868, ("Lytle-Holdcamper List"), by William M. Lytle and Forrest R. Holdcamper, revised and edited by C. Bradford Mitchell, (Staten Island, NY, 1975), p. 102
Wreck Diving in North Carolina, University of North Carolina, Sea Grant Publication, #78-13, p. 5

1864-1-US-NC-3: At daylight, January 11, 1864, an English built steamer was observed by the U.S. flagship *Minnesota*, beached and burning, one mile west of Lockwood's Folly Inlet, North Carolina. (Note One: The steamer was later identified as the blockade runner *Ranger*. She had been bound from Newcastle to Wilmington by way of Teneriffe and Bermuda with a government cargo when she was chased ashore by the U.S. gunboats *Governor Buckingham*, *Daylight* and *Aries*. The Confederates salvaged some muskets and carpenter tools before setting her afire and abandoning her on January 10, 1864.) (Note Two: The *Ranger* was also described as destroyed "off Old Inlet.") (Note Three: Dave Horner in his book *The Blockade Runners* states she "lies in about 20 feet of water about 200 yards offshore of Holden Beach, North Carolina." and adds "At the time of this writing, thousands of Austrian rifles still remain in the bottom of the *Ranger's* hull covered with sand. The muskets are packed in crates containing twenty-four guns each together with bayonets.") (Note Four: Artifacts recovered from the *Ranger* may be seen at the Southport Maritime Museum, Southport, North Carolina, and at the Fort Fisher Visitor's Center/Museum, Kure Beach, North Carolina.)

References for 1864-1-US-NC-3:
"Charleston Daily Courier," (Charleston, SC), Volume 62, #19667, January 16, 1864, p. 1, c. 4
"Charleston Mercury," (Charleston, SC), Volume 84, #11959, January 15, 1864, p. 2, c. 1

The "Real Rhett Butler" & Other Revelations

Annual Report of the Secretary of the Navy, 1864-1865, (Volume 6, #1, of Executive Documents, Washington, DC, 1865), p. 728

Official Records of the Union and Confederate Armies in the War of the Rebellion, (Washington, DC, 1891), Series 1, Volume 33, p. 1228

Official Records of the Union and Confederate Navies in the War of the Rebellion, (Washington, DC, 1899), Series 1, Volume 9, pp. 402-405, 409, 437

Official Records of the Union and Confederate Navies in the War of the Rebellion, (Washington, DC, 1900), Series 1, Volume 10, pp. 504, 518

Graveyard of the Atlantic: Shipwrecks of the North Carolina Coast, by David Stick (University of North Carolina Press, Chapel Hill, NC, 1952), p. 247

A Chart of Wrecks of Vessels Sunk or Captured Near Wilmington, NC, Circa 1861-65, compiled by Charles H. Foard, (Wilmington, North Carolina, 1962)

Wreck Diving in North Carolina, University of North Carolina, Sea Grant Publication, #78-13, p. 5

Lifeline of the Confederacy: Blockade Running During the Civil War, by Stephen R. Wise, (University Microfilms International, 1983), pp. 368, 607, 608

The Blockade Runners, by Dave Horner, (Florida Classics Library, Port Salerno, FL, 1992), Chapter 14, pp. 26, 37, 48, 218, 219

1864-1-US-NC-4: The fate of the steamer *Vesta*, Captain R.H. Eustace, which was wrecked near the South Carolina/North Carolina line on January 11, 1864, seems to have been sealed from the moment she left Bermuda. "For seven days she was chased over the seas by a number of Yankee cruisers; but succeeded in eluding them, and on the 10th (of January) made the coast in the vicinity of Wilmington. Being compelled to lay to she was decried by a Yankee cruiser, which gave chase; and in half an hour more than eleven Yankee vessels were pouncing down upon the suddenly discovered prey. The *Vesta*, although apparently surrounded, ran the gauntlet in splendid style, through one of the most stirring scenes which the war has yet witnessed on the water. Some of the cruisers attempted to cross her bows and cut her off; but she was too rapid for this maneuver, and at about half a mile's distance some of the cruisers opened their broadsides upon her, while five others in chase were constantly using their bow guns, exploding shells right over the decks of the devoted vessel. Fortunately, no one was hurt, and the vessel ran the gauntlet, raising her flag in defiance, suffering only from a single shot, which, though it passed amidships, above the water line, happily escaped the machinery." "But the trouble seems to have commenced with what the passengers, anticipated to be the triumphant escape from their captors; for the captain and the first officer, Tickler, are reported to have become outrageously drunk after the affair was over and the night had fallen. It is said that the captain was asleep on the quarter-deck, stupefied with drink, when he should have put the ship on land; and that at two o'clock in the morning he directed the pilot to take the ship ashore, telling him that the ship was above Fort Fisher, when the fact was that she was about forty miles to the southward of Frying Pan Shoals." In fifteen minutes she was run aground so hard, she could not be got off. The *Vesta* carried a cargo "of the most valuable description," including a "splendid uniform, intended as a present for General Lee from some of his admirers in London." Three fourth's of her cargo was "on government account, consisting of army supplies, and including a very expensive lot of English shoes." It had been her first attempt at running the blockade. One of her passengers was a paymaster for the Confederate Navy. The passengers and crew landed in lifeboats minus their baggage. The *Vesta's* fate was finalized when her inebriated captain ordered her fired and burned to the water's edge. The cruisers did not get up to the wreck until the afternoon of the next day when they were attracted to it by the smoke from the conflagration. Nothing of any account was saved from the wreck. Contemporary newspaper accounts stated that the wreck was at Little River Inlet at the South Carolina, North Carolina line. (Note One: Ship logs and official reports give a more precise location and show that the loss actually took place on the North Carolina side of the state line. Those reports show her as wrecked four miles south and westward of Tubb's Inlet, North Carolina. Her position is also given in some reports as at Little River Inlet, North Carolina. A Sea Grant publication put out by the University of North Carolina lists her as in ten feet of water off *"Vesta* Pier.") [Note Two: The *Vesta* was described as a "fine looking double propeller blockade runner," "exactly like the *Ceres*." She was "perfect in all appointments" and "worth about £300,000 to the Confederates." She had a long iron hull with an elliptical stern and was rigged as a hermaphrodite brig. Her smoke pipe and every thing forward was painted white, while the after part was painted a dark lead color. She was 500 tons (262 tons register) and drew eight feet of water. She was said to be "one of the finest steamers in the blockade running line" and measured 165'x23'x13'. The *Vesta* was built by J.&W. Dudgeon at London, England, in 1863, and was owned by Crenshaw, and Collie and Company. A penciled "Memo of loss by *Vesta*" in the Vessel File at the National Archives in Washington, DC, shows the *Vesta* as having lost 21 bales of blankets, 550 reams of paper, 127 cases of shoes, and 9 bales of cloth.]

References for 1864-1-US-NC-4:
"Charleston Daily Courier," (Charleston, SC), Volume 62, #19673, January 23, 1863, p. 2, c. 1
"Charleston Mercury," (Charleston, SC), Volume 84, #11966, January 23, 1864, p. 2, c. 1
Times, (London, England), #24798, February 18, 1864, p. 11, c. 2
"Memo of loss by *Vesta*," manuscript, United States National Archives, Washington, DC, Record Group 109, Vessel File, V-10-4
"Confederate Archives," NARS, Chapter 8-2-413, 437
Official Records of the Union and Confederate Armies in the War of the Rebellion, (Washington, DC, 1891), Series 1, Volume 33, p. 1
Official Records of the Union and Confederate Navies in the War of the Rebellion, (Washington, DC, 1899), Series 1, Volume 9, pp. 402-405, 409
Official Records of the Union and Confederate Navies in the War of the Rebellion, (Washington, DC, 1900), Series 1, Volume 10, p. 504
Graveyard of the Atlantic: Shipwrecks of the North Carolina Coast, by David Stick (University of North Carolina Press, Chapel Hill, NC, 1952), p. 247

The "Real Rhett Butler" & Other Revelations

A *Chart of Wrecks of Vessels Sunk or Captured Near Wilmington, NC, Circa 1861-65*, compiled by Charles H. Foard, (Wilmington, North Carolina, 1962)
"Vessel Papers" (manuscript records), United States National Archives, Washington, DC, Record Group 109, M909, roll 30, file V-10, frames 0921-0925
Spence's Guide to South Carolina, by E. Lee Spence, (Charleston, SC, 1972), p. 6
Wreck Diving in North Carolina, University of North Carolina, Sea Grant Publication, #78-13, p. 5
Lifeline of the Confederacy: Blockade Running During the Civil War, by Stephen R. Wise, (University Microfilms International, 1983), pp. 279, 368, 624
The Blockade Runners, by Dave Horner, (Florida Classics Library, Port Salerno, FL, 1992), Chapter 14, pp. 26, 217

1864-1-US-NC-5: The "notorious runner" *Advance* (a.k.a. *A.D. Vance*, ex-*Lord Clyde*) was run ashore on January 20 (or 17), 1864. Her crew escaped. The sidewheel steamer's location was described as well protected by the batteries of Fort Caswell and Bald Head, and not far from the Western Bar near Wilmington, North Carolina. She remained aground through January 24, 1864, but was got off with the help of large tugs or steamers which were sent to her aid by the Confederates. (Note One: This vessel has been included in this list, even though it got off, because the London *Times* reported that, although her cargo was expected to be saved, the steamer was "a total wreck." The *Times* gave her position as on the beach near the "entrance of the Wilmington River" and said she was run ashore by her captain to avoid capture.) (Note Two: She was eventually captured on September 10, 1864, and used as a blockader. She was "very fast" and had cost $175,000 in gold only two years before her capture. That much gold would have been over three million in today's dollars, which shows the importance and value of these vessels. Although rumors stated that she was supposed to have had a large shipment of gold aboard, none was found when she was captured, giving rise to speculation that her officers had stolen the gold and then let her be captured to cover its theft.)

References for 1864-1-US-NC-5:
"Charleston Mercury," (Charleston, SC), Volume 84, #11964, January 24, 1864, p. 2, c. 1
"Charleston Mercury," (Charleston, SC), Volume 84, #11965, January 25, 1864, p. 2, c. 1
"Charleston Mercury," (Charleston, SC), Volume 84, #11970, January 28, 1864, p. 2, c. 1
Times, (London, England), #24796, February 16, 1864, p. 12, c. 4
Times, (London, England), #24798, February 18, 1864, p. 12, c. 1
Times, (London, England), #24801, February 22, 1864, p. 12, c. 6
Official Records of the Union and Confederate Armies in the War of the Rebellion, (Washington, DC, 1895), Series 1, Volume 46, Part 2, p. 1007
Official Records of the Union and Confederate Navies in the War of the Rebellion, (Washington, DC, 1899), Series 1, Volume 9, p. 413
Official Records of the Union and Confederate Navies in the War of the Rebellion, (Washington, DC, 1900), Series 1, Volume 10, pp. 453-456

1864-1-US-NC-6: The "Charleston Mercury" of January 28, 1864, reported that the United States gunboat *Daylight* had been blown up and every man aboard her killed by a shell shot from Fort Fisher, North Carolina. [Note: Even if this report was true, she was not destroyed, as the *Daylight* continued in service until she was taken out of commission on May 24, 1865. The screw steamer *Daylight*,

Treasures of the Confederate Coast

was built in 1859 by Samuel Sueden of New York. She was 432 (or 682) tons and measured 170'x30'6"x13'.]

References for 1864-1-US-NC-6:
"Charleston Mercury," (Charleston, SC), Volume 84, #11970, January 28, 1864, p. 2, c. 1
Official Records of the Union and Confederate Navies in the War of the Rebellion, (Washington, DC, 1899), Series 1, Volume 9, pp. 499, 554, 579, 634, 720
Dictionary of American Naval Fighting Ships, (Washington, DC, 1963), Volume 2, p. 247
List of American-Flag Merchant Vessels that Received Certificates of Enrollment or Registry at the Port of New York 1789-1867, compiled by Forest R. Holdcamper, (U.S. National Archives, Washington, DC, 1968), Special List #22, Volume 1, p. 168

1864-1-US-SC/GA-1: The schooner *Sylvanus*, of Nassau, "after being repeatedly shelled and riddled (by the *U.S.S. Huron*), she was run ashore and sunk in one fathom water," in Doboy Sound, Georgia, on January 2, 1864.

References for 1864-1-US-SC/GA-1:
Times, (London, England), #24798, February 18, 1864, p. 12, c. 1
Times, (London, England), #24801, February 22, 1864, p. 12, c. 6
Report of the Secretary of the Navy, Second Session, 38th Congress, 1864-1865, (Washington, DC, 1865), p. 729.

1864-1-US-SC/GA-2: The sidewheel steamer *Dare*, bound from Bermuda to Wilmington, North Carolina, was chased ashore at North Inlet, near the south end of DeBordieu (aka DuBourdieu, or · DeBordeau) Island, South Carolina, on January 7, 1864. (Note One: Her position was also described as "beached six miles east of the Pee Dee" River. The *Dare*, captain Thomas B. Skinner, was burned by her own crew to prevent her capture. Two Federal boats "filed to their utmost capacity with the baggage of the officers and other plunder" swamped drowning between three and "fourteen of the Yankee sailors". The Yankees had broken into the *Dare's* liquor and had all gotten drunk. Twenty-four (or 25) Federals were afterwards captured on the beach by Major William P. White and two other men.) [Note Two: The *Dare* was also known as the *Virginia Dare*, and is incorrectly shown in some records as the *Dan* and as the *Adair*. The *Dare's* iron hull was designated yard #52, and was built at Kelvinhaugh Yard, Glasgow in September, 1863, by Alexander R. Stephen and Sons. She was schooner rigged. Her builders charged £12,860 for her construction and £4,720 for her engines, making them a profit of £3,500. The *Dare's* first registered owner was David McNutt. The vessel was operated by the Richmond Importing and Exporting Company at the time of her loss. The *Dare* measured 179.46 tons register, 553 12/94 tons BM (or 552 6/94), 217 (or 218') in length, 23' in breadth, and 9'6" in depth of hold to top of floors.] (Note Three: She carried a cargo of seventy-five tons, 50 tons of which was for the State of Virginia, and a considerable portion of that was intended for the Virginia Military Institute. Most of her cargo was expected to be saved.) (Note Four: A signal lantern and a porthole on display with a model

The "Real Rhett Butler" & Other Revelations

of the *Dare* at the "Ships of the Sea Museum" at Savannah, Georgia, were recovered by Master Diver Lawrence Wilde on June 11, 1962. Whether, the artifacts were actually recovered from the *Dare* is questionable, as a typed letter which was sent to the museum stated that the *Dare* lies "at the south end of Pawley's Island", which is factually incorrect. However, the blockade running steamer *Rose* was reportedly wrecked at the south end of Pawley's Island near the wreck of another unidentified steamer, and the museum's artifacts could have come from either of those two vessels. For more on the loss of the steamer *Rose* see entry 1864-6-US-SC/GA-1 of this book.) (Note Five: In 1966, Jim Batey, Ron Renau, and I dove on the wreck of a steamer at North Inlet. That wreck's position closely matches the location given for the *Dare* in contemporary documents. We recovered a number of Civil War era bottles and other artifacts. We also recovered an extremely rare and valuable pewter inkwell from just outside the broken iron hull of the wreck. A name and date had been scratched into the pewter. The inkwell was American made and dated from before the American Revolution, and may have been an heirloom or otherwise prized possession of one of the *Dare's* officers, or it may have come from a nearby wooden wreck, or even washed out of the creek. The inkwell is in excellent condition and has been valued at over $10,000. Portions of the steamer we dove on are exposed at low tide.] (Note Six: Stephen R. Wise in his book *Lifeline of the Confederacy: Blockade Running During the Civil War* gives the same date of loss, but incorrectly shows the *Dare* as having been wrecked off Lockwood Folly, North Carolina, on her first attempt through the blockade. Charles Foard's chart of Civil War wrecks of the Wilmington, North Carolina, area incorrectly shows the *Dare* as wrecked at "North Inlet, South Carolina (Little River)."] (Note Seven: The *Dare* was a sister ship to the *Fergus*. For additional information on the *Fergus* see entry 1864-2-US-SC/GA-1.)

References for 1864-1-US-SC/GA-2:

Charleston Daily Courier, (Charleston, SC), Volume 62, #19664, January 13, 1864, p. 1, c. 2
Charleston Daily Courier, (Charleston, SC), Volume 62, #19665, January 14, 1864, p. 1, c. 2
Charleston Daily Courier, (Charleston, SC), Volume 62, #19669, January 19, 1864, p. 1, c. 3
Charleston Mercury, (Charleston, SC), Volume 84, #11959, January 15, 1864, p. 2, c. 1
Charleston Mercury, (Charleston, SC), Volume 84, #11961, January 18, 1864, p. 1, c. 4
Charleston Mercury, (Charleston, SC), Volume 84, #12082, June 8, 1864, p. 2, c. 1
"Vessel Papers" (manuscript records), United States National Archives, Washington, DC, Record Group 109, files D-51, V-34
Report of the Secretary of the Navy, Second Session, 38th Congress, 1864-1865, (Washington, DC, 1865), p. 725
Official Records of the Union and Confederate Armies in the War of the Rebellion, (Washington, DC, 1891), Series 1, Volume 35, Part 1, pp. 272, 273
Official Records of the Union and Confederate Navies in the War of the Rebellion, (Washington, DC, 1899), Series 1, Volume 9, pp. 388-393, 409, 410
A Chart of Wrecks of Vessels Sunk or Captured Near Wilmington, NC, Circa 1861-65, compiled by Charles H. Foard, (Wilmington, North Carolina, 1962)
Typed 3x5 file cards, ("Ships of the Sea Museum," Savannah, Georgia), catalog cards #65:39, #65:40

Treasures of the Confederate Coast

Personal knowledge of E. Lee Spence of dive he made with Jim Batey and Ron Renau, circa summer, 1966.
History of Georgetown County, South Carolina, by George C. Rogers, (Columbia, South Carolina, 1970), p. 413
An Oceanographic Atlas of the Continental Margin, J.G. Newton, O.H. Pilkey, & J.O. Blanton, (Duke University Marine Laboratory, Beaufort, North Carolina, 1971), p. 17 chart symbol #87, p. 20 entry #87
Pawley's Island, A Living Legend, by Prevost and Wilder, (Columbia, South Carolina, 1972), p. 49
Lifeline of the Confederacy: Blockade Running During the Civil War, by Stephen R. Wise, (University Microfilms International, 1983), pp. 368, 551
Merchant Sailing Ships, 1850-1875, Heyday of Sail, by David R. MacGregor, (Lloyd's of London Press, 1984), p. 236

1864-2-US-NC-1: The steamer *Wild Dayrell*, of Liverpool, was discovered ashore at the mouth of Stump Inlet ("near Topsail Inlet about twelve miles north of Wilmington," North Carolina) by the *U.S.S. Sassacus* on February 1, 1864. [Note One: The Confederates had been unloading the *Wild Dayrell* when she was discovered. The blockade runner's iron hull was riddled with shot about her waterline by the *Sassacus* and she was set fire and burned by the *Sassacus* two days later. Over half of the *Wild Dayrell's* valuable cargo (reported as assorted merchandise, and as "shoes, blankets, and provisions") was destroyed with the vessel. A case of 270,000 percussion caps for muskets was taken from the wreck by the *U.S.S. Florida.* The value of the *Wild Dayrell* and her cargo was estimated at $200,000, which would have been today's equivalent of approximately $4,000,000.] [Note Two: The *Wild Dayrell* had made four successful runs through the blockade prior to her loss. She was built by Jones, Quiggin and Company at Liverpool, England, in 1863, and was owned by the Anglo-Confederate Trading Company. She measured 215'x20'x10.9' and was 320 (or 440) gross tons. She had two smokestacks and sidewheels.] (Note Three: Dave Horner in his book *The Blockade Runners* shows her name as the *Wild Darrell* and adds "Today the ruins of the *Wild Darrell* are well sanded in. However, anyone ambitious enough to search for a trace of her rusting relics may well stumble upon fragments of the Spanish galleon *El Salvador* which went down more than a hundred years earlier in the same vicinity. The Spanish ship also had a cargo of $200,000, but most of it was in silver.")

References for 1864-2-US-NC-1:
"Charleston Mercury," (Charleston, SC), Volume 84, #11978, February 6, 1864, p. 2, c. 1
Times, (London, England), #24802, February 23, 1864, p. 10, c. 6
Annual Report of the Secretary of the Navy, 1864-1865, (Volume 6, #1, of Executive Documents, Washington, DC, 1865), pp. 175-180, 729
Official Records of the Union and Confederate Navies in the War of the Rebellion, (Washington, DC, 1899), Series 1, Volume 9, pp. 437-439, 459-461, 465, 474, 476, 482, 483
Running the Blockade, by Thomas E. Taylor, (London, England, 1897), pp. 110-113
Graveyard of the Atlantic: Shipwrecks of the North Carolina Coast, by David Stick (University of North Carolina Press, Chapel Hill, NC, 1952), pp. 64, 247
A Chart of Wrecks of Vessels Sunk or Captured Near Wilmington, NC, Circa 1861-65, compiled by Charles H. Foard, (Wilmington, North Carolina, 1962)
An Oceanographic Atlas of the Continental Margin, J.G. Newton, O.H. Pilkey and J.O. Blanton, (Duke University Marine Laboratory, Beaufort, NC, 1971), p. 20 entry #130, p. 21 chart symbol #130
Lifeline of the Confederacy: Blockade Running During the Civil War, by Stephen R. Wise, (University Microfilms International, 1983), pp. 347, 348, 369, 628, 630 (misnumbered page)

The "Real Rhett Butler" & Other Revelations

The Blockade Runners, by Dave Horner, (Florida Classics Library, Port Salerno, FL, 1992), Chapter 14, p. 219

1864-2-US-NC-2: The *U.S.S. Underwriter*, Jacob Westervelt commanding, was captured, stripped, "burned to the water's edge," and blown up by the Confederates on February 2, 1864, while at anchor in the Neuse River off Foster's Wharf near the Federal fortifications above New Berne, North Carolina. Her officers and crew (about 80 or 90 in number) fought desperately until, overpowered by numbers, they were obliged to surrender. Captain Westervelt and eight men were killed, and twenty wounded. The attacking party was composed of about 300 well organized sailors, armed with rifles, revolvers, and cutlasses, commanded by John Taylor Wood. (Note One: Midshipman Scharf, who was among the attackers, later wrote in his *History of the Confederate States Navy*: "The enemy gathered in the ways just aft of the wheel-house, and as the Confederates came up they poured into them volley after volley of musketry, each flash of which reddened the waters around, enabling the attacking party to note their position. In spite of the heavy fire, the boarders were cool and yet eager, now and then one or more were struck down, but the rest never faltered. When the boats struck the sides of the *Underwriter*, grapnels were thrown on board, and the Confederates were soon scrambling, with cutlass and pistol in hand, to the deck with a rush and a wild cheer that rung across the waters, the firing from the enemy never ceasing for one moment." Lieutenant Benjamin P. Loyall was second in command and executive officer of the attacking force and was first to reach the deck, Scharf followed closely behind. Commander wood was promoted to captain and Lieutenant Loyall was subsequently appointed a commander in the Provisional Navy of the Confederate States of America by President Davis "for gallant and meritorious conduct" in that affair.) (Note Two: A contemporary map shows the wreck as located below Fort Stevens and across from Fort Anderson.) [Note Three: The *Underwriter* had been purchased by the Federal government at New York for $18,500 on August 23, 1861. The total cost to repairs while in government service was $47,294.12. She was a wooden hulled, sidewheel steamer of 341 tons. She was 170' in length, 23'7" in breadth, and 8'1" in depth. She was armed with two 8-inch guns of fifty-five hundredweight each (also described as one 6"-Dahlgren and one 8'-Dahlgren) and two 12-pounder howitzer's (also described as one 12-pounder rifle and one 12-pounder smoothbore). One of the howitzers was recovered. She had engines of eight hundred horse power. The *Underwriter* had been built at Brooklyn, New York, in 1852. She

Treasures of the Confederate Coast

was issued a certificate of steam enrollment at the port of New York on May 20, 1852.] (Note Four: A report from W.H. Macomb, commanding District Sounds, North Carolina Squadron, to Rear-Admiral D.D. Porter, dated November 27, 1864, refers to the boilers of the wreck of the *Underwriter*, as very valuable.)

References for 1864-2-US-NC-2:

"Charleston Daily Courier," (Charleston, SC), Volume 62, #19686, February 8, 1863, p. 1, c. 5

New York Times, (New York, NY), Volume 13, Supplement to #3860, February 6, 1864, p. 3, c. 2

Annual Report of the Secretary of the Navy, 1864-1865, (Volume 6, #1, of Executive Documents, Washington, DC, 1865), pp. 169-174

History of the Confederate States Navy From its Organization to the Surrender of its Last Vessel, by J. Thomas Scharf, (New York, NY, 1887), pp. 390, 393, 395-398, note on pp. 618, 619

Confederate Military History, edited by General Clement A. Evans, (Confederate Publishing Co., Atlanta, GA, 1899), Volume 12, pp. 76-77

Official Records of the Union and Confederate Armies in the War of the Rebellion, (Washington, DC, 1891), Series 1, Volume 33, pp. 50, 56, 91, 94, 103, 501, 511, 512

Official Records of the Union and Confederate Armies in the War of the Rebellion, (Washington, DC, 1897), Series 1, Volume 51, Part 2, p. 817

Official Records of the Union and Confederate Navies in the War of the Rebellion, (Washington, DC, 1899), Series 1, Volume 9, pp. 439-449, 453, 468

Official Records of the Union and Confederate Navies in the War of the Rebellion, (Washington, DC, 1900), Series 1, Volume 10, p. 72

Official Records of the Union and Confederate Navies in the War of the Rebellion, (Washington, DC, 1900), Series 1, Volume 11, p. 98

Official Records of the Union and Confederate Navies in the War of the Rebellion, (Washington, DC, 1901), Series 1, Volume 12, p. 181

Official Records of the Union and Confederate Navies in the War of the Rebellion, (Washington, DC, 1921), Series 2, Volume 1, p. 228

Graveyard of the Atlantic: Shipwrecks of the North Carolina Coast, by David Stick (University of North Carolina Press, Chapel Hill, NC, 1952), pp. 58, 247

List of American-Flag Merchant Vessels that Received Certificates of Enrollment or Registry at the Port of New York 1789-1867, compiled by Forest R. Holdcamper, (U.S. National Archives, Washington, DC, 1968), Special List #22, Volume 2, p. 696

An Oceanographic Atlas of the Continental Margin, J.G. Newton, O.H. Pilkey and J.O. Blanton, (Duke University Marine Laboratory, Beaufort, NC, 1971), p. 24 entry #280

Merchant Steam Vessels of the United States 1790-1868, ("Lytle-Holdcamper List"), by William M. Lytle and Forrest R. Holdcamper, revised and edited by C. Bradford Mitchell, (Staten Island, NY, 1975), p. 217

1864-2-US-NC-3: The new, sidewheel steamer *Nutfield* (or *Nutfield*), Captain Waller, was chased ashore at New River Inlet, North Carolina, on February 4, 1864, and burned by the *U.S.S. Sassacus*, Lt. Commander F.A. Roe. One of the unfortunate blockade runner's boats capsized and its crew drowned. One man was captured and the rest escaped. (Note One: The *Nutfield* was making her first attempt at running the blockade and carried an assorted cargo of merchandise, munitions of war, Enfield rifles, eight Whitworth guns, and pig lead. The Whitworth guns and lead were thrown overboard during the chase. The *Sassacus* saved the following items from the wreck: 529 Austrian rifled muskets with bayonets; 98 English rifled muskets with long bayonets; 100 English rifled muskets with regular bayonets; 40 English rifled muskets (short); 110 cavalry sabers; 23 boxes of needles, etc. The steamer's iron hull was riddled with shot to destroy her, and she was set afire.) (Note Two: The *Nutfield's* tonnage is given in various reports as "750 tons," as "420 tons, English Measurement," and as "402 tons register." She had one smokestack and foremast and was built by James Ash and Company at Cubitt Town, England, in 1862.) (Note Three: A typo on page 300 in Stephen Wise's excellent book, *Lifeline of the Confederacy: Blockade Running During the Civil War*, gives the year of loss as 1863 instead of 1864.) (Note Four: The London *Times* of March 2, 1864, listed a steamer *Hatfield*, as lost at Wilmington, but the report was undoubtedly referring to the loss of the *Nutfield*.)

References for 1864-2-US-NC-3:
Times, (London, England), #24809, March 2, 1864, p. 12, c. 4
Annual Report of the Secretary of the Navy, 1864-1865, (Volume 6, #1, of Executive Documents, Washington, DC, 1865), pp. 175, 180, 181, 727
Official Records of the Union and Confederate Navies in the War of the Rebellion, (Washington, DC, 1899), Series 1, Volume 9, pp. 459-461, 465, 482
Official Records of the Union and Confederate Navies in the War of the Rebellion, (Washington, DC, 1900), Series 1, Volume 10, p. 504
Graveyard of the Atlantic: Shipwrecks of the North Carolina Coast, by David Stick (University of North Carolina Press, Chapel Hill, NC, 1952), pp. 64, 247
A Chart of Wrecks of Vessels Sunk or Captured Near Wilmington, NC, Circa 1861-65, compiled by Charles H. Foard, (Wilmington, North Carolina, 1962)
An Oceanographic Atlas of the Continental Margin, J.G. Newton, O.H. Pilkey and J.O. Blanton, (Duke University Marine Laboratory, Beaufort, NC, 1971), p. 20 entry #131, p. 21 chart symbol #131
Lifeline of the Confederacy: Blockade Running During the Civil War, by Stephen R. Wise, (University Microfilms International, 1983), pp. 300, 368, 601

1864-2-US-NC-4: The steamer *Dee*, Captain George H. Bier, from Hamilton, Bermuda, was discovered ashore and on fire, opposite Mr. Thomas Hansley's plantation, about one mile to the southward of Masonboro Inlet, North Carolina, on February 5, 1864. Seven of her crew were captured. She was fired into and destroyed by the *U.S.S. Cambridge*. (Note One: The *Dee* had made six previous successful runs through the blockade. Captain Bier had formerly served as a Lieutenant on the *Dee* and had already made three successful trips. Her cargo consisted of bacon, a "proportion of lead" and a small quantity of coffee. "Portions" of the *Dee* were salvaged by the Confederate States Navy.) (Note Two: The *Dee* was built by J.W. Dudgeon of London, England, in 1863, and her engines were made by the Sun Iron Works. She had an iron hull and was a twin propeller steamer. The vessel was 165' in length, 23' in breadth, 13' in depth of hold and 215 registered tons. The first registered owner was F. Muir. The vessel was owned by Crenshaw and Collie and Company at the time of her loss.) (Note Three: David Stick in his book, *Graveyard of the Atlantic,* gives the location of the wreck as "Near Cape Fear" on one page and as "off New Inlet" on another. Dave Horner in his book *The Blockade Runners* says she "was loaded with guns and ammunition" and "a large number of heavy lead ingots." He further states "Several hundred bars of lead were thrown over the starboard side in a frantic effort to lighten the load" and "Today the pile of lead is still alongside the *Dee's* rusting

Treasures of the Confederate Coast

hull.) (Note Four: For more information on Captain Bier, please see note two of entry 1864-5-US-NC-2.)

References for 1864-2-US-NC-4:
"Charleston Mercury," (Charleston, SC), Volume 84, #11985, February 15, 1864, p. 2, c. 2
Times, (London, England), #24809, March 2, 1864, p. 12, c. 4
Annual Report of the Secretary of the Navy, 1864-1865, (Volume 6, #1, of Executive Documents, Washington, DC, 1865), pp. 175, 725
Official Records of the Union and Confederate Armies in the War of the Rebellion, (Washington, DC, 1891), Series 1, Volume 33, p. 1228
Official Records of the Union and Confederate Navies in the War of the Rebellion, (Washington, DC, 1899), Series 1, Volume 9, pp. 467, 468, 482
Official Records of the Union and Confederate Navies in the War of the Rebellion, (Washington, DC, 1900), Series 1, Volume 10, p. 504
Graveyard of the Atlantic: Shipwrecks of the North Carolina Coast, by David Stick (University of North Carolina Press, Chapel Hill, NC, 1952), pp. 64, 247
Lifeline of the Confederacy: Blockade Running During the Civil War, by Stephen R. Wise, (University Microfilms International, 1983), pp. 368, 551
The Blockade Runners, by Dave Horner, (Florida Classics Library, Port Salerno, FL, 1992), Chapter 14, p. 220 (references article in the Wilmington Journal of April 16, 1864)

1864-2-US-NC-5: On February 9, 1864, the Federals reported seeing the blockade runner *Spunkie* beached inside the bar, a short distance west of Fort Caswell, North Carolina. Her location was also given as under the guns of "Fort Campbell." [Note One: The wreck of the *Spunkie* (also spelled *Spunky*, or *Spunkey*) was said to have been broadside to shore with her bow headed westward and she was described broken in two. She carried blankets, shoes and provisions, most of which was saved by the Confederates. The *Spunkie* had succeeded in eight previous runs through the blockade.] [Note Two: The *Spunkie* was described as a long, low sidewheel steamer, painted white with one (or two) smokestack(s), and schooner rigged. She was also described as a "little Clyde steamer." She was built by Todd and McGregor at Patrick, Scotland, in 1857.] (Note Three: In his excellent book, *Graveyard of the Atlantic*, David Stick gives the location of the wreck as "Near Cape Fear" on one page but also reports it as described above on another page.)

References for 1864-2-US-NC-5:
"Charleston Mercury," (Charleston, SC), Volume 84, #11983, February 12, 1864, p. 2, c. 1
"Charleston Mercury," (Charleston, SC), Volume 84, #11984, February 13, 1864, p. 2, c. 1
"Charleston Mercury," (Charleston, SC), Volume 84, #11985, February 15, 1864, p. 2, c. 2
"Charleston Daily Courier," (Charleston, SC), Volume 62, #19692, February 15, 1863, p. 1, c. 2
Times, (London, England), #24809, March 2, 1864, p. 12, c. 4
Official Records of the Union and Confederate Navies in the War of the Rebellion, (Washington, DC, 1899), Series 1, Volume 9, pp. 153, 250, 341, 472, 473
Official Records of the Union and Confederate Navies in the War of the Rebellion, (Washington, DC, 1900), Series 1, Volume 10, p. 504
Graveyard of the Atlantic: Shipwrecks of the North Carolina Coast, by David Stick (University of North Carolina Press, Chapel Hill, NC, 1952), pp. 64, 247
A Chart of Wrecks of Vessels Sunk or Captured Near Wilmington, NC, Circa 1861-65, compiled by Charles H. Foard, (Wilmington, North Carolina, 1962)
University Marine Laboratory, Beaufort, NC, 1971), p. 17 chart symbol #44, p. 20 entry #44
Lifeline of the Confederacy: Blockade Running During the Civil War, by Stephen R. Wise, (University Microfilms International, 1983), pp. 369, 615, 616

1864-2-US-NC-6: The sidewheel steamer *Fanny and Jenny* (a.k.a. *Fannie and Jennie*, ex-*General Banks*, ex-*Scotia*), Captain Coxetter, five days out of Nassau, with coal and merchandise, was run ashore by the *U.S.S. Florida* and was destroyed near and above Masonboro Inlet, North Carolina, on February 9 (or 10), 1864. (Note One: At least one account attributed her loss to a case of mistaken identity. It stated that the officer in charge of a Whitworth battery, supposing her to be an enemy steamer opened fire on her and set her afire, completely destroying her. Captain Coxetter was nearly frozen to death and four or five men were drowned when their boat overturned. Among the dead was the former purser for the *Beauregard*. Twenty-five of her men were captured. A Confederate flag, a spyglass, her chronometer, her sextant, and her charts were taken from the wreck by the Federals. A "handsome sword, gold mounted, for General R.E. Lee" was destroyed with the vessel.) [Note Two: The steamer's iron hull was built by Wigram and Company at Blackwell, England, in 1847, and she was engined by Maudsley and Company of London. She was owned by Weir and Company. She had made two successful runs through the blockade under the name *Scotia* but was captured on a third voyage by the *U.S.S. Restless* on October 24, 1862. When she was condemned and sold she was documented as the *General Banks* on January 28, 1863. Shortly thereafter she was renamed *Fanny and Jenny* and put back into the blockade running business. She was 202'2" in length, 28'4" in breadth, and 13'7" in depth of hold. She was 479 gross tons (also shown as 727 tons). She was issued a certificate of steam registry at the port of New York on January 28, 1863. Some records show her as a steam propeller.] (Note Three: The book, *Graveyard of the Atlantic,* gives the location of the wreck as "north of Wrightsville Beach." A Sea Grant publication put out by the University of North Carolina places this wreck in 12' of water north of the Wrightsville Beach Jetty.) (Note Four: In his exciting book *Always Another Adventure*, Marx refers to research and local legend that said that the *Fanny and Jenny* "was carrying half a million gold sovereigns" and that the sword's hilt was "studded with jewels." During a conversation I had with Marx in 1967, he told me that the wreck he dove on and identified as the *Fanny and Jenny* was definitely that of a screw steamer and not a sidewheeler.) (Note Five: The London *Times* of March 2, 1864, incorrectly listed the loss of the *Fanny and Jenny* as being the loss of two separate vessels, the *Fanny*, and the *Jenny*.)

References for 1864-2-US-NC-6:
"Charleston Mercury," (Charleston, SC), Volume 84, #11984, February 13, 1864, p. 2, c. 1
"Charleston Mercury," (Charleston, SC), Volume 84, #11990, February 20, 1864, p. 2, c. 1, 2
"Charleston Daily Courier," (Charleston, SC), Volume 62, #19692, February 15, 1863, p. 1, c. 4
Times, (London, England), #24809, March 2, 1864, p. 12, c. 4

Treasures of the Confederate Coast

Annual Report of the Secretary of the Navy, 1864-1865, (Volume 6, #1, of Executive Documents, Washington, DC, 1865), pp. 175-178, 725

Official Records of the Union and Confederate Navies in the War of the Rebellion, (Washington, DC, 1899), Series 1, Volume 9, pp. 473-476, 482, 483

Official Records of the Union and Confederate Navies in the War of the Rebellion, (Washington, DC, 1900), Series 1, Volume 10, p. 504

"Ships that Tested the Blockade of the Carolina Ports, 1861-1865," by Marcus W. Price, (*The American Neptune*, July, 1948), p. 238

Graveyard of the Atlantic: Shipwrecks of the North Carolina Coast, by David Stick (University of North Carolina Press, Chapel Hill, NC, 1952), pp. 64, 247

A Chart of Wrecks of Vessels Sunk or Captured Near Wilmington, NC, Circa 1861-65, compiled by Charles H. Foard, (Wilmington, North Carolina, 1962)

Always Another Adventure, by Robert F. Marx, (World Publishing, Cleveland and New York, 1967), pp. 44-51

List of American-Flag Merchant Vessels that Received Certificates of Enrollment or Registry at the Port of New York 1789-1867, compiled by Forest R. Holdcamper, (U.S. National Archives, Washington, DC, 1968), Special List #22, Volume 2, p. 266

An Oceanographic Atlas of the Continental Margin, J.G. Newton, O.H. Pilkey and J.O. Blanton, (Duke University Marine Laboratory, Beaufort, NC, 1971), p. 17 chart symbol #92, p. 20 entry #92

The Treasure Diver's Guide, by John S. Potter, Jr., (Garden City, NY, revised edition 1972), pp. 487, 529

Merchant Steam Vessels of the United States 1790-1868, ("Lytle-Holdcamper List"), by William M. Lytle and Forrest R. Holdcamper, revised and edited by C. Bradford Mitchell, (Staten Island, NY, 1975), pp. 71, 79

Wreck Diving in North Carolina, University of North Carolina, Sea Grant Publication, #78-13, p. 7

Lifeline of the Confederacy: Blockade Running During the Civil War, by Stephen R. Wise, (University Microfilms International, 1983), pp. 369, 561, 562, 613

The Blockade Runners, by Dave Horner, (Florida Classics Library, Port Salerno, FL, 1992), Chapter 14, pp. 221-222

1864-2-US-NC-7: The screw steamer *Emily*, of London, bound from Bermuda, with a cargo of bacon and salt for the Confederate government, and a few barrels of merchandise, was accidentally run ashore 1/2 mile north of the wreck of the *Fannie and Jennie* above Masonboro Inlet, North Carolina, on February 9 (or 10), 1864. (Note One: The *Emily* was said to have been lost "through the incapacity of her pilot, who • • • was at once put in the army." She was making her first attempt through the blockade when she was lost. The wreck was burned by the *U.S.S. Florida*. There was speculation that something may have been hidden under the salt, but just what that might have been was never made clear.) (Note Two: The *Emily* had been brig rigged, but was stripped down to her two lower masts in preparation to run the blockade. She was 253 tons register and was owned by Thomas Sterling Begbie. Stephen Wise in his excellent book, *Lifeline of the Confederacy: Blockade Running During the Civil War*, states that the *Emily* was built by William Simons and Company in 1855. However, in contemporary records, the *Emily* was described as a new and "very handsome steamer, expensively fitted out.") (Note Three: Stephen Wise gives her location as "off Wrightsville Beach," while David Stick in his book, *Graveyard of the Atlantic*, calls her the *Emily of London*, and gives the location of the wreck as "north of Wrightsville Beach.") (Note Four: For more on the wreck of the *Fannie and Jennie*, please see entry 1864-2-US-NC-6.)

References for 1864-2-US-NC-7:

"Charleston Mercury," (Charleston, SC), Volume 84, #11984, February 13, 1864, p. 2, c. 1

Times, (London, England), #24809, March 2, 1864, p. 12, c. 4

The "Real Rhett Butler" & Other Revelations

Annual Report of the Secretary of the Navy, 1864-1865, (Volume 6, #1, of Executive Documents, Washington, DC, 1865), pp. 175, 725
Official Records of the Union and Confederate Navies in the War of the Rebellion, (Washington, DC, 1899), Series 1, Volume 9, pp. 132, 473-476, 482, 483
Official Records of the Union and Confederate Navies in the War of the Rebellion, (Washington, DC, 1900), Series 1, Volume 10, p. 504
Official Records of the Union and Confederate Navies in the War of the Rebellion, (Washington, DC, 1922), Series 2, Volume 3, p. 1084
Graveyard of the Atlantic: Shipwrecks of the North Carolina Coast, by David Stick (University of North Carolina Press, Chapel Hill, NC, 1952), pp. 64, 247
A Chart of Wrecks of Vessels Sunk or Captured Near Wilmington, NC, Circa 1861-65, compiled by Charles H. Foard, (Wilmington, North Carolina, 1962)
An Oceanographic Atlas of the Continental Margin, J.G. Newton, O.H. Pilkey and J.O. Blanton, (Duke University Marine Laboratory, Beaufort, NC, 1971), p. 17 chart symbol #93, p. 20 entry #93
Lifeline of the Confederacy: Blockade Running During the Civil War, by Stephen R. Wise, (University Microfilms International, 1983), pp. 368, 558

1864-2-US-NC-8: The "Charleston Mercury" of February 13, 1864, reported the steamer *City of Petersburg,* as wrecked trying to run the blockade off Wilmington, North Carolina. (Note One: The report was incorrect as all sixteen attempts she made to run the blockade were successful and she survived the war.) (Note Two: The *City of Petersburg* had two stacks, telescopic funnels, and sidewheels. She was 426 tons register, had an iron hull, and was 223'x25'x13'6". She was built by Caird and Company at Greenock, Scotland, in 1863, and was owned by the Virginia Importing and Exporting Company.)

References for 1864-2-US-NC-8:
"Charleston Mercury," (Charleston, SC), Volume 84, #11984, February 13, 1864, p. 2, c. 1
Official Records of the Union and Confederate Navies in the War of the Rebellion, (Washington, DC, 1899), Series 1, Volume 9, pp. 154, 341, 475, 476
Lifeline of the Confederacy: Blockade Running During the Civil War, by Stephen R. Wise, (University Microfilms International, 1983), pp. 296, 299, 362-367, 546

1864-2-US-SC/GA-1: The blockade runner *Presto* (a.k.a. *Fergus*), Captain Horsey, struck the wreck of the *Minho,* and got ashore nearly opposite Battery Rutledge on Sullivan's Island, South Carolina, on February 2 (or 4), 1864, and was lost. (Note One: At the time of her loss, the *Presto* was inbound from Nassau on her third run through the blockade, with a cargo of shoes, liquor, blankets, bacon, ham, etc. Most of her cargo was on government account, and only a small part of the cargo belonged to private individuals. Her crew escaped over the side taking their personal possessions with them. The Federals shelled the wreck with a 300-pounder Parrott and other heavy rifles. The third shot crashed into her and the steamer "was immediately deserted by the loiterers who jumped overboard, took to the shore, and then to their heels in an amusing manner." The next day the monitors shelled the wreck with their 15-inch guns and completed the destruction. The wreck was fired at one hundred and forty-two times and struck twenty-one times. The soldiers in the fort managed to brave the shelling and rescue a large part of the liquor. The Confederate soldiers got so

Treasures of the Confederate Coast

drunk that it threatened the security of the fort. The Federal commander later wrote that the Confederate troops had a "grand drunk" and he could have captured the entire island with a force of 300 men, if he had just known about the liquor in time. The *Presto* was afterwards reported as burned to the water's edge and broken up. (Note Two: The *Presto* was described as a very handsome, new steamer with sidewheels and two short funnels painted white, and of 164 tons register. This was probably the iron hulled steamer *Fergus*, 553 12/94 tons BM, which was built by Alexander Stephen & Sons at Kelvinhaugh Yard, Glasgow, in 1863. That vessel was a sister ship to the *Dare* and was built under a contracted price of £12,200. The price probably did not include her engines. Her builders made a profit of £3,500 on her construction. She was originally designated yard #48. For information on the *Dare* see entry 1864-1-US-SC/GA-2.) (Note Three: The remains of a wreck in the described location were located and tentatively identified as the *Presto* by Jim Batey and me in 1967.)

References for 1864-2-US-SC/GA-1:

Charleston Mercury, (Charleston, SC), Volume 84, #11975, February 3, 1864, p. 2, c. 1
Charleston Mercury, (Charleston, SC), Volume 84, #11976, February 4, 1864, p. 2, c. 1
Charleston Mercury, (Charleston, SC), Volume 84, #11977, February 5, 1864, p. 2, c. 1
Charleston Mercury, (Charleston, SC), Volume 84, #11979, February 8, 1864, p. 2, c. 1
"Charleston Daily Courier," (Charleston, SC), Vol. 62, #19682, February 3, 1863, p. 1, c. 3
"Charleston Daily Courier," (Charleston, SC), Vol. 62, #19683, February 4, 1863, p. 1, c. 4
"Charleston Daily Courier," (Charleston, SC), Vol. 62, #19684, February 5, 1863, p. 1, c. 4
"Charleston Daily Courier," (Charleston, SC), Vol. 62, #19685, February 6, 1863, p. 1, c. 2
Times, (London, England), #24800, February 20, 1864, p. 12, c. 1
Times, (London, England), #24802, February 23, 1864, p. 10, c. 6
Times, (London, England), #24804, February 25, 1864, p. 9, c. 4
"Vessel Papers" (manuscript records), United States National Archives, Washington, DC, Record Group 109, file P-22
Report of the Secretary of the Navy, Second Session, 38th Congress, 1864-1865, (Washington, DC, 1865), p. 728
Official Records of the Union and Confederate Armies in the War of the Rebellion, (Washington, DC, 1891), Series 1, Volume 35, Part 2, p. 40
Official Records of the Union and Confederate Navies in the War of the Rebellion, (Washington, DC, 1902), Series 1, Volume 15, pp. 262-266
The Navy in the Civil War, (Charles Scribner's Sons, New York, NY, 1905), Volume 2 ("The Atlantic Coast" by Daniel Ammen), p. 146
Lifeline of the Confederacy: Blockade Running During the Civil War, by Stephen R. Wise, (University of South Carolina, Columbia, SC, 1983), pp. 368, 605, 606
Merchant Sailing Ships, 1850-1875, Heyday of Sail, by David R. MacGregor, (Lloyd's of London Press, 1984), p. 236
Charleston's Maritime Heritage 1670-1865, by P.C. Coker III, (CokerCraft Press, Charleston, SC, 1987), pp. 271, 288, 303

1864-2-US-SC/GA-2: The United States gunboat *Housatonic* was attacked in twenty-seven feet of water approximately three and a half miles from Sullivan's Island, South Carolina, and five and a half miles E.N.E. of Fort Sumter, by the Confederate submarine/torpedo boat *H.L. Hunley* (or *Hunley*), commanded by Lieutenant George E. Dixon, on February 17, 1864, and both vessels were sunk. (Note One: Of the approximately one hundred and sixty men aboard the *Housatonic* only three crewman and two officers died, while the

The "Real Rhett Butler" & Other Revelations

entire crew of eight men aboard the *Hunley* died. The sinking of the *Housatonic* marked a new phase in naval warfare, as never before had a vessel been sunk by a submarine in actual warfare.) (Note Two: The paymaster's safe went down with the *Housatonic*. One of the *Housatonic's* men died trying to save $300.00 he had in his bag on the berth deck. Many of the survivors lost "quite large sums of money" that they had laid away to send home by the next mail.) (Note Three: The *Housatonic* was 1240 tons, 207' in length, 38' in breadth, 16'10" in depth of hold, and 7'7" in draft. She had two main boilers and one auxiliary boiler. All of the *Housatonic's* boilers were of Martin's tubular patent type. She had two horizontal, direct action engines, with 42" diameter cylinders and 30" piston stroke. Her armament consisted of one 100-pounder Parrot rifle, three 30-pounder Parrot rifles, one 11-inch Dahlgren smooth-bore, four 32-pounder 33 hundred weight guns, and one 12-pounder rifle. The *Housatonic* had a wooden hull and was built at the Boston Navy yard. Her machinery was manufactured by Globe Works. She was an "*Ossipee* Class" gunboat and was launched on November 20, 1861.) (Note Four: The *Hunley* was designed by Horace L. Hunley and was built at Mobile, Alabama. She was hand cranked and was capable of diving entirely under another vessel. The tiny submarine was transported to Charleston by railroad.) (Note Four: One of the *Housatonic's* boilers was removed by divers prior to June 17, 1873, and carried to Charleston. The remainder of the wreck was leveled to within seven feet of the sea floor under a government contract by Professor Maillefert's salvage company in the 1870's.) (Note Five: Lieutenant Dixon had been with the 21st Regiment of Alabama Volunteers. He had been issued "special orders No. 271" to "take command and direction of the submarine torpedo boat" and to "sink and destroy any vessel of the enemy" with which he could "come in conflict." Dixon had a free selection of targets, but both he and his men actually hoped to sink one of the Federal monitors, or the United States warship *Wabash*. Those vessels were the preferred targets because the blockade running firm John Fraser & Company had promised a $100,000 reward for the destruction of a monitor and $50,000 for sinking the *Wabash*, and "only" $25,000 for a wooden warship such as the *Housatonic*. The reward, in 1994 dollars, for sinking the *Housatonic* was the equivalent of half a million dollars. George Alfred Trenholm, who has been described as "the real Rhett Butler," was the senior partner in John Fraser & Company.) (Note Six: The mission was so secret that the original reports in the Charleston papers assumed the *Housatonic's* sinking

Treasures of the Confederate Coast

was the result of a gale. And, as late as February 29, 1864, the *Charleston Mercury* was reporting the *Hunley* and her crew as safe.) (Note Seven: The *Housatonic* is shown on the 1865 chart drawn by E. Willenbucher for the "Annual Report of the Secretary of the Navy," and is listed in Adrian Lonsdale's *Guide to Sunken Ships in American Waters*, as having been wrecked at latitude 32°43.1' North, longitude 79°46.5' West. However, when the 1865 chart was prepared, an error in the time differential between celestial time and Greenwich time was made. That error was used in calculating the longitude and resulted in the wreck's location being incorrectly shown on the chart. The actual location is several hundred yards from that shown on the 1865 chart. Due to the archeological and historical importance of these two wrecks, the exact locations of these wrecks have not been published in this list.) (Note Eight: In November of 1970, while diving from a boat captained by Joe Porcelli, I discovered wreckage which I tentatively identified as the *Hunley*. Using a magnetometer, I subsequently located additional wreckage which I was able to positively identify as the remains of the *Housatonic*.) (Note Nine: For more information on the *Hunley*, please see entries 1863-8-US-SC/GA-4 and 1863-10-US-SC/GA-1, and see Chapter Two of this book.) (Note Ten: There is a great deal of confusion over this famous shipwreck as evidenced by a recent book, published by the North Carolina Division of Archives and History, which shows the *Housatonic* as sunk by a German submarine during the First World War.)

References for 1864-2-US-SC/GA-2:
Charleston Mercury, (Charleston, SC), Volume 84, #11990, February 20, 1864, p. 2, c. 1
Charleston Mercury, (Charleston, SC), Volume 84, #11991, February 22, 1864, p. 2, c. 1
Charleston Mercury, (Charleston, SC), Volume 84, #11997, February 29, 1864, p. 2, c. 1
Charleston Mercury, (Charleston, SC), Volume 84, #12000, March 3, 1864, p. 2, c. 1
Charleston Mercury, (Charleston, SC), Volume 84, #12001, March 4, 1864, p. 2, c. 1
Charleston Mercury, (Charleston, SC), Volume 84, #12004, March 8, 1864, p. 2, c. 1
Charleston Mercury, (Charleston, SC), Volume 84, #12009, March 14, 1864, p. 2, c. 1
Charleston Mercury, (Charleston, SC), Volume 84, #12011, March 16, 1864, p. 2, c. 1
Charleston Mercury, (Charleston, SC), Volume 84, #12027, April 4, 1864, p. 2, c. 4, 5
Charleston Mercury, (Charleston, SC), Volume 85, #12227, November 26, 1864, p. 2, c. 1
"Charleston Daily Courier," (Charleston, SC), #19715, Vol. 62, March 14, 1863, p. 1, c. 3
New York Times, (New York, NY), February 27, 1864, p. 3 (marked supplement), c. 1, 2
Records of General Courts Martial and Courts of Inquiry of the Navy Department, 1799-1867, Court of Inquiry, #4345, February 26, 1864, NARS M-273, roll 169, frames 0488-0591
"Vessel Papers" (manuscript records), United States National Archives, Washington, DC, Record Group 109, file H-71
"General Map of Charleston Harbor, South Carolina, Showing Rebel Defenses and Obstructions," drawn by E. Willenbucher for the Annual Report of the Secretary of the Navy, (U.S. Coast Survey, 1865)
"Salvage Log," B. Maillefert, (in the collection of the South Carolina Historical Society at Charleston, SC), June 17, 19-24, 28 & 30, 1873; July 1, 1873; August 30, 1873; September 1, 1873; April 17, 1874; and August 29, 1874
History of the Confederate States Navy From its Organization to the Surrender of its Last Vessel, by J. Thomas Scharf, (New York, New York, 1887), pp. 760, 761
Confederate Military History, written by Brig. Gen. Ellison Capers, edited by General Clement A. Evans, (Confederate Publishing Co., Atlanta, Georgia, 1899), Volume 5, p. 300
Official Records of the Union and Confederate Armies in the War of the Rebellion, (Washington, DC, 1890), Series 1, Volume 28, Part 2, p. 553
Official Records of the Union and Confederate Navies in the War of the Rebellion, (Washington, DC, 1902), Series 1, Volume 14, pp. 229, 231, 238, 327-337, 692, 693

The "Real Rhett Butler" & Other Revelations

Official Records of the Union and Confederate Navies in the War of the Rebellion, (Washington, DC, 1921), Series 2, Volume 1, pp. 28, 104, 256, and illustration of *H.L. Hunley* opposite p. 256
The Navy in the Civil War, (Charles Scribner's Sons, New York, NY, 1903), Volume 1 ("The Blockade and the Cruisers" by James Russell Soley), p. 245
The Navy in the Civil War, (Charles Scribner's Sons, New York, NY, 1905), Volume 2 ("The Atlantic Coast" by Daniel Ammen), p. 147
Guide to Sunken Ships in American Waters, by Adrian L. Lonsdale and H.R. Kaplan, (Arlington, VA, 1964), pp. 60, 70
Shipwrecks of the Civil War: The Encyclopedia of Union and Confederate Naval Losses, by Donald Shomette, (Washington, DC, 1973), pp. 71, 72, 256
Miscellaneous dives and personal observations made by Edward Lee Spence, 1970-1990
Charleston's Maritime Heritage 1670-1865, by P.C. Coker III, (CokerCraft Press, Charleston, SC, 1987), pp. 203, 256, 262-267
Warships of the Civil War Navies, by Paul H. Silverstone, (Naval Institute Press, Annapolis, MD, 1989), p. 42
Ship Ashore!: The U.S. Lifesavers of Coastal North Carolina, by Joe A. Mobley, (Division of Archives and History, North Carolina Department of Cultural Resources, Raleigh, NC, 1994), p. 154

1864-2x-US-NC-1: The London *Times* of March 2, 1864, lists a blockade runner *Hatfield* as lost at Wilmington, North Carolina. (Note: The report was undoubtedly referring to the loss of the steamer *Nutfield* on February 4, 1864. Please see entry 1864-2-US-NC-3 for details of the loss of the *Nutfield*.)
Reference for 1864-2x-US-NC-1:
Times, (London, England), #24809, March 2, 1864, p. 12, c. 4

1864-2x-US-NC-2: The London *Times* of March 2, 1864, incorrectly lists the loss of the steamer *Fanny and Jenny* as though it was the loss of two separate vessels, the *Fanny*, and the *Jenny*. (Note: Please see entry 1864-2-US-NC-6 for details of the loss of the *Fanny and Jenny*.)
Reference for 1864-2x-US-NC-2:
Times, (London, England), #24809, March 2, 1864, p. 12, c. 4

1864-3-US-NC-1: The *U.S.S. Peterhoff* (or *Peteroff*) was sunk March 6, 1864, in a collision with the *U.S.S. Monticello* in five fathoms of water, one mile south of Sheep Head Rock, south of New Inlet Bar, North Carolina. Her officers and crew were saved. [Note One: The *Peterhoff* had been captured off St. Thomas as a blockade runner and had been sold to the U.S. Navy by the United States Prize Court at New York for $80,000. The United States Supreme Court overturned her condemnation, but she was sunk before she could be returned to her owners. The *Peterhoff* had been owned by Z.C. Pearson and Company at the start of the war and was owned by James Spence (of Bermuda) when she was captured.] (Note Two: She was 210' in length, 28' in breadth, 15' in depth, 800 tons, and 4th rate.) (Note Three: The "Charleston Mercury" of March 16, 1864, reported her as sunk in thirty feet of water, seven miles S.S.W. of Fort Fisher. The *U.S.S. Cherokee* struck what her captain believed to be the wreck of the *Peterhoff* on July 13, 1864. He reported the Mound light bearing by compass N. 1/2 W., and Bald Head light S.W. 3/4 W. A Sea Grant publication

Treasures of the Confederate Coast

put out by the University of North Carolina lists the wreck as in thirty-five feet of water two miles off Corncake Inlet, North Carolina.)

References for 1864-3-US-NC-1:
"Charleston Mercury," (Charleston, SC), Volume 84, #12011, March 16, 1864, p. 2, c. 1
New York Times, (New York, NY), Volume 13, Supplement to #3896, March 19, 1864, p. 4, c. 6, p. 6, c. 4
New York Times, (New York, NY), Volume 14, #4117, December 3, 1864, p. 2, c. 3
Official Records of the Union and Confederate Navies in the War of the Rebellion, (Washington, DC, 1899), Series 1, Volume 9, pp. 535-537, 561, 777, 781, 787
Official Records of the Union and Confederate Navies in the War of the Rebellion, (Washington, DC, 1900), Series 1, Volume 10, p. 275
Official Records of the Union and Confederate Navies in the War of the Rebellion, (Washington, DC, 1921), Series 2, Volume 1, p. 176
A Chart of Wrecks of Vessels Sunk or Captured Near Wilmington, NC, Circa 1861-65, compiled by Charles H. Foard, (Wilmington, North Carolina, 1962)
Wreck Diving in North Carolina, University of North Carolina, Sea Grant Publication, #78-13, p. 6
Lifeline of the Confederacy: Blockade Running During the Civil War, by Stephen R. Wise, (University Microfilms International, 1983), pp. 415, 416649

1864-3-US-NCx-1: The sidewheel steamer *Helen* (ex-*Juno*), Captain Philip Porcher, C.S.N., was lost when her iron hull broke in two amidships during a heavy gale on her second day out of Charleston, South Carolina. She sank in just three minutes, and, of twenty-two seamen and eight officers, only two of her officers Burke and Dent, survived by clinging to pieces of her bridge. They were rescued by the schooner *Petrel*, Captain Habernicht. (Note One: The *Helen* had sailed from Charleston on March 8, 1864, so the loss probably took place on March 10, 1864. She was bound to Nassau when she was lost on what would have been her second trip through the blockade. She was carrying 220 bales of cotton.) (Note Two: The *Helen* was built by Todd and McGregor in 1860. She was purchased for the Confederacy in December of 1863 for £21,000 and was registered under the name of George Wigg. She drew only four feet of water and was 185 registered tons.) (Note Three: This loss is included in this book because the London *Times* reported the *Juno* as "from Wilmington" and as lost in the Gulf Stream, which might lead one to believe she was wrecked off the North Carolina coast.)

References for 1864-3-US-NCx-1:
"Charleston Mercury," (Charleston, SC), Volume 84, #12036, April 14, 1864, p. 2, c. 1
"Charleston Mercury," (Charleston, SC), Volume 84, #12036 (sic), April 15, 1864, p. 2, c. 1
Times, (London, England), #24861, May 2, 1864, p. 14, c. 5
Official Records of the Union and Confederate Navies in the War of the Rebellion, (Washington, 1899), Series 1, Volume 9, p. 802
Official Records of the Union and Confederate Navies in the War of the Rebellion, (Washington, 1902), Series 1, Volume 15, pp. 369, 370, 429
Official Records of the Union and Confederate Navies in the War of the Rebellion, (Washington, 1921), Series 2, Volume 2, p. 745
Lifeline of the Confederacy: Blockade Running During the Civil War, by Stephen R. Wise, (University of South Carolina, Columbia, SC, 1983), p. 580

1864-3-US-SC/GA-1: On March 3, 1864, the schooner *Arletta* (also mentioned as the *Martha*, *Marthie* or *Mattie*), Captain John Wicks, of Nassau, went ashore on the south end of Tybee Island near a picket station of the Third Regiment Rhode Island Heavy Artillery.

(Note: The schooner was about fifty tons, with a crew of five, and carried a cargo of alcohol, coffee and pepper. Her cargo was taken out, but the schooner was not expected to be got off.)

References for 1864-3-US-SC/GA-1:
Report of the Secretary of the Navy, Second Session, 38th Congress, 1864-1865, (Washington, DC, 1865), p. 724
Official Records of the Union and Confederate Armies in the War of the Rebellion, (Washington, DC, 1902), Series 1, Volume 15, Part 1, pp. 354-356

1864-3-US-SC/GA-2: A Federal boarding party from the United States steamer *Dan Smith* discovered the blockade running schooner *Sophia* ashore on the north-east part of Egg Island, Altamaha Sound, Georgia, on March 3, 1864. (Note One: Finding her with no nautical instruments, other than binnacles, but otherwise in good condition, the Yankees claimed her as a prize and succeeded in getting her off. While taking her northwards, she got into a gale and began to sink. She was abandoned somewhere near latitude 38°30' North and longitude 69° West. The *Sophia* was under the command of Acting Ensign Paul Armandt U.S.N. when she was abandoned for the last time.) (Note Two: Her stern was painted white, and her sides and rail were painted "with a light lead color." Her name was newly painted. Contemporary reports described her as a British schooner "with a good cargo, for a Confederate port." It was also said that both the schooner and her cargo had been owned in Savannah, with the exception of a lot of blankets, which were the property of the State of Georgia.) (Note Three: The "Charleston Mercury" reported her as having been run ashore near Darien, Georgia, on March 1, 1864. That report described her as complete wreck. Donald Shomette's excellent book *Shipwrecks of the Civil War* lists the *Sophia* as lost at sea off the coast of Georgia in a heavy gale on May 8, 1864.)

References for 1864-3-US-SC/GA-2:
Charleston Mercury, (Charleston, SC), Volume 84, #12005, March 9, 1864, p. 2, c. 1
Official Records of the Union and Confederate Armies in the War of the Rebellion, (Washington, DC, 1902), Series 1, Volume 15, Part 1, pp. 349-354, 420
Shipwrecks of the Civil War: The Encyclopedia of Union and Confederate Naval Losses, by Donald Shomette, (Washington, DC, 1973), pp. 462, 463

1864-3-US-SC/GA-3: On March 22, 1864, the prize sloop *Buffalo*, valued at one thousand dollars, was beached by her crew after her sails blew out in rough weather. (Note: The *Buffalo's* crew took some things "of value" from the wreck before they abandoned her, and managed to get to shore safely. Her position was described as "well up on the beach" on Ossabaw Island, Georgia. She had been captured off St. Andrew's Sound, Georgia, by the *Braziliera* on February 1, 1864, with a load of cotton.)

References for 1864-3-US-SC/GA-3:
Report of the Secretary of the Navy, Second Session, 38th Congress, 1864-1865, (Washington, DC, 1865), p. 724

Treasures of the Confederate Coast

Official Records of the Union and Confederate Navies in the War of the Rebellion, (Washington, DC, 1902), Series 1, Volume 15, pp. 372-374, 420
"Log of the *Vermont*," March 14, 1864, National Archives, Record Group 24

1864-3-US-SC/GA-4: On March 24, 1864, the iron steamer *Little Ada* (or *Ada*), of Glasgow, was boarded in the creek at McClellenville, South Carolina, by a Federal expedition intending to destroy or capture her during a day time raid. A Confederate battery opened up with three rifled guns (believed to have been 12-pounder Whitworths). One shot penetrated the steam drum and another went through her boilers, destroying tubes, etc. "In fact, they had the range so perfectly that their shot completely riddled her." The Yankees then fled to escape capture or death. The *Little Ada* had a 6-pounder Whitworth gun mounted on her deck which she fired shell and shrapnel at the fleeing Yankees. (Note: A dispatch from the U.S. Consul at Glasgow described the *Ada* as a "screw steamer of 220 tons, speed 12 knots." She was 112'x18'6"x10', drew 5'6" forward and 8' aft, and was rated at 208 tons burden and 94 tons register. She had a crew of 22 officers and men, and was commanded by a Baltimorean named Martin. The vessel was not destroyed, and was quickly repaired. She was owned by the Importing and Exporting Company of Georgia and was registered in the name of Henry Lafone. The vessel made two successful trips through the blockade before being captured at sea off Cape Romain, South Carolina, on July 9, 1864, by the *U.S.S. Gettysburg*.)

References for 1864-3-US-SC/GA-4:

Official Records of the Union and Confederate Navies in the War of the Rebellion, (Washington, DC, 1900), Series 1, Volume 10, p. 245
Official Records of the Union and Confederate Navies in the War of the Rebellion, (Washington, DC, 1902), Series 1, Volume 15, pp. 374-380
Lifeline of the Confederacy: Blockade Running During the Civil War, by Stephen R. Wise, (University of South Carolina, Columbia, SC, 1983), p. 586
Warships of the Civil War Navies, by Paul H. Silverstone, (Naval Institute Press, Annapolis, MD, 1989), p. 104

1864-3-US-SC/GA-5: The United States bark *Kingfisher* was wrecked in St. Helena Sound on Combahee Bank on the south end of Otter Island, South Carolina, on March 28, 1864. (Note One: The wreck was said to be in two and one half fathoms of water, laying on her starboard side with her bow into the shoal. The Federal salvage crew managed to take out all of her ammunition, shot and shell from her magazine and such stores as could be got at. The Federal salvage team was apparently were able to save all of the *Kingfisher's* guns and at least some of her anchors. The salvage was conducted by the wrecking steamer *Mountain Home* and was assisted by the tug *O.M. Pettit*, the gunboat *Oleander*, and the gunboat *Dai Ching*.) [Note Two: The *Kingfisher* measured 451 (or 417) tons, 121'4" (or 121'6") in length, 28'8" (or 28'9") in breadth, 14'4" (or 16'6") in depth of hold, and drew 15' of water. She was built at Fairhaven, Maine, in 1857, of oak and was copper and iron fastened. She was purchased August 2, 1861, at Boston, Massachusetts, for the U.S. Navy by a board composed of J.M. Forbes and others at a cost of $17,000. She was commissioned on October 3, 1861, at the Boston yard, and was a "4th rate" sailing vessel. The cost of repairs while in government service was $15,349.02. Her armament consisted of four 8-inch Dahlgren smooth-bores, one 20-pounder rifle, and one light 12-pounder.]

References for 1864-3-US-SC/GA-5:

American Lloyd's: Registry of American & Foreign Shipping, (New York, New York, 1863), p. 185, #1701
American Lloyd's: Registry of American & Foreign Shipping, (New York, New York, 1865), p. 204, #2074
American Lloyd's: Registry of American & Foreign Shipping, (New York, New York, 1866), p. 207, #2216
"Log of the U.S. bark *Kingfisher*," March 28, 1864, National Archives, Record Group 24
"Log of the U.S. steamer *Oleander*," April 1-7, 1864, National Archives, Record Group 24
"Log of the U.S. steamer *O.M. Pettit*," April 3, 1864, National Archives, Record Group 24
"Log of the U.S. steamer *Dai Ching*," April 6-8, 1864, National Archives, Record Group 24
Records of General Courts Martial and Courts of Inquiry of the Navy Department, 1799-1867, Court of Inquiry, #4304, May 2, 1864, NARS M-273, roll 167, frames 0171-0224
Official Records of the Union and Confederate Navies in the War of the Rebellion, (Washington, DC, 1902), Series 1, Volume 15, pp. 383-388
Official Records of the Union and Confederate Navies in the War of the Rebellion, (Washington, DC, 1921), Series 2, Volume 1, p. 122
Warships of the Civil War Navies, by Paul H. Silverstone, (Naval Institute Press, Annapolis, MD, 1989), p. 142

1864-4-US-NC-1: The U.S. Army steamer *Bombshell* was sunk at her wharf at Plymouth, North Carolina, on April 18, 1864, after having received several shots from the Confederates in an earlier trip up the river the same day. The *Bombshell* was under the temporary command of Ensign Thomas B. Stokes when she was lost. (Note One: The vessel, which was immediately raised and put into service by the Confederates, was recaptured by the *U.S.S. Mattabesett* on May 5, 1864. By November 27, 1864, it was reported that she had been hauled up on the mud to keep her from sinking at New Berne, North Carolina. The same report stated that she had a "couple of locomotive engines on board which might be turned to account.") (Note Two: The *Bombshell* had two inclined, high pressure engines. Her cylinders were about 10" in diameter and had a 2'9" piston stroke. The cylinders were placed one on each side of the boiler and were connected at right angles to the shaft of the paddle wheels. She was armed with two rifled 12-pounders, one smooth bore, and one 20-pounder Brooke.) (Note Three: This may have been the floating battery *Bombshell* which first arrived in North Carolina as part of General Burnside's invasion fleet. That vessel was ninety-six feet in length and used JSDC as her signal letters.)

References for 1864-4-US-NC-1:

New York Times, (New York, NY), Volume 13, #3926, April 23, 1864, p. 1, c. 1, p. 4, c. 1
New York Times, (New York, NY), Volume 13, #3926 (misnumbered), April 24, 1864, p. 1, c. 1, 2, p. 4, c. 1
Times, (London, England), #24863, May 4, 1864, p. 14, c. 1

Treasures of the Confederate Coast

History of the Confederate States Navy From its Organization to the Surrender of its Last Vessel, by J. Thomas Scharf, (New York, NY, 1887), pp. 405, 406

Official Records of the Union and Confederate Navies in the War of the Rebellion, (Washington, DC, 1897), Series 1, Volume 6, pp. 472, 473

Official Records of the Union and Confederate Navies in the War of the Rebellion, (Washington, DC, 1899), Series 1, Volume 9, pp. 637, 644, 645

Official Records of the Union and Confederate Navies in the War of the Rebellion, (Washington, DC, 1900), Series 1, Volume 11, p. 98

Official Records of the Union and Confederate Navies in the War of the Rebellion, (Washington, DC, 1921), Series 2, Volume 1, p. 249

Confederate Military History, edited by General Clement A. Evans, (Confederate Publishing Co., Atlanta, GA, 1899), Volume 12, p. 83

The Navy in the Civil War, (Charles Scribner's Sons, New York, NY, 1905), Volume 2 ("The Atlantic Coast" by Daniel Ammen), p. 205

1864-4-US-NC-2: The *U.S.S. Southfield*, Acting Volunteer Lieutenant Charles A. French commanding, with 117 men, was rammed and sunk in the Roanoke River by the Confederate States ram *Albemarle* on April 19, 1864. [Note One: She sank in less than fifteen minutes in twenty-two feet of water near the Camphor Battery, Plymouth, North Carolina. She had been lashed to the *U.S.S. Miami* for their mutual protection when she was rammed. A report dated November 1, 1864, stated "We continued to advance to within a mile of the works (at Plymouth, North Carolina), when we discovered that the channel was obstructed at a point opposite the batteries by two schooners sunk one on each side of the wreck of the *Southfield*, which together formed a barrier which could only have been passed with great danger, if at all." A diagram showing the position of the schooners and the *Southfield* appears in Volume 11 of the "Official Records-Navy." Another report mentions three schooners rather than just two.] (Note Two: The *Southfield* was built in 1857 at Brooklyn New York by John English. She had been purchased for $65,000 by George D. Morgan from George Law at New York on December 16, 1861, for the U.S. Navy. She was fitted out for naval service by W.H. Webb at a cost of $4,820.80. Total cost of alterations and repairs while in the Government service was $37,179.19. She was a double ended sidewheel steamer with a wooden hull. She was 781 (or 751) tons, 200' in length, 34' in breadth and 11'8" in depth, and 6'6" in draft. She was armed with one 100-pounder Parrott rifle, five 9-inch Dahlgren smooth bores and one 12-pounder smooth bore. The 100-pounder Parrott rifle and at least two of the 9-inch Dahlgrens were raised by the Confederates. The *Southfield* was rated as a ferry boat. She had been issued a certificate of steam enrollment at the port of New York on July 2, 1857.) (Note Three: Reports filed in November of 1864 indicated that the *Southfield* could be raised, and said that her "engine was a very fine one.")

References for 1864-4-US-NC-2:
New York Times, (New York, NY), Volume 13, #3926, April 23, 1864, p. 1, c. 1, p. 4, c. 1

The "Real Rhett Butler" & Other Revelations

New York Times, (New York, NY), Volume 13, #3926 (misnumbered), April 24, 1864, p. 1, c. 1, 2, p. 4, c. 1

Times, (London, England), #24863, May 4, 1864, p. 14, c. 1

History of the Confederate States Navy From its Organization to the Surrender of its Last Vessel, by J. Thomas Scharf, (New York, NY, 1887), pp. 404, 405, 408, 409, 413

Confederate Military History, edited by General Clement A. Evans, (Confederate Publishing Co., Atlanta, GA, 1899), Volume 4, p. 224, 12, p. 83

Official Records of the Union and Confederate Navies in the War of the Rebellion, (Washington, DC, 1899), Series 1, Volume 9, pp. 638-642, 658, chart opposite 658

Official Records of the Union and Confederate Navies in the War of the Rebellion, (Washington, DC, 1900), Series 1, Volume 10, pp. 32, 49, 72, 73, 86, 306, 405, 406, 611, 640

Official Records of the Union and Confederate Navies in the War of the Rebellion, (Washington, DC, 1900), Series 1, Volume 11, pp. 12, 13, 19, 64, 65, 96

Official Records of the Union and Confederate Navies in the War of the Rebellion, (Washington, DC, 1921), Series 2, Volume 1, p. 212

The Navy in the Civil War, (Charles Scribner's Sons, New York, NY, 1903), Volume 1 ("The Blockade and the Cruisers" by James Russell Soley), pp. 101-105

The Navy in the Civil War, (Charles Scribner's Sons, New York, NY, 1905), Volume 2 ("The Atlantic Coast" by Daniel Ammen), pp. 202, 203, 214

Graveyard of the Atlantic: Shipwrecks of the North Carolina Coast, by David Stick (University of North Carolina Press, Chapel Hill, NC, 1952), pp. 58, 247

List of American-Flag Merchant Vessels that Received Certificates of Enrollment or Registry at the Port of New York 1789-1867, compiled by Forest R. Holdcamper, (U.S. National Archives, Washington, DC, 1968), Special List #22, Volume 2, p. 646

Naval History of the Civil War, by Howard P. Nash, (A.S. Barnes & Co., New York, NY, 1972), pp. 218, 219, 225

Merchant Steam Vessels of the United States 1790-1868, ("Lytle-Holdcamper List"), by William M. Lytle and Forrest R. Holdcamper, revised and edited by C. Bradford Mitchell, (Staten Island, NY, 1975), p. 201

C.S.S. Neuse: A Question of Iron and Time, by Leslie S. Bright, William H. Rowland, and James C. Bardon, (Raleigh, NC, 1981), Appendix IV, C.S.S. Albemarle, p. 145

1864-4-US-SC/GA-1: On April 5, 1864, a torpedo being laid by the Confederates near Rosedew Battery at Savannah, Georgia, exploded sinking the boat being used in the work. One man was injured and six others were killed.

References for 1864-4-US-SC/GA-1:
Charleston Mercury, (Charleston, SC), Volume 84, #12031, April 8, 1864, p. 2, c. 1

1864-4x-US-NC-1: The London *Times* of May 4, 1864, reported that in April of 1864, the Confederates "had sunk three Federal gunboats at Plymouth," North Carolina. (Note: See entries 1864-4-US-NC-1 and 1864-4-US-NC-2.)

Reference for 1864-4x-US-NC-1:
Times, (London, England), #24863, May 4, 1864, p. 14, c. 1

1864-4x-US-NC-2 and **1864-4x-SC/GA-1:** The London *Index* reported that during the period from January 1, 1863, through April, 1864, there were five hundred and ninety attempted trips (by steamers) through the blockade at Wilmington and Charleston, of those, four hundred and ninety-eight were successful. That figures out to be a success rate of just over eighty four percent. (Note: Because this entry applies to both Charleston and Wilmington, it has been assigned two SL Codes.)

Reference for 1864-4x-US-NC-2 and 1864-4x-US-SC/GA-1:
Times, (London, England), #24913, July 1, 1864, p. 10, c. 4

1864-5-US-NC-1: On May 7, 1864, the Confederate States ironclad ram *Raleigh*, Flag-Officer William F. Lynch (or Lieutenant Pembroke Jones), crossed Wilmington Bar, North Carolina, and

Treasures of the Confederate Coast

"attacked the enemy fleet, driving his vessels to sea." The Federal vessels involved in the engagement included the *Kansas, Mount Vernon, Howquah*, and *Nansemond*. In returning to port, the Confederate ram got struck and "broke her back" on the "New Inlet Rips" (interior bar). (Note One: An illustration in Volume 10 of the "Official Records-Navy" shows the position of the wrecked ram. One contemporary account described her as "• • • a monstrous turtle stranded and forlorn • • •." Her position was sometimes given as "ashore on Zeek's Island.") (Note Two: The *Raleigh* had been built in Wilmington in 1864, and was armed with four guns. A witness wrote: "The appearance of the vessel, is like a large vessel cut down to the waterline, and a house built on and plated. The sides of the house are arched, and having three ports on a side and one in each end. She has one smokestack and a small flag posted aft. Goes, I think, 6 to 7 knots, and turns very quickly. The guns fired at us during the night were not heavier than 30-pounders, but this morning she used much heavier ones; some think 10 inches." There was some question as to whether she drew 12' of water, or no more than 9.5' or 10'.) (Note Three: One account states "her guns, equipment, iron, etc. being saved.") (Note Four: David Stick's book, *Graveyard of the Atlantic*, states that she was "abandoned up the river.")

References for 1864-5-US-NC-1:

History of the Confederate States Navy From its Organization to the Surrender of its Last Vessel, by J. Thomas Scharf, (New York, NY, 1887), pp. 414, 415, 417

Official Records of the Union and Confederate Armies in the War of the Rebellion, (Washington, DC, 1893), Series 1, Volume 42, Part 2, pp. 1294, 1297

Official Records of the Union and Confederate Navies in the War of the Rebellion, (Washington, DC, 1900), Series 1, Volume 10, pp. 23, 24, 25, 80, 125 (illustration), 134, 203, 442, 460

Official Records of the Union and Confederate Navies in the War of the Rebellion, (Washington, DC, 1900), Series 1, Volume 11, pp. 619, 746

Official Records of the Union and Confederate Navies in the War of the Rebellion, (Washington, DC, 1921), Series 2, Volume 1, pp. 263, 273, 301, 302

Confederate Military History, edited by General Clement A. Evans, (Confederate Publishing Co., Atlanta, GA, 1899), Volume 12, pp. 85, 108

The Navy in the Civil War, (Charles Scribner's Sons, New York, NY, 1903), Volume 1 ("The Blockade and the Cruisers" by James Russell Soley), p. 96

The Navy in the Civil War, (Charles Scribner's Sons, New York, NY, 1905), Volume 2 ("The Atlantic Coast" by Daniel Ammen), p. 211

Graveyard of the Atlantic: Shipwrecks of the North Carolina Coast, by David Stick (University of North Carolina Press, Chapel Hill, NC, 1952), pp. 60, 247

Outer Banks of North Carolina, by David Stick, (UNC Press, Chapel Hill, NC, 1958, pp. 118, 132, 133, 141

A Chart of Wrecks of Vessels Sunk or Captured Near Wilmington, NC, Circa 1861-65, compiled by Charles H. Foard, (Wilmington, North Carolina, 1962)

An Oceanographic Atlas of the Continental Margin, J.G. Newton, O.H. Pilkey and J.O. Blanton, (Duke University Marine Laboratory, Beaufort, NC, 1971), p. 17 chart symbol #50, p. 20 entry #50

Iron Afloat: The Story of the Confederate Armorclads, by William N. Still Jr., (Vanderbilt University Press, 1971), p. 167 (note #34)

Lifeline of the Confederacy: Blockade Running During the Civil War, by Stephen R. Wise, (University Microfilms International, 1983), pp. 481, 483, 620

1864-5-US-NC-2: When the blockade runner *Greyhound* was captured by the *U.S.S. Connecticut* on May 10, 1864, she proved to be a very valuable prize. Besides carrying a cargo of 800 bales of

The "Real Rhett Butler" & Other Revelations

cotton, 35 tons of tobacco, and 25 casks of turpentine, the beautiful Confederate spy, Belle Boyd, was aboard and was taken prisoner. (Note One: The *Greyhound* had sailed from Wilmington, North Carolina, and was captured in latitude 33°3' N., longitude 75°55'W., 109 miles E. by S. of Cape Fear.) (Note Two: The *Greyhound's* captain represented himself as George Henry, but his real name was George H. Bier. He was formerly a lieutenant in the United States Navy and he was a lieutenant in the Confederate Navy. He had also served as captain of the blockade runner *Dee* when she was lost off Masonboro Inlet in February of 1864.) [Note Three: As the Federal gunboat approached, a keg containing $20,000 to $30,000 (and consisting of between 1,000 and 1,500 ounces of gold coins) was thrown overboard, and Belle Boyd burned her secret dispatches. Belle Boyd charmed handsome young Ensign Samuel Hardinge, who had been made prize master of the captured runner. With Hardinge's assistance, Miss Boyd escaped and the two were soon reunited and married in England. When Hardinge returned home the next month, he was immediately arrested, and due to his poor treatment in prison, he died shortly after his release.] (Note Four: For more on the loss of the *Dee*, please see entry 1864-2-US-NC-4.)

References for 1864-5-US-NC-2:
Official Records of the Union and Confederate Navies in the War of the Rebellion, (Washington, DC, 1900), Series 1, Volume 10, pp. 42, 43, 504
Belle Boyd in Camp and in Prison, by Harding, two volumes (Blelock & Co., London and New York, 1865), pp. 276-289
Blockade Runners of the Confederacy, by Hamilton Cochran (Bobbs-Merrill Co., Inc., Indianapolis, 1958), pp. 142-153
Civil War at Sea, by Virgil Carrington Jones (Holt, Rinehart, Winston, NY, 1960-62, in 3 volumes), Volume 3, pp. 204, 205
Spies for the Blue and Gray, by Harnett T. Kane, (Hanover House, Garden City, NY), pp. 150, 151
Miscellaneous records (including some of the above) provided as attachments to letter of Brad Sharmen to E. Lee Spence, June 27, 1988

1864-5-US-NC-3: A large flat, used for transporting grain, was destroyed in the Alligator River at Simmond's Mill, North Carolina, on May 12, 1864, by an expedition from the *U.S.S. Ceres*. The mill was also destroyed because the Yankees believed that the mill had "lately been engaged in grinding corn for the rebels."

Reference for 1864-5-US-NC-3:
Official Records of the Union and Confederate Navies in the War of the Rebellion, (Washington, D.C., 1900), Series 1, Volume 10, p. 58

1864-5-US-NC-4: The London *Times* of June 13, 1864, reported that a bottle was "picked up off Hatteras on the 20th (May, 1864) containing the record of the loss of the steamer *Manhattan* at sea, from Wilmington, North Carolina, bound to Bermuda." A large lot of cotton was picked up off Hatteras Inlet, North Carolina, on that day and on the following day.

Reference for 1864-5-US-NC-4:

Times, (London, England), # 24897, June 13, 1864, p. 5, c. 5

1864-5-US-SC/GA-1: The United States transport steamer *Boston* was run aground in the Ashepoo River, South Carolina, near a Confederate battery, on May 25 (or 26), 1864. She was shelled by the Confederates who hit her seventy times with 6-pounder shot and shell, setting her afire and destroying her. She was carrying three hundred men and had ninety-one horses on board. Half of the horses were killed by shot and half were burned to death. Two of her crew and sixteen soldiers were lost. (Note One: An extensive article on the loss of the Boston appeared in the June 3, 1864, issue of the *New York Times*. The loss was put at $250,000. Captain Faircloth lost $1,100 as the safe's side had been bent by a shot entering his stateroom and he couldn't get the safe's door open.) (Note Two: In 1856 the *Boston's* captain was listed as Charles O. Clark and she was owned by the New York and Philadelphia Steam Navigation Company, Oscar Coles of New York, President. In 1858 the vessel had been shown as running on the Boston and Bangor Line. The *Boston* was reported as chartered at New York on July 18, 1862, for $600 per day by Colonel D.D. Tompkins, from James T. Sandford for transporting troops and supplies. She could carry 800 troops.) [Note Three: The *Boston* was built by W.H. Brown at New York, New York, in 1850. Her hull was of oak and chestnut (or oak and cedar) and was copper and iron fastened. She had one deck, two masts, a scroll head, a square stern, and was of medium model. The *Boston* had one independent fire pump which was originally said to be "insufficient" security against fire. The vessel's fire rating had been upped to "good" by 1863, but whether that meant her equipment had been upgraded or that looser standards were being applied is not known. The steamer was classed A-2 for insurance purposes. She measured 574 41/95 (or 580) tons, 215' in length, 28' (or 29') in breadth, and 9'10" (or 9') in depth of hold. She drew 8'4" of water. Her hull was metalled in 1850 and she had a new bottom put on in 1859. She had a vertical engine with one 44" cylinder with an 11' piston stroke.] (Note Four: The *Boston* was discovered in 1965 by Jim Batey and Ron Renau of Charleston. They recovered a small safe, but the side was not damaged and they said they found no money inside, so it may have been a different safe than the one mentioned above. The wreck was later independently researched and discovered by Howard Tower and associates of Jacksonville, Florida. Tower's team worked the wreck under a contract and in cooperation with the Institute of Archeology and Anthropology at the University of South Carolina.)

References for 1864-5-US-SC/GA-1:

The "Real Rhett Butler" & Other Revelations

"Permanent Enrollment #43, (New York, NY), May 26, 1856, National Archives, Record Group 41
"Permanent Enrollment #44, (New York, NY), May 26, 1856, National Archives, Record Group 41
"Permanent Enrollment #46, (New York, NY), May 26, 1856, National Archives, Record Group 41
American Lloyd's: Registry of American & Foreign Shipping, (New York, New York, 1858), p. 336, #40
American Lloyd's: Registry of American & Foreign Shipping, (New York, New York, 1863), p. 568, #60
"List of Steamers Chartered by the U.S. and in the Service of the Quartermaster's Department at Port Royal, South Carolina, November 30, 1862," (manuscript list), National Archives, Record Group 92, entry 1407, Box 123
"List of Steamers Chartered by the U.S. and in the Service of the Quartermaster's Department at Port Royal, South Carolina, January 31, 1863," (manuscript list), National Archives, Record Group 92, entry 1407, Box 123
"Lost," (manuscript list of vessels), National Archives, Record Group 92, entry 1407, Box 123, Section "Vessels Wrecked and Lost"
"Report of vessels employed by the U.S. in the Department of the Carolinas which have been lost," (manuscript list), National Archives, Record Group 92, entry 1407, Box 123
Charleston Mercury, (Charleston, SC), Volume 84, #12074, May 30, 1864, p. 2, c. 1
New York Times, (New York, NY), Volume 13, #3961, June 3, 1864, p. 2, c. 1, 2, p. 4, c. 1
Official Records of the Union and Confederate Navies in the War of the Rebellion, (Washington, DC, 1903), Series 1, Volume 15, pp. 426, 459-462, 506, 690
Merchant Steam Vessels of the United States 1807-1868, ("Lytle List"), by William M. Lytle, (Mystic, CT, 1952), p. 21
List of American-Flag Merchant Vessels that Received Certificates of Enrollment or Registry at the Port of New York 1789-1867, compiled by Forest R. Holdcamper, (U.S. National Archives, Washington, DC, 1968), Special List #22, Volume 1, p. 88
Manuscript 3x5 file card for steamer *Boston* used in preparation of "Lytle-Holdcamper List," NARS, RG 41

1864-5-US-SC/GA-2: A sailboat capsized in the harbor off South Bay Battery, Charleston, South Carolina, on May 30, 1864, drowning Mrs. Julia A. Hoffman and her six year old daughter, Louisa.

Reference for 1864-5-US-SC/GA-2:
Charleston Mercury, (Charleston, SC), Volume 84, #12075, May 31, 1864, p. 2, c. 1

1864-5x-US-NC-1: The *New York Times* of May 10, 1864, reported that the *U.S.S. Sassacus* had attacked and sunk the Confederate States ram *Albemarle*. (Note One: The report was premature as the *Albemarle* not only survived the ramming, the *Sassacus* actually lodged in the side of the ironclad, which allowed the Confederate gunners to fire shot from its 100-pounder directly into the trapped Union vessel, blowing up her boiler and scalding her men. The men in the engine room of the Sassacus "wild with boiling steam, sprang to the ladder with pistol and cutlass, but ••• it would have been madness to send our crew on the grated top of the ironclad." The two vessels finally separated and both survived the battle.) (Note Two: On October 28, 1864, the *Albemarle* was attacked and sunk by a Federal torpedo boat. For more information on her loss, please see entry 1864-10-US-NC-7.)

Reference for 1864-5x-US-NC-1:
"Charleston Mercury," (Charleston, SC), Volume 85, #12214, November 10, 1864, p. 2, c. 1
"Charleston Mercury," (Charleston, SC), Volume 85, #12216, November 12, 1864, p. 1, c. 3, 4
New York Times, (New York, NY), Volume 13, #3940, May 10, 1864, p. 8, c. 3
Times, (London, England), #25031, November 16, 1864, p. 10, c. 1
History of the Confederate States Navy From its Organization to the Surrender of its Last Vessel, by J. Thomas Scharf, (New York, NY, 1887), pp. 402, 403 (diagram), 404-407
Official Records of the Union and Confederate Navies in the War of the Rebellion, (Washington, DC, 1900), Series 1, Volume 10, pp. 610-623
Official Records of the Union and Confederate Navies in the War of the Rebellion, (Washington, DC, 1900), Series 1, Volume 11, p. 64
Official Records of the Union and Confederate Navies in the War of the Rebellion, (Washington, DC, 1901), Series 1, Volume 12, pp. 9, 22, 75

Treasures of the Confederate Coast

Official Records of the Union and Confederate Navies in the War of the Rebellion, (Washington, DC, 1921), Series 2, Volume 1, pp. -31, 247, and illustration opposite p. 247
The Navy in the Civil War, (Charles Scribner's Sons, New York, NY, 1905), Volume 2 ("The Atlantic Coast" by Daniel Ammen, pp. 205-209
Graveyard of the Atlantic: Shipwrecks of the North Carolina Coast, by David Stick (University of North Carolina Press, Chapel Hill, NC, 1952), pp. 58, 248
Iron Afloat: The Story of the Confederate Armorclads, by William N. Still Jr., (Vanderbilt University Press, 1971), pp. 91, 213, 214
C.S.S. Neuse: A Question of Iron and Time, by Leslie S. Bright, William H. Rowland, and James C. Bardon, (Raleigh, NC, 1981), Appendix IV, *C.S.S. Albemarle*, p. 146

1864-6-US-NC-1: The British sidewheel steamer *Georgiana McCaw* (ex-*Dundalk*), of Liverpool, was chased ashore and bilged by the *U.S.S. Victoria*, Acting Master Alfred Everson, on June 2, 1864. The *Georgiana McCaw* had been bound from Nassau to Wilmington, North Carolina, on her first attempt through the blockade when she was lost. [Note One: She was variously reported as 373 tons register and as 700 tons burden. Her cargo consisted of sixty tons of provisions. She was owned by M.G. Klingender (possibly for George Alfred Trenholm). The Federal boarding party took two chronometers, one barometer, one sextant, and a clock from the wreck. Twenty-nine men (including the captain and three passengers) from the steamer, were captured, and another fourteen men escaped.] (Note Two: The *Georgiana McCaw's* position was said to have been in easy range of the guns of the Western Battery and Battery Cameron of Fort Campbell and Fort Caswell, North Carolina. She was listed by one source as on "Cape Fear - SW of Baldhead Light." The location of her loss was also described as "off Old Inlet" and simply as at "Cape Fear." One account said she was 1000 yards to the westward of Battery Campbell, and gave the depth of water at her location as 3.5 fathoms.) (Note Three: According to Dave Horner's book, *The Blockade Runners*, her pilot, Thomas Dryer, who had stayed aboard the vessel to guard "a quantity of gold" was murdered, and the money was never found.)

References for 1864-6-US-NC-1:
Times, (London, England), # 24939, August 1, 1864, p. 7, c. 3
Official Records of the Union and Confederate Navies in the War of the Rebellion, (Washington, DC, 1900), Series 1, Volume 10, pp. 114, 115, 379, 434, 448, 478, 504, 518
Official Records of the Union and Confederate Navies in the War of the Rebellion, (Washington, D.C., 1900), Series 1, Volume 11, pp. 50, 51, 385
Graveyard of the Atlantic: Shipwrecks of the North Carolina Coast, by David Stick (University of North Carolina Press, Chapel Hill, NC, 1952), p. 247
A Chart of Wrecks of Vessels Sunk or Captured Near Wilmington, NC, Circa 1861-65, compiled by Charles H. Foard, (Wilmington, North Carolina, 1962)
An Oceanographic Atlas of the Continental Margin, J.G. Newton, O.H. Pilkey and J.O. Blanton, (Duke University Marine Laboratory, Beaufort, NC, 1971), p. 17 chart symbol #57, p. 20 entry #57
Lifeline of the Confederacy: Blockade Running During the Civil War, by Stephen R. Wise, (University Microfilms International, 1983), p. 569
The Blockade Runners, by Dave Horner, (Florida Classics Library, Port Salerno, FL, 1992), Chapter 14, pp. 26, 222, 223

1864-6-US-NC-2: Two old boats were intentionally "blown to atoms" during a successful torpedo experiment in Albemarle Sound, North Carolina, on June 6, 1864. The experiment was conducted by

The "Real Rhett Butler" & Other Revelations

Captain Melancton Smith of the *U.S.S. Mattabesett* and the results were supposed to be confidential.

References for 1864-6-US-NC-2:
Official Records of the Union and Confederate Navies in the War of the Rebellion, (Washington, D.C., 1900), Series 1, Volume 10, pp. 144, 145

1864-6-US-NC-3: The blockade running steamer *Pevensey* (or *Penversey*), of London, was run ashore on June 9, 1864, nine miles (or seven miles) west of Beaufort, North Carolina, where she was blown up by her own crew. One man died and thirty-five were captured. (Note One: The *Pevensey* had been bound from Bermuda to Wilmington, and was loaded "on Confederate account." Her "valuable cargo" consisted of arms, blankets, shoes, cloth, clothing, lead, bacon and numerous packages marked to individuals. She had been chased by the *U.S.S. Quaker State* and the *U.S.S. New Berne,* and according to the blockade runner's own log book she had thrown thirty tons of lead and twenty tons of bacon overboard on June 7, 1864.) (Note Two: The *Pevensey* was 543 tons English register and was reportedly operated by Stringer, Pembroke and Company. Seven Whitworth tompions were found all tied together, suggesting that number of guns being under the musket boxes. The vessel and cargo proved to be a total loss. Stephen Wise in his fine book, *Lifeline of the Confederacy: Blockade Running During the Civil War*, shows the *Pevensey* as 485 tons register and states that she had made two previous runs through the blockade.) (Note Three: David Stick's book, *Graveyard of the Atlantic*, gives her location as at "Bogue Inlet.")

References for 1864-6-US-NC-3:
Official Records of the Union and Confederate Navies in the War of the Rebellion, (Washington, DC, 1900), Series 1, Volume 10, pp. 136-138, 504
Official Records of the Union and Confederate Navies in the War of the Rebellion, (Washington, DC, 1917), Series 1, Volume 27, p. 700
Graveyard of the Atlantic: Shipwrecks of the North Carolina Coast, by David Stick (University of North Carolina Press, Chapel Hill, NC, 1952), p. 247
Lifeline of the Confederacy: Blockade Running During the Civil War, by Stephen R. Wise, (University Microfilms International, 1983), pp. 368, 604

1864-6-US-NC-4: The United States screw steamer *Lavender* (ex-*May Flower*, a.k.a. *Mayflower*), Acting Master J.H. Gleason, was wrecked on Cape Lookout Shoals, North Carolina, on the night of June 11, 1864. (Note One: Her men clung to a small portion of the hull, which was just out of water, and remained on the wreck for four days and nights without food before they were rescued. Nine men were lost from exposure and drowning, the rest, fourteen in number, were saved at great risk by the men of the United States Army steamer *John Farron*, Captain J.F. Smallman. The wreck went to pieces within two hours after their rescue.) (Note Two: The steamer had been purchased at Philadelphia on May 25, 1864, for

Treasures of the Confederate Coast

$47,000 by Commodore C.K. Stribling from H.&W.D. Winsor for the U.S. Navy and her name was changed at that time. She was fitted out with two 12-pound rifles and two 24-pounder howitzers. Her hull was wood with copper fastenings. She was classed as an armed tug of the 4th rate. She was 173 tons, 112' in length, 22 in breadth, and 7'6" in depth. She had one vertical low pressure engine. Its cylinder was 30" in diameter and had a 30" stroke. She had one cylindrical boiler. She was newly built at Philadelphia and was intended to be used as a tender.)

References for 1864-6-US-NC-4:
New York Times, (New York, NY), Volume 13, #3978, June 23, 1864, p. 2, c. 3
"Charleston Mercury," (Charleston, SC), Volume 85, #12111, July 13, 1864, p. 2, c. 1
Official Records of the Union and Confederate Navies in the War of the Rebellion, (Washington, DC, 1900), Series 1, Volume 10, pp. 200, 201
Official Records of the Union and Confederate Navies in the War of the Rebellion, (Washington, DC, 1921), Series 2, Volume 1, p. 125
Merchant Steam Vessels of the United States 1790-1868, ("The Lytle-Holdcamper List"), by William M. Lytle and Forrest R. Holdcamper, revised and edited by C. Bradford Mitchell, (Staten Island, New York, 1975), p. 141

1864-6-US-NC-5: Of five schooners captured by the *U.S.S. Lockwood* at Mount Pleasant, Hyde County, North Carolina, on June 16, 1864, two were burned because low water prevented them from being taken away. No papers were found on board.

References for 1864-6-US-NC-5:
Official Records of the Union and Confederate Navies in the War of the Rebellion, (Washington, D.C., 1900), Series 1, Volume 10, p. 154

1864-6-US-NC-6: Despite an order by Captain Smith, U.S.N., dated at Albemarle Sound, North Carolina, in June of 1864, to send the prize schooner *Ann S. Davenport* to him, so he could sink it "in the cut-off between Middle and Roanoke rivers" the vessel was repaired and used as a coal hulk. (Note: The *Ann S. Davenport*, 45 tons, of Plymouth, North Carolina, with a load of 7,000 board feet of yellow pine, was seized on May 12, 1864, by an expedition from the *U.S.S. Ceres*. The schooner was said to have belonged to Samuel S. Simmonds, "a notorious rebel, having taken the oath of loyalty to the U.S. Government and violated same.")

References for 1864-6-US-NC-6:
Official Records of the Union and Confederate Navies in the War of the Rebellion, (Washington, D.C., 1900), Series 1, Volume 10, pp. 58, 115, 122, 142, 161, 213, 239, 439

1864-6-US-SC/GA-1: The British blockade runner *Rose*, Captain W. M. Hale, was chased aground on the south end of Pawley's Island, South Carolina, by the United States gunboat *Wamsutta* on June 2, 1864. The *Rose* carried an assorted cargo which included barrels and cases of liquor, small stores, etc., but most was believed to have already been unloaded on the beach at North Inlet, South Carolina, prior to her being spotted and chased. The Federals captured her register and other papers. The Federals set the steamer on fire and she was completely destroyed. (Note One: The "Charleston Mercury" of June 8, 1864, reported the *Rose* as having a cargo of coal for the Confederate government, and gave her position as off "Butler's Island, near Georgetown, and near the wreck of the *Virginia Dare*." For more on the wreck referred to as the *Virginia Dare*, please see entry 1864-1-US-SC/GA-2 of this book.) (Note Two: The *Rose* was a sidewheel steamer. Federal reports said she ran ashore near the wreck of another steamer, but did not say how near, or what the other wreck was called. It was the *Rose's* first attempt to run the blockade. The Federal troops were driven off by a company of seventy-five Confederates. Her crew lost all of their personal effects and baggage.)

References for 1864-6-US-SC/GA-1:
"Charleston Mercury," (Charleston, SC), Volume 85, #12082, June 8, 1864, p. 2, c. 1
Times, (London, England), #24909, June 27, 1864, p. 9, c. 6
Official Records of the Union and Confederate Armies in the War of the Rebellion, (Washington, DC), Series 1, Volume 15, Part 1, pp. 340, 409-411
Official Records of the Union and Confederate Navies in the War of the Rebellion, (Washington, DC, 1902), Series 1, Volume 15, pp. 467, 468, 513, 517
History of Georgetown County, South Carolina, by George C. Rogers, (Columbia, South Carolina, 1970), p. 413
Pawley's Island, A Living Legend, by Prevost and Wilder, (Columbia, South Carolina, 1972), p. 49
Lifeline of the Confederacy: Blockade Running During the Civil War, by Stephen R. Wise, (University of South Carolina, Columbia, SC, 1983), pp. 369, 609

1864-6-US-SC/GA-2: The sidewheel steamer *Etiwan* (variously spelled as *Etowan*, *Etowah*, *Etwan*, or *Hetiwan*), Captain W. McNulty, ran aground in Charleston Harbor, South Carolina, between Fort Johnson and Fort Sumter on June 7, 1864. She was immediately shelled by the "Yankee's heavy Parrott guns" on Morris Island. (Note One: Her position was also given as on "Fort Johnson reef." The wreck's location is shown on the 1865 chart drawn by E. Willenbucher for the "Annual Report of the Secretary of the Navy." She is listed in Adrian Lonsdale's *Guide to Sunken Ships in American Waters*, as having been wrecked at latitude 32°45.3' North, longitude 79°53.1' West.) (Note Two: She had been owned by Captain Ferguson. It was incorrectly assumed that she was entirely destroyed. However, the wreck was removed and repaired after the war. She was used by the United States Quartermaster's Department, and was later renamed and documented as the *Saint Helena*. She was built at Charleston in 1834 and was 132 tons. She had a wooden hull. Her official number was 22339.) (Note Three: The *Etiwan* had been wrecked once before, for more information on that wreck, please see entry 1863-4-US-SC/GA-3.)

References for 1864-6-US-SC/GA-2:
"Charleston Mercury," (Charleston, SC), Volume 84, #12082, June 8, 1864, p. 2, c. 1
"Vessel Papers" (manuscript records), United States National Archives, Washington, DC, Record Group 109, file E-26
General Map of Charleston Harbor, South Carolina, Showing Rebel Defenses and Obstructions, drawn by E. Willenbucher in 1865 for the "Annual Report of the Secretary of the Navy"

Treasures of the Confederate Coast

Official Records of the Union and Confederate Navies in the War of the Rebellion, (Washington, DC, 1901), Series 1, Volume 13, p. 823
Official Records of the Union and Confederate Navies in the War of the Rebellion, (Washington, DC, 1903), Series 1, Volume 16, pp. 388, 411, 412
Guide to Sunken Ships in American Waters, by Adrian L. Lonsdale and H.R. Kaplan, (Arlington, VA, 1964), p. 70
Shipwrecks of the Civil War: The Encyclopedia of Union and Confederate Naval Losses, by Donald Shomette, (Washington, DC, 1973), pp. 264, 265
Merchant Steam Vessels of the United States 1790-1868, ("Lytle-Holdcamper List"), edited by C. Bradford Mitchell, (Staten Island, NY, 1975), p. 67
Warships of the Civil War Navies, by Paul H. Silverstone, (Naval Institute Press, Annapolis, MD, 1989), p. 239

1864-8-US-NC-1: The United States steamer *Violet* (ex-*Martha*) was wrecked and lost "over the point of Reaper's shoal" near Western Bar Inlet, Cape Fear River, North Carolina, on August 7, 1864. Her "signal books, signals, glasses, gunlocks and equipment" and the men's "bags and hammocks" were saved. (Note One: The wreck was described as about 3/4 of a mile distant from Bald Head battery and about 1 1/2 miles from Fort Caswell. Bald Head Light was said to be bearing about East by North and Bug Light about North by West. A court of inquiry was held on August 8, 1864, to determine the circumstances of the loss.) [Note Two: The *Violet* was armed with two 12-pounder rifles and one 24-pounder. One of her 12-pounder rifles was thrown overboard and the other was spiked and left on the forecastle Her 24-pounder was over the magazine and was blown into the sea. The *Martha* was purchased by Rear-Admiral H. Paulding from E. Brandon & J. Briles, at New York on December 30, 1862, for $23,000 and her name was immediately changed to *Violet*. The total cost of her repairs while she was in naval service was $8,490.08. She was a wooden hulled screw steamer and was classed as a tug, 4th rate. She had one boiler and one direct acting engine with a 30" diameter cylinder and a 28" stroke. The *Violet* was 166 (or 146) tons, 85' in length, 19'9" in breadth, and 11' in depth. She was built at Brooklyn, New York, in 1862. Her first home port was at New York, New York, where she was issued a steam enrollment on December 24, 1862.]

References for 1864-8-US-NC-1:
Records of General Courts Martial and Courts of Inquiry of the Navy Department, 1799-1867, Court of Inquiry, #4320, August 8, 1864, NARS M-273, roll 167, frames 0696-0719
Official Records of the Union and Confederate Navies in the War of the Rebellion, (Washington, DC, 1900), Series 1, Volume 10, pp. 343, 344
Official Records of the Union and Confederate Navies in the War of the Rebellion, (Washington, DC, 1921), Series 2, Volume 1, p. 233
List of American-Flag Merchant Vessels that Received Certificates of Enrollment or Registry at the Port of New York 1789-1867, compiled by Forest R. Holdcamper, (U.S. National Archives, Washington, DC, 1968), Special List #22, Volume 2, p. 450
Merchant Steam Vessels of the United States 1790-1868, ("Lytle-Holdcamper List"), by William M. Lytle and Forrest R. Holdcamper, revised and edited by C. Bradford Mitchell, (Staten Island, NY, 1975), p. 137

1864-8-US-NC-2: The "Charleston Mercury" of August 31, 1864, reported that the "blockade runner *Hope*, a new and first class steamer, was run ashore, near Wilmington by the Yankees last week, near Fort Caswell. It is feared she will be a total loss. She belongs to Fraser & Co., and was making her first trip." [Note One: The *Hope* had a steel hull with water tight compartments and was built by Jones, Quiggin and Company, at Liverpool, England, in 1864. She was 281' (280') in length, 35' (30') in breadth, 15' in depth of hull, had a 9' (or 11') draft, and was 1698 gross tons. A sidewheeler, she was engined by James Jack and Company with two 72" cylinders with 6' piston stroke. She had a crew of 66 men.] (Note Two: The *Hope*, Captain William C. Hammer, was got off and safely brought into Wilmington where she safely unloaded her cargo which included two 150-pounder Armstrong guns and two 12-pounder Whitworth guns. She successfully ran back out of Wilmington on October 3, 1864, but was subsequently chased and captured on October 22, 1864, by the *U.S.S. Eolus* after being spotted off New Inlet, North Carolina, during what would have been the *Hope's* third run through the blockade.) (Note Three: Contemporary records show her as having been owned by Fraser, Trenholm and Company and as registered in the name of John Lafitte. Both Fraser, Trenholm, and Company in Liverpool, and Fraser & Co. in Charleston were headed by George Alfred Trenholm who was later used as the historical basis for Margaret Mitchell's fictional character Rhett Butler in *Gone With The Wind*.)

References for 1864-8-US-NC-2:
"Charleston Mercury," (Charleston, SC), Volume 85, #12153, August 31, 1864, p. 2, c. 1
Official Records of the Union and Confederate Navies in the War of the Rebellion, (Washington, DC, 1900), Series 1, Volume 10, pp. 477, 592-594
Lifeline of the Confederacy: Blockade Running During the Civil War, by Stephen R. Wise, (University Microfilms International, 1983), pp. 473, 474, 512, 576, 577

1864-8-US-SC/GA-1: The propeller steamer *Prince Albert*, bound to Charleston from Nassau, was accidentally run aground at Bowman's Jetty, near Fort Moultrie on Sullivan's Island, South Carolina, on August 9, 1864. (Note One: The *Prince Albert* was on her third run through the blockade when she was lost. A small portion of her cargo, consisting chiefly of medicines, was saved. The wreck was shelled and set on fire by the United States monitor *Catskill* and by the Federal batteries on Morris Island.) (Note Two: She was built by Denny at Dumbarton, Scotland, in 1849, and was engined by Caird and Company.) (Note Three: In late December of 1861, the *Prince Albert* was reported as "formerly of the Galway line" and as under the control of "Mr. Klingender, the advertised agent of Fraser, Trenholm & Co.'s line of Charleston steamers.") (Note Three: Stephen Wise's book *Lifeline of the Confederacy* shows the *Prince Albert* as a sidewheel steamer and gives her dimensions as 138.1'x16.7'x7'. Wise shows her as 132 gross tons

Treasures of the Confederate Coast

and 94 registered tons and says she ran onto the wreck of the *Minho*.) (Note Four: Divers examining the wreck immediately after the war found it to be badly sanded and impossible to save. Portions of the wreck were removed along with the seaward end of Bowman's Jetty during the harbor improvements of the 1870's. Sometime around 1967, the remains of a wreck in the described location were located and tentatively identified as the *Prince Albert* by myself with the aid of Ron A. Gibbs of the United States National Park Service.)

References for 1864-8-US-SC/GA-1:
Log of the U.S. monitor *Catskill*, August 9, 1864, National Archives, Record Group 24
Log of the U.S. ship *John Adams*, August 9, 1864, National Archives, Record Group 24
"Charleston Mercury," (Charleston, SC), Volume 85, #12135, August 10, 1864, p. 2, c. 1
"Charleston Mercury," (Charleston, SC), Volume 85, #12151, August 29, 1864, p. 2, c. 2
"Daily Morning News," (Savannah, GA), August 10, 1864, p. 2, c. 1
"Daily Morning News," (Savannah, GA), August 11, 1864, p. 2, c. 3, 4
"Vessel Papers" (manuscript records), United States National Archives, Washington, DC, Record Group 109, file P-79
Report of the Secretary of the Navy, Second Session, 38th Congress, 1864-1865, (Washington, DC, 1865), p. 730
Official Records of the Union and Confederate Navies in the War of the Rebellion, (Washington, DC, 1897), Series 1, Volume 6, p. 510
Official Records of the Union and Confederate Navies in the War of the Rebellion, (Washington, DC, 1900), Series 1, Volume 10, p. 477
Official Records of the Union and Confederate Navies in the War of the Rebellion, (Washington, DC, 1902), Series 1, Volume 15, p. 624
Official Records of the Union and Confederate Navies in the War of the Rebellion, (Washington, DC, 1903), Series 1, Volume 16, pp. 34, 37, 354
Lifeline of the Confederacy: Blockade Running During the Civil War, by Stephen R. Wise, (University of South Carolina, Columbia, SC, 1983), pp. 369, 606

1864-8-US-SC/GA-2: The blockade runner *Mary Bowers*, Captain Jesse DeHorsey (or Horsey), bound from Bermuda with an assorted cargo, struck the submerged wreck of the *Georgiana* in fourteen feet of water a mile off Long Island (the present day Isle of Palms, South Carolina) on August 31 (or September 1), 1864. She "went on with such force as to make immense openings in her bottom," and she sank in a "few minutes, most of the officers and men saving only what they stood in." The steamer's passengers and crew escaped with the exception of a boy, Richard Jackson, who was left on the wreck and later taken off by the Federals. [Note One: The *Mary Bowers* was a large, shallow draft, sidewheel steamer of approximately 680 tons (also shown as 750 tons burden and 220 tons register). She measured 226'x25'x10'6" and was built by Simons and Company of Renfrew, Scotland. She was owned in part by L.G. Bowers of Columbus, Georgia, and had been built especially for the purpose of running the blockade at a cost of approximately £22,682. The vessel was registered as owned by Henry Lafone. Her company owner was the Importing and Exporting Company of Georgia (which was sometimes called the Lamar Company).] (Note Two: The Federals misidentified the blockade runner in their initial reports calling her the *Mary Powers*.

The "Real Rhett Butler" & Other Revelations

The Federal boarding party took a bell and a few other items from the wreck. She had made two previous successful attempts through the blockade, on one of which, she was chased by the *U.S.S. R.G. Cuyler* and had been forced to throw overboard sixty bales of cotton to escape.) (Note Three: In 1967, while diving from a boat captained by Wally Shaffer, I positively identified a previously unidentified "hang" as the combined wreckage of the *Georgiana* and the *Mary Bowers*. That discovery was the result of research I had started years before I met Mr. Shaffer. For more on the *Georgiana* and *Mary Bowers*, please see Chapter One, and see entries 1863-3-US-SC/GA-2 and 1864-10-US-SC/GA-1, also see appendices C and F.)

References for 1864-8-US-SC/GA-2:
"Charleston Mercury," (Charleston, SC), Volume 85, #12155, September 2, 1864, p. 2, c. 1
"Charleston Mercury," (Charleston, SC), Volume 85, #12185, October 7, 1864, p. 2, c. 1
"Daily Morning News," (Savannah, GA), September 2, 1864, p. 2, c. 1
Times, (London, England), #24974, September 10, 1864, p. 8, c. 6
"Vessel Papers" (manuscript records), United States National Archives, Washington, DC, Record Group 109, file M-275
Official Records of the Union and Confederate Navies in the War of the Rebellion, (Washington, DC, 1896), Series 1, Volume 3, pp. 121, 127
Official Records of the Union and Confederate Navies in the War of the Rebellion, (Washington, DC, 1902), Series 1, Volume 15, pp. 658, 659, 660, 661, 670
Official Records of the Union and Confederate Navies in the War of the Rebellion, (Washington, DC, 1903), Series 1, Volume 16, pp. 8, 34, 37
"Salvaging the Cargo of the *Mary Bowers*," by E. Lee Spence, *The Conference on Historic Site Archeology Papers 1969*, (1971), Volume 4, part 1
Lifeline of the Confederacy: Blockade Running During the Civil War, by Stephen R. Wise, (University of South Carolina, Columbia, SC, 1983), pp. 338, 341, 345, 368, 593, 594
Charleston's Maritime Heritage 1670-1865, by P.C. Coker III, (CokerCraft Press, Charleston, SC, 1987), pp. 203, 214, 286, 304
The Blockade Runners, by Dave Horner, (Florida Classics Library, Port Salerno, FL, 1992), Chapter 14, pp. 223, 225

1864-9-US-NC-1: The sidewheel steamer *Badger* was reported by refugees as having been run ashore in Wilmington Harbor, North Carolina, about September 10, 1864. (Note One: The *Badger* had made one previous run through the blockade and was built of iron and steel. Her dimensions were 218'x24.3'x11.6'. She was 375 gross tons and 623 tons burden. The *Badger* was engined with two cylinders of 48" diameter and 5' piston stroke.) (Note Two: David Stick's book, *Graveyard of the Atlantic*, gives her location as on the "Cape Fear Bar.") (Note Three: The *Badger's* first registered owner was John B. Lafitte, but she was owned by Fraser, Trenholm and Company at the time of her loss. The vessel had been built by Jones, Quiggin and company in Liverpool, England, in 1864. Fraser, Trenholm and Company was a British firm headed by Charlestonian George Alfred Trenholm who was later used as the historical basis for Margaret Mitchell's fictional character Rhett Butler in *Gone With The Wind*.)

References for 1864-9-US-NC-1:
Official Records of the Union and Confederate Navies in the War of the Rebellion, (Washington, DC, 1900), Series 1, Volume 10, pp. 391, 394, 504

Treasures of the Confederate Coast

Graveyard of the Atlantic: Shipwrecks of the North Carolina Coast, by David Stick (University of North Carolina Press, Chapel Hill, NC, 1952), p. 247
An Oceanographic Atlas of the Continental Margin, J.G. Newton, O.H. Pilkey and J.O. Blanton, (Duke University Marine Laboratory, Beaufort, NC, 1971), p. 17 chart symbol #72, p. 20 entry #72
Lifeline of the Confederacy: Blockade Running During the Civil War, by Stephen R. Wise, (University Microfilms International, 1983), pp. 473, 535

1864-9-US-NC-2: Refugees reported that the sidewheel steamer *Florie* (or *Florrie*) had accidentally run onto an old wreck in Wilmington Harbor, North Carolina, about September 10, 1864. (Note One: The *Florie* was outbound when she was lost on her eighth attempt to run the blockade. Six of her previous attempts had proved successful.) (Note Two: The *Florie* was named for the daughter of John Newland Mafia, captain of the *C.S.S. Florida.* Contemporary records showed her as 215 tons register and as 320 gross tons. She was 220' in length, 25' in breadth, 10'6" in depth of hull, and a draft of only 7'6". Her engine had a 48" cylinder. She could run seventeen miles per hour. The *Florie* had been impressed by the Confederate Navy for use in the Point Lookout Expedition in August of 1864.) (Note Three: Stephen Wise's book, *Lifeline of the Confederacy: Blockade Running During the Civil War*, shows her as lost in October of 1864, and states that she was "run aground inside the Cape Fear River Bar." David Stick's book, *Graveyard of the Atlantic*, places the wreck on the "Cape Fear Bar." A report in the London *Times* of November 23, 1864, listed the *Florie* as "ashore outside of Charleston," but that report was probably referring to the *Flora* which was wrecked on Sullivan's Island on October 22, 1864. For information on the loss of the *Flora*, please see entry 1864-10-US-SC/GA-2.) (Note Four: The *Florie* was owned by Henry Lafone of the Importing and Exporting Company of Savannah, Georgia, and appears to have been one of the steamers contracted for by Henry Lafone in an agreement dated October, 1863. A copy of that agreement is given in Appendix F of this book.)

References for 1864-9-US-NC-2:
Times, (London, England), #25037, November 23, 1864, p. 7, c. 5
Official Records of the Union and Confederate Navies in the War of the Rebellion, (Washington, DC, 1900), Series 1, Volume 10, pp. 427, 504, 601
Graveyard of the Atlantic: Shipwrecks of the North Carolina Coast, by David Stick (University of North Carolina Press, Chapel Hill, NC, 1952), p. 247
An Oceanographic Atlas of the Continental Margin, J.G. Newton, O.H. Pilkey and J.O. Blanton, (Duke University Marine Laboratory, Beaufort, NC, 1971), p. 17 chart symbol #69, p. 20 entry #69
Lifeline of the Confederacy: Blockade Running During the Civil War, by Stephen R. Wise, (University Microfilms International, 1983), pp. 470, 512, 564, 565
Wreck of the Georgiana: Mystery Ship of the Confederacy, by E. Lee Spence, (Charleston, South Carolina, 1989 prepublication copy), Appendix C
High Seas Confederate: the Life and Times of John Newland Maffitt, written by Royce Shingleton, edited by William N. Still, Jr., (University of South Carolina Press, Columbia, SC, 1994), p. 81h

1864-9-US-NC-3: The armed sidewheel steamer *Lynx*, Captain Reid (or Reed), was chased ashore near the Half Moon Battery north of Fort Fisher, North Carolina, on September 25, 1864, by the United

The "Real Rhett Butler" & Other Revelations

States gunboats *Howquah, Niphon, Governor* and *Buckingham*. [Note One: The *Lynx* was bound from Wilmington to Bermuda with over six hundred bales cotton (half on government account), $50,000 in gold (on freight for the government), and a large amount of bonds. One of her men was wounded by a volley of musketry fired at the *Lynx*. She was burned by her own crew to prevent her from falling into the hands of the Federals. Thirty four bales of cotton which had been thrown overboard by the *Lynx* were picked up the following day. The following account of the *Lynx's* chase and capture is taken verbatim from the *London Times* of December 24, 1864. "Having passed safely over the bar, the pilot acquainted the captain with the fact, when he directed his course due east. The order had no sooner been given and the helm answered, when the night became brilliantly illuminated by rockets and blue lights from all quarters. Shot after shot was fired in quick and rapid succession near and over the gallant little ship. The first one, passing through the wheelhouse, wounded the man at the wheel, and threw particles of glass and splinters over a lady passenger who had taken refuge therein. Captain Reed directed his steamer through the narrow passages between the hostile ships. Speed alone could save the ship from the whizzing balls, for the calmness of the sea gave the enemy too great an advantage in firing. The little steamer leaped and trembled through the water, passing successively each of the enemy's ships, as each kept banging, banging away. A rifled shell soon passed through her cabin below the water-line, and again near the passenger who had descended from the wheelhouse. Seven more in rapid succession struck the ship, and each time she trembled like an aspen leaf. At one time the enemy were so near as to give the order for Captain Reed to heave to. 'Drive her Mr. Lake, drive her!' was the cool response of the captain. A whole broadside renewed the enemy's order, yet the *Lynx*, uninjured in hull, sped rapidly onward, with her immense power. 120 shots in all were fired at the ship, besides a volley of musketry, which, whistling through the air, rattled against her sides. Ten of the fleet were thus passed, amid the most rapid and effective fire yet directed against any blockade runner. The steamer, having now passed the blockaders, had her course changed direct, and Mr. Boggs, chief officer, was sent to ascertain the damage. He soon returned, and reported eight shots below the water line and the steamer sinking. The idea of running out and in the same night was objectionable in the extreme, and no one thought of surrender once entered the captain's head. Still, no fear or trepidation was felt by any one. All were subordinate and obedient to the captain's orders, and no breach of discipline once occurred to mar the management of the ship. The *Lynx* was headed for the beach, the cotton buoying her up. Fortunately the engine compartment was uninjured, and the motive power, pushed to its utmost, drove the sinking ship onward to her now certain end. Every preparation was made for the safety of the crew and passengers. The steamer at last struck - her steel hull sprung forward with the concussion, and on the next swell a few more yards were obtained. In the midst of perfect coolness, as if embarking for pleasure, Captain Reed directed the transfer of the coin and bonds himself, and the pilot left the ship with the purser and the passengers. No good boat was now left, yet all the crew in perfect discipline and obedience promised to stick to the last. The carpenter soon reported the (life) boat repaired. The rest embarked; Captain Reed and Chief Officer Boggs were the last on board. Six barrels of spirits of turpentine were poured over the equally combustible cotton, and almost with tears in his eyes and with a heavy, heavy heart, the captain applied the torch to his ship." Mrs. Louis H. DeRosset jumped ten feet into a small boat, and despite the breakers, caught her baby which a sailor tossed from the deck. The baby also ran the blockade aboard the *Owl*.] (Note Two: Her position was also described as five or six miles above Fort Fisher.) [Note Three: The *Lynx* was described as a long steamer, painted white, with two stacks and two masts. She had made nine previous successful runs through the blockade. She had been built by Jones, Quiggin and Company at Liverpool, England, in 1864. She was built of steel and was 220' in length, 24' in breadth, 11'6" in depth of hold. She was 372 tons gross and 233 tons register.) (Note Four: The *Lynx* was registered to Richard Wright and was owned by Fraser, Trenholm and Company (also shown as owned by John Fraser & Co.). Both the Charleston based Fraser & Co. and the Liverpool based Fraser, Trenholm and Company were headed by George Alfred Trenholm who was later used as the historical basis for Margaret Mitchell's fictional character Rhett Butler in *Gone With The Wind*.] (Note Five: In one account, her name was given as the *Linch*.) (Note Six: The $50,000 in gold, which was saved by Mr. Gordon, the steamer's purser, would have weighed 2,500 troy ounces or just over 208 troy pounds.)

References for 1864-9-US-NC-3:
"Charleston Mercury," (Charleston, SC), Volume 85, #12178, September 29, 1864, p. 2, c. 1
Times, (London, England), #25004, October 15, 1864, p. 12, c. 1
Times, (London, England), #25007, October 19, 1864, p. 10, c. 1
Times, (London, England), #25064, December 24, 1864, p. 12, c. 3
Official Records of the Union and Confederate Navies in the War of the Rebellion, (Washington, DC, 1900), Series 1, Volume 10, pp. 478-482, 492, 503, 504, 509

The "Real Rhett Butler" & Other Revelations

Official Records of the Union and Confederate Navies in the War of the Rebellion, (Washington, DC, 1900), Series 1, Volume 11, p. 743
Derelicts, An Account of Ships Lost at Sea in General Commercial Traffic and a Brief History of Blockade Runners Stranded Along the North Carolina Coast 1861-1865, by James Sprunt (Lord Baltimore's Press, Wilmington, DE, 1920), p. 451
A Chart of Wrecks of Vessels Sunk or Captured Near Wilmington, NC, Circa 1861-65, compiled by Charles H. Foard, (Wilmington, North Carolina, 1962)
An Oceanographic Atlas of the Continental Margin, J.G. Newton, O.H. Pilkey and J.O. Blanton, (Duke University Marine Laboratory, Beaufort, NC, 1971), p. 17 chart symbol #82, p. 20 entry #82
George Alfred Trenholm: The Company that went to War, by Ethel Trenholm Seabrook Nepveux, (Charleston, SC, 1973), p. 70
Lifeline of the Confederacy: Blockade Running During the Civil War, by Stephen R. Wise, (University Microfilms International, 1983), pp. 473, 590
The Blockade Runners, by Dave Horner, (Florida Classics Library, Port Salerno, FL, 1992), Chapter 14, pp. 33, 224 (references the *Wilmington Daily Journal* of October 3, 1864)

1864-9-US-NC-4: The English blockade runner *Night Hawk*, Captain Uriah Francis Smiley, was chased ashore by the *U.S.S. Niphon* on Federal Shoals, Cape Fear, North Carolina, on September 29, 1864. (Note One: The complement of the vessel was 42, 19 of whom eventually escaped to shore. She was boarded by a boat from the *U.S.S. Niphon*, in the charge of Acting Ensign E. N. Semon, a man said to be of ungovernable temper. Ensign Semon's conduct was severely criticized by the *Night Hawk's* crew and was officially protested by British diplomatic officials. According to sworn testimony, the vessel was fired into with musketry, wounding some of her crew, well after she was aground and even though the men were no longer trying to escape or otherwise resisting. It was said that Ensign Semon pistol whipped the steamer's chief engineer, and set fire to the vessel despite the fact that it could have been gotten off without danger to his men. As Ensign Semon left the burning vessel, he cursed the fourteen crew and officers, including three wounded who were lying on the deck, that he left aboard, saying they could all "go to Hell and be damned.") (Note Two: The *Night Hawk* carried a general cargo and was bound from Bermuda to Wilmington. She had sailed from Liverpool on August 27, 1864, in ballast and had taken on sixty pigs of lead, twenty-six bags of saltpeter and a large amount of provisions and liquor at Bermuda. Some of the liquor was used in torching the vessel.) [Note Three: The steamer was 300 tons burden and could make 14 knots. She cost £30,000 and could carry eight hundred bales of cotton. She was owned by Edward Lawrence of Liverpool (also shown as owned by M.J. Wilson and the Anglo-Confederate Trading Company). She was a long, low, iron hulled, sidewheeler, with two stacks and two masts. The *Night Hawk* measured 220'x21'6"x11'. She was built by McAndrew and Preston at Liverpool, England, in 1864. Her supercargo was a dashing young man named Thomas E. Taylor.] (Note Four: The location of the wreck was also given as half a mile from Fort Fisher

Treasures of the Confederate Coast

and as "on the North Breaker, about a mile from shore." Although the *Night Hawk's* woodwork had burned away, her engines and hull remained intact and the steamer was later got off and repaired at Wilmington. She eventually escaped through the blockade and arrived at Nassau on January 7, 1865.)

References for 1864-9-US-NC-4:
"Charleston Mercury," (Charleston, SC), Volume 85, #12193, October 17, 1864, p. 1, c. 1, 2
Times, (London, England), #25007, October 19, 1864, p. 10, c. 1
Records of General Courts Martial and Courts of Inquiry of the Navy Department, 1799-1867, Court of Inquiry, #4522, December 22, 1864, NARS M-273, roll 2, alphabetical card index 1861-1867
Official Records of the Union and Confederate Navies in the War of the Rebellion, (Washington, DC, 1900), Series 1, Volume 10, pp. 492-501, 504, 511, 531, 532, 536, 800
Running the Blockade, by Thomas E. Taylor, (London, England, 1897), pp. 116-127
A Chart of Wrecks of Vessels Sunk or Captured Near Wilmington, NC, Circa 1861-65, compiled by Charles H. Foard, (Wilmington, North Carolina, 1962)
Lifeline of the Confederacy: Blockade Running During the Civil War, by Stephen R. Wise, (University Microfilms International, 1983), pp. 439, 440, 449, 450, 599

1864-9-US-NC-5: The Confederate States sloop of war *North Carolina*, "her bottom eaten out by worms," sprang a leak and sank in the Cape Fear River while moored near Fort Caswell, North Carolina, in September, 1864. Within the month, a blockade runner "ran afoul of her wreck and immediately sunk." (Note: The ironclad steamer was armed with four guns and manned by one hundred and fifty men. The ram *North Carolina* had been built by Berry & Brothers at Wilmington, North Carolina, in 1863, and was 150' in length, 32' in breadth, 14' in depth and drew 12' of water. Her machinery had been taken out of the *C.S.S. Uncle Ben.*)

References for 1864-9-US-NC-5:
Official Records of the Union and Confederate Armies in the War of the Rebellion, (Washington, DC, 1893), Series 1, Volume 42, Part 2, pp. 1294, 1297
Official Records of the Union and Confederate Navies in the War of the Rebellion, (Washington, DC, 1900), Series 1, Volume 10, p. 509
Official Records of the Union and Confederate Navies in the War of the Rebellion, (Washington, DC, 1921), Series 2, Volume 1, pp. 262, 270
Graveyard of the Atlantic: Shipwrecks of the North Carolina Coast, by David Stick (University of North Carolina Press, Chapel Hill, NC, 1952), pp. 60, 247
A Chart of Wrecks of Vessels Sunk or Captured Near Wilmington, NC, Circa 1861-65, compiled by Charles H. Foard, (Wilmington, North Carolina, 1962)
Dictionary of American Naval Fighting Ships, (Washington, DC, 1963), Volume 2, p. 553
An Oceanographic Atlas of the Continental Margin, J.G. Newton, O.H. Pilkey and J.O. Blanton, (Duke University Marine Laboratory, Beaufort, NC, 1971), p. 17 chart symbol #53, p. 20 entry #53
Iron Afloat: The Story of the Confederate Armorclads, by William N. Still Jr., (Vanderbilt University Press, 1971), pp. 165, 166

1864-9x-US-SC/GA-1: The steamer *Clinch* is mentioned in Major General Sam Jones' letter of September 21, 1864, as having been raised from Charleston Harbor by her owner, Mr. McCormick. She had been discharged from government service after her sinking. McCormick was making repairs to her and hoped to use her to run the blockade, but General Jones did not want to let her go as she could carry about 1,000 men and was needed at Charleston.

Reference for 1864-9x-US-SC/GA-1:
Official Records of the Union and Confederate Armies in the War of the Rebellion, (Washington, DC, 1891), Series 1, Volume 35, Part 2, pp. 624, 625

The "Real Rhett Butler" & Other Revelations

1864-10-US-NC-1: The "huge" British steamer *Condor*, Captain Augustuis Charles-Hobart-Hampden, was chased ashore on Swash Channel Bar abreast of Fort Fisher, North Carolina, by the *U.S.S. Niphon* on October 1, 1864. (Note One: The *Condor* was inbound on her first voyage through the blockade when she was wrecked. Her location was also reported as being near the wreck of the *Night Hawk* on Federal Shoals, and one report attributed the *Condor's* loss to the fact that her captain had been fooled by the wreck of the *Night Hawk*. Part of the *Condor's* cargo was saved.) [Note Two: The *Condor* was described as of rakish build, long and low, three low funnels, two short masts, and light draft. She was a sidewheel steamer of 300 tons (283 tons register) and of "great" or "tremendous" speed. She had an iron hull, painted a light lead color, and her dimensions were 270'x24'x12'. She was built by Randolph, Elder and Company at Fairfield, England, in 1864, and her foredeck was covered with a "turtleback." She was insured by was Donald McGregor, of London, and was owned or operated by Alexander Collie and Company at the time of her loss, although some accounts show McGregor as her registered owner.] (Note Three: She had a crew of forty men, which would have required a payroll and expense account of over $80,000 per voyage. That much in gold would have weighed approximately 2,000 troy ounces and, if in United States coinage, could now have a numismatic value in excess of $12,000,000.) (Note Four: One of the *Condor's* passengers was the famous Confederate female spy, Rose O'Neal Greenhow, who had given General Beauregard the Union Army's plans for the First Battle of Bull Run. Mrs. Greenhow was drowned when the small boat she was in which she was fleeing to shore was overturned in the surf and the $2,000 in gold sovereigns she had hidden in her clothing carried her to the bottom. Another report gave the value of the gold she carried at six hundred pounds sterling. Both Mrs. Greenhow's body was found by Thomas E. Taylor, supercargo for the *Night Hawk*. She was buried at Oakdale Cemetery. Only 100 gold sovereigns were reported as recovered.) (Note Five: For more information on the wreck of the steamer *Night Hawk* see entry 1864-9-US-NC-4.) (Note Six: The wreck of the *Condor* appears to have been fairly close to that of a wrecked Federal vessel, as on December 3, 1864, Colonel Lamb, C.S.A., reported "Blockaders off to windward. Practiced with Armstrong 150-pounder rifle, with 30 pounds powder and steel shell. First shot struck rearmost chimney of *Condor*; second struck her forward smokestack; third shot, at 3 o'clock, struck wreck of blockader.")

Treasures of the Confederate Coast

(Note Seven: A Sea Grant publication put out by the University of North Carolina lists the wreck of the *Condor* as being in twenty feet of water offshore of a monument at Fort Fisher.) (Note Eight: Captain Hobart-Hampden was a dashing, colorful figure, tall and bearded, who's stirring words in 1854 as captain of a British warship facing the Russian fleet were: "Lads, sharpen your cutlasses!" Late commander of *H.M.S. Rinaldo*, he was still an officer in Her British Majesty's service on half pay. His exploits with women were legendary. As a blockade runner captain he used the aliases Roberts, Gulick, William N.W. Hewett, and Ridge. Samuel S. Ridge being the name Hobart used in conjunction with the *Condor*. He received the Victoria Cross for his distinguished heroism in the Crimean War, and once skippered Queen Victoria's yacht. He retired as a Vice-Admiral of the British Navy and served as Admiral-in-Chief of the Ottoman Empire's Navy. The fearless adventurer died in 1886, "a brilliantly representative type" of the Britisher who would go anywhere and do anything.)

References for 1864-10-US-NC-1:
Times, (London, England), #24950, August 13, 1864, p. 9, c. 5
Times, (London, England), #25007, October 19, 1864, p. 10, c. 1
"Charleston Mercury," (Charleston, SC), Volume 85, #12185, October 7, 1864, p. 1, c. 1
"Charleston Mercury," (Charleston, SC), Volume 85, #12193, October 17, 1864, p. 1, c. 2
"Charleston Mercury," (Charleston, SC), Volume 85, #12210, November 5, 1864, p. 1, c. 2
"Daily Morning News," (Savannah, GA), October 15, 1864, p. 1, c. 2
Official Records of the Union and Confederate Navies in the War of the Rebellion, (Washington, DC, 1900), Series 1, Volume 10, pp. 438, 477, 484, 531-533, 536, 552, 781, 782
Official Records of the Union and Confederate Navies in the War of the Rebellion, (Washington, D.C., 1900), Series 1, Volume 11, pp. 741, 743, 745, 787
Graveyard of the Atlantic: Shipwrecks of the North Carolina Coast, by David Stick (University of North Carolina Press, Chapel Hill, NC, 1952), pp. 60, 247
Blockade Runners of the Confederacy, by Hamilton Cochran (Bobbs-Merrill Co., Inc., Indianapolis, 1958), p. 142
A Chart of Wrecks of Vessels Sunk or Captured Near Wilmington, NC, Circa 1861-65, compiled by Charles H. Foard, (Wilmington, North Carolina)
An Oceanographic Atlas of the Continental Margin, J.G. Newton, O.H. Pilkey and J.O. Blanton, (Duke University Marine Laboratory, Beaufort, NC, 1971), p. 17 chart symbol #65, p. 20 entry #65
Wreck Diving in North Carolina, University of North Carolina, Sea Grant Publication, #78-13, p. 6
Lifeline of the Confederacy: Blockade Running During the Civil War, by Stephen R. Wise, (University Microfilms International, 1983), pp. 312, 314, 447-450, 512, 548
The Blockade Runners, by Dave Horner, (Florida Classics Library, Port Salerno, FL, 1992), Chapter 4, pp. 54-66

1864-10-US-NC-2: The steamer *Aphrodite*, Morgan master, chartered as a transport, was run aground October 3, 1864, twelve miles north of the light house at Cape Lookout, North Carolina. She carried 510 United States Navy recruits under Commander Clarey. At least two and possibly as many as eight lives were lost in the surf. Approximately twenty men were said to have deserted to the North Carolina shore. (Note One: Some damaged stores were saved from the *Aphrodite* which was described as broken in two and a total wreck. It was reported that it would require an organized wrecking party to save the anchors, cables, etc.) (Note Two: The *Aphrodite* was 1098 tons, had a wood hull, and was built at Mystic,

The "Real Rhett Butler" & Other Revelations

Connecticut, in 1864. Her first home port was New York, New York, where she was issued a certificate of steam enrollment on August 1, 1864.) (Note Three: The "Lytle-Holdcamper List" gives the date of sinking as October 15, 1864, and her location as Core Sound, North Carolina.) (Note Four: Underwater explorer Carter Leary reports that this wreck has recently been discovered in about thirty feet of water, and divers have salvaged some bars of lead and tin from the wreck.

References for 1864-10-US-NC-2:
New York Times, (New York, NY), Volume 14, #4124, December 12, 1864, p. 8, c. 3, 4
Official Records of the Union and Confederate Navies in the War of the Rebellion, (Washington, DC, 1900), Series 1, Volume 10, pp. 523, 524, 531
List of American-Flag Merchant Vessels that Received Certificates of Enrollment or Registry at the Port of New York 1789-1867, compiled by Forest R. Holdcamper, (U.S. National Archives, Washington, DC, 1968), Special List #22, Volume 1, p. 53
Merchant Steam Vessels of the United States 1790-1868, ("Lytle-Holdcamper List"), by William M. Lytle and Forrest R. Holdcamper, revised and edited by C. Bradford Mitchell, (Staten Island, NY, 1975), pp. 12, 242
Telephone interview of Carter Leary by E. Lee Spence, 1989, and October 22, 1994

1864-10-US-NC-3: Both sides routinely destroyed buoys and light-houses thought to be of greater service to their enemy. Such is the normal practice of war. The Confederates blew up and burned the light-house (the Croatan Light) at the entrance from Albemarle to Croatan Sound on October 4, 1864. However, a report of Commander Daniel Ammen, of the *U.S.S. Mohican*, dated November 28, 1864, suggested a plan of questionable morality and ethics in that it involved the display of false signal lights to purposefully cause the destruction of foreign merchant vessels (albeit blockade runners), and other passing vessels of all types. In his words: "The suggestion is, in placing close off Masonboro Inlet (North Carolina) two small vessels for the purpose of serving as (false) Mound and range light, and in the direction of the proper bearing, or nearly, a dim light could be hoisted on board of two fast chasers to pass as Bald Head light in the distance. The manner of occulting these various lights here could be observed nightly, and until their system becomes developed could be repeated the following night off Masonboro Inlet. By screening the light so as to hide them from the shore, many of the blockade runners might become victims before they are aware of the ruse." (Note: For actual orders regarding the display of false lights by Federal blockaders, please see Appendix G of this book.)

Reference for 1864-10-US-NC-3:
Official Records of the Union and Confederate Navies in the War of the Rebellion, (Washington, D.C., 1900), Series 1, Volume 10, pp. 529, 530
Official Records of the Union and Confederate Navies in the War of the Rebellion, (Washington, DC, 1900), Series 1, Volume 11, p. 100

1864-10-US-NC-4: The "Charleston Mercury" reported that a shell fired from Fort Fisher on October 7, 1864, struck a Federal gunboat

Treasures of the Confederate Coast

that had accompanied a Federal launch in to burn the wreck of the *Condor*. The report stated that the gunboat was run ashore on the south breaker of the bar and abandoned. Her crew set fire to her in several places, and before morning she was totally destroyed, her magazine having exploded and torn her to pieces. (Note: This report undoubtedly refers to the United States armed tug *Aster*, which was accidentally run aground while chasing a blockade runner. The article was probably the result of an erroneous report filed on October 11, 1864, at Wilmington, North Carolina, by Major-General W.H.C. Whiting, C.S.A., saying "a chance shot struck the gunboat and sunk her instantly." See also next entry.)

References for 1864-10-US-NC-4:
"Charleston Mercury," (Charleston, SC), Volume 85, #12193, October 17, 1864, p. 1, c. 2
Official Records of the Union and Confederate Navies in the War of the Rebellion, (Washington, DC, 1900), Series 1, Volume 10, pp. 541-546, 552, 782

1864-10-US-NC-5: The United States armed tug *Aster* (ex-*Alice*) accidentally went ashore on the eastern extremity of Carolina (or Caroline) Shoals, at the entrance of New Inlet North Carolina, on October 8, 1864, while attempting to cut off the escape of the blockade runner *Annie*. Although the *U.S.S. Berberry* immediately came to her aid, the *Berberry* was unable to get her off due to the parting of an eight inch hawser and the ebbing of the tide. The *Aster's* aft 24-pounder and numerous other items were heaved overboard in a futile effort to float the tug. The *Aster* was set fire to prevent her from falling into the hands of the Confederates. The *Annie*, bound from Halifax, had run aground nearby and one of the *Annie's* boats, with 15 men, was captured by the Federal sailors leaving the *Aster*. (Note One: The *Aster* was a screw steamer with a copper fastened wooden hull and was sheathed with "yellow metal." The tug was 285 tons, 122'6" in length, 23' in breadth, 10' in depth and drew 10' of water. She had one vertical, low pressure engine with a 40" cylinder and 7'4" piston stroke. Her single boiler was 15' by 12' and had three furnaces. She was purchased on July 25, 1864, at Philadelphia, by Commodore C.K. Stribling from Bishop Son & Co. for $75,000. She was commissioned on August 12, 1864. She was a new tug, well built of first-class material and sheathed with yellow metal. The cost of her repairs while she was in naval service was $616.66. The tug was armed with one 30-pounder Parrott rifle, and two heavy 12-pounder smoothbores.) (Note Two: The *Annie* was lightened of her cargo by the Confederates and got off the next day, "favored by an offshore wind.") (Note Three: See previous entry, and see entry 1864-10-US-NC-10.)

References for 1864-10-US-NC-5

The "Real Rhett Butler" & Other Revelations

Official Records of the Union and Confederate Navies in the War of the Rebellion, (Washington, DC, 1900), Series 1, Volume 10, pp. 541-546, 552, 782
Official Records of the Union and Confederate Navies in the War of the Rebellion, (Washington, D.C., 1900), Series 1, Volume 11, p. 30
Official Records of the Union and Confederate Navies in the War of the Rebellion, (Washington, DC, 1921), Series 2, Volume 1, p. 40
An Oceanographic Atlas of the Continental Margin, J.G. Newton, O.H. Pilkey and J.O. Blanton, (Duke University Marine Laboratory, Beaufort, NC, 1971), p. 17 chart symbol #78, p. 20 entry #78

1864-10-US-NC-6: A cutter from the *U.S.S. Tacony*, which had been sent on a reconnaissance of the Roanoke River, North Carolina, was ambushed by the Confederates on October 24, 1864. John Williams, quartermaster was killed, William G. Green, ordinary seaman, was seriously wounded in the head, and the boat was so badly shattered it sank. The boat had been commanded by Acting Ensign R. Sommers, who "after great exertion, and with his usual indomitable perseverance, succeeded in constructing a raft," on which he and two other men escaped. Three men were reported missing in the swamp, but it was hoped they might be saved.

References for 1864-10-US-NC-6:

Official Records of the Union and Confederate Navies in the War of the Rebellion, (Washington, DC, 1900), Series 1, Volume 10, pp. 595, 596

1864-10-US-NC-7: The Confederate States ram *Albemarle*, Commander J.W. Cooke (or A.F. Warley), was sunk in eight feet of water by a Federal torpedo boat (picket boat *No. 1*) commanded by Lieutenant W. B. Cushing, at Plymouth, North Carolina, on October 28, 1864. Cushing's boat was swamped and captured. [Note One: Cushing reported the action as follows: "The rebels sprung their rattle, rang the bell, and commenced firing, at the same time repeating their hail and seeming much confused. The light of a fire ashore showed me the ironclad made fast to the wharf, with a pen of logs around her about 30 feet from her side. Passing her closely, we made a complete circle so as to strike her fairly, and went into her bows on. By this time the enemy's fire was very severe, but a dose of canister at short range served to moderate their zeal and disturb their aim. Paymaster (Francis H.) Swan, of the *Otsego*, was wounded near me, but how many more I know not. Three bullets struck my clothing, and the air seemed full of them. In a moment we had struck the logs, just abreast of the quarter port, breasting them in some feet, and our bows resting on them. The torpedo boom was then lowered and by a vigorous pull I succeeded in diving the torpedo under the overhang and exploding it at the same time that the *Albemarle's* gun was fired. A shot seemed to go crashing through my boat, and a dense mass of water rushed in from the torpedo, filling the launch and completely disabling her. The enemy then continued his fire at 15 feet range, and demanded our surrender, which I twice refused, ordering the men to save

Treasures of the Confederate Coast

themselves, and removing my own coat and shoes. Springing into the river, I swam, with others, into the middle of the stream, the rebels firing to hit us. The most of our party were captured, some were drowned, and only one escaped besides myself, and he in another direction."] (Note Two: A Confederate soldier wrote: "The (*Albemarle's*) crew lost everything they had, bed clothing and everything. Some lost their hats and shoes, and some even came out in their shirts and drawers, barefooted.") (Note Two: The Confederates further blew up the wreck by detonating a torpedo inside the casemate. The additional damage prevented the Federal forces from quickly raising and using the ram. However, on March 18, 1865, she was finally refloated. She was later sufficiently repaired to be taken into the U.S. Navy.) [Note Three: The *Albemarle* was patterned after the famous ironclad steamer *Merrimack*. She was built at Edward's Ferry on the Roanoke River in North Carolina in 1864. She was an ironclad screw steamer built of yellow pine sills fourteen inches square and was fastened with iron and with treenails (wooden pegs). She was armed with two pivot guns, each designed to work out of three ports. The ram was 158' in length, 35'3" in breadth, 8'2" in depth and 9' in draft. She had two engines and two boilers. The boilers were 15'4" in length, 5'2" in height and 4'7" in width. Her furnaces were 4'6" in length and 4' in width. The slanting roof of the battery and all exposed parts were covered with five inches of pine, five inches of oak, and then plated with railroad iron.] (Note Four: See also entry 1864-6x-US-NC-1.)

References for 1864-10-US-NC-7:
"Charleston Mercury," (Charleston, SC), Volume 85, #12214, November 10, 1864, p. 2, c. 1
"Charleston Mercury," (Charleston, SC), Volume 85, #12216, November 12, 1864, p. 1, c. 3, 4
"Daily Morning News," (Savannah, GA), November 26, 1864, p. 1, c. 3
New York Times, (New York, NY), Volume 13, #3940, May 10, 1864, p. 8, c. 3
Times, (London, England), #25031, November 16, 1864, p. 10, c. 1
History of the Confederate States Navy From its Organization to the Surrender of its Last Vessel, by J. Thomas Scharf, (New York, NY, 1887), pp. 402, 403 (diagram), 404-407
Confederate Military History, edited by General Clement A. Evans, (Confederate Publishing Co., Atlanta, GA, 1899), Volume 12, pp. 81-85
Official Records of the Union and Confederate Armies in the War of the Rebellion, (Washington, DC, 1893), Series 1, Volume 42, Part 3, pp. 511, 560
Official Records of the Union and Confederate Navies in the War of the Rebellion, (Washington, DC, 1900), Series 1, Volume 10, pp. 610-623
Official Records of the Union and Confederate Navies in the War of the Rebellion, (Washington, DC, 1900), Series 1, Volume 11, p. 12, 15, 21, 26, 27, 39, 43, 61, 64, 65, 79, 93, 94, 96, 98, 102, 105, 161, 165, 722, 754
Official Records of the Union and Confederate Navies in the War of the Rebellion, (Washington, DC, 1901), Series 1, Volume 12, pp. 9, 15, 16, 22, 75, 143, 166
Official Records of the Union and Confederate Navies in the War of the Rebellion, (Washington, DC, 1921), Series 2, Volume 1, pp. 31, 247
Confederate Military History, edited by General Clement A. Evans, (Confederate Publishing Co., Atlanta, GA, 1899), Volume 12, p. 107
"The Confederate Ram *Albemarle*," by James Dinkins, (published in *Southern Historical Society Papers*, #30, 1902), pp. 205-214
"The *Sassacus* and the *Albemarle*," by Edgar Holden, (published in the *Magazine of History*, #5, May, 1907), pp. 266-274

The "Real Rhett Butler" & Other Revelations

The Navy in the Civil War, (Charles Scribner's Sons, New York, NY, 1905), Volume 2 ("The Atlantic Coast" by Daniel Ammen), pp. 211-214
Graveyard of the Atlantic: Shipwrecks of the North Carolina Coast, by David Stick (University of North Carolina Press, Chapel Hill, NC, 1952), pp. 58, 248
Battles and Leaders of the Civil War, edited by Robert U. Johnson and Clarence C. Buel, Volume 1 of 4 volumes (Century Co., New York, NY, 1884-87, reprinted by Thomas Yoseloff Inc. 1956), p. 629
Iron Afloat: The Story of the Confederate Armorclads, by William N. Still Jr., (Vanderbilt University Press, 1971), pp. 91, 213, 214
Naval History of the Civil War, by Howard P. Nash, (A.S. Barnes & Co., New York, NY, 1972), pp. 226, 227
C.S.S. Neuse: A Question of Iron and Time, by Leslie S. Bright, William H. Rowland, and James C. Bardon, (Raleigh, NC, 1981), Appendix IV, C.S.S. Albemarle, pp. 145, 146

1864-10-US-NC-8: When the blockade running steamer *Lady Sterling*, bound from Wilmington, North Carolina, to Nassau, with 980 bales of cotton and 3 tons of tobacco, was captured on October 28, 1864, off the Bald Head, North Carolina, light-house, "coin was found on board of her amounting to $3,415." Her "papers were left on board, and were under lock and key."

Reference for 1864-10-US-NC-8:
Official Records of the Union and Confederate Navies in the War of the Rebellion, (Washington, DC, 1900), Series 1, Volume 11, p. 7

1864-10-US-NC-9: A report dated November 1, 1864, stated "We continued to advance to within a mile of the works (at Plymouth, North Carolina), when (on October 31) we discovered that the channel was obstructed at a point opposite the batteries by two schooners sunk one on each side of the wreck of the *Southfield*, which together formed a barrier which could only have been passed with great danger, if at all." (Note One: A diagram showing the position of the schooners and the *Southfield* appears in Volume 11 of the "Official Records-Navy.") (Note Two: The *U.S.S. Southfield* had been rammed and sunk in the Roanoke River by the Confederate States ram *Albemarle* at Plymouth, North Carolina on April 19, 1864. For more information on the *Southfield* see entry 1864-4-US-NC-4.)

References for 1864-10-US-NC-9:
Official Records of the Union and Confederate Navies in the War of the Rebellion, (Washington, DC, 1900), Series 1, Volume 11, pp. 12, 13

1864-10-US-NC-10: The iron hulled, twin screw, English blockade runner *Annie* was captured off Cape Fear, North Carolina, on October 31, 1864, while attempting to run the blockade with a cargo of 540 bales of cotton weighing 650 to 700 pounds per bale, 30 tons of pressed tobacco, and 14 casks of spirits of turpentine. (Note One: "Her papers were all captured, showing that $50,000 in gold had been shipped in her; also a lot of Confederate bonds. The gold and bonds were thrown overboard after the *Annie* had stopped, and in view of Acting Master Arey, commanding the *Wilderness*, who endeavored, by firing a rifle, to prevent it. It was in 6 fathoms of water and bearings doubtful." An effort was to be made by

Treasures of the Confederate Coast

Lieutenant Commander Pend. G. Watmough of the United States gunboat *Kansas* "to recover the gold and mail bag". A diagram in Volume 11, of the "Official Records-Navy" shows the path of the *Annie* and the positions of the Federal vessels that participated in her capture. The vessels participating in her capture included the *Howquah, Wilderness, Kansas,* and *Niphon*.) (Note Two: The *Annie* had a large number of men dressed in dark clothing aboard at the time of her capture and it was thought that she had been intended as a privateer. Among her eleven passengers was a Mrs. Johnson and her daughter, of Nassau, New Providence.) (Note Three: $50,000 in gold would have weighed 2,500 troy ounces or just over 208 troy pounds, and if in United States coinage, could potentially have a numismatic value of in excess of $7,000,000.) (Note Four: This was the same vessel which had been chased aground by the *Aster* on the morning of October 8, 1864, but which had gotten off the next day.) (Note Five: The *Annie* had made thirteen successful runs out of fourteen attempts to run the blockade. Both the vessel and her engines were built by J. and W. Dudgeon, London, England, in 1863. She had a single smoke stack, and was schooner rigged. Her dimensions were 170'x23'3"x13'4.5" with a draft of 7' forward and 8' aft. The *Annie* was 428 gross tons and 263 registered tons and was owned by A. Collie and Company. She could average 13.5 knots.) (Note Six: See also entry 1864-10-US-NC-5.)

References for 1864-10-US-NC-10:

History of the Confederate States Navy From its Organization to the Surrender of its Last Vessel, by J. Thomas Scharf, (New York, NY, 1887), p. 465

Official Records of the Union and Confederate Navies in the War of the Rebellion, (Washington, DC, 1900), Series 1, Volume 10, pp. 541-546, 552, 781, 782

Official Records of the Union and Confederate Navies in the War of the Rebellion, (Washington, D.C., 1900), Series 1, Volume 11, pp. 31-38

A Chart of Wrecks of Vessels Sunk or Captured Near Wilmington, NC, Circa 1861-65, compiled by Charles H. Foard, (Wilmington, North Carolina, 1962)

Lifeline of the Confederacy: Blockade Running During the Civil War, by Stephen R. Wise, (University Microfilms International, 1983), p. 531

1864-10-US-SC/GA-1: The blockade runner *Constance*, bound from Halifax, with a valuable assorted cargo, mostly on government account, and quite possibly a large quantity of gold, struck the combined wreckage of the *Georgiana* and the *Mary Bowers* off Long Island (the present day Isle of Palms), South Carolina, on October 6, 1864, and sank in fifteen feet of water six hundred and forty yards south of the other wrecks. [Note One: Some reports show her as the *Constance Decima, Constance Decimo,* or *Constance Decimer* but most simply as the *Constance*. She was an iron hulled, British Clyde River sidewheel steamer, 201'4" in length, 20'2" in breadth and 9'4" in depth of hold, with a draft of

7'6". The *Constance* was 123 registered tons, 254 gross tons, and 345 (or 400 tons) burden. She was schooner rigged (also described as having two masts lightly rigged) no bowsprit, wide between the funnels (two smokestacks placed in line with the keelson) long and low, raking stem, top gallant fore castle extending far back and unusually round or oval, small rounded house far aft, drawing six feet, one hundred and twenty horsepower, built by John Scott and Sons at Glasgow, Scotland, captained by Duncan Stewart. The *Constance* cost £13,500 and was registered as owned by Duncan McGregor, who was an agent for Alexander Collie and Company. The *Constance* was launched at Greenock in 1864, sailed to Bermuda, underwent repairs in Halifax. The vessel was first reported as painted white, then black, then a light lead color, and an even later report stated that her stacks were painted red. She carried a crew of twenty-nine men.] (Note Two: In 1967, as part of my search for the *Georgiana*, I dove on this wreck and was able to positively identify it as the *Constance*. I had been researching these wrecks for years, and would have probably spent even more time finding them if it had not been for the aid and cooperation of commercial fisherman Wally Shaffer, who had hung up his nets on them years before while trawling for shrimp. I later secured the salvage rights to the wreck under the name Artifacts Inc. and salvaged numerous artifacts from it.) (Note Two: For more information on the gold on the *Constance*, please see Appendix E in this book. For more on the *Georgiana*, please see Chapter Three, entry 1863-3-US-SC/GA-2, and Appendix C. For more on the *Mary Bowers*, please see entry 1864-8-US-SC/GA-2 and Appendix F.)

References for 1864-10-US-SC/GA-1:
"Charleston Daily Courier," (Charleston, SC), October 8, 1864, p. 2, c. 3
"Charleston Mercury," (Charleston, SC), Volume 85, #12185, October 7, 1864, p. 2, c. 1
"Daily Morning News," (Savannah, GA), October 8, 1864, p. 2, c. 1
"Vessel Papers" (manuscript records), United States National Archives, Washington, DC, Record Group 109, file C-227
Report of the Secretary of the Navy, Second Session, 38th Congress, 1864-1865, (Washington, DC, 1865), p. 725
Official Records of the Union and Confederate Navies in the War of the Rebellion, (Washington, DC, 1900), Series 1, Volume 10, pp. 386, 406, 468
Official Records of the Union and Confederate Navies in the War of the Rebellion, (Washington, DC, 1903), Series 1, Volume 16, pp. 8, 9, 10, 34, 37
Official Records of the Union and Confederate Navies in the War of the Rebellion, (Washington, DC, 1922), Series 2, Volume 3, p. 1120
Lifeline of the Confederacy: Blockade Running During the Civil War, by Stephen R. Wise, (University of South Carolina, Columbia, SC, 1983), pp. 512 (b), 548
Charleston's Maritime Heritage 1670-1865, by P.C. Coker III, (CokerCraft Press, Charleston, SC, 1987), pp. 214, 304
The Blockade Runners, by Dave Horner, (Florida Classics Library, Port Salerno, FL, 1992), Chapter 14, pp. 114, 115, 225

1864-10-US-SC/GA-2: The fine sidewheel steamer *Flora*, Captain Gilmore, was destroyed on October 22, 1864, by the Federal forces

Treasures of the Confederate Coast

when they opened fire upon the blockade runner, causing her to run aground on Drunken Dick Shoals on the south side of Maffitt's (or Beach) Channel opposite Battery Rutledge on Sullivan's Island, South Carolina. [Note One: The *Flora* had sailed from Nassau on October 18, bound for Charleston, and soon after "was compelled to put into Elbow Key." On October 20 (shortly after she had left Elbow Key) she "was discovered and chased all day by a Yankee propeller, during which the *Flora* had to throw overboard what cargo she had, and only eluded her pursuer by dodging her at night. On Saturday night (October 22) off Dewees Island, fell in with several blockaders and at one time was cut off but managed to escape, and, off Beach Channel, fell in with Yankee picket boats, which threw up rockets, and it was while working clear of these obstacles at the mouth of the harbor that the steamer got ashore on the lump on the south side of Beach Channel. The crew got ashore in boats."] (Note Two: The wreck was said to have been 2700 yards from Fort Putnam, 2600 yards from Battery Chatfield, and 3500 yards from Fort Strong, all of which were located on Morris Island, South Carolina. The steamer was also fired upon by the United States monitors *Catskill* and *Patapsco*. Of the one hundred and forty-four shells fired at the *Flora*, ninety-eight actually hit her. The remains of a wreck at the described location were located and tentatively identified as the *Flora* by me and Jim Batey in 1967.) [Note Three: The *Flora* (ex-*Anna*) was described as a fine, large, shallow draft, steamer of 437 (or 700) tons. The vessel had an iron hull and was over two hundred feet in length, painted lead gray, and had two stacks. She was registered in the name of Henry Lafone of the Importing and Exporting Company of Georgia (sometimes referred to as the Lamar Company), but it was reported that she had "lately" been purchased by the State of Georgia.] (Note Four: This was probably the vessel listed in the London *Times* of November 23, 1864, as "ashore outside of Charleston." Her name was written as *Florie* in that report, so it is easy to confuse this wreck with the September 10, 1864, wreck of the *Florie* in North Carolina. See also entry 1864-9-US-NC-2 in this book.)

References for 1864-10-US-SC/GA-2:
Log of the U.S. monitor *Catskill*, October 22, 1864, National Archives, Record Group 24
Log of the U.S. ship *John Adams*, October 23, 1864, National Archives, Record Group 24
"Charleston Mercury," (Charleston, SC), Volume 85, #12199, October 24, 1864, p. 2, c. 1
"Charleston Mercury," (Charleston, SC), Volume 85, #12200, October 25, 1864, p. 2, c. 1
"Charleston Mercury," (Charleston, SC), Volume 85, #12201, October 26, 1864, p. 2, c. 1
"Charleston Mercury," (Charleston, SC), Volume 85, #12202, October 27, 1864, p. 2, c. 1
"Daily Morning News," (Savannah, GA), October 26, 1864, p. 1, c. 1
Times, (London, England), #25037, November 23, 1864, p. 7, c. 5
"Vessel Papers" (manuscript records), United States National Archives, Washington, DC, Record Group 109, file F-15
"General Map of Charleston Harbor, South Carolina, Showing Rebel Defenses and Obstructions," drawn by E. Willenbucher, (U.S. Coast Survey, 1865)

The "Real Rhett Butler" & Other Revelations

Official Records of the Union and Confederate Navies in the War of the Rebellion, (Washington, DC, 1900), Series 1, Volume 10, pp. 223, 601
Official Records of the Union and Confederate Navies in the War of the Rebellion, (Washington, DC, 1903), Series 1, Volume 16, pp. 29-32, 34, 37, 357
Lifeline of the Confederacy: Blockade Running During the Civil War, by Stephen R. Wise, (University of South Carolina, Columbia, SC, 1983), pp. 512, 563
Charleston's Maritime Heritage 1670-1865, by P.C. Coker III, (CokerCraft Press, Charleston, SC, 1987), p. 304
The Blockade Runners, by Dave Horner, (Florida Classics Library, Port Salerno, FL, 1992), Chapter 14, pp. 226-227

1864-10-US-SC/GA-3: The *Flamingo*, well known for her many successful trips through the blockade, was wrecked between Bowman's Jetty and Drunken Dick Shoals off Sullivan's Island, South Carolina, on October 23, 1864. (Note One: The *Flamingo* was described as a beautiful, black, sidewheel paddle steamer, with three forward stacks painted white, a covered fore deck and stern, and two masts lightly rigged. The *Flamingo* sailed under both British and Confederate colors. She was capable of making fifteen knots, and the trip from Bermuda to Charleston took her less than two days. The *Flamingo* was 283 registered tons, 270' in length, 24' in breadth, and 7' in draft. She was built by Randolph, Elder and Company at Fairfield, England, in 1864, and could carry one thousand bales of cotton at a time. She was owned by the Confederate government.) (Note Two: The *Flamingo* had a crew of forty-five men, which would have required a payroll and expense account of well over $80,000 per voyage. That much in gold would have weighed approximately 4,000 troy ounces and, if in United States coinage, could now have a numismatic value in excess of $12,000,000.) (Note Three: Stephen Wise in his book *Lifeline of the Confederacy* states that the *Flamingo* was owned by Alexander Collie and Company and that she survived the war.) (Note Four: About 1967, I discovered the remains of a wreck in the described location and tentatively identified it as the *Flamingo*. I was assisted by Ron A. Gibbs of the United States National Park Service, and Jim Batey of Palmetto Divers.)

References for 1864-10-US-SC/GA-3:
Log of the U.S. monitor *Catskill*, October 23, 1864, National Archives, Record Group 24
Log of the U.S. ship *John Adams*, October 23 & 24, 1864, National Archives, Record Group 24
"Vessel Papers" (manuscript records), United States National Archives, Washington, DC, Record Group 109, file F-65
"General Map of Charleston Harbor, South Carolina, Showing Rebel Defenses and Obstructions," drawn by E. Willenbucher, (U.S. Coast Survey, 1865)
Official Records of the Union and Confederate Navies in the War of the Rebellion, (Washington, DC, 1900), Series 1, Volume 10, pp. 427, 476
Lifeline of the Confederacy: Blockade Running During the Civil War, by Stephen R. Wise, (University of South Carolina, Columbia, SC, 1983), p. 562
Warships of the Civil War Navies, by Paul H. Silverstone, (Naval Institute Press, Annapolis, MD, 1989), p. 222

1864-11-US-NC-1: On November 20, 1864, Colonel Hedrick, C.S.A., telegraphed Captain Hardeman, at Smithville, to say "there is a large Yankee steamer on fire and standing in to the shore in the direction of Lockwood's Folly (North Carolina)."

Reference for 1864-11-US-NC-1:
Official Records of the Union and Confederate Navies in the War of the Rebellion, (Washington, D.C., 1900), Series 1, Volume 11, p. 768

1864-11-US-NC-2: On November 22, 1864, Colonel Lamb, C.S.A., visited General Whiting "on board steamer *Cape Fear*, ashore on Drum Shoal." (Note: The vessel definitely got off as on December 17, 1864, Colonel Lamb reported that he "came down the river with General Whiting in the *Cape Fear*.")

References for 1864-11-US-NC-2:
Official Records of the Union and Confederate Navies in the War of the Rebellion, (Washington, D.C., 1900), Series 1, Volume 11, pp. 744, 746

1864-11-US-SC/GA-1: A small sloop with cotton and turpentine was accidentally run ashore on the beach in front of Fort Moultrie, Sullivan's Island, South Carolina, on November 5, 1864. The sloop was shelled and set afire by the United States monitor *Patapsco* which hit her twice out of 13 shots with her 12-pounder Dahlgren and once out of 10 shots with her 150-pounder.

References for 1864-11-US-SC/GA-1:
Official Records of the Union and Confederate Navies in the War of the Rebellion, (Washington, DC, 1903), Series 1, Volume 16, p. 42
The Navy in the Civil War, (Charles Scribner's Sons, New York, NY, 1905), Volume 2 ("The Atlantic Coast" by Daniel Ammen), p. 151

1864-11-US-SC/GA-2: The schooner *Mary* was captured and burned by the Federals, off Morris Island, South Carolina, on November 5, 1864. The Confederates managed to save about thirty-five bales of cotton. Another one hundred bales of cotton and thirty-five boxes of tobacco were lost.

Reference for 1864-11-US-SC/GA-2:
"Charleston Mercury," (Charleston, SC), Volume 85, #12211, November 7, 1864, p. 2, c. 1

1864-11-US-SC/GA-3: The sidewheel steamer *Beatrice*, Captain J.E. Randle, from Nassau, was run ashore near the wreck of the *Flamingo* east of Bowman's Jetty on Sullivan's Island, South Carolina, while attempting to run past the blockade into Charleston on November 27, 1864. The steamer was heavily shelled by the blockade fleet and had almost made it to safety when she struck bottom in about six feet of water. [Note One: A contemporary news account stated: "While feeling her way into port, it seems the *Beatrice* was surrounded and fired into by the Yankee barges, which kept up a constant fire of grape and musketry upon the grounded vessel, preventing her officers and men from getting her afloat." The captain and eight of his men escaped but the remainder of the crew (some thirty in number) were captured. Her purser was among those who escaped. She was owned by English parties and was consigned

The "Real Rhett Butler" & Other Revelations

to Beach and Root. Many of her crew were Charlestonians. She had made two previous successful runs through the blockade. The blockade runner carried a crew of thirty men. The *Beatrice* carried an assorted cargo which included twenty 120-pounder Whitworth shells.] (Note Two: The *Beatrice* had an iron hull and was built by McNab at Greenock, Scotland, in 1863. She measured 167'6"x24'1"x12' and was 342 gross tons and 274 register tons. She drew 6'2" forward and 6'8" aft. She averaged 12 knots and could make a maximum of 14 knots.) (Note Three: In 1967, Jim Batey and I found the remains of a wreck in the described location. We tentatively identified the wreck as the *Beatrice*.) (Note Four: Stephen Wise in his book *Lifeline of the Confederacy* shows the *Beatrice* as a screw steamer and indicates that her registered owner may have been Edward J. Somnitz. She is also listed as a screw steamer in "Lloyd's Register" for 1864/65. "Lloyd's Register" also shows her as having four bulkheads.)

References for 1864-11-US-SC/GA-3:
"Charleston Mercury," (Charleston, SC), Volume 85, #12229, November 29, 1864, p. 2, c. 1
"Vessel Papers" (manuscript records), United States National Archives, Washington, DC, Record Group 109, files B-41a, O-1
Lloyd's Register of British and Foreign Shipping, from 1st July, 1864, to the 30th June, 1865, (London, 1864), entry B-86
"General Map of Charleston Harbor, South Carolina, Showing Rebel Defenses and Obstructions," drawn by E. Willenbucher, (U.S. Coast Survey, 1865)
Official Records of the Union and Confederate Navies in the War of the Rebellion, (Washington, DC, 1903), Volume 16, pp. 112-114, 354
Shipwrecks of the Civil War: The Encyclopedia of Union and Confederate Naval Losses, by Donald Shomette, (Washington, DC, 1973), pp. 406, 407
Lifeline of the Confederacy: Blockade Running During the Civil War, by Stephen R. Wise, (University of South Carolina, Columbia, SC, 1983), pp. 512, 537
Charleston's Maritime Heritage 1670-1865, by P.C. Coker III, (CokerCraft Press, Charleston, SC, 1987), p. 304

1864-11-US-x-1: In a letter to Rear-Admiral David D. Porter, dated November 18, 1864, United States Secretary of the Navy Gideon Welles wrote: "From reports of captures, it is inferred that in some instances articles are thrown overboard after the prize has yielded or surrendered. After a vessel has surrendered or has ceased to resist, either by abandoning further effort to escape or discontinuing hostile action, it is inadmissible for those in her to throw overboard papers, cargo, or other articles of importance or value, or to injure the vessel in any manner. By doing so they subject themselves to the danger of being fired into, and the captor is justifiable in resorting to such measures, should he perceive unmistakable indications that such a course is being pursued by those on board the captured vessel." (Note: For an example of gold and papers being thrown overboard from a blockade runner, please see entry 1864-10-US-NC-10.)

Reference for 1864-11-US-x-1:
Official Records of the Union and Confederate Navies in the War of the Rebellion, (Washington, DC, 1900), Series 1, Volume 11, p. 75

The sole survivor of the December 9, 1864, sinking of the Robert B. Howlet awaits rescue off Charleston, South Carolina. Illustration taken from "Harper's Weekly" of January 21, 1865.

The "Real Rhett Butler" & Other Revelations

Crew escaping off a blockade runner wrecked on Sullivan's Island, South Carolina.
Illustration from "Frank Leslie's Illustrated Newspaper," June 20, 1863.

This Confederate torpedo boat is probably buried under present day Tradd Street in Charleston, South Carolina. The mansion in the background still stands and it would be easy to pinpoint this wreck's location. 1865 photo by Matthew Brady.

The "Real Rhett Butler" & Other Revelations

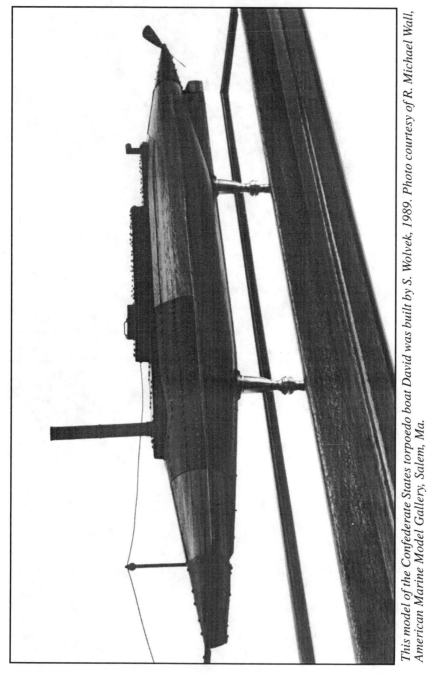

This model of the Confederate States torpoedo boat David was built by S. Wolvek, 1989. Photo courtesy of R. Michael Wall, American Marine Model Gallery, Salem, Ma.

Treasures of the Confederate Coast

Logos of some of the sponsors of the Constance expedition were displayed on the smokestack of the Research Vessel Fathom V. Photo by Jo Pinkard. (Note: The following corporations have financed or otherwise assisted me on my various underwater archeological projects: Allis Chalmers; Barringer Research; Bendix; Fisher Research; Gulf Oil; Ingersoll Rand; J.W. Fisher; Klein Associates; McKee Craft; Mercury Motors; Orca Industries; Rolex Watch Co.; Seagram's Classic Wines; Trimble Navigation; White's Electronics; and Zodiac.)

The "Real Rhett Butler" & Other Revelations

This decorative map was prepared by E. Lee Spence to show the general locations of the many Civil War shipwrecks in the vicinity of Charleston, South Carolina. The ship symbols show the approximate location and represent the different rigs of the wrecked vessels.

These large aluminum nozzles are propwash delection units (aka: PDU's). They are mounted on hinges and are kept in the upright position when the vessel is at dock or underway. Upon anchoring over the wreck site with a three or four point mooring, the PDU's are swung down (as shown), and locked in place so they can be used to divert the vessel's propwash downward and thus use the force of the wash for pumping the clearer surface waters down to the diver. The force of the flow can be adjusted for blowing off a thin layer of sand from the wreck, or for rapid removal of deep overburden. The PDU on the left makes a true 90° angle and is used for deep digging, while the one on the right is offset to help it blow sand off and away from the wreck. Photo by L. Spence.

This rectangular shaped PDU is shown in the upright position. It has a safety cage that encloses the propeller. Some people refer to PDU's as "mail boxes" due to their shape. Photo by L. Spence.

The "Real Rhett Butler" & Other Revelations

Lee Spence with a 6" water induction dredge which was loaned to him by Mel Fisher in 1969 for use on the Georgiana, etc. Note: This dredge was powered via a firehose fed by a pump on the surface. Water ran through the hose into a venturi pointed towards the discharge and mounted just above the intake. The intake has a circular guard to prevent artifacts and shells from getting clogged in the mouth of the dredge. The discharge was exhausted on the bottom and was not carried back up to the surface. The "garden" hose coming out of the handle is used for jetting. Photo by Gene West, courtesy of Shipwreck Archaeology Inc.

Treasures of the Confederate Coast

1864-11x-US-SC/GA-1: A letter from Rear-Admiral Dahlgren to Commander Egbert Thompson, dated November 5, 1864, mentions the apparently recent loss of a United States coal vessel at North Edisto, South Carolina. The loss was put at $30,000 (which would have been $600,000 in today's money).

Reference for 1864-11x-US-SC/GA-1:
Official Records of the Union and Confederate Navies in the War of the Rebellion, (Washington, DC, 1903), Series 1, Volume 16, p. 43

1864-12-US-NC-1: The sidewheel steamer *Ella* was driven ashore on Bald Head Beach, North Carolina, on December 3, 1864. Vessels participating in the chase or in her subsequent destruction on December 5, 1864, were the United States gunboats *Pequot*, *Emma*, *Maratanza*, *Britannia* and *Huron*. She was fired into, burned and blown up. Her complete destruction was accomplished by setting her on fire after placing 24-pound howitzer shells next to the engines to destroy the ship's machinery. (Note One: The *Ella* was bound from Nassau and carried gin, military goods, arms and ammunition. Part of her cargo consisted of a large quantity of 5 1/2 inch rifle shells in boxes.) [Note Two: The *Ella* had an iron hull with two stacks, iron masts and iron paddle wheel boxes. She was estimated to be 1000 tons burden but other reports gave her gross tonnage as 634, her register tonnage as 404, and her displacement as 1165 tons. She was 225' in length, 28' in breadth, 13' in depth of hold, and drew 9' of water. She was a "splendid vessel" built by William Denny and Brothers at Dumbarton, Scotland, in 1864. She was engined by Robert Napier and Sons, Lanceford Foundry, at Glasgow, Scotland. She was owned by the Importing and Exporting Company of South Carolina (a.k.a. the "Bee Company").] (Note Three: The *Ella's* position was variously given in contemporary reports as: on the south end of Marshal Shoal, Smith's Island, North Carolina, twelve hundred yards from the shore batteries; 1 1/2 miles south by west of Bald Head Point, North Carolina; and as on the south east end of Reeper Shoal, North Carolina. One author states that the steamer was chased ashore "while trying to enter Old Inlet," while another simply states she was lost at "Cape Fear." A Sea Grant publication put out by the University of North Carolina states that the wreck is in six feet of water and 1.3 miles from shore.) (Note Four: This wreck was partially salvaged by Charles V. Peery, MD, who is now living in Charleston, South Carolina. Artifacts recovered from the *Ella* may be seen at the Southport Maritime Museum, Southport, North Carolina, and at the Fort Fisher Visitor's Center/Museum, Kure Beach, North Carolina.)

The "Real Rhett Butler" & Other Revelations

References for 1864-12-US-NC-1:
"Charleston Mercury," (Charleston, SC), Volume 85, #12236, December 7, 1864, p. 2, c. 1
Times, (London, England), #25066, December 26, 1864, p. 7, c. 2
Official Records of the Union and Confederate Navies in the War of the Rebellion, (Washington, DC, 1900), Series 1, Volume 11, pp. 126-134, 151, 416
Graveyard of the Atlantic: Shipwrecks of the North Carolina Coast, by David Stick (University of North Carolina Press, Chapel Hill, NC, 1952), pp. 64, 248
A Chart of Wrecks of Vessels Sunk or Captured Near Wilmington, NC, Circa 1861-65, compiled by Charles H. Foard, (Wilmington, North Carolina, 1962)
An Oceanographic Atlas of the Continental Margin, J.G. Newton, O.H. Pilkey and J.O. Blanton, (Duke University Marine Laboratory, Beaufort, NC, 1971), p. 17 chart symbol #55, p. 20 entry #55
George Alfred Trenholm and the Company that Went to War 1861-1865, by Ethel Trenholm Seabrook Nepveux, (Charleston, South Carolina, 1973), pp. 42, 60
Wreck Diving in North Carolina, University of North Carolina, Sea Grant Publication, #78-13, p. 5
Lifeline of the Confederacy: Blockade Running During the Civil War, by Stephen R. Wise, (University Microfilms International, 1983), pp. 471, 472, 512, 556

1864-12-US-NC-2: When the blockade running steamer *Armstrong*, 630 tons, with 743 bales of cotton, was captured on December 4, 1864, by the United States gunboats *R.R. Cuyler* and *Gettysburg*, she had on freight about $25,000 in "Confederate scrip" or cotton bonds. Her captors also took "from the person of the master and purser $4,400 in American gold." (Note: This entry has been included to give an idea of what might be listed on a manifest. Because it was freight, the $25,000 in "Confederate scrip" should have appeared on a correctly drawn manifest. However, manifests for ships engaged in running the blockade were notorious for being incomplete or inaccurate. Rifles and cannons were frequently listed on manifests as "merchandise" or "hardware." In this particular case, the gold coins, not being freight, but rather ship's expense money, or private money, definitely would not have been listed. Additional gold and silver coins may have been in the possession or baggage of passengers, or may have been hidden in secret compartments or under cargo. Such money would not appear on a manifest.)

References for 1864-12-US-NC-2:
Official Records of the Union and Confederate Navies in the War of the Rebellion, (Washington, DC, 1900), Series 1, Volume 11, pp. 138, 139

1864-12-US-NC-3: Charles Foard's chart of Civil War shipwrecks in the Wilmington, North Carolina, area shows a wreck approximately 1.5 miles south of the tip of Cape Fear. Foard identifies the wreck as the *Phantom II* and shows it as having been lost on December 5, 1864. (Note: See also entry 1863-9-US-NC-2.)

Reference for 1864-12-US-NC-3:
A Chart of Wrecks of Vessels Sunk or Captured Near Wilmington, NC, Circa 1861-65, compiled by Charles H. Foard, (Wilmington, North Carolina, 1962)

1864-12-US-NC-4: A vessel identified as the *Pathfinder* is shown on Charles Foard's chart of Civil War shipwrecks in the Wilmington, North Carolina, as lost at New River Inlet on December 5, 1864. [Note: Checking the *Official Records for the Union and Confederate Navies in the War of the Rebellion* in an effort to locate an account

Treasures of the Confederate Coast

of a wreck by that name at that date produced no results. However, there was an English schooner called the *Pathfinder* that was run ashore, set on fire and destroyed, two miles to the westward of Little River Inlet, North Carolina, (which would have placed her off South Carolina) on November 2, 1862. That schooner was loaded with salt, boots, shoes, olive oil, liquors, cutlery, etc. For more on the loss of that vessel, please see entry 1862-11-US-SC/GA-1.]

References for 1864-12-US-NC-4:
Official Records of the Union and Confederate Navies in the War of the Rebellion, (Washington, DC, 1899), Series 1, Volume 8, pp. 175, 190
A Chart of Wrecks of Vessels Sunk or Captured Near Wilmington, NC, Circa 1861-65, compiled by Charles H. Foard, (Wilmington, North Carolina, 1962)

1864-12-US-NC-5: The blockade running steamer *Stormy Petrel* (or *Petrel*), Captain Donaly, was driven ashore by the United States gunboats at New Inlet, Cape Fear River, North. Carolina, on December 7, 1864. Her position was also described as "well out on the south breakers" near Fort Fisher. Once ashore the *Stormy Petrel* was fired upon and sunk. She was finally totally destroyed by a northeast gale. The steamer carried a large cargo of arms and munitions of war, all of which were lost, although the Confederates did succeed in getting two full boats loads of cloth from the wreck. (Note One: The *Stormy Petrel* was 225' in length, 25' in breadth, 11'6" in depth of hold, and 220 tons register. She was a sidewheel steamer and apparently was lost on her first attempt to run the blockade. She was built by William Simons and Company at Renfrew, Scotland, in 1864. The steamer was owned by John Lawrence and the Anglo-Confederate Trading Company. Her pilot's name was given as Sellers and her operator's name as Langham.) (Note Two: At least one report attributed the *Stormy Petrel's* loss to her having "struck a sunken vessel.")

References for 1864-12-US-NC-5:
Times, (London, England), #25073, January 4, 1865, p. 9, c. 2, p. 11, c. 4
Times, (London, England), #25076, January 7, 1865, p. 7, c. 2
Official Records of the Union and Confederate Navies in the War of the Rebellion, (Washington, DC, 1900), Series 1, Volume 11, pp. 195, 745
A Chart of Wrecks of Vessels Sunk or Captured Near Wilmington, NC, Circa 1861-65, compiled by Charles H. Foard, (Wilmington, North Carolina, 1962)
An Oceanographic Atlas of the Continental Margin, J.G. Newton, O.H. Pilkey and J.O. Blanton, (Duke University Marine Laboratory, Beaufort, NC, 1971), p. 17 chart symbol #77, p. 20 entry #77
Lifeline of the Confederacy: Blockade Running During the Civil War, by Stephen R. Wise, (University Microfilms International, 1983), pp. 467, 512, 617
The Blockade Runners, by Dave Horner, (Florida Classics Library, Port Salerno, FL, 1992), Chapter 14, p. 227

1864-12-US-NC-6: The United States gunboat *Otsego*, Lieutenant Commander Arnold, ten guns, 3rd rate, 974 tons, was destroyed by Confederate torpedoes (mines) on December 9, 1864. (Note One: She had just stopped her engines and was about to let go her anchor when a torpedo exploded under her on the port side, and shortly afterwards another exploded under her forward pivot gun, which was thrown over the deck by the concussion, the two explosions injuring her so badly that she sank in a few minutes, her spar deck being about three feet under water. The wreck took place at a sharp bend in the Roanoke River, six miles above Plymouth and just below Jamesville, North Carolina. Fortunately, no one was killed on board the *Otsego*, and with the exception of a few slight scratches no one was injured. The *Otsego* had spars rigged out ahead of her to which was fastened a net for the purpose of catching the torpedoes, and two were found in the net after she sank. She was thought to have stopped directly on top of a line of the "infernal machines." Six torpedoes were picked up after the explosion.) (Note Two: The U.S. tug *Bazely* was sunk right alongside the *Otsego* when a torpedo exploded under her as she tried to pass by.) (Note Three: The *Otsego's* guns and every article of value that could be reached was immediately salvaged and the remainder of the wreck destroyed by firing into her and by the purposeful detonation of two torpedoes in her engine room.) (Note Four: The *Otsego* was a "*Sassacus* Class," double ended, sidewheel steamer built at New York under a contract with the U.S. Navy at a cost of $157,000. The cost of her repairs while in the naval service was $4,929.91. Her hull was built by J.A. & D.D. Westervelt and her machinery was made by the Fulton Works. The *Otsego* had a single inclined, direct acting engine with a surface condenser. The diameter of the cylinder was 58" with an 8'9" piston stroke. She had two vertical tubular boilers. She was 974 tons and drew 9' loaded and 7'4" light. She could make a maximum of fourteen knots, was rigged as a schooner and classed as a 3rd rate. She was armed with two 100-pounder Parrott rifles, two 20-pounder Parrott rifles, four 11-inch smooth bore Dahlgrens, and two 24-pounders.) (Note Five: See also entries 1864-12-US-NC-7 and 1864-12-US-NC-8.)

References for 1864-12-US-NC-6:
"Charleston Mercury," (Charleston, SC), Volume 85, #12247, December 10, 1864, p. 2, c. 1
New York Times, (New York, NY), Volume 14, #4129, December 17, 1864, p. 1, c. 4
History of the Confederate States Navy From its Organization to the Surrender of its Last Vessel, by J. Thomas Scharf, (New York, NY, 1887), p. 768
Official Records of the Union and Confederate Armies in the War of the Rebellion, (Washington, DC, 1893), Series 1, Volume 42, Part 3, p. 1014
Official Records of the Union and Confederate Navies in the War of the Rebellion, (Washington, DC, 1900), Series 1, Volume 11, pp. 40, 160-165, 168-177, 180, 181, 193
Official Records of the Union and Confederate Navies in the War of the Rebellion, (Washington, DC, 1901), Series 1, Volume 12, p. 107
Official Records of the Union and Confederate Navies in the War of the Rebellion, (Washington, DC, 1921), Series 2, Volume 1, pp. 43, 45, 168
The Navy in the Civil War, (Charles Scribner's Sons, New York, NY, 1903), Volume 1 ("The Blockade and the Cruisers" by James Russell Soley), p. 247
The Navy in the Civil War, (Charles Scribner's Sons, New York, NY, 1905), Volume 2 ("The Atlantic Coast" by Daniel Ammen), p. 214

1864-12-US-NC-7: The United States tug *Bazely* (ex-picket boat #2, ex-*Beta*, aka-*J.E. Bazely*, or *Bazley*), Acting Ensign Curtis, was

Treasures of the Confederate Coast

destroyed by a Confederate torpedo (mine) in the Roanoke River on December 10, 1864, as it tried to pass by the wreck of the *Otsego* at a sharp bend in the Roanoke River just below Jamesville, North Carolina. Two of her men were killed in the explosion. (Note One: Thomas Scharf in his *History of the Confederate States Navy* calls the *Bazely* a "gunboat." The *New York Times* of December 17, 1864, shows her as the "*Basly, No. 5.*") (Note Two: The *Bazely* was a screw steamer purchased at Philadelphia on June 4, 1864, by Commodore C.K. Stribling from William Mallory for $15,500. She was classed as a picket boat and was rated as a tug. She was 50 tons, 70' in length, 16' in breadth, 6'6" in depth, and drew 7' loaded and 6' light. The *Bazely* was engined with one vertical high pressure engine with an 18" diameter cylinder with an 18" piston stroke.) (Note Three: See also entries 1864-12-US-NC-6 and 1864-12-US-NC-8.)

References for 1864-12-US-NC-7:
New York Times, (New York, NY), Volume 14, #4129, December 17, 1864, p. 1, c. 4
History of the Confederate States Navy From its Organization to the Surrender of its Last Vessel, by J. Thomas Scharf, (New York, NY, 1887), p. 768
Official Records of the Union and Confederate Navies in the War of the Rebellion, (Washington, DC, 1900), Series 1, Volume 11, pp. 39, 140, 141, 160, 161, 172, 177, 181
Official Records of the Union and Confederate Navies in the War of the Rebellion, (Washington, DC, 1921), Series 2, Volume 1, p. 43
The Navy in the Civil War, (Charles Scribner's Sons, New York, NY, 1905), Volume 2 ("The Atlantic Coast" by Daniel Ammen), p. 214

1864-12-US-NC-8: Thomas Scharf in his *History of the Confederate States Navy* wrote that the United States gunboat *No. 5*, was destroyed by a Confederate torpedo (mine) in the Roanoke River on December 10, 1864. (Note: Gunboat *No. 5* was a steam launch armed with one gun that was assigned to the sounds of North Carolina, but the report of her destruction was probably in error as she appears in a list of vessels in service on February 1, 1865. There was also a picket boat *#5*, a.k.a. *Epsilon*, but that vessel appears in the same list.) (Note Two: See also entries 1864-12-US-NC-6 and 1864-12-US-NC-7.)

References for 1864-12-US-NC-8:
Official Records of the Union and Confederate Navies in the War of the Rebellion, (Washington, DC, 1900), Series 1, Volume 11, pp. 598, 723
History of the Confederate States Navy From its Organization to the Surrender of its Last Vessel, by J. Thomas Scharf, (New York, NY, 1887), p. 768

1864-12-US-NC-9: Charles Foard's chart of Civil War shipwrecks of the Wilmington, North Carolina, area shows a steamer, identified only as having been lost December 10, 1864, as wrecked below Fort Fisher and east south east of the Mound. (Note: The "Mound" was an artificial one erected by Colonel Lamb, C.S.A., who commanded Fort Fisher. It had a conical shape and a light on it that served as a range for both blockaders and blockade runners alike.)

Reference for 1864-12-US-NC-9:

The "Real Rhett Butler" & Other Revelations

A Chart of Wrecks of Vessels Sunk or Captured Near Wilmington, NC, Circa 1861-65, compiled by Charles H. Foard, (Wilmington, North Carolina, 1962)

1864-12-US-NC-10: The disabled steamer *North Heath* was ordered stripped and sunk as an obstruction at the entrance of New Inlet Rip near Wilmington, North Carolina, on December 21, 1864. She was to be sunk with her stern and stem nearly with the flow of the tide. (Note One: The *North Heath* had made five trips through the blockade before she was declared unfit for that purpose after being very badly damaged on entering Wilmington in October of 1864. She was a sidewheeler of 343 tons register and was owned by Thomas Sterling Bigbie and the Universal Trading Company.) (Note Two: The actual sinking did not take place until January 15, 1865. Her location was also given as "in the Cape Fear River off Fort Strong.")

References for 1864-12-US-NC-10:
Times, (London, England), #25040, November 26, 1864, p. 9, c. 6
Official Records of the Union and Confederate Navies in the War of the Rebellion, (Washington, DC, 1900), Series 1, Volume 11, pp. 44, 785, 786
Graveyard of the Atlantic: Shipwrecks of the North Carolina Coast, by David Stick (University of North Carolina Press, Chapel Hill, NC, 1952), p. 248
A Chart of Wrecks of Vessels Sunk or Captured Near Wilmington, NC, Circa 1861-65, compiled by Charles H. Foard, (Wilmington, North Carolina, 1962)
An Oceanographic Atlas of the Continental Margin, J.G. Newton, O.H. Pilkey and J.O. Blanton, (Duke University Marine Laboratory, Beaufort, NC, 1971), p. 17 chart symbol #52, p. 20 entry #52
Lifeline of the Confederacy: Blockade Running During the Civil War, by Stephen R. Wise, (University Microfilms International, 1983), pp. 468, 513, 600

1864-12-US-NC-11: The United States gunboat *Louisiana* was disguised as a blockade runner, loaded with 235 tons of gun powder and was towed to within three hundred yards from the beach opposite Fort Fisher, North Carolina, on December 24, 1864, and, using clockwork time fuses, and a fire as a back up, was blown up in a futile effort to destroy the fort by explosion. One observer described it as follows "a few minutes after the explosion a cloud of dense black smoke rose up rapidly on the horizon, and stood out in sharp well defined outlines against the clear starlight sky. The cloud was of huge proportions, and as it rose rapidly in the air, and came swiftly towards us on the wings of the wind, presented a most remarkable appearance, assuming the shape of a monstrous waterspout, its tapering base seemingly resting on the sea. In a few minutes it passed us, filling the atmosphere with its suphurous odour, as if a spirit from the infernal regions had swept by us." [Note One: The screw steamer had an iron hull, with three masts, and was 295 tons burden. She was also described as 750 gross tons and as 205 tons burden. She was 143'2" (145.2) (150) feet long, 27'3" (27.32) (22) feet beam, and 8'1" (8.1) feet depth of hold. She had a draft of 8 to 8.5 feet of water when fully loaded. The

Treasures of the Confederate Coast

Louisiana had been built by Harlan and Hollingsworth at Wilmington, Delaware, in 1860 and had been purchased at Philadelphia, Pennsylvania, by Rear-Admiral Du Pont for the U.S. Navy on July 10, 1861, for $35,000. The total cost of her repairs while she was in the naval service was $20,374.92. On January 19, 1862, her armament was reported as one 8-inch Dahlgren smooth bore, one 32-pounder of 57 hundred weight; one 32-pounder of 33 hundred weight; and one 12-pounder Dahlgren rifle. She had a condensing, direct acting engine with a 32" diameter cylinder with a 28" piston stroke. She had one flue boiler in her hold,] (Note Two: Her guns, appurtenances, masts and part of the deck house had been removed and her deck and holds cleared of fittings in preparation for her use as a "powder vessel.") (Note Three: The "Lytle Holdcamper List" listed the *Louisiana* as a sidewheel steamer.)

References for 1864-12-US-NC-11:

Times, (London, England), # 25077, January 9, 1865, p. 10, c. 3
Times, (London, England), # 25079, January 11, 1865, p. 9, c. 2
Times, (London, England), # 25082, January 14, 1865, p. 7, c. 6
History of the Confederate States Navy From its Organization to the Surrender of its Last Vessel, by J. Thomas Scharf, (New York, NY, 1887), pp.
Official Records of the Union and Confederate Armies in the War of the Rebellion, (Washington, DC, 1893), Series 1, Volume 42, Part 1, pp. 988-993
Official Records of the Union and Confederate Navies in the War of the Rebellion, (Washington, DC, 1900), Series 1, Volume 11, pp. 78, 79, 207-245, 737
Official Records of the Union and Confederate Navies in the War of the Rebellion, (Washington, DC, 1921), Series 2, Volume 1, p. 129
Official Records of the Union and Confederate Armies in the War of the Rebellion, Atlas, (Thomas Yoseloff Inc., NY, 1958), plate LXVII, illustration #5
The Navy in the Civil War, (Charles Scribner's Sons, New York, NY, 1905), Volume 2 ("The Atlantic Coast" by Daniel Ammen), pp. 218, 221
Graveyard of the Atlantic: Shipwrecks of the North Carolina Coast, by David Stick (University of North Carolina Press, Chapel Hill, NC, 1952), pp. 59, 60, 248
An Oceanographic Atlas of the Continental Margin, J.G. Newton, O.H. Pilkey and J.O. Blanton, (Duke University Marine Laboratory, Beaufort, NC, 1971), p. 17 chart symbol #79, p. 20 entry #79
Naval History of the Civil War, by Howard P. Nash, (A.S. Barnes & Co., New York, NY, 1972), pp. 260-262
Merchant Steam Vessels of the United States 1790-1868, "The Lytle-Holdcamper List," by William M. Lytle and Forrest R. Holdcamper, revised and edited by C. Bradford Mitchell, (Staten Island, New York, 1975), p. 131
Lifeline of the Confederacy: Blockade Running During the Civil War, by Stephen R. Wise, (University Microfilms International, 1983), pp. 479-482, 655

1864-12-US-NC-12: The Confederate States ironclad floating battery *Arctic*, Lieutenant C.B. Poindexter, was sunk as an obstruction at the Rip at New Inlet, North Carolina, on December 24, 1864. (Note One: The *Arctic* had been built at Wilmington, North Carolina, in 1862, and had served as a receiving ship for Flag Officer Robert F. Pinckney's North Carolina defense force. The ironclad's machinery had been removed in late 1862 for use in the *C.S.S. Richmond* which was then being completed at Richmond.) (Note Two: Some records show her as burned by the Confederates at the fall of Wilmington in 1865, others simply as sunk in the Cape Fear River.) (Note Three: This may have been the ironclad ram mentioned in Lieutenant-Commander William G. Temple's dispatch of January 2,

The "Real Rhett Butler" & Other Revelations

1865, to Rear-Admiral David D. Porter, in which Temple states "the ironclad ram, formerly in the river, got aground and burst open and was dismantled of her engines and her armor".)

References for 1864-12-US-NC-12:
Official Records of the Union and Confederate Navies in the War of the Rebellion, (Washington, DC, 1900), Series 1, Volume 11, pp. 288, 786, 787
Official Records of the Union and Confederate Navies in the War of the Rebellion, (Washington, DC, 1921), Series 2, Volume 1, p. 248
Civil War Naval Chronology References for 1861-1865, (Washington, DC), Volume 6, p. 198
A Chart of Wrecks of Vessels Sunk or Captured Near Wilmington, NC, Circa 1861-65, compiled by Charles H. Foard, (Wilmington, North Carolina, 1962)
Dictionary of American Naval Fighting Ships, (Washington, DC, 1963), Volume 2, p. 499

1864-12-US-NC-13: On December 25, 1864, during the Federal assault on Fort Fisher, North Carolina, a launch, commanded by Acting Ensign John F. Merry, landing troops from the *U.S.S. Osceola* was "stove on the beach and afterwards burned by the crew, it being impossible to save her". "There were lost in the boat 9 cartridge boxes and belts, with 60 rounds of ammunition in each box for Sharps and Hawkins rifle, 1 box of ammunition containing 1,000 rounds for Sharps and Hawkins rifle, 1 revolver, 14 oars, 2 boat hooks, 14 rowlocks, 2 20 gallon water breakers, 1 ax, 2 boat grapnels, 1 half barrel of pork".

References for 1864-12-US-NC-13:
Official Records of the Union and Confederate Navies in the War of the Rebellion, (Washington, DC, 1900), Series 1, Volume 11, pp. 336, 337, 338

1864-12-US-NC-14: On December 25, 1864, the *U.S.S. Sassacus'* second cutter, commanded by Acting Ensign Whitman Chase, and a launch, commanded by Mr. Wilson (Oscar W. Allison?), were both swamped on the beach during the Federal assault on Fort Fisher, North Carolina. The cutter was immediately hauled up the beach, but she had started a plank and nothing could be done with her until the following morning. The next day the launch was got up and repaired. Despite Mr. Chase's protests, both the cutter and the launch were left on the beach under orders of General Curtis and were afterwards destroyed by order of General Butler.

Reference for 1864-12-US-NC-14:
Official Records of the Union and Confederate Navies in the War of the Rebellion, (Washington, DC, 1900), Series 1, Volume 11, p. 340

1864-12-US-NC-15: A report dated December 26, 1864, from Rear-Admiral David D. Porter, of the North Atlantic Blockading Squadron, to Secretary of the Navy, Gideon Welles, regarding in part a survey of the bar off Fort Fisher, North Carolina, stated "The great number of wrecks in and about the bar has changed the whole formation, and where the original channel was we found a shallow bar." Porter went on to report that while his men were searching and buoying the bar that "one boat belonging to the *Tacony* was sunk by a shell, and a man had his leg cut off. Still they stuck to their work

Treasures of the Confederate Coast

until ordered to withdraw for other duty." (Note: Visible wrecks, like buoys, were used as reference points. Just five days after Porter's report, Captain Daniel B. Ridgely, of the *U.S.S. Shenandoah*, reported anchoring "three ship's length outside of a wreck on the bar.")

References for 1864-12-US-NC-15:
Official Records of the Union and Confederate Navies in the War of the Rebellion, (Washington, DC, 1900), Series 1, Volume 11, pp. 258, 324

1864-12-US-NC-16: An entry dated December 27, 1864, in the log of the *U.S.S. Eolus* stated "at daylight made a schooner offshore and two blockade runners; one of them ashore near the wreck of the *McCaw* (*Georgiana McCaw*) and another on the bar under Fort Caswell." An entry for that same day in the log of the *U.S.S. Monticello* speaks of the *Monticello* acting in consort with the *Eolus* relative to the "blockade runners ashore". (Note One: Since one blockade runner was described as "ashore near the wreck of the *McCaw*" which was within the guns of Fort Caswell, and the other blockade runner was described as "on the bar under Fort Caswell" it is difficult to distinguish between the two. In any case, one of the stranded blockade runners appears to have been sidewheel steamer *Agnes Emily Fry*. However, since the stranded *Fry* was described as late as February 1, 1865, as "not bilged and is in first-rate order in every respect", she may not have been the blockade running steamer reported as destroyed by the guns of the *U.S.S. Monticello* on the Western Bar on December 27, 1864.) (Note Two: For more on the *Fry*, please see entry 1864-12-US-NC-17. For more precise information on the location of the wreck of the *McCaw*, please see entry 1864-6-US-NC-1.)

References for 1864-12-US-NC-16:
Official Records of the Union and Confederate Navies in the War of the Rebellion, (Washington, DC, 1900), Series 1, Volume 11, pp. 385, 725

1864-12-US-NC-17: The sidewheel steamer *Agnes Emily Fry* [or *Agnes E. Fry, A.E. Fry, Agnes C. Fry, Agnes C. Frey, Roe(II)*, ex-*Fox(II)*] was run aground below Fort Campbell, North Carolina, on December 27, 1864. Her position was also reported as off Old Inlet, and as two miles to the southward of Fort Caswell. Her cargo and machinery were expected to be saved, but the ship was lost. She was valued at $150,000. (Note One: Although she was eventually destroyed, the stranded *Fry* was described as late as February 1, 1865, as "not bilged and is in first-rate order in every respect.") (Note Two: The vessel was described as a fine, one thousand ton, blockade running steamer built of 5/8" iron, with splendid engines, handsomely fitted out. The *Agnes E. Fry* was named for the wife of the vessel's captain, Joseph Fry. He also writes that the vessel was

The "Real Rhett Butler" & Other Revelations

successful in four of her six attempts to run the blockade. She was 236.6'x25.2'x13.5' and was 559 gross tons. The *Agnes E. Fry* was owned by Crenshaw and Company and was built by Caird and Company, Greenock, Scotland, in 1864. Her engines were also built by Caird and Company and had two cylinders, 58"x69".) (Note Three: Blockade running must have been in Joseph Fry's blood as he later ran guns to the Cuban rebels and was caught and executed by the Spaniards on November 7, 1873. Fry was a, not so distant, relative of Margaret Mitchell who wrote about blockade running to the Confederacy and post war gun running to the Cubans in her novel *Gone With The Wind*.) (Note Four: A report in the London *Times* of November 23, 1864, incorrectly listed the *A.E. Fry* as "ashore outside of Charleston.")

References for 1864-12-US-NC-17:
Times, (London, England), # 25037, November 23, 1864, p. 7, c. 5
Times, (London, England), # 25099, February 3, 1865, p. 9, c. 2
Official Records of the Union and Confederate Navies in the War of the Rebellion, (Washington, DC, 1900), Series 1, Volume 10, pp. 477, 601
Official Records of the Union and Confederate Navies in the War of the Rebellion, (Washington, DC, 1900), Series 1, Volume 11, pp. 385, 416, 627, 725, 788
Gone With The Wind, by Margaret Mitchell, (Macmillan, 1936), pp. 223, 755, 839, 840
A Chart of Wrecks of Vessels Sunk or Captured Near Wilmington, NC, Circa 1861-65, compiled by Charles H. Foard, (Wilmington, North Carolina, 1962)
Saga of Felix Senac, by Regina Rapier, (Atlanta, Georgia, 1972), pp. 109, 154, 161, 171
Lifeline of the Confederacy: Blockade Running During the Civil War, by Stephen R. Wise, (University Microfilms International, 1983), pp. 512, 528
The Blockade Runners, by Dave Horner, (Florida Classics Library, Port Salerno, FL, 1992), Chapter 14, pp. 227-228

1864-12-US-NC-19: When the Federal fleet left Old Point, Virginia, in December of 1864, for Wilmington, North Carolina, to attack Fort Fisher, the United States gunboats *Wabash* and *Colorado* sailed "in advance, painted white, with Confederate flag. Troops concealed under deck." (Note: After the *Wabash* grounded on Frying Pan Shoals, North Carolina, on October 13, 1864, her captain described her crew of 400 as including "100 inferior plantation negroes and 50 reformed rebels from Forrest's and other armies, with the remainder of landsmen and boys. The few petty officers now on board were nearly all landsmen and boys when the old crew was discharged last June." During that incident her solid shot was heaved overboard to lighten the vessel.)

References for 1864-12-US-NC-19:
Official Records of the Union and Confederate Navies in the War of the Rebellion, (Washington, D.C., 1900), Series 1, Volume 10, pp. 564-566
Official Records of the Union and Confederate Navies in the War of the Rebellion, (Washington, D.C., 1900), Series 1, Volume 11, p. 784

1864-12-US-SC/GA-1: The schooner *Robert B. Howlett*, of Philadelphia, Captain James Brewer of Abescon, New Jersey, was wrecked on the Northern Bar (a portion of Charleston Bar, South Carolina) in a hurricane on December 9, 1864. (Note One: The schooner's mate was A.H. Dean. The crew consisted of Charles

Treasures of the Confederate Coast

Winslow of Port Richmond, Pennsylvania; Lewis Mulcott of Miliville, New Jersey; and John R. Cruse of Dorchester, New Jersey. John R. Cruse was the sole survivor and was rescued by Captain Post of the *Eliza Hancox*.) (Note Two: The schooner had been lying inside the Charleston Bar for over two months with a cargo of coal for the blockading fleet. The schooner had recently been anchored in the channel-way and was being used as the inside lightship when she was lost.) [Note Three: The *Robert B. Howlett* was built in 1860 in Mathews County, Virginia, (her place of construction was also reported as Boston). Her hull was of oak and was iron fastened. She was described as a strong, medium model vessel with two masts. The vessel measured 246 3/95 (or 120) tons, 106'6" in length, 27' in breadth, 9'7" in depth of hold, and drew 9' of water. She had an elliptic stern, no galleries, a plain head, and one deck with a poop for cargo. She was issued a bond and enrollment at Philadelphia on October 12, 1863.]

References for 1864-12-US-SC/GA-1:
"Temporary Register #41," (Portland, Maine), January 26, 1861, National Archives, Record Group 41
"Bond and enrollment," (Philadelphia, Pa.), October 12, 1863, National Archives, Record Group 41
American Lloyd's: Registry of American & Foreign Shipping, (New York, New York, 1863), p. 523, #3971
New York Times, (New York, NY), #4128, December 16, 1864, p. 5, c. 2, 3
"Harper's Weekly," January 21, 1865, article with picture

1864-12-US-SC/GA-2: The small Confederate States sidewheel steamer *Ida* was captured and burned at Argyle Island, Georgia, in the Savannah River by Federal cavalry, headed by Captain Henry A. Gildersleeve, of the 150th New York Volunteers, on December 10, 1864. (Note: The *Ida* was a former U.S. government vessel, and had been serving as a transport, and as a dispatch and tow boat, when she was destroyed. The Yankees captured thirteen men including Colonel Clinch of General Hardee's staff.)

References for 1864-12-US-SC/GA-2:
Official Records of the Union and Confederate Armies in the War of the Rebellion, (Washington, DC, 1893), Series 1, Volume 44, pp. 45, 158, 208, 215, 219, 222, 235, 239, 247
Official Records of the Union and Confederate Navies in the War of the Rebellion, (Washington, DC, 1903), Series 1, Volume 16, pp. 474, 479
Warships of the Civil War Navies, by Paul H. Silverstone, (Naval Institute Press, Annapolis, MD, 1989), p. 240

1864-12-US-SC/GA-3: The Confederate States sidewheel steamer *Resolute* collided with the Confederate States steamer *Macon* on December 12, 1864, about eight hundred yards from a bluff near the "mill at Tweedside" on the Savannah River and was run aground. (Note: The *Resolute* is described in some contemporary reports as burned and destroyed by the Federals, but she was not destroyed. Instead, she was captured and repaired. She had been used as a transport and as a tender and residence for the crew of the Confederate ram *Savannah*, and was armed with musketry only. She had 7 officers and 25 or 28 seamen.) (Note: The *Resolute* survived the war and was renamed and documented as the *Ajax* on July 8, 1867. She was built in Savannah in 1858, and had a wood hull with sidewheels. She was 322 tons and her official number was 1539.)

References for 1864-12-US-SC/GA-3:
Official Records of the Union and Confederate Armies in the War of the Rebellion, (Washington, DC, 1893), Series 1, Volume 44, pp. 45, 158, 208, 219, 222, 235, 238, 250-252, 328, 694, 697, 727
Official Records of the Union and Confederate Navies in the War of the Rebellion, (Washington, DC, 1903), Series 1, Volume 16, pp. 486, 489, 490
Official Records of the Union and Confederate Navies in the War of the Rebellion, (Washington, DC, 1921), Series 2, Volume 1, pp. 264, 273, 303
Civil War Naval Chronology 1861-1865, compiled by Navy History Division, Navy Department, (Washington, DC, 1971), pp. VI-292, VI-293
Merchant Steam Vessels of the United States 1790-1868, ("Lytle-Holdcamper List"), edited by C. Bradford Mitchell, (Staten Island, NY, 1975), p. 184
Warships of the Civil War Navies, by Paul H. Silverstone, (Naval Institute Press, Annapolis, MD, 1989), p. 241

1864-12-US-SC/GA-4: Research done by Frank and Paul Chance of Richmond Hill, Georgia, shows that the Confederate States steamer *Columbus*, two guns, was burned in the Ogeechee River, Georgia, in 1864. (Note: The propeller steamer *Columbus* had one deck, no masts, a square stern, no galleries, and no figurehead. The steamer measured 105 85/95 tons, 82' in length, 19' in breadth, and 7'6" in depth of hold. She had a wood hull and sidewheels. She was built at Wilmington, Delaware, in 1855, and her first home port was Philadelphia, Pennsylvania.)

References for 1864-12-US-SC/GA-4:
"Enrollment #3," (Savannah, GA), May 10, 1859, National Archives, Record Group 41
Merchant Steam Vessels of the United States 1807-1868, ("Lytle List"), by William M. Lytle, (Mystic, CT, 1952), p. 38
Merchant Steam Vessels of the United States 1790-1868, ("Lytle-Holdcamper List"), edited by C. Bradford Mitchell, (Staten Island, NY, 1975), p. 842
Interview with Frank and Paul Chance by E. Lee Spence, March, 1983, Richmond Hill, Georgia

1864-12-US-SC/GA-5: The United States steamer *Water Witch*, which had been captured in Ossabaw Sound, Georgia, at the beginning of June, 1864, was burned by the Confederates on December 19, 1864, to prevent her from being recaptured by the Federals. The destruction of the vessel took place in the Vernon River near White Bluff Plantation not far from Thunderbolt outside of Savannah, Georgia. (Note One: The *Water Witch* had been libeled in Admiralty in the Southern District Court of Georgia, C.S.A., on July 13, 1864.) (Note Two: The *Water Witch* was a sidewheel steamer and, when captured, was manned with a crew of eighty, and was armed with one 32-pounder rifle, one 12-pounder rifle, and two 12-pounder howitzers (some reports showed her as armed with three 100-pounders and three 12-pounders). The Confederates removed the steamer's pivot gun after her capture.] [Note Three: The *Water Witch* was built by the United States government at the Washington Navy Yard in 1852. The steamer's machinery was made by William M. Ellis. The *Water Witch* had a

Treasures of the Confederate Coast

wood hull. The vessel measured 378 tons (some reports state 1300 tons), 150' in length, 23' in breadth, 11'6" in depth of hull, and 10' in draft. She was capable of "moderate speed, probably not 9 knots." She took the first shot that opened the "Paraguay war" at the Itapine fort in South America. She was "for years cruising in command of Lieut. Page, the explorer."] (Note Four: U.S. Court of Inquiry #4333 held on November 3, 1864, and U.S. General Court Martial #3832 held on December 19, 1864, dealt with the cause and responsibility of her capture by the Confederates.)

References for 1864-12-US-SC/GA-5:
New York Times, (New York, NY), Volume 10, #2990, April 21, 1861, p. 3, c. 6
"Engines," (Plans of the Water Witch), 1852, National Archives, Record Group 19, 108-11-8-A
"Sheer, half breadth & body," (Plans of the Water Witch), 1852, National Archives, Record Group 19, 108-11-8-B
"Midship section," (Plans of the Water Witch), 1852, National Archives, Record Group 19, 108-11-8-C
"Inboard profile & upper deck," (Plans of the Water Witch), 1852, National Archives, Record Group 19, 108-11-8-D
"Masts & spars, profile," (Plans of the Water Witch), National Archives, Record Group 19, 108-11-8-E
"Lower cabins," (Plans of the Water Witch), 1856, National Archives, Record Group 19, 108-11-8-F
"Berth deck & hold," (Plans of the Water Witch), 1852, National Archives, Record Group 19, 108-11-8-H
"Berth deck & hold," (Plans of the Water Witch), 1861, National Archives, Record Group 19, 78-6-28
"Sail Plan," (Plans of the Water Witch), National Archives, Record Group 19, 107-14-13-A
"Charleston Mercury," (Charleston, SC), Volume 84, #12080 (but printed 12008), June 6, 1864, p. 1, c. 5, 6
"Charleston Mercury," (Charleston, SC), Volume 84, #12091, June 18, 1864, p. 1, c. 1
New York Times, (New York, NY), Volume 13, #3968, June 10, 1864, p. 1, c. 4
New York Times, (New York, NY), Volume 14, #4181, February 17, 1865, p. 4, c. 2
Times, (London, England), #25220, June 25, 1865, p. 14, c. 1
"Daily Morning News," (Savannah, GA), July 15, 1864, p. 2, c. 5, (advertisement)
"Daily Morning News," (Savannah, GA), July 18, 1864, p. 2, c. 5, (advertisement)
Records of General Courts Martial and Courts of Inquiry of the Navy Department, 1799-1867, Court of Inquiry, #4333, November 3, 1864, NARS M-273, roll 169, frames 0002-0147
Records of General Courts Martial and Courts of Inquiry of the Navy Department, 1799-1867, General Court Martial, #3832, December 19, 1864, NARS M-273, roll 2, alphabetical card index 1861-1867
History of the Confederate States Navy From its Organization to the Surrender of its Last Vessel, by J. Thomas Scharf, (New York, New York, 1887), pp. 274, 645, 648-651
Official Records of the Union and Confederate Armies in the War of the Rebellion, (Washington, DC, 1891), Series 1, Volume 35, Part 1, pp. 120, 404; Part 2, pp. 116, 125-128, 131, 137, 138, 521, 522, 611, 615
Official Records of the Union and Confederate Navies in the War of the Rebellion, (Washington, DC, 1903), Series 1, Volume 16, pp. 484, 487, 503
Official Records of the Union and Confederate Navies in the War of the Rebellion, (Washington, DC, 1921), Series 2, Volume 1, pp. 237, 271
Confederate Military History, edited by General Clement A. Evans, (Confederate Publishing Co., Atlanta, GA, 1899), Volume 12, pp. 78-80
"Ships Named Savannah," by Amy Chambliss, (typed manuscript in the collection of the Georgia Historical Society, Savannah, Georgia), p. 58
Civil War Naval Chronology 1861-1865, compiled by Navy History Division, Navy Department, (Washington, DC, 1971), p. VI-323
Warships of the Civil War Navies, by Paul H. Silverstone, (Naval Institute Press, Annapolis, MD, 1989), p. 24

1864-12-US-SC/GA-6: The Confederate States steamer *Kate L. Bruce* (a.k.a. *Kate Bruce* and *K.L. Bruce*) was scuttled as an obstruction in the Chattahoochee River in December of 1864. (Note: The *Kate L. Bruce* was 310 tons and drew 10' of water. She was originally rigged as a schooner and had been used in running the blockade. At least one source shows her as converted to a steam powered gunboat of two guns at Columbus, Georgia, in 1862.)

References for 1864-12-US-SC/GA-6:
Official Records of the Union and Confederate Navies in the War of the Rebellion, (Washington, DC, 1903), Series 1, Volume 17, pp. 120, 262, 357

The "Real Rhett Butler" & Other Revelations

Official Records of the Union and Confederate Navies in the War of the Rebellion, (Washington, DC, 1921), Series 2, Volume 1, p. 257
Shipwrecks of the Civil War: The Encyclopedia of Union and Confederate Naval Losses, by Donald Shomette, (Washington, DC, 1973), pp. 306, 307
Perilous Journeys: A History of Steamboating on the Chattahoochee, Apalachicola, and Flint Rivers, 1828-1928, by Edward A. Mueller, (Historic Chattahoochee Commission, Eufalia, Alabama, 1989), pp. 106, 107, 115
Warships of the Civil War Navies, by Paul H. Silverstone, (Naval Institute Press, Annapolis, MD, 1989), p. 240

1864-12-US-SC/GA-7: The Confederate States ironclad (or floating battery) *Georgia* was burned by the Confederates below Savannah, Georgia, during the Confederate evacuation of that city on December 21, 1864. (Note: The *C.S.S. Georgia* was 250' in length and 60' in breadth. The ironclad was also known as the *State of Georgia* and as the "Ladies' Ram." The ram was armed with two 9-inch Dahlgren smooth-bores, and two 32-pounder rifles. Realizing she would have to be destroyed the order had previously been given that her guns were to be "spiked and shots jammed" down the barrels. The steamer carried a crew of eighty-two men and twelve officers. Although the *Georgia* was steam powered, she was under engined and could barely move about.)

References for 1864-12-US-SC/GA-7:
History of the Confederate States Navy From its Organization to the Surrender of its Last Vessel, by J. Thomas Scharf, (New York, New York, 1887), pp. 637, 651, 653
Official Records of the Union and Confederate Armies in the War of the Rebellion, (Washington, DC, 1893), Series 1, Volume 44, p. 965
Official Records of the Union and Confederate Navies in the War of the Rebellion, (Washington, DC, 1921), Series 2, Volume 1, pp. 254, 273, 286, 287, and illustration opposite p. 254
Confederate Military History, edited by General Clement A. Evans, (Confederate Publishing Co., Atlanta, GA, 1899), Volume 12, p. 108
Civil War Naval Chronology 1861-1865, compiled by Navy History Division, Navy Department, (Washington, DC, 1971), p. VI-238
Warships of the Civil War Navies, by Paul H. Silverstone, (Naval Institute Press, Annapolis, MD, 1989), p. 237

1864-12-US-SC/GA-8: The small Confederate States gunboat *Isondiga* (or *Isandiga*) was unable to escape to the sea or to join Flag Officer Hunter after the evacuation of that city by the Confederates on December 21, 1864, and was burned by her crew in the Savannah River above Savannah, Georgia. (Note: The *Isondiga* had a wood hull and no masts. The gunboat was a stern wheel steamer. The vessel had a draft of 6'6" and a could make five knots. She was armed with three guns, including at least one 9-inch Dahlgren smooth-bore gun and one 6.4-inch Brooke rifle.)

References for 1864-12-US-SC/GA-8:
Official Records of the Union and Confederate Armies in the War of the Rebellion, (Washington, DC, 1893), Series 1, Volume 44, p. 965
Official Records of the Union and Confederate Navies in the War of the Rebellion, (Washington, DC, 1921), Series 2, Volume 1, pp. 256, 273, 288, 289
Civil War Naval Chronology 1861-1865, compiled by Navy History Division, Navy Department, (Washington, DC, 1971), p. VI-252
Warships of the Civil War Navies, by Paul H. Silverstone, (Naval Institute Press, Annapolis, MD, 1989), p. 238

1864-12-US-SC/GA-9: The Confederate States tender *Firefly* (or *Fire Fly*), unable to join Flag Officer Hunter as planned, was burned by

Treasures of the Confederate Coast

the Confederates at the wharf at Screven's Ferry at Savannah, Georgia, on December 21, 1864, to prevent her from falling into the hands of the Federals upon the evacuation of Savannah by the Confederates. (Note One: The *Firefly* served as a tender to the Confederate squadron at Savannah, had a complement of 15 men, and had been authorized to mount a "boat's gun" in August, 1863. She was an ex U.S. Coast Survey boat and had been seized on December 29, 1860. She was described as wooden side-wheel steam yacht.) (Note Two: See also entry 1862-11-US-SC/GA-2 of this book.)

References for 1864-12-US-SC/GA-9:
Official Records of the Union and Confederate Armies in the War of the Rebellion, (Washington, DC, 1893), Series 1, Volume 44, p. 965
Official Records of the Union and Confederate Navies in the War of the Rebellion, (Washington, DC, 1902), Series 1, Volume 14, pp. 748, 749
Official Records of the Union and Confederate Navies in the War of the Rebellion, (Washington, DC, 1903), Series 1, Volume 16, p. 484
Official Records of the Union and Confederate Navies in the War of the Rebellion, (Washington, DC, 1921), Series 2, Volume 1, pp. 252, 273, 285
Civil War Naval Chronology 1861-1865, compiled by Navy History Division, Navy Department, (Washington, DC, 1971), p. VI-236
Warships of the Civil War Navies, by Paul H. Silverstone, (Naval Institute Press, Annapolis, MD, 1989), p. 239

1864-12-US-SC/GA-10: The Confederate States ram *Savannah* was abandoned and burned by the Confederates in the Savannah River below Savannah, Georgia, during the evacuation of that city on December 21, 1864. (Note: The *Savannah* carried a crew of 27 officers and 144 men. She was armed with two 7-inch Brooke single banded rifles, and two 6.4" Brooke double banded rifles. She was built at Savannah, Georgia, by Henry F. Willink, could make a speed of 6 1/2 knots when under 15 pounds of steam. She was 150' between perpendiculars, 34' in breadth, 14' in depth, and 12'6" in draft.)

References for 1864-12-US-SC/GA-10:
History of the Confederate States Navy From its Organization to the Surrender of its Last Vessel, by J. Thomas Scharf, (New York, New York, 1887), p. 653
Official Records of the Union and Confederate Navies in the War of the Rebellion, (Washington, DC, 1903), Series 1, Volume 16, p. 484
Official Records of the Union and Confederate Navies in the War of the Rebellion, (Washington, DC, 1921), Series 2, Volume 1, p. 266
Georgia Historical Quarterly, (1934), Volume 18, pp. 163, 164
"Ships Named Savannah," by Amy Chambliss, (typed manuscript in the collection of the Georgia Historical Society, Savannah, Georgia), p. 58
Civil War Naval Chronology 1861-1865, compiled by Navy History Division, Navy Department, (Washington, DC, 1971), p. VI-298
Warships of the Civil War Navies, by Paul H. Silverstone, (Naval Institute Press, Annapolis, MD, 1989), p. 205

1864-12-US-SC/GA-11: The Confederate States ironclad steamer *Milledgeville*, which had just been built and launched by Henry Willink's shipyard at Savannah, Georgia, was burned and sunk by the Confederates in the middle of the Savannah River upon the evacuation of Savannah by the Confederates on December 21, 1864.

The "Real Rhett Butler" & Other Revelations

(Note: The *Milledgeville* was 175' in length, 35'3" in breadth, 12' in depth of hold, and 9' in draft. Her guns were never mounted.)

References for 1864-12-US-SC/GA-11:
History of the Confederate States Navy From its Organization to the Surrender of its Last Vessel, by J. Thomas Scharf, (New York, New York, 1887), pp. 637, 651
Confederate Military History, edited by General Clement A. Evans, (Confederate Publishing Co., Atlanta, GA, 1899), Volume 12, p. 108
Official Records of the Union and Confederate Navies in the War of the Rebellion, (Washington, DC, 1903), Series 1, Volume 16, p. 502
Official Records of the Union and Confederate Navies in the War of the Rebellion, (Washington, DC, 1921), Series 2, Volume 1, p. 260
Civil War Naval Chronology 1861-1865, compiled by Navy History Division, Navy Department, (Washington, DC, 1971), p. VI-271
Warships of the Civil War Navies, by Paul H. Silverstone, (Naval Institute Press, Annapolis, MD, 1989), p. 208

1864-12-US-SC/GA-12: The steamer *Swan* was burned by the Confederates at Screven's Ferry at Savannah, Georgia, on December 21, 1864. (Note One: The *Swan* was an iron hulled screw steamer and was built by Harlan and Hollingsworth at Wilmington, Delaware in 1856. Her official number was 23062 and she was 316 49/95 tons. She measured 135' in length, 27' in breadth, and 5' in depth of hold. She had one deck, no masts, a square stern, and no galleries.) (Note Two: The *Swan* was raised in less than three weeks in July, 1865. She was refitted as a passenger and freight steamer and was rated as A-1 for insurance purposes.)

References for 1864-12-US-SC/GA-12:
"Permanent Enrollment #16," (Savannah, GA), January 2, 1866, National Archives, Record Group 41
"Savannah Daily Herald," (Savannah, GA), #170, August 4, 1865, p. 3, c. 1, 2
"Savannah Daily Herald," (Savannah, GA), January 13, 1866, p. 3, c. 1
"Record of Metal Vessels Built in the U.S., No 1," (bound manuscript list), p. 17, National Archives, Record Group 41
Merchant Steam Vessels of the United States 1790-1868, ("Lytle-Holdcamper List"), edited by C. Bradford Mitchell, (Staten Island, NY, 1975), p. 206

1864-12-US-SC/GA-13: The *North America* (or *North American*) Captain Marshall, "a chartered sidewheel steamer of the first class, perfectly new," foundered in gale in latitude 31°10' North, longitude 78°40' West, on December 22, 1864. (Note One: At least one hundred and ninety-seven lives were lost. Sixty-two people were saved by the bark *Mary E. Libby*, Capt. Libby. The dead included several women, but consisted chiefly of sick and wounded soldiers from the United States hospital at New Orleans.) (Note Two: The *North America*, 1651 tons, was a screw steamer, had a wood hull, and was built in 1864 at Philadelphia, Pennsylvania, which was also the steamer's first home port. She was issued a certificate of steam register at the port of New York on September 12, 1864.) (Note Three: One report stated that she was lost in the Gulf of Mexico, but they apparently meant the Gulf Stream. Another account reported her as lost off Cape Hatteras, North Carolina.) (Note Four: The *North America* had barely survived a heavy gale in May of 1863 and the damage suffered in that earlier storm may have contributed to her

Treasures of the Confederate Coast

final loss. During that earlier storm, she had been bound from New Orleans to New York when she was discovered in a sinking condition forty five miles from Beaufort, North Carolina. The captain of the *U.S.S. Monticello* which towed her to safety said "her decks were started, sponsons gone, and four feet of water in her hold, the engineer being up to his waste in water; all pumps going to prevent her from sinking.")

References for 1864-12-US-SC/GA-13:
New York Times, (New York, NY), Volume 14, #4160, January 24, 1865, p. 5, c. 2
Times, (London, England), #25079, January 11, 1865, p. 9, c. 2
Times, (London, England), #25081, January 13, 1865, p. 10, c. 5
Official Records of the Union and Confederate Armies in the War of the Rebellion, (Washington, DC, 1900), Series III, Volume 5, pp. 228, 288
Official Records of the Union and Confederate Navies in the War of the Rebellion, (Washington, DC, 1899), Series 1, Volume 9, p. 27
List of American-Flag Merchant Vessels that Received Certificates of Enrollment or Registry at the Port of New York 1789-1867, compiled by Forest R. Holdcamper, (U.S. National Archives, Washington, DC, 1968), Special List #22, Volume 2, p. 514
Encyclopedia of American Shipwrecks, by Bruce D. Berman, (Boston, 1972), p. 137, #1459
Merchant Steam Vessels of the United States 1790-1868, ("Lytle-Holdcamper List"), edited by C. Bradford Mitchell, (Staten Island, NY, 1975), pp. 159, 285

1864-12-US-SC/GA-14: The "howitzers and other articles" aboard a launch commanded by Acting Master's Mate A.F. Rich, U.S.N., were believed to have been thrown overboard prior to its capture in Charleston Harbor, South Carolina, on December 31, 1864.

References for 1864-12-US-SC/GA-14:
Official Records of the Union and Confederate Navies in the War of the Rebellion, (Washington, D.C., 1903), Series 1, Vol. 16, pp. 139, 140

1864-12-US-SC/GAx-1: The London *Times* of February 3, 1865, reported the steamer *Julia* as "lost while trying to get out of Charleston." The *Julia* had been caught in a gale while escaping from Charleston in December of 1864, and was forced to seek shelter in the Santee River where she accidentally ran aground. She was soon discovered and captured by small boats from the United States gunboat *Acadia.* (Note: The *Julia* was an iron hulled, sidewheel steamer built by Simons and Company at Renfrew, Scotland, in 1863. She was 210' in length, 23.2' in breadth, 9.8' in depth of hull, 117 tons register, and 735 tons burden. She was owned by Donald McGregor and had made one previous run through the blockade.)

References for 1864-12-US-SC/GAx-1:
Times, (London, England), #25099, February 3, 1865, p. 9, c. 2
Lifeline of the Confederacy: Blockade Running During the Civil War, by Stephen R. Wise, (University of South Carolina, Columbia, SC, 1983), p. 580

1864-12-US-x-1: On December 6, 1864, S.R. Mallory, Secretary of the Confederate States Navy, issued the following instructions with regard to the sailing of the government owned blockade runner *Stag.* "Before leaving port you will station your crews for the different boats of the steamer, having placed in them water and provisions,

The "Real Rhett Butler" & Other Revelations

and also nautical instruments. When capture in your judgment becomes inevitable, fire the vessel in several places and embark in the boats, making for the nearest land. The (Navy) Department leaves to your discretion the time when and the circumstances that must govern you in the destruction of the *Stag* in order to prevent her falling into the hands of the enemy. You will obtain the best engineer officers and pilots, and make the vessel as thoroughly efficient as practicable for the service for which she is engaged. No passenger will be received on board without the authority of this Department."

Reference for 1864-12-US-x-1:
Official Records of the Union and Confederate Navies in the War of the Rebellion, (Washington, D.C., 1900), Series 1, Volume 11, p. 621

1864-12-US-x-2: A report dated December 15, 1864, from Rear-Admiral David D. Porter, of the North Atlantic Blockading Squadron, to Secretary of the Navy, Gideon Welles, stated "Blockade running seems almost as brisk as ever, and I suppose will continue so long as it is remunerative. The new class of blockade runners is very fast, and sometimes come in and play around our vessels; they are built entirely for speed. Within the last fifty days we have captured and destroyed $5,500,000 worth of the enemy's property in blockade runners. To submit to these losses and still run the blockade shows the immense gains the runners make and the straits the enemy are in." (Note: Those losses would amount to approximately $110,000,000 in today's money.)

Reference for 1864-12-US-x-2:
Official Records of the Union and Confederate Navies in the War of the Rebellion, (Washington, DC, 1900), Series 1, Volume 11, p. 195

1864-12x-GB-England-1: The London *Times* of January 31, 1865, reported that from the beginning of 1862 through the end of 1864 "no fewer than one hundred and eleven swift steamers were built on the Clyde for the purpose of running the blockade of the Confederate ports." The *Times* went on to say that "the average number of trips made by a blockade-runner does not, however, exceed five, so enormous profits must be realized per voyage to make this peculiar branch of adventure at all renumerative."

Reference for 1864-12x-GB-England-1:
Times, (London, England), # 25096, January 31, 1865, p. 8, c. 1

1864-12x-US-SC/GA-1: The United States coal vessel *Abby Allen* was driven ashore near Wassaw Sound, Georgia, in a "very severe northeaster" in late November or early December, 1864. She was expected to be saved, but the records make no further mention of her.

Reference for 1864-12x-US-SC/GA-1:

Treasures of the Confederate Coast

Official Records of the Union and Confederate Navies in the War of the Rebellion, (Washington, D.C., 1903), Series 1, Vol. 16, p. 124

1864x-12x-US-SC/GA-1: The *C.S.S. Spray* was scuttled by the Confederates in the St. Mary's River (Georgia/Florida line). (Note One: She was a steam tug and as late as November 5, 1864, she was reported as armed with two guns.) (Note Two: This may have been the 106 ton, wooden hulled, sidewheel steamer *Spray*, which was built at Wilmington, Delaware, in 1852. That vessel's first home port was Wilmington, North Carolina, and passed into Confederate control in 1861.)

References for 1864x-12x-US-SC/GA-1:
Official Records of the Union and Confederate Navies in the War of the Rebellion, (Washington, D.C., 1921), Series 2, Vol. 1, Part 1, p. 267
Merchant Steam Vessels of the United States 1790-1868, ("Lytle-Holdcamper List"), edited by C. Bradford Mitchell, (Staten Island, NY, 1975), p. 201

1864-12x-US-x-1: When large amounts of gold was being shipped (and it was actually shipped in and out of the blockade throughout the war) it was frequently hidden beneath heavy cargo or in secret compartments to prevent its discovery if, in the event of capture, the Yankees searched the vessel before scuttling it or setting it afire. Virtually all Civil War vessels, regardless of whether they were private, Federal, or Confederate, inbound or outbound, carried at least some specie (coin) as pay for crew, bribes or expenses. Confederate naval historian John Thomas Scharf's book, *History of the Confederate States Navy from its Organization to the Surrender of its Last Vessel,* compares the costs of operating a steamer for one month in peace time and for one month during the war. Scharf points out that wages and expenses were "paid in gold." The following list has been prepared from Scharf's breakdown of one month's expenses for a first class steamer carrying passengers and freight through the blockade.

Captain	$5,000
First Officer	600
Second Officer	250
Third Officer	170
Boatswain	160
Carpenter	160
Purser	1,000
Steward and Three Assistants (total)	330
Cook and Two Assistant Cooks (total)	270
Engineer and Three Assistants (total)	3,500
Twelve firemen & Coal Heavers (total)	2,400
Coal	4,800
Rations for Crew	2,700

Provisions for Passengers	3,000
Oil Tallow and Packing	1,000
Stevedores	5,000
Pilotage (Out and In)	3,000
Sea Insurance, Risks, and Interest	41,875
Wear and Tear	4,250
Incidental	1,000
TOTAL	$80,465

Blockade runner captains routinely carried a high percentage of the expected expenses in gold aboard the vessel. The captains often used this and other money they carried aboard their vessels to try bribe Federal officers to let their ships go if they were caught. (Note: Since many of the captures were being made on the high seas, where the Federal ships had questionable jurisdiction and where it was often hard to prove that a ship was intending to run the blockade, the bribes may have been accepted on more than one occasion. It would certainly explain why Federal ships let some of the blockade runners go after catching them. The "notorious" Captain Thomas J. Lockwood, who ran some of George Trenholm's ships, used to boast that his success lay in "arrangements with (Federal) naval officers" who had been bribed to let him through.

References for 1864-12x-US-x-1:
"Charleston Mercury," (Charleston, SC), Volume 83, #11892, October 26, 1863, p. 2, c. 1
"Charleston Mercury," (Charleston, SC), Volume 83, #11903, November 7, 1863, p. 1, c. 2
"Charleston Mercury," (Charleston, SC), Volume 83, #11911, November 17, 1863, p. 1, c. 6
"Charleston Mercury," (Charleston, SC), Volume 83, #11913, November 19, 1863, p. 2, c. 1
"Charleston Mercury," (Charleston, SC), Volume 83, #11917, November 24, 1863, p. 2, c. 1
"Charleston Mercury," (Charleston, SC), Volume 83, #11928, December 7, 1863, p. 2, c. 1
"Charleston Mercury," (Charleston, SC), Volume 83, #11945, December 29, 1863, p. 2, c. 1
"Charleston Mercury," (Charleston, SC), Volume 83, #12009, March 14, 1864, p. 2, c. 1
History of the Confederate States Navy From its Organization to the Surrender of its Last Vessel, by J. Thomas Scharf, (New York, New York, 1887), pp. 480, 481
Official Records of the Union and Confederate Navies in the War of the Rebellion, (Washington, DC, 1899), Series 1, Volume 9, pp. 248-251, 275, 277, 282, 284, 286-291, 341, 785
Official Records of the Union and Confederate Navies in the War of the Rebellion, (Washington, DC, 1900), Series 1, Volume 10, pp. 393, 394, 602
Official Records of the Union and Confederate Navies in the War of the Rebellion, (Washington, DC, 1902), Series 1, Volume 15, p. 267
The Navy in the Civil War, (Charles Scribner's Sons, New York, NY, 1903), Volume 1 ("The Blockade and the Cruisers" by James Russell Soley), pp. 166, 167

1865-1-US-NC-1: A report of Commander W.H. Macomb, U.S.N., to Admiral David D. Porter, dated January 6, 1865, advised the barricading of the Roanoke River, North Carolina. Macomb wrote "I think that this river should be barricaded, so as to prevent the enemy from bringing out his ironclad, which, from all accounts, is within five or six months of completion. This might be done in two ways - by sinking vessels in the river (twelve good sized schooners sunk stem upstream would be sufficient) or by building a regular causeway of cobwork across the stream, leaving sluices for the

Treasures of the Confederate Coast

water to flow through. The latter of these methods is perhaps the most effectual, but the former is much more easily accomplished."

Reference for 1865-1-US-NC-1:
Official Records of the Union and Confederate Navies in the War of the Rebellion, (Washington, D.C., 1900), Series 1, Volume 11, p. 414

1865-1-US-NC-2: During the evening of January 12, 1865, the *U.S.S. Eolus*, "in trying to cross a hawser from the *Fort Jackson* to a monitor, ran into the *Fort Jackson*, carrying away the gig and smashing a portion of the hurricane deck".

Reference for 1865-1-US-NC-2:
Official Records of the Union and Confederate Navies in the War of the Rebellion, (Washington, D.C., 1900), Series 1, Volume 11, p. 570

1865-1-US-NC-3: The second cutter from the *U.S.S. Cherokee* was abandoned on the beach near Fort Fisher, North Carolina, during the Federal assault of January 13, 1865.

Reference for 1865-1-US-NC-3:
Official Records of the Union and Confederate Navies in the War of the Rebellion, (Washington, D.C., 1900), Series 1, Volume 11, p. 567

1865-1-US-NC-4: On January 15, 1865, Acting Volunteer Lieutenant MacDiarmid of the *U.S.S. Governor Buckingham* sent a carpenter's mate and boat's crew on shore to repair a launch which had been damaged during the Federal assault on Fort Fisher. "They returned and reported her so badly stove and broken up that she could not be repaired; was condemned".

Reference for 1865-1-US-NC-4:
Official Records of the Union and Confederate Navies in the War of the Rebellion, (Washington, D.C., 1900), Series 1, Volume 11, p. 575

1865-1-US-NC-5: On the evening of January 15, 1865, the first and second launches from the *U.S.S. Pequot* were lost on the beach near Fort Fisher, North Carolina, when they were driven on shore by a heavy surf. The armed launches had been used to transport forty-two men and officers under the command of Acting Ensigns George Lamb and Anthony Smalley as part of the assault on Fort Fisher. The men took heavy casualties, and Smalley was afterwards recommended for promotion to acting master.

References for 1865-1-US-NC-5:
Official Records of the Union and Confederate Navies in the War of the Rebellion, (Washington, D.C., 1900), Series 1, Volume 11, pp. 479, 480, 482

1865-1-US-NC-6: The second cutter from the *U.S.S. Mackinaw* was lost on the beach near Fort Fisher, North Carolina, during the Federal assault of January 15, 1865, when "she got broadside on to the surf, filled, and capsized". Two swords, six swords with belts and frogs, seven revolvers, eight frogs, and four pistols and frogs were lost in the cutter.

Reference for 1865-1-US-NC-6:
Official Records of the Union and Confederate Navies in the War of the Rebellion, (Washington, D.C., 1900), Series 1, Volume 11, p. 523

The "Real Rhett Butler" & Other Revelations

1865-1-US-NC-7: The Confederate States gunboat *Tallahassee* was thought by the Federals to have been one of two steamers blown up, near Fort Caswell, in the Cape Fear River by the Confederates during the final Federal assault on Fort Fisher, North Carolina, January 15, 1865, to prevent their capture. (Note One: The *C.S.S. Tallahassee* escaped from Cape Fear and is listed in the "Official Records-Navy" as in England when the war ended, so there is definitely some confusion here.) (Note Two: The *Tallahassee* was bought at Wilmington in 1864. She was a twin screw steam sloop cruiser of 3 (or 5) guns. One report gave her armament as one 84-pounder, two 24-pounders, and two 32-pounders. She was 220' in length, 22' in breadth, and could make 17 knots. She was the former blockade runner *Atlanta*. Subsequently her name was changed to *Olustee* and then to *Chameleon*. The *Tallahassee* was not a privateer, but a regularly commissioned and officered vessel of the Provisional Navy of the Confederate States.) (Note Three: The second steamer was thought to have been the *C.S.S. Chickamauga*, but that vessel was not scuttled until February 25, 1865. For more information on the *Chickamauga*, please see entry 1865-2-US-NC-2.)

References for 1865-1-US-NC-7:
Official Records of the Union and Confederate Navies in the War of the Rebellion, (Washington, DC, 1900), Series 1, Volume 10, pp. 400, 445, 510, 782, 793, 801
Official Records of the Union and Confederate Navies in the War of the Rebellion, (Washington, D.C., 1900), Series 1, Volume 11, pp. 97, 441
Official Records of the Union and Confederate Navies in the War of the Rebellion, (Washington, DC, 1921), Series 2, Volume 1, p. 268
Graveyard of the Atlantic: Shipwrecks of the North Carolina Coast, by David Stick (University of North Carolina Press, Chapel Hill, NC, 1952), pp. 60, 248
An Oceanographic Atlas of the Continental Margin, J.G. Newton, O.H. Pilkey and J.O. Blanton, (Duke University Marine Laboratory, Beaufort, NC, 1971), p. 17 chart symbol #64, p. 20 entry #64

1865-1-US-NC-8: The Confederate transport *Cape Fear* (ex-*Flora*, ex-*Virginia*) was sunk by her crew in the Cape Fear River off Smithville, North Carolina, on the night of January 16, 1865, after transporting troops from Fort Holmes to Smithville during the evacuation of the Confederate defenses at Old Inlet. (Note: The *Cape Fear* had previously served as a blockade runner and had made eleven successful runs out of eleven tries. She was built and engined by J.&W. Dudgeon at London, England in 1862. She had a two cylinders of 26" with 21" piston stroke. The twin screw vessel was 161.3' in length, 22.5' in breadth, 12.4' in depth of hold, drew 7' of water, and was 434 tons burden. During her career the *Cape Fear* was variously owned by the Alexander Collie and Company, by Henry Hart of the Consolidated Steamship Company of Charleston, and by the Confederates States of America. The Confederate government reportedly paid $500,000 worth of cotton for the vessel

Treasures of the Confederate Coast

when they acquired her in the fall of 1863 from the Consolidated Steamship Company. The Confederate government used the vessel as a transport on the Cape Fear River.)

References for 1865-1-US-NC-8:

Official Records of the Union and Confederate Armies in the War of the Rebellion, (Washington, DC, 1895), Series 1, Volume 46, Part 2, p. 1088

Official Records of the Union and Confederate Armies in the War of the Rebellion, (Washington, DC, 1897), Series 1, Volume 51, Part 2, p. 1043

Graveyard of the Atlantic: Shipwrecks of the North Carolina Coast, by David Stick (University of North Carolina Press, Chapel Hill, NC, 1952), p. 248

A Chart of Wrecks of Vessels Sunk or Captured Near Wilmington, NC, Circa 1861-65, compiled by Charles H. Foard, (Wilmington, North Carolina, 1962)

An Oceanographic Atlas of the Continental Margin, J.G. Newton, O.H. Pilkey and J.O. Blanton, (Duke University Marine Laboratory, Beaufort, NC, 1971), p. 17 chart symbol #71, p. 20 entry #71

Lifeline of the Confederacy: Blockade Running During the Civil War, by Stephen R. Wise, (University Microfilms International, 1983), pp. 331, 513, 562, 563

1865-1-US-NC-9: The steamer *Pelteway* was destroyed by the Confederates during their January 17, 1865, evacuation of Smithville, North Carolina. The Confederates were under the command of Brigadier General Louis Hébert.

Reference for 1865-1-US-NC-9:

Official Records of the Union and Confederate Armies in the War of the Rebellion, (Washington, DC, 1895), Series 1, Volume 46, Part 2, p. 1088

1865-1-US-NC-10: A report of Commander W.H. Macomb, U.S.N., dated January 20, 1865, stated "the obstructions are about 3 miles above New Berne (North Carolina). In the main channel (of the Neuse River) there is about 12 feet of water, and in it are sunk a brig and a schooner. The rest of the barricade consists of spiling (pilings), rather weak in the shoal water". (Note: Macomb's report mentions a sketch of the obstructions made by Acting Master H.H. Foster of the *U.S.S. Ceres*, but it was not published with that report in the "Official Records.")

Reference for 1865-1-US-NC-10:

Official Records of the Union and Confederate Navies in the War of the Rebellion, (Washington, D.C., 1900), Series 1, Volume 11, p. 618

1865-1-US-NC-11: On January 26, 1865, Lieutenant-Commander J.H. Upshur, commanding the *U.S.S. A.D. Vance*, reported to the United States Secretary of Navy: "I am today informed that one of the crew of the prize steamer *Charlotte* asserts that there was on board that vessel at the time of her capture a safe (stowed under the cargo) containing a large amount of specie; also, that her letters and dispatches were thrown overboard from the paddle box in a bag, with a pig of lead attached to sink them. She was at anchor near Smithville (North Carolina), and I presume her position can be accurately ascertained." [Note One: The blockade running steamers *Charlotte* and *Stag*, bound from Bermuda and not knowing that Fort Fisher had fallen into Federal hands, had been decoyed into entering the harbor where they "quietly anchored near the (*U.S.S.*) *Malvern*, and were taken possession of." The *Charlotte* had brought in "five

English passengers, one of them an English army officer. They all came over (as they expressed it) 'on a lark,' and were making themselves quite jolly in the cabin over their champagne, having felicitated themselves on their safe arrival."] (Note Two: This entry has been included as an example of especially valuable items being hidden under the cargo of a blockade runner, and as an example of specie coming into the South rather than taken from it.)

References for 1865-1-US-NC-11:
Official Records of the Union and Confederate Navies in the War of the Rebellion, (Washington, D.C., 1900), Series 1, Volume 11, pp. 618, 620, 623, 624, 626-628

1865-1-US-SC/GA-1: The Confederate States ram *Columbia* (or *Ashley*) was run ashore at the rocks near Fort Moultrie, South Carolina, on January 12, 1865, to save her crew after she accidentally ran onto a sunken wreck. (Note One: Although they did strip the *Columbia* of some of her iron plating, the Confederates abandoned the city before they could raise her. She was raised in March, 1865, by the United States Navy Department under the supervision of Commander Matthews of Admiral Dahlgren's Staff. The vessel was not seriously damaged and was to be sent north.) [Note Two: The *C.S.S. Columbia*, six guns, was a propeller steamer. The steamer's hull was of yellow pine and white oak with iron fastenings. The vessel was 216' in length, 51'2" in breadth, 13' in depth of hold, and 13'6" in draft. She had two non-condensing steam engines with 36" diameter cylinders and a 24" piston stroke. Her three bladed propeller was 10'8" in diameter with a 12' pitch. The propeller shaft was 8" in diameter. She had 5 cylindrical flue boilers each 20' in length and 4' in diameter. The *Columbia* was built at Charleston, South Carolina, in 1864 at a total cost of $193,480 (which would be the equivalent over $2,000,000 today). The upper part of the vessel was clad with 6" of iron.]

References for 1865-1-US-SC/GA-1:
"Charleston Daily Courier," (Charleston, SC), #56, May 1, 1865, p. 2, c. 3
"Charleston Daily Courier," (Charleston, SC), #57, May 2, 1865, p. 2, c. 1
History of the Confederate States Navy From its Organization to the Surrender of its Last Vessel, by J. Thomas Scharf, (New York, New York, 1887), pp. 672, 706
Official Records of the Union and Confederate Armies in the War of the Rebellion, (Washington, DC, 1895), Series 1, Volume 47, Part 1, p. 1016
Official Records of the Union and Confederate Navies in the War of the Rebellion, (Washington, DC, 1903), Series 1, Volume 16, p. 23
Official Records of the Union and Confederate Navies in the War of the Rebellion, (Washington, DC, 1921), Series 2, Volume 1, p. 251
Confederate Military History, edited by General Clement A. Evans, (Confederate Publishing Co., Atlanta, GA, 1899), Volume 12, p. 108
The Navy in the Civil War, (Charles Scribner's Sons, New York, NY, 1905), Volume 2 ("The Atlantic Coast" by Daniel Ammen), pp. 156, 157
Civil War Naval Chronology 1861-1865, compiled by Navy History Division, Navy Department, (Washington, DC, 1971), pp. V-42, VI-214
Charleston's Maritime Heritage 1670-1865, by P.C. Coker III, (CokerCraft Press, Charleston, SC, 1987), pp. 232-234
Warships of the Civil War Navies, by Paul H. Silverstone, (Naval Institute Press, Annapolis, MD, 1989), p. 208

Treasures of the Confederate Coast

1865-1-US-SC/GA-2: The United States monitor *Patapsco*, Lieutenant Commander Stephen D. Quackenbush commanding, hit a torpedo (Confederate mine) and sank at the entrance to Charleston Harbor, South Carolina (600 yards from Fort Sumter and 1200 yards from Fort Moultrie), on January 15, 1865. Two feet of her smokestack stuck out of the water clearly marking her location. (Note One: The *Patapsco* had been acting as protection for a launch that was searching for "those nefarious machines." She struck the torpedo at a point 35' abaft of her port bow and directly under her ward room, and sank in 30' of water in 15-30 seconds. She carried a crew of 105 men and officers, 64 of whom died in the wreck. Two of her boats were reported as still lashed to the wreck. The dead included paymaster William S. Chevy and acting paymaster John White.) [Note Two: The *Patapsco* was a *"Passaic* Class" monitor and was built in 1862 by the Harlan and Hollingsworth shipyard at Wilmington, Delaware, under a contract with John Ericsson at a cost of $400,000. She was commissioned on January 2, 1863, at the Philadelphia Navy Yard. The total cost of repairs, sundries, and extra work while she was in service totaled $26,730.40. She was 844 (1,875) tons, and measured 190' in length, 37' in breadth, and 11'10" in depth of hold with a 12' draft (also shown as 241'x46'x11'10" with an 11'1" draft). The heavily built vessel could make only 6 knots. She was armed with one 15-inch Dahlgren smooth-bore, one 150-pounder Parrott rifle, one heavy 12-pounder smooth-bore, and one 12-pounder rifle.] (Note Three: The *Patapsco* was partially salvaged after the war and a monument to the *Patapsco's* dead is located near the main entrance of Fort Moultrie.) (Note Three: Charleston diver Jim Batey and I found and dove on the remains of this wreck while doing a magnetometer survey in 1971.)

References for 1865-1-US-SC/GA-2:
"Savannah Daily Herald," (Savannah, GA), January 18, 1865, p. 2, c. 1
New York Times, (New York, NY), Volume 14, #4168, February 2, 1865, p. 1, c. 5
New York Times, (New York, NY), Volume 14, #4170, February 5, 1865, p. 1, c. 5
Times, (London, England), # 25098, February 2, 1865, p. 12, c. 1
"Vessel Disasters, 1864-1865," (bound annotated clipping file, Atlantic Mutual Insurance Companies of New York), Volume 39, pp. 247, 254
Records of General Courts Martial and Courts of Inquiry of the Navy Department, 1799-1867, Court of Inquiry, #4349, January 16, 1865, NARS M-273, roll 170, frames 0002-0048
"Vessel Papers" (manuscript records), United States National Archives, Washington, DC, Record Group 109, file P-102
"General Map of Charleston Harbor, South Carolina, Showing Rebel Defenses and Obstructions," drawn by E. Willenbucher, (U.S. Coast Survey, 1865)
History of the Confederate States Navy From its Organization to the Surrender of its Last Vessel, by J. Thomas Scharf, (New York, New York, 1887), p. 705
Official Records of the Union and Confederate Armies in the War of the Rebellion, (Washington, DC, 1895), Series 1, Volume 47, Part 1, pp. 1068, 1134, 1135
Official Records of the Union and Confederate Navies in the War of the Rebellion, (Washington, DC, 1903), Series 1, Volume 16, pp. 171-180, 184, 205, 258, 296, 297, 311, 339, 344, 350, 352, 353, 365, 36, 376, 388, 404, 405, 407, 415-417, 432
Official Records of the Union and Confederate Navies in the War of the Rebellion, (Washington, DC, 1921), Series 2, Volume 1, pp. 170, 171

The "Real Rhett Butler" & Other Revelations

The Navy in the Civil War, (Charles Scribner's Sons, New York, NY, 1903), Volume 1 ("The Blockade and the Cruisers" by James Russell Soley), p. 249
The Navy in the Civil War, (Charles Scribner's Sons, New York, NY, 1905), Volume 2 ("The Atlantic Coast" by Daniel Ammen), pp. 148, 154
Memorial monument to the dead of the *U.S.S. Patapsco*, located at Fort Moultrie, Sullivan's Island, South Carolina
Guide to Sunken Ships in American Waters, by Adrian L. Lonsdale and H.R. Kaplan, (Arlington, VA, 1964), p. 70
Naval History of the Civil War, by Howard P. Nash, (A.S. Barnes & Co., New York, NY, 1972), p. 214
Shipwrecks of the Civil War: The Encyclopedia of Union and Confederate Naval Losses, by Donald Shomette, (Washington, DC, 1973), pp. 118-120
Charleston's Maritime Heritage 1670-1865, by P.C. Coker III, (CokerCraft Press, Charleston, SC, 1987), pp. 224-232, 234, 244, 249, 282, 265
Charleston's Maritime Heritage 1670-1865, by P.C. Coker III, (CokerCraft Press, Charleston, SC, 1987), p. 255
Warships of the Civil War Navies, by Paul H. Silverstone, (Naval Institute Press, Annapolis, MD, 1989), p. 8

1865-1-US-SC/GA-3: The blockade running steamer *John Randolph* was wrecked on Sullivan's Island on January 20, 1865. [Note One: The *John Randolph* was manufactured by John Laird at Birkenhead, Scotland, and sent to Savannah, Georgia, in pieces. The prefabricated pieces were assembled by John Cant at Savannah in 1834, making the *John Randolph* one of the first three iron hulled vessels built in the United States (she was predated by the steamer *Coduras* and an unnamed coal barge). Her distinction lies in the fact that she was the first "commercially successful" metal hull vessel used in the United States.] [Note Two: The *John Randolph* was 100' (or 108') in length, 22' in breadth (not counting her paddle wheels), 8' to 9' (or 7') in depth of hold, and 2'9" in draft. The bottom of the vessel's hull was of English rolled boiler plate iron 5/16" thick, with the upper strakes being 1/4" thick. She was 177 (or 122, or 155) tons, had one deck, a round stern, no galleries, no masts, and no figure head. She was powered by a thirty-six horsepower condensing steam engine manufactured by Fawcett, Preston and Company of Liverpool. Her engine cylinder was 30" in diameter and she had a 5' piston stroke. She was issued an Enrollment by the Confederate government at Charleston, South Carolina, on September 4, 1861. That enrollment showed her as owned by George W. Mansfield, and as captained by Daniel O'Leary. By September of 1864, she was still considered a good boat, but needed a new boiler and other repairs. She was then being used as a transport in Charleston Harbor by the Confederate government and could carry 500 men.]

References for 1865-1-US-SC/GA-3:

"Record of Metal Vessels Built in the United States," (bound manuscript prepared by the Bureau of Navigation), Volume 1, p. 3, National Archives, Record Group 41
"Enrollment #3," (Savannah, GA), June 28, 1860, National Archives, Record Group 41
"Confederate States Enrollment," (Charleston, SC), September 4, 1861, National Archives, Record Group 109, Vessel File, J-52-4
Official Records of the Union and Confederate Armies in the War of the Rebellion, (Washington, DC, 1891), Series 1, Volume 35, Part 2, pp. 624, 625
Official Records of the Union and Confederate Navies in the War of the Rebellion, (Washington, DC, 1901), Series 1, Volume 12, p. 787

Treasures of the Confederate Coast

Merchant Steam Vessels of the United States 1807-1868, ("Lytle List"), by William M. Lytle, (Mystic, CT, 1952), p. 102

Georgia Historical Quarterly, ("The John Randolph: America's First Commercially Successful Iron Steamboat"), June, 1952, Volume 36, #2, pp. 32-45

Georgia Historical Markers, by C.P. Scruggs, p. 70

Civil War Naval Chronology 1861-1865, compiled by Navy History Division, Navy Department, (Washington, DC, 1971), p. VI-290

1865-1-US-SC/GA-4: The United States gunboat *Dai Ching* was run aground in the Combahee River at the first bend below the Confederate battery at Tar Bluff, South Carolina and destroyed on January 31, 1865. (Note One: The grounding was attributed to the *Dai Ching's* pilot leaving his post to hide below during heavy shelling by the Confederates as she attempted to slip past Tar Bluff. The steamer still could have been saved if it had not been for the failure of the United States tug *Cloverleaf* to come to the aid of the gunboat when she was signaled. That failure was attributed to cowardice on the part of the *Cloverleaf's* master, acting master Howarth, who's actions were deemed "highly reprehensible" by a Court of Inquiry convened January 26, 1865. The *Dai Ching's* crew defended their vessel valiantly until her guns were completely disabled. Her men then rolled the smaller guns over the side, spiked the others, set the steamer afire and abandoned her. The men then escaped through the marsh but were forced to sludge through miles of deep mud in the freezing cold to get to safety.) [Note Two: The *Dai Ching* was a propeller steamer, built in New York in 1862 as a gunboat for the emperor of China, but was purchased by the United States government from R.B. Catherwood for $117,575. At the time of her purchase she was described as an "exceedingly pretty vessel." She was built under the direction of James C. Jewell (or Jewett), master builder, and measured 728 89/95 tons (520 tons burden), 175'2" in length, 29'8" in breadth, 14'10" in depth of hold, and had an 11' draft. The *Dai Ching* had three masts, a round stern, a round tuck, and a scroll head. Her hull was of oak and locust (or live oak), and was copper and iron fastened. Her hull was metalled in December, 1862. She had a direct acting low pressure steam engine with two 32" (or 20") diameter cylinders each having a 26" piston stroke. The vessel was considered to have good security against fire and was rated A-1 for insurance purposes. She was of medium model and was bark rigged. She carried a complement of 83 men. The *Dai Ching* was armed with four 24-pounder smooth-bores, two 20-pounder Parrott rifles, and one 100-pounder Parrott rifle.] (Note Three: A marsh island has since formed at the site of the wreck, and is appropriately named Gunboat Island. The late Civil War ordnance historian, Tom Dickey of Atlanta, Georgia, reported that his research indicated that this wreck had been completely salvaged.)

References for 1865-1-US-SC/GA-4:
"Permanent Register #49," (New York, NY), December 24, 1862, National Archives, Record Group 41
American Lloyd's: Registry of American & Foreign Shipping, (New York, New York, 1863), p. 572, #136
New York Times, (New York, NY), Volume 12, #3607, April 16, 1863, p. 8, c. 1
New York Times, (New York, NY), Volume 14, #4168, February 2, 1865, p. 1, c. 5
New York Times, (New York, NY), Volume 14, #4170, February 5, 1865, p. 1, c. 4
"Savannah Daily Herald," (Savannah, GA), February 7, 1865, p. 2, c. 4
Records of General Courts Martial and Courts of Inquiry of the Navy Department, 1799-1867, Court of Inquiry, #4344, January 26, 1865, NARS M-273, roll 169, frames 0476-0486
"Vessel Disasters, 1864-1865," (bound annotated clipping file, Atlantic Mutual Insurance Companies of New York), Volume 39, pp. 247, 254
History of the Confederate States Navy From its Organization to the Surrender of its Last Vessel, by J. Thomas Scharf, (New York, New York, 1887), pp. 704, 705
Official Records of the Union and Confederate Navies in the War of the Rebellion, (Washington, DC, 1903), Series 1, Volume 16, pp. 192-200, 223-225, 366
Official Records of the Union and Confederate Navies in the War of the Rebellion, (Washington, DC, 1921), Series 2, Volume 1, p. 70
The Navy in the Civil War, (Charles Scribner's Sons, New York, NY, 1905), Volume 2 ("The Atlantic Coast" by Daniel Ammen), p. 155
Merchant Steam Vessels of the United States 1807-1868, ("Lytle List"), by William M. Lytle, (Mystic, CT, 1952), p. 44
List of American-Flag Merchant Vessels that Received Certificates of Enrollment or Registry at the Port of New York 1789-1867, compiled by Forest R. Holdcamper, (U.S. National Archives, Washington, DC, 1968), Special List #22, Volume 1, p. 163
Interview with Tom Dickey by E. Lee Spence at Isle of Palms, South Carolina, August, 1976
Warships of the Civil War Navies, by Paul H. Silverstone, (Naval Institute Press, Annapolis, MD, 1989), p. 88

1865-1x-US-SC/GA-1: The twin screw steamer *Rattlesnake* was run aground and destroyed on the northeast side of Breach Inlet, South Carolina, while attempting to run the blockade into Charleston in January of 1865. It was her second failed attempt. (Note One: The *Rattlesnake* had an iron hull and was built and engined by John and W. Dudgeon of Cubitt-town yard and the Sun engineering works, at London, England, in 1864. She was owned by Alexander Collie and Company. She was 200' in length, 25' in breadth, 13'6" in depth of hold, and 615 tons builder's measurement. The steamer had two stacks, was "clipper looking," with two schooner rigged masts. She was described as "almost a copy of the *Tallahassee*," but she had a poop and a deck house amidships. She was fitted out with engines of 200 h.p., collectively, with a diameter of cylinders of 34" and a 21" stroke of piston. Her twin propellers were 9' in diameter with 17'6" pitch. During time trials, the *Rattlesnake* was clocked at over 17 knots.) (Note Two: Stephen Wise in his book *Lifeline of the Confederacy* gives her dimensions as 200'x13'4"x9'6" and shows her as 529 gross tons and 259 registered tons.) (Note Three: I visually spotted a wreck at this location on a day when the water was extremely clear, but rough, during the summer of 1968. I did not get to examine the wreck because, when the boat's owner, John Cranston Coleman, turned his boat around to go back to the site, the boat was virtually swamped by a large wave, and we were unable to anchor for safety reasons. John now lives in Jacksonville, Florida.)

Treasures of the Confederate Coast

References for 1865-1x-US-SC/GA-1:
Times, (London, England), #25053, December 12, 1864, p. 12, c. 1
Times, (London, England), #25054, December 13, 1864, p. 11, c. 1
Times, (London, England), #25055, December 14, 1864, p. 7, c. 3
"General Map of Charleston Harbor, South Carolina, Showing Rebel Defenses and Obstructions," drawn by E. Willenbucher, (U.S. Coast Survey, 1865)
Blockade Running in Confederate Times, by M.P. Usina, (George Nichols Press, Savannah, 1895), pp. 38, 39
Official Records of the Union and Confederate Navies in the War of the Rebellion, (Washington, DC, 1903), Series 1, Volume 16, p. 354
Lifeline of the Confederacy: Blockade Running During the Civil War, by Stephen R. Wise, (University of South Carolina, Columbia, SC, 1983), pp. 485, 486488, 512, 608
Charleston's Maritime Heritage 1670-1865, by P.C. Coker III, (CokerCraft Press, Charleston, SC, 1987), pp. 288, 304

1865-1x-US-SC/GA-2: A listing in the *Official Records of the War of Rebellion* incorrectly shows the *C.S.S. Stono* (ex-*U.S.S. Isaac Smith*) as "burned by the Confederates at the evacuation of Charleston in 1865." The *Stono* was actually wrecked on Sullivan's Island in June of 1863. (Note: See entry 1863-6-US-SC/GA-2 for additional information and references on the *Stono*.)

References for 1865-1x-US-SC/GA-2:
Official Records of the Union and Confederate Navies in the War of the Rebellion, (Washington, DC, 1902), Series 1, Volume 14, pp. 190, 219, 252, 494
Official Records of the Union and Confederate Navies in the War of the Rebellion, (Washington, DC, 1921), Series 2, Volume 1, pp. 109, 267

1865-1-US-x-1: An order issued on January 23, 1865, by Rear Admiral David D. Porter of the United States Navy to Lieutenant-Commander Barnes, commanding the *U.S.S. Bat*, at Cape Fear River, North Carolina, stated "You will proceed as soon as you get a pilot, and the water will permit, around to Western Bar, Cape Fear River, and cruise along there, inshore, down as far as Georgetown, S.C., and cruise off that place and endeavor to open communication with General Sherman in case he should come there. At the same time keep a lookout for blockade runners and prevent them going into that port. In case of capturing a prize the men (aboard the prize) will be drawn up on the quarter deck and no one permitted to go below on pain of death. Have all the liquors and wines on board secured and locked up. Have all the hatches secured and sealed up and provisions taken out enough to last the voyage. Send all prizes captured to me here." (Note: The sidewheel steamer *Bat* was a former British blockade runner, she having been captured off the Western Bar on October 10, 1864, with a cargo of machinery for manufacturing shoes. Her papers and log book were destroyed by her captain. She was 230' in length, 26' in breadth, 9'6" in depth of hold, and drew 6'6" of water. She had "double, powerful oscillating engines, 180 horsepower, 52-inch cylinders of 4 feet stroke; draft, when loaded, 6 feet 6 inches," and could make over 13 knots. She was built of molded steel by Messrs. Jones, Quiggin & Co., of Liverpool, and was captured on her first trip. At the time of her capture, she was struck in her covered forecastle, and a shot from a 30-pounder rifle took off the leg of one Match Madick, an Australian, serving on board of her. Madick, who had been captain of the forecastle on board the *Alabama* at the time she lost her famous duel with the *Kearsarge*, died of his wounds.)

References for 1865-1-US-x-1:
Official Records of the Union and Confederate Navies in the War of the Rebellion, (Washington, D.C., 1900), Series 1, Volume 10, pp. 545-549
Official Records of the Union and Confederate Navies in the War of the Rebellion, (Washington, D.C., 1900), Series 1, Volume 11, pp. 631, 632

1865-2-US-NC-1: The United States picket boat *No. 3* was cut adrift from her ship on the night of February 19, 1865, at the mouth of the Cape Fear River, North Carolina, and "drifted to sea." She was a screw steamer.

Reference for 1865-2-US-NC-1:
Official Records of the Union and Confederate Navies in the War of the Rebellion, (Washington, DC, 1921), Series 2, Volume 1, p. 178

1865-2-US-NC-2: The twin screw steamer *Chickamauga* (ex-*Edith*) was scuttled and burned, by the Confederates, across the narrow part of the channel at Indian Wells on the North West Branch of the Cape Fear River, North Carolina, on February 25, 1865. At least two of her guns were mounted on a bluff on the western bank of the river. (Note One: One report shows her as destroyed at Gray's Point in the Cape Fear River.) (Note Two: The steamer had previously made eleven successful trips through the blockade. She had been built and engined in London, England, in 1864, by J.&W. Dudgeon. The vessel was owned and operated as the *Edith* by Collie and Company until September, 1864, when she was sold to the Confederate Navy and renamed the *Chickamauga*. She was not a privateer, but a regularly commissioned and officered vessel of the Provisional Navy of the Confederate States. The vessel had an iron hull and she was 175' in length, 25' in breadth, and 15' in depth of hold. She drew 9' forward and 10' aft. She was 370 gross tons and 239 tons register. She carried a crew of thirty-two men and officers. The *Chickamauga* was also shown as 585 tons, with a complement of one hundred and twenty men. One report gave her armament as one 84-pounder, two 24-pounders, and two 32-pounders, while others stated she was armed with three rifled cannon.) (Note Three: According to one source the current swept her alongside the bank where she "lay at peace till some enterprising Yankee a few years later raised her hull and converted her into an inglorious West India fruiter." According to the London *Times*, the *Chickamauga* was raised in late 1865 and was towed to Wilmington, where her machinery was declared to be "nearly perfect, owing to its having been heavily greased before she was sunk.") (Note Four: The

Treasures of the Confederate Coast

Chickamauga had been credited with destroying "several fine vessels and some smaller ones.") (Note Five: See also note three of entry 1865-1-US-NC-7.)

References for 1865-2-US-NC-2:
The Times, (London, England), #25372, December 19, 1865, p. 11, c. 4
History of the Confederate States Navy From its Organization to the Surrender of its Last Vessel, by J. Thomas Scharf, (New York, NY, 1887), p. 426
Official Records of the Union and Confederate Armies in the War of the Rebellion, (Washington, DC, 1895), Series 1, Volume 46, Part 2, p. 783
Official Records of the Union and Confederate Navies in the War of the Rebellion, (Washington, DC, 1900), Series 1, Volume 10, pp. 416, 468, 509, 510, 606, 750, 751, 774, 783, 793, 794, 801, 802
Official Records of the Union and Confederate Navies in the War of the Rebellion, (Washington, DC, 1900), Series 1, Volume 11, pp. 97, 441, 743, 786, 787
Official Records of the Union and Confederate Navies in the War of the Rebellion, (Washington, DC, 1901), Series 1, Volume 12, pp. 17, 53, 57, 63, 71
Official Records of the Union and Confederate Navies in the War of the Rebellion, (Washington, DC, 1921), Series 2, Volume 1, p. 250, and illustration opposite p. 250
Dictionary of American Naval Fighting Ships, (Washington, DC, 1963), Volume 2, p. 508
Lifeline of the Confederacy: Blockade Running During the Civil War, by Stephen R. Wise, (University Microfilms International, 1983), pp. 455, 456, 459-464, 485, 513, 556

1865-2-US-NC-3: The Confederate states gunboat *Yadkin*, Lieutenant Commander W.A. Kerr, was burned by the Confederates in the Cape Fear River in anticipation of the fall of Wilmington, North Carolina, in February, 1865. (Note: The *Yadkin* was built at Wilmington, North Carolina, in 1863-64. She was a small screw steamer with a wooden hull of about 300 tons and was armed with one gun. She served as flagship for Commodore W.F. Lynch and was described as a "small river steamer.")

References for 1865-2-US-NC-3:
History of the Confederate States Navy From its Organization to the Surrender of its Last Vessel, by J. Thomas Scharf, (New York, NY, 1887), p. 414
Official Records of the Union and Confederate Navies in the War of the Rebellion, (Washington, DC, 1921), Series 2, Volume 1, p. 272
A Chart of Wrecks of Vessels Sunk or Captured Near Wilmington, NC, Circa 1861-65, compiled by Charles H. Foard, (Wilmington, North Carolina, 1962)
Dictionary of American Naval Fighting Ships, (Washington, DC, 1963), Volume 2, pp. 582, 583
Iron Afloat: The Story of the Confederate Armorclads, by William N. Still Jr., (Vanderbilt University Press, 1971), p. 166

1865-2-US-NC-4: The Confederate States torpedo boat *Squib* (also called the *Infanta*) was destroyed in the Cape Fear River, North Carolina, by the Confederates to prevent her capture at the fall of Wilmington in February 1865. (Note: She was 46' in length, 6'3" in breadth, and 3'9" in depth. She was armed with a percussion torpedo on an 18' spar and was built for a crew of six men.)

References for 1865-2-US-NC-4:
Official Records of the Union and Confederate Navies in the War of the Rebellion, (Washington, DC, 1921), Series 2, Volume 1, p. 267
Official Records of the Union and Confederate Navies in the War of the Rebellion, (Washington, DC, 1899), Series 1, Volume 9, p. 602 (picture)
A Chart of Wrecks of Vessels Sunk or Captured Near Wilmington, NC, Circa 1861-65, compiled by Charles H. Foard, (Wilmington, North Carolina, 1962)
Dictionary of American Naval Fighting Ships, (Washington, DC, 1963), Volume 2, p. 567

1865-2-US-NC-5: The Confederate States tender *Caswell*, thirty-two men, was burned by her crew to prevent her from falling into the hands of the Federals during the fall of Wilmington, North Carolina,

The "Real Rhett Butler" & Other Revelations

in February of 1865. (Note: She was a sidewheel steamer and served as a tender on the Wilmington station. She had a wooden hull.)

References for 1865-2-US-NC-5:
Official Records of the Union and Confederate Navies in the War of the Rebellion, (Washington, DC, 1921), Series 2, Volume 1, p. 250
Dictionary of American Naval Fighting Ships, (Washington, DC, 1963), Volume 2, p. 506

1865-2-US-NC-6: Thomas Scharf in his *History of the Confederate States Navy* wrote that the United States launch *Shawmut* was destroyed by a Confederate torpedo (mine) in the Cape Fear River on February 20, 1865. (Note One: In actuality it was not the *Shawmut*, but one of the *Shawmut's* boats that was lost. Two men were killed and two wounded when a torpedo went off under the boat's bow.) (Note Two: The screw steamer *Shawmut*, 593 tons, was decommissioned at the New York Navy Yard on April 17, 1865.)

References for 1865-2-US-NC-6:
History of the Confederate States Navy From its Organization to the Surrender of its Last Vessel, by J. Thomas Scharf, (New York, NY, 1887), p. 768
Official Records of the Union and Confederate Navies in the War of the Rebellion, (Washington, DC, 1901), Series 1, Volume 12, pp. 44, 73, 74
Official Records of the Union and Confederate Navies in the War of the Rebellion, (Washington, DC, 1921), Series 2, Volume 1, p. 206

1865-2-US-NC-7: The schooner *Spray*, of Egg Harbor, New Jersey, Israel G. Adams master, bound from Fortress Monroe to Beaufort, with coal for the United States Army, was wrecked on the shoals about eleven miles SSE from Cape Lookout, North Carolina, on February 27, 1865. (Note: Because her stern was washed in and she was going to pieces very fast, her crew took refuge on the bowsprit and jib boom, from which they were rescued by a boat from the *U.S.S. Rhode Island* on March 2, 1865. Captain Adams reported that during the time they were on the wrecked schooner, "several vessels passed so near that he could see their signal for pilots without rendering any assistance.")

References for 1865-2-US-NC-7:
Official Records of the Union and Confederate Navies in the War of the Rebellion, (Washington, D.C., 1901), Series 1, Volume 12, p. 61
List of American-Flag Merchant Vessels that Received Certificates of Enrollment or Registry at the Port of New York 1789-1867, compiled by Forest R. Holdcamper, (U.S. National Archives, Washington, DC, 1968), Special List #22, Volume 2, p. 649

1865-2-US-NC-8: The steamer *North Easter* was scuttled by the Confederates as an obstruction near Fort Strong, Cape Fear, North Carolina, in February of 1865.

Reference for 1865-2-US-NC-8:
Official Records of the Union and Confederate Navies in the War of the Rebellion, (Washington, DC, 1901), Series 1, Volume 12, p. 45

1865-2-US-SC/GA-1: The blockade runner *Celt* (also shown as the *Colt*, or *Sylph*) was wrecked on the east side of Bowman's Jetty

Treasures of the Confederate Coast

near Fort Moultrie, Sullivan's Island, South Carolina, on February 14, 1865, after being impressed for use of the government. She was carrying a "valuable cargo of cotton." [Note One: The *Celt* was a sidewheel steamer launched from the ship yard of F.M. Jones at Charleston, South Carolina, on May 15, 1862. The *Celt* was described as "a beautifully modeled vessel of light draught, built in the most substantial manner with white oak and yellow pine." The vessel was 160' in length, 25' in breadth, and 9' in depth of hold. The *Celt* was designed to be used as either a cargo vessel or as a gunboat. She was capable of carrying 1,500 men "at a trip." The vessel had low pressure steam engines of about 250 horsepower. The *Celt* was owned by Captain John Ferguson (or Furguson) (also reported as owned by the Steamer *Celt* Company of Charleston). She was meant as a replacement for the steamer *Planter* which had been stolen from Captain Ferguson and run away with to the Federals by a black man named Robert Smalls.] (Note Two: There was a larger English steamer, also named *Celt,* that operated between Nassau and Matamoras during the Civil War, but it never attempted to run the blockade.) (Note Three: One hundred and ninety bales of cotton were salvaged by the Federals who also hoisted the United States over the wreck claiming it for the government. "A strict and careful survey" reported her "back broken, and full of water, and decks ripped up. The machinery is in an irreparable condition, some few pieces might be removed and be of service. Boilers are mostly below water, but judging from the condition of those parts visible, we are of the opinion they are not worth the expense of removing.") (Note Four: Using a copy of an 1865 photograph showing the wreck, National Park Service historian Ron Gibbs and I located and positively identified the remains of this vessel in 1965. A small part of the steamer still sticks out of the water at low tide but, due to marine growth, simply appears to be part of the scattered rocks from Bowman's Jetty. Bowman's Jetty is the jetty near Fort Moultrie that has a red nun buoy anchored at the offshore end of it.)

References for 1865-2-US-SC/GA-1:

"Charleston Daily Courier," (Charleston, SC), #19162, May 16, 1862, p. 1, c. 4

"Vessel Papers" (manuscript records), United States National Archives, Washington, DC, Record Group 109, file C-40

Official Records of the Union and Confederate Armies in the War of the Rebellion, (Washington, DC, 1891), Series 1, Volume 35, Part 2, p. 624

Official Records of the Union and Confederate Navies in the War of the Rebellion, (Washington, DC, 1903), Series 1, Volume 16, pp. 246, 256, 257, 258, 369

Photographic History of the Civil War, edited by F. T. Miller, (New York, New York, 1957), p. 103

Civil War Naval Chronology 1861-1865, compiled by Navy History Division, Navy Department, (Washington, DC, 1971), pp. V-39, V-42

Lifeline of the Confederacy: Blockade Running During the Civil War, by Stephen R. Wise, (University of South Carolina, Columbia, SC, 1983), pp. 488, 543, 544

The Blockade Runners, by Dave Horner, (Florida Classics Library, Port Salerno, FL, 1992), Chapter 14, pp. 25, 228

1865-2-US-SC/GA-2: The Confederate States receiving ship *Indian Chief*, Lieutenant Ray commanding, was burned by the Confederates at Charleston, South Carolina, during the evacuation of that city on February 18, 1865, to prevent her from falling into the hands of the Federal Navy. [Note: The vessel had also been used in support of the Charleston harbor torpedo (mine) operations, and in posting picket boats in the harbor at night.]

References for 1865-2-US-SC/GA-2:
History of the Confederate States Navy From its Organization to the Surrender of its Last Vessel, by J. Thomas Scharf, (New York, New York, 1887), pp. 674, 688, 692, 760
Official Records of the Union and Confederate Armies in the War of the Rebellion, (Washington, DC, 1895), Series 1, Volume 47, Part 1, pp. 1016, 1017
Official Records of the Union and Confederate Navies in the War of the Rebellion, (Washington, DC, 1921), Series 2, Volume 1, pp. 257, 273, 288
Dictionary of American Naval Fighting Ships, (Washington, DC, 1963), Volume 2, p. 536
Civil War Naval Chronology 1861-1865, compiled by Navy History Division, Navy Department, (Washington, DC, 1971), p. VI-251
Warships of the Civil War Navies, by Paul H. Silverstone, (Naval Institute Press, Annapolis, MD, 1989), p. 240

1865-2-US-SC/GA-3: The Confederate ironclad *Charleston* was stripped and burned at Charleston, South Carolina, during the evacuation of that city on February 18, 1865, by the Confederates to prevent her from falling into the hands of the Federal Navy. Her position was described as "at her anchorage opposite Mount Pleasant ferry wharf, in the Cooper River." [Note: The *Charleston* was built at Charleston in 1862 and was a source of pride to area residents. She was known as the "Ladies Gunboat" as she had been partly paid for through donations made by the women of Charleston. The *Charleston* carried a crew of 150 (or 140) men and was armed with four rifled guns (also shown as six 8-inch rifled guns, and as two 8-inch rifles and four rifled 42-pounders), and was sometimes referred to as a sloop of war. The ironclad steamer was 180' in length, 34' in breadth, and 14' in depth of hold. The *Charleston*, Captain Brown, served as Commodore Tucker's flagship for the Confederate squadron at Charleston, and was capable of 6 or 7 knots.]

References for 1865-2-US-SC/GA-3:
"Vessel Papers" (manuscript records), United States National Archives, Washington, DC, Record Group 109, file C-41
History of the Confederate States Navy From its Organization to the Surrender of its Last Vessel, by J. Thomas Scharf, (New York, New York, 1887), pp. 671, 706
Official Records of the Union and Confederate Armies in the War of the Rebellion, (Washington, DC, 1895), Series 1, Volume 47, Part 1, pp. 1016, 1019
Official Records of the Union and Confederate Navies in the War of the Rebellion, (Washington, DC, 1903), Series 1, Volume 16, pp. 23, 355, 372, 387
Official Records of the Union and Confederate Navies in the War of the Rebellion, (Washington, DC, 1921), Series 2, Volume 1, pp. 250, 273-282
Confederate Military History, edited by General Clement A. Evans, (Confederate Publishing Co., Atlanta, GA, 1899), Volume 12, p. 108
The Navy in the Civil War, (Charles Scribner's Sons, New York, NY, 1905), Volume 2 ("The Atlantic Coast" by Daniel Ammen), p. 157
Civil War Naval Chronology 1861-1865, compiled by Navy History Division, Navy Department, (Washington, DC, 1971), pp. V-42, V-43, VI-208

Treasures of the Confederate Coast

Warships of the Civil War Navies, by Paul H. Silverstone, (Naval Institute Press, Annapolis, MD, 1989), p. 207

1865-2-US-SC/GA-4: The Confederate ironclad ram *Chicora*, Commander John R. Tucker (or Captain Hunter), was stripped and burned at Charleston, South Carolina, during the evacuation of that city on February 18, 1865, by the Confederates to prevent her from falling into the hands of the Federal Navy. [Note One: The *Chicora* carried a crew of one hundred and fifty men (or 60) and was armed with two (or four) 8-inch (or 32-pounder) rifles forward and aft, and two 9-inch Dahlgren smooth-bores on each side. The 32-pounders had been banded and were said to have been altered to allow them to fire a 62-pound projectile. Her armament was also reported as six 8-inch rifles. The ironclad steamer was 150' in length, 35' in breadth, and 12' (or 14') in depth of hold. The *Chicora* was built at a cost of $263,892. She was said to have had 500 tons of iron in her armour. Although one account stated that she could make four knots "with a clean bottom," another said her engines were so weak that she could "hardly stem the tide."] (Note Two: The top of her casemate was above water at low tide.)

References for 1865-2-US-SC/GA-4:
"Vessel Papers" (manuscript records), United States National Archives, Washington, DC, Record Group 109, file C-66
History of the Confederate States Navy From its Organization to the Surrender of its Last Vessel, by J. Thomas Scharf, (New York, NY, 1887), pp. 670-672, 678, 691, 698-701, 706
Official Records of the Union and Confederate Armies in the War of the Rebellion, (Washington, DC, 1895), Series 1, Volume 47, Part 1, p. 1016
Official Records of the Union and Confederate Navies in the War of the Rebellion, (Washington, DC, 1903), Series 1, Volume 16, pp. 23, 355, 372, 387
Official Records of the Union and Confederate Navies in the War of the Rebellion, (Washington, DC, 1921), Series 2, Volume 1, pp. 250, 273, 283, 284
Confederate Military History, edited by General Clement A. Evans, (Confederate Publishing Co., Atlanta, GA, 1899), Volume 12, p. 107
The Navy in the Civil War, (Charles Scribner's Sons, New York, NY, 1905), Volume 2 ("The Atlantic Coast" by Daniel Ammen), p. 157
Civil War Naval Chronology 1861-1865, compiled by Navy History Division, Navy Department, (Washington, DC, 1971), pp. V-42, V-43, VI-211, VI-279
Charleston's Maritime Heritage 1670-1865, by P.C. Coker III, (CokerCraft Press, Charleston, SC, 1987), pp. 224-232, 234, 244, 249, 282, 265
Warships of the Civil War Navies, by Paul H. Silverstone, (Naval Institute Press, Annapolis, MD, 1989), p. 205

1865-2-US-SC/GA-5: The Confederate States ironclad ram *Palmetto State*, Lieutenant Rochelle commanding, was stripped and burned at Charleston, South Carolina, during the evacuation of that city on February 18, 1865, by the Confederates to prevent her from falling into the hands of the Federal Navy. (Note: The *Palmetto State* was armed with ten 7-inch rifles, four being on each side and one on the bow and one on the stern. One account stated she was armed with only five guns, and another says she carried just four guns, one being an 80-pounder, one a 60-pounder, and two 8-inch shell guns. The ram was built by Cameron and Company at Charleston in 1862 under the supervision of flag officer D.N. Ingraham. The ironclad

The "Real Rhett Butler" & Other Revelations

could make six knots and measured 150' in length, 34' in breadth, 14' in depth, and 12' in draft.)

References for 1865-2-US-SC/GA-5:

"Vessel Papers" (manuscript records), United States National Archives, Washington, DC, Record Group 109, file P-28

History of the Confederate States Navy From its Organization to the Surrender of its Last Vessel, by J. Thomas Scharf, (New York, New York, 1887), pp. 670, 689, 698, 701, 706

Official Records of the Union and Confederate Armies in the War of the Rebellion, (Washington, DC, 1895), Series 1, Volume 47, Part 1, p. 1016

Official Records of the Union and Confederate Navies in the War of the Rebellion, (Washington, DC, 1903), Series 1, Volume 16, pp. 23, 355, 372, 387

Official Records of the Union and Confederate Navies in the War of the Rebellion, (Washington, DC, 1921), Series 2, Volume 1, pp. 141, 258, 262, 273, 298, and illustration opposite p. 262

Confederate Military History, edited by General Clement A. Evans, (Confederate Publishing Co., Atlanta, GA, 1899), Volume 12, p. 107

The Navy in the Civil War, (Charles Scribner's Sons, New York, NY, 1905), Volume 2 ("The Atlantic Coast" by Daniel Ammen), p. 157

Civil War Naval Chronology 1861-1865, compiled by Navy History Division, Navy Department, (Washington, DC, 1971), pp. V-42, V-43, VI-279

Charleston's Maritime Heritage 1670-1865, by P.C. Coker III, (CokerCraft Press, Charleston, SC, 1987), pp. 203, 224-230, 232, 244

Warships of the Civil War Navies, by Paul H. Silverstone, (Naval Institute Press, Annapolis, MD, 1989), p. 205

1865-2-US-SC/GA-6: Three Confederate torpedo boats (called "Davids") were discovered sunk in the Cooper River (two were later raised) shortly after the February 18, 1865, evacuation of Charleston. The vessels were described 64' in length and 5'6" in diameter (and as 50'x6'x5'). They had apparently been scuttled by the Confederates to prevent them from falling into the hands of the Federal Navy. (Note One: The original *David* was built at Stoney Landing near Monks Corner, South Carolina. According to its builder, David Ebaugh, he named it for himself, and not for David in the biblical story of David and Goliath. The *David's* 1863 attack on a Federal gunboat *New Ironsides* failed, but earned the craft a place in the books as "the most important development in naval warfare in over 2,000 years.") (Note Two: During and after the war, many Confederate and Federal navy officers classed the Confederate submarine *H.L. Hunley* as a "David.") (Note Three: Long after the war ended, at least two of these cigar shaped, semi-submersible boats were reported as still sitting abandoned and rotting in the mud along Chisolm's causeway. This area has since been filled and paved as an extension of Tradd Street in Charleston.)

References for 1865-2-US-SC/GA-6:

"Charleston Mercury," Volume 83, #11892, October 26, 1863, p. 1, c. 4, 5 and J.T. Scharf (1887) p. 758-761

"Charleston Daily Courier" Volume 61, #19626, November 18, 1863, p. 1, c. 3

Official Records of the Union and Confederate Armies in the War of the Rebellion, (Washington, DC, 1890), Series 1, Volume 28, Part 1, pp. 141, 404, 680, 681, 731-735

Official Records of the Union and Confederate Armies in the War of the Rebellion, (Washington, DC, 1890), Series 1, Volume 28, Part 2, pp. 462, 500, 504, 510, 525

Confederate Military History, edited by General Clement A. Evans, (Confederate Publishing Co., Atlanta, GA, 1899), Volume 12, pp. 75, 76

The Navy in the Civil War, (Charles Scribner's Sons, New York, NY, 1905), Volume 2 ("The Atlantic Coast" by Daniel Ammen), p. 157

"David C. Ebaugh on the building of the *David*," in the *South Carolina Historical Magazine*, (Charleston, South Carolina

Dictionary of American Naval Fighting Ships, (Washington, DC, 1963), Volume 2, pp. 513, 514

Treasures of the Confederate Coast

Charleston's Maritime Heritage 1670-1865, by P.C. Coker III, (CokerCraft Press, Charleston, SC, 1987), pp. 203, 256-262
Warships of the Civil War Navies, by Paul H. Silverstone, (Naval Institute Press, Annapolis, MD, 1989), p. 219

1865-2-US-x-1: A report from the Bahamas dated February 3, 1865, stated "Nassau is a doomed city so far as the contraband trade • • • 30 of her fleet of law defying steam vessels, idle and without employment" and "sailing craft which can be counted by the hundred." Her warehouses were said to be filled with goods for which there was no market. Subsequent reports told of the return of the blockade runner fleet to England.

References for 1865-2-US-x-1:
Times, (London, England), # 25123, March 3, 1865, p. 9, c. 6
Times, (London, England), # 25179, May 8, 1865, p. 9, c. 6

1865-2x-US-NC-1: The Confederate States gunboat *Equator* was burned by the Confederates in the Cape Fear River to prevent her from falling into the hands of the Federals in January or February, 1865, in anticipation of the fall of Wilmington, North Carolina. (Note: The *Equator* was a small, sidewheel, river steamer with a wooden hull and was formerly a tug. She was armed with only one gun.)

References for 1865-2x-US-NC-1:
History of the Confederate States Navy From its Organization to the Surrender of its Last Vessel, by J. Thomas Scharf, (New York, NY, 1887), p. 414
Official Records of the Union and Confederate Navies in the War of the Rebellion, (Washington, DC, 1921), Series 2, Volume 1, pp. 252, 273
A Chart of Wrecks of Vessels Sunk or Captured Near Wilmington, NC, Circa 1861-65, compiled by Charles H. Foard, (Wilmington, North Carolina, 1962)
Dictionary of American Naval Fighting Ships, (Washington, DC, 1963), Volume 2, p. 518
Iron Afloat: The Story of the Confederate Armorclads, by William N. Still Jr., (Vanderbilt University Press, 1971), p. 166

1865-3-US-NC-1: The United States transport steamer *Thorn* (or *Thorne*) was blown up by a Confederate torpedo and sunk in just two minutes on March 4, 1865, in the Cape Fear River just below Fort Anderson, North Carolina. Her crew barely escaped with their lives. (Note: The *Thorn* had a wooden hull, was 403 tons and was built at Mystic, Connecticut, in 1862. Her first home port was Stonington, Connecticut. She was issued a certificate of steam enrollment at the port of New York on December 3, 1863.)

References for 1865-3-US-NC-1:
"Savannah Daily Herald," (Savannah, GA), Volume 1, #50, March 20, 1865, p. 4, c. 3
History of the Confederate States Navy From its Organization to the Surrender of its Last Vessel, by J. Thomas Scharf, (New York, NY, 1887), p. 768
Official Records of the Union and Confederate Armies in the War of the Rebellion, (Washington, DC, 1895), Series 1, Volume 47, Part 3, p. 729
A Chart of Wrecks of Vessels Sunk or Captured Near Wilmington, NC, Circa 1861-65, compiled by Charles H. Foard, (Wilmington, North Carolina, 1962)
List of American-Flag Merchant Vessels that Received Certificates of Enrollment or Registry at the Port of New York 1789-1867, compiled by Forest R. Holdcamper, (U.S. National Archives, Washington, DC, 1968), Special List #22, Volume 2, p. 680
Encyclopedia of American Shipwrecks, by Bruce D. Berman, Mariners Press, (Boston, MA, 1972), p. 147, #1923

The "Real Rhett Butler" & Other Revelations

Merchant Steam Vessels of the United States 1790-1868, ("Lytle-Holdcamper List"), by William M. Lytle and Forrest R. Holdcamper, revised and edited by C. Bradford Mitchell, (Staten Island, NY, 1975), pp. 212, 301

1865-3-US-NC-2: The Confederate States ironclad sloop-of-war *Neuse* was scuttled and set on fire by the Confederates on March 12, 1865, in the Neuse River, near Kinston, North Carolina, where she had been aground for some time. She was destroyed on the retreat of General Hardee after the battle of Kinston, to prevent her from being captured by Sherman's advancing army. [Note One: The *Neuse* had been built at Kinston in 1863-64 by Elliot, Smith and Company. She was 152' in length, 34' in breadth, and drew 9' of water. She was armed with two 6.4" guns (also reported as two 8" guns).] [Note Two: Her guns, armor plating, and machinery were salvaged in the 1800's but the hull remained relatively undisturbed until late 1961 when Henry Clay Casey, Lemuel Houston, and Thomas Carlye initiated efforts to raise her. The vessel (along with approximately 15,000 artifacts) was finally pulled from the water in late 1963, and is now housed at the Richard Caswell Memorial Park (Caswell/Neuse State Historic Site) at Kinston. The definitive book on the vessel is the *C.S.S. Neuse: A Question of Iron and Time*.] (Note Three: Some sources incorrectly show the *Neuse* as sunk in the Cape Fear River.)

References for 1865-3-US-NC-2:

History of the Confederate States Navy From its Organization to the Surrender of its Last Vessel, by J. Thomas Scharf, (New York, NY, 1887), p. 414
Confederate Military History, edited by General Clement A. Evans, (Confederate Publishing Co., Atlanta, GA, 1899), Volume 12, p. 108
Official Records of the Union and Confederate Navies in the War of the Rebellion, (Washington, D.C., 1901), Series 1, Volume 12, pp. 166, 191
Official Records of the Union and Confederate Navies in the War of the Rebellion, (Washington, DC, 1921), Series 2, Volume 1, pp. 261, 273
"The Career of the Confederate Ram Neuse," by L.V. Archbell, (published in the *North Carolina Historical Review*, #43, 1966), p. 1-13
"The Confederate Ram Neuse," by L.V. Archbell, (published in the *Carolina and the Southern Cross*, November, 1913), pp. 3-5
"The Confederate Navy Yard at Charlotte, North Carolina, 1862-1865," by Alexander Violet, (published in the *Southern Historical Society Papers*, #40, 1915), pp. 184-192
Dictionary of American Naval Fighting Ships, (Washington, DC, 1963), Volume 2, p. 552
"Operation Ram Neuse," by David H. Pierce, (unpublished manuscript, Virginia Military Institute, Lexington, VA, 1963)
A Chart of Wrecks of Vessels Sunk or Captured Near Wilmington, NC, Circa 1861-65, compiled by Charles H. Foard, (Wilmington, North Carolina, 1962)
Iron Afloat: The Story of the Confederate Armorclads, by William N. Still Jr., (Vanderbilt University Press, 1971), p. 221
C.S.S. Neuse: A Question of Iron and Time, by Leslie S. Bright, William H. Rowland, and James C. Bardon, (Raleigh, NC, 1981), pp. vii, 17, 19, 25, 37

1865-3-US-NC-3: The sternwheel steamer *Caldwell*, fifty-one tons, was burnt at Fayetteville, North Carolina, on March 14, 1865. (Note: She had a wood hull and was built at Fayetteville, North Carolina, in 1859. Her first home port was Beaufort, North Carolina.)

References for 1865-3-US-NC-3:

Encyclopedia of American Shipwrecks, by Bruce D. Berman, Mariners Press, (Boston, MA, 1972), p. 111, #279

Treasures of the Confederate Coast

Merchant Steam Vessels of the United States 1790-1868, ("Lytle-Holdcamper List"), by William M. Lytle and Forrest R. Holdcamper, revised and edited by C. Bradford Mitchell, (Staten Island, NY, 1975), pp. 28, 247

1865-3-US-NC-4: The sidewheel steamer *Chatham* was burned at Fayetteville, North Carolina, on March 14, 1865. (Note: The *Chatham* was built in 1850 at Newbern, North Carolina, which was also her first home port. She had a wood hull and was 57 tons. She went to Confederate registry in 1861.)

Reference for 1865-3-US-SC/GA-4:
Merchant Steam Vessels of the United States 1790-1868, ("Lytle-Holdcamper List"), by William M. Lytle and Forrest R. Holdcamper, revised and edited by C. Bradford Mitchell, (Staten Island, NY, 1975), p. 34 (entry for *Chatham*, and note 5)

1865-3-US-NC-5: The United States government transport *General Lyon* caught fire and wrecked on the coast of North Carolina, on March 25, 1865. [Note One: She was a wooden hulled, screw steamer of 1,026 tons. She was built at East Haddam, Connecticut, in 1864, and was first home ported at Middletown, Connecticut. Some reports stated that she was sixty miles off Cape Hatteras when she caught fire but that she eventually drifted into the breakers where she was totally lost. The steamer had been bound from Hilton Head, South Carolina, (one report says Smithville) to Fort Monroe, Virginia. Her captain became crazed with fear and despite the assistance of the U.S. transport *General Sedgewick*, Captain Starkey, nearly all of between 550 and 600 troops and refugees aboard the steamer perished in the flames. Only twenty-nine people were believed to have been saved. The vessel was entirely destroyed. The unfortunate screw steamer was formerly a blockade runner. Her passengers consisted of discharged and paroled soldiers, escaped prisoners, and refugees, among them about thirty women and twenty-five children. There were two freed slaves among the refugees. "There were several barrels of oil (kerosene) in the engine-room, and the wind blowing a hurricane, some of these rolled upon the boiler and ignited. When the engines stopped, the vessel swung round with her broadside to the wind, and the flames spread with fearful rapidity. Two vessels which hove in sight could render no aid, the storm raging fiercely, and the burning steamer having drifted in towards the breakers. The captain, who (was) described as 'crazed with fear,' leapt into the first boat launched; she drifted instantly under the stern of the vessel, struck the screw, and went down with the captain and all but three of the ten men in her. A second boat with 27 persons, succeeded in reaching the *General Sedgewick* ••• but was dashed violently against the side of that ship and went down, seven only of her passengers escaping. A number of men threw themselves overboard, with doors or spars or the like

The "Real Rhett Butler" & Other Revelations

for support, and a cavalry soldier was saved by being picked up after thus floating for three hours. There were 200 men of the 56th Illinois Regiment on board, and it is not known that more than five of them were saved." "The frightful shrieks of the women and children, and their piteous supplications for help, were drowned by the roaring of the storm. Several of the paroled soldiers were sick and confined to their berths. Some of them managed to crawl on deck, and clung there until washed overboard by the waves." Despite valiant efforts by the crew, who had remained calm even after the captain's display of cowardice, "many of those below were ••• suffocated. The shrieks and moans of the dying came up to those on the deck, and they could do nothing to save them."] (Note Two: Some accounts put the total loss of life at four hundred people.)

References for 1865-3-US-NC-5:
New York Times, (New York Times, NY), Volume 14, #4219, April 3, 1865, p. 5, c. 1
New York Times, (New York Times, NY), Volume 14, #4229, April 14, 1865, p. 1, c. 2
"Savannah Daily Herald," (Savannah, GA), Volume 1, #72, April 11, 1865, p. 1, c. 1-3
Times, (London, England), # 25160, April 15, 1865, p. 9, c. 3
Times, (London, England), # 25166, April 22, 1865, p. 12, c. 2
Times, (London, England), # 25170, April 27, 1865, p. 6, c. 4, 5
Annual Report of the Supervising Inspector of Steamboats, Volume 6, #3, p. 215, serial doc. #1254
Official Records of the Union and Confederate Armies in the War of the Rebellion, (Washington, DC, 1900), Series III, Volume 5, pp. 228, 288
Encyclopedia of American Shipwrecks, by Bruce D. Berman, Mariners Press, (Boston, MA, 1972), p. 121, #745
Merchant Steam Vessels of the United States 1790-1868, ("Lytle-Holdcamper List"), by William M. Lytle and Forrest R. Holdcamper, revised and edited by C. Bradford Mitchell, (Staten Island, NY, 1975), pp. 81, 263

1865-3-US-NC-6: A report from Superintendent G.J. Rains, of the Confederate Torpedo Bureau, to the Confederate Secretary of War, Honorable J.C. Beckinridge, dated March 31, 1865, stated that six United States vessels were destroyed by Confederate torpedoes (mines) while they were ascending the Roanoke River in North Carolina.

Reference for 1865-3-US-NC-6:
Official Records of the Union and Confederate Armies in the War of the Rebellion, (Washington, DC, 1895), Series 1, Volume 47, Part 3, p. 729

1865-3-US-SC/GA-1: On March 1, 1865, while the United States gunboat *Harvest Moon*, was going up the river to Georgetown, South Carolina, a torpedo (Confederate mine) exploded near her, shattering her wheel house and injuring her hull so badly that she quickly sank in Winyah Bay. Her ward room steward was killed, but the remainder of her officers and men were saved. [Note One: The *Harvest Moon* was a sidewheel steamer measuring 193' in length, 29' in breadth, and 10' in depth of hold, with a draft of 8'. She was serving as Admiral Dahlgren's flagship when she was lost. The vessel was launched at Portland, Maine, on November 22, 1862, and was completed in 1863. Her first home port was at Boston. She was purchased at Boston on November 16, 1863, by

Treasures of the Confederate Coast

Commodore J.B. Montgomery from Charles Spear for $99,300. She was commissioned at Boston Navy Yard on February 12, 1864. The *Harvest Moon* had a wood hull with a vertical beam engine (41" diameter cylinder with a 10' piston stroke). She averaged nine miles an hour and could make a maximum of fifteen miles per hour. She was armed with one 20-pounder Parrott rifle, four 24-pounder howitzers, and one 12-pounder rifle. She carried a complement of 72 men.] (Note Two: The *Harvest Moon's* logbook is in the National Archives, and apparently includes some data on salvage efforts as covers the period February 12, 1864, through April 20, 1865. She "was abandoned, after taking out machinery, etc.) (Note Three: Drew Ruddy, Steve Howard, John Coleman and I visited this wreck in the mid 1960's. We tied up to her stack which stuck out of the water. Ruddy, who was then about fifteen and still a novice diver, was extremely safety minded and recited a long list of signals and things to do if anyone got into trouble on the wreck. As he went to go overboard, he tripped and fell head first into the murky waters. Seconds later he reappeared. His head was covered with sticky black mud, and he quipped "if you get in trouble, just stand up." The wrecked gunboat was almost entirely buried in mud and sand. Her stack stuck out of the water which, due to heavy silting, was only about three feet deep. Ruddy later held the record for deep diving in a mechanical suit, and made international news when he found the Bank of Rome safe on the wreck of the *Andrea Doria*.)

References for 1865-3-US-SC/GA-1:
"Steam Vessels #1, 1850's," (bound manuscript, Atlantic Mutual Insurance Companies of New York), entry for *Harvest Moon*
"Savannah Daily Herald," (Savannah, GA), #41, March 7, 1865, p. 2, c. 1
Times, (London, England), #25136, March 18, 1865, p. 14, c. 1
Records of General Courts Martial and Courts of Inquiry of the Navy Department, 1799-1867, Court of Inquiry, #4319, NARS M-273, roll 167, frames 0647-0695
"Vessel Papers" (manuscript records), United States National Archives, Washington, DC, Record Group 109, file H-106
"Description and Disposition of U.S. Vessels, Navy Dept.," (bound manuscript), Volume 1, National Archives, Record Group 45, entry 287
History of the Confederate States Navy From its Organization to the Surrender of its Last Vessel, by J. Thomas Scharf, (New York, New York, 1887), p. 705
Official Records of the Union and Confederate Armies in the War of the Rebellion, (Washington, DC, 1895), Series 1, Volume 47, Part 1, pp. 1008, 1009
Official Records of the Union and Confederate Navies in the War of the Rebellion, (Washington, DC, 1903), Series 1, Volume 16, pp. 282-284, 366, 371, 386
Official Records of the Union and Confederate Navies in the War of the Rebellion, (Washington, DC, 1921), Series 2, Volume 1, p. 99
The Navy in the Civil War, (Charles Scribner's Sons, New York, NY, 1905), Volume 2 ("The Atlantic Coast" by Daniel Ammen), p. 148
Logbooks of the United States Navy Ships, Stations and Units 1801-1947, p. 126
Merchant Steam Vessels of the United States 1790-1868, ("Lytle-Holdcamper List"), edited by C. Bradford Mitchell, (Staten Island, NY, 1975), p. 92
Warships of the Civil War Navies, by Paul H. Silverstone, (Naval Institute Press, Annapolis, MD, 1989), p. 84

1865-3-US-SC/GA-2: The sidewheel steamer *Cosmopolitan* which left Savannah on March 3, 1865, for Hilton Head, went ashore on

The "Real Rhett Butler" & Other Revelations

the lower end of the North Breakers, six miles due north of Tybee Light, Georgia. The steamer was later reported off. (Note: The 774 ton steamer had a wood hull and was built at New York, New York, in 1861. She was launched as the *Zouave*, but was documented *Cosmopolitan*. She was renamed and documented as the *Havana* on January 28, 1871; renamed *Paul Koch* on April 20, 1897; and renamed *Edmund Butler* on September 26, 1899.)

References for 1865-3-US-SC/GA-2:
"Savannah Daily Herald," (Savannah, GA), #44, March 4, 1865, p. 2, c. 3
"Savannah Daily Herald," (Savannah, GA), #46, March 6, 1865, p. 2, c. 3
List of American-Flag Merchant Vessels that Received Certificates of Enrollment or Registry at the Port of New York 1789-1867, compiled by Forest R. Holdcamper, (U.S. National Archives, Washington, DC, 1968), Special List #22, Volume 1, pp. 154, 155 note 2
Merchant Steam Vessels of the United States 1790-1868, ("Lytle-Holdcamper List"), edited by C. Bradford Mitchell, (Staten Island, NY, 1975), p. 46

1865-3-US-SC/GA-3: On March 4, 1865, the ship *Lawrence*, of New York, Captain N.C. Johnson, bound to New York with 2376 bales of cotton, drifted on the North Breaker near Tybee, Georgia, where she lost most of her false keel and suffered a "fair amount of damage" before being towed off by the steamer *Resolute*. (Note One: The *Resolute* towed her into Cockspur Roads, Georgia, where she was beached on a mud flat with ten feet of water in her hold. The *Lawrence* was repaired by divers from the schooner *Compromise*, Captain Brown, using a "steam pump, diving armor, and the necessary wrecking apparatus and operatives.") [Note Two: The *Lawrence* was about one thousand (998) tons burden and was owned by Messrs. Lawrence, Giles and Company. She was built at Damariscotta (sic), Maine, in 1861, and was issued a certificate of register at the port of New York on March 18, 1862.]

References for 1865-3-US-SC/GA-3:
"Savannah Daily Herald," (Savannah, GA), #46, March 6, 1865, p. 2, c. 4
"Savannah Daily Herald," (Savannah, GA), #60, March 22, 1865, p. 2, c. 3
"Savannah Daily Herald," (Savannah, GA), #90, May 1, 1865, p. 2, c. 2
"New York Journal of Commerce," (New York, NY), #2569, March 20, 1865, p. 3, c. 5
List of American-Flag Merchant Vessels that Received Certificates of Enrollment or Registry at the Port of New York 1789-1867, compiled by Forest R. Holdcamper, (U.S. National Archives, Washington, DC, 1968), Special List #22, Volume 2, p. 410

1865-3-US-SC/GA-4: The Confederate States gunboat *Pee Dee* (or *Peedee*, or *Pedee*) was burned and sunk along with several other vessels about March 15, 1865, by the Confederates to prevent their falling into the hands of the rapidly advancing Federal Army. The *Pee Dee's* location was given as just below the railroad bridge on the west side of the Great Pee Dee River, South Carolina. [Note: The *Pee Dee* was described as the best wooden ship constructed by the Confederacy. She had a single engine, twin propellers, and was schooner rigged. Her hull was 170' in length, 26' in breadth, 10' in depth of hold. The *Pee Dee* was armed with two 3-inch pivot guns (bow and stern) and a 9-inch Dahlgren mounted as a pivot gun

Treasures of the Confederate Coast

amidships (one report said she was to have been armed with four 32-pounders and two pivots). She was built in January of 1865 at the Confederate Navy Yard at Mars Bluff, just above the railroad trestle on the Pee Dee River. In 1926 the Ellison Capers and Maxcy Gregg Florence chapters of the United Daughters of the Confederacy salvaged the ship's propellers which are now displayed on the grounds of the Florence Museum in Florence, South Carolina. In 1954 the remainder of the vessel was salvaged and displayed at the South of the Border tourist center in Dillon County, South Carolina. The *Pee Dee* was commanded by Lieutenant Oscar Johnson. Her guns may have been salvaged immediately after the war. The other vessels, which were scuttled and burned, were all sunk at the shipyard above the railroad bridge. They included a "Tender," described as a new boat 128' in length and 22' in breadth.]

References for 1865-3-US-SC/GA-4:
Manuscript letter from William Radford to the Chief of the Bureau of Construction and Repair, (August 17, 1865), National Archives, Record Group 45, Subject File AX, Box 87, (0-1910), #15
Manuscript letter from R.L. Law to Gideon Welles, (October 20, 1865), NARS Microfilm M-89-roll 246, p. 14
"Vessel Papers" (manuscript records), United States National Archives, Washington, DC, Record Group 109, file P-100
Official Records of the Union and Confederate Navies in the War of the Rebellion, (Washington, DC, 1903), Series 1, Volume 16, p. 511
Official Records of the Union and Confederate Navies in the War of the Rebellion, (Washington, DC, 1921), Series 2, Volume 1, p. 262
Theodosia and Other Pee Dee Sketches, by James A. Rogers, pp. 3-5 *Civil War Naval Chronology 1861-1861*, compiled by Navy History Division, Navy Department, (Washington, DC, 1971), p. VI-281
Warships of the Civil War Navies, by Paul H. Silverstone, (Naval Institute Press, Annapolis, MD, 1989), p. 218

1865-3-US-SC/GA-5: On March 26, 1865, the United States Coast Survey steamer *Bibb*, C.O. Boutelle, struck a Confederate torpedo (mine) in 25' of water, while sounding the channel off Battery Bee on Sullivan's Island, South Carolina. The force of the concussion threw the bow out of the water and did considerable damage, but she did not sink. None of her men were injured. (Note One: By December 18, 1865, she was already repaired and engaged in surveying the obstructions in the Savannah River.) (Note Two: The *Bibb* was 409 tons burden, 143' between perpendiculars, 23' in breadth and drew 10'. Built for the Revenue Marine by Knapp at Pittsburgh and launched as the *Tyler* on April 10, 1845, she was originally fitted with Hunter's Wheel propulsion, but was converted to sidewheels.)

References for 1865-3-US-SC/GA-5:
"Savannah Daily Herald," (Savannah, GA), March 27, 1865, p. 2, c. 3
"Savannah Daily Herald," (Savannah, GA), December 18, 1865, p. 3, c. 1
"General Map of Charleston Harbor, South Carolina, Showing Rebel Defenses and Obstructions," drawn by E. Willenbucher for the Annual Report of the Secretary of the Navy, (U.S. Coast Survey, 1865)
Official Records of the Union and Confederate Navies in the War of the Rebellion, (Washington, DC, 1903), Series 1, Volume 16, pp. 295-297, 385
Warships of the Civil War Navies, by Paul H. Silverstone, (Naval Institute Press, Annapolis, MD, 1989), pp. 187, 195

The "Real Rhett Butler" & Other Revelations

1865-4-US-NC-1: A Confederate "floating battery" was sunk in the Roanoke River about eight miles above Plymouth, North Carolina, on April 5, 1865. (Note One: It was thought that the craft had been set adrift at Halifax due to the advance of Union troops and that it had struck one of the torpedoes placed in the river by the Confederates. It was said to have been sunk on a sand bar, nearly in the middle of the river, in a depth of 2.5 or 3 fathoms water with only about two feet of the casements being visible. It was described as a "four-sided box, 20 feet square on top, with sides sloping at an angle of about 45°. Height between decks, 8 feet, the box composed of heavy timber frames with a layer of yellow pine 1.5 feet thick. On two of the sides this pine had been covered with 6-inch oak, bolted athwartships." There were two ports on either side. The Federal forces set the exposed wood on fire.) (Note Two: Her position was also described as between Jamesville and Plymouth.)

References for 1865-4-US-NC-1:
Official Records of the Union and Confederate Navies in the War of the Rebellion, (Washington, DC, 1901), Series 1, Volume 12, pp. 107, 108, 116

1865-4-US-NC-2: Two barges and the sidewheel steamer *Minquas* (or *Minquass*), 160 tons, all loaded with quartermaster's and commissary stores, were captured and destroyed (burned) by the Sixty-seventh North Carolina Infantry, in the Neuse River, North Carolina, on April 7, 1865. Very little was saved. (Note: The steamer had a wood hull and was built at Wilmington, Delaware, in 1864. Her first home port was Philadelphia, Pennsylvania.)

References for 1865-4-US-NC-2:
Encyclopedia of American Shipwrecks, by Bruce D. Berman, Mariners Press, (Boston, MA, 1972), p. 135, #1368
Merchant Steam Vessels of the United States 1790-1868, ("Lytle-Holdcamper List"), by William M. Lytle and Forrest R. Holdcamper, revised and edited by C. Bradford Mitchell, (Staten Island, NY, 1975), pp. 146, 282
Official Records of the Union and Confederate Armies in the War of the Rebellion, (Washington, DC, 1895), Series 1, Volume 47, Part 1, p. 1134

1865-4-US-NC-3: A report dated April 13, 1865, from Commander W.H. Macomb, to Rear-Admiral David. D. Porter, stated his belief that "the rebels have evacuated Weldon (North Carolina), burning the bridge, destroying the ram at Edwards Ferry, and throwing the guns at Rainbow Bluff (Fort Branch) into the (Roanoke) river." [Note One: Subsequent reports stated that only three guns had been recovered at Rainbow Bluff from "under the embrasures from which they were thrown," and said "the others have launched out into deep water, and if sunk in the mud, will • • • never be recovered. • • • There were originally fourteen or fifteen guns of all classes in the fort; two were burst, one of which was a 32-pounder; one, a Blakely, carried to Weldon; one 12-pounder, carried away by

Treasures of the Confederate Coast

Captain Lee; one 12-pounder, sent to Plymouth; leaving nine or ten in the river (less the three saved). The three guns that were saved consisted of one rifle-gun 6-inch caliber, one smoothbore 32-pounder, and one 12-pounder. After dragging the river and talking with locals Commander Macomb was convinced that most had been carried off and that it was questionable that even one gun still remained, and if so it was buried in the mud in deep water.] (Note Two: The ram mentioned as destroyed at Edward's Ferry on the Roanoke River, North Carolina, was still under construction by Elliot, Smith & Co., and was burned on the ways, rather than scuttled and sunk. She was a "wooden gunboat of light draft, and ready for launching, to mount two guns, and suitable for operating on the Roanoke." This was probably the same ram that the Federals had hoped to burn in their expedition of January 19, 1865.) (Note Three: The late Ron Reneau and I found the guns at Rainbow Bluff in 1967, but gave up trying to recover them after I was almost crushed to death by a giant raft of logs which was being floated down the river. It is my understanding that some of the guns were subsequently recovered by the late historian Tom Dickey of Atlanta, Georgia. The remainder have been recovered by the State of North Carolina.)

References for 1865-4-US-NC-3:
Official Records of the Union and Confederate Navies in the War of the Rebellion, (Washington, D.C., 1901), Series 1, Volume 11, pp. 618, 755
Official Records of the Union and Confederate Navies in the War of the Rebellion, (Washington, D.C., 1901), Series 1, Volume 12, pp. 116, 123, 150, 151, 166
Personal knowledge of search expedition conducted by E. Lee Spence and the late Ron Renau ca. 1967
Conversations with Tom Dickey by E. Lee Spence, year not recorded

1865-4-US-NC-4: A report by Lieutenant-Commander Thomas S. Phelps, commanding the *U.S.S. Lenapee,* dated April 15, 1865, at Wilmington, North Carolina, stated "we have succeeded in raising the hull of the small steamer *General Whiting.* The hull is badly burned amidships, and the machinery has never been set up.

Reference for 1865-4-US-NC-4:
Official Records of the Union and Confederate Navies in the War of the Rebellion, (Washington, D.C., 1901), Series 1, Volume 12, p. 118

1865-4-US-SC/GA-1: The Confederate gunboat *Chattahoochee* was soaked with ten barrels of kerosene and set afire by her own crew in the Chattahoochee River, on April 16, 1865, to prevent her from falling into the hands of the advancing federal forces. The fiercely burning gunboat drifted ten to twelve miles below Columbus, Georgia, where it grounded at Race Path Landing. [Note One: The *Chattahoochee* was a wooden hulled, twin screw, steamer. She was initially rigged as a three-masted fore and aft schooner. One report shows her as a "type of barkentine." She was armed with one 9-inch

The "Real Rhett Butler" & Other Revelations

Dahlgren smooth-bore aft, four 32-pounder smooth-bores of 41-cwt. in broadside, and one rifled and banded 32-pounder, forward. She had a crew of approximately 120 men and officers. The vessel was built by William O. Saffold and David S. Johnston at Saffold Landing, Early County, Georgia, between October, 1861, and January, 1863, under a contract with the Confederate government that originally called for her to be finished in 120 days at a cost of $47,500. Her measurements are variously given as 150' in length (or 130' between perpendiculars), 25' in breadth (or 30' molded), 10' in depth of hold, and 8' (or 7'3") in draft. Her speed during trials was reported as 12 knots. The *Chattahoochee's* first commander was Lieutenant Catesby ap R. Jones, who had assumed command of the *C.S.S. Virginia* (ex-*U.S.S. Merrimack*) when Captain Buchanan was wounded during her legendary duel with the *U.S.S. Monitor*. Because it was found impossible to get her out of the river, the] (Note Two: Some reports incorrectly show the *Chattahoochee* as destroyed by the Federal Army about the middle of December, 1864.) (Note Three: The *Chattahoochee* had previously been sunk in the Chattahoochee River, at Blount's Bar, Blountstown, Florida, when her boiler exploded on May 27, 1863. Fifteen or sixteen men were killed in that accident, but she was afterwards raised and towed up the river to Columbus, Georgia, for repairs.) (Note Four: A thirty foot stern section of her wooden hull, with her steam engines, shafts and propellers, was raised in 1964, and is currently on display at the James W. Woodruff, Jr., Confederate Naval Museum. The museum's address is 202 4th Street, PO Box 1022, Columbus, Georgia, 31902. The hours are 10:00 a.m. to 5:00 p.m. Tuesday through Friday, and 1:00 p.m. to 5:00 p.m. on Saturdays and Sundays. It is closed every Monday and on most major holidays. For more information call area code 706 phone number 327-9798.)

References for 1865-4-US-SC/GA-1:
"Charleston Mercury," (Charleston, SC), Volume 82, #11770, June 2, 1863, p. 2, c. 1
"Charleston Mercury," (Charleston, SC), Volume 82, #11774, June 6, 1864, p. 1, c. 2
"Daily Morning News," (Savannah, GA), #128, June 1, 1863, p. 1, c. 1
"Daily Morning News," (Savannah, GA), #130, June 3, 1863, p. 1, c. 2
"Daily Morning News," (Savannah, GA), #131, June 4, 1863, p. 2, c. 3
New York Times, (New York, NY), Volume 12, #3666, June 24, 1864, p. 8, c. 1
History of the Confederate States Navy From its Organization to the Surrender of its Last Vessel, by J. Thomas Scharf, (New York, New York, 1887), pp. 48, 617, 622
Official Records of the Union and Confederate Armies in the War of the Rebellion, (Washington, DC, 1897), Series 1, Volume 49, p. 365
Official Records of the Union and Confederate Navies in the War of the Rebellion, (Washington, DC, 1921), Series 2, Volume 1, pp. 250, 273, 283
Perilous Journeys: A History of Steamboating on the Chattahoochee, Apalachicola, and Flint Rivers, 1828-1928, by Edward A. Mueller, (Historic Chattahoochee Commission, Eufalia, Alabama, 1989), pp. 105-115, 117; illustrations on pp. 126-3, 126-4
Warships of the Civil War Navies, by Paul H. Silverstone, (Naval Institute Press, Annapolis, MD, 1989), p. 218
The Confederate Navy: A Pictorial History, by Philip Van Doren Stern, (Da Capo Press, New York, NY, 1992), p. 83

Treasures of the Confederate Coast

"The Confederate Gunboat *Chattahoochee*," (undated print, drawn by Robert Holcombe)
"Data Sheet, *Chattahoochee*" provided to E. Lee Spence by the James W. Woodruff, Jr. Confederate Naval Museum, Columbus, Georgia, July 7, 1994
"James W. Woodruff, Jr. Confederate Naval Museum, Columbus, Georgia, An Inland Port," (three fold, rack card), provided to E. Lee Spence by the James W. Woodruff, Jr. Confederate Naval Museum, Columbus, Georgia, July 7, 1994

1865-4-US-SC/GA-2: The Confederate States ironclad ram *Jackson* (a.k.a. *Muscogee*) was captured and set afire by the Federal troops in the Chattahoochee River at the Columbus Navy Yard at Columbus, Georgia, on April 17, 1865. The burning hulk drifted thirty miles downstream before grounding and burning to her waterline. The troops were a wing of General Sherman's army and were under the command of General James H. Wilson. [Note One: The *Jackson* is variously reported as a propeller steamer and as having a "center wheel," due to her having been altered from a paddle wheel to a twin screw system. She was armed with four 7" Brooke rifles (two mounted in the forward corners of her casemated gun room and two mounted in the aft corners, so they could fire broadside as well) and two 6.4" Brooke rifles (mounted strictly in broadside). She may have also been meant to carry one or two 12-pounder boat howitzers on her spar deck. The vessel was powered with two horizontal, direct-acting, high-pressure engines, fed by four boilers. Each engine had a single 3' diameter cylinder with a 3' piston stroke, and each drove a 7'6" propeller. Her machinery was manufactured by the Confederate States Naval Iron Works at Columbus. Her measurements were 208'6" length between perpendiculars (also shown as 250' long, and as 223'6" overall); 56'6" breadth molded (also shown as 45' wide, and as 59' extreme); and 10' in depth of hold. She drew 6'6" to 7'6" (or 8') of water. Her hull was built of live oak, was 2' thick, and had a solid ram (also of oak) protruding 15' from her bow. Although the armor on her gun room was incomplete, she was within two weeks of completion, when she was destroyed. Her casemated gun room was 40' long and 20' wide, and was pierced with 10 ports for her heavy guns. The gun room's sides sloped at a 40° angle and were armored with 4" of rolled iron plate, backed with approximately 20" of wood. The iron on her spar deck and flush decks was 2" thick, and was doubled over the knuckle.] (Note Two: The *Civil War Naval Chronology* compiled by the Navy Department incorrectly lists the *Muscogee* as destroyed in December of 1864.) (Note Three: Donald Shomette in his book on Civil War shipwrecks states she was launched too late in the war to be of any value to the Confederacy, and he quotes a contemporary newspaper account describing her as a perpendicular looking craft, reminiscent of Noah's ark, and

The "Real Rhett Butler" & Other Revelations

"nothing short of a flood" would float her.) (Note Four: According to curator Robert Holcombe, the wreck was located in 1960. It was raised in 1963 and is now on display at the James W. Woodruff, Jr., Confederate Naval Museum at Columbus, Georgia. Please see note four of the previous entry for specific information on the museum's operating hours, address, and phone number.)

References for 1864-12x-US-SC/GA-1:
Official Records of the Union and Confederate Armies in the War of the Rebellion, (Washington, DC, 1897), Series 1, Volume 49, pp. 34, 352, 365, 384, 392, 482, 485, 487
Official Records of the Union and Confederate Navies in the War of the Rebellion, (Washington, DC, 1921), Series 2, Volume 1, p. 260
"The Saga of the *Muscogee*," by Joel Turner, (published in *Georgia Magazine*, February-March issue, 1966), pp. 16-19
Civil War Naval Chronology 1861-1865, compiled by Navy History Division, Navy Department, (Washington, DC, 1971), p. VI-273
Shipwrecks of the Civil War: The Encyclopedia of Union and Confederate Naval Losses, by Donald Shomette, (Washington, DC, 1973), pp. 326, 327
Warships of the Civil War Navies, by Paul H. Silverstone, (Naval Institute Press, Annapolis, MD, 1989), p. 207
C.S.S. Neuse: A Question of Iron and Time, by Leslie S. Bright, William H. Rowland, and James C. Bardon, (Raleigh, NC, 1981), Appendix IV, *C.S.S. Albemarle*, p. 156
Perilous Journeys: A History of Steamboating on the Chattahoochee, Apalachicola, and Flint Rivers, 1828-1928, by Edward A. Mueller, (Historic Chattahoochee Commission, Eufalia, Alabama, 1989), pp. 110-113, 116, 117; illustrations on pp. 126-5, 126-6, 126-7
"The Confederate Ironclad Ram *Jackson*," (undated print, drawn by Robert Holcombe)
"Data Sheet, *Jackson* (*Muscogee*)" provided to E. Lee Spence by the James W. Woodruff, Jr. Confederate Naval Museum, Columbus, Georgia, July 7, 1994
"James W. Woodruff, Jr. Confederate Naval Museum, Columbus, Georgia, An Inland Port," (three fold, rack card), provided to E. Lee Spence by the James W. Woodruff, Jr. Confederate Naval Museum, Columbus, Georgia, July 7, 1994

1865-4-US-SC/GA-3: The United States steamer *Enoch Dean*, employed by the Freedman's Bureau and carrying freedmen, their families and effects, struck a snag while passing through a creek leading into St. Catherine's Sound, Georgia, and sank on April 19, 1865. The people were saved. The steamer also carried seeds and farming utensils. (Note One: The *Enoch Dean* was a wooden hulled sidewheel steamer and was acting under the direct orders of General Saxon, and was used by him "to further, in various ways, his philanthropic endeavors to elevate the condition of the freedmen." The *Enoch Dean* had left Savannah to carry the former slaves to some of the sea islands of Georgia where the people were to be settled in comfortable homes on lands which had been confiscated from the rightful owners.) (Note Two: The *Enoch Dean* had one deck, no masts, no galleries, a round tuck, and a billet head. She was built at Keyport, New Jersey, in 1852. The steamer's first home port was New York, New York. She was transferred to the War Department in 1863. She was 135'8" in length, 25'10" in breadth, 7' in depth and was 194 33/95 tons.)

References for 1865-4-US-SC/GA-3:
"Permanent Enrollment #115," (New York, NY), October 17, 1855, National Archives, Record Group 41
"Permanent Enrollment #93," (New York, NY), August 21, 1860, National Archives, Record Group 41
"Savannah Daily Herald," (Savannah, GA), March 23, 1865, p. 3, c. 3
"Savannah Daily Herald," (Savannah, GA), April 23, 1865, p. 2, c. 4
"Vessel Disasters, 1865," (bound annotated clipping file, Atlantic Mutual Insurance Companies of New York), Volume 40, p. 176

Treasures of the Confederate Coast

"Report of vessels employed by the U.S. in the Department of the Carolinas which have been lost," (manuscript list), National Archives, Record Group 92, entry 1407, Box 123
Merchant Steam Vessels of the United States 1807-1868, ("Lytle List"), by William M. Lytle, (Mystic, CT, 1952), p. 58
List of American-Flag Merchant Vessels that Received Certificates of Enrollment or Registry at the Port of New York 1789-1867, compiled by Forest R. Holdcamper, (U.S. National Archives, Washington, DC, 1968), Special List #22, Volume 1, p. 215

1865-4-US-SC/GA-4: The United States steamer *Oliver M. Pettit* (a.k.a.: *O.M. Pettit* or *Pettit*) Captain Smith, struck a snag or a sunken flat opposite the wreck of the steamer *General Lee* at Williamson's Landing on the Savannah River on April 24, 1865, and sank. The officers and crew saved themselves in the ship's boats. (Note One: A court of inquiry held on May 6, 1865, cleared her officers and crew of any blame for her loss. It was originally considered doubtful that she could be raised. However, the *Pettit* was later reported as raised and sold at Bay Point, South Carolina, for $8,200 on September 2, 1865. The *Pettit* had been purchased by the United States government at New York on August 17, 1861, for $15,000. The *Pettit* was a fourth rate, wood hulled, sidewheel steam tug. The *Pettit* was 165 tons, 106' in length, 24'4" in breadth, 7' in depth of hold, and 6' in draft. The *Pettit* could make eight knots. The *Pettit* was armed with one 30-pounder gun, and one 20-pounder Parrott rifle.) (Note Two: At least one contemporary account incorrectly gives the name of the *Pettit*, Captain Smith, as the *Petit Smith*.) (Note Three: For more information on the wreck of the *General Lee*, see entries 1865-8-US-SC/GA-1 and 1865-12x-US-SC/GA-1 of this book.)

References for 1865-4-US-SC/GA-4:
"Savannah Daily Herald," (Savannah, GA), April 25, 1865, p. 2, c. 1
Records of General Courts Martial and Courts of Inquiry of the Navy Department, 1799-1867, Court of Inquiry, #4336, May 6, 1865, NARS M-273, roll 169, frames 0292-0309
"Vessel Disasters, 1865," (bound annotated clipping file, Atlantic Mutual Insurance Companies of New York), Volume 40, p. 176
Official Records of the Union and Confederate Navies in the War of the Rebellion, (Washington, DC, 1921), Series 2, Volume 1, p. 164
List of American-Flag Merchant Vessels that Received Certificates of Enrollment or Registry at the Port of New York 1789-1867, compiled by Forest R. Holdcamper, (U.S. National Archives, Washington, DC, 1968), Special List #22, Volume 2, p. 527
Merchant Steam Vessels of the United States 1790-1868, ("Lytle-Holdcamper List"), edited by C. Bradford Mitchell, (Staten Island, NY, 1975), p. 163

1865-5-US-SC/GA-1: On May 7, 1865, the steamer *Sylph*, bound from Hilton Head, with passengers and government stores, went ashore in the Savannah River, above and north of Fort Pulaski, below Savannah, Georgia. The steamer's condition was said to be critical. (Note: The steamer *Celt*, which was wrecked on Sullivan's Island in February of 1865 was referred to in some accounts as the *Sylph*. For more information on that wreck, please see entry 65-2-SC/GA-1.)

Reference for 1865-5-US-SC/GA-1:
"Savannah Daily Herald," (Savannah, GA), #96, May 8, 1865, p. 4, c. 1

The "Real Rhett Butler" & Other Revelations

1865-5-US-SC/GA-2: A black man was drowned between Poor Robin and Two Sisters ferries on the Savannah River in May of 1865 while attempting to board the steamer *Jeff Davis* from his bateau. From the bulky appearance of his clothing it was thought that the man was trying to conceal a large amount of coin.

Reference for 1865-5-US-SC/GA-2:
"Savannah Daily Herald," (Savannah, GA), May 24, 1865, p. 4, c. 1

1865-5-US-SC/GA-3: On May 28, 1865, the steamer *Governor Troup*, Captain Davis, which left Augusta for Savannah with over two hundred crew and passengers, took aboard three hundred bales of cotton from the steamer *Amazon* which lay snagged at Sand Bar Ferry. On the following day, nine miles below Augusta, Georgia, it was discovered that the cotton was on fire and the *Governor Troup* was rounded and run into the South Carolina bank of the river. The *Governor Troup* was burned to the water's edge. Forty lives were lost, including that of Dr. Alexander of Savannah, Georgia. Three small bags or pouches of the U.S. mails were lost. The crew and passengers lost all their baggage and effects, but Mr. A.A. Rice, superintendent of Adams Express, was on board and saved the Express mail pouch. (Note One: The *Governor Troup* had been purchased in 1863 by the Confederate government for $16,000 and had been rebuilt and used for the collection of tithes. The *Governor Troup* was built at Dublin, Georgia, in 1859, and her first home port was Savannah. The *Governor Troup* had a wood hull, sidewheels, a square stern, and no galleries. The vessel measured 122'6" in length, 25' in breadth, 5'6" in depth of hold, and was 154 82/95 tons.) (Note Two: The steamer *Amazon* got off the sand bank and was later reported as arrived at Savannah.)

References for 1865-5-US-SC/GA-3:
"Enrollment #2," (Savannah, GA), September 2, 1859, National Archives Record Group 41
"Savannah Daily Herald," (Savannah, GA), #117, June 2, 1865, p. 4, c. 2, 3
"Savannah Daily Herald," (Savannah, GA), #118, June 3, 1865, p. 2, c. 1
Times, (London, England), #25221, June 26, 1865, p. 10, c. 4
Merchant Steam Vessels of the United States 1790-1868, ("Lytle-Holdcamper List"), edited by C. Bradford Mitchell, (Staten Island, NY, 1975), pp. 88, 265

1865-6-US-NC-1: The ship *Empire*, of Liverpool, bound from Lagua La Grande to New York, was lost on the outer dam (bar) of Cape Hatteras Shoals, North Carolina, on June 12, 1865. The captain of the *Empire* was sick and her crew asked to be taken aboard the steamship *Carolina*, but their request was refused as the "sea was smooth, and the vessel lay only four or five miles from shore." The people took to their boats and were seen landing on the beach.

Reference for 1865-6-US-NC-1:
"Savannah Daily Herald," (Savannah, GA), Volume 1, #130, June 17, 1865, p. 2, c. 2

Treasures of the Confederate Coast

1865-6-US-SC/GA-1: A craft identified as steam launch *#3* was wrecked on St. Helena Shoals, South Carolina, on June 8, 1865. The launch was attached to the United States fleet at Port Royal, South Carolina.

Reference for 1865-6-US-SC/GA-1:
Official Records of the Union and Confederate Navies in the War of the Rebellion, (Washington, DC, 1903), Series 1, Volume 16, p. 343

1865-6-US-SC/GA-2: A sloop containing five men capsized "an extreme distance from shore" off Seabrook Island, South Carolina, in a squall in early June, 1865. The men were rescued in a drowning condition by Captain Briggs of the steamer *U.S. Grant.* The report stated that Capt. Briggs deserved "more than thanks from those who were rescued from a watery grave."

Reference for 1865-6-US-SC/GA-2:
"Savannah Daily Herald," (Savannah, GA), Volume 1, #130, June 17, 1865, p. 2, c. 2

1865-6-US-SC/GA-3: The steamer *Leesburg*, partially loaded with cotton, hit a snag and sank in the Savannah River about fifteen miles below Augusta, Georgia, on June 22, 1865. Two lives were lost. (Note: The *Leesburg* had served as a Confederate transport on the Savannah River during the period 1862-1865.)

References for 1865-6-US-SC/GA-3:
"Savannah Daily Herald," (Savannah, GA), #135, June 23, 1865, p. 4, c. 1
"Daily National Intelligencer," (Washington, DC), #16493, June 28, 1865, p. 3, c. 4
Official Records of the Union and Confederate Armies in the War of the Rebellion, (Washington, DC, 1885), Series 1, Volume 14, p. 10
Warships of the Civil War Navies, by Paul H. Silverstone, (Naval Institute Press, Annapolis, MD, 1989), p. 240

1865-6-US-x-1: On June 13, 1865, President Andrew Johnson ordered the immediate lifting of the Federal blockade of Southern ports. Although the order formally re-opened the ports, it specifically prohibited the importation of "arms, ammunitions, all articles from which ammunition is made, and gray uniforms and cloth" into the South, in apparent fear that the South might rise again.

Reference for 1865-6-US-x-1:
Times, (London, England), # 25221, June 26, 1865, p. 10, c. 3

1865-6x-US-NC-1: A report by Acting Rear-Admiral William Radford, dated at Norfolk, Virginia, on June 19, 1865, stated "Picket launch *No. 1* has been lately raised by Commander W.H. Macomb and will be sent to Norfolk as soon as sufficiently repaired." There was no indication of how or when she was sunk. An enclosure showed her duty or station as in the Sounds of North Carolina. (Note: Because the designation "No. 1" was used for more than one vessel put to picket duty, it isn't clear which one was raised. Because of both her and Macomb's duty station, the most

The "Real Rhett Butler" & Other Revelations

likely candidate was United States picket boat *No. 1*, which had been captured by the Confederates during Lieutenant Cushing's successful raid against the *C.S.S. Albemarle* in the Roanoke River. That vessel was a wooden hulled, screw steamer and was delivered at the New York Navy Yard on August 22, 1864. She was 40' in length, 9'6" in breadth, and 4'6" in depth of hull. She had a double piston, reciprocating, condensing engine that cost $4,117.32. Her repairs at Norfolk on June 30, 1867, were $545.84. She could make a maximum of 7 knots. Her armament consisted of a single howitzer. For more on the sinking of the *Albemarle*, see entry 1864-10-US-NC-7.)

References for 1865-6x-US-NC-1:
Official Records of the Union and Confederate Navies in the War of the Rebellion, (Washington, D.C., 1901), Series 1, Volume 12, p. 160, 166
Official Records of the Union and Confederate Navies in the War of the Rebellion, (Washington, D.C., 1921), Series 2, Volume 1, p. 177

1865-7-US-NC-1: The United States transport *Quinebaug* (or *Quinnebaug*) bound from Moorehead City to Baltimore (or Philadelphia) with 280 (or 350) discharged soldiers and sixteen horses was driven ashore and wrecked on the Beaufort bar or reef off Shackleford Banks, near Beaufort, North Carolina. Her location was also described as stranded at Moorehead City, North Carolina, on July 20, 1865. [Note One: Between thirty and forty passengers were initially reported missing and at least twenty-five lives were lost. One report stated "31 men of the 76th Pennsylvania Regiment, Lieutenant Danan (or Denning), of the 9th Maine, and all the horses; were drowned. The remainder were saved by the schooner *Benjamin Adams* and a gunboat, and taken into Beaufort. Her captain "set her colors half-mast, union down" and aid was immediately rendered by the United States Coast Survey steamer *Corwin* and the army tug *Goliah*. Contemporary news accounts stated "The *Quinebaug* is an old boat, built probably before some of its ill-fated passengers were born, and might have done well enough as a transport for cattle; but human beings, particularly discharged soldiers, who have fought through the battles of their country, and are returning home after a long absence, should be furnished something more secure."] (Note Two: The *Quinebaug* was built at Norwich, Connecticut, in 1844, and by the time of her loss was described as a "frightfully horrible" old boat. Her first home port was New London, Connecticut. She was a screw steamer of 186 tons and had a wooden hull.) (Note Three: The wreck of the *Quinebaug* has been discovered, and is presently being worked by divers.)

References for 1865-7-US-NC-1:
New York Times, (New York Times, NY), Volume 14, #4314, July 24, 1865, p. 1, c. 4

Treasures of the Confederate Coast

New York Times, (New York Times, NY), Volume 14, #4316, July 26, 1865, p. 1, c. 4
Times, (London, England), # 25257, August 7, 1865, p. 4, c. 3
"Savannah Daily Herald," (Savannah, GA), Volume 1, #167, August 1, 1865, p. 2, c. 4
Official Records of the Union and Confederate Navies in the War of the Rebellion, (Washington, DC, 1901), Series 1, Volume 12, pp. 170, 171
Encyclopedia of American Shipwrecks, by Bruce D. Berman, Mariners Press, (Boston, MA, 1972), p. 141, #1625
Merchant Steam Vessels of the United States 1790-1868, ("Lytle-Holdcamper List"), by William M. Lytle and Forrest R. Holdcamper, revised and edited by C. Bradford Mitchell, (Staten Island, NY, 1975), pp. 179, 291
Telephone interview of Carter Leary by E. Lee Spence, October 22, 1994

1865-7-US-SC/GA-1: The Savannah Daily Herald of July 10, 1865, reported that the remains of the "Confederate ram," lying submerged in the Savannah River opposite the "lower Rice Mills" were gradually shifting and becoming dangerous to navigation.
Reference for 1865-7-US-SC/GA-1:
"Savannah Daily Herald," (Savannah, GA), July 10, 1865, p. 3, c. 1

1865-8-US-SC/GA-1: The steamer *General Lee*, which had been variously reported in the Savannah papers as sunk in the Savannah River at Stiles Landing, at Williamson's Landing, or opposite McAlpin's Landing, was sold at auction to W.S. Johns, agent of H.B. Plant of Augusta, Georgia, on July 19, 1865, for $2000. On August 4, 1865, the "Savannah Daily Herald" reported that the steamer's brass and rods had been stolen and sold, but that it was still expected that she would be raised and repaired. The "Savannah Daily Herald" of September 13, 1865, stated that the vessel had not been raised and that the engines had been removed from the wreck. The *General Lee* was built in 1862 by Krenson and Hawkes and was used as a Confederate transport until her capture. (Note One: Salvage master Jim Batey reports that he destroyed the wreck of an old sternwheel steamer, said to have been a Confederate vessel called the *Robert E. Lee,* near a boat landing on the Savannah River. Although this may have been the steamer *General Lee* it may have been the steamer *Robert Lehr.* According to Batey the destruction of the wreck took place in the late 1970's and was done in accordance with requirements set down by the United States Army Corps of Engineers as part of a river clearance project. Batey reports that he bought the wreck from a Mr. Simkins.) (Note Two: See also entries 1865-4-US-SC/GA-4, 1865-11-US-SC/GA-5, and 1865-12x-US-SC/GA-1 of this book.)

References for 1865-8-US-SC/GA-1:
"Savannah Daily Herald," (Savannah, GA), April 20, 1865, p. 2, c. 5
"Savannah Daily Herald," (Savannah, GA), #153, July 15, 1865, p. 4, c. 1
"Savannah Daily Herald," (Savannah, GA), #156, July 19, 1865, p. 4, c. 4
"Savannah Daily Herald," (Savannah, GA), #170, August 4, 1865, p. 3, c. 2
"Savannah Daily Herald," (Savannah, GA), #204, September 13, 1865, p. 3, c. 1
Personal interview of James Lee Batey conducted by E. Lee Spence, September, 1994
Warships of the Civil War Navies, by Paul H. Silverstone, (Naval Institute Press, Annapolis, MD, 1989), p. 240

The "Real Rhett Butler" & Other Revelations

1865-8-US-SC/GA-2: The brig (or schooner) *Fanny*, (or *Fannie*) Captain Crocker, bound from Philadelphia, for Savannah, with an assorted cargo, went ashore on the South Breaker of Tybee Beach, Georgia, about August 25, 1865, and was expected to be a total loss. The strong easterly winds had driven the *Fanny* high up on the breakers and were said to "preclude all possibility of any attempt to save either vessel or cargo." (Note One: Despite such expressed pessimism the *Fanny* was lightered, got off and brought to Savannah on September 6, 1865.) (Note Two: The *Fanny* was consigned to Hunter and Gammell. She was 363 tons and was built at Greenpoint, Long Island, New York, in 1853, and was issued a certificate of register at that port on November 16, 1853. The vessel was rated A-2 for insurance purposes.)

References for 1865-8-US-SC/GA-2:
"Savannah Daily Herald," (Savannah, GA), #199, September 7, 1865, p. 3, c. 1
"Savannah Daily Herald," (Savannah, GA), #204, September 13, 1865, p. 3, c. 1
"Vessel Disasters, 1865," (bound annotated clipping file, Atlantic Mutual Insurance Companies of New York), Volume 41, p. 82
List of American-Flag Merchant Vessels that Received Certificates of Enrollment or Registry at the Port of New York 1789-1867, compiled by Forest R. Holdcamper, (U.S. National Archives, Washington, DC, 1968), Special List #22, Volume 1, p. 236

1865-8-US-NCx-1: 1865-8-US-SC/GAx-1: The United States steamer *Commodore McDonough* sprang a leak, filled rapidly, and sank about 10:30 a.m. on August 22 (or 23), 1865, while being towed from Port Royal, South Carolina, to New York (also shown as bound from Charleston to Baltimore). [Note One: The *Commodore McDonough* was a wooden hulled side wheel ferry boat of 532 tons, with an inclined engine (38" diameter cylinder with a 10' piston stroke). She drew 8'6" of water and could make eight knots. Her battery was last reported as consisting of one 100-pounder rifle, one 9-inch Dahlgren smooth bore, two 50-pounder Dahlgren rifles, and two 24-pounder howitzers. She had been purchased by Rear Admiral H. Paulding from the Union Ferry Company at New York for $42,409.40. The total cost of her repairs while in government service was $27,790.48. Under normal circumstances she carried a complement of 75 men.] (Note Two: The actual location of the wreck has not been determined at this time and the loss is included in this list solely to alert the reader that she may have been lost off the Confederate Coast.)

References for 1865-8-US-NCx-1:
"Savannah Daily Herald," (Savannah, GA), Volume 1, #190, August 28, 1865, p. 3, c. 5
Official Records of the Union and Confederate Navies in the War of the Rebellion, (Washington, DC, 1921), Series 2, Volume 1, p. 63
Warships of the Civil War Navies, by Paul H. Silverstone, (Naval Institute Press, Annapolis, MD, 1989), p. 100

1865-9-US-SC/GA-1: The bark *Iddo Kimball*, bound from New York to Savannah, got ashore in the Savannah River at the Oyster

Treasures of the Confederate Coast

Beds near Fort Pulaski below Savannah, Georgia, about September 27, 1865. (Note: The *Iddo Kimball* was built at Rockland, Maine, in 1851, and was 474 tons. She was issued a certificate of register at the port of New York on January 13, 1859.)

References for 1865-9-US-SC/GA-1:
"Savannah Daily Herald," (Savannah, GA), #218, September 29, 1865, p. 3, c. 1
List of American-Flag Merchant Vessels that Received Certificates of Enrollment or Registry at the Port of New York 1789-1867, compiled by Forest R. Holdcamper, (U.S. National Archives, Washington, DC, 1968), Special List #22, Volume 1, p. 336

1865-10-US-NC-1: Conflicting data in the "Lytle Holdcamper List" shows the screw steamer *Alpha* as destroyed in Albemarle Sound, North Carolina, by an explosion on October 7, 1865, and as lost in 1868. (Note One: The *Alpha*, official number 890, was built at Brooklyn, New York, in 1858. She was issued a certificate of steam enrollment on August 26, 1858, at New York, New York, which was also her first home port. She had a wood hull and was 107 (or 170) tons.) (Note Two: Bruce Berman's *Encyclopedia of American Shipwrecks* also gives the date of loss as October 7, 1865, but shows her as built in 1857.)

References for 1865-10-US-NC-1:
Merchant Steam Vessels of the United States 1790-1868, "The Lytle-Holdcamper List," by William M. Lytle and Forrest R. Holdcamper, revised and edited by C. Bradford Mitchell, (Staten Island, New York, 1975), p. 34
Encyclopedia of American Shipwrecks, by Bruce D. Berman, Mariners Press, (Boston, MA, 1972), p. 106, #75
Merchant Steam Vessels of the United States 1790-1868, ("Lytle-Holdcamper List"), by William M. Lytle and Forrest R. Holdcamper, revised and edited by C. Bradford Mitchell, (Staten Island, NY, 1975), pp. 8, 241

1865-10-US-SC/GA-1: The steamer *Annie*, Captain Clark, was run ashore on the south side of Fig Island, Georgia, in the Savannah River, about October 22, 1865, to prevent her from sinking in deep water. The *Annie* had left Darien, Georgia, with a heavy load of cotton, and had run afoul of something which punched a hole in her bottom. [Note One: The vessel was raised by Captain Conklin of the Coast Wrecking Company of New York after only two hours of pumping with his centrifugal wrecking pump. She was owned by her captain. Contemporary accounts stated that the *Annie* had been built especially for the running of the blockade and was claimed she had made seventeen successful trips prior to her capture and subsequent sale at Key West. However, they were probably confusing her with another blockade runner named *Annie*. This *Annie* was built in 1844, and ran the blockade only once, and then it was under the name *Dolphin*, and she was captured before she could get in. She was a sidewheel steamer of 357 tons (also shown as 238 gross tons) and measured 162' in length, 21' in breadth, and 11' in depth of hold (also shown as 170.2'x21.2'x10.5'). She was built by Robert Napier at Glasgow, Scotland. Her engine had a single cylinder 53.3" in diameter, with a 4' piston stroke. She was issued a certificate of registry at the port of New York on September 29, 1863. The steamer had an iron hull with two water tight bulkheads, an enclosed forecastle, and a poop cabin. For insurance purposes the vessel was classed A-2 for rivers and A-3 for the open ocean. The *Annie* was considered a poor sea risk.] (Note Two: A clipping contained in the files of the Atlantic Mutual Insurance Companies of New York lists a steamer *Emma Valeria* as lost in the Savannah River in 1865 and states that the steamer was the former blockade runner *Annie*. The clipping may mean that she was sunk a second time in 1865. The "Lytle-Holdcamper List" shows her as "lost" in 1866, but does not give a specific date, cause, or location.)

References for 1865-10-US-SC/GA-1:
"Savannah Daily Herald," (Savannah, GA), #238, October 23, 1865, p. 3, c. 1
"Savannah Daily Herald," (Savannah, GA), #268, November 27, 1865, p. 3, c. 1
"Savannah Daily Herald," (Savannah, GA), November 30, 1865, p. 3, c. 1
"Steam Vessels #1, 1850's," (bound manuscript, Atlantic Mutual Insurance Companies of New York), clipping after entry 370, and entry 432
List of American-Flag Merchant Vessels that Received Certificates of Enrollment or Registry at the Port of New York 1789-1867, compiled by Forest R. Holdcamper, (U.S. National Archives, Washington, DC, 1968), Special List #22, Volume 1, p. 51
Merchant Steam Vessels of the United States 1790-1868, ("Lytle-Holdcamper List"), edited by C. Bradford Mitchell, (Staten Island, NY, 1975), pp. 11, 242
Lifeline of the Confederacy: Blockade Running During the Civil War, by Stephen R. Wise, (University of South Carolina, Columbia, SC, 1983), p. 553

1865-10-US-SC/GA-2: The beautiful river steamer *Alice*, Captain Wingate, heavily laden with freight for Columbus, Georgia, was sunk near Ricoe's Bluff on October 25, 1865. She had just left the wood yard when she struck something in the stream, careened, and sank in fifteen feet of water. Her captain, watchman, and two deckhands were drowned.

Reference for 1865-10-US-SC/GA-2:
"Savannah Daily Herald," (Savannah, GA), November 1, 1865, p. 2, c. 4

1865-10-US-SC/GA-3: A dispatch from Darien, Georgia, which was published in the October 31, 1865, "Savannah Daily Herald," stated that the schooner *Island Queen*, Captain R.J. Conary, bound for Savannah, was on fire in that port.

Reference for 1865-10-US-SC/GA-3:
"Savannah Daily Herald," (Savannah, GA), October 31, 1865, p. 1, c. 3

1865-10-US-SC/GAx-1: The schooner *Thomas Martin*, Captain Leighton, which sailed from New York for Charleston in October, 1865, with a cargo of lumber consigned to Mr. D.J. Sturges, was hit by a terrible gale or hurricane on October 23, 1865, between Cape Lookout and Frying Pan Shoals, North Carolina. During the gale the schooner sprang a leak and, while the crew was throwing her deck load overboard, she was knocked on her beam ends (her sides). The schooner's mainmast broke into three pieces and, when the rigging was cut away to lighten the vessel, her foremast went

Treasures of the Confederate Coast

overboard. The vessel then righted. But, she came up full of water, and her decks remained awash. The schooner having drifted into shoal water her anchors were dropped. But the derelict drug past Frying Pan Shoals and, after seven days of severe suffering on the part of her men and officers, she finally drifted ashore "on Folly Island Beach, north of Georgetown," South Carolina. (Note One: Although there is a Folly Island in South Carolina, it is located near Charleston and is well south of Georgetown, so there was obviously some confusion as to her location. It is more likely that the wrecked schooner actually washed ashore near Lockwood's Folly Island, North Carolina, as that island is located south of Frying Pan Shoals and north of Georgetown.) (Note Two: This was probably the schooner *Thomas Martin* that was built at Lodi, New Jersey, in 1839. That schooner was 156 tons and was issued a certificate of enrollment at the port of New York, New York, on March 25, 1851.)

References for 1865-10-US-SC/GAx-1:
"Charleston Daily Courier," (Charleston, SC), #220, November 9, 1865, p. 1, c. 1
List of American-Flag Merchant Vessels that Received Certificates of Enrollment or Registry at the Port of New York 1789-1867, compiled by Forest R. Holdcamper, (U.S. National Archives, Washington, DC, 1968), Special List #22, Volume 2, p. 679

1865-11-US-NC-1: The screw steamer *Twilight*, 644 tons, was lost by stranding in the Cape Fear River, North Carolina, on November 14, 1865. (Note: The *Twilight* had a wood hull and was built at Mystic, Connecticut, in 1865, and was first home ported at Stonington, Connecticut.)

References for 1865-11-US-NC-1:
Encyclopedia of American Shipwrecks, by Bruce D. Berman, Mariners Press, (Boston, MA, 1972), p. 148, #1946
Merchant Steam Vessels of the United States 1790-1868, ("Lytle-Holdcamper List"), by William M. Lytle and Forrest R. Holdcamper, revised and edited by C. Bradford Mitchell, (Staten Island, NY, 1975), pp. 216, 302

1865-11-US-NC-2: The large ship *Alcyone*, Captain Leavitt, of St. Johns, N.B., went ashore thirty-five miles north of Hatteras, North Carolina, about November 27, 1865, and was abandoned by her crew, after every means were tried by the steamer *Washington* to get her off. Her crew was carried into Wilmington.

References for 1865-11-US-NC-2:
"Savannah Daily Herald," (Savannah, Georgia), December 20, 1865, p. 1, c. 3

1865-11-US-SC/GA-1: A flat loaded with cotton was reported to have sunk at Hershman's Lake on the Savannah River during the first week of November, 1865.

Reference for 1865-11-US-SC/GA-1:
"Savannah National Republican," (Savannah, GA), #15, November 7, 1865, p. 3, c. 1

1865-11-US-SC/GA-2: The steamer *Savannah*, Captain Silas Spicer, bound from Savannah to Augusta, Georgia, with a cargo valued at

The "Real Rhett Butler" & Other Revelations

$125,000 (also given as valued at $250,000, which would be about $5,000,000 in 1994 dollars), was run into by the steamer *Mayflower* on November 5, 1865, and sunk at Hickory Bend, twenty-eight (or thirty-five) miles above Savannah, Georgia, and four miles above (or at) Purrysburg, South Carolina. The *Savannah* sank in about twenty minutes and no lives were lost on either vessel. She was sunk in twenty feet of water with only her pilot house showing above water. (Note: The *Savannah* had been taken as a prize of war by the United States government and had been purchased the week before the sinking for $5,200. The steamer was on her first trip for her new owners when she was sunk. The vessel had originally been built as a river transport by the Confederate States and had been clad with sheet iron pierced with rifle loops for sharpshooters and had mounted two howitzers, but her armor had been taken off prior to her sinking. Although it was originally reported that neither the vessel nor her cargo were expected to be saved, she was afterwards raised. One account stated that the *Savannah* was designed and constructed by Norman Wiard of New York and was 160' in length, 37' in breadth, and 3' in draft. The *Savannah* was a double ended steamer.)

References for 1865-11-US-SC/GA-2:
"Savannah Daily Herald," (Savannah, GA), May 15, 1865, p. 2, c. 1
"Savannah Daily Herald," (Savannah, GA), #251, November 7, 1865, p. 3, c. 1
"Savannah Daily Herald," (Savannah, GA), #254, November 10, 1865, p. 1, c. 3
"Savannah Daily Herald," (Savannah, GA), #257, November 14, 1865, p. 3, c. 1
"Savannah Daily Herald," (Savannah, GA), #263, November 21, 1865, p. 3, c. 1
"Savannah Daily Herald," (Savannah, GA), #273, December 2, 1865, p. 3, c. 1
"Savannah Daily Herald," (Savannah, GA), #290, December 23, 1865, p. 3, c. 2
"Savannah Daily Herald," (Savannah, GA), #294, December 29, 1865, p. 3, c. 1
"Savannah Daily Herald," (Savannah, GA), January 12, 1866, p. 3, c. 1
"Savannah National Republican," (Savannah, GA), #15, November 7, 1865, p. 2, c. 2
"Vessel Disasters, 1865," (bound annotated clipping file, Atlantic Mutual Insurance Companies of New York), Volume 42, pp. 129, 131, 237
Georgia Historical Quarterly, (Savannah, 1934), Volume 18, pp. 159, 160
"Ships Named Savannah," by Amy Chambliss, (typed manuscript in the collection of the Georgia Historical Society, Savannah, Georgia), pp. 59-61

1865-11-US-SC/GA-3: The British ship *Marianna*, Captain J.J. Coombes, bound from London to Savannah in ballast, was wrecked on November 14, 1865, when a gale drove her ashore and she was totally destroyed near the second outer buoy of Tybee Bar, Georgia. The ship's captain and crew were rescued and carried to Savannah by the brig *Rush* from New York. (Note: The *Marianna* was a first class ship of one thousand tons burden.)

References for 1865-11-US-SC/GA-3:
"Savannah Daily Herald," (Savannah, GA), #259, November 16, 1865, p. 2, c. 3

1865-11-US-SC/GA-4: The sidewheel river steamer *Fannie Lehr*, Captain H. Lewis, which ran on a snag during her first trip to Augusta, Georgia, and which was beached five miles above Purrysburg, South Carolina, on November 19, 1865, was raised by

Treasures of the Confederate Coast

Captain Thomas Conklin of the Coast Wrecking Company of New York. (Note One: The *Fannie Lehr*, official #9050, was built at Baltimore, Maryland, in 1863. The *Fannie Lehr* had a wood hull and was a sidewheel steamer of 306 tons. Her first home port was Baltimore.) (Note Two: Captain Conklin had previously raised the steamer *Annie* which had been sunk at Fig Island near Savannah. For information on the *Annie* see entry 1865-10-US-SC/GA-1 of this book.)

References for 1865-11-US-SC/GA-4:
"Savannah Daily Herald," (Savannah, GA), #263, November 21, 1865, p. 3, c. 1
"Savannah Daily Herald," (Savannah, GA), #267, November 25, 1865, p. 1, c. 2
"Savannah Daily Herald," (Savannah, GA), #272, December 1, 1865, p. 3, c. 2
"Savannah Daily Herald," (Savannah, GA), #281, December 13, 1865, p. 3, c. 2
Merchant Steam Vessels of the United States 1790-1868, ("Lytle-Holdcamper List"), edited by C. Bradford Mitchell, (Staten Island, NY, 1975), p. 70

1865-11-US-SC/GA-5: The steamer *Robert Lehr*, of Baltimore, Captain J. Cottrell, bound from Savannah to Augusta, with a "very full freight," was snagged and sunk in the Savannah River one mile above Burton's Ferry on November 22, 1865. The first deck was entirely submerged. (Note One: The *Robert Lehr* apparently was raised, as she was issued "Temporary Register #7" at Savannah, Georgia, on December 26, 1865, with a note that she had been re-admeasured at Savannah by William Kine, acting surveyor. But the steamer must have sunk again as that document was surrendered at Baltimore, Maryland, on May 11, 1866, with the note that she had been lost. The *Robert Lehr* had two decks, no masts, a round stern and a plain head. The vessel was 130' in length, 22'6" in breadth, 8' in depth of hold and 434.85 gross tons. The steamer was 153.75 tons capacity under her tonnage deck, 281.10 tons capacity between decks above tonnage deck and in enclosures on her upper deck. The *Robert Lehr* was built at Wilmington, Delaware, in 1854, and she was owned by Robert Lehr; Jacob Brandt, Jr.; and Washington Booth.) (Note Two: See also entry 1865-12x-US-SC/GA-1 of this book.)

References for 1865-11-US-SC/GA-5:
"Savannah Daily Herald," (Savannah, GA), #267, November 25, 1865, p. 1, c. 2
"Temporary Register #7," (Savannah, GA), December 16, 1865, National Archives, Record Group 41

1865-11-US-SC/GA-6: The steamer *Comet*, official #5691, Captain N. King, was snagged and lost in November, 1865, in the Ocmulgee River at Hawkinsville, Georgia. No lives were lost. (Note: The *Comet* was built in 1865 at Savannah, Georgia, which was also her first home port. She had a wood hull, sidewheels, one deck, no masts, and a square stern. The vessel was 131' in length, 26'3" in breadth, 5'5" in depth of hold, and 496 gross tons. The *Comet's* enrollment papers show that she had a capacity of 307.63

The "Real Rhett Butler" & Other Revelations

tons below her tonnage deck and 189.13 in enclosures on her upper deck. The *Comet* was owned by the Ocmulgee and Altamaha Steam Navigation Company.)

References for 1865-11-US-SC/GA-6:
"Permanent Enrollment #7," (Savannah, GA), September 7, 1865, National Archives, Record Group 41
"Official Number Book," (bound manuscript list), Volume 2, p. 225, #5691, National Archives, Record Group 41
"Vessel Disasters, 1865-1866," (bound annotated clipping file, Atlantic Mutual Insurance Companies of New York), Volume 43, p. 73
Merchant Steam Vessels of the United States 1790-1868, ("Lytle-Holdcamper List"), edited by C. Bradford Mitchell, (Staten Island, NY, 1975), pp. 42, 252

1865-12-US-NC-1: The screw steamer *Constitution*, 944 tons, was lost by stranding at Cape Lookout, North Carolina, on December 26, 1865. Forty lives were lost. (Note One: She had a wood hull and was built at Mystic Bridge, Connecticut, in 1863 and was first home ported at New York, New York, where she was issued a steam enrollment on August 8, 1863.) (Note Two: Although her official number was #4864, the number appears to have been assigned after her loss.)

References for 1865-12-US-NC-1:
Merchant Steam Vessels of the United States 1790-1868, "The Lytle-Holdcamper List," by William M. Lytle and Forrest R. Holdcamper, revised and edited by C. Bradford Mitchell, (Staten Island, New York, 1975), p. 149
Encyclopedia of American Shipwrecks, by Bruce D. Berman, Mariners Press, (Boston, MA, 1972), p. 114, #417
Merchant Steam Vessels of the United States 1790-1868, ("Lytle-Holdcamper List"), by William M. Lytle and Forrest R. Holdcamper, revised and edited by C. Bradford Mitchell, (Staten Island, NY, 1975), pp. 45, 253

1865-12-US-SC/GA-1: The schooner *Israel R. Snow* (also shown as the *Israel L. Snow*), Captain Achorn, which sailed from Rockland, Maine, on November 26, 1865, with a cargo of eight hundred bushel barrels of lime and one hundred bushel barrels of potatoes consigned to W.F. Sims and Company of Savannah, was forced to beach herself on Tybee Island, Georgia, on December 18, 1865. The schooner had sprung a leak and had started her upper seams, and her cargo was on fire necessitating running her ashore to save the crew and as much property as possible. The schooner's masts were cut away before she was beached. [Note: The *Israel R. Snow* was built of oak and hackmatack, fastened with iron, at Owlshead (or Thomaston), Maine, in 1853. The vessel was owned in Rockland, Maine, by Snow and others. The *Israel R. Snow* was a full model schooner with one bow port, and a "break to deck." The vessel was 95 (or 94) tons and drew 8'6" of water. She was issued a certificate of register at the port of New York on May 5, 1855. On April 28, 1865, she had made history by becoming the first vessel to arrive at Savannah directly from New York on a strictly commercial voyage since 1861.]

References for 1865-12-US-SC/GA-1:
"Savannah Daily Herald," (Savannah, GA), April 29, 1865, p. 2, c. 1
"Savannah Daily Herald," (Savannah, GA), December 19, 1865, p. 3, c. 1

Treasures of the Confederate Coast

American Lloyd's: Registry of American & Foreign Shipping, (New York, New York, 1865), p. 493, #2379
"Vessel Disasters, 1865-1866," (bound annotated clipping file, Atlantic Mutual Insurance Companies of New York), Volume 43, p. 142
List of American-Flag Merchant Vessels that Received Certificates of Enrollment or Registry at the Port of New York 1789-1867, compiled by Forest R. Holdcamper, (U.S. National Archives, Washington, DC, 1968), Special List #22, Volume 1, p. 349

1865-12-US-SC/GA-2: A flat loaded with wood, bound down the Savannah River to Savannah, Georgia, was sunk a short distance from that city on December 20, 1865. It was thought that all hands were drowned. The wood floated down the river.

Reference for 1865-12-US-SC/GA-2:
"Savannah Daily Herald," (Savannah, GA), #288, December 21, 1865, p. 3, c. 2

1865-12-US-SC/GA-3: On Christmas day, 1865, J.P. Blake of New Haven, Connecticut, and Miss Myra Stanton and Miss Helen Kempt of New Bedford, Massachusetts, all missionary teachers who had come to South Carolina to teach the freed slaves, were drowned when their boat sank near Edisto Island, South Carolina, while they were traveling from one plantation to another. (Note: It was reported that the dead were buried in the "far corner of the Presbyterian churchyard" on Edisto Island.)

Reference for 1865-12-US-SC/GA-3:
Tales of Edisto, by Nell S. Graydon, (Columbia, South Carolina, 1968), p. 155

1865-12x-US-NC-1: The "Lytle Holdcamper List" shows the vessel *Etta* as lost at Cape Hatteras, North Carolina, in 1865. The *Etta* was the ex-Confederate privateer schooner *Retribution* which was originally the screw steamer *Uncle Ben*. (Note: The *Uncle Ben* had been built at Buffalo, New York, in 1856. Buffalo was also the vessel's first home port. She was 95' in length, 20'5", and 9' in depth of hold. She had a round stern, no galleries, and no head. The *Uncle Ben* had seen service as a Confederate transport with one gun, but her engines had been taken out for use in the Confederate ironclad *North Carolina*. The *Etta* was 155 31/95 tons and had a wooden hull.)

References for 1865-12x-US-NC-1:
"Permanent Enrollment #115," (New York, NY), December 31, 1859, National Archives, Record Group 41
Official Records of the Union and Confederate Navies in the War of the Rebellion, (Washington, DC, 1921), Series 2, Volume 1, p. 270
List of American-Flag Merchant Vessels that Received Certificates of Enrollment or Registry at the Port of New York 1789-1867, compiled by Forest R. Holdcamper, (U.S. National Archives, Washington, DC, 1968), Special List #22, Volume 2, p. 695
Merchant Steam Vessels of the United States 1790-1868, ("Lytle-Holdcamper List"), by William M. Lytle and Forrest R. Holdcamper, revised and edited by C. Bradford Mitchell, (Staten Island, NY, 1975), pp. 67, 217

1865-12x-US-SC/GA-1: On December 1, 1865, the "Savannah Daily Herald" reported that Captain Thomas Conklin of the Coast Wrecking Company of New York was planning to raise the steamer *Robert Lee* which was sunk in the Savannah River. (Note One: The paper may have been referring to the *Robert Lehr*, the *General Lee* or even another vessel altogether.) (Note Two: See also entries 1865-4-US-SC/GA-4, 1865-8-US-SC/GA-1, and 1865-11-US-SC/GA-5 of this book.)

Reference for 1865-12x-US-SC/GA-1:
"Savannah Daily Herald," (Savannah, GA), #272, December 1, 1865, p. 3, c. 2

Final Entry

Note: A number of additional vessels, which played significant roles in the War, were later sunk in South Carolina waters. Two of those were the *Princess Royal* and the *Planter*.

The British blockade runner *Princess Royal*, which was captured off Charleston and converted to a Federal gunboat, was lost off Cherry Grove, South Carolina, on January 10, 1874. The $1,000,000 cargo (equivalent to $20,000,000 in today's dollars) that she carried when captured had been owned by George Alfred Trenholm. (Note One: Trenholm was the historical basis for Margaret Mitchell's Rhett Butler character in *Gone With The Wind*.) [Note Two: The *Princess Royal* was a 619 ton screw steamer and was built at Glasgow, Scotland, in 1861. She was sold to private parties after the war and was registered under the name *Sherman* (official #22267 ex #43681) at Philadelphia on September 23, 1865. Due to the name change, divers and fishermen incorrectly refer to the wreck as the "General Sherman." The *Princess Royal's* captured log showed her as 494 tons register.]

The Confederate steamer *Planter*, which made history after being high-jacked out of Charleston Harbor by its black pilot, Robert Smalls, was wrecked on Cape Romain, South Carolina, on July 1, 1876, while going to the rescue of another vessel. [Note: The sidewheel, wooden hulled, *Planter* (official #19658) was built in 1860 at Charleston, South Carolina. She was 147.4' in length, 30.8' in breadth, 7.7' in depth of hold, and was 209.62 (or 313) tons.]

References for Final Entry
"Charleston Daily Courier," (Charleston, SC), Volume 61, #19379, January 30, 1863, p. 2, c. 2
"Charleston Daily Courier," (Charleston, SC), Volume 61, #19380, January 31, 1863, p. 2, c. 2
"Charleston Daily Courier," (Charleston, SC), Vol. 61, #19406, March 3, 1863, p. 2, c. 2
New York Times, (New York, NY), Vol. 12, #3550, February 9, 1863, p. 1, c. 1, 2
New York Times, (New York, NY), Vol. 12, #3551, February 10, 1863, p. 1, c. 3, 4
"Log of the *S.S. Princess Royal*," December 6, 1862, to January 10, 1863, contained in the collection of the Philadelphia Maritime Museum, listed as logbook #67.296
"Permanent Enrollment #7," (issued for the *Planter* at Charleston, SC), April 17, 1872, National Archives, Record Group 41
Merchant Steam Vessels of the United States 1790-1868, ("Lytle-Holdcamper List"), edited by C. Bradford Mitchell, (Staten Island, NY, 1975), pages 198 and 297 for *Sherman*, and pages 175 and 290 for *Planter*

• • •

Treasures of the Confederate Coast

The C.S.S. Planter, hi-jacked by her black pilot, steals her way out of Charleston Harbor under the cover of night. The pilot, Robert Smalls, was much respected and became a successful politician after the war. The Planter was lost on Cape Romain, South Carolina, in 1876. Illustration copied from the "Official Records of the War of the Rebellion, Union and Confederate Navies."

APPENDIX A
SL Codes™ Explained

SL Codes™ are alpha-numeric codes used to organize shipwreck data in various versions of *Spence's List*™. You do not need to understand them to enjoy this book. However, for the more serious researcher, the following information is provided. *SL Codes*™ are based on an easy to understand system. *SL Codes*™ are divided into five sections and are designed to answer five different questions at a glance. Each of the five sections of the *SL Code*™ is separated by a dash. The *SL Code*™ for the wreck of the steamer *Georgiana* is 1863-3-US-SC/GA-2. The first section tells the year of loss (1863); the second the month of loss (In this case, March, which is designated numerically as 3.); the third is the general coastal area (US for the country); the fourth pinpoints the region (Each region has been assigned a particular code. In this case the wreck lies the region designated as SC/GA. A partial listing of country and regional codes used in assigning *SL Codes*™ for other areas follows for informational purposes only.); and the fifth section would be a sequential number in case the *SL Code*™ data in the first four sections is identical for two or more wrecks (In this case it is, so it has been assigned the number 2.). When data for any part of the file number is not known, or when there is unresolvable conflicting data, the cataloger simply enters an arbitrary or best guess followed by an "x" for that section. Wrecks or other entries taken from a source which failed to give the month are shown by the number for the most logical month followed by an "x," or if there is no clue at all to the month, December may be arbitrarily selected, and 12x placed in the month section. *SL Codes*™ containing sections with an "x" are meant as preliminary designations until better information can be located. In some cases a vessel may be accessed through more than one *SL Code*™. This is intentionally done in cases of multiple sinkings, updating of *SL Codes*™, or in cases where existing published data might otherwise be confusing and cause you to look in the wrong spot. If you think of *SL Codes*™ as being assigned to "data packages" rather than being assigned to individual or particular wrecks, it may be less confusing. In fact, in some cases such data packages will not refer to a wreck at all, but may instead contain data on something else which might be of interest to researchers. An entry may give a detailed listing of all of the vessels that sailed in a particular fleet (and some of those vessels may also have separate individual listings) or an entry may simply give data on the passage of a law involving salvage. In any case, whenever possible, multiple listings

Treasures of the Confederate Coast

will be cross referenced. When an *SL Code*™ containing one or more x's is updated with a more accurate *SL Code*™, the old *SL Code*™ will be removed from future editions of *Spence's List*™ and the data will appear only under the new more accurate *SL Code*™. When organizing entries by *SL Codes*™, section two is considered a subsection of section one, section three a subsection of section two, etc. It should also be noted that, for organizational purposes, an "x" in any section of an *SL Code*™ causes that particular section to treated as a further subsection. Therefore, an entry with an "x" in its *SL Code*™ would be placed after an entry with an otherwise identical (up to that point) *SL Code*™ without an "x" in that section. Advantages of this system should quickly become obvious.

Researchers using this book (or any other volume in the *Spence's List*™ series of books.) should use the *SL Code*™ in citing the source. It is not correct or fair to the original compiler for users of this list to show the "references" given with the entry as "their" source. By including the *SL Code*™ in the citation, future readers will be able to locate additional information, not only by returning to the original list, but by looking up the same *SL Code*™ in future revisions of the list. The correct form of citation for information on the *Georgiana*, taken from this particular list would be: *Treasures of the Confederate Coast: The "Real Rhett Butler" & Other Revelations* by Edward Lee Spence, (Narwhal Press Inc., Miami/Charleston, 1994), pages 221-225, *Spence's List*™ entry #1863-3-US-SC/GA-2. Or, for less formal purposes, you might record that citation as: *SL Code*™ 1863-3-US-SC/GA-2.

SL is simply an abbreviation for *Spence's List*™. *SL Codes*™ for the East Coast states are: ME/NH-Maine, New Hampshire; MA/RI/CT-Massachusetts, Rhode Island, & Connecticut; NY/NJ/DE-New York, New Jersey, & Delaware; MD/VA-Maryland & Virginia; NC-North Carolina; SC/GA - South Carolina & Georgia; FL - Florida.

Compilation of this book took over twenty-five years and cost many thousands of dollars. To protect that investment in time and money, actual and punitive damages, etc., will be sought in the event of any copyright infringement, including, but not limited to the inclusion of portions of *Spence's List*™ in any book or computerized list.

• • •

Research vessel Sea Raven, anchored over a wreck off the South Carolina coast. Photo courtesy Shipwrecks Inc.

Cannon being hoisted from the Roanoke River, below Fort Branch, Rainbow Bluff, North Carolina, as part of a Field School with the University of North Carolina at Wilmington that was sponsored by the Underwater Archeology Unit of the North Carolina Department of Cultural Resources. This gun had been rolled off the bluff, along with a number of others, in an effort to prevent them from being captured by the rapidly advancing Union Army. (Note: In 1967, I was almost crushed to death by a giant raft of logs while Ron Renau and I were searching for these guns during a night dive. Although we had already located several guns, still attached to their carriages and sitting upside down in the mud, we immediately called off the expedition. Photo courtesy of the Fort Fisher Museum & Visiter's Center.

APPENDIX B
Abandoned Ordnance &
Ordnance Stores

As the "War Between the States" wound to a close the United States captured thousands of tons of ordnance and ordnance stores abandoned by the retreating Confederate forces. Like the Confederates, the Union Army found it logistically impossible to take it with them. Afraid that this vast store of material might fall back into "rebel" hands, the orders were repeatedly given to destroy the captured material. The most expedient way to dispose of it was to simply dump it in the nearest available river. This tactic was actually employed by both sides, effectively building a vast storehouse of military goods that is just now being recovered.

Inventory A: On November 23, 1864, the Federal troops at Milledgeville, Georgia, destroyed the following items, by either burning them or dumping them in the river.

Ammunition (.69 caliber, for smoothbore)	10,000
Ammunition (artillery, fixed, boxes)	170
Cutlasses	1,500
Infantry accouterments (sets)	300
Lances or John Brown Pikes	5,000
Muskets, smoothbore (.69 caliber)	2,300
Powder (kegs)	200
Salt (hogsheads)	16
Weights and measures (U.S. standard, boxes)	15

Inventory B: The following is a list of ordnance and ordnance stores captured in the city of Columbia, South Carolina, February 16/17, 1865, and dumped into the "river." After ten years of archival and field research, (including hundreds of hours diving in the dark, polluted waters of the Saluda, Broad, Congaree rivers), E. Lee Spence located the main portion of the remains of this "dump" in 1976 with the assistance and financial backing of E.D. (Ned) Sloan, Jr., of Greenville, South Carolina.

Ball cartridges (musket balls, no caps)	1,200,000
Cannon powder (kegs and boxes) pounds	8,750
Cartridge-box belts and plates	2,500
Cartridge-box plates	3,500
Percussion caps	100,000
powder (meal, in kegs and boxes) pounds	3,800

Treasures of the Confederate Coast

powder (rifle, in kegs) pounds	13,000
Waist-belt plates	3,000
Waist-belts	2,900
Artillery sabers	220
Cavalry sabers (all kinds)	2,700
Naval cutlasses	175
Saber belts	800
Saber knots	700
Austrian rifled muskets (old at the time)	560
Enfield rifled muskets	1,200
Enfield rifles (short, sword bayonet)	2,000
Mississippi rifles	200
Morse rifles (South Carolina)	400
Musket barrels and stocks, unfinished	6,000
Palmetto rifles	500
Remington rifles	100
Springfield rifled muskets.	100
U.S. muskets, caliber .69	1,740
Whitney rifles (old at the time)	50
Yager muskets	960
Pikes	4,000
Canister, fixed, 6-pounder gun	1,250
Canister, fixed, 12-pounder gun	148
Canister, fixed, 24-pounder gun	314
Case, fixed, 6-pounder gun	550
Case-shot, fixed, 12-pounder gun	183
Fuse-shell, fixed, 6-pounder gun	372
Fuse-shell, fixed, 12-pounder gun	216
Grape-shot, 12-pounder gun	460
Shell, fixed, 8-inch	64
Shell, fixed, 24-pounder gun	120
Shot and shell, not fixed, 8-inch	2,280
Shot and shell, not fixed, 10-inch	1,320
Shot, fixed, 6-pounder gun	1,680
Shot, fixed, 24-pounder gun	112
2-pounder gun (bronze)	1
3-inch gun (rifled, iron)	1
4-inch gun (rifled, iron)	1
4-inch mortars	2
6-pounder guns (bronze)	10
6-pounder guns (iron)	4
10-pounder gun (rifled, iron)	1
10-pounder Parrot guns	2

12-pounder mountain howitzers (probably bronze)	4
18-pounder gun (reinforced, iron)	1
18-pounder gun (rifled, iron)	2
20-pounder gun (iron)	1
Blakely guns (rifled, iron)	2
breech-loading gun (caliber 1.5")	1
bronze guns (caliber 1.5")	2
Coehorn mortar (bronze)	1
James guns (rifled, bronze)	2
Repeating battery (caliber 1")	1
Gun carriages	9
Gun caissons	14
Mountain howitzer caissons	3
Forges	2
Sponges and rammers	1,125
Blacksmith vises	20
Anvils	11
Artillery harness	11
Cavalry-pistol holsters (pairs)	300
Bayonet scabbards	4,000
Cartridge-boxes, caliber .54	2,450
Cartridge-boxes, caliber .69	1,400
Cartridge-boxes, caliber .58	300
Ball screws	2,000
Pistol-cartridge boxes	550

Inventory C: Ordnance and ordnance stores captured in the city of Cheraw, South Carolina, by the Army of the Tennessee (United States forces, not Confederate) on March 3, 1865.

6-pounder smooth-bores (brass)	6
12-pounder howitzer	1
12-pounder howitzers (navy)	5
12-pounder smooth-bore (iron)	1
16-pounder Blakely rifles (caliber 3.5 inch)	1
20-pounder Blakely rifles (caliber 3 9/16 inch)	2
24-pounder howitzer	1
Rifled guns (banded, caliber 3 inch)	2
Rifled guns (banded, caliber 3.75 inch)	2
Rodman rifles (caliber 3 inch)	2
Short howitzer (caliber 5 7/8 inch)	1
Smooth-bore gun (caliber 3 5/8 inch)	1
Caissons complete	12
Battery wagons without limbers	3

Treasures of the Confederate Coast

Limber carriage without chest	1
Limbers	10
Gun carriage without wheels	1
Gun carriage, (3.75 inch caliber rifle)	2
Gun carriage, 3-inch rifle (navy)	2
Gun carriage, 3-inch Rodman rifle	2
Gun carriage, 6-pounder	1
Gun carriage, 12-pounder howitzer	1
Gun carriage, 12-pounder smooth-bore	1
Gun carriage, 16-pounder Blakely rifle	1
Gun carriage, 20-pounder Blakely rifle	2
Gun carriage, 24-pounder howitzer	1
Gun carriage, short howitzer	1
Gun carriage, smooth-bore gun (caliber 3 5/8 inch)	1
3-inch rifle ammunition (fixed, rounds)	180
3.75 rifle ammunition (fixed, rounds)	190
6-pounder shell (fixed, rounds)	40
12-pounder howitzer ammunition (fixed, rounds)	160
12-pounder light Napoleon ammunition (fixed, rounds)	1,375
12-pounder shell (fixed, rounds)	1,000
24-pounder howitzer ammunition (fixed, rounds)	7
Blakely rifle ammunition (fixed, rounds)	92
Austrian muskets (caliber .69)	663
Belgian muskets (caliber .69)	33
Enfield muskets (caliber .577)	200
Muskets (various kinds and calibers)	500
Springfield muskets (caliber .69)	2,345
U.S. rifles (caliber .58)	8
Artillery sabers and scabbards	200
Cavalry sabers and scabbards	150
Bayonet scabbards	1,000
Bayonet scabbards (saber)	500
Powder and cartridges (pounds)	43,700
Elongated ball cartridges, various calibers, (rounds)	30,000
Whitworth rifle cartridges (rounds)	250
Signal Rockets	25

References for Appendix B:
Official Records of the Union and Confederate Armies in the War of the Rebellion, (Washington, DC, 1893), Series 1, Volume 44, Part 1, pp. 239, 248, 249
Official Records of the Union and Confederate Armies in the War of the Rebellion, (Washington, DC, 1895), Series 1, Volume 47, Part 1, pp. 180-182, 475, 486, 487, 502, 503, 700, 701

• • •

Lee Spence with one of two iron cannons salvaged from a wreck he discovered off Cape Romain, South Carolina. Photo by Steve Howard, courtesy of Shipwrecks Inc.

Lee Spence examines a pile of cannon balls which have become encrusted with marine growth. Photo by Ray Lunsford.

This 2.9-inch Blakely's patent rifled gun was part of the Georgiana's cargo. It was one of two guns salvaged by Lee Spence from underneath the hull of the Mary Bowers. Both guns were sold to Fred Hack of Hilton Head Island who then donated them to the Fort Jackson Museum in Columbia, South Carolina. Photo courtesy of the Fort Jackson Museum.

Appendix C: Technical Report on the *Georgiana*

APPENDIX C
Technical Report on the *Georgiana*
(Based on the Archeological and Historical Records)

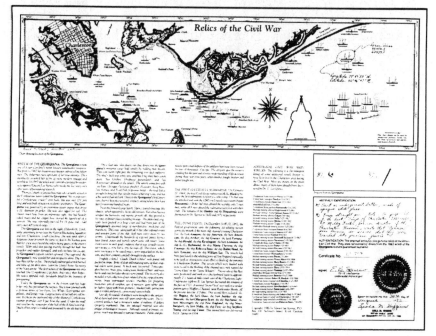

Notarized certificate with artifacts from the Georgiana.

SITE LOCATION

This unique archeological site was discovered by E. Lee Spence in 1969 and is located at latitude 32°46'47" North, longitude 79°45'35" West. The wreck site is entirely within the Atlantic Ocean and is approximately 0.9 nautical miles in a south easterly direction off the Isle of Palms, South Carolina, and 2.12 nautical miles from the eastern end of Breach Inlet, South Carolina.

"Loran C" lines of position crossing the site are 45498.3; 60454.1; 14561.4; and 31894.1. It is usually sufficient after the first visit to the site to use visual ranges and dragging of a grappling hook to relocate the wreck. The wreck of the *Constance Decimer* lies approximately 640 yards due south of the *Georgiana* Site.

LEGAL STATUS

The actual legal status, and therefore the ownership, of the *Georgiana* is unclear. Spence claimed ownership of the *Georgiana* and the surrounding wrecks in 1969 and has never formally

Treasures of the Confederate Coast

renounced that claim. However, the Federal government may have had a prior legal claim of ownership based on the Federal Navy's actions during and immediately after the Civil War. The Federal government also may hold title to Civil War wrecks through the "Abandoned Properties Act of 1876," which claimed title to certain captured and abandoned Confederate properties. The Federal government may have given up any claim it has to the site by assignment of title through salvage contracts awarded in the late 1800's or through the passage of a new act which transfers title to certain wrecks in State controlled waters to the individual States. Constitutionality of the new act has not yet been tested in Federal court. The State of South Carolina very definitely claims title to the *Georgiana* and many of the other wrecks discussed herein.

The State of South Carolina underwater antiquities act of 1969 (Spence was the primary mover behind the original legislation which is meant to protect both public and private interests in the wrecks), and its subsequent revisions and associated rules and regulations, provides for the issuance of hobby and commercial licenses, which allow the diver, the salvor and/or the archeologist to conduct his or her explorations within the framework of State law. The State underwater antiquities act, as it applies to shipwrecks, is currently administered by the State Archeologist (and his staff) at the Institute of Archeology and Anthropology at the University of South Carolina.

On March 27, 1989, Spence officially filed an application for a license to return to the *Georgiana* Wreck Site to conduct salvage operations. This was meant partially as a "holding action" to protect the site from looters Spence had heard were planning to visit the site. In fact, Spence would officially assign to the State, any claim Spence has (real or imagined) to ownership of the *Georgiana* and the associated wrecks, if Spence could be assured that the archeological and historical integrity of the wrecks would be protected and that Spence would be treated fairly as their original discoverer.

SITE HISTORY

The site was located in January, 1968, through the efforts of E. Lee Spence, who tentatively identified the site as the wreckage of the *Georgiana* and *Mary Bowers*. A second wreck site was located about a half mile inshore of the first site and was tentatively identified by Spence as the wreck of the *Norseman*. A third wreck site was located 640 yards due south of the first wreck and was tentatively identified by Spence as that of the *Constance Decimer*. Spence's preliminary identifications were based primarily on historical data he had gathered relating to losses of those particular

The "Real Rhett Butler" & Other Revelations

vessels. All four vessels were iron or steel hulled steamers lost while attempting to run the Federal blockade during the Civil War. Historical and archeological data gathered by Spence has confirmed the identification of all of the wrecks. Efforts were made at that time to begin commercial salvage efforts at the site. During the first year after the discovery, fewer than six dives were conducted on the site. Those efforts concentrated entirely on locating and raising easily accessible portions of the *Georgiana's* cargo.

In an effort to secure exclusive salvage rights to the wreck site, a company called Shipwrecks, Inc., was formed by Spence, Captain Walter Shaffer, and George Campsen. (Note: Mr. Campsen is a Charleston attorney and businessman. Captain Shaffer is a commercial fisherman. Spence had approached Captain Shaffer for help after learning that Shaffer was familiar with several unidentified obstructions in the general area Spence had identified, through research and visual search from the air, as the location of the *Georgiana's* destruction. One of those obstructions indeed proved to be the *Georgiana*.)

Legislation, drafted by Spence and Campsen, was subsequently passed and Shipwrecks, Inc. was immediately granted South Carolina State Salvage License #1, which gave them the exclusive rights to salvage the wrecks Spence had identified as the *Georgiana* and *Mary Bowers*. The license allowed the State a 25% share of the gross recovery.

Jurisdiction over the site was originally placed in the hands of the South Carolina Department of Archives and History, but subsequent legislation shifted supervision to the office of the State Archeologist and the Institute of Archeology and Anthropology at the University of South Carolina.

Shipwrecks, Inc. then subcontracted the work on the site to Real Eight Co., Inc., of Florida, with the agreement that the two companies would share in both the publicity and in the sale of any artifacts recovered from the site. Although Real Eight Company brought both men and equipment to South Carolina and stayed for a period of time, made relatively few dives before it abandoned the project due to poor visibility and adverse weather conditions. A contract was then signed between Shipwrecks, Inc. and Palmetto Divers, a two man, Charleston based company, made up of divers Jim Batey and Drew Ruddy. Palmetto Divers agreed to work the site on a salary basis and proceeded to do so for a period of weeks during the summer of 1969. Although Palmetto Divers, using capital equipment of less than $20,000, and expending less than $2,000 in operating costs, succeed in recovering a significant amount of

Treasures of the Confederate Coast

artifacts (estimates at the time placed the value at over $150,000) their contract was not renewed at the end of the contract period due to internal management problems in Shipwrecks, Inc.

Shortly afterwards, Spence, who had been president of Shipwrecks, Inc. formed another company, Artifacts, Inc., and began to concentrate his efforts on organizing the archeological excavation and salvage of the *Constance*. Spence eventually sold his stock in Shipwrecks, Inc. to his friend John W. (Jack) Thomson, an insurance adjuster who was both a diver and an excellent historian (he is now a Charleston tour guide specializing in Civil War related tours). Then in the early summer of 1970, Bill Alge, Dr. Jerry Crosby, and several of their friends (all experienced divers, and owners of the "Wet Shop" in North Charleston) purchased the remainder of the company from Shaffer and Campsen. Salvage efforts, under the direction of Dr. Crosby who had been elected president, were then resumed. Unfortunately, due to job commitments, their diving was limited to occasional weekend forays with insignificant results. Work finally ceased altogether on the site. Despite Shipwrecks, Inc.'s, failure to actively work the site their State salvage license was periodically renewed by the State Archeologist. Then, in November of 1973, Shipwrecks, Inc., signed a contract with Spence, hiring him for $1.00 per year as "Marine Archeologist and Director of the *Georgiana* Project." Shipwrecks Inc. was to get 25% and Spence was to pay the state the previously agreed 25% "share" called for in Shipwrecks, Inc.'s, State license. Spence also agreed to direct the project and to arrange all of the funding by further dividing the recovery. Funding for the project was received from Shipwreck Archaeology, Inc., an archeologically oriented salvage company which was entirely owned by the Hack family of Hilton Head Island, South Carolina. The company had previously been formed by the Hacks in connection with Spence's work on the *Constance*. An estimated total of $80,000 was spent for salvage and archeology on the site.

Over one million individual artifacts (ranging from common sewing pins to rare rifled cannon) were recovered. Most of the artifacts were donated to various museums by the Hack family. Since the bulk of the artifacts were never actually sold, it is impossible to put a dollars and cents value on the total recovery, but at today's prices it would easily amount to over twenty million dollars.

SITE DESCRIPTION

The *"Georgiana* Site" is actually a duel shipwreck site. The wreck of primary interest has been identified by Spence as that of the *Georgiana*, the second wreck has been identified as the wreck of the *Mary Bowers*.

The site is situated at mean low water at a depth of 14 feet with a mean diurnal tide rise of 5.2 feet. When originally discovered by Spence, the remains of part of the sheet metal covering of the forward end of the starboard boiler of the *Mary Bowers* sat within 3.5 feet of the surface at low tide. But, the effects of the sea have since rusted and collapsed that remaining portion to a point several feet further down.

Horizontal water visibility on the bottom is generally zero to three feet during the summer months, occasionally clearing to fourteen feet. Vertical visibility is usually less. During the winter months the visibility is slightly increased on the good days. However, the winter months also have a higher percentage of bad days. On extremely bad days there is not only zero visibility, there is often zero light penetration. Since surface water over the site is generally several feet clearer than water near the sand level, visibility can be dramatically increased by the use of a prop-wash deflection system. Visibility appears to be at its greatest shortly before and after high tide. Rains appear to have a greater affect on visibility than the wind, although high winds are capable of dropping the visibility to absolute zero for days at a time. Bottom dragging fishing trawlers working in the area present no safety hazard to the diver as they avoid the specific area, but silt stirred up by their trawl nets and trawl net doors causes considerable visibility problems on otherwise perfect days. Silt and mud on the wreck are easily stirred up by the divers, frequently preventing the use of water induction dredges on the site without the unwanted destruction or loss of numerous small artifacts which litter the wreck site.

The *Georgiana* appears to run north north west, while the *Mary Bowers* sits on top of her and crosses her in a westerly direction. The *Georgiana* was evidently headed towards shore when she was grounded, while the *Mary Bowers*, which was wrecked more than a year later, had apparently been following a course roughly parallel to shore when she struck the earlier wreck. The direction of the physical orientation of both wrecks matches well with historical accounts of their losses.

The *Georgiana's* stern is unmistakable, as the rudder, rudder-post, propeller shaft, and propeller are still in place. The topmost extant portion of the rudder post comes to within six feet of the surface at low water. The propeller is approximately twelve feet in diameter and is made of iron. One of the propeller's three blades is missing approximately one third of its length. Such damage was expected, as contemporary accounts of her loss said she was damaged when an exploding shell went off under her stern. It was this crippling damage which lead directly to her loss. The rudder, which appears to have either been hollow or made of wood sheathed with iron, is turned to the port side and is also damaged. We were unable to determine if the position of the rudder was intentional or if it was the result of gravity and the *Georgiana's* current list to her port side.

The *Georgiana* has one rectangular boiler. It is approximately nine feet wide, ten feet long, and ten feet high, with three fireboxes running longitudinally through her base. Most of the sheet metal covering over the boiler has deteriorated exposing the boiler tubes. The boiler is sitting upright and inside of the main hull of the *Georgiana*, and is approximately ten feet aft of the point where the *Mary Bowers* crosses the *Georgiana*.

The *Georgiana* is heeled over on her port side at both her stem and her rudder post, but (from the appearance of her boiler) is apparently sitting upright amidships, indicating that her keel has broken in at least two places.

The *Georgiana* is constructed of one quarter inch iron plates or strakes riveted to 2.5" by 1/8" angle iron frames. All frames are on eighteen inch centers. The frames have reverse frames attached and on casual observation appear to be Z-bar. Reverse frames face forward in the forward sections and aft in the after sections of the *Georgiana*.

Major strakes on the *Georgiana* are 2' by 28' by 1/4" with countersunk flat rivet heads with hammered points. The plates or strakes in the ship's shell plating are arranged in the sunken and raised system with parallel liners. The *Georgiana's* register had shown her as "clincher built," which is a similar although technically different type of construction. Her seams are lapped with double rows of alternating rivets. The ends of the plates are butted and fastened with single butt straps. The butt straps are fastened with double alternating rows of rivets on each side of the butt joint, making a total of four vertical rows of rivets on each butt strap.

Stealer plates changing to drop strakes, are found in both the bow and stern portions of the *Georgiana* and can be located by looking for strakes that suddenly become both an inner and an outer, or a clincher (clinker) strake, instead of entirely an inner strake or an outer strake. The *Georgiana* appears to have a bar keel.

Flooring (correctly called "ceiling") in the cargo holds is of heavy pine planking of varying widths. Eight inch by four inch pine planks (cargo battens) were attached to the transverse frames in the cargo holds. The cargo battens were fastened on sixteen inch centers and ran longitudinally. Decks were of wood set on iron deck beams which supported by vertical iron stanchions or deck pillars. Four of these pillars were still in place when Spence first discovered the wreck, only one remains. The other pillars collapsed (probably in a storm) during one of the lengthy periods when divers were not working the wreck. The pillars are three inches in diameter and appear to have been of solid wrought iron construction. Three were mounted on the center-line or keelson of the *Georgiana*. The first pillar was mounted at a point twelve feet forward of the after bulkhead of the forward cargo hold, the second thirty feet forward of the bulkhead, the third thirty-six feet forward of the bulkhead. That bulkhead is braced with angle iron bulkhead stiffeners on its after side. There are four bulkhead stiffeners which are visible. Measuring from the lowest exposed portion of *Georgiana's* starboard hull, the stiffeners are located at 36", 70", 102" and 136". Past that point the bulkhead is obscured by the wreckage of the *Mary Bowers*. The fourth visible deck pillar is mounted at the same frame as the first deck pillar mentioned above, but is six feet to the starboard and six feet from the starboard side of the *Georgiana's* hull. It appears that deck pillars were located every six feet along the keelson with a deck girder running along top of them. A single deck girder was located that was still attached to the first deck pillar mentioned above. The iron girder runs under the collapsed lower hull of the *Mary Bowers*.

The forward cargo hold is 67.5' in length as measured between the forward and after bulkheads of that hold. Running from the after end of the forward cargo hold on the starboard side one finds the hull to protrude four to five passing strakes from the sand for a distance of thirty-two feet where the remaining exposed portion of the hull drops to two to three passing strakes. The exposed remains of the starboard side of the *Georgiana* continues at that level until just past the forward bulkhead of the forward cargo hold, at which point the bow is twisted and definition is lost. The sand level inside the hull on the starboard side is slightly higher than the sand level on the outside which appears to be more vulnerable to the scouring action of the sea.

No visible strakes are attached to the stem of the *Georgiana* which is a solid bar and protrudes six feet from the sand. The stem is heavily raked and leans to the port side. Turning and swimming aft from the stem of the *Georgiana* one finds two to three passing strakes exposed, with additional upper strakes visible in the sand outside of the hull where they have broken outwards from the main body of the ship. Forty-five feet aft of the forward bulkhead of the *Georgiana's* forward cargo hold, the lower hull of the *Mary Bowers* obscures the port side of the hull of the *Georgiana*. Crossing the bilges of the *Mary Bowers* one again picks up the port side of the *Georgiana* at a point approximately twelve feet aft of the forward cargo hold. Passing the *Georgiana's* boiler going aft, one comes to the forward bulkhead of the after cargo hold.

Immediately aft of the forward bulkhead of the *Georgiana's* after cargo hold are several boxes of tinned iron sheets. The tinned sheets are in wooden boxes, now heavily impregnated with iron oxide. The sheets of tinned iron were probably intended for the manufacture of canteens, cups, cans, etc. Identical boxes of tinned sheet iron were found in the *Georgiana's* forward cargo hold, stacked in rows, nine boxes high, along the after bulkhead.

The *Georgiana's* keel and hull are broken at the forward bulkhead of her after cargo hold. From that bulkhead aft, the port side of the *Georgiana* is laying in the sand with her deck beams now standing vertical rather than horizontal. Two rows of deck beams protrude from the sand. Deck girders are still attached to some of the deck beams. Some of the diagonal tie plates, longitudinal tie plates, and stringer plates are also still attached and in place. The upper and lower decks are approximately seven feet apart, which would have left her about seven feet in the hold as *Lloyd's Register of Shipping* for 1873 gives the *Georgiana's* "depth moulded" as fourteen feet.

A ten inch diameter brass framed porthole with glass intact was located on the port side, one foot below the upper deck, between the third and fourth frame aft of the forward bulkhead of the after cargo hold of the *Georgiana*. The porthole was still set in an open position when it was found. The porthole has since been removed.

The port side of the *Georgiana's* hull (which, as mentioned earlier is broken outwards and is laying in the sand) is visible for three frames past the aforementioned porthole, but from there to the stern it is buried except for part of an occasional deck beam protruding upwards from the sand. Approximately one thousand Enfield rifle bullets were found buried in the sand between the frames of the hull in this area.

Reaching the *Georgiana's* stern one finds a transverse bulkhead which probably served as the after bulkhead to the after cargo hold and as the forward bulkhead to the lazarette. The propeller shaft is visible in this area going aft through the hull, but the forward part of the shaft is missing at a large coupling, which probably indicates heavy salvage work done at some time prior to

The "Real Rhett Butler" & Other Revelations

Spence's discovery and identification of the wreck. Most likely that salvage would have taken place in the early 1870's when the location of the wrecks was still marked by wreckage exposed at low tide, and before the knowledge of their identity had faded into history. The shaft, coupling, and hull are all made of iron. Turning and swimming forward along the starboard hull of the *Georgiana*, one finds four or five passing strakes intact and sticking out of the sand. The whole after cargo hold is cocked heavily to the port side. Thirty-five feet forward of the lazarette bulkhead, one comes onto several large iron water tanks built to the contours of the hull. Two of the water tanks still have lead piping running into their tops.

A large crate was recovered from just past the water tanks. The crate contained the encrusted remains of one thousand folding knife and spoon sets. The spoons were made of hallmarked "German Silver" and were in perfect condition. In fact some of the spoons were still shiny where they had been protected from the sea by the cathodic action of the steel knife blades. The steel was almost entirely eaten away. Similar loose spoons have been found in the *Georgiana's* forward cargo hold so it is thought that she was carrying at least one more crate of the spoons.

Swimming outside of the starboard side of the ship in this area one finds the upper portion of the *Georgiana's* starboard hull. The strakes are partially buried in the sand with the deck beams of both upper and lower decks sticking up in rows. It appears that the upper portion of the starboard side of the *Georgiana's* after cargo hold must have broken and fallen outwards prior to the vessel being struck (probably by the *Constance*) near its stern and rolled over on its port side. Two large, brass framed portholes were observed. They did not appear to be attached to the hull other than by recent marine encrustation. No other portholes or ports of any kind have been observed on the *Georgiana*. Returning to the water tanks, one swims forward to find that he is passing the boiler on his left. The *Georgiana* appears to be sitting upright in this area but the hull is broken flush to the level of her floor plates. The upper hull strakes are laying flat and are normally covered with less than one inch of sand.

Forward of the boiler one finds a considerable amount of presently unidentified wreckage consisting largely of iron pipe. A few brass valves and grates are visible, but there is nothing that appears to actually be the *Georgiana's* steam engines. Her engines may lie underneath other wreckage but were more likely salvaged after the war.

Treasures of the Confederate Coast

Next one crosses the flattened out hull of the *Mary Bowers* just forward of her starboard boiler and returns to the forward cargo hold. In the forward cargo hold of the *Georgiana* one can see the exposed edges of crates and barrels. Some of the crates held assorted sizes of hand finished brass straight pins. Many of the pins had wire wrapped and hammered heads. The pins were in excellent condition with some showing traces of a silver or tin plating. Other crates held opaque white glass buttons (both three hole and four hole varieties of several sizes and shapes). The buttons were found in perfect rows, having apparently been strung for packing, but there was no trace left of the thread which had disintegrated over the years. The upper portions of the crates, which had stuck completely out of the sand, had already been completely eaten away by sea worms (teredo navalis). Twelve crates containing easily destroyed items such as spools of thread, bolts of cloth, and rolls of seam tape were left undisturbed by the divers. There may be additional cargo under the undisturbed crates. Layers of cargo were originally separated by dunnage consisting of 2 by 4's, 4 by 4's, assorted wedges, etc. Both crates and barrels are packed side by side. Barrels are packed on their side, lengthwise in the hold, and are braced in place by wooden wedges. Crates are also packed lengthwise along the center-line of the ship.

Two small cast iron, rifled guns, 2.9" bore, stamped "BLAKELY'S PATENT" on the wrought iron reinforcing band on the breech, and marked "VAVASSEUR 1862 LONDON" on the trunions, were found just forward of the two rows of boxes of tinned sheet iron along the aft end of the forward cargo hold. Shot and shell for these guns, as well shot and shell for a 3.5" version of the gun, were found nearby, as was a brass breech site believed to have been meant for a Whitworth gun. The other guns were not located. The two 2.9" guns were recovered and are now on display at Fort Jackson Museum at Columbia, South Carolina. The 2.9" shells had pewter fuses while the 3.5" shells had brass fuses. All of the shot and shell had lead sabots. Although unique in their appearance for Blakely guns, the cannon bores had the distinctive ratchet rifling (the *lands* having a smooth transition from the edge of the groove to the opposite edge of the *land*) which had been designed and patented by Blakely and are characteristic of his guns.

The two Blakely guns were found hanging from the bottom of the *Mary Bowers*. The guns had apparently been sitting on top of the *Georgiana's* cargo (which is supported by the reports of the Federal sailors who boarded the *Georgiana* shortly after the wreck) when the *Mary Bowers* crashed across the wreck of the *Georgiana*.

The "Real Rhett Butler" & Other Revelations

Over the years the cannon became encrusted with a matrix composed of sand, marine growth and iron oxide which fused them to the underside of the *Mary Bowers*. As time elapsed, the cargo sitting under the Blakely guns was eventually dislodged, eaten, or washed away, leaving the guns hanging almost three feet above the present day level of sand.

It would have been impossible to hammer the guns from their binding matrix without damaging them, and without endangering the lives of the divers who would have had to chip them loose while lying underneath them, so the two guns were removed, without damage, by the judicious use of detonating cord. (Note: Detonating cord is an explosive that is commonly used by divers to remove the propellers of yachts at the dock. Commercial divers use the cord because, properly used, it does less damage to the expensive bronze propellers, and shafts, than would a hammer or a gear puller. This is not in any way to endorse the use of detonating cord or any other explosive on an underwater site as a first choice method, but rather to point out that it may be the best choice. Any explosive device should only be used when absolutely necessary and then only as a last resort by experts. Despite emotional responses to the contrary, appropriate controlled explosive devices do have a valid place in underwater archeology. For the record, this underwater archeologist has never used dynamite on an archeological site and has yet to hear of a situation where such use would be appropriate.)

The *Mary Bowers* rammed the wreck of the *Georgiana* with such force that she broke entirely through both sides of the *Georgiana*. The forward end of the *Mary Bowers'* starboard boiler is in line with the starboard hull of the *Georgiana* and is only twenty-two inches aft of the after bulkhead of the *Georgiana's* forward cargo hold. From there the *Mary Bowers* crosses the *Georgiana*, forming a ledge across the aft end of the cargo hold. That ledge runs diagonally from the starboard side of the *Georgiana*, just aft of the aft of the after bulkhead of the forward cargo hold to a point on the port side twenty-one feet forward of the same bulkhead. The sides of the hull of the *Mary Bowers* in this area have broken outwards from the vessel at a point just below the level of the ship's floor plates near the turn of the bilge. No wreckage associated with the *Mary Bowers* has been located aft of her boilers. Her port boiler has rolled away from the starboard boiler and is largely buried in the sand with her expansion tank still mounted in place. The boilers are cylinder shaped tube boilers, 8.5' in diameter, 14' long, with twin

3' diameter fireboxes running longitudinally. The expansion tank on her port boiler is seven feet in diameter.

Running forward from the starboard boiler one finds the frames in the *Mary Bowers* to be on eighteen inch centers, as are those on the *Georgiana*. Both side stringers and bilge stringers are visible on the *Mary Bowers*. She is built with deep floor plates without lightening holes. The ship has a flat plate keel with a center vertical keel or keelson. The condition of the *Mary Bowers* seems to improve as one leaves the vicinity of the *Georgiana*. In the *Mary Bowers'* forward cargo hold one finds both the starboard and port sides of the vessel intact for a level of two passing strakes above the floor plates. Heavy pine flooring (correctly called *ceiling*) is visible in some areas but must frequently be covered with shifting sand or the planks would have already been destroyed away by the sea worms.

The hull has broken outwards along the entire length of the forward section of the *Mary Bowers* and there is little evidence of her cargo as the hold has been fully exposed to the force of the currents which have left little in place. Presumably, the *Mary Bowers'* cargo (and there is a question as to whether or not she carried a full cargo of merchandise or whether she carried primarily a cargo of coal) is now buried in the sand outside of the wreck. Two brass framed portholes have been located on the port side of the forward part of the *Mary Bowers*. Both portholes have their glass intact and were found set in an open position. The port holes are set between the transverse frames and are mounted with their upper edge at a level one foot below the iron deck beams. On the port side of *Mary Bowers* the flattened out sides are buried under a shallow layer of sand and the broken deck beams form a row of upright posts.

The forward bulkhead of the *Mary Bowers'* forward cargo hold is clearly visible, but unlike that of the *Georgiana* it is set well aft of the bow stem. The wreck is extremely narrow. The extreme bow and bow stem were not identified due to considerable wreckage in the area. Presumably the wreckage is associated with the "turtle deck" that covered the bow of the *Mary Bowers*.

ARCHEOLOGY ON THE SITE

As can be deduced from the foregoing site description, a considerable amount of archeological investigation has taken place on the wreck site. True archeology on the site was first made possible in November of 1973 through private funding received from the Hack family of Hilton Head Island, South Carolina. Unfortunately, no matching support was received from the Office of the State Archeologist, or from the Institute of Archeology and Anthropology, in the form of money, equipment, personnel, or pertinent advice. (Management, staff and rules at the Institute have since changed, so this is not meant in any way as a criticism of the current management, staff or rules of the Institute as it is currently organized, staffed and managed.)

All archeology on the site was conducted by E. Lee Spence, or by students from Sea Research Society's College of Marine Arts, working under Spence's direction.

To this date no State official has ever visited or dived on the *Georgiana* site (unless one counts dives made by sport divers or commercial salvors who were later employed by the State). This is despite the fact that the State has consistently claimed and taken a share of all artifacts recovered by privately funded commercial salvors and archeologists working the site. Such failure by the Institute to have even one of its staff visit the *Georgiana* Site is as surprising as it is distressing, as South Carolina law clearly mandates that no licenses be issued except those that can be properly supervised. The license for the *Georgiana* Site was State salvage license #1, and the Institute's failure to make even one visit to the *Georgiana* Site, during the seven years the license was in effect, combined with the State's history of issuing numerous other licenses (for both commercial and hobby purposes), clearly demonstrates a lack of regard for the law and a lack of due diligence with respect to the proper supervision of licenses. In all fairness, as hinted at above, it should be noted that the Institute of Archeology and Anthropology is now headed by a new director, who seems to be very able, competent, and diligent. The current State Archeologist (who serves as the director of the Institute) has hired a new underwater archeologist, and it is hoped that this new staffing will result in more State interest and involvement in the *Georgiana* Site in particular, and in more cooperation between the State and private salvors in general.

Further archeology on the *Georgiana* Site is both necessary and desirable as there are still many things to be learned from and about the *Georgiana*. and the associated wrecks

Archeological tools, salvage equipment and diving gear used on the *Georgiana* Site were limited to: two chipping hammers; two brick chisels; one cold chisel; one pry bar; two aluminum yardsticks; a five hundred pound capacity lift bag; a small quantity of detonating cord; a one ton winch; two underwater writing pads; six rolls of colored survey flagging; plastic storage jars; small self sealing sample bags; specimen jars; graph paper; one Nikonis underwater camera with flash attachment; one aluminum survey pole (metric); serially numbered plastic identification tags; one waterproof level; two sets of underwater communications gear; two sets of cold water diving gear; six complete sets of SCUBA gear; two six inch water induction dredges; one 1.5" water jet; hookah gear sufficient to support four divers; and two boats (one twenty seven feet in length, gas powered; the other forty-two feet in length and diesel powered), each complete with dive ladders and prop-wash deflection systems.

The majority of the detailed archeology on the site has taken place in the forward cargo hold of the *Georgiana* (as can be seen from the foregoing Site Description). Some preliminary archeological investigation has taken place at the stern of the *Georgiana* and at various points along the *Mary Bowers*. A sight survey has been made of the entire wreck site but was limited in its results due to consistently poor visibility.

The transverse framing of the *Georgiana* was adopted as a ready made grid system. The frames are uniformly mounted on eighteen inch centers and those in the forward cargo hold were marked with serially numbered tags for use as reference points. Using the after bulkhead of the forward cargo hold as frame #1, all frames were numbered consecutively towards the bow on both the port and starboard sides of the ship. Significant features such as stanchions, deck beams, deck girders, transverse bulkheads, butt straps, machinery, valves or other archeological features were noted with respect to the grid and their respective distances from the hull or other significant features that had already been plotted. A master diagram was made of the grid (i.e. the wreck) and all features carefully recorded on a scale of 1" to 18". Crates and barrels were recorded as to their size, contents, and relative positions. All wooden artifacts, including barrels staves, crating, and dunnage were brought to the surface, photographed, drawn and measured. Fiberglass tanks were constructed for the storage and preservation of artifacts.

The complexity of the *Georgiana* Site, due to its being a duel wreck site, offers both challenges and opportunity, to the archeologist. The challenges should be obvious, but opportunities are more subtle. The major opportunity being the chance to work on two vessels of the same age, but entirely different construction, at one location. This writer heartily recommends that the archeological salvage of the *Georgiana* site be resumed to take advantage of the opportunities the site offers. The work should be resumed before the site is further destroyed by the natural forces of the weather and the sea.

DAMAGE TO THE SITE

Artifacts which required the destruction of surrounding artifacts for their recovery were normally left in place. But, when such removal was deemed necessary, those artifacts were raised only after the surrounding artifacts were completely examined and recorded.

Although it was originally assumed by Spence that the wreck site had achieved a stabilized state, where deterioration was slow or non-existent, Spence has since realized that the process of deterioration still goes forth with vigor. The iron hulls and frames of the two vessels are continually being reduced by the nonstop electrolysis and oxidation on the site. The hulls are continuing to collapse under the combined forces of their own weight and wind and tide driven currents. The *Georgiana* Site could be compared to a gigantic galvanic battery composed of tons of dissimilar metals (brass, tin, lead, zinc, copper, wrought iron, cast iron and steel) in an electrolytic bath (salt water). The battery is slowly consuming itself, with the baser metals (those metals further down the Galvanic Scale) being destroyed first. As the remaining portions of the hulls of the two vessels further collapse, they expose any cargo which remains inside of the wrecks to ever increasing destructive forces in the form both marine borers and currents. Any artifacts thus exposed to the full force of the sea may be swept entirely outside and away from the wrecks never to be observed, recorded, or recovered. Surviving wooden portions of both the *Georgiana* and the *Mary Bowers*, such as flooring and longitudinal battens, and containers such as crates and barrels are frequently exposed to teredo navalis and other marine borers as sand is scoured from the wrecks during storms. The damage is temporarily halted each time the sand washes back over the wood, but the damage is cumulative, and it is obvious that a great deal has taken place since the wreck was first discovered in 1967.

IS THERE GOLD?

Perhaps surprisingly, Spence's interest in the reputed gold on these wrecks has always been minimal and he has never made a concerted effort to locate the gold or to even conclusively confirm its existence. Part of the lack of interest in the *Georgiana's* gold is that when Spence first began researching the wrecks he was unaware of its possible existence. Later, when Spence did realize that some gold might have been lost with one or more of the wrecks, he still wasn't impressed. The price of gold, at the time of Spence's original research, was only thirty-two dollars a troy ounce (for a total bullion value of less than $140,000) and the numismatic values were barely higher, so the high cost of salvage certainly could not have been justified, at that time, solely on the basis of a hunt for the coins. However, the main reason for the lack of interest, then and now, is that Spence has always been far more fascinated by the history and archeology of the *Georgiana* than the monetary potential of the wreck. Despite this relative lack of monetary interest in the gold, Spence very definitely believes gold was carried on each of the four steamers, and he believes that most, if not all, of the gold was lost and has never been recovered.

Confederate naval historian John Thomas Scharf's book, *History of the Confederate States Navy from its Organization to the Surrender of its Last Vessel,* compares the costs of operating a steamer for one month in peace time and for one month during the war. Scharf points out that wages and expenses were "paid in gold." A list has been prepared from Scharf's breakdown of one month's expenses for a first class steamer carrying passengers and freight through the blockade has been given in the Spence's List section of this book.

The steamers *Mary Bowers*, *Norseman*, and *Constance Decimer*, certainly carried gold for expenses such as those listed above. The amounts of gold actually carried would have varied according to the respective sizes of the vessels and their crews. The passengers would also have carried gold to cover their expenses on the voyage as well as for other purposes.

The *Constance Decimer's* cargo was described as "on government account". It is mere speculation that she carried gold to purchase an outbound cotton. It is just as likely that the *Constance Decimer* outbound cargo would have been cotton "on government account."

The possibility of the *Norseman's* having gold hidden underneath her cargo of cotton comes from a Federal report at the end of the war. But that report merely mentioned a rumor of "something" hidden under her cargo of cotton. The report did not specify that the "something" was gold. However, the Confederate government was shipping gold out of the Confederacy on a fairly regular basis, throughout the war, and gold was often hidden where it could not be easily retrieved. One ship, that had been captured by the Federals, was later reported to have had gold hidden in the keelson, and the Confederate owners were trying to buy the vessel back from the Federal government before the gold was discovered. The Confederates knew that the Federal Navy often found itself in the position of having to destroy a ship and its cargo rather than let it be recaptured by the Confederates. By hiding the gold, the

Confederates may not get the gold, but then, neither would the Federals. Many of the wealthy people in the South simply sold everything they owned (taking payment in gold when possible) and fled the war. Such outbound passengers could have carried significant amounts of gold.

The story of $90,000 in gold coin carried on the Georgiana comes from a Confederate dispatch directing that sum be issued to the "cruiser" which was nearing completion and almost ready to sail. The money was to have been used as pay for the crew and for expenses. The vessel was not actually named, but the "cruiser" appears to have been the Georgiana. Additionally, the figures given by Scharf, and recounted above, were for a thirty man crew. The Georgiana's crew apparently was much larger as reports gave it's size as anywhere from 44 to 140 men. A larger crew would have meant even more gold was necessary. The idea of the Georgiana's crew leaving behind $90,000 in gold is not in the least far fetched, as the Georgiana's crew were already abandoning a vessel and cargo worth over $1,000,000. Besides, the Federals were in hot pursuit, and attempting to delay escape, while the gold was taken out of hiding, brought up on deck, and lowered over the side, would have been an unwarranted risk to the lives of Georgiana's men.

Although the paper price of gold fluctuated, a twenty dollar U.S. "Double Eagle" gold piece (which was probably the denomination and type of gold coin shipped) contained 0.9677 troy ounces of gold. Figuring that the price of gold (at the time of this writing) is just under $400.00 per troy ounce, gold coins having a face value of $90,000 would now have a bullion value of approximately $1,741,860. Numismatic value would, of course, be higher and would depend on dates, mints, and condition. Gold is not affected by immersion in salt water and the coins should be in the same condition as the day they were lost which would probably be uncirculated or MS-60 condition. If the coins were all minted at Philadelphia in 1862 and they were in MS-60 condition, the current total numismatic book value would be $15,750,000. Even if the coins were much older, they would probably still have been in uncirculated condition, as gold coins were normally boxed and shipped from place to place to meet major trade needs and, although legal tender, were not commonly used in general circulation (except during wartime), as were silver coins.

A schedule of pay rates for the men and officers of the Confederate Navy may be found in the book, The Confederate Navy: A Study in Organization, by T.H. Wells. Those pay rates, although lower than those paid to "merchant crews" would (due to the larger crews) have still meant a significant quantity of gold was needed to meet payroll and other expenses.

Fisher Research Laboratories, a California company which manufacturers sophisticated hand held underwater metal detectors that can discriminate between gold and iron, has been working with Spence to help develop a workable plan to locate any gold that might be on the wrecks.

CRUISER OR MERCHANT SHIP?

The mystery: There has always been a major question as to whether or not the *Georgiana* was built as a cruiser or as merely a merchant ship. The *Georgiana's* true character was open to question in 1863, just as it is today.

Ordnance and stores: There is no question at all as to whether or not the *Georgiana* carried ordnance and ordnance stores, as two guns and a large amount of shot and shell was recovered. The recovered guns were 2.9" Blakely rifles. The guns were found in the cargo hold and from the rope slings tied around their balance points it was obvious that they had not been mounted at the time of the *Georgiana's* sinking. The question thus arises as to whether the guns were intended as armament for the *Georgiana* or whether they were merely cargo. Due to the small caliber of the recovered guns it has been suggested that the guns were intended as field pieces (and newspaper accounts in the Charleston papers in the days following the wreck stated that the *Georgiana* carried "six pieces of field artillery of the Whitworth and Blakely patterns"), but the loop on the cascabel seems to indicate that they were made for shipboard use.

Class: Cruisers are actually intended to seek out, capture and destroy enemy merchant vessels, which are seldom armed. Cruisers are not meant to have to fight it out with their prey so heavy caliber guns are not necessarily a part of their armament. Cruisers are normally designed light and fast to outrun heavy warships, and the use of small caliber guns would help allow a cruiser to keep its weight down. Besides, the *Georgiana* apparently was carrying heavier guns. In addition to the 2.9" Blakely shot and shell, some 3.5" Blakely shot and shell was recovered. There was also a brass breech sight recovered which appears to have been from a Whitworth gun of unknown caliber.

Armament: One contemporary newspaper account described the *Georgiana* as pierced for fourteen guns. The steamer was also reported as having a crew of 140 men, and as going into Charleston to pick up yet more men. If true, this would match with Confederate naval historian John Thomas Scharf's description of her in his book, *History of the Confederate States Navy from its Organization*

The "Real Rhett Butler" & Other Revelations

to the Surrender of its Last Vessel, as the "most powerful (Confederate) cruiser then afloat." Scharf, who had actually been an officer (albeit a midshipman) in the Confederate Navy, was certainly familiar with the better known Confederate cruisers, *Alabama*, *Florida*, and *Shenandoah*, which were all still afloat at the time of the *Georgiana's* destruction. Scharf was clearly saying that the *Georgiana* was the most powerful Confederate cruiser ever built. The *Alabama*, normally thought of as the most powerful Confederate cruiser, was certainly better known than the *Georgiana*, but the *Alabama* carried only eight guns and her full complement of men was put at 145. Furthermore, the *Georgiana* was of iron construction while the *Alabama* was constructed of wood. Iron construction alone doesn't make for a fighting ship but it certainly helps to make a better one. Less weight in materials is required, when building a hull of iron versus wood, to achieve the same hull strength. A lighter hull can mean a faster ship. Iron doesn't catch fire and burn in battle, and iron doesn't splinter like wood. Fire and wood splinters were frequently cited as major causes of deaths aboard wooden ships in battle.

Iron plating: Another contemporary account stated that the *Georgiana* was carrying iron plating in her hold. The iron plating was to have been added to the *Georgiana* for extra protection. Such plates have not been found in the wreck, but may have been salvaged after the war. Previous salvage of the wreck is indicated archeologically through the absence of the *Georgiana's* main propeller shaft and steam engines. Iron plates, if they did exist, would have been easily salvageable targets for late 19th century salvors. Such salvage might also explain why additional cannon have not been found. (Note: It is actually thought that some additional cannon remain buried under the wreckage of the *Mary Bowers* where they would not have been easily accessible to salvors.)

Consular dispatch (Liverpool): A United States consular dispatch dated at Liverpool on January 6, 1863, had stated "The steamer *Georgiana*, just arrived at Liverpool from the Clyde. She is new and said to be a very superior steamer. She arrived at this port on the 4th instant (January, 1863). Yesterday while lying here she had the Rebel flag flying at her mast. She has not as yet been entered to load at the customs, but by the advertisement on the slip enclosed is to load and clear for Nassau. 'Brig Rigged steamer *Georgiana* s.s. - Liverpool 580 tons, Capt. Davis - Hull painted black - built of iron - round stern, carvings and name on the same gilt - bust female figurehead - painted white - poop deck, iron railings around same

Treasures of the Confederate Coast

painted white - draws when loaded 15 feet aft and 14 feet forward - steams 12 knots.' The *Georgiana* was purchased expressly to run the blockade and was reported as bound to Charleston."

Detective report: A report by two detectives from the Liverpool Police Department who, at the demand of the U.S. Consul, physically inspected the *Georgiana* to determine her nature, reported that she was so lightly built that if a gun were fired from her decks that she would "shake from stem to stern." To many, such an official report would seem to settle the matter once and for all, but it isn't all that easy. The *Alabama* had been described as a lightly built merchant vessel before her sailing, yet such reports are now laughed at in view of her well known history. The U.S. Consul had apparently seen the *Georgiana,* and he was convinced she was intended to fight. The Consul's demand for an official inspection was not a simple attempt to learn her character, it was a required step that had to be gone through to get the vessel condemned. The two detectives may have been Confederate sympathizers or may have simply been bribed. The *Georgiana* sailed the day after the inspection by the detectives. The fact that the *Georgiana's* captain chose to sail on a Sunday, when his ship was still not completely loaded and fitted out, tends to support the idea that delay (and the additional time for investigation such delay would have allowed) might have ended in the *Georgiana's* seizure. The *Georgiana's* Sunday sailing effectively prevented any further official inspection.

Consular dispatch (Teneriffe): On February 13, 1863, the U.S. Consul at Teneriffe wrote that "from her appearances and the circumstances of her officers wearing gold lace on their caps, coupled with the description of her in the *London American* of January 28, I fear that she is an armed vessel, intended as a cruiser against our merchantmen. Two weeks later the U.S. Consul at Nassau wrote "also arrived the brig-rigged iron propeller *Georgiana*, another confederate to the pirate *Alabama*. * * * a formidable addition to the rebel fleet."

Officers: The *Georgiana's* captain was probably A.B. Davidson, who was described as a "retired" British naval officer. One report gives the captain's name as Davis, while other reports state that Lt. George Terry Sinclair of the Confederate Navy was meant to be the *Georgiana's* commander, so Davidson may have only held temporary command (for the voyage to Charleston). A third man by the name of Hudson, also appears in some reports as the *Georgiana's* captain. These discrepancies are more easily explained on a military vessel than aboard a merchantmen as often a military vessel would have a captain and a commander. The commander

The "Real Rhett Butler" & Other Revelations

would also be shown as captain, but his duties would have been primarily military. It may also be of significance that a man who had served as a gunner in the Crimean was among those reported as enrolled as crew aboard the *Georgiana*.

Ownership: Ownership of the *Georgiana* is shown in some records simply as "English parties" but her register listed Neal Mathewson, who was then head of the Confederate Aid Society. The Navigation Company, a firm owned by J. and T. Johnson and Company of Liverpool, has also been mentioned as an owner. The vessels of the Navigation Company were frequently reported as "owned" by George Wigg, who was an active steamship agent working out of Nassau. Contemporary Charleston newspapers reported the *Georgiana's* cargo as consigned to "Messrs. John Fraser & Co.", of Charleston. If the vessel was indeed meant as a Confederate cruiser, it would logically follow that the financing and construction of the *Georgiana* would have been arranged through Fraser, Trenholm & Co., of Liverpool, for the reasons stated below.

Trenholm connection: Contemporary newspaper accounts state that the *Georgiana's* cargo was consigned to Fraser & Co., a Charleston based blockade running firm headed by George A. Trenholm. Trenholm was also the principal owner of the Liverpool based firm, Fraser, Trenholm & Co. The two companies jointly served as "the bankers of the Confederacy." The moneys for the construction of the cruisers and the elusive $90,000 in gold coin were all funneled through Trenholm's Liverpool accounts. James D. Bullock, who was in charge of the Confederacy's secret service operations in Europe, actually worked out of Trenholm's Liverpool offices. It was Bullock's job to arrange for the clandestine construction and outfitting of cruisers (like the *Georgiana*), and it was Trenholm's job to see that Bullock had the funds to succeed.

Trenholm was the absolute master of blockade running, and was the historical basis for Margaret Mitchell's fictional Rhett Butler in *Gone With The Wind*. Trenholm was tall and handsome with a distinctive smile, and a sharp mind for business. His companies made today's equivalent of over a billion dollars from blockade running. Having served as Treasurer of the Confederacy, Trenholm was accused of making off with and hiding hundreds of millions of dollars in government funds. He was charged with high treason and thrown in jail under threat of death at war's end. In jail he had a beautiful, but "fast," young widow visit him. She cried at seeing him locked up. Fabulously wealthy and brave, he was both admired and feared and quickly received a presidential pardon. His postwar

Treasures of the Confederate Coast

friendships with Yankee carpet baggers and scalawags earned him a questionable reputation, but his endowments of Southern churches, hospitals and orphanages insured acceptance into polite society. For more on Trenholm see Chapter One in this book.

What's in a name ?: By first calling the vessel *Louisiana*, yet hiring people for the *Georgiana*, it confused Union spies in Liverpool who didn't immediately realize they were the same vessel. The name *Georgiana* could have been symbolic of the State of Georgia. Such a possibility is supported by a report from the Union Consul at Nassau, James Samuel Whitney, that by the time of the *Georgiana's* arrival at Nassau her name had been altered to read *Georgia*. Whitney also believed that she was to be renamed *South Carolina*. However, because of the Fraser, Trenholm & Co. connection, mentioned above, it is more likely that the name *Georgiana* was named for the infant daughter of George and Anna Trenholm, who's name had been derived from combining the first names of the child's parents. Georgiana died as an infant and was buried at Magnolia cemetery in Charleston. There is also the possibility that the vessel was named for Georgiana Moore, wife of Felix Gregory DeFontaine. DeFontaine was co-editor (with William Gilmore Simms and Henry Timrod) of the *Columbia Daily South Carolinian*, which was largely owned by George Trenholm. DeFontaine, who wrote under the name *Personne* has been described as "one of the two outstanding reporters of the South" and "provided vivid, first hand descriptions of the battles".

Hull strength: Archeological investigation of the *Georgiana's* wreckage showed that the upper strakes of her hull were made of one quarter inch iron plates. Lower strakes would have been much heavier. That is double the one eighth inch iron planks used for similar strakes in the construction of both the *Mary Bowers* and the *Constance*. Additionally, although the frames in both the *Constance* and the *Mary Bowers* are single frames, the frames in the *Georgiana* are strengthened with attached reverse frames. The *Georgiana's* doubled frames and hull thickness appear much the same as those observed, by this archeologist, on the wreck of the *Sherman*. (Note: The *Sherman*, which wrecked off South Carolina in 1874, had been captured as a blockade runner, and had been successfully used during the war by the United States Navy as the United States gunboat *Princess Royal*. No report has been found that would indicate that the *Princess Royal* shook from "stem to stern" when a gun was fired from her deck. In fact contemporary descriptions of the *Princess Royal* speak of her in glowing terms.).

The "Real Rhett Butler" & Other Revelations

Draft: Although deep draft sea going vessels already in existence were certainly purchased and pressed into service as blockade running merchant ships, they were not well suited for the purpose. By the time the *Georgiana* was being designed and built, the British shipyards were already turning out vessels suited for running the blockade. The British were building steamers with large cargo holds, yet of extremely shallow draft to allow them to run close into shore where the deeper draft warships couldn't go. The ideal blockade runner was built along the lines of the *Mary Bowers* (which was built specifically for running the blockade). The *Mary Bowers* was a side-wheel steamer and, although rated to carry 680 tons, drew only six to eight feet of water. The *Georgiana* drew fourteen feet of water, yet could only carry 407 tons. If the *Georgiana* was built as a "merchant vessel" intended to run the blockade why was she built to draw so much water and to carry so little tonnage for that draft? A cruiser, expected to spend long periods of time at sea, and unable to enter just any port in a storm, would have needed the added stability of a deep keel.

The China syndrome: If the *Georgiana* was as innocent as some people have claimed, there would have been no need to have represented herself as built for the Emperor of China when she left Great Britain. The Emperor of China was building and purchasing vessels for his navy at the time of the *Georgiana's* sailing so such a representation did not automatically sound absurd, and reports of Chinese ownership would certainly have confused the facts, been hard to refute, and given the *Georgiana* a cover story, if she did indeed need one.

Privately armed: Once the *Georgiana* arrived at Nassau, it would have been obvious that she wasn't headed to China. A new cover would have been needed. At Nassau the *Georgiana* simply listed herself as a privately armed merchant vessel. It would have been highly unusual for a merchant ship running the blockade to have risked having guns mounted on her deck, as such armament would never have been sufficient to mount a successful defense against a full fledged warship, yet would have taken away all claim the merchant had of being a neutral vessel. Mounted guns would have subjected a captured blockade runner's crew to possible long term internment as true prisoners of war or, even worse, open them to charges of piracy with a potential penalty of hanging.

Mounted guns: An article in the *New York Times* of March 27, 1863, reported that the *Georgiana* had two guns mounted on her deck and that she fired at the Federal gunboats as she attempted to escape them. The reports of the various ships involved in the

Treasures of the Confederate Coast

destruction of the *Georgiana* make no mention of her firing back at them, but the existence of guns on her deck is supported by Confederate reports. The Confederate commander at battery Marshal on Sullivan's Island, who would have certainly had a chance to speak with the crew and officers of the *Georgiana*, reported that his efforts to go out and get the guns had failed. The Confederate commander said that despite the intact appearance of the *Georgiana* (her wire rigging was still standing), her wooden decks had burned, and that the guns had apparently tumbled into her hold. Since the 2.9" Blakely guns which were recovered from the *Georgiana* were still tied with (unburned) rope slings when found, they could not have been the guns that had been on the deck.

Gideon Welles' opinion: Possibly the most informed authority on the true nature of the *Georgiana* was President Abraham Lincoln's Secretary of Navy, Gideon Welles. It would have been his job to know, and he sent a dispatch to Rear-Admiral Samuel F. Du Pont, Commanding the United States South Atlantic Blockading Squadron, that said "the destruction of the *Georgiana* not only touched their pockets, but their hopes. She was a splendid craft, peculiarly fitted for the business of privateering."

CONCLUSIONS & RECOMMENDATIONS

Spence's conclusion, based on his "in depth" examination of both the historical and archeological record of the *Georgiana*, is that the *Georgiana* was not a mere merchant vessel. Spence believes the *Georgiana* was intended either as a privateer or as a cruiser. Spence also believes, that if the *Georgiana* had been fully fitted out she would indeed have deserved the title as the "most powerful" Confederate cruiser. It is Spence's further conclusion that the *Georgiana* Site is still extremely important and needs protection until further archeological investigation can be conducted. Spence recommends that the *Georgiana* Site be placed upon the *National Register of Historic Places*, and that the Institute of Archeology and Anthropology make resumption of work (whether conducted by themselves or Spence) a major priority.

IMPORTANT FINAL NOTE

Despite the obvious importance of the *Georgiana*, and the fact that the first salvage license issued in the State of South Carolina was for work done by Spence on the wreck of the *Georgiana*, over twenty-five years have passed since Spence first discovered the wreck without a single state official ever even visiting the wreck site. It makes one wonder how the Institute of Archeology and Anthropology has carried out the rest of its job, since in the mean time it has issued thousands of permits and licenses relating to diving, despite the fact that the law clearly states that it shall not issue more licenses than it can properly supervise.

Spence says the most important lesson learned from his discovery of the *Georgiana* was: "Don't ever assume that a public official is above petty jealousies, and never think that he is automatically knowledgeable, right, competent or trustworthy. Never expect any bureaucrat to do his job in a timely manner. Always realize that it is usually only with great reluctance that any government official will acknowledge or credit you for the discoveries you have made or for the work you have done, and if he does acknowledge you, he will usually damn you with faint praise." • • •

This brown and tan storage jar was manufactured by Powell & Co. of Bristol. It was salvaged from the Georgiana. The number 64 is a model number, not a date. Several sizes of these jars were recovered. Photo by the Institute of Archaeology & Anthropology, University of South Carolina, courtesy of Shipwrecks Inc.

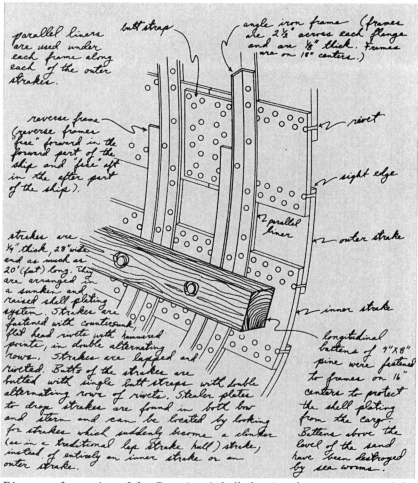

Diagram of a section of the Georgiana's hull showing the arrangement of the inner and outer strakes, forward and reverse frames, longitudinal battens, rivet patterns, etc. Prepared by L. Spence.

Brass steam valve removed from the base of the boiler on the Georgiana. Photo by L. Spence.

2.9-inch Blakely's patent solid shot with lead sabot, recovered from the forward cargo hold of the Georgiana, stands surrounded by a diver's weight belt. Photo by L. Spence.

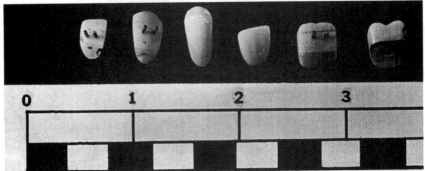

These realistic false teeth were part of the Georgiana's cargo. Photo by the Institute of Archaeology & Anthropology, University of South Carolina, courtesy of Shipwrecks Inc.

These projectiles are of the Blakely patent type and were shipped with four matching Blakely patent guns aboard the Georgiana. The one on the left is a 3.5-inch exploding shell, while the one on the right is a 2.9-inch solid shot. Both have lead sabots designed to expand into the rifling upon firing and thereby act as a gas seal and enhance the spin. Note the brass fuse plug in the nose of the shell. Photo by L. Spence.

Appendix C: Technical Report on the *Georgiana*
Page 440

This was one of seventy-two cobalt blue glass bottles packed in a single barrel on the Georgiana. The bottles contained castor oil and were corked and sealed with pewter foil. The barrel was found on the port side of the forward cargo hold, just forward of the path of the Mary Bowers. Photo by L. Spence.

This brass lifting lug for a hatch cover, and this eyepiece end of a telescope were both recovered from the Georgiana Site. Photos by the Institute of Archaeology & Anthropology, University of South Carolina, courtesy of Shipwrecks Inc.

Polychrome earthenware cup (pearlware) found on the Georgiana. Photo by the Institute of Archaeology & Anthropology, University of South Carolina, courtesy of Shipwrecks Inc.

Lee Spence, wearing an old style double hose regulator, surfaces from a dive on the Georgiana/Mary Bowers wreck site. Photo by Stu Gregg, courtesy of Shipwrecks Inc.

Appendix C: Technical Report on the *Georgiana*
Page 443

Boxes of silver plated brass pins and opaque white buttons were found in the forward cargo hold of the Georgiana. Some of the pins, which came in a wide range of sizes, had wire wrapped heads, while others had machined heads. The glass buttons were in perfect condition. Some of the buttons had three holes instead of the standard four holes. Also found were hooks and eyes, and rolls of binding tape and bolts of cloth. Photo by L. Spence.

APPENDIX D
"Sundry Clues"
(The *Georgiana's* pins & buttons)

Note: It was only after salvaging thousands of small sundries (glass buttons, brass straight pins, sewing needles, and spools of thread) from the wreck of the steamer *Georgiana* that I began to suspect that George Trenholm was the "real Rhett Butler." The *Georgiana's* cargo was consigned to John Fraser and Company in Charleston. John Fraser and Company was the most important blockade running company in the South. George Trenholm, a tall, handsome man from Charleston, South Carolina, was the head of this amazingly successful blockade running firm. My surprise at finding the sundries, shipped along with tons of war supplies, led me to continue his research and eventually uncover the spectacular truth behind *Gone With The Wind*. Trenholm's Liverpool based company, Fraser, Trenholm & Co., had purchased the cargo in England. Even in 1863, the *Georgiana's* cargo was valued at over one million dollars.

Rhett Butler "blockaded in at risk of his life - papers of pins and needles, buttons, spools of silk thread and hairpins." - excerpted from page 219 of *Gone With The Wind*.

Scarlett knew Rhett wasn't being patriotic and knew she should refuse his gifts, but "with prices as high as they were, where on earth could she get needles and bonbons and hairpins." - excerpted from page 236 of *Gone With The Wind*.

For Christmas Scarlett gave Ashley "the whole precious pack of needles Rhett had brought her from Nassau." - excerpted from page 266 of *Gone With The Wind*.

In a fit of anger, Scarlett ordered Rhett out of her house saying "Don't you ever come back here with any of your piddling papers of pins and ribbons, thinking I will forgive you. I'l! - I'll tell my father and he'll kill you!" - excerpted from page 336 of *Gone With The Wind*.

"Common pins became so scarce that they were hoarded like precious jewels." - excerpted from *The Siege of Charleston 1861-1865*.

"The loss of a sewing needle became a household calamity" - excerpted from page 26 of *The Women of the South in War Times*.

Treasures of the Confederate Coast

"Pins and needles were scarce. A half-dozen pins did duty for a year or two, and were stuck away carefully in a secret hiding place. Needles were borrowed from each other. One old lady I knew, who had but one needle, kept it hid away in the clock - she said from meddlesome busy-bodies." - excerpted from page 363 of *South Carolina Women in the Confederacy.*

• • •

This roll of binding or sewing tape was part of the Georgiana's cargo. Spools of thread (manufactured by Coates), bolts of cloth, and other sundries were also found. Photo by L. Spence.

APPENDIX E
"Gold on the *Constance*"
or
"The Mystery of the Boatswain's Whistle"

The discovery of a pewter boatswain's whistle in the stern area of the wreck of the British blockade runner *Constance Decimer* gives us a unique clue to speculate about.

A boatswain's whistle is the symbol or badge of office carried by the ship's boatswain (warrant officer or petty officer in charge of the deck crew, rigging, etc.). The whistle is commonly worn on a lanyard or chain around the boatswain's neck. Unless one accepts the hypothesis that this particular whistle was a spare, one is forced to conclude that the boatswain either lost the whistle during the excitement of the sinking or that the boatswain drowned wearing it.

Government documents and newspaper articles written in the days immediately following the loss of the steamer tell us that the *Constance* was in the process of running the blockade on the night of October 5, 1864, when it ran afoul of the wreckage of the *Georgiana* and *Mary Bowers*. The records state that the runner then turned offshore and sank in five minutes with the loss of one life.

It can be safely assumed that her captain, Duncan Stewart, was ignorant of the extent of the damage caused to the *Constance* at the time of the collision, for Stewart turned the *Constance* offshore to head for deeper water, where presumably he thought his ship would be safe further groundings. If Captain Stewart had been aware of his ship's immediate and certain danger of sinking, he would certainly have turned hard to starboard and headed the steamer for the nearby beach (present day Isle of Palms) where her grounding would have prevented the loss of life and would have helped insure the salvage of the cargo by the Confederates.

We can pretty much rule out the possibility of the lone drowning victim having perished at the instant of the collision, for this would surely have tipped off the captain as to the seriousness of the damage. Furthermore, since the vessel was actually in the process of running the blockade, all of the crew except for those needed to operate the ship's machinery would have been topside standing watch for enemy ships. Since the engine crew would have certainly been in voice contact with the captain it can be reasoned that the damage was not immediately apparent to them. Once the damage was apparent to the engine crew, they would have immediately warned the captain, and should have had ample time to make it topside (remember this vessel had only one deck, so there would have been very little distance to run for safety). Therefore, whoever died, either drowned topside or lingered below for some reason. The chance of a person drowning topside would be relatively remote due to the shallowness of the water and the size of the vessel. At the location where the *Constance* was lost, the water is only fourteen feet deep and the steamer's stacks, masts, rigging, and deck houses should have offered safety to non-swimmers who failed to make it to the life boats.

The *Constance* was found 640 yards from the other wrecks, a distance that would have taken less than two minutes to travel at a rate of ten knots. I used the ten knot figure even though she was capable of making at least fourteen knots, as her speed would have been reduced while operating in strange waters at night. That would have left her an additional three minutes for the crew to abandon ship. Three minutes would certainly have allowed adequate time for the crew to man their stations and launch lifeboats, but would not have allowed time to rescue baggage or personal effects, which the papers specifically said were not saved.

The papers and government documents stated that the *Constance* carried a valuable cargo on government account. The vessel would have also carried a fair amount of gold for payment of the crew, and for the purchase of emergency supplies and payment for repairs needed on the voyage while in foreign ports. A typical amount that would have been carried would have been in excess of $40,000. At today's prices, the bullion value alone would be around $8,000,000. The numismatic value could be far higher.

All of the ship's officers would have been aware of the gold and would have known where it was stored in the captain's cabin.

The captain's cabin is customarily located in the stern of the ship. While working in this area the divers realized that the ship had broken in such a way that any artifacts that had been in the captain's cabin would certainly have spilled out of the wreck, they therefore began to excavate immediately outside of the wreck on the port side by a break in the hull. Several silver spoons, a small brass bell, a pair of silver sugar tongs, a single coin, and an ornate, gimbaled, brass lamp were found. The quality of the artifacts, as well as their location when found, convinced the divers that they had indeed located the remains of the captain's cabin. A pewter boatswain's whistle, in the shape of a cannon, was found along with the other artifacts.

The "Real Rhett Butler" & Other Revelations

We have already presented a logical case against anyone drowning, and yet the historic records say that someone did drown. The boatswain's whistle should have been around his neck, and his job was topside, yet a boatswain's whistle was found with the artifacts from the captain's cabin. Nothing was saved from the wreck at the time of the sinking, yet, as stated earlier, there certainly must have been a large amount of gold aboard. Taken together, one might logically conclude that the boatswain died a hero while trying to save gold hidden in the captain's cabin. Speculation? Maybe, but it does have the ring of truth.

Our salvage contract with the State expired before we could finish excavating the wreck, and we never found the gold.

• • •

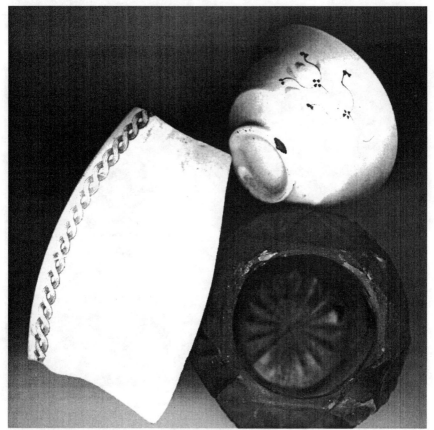

These artifacts were recovered from the stern section of the Constance. Note the rope border on the fragment of ironstone china. Like those found on the Georgiana, the handless cup appears to date from well before the Civil War. Also note the weathering on the glass inkwell. Photo by L. Spence.

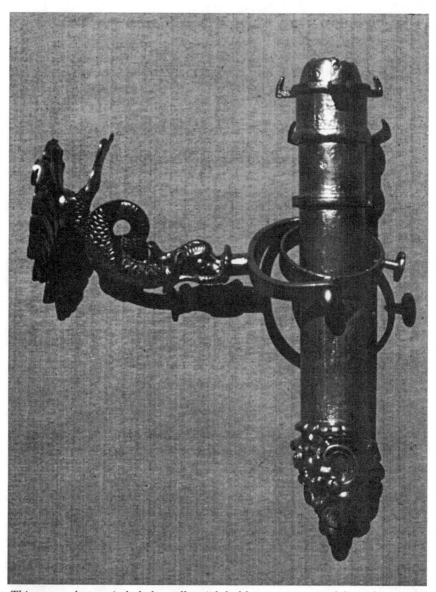

This ornate brass gimbaled candle stick holder was recovered from the area of the Captain's cabin on the wreck of the Constance. The wall mount was in the shape of a scallop shell. Photo by L. Spence, courtesy of Shipwreck Archaeology Inc.

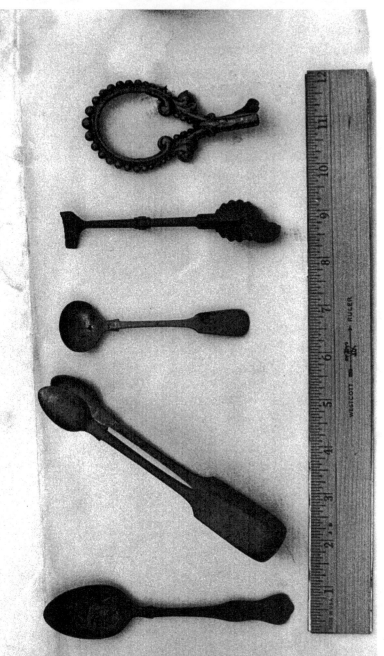

These items were found in the vicinity of the ship's galley on the blockade runner *Constance.* The item at the top appears to have been a decorative handle, possibly for a condiment caddy. The item immediately below it is a pie wheel used for trimming pie crusts. Photo by L. Spence.

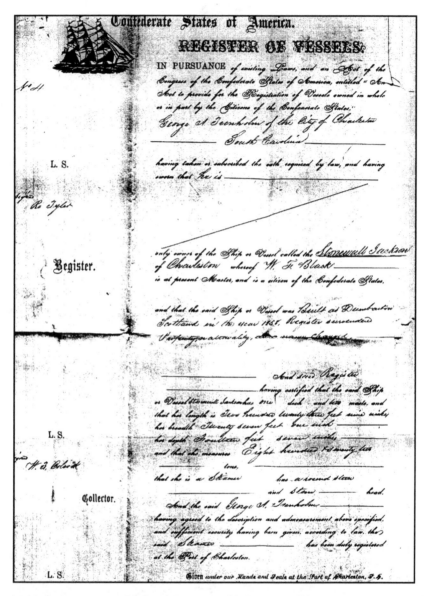

An important source of information on a ship's measurements, rig, captain, and owners are the ship's papers. This "certificate of register" belonged to the Confederate steamer Stonewall Jackson, which was one of the many blockade runners owned by George Trenholm. Courtesy of the United States National Archives.

APPENDIX F
Construction Agreement for the *Mary Bowers*

(Note: Question marks have been inserted for illegible words in the original hand written agreement, which was made available courtesy of L.G. Bowers, III.)

Articles of Agreement made this 29th day of October, 1863, between Charles Augustus Lafayette Lamar, J.H. Phinizy, W.G. Foote, John E. Ward, each of Savannah, Lloyd Guyton Bowers of Columbus, John F. McCauley of Virginia, of the one part and Henry Lafone of Liverpool of the other part.

Henry Lafone agrees to purchase for the joint account of himself and C.A.L. Lamar & others above mentioned, the (?) boat he can find for immediate use, the same to meet (?) approbation in all respects of Captain J.N. Maffitt, (?) is to take command of her.

Henry Lafone also agrees to furnish a first class iron Steamer of the following dimensions viz 220 feet long, 25 feet Beam, 10 feet 6 inches deep, 48 inches Cylinder, (?) being built, and to be ready in 14 weeks from the (?) October last and guarantees her to run 17 miles per hour with 200 Tons dead Weight and not to draw with (?) weight exceeding 7 feet 6 Inches of Water at the price of £25,000 Sterling.

Henry Lafone further agrees to furnish a first class iron Steamer now in the process of being built of the following dimensions viz 226 feet long 26 feet beam, (?) feet deep 51 inches Cylinder and guarantees her to run (?) less than 17 Miles per hour with 200 Tons Dead weight on 7 feet 6 inches draft and to be ready for (?) within 4 Months from the 22nd day of October last, at the price of £24,000 Sterling.

(?) the completion of the first Boat viz on the 19th January.

(?) Henry Lafone agrees to send her to Bermuda or any other port that may be agreed upon, and there turn her over to Captain J.N. Maffitt or such other commander as said C.A.L. Lamar may appoint to take her - Henry Lafone then agrees to take the Boat purchased for immediate use off the hands of said C.A.L. Lamar & others at cost price if she is in fair seagoing condition, or to let her remain working on joint account as Lamar may elect.

Upon completion of the second Boat on the 22nd February Henry Lafone agrees to send her to Bermuda or such other Port as C.A.L. Lamar may direct, and there turn her over to such Commander as may be appointed by the said C.A.L. Lamar.

All the Boats to be registered in the joint names of Charles Augustus Lafayette Lamar and Henry Lafone and the Nett (sic)

Treasures of the Confederate Coast

Profits from their workings are to be apportioned as follows, one Half to the said C.A.L. Lamar and others as before mentioned, and one half to the said Henry Lafone.

C.A.L. Lamar for himself and others agrees to pay said Henry Lafone the sum of £10,000 Sterling or more in payment or part payment of their Interest in the Boat for immediate use.

C.A.L. Lamar and others agree to give Henry Lafone a lien on £15,000 Sterling worth of good average cotton estimated at Sixpence per lb for their one half Share in Boat Building No. 1 which is to be completed on the 19th January next.

C.A.L. Lamar and others agree to give Henry Lafone as part payment of their half interest in boat building No. 2 which is to be completed on the 22nd February next, £5000 Sterling worth of 7% Bonds of the Confederate States Government valuing the Dollar at Thirteen pence Sterling, and said Bonds to be delivered within four months from this date. They further agree to give £10,000 worth of good average Cotton estimated at Sixpence per lb as additional payment of any balance, subject to the same terms and conditions as above.

C.A.L. Lamar and Associates are to be responsible for their one half Interest in said Boats, it being understood that all Cotton brought out by one or of the Boats, are to go towards the payment of what may be due said Henry Lafone upon their one half interest until he is paid in full, when he relinquishes his claim upon the said Cotton.

It is understood and agreed that these boats to be fitted for Sea with every requisite usual to sea going Steamers without additional charge of any kind save and except Stores, Coals and Nautical Instruments.

The Boats to bring out 1000 Bales of Cotton for account of Henry Lafone, but at no time to (?) more than one half the Stowage capacity. (?) which he is entitled on each Boat).

Statements of account of each is to be sent to all the interested parties, also Statements of Sales of each Cargo of Cotton, or other Merchandise, and all the Books and accounts connected in any way with this enterprise shall be subject at any time to the inspection of either of the parties above named upon application.

The amounts subscribed by C.A.L. Lamar and associates are as follows.

C.A.L. Lamar	£3,500	J.H. Phinizy	£3,000
Wm. G. Foote	£1,500	John E. Ward	£1,000
Lloyd Guyton Bowers	£1,500	John F. McCauley	£2,000

• • •

Appendix F: *Mary Bowers*
Page 454

APPENDIX G
INSTRUCTIONS TO
BLOCKADERS

(Note: This appendix relates to the establishment of a blockade of the Southern Ports. It includes some of the orders issued to the commanders of Federal ships engaged in the blockade of Confederate ports. You may note that some of the orders were in violation of international law, but war was war, and neither side followed all of the rules.)

On April 16, 1861, President Lincoln proclaimed that the "inhabitants of the Southern States" were in a "state of insurrection" and forbade "all commercial intercourse with same." Lincoln further ordered that after fifteen days "all ships and vessels belonging in whole or in part to any citizen or inhabitant of any (of the rebelling states) found at sea or in any port of the United States" be forfeited to the United States. Lincoln also announced that a blockade of the ports within the rebelling states would be put in place, and that any vessels attempting to leave any of said ports were to be "duly warned by the commander of one of the said blockading vessels, who will indorse on her register the fact and date of such warning; and if the same vessel shall again attempt to enter or leave the blockaded port, she will be captured."

New York Times, (New York, NY), Volume 10, #2989, April 20, 1861, p. 1, c. 1
Official Records of the Union and Confederate Navies in the War of the Rebellion, (Washington, DC, 1897), Series 1, Volume 6, pp. 90, 91

In a lengthy letter to President Abraham Lincoln, dated August 5, 1861, Gideon Welles, Secretary of the United States Navy, discussed the ramifications of imposing a blockade on the southern ports. Welles stated that, if the Federal government closed the ports by blockade, the rules and principles of international law would govern. The Confederate States would be considered and treated as a distinct nationality, and their customs collectors, revenue officers, clearances, registers, etc., would be recognized as legitimate. Welles pointed out that the Federal government had been trying to show the Confederacy as an illegal rebellion and warned of the serious consequences of effectively recognizing the Confederate government as legitimate by the declaration of a formal blockade rather than simply closing them by act of civil law and then seizing vessels sailing to or from them as smugglers.

Official Records of the Union and Confederate Navies in the War of the Rebellion, (Washington, DC, 1897), Series 1, Volume 6, pp. 53-56

Treasures of the Confederate Coast

The following instructions by David D. Porter, Rear-Admiral, Commanding North Atlantic Squadron, dated October 22, 1864, were "issued for the guidance of blockading vessels, and must be observed as nearly as possible, except in cases where there is a chance of losing a vessel by too close adherence to orders. While it is desirable to observe some system in blockading , still there are times when officers must deviate from their orders to insure success; and when success follows, or the officer shows the necessity of deviating from general orders, I will approve. A few vessels properly arranged will do more than a crowd of vessels with no system.

To enable me to the better to form a correct idea of the situation of things at the bars, senior officers blockading are directed to give me their views and experience on the subject, and for the future the following order will be carried out as nearly as possible:

An equal division of vessels must be made at the Eastern and Western bars, and there must be established an inner and outside line. The slower vessels of the divisions are to be stationed near the bars ready to fire on the blockade runners as they attempt to pass in or out, and one or two fast vessels furnished with calcium lights are to be ready with steam up to chase. The slow vessels stationed at the bar are not to chase offshore, but the fast chasers are to pursue as long as there is any chance of catching the blockade runner. The moment a chase commences the chasers must, at night, carry a red light over the stern so that there will be no danger of our vessels firing into each other. These lights must be protected on the sides that they may not show abeam.

Whichever vessel sights a blockade runner and chases her at night must indicate by signal the course the blockade runner is steering, according to the following table:

Course Signals

1 rocket - Northward
2 rockets - Northeastward
1 rocket and white Coston - Northwestward
1 rocket and green Coston - Eastward
1 rocket and red Coston - Westward
2 rockets and white Coston - Southward
2 rockets and red Coston - Southwestward
2 rockets and green Coston - Southeastward

And rockets will be thrown horizontally in the direction of the chase from time to time.

Course signals by steam whistle

1 short whistle - Northward
1 long whistle - Northeastward

The "Real Rhett Butler" & Other Revelations

2 short whistles - Northwestward
2 long whistles - Eastward
3 short whistles - Westward
3 long whistles - Southward
1 long and 1 short whistle - Southeastward
1 short and 1 long whistle - Southwestward

The vessels blockading the bars must not go in until twilight, and must then lie in as close as they can. The picket boats will cruise inside of them over the bar. No lights will be shown by bar blockaders, nor will any noise be allowed on board.

Each bar vessel will keep out a good, swift boat in fair weather, well armed, and provided with a bright red lantern, enclosed in a box, and the light is to be shown only toward the bar blockaders when anything is seen coming out. The picket steam launches will be provided in the same way.

Vessels lying at the bar will be careful to ascertain the position of each and every blockader, so that there will be no danger of collision or firing into each other.

Those vessels that are not to chase will (when signal is made that a blockade runner has passed the bar) hold a red light over the side opposite the batteries; these lights always to be kept lit on deck. It is to be remembered that the inshore line is not to chase, but to fire on blockade runners as they go in or out.

The moment a blockade runner is signaled the bar vessels will endeavor to get in between her and the bar and turn her off. If a vessel supposed to be a blockade runner does not show a red light at once, and attempts to run, she must be fired into immediately, and any vessel making doubtful movements must be brought to. If a vessel moves while being boarded, the boarding boat must be left to take care of itself and the vessel pursued and fired at. The chase must lie with her broadside bearing on the blockade runner and make her blow off her steam.

The following are the signals to be made when a vessel is sighted, and every commander will study them and strictly observe them:

Day of month	Vessel making signal first	Answer
1	1 flash white	3 flashes red
2	2 flashes white	1 flash red
3	3 flashes white	2 flashes red
4	1 flash red	1 flash red
5	2 flashes red	1 flash white
6	3 flashes red	2 flashes white
7	1 flash white, red burning	3 flashes red, white burning
8	2 flashes white, red burning	1 flash red, white burning
9	3 flashes white, red burning	2 flashes red, white burning

Treasures of the Confederate Coast

10	1 flash red, white burning	3 flashes white, red burning

Day of month	In fog, vessel making signal first	Answer
1	1 short whistle	4 long whistles
2	2 short whistles	1 long whistle
3	3 short whistles	2 long whistles
4	4 short whistles	3 long whistles
5	1 short, 1 long	4 long, 1 short
6	2 short, 1 long	1 long, 1 short
7	3 short, 1 long	2 long, 1 short
8	4 short, 1 long	3 long, 1 short
9	1 long, 1 short	1 short, 1 long
10	2 long, 1 short	1 short, 2 long

Day of month	Vessel making signal first	Answer
1	Coston's No. 1	Coston's No. 2
2	Coston's No. 2	Coston's No. 3
3	Coston's No. 3	Coston's No. 4
4	Coston's No. 4	Coston's No. 5
5	Coston's No. 5	Coston's No. 6
6	Coston's No. 6	Coston's No. 7
7	Coston's No. 7	Coston's No. 8
8	Coston's No. 8	Coston's No. 9
9	Coston's No. 9	Coston's No. 0 (10?)
10	Coston's No. 10	Coston's No. 1

This system to be recommenced at the end of every ten days of the month. It is not intended by it to particularize any vessel or ship, but to serve as a password to any vessel which may be moving within or about the blockading line or suddenly sighting a friendly vessel at night; the Coston signals to be the last resorted to. Should either of the vessels thus interchanging signals desire to communicate by hail or by boat, the vessel so desiring will "wave" a white light until it be answered by a similar movement from the other vessel. But should the vessel thus summoned be upon urgent duty admitting no delay, she will, after answering, burn a Coston "A." The challenge for the 31st day of the month will be the same as on the 1st. To signalize to the blockading fleet the presence of a blockade runner, a gun will be fired by the vessel sighting her and signals made to show the direction she is going. Care should be taken, however, that the runner be not prematurely alarmed, and if coming out or going in the vessel seeing her should endeavor to get, if possible, between her and the bar before alarming her or the fleet. The signal for danger will be the firing of a gun and the burning of a blue light.

The "Real Rhett Butler" & Other Revelations

One or two fast vessels will be kept 40 miles to the eastward and westward of the bar, and cruise alongshore in the daytime to see if any vessels are anchored ready to run in at night. The vessels to the eastward and westward of the bar will sometimes, at night, burn false lights corresponding as nearly as possible to the lights shown by the lighthouses at the entrances to Cape Fear River. This may lead the runners astray. In doing this the same position must not always be taken.

There will be a line of outside blockaders, who will observe the following general rules, deviating from them only when there is a chance of losing a blockade runner. These vessels must lie off Cape Fear at such a distance as would allow the outward-bound blockade runner to make 13 miles per hour from sundown until daylight, remain with low steam after 10 o'clock in the morning, to keep everything in working order, the lookouts aloft to dress in light colored clothes. Before daylight full steam must be got up to chase the moment a blockade runner appears.

The position for the senior officer to take will be about the latitude of 33°15', longitude 75°50'. A line of vessels will then stretch in a N.N.W. line for Cape Lookout, keeping in signal distance of each other if possible. Another line will stretch N.E. by E., keeping within signal distance. Vessels and diagrams will be sent to these stations as soon as possible.

The blockade runners will likely try to cross the bar after dark or in the twilight. By allowing 13 knots an hour, they will also start from about that point at night to make the bar at daylight. If seen by the outside line, they must be chased until lost sight of; and commanders will keep on hand a supply of pine wood to enable them to run their steam up quickly.

If nothing is in sight at daylight, the vessels on the N.E. by E. line will steer in calculating to meet blockade runners that left as late as 12 o'clock of that night. After running in about 20 miles, and not meeting anything, they will return to their stations, looking out for inward-bound blockade runners. These will likely make their appearance from 2 o'clock p.m. until sunset, at such a distance from Cape Fear inlets as will enable them to cross the bar by or before daylight.

Blockade runners will try to get head to wind and sea on account of draft and steady running. If two vessels are chasing them, try and keep them in the trough of the sea and not let them get before or off the wind to enable them to carry sail. Other directions will be issued as occasions offer and I become more familiar with the tricks of these blockade runners.

Treasures of the Confederate Coast

Every officer will keep a small chart or diagram, including Cape Lookout and Cape Fear, and 40 miles each side of both those places. The position of vessels seen and the line on which they are chased will be marked down and sent to me at such times as may be most convenient. This will best enable me to lay down general rules for the capture of vessels.

When blockade runners are run on shore at the bar, or beached, they must be destroyed at all hazards, unless they are in a position where they can certainly be got off.

Every officer must keep a close account of the tides, as the runners will often be governed in their movements by high water, especially at night; but the tides must not be relied on to govern their movements, as the class of vessels now employed in illicit trade do not draw much water and can run in and out at any time.

When calcium lights are supplied they will be kept at night in readiness on the forecastle, and when chasing be kept turned to the runner. Certain vessels on the bar will be supplied with calcium lights, and they will turn them on the bar when a runner is trying to get out or in. As these lights require nice management, they will only be intrusted (sic) to competent persons.

The pipes, hulls, and all parts of the blockaders should be painted one uniform color. As the fog signals and course signals will be used at different times, the latter only in clear weather, the former only in fogs, there can be no confusion."

Official Records of the Union and Confederate Navies in the War of the Rebellion, (Washington, DC, 1900), Series 1, Volume 10, pp. 579-583

The following instructions by Gideon Welles, Secretary of the Navy, dated Navy Department, May 9, 1864, "will hereafter be observed with regard to the disposition of persons found on board vessels seized for breach of blockade:

1st.   Bona fide foreign subjects captured in neutral vessels, whether passengers, officers, or crew, can not be treated as prisoners of war unless guilty of belligerent acts, but are entitled to immediate release. Such as are required as witnesses may be detained for that purpose, and when their testimony is secured they must be unconditionally released.

2nd.   Foreign subjects captured in vessels without papers or colors, or those sailing under the protection and flag of the insurgent Government or employed in the service of that Government, are subject to treatment as prisoners of war, and if in the capacity of officers or crew are to be detained. If they were passengers only, and have no interest in the vessel or cargo and are in no way connected with the insurgent Government, they may be released.

3d.   Citizens of the United States captured either in neutral or rebel vessels are always to be detained, with the following exceptions: If they are passengers only, have no interest in vessel or cargo, have not been active in the rebellion or engaged in supplying the insurgents with munitions of war, etc., and are loyally disposed, they may be released on taking the oath of allegiance. The same privilege may be allowed to any of the crew that are not seafaring men, of like antecedents, and who are loyally disposed.

4th.   Pilots and seafaring men, excepting bona fide foreign subjects, captured in neutral vessels are always to be detained. These are the principal instruments in maintaining the system violating the blockade and it is important to hold them. Persons habitually engaged in violating the blockade, although they may not be serving on board the vessels, are of this class and are to be likewise detained.

5th.   When there is reason top doubt that those who claim to be foreign subjects are in reality such, they will be required to state under oath that they have never been naturalized in this country, have never exercised the privileges of a citizen thereof by voting or otherwise, and have never been in the pay or employment of the insurgent or the so-called Confederate Government. On their making such statement they may be released, provided however you have not evidence of their having sworn falsely. The examination in cases that are doubtful should be rigid.

6th.   When the neutrality of a vessel is doubtful, or when a vessel claiming to be a neutral is believed to be engaged in transporting supplies and munitions of war for the insurgent Government, foreign subjects captured in such vessel may be detained until the neutrality of the vessel is satisfactorily established. It is not advisable to detain such persons under this instruction unless there is good ground for doubting the neutrality of the vessel

7th. Parties who may be detained under the foregoing instructions are to be sent to a Northern port for safer custody, unless there is a suitable place for keeping them within the limits of your command, and the Department furnished with a memorandum in their cases, respectively."

Official Records of the Union and Confederate Navies in the War of the Rebellion, (Washington, DC, 1900), Series 1, Volume 10, pp. 61-62

In a letter to Rear-Admiral David D. Porter, dated November 18, 1864, United States Secretary of the Navy Gideon Welles

Treasures of the Confederate Coast

wrote: "From reports of captures, it is inferred that in some instances articles are thrown overboard after the prize has yielded or surrendered. After a vessel has surrendered or has ceased to resist, either by abandoning further effort to escape or discontinuing hostile action, it is inadmissible for those in her to throw overboard papers, cargo, or other articles of importance or value, or to injure the vessel in any manner. By doing so they subject themselves to the danger of being fired into, and the captor is justifiable in resorting to such measures, should he perceive unmistakable indications that such a course is being pursued by those on board the captured vessel." (Note: For examples of gold and/or papers being thrown overboard from blockade runners, please see entries 1864-10-US-NC-10 and 1865-1-US-NC-11.)

Official Records of the Union and Confederate Navies in the War of the Rebellion, (Washington, DC, 1900), Series 1, Volume 11, p. 75

An order issued on January 23, 1865, by Rear Admiral David Porter of the United States Navy to Lieutenant-Commander Barnes, commanding the *U.S.S. Bat,* at Cape Fear River, North Carolina, stated "You will proceed as soon as you get a pilot, and the water will permit, around to Western Bar, Cape Fear River, and cruise along there, inshore, down as far as Georgetown, S.C., and cruise off that place and endeavor to open communication with General Sherman in case he should come there. At the same time keep a lookout for blockade runners and prevent them going into that port. In case of capturing a prize the men (aboard the prize) will be drawn up on the quarter deck and no one permitted to go below on pain of death. Have all the liquors and wines on board secured and locked up. Have all the hatches secured and sealed up and provisions taken out enough to last the voyage. Send all prizes captured to me here." (Note: The sidewheel steamer *Bat* was a former British blockade runner, she having been captured off the Western Bar on October 10, 1864, with a cargo of machinery for manufacturing shoes. Her papers and log book were destroyed by her captain. She was 230' in length, 26' in breadth, 9'6" in depth of hold, and drew 6'6" of water. She had "double, powerful oscillating engines, 180 horsepower, 52-inch cylinders of 4 feet stroke; draft, when loaded, 6 feet 6 inches," and could make over 13 knots. She was built of molded steel by Messrs. Jones, Quiggin & Co., of Liverpool, and was captured on her first trip. At the time of her capture, she was struck in her covered forecastle, and a shot from a 30-pounder rifle took off the leg of one Match Madick, an Australian, serving on board of her. Madick, who had been captain

The "Real Rhett Butler" & Other Revelations

of the forecastle on board the *Alabama* at the time she lost her famous duel with the *Kearsarge*, died of his wounds.)

Official Records of the Union and Confederate Navies in the War of the Rebellion, (Washington, D.C., 1900), Series 1, Volume 10, pp. 545-549
Official Records of the Union and Confederate Navies in the War of the Rebellion, (Washington, D.C., 1900), Series 1, Volume 11, pp. 631, 632

On June 13, 1865, U.S. President Andrew Johnson ordered the immediate lifting of the Federal blockade of Southern ports. Although the order formally re-opened the ports, it specifically prohibited the importation of "arms, ammunitions, all articles from which ammunition is made, and gray uniforms and cloth" into the South, in apparent fear that the South might rise again.

Times, (London, England), # 25221, June 26, 1865, p. 10, c. 3

• • •

Bowie knives off the Modern Greece. Photo courtesy of the Underwater Archeology Unit, North Carolina Department of Cultural Resources.

These artifacts are part of the extensive shipwreck collection at the Southport Maritime Museum at Southport, North Carolina. The bottle and pig bone were recovered from the Civil War blockade runner Ella. Photo by L. Spence, courtesy of the museum.

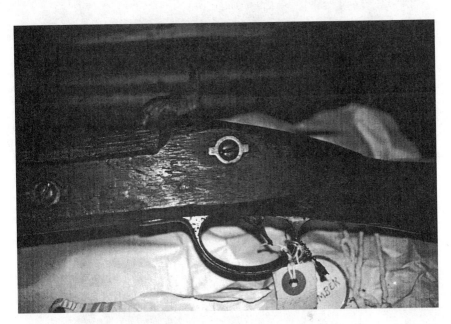

The musket above and the bayonet handles below are some of the many Civil War era shipwreck artifacts processed at the Underwater Archeology Unit at the Fort Fisher Historical Site. The Unit is part of the North Carolina Department of Cultural Resources. Photos by L. Spence, courtesy of the Underwater Archeology Unit.

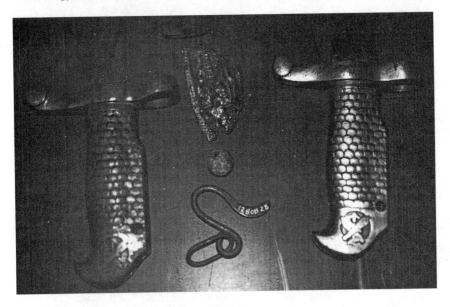

United States Navy photo of Civil War blockade runners at dock, courtesy of the United States National Archives.

Admiral Dahlgren's flag ship, U.S.S. Harvest Moon, was sunk in Winyah Bay, South Carolina. Illustration from the "Official Records of the War of the Rebellion, Union & Confederate Navies."

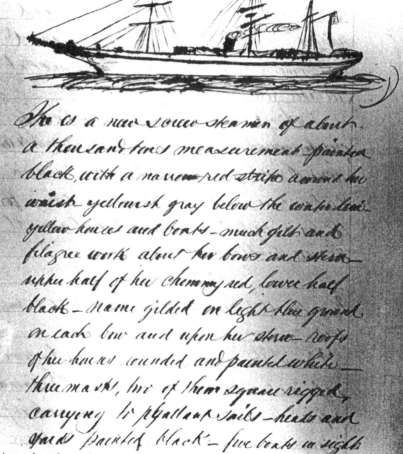

Dispatches from the consuls of various countries are an excellent source of information on shipping. This one, directed to the United States Secretary of State from the United States consul to Great Britain, describes a suspected blockade runner. Photo by L. Spence, courtesy of the United States Nation Archives.

BIBLIOGRAPHY

Note: The following books are suggested reading for learning more about the Civil War, the Southern Confederacy, the Federal blockade of the South, George Alfred Trenholm, shipwrecks, and underwater archeology. Realizing that most of my readers will not be familiar with the authors of these works, I have intentionally disregarded tradition, and have listed the books alphabetically by title (minus the first word "A" or "The") for convenience, rather than listing books by the author's last name. Some of the entries have been annotated to provide additional information.

Activities of a Confederate Business Man, Gazaway B. Lamar, by Edwin B. Coddington (Volume 9, of the Journal of Southern History, Feb.-Nov., 1943)

Advance and Retreat, by John Bell Hood (New Orleans, 1880)

Adventures of a Blockade Runner, or Trade in Time of War, by William Watson (McMillan & Co., 1893)

Archeology Under Water, by George F. Bass, (Frederick A. Praeger, New York, 1966)

Arms and Equipment of the Civil War, by Jack Coggins, (Doubleday, New York, NY, 1962)

Artillery and Ammunition of the Civil War, by Warren Ripley, (Van Nostrand and Reinhold Co., New York, NY, 1970)

Artillery Through the Ages: A Short Illustrated History of Cannon, Emphasizing Types Used in America, by Albert Mauney, National Park Service Interpretative Series History, #3, (Government Printing Office, Washington, DC, 1949)

Atlanta and its Builders, by Thomas H. Martin (Atlanta, 1902; 2 volumes.)

Baffling the Blockade, by J.M. Oxley, (Nelson, London, 1896)

Basic History of the Confederacy, by Frank E. Vandiver (Princeton, NJ, 1962)

Battles and Leaders of the Civil War, edited by Robert U. Johnson and Clarence C. Buel, 4 volumes (Century Co., New York, NY, 1884-87)

Belle Boyd, Confederate Spy, by Louis A. Siguad, (Dietz Press, Richmond, VA, 1944) - Belle Boyd was a beautiful Confederate spy, who talked her Yankee captor into letting her escape. The two were later married.

Belle Boyd in Camp and in Prison, by Harding, two volumes (Blelock & Co., London and New York, 1865)

Belle of the Fifties, by Virginia Tunstall Clay-Clopton (New York, 1904)

Belles, Beaux and Brains of the 60's, by Thomas C. DeLeon (G.W. Dillingham, NY, 1909)

Bible Publication and Procurement in the Confederacy, by Daniel W. Harrison, (published in the Journal of Southern History, Volume 24, Feb.-Nov., 1958)

Blockade: The Civil War at Sea, by Robert Carse, (Rinehart & Co., New York, NY, 1958)

Blockade and Contraband, by Alfred M. Low (Columbian Printing, Washington, 1916)

Blockade and the Cruisers, by James Russell Soley (Scribner Brothers, 1883)

Blockade Family: Life in Alabama During the Civil War, by Parthenia Hague (Houghton, Mifflin, Boston, 1885)

Blockade Runner Modern Greece and Her Cargo, by Leslie S. Bright, (Division of Archives and History, North Carolina Dept. of Cultural Resources, Raleigh, NC), 1977

Blockade Runners, by Dave Horner, (Florida Classics Library, Port Salerno, FL, 1992)

Treasures of the Confederate Coast

Blockade Runners of the Confederacy, by Hamilton Cochran (Bobbs-Merrill Co., Inc., Indianapolis, 1958)

Blockade Runners, True Tales of Running the Yankee Blockade of the Confederate Coast, by Dave Horner (Dodd Mead, 1968)

Blockade Running During the Civil War, and the effect of Land and Water Transportation on the Confederacy, by Francis Bradlee (Essex Institute, Salem, MA, 1925)

Blockade Running in Confederate Times, by M.P. Usina (George N. Nichols Press, Savannah, 1895)

"Building a Warship in the Southern Confederacy," (published in *United States Naval Institute Proceedings*, August, 1923), pp. 1299-1307

Burckmyer Letters, (Columbia: The State Company, 1926)

Burning of Columbia, SC: A review of Northern Assertions and Southern Facts, by D.H. Trezevant (SC Power Press, Columbia, SC, 1866)

Butler's Book, by Benjamin Butler (A.M. Thayer & Co., Boston, 1882) - Butler was a general in the Union Army, and was known by the Confederates as "Beast Butler" and as "Silver Spoons Butler" because of his encouragement of the ill treatment of Southern women, and the theft of private silver by his troops. His forces participated in numerous river battles and in the first assault on Fort Fisher, North Carolina. Some people believe that Margaret Mitchell used his name for her blockade runner captain to add a sinister connotation to that character.

By Sea and By River, by Bern Anderson (Alfred A. Knoft, NY, 1962)

By Valour and Arms, by James Street, (Dial Press, NY, 1944) - This book recounts the story of the *C.S.S. Arkansas.*

C.S.S. Neuse: A Question of Iron and Time, by Leslie S. Bright, William H. Rowland, and James C. Bardon, (Raleigh, NC, 1981)

C.S.S. Shenandoah, The Memoirs of Lieutenant James I. Waddel, edited by James D. Horan (Crown Publishers, NY, 1960)

Campfire Sketches and Battlefield Echoes of the Rebellion, by W.C. King, (Springfield, MA, 1887)

Captain Fry, The Cuban Martyr, by Jeanie Mort Walker (Hartford, 1875) - Note: Captain Fry earned fame during the Civil War as a fearless blockade runner captain. Although he was executed before she was born, he was a relative of Margaret Mitchell, author of *Gone With The Wind.*

"Captain William Sharp of Norfolk, Virginia, U.S.N.-C.S.N.," by Richard Southall Grant, (published in *Virginia Magazine of History and Biography*, #47, January, 1949), pp. 48-53

"Career of the Confederate Ram Neuse," by L.V. Archbell, (published in the *North Carolina Historical Review*, #43, 1966), p. 1-13

Cease Firing, by Mary Johnston (Boston and NY, 1912)

Centennial Address Before the Charleston Chamber of Commerce, by William L. Trenholm (News and Courier Presses, 1884)

Charleston, A Gracious Heritage, by Robert Molloy, (Appleton-Century Co., New York, NY, 1947)

Charleston Come Hell or High Water, by Whitelaw and Levkoff (Columbia, SC, 1975) - This is a pictorial book of Charleston, South Carolina.

"Charleston Daily Courier" (Charleston, SC)- This daily newspaper is an excellent source of additional contemporary information on wrecks and is available on microfilm through interlibrary loan. In most cases if you start searching a day or two before the date of the wreck and continue searching for at least two weeks following the last account you find of the wreck you will get most if not all of the articles relating to the wreck.

The "Real Rhett Butler" & Other Revelations

"Charleston During the Civil War," by Theodore D. Jervey, contained in the *Annual Report of the American Historical Association*, Volume 1 (Washington, DC, 1913)

Charleston Orphan House, 1860-1876, by Newton B. Jones, published in the South Carolina Historical Magazine (October, 1961)

Chronicles of the Cape Fear River, 1660-1916, by James Sprunt (Edwards and Broughton Printing Company, Raleigh, 1916)

Civil War and Reconstruction, by J.G. Randall and David Donald (D.C. Heath and Co., Lexington, MA)

Civil War at Sea, by Virgil Carrington Jones (Holt, Rinehart, Winston, NY, 1960-62, in 3 volumes)

Civil War Collector's Encyclopedia, by Francis A. Lord, (Stackpole Co., Harrisburg, PA, 1963)

Civil War Digest, by Ralph Newman and E.B. Long, (Grosset & Dunlap, New York, NY, 1956)

Civil War Dictionary, by Mark Mayo Boatner III, (David McKay, New York, NY, 1959)

Civil War Explosive Ordnance, by John D. Bartleson, (U.S. Naval Ordnance Station, Indian Head, 1972)

Civil War Guns, by W.B. Edwards, (Stackpole Co., Harrisburg, PA, 1962)

Civil War in North Carolina, by John G. Barrett, (University of North Carolina Press, Chapel Hill, NC, 1963)

Civil War in Song and Story, by edited by Frank Moore, (P.F. Collier, NY, 1889)

Civil War Ironclads: The Dawn of Naval Arrmor, by Robert MacBride, (Chilton Press, Philadelphia, PA, 1962)

Civil War Naval Chronology References for 1861-1865, (Government Printing Office, Washington, DC, 1971), 6 volumes - This is a rather useful set of books taken largely from the *Official Records of the War of the Rebellion for the Union and Confederate Navies*. It is a quick and easy reference for beginning the research on most civil war vessels.

Civil War Naval Chronology, 1861-1865 (Washington, DC, 1971)

"Civil War Naval Ordnance - Weapons and Equipment," by Jack Coggins, (published in *Civil War Times Illustrated*, November, 1964), pp. 16-20

Colin J. McRae Confederate Financial Agent, by Charles S. Davis, contained in Confederate Centennial Studies #17 (Tuscaloosa, AL, 1961)

Colonel Joseph Glover and His Descendants, by William L. Glover (published in the South Carolina Historical and Genealogical Magazine, January, 1939)

Compilation of Messages and Papers of the Confederacy, Including Diplomatic Correspondence, 1861-1865, by James D. Richardson (U.S. Publishing Co., Nashville, 1905)

Confederacy, by Charles P. Roland (University of Chicago Press, 1960)

Confederate Arms, by William A. Albough III and Edward N. Simmons (Bonanza Books, NY, 1957)

Confederate Blockade Running Through Bermuda, 1861-1865, by Frank E. Vandiver (University of Texas Press, Austin, TX, 1947)

Confederate Congress, by Wilfred B. Yearns, (University of Georgia Press, Athens, GA, 1960)

Confederate Edged Weapons, by William A. Albaugh, (Harper & Brothers, New York, 1960)

Confederate Finance, by Richard Cecil Todd (University of Georgia Press, 1954)

Confederate Girl's Diary, by S.M. Dawson, (Houghton, Mifflin Co., New York, NY, 1913)

Treasures of the Confederate Coast

Confederate Ironclads, by Maurice Melton (Thom Yoseloff Publishers, Cranbury, NJ)

Confederate Military History, Volume 1 (Atlanta, GA, 1899)

"Confederate Naval Strategy: The Ironclad," by William N. Still, Jr., (published in the *Journal of Southern History*, #27, 1961), pp. 330-343

"Confederate Naval Policy and the Ironclad," by Jack Coggins, (published in *Civil War History*, #9, June, 1963) pp. 153-159

Confederate Navy, A Pictorial History, by Philip Van Doren Stern, (Doubleday, New York, NY, 1962)

Confederate Navy, A Study in Organization, by Tom Henderson Well (University of Alabama Press, 1971)

"Confederate Navy Yard at Charlotte, North Carolina, 1862-1865," by Alexander Violet, (published in the *Southern Historical Society Papers*, #40, 1915), pp. 184-192

Confederate Privateers, by William Morrison Robinson, Jr. (Yale University Press, 1928). (Note: This book was republished by the University of South Carolina Press in 1990 at Colombia, SC.)

Confederate Propaganda in Europe, by Charles P. Cullop, (University of Miami Press, 1969)

Confederate Purchasing Operations Abroad, by Samuel Bernard Thompson (University of North Carolina Press, 1935)

"Confederate Ram *Albemarle*," by James Dinkins, (published in *Southern Historical Society Papers*, #30, 1902), pp. 205-214

"Confederate Ram *Neuse*," by L.V. Archbell, (published in the *Carolina and the Southern Cross*, November, 1913), pp. 3-5

Confederate Shipbuilding, by William N. Still, Jr., (University of Georgia Press, Athens, GA, 1969)

Confederate States of America, by E. Merton Coulter (Louisiana State U. Press, 1950)

Confederate States of America, The Financial and Industrial History of the South During the Civil War, by John Christopher Schwab (Charles Scribner, 1901)

Confederate Success in Europe: The Erlanger Loan, by Edith Fenner Gentry (published in the Journal of Southern History, May, 1970)

Confidential Correspondence of Gustavus Vasa Fox, Assistant Secretary of the Navy, 1861-1865, by G.V. Fox, edited by Robert Means Thompson and Richard Wainwright (NY)

Congress, by Wilfred Buck Yearns (University of Georgia Press, 1960)

"*Constance* Expedition," professional paper by E. Lee Spence, presented at the *12th Annual Conference on Historic Site Archeology*, Macon, Georgia, 1971. - The *Constance* was one of the blockade runners which wrecked on top of the Confederate cruiser *Georgiana* outside of Charleston harbor.

Contemporary University Project Report: Constance Expedition, Confederate Shipping Losses, by E. Lee Spence, (Columbia, South Carolina, 1972) - Deals with the research and salvage of the blockade runner *Constance*, and the various state laws relating to salvage. Includes a fairly comprehensive list of vessels and cargoes captured by the Federals and adjudicated at various United States prize courts.

Crisis of the Union, 1841-1877, by Dumas Malone and Basil Rauch (Appleton-Century-Crofts, NY, 1960)

Daring Deed in Saving the David, by James Lachlison, published in the *Confederate Veteran*, Volume 16

Deck and Field, by Frank W. Hackett, (W.H. Lowdermilk & Co., Washington, DC, 1909)

The "Real Rhett Butler" & Other Revelations

Defense of Charleston Harbor including Fort Sumter and the Adjacent Islands, 1863-1865, by John Johnson (Walker, Evans, and Cogswell Co., Charleston, SC, 1890)

Derelicts, An Account of Ships Lost at Sea in General Commercial Traffic and a Brief History of Blockade Runners Stranded Along the North Carolina Coast, 1861-1865, by James Sprunt, (Lord Baltimore Press, Wilmington, 1920)

Destruction and Reconstruction, by Richard Taylor (D. Appleton, NY, 1879, 1900)

Diary from Dixie, by Mary Boykin Chesnut (D. Appleton and Company, NY, 1905) - This book provides an excellent view of the life of a southern woman during the Civil War.

Diary of a Refugee, edited by Frances Hewitt Fearn (New York, 1910)

Dictionary of American Biography (1944, Supplement) - Contains brief entry on George Alfred Trenholm, but makes no mention of his being "the real Rhett Butler".

Dictionary of American Naval Fighting Ships (Government Printing Office, Washington, DC), - This multi-volume set is an excellent quick reference for American vessels of war from 1776 to the present. It also includes Confederate war vessels. Typical data includes origin of name, date and place of construction, dimensions, and brief history.

Diplomatic History of the Confederacy, by James Morton Callahan (John Hopkins Press, Baltimore, 1901)

Diplomatic History of the Southern Confederacy, by James Morton Callahan (Fred Ungar Publishing Co., NY, 1964)

Diving for Treasure, edited by James McNutt, (Hydrodyne Company, 1987), E. Lee Spence wrote two of the chapters in this book.

Dixie After the War, by Myrta Lockett Avary of Atlanta (reprint by Houghton, Mifflin)

Economic Aspects of Southern Sectionalism, 1840-1861, by Robert Royal Russell (University of Illinois Press, Urbana, 1924)

Education in Underwater Archeology, professional paper by E. Lee Spence, presented at *I.Q.-5*, an international conference jointly sponsored by the National Association of Underwater Instructors, Harvard University and the Massachusetts Institute of Technology, Boston, Massachusetts, 1973.

Encyclopedia of American Shipwrecks, by Bruce D. Berman, Mariners Press, Boston, MA, 1972. - This excellent book is arranged alphabetically by name of vessel under general geographic area of loss. It is best used as a quick index to look up dates, causes and places of loss.

"Enrollments" - Vessels engaged in coastwise trade between American ports were required to have a certificate of enrollment. These were issued as "Temporary" or as "Permanent" documents. A new certificate was supposed to be issued each time ownership, home port, rig, or use of the vessel changed. These contain information on the dimensions of the vessel, date and place of construction, rig, master, owners, etc. The best source for these documents is the U.S. National Archives.

Experiment in Rebellion, by Clifford Dowdey (Doubleday, Garden City, NY, 1964)

"Facilities for the Construction of War Vessels in the Confederacy," by James Dinkins, (published in *Journal of Southern History*, #31, 1965), pp. 285-304

Fifty years on the Mississippi; or, Gould's history of river navigation. Containing a history of the introduction of steam as a propelling power on ocean, lakes and rivers - the first steamboats on the Hudson, the Delaware, and the Ohio rivers - navigation of western rivers before the introduction of steam - character of the early navigators - description of first steamboats - steamboat New Orleans in

Treasures of the Confederate Coast

1811, and sixty consecutive boats, when and where built - their effect upon the settlement of the valley of the Mississippi - character and speed of boats at different periods - appropriations by Congress for the improvement of Western water ways - floods in the Mississippi Valley for 150 years - Mississippi River Commission and its work. Rapid increase and decline of river transportation, causes of the decline - destruction of steamboats on Western waters - biographies of prominent steamboatmen - illustrated by photographs and cuts of steamboats at different periods, by E.W. Gould, (750 pages, Nixon-Jones Printing Company, St. Louis, MO, 1889, also LAC microfiche 10341)

"Fighting in North Carolina Waters," by Roy Nichols, (published in *North Carolina Historical Review*, #40, Winter, 1963), pp. 79-82

First Lady of the South, by Isabel Ross (Harper and Brothers, NY, 1958)

Flight From the Flag, The Continuing Effect of the Civil War Upon the American Carrying Trade, by George W. Dalzell (University of North Carolina Press, 1940)

Flight Into Oblivion, by A.J. Hanna, Indiana University Press,

Four Years in Rebel Capitals, by T.C. DeLeon (Gossip Printing, Mobile, 1890, 1892)

Four Years in Rebel Capitals: an Inside View of Life in the Southern Confederacy, from Birth to Death, by T.C. DeLeon, (Gossip Printing Co., Mobile, 1890)

Four Years in the Confederate Navy, the career of Captain John Low on the C.S.S. Finigal, Florida, Alabama, Tuscaloosa, and Ajax, by William Stanley Hoole (University of Georgia Press, 1964)

France and the Confederate Navy, 1862-1868, by John Bigelow (Harper & Brothers, NY, 1888)

Freemantle Diary, by Lt. Col. James Freemantle, (Little Brown & Co., Boston, London, 1863)

From Flag to Flag, by Eliza Moore Chinn McHatton Ripley (New York, 1889)

From Manassas to Appomattox, by James Longstreet (J.B. Lippincott & Co., Philadelphia, 1895)

From Reefer to Rear Admiral, by Benjamin Sands (Frederick A. Stokes, NY, 1899)

From Sail to Steam, by A.T. Mahan, (Harper Brothers, NY and London, 1907)

General Butler in New Orleans, by J. Parton, (Mason Brothers, NY, 1864) - Butler was a general in the Union Army, and was known by the Confederates as "Beast Butler" and as "Silver Spoons Butler" because of his encouragement of the ill treatment of Southern women, and the theft of private silver by his troops. His forces participated in numerous river battles and in the first assault on Fort Fisher, North Carolina.

General Forrest, by J. Harvey Mathes (New York, 1902)

George Alfred Trenholm and the Company That Went to War 1861- 1865, by Ethel Trenholm Seabrook Nepveux (Charleston, SC, 1973) - This is an excellent work on the life of Trenholm and his companies, but it fails to make any connection between Trenholm and the fictional Rhett Butler. However, it is thoroughly referenced and indexed and was of immense use to me in the preparation of Chapter One of this book.

Georgia Land and People, by Francis Letcher Mitchell (Franklin Publishing Co., Atlanta, 1893)

Georgia, Land and People, by Frances Letcher Mitchell (Atlanta, 1934)

Ghost Ship of the Confederacy, The Story of the Alabama and her Captain Raphael Semmes, by Edward Boykin (Funk and Wagnalls Co., NY, 1957)

Gone With the Wind, by Margaret Mitchell, (MacMillan Company, NY, 1936)

The "Real Rhett Butler" & Other Revelations

Gone With The Wind: The Definitive Illustrated History of the Book, the Movie, and the Legend, by Herb Bridges and T. C. Boodman, (Simon & Schuster, NY, 1989)

Graveyard of the Atlantic, by David Stick, (University of North Carolina Press, Chapel Hill, NC, 1952)

Great Britain and the American Civil War, by Ephraim Douglas Adams (Russell and Russell, NY, 1924)

Great South, by Edward King, 2 volumes (Burt Franklin, NY, 1875)

Greyjackets (Jones Brothers and Company, Richmond, 1867)

Heavy Artillery Projectiles of the Civil War, 1861-1865, by Thomas S. Dickey and Sydney C. Kerksis, (Phoenix Press, Kennesaw, GA, 1972)

High Seas Confederate: the Life and Times of John Newland Maffitt, written by Royce Shingleton, edited by William N. Still, Jr., (University of South Carolina Press, Columbia, SC, 1994). During the Civil War Maffitt distinguished himself as the very successful commander of the Confederate cruiser *Florida*. This book is excellent reading and accurately carries the reader from Maffitt's birth all of the way through his death in 1886.

Histories of the Several Regiments and Battalions from North Carolina in the Great War, 1861-1865, 5 volumes, edited by Walter Clark, (Nash Brothers Printers, Goldsborough, NC, 1901)

History of a Work of Faith and Love in Charleston, South Carolina, Which Grew Out of the Calamities of the Late Civil War and is a Record of God's Wonderful Providence, by A. Toomer Porter (Appleton and Co., NY, 1882)

History of Atlanta and its Pioneers, by the Pioneer Citizens Society of Atlanta, (Byrd Printing Company, 1902)

History of Atlanta, by Wallace P. Reed, (D. Mason & Co., NY, 1889)

History of early steamboat navigation on the Missouri River; life and adventures of Joseph La Barge pioneer navigator and Indian trader for fifty years identified with the commerce of the Missouri valley, by Hiram Martin Chittenden, (F.P. Harper, New York, 1903, also LAC microfiche 2003). This book gives some good insight into the realities of early steam navigation on the Missouri River. It was a limited edition of only 950 copies so it is quite rare. It has a number of interesting illustrations.

History of Georgia, by Clark Howell (Chicago, Atlanta, 1926; 4 vols.)

History of North Carolina, Volume 2, by Samuel F. Ashe

History of North Carolina in the War Between the States, by Daniel H. Hill, 2 volumes, (Raleigh, NC, 1926)

History of South Carolina, by David W. Wallace, Volume 3, (American History Inc., NY, 1934)

History of the American Privateers, by Edgar Stanton Maclay (Sampson, Low, Marsten & Co., London, 1900)

History of the Civil War in America, by John S.C. Abbott, (New York, 1866)

History of the College of Charleston, by J. Harold Easterby (1935)

History of the Confederate States Navy, by John Thomas Scharf (Rogers and Sherwood, NY, 1887)

History of the Confederate Treasury, by Ernest A. Smith, Southern History Association (Volume 5, 1901)

History of the Southern Confederacy, by Clement Eaton, (Macmillan Co., New York, NY, 1954)

History of the State of Georgia from 1850 to 1881, by Colonel I.W. Avery (Brown and Derby, New York, 1881)

Home Letters of General Sherman, edited by M.A. DeWolfe Howe (Charles Scribner's Sons, NY, 1909)

Treasures of the Confederate Coast

I Remember Margaret Mitchell, by *Yolande Gwinn* (Copple House Books, Lakemont, GA, 1987)

I Road With Stonewall, by H.K. Douglas, (University of North Carolina Press, Chapel Hill, NC, 1940)

In and Out of the Lines, by Frances Thomas Howard (New York and Washington, 1905)

In South Carolina Waters, 1861-1865, by Maxwell Clayton Orvin (Nelson's Southern Printing and Publishing Company, Charleston, SC)

Incidents and Anecdotes of the Civil War, by David D. Porter (D. Appleton and Co., NY, 1886) - Porter was an admiral in the Federal Navy.

Incidents of the Blockade, by John J. Almy, (War Papers 9, Military Orders of Loyal Legion, Washington, DC, 1892)

Index, Confederate weekly published by Henry Hotze (London, May 1, 1862 through August 12, 1865) - Hotz worked for George Trenholm ("the real Rhett Butler") and married Ruby Senac.

Infernal Machines: The story of Confederate Submarine and Mine Warfare, by Milton F. Perry, (Louisiana State University Press, Baton Rouge, LA, 1965)

Inscriptions on the Tablets and Gravestones in St. Michael's Church and Churchyard, Charleston, S.C., compiled by Clare Jervey (State Co., Columbia, SC, 1906)

Inside the Confederate Government, by Robert Kean, (Oxford University Press, NY, 1957)

Introduction of the Ironclad Warship, by James P. Baxter III, (Harvard University Press, Cambridge, MA, 1933)

Invisible Empire: the story of the Ku Klux Klan, 1866-1871, by Stanley Horn (Boston, 1939)

Iron Afloat, The story of the Confederate Ironclads, by William N. Still (Vanderbilt University Press, 1971) - Excellent account of the development of the Confederate ironclad navy.

Ironmaker to the Confederacy: Joseph R. Anderson and the Tredegar Iron Works, by Charles B. Dew, (Yale University Press, New Haven, CT, 1966)

Jacket of Gray and Other Fugitive Poems, by Caroline Rutledge Ball (Charleston, 1866)

Jefferson Davis and his Cabinet, by Rembert W. Patrick (Louisiana State University Press, 1944)

Jefferson Davis and the Confederate State, by Frank E. Vandiver (Oxford, Claredon Press, 1964)

John Slidell and the Confederates in Paris, by Beckles Willson, (Minton, Balch & Co., NY, 1932)

Journal of a Residence on a Georgian Plantation in 1838-1839, (New York, 1863)

King Cotton Diplomacy, by Frank Laurence Owsley (University of North Carolina Press, 1940, University of Chicago Press, 1953))

King Cotton Diplomacy, by Frank Lawrence Owsley (University of Chicago Press, 1969)

Kinston, Whitehall, and Goldsboro Expedition, December, 1862, by W.W. Howe, (New York, 1890)

Last of the Confederate Privateers, by David and Joan Hay (Crescent Books, 1977)

Last Years of Henry Timrod, by Jay B. Hubbell (Duke University Press, 1941)

Leaves from a Lawyer's Life Afloat, by Charles Crowley (Lee and Shepard, 1879)

Led On Step By Step, An Autobiography, by A. Toomer Porter (G.P. Putnam and Sons, NY, 1898) - Porter was a the pastor of Trenholm ("the real Rhett Butler").

Lee's Lieutenants, by Douglas Southall Freeman, (Charles Scribner's Sons, New York, NY, 1942)

The "Real Rhett Butler" & Other Revelations

"Licenses" - Frequently, vessels engaged in fishing or other limited area coast bound trade were issued licenses. Like registers and enrollments, these documents often contain information on the dimensions of the vessel, date and place of construction, rig, master, owners, etc., but also tell the trade for which the vessel was licensed. The best source for these documents is the U.S. National Archives.

Lee and Longstreet at High Tide, Gettysburg in the Light of the Official Records, by Helen Dortch Longstreet, (Gainesville, Ga., 1904)

Life and Services of John Newland Maffitt, by Emma Martin Maffitt (New York, Neale Publishing Company, 1906) - Maffitt was one of the most famous blockade runner captains and was the son-in-law of George Trenholm who was "the real Rhett Butler".

Life and Times of C.G. Memminger, by Henry D. Capers (Richmond, 1893)

Life in Dixie During the War, by Mary Ann Harris Gay (Foote and Davies, Atlanta, 1897) - This book gives insight into the life of Southern women during the Civil War and was undoubtedly used by Margaret Mitchell in the writing of *Gone With The Wind.*

Life in the South During the War, by Catherine Hopley, (London, 1863)

Lifeline of the Confederacy, Blockade Running During the Civil War, compiled and written by Stephen R. Wise, edited by William N. Still, Jr., (University of South Carolina Press, Columbia, SC, 1988) - This is undoubtedly the finest book that has been written on the steam blockade runners.

Lincoln's Commando: The Biography of Commander W.B. Cushing, U.S.N., by Ralph J. Roske and Charles Van Doren, (Harper, New York, NY, 1957)

List of American-Flag Merchant Vessels that Received Certificates of Enrollment or Registry at the Port of New York 1789-1867, also called "Special Lists Number 22," compiled by Forest R. Holdcamper, U.S. National Archives, Washington, DC, 1968. - This list contains the names of more than 26,000 American-flag merchant vessels that received certificates at the port of New York during the years 1789-1867. Because of its prominence as a major commercial center, many vessels documented at other ports stopped at New York on their inward or outward voyages and were required to get new certificates because of a change in ownership or in type of trade (coastwise or foreign) in which the vessels were to engage.

Look at South Carolina's Underwater Heritage, by E. Lee Spence (Nelson's Southern Printing, Charleston, South Carolina, 1974) - Booklet gives a brief overview of the importance of South Carolina's shipwrecks and includes a copy of South Carolina's law on the salvage shipwrecks, which was passed as the result of Spence's discovery of the wreck of the *C.S.S. Georgiana.*

Long Roll, by Mary Johnston (Boston and NY, 1911)

Man Who Almost Signed His Life Away, by Horace Knowles, *Saturday Evening Post,* (February 7, 1961)

Marching Through Georgia, by H.Y. Hedley, (M.A. Donahue & Co, Chicago, 1884)

Margaret Mitchell of Atlanta, by Finis Farr (New York, 1965)

Margaret Mitchell's Gone With The Wind Letters, 1936-1949, edited by Richard Harwell (Collier Books, NY, London, 1976)

Medical and Surgical History of the War of the Rebellion, Medical Volume I, part 2 (Washington, 1879)

Memoirs, by General William T. Sherman, 2 volumes, (New York, 1875)

Memoirs of a South Carolina Plantation During the War, by Mrs. E.A.S. Cox (in the collection of the Charleston Library Society)

Treasures of the Confederate Coast

Memoirs of General Turner Asby and his Compeers, by Reverend James B. Avirett, (Selby & Dulany, Baltimore, 1867)

Memoirs of Paul Henry Kendricken, by Paul H. Kendricken (Boston, 1910)

Memoirs of Service Afloat During the War Between the States, by Admiral Raphael Semmes (Kelly, Piet and Co., Baltimore, 1869)

Merchant Steam Vessels of the United States 1790-1868 ("Lytle-Holdcamper List"), by William M. Lytle and Forrest R. Holdcamper, revised and edited by C. Bradford Mitchell, Staten Island, NY, 1975. - This is an update of the original "Lytle List." Virtually any steam powered vessel built in the United States prior to 1869 is listed in this very useful book. It gives the tonnage, hull material, date of construction, disposition, first home port, etc.

Middleton Correspondence, edited by Isabelle Leland, South Carolina Historical Magazine (May, 1962)

Military Memoirs of a Confederate, by E.P. Alexander, (Charles Scribner's Sons, New York, 1907)

Military Operations of General Beauregard, by Alfred Roman (Harper and Brothers, 1883)

Mr. Lincoln's Navy, by Richard S. West (Longmans, Green and Company, New York, London, and Toronto, 1957)

My Diary North and South, by William Howard Russell, 2 volumes (Bradbury and Evans, London, 1863)

Narrative of a Blockade Runner, by John Wilkinson, Captain of the Late Confederate Navy, (Sheldon & Co., New York, NY, 1877)

Narrative of Military Operations, by General Joseph E. Johnston (Appleton publishers, 1874)

Narrative of the Confederate Navy, by William Force Clayton (Harrell's Printing House, Weldon, 1910)

Naval History of the Civil War, by Admiral David D. Porter (Sampson, Low, Searle & Rivington, London, 1887)

Naval History of the Civil War, by Howard P. Nash, (A.S. Barnes & Co., New York, NY, 1972)

Navy in the Civil War, by Alfred T. Mahan, (Charles Scribner's Sons, New York, NY, 1895)

Never Caught, by Augustus Hobart-Hampton (John Camden Holton, London, 1867)

Nine Men in Gray, by Charles Dufour (Doubleday & Company, Garden City, NY, 1963)

North Carolina in the War Between the States, by James R. Sloan, (Washington, NC, 1883)

Oceanographic Atlas of the Carolina Continental Margin - This book contains charts and overlays which will give you a feeling for the sheer number of shipwrecks along the North Carolina coast, but it is frequently incorrect in locations and other details. Wreck information appears to have come primarily from secondary sources. Although very useful, it should definitely not be used as a final authority.

Official Atlas of the Civil War, (Thomas Yoseloff, New York, NY, 1958)

Official History of Fulton County, by Walter G. Cooper

Official Records of the Union and Confederate Armies in the War of the Rebellion - This is a set of some one hundred and twenty-eight volumes (138,579 total pages) of official dispatches, reports and letters dealing with the day to day events of the Civil War. Published by the United States government between 1881 and 1901. It is poorly indexed, but it is one of the best sources of first hand information on vessels lost or destroyed in inland and coastal waters of the

The "Real Rhett Butler" & Other Revelations

South during the Civil War. Original or reprints of complete sets can be found in most large public libraries and are also available on microfilm.

Official Records of the Union and Confederate Navies in the War of the Rebellion - This is a set of thirty-two volumes of contemporary reports and letters dealing with the blockade of the South and other naval actions during the Civil War. It is indexed more thoroughly than the companion set of 128 volumes of army records, and is easier to use because of its smaller size, but it also lacks a lot of valuable information on Army transport losses, vessels sunk as intentional obstructions, etc.

Old times on the upper Mississippi; the recollections of a steamboat pilot from 1854 to 1863, by George Byron Merrick, (A.H. Clark Company, Cleveland, OH, 1909, also LAC microfiche 16468)

"Operation Ram *Neuse*," by David H. Pierce, (unpublished manuscript, Virginia Military Institute, Lexington, VA, 1963)

Our Women in the War: the Lives They Lived: The Deaths They Died (News and Courier Book Presses, Charleston, SC, 1885)

Outer Banks of North Carolina, by David Stick, (UNC Press, Chapel Hill, NC, 1958

Perilous Journeys: A History of Steamboating on the Chattahoochee, Apalachicola, and Flint Rivers, 1828-1928, by Edward A. Mueller, (Historic Chattahoochee Commission, Eufalia, Alabama, 1989)

Prelude to Civil War, The Nullification Controversy in South Carolina, 1816-1836, by William W. Freehling (Harper and Row, NY, 1965)

Private and Official Correspondence of General Benjamin F. Butler during the Period of the Civil War, by Benjamin Butler, 5 volumes, (Norwood, MA., 1917) - Butler was a general in the Union Army, and was known by the Confederates as "Beast Butler" and as "Silver Spoons Butler" because of his encouragement of the ill treatment of Southern women, and the theft of private silver by his troops. His forces participated in numerous river battles and in the first assault on Fort Fisher, North Carolina.

Public Life and Diplomatic Correspondence of James M. Mason, with some Personal History, edited by Virgia Mason (Stone Printing, Roanoke, 1903)

R.E. Lee, by Douglas Southhall Freeman, 4 volumes (New York)

"Rams and Gunboats," by Herbert Gambrell, (published in the *Southwest Review*, October, 1973), pp. 46-78

Rebel Brass: The Confederate Command System, by Frank E. Vandiver, (Louisiana State University Press, Baton Rouge, LA, 1956)

Rebel Recollections, by G.C. Eggleston, (G. Putnam & Sons, New York, NY, 1905)

Rebel Rose, by Ishbel Ross, (Harper Brothers, NY, 1954) - An account of the life of Confederate female spy, Rose O'Neal Greenhow, who died when the blockade runner *Condor* wrecked off Fort Fisher in 1864.

Rebel Shore: The Story of Union Sea Power in the Civil War, by James M. Merrill (Little, Brown, and Co., Boston, Toronto, 1957)

Rebel War Clerk's Diary at the Confederate States Capital, by John B. Jones (J.B. Lippincott, Philadelphia, 1866)

Recollections of a Rebel Reefer, by James Morris Morgan (Houghton Mifflin Co., Boston and NY, 1917) - Morgan served as a midshipman in the Confederate Navy and married one of the daughters of George Trenholm ("the real Rhett Butler").

Reconstruction of Georgia, by Edwin Campbell Woolley (New York, Columbia University Press, 1901)

Refugee Life in the Confederacy, by Mary Elizabeth Massie (Louisiana State University Press, 1964)

Treasures of the Confederate Coast

"Registers" - Vessels sailing from an American port to a foreign port were required to have a certificate of registry. These were issued as "Temporary" or as "Permanent" documents. A new certificate was supposed to be issued each time ownership, home port, rig, or use of the vessel changed. These contain information on the dimensions of the vessel, date and place of construction, rig, master, owners, etc. The best source for these documents is the U.S. National Archives.

Reminiscences of Confederate Service, by Francis W. Dawson (Courier Presses, Charleston, SC, 1882)

"Richmond Whig," (Richmond, Virginia) - Contemporary Confederate newspaper with the usual accounts of the day to day affairs of the war and of losses of vessels lost while attempting to run the Federal blockade of the various Southern ports.

Rise and Fall of the Confederacy, by Jefferson Davis (Thomas Yoseloff, NY, London, 1881)

Road to Tara, The Life of Margaret Mitchell, by Anne Edwards (Tickner & Fields, New Haven and NY, 1983)

Robert Barnwell Rhett, Father of Secession, by Laura W. White (NY and London, 1931) - This man was a close friend of George Trenholm ("the real Rhett Butler").

"Running of the Blockade," by James Sprunt (published in the *Southern Historical Society Papers*, Volume 24, Richmond, VA)

Running the Blockade, by Thomas Taylor (John Murray Co., London, 1896)

"Saga of the *Muscogee*," by Joel Turner, (published in *Georgia Magazine*, February-March issue, 1966), pp. 16-19

Saga of Felix Senac Being the Legend and Biography of a Confederate Agent in Europe, by Regina Rapier (Atlanta, GA, 1972) - Felix's daughter was unsuccessfully pursued by Alfred Glover Trenholm, son of George Alfred Trenholm ("the real Rhett Butler").

Sailor of Fortune: Personal Memories of Captain B.S. Osborn, edited by Albert B. Paine (Doubleday, NY, 1906)

Salvaging the Cargo of the "Mary Bowers", professional paper by E. Lee Spence, presented at *The Ninth Annual Conference on Historic Site Archeology*, University of Tennessee, Knoxville, Tennessee, 1968. Republished in *The Conference on Historic Site Archeology Papers 1969*, Volume 4, Part 1, 1971. - The *Mary Bowers* was one of the blockade runners that ran onto the wreck of the C.S.S. *Georgiana*.

"The *Sassacus* ãnd the *Albemarle*," by Edgar Holden, (published in the *Magazine of History*, #5, May, 1907), pp. 266-274

Savannah newspapers published during the Civil War, such as the "Daily Morning News," and "Savannah Daily Herald," and "Savannah Republican," often carried verbatim accounts of those in the "Charleston Daily Courier," and the *New York Times*, but is not as readily available. The Savannah papers do have the added advantage of having been partially digested and indexed during the WPA days, but copies of the index are both bulky and scarce.

Sea Devil of the Confederacy, The Story of the Florida and her Captain, John Newland Maffitt, by Edward Boykin (Funk and Wagnalls Co., NY, 1959)

Sea Dogs of the Sixties, by Jim Dan Hill, (U. of Minnesota Press, Minneapolis, MN, 1935)

Secret Service of the Confederate States in Europe, by James Bullock, 2 volumes, (Thomas Yoseloff, NY, 1884)

Selected Essays by Gideon Welles, Civil War and Reconstruction, compiled by Albert Mordell, (Twayne Publishers,, NY, 1959)

The "Real Rhett Butler" & Other Revelations

Service Afloat, by Admiral Raphael Semmes, (P.J. Kennedy, New York, NY, 1903)

Sherman's March Through the Carolinas, by John G. Barrett, (University of North Carolina Press, Chapel Hill, 1956)

Sherman's March, by Richard Wheeler, (Thomas Y. Crowell Publishers, NY, 1978) - Extremely interesting account, but definitely glosses over Sherman's role in ordering the looting and burning of the homes and plantations of private citizens in the South.

Sherman's March Through the South, by David Conyngham (Sheldon & Co., NY, 1865)

"Ships That Tested the Blockade of the Carolina Ports, 1861- 1865," by Marcus W. Price, *The American Neptune* (Volume 8, #8, July, 1948)

"Ships That Tested the Blockade of the Gulf Ports, 1861- 1865," by Marcus W. Price, *The American Neptune* (Volume 9, #4, 1949)

"Ships That Tested the Blockade of the Georgia and East Florida Ports, 1861- 1865," by Marcus W. Price, *The American Neptune* (Volume 15, #2, 1955)

Shipwreck Encyclopedia of the Civil War: North Carolina, 1861-1865, by E. Lee Spence, (Shipwreck Press™, Sullivan's Island, South Carolina, 1991) - Virtually the entire book is contained in this current volume.

Shipwreck Encyclopedia of the Civil War: South Carolina and Georgia, 1861-1865, by E. Lee Spence, (Shipwreck Press™, Sullivan's Island, South Carolina, 1991) - Virtually the entire book is contained in this current volume.

Shipwreck List for the years 1812-1816 (All Areas), by E. Lee Spence, (Shipwreck Press™, Sullivan's Island, South Carolina, 1991) - primarily deals with British and American losses during the War of 1812.

Shipwrecks and Shark Attacks: South Carolina and Georgia 1784-1821, by E. Lee Spence, (Shipwreck Press™, Sullivan's Island, South Carolina, 1991)

ShipWrecks™: Only three issues of this magazine, edited by E. Lee Spence, were published. It was designed to reach both amateurs and professionals interested in the field of historic shipwrecks and underwater archaeology. Each issue was illustrated with maps, charts, drawings and photos (both candid and technical).

Shipwrecks of Charleston Harbor, (magazine article reprinted from *Atlantic Coastal Diver*), Shipwreck Press™, Sullivan's Island, South Carolina, 1980. - Brief listing of shipwrecks around Charleston, South Carolina.

Shipwrecks of Charleston Harbor (South Carolina), professional paper by E. Lee Spence, presented before the Atlantic Alliance for Maritime Heritage's *First National Shipwreck Conference* (co-sponsored by the North Carolina Marine Education & Resources Foundation and the Year of the Ocean Foundation) at Nags Head, North Carolina, October 20, 1984. This paper was later re-edited and republished in the 1986 edition of the Alliance's journal, *Seafarers.*

Shipwrecks of the Ante-bellum South: South Carolina & Georgia, 1822-1860, by E. Lee Spence, (Shipwreck Press™, Sullivan's Island, South Carolina, 1991) - Detailed list of shipwrecks, heavily footnoted.

Shipwrecks of the Civil War, South Carolina and Georgia, professional paper by E. Lee Spence, presented before the annual shipwreck conference of the Atlantic Alliance for Maritime Heritage held at Atlantic City, New Jersey, December 14, 1986. This paper is also to appear in a future edition of *Seafarers.*

Shipwrecks of the Civil War: the Encyclopedia of Union and Confederate Naval Losses, by Donald G. Shomette, (Donic Ltd., Washington, DC, 1973)

Shipwrecks of the Era of Colonization: South Carolina and Georgia 1521-1762, by E. Lee Spence, (Shipwreck Press™, Sullivan's Island, South Carolina, 1991) - Detailed list of shipwrecks, heavily footnoted. Contains interesting overview applying to shipwrecks of all time periods.

Treasures of the Confederate Coast

Shipwrecks of the Era of Revolution: South Carolina and Georgia 1763-1783, by E. Lee Spence, (Shipwreck Press™, Sullivan's Island, South Carolina, 1991) - Detailed list of shipwrecks, heavily footnoted, with overview.

Shipwrecks of South Carolina and Georgia, (includes Spence's List, 1520-1865), by E. Lee Spence, (Sea Research Society, Sullivan's Island, South Carolina, 1984) - Detailed list of shipwrecks, heavily footnoted. Contains overview applying to shipwrecks of all time periods, and introductory chapters and appendices on specific wrecks. Prepared under grant from the South Carolina Committee for the Humanities, the National Endowment for the Humanities, and the Savannah Ship's of the Sea Museum.

Shipwrecks, Skin Divers, and Sunken Gold, by Dave Horner, (Dodd, Mead & Co., New York, NY, 1965)

Siege of Charleston 1861-1865, by Milby E. Burton,(U. of South Carolina Press, Columbia, SC, 1970)

Sketches From My Life, by Hobart Pasha, (D. Appleton & Co., New York, NY, 1887)

South Carolina and the Sea: Day by Day Towards Five Centuries, 1492-1976 A.D., edited by J. Percival Petit, (South Carolina Bi-Centennial Commission, 1976) - The section by E. Lee Spence on shipwrecks is taken almost directly from his book *A look at South Carolina's Underwater Heritage*.

South Carolina During Reconstruction, by Francis Butler Simkins and Robert Hilliard Woody (Chapel Hill, 1932)

South Carolina Goes to War, 1860-1865, by Charles E. Cauthen (University of North Carolina Press, Chapel Hill, NC, 1950)

South Carolina Rice Plantations, by J. Harold Easterby (University of Chicago Press, 1946)

South Carolina Women in the Confederacy, (section by Malvina S. Waring)

South Reports the Civil War, by J. Cutler Andrews (Princeton University Press, 1970)

Spence's Guide to South Carolina, by E. Lee Spence, (Nelson's Southern Printing, Charleston, South Carolina, 1976) Gives information on hunting, fishing, shipwrecks, etc.]

Spies for the Blue and Gray, by Harnett T. Kane, (Hanover House, Garden City, NY)

S.S. "Georgiana", professional paper by E. Lee Spence, published by the Sea Research Society for distribution at the *International Conference on Underwater Archeology*, Charleston, South Carolina, 1974.

Standard History of Georgia and Georgians, by Lucian Lamar Knight (Chicago, New York, 1917; 6 vols.)

State Records of South Carolina, Journals of the South Carolina Executive Councils of 1861 and 1862, by Charles E. Cauthen (Columbia, SC, 1956)

Statesmen of the Lost Cause, by Burton J. Hendrick (Little - Brown & Co., Boston, 1939)

Steamboat Bertrand: History, Excavation and Architecture, by Jerome E. Petsche, publications in Archeology, #11, (NPS, Washington, DC, 1974)

Stephen R. Mallory, Confederate Navy Chief, by Joseph T. Durkin (University of North Carolina Press, 1954) - Mallory was a relative of *Gone With The Wind* author Margaret Mitchell's maternal grandmother.

Stonewall Jackson and the American Civil War, by George Francis Robert Henderson, 2 volumes, (London, New York, 1898)

Stories of Charleston Harbor, by Katherine Drayton Simons (State Company, Columbia, SC, 1930)

Story of the Confederacy, by Robert Selph Henry (Indianapolis, 1931)

Story of the Great March, by George Ward Nichols (Harper & Brothers, NY, 1865)

The "Real Rhett Butler" & Other Revelations

Supplies for the Confederate Army, by Caleb Huse (Boston, 1904) - Major Huse sought and received emergency funding through the New York offices of Trenholm Brothers, and he subsequently served in Europe as a Confederate purchasing agent.

Surry of Eagle's-Nest, by John Esten Cooke (New York, 1866)

Tales and Traditions of the Lower Cape Fear, 1661-1898, by James Sprunt (LeGwin Brothers, Wilmington, 1898)

Tales of the Cape Fear Blockade; Being a Turn of the Century Account of Blockade Running, by James Sprunt, (Capital Printing, 1902)

"The case of the United States to be laid before the Tribunal of Arbitration to be convened at Geneva under the United States of America and Her Majesty the Queen of Great Britain Concluded at Washington, May 8, 1871" (Government Printing Office, Washington, 1872)

Torch on the Hill, by Michael Kenny (The American Press, NY, 1931)

Trenholm Family Chart, prepared by W. de Sausssure Trenholm, (NY, 1930)

Trenholm Family, by Henry Shultz Holmes (South Carolina Historical and Genealogical Magazine, October, 1915)

Underwater Archeology on the "Georgiana", professional paper by E. Lee Spence, ("Salvage of the *Georgiana*"), presented before the *International Conference on Underwater Archeology*, Charleston, SC, 1974. - The *Georgiana's* cargo was consigned to a company headed by George Trenholm, who Spence has determined was the "real Rhett Butler."

Underwater Exploration in South Carolina, professional paper by E. Lee Spence, presented at the *Eleventh Annual Conference on Historic Site Archeology*, University of South Carolina, 1970. Republished as *Underwater Archeology in South Carolina* in the *Conference on Historic Site Archeology Papers 1970*, Volume 5, Part 1, 1971. *A Comment on Diving Operations in South Carolina*, published as part of the *Historical Archeology Forum*, contained in the *Conference on Historic Site Archeology Papers 1969*, Volume 4, Part 2, 1971. The forum was a series of papers centered around Lee Spence's discovery and salvage of the *Mary Bowers*.

"United States versus John Fraser & Co. et al, In the circuit court of the United States for the District of South Carolina, Report of S. Lord, Jr., Referee as to Counsel Fees," (Walker, Evans, and Cogswell, Printers, Charleston, SC, 1873) - Gives list of properties seized. The senior partner in the firm of John Fraser & Co. was George Trenholm, "the real Rhett Butler." This firm was the most successful blockade running company in the Confederacy.

Virginia Girl in the Civil War 1861-1865, by M.S. Avary, (Appleton & Co., New York, NY, 1903)

War Time Journal of a Georgia Girl, 1864-1865, by Eliza Frances Andrews (Appleton and Company, NY, 1908) - This was definitely one of the books used by Margaret Mitchell in her writing of *Gone With The Wind*.

Way's Packet Directory 1848-1983, by Frederick Way, Jr., (Ohio University, Athens, Ohio, 1983) - Although its primary topic is river packet steamers (vessels used for both freight and passengers), this book contains information on approximately 500 steamers sunk during the Civil War. Entries are arranged by name of vessel.

When the Guns Roared - World Aspects of the American Civil War, by Philip Van Doren Stern (Doubleday and Co., Garden City, 1965)

"Wilmington During the Blockade," by John Johns, (published in *Harper's New Monthly Magazine*, September, 1866), pp. 497-502

Treasures of the Confederate Coast

Woman's Wartime Journal, by Dolly Sumner Lunt (J.W. Burke Co., Macon, GA, 1927)
Women of the South in War Time, by Matthew Page Andrews (Norman, Remington Company, Baltimore, 1920, 1924) - This was probably one of the books used by Margaret Mitchell in her writing of *Gone With The Wind*.
Wreck Diving in North Carolina, University of North Carolina, Sea Grant Publication #78-13. - This booklet is on some of the better known shipwrecks of North Carolina.
Wreck! The North Carolina Diver's Handbook, by Jess Harker (pseudonym for Dr. Donald Keith), (Marine Graphics Inc., Chapel Hill, NC, 1977)

• • •

These solemn looking men were the gun crew of the U.S.S. Wissahicken, which sank the Confederate cruiser/blockade runner Georgiana. Photo courtesy of the United States National Archives.

The U.S.S. Winfield Scott survived this storm off North Carolina, but was eventually sunk at Hilton Head Island, South Carolina.

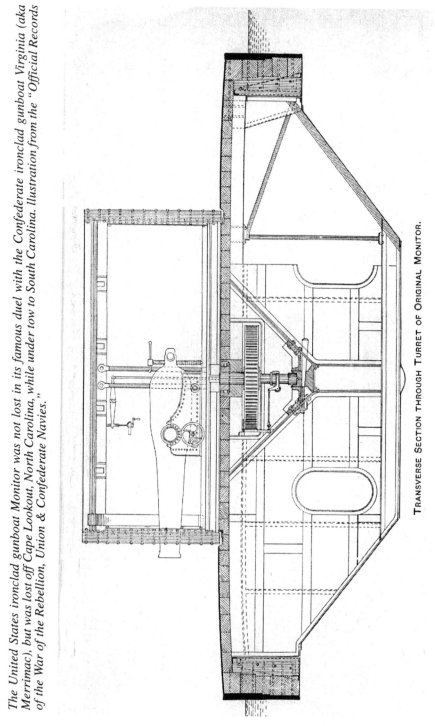

TRANSVERSE SECTION THROUGH TURRET OF ORIGINAL MONITOR.

The United States ironclad gunboat Monitor was not lost in its famous duel with the Confederate ironclad gunboat Virginia (aka Merrimac), but was lost off Cape Lookout, North Carolina, while under tow to South Carolina. Illustration from the "Official Records of the War of the Rebellion, Union & Confederate Navies."

Civil War cannon on display at the Confederate Naval Museum at Columbus, Georgia. Photo by L. Spence, courtesy of the museum.

Most people incorrectly believe that all Civil War cannon balls were round. They actually came in a wide range of sophisticated designs. Many had time delay, and/or waterproof fuses.

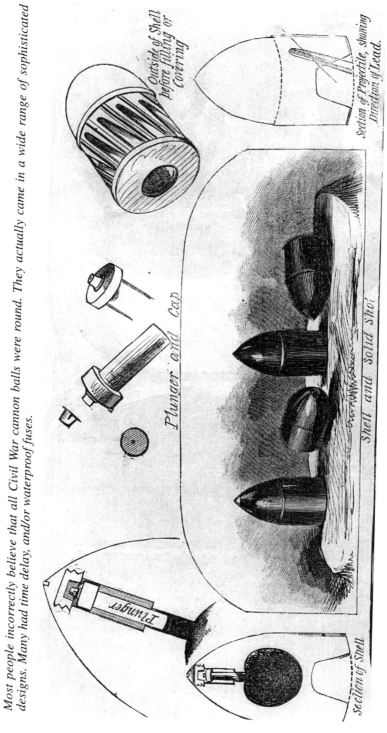

Outside of Shell before filling or covering

Section of Projectile, showing Direction of Lead.

Plunger and Cap

Shell and Solid Shot

Section of Shell

Plunger

INDEX

Note: To find information on the blockade running steamer *Hebe* look under *Hebe*. Doing so, we find the following three entries: 63-8-2, 63-10-1, and 63-10-3. This means you need to look under entries marked with SL Codes™: 1863-8-US-NC-2, 1863-10-US-NC-1, and 1863-10-US-NC-3. Just remember, all SL Codes™ in this index have had the century (18) and the letters US removed for brevity. Names of vessels have been italicized. Although, some major topics have been indexed for other sections, this is meant primarily as an index to the Spence's List section of this book.

#3, US picket boat: 65-2-NC-1
#5: 64-12-NC-8
#3: 65-6-SC/GA-1
#19: 61-11-SC/GA-4
$1,100 lost: 64-5-SC/GA-1
$2,000 in gold sovereigns: 64-10-NC-1
$3,415 in coin: 64-10-NC-8
$20,000 to $30,000 in gold: 64-5-NC-2
$30,000 "in cash": 62-2-NC-5
$50,000 in gold: 64-9-NC-3
$60 to $70,000 in gold: 63-12-NC-3
$90,000 in gold coin: 63-3-SC/GA-2
$250,000 cargo: 65-11-SC/GA-2
$500,000 in silver: 63-7-NC-4
$$$$ (see gold, money, paymasters, specie, and valuable cargoes, also see chapters one, three, and four)
9th Maine: 65-7-NC-1
14th New York Militia: 61-11-NCx-2
29°50'N/79°50'W: 63-4-SC/GAx-1
31°10'N/78°40'W: 64-12-SC/GA-13
32°41.6'N/79°51.6'W: 63-4-SC/GA-5
32°43.0'N/79°50.9'W: 63-12-SC/GA-1
32°43.1'N/79°46.5'W: 64-2-SC/GA-2
32°44.5'N/79°49.9'W: 63-3-SC/GA-2
32°45.3'N/79°53.1'W: 63-4-SC/GA-3
32°45.3'N/79°53.1'W: 64-6-SC/GA-2
32°46'47"N/79°45'35"W: 63-3-SC/GA-2
33°08'12"N/79°14'W: 63-3-SC/GA-1
33°39'N/71°29'W: 63-6-SC/GA-3
38°30'N/69°W: 64-3-SC/GA-2
56th Illinois Regiment: 65-3-NC-4
76th Pennsylvania Regt.: 65-7-NC-1
99th New York Regiment: 63-10-NC-4
300-pounder Parrott: 64-2-SC/GA-1
45333.5/59483.5: 61-11-SC/GA-5
45498.3/60454.1: 63-3-SC/GA-2
A.B. Thompson: 62-12x-SC/GA-1; 62-12x-SC/GA-4
A.C Williams, schooner: 62-1-NC-11
A.D. Vance, steamer: 64-1-NC-5

A.E. Fry, steamer: 64-12-NC-17
Abby Allen, coal vessel: 64-12x-SC/GA-3
accouterments: 63-8-SC/GA-5
Ada: 64-3-SC/GA-4
Adair (steamer): 64-1-SC/GA-2
Adair, Captain: 63-4-SC/GAx-1
Adair, Captain W.F.: 61-12-SC/GA-10
Adams Express: 65-5-SC/GA-3
Adams, Samuel: 62-4-SC/GA-6
Adelaide, schooner: 62-10-NC-2
Advance, steamer: 64-1-NC-5
Agnes C. Fry, steamer: 64-12-NC-16; 64-12-NC-17
Agnes E. Fry: 64-12-NC-16
Agnes E. Fry, steamer: 64-12-NC-17
Agnes Emily Fry: 64-12-NC-16; 64-12-NC-17
Alabama, privateer: 63-3-SC/GA-2; 65-1-x-1
Albatross' gig: 61-10-NC-1
Albemarle and Chesapeake canal, NC: 62-2-NC-13; 62-2-NC-14; 62-2-NC-15; 62-2-NC-16; 62-4-NC-3
Albemarle Sound, NC: 62-2-NC-11; 64-6-NC-2; 65-10-NC-1
Albemarle, CS ram: 64-5x-NC-1; 64-10-NC-7; 64-10-NC-9; 65-6x-NC-1
Albemarle, steamer: 62-3-NC-4
alcohol: 62-5-SC/GA-3
ale: 62-10-SC/GA-1
Alexander Cooper, schooner: 63-8-NC-5
Alexander, John, schooner: 61-12x-NC-1
aliases used by blockade runners: 64-10-NC-1
Alice: 65-10-SC/GA-2
Alice (later *U.S.S. Aster*): 64-10-NC-5
Alice L. Webb, schooner: 63-11-NC-1
Alice Provost: 63-12-SC/GA-3
Aligator: 63-SC/GA-4-SC/GAx-1
All Saints Parish, SC: 62-6-SC/GA-1

Treasures of the Confederate Coast

The "Real Rhett Butler" & Other Revelations

Battery Chatfield, SC: 64-10-SC/GA-2

Battery Rutledge, SC: 64-2-SC/GA-1; 64-10-SC/GA-2

bayonets (long and short): 63-3-SC/GA-2; 64-2-NC-3

Bazely, US tug: 64-12-NC-6

Bazley: 64-12-NC-6; 64-12-NC-7

Beach Channel, SC: 64-10-SC/GA-2

Beacon Island, NC: 61-9-NC-1

beam engine: 63-6-SC/GA-2

Bear Inlet, NC: 63-12-NC-4

Beatrice: 64-11-SC/GA-3

Beaufort, NC: 61-11-NC-2; 61-11-NC-9; 62-3-NC-3; 63-11-NC-1; 64-6-NC-3; 65-7-NC-1 (see also Beaufort, SC)

Beaufort, SC: 61-11-SC/GA-6; 63-7-SC/GA-1 (see also Beaufort, NC; Hilton Head, SC; and Port Royal, SC)

Beauregard's ironclads: 63-1-SC/GA-3

Beauregard, steamer: 63-12-NC-3

bell: 64-8-SC/GA-2

bell rung: 63-10-NC-3

Belle Boyd: 64-5-NC-2

belt buckles: 61-11-SC/GA-5

belts with boxes lost: 64-12-NC-13

Bendigo , steamer: 64-1-NC-1; 64-1-NC-2

Bermuda: 62-10-SC/GA-1; 64-8-SC/GA-2

Berosa: 63-4-SC/GAx-2

Beta: 64-12-NC-7

Bibb: 65-3-SC/GA-5

Bibbey, Sarah (schooner): 61-12x-NC-1

Bier (George H., aka George Henry): 64-2-NC-4; 64-5-NC-2

Bigelow, G.O., schooner: 63-12-NC-4

binnacles: 63-3-SC/GA-1; 63-7-NC-1; 64-3-SC/GA-2

Black River, NC: 62-5-NC-4; 62-5-NC-5

Black Squall, brig: 61-4-NC-1

Black Warrior, CS schooner: 62-2-NC-6

black man (drowned): 65-5-SC/GA-2

black man: 61-10-SC/GA-3

black men (heroics of): 62-2-SC/GA-7; 65-5-SC/GA-2 (see also final entry)

blacks (enlistment): 61-9-NC-4

blacks (described): 64-12-NC-19

blacks (freed): 65-4-SC/GA-3

Blackwater River, NC: 62-5-NC-4; 62-5-NC-6

blankets: 61-10-SC/GA-1; 62-10-SC/GA-2; 63-11-NC-2; 64-1-NC-4; 64-2-NC-

1; 64-2-NC-5; 64-2-SC/GA-1; 64-3-SC/GA-2; 64-6-NC-3

blockade established: 61-4-x-1

blockade lifted: 65-6-x-1

blockade raised: 63-1-SC/GA-3

blockade runners: 63-6x-SC/GA-1; 65-2-x-1

blockade runners (aliases used by): 64-10-NC-1

blockade runners built: 64-12x-GB-England-1

blockade runners (built entirely for speed): 64-12-x-2

blockade runners ($110,000,000 worth destroyed): 64-12-x-2

blockade runners ($5,500,000 worth destroyed): 64-12-x-2

blockade runners (immense gains): 64-12-x-2

blockade runners (new class): 64-12-x-2

blockade runners (play): 64-12-x-2

blockade runners (very fast): 64-12-x-2

blockade running: 65-2-x-1

blockade running (brisk): 64-12-x-2

blockade running (remunerative): 64-12-x-2

blockade running expenses: 64-12x-x-1

blockade running orders: 64-12-x-1

blockade running trips: 64-4x-NC-2

Blount's Bar, FL: 65-4-SC/GA-1

Blountstown, FL: 65-4-SC/GA-1

blown to atoms: 64-6-NC-2

blunderbuss: 61-10-SC/GA-1

Bodie Island, NC: 62-5-NC-1; 63-8-NC-1

Bodie Island light-house, NC: 61-8-NC-1

Bogota: 62-1-SC/GA-4

Bogue Inlet, NC: 61-10-NC-1; 62-1-NC-8; 64-6-NC-3

Bogue Island (banks), NC: 61-11-NC-2

Bogue Island, NC: 61-12-NC-2

Bogues Beach, NC: 61-11-NC-2

bomb-proof: 63-12-SC/GA-4

bombs: 62-1-NC-4; 62-1-NC-5

Bombshell, US Army steamer: 64-4-NC-1

boots: 62-11-SC/GA-1; 64-12-NC-4

Boston: 64-5-SC/GA-1

bottle with note: 64-5-NC-4

bottles: 62-6-NC-5; 62-10-SC/GA-1

Bowers, L.G.: 64-8-SC/GA-2

Bowers, Mary: 63-3-SC/GA-2; 64-8-SC/GA-2; 64-10-SC/GA-1

Treasures of the Confederate Coast

Cape Lookout Shoals, NC: 64-6-NC-4

Cape Romain (lighthouse): 62-3-SC/GA-7; 62-10-SC/GA-3

Cape Romain (Mill Island, SC): 62-3-SC/GA-4

Cape Romain (see also Bull's Bay)

Cape Romain (see final entry)

Cape Romain: 62-4-SC/GA-8; 63-6-SC/GA-3

captain's gig (*U.S.S. Albatross'*): 61-10-NC-1

Carlton's Wharf: 61-1-SC/GA-3

Carolina Beach, NC: 63-8-NC-2; 63-12-NC-3; (see also Cape Fear)

Carolina Shoals, NC: 64-10-NC-5

Carolina, steamer: 62-11-NC-8

carpenter tools: 64-1-NC-3

Carter, schooner: 62-1-NC-13

Caswell, CS tender: 65-2-NC-5

Catawba: 62-5-SC/GA-6

Catinat, French corvette: 61-11-NC-8

cattle: 61-11-SC/GA-3

caustic soda: 62-8-NC-1

cavalry gilt buttons: 62-10-SC/GA-1

cavalry sabers: 64-2-NC-3

cavalry swords: 62-10-SC/GA-1

Cawtawba: 62-5-SC/GA-6

ceiling (flooring): 61-9-SC/GA-1

celebrations (premature): 64-1-NC-4; 65-1-NC-11

Celt: 65-2-SC/GA-1

centrifugal wrecking pump: 65-10-SC/GA-1

Ceres, steamer: 63-12-NC-2

Chace: 62-1-SC/GA-3

chains: 63-12-SC/GA-2

Champagne: 62-10-SC/GA-1; 65-1-NC-11

Chance, Frank and Paul: 62-4-NC-2; 63-2-SC/GA-7; 64-12-SC/GA-4

Charleston, SC (see also Ashley River, Cooper River, Folly Island, James Island, Isle of Palms, Morris Island, Mount Pleasant, and Sullivan's Island)

Charleston, SC: 64-4x-NC-2; 64-4x-SC/GA-1; 61-1-SC/GA-2; 61-11-SC/GA-1; 61-11-SC/GA-4; 61-11-SC/GA-5; 61-12-SC/GA-1; 61-12-SC/GA-2; 61-12-SC/GA-3; 61-12-SC/GA-4; 61-12-SC/GA-5; 61-12-SC/GA-6; 61-12-SC/GA-8; 61-12x-SC/GA-1; 61-12x-SC/GA-2; 61-12x-SC/GA-3; 61-12x-SC/GA-4; 62-1-SC/GA-1; 62-1-SC/GA-2; 62-1-SC/GA-4; 62-1x-SC/GA-1; 62-1x-SC/GA-2; 62-1x-SC/GA-3; 62-1x-SC/GA-4; 62-3-SC/GA-1; 62-5-SC/GA-3; 63-1-SC/GA-2; 63-4-SC/GA-2; 63-5-SC/GA-3; 63-8-SC/GA-4; 63-10-SC/GA-1; 64-5-SC/GA-2; 65-2-SC/GA-2; 65-2-SC/GA-3; 65-2-SC/GA-4; 65-2-SC/GA-5; 65-2-SC/GA-6; 65-8-SC/GAx-1

Charleston: 65-2-SC/GA-3

Charleston Bar, SC: 61-1-SC/GA-1; 62-4-SC/GA-6; 63-8-SC/GA-3; 64-12-SC/GA-1

Charleston Harbor, SC: 62-2-SC/GA-7; 62-10-SC/GA-1; 63-2-SC/GA-4; 63-4-SC/GA-3; 64-6-SC/GA-2; 64-12-SC/GA-14; 65-1-SC/GA-2

Charleston Light, SC: 61-12-SC/GA-8

Charlotte, prize steamer: 65-1-NC-11

charts (saved): 64-2-NC-6

charts: 62-1-SC/GA-4

Chase: 62-4-SC/GA-8; 62-4-SC/GA-9

Chattahoochee: 65-4-SC/GA-1

Chattahoochee River (AL, GA, & FL): 64-12-SC/GA-6; 65-4-SC/GA-1; 65-4-SC/GA-2

cheese: 62-5-SC/GA-3

Cherry Grove (see final entry)

Chesapeake (and Albemarle) canal: 62-2-NC-13; 62-2-NC-14; 62-2-NC-15; 62-2-NC-16; 62-4-NC-3

Chesterfield.: 63-8-SC/GA-5

Chickamauga, C.S.N. steamer: 65-2-NC-2

Chicora: 65-2-SC/GA-4

Chicora, steamer: 62-11-NC-8

china: 62-6-NC-5

Chisolm's causeway: 65-2-SC/GA-6

Chisolm's Island: 63-4-SC/GA-6

Chowan River, NC: 62-5-NC-2

chronometers: 62-1-SC/GA-4; 62-6-NC-4; 63-1-NC-1; 63-6-SC/GA-3; 64-2-NC-6; 62-2-NC-19

churchyard: 65-12-SC/GA-3

cigar boats: 65-2-SC/GA-6

cigar lighters: 62-10-SC/GA-1

cigars: 62-10-SC/GA-1; 63-9-SC/GA-1

City of New York, US transport: 62-1-NC-5; 62-1-NC-6

City of Petersburg, steamer: 64-2-NC-8

City of York, US propeller: 62-1-NC-4

Treasures of the Confederate Coast

The "Real Rhett Butler" & Other Revelations

Treasures of the Confederate Coast

Edisto River, SC: 63-2x-SC/GA-1; 63-7-SC/GA-1
Edith, steamer: 65-2-NC-2
Edward: 62-1-SC/GA-4; 62-1x-SC/GA-2
Edwards Ferry, NC: 65-4-NC-3
Edwin: 62-5-SC/GA-3
Egg Island, GA: 64-3-SC/GA-2
Elisabeth, steamer: 63-9-NC-3
Elite: 61-4-SC/GA-1
Elizabeth: 62-2-SC/GA-4
Elizabeth City, NC: 62-2-NC-5; 62-2-NC-6; 62-2-NC-7; 62-2-NC-8; 62-2-NC-9; 62-2-NC-10; (see also Albemarle and Chesapeake canal)
Elizabeth, steamer: 63-9-NC-3; 64-1-NC-1
Eliza Hancox: 64-12-SC/GA-1
Ella, steamer: 64-12-NC-1
Ellen Goldsborough, schooner: 61-12x-NC-1
Ellen, schooner: 62-6-NC-3
Ellis, US steamer: 62-11-NC-11
Emerald: 62-1-SC/GA-1; 62-1-SC/GA-4
Emily, schooner: 62-6-NC-4
Emily, steamer: 64-2-NC-7
Emma: 62-8-SC/GA-1
Emma Valeria: 65-10-SC/GA-1
Empire: 62-3-SC/GA-2
Empire, ship: 65-6-NC-1
Enfield muskets: 62-6-NC-5
Enfield rifles: 63-3-SC/GA-2; 64-2-NC-3
enlistment (blacks): 61-9-NC-4
enlistment (contrabands): 61-9-NC-4
Enoch Dean: 65-4-SC/GA-3
Epsilon, US picket boat: 64-12-NC-8
Equator, CS steamer: 65-2x-NC-1
Ericsson vibrating engines: 63-12-SC/GA-1
Etiwan: 63-4-SC/GA-3; 64-6-SC/GA-2
Etowah: 63-4-SC/GA-3; 64-6-SC/GA-2
Etowan: 63-4-SC/GA-3; 64-6-SC/GA-2
Etta, ex steamer: 65-12x-NC-1
Etwan: 63-4-SC/GA-3; 64-6-SC/GA-2
Evans and Cogswell: 61-10-SC/GA-1
Everglade: 63-8-SC/GA-2
excellent assortment of goods: 63-2-SC/GA-5
Experiment: 62-4-SC/GA-2
explosions: 63-8-SC/GA-1; 64-12- NC-12
express mail pouch: 65-5-SC/GA-3
extravagant prices: 62-5-SC/GA-6

false compartment: 63-3-SC/GA-2
false signal lights: 64-10-NC-3
Fannie: 65-8-SC/GA-2
Fannie and Jennie, steamer: 64-2-NC-6; 64-2-NC-7
Fannie Lehr: 65-11-SC/GA-4
Fanny: 65-8-SC/GA-2
Fanny and Jenny, steamer: 64-2-NC-6; 64-2x-NC-2
Fanny Lewis, brig: 62-11-NC-6; 62-11-NC-7
Fanny, CS steamer: 62-2-NC-10
Fanny, steamer: 64-2-NC-6; 64-2x-NC-2
Farmer, Delaware (schooner): 61-12x-NC-1
farming utensils: 65-4-SC/GA-3
Fayetteville, NC: 65-3-NC-3
fear: 65-3-NC-4
Federal Shoals: 64-9-NC-4; 64-10-NC-1
female spies: 64-5-NC-2; 64-10-NC-1
Fergus: 64-2-SC/GA-1
Ferguson, Captain: 64-6-SC/GA-2; 65-2-SC/GA-1
Ferguson, Captain John: 63-2-SC/GA-2
ferry: 61-10-SC/GA-2; 62-5-NC-2
ferry boat: 61-10-SC/GA-3
fictitious name: 64-5-NC-2
field artillery: 63-4-SC/GA-7
field pieces (brass): 62-11-NC-1
Fig Island, GA (Savannah River): 65-10-SC/GA-1
figurehead of a woman: 62-10-SC/GA-1
Fingal: 63-6-SC/GA-5
Fire Fly: 62-11-SC/GA-2; 64-12-SC/GA-9
fire (caused by wet lime): 65-12-SC/GA-1
fire: 61-10-SC/GA-3; 61-11-SC/GA-10
Firefly: 62-11-SC/GA-2; 64-12-SC/GA-9
fish: 62-5-SC/GA-3
Five Fathom Hole, GA (see also Savannah River)
Five Fathom Hole, SC (see also Charleston and Sullivan's Island)
flags (Confederate used by U.S. ships): 64-12-NC-19
flags: 61-9-SC/GA-1; 61-10-SC/GA-1; 63-1-SC/GA-2 (first Confederate flown); 63-3-SC/GA-2; 64-2-NC-6; 64-10-SC/GA-3
flagship (Lynch's): 65-2-NC-3
flagship: 65-2-SC/GA-3

Treasures of the Confederate Coast

The "Real Rhett Butler" & Other Revelations

Treasures of the Confederate Coast

The "Real Rhett Butler" & Other Revelations

Treasures of the Confederate Coast

1; 64-6-SC/GA-1; 64-9-NC-4; 64-12-NC-4; (see also brandies, and whiskey) liquors and wines secured & locked up: 65-1-x-1

Little Ada: 64-3-SC/GA-4

Little River (inlet at NC SC state line): 61-11-SC/GA-5; 62-6-SC/GA-1; 62-11-SC/GA-1; 63-3-NC-1; 63-4-SC/GA-1364-1-NC-4; 64-12-NC-4

Little Washington, NC: 63-4-NC-2

Liverpool: 62-4-SC/GA-4

Lizzie, English sloop: 62-8-NC-1

lock and key: 64-10-NC-8

locks: 62-10-SC/GA-1

Lockwood, Captain Thomas J.: 64-12x-US-x-1

Lockwoods Folly Inlet, NC: 62-1-NC-1; 62-4-NC-1; 63-4-NC-1; 63-9-NC-3; 64-1-NC-1; 64-1-NC-2; 64-1-NC-3; 64-11-NC-1

Lockwoods Folly Island, NC: 63-9-NC-3; 65-10-SC/GAx-1

Loggerhead Inlet, NC: 61-12x-NC-1

Long Island (present day Isle of Palms, SC): 62-1-SC/GA-4; 62-4-SC/GA-6; 62-5-SC/GA-6; 63-3-SC/GA-2; 63-4-SC/GA-7; 63-5-SC/GA-2; 64-8-SC/GA-2

Long, Captain Billy: 61-11-SC/GA-5

loot (stolen): 62-4-SC/GA-3

Lotus: 63-1-SC/GA-1

Louisa, schooner: 61-8-NC-2

Louisiana, US gunboat: 64-12- NC-12

Louisiana, US transport: 62-2-NC-17

Louisiana, US transport: 63-4-NC-2

Lucy C. Holmes, schooner: 62-4-NC-1

lumber: 65-10-SC/GAx-1

Lydia Francis, brig: 61-5-NC-1

Lydia French, brig: 61-5-NC-1

Lynx, CS steamer: 64-9-NC-3

machinery: 61-10-SC/GA-1

mackerel (sic): 62-5-SC/GA-3

Madgie, US steamer: 63-10-NC-2

Madgil, US steamer: 63-10-NC-2

Madick, Match (Austrian crew member): 65-1-x-1

Maffitt's Channel, SC: 62-1-SC/GA-1; 62-1-SC/GA-2; 62-1-SC/GA-4; 62-1x-SC/GA-2; 62-1x-SC/GA-3; 62-1x-SC/GA-4; 64-10-SC/GA-2

magnetometer survey: 63-7-SC/GA-3; 65-1-SC/GA-2

Magnolia: 62-2-NC-17

Magnolia Beach: 63-4-SC/GA-13

Magnolia Cemetery, SC: 63-10-SC/GA-1

Maillefert's salvage company: 63-12-SC/GA-1; 64-2-SC/GA-2

mails: 63-6-SC/GA-4; 65-5-SC/GA-3

Maine (9th Regiment): 65-7-NC-1

Maine Regiment (4th): 62-1-NC-4

Majestic: 62-1-SC/GA-4

Major Anderson: 63-12-SC/GA-4

mammoth ship *Great Republic*: 61-11-NC-7

Manhattan, steamer: 64-5-NC-4

Manns Harbor, NC: 62-2-NC-4

Marcia: 62-1-SC/GA-2; 62-1-SC/GA-4

Margaret Scott: 62-1-SC/GA-4

Maria Theresa: 61-12-SC/GA-8

Marianna: 65-11-SC/GA-3

marines: 61-11-NCx-2

Marion: 63-4-SC/GA-2

Mars Bluff, SC: 65-3-SC/GA-4

Marshal Ney: 62-1-NC-7

Marshal Nye: 62-1-NC-7

Marshal Shoal, NC: 64-12-NC-1

Martha: 64-3-SC/GA-1

Martha, steamer: 64-8-NC-1

Marthie: 64-3-SC/GA-1

Martin boilers: 63-12-SC/GA-1; 64-2-SC/GA-2

Martin's Industry, SC: 61-11-SC/GA-8; (see also Port Royal)

Martin, B.T. (brig): 61-7-NC-3

Marx, Sir Robert F. (undersea explorer): 62-12-NC-2; 64-2-NC-6

Mary: 64-11-SC/GA-2

Mary and Hetty, schooner: 61-12x-NC-1

Mary Bowers (see also *Constance* and *Georgiana*)

Mary Bowers: 63-3-SC/GA-2; 64-8-SC/GA-2; 64-10-SC/GA-1

Mary Frances, schooner: 61-12x-NC-1

Mary Louisa: 62-3-SC/GA-7

Mary Powers: 64-8-SC/GA-2

Masonboro Inlet, NC: 62-7-NC-1; 62-11-NC-1; 62-11-NC-3; 63-1-NC-1; 63-8-NC-2; 63-10-NC-1; 64-2-NC-4; 64-2-NC-6; 64-2-NC-7; 64-10-NC-3

matches: 62-10-SC/GA-1

Mattie: 64-3-SC/GA-1

May Flower, steamer: 64-6-NC-4

Mayflower, steamer: 64-6-NC-3

Mayflower, US steamer: 61-11-NC-4

Maynard rifles: 61-9-NC-6

McAlpin's Landing (Savannah River): 65-8-SC/GA-1

McCaw, steamer: 64-6-NC-1; 64-12-NC-16

McClellenville, SC: 64-3-SC/GA-4; (see also Bull's Bay and Cape Romain, SC)

McCormick, Randy: 61-11-SC/GA-5

McDonough, Commodore (US steamer): 65-8-NCx-1

McNutt, David: 64-1-SC/GA-2

Mechanic: 62-1-SC/GA-4

medicines: 62-5-SC/GA-6; 62-10-SC/GA-1; 63-3-SC/GA-1; 63-9-NC-2; 64-8-SC/GA-1

Meherrin River: 62-5-NC-3

Mercedita: 63-1-SC/GA-3

merchandise: 61-10-SC/GA-1; 62-5-SC/GA-6; 62-10-SC/GA-2; 63-4-SC/GA-7; 63-7-NC-1; 63-12-NC-4; 64-2-NC-1; 64-2-NC-3; 64-2-NC-6; 64-2-NC-7

mercury: 61-9-NC-6

Merrimac, CS ram: 64-10-NC-7

Merrimack, U.S.S.: 62-12-NC-2

Messenger: 62-1-SC/GA-4

Meteor: 61-12-SC/GA-2; 61-12-SC/GA-8

Mexican Republic: 61-11-SC/GA-5

military goods: 64-12-NC-1

Mill Island, SC: 62-3-SC/GA-4

mill on Savannah River: 64-12-SC/GA-3

Milledgeville: 64-12-SC/GA-11

Milly, steamer: 64-1-NC-1

mines (torpedoes): 63-2-SC/GA-6; 63-4-SC/GA-2; 65-1-SC/GA-2; 65-3-SC/GA-1; 65-3-SC/GA-5

Minho: 62-10-SC/GA-1; 64-8-SC/GA-1

Minquas, steamer: 65-4-NC-2

Minquass, steamer: 65-4-NC-2

missionary teachers: 65-12-SC/GA-3

Modern Greece, steamer: 62-6-NC-5

money ($30,000): 62-2-NC-5

money (hidden in keelson): 63-11-NC-2

money: 62-2-NC-6; 63-7-NC-4; 63-10-NC-3; 64-2-SC/GA-2; 64-9-NC-3; 64-10-NC-1; 65-1-NC-11; 65-1-SC/GA-2; 65-5-SC/GA-2

monitor Patapsco: 65-1-SC/GA-2

monitor Weehawken: 63-12-SC/GA-1

monitor(s): 63-2-SC/GA-6; 63-4-SC/GA-5; 63-12-SC/GA-6; 64-2-SC/GA-2

Monitor, US ironclad: 62-12-NC-2

Monks Corner, SC: 65-2-SC/GA-6

Montauk: 63-2-SC/GA-6

Montezuma: 62-1-SC/GA-4; 62-1x-SC/GA-3

Moodna: 63-4-SC/GA-5

Moorehead City, NC: 65-7-NC-1

morphine: 62-10-SC/GA-1; 63-3-SC/GA-1

Morris Island (see also Charleston, SC)

Morris Island, SC: 61-12-SC/GA-1; 61-12-SC/GA-2; 61-12-SC/GA-3; 61-12-SC/GA-4; 61-12-SC/GA-5; 61-12-SC/GA-6; 61-12x-SC/GA-1; 61-12x-SC/GA-2; 61-12x-SC/GA-3; 61-12x-SC/GA-4; 62-5-SC/GA-3; 63-4-SC/GA-3; 63-4-SC/GA-4; 63-4-SC/GA-5; 63-6-SC/GA-4; 63-7-SC/GA-2; 63-8-SC/GA-5; 63-12-SC/GA-4; 64-6-SC/GA-2; 64-11-SC/GA-2

Mound (Cape Fear, NC): 64-12-NC-9

Mount Pleasant, NC: 64-6-NC-5

Mount Pleasant, SC: 61-10-SC/GA-2; (see also Charleston)

Mountain Home (wrecking steamer): 64-3-SC/GA-5

munitions: 63-3-SC/GA-2; 64-2-NC-3; 64-12-NC-5

munitions carrier: 63-8-SC/GA-5

Murray's Inlet, SC: 63-4-SC/GA-11; (see also Murrell's Inlet, SC)

Murrell's Inlet, SC: 63-4-SC/GA-11; 63-4-SC/GA-12; 63-5-SC/GA-1; 63-10-SC/GA-2; 63-12-SC/GA-5; (see also Murray's inlet)

Muscogee: 65-4-SC/GA-2

museums (see Cape Fear Museum, Confederate Naval Museum, Florence Museum, Fort Fisher Visitor's Center/Museum, Savannah Ships of the Sea Museum, Southport Naval Museum)

musket boxes: 64-6-NC-3

muskets: 62-2-NC-6; 62-6-NC-5; 62-10-SC/GA-1; 64-1-NC-3; 64-2-NC-1

Nag's Head, NC: 62-2-NC-19

Nashville: 62-4-NC-2; 63-2-SC/GA-7

Nassau (a doomed city): 65-2-x-1

Nasworthy, John: 63-2-SC/GA-7

nautical instruments: 61-10-SC/GA-1; 64-12-x-1

Navigation Company: 62-10-SC/GA-1

Navy recruits (US): 64-10-NC-2

needles: 62-10-SC/GA-1; 64-2-NC-3

Treasures of the Confederate Coast

The "Real Rhett Butler" & Other Revelations

Rattlesnake (C.S.N. schooner): 62-3-SC/GA-1
Rattlesnake (C.S.N. str.): 63-2-SC/GA-7
Rattlesnake (screw str.): 65-1x-SC/GA-1
Rattlesnake Shoal, SC: 62-1-SC/GA-1; 62-1-SC/GA-2; 62-1-SC/GA-4; 62-1x-SC/GA-2; 62-1x-SC/GA-3; 62-1x-SC/GA-4
Reaper's shoal (Reeper Shoal): 64-8-NC-1; 64-12-NC-1
Rebecca: 61-12-SC/GA-8
Rebecca Sims: 61-12-SC/GA-8
Rebel: 63-8-SC/GA-5
Rebel flag: 63-3-SC/GA-2
rebels (reformed): 64-12-NC-19
receiving ship Indian Chief: 65-2-SC/GA-2
recruits, US Navy: 64-10-NC-2
Reeper Shoal (Reaper's Shoal), NC: 64-8-NC-1; 64-12-NC-1
reference points (wrecks used as): 64-12-NC-15
reformed rebels: 64-12-NC-19
Regia (Neustra Señora de) Spanish steamer: 61-11-NC-6
Reliance: 63-10-SC/GAx-1
Renau, Ron: 65-4-NC-3
Renaudin: 63-2-SC/GA-4
Resolute: 64-12-SC/GA-3
Retribution, CS privateer: 65-12x-NC-1
Revenue cutter (U.S.): 63-4-SC/GA-10
Revenue cutter: 63-4-SC/GA-10
Reverend Wm. B. Yates: 63-8-SC/GA-4; 63-10-SC/GA-1
revolvers: 62-1-NC-4; 63-9-SC/GA-1; 64-12-NC-13
revolving turret: 63-12-SC/GA-1
reward offered: 64-2-SC/GA-2
Rhode Island battery: 62-1-NC-4
Rice Mills (lower): 65-7-SC/GA-1
rice: 62-2-SC/GA-2; 62-2-SC/GA-3; 62-2-SC/GA-4; 62-2-SC/GA-5; 62-2-SC/GA-6; 62-3-SC/GA-4; 62-3-SC/GA-7
rice meal: 62-3-SC/GA-4
Riceborough River, GA: 62-4-SC/GA-7
Rich Inlet, NC: 63-2-NC-2; 63-9-NC-2
Richmond: 61-12-SC/GA-8
Richmond Importing and Exporting Company: 64-1-SC/GA-2
Ricoe's Bluff: 65-10-SC/GA-2
Ridge, Samuel S. (captain): 64-10-NC-1

rifles: 62-1-NC-4; 62-1-NC-5; 62-6-NC-5; 62-10-SC/GA-1; 63-11-NC-2; 64-2-NC-3
rifles (Austrian): 63-11-NC-2; 64-2-NC-3
rifles (Enfield): 64-2-NC-3
Rio, schooner: 62-1-NC-16
river steamer: 63-2-SC/GA-1
riverboat: 61-11-SC/GA-6
Roanoke Island, NC: 61-12-NC-3; 62-1-NC-3; 62-1-NC-12; 62-1-NC-13; 62-1-NC-14; 62-1-NC-15; 62-1-NC-16; 62-1-NC-17; 62-1-NC-19; 62-2-NC-1; 62-2-NC-2; 62-2-NC-3; 62-2-NC-11
Roanoke River, NC: 64-4-NC-2; 64-10-NC-6; 64-10-NC-9; 64-12-NC-6; 64-12-NC-7; 64-12-NC-8; 65-3-NC-5; 65-4-NC-1; 65-4-NC-3; 65-6x-NC-1
Robert B. Howlett: 64-12-SC/GA-1
Robert E. Lee: 63-7-NC-4
Robert E. Lee: 65-8-SC/GA-1; 65-12x-SC/GA-1
Robert E. Lee, CS steamer: 63-11-NC-2
Robert Habersham: 63-8-SC/GA-1
Robert Haversham: 63-8-SC/GA-1
Robert Lehr: 65-8-SC/GA-1; 65-11-SC/GA-5; 65-12x-SC/GA-1
Roberts (captain): 64-10-NC-1
Robin Hood: 61-12-SC/GA-8
rockets: 64-10-SC/GA-2
Roe(II): 64-12-NC-17
Rogues Beach (sic): 61-11-NC-2
Romain light: 62-4-SC/GA-8
Rose: 64-6-SC/GA-1
Rose O'Neal Greenhow, female spy: 64-10-NC-1
Rosedew battery, GA: 64-4-SC/GA-1
Rosetta stone: 63-3-NC-2
rosin: 62-11-NC-9; 63-10-NC-1
Rover: 63-10-SC/GA-2
Ruby: 63-6-SC/GA-4
Ruddy, Drew: 63-5-SC/GA-2; 65-3-SC/GA-1
rum: 62-4-SC/GA-6
rumor: 63-2-SC/GA-3
sabers: 63-3-SC/GA-2
safe: 64-5-SC/GA-1; 65-1-NC-11
sailboat capsized: 64-5-SC/GA-2
sails: 63-12-SC/GA-2
St. Andrew's Sound, GA: 64-3-SC/GA-3
St. Catherine's Island, GA: 63-8-SC/GA-2
St. Catherine's Sound, SC: 65-4-SC/GA-3

Treasures of the Confederate Coast

Treasures of the Confederate Coast

The "Real Rhett Butler" & Other Revelations

Treasures of the Confederate Coast

ABOUT THE AUTHOR
Dr. E. Lee Spence

By
Charles King

Lee Spence points to a silver wedge marking the location of a shipwreck.

Spurred on by childhood tales of pirates and adventure, shipwreck expert, Edward Lee Spence, found his first shipwrecks at the age of twelve. He has since found hundreds of wrecks and has worked on everything from Spanish galleons and pirate ships, to blockade runners, and Great Lakes freighters.

Always an adventurer, Spence has traveled to a wide range of countries including such places as Hong Kong, Vietnam, the Philippines, the Bahamas, the Cayman Islands, the Dominican Republic, El Salvadore, Jamaica, Haiti, Mexico, Colombia, Honduras, Costa Rica, Panama, Nicaragua, Canada, England, Holland, Italy, Germany, Spain, and France. He has explored castles, palaces, shipwrecks, ancient ruins, secret tunnels, and subterranean and underwater caves.

Treasures of the "Real Rhett Butler"

He has been shot at, buried in cave-ins, trapped in fishing nets, pinned under wreckage, run out of air, lost inside a wreck, and bitten by fish while pursuing his quests.

Finding himself the target of an extortionist, Spence "borrowed" over a million dollars worth of original prints by famed wildlife artist John James Audubon in an unsuccessful effort to save the life of his child. Afterwards, he voluntarily turned himself in along with the art which was the only concrete evidence against him. Charged with theft, he was unjustly imprisoned, but was finally pardoned. Legally, the pardon means he was never convicted.

A man of action, Spence has saved the lives of others on more than a dozen occasions, sometimes at great risk to his own. He freely admits to having worked undercover for our government. However, he says it was many years ago when he was "young, invisible, and bulletproof." He refuses to say which agency.

His tools of discovery have ranged from primitive grappling hooks to highly sophisticated side-scanning sonars. Over the years, he has worked out of tiny sailboats, beautiful yachts, and ocean going research vessels.

He first made local and national news when he was a teenager. His work has since been written up in *Life*, *People Weekly*, the *London Sun* and hundreds of other periodicals all over the world. You may have seen him on the *Today Show* or heard him on Talk Net Radio.

Having extensively researched ships lost in hurricanes, Spence was not surprised when his home on Sullivan's Island, South Carolina, was destroyed by Hurricane Hugo.

Spence's initial, but very brief announcement in 1989 of the identity of the "Real Rhett Butler," made international news. He had discovered (what one of the editors for *Life* magazine later characterized as "overwhelming evidence") that Margaret Mitchell based her famous *Gone With The Wind* character on a 19th century Charlestonian named George Alfred Trenholm. This book represents the first time that detailed information relating to that discovery has been made available to the public.

Spence has actually located several steamers and sailing ships once owned by Trenholm. Trenholm's blockade running activities earned him today's equivalent of over one billion dollars in less than five years time. Spence is currently working on a book specifically on Trenholm.

Although long considered one of the "founding fathers" of underwater archeology, at age 47, Spence is still a relatively young man.

About the Author: Dr. E. Lee Spence
Page 516

Shipwrecks of the Confederate Coast

In June of 1992, Spence was appointed chief of underwater archeology for Providencia, an archipelago owned by the country of Colombia and covering more than 43,000 square miles in the Western Caribbean. As part of the arrangement, Spence's company was granted the exclusive salvage rights to the entire area for 25 years. His primary target was a treasure fleet which was lost in 1605 with over 250 tons of silver, gold, and precious jewels. Spence's expected share would have made him richer than Ross Perot.

When word leaked out that Spence had discovered the location of one of the fleet's richest galleons, he suddenly found himself threatened with trumped up charges of treason. The charges were absolutely absurd, but definitely were not laughable, as they could have meant the death penalty. When Spence didn't immediately flee the country and seemed to be winning major political support, he was told that one of the drug cartels wanted his salvage rights and was going to have him killed. The man who passed the word was one of the wealthiest and most powerful men in the archipelago. Knowing that the man didn't make idle threats, and had previously shot and killed a government official in front of witnesses, Spence wisely said good-by to Colombia. He has no immediate plans to return.

Spence is a member of Mensa and the even more elite Intertel, both organizations are widely known as societies for geniuses. He has a Doctor of Marine Histories and has served as a consultant for numerous "for-profit" and "not-for-profit" organizations, including the College of Charleston and the National Endowment for the Humanities. He is actively working on more than a dozen new books relating to shipwrecks and treasures of various eras and localities. He also serves as an editor and writes regular columns and articles on shipwrecks for several nationally distributed magazines.

Not only an historian, cartographer, and an underwater archeologist, Spence is a successful treasure hunter. He has raised hundreds of thousands of valuable artifacts (with a total estimated retail value well in excess of $50,000,000) from the ocean floor. He says most of it went to the government and to his partners.

As an historian, Spence believes the biggest key to success on any expedition is the archival research that precedes it. Spence calls historical research "his drug of choice" and says, "In today's world, time is the most expensive part of an expedition. Man-hours spent in the archives can cut hundreds of thousands of dollars worth of time from the field phase of most projects."

• • •

About the Author: Dr. E. Lee Spence
Page 517

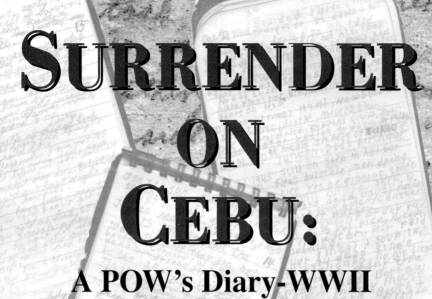

SURRENDER
ON
CEBU:
A POW's Diary-WWII

LTC William D. Miner

*Researched and edited
by Lewis A. Miner*

TURNER PUBLISHING COMPANY

412 Broadway • P.O. Box 3101
Paducah, Kentucky 42002-3101
(270) 443-0121

Copyright © 2001 Lewis A. Miner
Publishing Rights: Turner Publishing Company

Turner Publishing Company Staff:
Editor: Dayna Spear Williams
Designer: Lyndsi F. Hall

Library of Congress Control Number:
2001096097
ISBN: 1-56311-711-8

Printed in the United States of America.
Additional copies may be purchased directly from the publisher.
Limited Edition

TABLE OF CONTENTS

DEDICATION

To my children and grandchildren... This document contains a copy of the diary which I wrote during events of World War II while I was a Japanese Prisoner of War. I made and kept the diary at the risk of torture and death.

I am giving you a copy of this diary along with my personal accounts, with the hope that you will keep it as a family heirloom and give copies to your children and families...

Lovingly, father and grandfather
William Dilworth Miner
1994

FOREWORD

Surrender on Cebu...is a story that has been waiting patiently to be told. The book is a story of Bill Miner during World War II. It is a series of accounts, from May 1941 to October 1945, describing the authors service on the island of Cebu and his subsequent capture and imprisonment by Japanese forces. It is a forceful and disturbing story that encompasses adventure, courage, persecution, death and liberation. The effects of imprisonment for 39 months, with torture and deprivation being central to that imprisonment, are clearly marked. The authors ability to have survived and transcend the experience, and further, to have gone on to a substantial academic career and meaningful retirement are all enormous accomplishments. "I am lucky." Bill Miner writes. "People fell beside me and people were blown apart beside me. Anywhere I went as a prisoner, I tried to be aware of the situation and use it the best I could to survive."

The author has set forth at some length the people that he encountered during his tour of duty in the Philippines. The people mentioned in this book are factual. He has introduced from time to time elements of individuals personalities and what happened to them. I have endeavored to keep the journal intact as much as possible to clearly reflect what the author had in mind as he experienced events. Some accounts were written down on Japanese toilet paper and carried on the author's person. A small, pocket size memo pad was also used to tally the days of captivity and record events.

In September 1945, the author reflected: "I have lost every close friend I had out here - have been through filth, destruction, near death many times, and lived under conditions that would warp men's souls..."

Lewis A. Miner

ACKNOWLEDGMENTS

Without the time and effort of many people, this book would have never been possible. Beginning with Clara Miner (Bill's wife), in the late 1940s, typed part of the original manuscript, on frail, onion skin paper, using the manual, ribbon typewriter of those days...

I am under deep obligation to my brother, Charles Miner, for his review of the journal and for providing pictures and supporting documentation. My sincere thanks to my sister, Georgia, for providing the original diary. Without it the book would not have been complete.

Thanks to my editor, Dayna Williams, and to Turner Publishing for undertaking this project.

Special thanks to Bill Lair, Carol Kelly-Larson and Jack Robinson for their time, interest and devotion to this work.

I would be remiss not to thank the author for his perseverance in setting down the accounts as they occurred. Rarely does someone get to interact with an historical figure over a long period and be so profoundly influenced by their example. His courage and sacrifice was the inspiration for this book. It would have been a shame for these accounts to be left on a shelf, only to be moved from time to time and eventually be discarded. As I put the final touches to the page, I am subtly reminded of the great sacrifices that he and his fellow soldiers made by the sounds of his grand children playing in the yard. On this day, no bombs are falling from the sky and no invading army threatens their well being. Thank you, Dad!

Finally, thanks go to my family. My wife Lynn was very patient with me as I poured over the text night after night and ran out to get photos made on the spur of the moment. She never failed to lend me her time and attention. It would be difficult for me to convey to her how much inspiration I draw from her love and her support of me.

Lewis A. Miner
Knoxville, TN

PROLOGUE

The spring of 1941 was portentous of coming events. Already the war in Europe had reached critical stages. Germany had overrun all of western Europe except Spain and Turkey, the former was pro-axis and the latter strictly neutral. The German forces in Russia had penetrated almost to Moscow and the battle of Stalingrad was fluctuating day by day. In Britain the air arm was blitzing as wide a swath of destruction in a series of "Coventry Raids" as her ground troops were in Russia.

In the United States Roosevelt was getting the Lend-Lease Program under way with much opposition. The Selective Service Act of 1940 was slowly getting under way. Senators Burton K. Wheeler and Gerald Nye were gratifying their ego for prominence and sowing seeds of shame by becoming leaders for a policy of Isolationism when they had the chance to be leaders of a "Cooperation for National Defense" movement. Any clear thinking citizen could see what was in the air; why these men, supposedly leaders and statesmen, could be so blind I'll never understand. Those two men by their hindrance to national defense are responsible for more dead and wounded American soldiers than any other Americans at home or in the field. Soldiers were using trucks marked "Tanks" in Army training, throwing stones as substitutes for hand grenades, you know the rest of the story.

The public in general was doing a lot of wishful hoping and desperately shutting its ears and eyes to cold facts that the last remaining great power, the US, would sooner or later be forced into the war. Americans have had such an easy life in the last two generations that they have developed the philosophical characteristic of shutting their minds to unpleasant situations and letting somebody else work the situation out for them, that is, until the situation gets personal, then they go into action.

On the Indiana University campus life was pretty sedate and untouched by the outside momentous events soon to affect the entire campus. A few of the men students were complaining because they would have to go into the Army via draft in June 1941.

Steven Skalskie, 1941, when asked what he was going to do on graduation, replied he was going to work for a commercial company. The young man was an ROTC graduate, so I asked him what about going into the Army and being in on the ground floor, as a war was coming. "Hell!" he replied, "the war and the Army are the least of my worries."

Rovert Schilling, 1941, when asked his opinion of the nearness of war, remarked that he "hoped to spend next Christmas at home."

Robert Irrnann, a graduate student in history, said "I don't see how it can be avoided, but we can hope for the best."

Dennis Volonopolo, also a graduate student in history, said, "Let's worry about it if it comes."

In general it seemed that the people, even the thinking people, were prone to shut their minds to the fact that war was inevitable. Instead of preparing for events that common sense and logic told them were inevitable and soon to come, they chose to prepare for the situation after the "horse had been stolen."

STUDENT DAYS AT INDIANA UNIVERSITY

From a much more personal standpoint spring and final exams were in the campus air by May 15. On returning from classes at noon, Thursday, May 15, 1941, I found a letter from the War Department headquarters at Indianapolis informing me that I was being considered for duty in the Philippine Islands and to be prepared for immediate assignment.

This letter rather upset my daily schedule. I spent the afternoon informing my professors that likely I was leaving soon for the Philippines in spite of the fact that I was still in school.

I also had some civilian affairs that I would have to take care of if I were going away. It looked like (and felt like it, too) I was on the jump.

On Friday, May 16, I cut classes. I rose early, ate breakfast as soon as possible and started to Indianapolis via hitch-hiking. As I remember it, I made fair time and was soon in the city. Once there I went to the War Department office under Col. F.M. Armstrong, assisted by the Adj. Capt. Floyd Fix.

On meeting the colonel and showing him the letter the conversation went something like this.

Colonel: "First lieutenant and single, eh."

"Yes sir, colonel, just how definite is it that I will receive this assignment?"

Colonel: "Pretty certain. Captain will you get the lieutenants 201 file? You see half of our reserves have already been ordered to active duty, many of them married men with children. We have the policy of not sending married men out of the continental limits of the US."

Capt. Fix appeared with my 201 file and another officer, a captain. The captain had volunteered for duty in the Philippines and apparently been turned down. The captain immediately started talking to Col. Armstrong as soon as he entered.

"Colonel," the captain said, "I thought I was being called to active duty and assigned to the Philippines. Now I receive this letter telling me I am not. What is the trouble?"

The colonel, "I am sorry, we can't use you."

"But sir, I was told by one of the staff of this headquarters that my name was on the list to go," the captain cried, "and what's more I want to go and I volunteered for the detail!"

"I can't help that, captain," the colonel replied. "The cold turkey is that we are not sending any married men over to the Philippine Department now. You are married and have a family and that disqualified you for the PI Dept. We are sending only single men out there now. In spite of what some of my staff may have told you, you are not going. That's final!"

Turning to Capt. Fix, his adjutant, he said, "Fix, if this man's name is on the list to go, scratch it! Good day, captain."

The colonel then picked up my 201 file and leafed through it murmuring, "single, within the age limit, qualified, da da da. Capt. Fix, is this lieutenant's name on the list?"

"It is, colonel," responded the adjutant.

"Well, son," said the gray-haired colonel, "I guess you're one of them. It's a wonder we haven't called you before. If you hadn't been in school you would already be in the Army."

"Colonel," I said, "it's dead sure I am going?"

"I'm afraid it is," he smiled.

By this time I was wringing wet with sweat and the pit of my stomach felt like it was about to upset. I felt my fate was being decided before my eyes and within my hearing, yet I couldn't stop it for one second. How little did I realize standing there, that many, many times during the next four and a half years I was going to experience that same sick feeling in the pit of the stomach. Experience it so often that I would grow used to it. Nor did I expect later, time and time again, to watch unmoved a group of barbarian sadists decide my fate and thousands of others.

After being told I was certain to be shipped I left the colonel's office and hitch-hiked over to New Castle, IN to see H.G. Ingersoll and family. Hitch-hiking was good in those days and I made good time. By noon I was out at the Ingersoll Steel Plant having lunch with Harold. After lunch I straightened up my business with him, I called on Victor Payne of the American Security Co. of New Castle. From Payne's I went over to the New Castle High School and visited Herbert Heller between class. Herb was later Lt. (Sr. Gr.) Herbert Heller, USNR, in radar work, stationed on New Caledonia along with Robert Hamilton, who was a Seabee there.

Lt. Heller and I had quite a talk in those few minutes. We agreed that the trend of the times was straight toward war and we did not see how it could be avoided. To us we could not see how John Q. Public could be so indifferent to conditions concerning his welfare, but he was and still is after fighting the greatest war of our national history. Herb bid me a fond farewell and wished me the best of luck. I remember later in prison I often thought of our last talk and that I sure need all the luck he could wish me.

By this time it was just about 3:00 p.m. and there was a 3:15 p.m. bus running from New Castle to Indianapolis. I wanted to take that bus, I remember, so I had to run for it because I stopped on the way out to see Miss Florence Smith whom I had dated in the past. She was busy when I walked into her classroom and I guess hesitated about talking to me during the class period because it would only increase the commotion I had already caused in the classroom. Realizing that she was waiting for the class to be dismissed at 3:00 p.m., I commandeered a sheet of paper from a nearby notebook, wrote a note, folded it up and left it on the desk of the seat on which I was sitting. Then I left.

I arrived back at Bloomington about 7:00 p.m., worn out and dirty. On the way back to the dormitory I stopped at Westminster Inn to tell Miss Treva Rousch that I would be late for our date. On reaching my dormitory room I cleaned up and laid down on the bed for "just a minute." This was shortly after 7:00 p.m. When I awakened from the "minute's" relaxation, the clock said 11:30 p.m. Consternation reigned in my mind about a broken date. I thought the hour too late to make amends that evening, so went to bed. The next morning I made my peace with the young lady via phone.

The next morning I spent calling on my professors, Kohlmeger, Winther, Franzen, Thurston, Dean Smith and the professor of economics. Everyone that I saw promised and did give the most cooperation that was possible. I was to report the next Thursday, May 22, at Fort Hayes, Columbus, Ohio. Each professor gave me a special exam on the next Monday or Tuesday, depending on when I could find time to take it. I had to take these exams without doing any reviewing as there was so little time to completely tie up all affairs in civilian life, pack my things, purchase some luggage, etc. May 19 and 20, Monday and Tuesday, I took exams in 15 hours of subjects. I drew a straight B in all those exams. I think my professors must have been prejudiced in my favor because such good grades without any traditional cramming and reviewing was not for the likes of me, for a Phi Beta Kappa perhaps, but not for the ordinary student.

On May 21, Dad and Mother came down to Indiana University bringing with them my youngest sister Ruth who was a senior at Knox College. I got to visit with them for about four hours on Wednesday. They departed taking all my worldly goods that I wasn't going to take into the Army with me. My other sister was in Chicago and I never got to see her until years later, after I returned from overseas. When my family drove away from Indiana University on May 21, 1941, I was just leaving for two years. By that time in 1943 I was to have seen them again. The infinite little spark of life called man never dreams what the future may make reality. It was 54 months, four and a half years, before I saw my folks again. During that 54 months, I was to live more experiences than the ordinary man would ever dream of in his lifetime.

FORT HAYES

Early Thursday morning, May 22, 1941, I climbed aboard the bus at Bloomington, IN en route to Fort Hayes at Columbus, OH. The trip was uneventful except for meeting Mrs. Floyd Fix, wife of Capt. Floyd Fix, stationed at Fort Hayes. In the following days I called on the captain at his office asking for pointers and advice about my coming trip.

I suppose my experiences at the reception center were similar to that of all incoming personnel: physical exams to be taken, forms to fill out, insurance to get, etc. We were issued no clothing as the post told us we would get all of that once we were at our post in the Philippines. Everything ran smoothly and we were soon through with our routine. The group slated for the Philippines was the only casual group around the post at that time and we were all reserve officers. We were assigned to companies for duty in name only and after a few days we were aboard the trains for the West Coast port of San Francisco.

At this late date I don't recall whether I met the following men at Fort Hayes or on the train to San Francisco, yet they are the first of the men I knew who were later to be prisoners in the Philippines. Most of them never survived the hideous days.

About the first lad was 1st Lt. Jack McCoffrey of Logansport, IN and with him was a lad named 2nd Lt. Robert Emerson also from Logansport. Jack was tall, slim, fair complected, wore a little mustache and looked extremely handsome. Better than that, he was excellent company. During those first few days we struck up quite a friendship. He and Emerson were quite good friends. Jack lived in Emerson's home, having no parents and was a draftsman for one of the local Logansport companies.

Emerson was not quite 6 feet tall, reddish complected, red headed and had a tendency to be heavy set. He must have weighed from 170 to 180 pounds. When he came to Davao Prison Camp 18 months later, he weighed 100 pounds less and looked like a ghost. Emerson also worked at Logansport and lived with his family. These two boys left for San Francisco via Logansport for a few days and then Chicago where they took the transcontinental train. After they left me at Fort Hayes, I didn't see them until they were on the President Pierce sailing out of the Golden Gate.

1st Lt. William Nels was also at Fort Hayes with me. He was about 6 feet tall, slender, semi-bald, around 35 years of age, a schoolteacher by profession, a principal in some West Virginia high school, if my memory is correct. He was single and I believe all the family he had was a mother. I did not know him so well and after he got off the President Pierce in Manila I remember seeing him only once when I ran into him at the Army and Navy Club in Manila. Nels was killed early in the war before things really got bad.

Another West Virginia boy was 1st Lt. Paul Schultz, also a schoolteacher by profession. Paul was about 5'6" in height and didn't weight over 150. He was slender and slightly built. I remember I talked to him about the teaching profession at Fort Hayes and months later, three years later in fact, while in Bilibid Prison in Manila, when we were waiting to be placed on the ill-fated Oryoku Maru in December 1944. During that intervening time while I was in the southern islands, he had seen service in Bataan, survived the Death March, dysentery while in Cabantuan Prison and a number of other things. Paul never survived the second bombing on that trip north.

There were about six or eight officers on the Santa Fe train from St. Louis to Frisco. I don't remember their names with the exception of William F. O'Connor, 1st lieutenant, infantry, from Massachusetts not far from Boston. Bill and I got acquainted real well on that train "out" and we were together all through our military careers from then on; until Bill went out on the Lasang detail, March 2, 1944 and I remained behind with the main Davao detail.

Bill O'Connor must have been about 5'8 or 9", very thin, a tendency to be bald and knew the Army thoroughly. He had been an enlisted man in Hawaii, a sergeant in a motor pool while holding a reserve commission. With the expansion of our armed forces, he had gone to active duty in the States and then ordered out to the Philippines. Bill was to marry a nurse the next September and this was June and he was on the "way-out." Out to the places where no more women were allowed and all Army wives and children were being sent home. He was pretty discouraged about having to leave his fiancee behind. Bill was a devout Catholic and the next Easter he was the only white man to go to a Filipino Easter Service with me, just before all hell broke loose. O'Connor and I had long conversations on the train about the coming war which both of us did not see how it could be avoided. I shall leave Bill for the moment and refer to him time and again later, as our trails criss-crossed the rest of his life.

At this point I shall drift away from the military passengers of this train trip to others some of whom were far more interesting at the moment.

One of the civilians was a high official of the Santa Fe Railroad. I wanted to know if he knew my Knox College friend, Tommy Willard, son of the Santa Fe executive in Chicago. Another was an ex-actress and dancer who had twin daughters that were the idols of the entire train.

Finally, the most interesting were not Americans at all. They were Germans and the party consisted of a man, his wife and two little boys. The man was part of the German Diplomatic Corps stationed in Washington, D.C. or New York. By this time the war in Europe had been on almost two years and of course our relations with Germany were becoming more strained as time went on. As a result he had been called home and was taking his family back by the long road home. The man was around 5' 10" tall, blonde and rather flashy. He stayed mostly in their stateroom by himself, but his wife and family would by day come out and occupy an ordinary seat with the rest of the passengers. Once in awhile the boys would get noisy and he would come out and speak very sharply to them and often to his wife in the same manner. Mostly he spoke in German, but sometimes he spoke in beautiful English with just a trace of an accent. He was distinctly unfriendly to all the rest of us.

His pretty wife was slender, good-looking, had a pleasing personality, spoke English with a delightful accent and had plenty on the ball. She managed the two boys fairly well and spoke very sharply to them if they spoke German instead of English. I asked her why one time and she said it was a family policy that the children must speak the English language as long as they were in the US, else how would they learn to speak it properly? She was very friendly to everybody on the train, or tried to be.

The first day or two she didn't pay much attention to the soldiers in uniform, but as the trip progressed, she turned her attentions more and more to us. Her husband was noticeably absent when she was conversing with one of us and it didn't take any brains for us to see that she was trying to pump us for whatever information she could get. Of course we knew nothing of military value at that time and it was no state secret as to where we were going. Some of our baggage was checked clear through to Manila. The last day before we arrived in Frisco, she had an hour's conversation with me. I found it mentally stimulating to parry her questions and leading statements by the same methods she was using. I had the satisfaction at the end of the conversation to know I had gained as much or more information from her as she had gotten from me. Three days after I got off the train in San Francisco and a day later I saw them again at the baggage room in the railroad station. She told me then that they were taking the Japanese luxury liner Tasuta Maru for Tokyo about June 4, 1941. The next day as a guest of Lt. Col. George B. Jones, MC, retired, dining at the Inn at the San Francisco end of the Golden Gate bridge, I watched that ship sail out of the bay under the Golden Gate bridge and put out to sea while Mrs. Jones told me the morning paper had an article in it saying that the Japanese liner had lain outside the harbor limit until it had assurance it could enter the harbor and leave with Japanese nationals. The captain was afraid he might be detained and it was possible that it would be the last Japanese ship to enter our ports for sometime. I remember we speculated whether those Germans would ever reach their homeland.

Lt. Col. Jones showed me around San Francisco, gave me some addresses in the Philippines and some tips on the customs in the Islands.

I didn't stay downtown, but moved into the Hostess House at Fort Mason, Port of Embarkation. While out there I met several more officers slated for the Philippines. I shared my room with a chaplain, 1st Lt. Albert Talbot. He was a young Catholic Father being sent out for duty with troops in the Islands. He and I became quite close friends on the trip over. After he left the boat I don't recall seeing him again until around July 1944 when my group of American prisoners were moved from Davao up to Cabanatuan, Luzon. At this stage Al was just a shadow of his former self, but still in good spirits and still doing his duties as chaplain.

The room directly across the hall from Chaplain Talbot's room and mine in the Hostess House was occupied by two tall Army nurses. The chaplain knew one, then the other and introduced me to them both as we met in the hall one morning. I talked several minutes to one whose name was Black. It turned out that they were going over on our boat and I saw them several times aboard ship. I never saw Lt. Black, ANC, after she left the Pierce. She went to duty in the hospital on the Fortress of Corregidor and I heard about her from fellow prisoners in the early part of our imprisonment.

Fate moves in strange circles and makes life extremely interesting, you never know who you will see or where! Five years later, lacking a month, as I write this tale, I met a Lt. Col. Harry Harding in BOQ No. 5 at the Armored School, Fort Knox, KY. On the young colonel's desk, Col. Harding had also been a POW of the Japanese, was the photograph of a strikingly pretty Army nurse in full uniform. One look at the picture strikes a familiar chord and I say, "The girl friend, Harding?"

"Yes," he replied.

"I know her." I answered.

"You do," he asked, looking startled.

"Yes! Her name is Black, Lt. Black. She is tall and dark and just as good looking as her picture."

"Where did you know her?" Harding inquired of me instantly.

"She went over on the boat with me, but I didn't know what had happened to her other than that she lived to be released."

While I was giving him this information he dug up another picture, a large snapshot this time and showed me. It was Lt. Black all right and was so startlingly natural that it fairly took my breath away. I told Harding and again he looked at me intently, where upon I laughed again.

The first day I was at Fort Mason embarkation office, I was standing in line, yes, the usual Army line without which the Army wouldn't be the Army! The man immediately ahead of me wore captain's bars on his shoulders and during the tiresome wait, he stepped on my toe by accident.

"Pardon me," he said, quickly retreating from the injured member.

"I stand on it too," I smiled, "So let's forget it."

"My name is Hughes, Joseph Hughes," he said extending his hand by the way of introduction. I looked at the man closely and saw before me a well built man about 5'9," round-faced, dark-haired and the dark stubble of a beard showing on his face and giving him the appearance of being travel-worn and tired. Yet despite that weariness there was a spirit of friendliness gleaming in his eye and he had the bearing of a man who could take what life handed him. A few months later in the jungles of Bataan he was proving what sterling steel he was made of.

"Miner is the name," I replied as I shook hands with him. "Bill Miner. Are you also going out to the Philippines captain?"

"Yes, I am. I don't know what the detail is yet, but I'm definitely on the way. Where is your home, lieutenant?"

"Illinois, captain, 200 miles southwest of Chicago near the small town of Vermont. What part of the US do you come from?"

"Near Boston," he replied. "I was an instructor in a military school not far outside the city. I have a wife and five children."

At that last remark I opened my eyes and looked surprised. "You look quite young to be so happily married, captain," I said in the way of a compliment.

There was pride in the captain's voice as he replied, "I am happily married, lieutenant and I wish I were just starting married life again instead of starting to the Orient. I would like to believe this situation would clear up but common sense says it just can't clear up until our country steps in and clears them up. If you are just here to report in like myself, it won't take long and then if you like, come upstairs with me. I know a captain in the Port Quartermaster Corps and we can go out for lunch. He will show us around and you can get an idea of the things just beginning."

We checked in and then looked up Joe's friend whose name I now forget but the things I learned I didn't forget. This was June of 1941 and in that San Francisco Office of the Army Transport Service I saw the signs of a great nation belatedly beginning to prepare for its own security. Troops and supplies were to be sent to Alaska, but there were no boats to take them, no roads after they reached Alaska, no facilities to take care of the men after they were landed, yet Alaska must be fortified quickly. Just how quick that need was to become a battle reality we little realized. The ATS was chartering commercial vessels as fast as it could to move supplies and men to Alaska, Hawaii, Philippines, Wake, etc.

"We need this, we need that," the ATS man said listing a dozen items, "But we just can't get them, Congress won't give them to us. It's going to cost us lives before this is over, perhaps your lives and remember this, if you get caught out there without equipment it's not the Army's fault. It's the fault of Congress and the people!"

Hughes and I looked at each other in consternation. We had the feeling that the ATS man was barely scratching the surface of conditions. I had that funny, sickly feeling in my stomach again. The feeling I always got when I saw my fate being decided and I was helpless to defend myself. As Hughes and I looked at each other we saw the same question in the other's eyes. "Will I come back? Will we come back?" I personally felt like I was a pawn in a game of chess where the players were drunken fools who were deliberately playing with their eyes shut, because they were afraid to open their eyes and look at the board to see how bad the situation really was. I write this now while many of those same Congressmen have spent many months and countless millions trying to fix the blame of Pearl Harbor on someone in the Armed Forces. A simple child knows the answer, better all this time and money had been spent on how to prevent such an event occurring again. After fighting two world wars we still haven't learned to take care of ourselves. Less than a year after V-J Day we don't have enough left of our Armed Forces to clean up the litter after a good Kansas cyclone. I am alive today, Maj. Joseph Hughes is dead, dead of starvation after months of grim prison life and his heart rending question in prison still rings in my ears, "Bill, why did Congress and our people ever let this country get caught so unprepared? I hope to God they learn this time!" Today I am back on American soil and the answer is, "Nobody has learned the lesson."

We left the ATS man with the finishing of our lunch. I remember we were silent as we left. The very air of that office was filled with coming events and it took us an hour to shake off the spell of tragedy to come.

I met more officers at Fort Mason and by June 5 there were quite a few bound for the Philippines. Nobody was very happy and almost without exception we felt that we were going to have a grandstand seat on an oriental fracas. Just how grand it was going to be we couldn't even dream.

At Sea

A t 2:00 p.m., June 5, 1941, the President Pierce pulled away from the pier in San Francisco Bay and headed toward the Golden Gate. Its cargo was almost a thousand sad hearts. Of over 250 officers, there were six who came back on the Storm King with me. There were others of course, but very, very few.

The President Pierce had about 800 casual troops, of which around 250 were officers, 150 were Air Corps lieutenants, most of them pilots. In addition there were 13 Army nurses and about a score of civilians who were airplane technicians headed for China. Rumor had it that they were going out to join the Flying Tigers and keep their planes in the air. All these men lined the railings and decks of the ship as we slowly moved out of the harbor into the bay. Minute by minute the piers and shore objects grew smaller and faded away. New objects and familiar landmarks appeared, grew large, grew small and disappeared. The Golden Gate bridge drew near and soon was directly overhead. We could look up at the bottom of the roadway, see the great rivets and braces of the massive structure.

Soon they too faded away and the whole bridge span again became a comprehensive view growing smaller and smaller, fading, as the ship left the land behind. Soon the coast line became an extended view lying low and dark on the horizon, its dark outline contrasted with rising and falling waves and clouds of white spray. The afternoon grew cloudy and gray, the sun became lost behind the clouds, the wind sprang up and grew into a small gale, the sea became rough, the air very chilly and night settled around our ship as she rolled through the waves toward Hawaii, the Philippines taking us to the scenes of destruction, death, imprisonment, torture and hate, leaving behind the US, a land of beauty, quiet and peace.

Jack McCoffrey had joined upon the upper deck soon after we left the pier and watched with me the departing of the ship. Jack not having had the glimpse of the future through the eyes of the ATS officer was in high spirits. He wanted to see the Philippines, Singapore, Indo China, China and the East Indies. He was already straining at the leash to go. My sense of foreboding grew and it was with a heavy heart that I followed Jack below to our stateroom from our post of observation of our departure.

All my life I shall remember Jack McCoffrey as he stood at the railing looking west into the night. To me he was the spirit of American youth, clean cut, vigorous, adventurous, dauntless, unafraid of life and eager for the events of tomorrow.

As night came on the ship began to roll pretty badly. I ate my dinner, but three hours later upchucked it all. Following that unpleasantness I went to bed and slept fairly well. The next morning I ate a moderate breakfast and felt half secure. By the end of the first 24 hours, I was back to normal and began to take an interest in the people and the happenings around me.

The staterooms were pretty crowded, four men where two should have been. In my cabin was 1st Lt. Marmon, MC and 1st Lt. James Pinnick from southern Indiana. Pinnick was a graduate of Indiana University Law School and had done some practicing in law. The third member of my cabin I do not recall his name nor did I see him after he left the boat at Manila.

Young Doc Harmon, as we called him, was stationed at Sternberg General Hospital in Manila. He got some strange malady and was sent home in October or November of 1941. I never did hear exactly what his trouble was; the Med Corps wouldn't talk about him.

Young Pinnick was a card. He had more energy than a bushel of kittens. In stature he was around 5'10", heavy set, but not fat, round faced, dark haired, had a pleasant disposition, a ready wit, an easy laugh, was good company and liked to smoke cigars. His favorite pastime on the boat was to lie on his bed, smoke cigars and read. None of us had brought too many magazines along and by the evening of the third day out, Pinnick was lying on his bed smoking a long cigar and staring at the ceiling of the stateroom. Every once in awhile he would blow smoke rings into the air. All of a sudden he swung his feet off the bed saying, "Well, boys, I can't take this inactivity any longer. See you later!" He walked out of the room leaving us staring after him with open mouths.

"Yeah? Well, stay away from Charley's Steak House," I called after him as his footsteps retreated down the corridor.

Midnight came and we all went to bed. About 2:00 a.m. the lights suddenly came on and Pinnick stomped into the room. His white shirt was soaked, there wasn't a dry stitch in it; its front was stained with cigar ashes and its front pockets were bulging. Pinnick was without his cigar. We three raised upon our elbows and gawked at him in sleepy amazement.

In his left hand he had a wad of greenbacks which he threw on his bed. Next he emptied his shirt pockets of the same green stuff. From there he started to his trouser pockets, emptying each with much ceremony. By this time all three of us were sitting up and pouring out a stream of questions. "What bank did you rob? Is there anything left in the vaults at Fort Knox? Lend me a thousand? Better give us a cut on that loot or we'll snitch on you."

"Boys," he said, "I got in a crap game with the Air Corps. Those babies are plenty wild, but they aren't good!"

From there he proceeded to his hip pockets which we now observed were also bulging. From them came more greenbacks. He had the biggest pile of crumpled greenbacks I had yet seen lying on the middle of that bed. We gathered around while he counted, "one, two, five, da da, da da 25, da da 50, 100, 150, 200, 250. Well boys, that's quite a haul." He stood back looking at the piles of money. "Boy, does my back hurt," he said, rubbing it. "Hell," he exclaimed; tore open his shirt and pulled out another bunch of greenbacks. "Let's see if there are any more!" he said as he felt his anatomy. He rubbed his watch pocket and then extracted some more bills. These he also counted.

"Not bad for a night's entertainment?" he said as he totaled up about $275. He then stripped the pillow case off his pillow, stuffed the money in it, tied a knot in the end and tossed it on the head of his bed for a pillow.

With that remark he undressed, took a shower, came back and said to us in general. "Now if you boys will let me, I'll catch up on my beauty sleep."

"Let you! Hell's bells!" young Doc came back at him. "Just who is keeping who awake?" and threw a pillow at Pinnick.

Pinnick ducked, snapped out the light and we heard him crawl into bed. A few minutes later he was snoring.

Pinnick slept most of the next day and the next evening he again lay on his bed after the evening meal. We looked at one another and waited. After he finished his cigar he got up, took off his tie and said, "Guess I had better go and give the Air Corps their revenge!"

We saw no more of him until long after midnight when he again came in loaded to the gills with greenbacks and wringing wet with sweat. This time Pinnick had around $200. He took the sum of about $400 down to the safe the next morning. When we got to Honolulu a couple of days later he cabled around $400 back to his wife, saying, "I don't have any use for it and she'll save it."

After two such nights he turned his attention to the slot machines. For a couple of days he sat in the barroom observing how the slot machines paid off; then after the quarter machine had been played almost continuously for three hours he walked over and started playing too. Before he quit he got the jackpot of about $27.50. Three days later he repeated his performance. By now he had the reputation of being "good" and he decided to find some other outlet for his excess energy for diplomatic reasons. Somebody had a law book which he borrowed to keep himself occupied.

Pinnick, I was told, was killed early in the war. I know he went to troop duty with a Philippine scout outfit, but I never saw him after he left the boat in Manila. I am afraid today his widow has good use for that $400 he sent home.

Col. William F. Sharp, later major general, in command of the Mindanao Force, was our troop commander aboard the Pierce. On his shipboard staff were captain, later major, Albert Kircher, Al for short; Maj. Knowles, then a warrant officer; Capt. Joe Hughes and naturally a few more whose names I don't remember.

There were four companies of enlisted men in the holds of the ship. On the second day out I was assigned to CO duty under Capt. Truesdale who I shall mention later.

Another company commander was Capt. James (?) O'Donnovan. O'Donnovan was tall, dark, slender, thin in figure and face, wore a very small black mustache and was very intelligent. I used to visit with him a lot and we became good friends. He had a lot of originality and used to debunk the international situation. Time and again he told me going over, "We are all dead heroes. There is no other way out!" When the war did come, he was a battalion commander in the 31st Infantry and made a wonderful record for himself with his men. I am told he wore two guns and had several snipers to his credit. He died of dysentery while in prison shortly after the surrender.

Capt. Truesdale had another lieutenant to help with the company of casuals. He was 1st lieutenant James Franz. Jimmy came from southern Indiana or Kentucky. I first met him at Fort Hayes, but it was not until our crossing that we really got acquainted. He was assigned to Fort McKinley when we reached the Philippines. Jimmy was another who never survived the Luzon campaign to become a prisoner.

Capt. Truesdale was married and in civilian life had worked for the Bell Telephone Co. Upon reaching Manila he was assigned to the 31st Infantry as PX officer in the Cuartel De Espana. This assignment he held until the war began, when he was transferred to the Signal Corps and set out with, I believe, the Luzon forces. He lived through the campaign to become a prisoner and died of malnutrition and dysentery on board a prison ship to Japan in late 1942.

One of the most interesting friends I made on that boat trip over was a man named Capt. Albert J. Kircher. Kircher was heavy set, round faced, wore a black mustache, had dark hair and dark eyes. His Army branch was Field Artillery, but in civilian life he had been a mining engineer for British interests in central or northern South America. His versatility was remarkable and he had a common sense about him that comes only from wide experience and a deep study of human races. Kircher's duty aboard ship was police officer; he did have a little activity once in awhile. I got to know him through company duty. At this point I'll drop him from the picture and pick him up again down in the southern island city of Cebu at the beginning of the war. I followed his career all through and he always took an exceptionally friendly interest in me.

To date I haven't mentioned the trials and tribulations of the trip. To us it was just the bad beginning of a bad ending. Three days out of San Francisco we entered the tropics and the ship began to warm up. Shortly after pulling out from Honolulu the weather became really sweltering and the wind came from the east at the rate of about 16 knots, so that we didn't have a breath of air aboard the ship for days at a time. The smoke from the engines rose straight into the sky and soot fell straight down on us below. The ships' dining room was just above the overheated engine room, from the feel of it at least. Every meal in the room was stifling hot, but the evenings were the worst. We couldn't enter the dining room unless we had on a tie and a uniform blouse. Neither could we use summer civilian clothes and most of us had the heavy winter Stateside uniform. To enter that dining room was torture, but we did have to eat. Certainly adapting our uniform to the climate would have been sensible, yet it wasn't done. Looking back I remember those furnace evenings even more than the tortuous heat in the holds of some prison ships. Once I remarked, "God help us if a war breaks out. The rule book won't cover the situation!" It didn't! We had to make the rules as the moment demanded. To top things off, the ship was so overcrowded that we ran out of fresh water for all purposes except drinking. Even the salt water showers were turned off part of the day. Laundry was quite a problem too. When you added things up the trip was unpleasant for everybody—officers and enlisted men alike. I went over on a luxury liner and I came back on an ordinary transport. The latter was much more enjoyable, being business like and without unnecessary spit and polish.

Another friend I made was an Air Corps 2nd. Lt. Daniel Blase. Blase had just finished training when he was ordered overseas. His family and his fiancee had driven him out to San Francisco to see him off. Blase was assigned to duty with the same company that I was executive officer for. We used to go as far forward as one could get and lean over the railing to watch the spray rise from the bow of the ship below us. This consumed hours of our time, just leaning over the railing and talking about everything under the sun. Sometimes we just leaned and looked at the sea. Occasionally, the ocean was so calm that it looked like deep blue oil gently stirring. There wasn't a ripple on its glassy surface. It amplified the meaning of the name "Pacific." The laundry woman on the ship said that in 35 crossings, this was her smoothest. Blase and I actually seemed at times to become part of this vastness. The only moving thing in that wilderness of water was the ship. Now and then flying fish would break the surface and skim over the water from a few feet to 150 yards. Going over we saw lots of flying fish and there were many in the Islands before the war. After the fighting had been on for a year I don't remember seeing many. Coming home across the Pacific many people made the remark, "There are no flying fish this trip." Somehow I wonder if our high explosive sea warfare might be responsible?

Our first stop was a few hours layover in Honolulu. The famous Diamond Head is visible from way out at sea. Its appearance was barren, like the coast of Southern California. As we drew near the port the Royal Hawaiian Moana Hotels on Waikiki Beach were pointed out. They were beautifully nestled in the palm-clad shore back of the narrow white beach. Yet somehow I felt a vague disappointment in the scenic beauty, the wildness, grandness and lushness that I expected was not there. My expectations weren't even satisfied when I went over the Pali. It wasn't until the Philippine Islands that the large white beaches, gentle seas and tremendous forest giants that I had expected to see, became a part of the scenery.

As the big liner drew up to a pier near the Aloha Tower, the little Hawaiian boys swam out to meet the ship and dive for coins thrown to them from the decks. These dark skinned water wizards would dive for silver only. If someone tossed a penny, they ignored it. A band was playing on the pier and Hawaiian beauties decked in leis stood nearby waving to us and signing Aloha. Truly this was tropical atmosphere.

The sun was setting, lighting up the sky to the west over the shoulders of the mountains. To the north the Wianale mountains were standing dark and cloud covered behind the city. Shore leave was at hand!

Six of us, among whom were Capt. Joe Hughes; a Capt. Genough, Dental Corps; Father Talbot; two other lieutenants; and myself hired a taxi to see the city. It was filled with Navy men. We drove around the downtown part of

Honolulu, dined at the Alexander Hotel, went to a series of native dances in a park not far from the YMCA and then took off for the Royal Hawaiian Hotel.

At the Royal Hawaiian we drank Dole pineapple juice, looked around the place for atmosphere native to Hawaii. Instead there was evidence of Dorothy Lamour. In the dining room by the beach sat two acquaintances I had made on the Santa Fe train from St. Louis to San Francisco. I stopped at their table to pass the time of day and then rejoined my friends.

The Moana Hotel was next on our list. Again we looked around and then passed on. We had not long to stay and we wanted to look at all the places of interest that we could. Late that night we ended up back at the Royal Hawaiian drinking pineapple juice. From there we went back to the ship.

There wasn't much to do on board the ship going over. Some of the nurses had a fine time and several romances blossomed forth. There were only 13 of them and at least 250 officers.

Half of the latter were young Air Corps lieutenants and many of them single. The sun deck was the favorite place on the ship at all times because it was usually coolest there. At night some of the portable radios could reach commercial stations ashore and we used to congregate around the music and news broadcasts. Not far out of Honolulu the sundeck became forbidden territory after sundown. It seems that the romancers liked the sundeck in the dark hours the same as the radio listeners and the lads who couldn't sleep because of overheated quarters, but lest the sundeck become the "sin deck." It became "off limits after sunset."

And so we sailed westward, ever westward. Each day saw us a little farther out and each day was just a little warmer, each night a little sweatier and a little stickier. Each morning the red ball of a sun rose out of a clear sky behind us and each night that same red ball set in the seas ahead of us. Our ship was the only black thing on the surface of the deep blue sea.

Once or twice we met a ship. The captain chased all the men below and ran all the nurses up on sundeck so the petticoats would fly in the wind and give the impression of our being only a passenger ship. On reaching Manila, we found out that the ship had been a British battleship, damaged by German bombs in the battle for Malta, on her way supposedly to Mare Island for repairs.

About the 16th day out we passed through the Japanese mandated Marianas. The ship sailed just south of Agrihan Island, yet close enough we could see the squat red roofed buildings nestling among the tall coconut palms. This island began to look something like what I had expected a tropical isle to look like. That morning the steward told us we were within "spitting distance" of Manila, within 1,000 miles.

Many hours and several hundred miles later, fairly early in the morning, it was whispered about that we should soon see land. By mid-morning a low dark cloud appeared on the southern horizon. An hour or so later we could see that this was dark mountains. At mid-day we were within sight-seeing distance of the north shore of Samar and were passing numerous tiny islands. Even though small, some of them were mighty rugged and precipitous. One or two looked as though they rose a mile or more above the sea and most were heavily covered with vegetation. The mountains on the main shore of Samar were covered with a tremendously magnificent jungle forest. The scrawny brush on Oahu did not begin to compare with these forest giants!

As we stood and looked at those jungle covered slopes, down the railing of the ship went a string of comments, "Unchanged for a hundred million years." "A new world, boys." "Pythons, fever and dysentery." "One hell of a place to be." "Take me away from nature in the raw."

Little did we think that less than six months later those same fever infested jungles were going to hide us, conceal us, give us food and water and that slightly later we were going to eat those hated pythons and compare their white meat with the white meat of a chicken's breast in respect to taste and tenderness. Truly it was a new world. Very soon it was to be the scene of battle.

Late that afternoon we passed through San Bernadino Straits and as night fell proceeded up the west coast of southern Luzon. I was still at the rail looking at the dark line of the shore, the fires of the Filipino villages, the stars, listening to the strange new night sounds and smelling the strange tropical odors. Finally I went to bed, sometime the next morning we were to be in Manila.

Very late in the night or early in the morning I woke up to the sound of low voices and extremely suffocating heat. The voices whispered, "Wake up Joe, we're in." "Yeah Joe, we're in Manila Harbor."

"The hell you say. You're sure? Yeah you must be right, we're stopped and it's hellish hot. I wonder if old Dante ever knew anything like this."

I drifted back into an exhausted sickly sleep thinking, "Manila, I'm in Manila now, I wonder what it's like."

TENDERFOOT IN THE ISLANDS

J une 24, 1941 dawned, a very hot day with a beautiful Manila sunrise. By daylight there was feverish activity to repack and debark from the ship. We left the ship in alphabetical order by rank and on the way down the gangplank we were told the name of our assignment post. Our first solid footing in 19 days was the upper deck of Pier 7, then the largest in the world. We followed the ramps downstairs, located our baggage and went through the customs inspections. Meanwhile via word of mouth, word got around that representatives from the various department posts were there to pick up the new men slated for their posts.

A Capt. Al Thayer located me and said where to take my baggage for transportation to my quarters. I was assigned to the 31st Infantry stationed at the Post of Manila. After getting my baggage and myself into the truck I waited. Shortly afterward Capt. Fred Small of Denver, CO; Lt. Robert Emerson, I mentioned before; Capt. Packham; Capt. O'Donnovan and several others, all assigned to the 31st Infantry joined me. When the entire group was assembled, we were taken to the Army and Navy Club in Manila for lunch, after which we reported in to the headquarters of the 31st Infantry, Post of Manila. The post was located at the Cuartel De Espana in the old Walled City area of Manila.

I was assigned to the Service Co. of the 31st Infantry, which was located in Santa Lucia barracks. These barracks nestled in a rectangular part of the old City Wall. This area had evidently been used by the Spanish as a soldier's barracks and fortification point. The whole barracks area was built against the outside of the main city wall so that when one stood on the wall of the barracks he faced open ground on three sides and the outside of the main walls would be subject to gunfire or archery. At regular intervals these fortified areas jutted out from the main wall of the city. To get into this fortified area one had to pass through an arched gateway some 12 to 15 feel tall and about 15 feet thick. These old Spaniards really believed in stone masses for security.

It was June 24 that I arrived in Manila. The next day I reported to my company and met my company commander, Capt. Robert Johnston and the other company officers consisting of Lt. Gordon Meyers of Wisconsin, 2nd Lt. James K. Smith from Georgia or South Carolina and 1st Lt. Charles Y. Garett from Kentucky.

During the next few days I met many other officers and men of the 31st Infantry. Garett ran into a Lt. Harold (?) Tuggle from Kentucky. Both Garett and Tuggle had gone to college together at Bowling Green, KY. When Tuggle and I got acquainted we found that he had been in college with a girl named Elizabeth Harrington whom I later knew as Dean of Girls in the high school of New Castle, IN. This small link of a mutual acquaintance established a firm friendship between us. Among the others that I became good friends with was 2nd Lt. Homer Martin from Kentucky. Someone else who had, I believe, been in college at Bowling Green, KY. Another of the lads was a happy go lucky kid from North Dakota named Joseph Stienzland. Joe liked the west and always figured, even up to the last, on going back to the Big Horn country in Wyoming and owning a horse ranch.

Before we newcomers had gotten settled, we were thrown in to a concentrated training course of tactics and small arms weapons in preparation for the assignment of becoming instructors with the Philippine Army (PA). We arrived the last of June. The first of July Gen. Douglas MacArthur was made commander of the newly created USAFFE (United States Army Forces in the Far East) which was to consist of American and Philippine Army units. I will not go into the routine details of Army life with the troops, but will pass on to more interesting personal experiences.

As was mentioned before, when in San Francisco, I got a dim impression of things to come. In Hawaii this foreboding was increased and after reaching Manila it was obvious within the first hundred hours that an ill wind was blowing. In less than a week I decided that the Philippines was no place for my money, so I made an allotment to my mother of every spare dollar not needed for living expenses. As a result, when the war did start, I had a total of $5 in the Manila banks that I lost.

Everywhere that I have gone it has always been my idea that the inhabitants of a place furnish 90 percent of the interest. If you have friends and know interesting people, you can have a good time regardless of unpleasant surroundings. With this in mind I gathered addresses of people in the Philippines before leaving the States and on the way out.

When my father had been in college at Macomb, IL during the early part of the century, there had been six Filipino boys attending. At least two of these six had risen high in the life of the Philippines. One was Dr. Camille Oseis. The other was Dr. Francisco Benitez, then dean of education at the University of the Philippines. Dean Benitez and his family remained quite loyal to the Philippine Commonwealth and the U.S. all through the Japanese occupation. He and his family survived the siege of Manila in early 1945 and when the Americans retook the Philippines, Dean Benitez became director of the Bureau of Education under President Osmena. Because of lack of transportation I didn't get to see Dean Benitez in late 1945 when I was in Manila, but he did answer my letter.

Shortly after my arrival in Manila I called upon Dean Benitez and his family in their home on the outskirts of the city. He had a charming wife and family and a very beautiful home. The visit was both enjoyable and enlightening. From what he told me of the various people, dialects and languages, I knew the Philippines were going to be extremely interesting. He too had something to say on the imperialistic tendencies of Japan and the increasingly arrogant attitude of the Japanese people living in the vicinity. I saw Dean Benitez several times before I left for the Visayan Islands.

Another person on my list to look up was a Miss Lenora Jones, sister of Miss Maude Jones, English professor at the University of Indiana. Miss Lenora

Jones had been a teacher in the islands for several years so she knew people and places.

Harold Ingersoll of the Ingersoll Steel and Disc Co. had given me a letter of introduction to their company representative in Manila, Spike Wilson. Spike was an old timer, he had come out to the islands in the Spanish-American War and had stayed after it was over. Spike was a member of the Elks Club in Manila and had a great many contacts who proved exceedingly entertaining.

The most permanent civilian friend was accidentally made through Miss Lenora Jones. This man was another teacher, L.W. Jacobs. Milwaukee was his home originally. Jacobs had been in the islands 17 years by the time I met him and exceedingly well educated. He had traveled through Burma, Saigon, Indo-China, Dutch East Indies, been to all the great cities of China near the coast or within sailing distance on the large rivers of China and had studied at the Imperial University at Tokyo, Japan.

Jacobs was quite well versed in oriental arts and goods. He knew good silver work from India or bronze from Japan. One glance at an oriental rug was enough to tell him whether or not it was authentic. He knew good ivory or jade when he saw it, or wood carving from Bali. Not only did he recognize genuine articles, but had at his fingertips the history and background of these things and the designs on them. Jacobs was also quite an authority on Philippine customs and weaving. Personally he was likable, mentally he was stimulating and the amount of knowledge he had was tremendous.

In these few weeks, I undoubtedly saw more of the "real Manila" than many people who had lived there for years. I rarely went to a night club. A night club is a night club whether you find it in New York, Chicago, San Francisco, Honolulu, Manila, Shanghai or Makden. Jacobs would meet me when off duty, and we would go off to some native part of the city and penetrate into its heart and see life where I didn't have the knowledge to even dream existed.

Once we saw a Chinese measuring raw gold stolen from a mine near Baguio and smuggled into Manila. One other night he took me into the shop of a Chinese merchant and called for the proprietor himself. From the depths of the interior came an ancient and stately Chinese man in a silken kimono. Ceremoniously they greeted one another and then Jacobs told the old merchant I would like to see some of his treasures. We went through the dirtiest storehouse I ever saw into a storeroom which was fixed up into living quarters. There, from some gorgeous mahogany chests were brought some silks, jade statues and some old ivory carvings. These were museum pieces, even my unpracticed eye could tell that.

We went through Chinatown, to the Japanese area, to all the old stately cathedrals of Manila. To the Tonde district, to the Yanka Market area, which was filled with every type of Philippine ware, to Gondarra Street or Thieves Row where you could find everything from Cleopatra's girdle or Brunhild's sash to Caesar's ghost. There were things hundreds of years old and up to modern vintage and there was a price on everything. Jacobs said if some of the old established shops did not have what you wanted, just describe what it was you wished, and they would name a date for you to come and get it regardless of whatever it was; a diamond from India or a slave girl from China.

He took me to an ancient part of the city where the streets had been paved with headstones from ancient graves and you could still see the dialect inscriptions out in the stones.

Another time we went to an ancient part of the city to a Chinese house where the door knocker was the most exquisite bronze, feminine hand I have ever seen. The fingers were long, slender, tapered and gracefully curved. The hand swung from the forefinger and the wrist was the base of the knocker. The old Chinese had refused to place a price on it, it wasn't to be sold.

I could go on and on for hours about our excursions around the city of Manila. Everywhere we went I was introduced as a special friend of Jacobs and if I ever went back to one of these places, I called for the person in charge to whom Jacobs had introduced me. If I desired to buy anything, my personal check was accepted without question and I was shown nothing but worthwhile, genuine goods.

I went to the Union Protestant Church while in Manila. Rev. Walter Felley Brooks, I believe, was the pastor and several nationalities of white people went there. One member was an American Negro. Everywhere were interesting people, interesting things and interesting friends. I was out to get as broad an experience as possible. The old timers were glad to find somebody showing appreciation for something other than the conventional tourist lines.

Old Manila with its sights, its smells, its contracts, its magnificent Dewey Boulevard and Taft Avenue in contrast with the Tondo slums (Lake Shore Drive versus Maxwell or Halstead streets in Chicago); its mixture of races both occidental and oriental; its mixture of cultures, atmospheres and backgrounds was quite a place. There was hardly a race or religion on the face of the earth that wasn't represented in the city. One had only to look and recognize in order to find Chinese, Japanese, Javanese, Malinese, Burmese, Korean, Russian, Polynesian, Dutch, British, French Portuguese, Spanish, Indian (East) and any other race you can think of. There was the modern occidental part of the city, there were the various Oriental areas and then there was the old Spanish walled city with its magnificent cathedrals and homes surrounded by narrow streets and filth where little naked Filipino boys ran the streets and held up their hands crying, "Give me a penny, Joe." It wasn't safe at night to walk down the sidewalks of the walled city because, like many of the European medieval towns, the second stories of the shops and houses extended out over the street. Unless one walked a chalk line down the exact center of the thoroughfare you were apt to be drenched by someone emptying his night can out the window on you. Even with all precautions you were not safe from splattering. Robbery and murder was not uncommon. There were certain areas that we always went in groups of at least three for safety's sake.,

Time passed quickly, the days were filled with duty or outside interests. One event shows how ironical things can be. Back at Indiana University I had a roommate named James F. Coffee, 2nd lieutenant, FA Reserves. Jim gave me the merry ha ha about being sent out to the Philippines. Six weeks later Lt. Coffee walked down the gangplank at Manila.

I didn't get to greet him when he arrived because I was on a reconnaissance trip in Bataan; however I did send him a letter via courier which was delivered to him personally. Two weeks later, about August 15, I tried to visit him at his post in Fort Stetsenbrug. I missed him then and after we were taken prisoner, reports on him were vague and uncertain. After sifting through what news I could, I gathered he was a prisoner and had been taken to Japan early in the war, sometime late in 1942. Many months later, over three years to be exact, when I was liberated and back in the 29th Replacement Center near Manila, I was walking from the orderly room to my tent when I found myself face to face with Jim. Our reunion was like that of long separated brothers. We were both happy and going home.

Toward the last of August 1941, all the people from the various forts in the Philippines, who were slated to go out to the PA (Philippine Army) as instructors, at its various posts and camps, were assembled in the theater of the Post of Manila and briefed as to their assignments and the location of their respective posts. I drew an Army camp at Calape on the Island of Bohol. Bohol is the first sizable island west of Leyte. I was the only American officer assigned and was to be assisted by an American corporal, Curtis Sizemore, of the 31st Infantry and a Philippine Scout, Sgt. Jose Bosco of the 26th Calvary. That's all my orders told me, not a thing about where it was, how to get there, or what to take with me. This last was important because in some areas a white man had to make his own food and the means to prepare it. Therefore I went up to the major who was putting out the dope and said, "Major, where is the Island of Bohol?"

Major: "It's in the Southern Islands not far from Cebu."

"What installations are at this camp, what am I to expect?"

Major: "I don't know, our maps have an Army post located there and that's all I can tell you about it!"

I was completely nonplused. Here was the boy from the big headquarters and he didn't know anything about it, it was just a spot on the map.

"This can't happen to me" my comprehension cried and cold logic would pipe up the next moment, "but it is. That spot on the map, no matter where it is or what it is, is where you are going to live for the next three months at least." It was as though a stone wall had hit me on the head. It wasn't until the noon meal that my numbed brain started to function. This was just the beginning. Many times later I was to say to myself, "This can't happen to me, but it is! Now what in the hell are you going to do about it? Are you going to go to hell, or are you coming out of it?" The answer always was, "I'm coming out of it!"

The cogs began to whir. If the Army couldn't tell me where it was sending me perhaps my friend Jacobs could. If he himself couldn't tell me, he would know someone who could. We had been relieved from company duty to get ready for our new assignments. I took off. This was the first step.

I located Jacobs at lunch in the Oriente Hotel where he lived.

"Jacobs," I said, "I have been ordered to take charge of an Army training post at Calape, Bohol. The Army can't tell me the first thing about it! Can you give me some idea about the place and what to expect?"

"Yes, I can! I did some archeological work on the island one time. It's in the Visayan Islands between Cebu and Leyte. I don't remember the town of Calape very well except I have been through it and it must have a population of at least 5,000 inhabitants. The Visayans are a friendly people and I think you will grow to like them. You certainly get to know the real life and culture of the Filipino people. In fact I rather envy you having the chance to go to the province of Bohol. It is far enough south that it has an even climate, no hot dry season or cold, damp rainy season, very nice weather, a nice climate all told."

"What should I take in the way of equipment?"

"Everything, canned food, oil stove, Coleman lantern, cooking utensils, etc. You might have to live in a nepa house. Before you go, I'll give you the address of a friend named Dart Wiliams who is the provincial superintendent of schools for Bohol. Dart is a handsome, friendly man and we call him "God's gift to the women!"

Before I left I got that address and later I did look up Dart. We grew to be good friends and before this war was over Dart became quite active in the guerrillas, but that is getting ahead of my story.

I left Jacobs and went about my preparations. As a result of his advice I knew where I was going, what possible routes, what to expect when I arrived and what to take in the way of equipment for living conditions. Once there I did live in a nepa house and cooked my own food, etc., but I didn't suffer.

On Aug. 28, 1941 I boarded the inter-island luxury liner, Mayon, bound for Tagbilaran, Bohol, via Cebu City where I was to leave the luxury liner and take a local ferry going from Cebu City to Tagbilaran, Bohol, for a five hour trip.

We went via Iloilo, the provincial capital of the island province of Panay. Jacobs had given me the address of Mr. and Mrs. C.M. Hodges in Iloilo City. The Hodges were extremely wealthy and were formerly from Lubbock, TX. Since the ship stopped at Iloilo several hours, I planned to look up the Hodges.

The Mayon was filled with Filipino soldiers and officers who lived or worked around Manila and were reporting to their various posts for duty. Talk about overloading, Filipinos slept in corridors, in the life boats and all over the ship. My baggage had been put on board by the Army and it was all mixed up with other luggage on the deck. Passengers were sitting on it, tramping it and otherwise abusing it. By this time I had learned that the flash of money flying through the air does wonders. I flipped a silver coin high a couple of times and then approached a deckhand who was watching with glistening eyes.

"Hello Joe!"

"Where's number one stevedore boy?" I asked and flipped the silver coin where he could catch it, which he neatly did.

"I go get him, sir," he replied and disappeared in the mass of passengers. I stuck my hand back in my pocket, pulled out another silver coin and started flipping it.

Shortly the Filipino deckhand returned with another man whose bearing revealed some authority.

I flipped the second coin to the Filipino deckhand, reached in my pocket pulled out several more and started jingling them as I spoke to "number one boy."

"Benor, I have four pieces of baggage in that pile which I want to have placed inside where it will not get wet and where I can have you get it quickly when we reach Cebu. Do you know of a place to stow it?"

"Yes sir, I know just the place, sir," and I tossed him a coin. He whistled to a couple of other deckhands and they retrieved the luggage as I pointed it out. The number one boy placed it in a little room just below deck which had one bunk. "It will be safe here, sir. This is my bunk. Any time you want it we can get it quickly."

I rewarded all for their work and left them happy. Later, at Cebu, the number one boy took care of my baggage very efficiently.

Early the next day, we arrived at Iloilo. I went ashore, located the Hodges and was taken on a sight seeing tour all around the small city.

The boat left late that same afternoon and went over to Pulpandan, Negros. The next port of call after Pulpandan was Cebu City at which we arrived about 1600 on Aug. 28, 1941. After checking the bags on the ferry I started out to see that city and a man in business there by the name of K.L. Morrison.

Morrison was vice president and treasurer for the importing firm of Erlanger and Gallager in the Philippines. The Cebu office was under his charge and I found him at his work. He laid that aside, visited with me and then phoned his wife. Mrs. Morrison drove down and took me on a tour of the city.

Cebu City is about the oldest spot in the white man's history of the Philippines. Magellan landed there and he was killed on Mactan Island which lies in the harbor of Cebu City. They showed me that day the oldest street in the Philippine islands. It was an old world looking passageway, narrow, cobble stoned; the second stories of massive stone dwellings on each side extended out over the street. The walls of these dwellings were solid for the height of the first story. The upstairs had iron grilled windows. It had a typical medieval atmosphere all through. Like Manila, Cebu City had a beautiful occidental area and then a large Nepa area where the majority of the Filipinos lived. The total population was about 150,000. Outside of the Spanish, the white colony numbered only about 70. It consisted of mostly American and British. There were a few Dutch, Portuguese, Germans, etc. All of these people were representatives of commercial interest, generally of their respective countries. After this quick tour of the city I went back to board the ferry for the Island of Bohol. The family gave me a standing invitation to make the Morrison home my headquarters at any future date I might happen to be in Cebu.

By the time I returned, the ferry was about ready to sail. On it were Corp. Curtis Sizemore and the scout sergeant Jose Bosco. I had never seen these two individuals before, so it was with a sharp eye that I scrutinized them both. I liked what I saw.

The Filipino scout sergeant knew the language, had been raised on Bohol and in general knew his way around. He decided he could take a smaller boat and arrive at Calape ahead of me. Once there he would look for a place to locate the three of us until we could get permanently settled. I sent him on ahead and then went above to see the other American officers who were going to be on the Island of Bohol with me for the next three months. There were six of them, all strangers except one it proved.

I walked out on to the upper front deck of the little ferry where the six American officers were watching our withdrawal from the pier into the harbor. The first form I laid eyes on was the tall thin figure of Capt. Bill O'Connor. Was I glad to see him and he me! We were friends meeting in a far away, strange land. O'Connor then introduced me in turn to the following officers: Capt. Paul D. Wood to be in charge of the Officer School at Tubigon, Bohol. Wood was a West Point man.

First Lt. Duane L. Casper from Walla Walla, WA. Casper was one of Wood's assistants. Capt. Hoyt, another West Point man and second in command of the Tubigon School. Lt. Pratt, whom we soon named Donald Duck because he talked all the time and in a very hoarse voice. Last was 1st Lt. Gorden Utke from the Dakotas. Utke had been in the islands for a year or so and was married to Col. Carter's daughter. Utke, although stationed at the Tubigon Cadre was not part of the school. He was the instructor for the machine gun company of the 81st Infantry, Philippine Army, stationed there.

There we were, the eight American officers who were to be stationed on the Island of Bohol for the next three months, six at the Cadre School at Tubigon, Capt. O'Connor to be at the Tagbilaran Cadre with two rifle companies and myself to be in charge of one rifle company and a battalion headquarters unit at Calape. We all looked at each other with the friendly eyes of pilgrims in a foreign land and headed for the unknown. We all felt it was to be quite an adventure ahead of us.

It was five hours from Cebu to Tagbilaran. Our little ferry skirted around several sand bars and coral reefs which were only a few feet in height. Several were a few inches above the smooth surface of the "blue to green" sea. Flying fish frequently broke the calm surface of the water. The bow of the boat was low and we got some excellent views of the little fish.

At other times we went between narrow passes or defiles between small but heavily forested islands. Coconut palms and mangrove trees extended clear out into the sea water in many of these narrow lanes of water. At other places we saw wide, white sandy beaches fringed in the rear by thick growths of tall coconut palms. To me there was more charm possessed by these beaches than the famous Waikiki Beach at Honolulu.

Most of us stood at the bow railing watching the described scenery. Lt. Casper, however, was an exception. Casper sat at a table on the lower deck drinking hot beer (there was no ice in these waters or on this type of boat, nor was there drinking water) and writing postcards. He said the post cards were to help him catch up on his correspondence. Considering that we didn't know how much time we would have in the future for such chores, I thought his policy a good one and followed suit.

E.L. Morrison had telegraphed Dart Williams of Tagbilaran, Bohol, that I was arriving that evening and would he please meet me at the dock. About 1700 our ferry rounded the palm fringed coast of Bohol and pulled into a large bay. As the boat approached the dock, I stood on the bow deck and saw one lone white man standing beside a black Packard sedan, observing our approach. There was a look of bewilderment on his face as he counted eight American officers in uniform plus two non-coms, instead of one lone American lieutenant.

We docked, I stepped ashore and inquired if he was Williams. He was. Then followed introductions all around. In the end Williams took us all out to the PA cadre where we found a maintenance crew. Of course they didn't know we were coming, but we managed to get them to send transportation down to the pier and get our baggage. Williams having delivered us, left promising to see me later. There was a lot of confusion and he undoubtedly was glad to escape.

The group of us took inventory of the situation and surroundings and then we took over, Capt. Wood in command. The first thing to do was to get some chow, as it was late. Taking the cadre truck we all piled in and went back downtown. Tagbilaran is built around a square which contains the vendor's market booths on market days. It was almost 2100 by that time and not a single eating place appeared open. Finally one of the Filipinos directed us to a Chinaman's restaurant. We stopped at that building and looked at it in consternation. There were some wooden steps leading up to the second story where a weather beaten sign said "Restaurant" in English. The building itself was square, supported by four pillars about 10 feet high. The floor was on top of these four pillars. The walls were of woven swalai, pronounced swa lee, with Nepa palm thatching for a roof. Underneath that house were two pens made of woven bamboo. In one were two poor razorback pigs (these razorbacks would "out-razorback" our Arkansas variety) and a flock of droopy chickens. It smelled worse than the Chicago Stockyards in mid-August. If this were a restaurant, we were angels! But it was a restaurant and we weren't angels. The Chinaman came down the stairs dressed in dirty white trousers and an undershirt. We had to eat, so we told him we wanted something to eat and we wanted "Americano chow outta tin cans." Could he fix? I think everyone of us chimed in saying we wanted Americano chow. He gravely listened to us all with an inscrutable face and then said, "Okay, me fix" and motioned us to follow him.

We trailed up the stairs and sat down at a long table with benches beside it for seats and waited. Sights and smells were prevalent. Pretty soon the odor of cooking drifted into the room from behind a movable panel. Shortly afterward a comely looking Chinese girl gaudily dressed in calico began bringing out the dishes of soup. The dishes were dirty and greasy. The soup was hot, greasy, had eggshells and pinfeathers in it. Not many of us ate much of our soup.

Next the Chinese girl brought out a platter of rice with some pieces of boiled chicken in it. She then proceeded to take each dish of our uneaten soup and throw it through a hole in the floor. The pigs awoke immediately and started an awful squealing. Dish after dish was emptied and the empty dish placed in front of us. The Chinaman then passed the platter of rice and chicken to Capt. Wood. The Captain gingerly took a little of the rice and chicken and passed it on to O'Connor. When it came to Capt. Hoyt he made some remark about still being seasick and passed it on. Nobody said anything, but this was the first we had heard of Hoyt being seasick on the trip down. The platter passed from hand to hand, nobody taking more than a few small spoons of the rice and chicken. I was no different from the rest.

Not one of us dreamed that less than a year later every single one of us would have eaten that entire platter of rice at a single sitting declaring all the while that it was a "feast fit for a king."

We ate what we were going to of the rice and chicken. Then we told the Chinaman we wanted some fruit for dessert. He brought out two quart cans of Queen Anne cherries and opened them right at the table. He passed the cans to us and we passed them around. When an almost empty can reached Wood, he just ate out of the can, remarking "If any of you boys want to do the same, just tell him so" and pointed at the Chinaman. I think everyone of us called for an individual can of cherries and ate out of the cans. That Chinaman's eyes bugged out. You could almost see the thoughts flashing in his face about the uncouth, barbaric Americans who wouldn't eat rice and ate cherries out of a can.

By this time the only kerosene lamp was about to flicker out and several of the boys were exceedingly squirmy. I was too, I thought I felt things crawling on my legs. I reached down and picked something off my leg. It squashed between my thumb and forefinger. I looked at it in the flickering lamplight. It had been a bug and it had a characteristic odor I was soon to become well acquainted with. Yes, it was a squashed bed bug with its pungent odor of almonds.

We left immediately and once we got outside of that filthy, stinking place we felt like we had a new lease on life. Everyone of us was scared stiff we were going to get dysentery from that meal!

We drove back to the cadre and started looking for places to sleep. We all had our bed rolls, but nobody had thought to bring along any twine to hang our mosquito nets on. As a net result we spent the entire night slapping mosquitoes. Slap! Slap! Slap! What a night it was. I think every mosquito on the Island of Bohol entered that room, took a bite out of us and flew out to make way for another. I never heard such cursing in all my life. In the morning Wood's face was so welted and swollen from mosquito bites that I hardly recognized him.

The next morning we tore open somebody's box of canned chow and got some canned goods for breakfast. After that we went to our various post locations via the cadre truck. My post at Calape was on the road to Tubigon where Wood and his six officers were going. They dropped me off on the way.

Calape, Bohol, a strange new place to me, yet I was lucky. I walked into a good barracks on a level parade ground. It had running water, electric lights, flush toilets and bunks enough for all the men I was to have in my camp. O'Connor at Tagbilaran had the same facilities I did, but only for a quarter of the number of men he was to have. Capt. Wood was even worse off than O'Connor.

What I didn't have was a typewriter for all the Army paperwork that had to be done, paper for it, field manuals for training programs and equipment of any type for training soldiers. That barracks was absolutely barren of all equipment except one small desk, some built in brick stoves and the heavy iron caldrons for boiling rice in. There were no facilities for washing mess gear or even heating water.

With the cadre buildings were five Philippine Army regular soldiers who were the caretakers. Through them I gained knowledge of the PA system of contracting locally for needed food and supplies. This I did. I had five days grace before my troops arrived to scare up the minimum necessities to start my camp with. There wasn't even a stick of wood to build a fire around that place. I used quite a bit of my own money in order to be able to function when the time came. It was a great life. There was so much to do that I didn't have a chance to think.

Calape, Bohol, was a friendly little Filipino city 41 kilometers north of the Provincial capital, Tagbilaran. It lay on the west coast between the mountains and the sea. About two miles east of it the mountains rose sharply to the height of about 1400 feet. Once you were on the mountain slopes you ran into thick jungle. Though jungle covered the mountains there were numerous trails through it because there were valleys on the other side of the coast range which were heavily populated. To the west of the town lay a sizable bay sheltered from the open sea between Bohol and Cebu by Panganhan Island.

My camp lay at the north side of Calape. Its grounds consisted of a level grassy plot of about five acres. It was surrounded on all, but the town side, by small coconut plantations. These plantations were small, very close together and very numerous. To the casual observer they appeared to be one continuous plantation stretching for miles. The trees were very thick and about 80 feet tall. To the west side of my camp, about a mile away, lay the sea. Between the camp and the sea lay coconut plantations, rice paddies and mangrove swamps. Farther away to both north and south lay beautiful sandy beaches with beautiful tall palms growing right out of the sand. In some places the white sandy beaches were 100 yards wide. At other places the coconut palms had been planted in the sand clear to the roller's edge.

My camp was on the edge of a grassy meadow that lay in the midst of a forest of coconut palms. A white crushed coral road ran through the forest and past my camp.

Capt. Wood left me at my cadre barracks. I watched his group disappear in the coconut forest and turned to look at my surroundings.

Sgt. Bosco came out of a house in a nearby coconut grove.

Sgt. Bosco, saluting, "Good morning sir, lieutenant. I hope the lieutenant had a good trip yesterday."

"Yes, sergeant, we had a wonderful trip." I glanced at Sizemore as I said this and he grinned in a sickly manner.

"Everything is all hunky-dory lieutenant."

"How's that, sergeant?"

"I contracted for a house for the lieutenant and Corp. Sizemore, a lavandero to wash the uniforms and a cook who can cook Americano chow!"

"Hells bells, sergeant. How did you do all of that?"

"It's easy, lieutenant, if you know the methods."

"Where's the house?"

"There, sir," pointing to a large spacious looking Nepa house across the road. It was sheltered by coconut palms and the bottom floor stood on four slender pillars 12 feet above the ground. At the back under the house I could see a pen with a pig in it!

"And the lavandero, sergeant, where does she live?"

"There sir," pointed to a small Nepa shack 100 yards from my dwelling. It was so poor looking that it wasn't built high enough to have the usual pig pen. Again I looked at Sizemore whose face was a study in a mixture of emotions.

"And the cook, sergeant? When does he come to begin work?"

"Very soon, lieutenant. In time for noon chow." I tried to conceal my feelings at this stage. This sergeant was a "hot potato" and right on the ball. He had me all fixed up one way or another. He either had me fixed up in fine shape or he had me in one hell of a mess.

"Well, sergeant, how soon will the people move out of the house and I can move in?"

"Already sir, they have moved. Last night they went to live with their son." I sat down on my bed roll, took off my cap and wiped my forehead. This boy was too much for me, he had all the answers.

(Weakly) "That's a very big house, sergeant and we don't have any furniture."

(Quickly) "Oh, but Sir, that is hunky-dory. I knew the lieutenant had only his bedroll so I contracted for the furniture too."

"But, sergeant, won't this be pretty expensive?"

"Fifteen pesos a month, sir. It is really a very nice house, Sir." The sergeant looked very worried at this remark.

"Fifteen pesos, "I muttered in amazement. "That's $7.50 gold. I'd give a lot more than $7.50 for a roof over my head in this country."

I didn't want to live in the barracks with the Filipino soldiers.

"Sergeant, I guess you have taken care of everything. I am sure glad you are the scout detailed with me. Can my cook speak English and cook American chow?"

"Yes sir, lieutenant. He lived in Hawaii 15 years and worked for the Army."

By this time I decided I was lucky. This Filipino sergeant was plenty bright, he had been around white men and knew what they wanted. He certainly had been a quick worker here and he had the air of one who knew his stuff.

"Okay, sergeant. You go get the cook and better get me a house boy too."

"His son is the house boy, sir."

"Get them here on the double, I want to get settled before tonight."

"Yes Sir!" and scuttled off into the coconut palms.

I turned to Sizemore and said, "Well! Can you beat that?" I was flabbergasted.

"No, lieutenant, I can't. I didn't know there were Pinos like that."

I got up and walked for a few minutes, looking around and thinking. Here was a new situation, so far I was master of it. The sergeant's manner had been that he expected me to expect of him what he had accomplished. I wasn't going to change that attitude. Here was a horse that wanted to travel and I might as well travel as far as I could while moving was good. I decided the best policy was to express a desire or wish to the sergeant and then shut up and watch what happened until I got my feet on the ground and knew what the score was. It worked!

In a few minutes the sergeant came out of the coconuts on the double. Ten feet behind him dog-trotted a middle-aged Filipino man in a dirty white undershirt and white duck pants and 50 feet behind the man, on the run, was a boy about 12 years of age. These two were cook and houseboy respectively.

"Lieutenant, this is Alejandro, your cook, and his son Pablo, your house boy."

"Alejandro, I am glad you and Pablo are going to work for me. Right now move this baggage over to my house," and pointed to the house I was to occupy. "Sergeant, have a couple of the soldiers here bring over those two iron bedsteads from the cadre office. We don't want to sleep on the floor."

I won't go into the task of housecleaning around the kitchen. The extent, quality and type of filth was in accordance with the rest of the things I have mentioned in regard to sanitation. Strange to say, but circumstances alter opinions. One year later if I could have walked into that house I would have said, "Isn't this the height of luxury and sanitation?" That house, on looking back, was about 900 percent more sanitary than the places where we lived in Japanese prisons. This first day I got my quarters cleaned up and in order, we even got the kerosene stove and Coleman lantern working before nightfall.

In a day or two I was able to get the house owners to remove their pig and big two-wheeled cart. In a few days more the swine odor began to disappear. The cook and houseboy lived in their own home which was not far way and came to work early each morning.

While all these glittering generalities were taking place, small individual events were happening which concerned me. One in particular that I remember occurred one morning shortly after 7:00 a.m. I was in the toilet sitting on the stool when a loud banging occurred at the front door of my quarters.

"Wait a few minutes and I will be there," I said, expecting it to be one of my orderlies. The knocking sounded again, louder this time. "All right, damn it, I will be there, but you will have to wait until I am through here."

Upon my finishing that sentence, the door opened and I heard somebody come in. At that sound, I reached for my gun which I always kept near me, cocked it, got off the stool and moved towards the door with the gun leveled. As I reached the door Filipino Col. David was advancing across the center of my living room. Behind him were other Filipinos. At the sight of me, with a leveled gun in my right hand and holding up my pants with my left hand, the whole group stopped.

"Colonel, when people come into my house they identify themselves first. I have already shot at one thief in the night and I never know when to expect another. I came out here prepared to use this gun and I find you and your friends. Don't you think you should have told me who you were before you came in and eliminated this danger?" With that I put the safety on my gun and returned it to my holster.

"But the vice president of the Philippines, Senor Osmena is coming here to stay, so I brought him right in."

"The vice president of the Philippines is certainly welcome to occupy my quarters with me and I will do everything I can to make him comfortable. You, sir, were most unwise to bring him into this place without warning me of your identity. Won't you bring him in, sir?"

"This is the vice president," and he pointed to the man in the doorway behind him.

I looked at the calm face of the elderly Filipino standing in the doorway of my quarters. Sure enough, it was Vice President Osmena. Behind him stood various members of his staff and some soldiers carrying their baggage.

"Won't you come in, sir and share my poor quarters?" I then started to pull up my pants and stuff in my shirttail. Talk about being caught with your pants down, I certainly was in this case and by no other than the vice president of the Philippines.

"You will pardon my appearance, Mr. Vice President. I was not expecting visitors at this hour of the morning. I don't usually greet my guests with a .45 in my hand. However, someday I do expect to have some guests on which I will use the weapon. Breakfast should be ready in about 15 minutes. Won't you join me?"

"We are sorry to have frightened you, captain, and we really had no chance to give you warning of our coming."

With that speech, the stern face of the old man relaxed into a smile and he stepped forward with outstretched hand to shake hands with me. I saluted him and then shook hands with him. When he moved forward, the rest of the group moved in and they deposited the baggage on the floor inside the door.

On Sept. 1, 1941, most of my quota of 140 troops came in from Tagbilaran. They brought with them their equipment in the way of blankets, uniforms, canteen and mess kits. They didn't have any weapons, those were yet to come.

Out of the regular PA crew of five men, one could run a mess after a manner, another could do the clerical work if he had a typewriter (I borrowed one from the local Provincial High School), another knew how to operate the diesel engine for lights, etc. Under these men I had to assign soldiers to learn the duty from the ground up. It was a hard job selecting men capable of doing these jobs because they demanded some education in reading, writing and arithmetic. After examining these men I decided that if a man had completed the third grade he was well educated!

Those first two days were a nightmare. The lads couldn't understand me and I couldn't understand them. There were men from several different islands. Often a different island meant a different tribe and a different dialect spoken. Both the commissioned and non-commissioned officers, in most cases, had been assigned their commission and rates through the influence of political connections and not through their qualifications for the detail. There were some instances where a Tagalog corporal could speak only his own dialect. To give an order he spoke to a member of his squad in Tagalog who understood him, who in turn translated the command in English to a third member of the squad. This third member than translated the command from English to Visayan for the remainder of the squad. This command had to pass from the non-com through two interpreters before his squad could understand the order. With their knowledge of languages the percentages of error were practically 100 percent. To begin with that non-com couldn't understand me and he gave his order by watching what the other squads did. The whole set up seemed to run backwards. I had to sift all these things out for myself.

What about the Filipino officers, you ask? They were pretty bewildered. All were young, inexperienced, afraid they would do something wrong, unable to fully understand English or to translate English to their troops. Those first few days I told them to watch and I didn't work them too heavily. Slowly they gained confidence and grew used to assuming command.

Cpl. Sizemore was just as bad off as I in the language difficulties. He practically sweated blood daily. Each night he was exhausted. My savior through all of this chaos was Sgt. Bosco. He could speak several dialects and he knew the routine of the training backwards, forward and sideways. For hours at a time he would keep five or six officers busy with their troops. These officers had to learn with their men. He could teach them their administration work at night.

Each night after the troop duty was over and the troops fed, the corporal, the sergeant and myself held night classes for the officers and noncoms. The classes were on the mistakes of the day and the training for the next day.

I had to know everything, oversee everything, be everywhere at once and try to keep the officers and men in good spirits. All of them were like a group of children, most of them had never been away from home and family before and they got homesick. Many of them had never had so many clothes before. The uniforms were ill fitting and the shoes were hot tennis shoes that didn't fit. We gave them 10 minutes rest out of each hour. When they would fall in at the end of the rest period 75 percent of them were barefooted and carrying their shoes. They were like a bunch of children, you got the most out of them when you had them laughing and pulling with you.

The training was a 13-week basic training schedule worked up at Fort Benning, GA, calling for 44 hours training a week. We had to break this master schedule down into a daily schedule for each week. The authorities at the headquarters in Cebu City demanded that the training schedule should list the training manual and the paragraphs in the training manual concerning the training for each hour of the day. If our daily schedule said that 2:45 p.m. we would be in the field simulating advance by infiltration, woe be us if we were not doing that at 2:45 p.m. Often those troops were in the mud and water because there was a tropical downpour at that time of day. They had only one change of clothes and these were usually wet and dirty. Those rains didn't last long as a rule and if we had been permitted to take our 4:00 p.m. subject, which was an inside lecture while it rained and then resume the 2:45 training subject when the rain was over, the troops would not have been so miserable and they would have gotten 100 percent more out of the training with half the effort. In the first place, a Fort Benning training schedule should have been revised before being used in the Philippines. It didn't have a word about jungle fighting and in the second place, we weren't permitted to use it sensibly. Orders were orders.

I arose at 6:00 a.m. and turned in around midnight after conducting night schools and later doing my paperwork. The corporal and the sergeant had pretty much the same schedule. I watched them grow thin and tired. It was killing work. Looking back I wonder if I wasn't too conscientious about my duty for my own good. I had to see to two training schedules, a battalion headquarters and a rifle company, to daily take care of the camp supplies, administration and sanitation. This last was not easy. You don't get a race to give up personal habits and customs just because you induct them in an Army, put them into clothes and call them soldiers. It was a great life if you didn't weaken. I pushed my assistants and drove the Filipinos those first few weeks. The last, poor devils, were just like lost children that didn't know what to do. The rapidity of advance, demanded by the master schedule, kept them in a complete state of bewilderment. I never had more willing students though.

The whole set-up was a vicious circle and somehow I felt I must fit the training more to the Filipino psychology.

One of the men I later knew in prison, Maj. Campbell Snyder of Louisiana, often recited a piece of poetry which I think covered the situation fairly well; quoting from a dim memory:

"It is not good for the Occidental fair
To hurry the Easterner mild,
For the brown man smiles,
And the white man riles,
And it wears the white man down.
The end of the fight is a tombstone white,
Which bears the inscription:
'Here lies a fool
Who tried to hurry the East.'"

By the end of the first two weeks the officers were beginning to feel more at home with their men. I had gotten them bored enough with standing around that they wanted to do something. A few well-placed words stirred up the spirit of rivalry among them, words such as "I believe Lt. Reyes from Manila is going to be the best officer in the company. He does 'that' better than all the officers from Cebu. Of course he works very hard to get his men to learn." The Cebu officers standing nearby took the bait.

At the end of the two weeks I called a council of all my Filipino officers. All could understand English more or less. We held a conference, exchanged views on the training schedule, equipment, language difficulties, etc. When I had gotten as many ideas as possible I dismissed them with the promise to have some alterations pertaining to the training for them Monday. Then I gave the whole camp weekend leave.

Monday morning, I presented the Filipino officers a plan with the following points to it:

l. Teach the troops what was expected of them by observation.

2. Substitute explanation for demonstration.

3. Use the native dialects whenever possible.

4. Gather the best educated men into a demonstration team.

5. Lead the troops themselves.

That was to be my contribution to the camp that Monday morning in the middle of September 1941.

What about the contribution of the troops? That was conspicuous by its omission. To be exact, "by their omission." Two thirds of the entire camp had taken leave. All knew that they would have to be back to camp by midnight Sunday. Came time to fall in at 0700 Monday morning, the troops fell in and great gaps appeared in the ranks. The sergeants reported one by one to their platoon leaders.

"Sir, 10 men absent."

"Sir, men absent."

"Sir, men absent."

The company commander reported to the battalion CO. The results were appalling, more than a third of the camp was AWOL. By this time the face of every man in camp was on me. The platoon lieutenants were so scared that they were almost white. The company commander was visibly trembling and the battalion commander seemed to have lost his tongue and couldn't talk enough to make his report.

I was fit to be tied. I was so astonished that I was speechless. I didn't know what to say and the men couldn't have understood me if I had started sulfur fumes rolling toward them. I just stood and looked them up and down and after three minutes or so of silence, I turned my back on the whole scene and left them standing there staring after me. There was a dead silence. I walked into the office and wrote a letter in long hand. After about 10 minutes the battalion CO tiptoed in and asked what he should do. I laid down my pen and walked over to the door. The men were still standing at attention while the officers were standing in a sickly group. Cpl. Sizemore and Sgt. Bosco were just outside the office door discreetly saying nothing, yet in quick call.

"Sergeant, corporal," I called in a funny voice.

"Yes Sir," they answered in unison and saluted.

"Explain our new lesson plan to the officers, explain the lesson subjects and get under way with the Filipino officers instructing the platoons." I answered their salutes and again walked inside. I heard their voices start the program as I finished my letter. I then called an orderly and had him personally take this letter to the post office. This was a personal letter addressed to Col. Theodore Sledge, CO, 8th Military Area, Cebu City, Cebu. (It asked for field manual).

I then left the office and went to my quarters across the street. Once there I sat down on my bunk and laughed! This wasn't the American Army, the more I thought about it the funnier it got and I started laughing. I had a good laugh when I remembered the consternation in those faces. After an hour or so I returned to the training ground to see how things were going. I still held my silence. A few of the late soldiers came into camp from off the bus as it went by. I told the battalion CO to put all AWOL men in fatigue clothes and have them start to work on various police details around camp. I don't know what those Filipino officers told these men, but it was pretty rough from the sound.

At noon the corporal and sergeant told me things had gone well with the training that morning and that I had them all guessing what I was going to do about the situation. I just sat tight, ignored the situation and observed reactions. I decided by the time the day was over that as long as I kept silent the more they would toe the line. That I did. As these men who were AWOL returned, they were put to work cleaning up the camp. They cleaned up a lot that day. At retreat most of the men had returned and the next morning none were AWOL. Tuesday I carried on the regular training hours. At retreat I ordered all the men who had been AWOL to fall in at 6:00 p.m. They lined up at 6:00 p.m. and I looked them over. Pausing in front of a private who could speak English I said, "Why were you AWOL?"

"Sir, I went to see my family."

"Why did you not return by midnight?"

"Sir, I could not."

"Why not?"

"Sir, the lieutenant said I could go visit my family. He signed my pass. I take the boat to Cebu City. I take the provincial bus to Santandar. I take banca to Siguehor (Siquijor) Island. I get home Sunday morning and I stay with my family all day and all night. Monday morning I take banca back to Santandar. I come back to camp last night!"

I said nothing more. I knew family ties were very close, a lot closer in some ways than ours. I went on down the line. All of them had gone home or to see some relative at some place too remote for the time. The fact that all had returned after only a short visit showed that they did not intend to desert. I gave them an hour of grounds police and dismissed them. Privately I had decided to dismiss the whole episode and nothing more was said on my part. As a result the extra fatigue had disgraced the AWOL boys in the eyes of the rest of the camp and I had my camp looking real neat and tidy. When the district inspector came around later in the week my camp was rated excellent and the best on the island. The Filipinos thought the district commander had come around to investigate the AWOLs. I didn't disillusion them. The whole episode was a stumper at the moment but it resulted in establishing me more securely in charge of the camp.

On such a detail, with different races that way, you have to feel your way around and it is best not to be hasty. Study the people involved and bend their psychology to attain the ends you desire. More and more I applied this to my training and I found things becoming more organized.

I don't remember the names of all the Filipino officers. The ones that I do remember include 1st Lt. Valentine Velasco. Velasco was right on the ball. I am not sure that he didn't know more about the Army than I since he was a Philippine regular. He was invaluable during those first weeks in getting the camp organized. Somewhere he had been in training with American troops and he would cushion the occidental and oriental differences between myself and the troops. Ricardo Estralla was my supply officer. He was a likable chap and very helpful. His name was Spanish; translated into English, it mean Richard Star. Estralla was a reservist and a Philippine government employee in civilian life. He had charge of the National Forestry Office in Cebu City, Cebu. He also was familiar with white men.

Lt. Ignacio Javier was the commander of troops. He was young and with too much experience in handling men at the time. He improved as time went along. His father worked for the Shell Oil Co. in Cebu City.

Lt. Jose Momonana was another of the young officers. He likewise was young and an Army career man. He came from Luzon and belonged to the Tagalog tribe. Momonana didn't know too much about white men and he had a very violent temper which made it hard to get along with him. He was either all for something or all against it. There was no medium road for him.

The last I remember was 1st Lt. Perfecto Mabugat. As far as I became concerned his name should have been Imperfecto and not Perfecto. Velasco was transferred to the district headquarters in Cebu City to take the job that Mabugat had. Mabugat was sent to my camp, which made the two just trade places. Mabugat was as bad as Velasco was good. He was a regular in the PA, his branch was infantry. He was a licensed physician who evidently had gotten through the Medical School somewhere, but didn't make a good living so he joined the Army. My troubles really began when he appeared. The four previous years he had been a battalion commander and commanding officer of this Calape camp. In fact, I lived in his house and it still bore his wooden name plate. Now instead of being the big dog in a little puddle he was just another Filipino lieutenant under the American officer. This was quite a social comedown for him and he resented my presence very much. He was quite well known socially among the townspeople and it galled him not to be the CO in their presence. He was unreliable and inefficient.

The training went merrily on, the rifles were the old Enfield, long obsolete for the U.S. Army. When it came to hand grenades there were none to be had. I taught the soldiers to use stones in their throwing exercises. At first I made them use the U.S. way of heaving a grenade, then upon experimentation I found they could throw it twice as far in their natural way. Training regulations or no training regulations, in the heat of a battle those Filipinos would forget the white man's method and revert to their own. Better to get the idea across to them what the grenade would do if they pulled the pin and threw it in whatever manner they could throw it farthest.

In the jungle training those boys were plenty good, they were right at home and with plenty of ingenuity. They took to the art of camouflage with no difficulty. They weren't such good shots though. They were afraid of the recoil of that rifle. With no more time and ammunition that we had I never did get some of those boys over shutting their eyes and jerking the gun when they fired. One lad in the rapid fire exercises shut his eyes and fired his whole five shots before he opened them again. Where those bullets went I have no idea, except they didn't go into the target.

The first firing exercise was held in a farmer's valley cornfield. When the second firing exercise was due the cornfield was planted and we couldn't use it. Accordingly I had to search the foothills until I found a suitable place for a range and then get the owner's permission for using it. Once the permission was gained I had to build a whole new set up, pits for safety, frames for the targets, rope, cloth, paste, etc. all had to be bought. I paid for it out of my own pocket. As a result of that practice those boys riddled a farmer's banana plantation by their overshoots, the trees were so riddled that they died. I paid for two in order to do away with any possible hard feelings.

Those were long, hard exhausting days. Often I was too exhausted at night to anymore than take off my shoes until I woke up late sometime in the night, when I would undress and go to bed.

Col. Theodore Sledge was the CO of the 8th Military District which was composed of the islands of Cebu and Bohol. Every once in awhile, Col.

Sledge would ship his car over on the ferry and take a night boat to Bohol. Then he would make a personal tour and inspection of the camps at Tagbilaran, Calape and Tubigon. On one trip he brought Col. Callahan or Monahan from department headquarters in Manila. They had diner with me. I was always glad to see these inspectors because they often were the only white men I would see for days or even weeks at a time. Col. Sharp, later Maj. Gen. Sharp, CO of the Southern Islands, stopped very briefly one afternoon. He found me out in the field with the troops.

After I got the camp started, I received a 1-1/2 ton truck and a station wagon for camp use in getting supplies and transporting the soldiers to and from the boats when they went on leave. Because supplies were so short, often the three camps had to lend each other equipment. I managed to visit the other camps now and then and exchange ideas and notes. Sanitation was the chief problem we had in common. The flies were incubating in the latrines, around the kitchens and in the water ditches in the camps. Capt. Woods was having his hands full with his school. In that school there were quite a number of field officers and they resented the strict discipline of the school. In our sense of the word it wasn't strict discipline but in comparison to what they were used to, it was strict. It took all of Paul D's diplomacy to keep everybody on good terms.

I went down to O'Connor's camp one day for supplies at the small depot there. I found Bill in a blue mood. I only needed to use the stock phrase, "well how are things going?" to set him off.

"Going? Why things are going to hell! Do you know what I am doing? I'm building, houses (latrines to you)! I was in the first World War and all I did there was build houses and clean stables. I later served in Hawaii and all I did there was wash and grease cars. Now I come to the Philippines and what do I do? I build more houses. No wonder this Army is going to hell when all it does is build houses!!"

He paused and bit a cigarette. I noticed his hands shook as if he had the palsy. I looked at the man sharply to note that his face was haggard, his eyes sunken and that he had lost about 20 pounds.

"Whoa here, old timer, take it easy. You have been working too hard. It's noon time now, how about knocking off and let's go eat?"

"Okay, I just got a house rented and a couple of Filipino girls to take care of it and cook."

"I thought you stayed here at the barracks and ate at the mess here."

"I did for about 15 days but I couldn't stand it. I didn't have one single minute's privacy, the Filipinos were always bothering me even when I was in bed. The food was mostly rice and it was very unappetizing. One day they had some soup which smelled rotten so I investigated the kitchen. The cooks had a hog for that day and they had made the soup out of the entrails. The whole mess was rotten, I became very sick at my stomach and vomited. After that I couldn't eat at the mess there without getting sick from the thoughts of that stinking mess! Now I have a good mess, but I have lost my appetite."

I ate with O'Connor and he did have a good mess considering the situation and location. O'Connor had been at that camp about a month and most of that time he hadn't been able to eat. It was no wonder the man was a wreck physically. The next time I saw Col. Sledge I told him something ought to be done about Bill as he was in pretty bad shape. The colonel looked the situation over and made his own opinion about Bill. Shortly afterwards, Bill was transferred to the district headquarters in Cebu City. There he got back on his feet somewhat as he lived like a white man.

The man who took O'Connor's place was 1st Lt. Myron Sharp. Myron like the rest of us had his troubles.

The Army camps were fairly free from disease. There was some malaria, dysentery and typhoid. I lost one man, Sgt. Delatar from the Island of Cebu. I gave blood for a transfusion for him but even then he died. O'Connor helped me out with that mess. He took the body to Cebu while I went to the hospital exhausted. I stayed there three days and was very fortunate to be able to have a hospital to go to.

The hospital was a Presbyterian Mission Hospital at Tagbilaran, Bohol. It had been established by a missionary physician named Graham back before the turn of the century. The old Dr. Graham was dead but his daughter, Miss Graham, still lived there and carried on her father's missionary work. Three Filipino doctors carried on the medical end of it. Living with Miss Graham at that time were two young middle aged missionaries, Mr. and Mrs. Joseph Livesey. They had just recently been run out of Korea by the Japanese. I saw them several times while on Bohol and got to be quite friendly with them. I asked them a lot of questions about the Japanese and their answers were not what I liked to hear. During the war I believe Miss Graham and the Liveseys lived with the natives all the time. I heard they got through alive.

About Oct. 1, 1941, I spent a weekend over at Cebu City on the Island of Cebu. Cebu was the second city in size in the Philippine Islands and the metropolis of the southern islands, having about 150,000 population. To make the trip I drove 15 kilometers to the small port of Tubigon and took an inter-island ferry to Cebu, about three hours away. When I speak of a ferry here, I don't mean the flat-ended boats you find in our bays and harbors. I mean a sharp bowed, often sea going boat of 75 to 100 feet long. It was built to carry cargo and passengers, cargo below the water line and passengers on the two decks above the water line.

This boat was packed with soldiers and civilians going to Cebu. Filipinos were perched on the railing, rigging, steps, everywhere. There were very few benches or seats aboard. I wondered if we were going to have to stand for the next few hours. This was all new and strange to me so I was content just to stand at the railing and watch.

As the boat drew away from the pier some of the deck hands began to shove people aside and set up canvas cots on the deck. As fast as the cots were set up people sat and lay down upon them, sometimes a whole family of several children all settled themselves on one cot. The people that were standing disappeared as if by magic. Soon everybody was lying down except a few leaning against the rail. Most of the people went to sleep. I got a cot in the scramble, sat in it awhile and then moved around some to see what was going on. I wandered up to the pilothouse and there I found lieutenants Casper, Herr, Pratt, Utke and Capt. Hoyt. I joined the group. From the pilothouse or compass deck we watched the small islands slip by. The large island of Bohol sank into the green sea and its mountains dim in the purple haze. The dim Island of Cebu became more distinct as we approached. Several times our ship altered its course as it went by a sand bar or a coral reef, which rose a few inches out of the sea. I enjoyed the trip immensely and I enjoyed the company of my fellow Americans more.

Before leaving Calape I had sent a telegram to K.L. Morrison, manager of Cebu branch of Erlanger and Gallager, that I was coming over. He replied that his car would be waiting for me. As the ferry drew into the harbor of Cebu I took a keen interest in all the harbor activity and in trying to locate Morrison's dark Buick sedan. There were several inter-island boats in the harbor, the Mayon, Elcano and one or two more were there. The first two, fast passenger boats making the ports of Manila, Iloilo, Cebu, Zamboanga and lesser ports. The others were more cargo boats than passenger. Their chief cargo was copra, hemp, rice, etc. There were all sorts of bancas, fishing boats and quite a number of Japanese fishing boats. These latter were better equipped than the Filipino boats. Our little ferry sailed in and out among the various craft and finally approached a pier and slid alongside. It anchored and the mad scramble began as the Filipinos went down the gangplank. I remained on deck to watch and to see if I could locate the dark sedan. I didn't but by and by a well-dressed Filipino attracted my attention by shouting "Lieutenant!" and pointing toward a group of cars. I recognized him as Morrison's chauffeur, Adolpho. I waved in reply and went to get my baggage. On leaving the boys I made plans to see them later in the evening.

Morrison's Buick and chauffeur were at my disposal until late in the afternoon. Immediately I reported in at the 8th Military Headquarters to see what the latest dope was. I talked a short time with my CO, Col. Sledge and met Capt. Roy D. Gregory, Col. Sledge's assistant. Gregory was a West Point man and before coming to the southern islands he had been stationed at Fort McKinley with Philippine Scout troops. Originally he had come from a small town not far from Decatur, IL, which is the home of Millikin University. We had several mutual acquaintances we found out during the course of our conversation. The fact that we came from the same part of the country was enough to make us friends, let alone the fact that we were similar in character and had similar likes and dislikes. Roy was a pretty quiet fellow but he had plenty of gray matter upstairs. He made a wonderful record for himself during the war and rose to the rank of lieutenant colonel. Many a later day, in prison, we worked side by side in the Davao rice fields, on the logging detail or the farm or some other back breaking, heart rending work. I can still see him in my mind's eye standing in a rice paddy, covered with mud, wearing a battered old Filipino hat with a hole in the crown and g-string. There was a quiet grin on his face and a twinkle of dry humor in his eye even when going was the hardest. His is one of those pictures which will live with me to the end of my days.

From the headquarters I went downtown shopping for cooking utensils and canned food. I found some wonderful candied yams, a haircut, shampoo and shave. From there I went out to Morrison's house for a shower and back downtown to meet Morrison. The first thing we did was to find a botica (drug store to you) and get some ice cream and cokes. (I had been living on boiled water for the last month and bathing out of a five-gallon gasoline can).

I spent the evening with Morrison, his wife Buster and little boy, Kenneth. They had a beautiful home out on the lower slopes of the mountains, looking to the mountains and over the city. Their home was quite palatial and very, very comfortable.

I didn't realize how much I had missed ice water, easy chairs, screens from mosquitoes, the latest magazines, electric lights and a large nice soft bed. This was the first time in five weeks I had relaxed enough to think about all these luxuries. Yes, that shave, haircut and shampoo were first class luxuries. Anybody who has really been around would agree with me that it is only the softies who take even those ordinary things for granted.

Later that evening K.L. took me to the only air-cooled theater in town and I almost froze. After that we went out to the Country Club where I met several other Army men whom I had heard of but hadn't met.

First Lt. Russell Cracraft was one of the first of these Army men I met at the club. I don't remember where he came from but he had charge of a PA camp at Argao, Cebu which was directly across the strait from my camp. Like myself he was out all alone.

The second lad I met resembled myself in stature and build. To make things more confusing his name was Miner and it was spelled just like mine. He was 1st Lt. John S. Miner from Pomona and Laguna Beach, CA. John was called Jack part of the time and "Buck" at other times. I was called Bill and often we were mixed up, both of us being called "Buck" at times. We tried to figure out if we were any relation to each other. We finally gave it up as a bad job, but both of us always suspected that we were distantly related. Never at anytime yet have I come across somebody of my name who was not distantly related to me somehow. Jack was in charge of a camp near Medellian, at the north end of the Island of Cebu.

Another lad was 1st Lt. Robert P. Chrisman from Los Angeles. Chrisman, along with Jack Miner, was one of the few who had been able to bring their own cars with them. Chrisman was stationed at a PA camp right at the edge of Cebu and had his mess and quarters with the headquarters at Cebu.

Second Lt. Dick McKawn was another stationed in the PA camp at Cebu. I don't remember much about his background, but I dimly recall that he was an orphan and lived somewhere in the bay region of San Francisco.

At the Cebu camp was also stationed a 2nd Lt. Howard Humphreys. Humphreys claimed two homes. One was in the Virgin Islands where his parents lived. His father was a Navy officer, I believe. The other was his legal address which he gave as McLean County near Bloomington, IL. Later I found out he owned 335 acres of the finest cornbelt land in the US and had a fiancee standing by. He will appear from time to time in my events until he died in faraway Moji, Japan.

Somewhere about this time I met a Maj. Howard J. Edmands. Edmands was a Philippine Scout officer and had been in the islands for years. He knew the islands well and the natives too. His wife, Jane, was back in the States somewhere and his daughter, Shirley, was attending Knox College, from which I graduated five years before. Edmands had lived a colorful life up to the time I met him and he lived an even more colorful one after the war broke, until he died, a prisoner on the white sand dunes of the beach of San Fernando La Union, Luzon.

At another time at the headquarters of the Southern Forces, I met a young Capt. William L. Robinson. He was West Point 1937 and seemed to be right on the ball at the time. During the war, before the surrender, he rose to be a lieutenant colonel on Gen. Sharp's staff. Later in prison he was one of the administrative officers in the Davao colony. I never got to know him very well as he never went out on work details, that I know of. On board the ship taking the Southern Island prisoners from Bugo, Mindanao to Davao he was slapped on the face by the Nips. Later in prison when his eyes went bad it was rumored that the Nips had injured one of the optical nerves. Later one half the people in the camp had their eyes go bad, so it was generally attributed to malnutrition.

Also in General, then Col. Sharp's office, I met a Capt. William Halloway, cook, an Englishman by birth. Sometimes he was called Dash Cook. His branch was in the adjutant general's department, as I remember. He became a lieutenant colonel on Gen. Sharp's staff. There were some who made fun of him in various ways, but when it came to the final stand I will eagerly say that he showed himself a hero during the second bombing of our prison ship, on the trip from Manila to Moji, Japan. He should be awarded a citation for his efforts and the service he rendered the wounded during and after that bombing and strafing. When most people were huddling in groups on the floor of the hold he was up asking everybody who could spare a rag, torn undershirt, handkerchief, etc. to let him have it for the wounded. If someone had a rag he would wade through the blood, torn bodies, the dead and debris to get it and then he would take it to a wounded soldier. He did that for others regardless of danger to himself and he did not husband his strength while doing his good deed. Often to stir around and exhaust yourself proved fatal because there was no food to restore your strength. Col. Halloway, cook, died of exhaustion and malnutrition a few days after we landed in Moji. I wonder how many people are now alive because of his efforts. It's people like him and his deed that make me proud that I am an American. Time and again I saw little deeds of kindness turn the tide of a man's life.

In this same headquarters I met MSgt. Iphriam Iglewitz. Iglewitz had been stationed on Corregidor under Lt. Col. Clair M. Conzelman of Barrie, VT. I first new Iglewitz and later in prison I became very close friends with Col. Conselman. Iglewitz was very helpful in some of my administrative work.

Another officer that I met at this headquarters, was Col. Braddock, MC. Col. Braddock was a gentlemen and a scholar. He was an active physician and surgeon and regardless of the occasion he was always courteous. I remembered the first time he spoke to me he used the word "Sir." I was just a 1st lieutenant and he was a colonel. Before that conversation was over I understood why he was so well-liked by those around him. Years later in Muken prison I saw him give his few spare clothes away, in the face of an approaching semi-Arctic winter, to American soldiers with far less than he. I am glad to acknowledge receiving a woolen blouse from him. I saw Col. Braddock several times before the war.

Each time I was in Cebu I called to see Col. Sharp. Sometimes I saw the colonel and sometimes I didn't. Since he was the CO of the Southern Islands he was often out on an inspection somewhere. I think he visited my camp twice.

A little later than this about the middle of October 1941, there were at least two other officers who came to Cebu and I got to know them before the war.

The first was 1st Lt. Lyles G. Hardin from Rock Hill, SC. Hardin's father had been a minister and died when he was still young. His mother was then Dean of Women, not far from Rock Hill. Hardin was about six feet one and weighed over 200 pounds, had a wonderful disposition and a keen sense of humor. We soon nicknamed him "Tiny" and "Tiny" he remained to us until he went down on the prison ship. Tiny was stationed at Argao, Cebu, with Lt. Cracraft.

The second was 2nd Lt. Lee Johnson of Scotland Neck, SC. This Lee Johnson should not be confused with Maj. Lee Johnson who was an older man. Johnson had a southern accent so thick you could cut it in slices and butter your bread with it. He was in charge of guarding of military supplies on Mactan Island in the harbor of Cebu.

Another officer I met about this time was 1st Lt. Calin B. Whitehurst. One of the first things he did was to show me a picture of his wife Rose. Whitehurst was in the 8th District Headquarters with Capt. Gregory and Col. Sledge before the war started.

Prior to the war, it usually at some social gathering in Cebu City on a weekend that all these officers would get together. Not all I have mentioned were together any one time. It took two or three weekends in Cebu before I met them all. I remember the first weekend there because it was my first return to civilization after living in what was a foreign land for a month. I had a good visit with my old company commander, Capt. Robert Johnston, who was then Col. Sharp's S-4 and Capt. Al Kircher who was the engineer for Col. Sharp's staff.

In addition to these Army men, I met quite a number of civilians both Spanish and American. Of the first was Edward Aboitez whose family owned the La Naviera Filipinas Steamship Co. and some of his friends. Among the civilians were Capt. and Mrs. C.J. Martin, manager of Cebu Stevedoring Co.; Mr. William Ogan, owner of bus lines on Cebu and Bohol and who had been a soldier in the Spanish-American War; Mr. William Noble, son of Fredrick Noble, both of Standard Oil in the Philippines. Mr. and Mrs. Self, Mr. and Mrs. Miller, Mr. and Mrs. Edward Short of the Goodyear Rubber Co., Mr. Dave Offleck of Proctor and Gamble, Dr. Hawks of the US Public Health Service and others.

There was a dance at the club that night and I met several Spanish girls, Maria Theresa Aboiter, Carmen Godenez, Ester Moro, daughter of the Cebu harbor master, Sofita Pastuer. About midnight the Morrisons and I left the club and returned to their residence.

That night I slept in a real honest bed, the first since I had left the States some three months before. Since that time I had slept on Army cots or less. It was a wonderful feeling to be between clean white sheets in a wide bed. A bed so large that it would be large for two. Large enough you didn't feel cramped by the mosquito net around it and there was a light at the head! I felt like a white man again and read myself to sleep with a two-month old American magazine, new to us out there in the Orient.

The weekend was over far too soon. By noon the next day I was back on that ferry to Tubigon. Col. Sledge and his adjutant, Perfecto Mabugat, who was later to be transferred to my camp and I have spoken of elsewhere, were aboard. Col. Sledge was going over on an inspection tour of the Bohol camps. I visited with him all the way over, mostly catching up on the trend of things concerning our training and the world situation. He, like myself was wondering how many days of peace we had left. Things were looking black for Russia.

I resumed my schedule of training on return from Cebu. A few days later came a memorandum from the Southern Headquarters to the effect that at the end of the first six weeks training, a party for the troops would be held. This was more grief, but orders were orders. Theoretically we were supposed to persuade the community to throw the party for the troops. Well, that was the American way, not the Filipino way. I was already out of pocket for expenses and I just dug down some more. I assessed every officer in camp, the scout sergeant, the corporal and myself 10 Pesos. I appointed Lt. Estralla chairman of the party committee and told him, "take over."

The Filipinos under Lt. Estralla decided they wanted to throw a dance and serve ice cream for refreshments. This was growing interesting. The boys would have to have girls if they danced. Problem, how to get the girls? You don't just invite the girls and they come. The Filipino priest frowned on dancing in Calape so I had to pay a personal call to the Father inviting him to attend our Army dance in order to get his blessing on the party. The same thing for the major in order to get more community support, then the school teachers of the high school where the girls were and via the teachers send invitations to the duennas of the girls. As it turned out the duennas were often the whole family; papa, mamma and all the children. By this time I was tearing my hair. Oh, for the good old American way of living. If you wanted to take a girl to a dance you simply called her and the two of you went out to your dance! Right then and there I decided if I ever courted a girl I was going to do it in the USA. I went through the same procedure at another nearby town. Give me a few more years of this and I would become a first rate politician. I had to agree to furnish transportation for town dignitaries and many of the girls, plus duennas. Hiring an orchestra was the smallest and simplest item. Finally there was the ice cream for refreshments. I had to send Lt. Estralla to Cebu City to arrange to have that especially packed and sent over by boat to Tubigon the day of the party. He met the boat for delivery of it. That had to be well taken care of, ice cream melts, particularly in the tropics and you have it out in the provinces about as often as you find a chicken with a mouth full of teeth. I really believe the ice cream was about the most important item of the evening to those boys.

The party was a success; there were enough girls for the boys to dance with, around 80 with various members of their families. All in all there must have been 250 guests, only 80 of which entertained the soldiers. The rest were, shall we say, the "overhead." Where those girls got their dresses and why they had them I don't know. These weren't the south sea island girls I was used to seeing under a palm tree or in a Nepa house. Everyone came in an up-to-date American dress. Some were long formals and others were conventional dresses appropriate for evening wear. I could have easily imagined myself back in a high school gym at a community party as far as those girls were concerned. They danced American or Spanish dances, except for special numbers, to American or Spanish tunes. I was learning things. From the dance floor I let my eyes wander to the townspeople on the side lines. Men and women and a few young children in colorful Filipino and Filipina garbs. The old hillman who was squatting on his haunches wearing a pair of dark shorts and a pink flowered embroidered tunic so thin you could see through it. He was bare legged, barefooted and he was chewing betel nut. His wife was standing beside him in a long embroidered dress of some strange thick material unfamiliar to me. I wondered which one of those dusky beauties on the dance floor was their daughter. In contrast to this couple was the mayor of Calape and his wife, both in up-to-date white American clothes. He in a white suit and she in a white formal. This was truly a land of contrasts; south sea island and occidental cultures were mixing here. To me the native dances were more interesting than our own. Shortly before midnight we served the ice cream which luckily was still nice and solid. Everybody was served. The party then ended and I sent the girls and their duennas home, the dignitaries and finally the orchestra. I turned in about 2:30 a.m. a physical wreck. It may have been fun for the soldiers, but it was work to me! About 4:00 a.m. one of my lieutenants woke me up to tell me the truck taking the orchestra back to Tagbilaran had turned over. There was no rest for the weary. I had to go see about it. Luckily nobody was killed and I was able soon to get the truck repaired so it would again run.

There are always some amusing things about any detail if one has a sense of humor. I made an inspection of the grounds one day about two months after the camp began. There was too much paper around the Guard House rooms, so I gathered it up as evidence when I jumped somebody. Returning to the office I sat down at my desk and idly looked at the scraps. On one of the pieces, in pencil writing, I found a perfect gem of a love letter written to some Filipina girl by one of the soldiers. It ran something like this:

"Guard House
This date

Senorita Meo:
Today you have walked past the guard house so many times that I fell in love with you. You look so pretty with the hibiscus in your dark hair. You don't know my name, but you will when you read this letter and "poco" Jose will give it to you when you return. I will meet you tonight under the palm tree near this place."

I remember thinking that the Americans didn't have anything on the Filipinos. The way of a man with a maid is the same regardless of the land or the language.

There is a custom of the Filipinos that I like very much. In the daytime you can walk through the streets of the towns and hardly anybody speaks to you. Yet when evening comes, a feeling of friendliness floats through the air. The work clothes disappear and the evening or holiday clothes appear. The older people sit around their houses, but the younger people stroll through the streets or under the palm or banana trees. Whenever you meet them on the street singly or in a group, or if you pass a house surrounded by middle aged or elderly people the greeting is sure to come, "Good evening, Sir" or Buenos Noches, Señor." You reply with a similar greeting. If you show any inclination to visit they will invite you to a seat and bring out some coconut milk, beer or tuba (a native liquor made out of fermented coconut palm sap). The white man has made his reputation with the islanders, the reputation of drinking constantly.

In some places the funeral custom of the Filipinos is quite different from ours. We mourn our dead indefinitely. In the Philippines they have the funeral and mourn the dead. After a short period of mourning, two days or two weeks, the family and friends dress up in their best and have a party celebrating the new life the recently deceased has entered into. This is a happy occasion. After the celebration is over they then act like normal people without sorrow in the family.

Some interesting things happened in the field in the line of training. We had series of night marches. One night I had the troops start down the road. Knowing that some didn't want to go, I was making a check on who was in camp. The camp was deserted except for the guard detail, so I took off down the road through town after the troops. About 100 yards from camp I ran into two Filipino soldiers carrying their canteens.

"Where in the hell have you been? Don't you know you are supposed to be on the march?"

"Yes sir, er, but sire we have been to fill our canteens!"

"Couldn't you fill them at the water faucet at the barracks?"

"But sire, my friend had the canteens."

"Sire, we left the "cuan" at the house of his friend last night. We went to get them tonight and did not get back before this!"

About this time I began to smell something besides a rat. "Let me see those canteens!" and snatched them away before the surprised soldier knew what was happening. I unscrewed the cap of a canteen and took an incautious sniff. That full breath made me sneeze so hard I lost my cap and one of the Filipinos snickered.

"What in the devil do you have in there?"

"Tuba, sire," he answered quivering.

"Hell, I thought it was TNT the way it knocked my hat off," I muttered too astonished to do other than pick up my hat.

"Officer of the Day, Lt. Gonzaga!" shouting.

"Yes sire! coming." answered Gonzaga from the guard house.

"Put these men in the guard house." I then emptied both canteens (two quarts of tuba) and handed the canteens back to their owners.

This episode resulted in such a delay that I had to commandeer a carameda driver and his pony to trot three miles down the road to catch up with the troops.

Another time we were having a night problem up in the jungle-covered mountains. To get up to the foot of the mountains we had been following ridge tops. Traveling these ridge tops under a full tropical moon is an experience few people could have and ever forget. The night air is soft and balmy and often on the breezes float the rich, sweet perfume of the night-blooming cereus. That perfume itself is unforgettable. The moon overhead pales the stars by its brilliance. Small, fleecy, white, clouds float gently over it now and then, momentarily dimming its brilliance. At times we walked under palm trees or thick tropical ferns, in other places we passed through small areas of jungle. In other places the ridge was so sharp that it was barren and we could look for miles in all directions. With the brilliant moon we could distinguish the different shades of green in the forests below, at times we saw night blooming flowers and in areas of the forest there were flocks of lightning bugs flicking their little lights on and off. Off to the west below us was a low even forest of coconut trees, a strip of white sandy beach, beyond that the deep dark blue, almost black arm of the sea and miles away rising out of the sea in a black, broken, line was the Island of Cebu. Behind us to the east rose the nearby jungle-covered mountains. On either side of us running parallel, were deep ravines and other ridges running from the mountains to the sea. They were spotted with the deep, dark green of the jungle.

We were having a rest stop on the high, bare top of a ridge where we could enjoy the beauty of the night. I lay on my stomach, my chin cupped in my hands drinking in the beauty of the night. Suddenly I felt something icy cold crawling up my pants leg. I stood up and stomped. From out of that pant's leg tumbled a centipede nine inches long and bigger around than my thumb. It was coal black and started to wiggle away. I cursed and stomped on it. Then I lay down again after looking over the ground carefully.

At this time one of my Filipino officers came and asked if the soldiers could sing. I affirmed so the soldiers sang their native songs there above the moonlit jungles. One sergeant had a very melodious voice.

"Sergeant, you have a very good voice and sing well."

"Thank you sir. Would the lieutenant like me to sing a song for him?"

"Yes, indeed."

The sergeant spoke to some soldiers in dialect. To my astonishment, in almost perfect English, he sang the American song, I Understand, to the background of humming by his companions. This blending of cultures continued to amaze me. Each time I found something new.

I had another exhibit by the soldiers. This time it was pure Filipino art. One afternoon after a day's heavy training in the jungle we came back to the edge of a coconut plantation where it was so pleasant that I gave the company a rest period. The soldiers started to sing. To break the monotony, I had one of the officers break them into two groups and started some competition. From singing it went to other things and finally to what I would call "bolo fencing." Up to that time I thought I had seen some fancy fencing. These lads took a bayonet in each hand and started some intricate knife work. They were so fast and came so close to each other that I stopped the use of bayonets and made them use straight sticks. Those boys went to work then and really out did themselves. Right then and there I made a mental reservation never to get within reach of one of those knives. What I saw there convinced me that the boys in the "Three Musketeers" were amateurs to the best of these lads of mine. I learned something new about my men.

Another amusing incident occurred in my camp office. A Filipino solider, who for obvious reasons I shall call Joe, walked into my office and saluted.

"Sire, lieutenant, may I a..use the cuan?" and pointed to the typewriter. (Remind me to explain this word cuan). Joe lived on Luzon, had a wife and several children and was well set in the Army for a career.

"Sure, here's some paper." Joe sat down and started clicking the machine. I was curious because the boys didn't usually come in and ask to use the machine. I noted that he took the usual number of carbon copies. As he typed I got more and more curious. He would type a few words, think a bit, type some more, etc. He wasn't running true to form. Joe finished, took the original and the first carbon, tore them up and threw them away. This was too much for me. As he covered up the machine:

"Joe, what in the devil are you up to?"

He looked startled and then sheepish, but made no move to show it to me.

"Here, let me see that, you rascal!" and grinned at him to take the sharpness out of the words.

"Just a cuan, sire," and grinned weakly as he handed it to me. I looked at the carbon copy. It was a letter in the following form of military correspondence:

Subject: Marriage

To: Commanding General of the Army, Manila, PI

Paragraph No. I. The undersigned was a ... in the Army, so many years service, drew such and such pay, was single, etc.

Paragraph No. 2. Under A.R. dash dash dash a soldier of his standing was qualified to marry.

Paragraph No. 3. Request the undersigned to granted permission to marry Miss ...

"What the hell Joe, you're married!" I said looking at him in amazement.

"Oh, but sire, my wife, she is in Luzon and I must have a girl friend here."

"But Joe, you don't need this to get a girl friend, do you?"

"But sire, she is a school teacher and she wants to get married. I got one wife already, sire and she is very good. I don't want two wives. I just want a girl friend here."

"Well?"

"Sire, I take this carbon copy to give to my girl friend. I tell her only the commanding general in Manila can give me permission to marry. I tell her it will take three months for the answer to come from Manila. We move to Carmen one month. I give her this letter and it makes things okay with her."

I was too nonplused to do anything but try to hide a grin. Talk about a wolf. I made it a policy never to interfere with the private lives of my troops except to help them.

Joe took the letter to his pretty little school teacher and the following night her friends gave her a betrothal party.

I mentioned the word "cuan." It is of Spanish origin and the Filipinos use it to fill in when they lack a word, regardless of the language. It's used in every dialect I came in contact with and can mean everything under the sun. It's pronounced "Quon." I have had it used four times in one sentence and it meant a different thing each time. Example, by one Filipino in my office, "put the cuan, on the cuan and Jose is getting the cuan and Fredrico has the cuan." This was accompanied by various gestures. When I got it all boiled down, it meant simply this, "I put the typewriter on the table, Jose is getting the paper and Fredrico has the cover!"

It was a merry life trying to comprehend a dozen languages.

Toward the first of November I made another one of my visits to Cebu City. It stands out in my memory for two different things. One, my first meeting with a little man named V.R. Brown and second, it was my last free vacation or day off for almost exactly four years, 1941-46.

I again went to Tubigon and took the little ferry over to Cebu City. The Morrison car met me and at his home during dinner I met Dr. V.R. Brown. We called him Doc because he had three PhDs from various parts of the world. These doctorates came from the University of New Zealand, University of Peru at Lima and the Royal Academy at Madrid, Spain. Knowledge was, as he expressed it, his "stock in trade." Doc had traveled all over the world, not as a tourist but as a scientist. He was at home in the East Indies, South America and at the outbreak of the war he had been doing some forestry research in Rio Muni or Spanish Guinea in central Africa. Somehow or another he got a car and drove clear across equatorial Africa to the Indian Ocean, took a boat for India and from there he got to the Philippines. He was then at Cebu teaching English when I met him. He was "good" in any subject from Shakespeare to chemistry. Before the surrender came, he was making hand grenades for the Army. I have met many people with knowledge galore in their heads, but few who had a practical application for all their knowledge. Doc was practical to the last degree. When we were imprisoned by the Japanese it was Doc Brown more than anybody else who upheld the morale of all of us. He took over the prison kitchen and made "food out of nothing." We owe Doc for making the unpalatable food edible.

The other highlight of that visit was the picnic Sunday. Maria Thresa, her cousin, Sofita Pasture and Ester Moro were the girls. Edward Aboitex, lieutenants Gordon Utke, Howard Humphrey, Herr and myself were the boys. The girls took us out to the country home of the Aboitex, which nestled under the coconut palms on Lillion Beach, north of Cebu City. There they served a complete picnic of both Spanish and American foods. Later we went banca riding. I was in one with Ester Moro and ventured out to where the rollers were fully eight feet between the crest and pit. We got swamped. I remember how she laughed and instructed me how to assist her to empty the water from the banca. Once emptied, we climbed in, she took the paddle and we continued on our way over the waves.

On Nov. 23, 1941, all the elements of the 81st Infantry were assembled in the 81st Div. cantonment at Carmen, Bohol. Some of the other elements of the 81st were there at that time. The concentration brought the following Americans together: Capt. Colin B. Whitehurst; Lts. Melvin Herr, Duane Casper of Walla Walla, WA; Richard Cook, Robert H. Pratt, Eldon McKown, Gordon Utke, William F. O'Connor, Howard Humphreys, John S. Miner, Robert P. Chrisman, Joseph Stensland, Russell H. Cracraft, Lyes G. Hardin, and Capts. Roy D. Gregory and Charles Hoyt. In addition to the above were Sgt. Pizonka, Cpl. Curtis L. Sizemore and Cpl. Smith. Also Capt. Jack Fritts of Galesburg, IL and Col. Woodbridge were present with a FA unit. There were a few others that arrived a little later after I left on a special mission to Cebu.

Comparing those first few days in the division cantonment with what I heard about similar areas in the States, I am convinced that the States areas were picnic. I never saw more flies in my life except once later on a prison ship. This area was quite large in its building area. The buildings were all new and hundreds of natives were still working in the area. The sanitation was such that you had to watch where you stepped or you had to wash your shoes.

The American officers were assigned in advisory capacity to the various units even down to the companies. Stensland, Utke, John S. Miner, Cracraft, Hardin and myself were all battalion advisers. The others were placed at key points around the division. Lt. McKown was division supply officer, Pratt was the transportation officer and I don't remember the posts or who was assigned to them.

There is an old saying that nothing remains the same very long in the Army. That was certainly true in those days. I had just gotten things semi-organized in my battalion when I was called into division headquarters one morning at 0715.

"Miner, in 20 minutes Col. Woodbridge is going down to Tagbilaran. You are to accompany him that far and then take the boat for Cebu. Once in Cebu you will receive two more battalions, receive their equipment and bring them back to Tagbilaran. I will have transportation awaiting you at Tagbilaran on your return. Who do you want to help you?"

"Lt. Stensland, sir."

"All right, I'll get a hold of Stensland and inform him. You go get your bedroll."

Saluting, "Yes sir," and walked out. I double timed to my quarters and started furiously rolling my bed.

Sure enough, in 20 minutes Col. Woodbridge sounded his horn outside my quarters. Stensland was already in. After dumping my bedroll on a fender, I climbed in the car and we started to Tagbilaran.

The drive down to Tagbilaran was very beautiful in jungle-mountain scenery. Some of the canyons were deep and sheer and the streams at their bottoms were white and rushing. I remember thinking, "I would hate to have to walk through those jungle covered mountains." In just a few short months afterwards I was "thanking God" for similar jungle covered mountains in which to find concealment from the Japanese.

Joe and I arrived in Tagbilaran in time to sail on the noon boat for Cebu City. This was a quiet five-hour cruise. We were the only Americans on the boat and there were practically no Filipinos on board. I remember how we loathed the steamed rice dinner with burned chicken soup, yet in just a few days the war was to start, this was around November 28 or 29.

On arriving at Cebu, Joe and I took a taxi out to the district headquarters at Lahug Field and reported in. Once there we found the troops would not arrive for 36 hours. We then took off for a day's rest.

I called on the Morrisons that evening and had another wonderful visit. The next morning I went down to the Southern Island Headquarters to see Col. Braddock, Force doctor and surgeon, about some stomach infection I had had for a number of weeks. After examining me thoroughly he decided to send me to Sternberg Hospital in Manila for observation and treatment. We were afraid of appendicitis. This was Friday morning; on Sunday night one of the inter-island boats, the Elcano, left for Manila. He told me to be ready to sail on it. On the way out I ran into Capt. Al Kircher. I told him the latest developments concerning myself.

Kircher said, "Bill, stop down at La Noviera Filipinas Steamship Co. office and tell Don Ramon Aboitez to put you in the same cabin with me. I have to return to Luzon to an engineering detail in Gen. MacArthur's headquarters in USAFFE (US Armed Forces in the Far East). This I did, glad to have him for the company.

The next two days were just routine checking of troops and equipment. Again our chief difficulties arose from the lack of comprehension of English on the part of a Filipino. Here is just one episode of the day. I get a Filipino corporal to run an errand for me.

"Corporal, take this note over to Lt. Stensland, the American lieutenant in building number 15. To get to building 15 take this road (pointing), go down to the second street, turn left and it is the second building on the right. There is a big black number 15 on the front of it. Now tell me what you are going to do."

"Sir, I am going to get somebody who can understand English."

By this time I knew never to be surprised at what happened. You'd send one after a book and he would bring you his neighbor's hat. I finally sent a sergeant who was familiar with the post to deliver the note to Joe.

By Sunday night at 7:00 p.m. I had helped Joe Stensland and Capt. Roy Gregory get all the troops on the boat and it sailed away. Two hours later, thoroughly exhausted, I was aboard the Elcano standing beside Al Kircher. We watched from the sun deck railing the busy turmoil below us as the ship's crew cast away the moorings and we put out to sea. We remained silent at the railing as we watched the harbor slip away from us and the shores of Mactan Island slide past us. The lights of Cebu City faded and were lost behind the palms on the shore. The ship rapidly passed the beacon light on the north tip of Mactan Island (where Magellan was killed) and then turned north. When we turned north we left Mactan behind, glided into the open sea and were struck by the full force of the low, rising, tropical full moon. The night was almost as light as day. After a few minutes of drinking in the beauty of the night, the clam, dark, flashing seas and the purple mountain peaks of Cebu behind us, we left the railing and Al took me over by the captain's cabin where he introduced me to Capt. Arondo, the ship's captain and a beautiful Spanish girl, named Romana Corominas. Senorita Corominas' family was part owner of the boat and the steamship line. The four of us fell to talking.

The next morning we spent the time sitting on the main deck talking, Kircher and myself.

Kircher said, "We're sitting on a bubble out here, a bubble called peace, which in turn is sitting on a base of TNT and there's little yellow b ... playing with a lighted match and the fuse to the whole setup. One of these days soon the whole thing is going to burst under us and we'll never know exactly what happened! (This was Dec. 2, 1941). The entire world will be in the fracas. As things now stand there is only one major power on the face of the earth which is not at war. That is the U.S. We can't stay out of it; it's impossible, regardless what the fools at home think about living in isolationism. We have got to get in the war and win it if we expect to preserve our way of living. All of Europe has been conquered but Russia who has her back to the wall and is almost exhausted. She has got to be given a breather and some equipment. The British don't have what it takes. They lack the resources in material, their ordinary cockney soldier is underfed, undernourished and doesn't have the physical lasting qualities that it takes to overcome the crack German armies. The British lost most of their equipment at Dunkirk. We will have to resupply it to them or they will fall whenever Hitler decides to invade England. I tell you, Bill, we sit here in the cool, calm luxury of the sea breezes, but the calm is the calm before the storm. A storm such as the human race has never seen before will sweep across the face of the entire earth. It's going to make the fracas in Europe to date look small; the U.S. is going to play the major role in it. The days of peace are over and the war is at hand. It's near, far nearer than most people realize."

I sat in silence trying to imagine such chaotic events and wondering how soon the tragedy would strike. Little did I dream that before the week was out, the bubble would have exploded and we were in the midst of war. Many, many times later at war and in prison I though how literally Al Kircher hit the nail on the head. I never knew him to be wrong in his common sense, matter of fact judgment.

The rest of the morning I spent visiting with the few other passengers aboard. Of these were a man and wife, Americans both extremely tall and refined looking who lived in Manila. They had been on a short business trip to the southern Philippines. He was the U.S. Steel representative in the Philippines. I asked her one time why she hadn't gone home while she could. Her reply was that she decided to stay with her husband and "risk it." She hadn't long to wait.

Kircher and I were eating lunch in the dining room about 1300. Kircher said "Wonder what the trouble is? The engines just shut down, the ship is losing speed and the breeze is fading out."

Looking out the window I said "You're right and there's a big island right off our starboard." I walked over to the doorway and out over the deck to the railing. There I stared at a tall peak rising out of the sea about a quarter of a mile away. It rose steeply from the water line to its pinnacle top. I took a good look and returned to our table.

"It's a fair-sized island with a sheer jungle clad peak rising in its middle. It must be a mile high. I'd hate to have to climb that baby."

"I hope we don't lie here long or it will be hot and we're short on water, according to the captain. Let's go see what the trouble is when we finish lunch."

On finishing our lunch we went up on the bridge to see Capt. Arondo. We found him perspiring freely and cursing his luck.

"What's the delay, captain?" asked Kircher.

"A broken tooth on one of the drive shaft gears and we can't turn the engine over without danger of tearing up the whole gear assembly. I have just radioed our Manila office for help. It will be 12 or 14 hours before a tug can arrive to tow us."

"Well, that isn't too bad, is it?" asked Kircher.

"We are very close to that rocky shore there (pointing to the breakers less than a quarter of a mile away). We have a fishtail wind and if it settles down to a steady blow from our port side it will cause us to drift right on to the rocks. It's too deep to anchor here off Sibouyan Island."

"That will be my first time for such an experience, so let's hope the wind turns to our favor. Come on, Bill, let's get in the shade and get what breeze we can. It's too hot up here."

Kircher and I found a couple of deck chairs, moved them into the shade on the starboard side of the deck and relaxed in them with our feet on the rail. We watched the breakers a short distance away to our front and tried to keep cool. By and by I fell asleep. When I awoke there was a cool, steady breeze in my face. The island with the mountain was definitely farther away than when I fell asleep. Time and nature had solved another problem which involved me. Before many months I was to find that time and nature were great friends of mine.

Time passed swiftly. After dinner there was a gorgeous sunset, the sun sinking into an island-infested sea far off to the west. As the sun set, a full moon became bright in the eastern sky. Soon the whole world was again bathed in brilliant white moonlight. Sibouyan Island stood stark and dark in the sky.

To our south and west was a dark silver sea bordered on the low horizon in the west by dark, low islands.

I climbed up on the sun deck. Near the wheelhouse was Kircher and Capt. Arondo. Several feet away seated near the railing with an empty chair beside her was Ramona Caromenas. This was sweet! Here was a charming senorita all alone on the sundeck of a ship afloat on a calm sea. Overhead was a lover's moon bringing out the beauty of the nearby forested island and the surrounding sea. Clearly it was a night for romance and there was no competition! I pulled a deck chair near Ramona, sat down and put my feet on the railing beside hers.

About 2:00 a.m. Wednesday morning I was awakened by a shout coming through my porthole. I arose and looked out. There was a tugboat coming alongside via the aid of a search light. I dressed and hurried topside to watch the tug toss us a line and slowly get the ship under way. After a loss of about 14 hours we resumed our journey in tow at the rate of about seven knots an hour instead of our usual 15. This delay caused us to arrive in Manila about 2000 Thursday night instead of noon that day. The next two days were slow but enjoyable, a repetition of Monday night and Tuesday. Thursday night I bade the U.S. Steel couple good luck, met Ramona's sister, Curly, as I said "adieus" to her and watched the unloading of the ship's cargo.

Kircher and I slept aboard that night.

The next morning I arose late and found a note from Kircher saying he was going after transportation for us and our baggage.

I went down to the dining room for breakfast and there to my amazement was Morrie Cleland of Cebu City, the diesel engineer of the La Naviera Steamship Co. I had seen Morrie at the club the evening I had boarded the Elcano in Cebu. Here he had arrived in Manila ahead of me via boat and was on hand to take care of the ship's repairs.

This was getting to be a small world after all. I sat down and we had ham and eggs together. After a short visit I took off to finish my packing. Al Kircher arrived shortly with an Army truck; we loaded our baggage and shoved off. He for MacArthur's headquarters and I for Sternberg General Hospital. I left him downtown on the Escolta Street to make some purchases and he was later to bring my baggage to Sternberg Hospital. It was Friday morning, Dec. 5, 1941. After taking care of some business affairs, I reported in at Sternberg Hospital. On being assigned to a ward, I relaxed and took it easy while I looked over the patients in the surrounding beds.

I heard a voice from the other end of the room, "Hello Miner! What do they have you in here for?"

Recognizing the individual, "Hello yourself! What do they have you in here for Magers?"

"Malaria, I picked up the bug shortly after we landed."

"I just can't understand it! Here you are, a 2nd lieutenant in the Air Corps with malaria. I thought they kept you guys so far up in the air all the time that you never had a chance to come in contact with the ground maladies."

"They can't do it without some planes! I've been over here five months and the planes we're supposed to have haven't arrived yet. We were told when we sailed in June that they were on the way. Somebody is asleep at home. Who is holding up the works, Congress or the public in general? It looks to me like Tojo is going to take over pretty soon. One of our boys was up a week ago and he swears he saw some Nip planes over northern Luzon. He says we sure as hell don't have any like them, so they couldn't be ours."

"Hold on here and give me a chance to get my breath before you start taking it completely away! Who else is in here that I know?"

"None of the boys that came over on our boat. Remember that pretty, blond, good-looking nurse that came over on the boat with us? She is here on duty in this ward. You'll see her when they make the rounds."

With that, Lt. Magers went back to his bed and I started to unpack what little I would need for a protracted stay.

"Can I help you with that, lieutenant?" came a voice from my back across an empty bed. I turned around to meet the friendly smile of a slender, dark young lieutenant.

"My name is Montoya," he continued and walked around to meet me with an outstretched hand. I shook hands.

"I hardly think I need any help, but I am glad to meet you. Where are you from?"

"Santa Fe, New Mexico, and its a mighty fine place to be from!"

"No doubt it is. I imagine the least you could say against it is that the climate is a lot cooler! What are you in for, malaria?"

"No, not malaria. I hurt my back some time ago and it hasn't cleared up so they sent me in here to give it a rest." He grinned and so did I.

"Well, are you?"

"Sort of. At least I have caught up on my sleep."

By the end of the afternoon I had met all the men in my ward and had found out that my recent CO, Col. Theodore Sledge was in a nearby ward. I paid him a short visit and returned to my ward in time for the evening's rounds by the doctor.

The longer I live the smaller the world becomes. I sat on my bed and waited for the doctor and nurse. In they walked after a short delay. The first in, carrying the chart was the good-looking blonde nurse. I recognized her as one of the 13 nurses who had come over on the boat with me. The doctor who followed was tall, slender and familiar looking. He stopped in front of my bed.

"Hello, Miner, when did you come to town? I thought you went to the Southern Islands?"

"Fancy seeing you here. I had forgotten that Bill (Harold) Bertrand worked here. I always though he spent his time over at Santa Monica Courts drinking Cokes." (Bill grinned and the nurse smiled). "Seriously, though, Doc, I have a pain in my tummy, so they sent me up for observation and treatment."

"Hard to say just now what the trouble is. You'll likely spend Christmas here, because we'll give you a complete checkup."

Bill Bertrand and I had become friends in the Santa Monica Courts where both of us had lived a few months before. I saw him briefly the next day or two as he went about his duties at Sternberg Hospital. Before I had a good visit with him the war had started and I was on my way back to the Southern Islands. I never saw Bill again until October 1944 when I found him working in the Bilibid Prison Hospital. I came upon him going through his wards one day shortly after I arrived. He was part of the hospital detail and I was part of a large group of prisoners waiting to be shipped to Japan. Bill was much thinner then, but he still had his good humor and his same flashing smile for his patients. He had practically no medicine or equipment to work with and as I watched him I saw that often all he could give his patients was his flashing smile. On observing some of the live skeletons, I imagine this last was often pretty hard to do. Bill was still a member of the hospital detail when I left aboard the Oryoku Maru. Six weeks later he was rescued and taken back to the U.S.

The next two days were uneventful. On Saturday, December 6, Col. Carrol came through making an inspection. He told me to put my pajama top on because I might be seen from the outside. This burned me up. Which was the most important? The patients' comfort or the fact some Filipino might look into the hospital window? There is only one sensible answer, the patient's comfort. The next day was Sunday, December 7. I went to church in the morning and in the afternoon Al Kircher came to see me. The two of us visited all afternoon with Col. Sledge. Things were calm in the hospital that evening and night.

After darkness settled, a beautiful tropical full moon bloomed in the night from behind the nearby palm trees. The soft night breezes blew over us as we sat on the porch of the ward.

Everything was quiet and peaceful in Sternberg Hospital.

A few minutes to 0600 on Monday morning, Dec. 8, 1941, everybody was quietly sleeping. Two or three minutes to six a woman's shrill voice pealed through the ward.

"My God, get up!! Pearl Harbor has been bombed!" There stood our blonde ward nurse. Every man in the ward roused up and stared at her and the men around her. The voice had awakened them and the ringing words slowly penetrated through the minds of some. Others were sleeping too soundly to do more than stare stupidly. Mutters followed.

"Oh yeah?"

"The hell you say."

"If you want to wake us, you at least don't have to do this to us, do you?"

"No kidding?"

"Will you say that again, Nurse?'

"Did you say what I think you said?"

"Will you guys shut up! I want some sleep!"

The nurse said "Pearl Harbor has been bombed!!" She looked frightened.

"Will somebody turn on a radio! Tony (Antonio Montoya), turn on your radio. We'll find out if it's true."

Tony jumped out of bed and almost lost his oversized pajamas. I started to laugh at him. He grabbed his receding pants and pulled them up while he turned on the radio. It began to sputter. He found a station over which an excited babble of voices could dimly be heard. Suddenly the voice of Don Bell, local Manila radio commentator, burst out startlingly clear.

"...most distressing incident has occurred. News just now flashed from Hawaii says Pearl Harbor has just been bombed. As yet we have no details about this, but indications are that the news is true. As soon as we get the details we will broadcast them, so just stand by for the details any moment..."

No one was asleep any longer. All were out of bed in various disarray, huddled around the nurse, Tony and Tony's little radio. There was a breathless hush in the ward and the men looked from face to face trying to realize just what the future meant, as Don Bell's voice ceased. Some looked white and sick, others stunned and uncomprehending. Somebody relaxed and said, "Well, boys, this is it!"

Nobody said anything for just a minute, then I heard Magers mutter...

"Damn it, we don't have any planes, not enough, not near enough! I feel like a fish in the rain barrel."

The radio announcer, Don Bell said, "We have a little news now." (There was a general scurry back to Tony's radio). "It seems that early this morning a large number of strange planes suddenly attacked Pearl Harbor. We haven't heard yet as to where they came from, but reliable sources think they came from Japan. Just how much damage they did at Pearl Harbor we don't know. All reports are very vague..."

"It won't be long now," said Tony, "I am going to pack and get ready to go back to my unit. Its those damned Nips, I'll bet. They'll be here before the day is out!"

Tony was right.

The ward went to breakfast about 0700 and was back by 0800. Meantime, there were continuous news flashes coming in over the radio. They were not much, but if one would assimilate them and sift them, a trend could be seen. Something dire had happened at Pearl Harbor; it had caught our forces by surprise, our Air and Naval forces had suffered badly and finally we could expect an attack on the Philippine Islands at any moment. That was the gist of it. Shortly after 0800 the music suddenly stopped. It was interrupted, and Don Bell came on the air.

"We have just had word from Baguio that they are under a bombing attack up there. Before we could get any of the details our source of communication quit on us."

The boys in the ward, huddled around the radio, looked at each other. One lieutenant said, "that's getting close. They may be down here to bomb the harbor pretty soon. I am going to ask to go back to my unit."

For the next hour or so the radio kept bringing intermittent news flashes about the current situation in the Philippines, Hawaii and the U.S. We knew definitely that the Japs had attacked us in Hawaii, around Pearl Harbor and in the Philippines. Just what other points in between we did not know at that time.

Sometime after 1000, word came over the radio via Don Bell. "Our Army Forces are now undergoing a heavy air attack at Clark Field and Fort Stotsenburg. There seems to be a large number of enemy bomber concentration on our airfields and we can expect some of them any moment at Nichols Field." (five to 10 kilometers from Manila). "Everybody should stand by in case the city should be attacked."

Shortly after that the radio quit giving new details as it received them. It became more vague and confused. It didn't follow up the threads it had started to spin in the early morning. The censorship was beginning to function, leaving people up in the air as to what really was happening. I will never forget those first few hours of the war. Everything was in confusion, it seemed. In the matter of a few hours our entire civilization out there had to change from peacetime routine to defensive war conditions. The war was a surprise to most people and the realization that we were at war and under attack left many people mentally stunned. This in turn left them helpless and confused, particularly the latter. The streets of the city became filled with native carameda carts full of worldly goods of people trying to get out of Manila. When an air raid alarm sounded, the people just disappeared off the streets. Where they went I never could decide.

Inside the hospital there was a lull in routine activity. The doctors and nurses disappeared shortly after breakfast and it was almost noon before we saw them again. The rumor got around that they were being briefed as to their new war time organization within the hospital.

Meantime, we in the war, hung around the radios eagerly listening to every scrap of news that came over it.

About an hour after the news came over the radio that Clark Field was being bombed, news flashed through the hospital that the airfield was completely destroyed with tremendous losses. Some of the doctors and nurses were going up to help take care of the wounded and dead, of which there were so many the hospitals there could not take care of them. They were taking some ambulances and buses up to bring back the overflow of wounded who could travel. This, as countless other rumors were proved, was not quite as bad as it sounded. I think they failed to injure one or two percent of our Air Force and there were some survivors of the attack. It was perfectly true, though, that there were so many dead and wounded that the Clark Field and Stotsenburg hospitals could not take care of them. When the buses and ambulances returned, they brought men who should have never been moved, but it was bring them or leave them outdoors exposed to the elements.

Col. Sledge, Lt. Tony Montoya and myself stood by the gateway and watched the Clark Field convoy roll out of the hospital.

Col. Sledge said, "I hope it gets there safely without an air attack."

"I hope so too, colonel; those boys up there must need help pretty bad," said Lt. Montoya.

If I remember correctly, there was another air attack somewhere in Luzon that afternoon. The radio reports were very vague and nobody could make out many details. The only thing that seemed certain was that there was a war on and we were on the receiving end of it. Two or three of the patients of the hospital had gone down to some of the various headquarters to see if they could find out how things were going and how much damage had been done to our forces in Hawaii. The general feeling was that catastrophe had hit and shaken the very foundation of our defense. A great many wondered if Hawaii was to be the initial invasion point and the Philippines bypassed. All of us feared that the harbor at Manila would be bombed before the day was over. Toward the middle of the afternoon somebody came in with some news from MacArthur's headquarters. This news was that the real news was so bad that it wasn't being put out even at the headquarters. Only two or three men were supposed to know and they were supposed to be sworn to secrecy. To make a long story short, "Things were in a hell of a mess!"

During the day the city of Manila had several air alarms. No plane came over the city, but there were undoubtedly hostile planes not very far away. To my memory Nichols Field had not yet been bombed. During the first day the crowds on the city streets would fluctuate greatly. The streets would be filled with people and then the air raid siren would sound and the people would suddenly scurry for cover.

The evening meal was over before dark because the city was going into an absolute blackout. At the hour just before dark I was out on the ward porch which faces the street and looks across into the park in Manila. There were several field officers sitting there, among them Col. Sledge, discussing the situation in hushed voices. At this time Capt. Al Kircher came out onto the ward porch and inquired for me. He had some of my baggage with him.

He was mobbed when he was recognized as not being a patient of the hospital. He carried a gas mask and wore a .45 caliber. Questions were poured into him.

"How many raids on Clark Field? Did any Army planes survive the raid?"

"What was the truth about Hawaii and Pearl Harbor?"

"Was there any truth that 3,000 men had died in the Pearl Harbor raid this morning?"

"Was there help on the way?"

"What were Congress and the War Department doing?"

Of course these were all questions the captain could not answer. I remember I sat back and listened. I felt that I was very young and had a lot to learn. This was a new game to me and I could perhaps learn something if I just listened and observed older and wiser men. Yet at the same time I noted from the type of questions they asked that they were no better off than I, that on some of the questions my answers were just as good as theirs. The time had come for common sense and straight thinking. Originality was at a premium.

Somewhere around 2100, Al rose to go. I went to the gate with him. Just before we parted I said, "Al, everything you have told me about this situation has come true. Now just between us, what is your personal opinion about what happened in Hawaii and what is in store for us here?"

"Bill, that would be hard to say. A wire came into headquarters this morning. Only two or three people know what it said. I have no idea what it was, but it apparently is such bad news the men are sworn to secrecy. It's got to be bad news, Bill. Japan has jumped us. The nature and psychology of the nation is such that they were sure of themselves when they started. This wasn't a cat and mouse game. Japan is the tiger and our forces in Hawaii the mouse. Therefore, Japan used a tremendous force when she hit us. She hit us on Sunday morning when everybody would still be in bed drunk from the Saturday night parties. God! She must have struck us an awful blow. She must have hit our airfields with the same devastating effect she did Clark Field. She must have found half our Navy in Pearl Harbor and sunk it. You ask me what I think, I think we caught Hell in Hawaii worse than we did here. They caught our forces on Sunday morning with their pants down and shot the ass off of them. If the Navy is as bad off as I think it is, it will be a year before we can replace our losses. By that time Japan will have conquered all the world she wants, likely ending up with the East Indies and Australia. Boy, we are left out here in the middle of the ocean and a tidal wave is soon going to sweep over this place that is worse than we ever dared to dream. Today when they caught our air force on the ground at Clark Field, the Japanese gained almost complete air superiority. All we have left are a few fighters based at Nichols Field and a few other odd planes. Anytime the Japs desire to come in now, they can. Their bombers can knock out our Asiatic Fleet at will and then their transports can steam into the Philippines at will. We are soon going to be attacked on all sides and there will be no help from the States. We don't have the planes, ships, men or other equipment to save these islands. The US has been caught asleep and the lives of the American sons and many of the Filipinos will be the price for this unpreparedness. Everytime you see a man die out here due to the Japanese just remember that it is because the American public would rather drink cocktails and play bridge when it should be thinking of its security. You are now going to see what the price is for our national pastime. We may last a few months, but not longer than that. It won't be possible for our men to last. If you ever wanted to see adventure you are going to have your chance. Within a few days the Nip Air Force will destroy Nichols Field, our Navy out here and then walk in. We haven't seen anything yet, but it is coming. You had better go to bed now and get some sleep. There won't be many more nights, if any, that you can sleep uninterrupted. (How right he was!) Good night, Miner. When do you leave here?"

"I leave the hospital tomorrow morning in order to make room for incoming wounded. Then I am going to try to get a boat back to my troops in the Southern Islands."

"It may take several days to get a boat out. Do you have a place to stay? If not, come over and stay with me."

"Thanks, Al, I'll bring my stuff over when I leave tomorrow. Goodnight and many thanks for coming down." With that, Capt. Kircher set off through the dark Manila streets and I returned to sit beside Col. Sledge.

"Its been coming, boy, its been coming. Wasn't that what we tried to tell those Philippine Army troops you had on Bohol?"

"That's right, sir. Only it came quicker than I thought it would."

"Do you have a place picked out to go to in case of an air raid? If you haven't, that curb along the side of the street is as good protection as there is here."

"Hope we don't have to use it soon. I think I shall turn in and get some sleep while things are quiet.

With that I left the colonel still sitting in his chair on the ward porch. Soon I was asleep due to unused-to mental strain. Sometime after midnight I was awakened by the sound of the air raid sirens. All of us got out of bed and got more or less dressed. A few minutes later we heard airplane motors in the north. That was the signal for us to leave the ward for the more open parts of the hospital grounds. I went down to the ward porch and found Col. Sledge and some other officers. As the motors of planes increased their roar, we heard explosions off to the north. That was the signal for us to leave the porch. Col. Sledge and I went across the lawn and sat down on the street curb where it would only take an instant for us to lie down in the shelter of the curb.

It was a beautiful night. The moon was high and full, its brightness dimming out all but the larger stars. There were no lights in the city, but because of the bright moon, the buildings stood out with more clarity than they did on a rainy day. The streets were pathways of white light bordered by glistening palms, which cast their dark shadows along the sides of the streets and around the buildings. That moonlight was bright enough to read a newspaper with. To us huddled down there listening to the planes overhead it seemed like they were coming straight over us. In the moonlight the Passig River, a few hundred feet away, showed up against the dark of the ground like the white center stripe on a tar highway. The enemy planes had only to follow that river down to where it joined the sea and they knew where the heart of the city was. As the motor drew overhead we flattened out in the street and waited until the planes had passed far enough beyond us for any bombs they might have dropped to have landed or would land beyond us. Then we sat up and breathed a sign of relief. We were safe for the moment although we did not know for how long. As things remained quiet, we gradually drew back into the hospital edges where we could sit and lean against the building. There we waited for the two blasts of the siren to tell us all was clear.

Sometime around 0200 or 0230 there was a commotion outside the main gate of the hospital.

"The ambulances and busses have returned from Clark Field. They are full of dead and wounded."

"Stand back, make room so they can get in. MAKE ROOM!"

There was a general rush of patients to the area where the transportation was driving into the open courtyard.

"Get back, damn you! Make room, so we can attend the wounded. We don't have room to get the litters off the ambulances."

Right then began my education in blood and broken bodies. The characteristic stench was drifting over the hospital area. This was just the primary course for the heavy stuff to come later.

"Will 10 patients volunteer to carry litters with wounded on them from the ambulances to the hospital?" I was in front, so I stepped forward to the open door of an ambulance. There the sight that met my eyes I'll never forget.

On the floor of the ambulance was a stretcher and on the stretcher was an almost naked figure of a man. His clothes had been shot and torn away until they lay in streamers. One leg had a very bloody bandage around it, the other had several dark spots in it that looked like holes. A pool of blood had soaked into the stretcher under the legs. A little further up were more dark bloody spots on the white flesh of the thighs. Around his middle was more red blood-soaked bandage which was dripping; one hand and arm was bound to a bamboo piece to act as a splint and around his forehead was another bloody bandage. His eyes were open and glassy and he moaned as I placed a hand on the stretcher handle. By all the laws of nature this man should have been dead judging from his looks, yet he had survived a trip of more than 100 kilometers over bumpy roads.

Seated along the side of the ambulance were other drooping figures swathed in bloodstained bandages and splints. In the dim light they looked like ghastly apparitions from out of this world. I still think that man on the stretcher was almost out of this world. I didn't recognize any of these men, they were too ghostly. The first scene made a big impression on me, yet the time was to come before long when I was to see far worse and become so used to it that I regarded it as commonplace and part of the game we were playing.

I took hold of one side of the stretcher, another man the other and slowly we drew the moaning, bleeding man from that ambulance until all but the opposite end of the stretcher had cleared the end of the ambulance. Then two more caught the opposite end of the stretcher and we slowly and carefully made our way through the crowd until we had him inside a ward where the corpsmen and a nurse took over.

On the way out we passed other stretchers being brought in. Their burdens were just as ghastly as the one we had brought in. Less severely wounded were being helped into empty beds nearby. The odor of raw flesh and fresh blood became prevalent through the hospital.

Everywhere there was an empty bed a wounded man was put in it. There were more wounded than the hospital could take care of. I don't remember how many wounded came down that night. I have a vague impression there were at least 80. Some died on the way down and some died shortly after they arrived.

During all this time the air raid was still on and we had to work under blackout conditions. Flashlights were used to see our way inside the hospital corridors. After placing our litter with the wounded man in the ward, I went back to help some more. This time I found an Air Corps lieutenant, HuGay, by name, whom I helped under the guidance of a nurse to a bed in a ward adjacent to mine. She told me to stay with him while she went after some bandages. HuGay was in pain, although he tried to make light of his wounds.

"Do you have a cigarette, Pal? I lost mine."

"Looks like you damn near lost more than your shirt, Buddy." They were somewhat crushed, as I had put my hand on them as I helped him through the door. Finding a match nearby, I lit the cigarette and passed the lighted cigarette to him, holding the still lighted match so that its light shown on his face.

He looked drawn and haggard and there was agony in his eyes. His breath came in irregular gasps and his sentences were irregular while the words were broken.

"Did they hit you down here?"

"On the outskirts perhaps, but not in the city. The hospital is uninjured and can easily take care of you."

"That's good. They took us by surprise and we lost practically everything. Most of our planes burned on the ground" (here he knotted up and groaned). "It was a close call for me. They got me in the ankle and on the arm."

"Did you manage to save any planes?"

"Only a few. No enough to do anything with." He groaned again.

I said nothing more. There was nothing I could say. There was no use in my saying empty, useless words trying to assure him into false security. We would both know I was lying. His cigarette burned out. I lit another for him and one for myself. We smoked in silence until the nurse returned.

"Relax now and I will see if we can fix you up. Where are you hurt?" asked the nurse.

"My ankle and my upper arm. They got me both places."

"Will you hold the flashlight for me while I clean him up and put on the bandages?" she asked me.

"Sure, I'll be glad to. Will another light help? Yours is pretty dim."

"Yes, if you have one. Let's see his ankle."

I turned both flashlights on the ankles. One was large and swollen with a small blue hole in one side of it. I couldn't see the other side to tell if the object has passed clear through it. I didn't ask any questions for obvious reasons.

"Not too bad. Now turn the lights on the arm."

I obeyed. The shirt sleeve was in tatters and stiff with blood. There was a large piece of it stuck in the middle of a three inch circle of raw muscle on the biceps. The nurse gave this a tiny jerk and it came loose. HuGay groaned and went limp. I thought for a moment he had fainted. Then he rallied.

"There are a few more fragments of shirt we must get out or it will become infected. This will hurt a little, but you can take it soldier." With that, she took a pair of forceps from among her things and one by one she pulled the pieces of cloth out. HuGay squirmed. I could hear his teeth as he ground them together to keep from crying out. Finally the ordeal was over.

"You can relax now, lieutenant. This isn't how the book says to do it, but it gives you a clean wound. A few more hours and it would be infected. Tomorrow there will be more wounded come in. It is best we clean your wounds at once."

She then poured some solution over the wound to wash it out. The wound was now raw and red. The room stunk of raw "beef" and fresh blood which completely obliterated the smell of drugs prevalent in the hospital. HuGay retched at his stomach.

"It's about over, soldier. You have a clean wound which should be free of infection. You are one of the luckier ones. Now for a bandage son."

The nurse continued to doctor and bandage the arm. Soon she was through. Then she said, "Now, let's fix up your ankle."

She asked me to take off his shoes and socks so she wouldn't get her hands dirty. I obeyed and she went to work cleaning up the wounded ankle. She bathed it and then bandaged. Soon she was ready to go.

"You are all right now, lieutenant. I'll give you something so you will go to sleep and rest."

"Thanks for doing me up. Is there a cigarette left for the nurse?"

"Yes, there's plenty, enough for all of us." The three of us smoked our cigarettes in silence and darkness.

"Goodnight now, lieutenant. I'll see you tomorrow."

Looking at me she said, "Let's go."

I followed her out into and down the corridor.

"Thanks for holding the flashlights. It would have been hard without you. Just think, this mess is only the beginning; much much worse is yet to come I am afraid. I must go now and see if there are more yet to care for. You had better get some sleep if you can."

"Goodnight nurse, I wish I could do more."

She walked down the dark corridor and out of my life. I never saw her again that I know of. I only saw her face in the shadows cast by the flashlights. Her face was grim and tight and her hair was disarranged. I would not know her in the good daylight. As the weeks went by and report on report told of the mounting casualty lists in Bataan and Corregidor, I often thought of her as one of those heroic nurses who were the angels of mercy to our wounded and weary soldiers. Those angels who day and night with pitifully inadequate medicine and facilities, willingly gave their service, strength and courage to our men. I can still see her there in the blacked out hospital room working over this lieutenant. Her face was grim, she was hurting him and she knew it, but she went on, her movements swift and sure. I think tearing those pieces of cloth out of that wound hurt her as much as it did HuGay. Those nurses had a tremendous job on their hands and they did it heroically.

I went back to my ward, although the all clear siren had not sounded. I was exhausted from nervous strain. Flopping on my bunk, I fell into a troubled sleep. The war was on and I was right in the middle of it. GOD HELP US ALL.

The next morning we all awoke early and listened to the radio again. "...during the night Nichols Field had been bombed. Not much damage had resulted. Feverish preparations were being made against future attacks that would be sure to come..." The radio told of attacks elsewhere over the Pacific. "...not much more has been learned about the details of Pearl Harbor. It seems that our forces have really been hard hit there..."

We all had breakfast hunched around the dining room table talking in hushed voices. Some of the people didn't have very good appetites, I am afraid I was one.

After breakfast I went back to my ward and packed. I had decided to try to get back to my unit in the Southern Islands while getting was possible. If it were still possible. As soon as I was packed, I left my baggage under the care of the blonde nurse, St. Sally Durett, I believe that's what her name was. Then I took off for the port area and Fort Santiago. The latter was the headquarters of the PI Department. There I presented my orders for my return to the Southern Islands and they cut some new ones sending me to Wright, Samar, as my unit had left its cantonment area at Carmen, Bohol. There they told me I would be lucky to find a single boat going south. After waiting an hour for my orders to be cut, I received them.

While waiting that hour I tried to see what was going on there at the headquarters of the Philippine Department. Everybody was extremely nervous, nobody seemed to know much of anything. A great many of the desks were vacant. There was little or no activity among the civilian employees. Most of them were just sitting around talking in hushed tones. Only when somebody like myself came in and wanted something short and simple done, was there any activity. Everybody seemed to be waiting for something, a bombing raid most likely.

As soon as I received my orders I took off for the headquarters of the Port Area. There I was informed that all sea traffic was at a standstill. I was told to go down to Pier No. 7, then the largest pier in the world, there might be an ammunition boat going south soon.

Over to Pier No. 7 I go. I find one ship alongside and they are loading bombs on it. I walk into the office and recognize a Lt. Rothblatt from Chicago, standing before a major's desk.

"Hello, Bill, what do you know?"

"Not a damn thing, except we are in a hell of a shape. Do you?"

Rothblatt and I had gotten to be good friends in Santa Monica Courts on Dewey Boulevard when we both lived there. I hadn't seen him since I went south.

"Can I help you?"

"Can you tell me who to see about finding some transportation south to Cebu at least?"

"See the major here. He has charge of all the shipping going out. This boat alongside is going south with some cargo in a day or two, I think. I have to hurry back to my post now. I don't like to be away too long and the major is delayed for some reason. Look me up if you think I can help you."

"Many thanks, pal. I'll wait here for the major. Good luck if I don't see you again."

"Good luck, Bill. I don't envy your trip on this boat." With that he walked out the door waving his hand to me.

I lost track of Rothblatt after that for several months. Later along in February or March, while in the Censor's office in Cebu looking over some radio messages from Bataan, brought in by a P-40 pilot, I saw one from Rothblatt to his parents in Chicago. It stated he was still all right. I sent it on via RCA. Later I believe an answer came back via RCA and I tried to send it on up to Bataan via a P-40 pilot. I don't know if he ever received it. About two years later, August 1944, after I had been moved as a prisoner from Mindanao to Cabanatuan, Luzon, I ran across Rothblatt working in an adjacent rice paddy from me. Later that night in prison camp we got together and talked over old times. Shortly after that the Japanese started moving American POWs to Japan. Rothblatt was on either the October 10 boat, which was torpedoed and sunk with only seven survivors or he was on the Oryoku Maru with me and died on the trip north. I think it was the latter and that he died in early January 1945.

I waited a few minutes longer until the major returned to his desk.

"What can I do for you, lieutenant?"

"I have orders to go to Wright, Samar, to rejoin my unit. The QM HQ sent me over to see you about a possible ship going south as far as Cebu City. Have you anything?"

"The ship outside that we are loading with ammunition and bombs is going south in a few days. You can go on it. It's the only thing I know of now that will be going."

"Hummm. That's hot cargo! I sure won't rest easy on that!"

"Only the Devil himself would rest easy on that ship. Sorry."

I took off. I had done all I knew to do at the moment. I found a taxi in front of the QM office and hired him to take me downtown to the Philippine Trust Company Bank. On arriving downtown I found I couldn't get within a quarter of a block of the bank door. There was a run on the downtown branch of the Philippine Trust Bank and they had closed their doors. I couldn't get in to cash a $10.00 check. I told my taxi driver to take me on back to the hospital. Once at the hospital I went in to talk to Col. Sledge. I found him in the company of a Lt. Col. Connally.

"Well, what do you know, boy?"

"Nothing of general interest. I found a ride back to Cebu City on an ammunition boat in a few days."

"Ammunition boat! Can't you find anything better than that?"

"No sir, the QM HQ told me I was lucky to find that. There is only one boat scheduled to leave the harbor for the Southern Islands. There is a run on the Philippine Trust Company Bank downtown. I couldn't get near the doors which were locked."

"I am going out to Fort McKinley in less than half an hour. If you need some money I can fix it up so the Philippine Trust Company branch bank will cash your check." said Connally.

"Thanks, Colonel. I'll go out with you as I need some expense money in order to get back to my post in the Southern Islands."

"A staff car will be here in a few minutes to take me back to my regiment at Fort McKinley. You can ride out with me."

Shortly Lt. Col. Connally's staff car did arrive and I accompanied the colonel out to Fort McKinley where he took me to the bank and fixed it so I could get some money. Thanking the colonel, I left him.

"Good luck, Colonel, I hope this doesn't last too long."

"Good luck to you, lad, on your boat trip. Bon Voyage." I never saw the colonel again and I never have found out what happened to him. I remember him as a kindly gentleman who went out of his way to do a stranger a good turn when times were trying.

I left the colonel at the bank door and walked over to a taxi which I hired to take me to Manila. Winding in and out through the streets of Ft. Kinley, rounding one corner my taxi almost ran into a formation of scout MPs. In charge of them was an American officer. I recognized him as Lt. Jack McCoffrey from Logansport, IN who had come over on the boat with me.

"Stop, driver, I want to talk to that American officer back there."

"Yes, sire!"

Stepping out the cab, "Hello, Jack. This is a surprise to see you again. Do you have time to talk?"

"Sorry, Bill I don't. I have to march this relief over to the other side of the post and I am a little overdue."

"Well, good luck, old timer. I hope we see each other back home again before the next year is out."

"Best of luck to you also. The dinner's on me when you get back."

We shook hands and I climbed back into the taxicab. This was the last time I ever saw Lt. McCoffrey. Though neither one of us knew it, Jack was to be alive only 17 more days. Months later when in the Davao prison, a group of American prisoners from Luzon arrived there October 1942. Among those to arrive was 2nd Lt. "Red" Emerson, whom I have mentioned before. Jack lived with Emerson and his family back in Logansport, IN and both had come over on the President Pierce with me. Lt. Emerson told me the following story:

"On New Year's Eve we were down in Bataan in a quiet sector. There was a beautiful tropical moon shining this night and several of us were on a hill top under a palm tree drinking a bottle of good whisky as our celebration of New Year's Eve. I was forgetting the war and we were talking of things back home. One of the boys idly mentioned the name McCoffrey. I picked up my ears and asked if he knew him. He said Mac had been ambushed and killed on the evening of December 24 while on a motorcycle reconnaissance. Jack had ridden past a road junction in supposedly safe territory, but as luck would have it, a Nip patrol had penetrated to the road junction and lay in wait for a target. Jack was riddled and they didn't even get his body. This news just laid me low. I had been enjoying myself up to that time, but when I heard that Jack was dead, the evening was spoiled for me. Jack was just like a brother to me."

After leaving Jack McCoffrey, I went on into Manila and back to Sternberg Hospital where I looked up the blonde nurse and got my baggage. From the hospital I took my baggage out to the address Capt. Al Kircher had given me on Synagoga Street. Finding nobody at home at Al's apartment, I left my baggage with the next apartment neighbor (wife of a British officer in Singapore who had come to Manila on her way back to England and got caught). Then I went down to MacArthur's Headquarters on Street Calle No. 1 where I found Capt. Kircher.

"Al," I said, "my baggage is now at your neighbor's apartment. I have left the hospital, gotten orders cut at HPD (Headquarters Philippine Department) sending me back to my unit now at Wright, Samar. The boat is the Don Estaban and she is being loaded with ammunition and bombs. Some of these bombs are 100 pounds in weight and some are 500-pound affairs. I don't relish a two-day trip on that boat. Have you any suggestions as to alternatives?"

"No, Bill I don't. Not much is going out now and not much is going to get out. Reports today indicate that the Nips have air superiority now and their Navy is far superior to ours. By this time they must have a pretty good blockade around this island."

"What do you think about going back to Department Headquarters telling them the situation and asking them for an assignment here on this island?"

"If you have orders to go back, you take the ship and start back. Its going to be the same answer in the end. Annihilation! If you get back to Cebu, okay, if you don't it's too bad. A boat load of bombs means a quick death.

There is no telling what you will run into up here. Luzon is going to have her turn in hell before this thing ends out here. The best thing you can do is take the chance and start out on the ship. It is now past 1700. Let's go eat!"

As we left MacArthur's headquarters, he remarked, "Did you hear or see anything interesting today?"

"I was out to McKinley this afternoon. On the way back I saw a big bomb crater next to the Fort McKinley radio station, which was the result of last night's air raid. The bomb only missed that radio tower about 20 feet. The crater was about 20 feet in diameter and around eight feet deep. Was there anything of interest at your end?"

"Plenty, the Nips seem to be moving in all directions, Siam, Wake and several other points. Nobody seems to know when and where they are going to strike next. They just expect the worst very soon. Their bombers hit our airfields again today and our shipping along the coast. It's going to get interesting soon!"

"Yes, too interesting. Where do we eat? I haven't had much to eat in the last two days and now my system begins to demand something."

"We'll stop by the Army and Navy Club and then let's go on out to the house. I need some sleep."

"I do too," and related my experience of the night before concerning the bringing of the wounded down from Clark Field and my holding the flashlights for the nurse while she dressed the wounds of Lt. HuGay.

"You'll see a lot more of that before we are through with this. Here we are at the club. I'm going to have a steak if possible. We won't be having them much longer."

We dined at the Army and Navy Club, which was blacked out with black curtains over the windows. The lights were few, so that the effect was of dimness inside the club. The air was hot and stuffy and the sweat streamed off of us. We were very nervous as it was, so the dinner was something of an ordeal instead of something to be enjoyed. As soon as we were finished, we got outside into the cool of the night where there was a soft breeze blowing.

It was dark outside when we came out of the club. The city was in almost total blackness right then. Later on, the moon would rise and light up the city again. It took Al and me half an hour walking through the dark streets to get to his apartment on Synagoga Street. There were mobs of people moving about and we collided with other pedestrians several times. In the streets we could hear and dimly see cars creeping along. Several times we heard the noise of collisions followed by angry voices. Sometimes the dialects would be interspersed with English cuss words. I had to laugh at the sound.

On arriving at the apartment, Al and I got my baggage from the British officer's wife, stopping to visit with her and to listen to her radio for news reports. She had a good one and we heard broadcasts from Singapore where her husband was, London and San Francisco, as well as local reports. None of them were very encouraging. We left her soon, went to Al's apartment and got ready for bed. God only knew when we would again have a chance for a full night's rest. I simply unrolled my bedroll in the middle of the living room floor and crawled in. The last thing I remember thinking was, "this is a safe place. It is just another building lost in the mass of the city and it is not near a military installation. I can relax and sleep."

I awoke in the morning to find it broad daylight and Al kicking the end of my bed with his bare foot. I was still flat on my back with one arm thrown over my head. I don't think I had ever changed positions in something over 10 hours. I was still so exhausted that I could hardly bring myself to get up.

"Better get up and we can get a ride down to the headquarters with another officer who lives here," my host insisted. "You can take your bedroll down to the ship when we go."

"Okay, will be right with you." I sat up and stretched. I was very regretful to get up and face reality. That was my trouble! I was afraid of reality! This was Wednesday, December 10 in Manila, December 9 in the US. What events reality had in store for us that day!!

The day started out quietly enough. Breakfast at the Army and Navy Club; taking my baggage down to the Dan Estaban; saying good-bye to Al Kircher again and reported to Maj. Virgil Kerr, the Army officer in charge of the ship. All this was very quiet, taking up to about 1145 or 1200. About noon I went back to the Cuartel De Espana, HQ, 31st Infantry to see Capt. Truesdale with whom I was leaving my large camphor wood chest with my extra things and equipment. We ate our noon meal at the PX restaurant.

Capt. Truesdale said, "Let's go over to my room and listen to Don Bell the commentator at 1245."

"We had better get started then."

On the way to his quarters the air raid siren sounded.

"I'll have to leave you and go to my post. Good-bye and good luck." Capt. Truesdale left at a run.

"Good luck, captain, take it easy."

I ran to the nearest place where I could climb onto the top of the old fort stone wall about 15 feet high and 10 feet wide on top. I wanted to get a look at raiding planes. I had been afraid of a raid and I didn't intend to stick around that ship loaded with bombs until I had to. In case the harbor was raided and those bombs went off, I was going to be far enough away that I wouldn't be crowding my luck. Here the raid was.

From my point on the wall, I could look out over a small park and get a good view of the sky fairly low down in all directions. At first I saw nothing, so I waited, scanning the sky. Soon from the direction of Manila Bay I heard a few loud explosions. That meant planes somewhere. Looking again at the sky, I found them, enemy bombers. When I first saw them, they were in two v-shaped flights of 27 planes, a total of 54. They were so high up that they looked small, much smaller than I expected and they were a silvery white. Being so high and the color they were, they were hard to see until you were familiar with what to look for.

There they were, almost straight over me, yet not quite. Their line of flight would not take them over me, so I stood my ground and watched. Beautiful, majestic, silver birds they seemed to be, floating slowly over the city. I would guess they must have been at an altitude of 25,000 to 30,000 feet up. Suddenly our anti-aircraft opened up and little balls of white smoke appeared in the sky. These little puffs of smoke seemed to reach only halfway up to the planes and they burst behind the formation. Our boys were trying, but they didn't have the equipment equal to the job. We missed those formations so far it was pitiful. As the planes floated over other sections of the city, other of our AA guns opened fire. It was all the same. Beautiful silvery white birds in formation, floating through the skies unopposed and spreading terror through the city below. Little balls of smoke appeared in the skies halfway up to the silvery birds and far behind them.

There was a rattle of heavy objects striking the ground near me. I looked down. Ten feet away was a jagged fragment of an AA shell. I ducked down under a thick stone ledge of the wall top not far away. That splinter was sharp and jagged weighing over a pound, it looked like to me, I didn't want any of that stuff bouncing on my head.

The Nip planes passed on over Manila without dropping their bombs, passed out over part of Manila Bay toward Cavite Navy Yard. From that direction I heard dull explosions. In a few minutes a dark cloud of smoke arose from that area. Plainly there was an oil fire over near Cavite. The show was over from my balcony. I went back to the 31st PX for a drink of chocolate milk.

There were several officers in there like myself. Pretty soon Capt. O'Donnovan whom I have mentioned before, came in and spoke to us.

In answer to our inquiries, he gave out the information. "I guess they hit the Cavite Naval Yard this time. We don't know how bad, but reports indicate that it was pretty well wrecked."

"First the airfields, now the Navy Yard; what next, our ships in the various ports? At this rate they'll have us paralyzed within a week!"

Soon I left the post, found a taxi and went out to the Santa Monica Courts where I used to live. These courts are on Dewey Boulevard which runs along the bay shoreline and I could look across an arm of the bay toward Cavite Naval Yard. Standing on the sea wall, looking over the bay, I could see a tremendous stream of smoke rising seemingly off the surface of the sea. It covered quite a large area from my viewpoint. Some oil supplies had definitely been set on fire. More than that I could not see or comprehend.

Late in the afternoon before dark and the blackout, I returned to Pier No. 7 and found the Dan Estaban alongside and still loading. After eating, I walked out onto the pier, up to the gate to the street, through the gate, onto the base of the pier in the street and promptly lost my evening meal. It rolled out so suddenly I almost splattered my toes. Why?

There before me was a pile of 10 or 12 corpses stacked every which way. On top was the body of a beautiful little Filipino girl, I say body, but in reality it was only half a body. The head and trunk was intact, but from the waist down, there was only a mass of dark strings and ribbons. The face was peaceful and reposed, below the waist only a bloody mass of strings trailing over the pile of corpses, some of them a dozen feet long. The rest of the pile consisted of bodies in a less severed state. I staggered back and leaned against the wall of the pier building where the stench of raw flesh and blood was not so great. As soon as I felt better, I looked around. On the opposite side of the pier from my ship was a Navy ferry or small cargo boat of some type. There were several large holes in her and the glass of every window had been shattered out of their frames by concussion. The masts were bent and her frame looked twisted. There was a list to her. She was afloat, that was all, the boat was useless. Spying a soldier, I walked over to him.

"What's going on around here?" pointing to the heap of bodies and the wrecked ship."

"They are bringing the wounded and the bodies of the dead over from the Cavite Navy Yard by the use of a small speed boat, sir. They really caught hell over there this afternoon. The whole Navy Yard is destroyed and a great many are dead. Here comes the Navy ferry now, sir."

I looked the way he pointed. Sure enough, there was a long, sleek, gray looking boat plowing through the bay toward us. I stood by and watched. On reaching the pier edge, the boat drew alongside and some of the crew scrambled ashore. They were a horrible looking lot. Their clothes were half torn off of them, they were covered with blood and one or two had bloody bandages.

A Navy man was on the shore, "Hurry up and get this cargo ashore. Shove it up."

The crew below shoved up a dark smeared box of some kind. It was filled with bodies. Several bodies were lifted out by hand. The boat had some wounded which were being helped off the other end into a nearby truck or ambulance of some kind. When the unloading was completed, the crew scrambled on again. As it started to pull away, one of the sailors stooped to the floor of the boat, picked up something and threw it toward the soldier standing guard over the area, shouting as he did so, "Here's a present for you." The object fell at the guard's feet. It was a bare white woman's leg, the shoe was still on. I turned away.

"Soldier, how many trips has that boat made?"

"The 'bloodwagon' you mean, sir?"

"Yes, that 'bloodwagon'."

"I don't know, sir. It was making trips when I came on duty and one of the sailors said last trip they still couldn't see the end of the job."

"I'm going to get out of here. I can't take too much of this."

I walked away. The soldier was right. I did get used to it. I got so used to it that I could stand amid worse, eat and joke while I was standing there. Not only did I become that way, but the men with me that were alive became that way. It was a matter of "get used to it or go stark raving mad," but that comes a little later.

I got back on the Don Estaban. I had seen enough for one night. I felt sick, dizzy and weak. After lying down for an hour I got up and went down to the Oriente Motel in the walled city of Manila where I found my old friend

L.W. Jacobs. I visited with him an hour before we walked downtown over the Janes bridge to the Escolta (the Escolta was the main business street in Manila). It seemed strange to see the thriving business center all blacked out. There were scads of people near the entrance of some nightclub. In other parts the streets were almost deserted. We could dimly see the cars and caromeda carts. There were quite a few taxis cruising around without lights. Jacobs and I got one, went over the Army and Navy Club for some ice cream and about 2100 we walked home. I went on back to the boat when I left Jacobs. This was December 10 (9 in the States). I never saw my friend again until around Jan. 6 or 7, 1946, when I was visiting in Milwaukee. During prison days I heard twice that he was okay.

On board the ship full of bombs, I got a blanket, went up on deck, spread it out in a cool breeze and tried to sleep. Sleep? Sleep is brought by Morpheus, and Morpheus was hours away. I think he must have gone to Chicago for the late show. When he did come, he was accompanied by a helper, exhaustion. It was the helper who finally did the work!

I awoke at dawn the next morning, went back to my cabin which was now cool and slept late. I found Maj. Kerr at breakfast when I entered the dining room. He told me to stick around today, we could leave anytime now. I remained on board ship or in the shade of the nearby pier room until noon when I went to the ship's dining room.

The major and I were sitting at the dining table at about 1240 when the air raid siren sounded.

We both jumped up and rushed to the top deck. Maj. Kerr found the ship's captain there.

"Captain, get this ship out in the bay immediately. It's got all its cargo here. Go way out in the bay until you are the farthest ship out in the bay away from all other shipping. Then anchor. I am going ashore for final orders and will come aboard out in the bay. You have perhaps a short five minutes before the Nip planes arrive. NOW MOVE!" With that he ran to the pier and disappeared.

The ship's crew was all standing on deck waiting for orders.

The ship's captain ordered "Cut the shoreline fore and aft. Ziggay now!!!" He disappeared into the wheelhouse. I immediately heard him shouting in there and ship's bells began to ring far below inside the ship. The ship began to back away from the pier. I have read in books where they cut away the shorelines, but I had never expected to see it done. Standing on the wheelhouse deck, I saw two deck hands spring to the bow shoreline and begin to slash away at the big two-inch rope. Where those ragged devils got those two wicked-looking knives, I don't know, but they had carried them on their bodies somewhere. Before those men had slashed that rope in two, the ship was moving and had the rope taut. It parted with a snap like a rifle shot. I ran around to where I could look at the stern. I saw that rope snap, knocking the knife out of one of the men's hands slashing it. The ship was free in less than a minute and moving in reverse away from the pier as fast as I could walk. About three ship's lengths out in the bay from the pier, there was more ringing of bells, the ship swung in a circle, came to an abrupt stop for a ship and immediately started to move ahead. In only three minutes or so that little liner was racing around the breakwater wall into the open bay at what seemed to me her full speed of at least 15 knots (I am no sailor). I looked at my watch, the five minutes was not quite up, the ship was out in the bay rushing between anchored liners and cargo ships with a great white wave of water rising on either side of her bow. I didn't know a ship could move so fast. It took her sister ship half an hour to perform the same operation in peacetime. I still think of that feat in amazement. Of course we had expected air raids at any time after daylight. We had really been sweating them out. Another thing that might have encouraged that ship to move fast, we had a load of 500-pound bombs aboard, 400,00 pounds of them. That would make anybody move, in my estimation!

Now that we were free from the pier, I turned my attention to the skies. There was no use in going below with that cargo of hot eggs. One good jolt would send me into eternity. I might as well watch the show.

I saw no formation of Nip planes that day. I saw what I thought were some Jap bombers high in the sky. The sky was sort of hazy and high up in a brassy were some fluffy, small bunches of clouds. I definitely saw four of our P-40 planes from Nichols or Nielson Field climbing hell bent through the skies and searching around the cloud massed for the enemy bombers. I heard later that our boys had been alerted that the Nips were on the way and broke up the formation of the Jap planes. It was a brave thing to see those little P-40s tearing through the skies searching for the enemy. They knew they were hopelessly outnumbered if they ever ran into a group of Nip fighters. Yet there they were, winging around as if they owned the skies. The memory of them diving through the cloud masses, climbing and diving still stirs my heart. This day, thanks to them, there was no formation raid over Manila!

The *Don Esteban* continued on out into the bay at its high speed all through this air raid. The planes disappeared out of the sky, but the ship continued to speed far out into the bay until it was well beyond all the other ships and the Island of Corregidor loomed in sight. Then the ship slowed down and stopped.

We had to wait several hours until Maj. Kerr finally came out in a speed boat. All this time an American doctor, two sergeants and myself were on deck anxiously scanning the skies for hostile planes. We were now a lone ship way out in the bay. Any hostile planes which might happen to spot it would guess that it was something special. It was especially hot, we thought. The four of us anxiously awaited the major at the rail. He came aboard noting our anxious faces.

"Take it easy, boys. We don't move very far today!" Somebody groaned, but nobody asked a direct question. "Later tonight we'll move out to the pier at Merivales and be prepared to pick up some more cargo tomorrow."

"Any news of the air raid today, major?"

"I didn't hear of any raids around Manila today. The report is that there was one on the way, but our P-40s broke it up just before it arrived over Manila." With that the major went below.

The fact that we were to stay around that area longer was a great blow to us. Since we were going south, we wanted to get under way. We had been under a terrible nervous strain all afternoon; our clothes were dripping with sweat and the idea of remaining around on the boat load of bombs was enough to make one want to jump overboard.

I went downstairs and stood in my shower for 30 minutes or more trying to cool. Even the cold water was lukewarm, so I didn't get very cooled off. After that I dressed and went up on deck to wait for the evening meal.

Most of us ate the meal in silence, each contained by his own thoughts. As night came on, the weather became somewhat hazy. An hour after dark the ship slowly got under way, moving out toward the Island of Corregidor. We proceeded slowly in the darkness without a single light. I was up on the wheelhouse bridge with the major and the captain of the ship. Suddenly out of the darkness loomed the big hulk of a cruiser (it might have been a destroyer, but it looked too big in the night to be a mere destroyer). The ship's captain moved quickly, spoke into something (speaking tube, I guess) and the ship's bells jingled. The ship came to a sudden stop as the sound of the engines rose high and then began to back up in the water.

Fear gripped us all. We thought we were going to be rammed by the Naval vessel. To us standing on the bridge, we thought the end had come. For those 500-pound bombs to be rammed by that vessel meant "good-bye dear old Earth." The Naval vessel stopped, we stopped and the two vessels continued on our course after the Navy turned around.

"That was close! Almost head on. They had been notified to expect us, but I didn't expect to bump noses. We aren't out of the woods yet. That boat is now going to guide us through the minefields to Merivales," said the major.

I leaned against the rail. "This is enough to drive a man to drink and cigars!"

"If I catch you smoking on this boat, I'll personally throw you overboard!"

I gasped. The major was under far greater strain that I had realized. I said no more.

The next few hours our boat crept through the water bit by bit. Finally I went to bed on deck again where it was somewhat cool. There was nothing I could do and the sensible thing to do was sleep, if I could.

Shortly after dawn the movement of the ship awoke me. On sitting up I saw a rocky, jungle-covered mountain wall on three sides of me. Getting up, I looked to the back. A few miles away lay the green island of our fortress Corregidor. Turning again to the front, I found our ship was moving toward a long, low pier that extended out into the bay. A quarter of a mile from the pier the ship stopped. I soon found that the sea was too shallow here for the ship to go any closer. The cargo of bombs would have to be brought out by barge and then loaded via the winches. The loading got under way fairly early.

After breakfast I got to see several PT boats cruise around the bay while I was standing on deck. One of them approached alongside our ship and hailed us.

"Ahoy!"

"Good morning," said Maj. Kerr.

"Do you have any bread you can give us and some butter? We have been out from our base since Monday morning (this was Friday morning) and are running low on supplies. Most anything would help."

"Come aboard and I'll have the steward fix you up with something."

Standing at the railing I conversed with the PT boat crew and questioned them about their boat. These boats looked like "powerful hornets" to me. When their crew member came back with his load of chow, they took off. They told me their base was on Corregidor, but that they were temporarily stationed in Bataan not far from Merivales. They were patrolling.

I stayed on the boat and made no attempt to go ashore, that is, until the Nip bombers came. Because we were in the Merivales bay we could only see the mountains surrounding the bay and look over to the Island of Corregidor. All of a sudden a plane came swooping low across the front of the bay and went on toward Manila. Further out toward Corregidor were more Nip planes and the AA guns on the island were shooting at them. The little puffs of smoke from the shell bursts were just behind the Nip formation. Suddenly one faltered and dipped toward the sea with a trail of smoke behind it. That was one that wouldn't bother us again.

We heard from around the point of land to the stern of the ship just a few hundred yards away, the howl of airplane motors. Immediately I heard a burst of .50 caliber machine gun fire followed by the roar of the twin engines on a PT boat. The PT boat was in action and this was just over the hill out of sight. What the hell were they waiting for, the Nip plane?

"Captain, order the boats lowered and we will go ashore until the raid is over," said Maj. Kerr.

All of us took to the boats in record time and started for the nearest point of the rocky coast. The plane zoomed over the mouth of the bay and disappeared again. We heard more firing, but who and what we could not tell. It took us several minutes to cross that open stretch between the boat and the shore. Those minutes were lifetimes it seemed. The Nip plane and the PT boat were just over the hill and over Corregidor we again saw AA bursts in the air. When we finally reached the shore, we scuttled like frightened rabbits for the shelter of large boulders in the sandy beach. Once there behind the boulder, I then stuck my head out to see what was going on. As usual when I had reached a grandstand seat, the show was over.

Up to this time I have failed to remember that there were two other American officers on the boat going to the Southern Islands. One was Capt. Robert V. Nelson (later major), D.C. He was going down to be the chief dentist for Gen. Sharp's forces. The other was Capt. (later major) Oliver W. Orson, VC. Nelson was more like myself, just average, but Orson was made of a little sterner stuff. He didn't excite so easily and he liked adventure. What makes me remember him at this time was that he was in no hurry to leave our ship. He wanted to see the show and his boat was the last one to reach the beach.

As things reached a quiet stage, Orson, Nelson, Maj. Kerr and myself walked around the shore to the pier. Maj. Kerr stayed at the pier, but the other three of us wandered around the little Filipino town located in the coconut palms not far from the base of the pier. Its name was Marivales and it consisted of a string of Filipino nepa houses along each side of the shore road that ran around the bay. There wasn't much to see. I took some pictures with a little Kodak I wore on my belt. This took an hour or so. We then wandered back to the pier.

There at the pier we watched the operations. The bombs were brought by American trucks from their dumps high on the jungle covered slopes of Mt. Merivales. From the truck the bombs were loaded by cargadores onto the barges. The barges were then towed out alongside the ship where the bombs were unloaded. After talking with some of the truck drivers who had no news, we went back to the ship via a loaded barge. It was mealtime, so we went to the dining room. The crew had returned and our noon meal was waiting.

The loading continued all afternoon and late into the evening. Late in the afternoon the major received a radio message which told him to stand by to receive a Naval pilot who would guide us through the mine field and out into open sea during the night. This announcement brought joy to all our hearts. We had a dangerous, fragile cargo on board and the areas we had been in since the war started were areas of enemy targets. When the loading was finally finished, we had 500,000 pounds of 100-pound bombs. This made a total of 250 tons of bombs aboard our little ship. There was enough TNT in that cargo to level a city, let alone blow up our ship. Everybody aboard was anxious to scram.

The group of us ate our evening meal as the Filipino captain and crew got the ship ready to sail. Afterward, on deck, we watched a small Naval boat approach with the Naval officer in it. He drew alongside and climbed the rope ladder that was tossed to him. He went directly to the bridge where he stayed until dark.

I was up on the bridge after darkness watching and waiting for the experience of passing through our minefields. From the way the Naval officer talked, I did not doubt that he knew where he was going to guide us.

Suddenly a search light on the Island of Corregidor flashed its beam out across the water near us. It didn't flash its beam directly on us, just near us. The pilot spoke to the ship's captain.

"We are ready, captain. Move ahead slowly."

"Aye, aye sir."

"Right, left, stop, move ahead," etc.

I am not familiar with Naval terms, So I won't describe the language, but word by word and bit by bit, the pilot slowly guided us through the minefields. We passed several buoys anchored in the sea and every time we neared one of those, we turned in some direction. From time to time the searchlight switched its beam as we drew near its edge. At no time were we ever directly in the beam, always we moved in the outer fringes of its reflected light. I lost all track of direction during our twisting and turning. Finally the pilot spoke to the ship's captain who responded by using the speaking tube. The ship's bells jingled and the ship came to a stop. A small Naval boat came alongside and waited.

"You are now through the field, major. I'll go over side now." With that the pilot left the bridge and was soon riding over the waves back toward the searchlight. The light suddenly went out. The darkness was terrible for awhile, but all of us breathed a sign of relief, we had passed through the minefield. Another event had passed and we were still alive.

Looking back on those days I laugh at my fears. In comparison to events that took place later we were well off, but in those days the war was young and the constant fear of death was new to us. The time came when the day was done and you would hear remarks like, "Who got knocked off today?"

"Nobody I know of!"

"Hell! This isn't any ordinary day! Nobody dead, they can't do that to us!"

Maj. Kerr decided that each American officer should take turns standing guard upon deck. I don't remember what turn I drew, but I do remember the night was pitch black and slightly raining at times. We ran into squalls off and on all night. During one of the squalls I was standing on the bridge just under a bit of shelter out of the light drizzle. The sea was choppy and the wind was considerable. The visibility was practically zero. Suddenly in the blackness of the night loomed a blacker shape. Terror struck me. I recognized it as the dark hulk of a ship as large as ours. I thought we were going to crash head on. Then I realized that would have happened before I saw the dark looming hulk if we were going to. Our lengths overlapped already. There wasn't a single light on that whole dark hulk (neither was there on our ship). Nobody made a sound on it and nobody made a sound on our ship, yet the two passed within 15 feet of each other, with the whole China Sea to navigate in. I saw no watchman on the other ship. There was only the sound of the wind in the riggings and the waves. Surely the watchman on the other ship saw ours in the passing. Yet each of us, fearing the other might be the enemy, was willing to let the other pass unchallenged. Perhaps the other ship, like ours, didn't have any guns on aboard except the pistols worn by the passengers. There we were, two blacked out ships passing so close to each other one could almost jump to the other. To this day I don't know if that was a friendly ship. Knowing the Japs as I do, I think it was another unarmed American ship trying to slip into Manila harbor hoping for safety. If it had been a Jap ship at that time, I think they would have opened fire.

I remember watching that black hulk disappear expecting to hear the jingle of its bells and a burst of gun fire. It never came and we continued on our way. I was wringing wet with sweat. With that I decided to go below, undress and await my turn as guard.

Morning came and we were sailing south with the coast of Luzon low on our left horizon. Soon we lost it. The day was beautiful and bright.

I shall now attempt to make a list of the American soldiers on the boat. There were Maj. Virgil Kerr, officer in charge of the ship; a captain, doctor for the ship; Capt. Robert V. Nelson, DC, reporting to Gen. Sharp in the Southern Islands; Capt. Oliver W. Orson, VC, reporting to Gen. Sharp in the Southern Islands; Sgt. George T. Holmes, attached to the ship in QM capacity; Sgt. Paul Snowden and assistant, reporting to Gen. Sharp in the Southern Islands.

Sgt. Wilson, assigned to the ship in QM capacity and myself, returning to my unit.

There were several other non-coms attached to the ship in QM capacity. Prior to the war this ship had been transporting ammunition to Australia and other points. The Americans assigned to the ship had been in charge of the cargo. I don't remember their names, or much about them. Some I don't remember at all, the doctor for example.

While back at Manila, Maj. Kerr had secured two .30 caliber machine guns to mount on the ship for air protection, one on the bow and another on the stern.

All day Saturday, Holmes, Snowden and myself worked to build platforms in order that we could mount these guns. It fell to my lot to be in charge of this operation since I was the only line officer on board. Placing the gun on the bow deck was simple because it was flat and level. The stern gun was another matter, though. The only place we could get a clear field of fire back there was from the top of a stack of life rafts. First we had to lash the rafts more securely. Second we had to build a level platform on top of the life rafts that was large enough for a man to operate the gun. Third, we had to tie the machine gun down. Before the day was over, we had the job done. After the job was finished, I looked at that set up and felt like the farmer whose farm machinery is held together with bailing wire. It was a good job considering what we had to work with. I'll have to give all the credit to Snowden, Holmes and Snowden's assistant (whom I can't remember).

We moved steadily south all that day. Most of the times we were out of sight of land, or it was just a low line on either side of the horizon. Much to our pleasure the day passed and we saw no Jap planes in the air (we didn't expect to see any of ours, we didn't have any left).

Late in the afternoon, I inquired at the wheelhouse about our position and the name of the island that kept looming closer on our left.

"Where are we now?"

"At the end of the Negros, sir. That low land far to the left front is the north end of Cebu Island," said the wheelman.

I had to pass through Cebu City to get to Wright, Samar, but my boat wasn't going that way. This load of bombs had the first priority. We were going directly to Bugo in northern Mindanao. From there the ship would return via Bohol, Cebu City and to Manila.

On seeing the Island of Cebu, I remember thinking, "I wish to hell I could get off at Toledo tonight." (Toledo City being a small port on the west side of Cebu Island). I didn't think there was a chance in the world of ever doing that but as things developed, I almost did. I actually was in Toledo 48 hours later, but I landed that night at San Carlos, Negros directly across the straits from Toledo.

I stood on the upper deck after dinner that evening with Orson and Nelson. Maj. Kerr was resting as he expected to be up all night. Together we watched the straits narrow while our boat kept to the middle of them. The sun set leaving the near shore of Negros dark with the skyline of the island sharply outlined against a rose background. The black island loomed dark against the sky.

On the opposite side was the Island of Cebu. The slanting rays of the sun were fast creeping up the shores and slopes of its mountains. Soon the shore was dark leaving only the sun clad mountains etched with shadows. Finally, they too lost the last of the sun's rays. Then both of the islands stood dark against the sky. I remember the three of us watched that sun set as if it were to be our last. I don't remember that we talked much.

My turn for the night watch was early, so I didn't retire. I stayed up in the wheelhouse looking out the open window to the south. The strait was clear and the water clam.

"Sir, I have a message I think Maj. Kerr ought to have."

"He is resting, I don't want to disturb him unless it is very important."

"Sir, I intercepted a message from a radio station in southern Negros that five Jap transports and two cruisers are sailing around the southern end of the island toward Cebu."

The radio operator had been told to monitor all messages he could pick up.

"All right, I'll get him."

I had no answer for the problem. Our boat was scheduled to pass the southern end of Cebu a little after midnight. If it were true, we would likely run smack into the hostile ships. This was a decision for the major. Rapping on the major's door, I called, "Urgent message for you, Sir."

"Come in."

I opened his door and walked in.

"Sir, the radio operator just picked up a message of five Jap transports and two destroyers off the southern end of Negros heading this way. It looks like we are running directly into them."

"Go back to your post and I'll be up immediately."

I went back to my post and shortly Maj. Kerr passed by and went into the radio station. In a few minutes he came out.

"Call the captain," Maj. Kerr told the sailor on watch.

The helmsman spoke into a phone and the captain shortly appeared hastily stuffing his shirt into his trousers. He too, looked pretty sleepy.

I think everybody aboard ship had turned in shortly after dark. None of us had gotten much sleep in the Manila and Corregidor areas amidst the air raids. Last night we passed through the minefields and all of us were awake for that. As a result of the events of the week, lack of sleep and rest and due to the mental strain and fatigue, everybody including the crew, was dead tired. Tonight after darkness settled down and a cool breeze spring up a light feeling of security had settled aboard the ship and everybody had gone to bed. It was now somewhere near 2200. This ship was plowing steadily south between the islands of Negros and Cebu and the night was dark, yet clear. The moon would not rise for several hours yet.

The ship's captain conferred with the major a minute and then came back into the pilothouse. What he did, I didn't see, but suddenly the ship's bells rang out quite a number of times, giving us a prearranged alert signal.

When the bells ceased ringing, there seemed to be an eternity of silence in which the only sound was that of the ship plowing through the sea. Then pandemonium broke loose and the sound of subdued voices arose from all parts of the ship. There were cries and curses followed by the sound of human bodies being forced against hard unyielding obstacles. I could not see what was going on, I could only imagine the crew and the various other officers and men stumbling and fumbling around in the darkness of rooms, stairways and over decks littered with objects hidden by darkness. Each man carrying a little blanket roll of personal belongings quickly tried to reach his alert post. A feeling of the unknown and fear seemed to pervade the atmosphere.

In the meantime, the ship continued her way steadily southward. As the minutes went on, it seemed to me that we were rushing headlong into the jaws of the enemy. In a way, the alert brought mental relief.

I was no longer the only officer on watch and the responsibility had been taken from my shoulders. Since Maj. Kerr had taken over, I went to my alert post by one of the lifeboats. The major must have had a time making up his mind as to what to do. His orders were to deliver his cargo immediately to the Port of Bugo, Mindanao. Only a dire emergency could cause him to change those plans. As the ship continued southward toward the straits where the enemy was supposed to be heading, it became evident that the major could not decide whether to continue on the course or turn aside.

I lay down on the deck next to the lifeboat clutching my little musette bag of personal belongings and a gunnysack of some confidential documents the major had given me to destroy in case of capture by the enemy. With my head on the gunnysack and my arms around it, I fell asleep from exhaustion. I remember the last thought in my mind was that I had better get some rest, as that rest might mean the difference between having and not having the strength to survive the coming ordeal. Sometime later, how long I do not know, but certainly less than an hour, I awoke to a different feel of the ship. Rousing myself and looking into the night, I sensed that the ship was turning about. A few seconds later somebody coming from the direction of the wheelhouse, stumbled over me, and started talking to another person.

"What's up?"

"The major had the captain turn the ship around and they are going back to try to hide behind an island before dawn."

"What a relief! Why didn't he do that in the beginning?"

"Yours not to reason why, yours but to do..."

"Blast you; go to hell!"

That news brought a feeling of relief to all of us. We could hear people beginning to stir around again in the darkness. These were the hours just before the moon rose and the night seemed to get blacker as time went on. It was so dark that it was impossible for us to see the shore, even though we knew it could not be far off. How that Filipino captain sensed his way back up the coast of the Island of Negros, for a couple of hours, through the stygian blackness of the night, to anchor his ship behind a small island a couple hundred yards off shore from San Carlos, Negros, is incomprehensible to me. I remember that we all expressed fervent hopes that the old boy knew what he was doing. If he hit the wrong place and ran aground, it would not be hard to guess what the likely result would be.

By and by, the ship almost stopped and we could see land close on our right. Shortly afterwards, the ship seemed to stop and we heard the rumble of the anchor chain. A little later, we heard the major saying, "Well, boys, we'll stop here and go ashore."

"Miner and Snowden report to number one lifeboat," said Maj. Kerr.

I scrambled through the darkness over some men and made my way to the number one lifeboat.

"Lt. Miner reporting, Sir."

"Okay, where is Snowden? Is he here?"

"Coming up, Sir."

Presently, Sgt. Snowden bumped into me.

"Sergeant, you and Miner, along with some others will go ashore with me to see what we can find out about a place to unload the cargo in the morning if necessary."

We both replied that we understood. A Filipino captain and some of his crew were in the meantime lowering the lifeboat. Maj. Kerr, Snowden, a couple of other Americans (I have forgotten just who they were) and I entered the lifeboat.

While various individuals were groping their way down the rope ladder to the lifeboat, a rifle shot sounded in our mist.

"Quiet, you damn fools. Do you want to alarm everybody on shore? Who is responsible?" asked Maj. Kerr.

There was dead silence. No one answered.

"Who did that?"

"I, Sir."

"Who are you?"

"Sgt. Snowden, Sir. I bumped my rifle and it went off."

"Don't you know that such mistakes may cost lives? Don't let it happen again. Now, get aboard at once."

With no more mishaps, we got aboard the lifeboat and started toward the shore, which we could now dimly see.

"We had better shout and tell the townspeople who we are, or they may open fire on us. After all this noise and the rifle shot, some of the Filipinos may think we are Japs. Have some of the crew shout 'Americanos' in their dialect."

As the boat approached the shore, all of us shouted as to our identify in all the languages that we knew. Shouts of "Americans," "Americano," "Amigo" and other dialects meaning friends and Americans rang through the night from our boat. By the time we were 100 feet from the shore, we could hear people running up and down the beach and over boards, although we could not see them. Their excited voices rang sharply through the night. Very cautiously, we nosed our boat in the direction where the voices were loudest.

"If anyone understands English on shore, please answer our hale. We are Americans from an American ship. Do not shoot at us. If you have a light, flash it on us so you may see who we are."

There was no answer.

"Stop rowing men. Don't go any closer as we do not want to be shot."

The major repeated his instructions to the people on the shore. Finally, a flashlight was turned on us and we could hear excited muttering.

"As you can see, some of us are American soldiers. You have no need to be afraid of us. We come from an American ship out next to the island and we want to get help from the Americans in the American headquarters in Cebu. We want to come ashore to see about making these arrangements."

Voice from shore, "Okay, American. Come ashore. We will help you."

Our boat pulled up to the pier and all of us scrambled up except the Filipino crew. We were at once surrounded by natives, both men and women, who thrust flashlights in our faces, and peered closely at us. There were excited mutterings running through the crowds.

The men were dressed to a varying degree, from a pair of shorts to a policeman in full uniform. I believe even the mayor was there dressed in a pair of pants and an undershirt. The policeman and mayor revealed their identity and community offices, offering at the same time to help us in any way they could.

"Will you show us the telegraph office at the bureau of posts?"

"I, myself will take you there. It is not far, sire," said the mayor.

All of us including the surrounding townspeople started through the town at the mayor's heels. Upon arriving at the building, which contained the telegraph office, we found there was no operator at that late hour. The mayor dispatched one of his townspeople to the home of the operator asking him to come at once to the telegraph office. We had to wait a half-hour or so for the operator to appear. Then Maj. Kerr sent a telegram to Gen. Sharp in Cebu explaining the situation. While we had been waiting for the telegraph operator, the major learned that there was a large Sugar Central located at San Carlos, Negros, and that it was managed by a man named Roberts. After sending the telegram to Gen. Sharp, Maj. Kerr told me to go out to the Central and enlist the help of Mr. Roberts. I found a Filipino with a car and started out.

That drive through the night, twisting and turning through the palm trees, among which were Filipino houses, still seems like a dream. The night was murky black and how our Filipino driver found his way out to the Sugar Central I do not know. Finally after much twisting and turning, we came out of the palms into an open space. After driving through the clearing, the Filipino drove into the palms again and stopped.

"This is the Sugar Central, sir."

He pointed into the blackness. I looked and could make out the dim black bulk of a house.

"Show me the way to the door. I can't see in the dark."

I didn't want the Filipino to leave before I was ready for him to go.

"Yes, sir," and he led the way.

We moved through the darkness around the house until we came to a broad veranda. Here the Filipino hesitated and I moved on ahead on to the veranda and started pounding on the door. My pounding on the door seemed terribly loud in the stillness of the night. The noise seemed loud enough to wake the devil himself, yet, there was dead silence within the house. I banged again. Finally, from out of the silence, came a hard voice saying, "Who is it?"

"I am an American officer off of a ship down in the harbor. Some of the Filipinos said that an American named Roberts runs the Sugar Central here and I came to talk to him about disposition of our cargo. If you will come down where you can see me, I can further identify myself."

"Wait where you are and I will be down."

It was a relief to me to have somebody answer my knocking. In that country, it isn't always wise to go knocking around white men's doors in the dark of night. From the sound of that voice, I felt certain that there was a gun around. Later, I was told that this was true. I waited at the door of the veranda until the figure of a man appeared. There was still no light in the house and I could see that the man was taking no chances in being silhouetted against the light.

"What is your name?" (just inside the door).

"Lt. Miner and I came off the ship *Esteban* which is anchored off the municipal pier. Are you Mr. Roberts?"

"Yes."

With that a flashlight was turned on me and it scanned me from head to foot. I knew that I was getting a thorough check upon identification by appearance. Roberts then opened the door and I stepped inside. By the aid of the flashlight, we found chairs on the veranda and sat down.

"Maj. Kerr, the officer in charge of the ship, sent me down to contact you about the disposition of some our cargo for Cebu City while he is contacting Gen. Sharp's headquarters in Cebu. We have some officers and radio equipment which Maj. Kerr wants to unload here before he continues on his voyage. He has directed me to find out what facilities you have for the handling of and storage of this equipment for a short time."

"The Central has its own pier running out into the bay from the bodega. We can't get any men until daylight, but as soon as it is light, I'll send one of my men to get some boys to help. In the meantime, we can have your ship move up to the vacinity of my pier in order that you may unload your equipment in a minimum loss of time at daybreak. I have a motor boat and I'll take you back to the municipal pier where we can find your commanding officer. Wait until I get some clothes on.

With that, Mr. Roberts disappeared into the house and I turned to the Filipino boy who drove me out.

"Thank you very much for bringing me out and helping me to find Mr. Roberts. I shall go with him now. You may return to your house and get some sleep.

"Very good sir, but I shall go back to the pier."

"Okay, I'll see you back at the pier."

After a few moments of waiting, Roberts appeared fully clothed and led the way from the house down to the pier where his motor boat was tied up. He started up the boat and we puttered away through the darkness for several minutes. At the end of this time, we slowed down and Roberts said, "Well, here we are."

The boat bumped something and immediately I made out the vague outlines of the pier. He climbed on the pier and tied the boat while I followed.

"Where will the major be?"

"At the telegraph office is where we agreed to meet."

Roberts turned away without reply. I followed him through the darkness. We passed off the pier and for several minutes went through streets where few people were moving until we came to the telegraph office.

Here we found a small group talking in low tones. Passing through them into the telegraph office, we found the major still busy sending his telegrams. A few minutes later he finished and turned to us.

"Maj. Kerr, this is Mr. Roberts, the manager of the Sugar Central. Mr. Roberts has promised to help us in our present difficulty."

"I am glad to know you, Maj. Kerr, and I'll do all I can to help. I suggest that you tell me of the difficulty and then we will see what can be done with my facilities."

"I have an inter-island boat anchored out alongside the island with a small amount of radio equipment and several men which I want to take off the boat. I want to store the equipment, leaving the men in charge until they receive instructions from Gen. Sharp in Cebu as to its disposal. I wonder if you could furnish storage for this equipment and shelter for the men. They have their own bed rolls, but they will need food. The ship's crew can unload the equipment on the pier but we will need several men to carry the equipment once it is ashore."

Roberts said, "I suggest you move the ship over to my pier right away and then as soon as it's light, the crew can unload the equipment on to the pier. You can then move the ship away from the pier at the earliest possible hour. As soon as it is light, one of my men will get several Filipino boys and move the equipment from the pier into a nearby sugar bodega.

"All right, we will get under way at once."

With that, the major arose and the rest of us followed him back through the town and down to the pier.

"I'll take my own boat and guide your ship over to my pier," said Roberts.

"All right, I'll go out to the ship and tell the captain he is to follow you."

The next hour or so was spent cautiously moving the boats around in the dark, accompanied by much subdued talking. By dawn, the *Don Esteban* was moored close enough to the Sugar Central pier that our cargo could be transferred to the pier. After an hour or so of labor, this was accomplished and the *Don Esteban* withdrew from the pier and sought shelter on the west side of the small island just east of the town of San Carlos. There the ship remained the rest of the day. The equipment had been moved to the pier by shortly after dawn. True to his word, although it was Sunday, Roberts had a crew of Filipino boys who moved the radio equipment into the shelter of a large sugar bodega nearby.

By this time it was the middle of the morning, so Roberts took the Americans up to his house where we met the rest of his family and got something to eat.

The next few hours after breakfast, everybody relaxed and tried to sleep. In my own particular case, I went back to the *Don Esteban*, got my bedroll and had it carried into the sugar bodega. There I spread it on the floor beside a large pile of filled sugar sacks and went to sleep. The last thing that I remember before falling to sleep was how could there be so much sugar in one spot and no ants around it.

By mid-afternoon, a representative from Gen. Sharp's headquarters in Cebu arrived in the person of Capt. William L. Robinson. He had at his disposal a ferryboat running between the cities of San Carlos, Negros, and Toledo, Cebu, some 20 miles across the strait. Maj. Kerr and Robinson, after a short conference, made their respective arrangements for the transfer of the radio equipment to Capt. Robinson's ferryboat. Robinson then told Capt. Orson and Nelson that they could go back to Cebu with him that afternoon. To me, he gave instructions to see that the radio equipment with its attached personnel were put aboard the ferry and that I was to be in charge of that detail until I delivered it to Gen. Sharp's headquarters in Cebu.

With the help of Roberts' crew and one of his trucks, I transferred the radio equipment to the ferry alongside the municipal pier. By the time this tedious task had been accomplished, Capt. Robinson and the rest were aboard and anxious to sail. The ferry pulled out about 3 p.m. in the afternoon and headed for Toledo, Cebu. It was good to have a respite from duty and relax. As the ferry pulled away from the pier, Capt. Robinson, whom I had known while stationed in Bohol and whom I have previously mentioned in this journal, called to me to have a cup of coffee with him. We seated ourselves at a dining room table on the lower deck of the ferry.

"Well, Miner, what do you think of all of this?"

"I don't think much of it."

Then I proceeded to relate what I knew of the bombings on the Island of Luzon, mainly those of Clark Field, Nichols Field, Cavite Naval Yard and the ships in Manila harbor.

"Doesn't sound so good to date. There has been no action in Cebu. There have been some landings, however, by the Japanese at Davao." said Robinson.

"Well, it is only a matter of time until they take a crack at us here. Once on land at Toledo, how do we get this outfit over to Cebu City?"

"We have a detachment under Lt. Fossum stationed in Toledo. He will meet us when we arrive at Toledo. You can arrange to stay overnight with him. Borrow one of this trucks tomorrow morning and bring the radio and its crew over to Cebu."

"Well, that is a relief. I know where I am going to get the equipment to operate with now."

The rest of the two-hour trip, Capt. Robinson, Capt. Nelson and myself visited and talked of various subjects. Somewhere around 5:00 p.m, our ferry pulled into the dock at Toledo. There the three captains departed for Cebu City in Capt. Robinson's transportation.

I was left with the radio, which was charged to Snowden and his crew of technicians at the pier in Toledo.

As Robinson left, an American lieutenant in a truck drove on to the pier. The truck drove up and stopped by the ferry. The American lieutenant introduced himself as Lt. Orville Fossum.

"I am Bill Miner and I am sure glad to see you. I hope you have a piece of coconut to nibble on and a palm tree that is safe to sleep under."

"I can do better than that. I can give you a boiled egg to eat and a school house floor to sleep on."

"Wonderful! I am going to think I am in paradise with all of that."

"Capt. Robinson told me this morning to bring the truck down to meet the ferry and that he had some supplies coming over from Negros. He didn't say what it was. Do you know anything about it?"

"Yes, I do. I have a radio here, which is charged to Sgt. Snowden. He will need some help to load it into the truck."

"My truck driver will get several of the boys (pointing to a crowd of Filipinos on the pier) to help you."

"Okay, lets get some of the boys over there to help with the cuan on the ferry."

Fossum's truck driver sprang out of the truck and started arranging a group of Filipino men on the pier. In no time at all, half a dozen of them were leaping aboard the ferry.

"Sgt. Snowden, here are some men to help you. The crew of the ferry will also help, so load your radio on the truck as fast as you can and we will go to Lt. Fossum's camp."

The work got under way and in a short time, the equipment was loaded. Sgt. Snowden, his crew, another lieutenant and his crew, Lt. Fossum and myself all got aboard the truck and set out for the camp. Upon arrival at the camp, which consisted of a company of Filipino soldiers sheltered in a municipal school building at Toledo, Cebu, we left the equipment aboard the truck and under guard. Lt. Fossum, Sgt. Snowden's crew and myself then took our bed rolls from the truck and prepared to spend the night in the schoolhouse.

Lt. Fossum and I became well acquainted that night. He was quite lonesome, having been the only white man stationed in Toledo for several weeks. He practically gave me his life history. His home was in Fargo, ND where his parents had a store, the name of which (I believe) was the Fargo Rubber Stamp Co.

During the course of conversation, I found out he liked to hunt and fish, so we spent most of the evening talking about our respective fishing grounds. Of course, I also gave him all the news I had of the war. We all turned in early as this was the first night in a week that we felt we could go to sleep in safety. I remember that I became dead to the world shortly after nightfall and it was daylight when I awoke. My arms were still flung over my head when I awoke as they had been when I had gone to sleep. I was so deeply exhausted that I doubt I stirred the entire night.

The next morning, Fossum took me over to the home of one of his lieutenants for breakfast. There I had a complete meal of steamed rice, stewed chicken and coffee. I remember that I thought the meal very tasteless and found it hard to eat. Yet just a few months away I and all the American officers on the Island of Cebu would have given a small fortune for all we could eat of that same meal. After breakfast was over, Sgt. Snowden, his crew and myself with our equipment climbed aboard the truck with the radio and started over the mountains to Cebu City and Gen. Sharp's headquarters.

I enjoyed the trip across the island. I was much refreshed after a good night's rest and a substantial breakfast. The day was bright and cloudless. Our truck continually passed in and out of coconut palm groves. It seemed good to be alive and driving over beautiful mountains. As we climbed higher, we could look down on the green coastal plains of the island across the straits to the high mountains rising on the Island of Negros. There was a myriad of colors, greens of the vegetation, yellows of the corals and sand, deep blue of the sea and the distant smoky mountains of the dark Island of Negros. It didn't seem possible that there were such things as a war going on or that 400 miles away to the north on the Island of Luzon events were swiftly culminating into destruction and death for so many of the people and friends I knew there.

As our truck rolled over the mountains and down the east slope of the island, we ran into various troop movements on the highway.

I reported into Gen. Sharp's headquarters shortly after noon and found upon arrival that everyone there was filled with excitement. About half an hour before our arrival, two or three Nip planes had dive-bombed and strafed some oil installations and storage plants on Shell Island in Cebu Harbor. They had missed their objective and no damage was done. They told me that I had missed the fun. I wasn't the least bit sorry, for I had just had my fill of excitement in Manila and on the way down.

I reported to the adjutant, Capt. William T. Holloway Cook.

"Hello, Miner. Glad to see you again. Where do you come from? I thought you were in Sternberg Hospital."

"I was until 24 hours after the war broke out. By that time, the hospital was so full of seriously wounded that they expelled the less serious among us. I came down to San Carlos, Negros, on the *Don Esteban*. Across from there to Toledo, Cebu, with Capt. Robinson yesterday, bringing a radio and its crew of technicians. They are outside on the truck now. Whom do they report to?"

"I'll send a man down to take care of them. I expect you had better wait and see the general."

I sat down in a chair near the general's office and waited. After a short time, out of the office of the general walked a full colonel. On seeing me he stopped.

"Hello, what can I do for you?"

"Capt. Cook told me to wait and see the general, so I am waiting."

"I am Col. Thompson, his chief of staff, and I'll take you in to see the general at once."

"Thank you, sir."

I followed the colonel into Gen. Sharp's office.

"Here is a young man to see you."

"Capt. Cook, adjutant told me he thought the general would like to speak to me."

For the next few minutes I related to the general and his chief of staff what I knew concerning the events on Luzon. I told them I had gotten this far on the way back to my unit stationed in Wright, Samar. The general and his chief of staff sort of smiled.

"I think we can use you here, Miner. You wait outside the door and Col. Thompson will tell you what to do very shortly."

That was as close as I ever got to my unit. Col. Thompson appeared shortly.

"Miner, you report to Capt. Humber over in San Carlos College. He will tell you what to do."

I saluted and took off. Once outside the general's headquarters, I ran into Capt. Cook again.

"Capt. Cook, I was told to report to Capt. Humber for duty. Can you tell me where my quarters will be and where I will mess?"

"There is an empty room upstairs here and we mess here also. You can put your equipment in that empty room."

"Yes, thank you, sir." Then I moved on.

San Carlos College was only two or three blocks from Gen. Sharp's headquarters in old Fort San Pedro de Cebu. I walked over to San Carlos College and inquired of the guard at the door for Capt. Humber's office. The guard had an orderly show me the way and presently, after winding through various stone corridors of the old Spanish college building, I found myself in the presence of a captain who was surrounded by an office staff of Filipino men.

"I am Capt. Humber, who are you?"

"Lt. Miner. Gen. Sharp told me to report to you for duty."

"I am sure glad to see you, Miner. Aren't you the old S-4 man of the 2nd Battalion of the 34th Infantry?"

"That is correct. We worked together on a problem up at Fort Stottenburg last July."

"They have given me the G-2 office here and I need an assistant badly. I guess you are it."

"I'll do my best and I am glad to work under somebody I already know."

The next few hours were spent in becoming familiar with the duties of the G-2 office. There were large maps hung on the walls which showed all the islands of the Philippines in detail. On them were plotted the positions and composition of the various units of Gen. Sharp's command. In addition, we received reports of Japanese plane flights, which we traced by the use of pins and ribbons on these maps. Any ships reported, we also plotted on the maps. The work became quite interesting. Due to the air-warn system, which had been set up, we could receive reports of hostile planes when they were miles away. After we received several reports on them, we could establish, with reasonable certainty, their course and objective. Once those had been determined, if possible, we radioed or telegraphed a warning to that unit or installation. Late in the afternoon, Lt. Duane Cosper came in the office and asked for me.

"Hello, Duane, glad to see you. Where did you come from?"

"Wright, Samar. I just came from Gen. Sharp and he said to tell you to report to Lt. Bowers in the Bureau of Posts Office of the Customs Building. Lt. Bowers will tell you what your assignment is. The general said that I was to take over your job here.

"Things sure change fast, don't they? Here I am just becoming familiar with the job and they say, move on. I'll introduce you to Capt. Humber."

After introducing Lt. Cosper to Capt. Humber, I got my things and went over to the Bureau of Posts where I found Lt. Bowers. Bowers had charge of the censorship for Gen. Sharps' command. The rest of the day and part of the night I spent becoming acquainted with the details of the censorship. The censorship duty there consisted of establishing censorship on all newspapers, radio programs and commercial radio, telegrams, telephone services and cable services. In the telephone, telegraph and commercial radio services, government priorities had to be established and maintained. After that various types of civilian priorities were established. This too proved to be interesting work and had a wider scope than the phase of G-2 work that I had experienced under Capt. Humber. The reason that I was relieving Lt. Bower was that he was being transferred to Luzon. Prior to my coming, yet after the start of the war, while in harbor patrol duty, Bowers had shot a Filipino and for that reason, though just, he was being sent back to a unit in Luzon. His boat was due to leave that night. Bowers got back to Luzon and somewhere during the campaign of Bataan, was killed in action.

I don't remember all the members of Gen. Sharp's staff or his headquarters. I'll mention them and their duties as correctly as I can remember them. The rank mentioned from here on is the rank they attained at the end of the war or as I have known them. At the time of events some individuals may be a grade or two lower than their final grade.

On Gen. Sharp's staff were the following members:

Lt. Col. Floyd F. Forte, often called Sammy Forte. My friendship with Forte was very brief. He did not arrive at Cebu until around Dec. 1, 1941. After the war started, he was busy running secret missions for Gen. Sharp on various parts of the Southern Islands. He got over on the Island of Negros on one of these missions and contracted dysentery. This disease caused him to be laid up for several weeks. I saw him in Cebu City on his way to Mindanao from Negros. He asked me at that time how the war was coming in our favor. I remember telling him it was all going against us. Sammy was quite a boy and well liked by all who knew him. After he got to Mindanao he saw action against the Nips several times. During these actions, he showed plenty of intestinal fortitude. The details as to his death are not known. He was reported killed in action at Lanao, Mindanao. When he was last seen he was attacking single-handed a large number of Japs.

Another at Gen. Sharp's headquarters who met a similar fate was Capt. Charles Bucher. Bucher and I were together in the headquarters on Cebu. I knew him rather well. Bucher sweated out several secret missions from island to island with a narrow escape or two as I heard about him. He then went to Mindanao with Gen. Sharp while I stayed in Cebu. Bucher was killed in action by Japanese artillery somewhere on the Island of Mindanao.

Col. John W. Thompson was Gen. Sharp's chief of staff. During the early part of the war, while in Cebu, I got to know Col. Thompson very well. He was an earnest, hard-working man with inadequate facilities at hand for his tremendous job. He went to Mindanao with Gen. Sharp and surrendered with the general at Malaybalay in May 1942. Shortly after the surrender, he was among the group of full colonels and generals sent north to Formosa. After remaining a number of months at Formosa, they were moved to Manchuria and in June 1945 arrived at the Hoten Prison Camp in Mukden, Manchuria, where they remained until the end of the war. When I last saw Col. Thompson, he was in good health.

Col. William E. Braddock was force surgeon for Gen. Sharp. After organizing the hospital facilities and medical troops on the Island of Cebu, Col. Braddock went to Mindanao with Gen. Sharp where he continued to function as force surgeon. Col. Braddock likewise surrendered with Gen. Sharp and ended up in the Hoten Prison Camp at Muken, Manchuria.

Col. Archibald M. Mixon was Gen. Sharp's force communications officer. Col. Mixon was among those that went to Mindanao with Gen. Sharp to organize the defense of the island. He was rescued in Hoten Prison Camp in August 1945.

Lt. Col. William T. Halloway Cook was Gen. Sharp's adjutant general. He was a friendly sort of man whenever I was around him. He functioned in Mindanao headquarters until the surrender in May 1942.

After a few months imprisonment at Malaybalay, he was moved to the Davao Prison Camp where he, with numerous officers and enlisted men, did coolie labor for the Japanese. In June 1944, he was moved from Mindanao to Cabanatuan Prison Camp where he stayed a number of months. Finally, he was moved to the Bilibid prison and was placed on *Oryoku Maru* Dec. 13, 1944. He survived the bombings by American Naval dive-bombers. He was placed in a second ship in Linguayan Gulf and taken to Tokyo Harbor in southern Formosa. There he survived a second bombing during which and immediately afterwards he did heroic work in the relief and care of the wounded. When I think of the din and chaos of that wrecked prison ship, I can still hear his voice calling out to all who could hear to give of their clothes, food and water for the relief of the wounded. The man exhausted himself in their behalf and died later in the trip as a result of exhaustion, malnutrition, exposure and dehydration. This was a hero who might be alive today had he not been quite so unselfish.

Lt. Col. Charles I. Humber, commonly called Polly, was the G-2 on the staff. Humber was a big man with a lot of good humor. One of the sidelights of his experience in the Southern Islands was the securing of some Filipino straw mats of a special design while on one of his trips through the islands. Off the coast of either Samar or Leyte was a small island whose inhabitants wove these special mats. Having the time to make the trip across the water to this small island, Polly secured the services of a native with a banca to paddle him over to the island. On the shore, Polly said to the native, "Joe, how much to paddle me out to that island?"

"Five centavos, sir." (Equal to 2-1/2 cents in American money).

"Okay, Joe. Let's go."

He climbed into the boat producing the five centavos. In due time he landed on the other shore.

"Okay Joe, you wait for me. I come back pretty soon."

Polly secured his mats, came back to the shore and found the native waiting with his banca. Polly tossed his mats in, climbed in and said, "Okay Joe, let's go back."

Filipino (without lifting his paddle) "You give me five pesos, sir." (Equal to $2.50 in American money).

Polly exploded for about five minutes, calling the native all the good names this side of heaven. In the end, however, he paid the five pesos in order to get back to the mainland without missing his conference.

Polly likewise surrendered at Malaybalay in May 1942 and spent time in Davao, Cabanatuan and Bilibid prison. He died on the road to Japan Jan. 26, 1945. His death was due to exposure, malnutrition, dysentery and dehydration, because he had no serious wounds from either of the two bombings.

Lt. Col. Robert D. Johnston was the G-4 for the Mindanao force. Col. Johnston, when I first knew him, was my company commander of the Service Company of the 31st Infantry. We went south together in the latter part of August 1941 to assume posts with the Philippine Army. Col. Johnston surrendered at Malaybalay and as a POW worked as coolie laborer in Davao and Cabanatuan. At the time the last of the prisoners were shipped out of the Philippines by the Japs, Col. Johnston was in the hospital at Cabanatuan. A few weeks later, around February 1944, he was rescued along with the rest of the Cabanatuan prisoners by the rangers.

Lt. Col. William L. Robinson was another member of the headquarters. He was on duty with the Philippine Army Sept. 1, 1941. I found him very likable in the line of duty. He was with Gen. Sharp all the way through until the surrender. Robinson was part of the group that went to the Davao Penal Colony. While aboard the prison ship, which was taking us from northern Mindanao to Davao, he served as one of the executive officers for a group of prisoners. While trying to win some concessions from the Japs in the way of food and water for American POWs he was violently slapped around the head and eyes by one of the Japanese. He was the first officer of any rank in our group to be beaten by the Japanese. This action by the Jap solider caused a great comment among our ranks. This was worse than some prankster sawing the legs off the college president's chair, almost in two, so that the chair collapsed, spilling the college president on the floor of the chapel stage. However, no hostile movements were made by the POWs. Later in the Davao prison, he served as farm detail coordinator for a short time. Robinson spent a great deal of his time in the sick barracks or the hospital because of almost total blindness. It was rumored that one of the blows Robinson received from the Nip while on board ship injured an eye nerve causing the blindness. Very little food and a vitamin deficiency failed to improve his eyes. Regardless of the reason, he could hardly see to walk around the camp. He was moved from Davao to Cabanatuan and finally to Bilibad prison. On Dec. 13, 1944 he was among those placed on board the *Oryoku Maru*. He survived the two bombings to die of malnutrition exposure and dehydration about Jan. 25, 1945, on board ship in route to Japan.

Maj. Coleman T. Caruthers was another of Gen. Sharp's staff. Maj. Caruthers had joined Gen. Sharp's staff at the beginning of his Philippine Army assignment and remained with him all through the war. His earliest imprisonment was at Malaybalay. He was later in Davao where he, like everyone else, had his share of the work as a coolie laborer. He and Maj. Chrisman used to spend quite a bit of their spare time in prison talking of their families and friends in the Los Angeles area.

Maj. Robert P. Chrisman was in command of Gen. Sharp's message center during the war. As I mentioned before, Chrisman had been stationed in Cebu City training Filipino troops prior to the war. He knew all the American soldiers on duty with the Philippine Army on the islands of Cebu and Bohol. He had quite a number of friends among the civilians, Spanish and Filipino families. I had met him socially in Cebu City prior to the war. Picture taking was a great hobby of his. Prior to the war and during the war he gathered a great many pictures of interesting people and events on the islands of Cebu and Mindanao. Even after he became a prisoner, he still had some snapshots of pre-war days although he had no negatives with him. His negatives and private papers he had made some disposal of either by burying them or giving them to a Filipino for safe keeping. Chrisman was another that started out on the ill-fated prison ship *Oryoku Maru*. He was one of about 105 field officers instantly killed when our Naval dive bombers dropped a bomb into the hold of the ship. The date of his death was Dec. 15, 1944. He was another of the Los Angeles boys in our prison.

Maj. Robert v. Nelson was the force dental officer. I have previously mentioned him as one of my companions aboard the *Don Estaban* on my peerless voyage from Manila to Cebu. Maj. Nelson went to Mindanao and after the surrender, he became the chief dental officer in our prison camp

Lt. Col. Paul D. Phillips was a 2nd lieutenant when I knew him at the beginning of the war. He was a bright, likable, young fellow and seemed to be right on the ball. He soon became aide to Gen. Sharp, an assignment which he held throughout the war. He went to the Davao prison with the rest of the boys. I'll mention him later while dealing with prison life. He survived the war.

Capt. Duane L. Cosper was one of the assistant G-2s under Col. Humber. He went to Mindanao with Gen. Sharp's headquarters and was one of the boys who did not surrender at the appointed time. Duane took off to the hills near Malaybalay when it came time to surrender. Because of the loose guard on the camp at Malaybalay, there was a little freedom of movement of Americans in and out of the prison area. Somehow or another word got down to camp as to where Duane was staying and he was contacted. He was found to be very thin and practically without food. He was living in a little one room house belonging to a Filipino. He had a couple of poor, lean, native chickens tied to a bush out in front of the house. The boy was in bad shape with an infected tooth. The whole side of his face was swollen and quite painful. At that particular time, the American prisoners at Malaybalay were living well. They had plenty of food and a fair degree of medical care. One of the colonels who talked to the boy told him that under the circumstances he thought he would be wise to return to prison where he could get food and medical care. At that time, this looked like a wise move, but in view of later events, the colonel told me he was sorry he had ever helped to persuade the boy to come in. As a result of this advice, Cosper did turn in. After about three years' imprisonment at Davao, Cabanatuan and Bilibid prisons, he died on board ship en route to Japan and was buried at sea. The reason for his death was malnutrition, dehydration and exposure from years in prison.

Capt. Roy B. Gray was another of Gen. Sharp's headquarters staff. He was a six-foot, good looking, young fellow of a quiet temperament. You hardly knew he was around except when he appeared in line of duty. I don't remember what his assignment was, but I do know he was well liked by all who came in contact with him. Capt. Gray will again appear later in this story when he served as one of Gen. Sharp's emissaries for surrender of his various units during the fall of the Southern Islands.

Capt. William F. O'Brien was one of the American officers stationed in Cebu. I think I mentioned him as one of the men I met prior to the war. At that time he was with Headquarters, 8th Military District of the Philippine Army located in Cebu City. Being Irish and liked to eat, I remember his coming in for a lot of razzing the night or two that I ate at the 8th Military District HQ officer's mess. He was the mess officer, but he took it very gracefully. He went to Mindanao with Gen. Sharp and I didn't see him again until after the surrender when we were both at Davao. O'Brien and I went on the same work details together at Davao and we often planted rice together while there. On Feb. 24, 1944, part of our Davao camp was taken to Lasang by the Japanese to work on an air strip. This detail numbered 650 men and it was joined by a previous detail of 100 men. This made a total of 750 men working on the Lasang air strip. On Sept. 8, 1944, the Lasang detail was aboard a prison ship just north of Zamboanga that was torpedoed by an American submarine about 4 p.m. in the afternoon. As to Capt. O'Brien's fate, I only know that he went to Lasang Feb. 24, 1944.

Maj. Oliver W. Orson was the force veterinarian. I mentioned him previously as being one of the passengers on the *Don Esteban* when I came down from Manila during the first few days of the war. Maj. Orson went to Mindanao and surrendered with the group at Malaybalay. I will refer to him later when he was camp veterinarian at Davao.

Maj. Jefferson W. Speck, like Maj. Chrisman, came from Los Angeles. Speck was on Gen. Sharp's staff with the assignment of assistant to Col. Mixon. Speck was the man who did a lot of the wire laying, telephone and radio installation on Mindanao. He surrendered with the general and later went to Davao with the rest of the group. He survived the fearful trip on board the *Oryoku Maru*.

The final man, that I remember as a member of Gen. Sharp's staff, was Maj. Max Weil from Detroit. In civilian life, Maj. Weil had been a postal inspector. As I recall from several accounts, he found the work interesting, however, being a reserve officer, he was called to active duty and sent to the Philippines. His assignment at the beginning of the war was headquarters commandant for Gen. Sharp. Max was an interesting character and, during the first days of the war, because of common interests, I got to know him fairly well. Later in the Davao prison, we became very good friends.

After I took over the censorship office in Cebu City from Lt. Bowers, things began to grow interesting mighty fast. To begin with, a great deal of the work had to be done at night. As previously mentioned the work concerned all phases of communication with the public radio, telegraph, RCA, telephone and newspapers. There were two or three daily newspapers published in Cebu City when the war began. The papers gathered their news for the morning edition any time up to 11:00 p.m. at night. The censorship demanded that I proofread the entire issue before it went to press. The same thing occurred around noon for the evening edition. Often the Filipino editors would fail to send in their proofs and I would have to send a soldier over to the newspaper office with a threat to stop the press unless the proofs were immediately sent to me. It took several weeks and the loss of a lot of sleep to get those editors to send their proofs without fail.

Another duty of my censorship, in regard to the radio program in the city of Cebu, was a semi-daily censorship of all news broadcasts and commercial announcements.

Albert Fienstein commonly called Al Fenton was in charge of this radio station. Under my supervision, he did most of the actual censorship, but I required a copy of everything that went out over the air. A few commercial announcements prior to the war had been made in Chinese and Spanish. I required that everything be made in English. Shortly after the sinking of the inter-island boat *Corregador*, we had quite a few requests for commercials offering rewards as to the knowledge of individuals who were believed to have been aboard the *Corregador*. The originators of these announcements sometimes wanted them in a dialect. People were persuaded to use English. It was the same way with the newspaper. There was one rich Chinaman in particular who for days and days after the sinking of the *Corregador* became known, ran an ad accompanied by a picture offering 1,000 pesos reward for knowledge of the whereabouts of his son who was believed to have been aboard the Corregador.

I mentioned the telegraphic system. Cebu City being the largest city of the Southern Islands and centrally located in the Archipelago, was chosen for the telegraphic central for the Southern Islands. (The telegraphic system in the Philippines was called Bureau of Posts). The system varies from ours in that it makes use of both wire and radio. On the larger islands, there were telegraph wires strung between the larger towns. These wires were all connected with the main office for that district or island. In this main office was a short-wave radio set operating on a frequency designated by the Bureau of Posts. When a telegram was sent from one island to another, the short-wave radio would send it to the main office of the respective island or district. The radio operator there would receive it, transfer the message to the wire system again and the message would be delivered to its destination. The Cebu Office of the Bureau of Posts seemed to be the clearinghouse for all the Southern Island stations. Telegrams originating in Tacloban, Leyte, designated for Iloilo, Panay, would be radioed from Tacloban to Cebu City and Cebu City would relay the message to Iloilo. It was the same way with message from Zamboanga to Manila. The message would be relayed through the Cebu City office of the Bureau of Posts. My duty called for 24 hours a day censorship of all messages relayed through Cebu. This duty consisted not only of the censorship of the content of the messages, but it also smooth organization to see that all priorities were duly observed, that the wires did not become jammed with non-essentials and that speedy, efficient service was maintained every minute of the day and night.

Another phase of the job was the RCA radiograms. For a short time after the war started, we had contact with the Manila office. Prior to the war, the RCA traffic between the Philippines and the States was handled by the Manila office. When Manila fell, the islands were temporarily out of commercial contact, because the Manila equipment fell into the hands of the Japs. Immediately after Manila fell, the Cebu RCA office under the Army censorship set about contacting RCA, San Francisco. In a short time, this contact was made and a traffic schedule was established. This traffic schedule was experimented with and developed until a fairly satisfactory contact was maintained; up until within a few short hours of the fall of the city of Cebu. The equipment was then destroyed to prevent its falling in the hands of the Japs and being put to use against us. The biggest difficulty that we had with the RCA traffic was not a case of breaking rules or military laws, but the getting of messages accepted collect by the RCA. They had a rule that all messages had to be paid for. At our end of the line it was impossible to pay for all messages sent. Those poor devils up on the battlefields of Bataan and Corregidor didn't have any money of their own and spent most of what they had, if any, to buy food and other physical comforts. On the battlefields, paychecks were non-essentials. Our boys knew that there were some contacts with the outside world and that RCA Cebu was one of them. They would send messages down to Cebu by every possible ship or plane. These messages all had to be sent collect to the soldier's family, if the family were to get the message. A plane would come down from Luzon bringing a whole bundle of radiograms to be sent collect to the families. Then we could not send the radiographs because they were collect. Like them we didn't have any money to pay for these numerous messages. It was finally ironed out whereby they could be sent collect. This was not until late in the game, however. After the messages were sent, we still had no knowledge that upon being received by RCA, San Francisco, they would be delivered. As censor and with the burden of all these details, I made an effort to find out if they were being delivered. RCA, San Francisco said they were being delivered provided the censor permitted. There again was a ball up. These messages were strictly censored before they went on the air in clear English. There wasn't anything that went out over the line from my end that the Japs didn't already know and that the people back home shouldn't know.

We were in touch first hand with the situation while the States didn't comprehend. It seemed a pity when the boys on the battlefield would risk their lives to send a message home, saying they were alive and okay, that the people sitting in safety failed to give immediate action to such morale-building factors in our troops. RCA failed to inform their operators that messages could be sent to the men in the islands from their families. One member of my own family after receiving several messages from me, finally got one back to me, but it was only after I sent her an RCA message with instructions to reply through RCA. Even in the face of that, the local operator said the message would not go through. Finally, she got him to accept the message on the grounds that if she paid for it he would send it to RCA, San Francisco, and let that office decide what to do with the message. Of course, the message came on through.

A lot of the boys in Bataan would have felt better if they could have had more home contacts. An agency such as the Red Cross could have performed such a service Stateside and the public would never have known how the traffic was routed. The last six weeks before the surrender came, a lot of the boys got messages from home which were never delivered to them. By that time, all our ships had been sunk and all our courier planes had been shot out of the skies.

On April 10, RCA, Cebu, went out of service as the Japs came into the city. It was intended to take the equipment, which had been made semi-mobile, into the hills with us as we fell back into the jungle. The Jap forces, however, were too strong and they advanced too fast for it to ever be rein-stalled after the invasion of Cebu.

The Bureau of Posts was the communication net around which our air warning system was set up. Maj. Ernest V. Jordan from Milledgeville, Georgia, was in charge. Because both our duties lay around the traffic of the Bureau of Posts, we decided to have a common office and to arrange and organize our work where each could relieve the other, thereby giving us time for such necessities as eating, sleeping and other physical needs. Because there was such a tremendous lack of American personnel in all ranks, many of the men and officers got hardly any sleep for weeks at a time. By mutual cooperation, Maj. Jordan and I could run the combined offices in shifts. One of the most interesting phases of the duty was tracing flights of Jap planes across the Southern Islands and their inland seas. The air warning system was arranged so that any government or city official, postmaster, Bureau of Posts operator, etc., who received a reliable report of planes flying over his locality would report the number and direction in which they were flying. As the planes passed over various towns and islands, these reports were telegraphed and radioed into our headquarters. This system would forewarn us of an air raid anywhere from 15 to 40 minutes. Anytime a group of planes came near any part of this net, the islands of Mindora, Panay, Negros, Cebu, Bohol, Leyte, Samar, Masbate and Mindanao, they would immediately be reported and as their flight progressed we would receive a whole flock of telegrams reporting their location and direction of movement. We had a supply of Shell Oil maps, some of which we always kept stored in the desk. As military maps, there were very poor, but they did have all the roads and principal towns on the coast and inland marked on them. By taking the wires that came in concerning a flight of planes and putting pins in the map at the point of origins from the telegrams, we could soon plot the course of the incoming enemy planes. As soon as the course began to shape itself, we sent warning messages to any military object over which they might pass. There was never any doubt as to the identity of a large group of planes. The Japanese were the only ones who had any planes in numbers in that area. If we got a report of just a single plane or perhaps two at the most, we would stand by after warning Gen. Sharp's headquarters for the possibility that it was one of our courier planes.

It was rather an exciting game to plot the course of those incoming planes, but the big trouble was that the city of Cebu was very often their objective.

The Bureau of Posts in Cebu was located in the Customs Building, which stood right on the waterfront. Directly across a few hundred feet of water lay Shell Island, so named because it had the Shell Oil refinery and storage tanks on it. This was a prime objective of Japanese bombings and strafing during the early days of the war. Other military objectives were ships lying in the harbor and harbor installations. There was no guarantee that raiding Japanese planes could hit Shell Island and miss us. As time went on, we found by experience that the Japs more often missed their target than they hit it. Our office being right on the waterfront was one of the hot spots of the harbor. Things were always interesting there.

One afternoon a priest named Father Sheridan, who had donned the uniform to become a chaplain, was in the office about 4:00 p.m. A Filipino hurriedly brought in a stack of telegrams while we were talking. I received them and started to lay them aside, however, on the top telegram I caught a fleeting glance of the words "24 planes." I immediately directed most of the attention to the telegrams. Twenty-four planes had appeared over the northern end of the Island of Negros. The next two telegrams came from points a little farther down the coast, nearer Cebu. The soldier appeared again with another telegram. This time the figure was 18. Others of the telegrams had just said many. I knew all I wanted to know by this time.

Large group of planes – Japanese of course – were headed toward Cebu.

"Father, you mentioned earlier in our conversation, did you not say that you had to hurry to a wedding?"

"No, I..."

"I am quite certain you said you were in a hurry to get away from here in the next 10 minutes."

"If you are busy, I'll leave."

"Take a look at this telegram."

I showed him the telegram that mentioned the large number of planes. Meantime, I picked up the phone connected with Gen. Sharp's G-2 office and Capt. Cosper answered.

"Hello, Duane. Got a surprise for you. A package of 24 pigeons just flew over the north end of Negros headed for the coop on top of your office. From the rate they are flying, you had better spread your umbrella in about 10 minutes to catch the droppings. Get me?"

"I get you."

Bang went the receiver and I looked at Father Sheridan.

"Captain, I think you are right. I do have a wedding and I am leaving at once."

With that the chaplain took off and I received another stack of telegrams concerning the oncoming planes. The last report we had of those planes, they had left the east coast of Negros just opposite the north end of Cebu and were headed straight east. Those planes never did attack Cebu City. Since it was only about an hour until dark, we believed that they must have headed back to a possible base in the Pelau Islands, 600 miles east of Mindanao.

One of the chief troubles we had during these air raids was to keep radio operators at their posts. As soon as one operator got hold of a message saying planes were approaching, it got around to all of the other operators and they would want to leave. The time came when I found it necessary to go stand in the door of the operator's room. Under my supervision, they would remain at their posts.

For assistants on this job, I had two American enlisted men, Cpl. Eckhart and Sgt. Dale E. Dyches. They were both good men and performed their work excellently. I put them in charge of the operating room and they divided the 24 hours of duty between themselves. The way those two lads worked together was a grand lesson in cooperation between individuals. One or the other of them was in the operations room all of the time. I helped them when I could, which wasn't often as my day was 18 to 20 hours in length. It was they who actually read the telegrams, marked them as to priorities and eliminated the excess ones, preventing jamming of the wires. If there was anything that they were in doubt about, they brought it to me and I made the decision.

During these first days of the war, some of the civilian population were frantic and attempted to send all manner of messages of this and that to relatively all over the islands. Many of the messages were about non-essentials. The message that I remember distinctly had originated in Cebu City, it had gotten as far as the operations room where it was stopped. It was from some local politician concerning the arrival of two fighting cocks from one of the other islands. Somehow or another through the native operators, the old boy had found out that the message had been stopped, so he came to see me about it. I assured him the message would go through with his priority classification. The truth of the matter was that the wires were so jammed with essentials that the priority rating, under which his message was classified, was never used. These telegrams were filed away and later sent after the rush was over. In order to get rid of him, I took him into the operator's room, found his message and placed it at the top of the priority list, which as I said before was not acted upon until some time later. He then went away happy with my personal assurance that his message would be sent as soon as possible. Of course before the day was over it had been buried by other messages of that same priority rating.

As soon as I got rid of this local politician, I immediately traced down the channels through which he had learned that his telegram had been held up. Upon asking the people involved, all of them Filipinos, why they gave out such information to the public, I got the answer, "but, Sir, we do not give information to the public. This man is a politico and a great friend of assemblyman in Manila. We do not dare make him angry or we will lose our jobs." I assured them they would lose their jobs a lot faster if they committed that offense again. I went back to my office muttering something about Filipino politics being as foul as American politics.

Another instance I had of information appearing through the grapevine which authorities wanted suppressed, was concerning the sinking of the inter-island liner named *Corregador*. This ship was the second ship loaded at Manila with supplies for the Southern Islands. In addition to the Army personnel, there were a large number of civilians aboard the ship who were trying to get out of Luzon to some safer area.

No one knew just how many souls were aboard. The ship started out from Manila one afternoon and on reaching the mine field off the Island of Corregidor, hit a mine which blew its bottom out, causing it to sink within a period of a very few minutes. There were a few survivors who were able to swim ashore after being in the water for several hours. They told a tale of swift destruction and sudden death in the waters of Manila Bay. Nobody seems to know just who was responsible, but to say the least, this ship packed to almost standing room sank with almost 100 percent loss of life. Naturally, this was considered a terrible tragedy by the entire island. The message was flashed from Manila to Cebu over the Bureau of Posts wires, where it was immediately handed to me. Realizing the commotion this news would cause, in this already chaotic situation, I immediately censored the message except for the proper military authorities and sent the copy to Gen. Sharp's headquarters. In a few minutes, I received a call form the G-2 office.

"Miner, what in the hell do you mean by letting news of the Corregador sinking get by you?"

"That message was brought to me as soon as it arrived in this office. It was a personal message from individual to individual and I stopped it at once with instructions to my entire force to say absolutely nothing about it, since there was enough bad news and rumors floating around as it was. I shall immediately look into the matter and warn all personnel that severe punishment will be dealt to any and all who give out restricted information. The only way I can account for this news being aboard so early is the fact it may have been broadcast in a news flash over one of the Manila radios, since it is known to the public up there. There is no reason why it couldn't be broadcast in the news."

Wherever that news came from, I don't know. But it must have been a news broadcast, because very shortly a large number of telegrams came through from various places to relatives in Manila asking if certain individuals were on the Corregador or were safe, etc. We did what we could to keep the situation in hand, but it was several days before we let the newspapers carry the stories.

Previously, I have mentioned two enlisted men in the Bureau of Posts office who helped me as assistant censors. They were Sgt. Eckhart and Sgt. Dale Dyches. I don't remember much about Sgt. Eckhart other than he was a handsome young fellow, likable and a good soldier. I may be wrong, but I have the impression that he was assigned to the 31t Infantry of Manila. Sgt. Eckhart went to Mindanao with Gen. Sharp. He surrendered at Malaybalay, worked in the rice fields and on the plantations of Davao until Feb. 24, 1944 when he was sent out on the Lasang detail. The Lasang detail was aboard a prison ship north of Zamboanga Sept. 8, 1944 when the ship was torpedoed by one of our subs. There were 83 survivors out of 750 officers and men. I do not know what the fate of Sgt. Eckhart was other than he was supposed to be aboard this ship at the time of its sinking.

The other, Sgt. Dale D. Dyches was tall, lean and a Texan. His father was a minister at Goldwaithe, TX. I believe Dale was a career man in the Army, but what his unit was in the Philippines, I do not know. Sgt. Dyches also went to Mindanao with Gen. Sharp and surrendered at Malaybalay. He was with the group at Davao, but instead of going to Lasang, he was one of the enlisted men that remained with the main group of Davao POWs. He was shipped to Luzon with the main group in June 1944. Instead of going to Cabanatuan, he went with the group of enlisted men who were shipped on north to Japan. He survived our air attacks on the Japanese mainland and got back to the Philippines after the war was over. I saw him once at the 29th replacement center near Manila. He was looking fine considering that he was a POW. I later heard from him back in the States and he was then happily married and on leave at Fort Worth, TX.

It didn't take long after I became censor to see that our location on the waterfront was a bad one in every way concerned, whether we looked at it from the standpoint of continued operation or personal safety. It was in the tallest building on the Cebu waterfront and from its appearance, a most likely target for raiding by Japanese planes. Although the Bureau of Posts was on the second floor and there were two and perhaps three floors above it, I did not consider the Bureau of Posts office very well protected. The thing to do then was to move it away from the waterfront into some less conspicuous building back in the city. Maj. Jordan agreed wholeheartedly with me after our first air raid. Accordingly, we both got busy, located a place in one of the downtown theaters and Maj. Jordan arranged with the quartermaster to take over the theater for government use.

Maj. Jordan came into the office one noon and said, "Well, Miner, we sure are lucky. We are going to move off of the waterfront pretty damn quick."

"It can't be too quick for me. I can just see those red ... pigeons dropping eggs around this place. I for one, don't want to get splattered with what falls. It isn't healthy."

"Well, we can get under way this afternoon."

"Okay, when you go downstairs, see the man in charge of the B of P will you, and persuade him now is the time to move, not mañana."

"Will do. I am on my way."

"Okay, see you after chow."

The next few days were full of feverish haste. We had to prepare the theater in the center of the city to receive the equipment. We had to lay wires, both telephone and telegraph and have them prepared before we moved the sets form their present seat of operations. We arranged to setup in this manner. The radio and telegraph key receivers and transmitters were placed down on the main floor of the theater. Maj. Jordan and I had our offices on the Mezzanine floor. The lobby was used for the public in sending telegrams. When we finally completed the transfer, we had a very comfortable setup in spite of the hardships under which we operated.

Those few days while we were moving were days of anxiety. The enemy planes would appear every once in awhile or by the messages we censored and received through the air warning system, we knew that enemy planes were daily at work somewhere in the islands. Sometimes, they dropped their bombs not too far away. I thought we would never get the B of P moved to its new location. The Filipinos in charge were not inclined to be in much of a hurry, for we would ask them to get something accomplished before the end of the day and he would reply, "Oh, tomorrow, tomorrow." this would make the major and me as mad as hornets. He didn't seem to realize that his office was in danger. His attitude shows the typical philosophy of the tropics. If you don't get something done today, don't worry about it, there is always a to-morrow. He was right. There was a tomorrow, but it was filled with dead men, thousands of his kind, and the reason for their death was procrastina-tion. They were simply to slow to move out of the way of oncoming, clearly perceived attacks.

It was with a sigh of relief that we finally accomplished the task of mov-ing our offices.

About the time that we got our Bureau of Posts moved into the theater, Christmas 1941 arrived and what a Christmas! I think all of us had the feel-ing that it would be our last Christmas. It was for several. In spite of the feeling of foreboding, there was a Christmas dinner under way. Charlotte Martin, wife of Capt. C.J. Martin, both of them old-time residents of Cebu, prepared the turkey dinner for Gen. Sharp and all of his staff. Charlotte had been doing some work in Gen. Sharp's office and she felt so sorry for all the boys that she threw a grand and glorious party. It really was a grand and glorious party to us, since we had been out in the jungle and were going back to the jungle. All of us carried on our duties during the day, left our posts of duty in proper care and slipped away to the party for an hour or so. Many of us had arranged to attend in relays in exactly the same manner in which we would have gone to the ordinary mess hall for our evening meal. This was an old fashioned American Christmas dinner with turkey and cranberry sauce. It was served by Filipinos and the lights were candles.

There was only one emblem of American womanhood present, Mrs. Martin. I think every man there saw in her a resemblance to his wife or sweetheart back in the States. Not all the evening was devoted to pleasure. Officers would slip in, remain a little while and slip away again. Others would come in and take their places. At this stage of the game, with Jap landings occurring in Luzon, we felt we could expect a landing anywhere in the South-ern Islands at anytime. In my own case, I had been trying for several days to get some transportation in the form of a truck, so that when the invasion came, I could get some of my equipment away for use in the hills. At this time, there was working in the quartermaster motor pool, an Englishman named Fred Pipe. He had become a good friend of mine and before the dinner was over, I was telling him my troubles.

"You know I'd hate to see that invasion occur tonight. I don't even have a bicycle on which to make a get-away with any of the equipment. There are several good transmitters and receivers among the radio sets. I guess I'd have to evacuate them on my back from the looks of things."

"Do you expect an invasion tonight?"

"No, I don't. There was a new invasion in northern Luzon today, which you already knew about. There are no reports of any boats within unloading distance of here tonight. Yet, the general seems to be as jittery as a butterfly on a cake of Jell-O. I am just a lowly captain, so what I expect doesn't count, I guess. I still wish I could get some transportation. Since you work there, why don't you fix me up with something?"

"We do have a truck down at the pool which consists of a cab and a flat bed. There are no sides to it. We have a driver with it and if you think it would do you any good, we will go get it and have it standby at the theater."

"It would certainly take a load off my mind to have that truck parked in front of the theater."

"We can go get it at once and be back only slightly late for the next course. The motor pool isn't far from here."

"Let's go."

Arising, I excused us to Mrs. Martin by saying, "Will you please excuse us for about 15 minutes as we have some work to check on. We will be back before the next course is over."

With that, we left the dinner, passed through the double set of blackout curtains and into the night.

"Dong, Sssss! Jose, this is Pipe."

"Here, Sir."

"Count to 10 out loud, so we can tell where you are. We want to use your car."

"Uno, dos, tres..."

By the time the Filipino had counted to 10, Pipe and I had found the car. A blacker shadow in the black of the night.

"Jose, drive us back to the Motor Pool and go slowly. Don't run over anybody."

"Yes, Sir."

For the next five minutes or so, we slowly twisted and turned through the dark streets of Cebu, ending up at the Motor Pool. Pipe located the truck with its driver seated in the cab. He awoke the driver and said, "You follow us to the theater. If you get separated from us in the dark, you go to the theater...ziggay, zaggy. We will meet you there soon. You wait for us. Understand? Wait for us."

"Yes, Sir, I understand."

"Okay, you follow."

We again took off through the night in Pipe's car with the truck following us. We soon arrived at the theater and found the truck was still with us.

"Driver, you will park your truck here in front of this theater all night. You are a standby here. You can sleep, you can lie down on the back of the truck, but you stay here all night. Perhaps very suddenly Capt. Miner will want to move some boxes to a bodega. You then take Capt. Miner where he wants to go. Understand?"

"Yes, Sir, I stand by for Capt. Miner."

"That is good. You understand. You stand by for Capt. Miner. If he doesn't come, you sleep all night. If he does come, he will tell you where to go. Only Capt. Miner will tell you where to go. If anyone wants your truck, you tell them to go find Capt. Miner. If you leave before Capt. Miner tells you to, you will go like the Maro 'hermantodo'. That would not be good for you. Understand?"

Hermantodo is the word used for the fanatical insanity the Muslims work themselves into when they run 'amok' killing people, anybody in sight until they in turn are killed. The victims are usually non-Muslims. The Muslims believe they will go to the Muslims heaven if they die killing infidels.

With that warning, Pipe and I returned to the Martins' Christmas dinner, having been gone a total of 30 minutes.

During the next hour we finished Christmas dinner after which Gen. Sharp offered a prayer and there was a sad attempt at singing. The general called the party off very early, much to the disappointment of all concerned. We then returned to our various posts thankful that we had had an old-fashioned Christmas dinner in the atmosphere of Christmas carols instead of a prayer on the battlefield as a great many of the boys in Bataan had for their Christmas.

There were several local air raids in Cebu during the first days of the war. Most of the air raids had two military objectives. First, the gasoline and oil supplies by the various international oil companies such as the Shell Co. The second objective was the boats in the harbor and their harbor installations. There was also a Procter and Gamble Copra factory at Opon, Mactan Island. The Nips never made Cebu a constant objective of raids, but every few days, they would send a photo ship down to take pictures. If there was an inter-island ship in the harbor or quite a bit of small shipping, likely as not, 24 to 48 hours after photo Joe had made his rounds, a bunch of Nip bombers would come over and bomb the port area.

One day shortly after we had finished moving the Bureau of Posts to its new location in the theater, I viewed a light bombing and strafing attack from the roof of the theater. I had worked the night shift the night before and had just gotten to sleep around 10 a.m. That was the signal for the air raid. Shortly after the air raid siren sounded, I heard the sound of the planes. I knew that there would be no sleep for me during the raid. Once up, I climbed to the roof of the theater where I could get a view of the city from the mountains to the harbor. At my back, lying at the foot of the mountains was the Lasang Air Field. To the front, I could see the curve of the harbor with Shell Island on the right and away to my left in front lay Mactan Island and the Proctor and Gamble Copra Factory at Opon. In this particular raid there were three light bombers. After dropping their bombs around Opon and circling the harbor a few times, they headed across the city for Lasang Air Field, strafing the city as they went. Once over the airport, they proceeded to fly low over the field and strafe all installations on and around the field. I could see the planes swoop each in their turn and level off just about even with the roofs of the city. Then they would climb until they reached altitude enough to make another swoop on the airfield. About the time the planes would level off and begin to climb, I would hear the sound of their machine guns. About an hour after the bombing raid was over, I went out to the airfield to have a look at the damage. The hangers, the barracks and dummy installations were all riddled with machine gun holes. Luckily, the Philippine Air Corps with its two or three little training planes had moved out lock, stock and barrel and was now located under some tall trees half a mile away. No damage was done to either planes or personnel. This was just a minor raid, nevertheless, it had its effort on morale.

Toward the last of December, Gen. Sharp moved his headquarters from Cebu City to a place designated as Camp X located on the Talisay-Toledo road. The forestry maps had this area designated as Camp T. There in the high valley just under the divide on the western side, the Philippine Forestry had an experimental area. Gen. Sharp moved his headquarters to this area as it had cover from observation from both the air and ground and plenty of water. The place could be reached from either side of the island by this one highway. On the western side, the road up the mountain was more or less gradual, though full of hairpin turns. The road on the eastern slope was of altogether a different nature. It was carved out of the side of a very narrow precipitous, winding canyon. Three-fourths of this highway up the canyon was only a one-way road. There were control stations at each end with one in the middle. The traffic was controlled by the use of telephones connecting the three control stations. We generally had to wait at one of these stations, both going up and coming down. All in all, the place was fairly inaccessible as far as motor transportation was concerned. By foot, it could be reached from all four directions.

Gen. Sharp moved his headquarters up to Camp X leaving Col. Irving C. Scudder in command of the Cebu Provisional Brigade which was formed for the defense of the Island of Cebu. During all of this shifting of personnel, I continued as censor of the Island of Cebu.

Since the general had moved out into the mountains, a courier service had to be established between Gen. Sharp's headquarters and Cebu City, still the seat of communication. This courier service was established and operated by 2nd Lt. Paul D. Phillips. Paul had quite a lot of fun, or should we say grief, keeping an efficient messenger service operating over the 24 miles of dangerous, steep canyon road to Gen. Sharp's camp. He evidently did a good job, because he survived the war and was promoted to a lieutenant colonel.

The middle of the morning around Jan. 1, 1942, I got a message to report to Gen. Sharp at Camp X. Nothing more was said, no more, no less. I was in a quandary. Should I or should I not take all my baggage. If the general wanted to see me concerning the censorship as he frequently had in the past, I would be back to my post of censorship duty within a matter of a few hours. If he wanted me for something else, God alone knew where I would go. When I reported to Gen. Sharp, I took all my belongings with me. Luckily I did, for within a few minutes I found myself operations officer of a

Filipino Corps Message Center located in Camp X. There was a tense air of secrecy about the place. Nobody would say anything, yet anybody bright enough to run a Message Center could see that a move was imminent.

Capt. Chrisman who had been running the Message Center showed me how to operate the encoding and decoding devices.

"Well, Chris, is that all there is to it? Just simply substituting words for letter combinations on this little cylinder?"

"Yep, that's all there is to it. It is all very simple."

"Did you see that loaf of bread on the table at breakfast this morning? It is all very simple to cut and eat a slice of bread, yet a hell of a lot went on to make that loaf of bread. What is the background of all this Message Center work? I need a background to understand this, Capt. Chrisman."

"The best I can do for you is to leave you this field manual and tell you to read up on cryptography in the front of the Philippine Army code book. The Filipino boys here will show you the rest."

"Okay, if that is all there is to it, I'll see what I can do."

The next day at noon, I found myself in full charge of that Message Center. In fact, I was soon to be commanding officer of Camp X.

I learned my cryptography the hard way, by experience only. Because of the nature of the Filipino people and their inadequate use of our language, I had to check everything that came and went out for accuracy.

Gen. Sharp had moved to Mindanao leaving me in charge of his Force Communications Station on the Island of Cebu. At that time, this communications station was his only contact with Gen. MacArthur.

Capt. Chrisman had gone with Gen. Sharp to run the Message Center at the forward command post designated as Camp Y. These first few days of running that Message Center with Filipino soldiers and not knowing anything about the job, gave me merry hell. It took a lot of intensive work and long hours to get used to the ordinary procedure.

Gen. Sharp soon decided that Cebu was far too small an island on which to carry or wage a defensive campaign. Naturally, the most logical place was Mindanao directly to the south. Mindanao was the second largest in the Philippine group. It is quite mountainous and has quite a variety of vegetation as well as a variety of terrain. He had left Cebu City because it was a military objective that was illogical to defend and he was determined to leave the Island of Cebu in secrecy.

With Gen. Sharp's headquarters and most of the troops on Mindanao, the Visayas assumed a secondary importance in the defense of the south. In the event of attack it would be virtually impossible to reinforce any of the islands in that group from Mindanao. Each of the six defended islands – Cebu, Panay, Negros, Leyte, Samar and Bohol—was now dependent upon its own garrison and resources to meet a Japanese invasion. The organization of the Visayan-Mindanao Force established early in January lasted only about one month. In early February, in an effort to facilitate the delivery of supplies expected shortly from Australia, USAFFE assumed direct control of the garrisons on Panay and Mindoro, both a part of General Sharp's command. A month later, the remaining Visayan garrisons were separated from Gen. Sharp's command. The five garrisons in the Visayas were then organized into the Visayan Force and placed under Brig. Gen. G. Chynoweth, who had commanded on Panay. Gen. Sharp and Gen. Chynoweth reported directly to higher headquarters on Corregidor.

From time to time, I have mentioned the use of government transportation. This transportation was not regular Army, but consisted of civilian trucks and cars acquired by the quartermaster for military purposes. In Cebu, the Army had taken over whole lines of buses and equipment, trucks from commercial companies and passenger cars from individuals. It was the same on all other islands. In that manner, the Army was able to move supplies and troops from place to place.

Immediately after the beginning of the war, Gen. Sharp started moving all types of supplies back into the interior of the island. He concentrated heavily on food and clothing. He couldn't concentrate on such military supplies as guns and ammunition because these weren't to be had. I have the impression that by January 10, the troops on the Island of Cebu had about 10 rounds of ammunition each. A lot of food and clothing was moved into the mountains and was just taken over by the government and held in warehouses so that it would be easily available for shipping to the Southern Islands.

Lt. Col. Marcus Boulware was in charge of the food transportation into the hills. He worked day and night from around December 15 until after Christmas to accomplish this. He ended up going to the hospital due to exhaustion.

The job was too big for just one man. He had to transport the goods by Filipino labor on Filipino time with an American Army in back of him saying you will have this accomplished by such and such a date, and that accomplished by such and such a date. An American battalion under American officers could have accomplished the work under American schedule, but one man using Filipino labor was just out of luck. The colonel never fully recovered from the strain of this period of duty. It seemed to have affected his heart and it troubled him all through prison. His bad heart was undoubtedly a contributing factor to his death en route to Japan.

Shortly after Col. Boulware had gotten a lot of the food back into the hills, they had to go get it again, bring it back to Cebu and ship it to Mindanao. He had some fun.

Another American officer who had been connected with supplies was Lt. Col. Rufus H. Rogers. He came into the Finance Office shortly after January 1942 in order to get some pay so he could live. Gen. Sharp was in conference with Lt. Col. Paul S. Beard of the Finance Office. Col. Rogers used to tell this story in prison camp.

"I found Gen. Sharp in there with Col. Beard, the finance officer. They were talking in low tones. They looked up and saw me and went into a closer huddle. Pretty soon the general beckoned to me to come over to where they were. I went."

"You are it."

"I am what?"

"The new finance officer."

"You have the wrong man. My branch is the infantry."

"You are the new finance officer now."

"I don't know finance from flour sacks."

"Col. Beard will tell you about finance."

"Yes, Sir."

Col. Rogers concluded, "That is the way that I became the finance officer of Cebu Island. I just walked into the room and presto I became a Buck Rogers finance officer."

Col. Beard taught finance to Col. Rogers the rest of that forenoon and then took off for Camp X with several bags and trunks full of pesos to accompany Gen. Sharp.

On the night that Gen. Sharp left, among the officers left to follow him was Maj. Max Weil. He was headquarters commandant for Gen. Sharp. He was to follow in a day or two with the headquarters troops. The night that Gen. Sharp left, I spent it in the company of Maj. Weil. He was very kind in telling me all that he could about the installations at Camp X regarding the caves, tunnels and supplies since I was to take over when he left. After he finished discussing business, we talked about our future and the immediate war. We both agreed it looked pretty dark. I am afraid I was pretty blue that night, although I had been left behind to run a vital installation. I had the feeling of being deserted and left in one of the hottest spots in the Philippines. It took me some weeks to get used to the idea of "Well, what the hell! You got to go sometime. If I go now, early in the game, I am going to miss a lot of grief and I never did like trouble."

In the days that followed, I was very thankful that my new work of communications officer kept me mentally occupied every minute of the day. When I did sleep, it was because of exhaustion. More than one night I fell asleep at my desk and awoke in the dim hours of the morning slumped in my chair stiff and cold. I have found that physical labor is often the answer to a mind under mental stress. One of the other men Gen. Sharp left behind for a few days was his chief of staff, Col. John W. Thompson. While Col. Sharp was moving to Mindanao, there were other troop movements to Mindanao from other Southern Islands. Among these movements was the shifting of the 81st Infantry Regiment from Wright, Samar, to Surigao, Mindanao. I believe that Col. Ben Hur Chastine was in command of this operation. The troops had to be loaded on a boat at or near Catbalogan, Samar, where they sailed down the straits between Samar, Leyte, to some point on the Surigao Peninsula. Because of a late start, practically all of this troop movement was made in the daylight by a convoy of two boats. All of us, Col. Thompson particularly, were on pins and needles the entire day. About 11:00 a.m. as I remember, we got a report of three Nip planes flying back and forth along the north coast of Leyte and then down the west coast of the same island. They did this for about an hour and then went back north to Luzon. They didn't appear again that day. From the reports of these three planes flying back and forth along the Leyte coast we knew they were out scouting for something. They had evidently expected troop movements in the Southern Islands. They even guessed the unit and the island involved (or was it guessing). But they didn't guess the right route of the troop movement.

Col. Thompson really sweat blood all that day and night. Early the next morning, one of the first radiograms we received was the following, "Two units of transportation safe at Surigao. Signed, Ben Hur Chastine."

Col. Thompson wiped the sweat off his brow as he read that radiogram and said, "Well, this is what I have been waiting for. Yesterday when those planes were flying up and down the coast I was afraid they might find these boats."

On the third day after the departure of Gen. Sharp, I started sending out call signals for his Mindanao radio station. Late in the afternoon we got an answer. After an hour or so of traffic between the two stations for adjustment, the new station 6RC was ready for business. I wasn't satisfied that this was the station I was seeking. Therefore, I determined to make it identify itself in a manner that would satisfy me. To do this I required from the new station some inconsequential non-military information. There was still at Camp X an American corporal left behind because he was in Cebu drawing his pay when the headquarters left. He was to follow on the next boat. I reasoned that somebody in the headquarters would know who was left behind at Camp X and why. Accordingly, I wired to 6RC the following message. "For purpose of identification, what is the name of the American corporal left in Camp X because he was drawing his pay in Cebu."

The new station, 6RC, was silent for something over an hour. I began to think that it was an enemy station. Finally the radio silence was broken with the following message, "Cpl. Fitzjohn was left in Camp X because he was in Cebu after his pay." This answer established their authenticity with me and I then permitted military traffic to pass over the keys.

The next few days were full and busy ones for me, I was learning a new business. Maj. Max Weil had left with the headquarters troops. Col. Thompson had left to join Gen. Sharp and Col. Scudder, who had been at Camp X for only a day or so until Gen. Sharp left, going back to Cebu City. I now found myself alone, in charge of a Force Communication Station and commander of Camp X installations and supply dump.

I spent most of my time with the radio work, as that was what I was there for. All other things were mere incidentals. For quite sometime I did all the coding and decoding work for Col. Scudder in addition to my regular traffic for Gen. Sharp. As the weeks went by Gen. Sharp would radio for one by one of my Filipino Army signal corpsmen. I got so low on technical help that I finally complained. The result was that the cryptography work was done in the Cebu headquarters and I was handling only traffic for Gen. Sharp. As he got other contacts with Gen. MacArthur on Corregidor, my traffic lessened.

As the military personnel under me were transferred to Gen. Sharp's installations in Mindanao, I had to find civilian personnel to help me operate.

To do this I got hold of four men. Three were English and one Scottish. Naturally with their background, they were all dependable. One by the name of Fred Pipe, a big, six footer, was more American than English. He worked for the Lever Brothers Co. out of their New York office. Pipe had worked for the Motor Pool in Cebu City up to the time that Gen. Sharp left. He was now very willing to join me. The other Englishman, William L. Hocking, was a graduate of Oxford and was working for a commercial company in the islands. The third Englishman was a British first lieutenant Lawrie-Smith. Lawrie-Smith likewise had been a civilian with a commercial job before the beginning of the war. All three British at the beginning of the war had contacted their country's agency asking to be assigned to duty with the U.S. Army in the Philippines. This, of course, was quite an unusual request to make of the hide-bound British army. However, the men held the rank in the British reserve and white officers were at a premium in the islands. I don't know whether these assignments became official or not in the British army, but I do know the men performed the services commensurate with their rank.

A little later, I got two Norwegians to come and work for me at the camp. One was a cook and the other named Jens K. Jensen had been a ship's carpenter. These two men had been aboard a Norwegian freighter shortly after the war started which was sailing in the Pacific about 200 miles east of the Surigao Peninsula in northern Mindanao. Some Jap planes came over and bombed the ship, sinking it. They did not even know that there was a war on. The ship didn't go down too fast so most of the crew got aboard lifeboats and set sail for Mindanao. In due time, they reached the island and finally Cebu City. At Cebu City, there was a Norwegian consul who took care of the sailors. Most of them expressed their desire to help the American war effort against the Japs. They were used in small groups here and there around the island.

Returning to the British subjects, I don't know what happened to the Scotchman after the surrender of the islands. Lt. Lawrie-Smith was killed during the invasion of Cebu on duty with Filipino troops. Lt. Bill Hocking escaped to the Island of Leyte during the invasion and later surrendered on Leyte with the American officers. Capt. Fred Pipe remained in my service at Camp X until he was called to Mindanao to work under, I believe, Lt. Col. Robert Johnston whom I have mentioned before. Pipe surrendered with the Americans in Mindanao, but because of some technical standing concerning his commission, he was interned by the Japs as a civilian instead of a prisoner of war. Pipe survived the war. I don't know what happened to my Norwegian cook, but I do know what happened to the ship's carpenter Jens K. Jensen. He worked for me as civilian in charge of Camp X up to a few days before the invasion of Cebu. At that time Capt. William English, headquarters commandant, took over the camp and I became communications officer of the Visayan Force. Jensen worked for Capt. English until after the invasion. During the invasion and later, he became engaged in guerrilla activities. Jensen assumed responsibility and was commissioned 1st lieutenant quartermaster in the American Army by Gen. Chynoweth. Lt. Jensen shared my quarters with me at Camp X for weeks before the invasion. During the evenings and at mealtime we got to know each other quite well. He often expressed the desire to become a U.S. citizen, even in those dark days following the American defeat, this Norwegian stoutly maintained that there was only one end to the war, namely American victory. He often said that he wanted to be in on the finish. During the course of the war, there were two supply ships from Australia that succeeded in getting into Cebu with supplies. Both were unloaded and got safely out.

Jensen had an opportunity to get to Australia when each of these ships sailed. He refused to go on the grounds that he was needed by the American Army. From my point of view, he certainly was needed. To this day, I don't know what I would have done without him. He was efficient, reliable and responsible. When the Island of Cebu surrendered, he surrendered as a 1st lieutenant in the American Army and took the following years of imprisonment as any other American officer. He survived the war and came back to the U.S. on board the same transport with me. He was still a Norwegian citizen and his rank as a 1st lieutenant in the American Army had been authenticated. He was all set to go all out to secure his American citizenship once he landed in the States. To this end, I gave him a statement of service and the highest personal recommendations. I can only say that I wish the average American had as much patriotism and stability of character as Lt. Jensen had. The U.S. should be proud to have Lt. Jensen for a citizen.

With Gen. Sharp's departure to Mindanao around the first week in January 1942, Col. Irving C. Scudder became commander of the Island of Cebu with a provisional brigade of Filipino troops under him. With the exceptions of my Force Communications Station, every military and civilian installation on the island was directly under his command in respect to defense. Col. John D. Cook, IMC, was in command of the port area for operation and I was responsible directly to Gen. Sharp for the operation of my Force Communications Station.

Col. Scudder's staff consisted of Maj. Ernest V. Jorden, Maj. Lyles V. Hardin, Lt. Col. Marcus Boulware, Capt. William English, Capt. Russell H. Cracraft and assistants to his staff 2nd Lt. George M. Wightman, British, 1st Lt. (then sergeant) Doyle R. Armstrong. Maj. Ernest V. Jorden was a reserve officer whose home was in Milledgeville, GA.

Maj. Jorden had worked with me as the air-warning officer in Cebu. When Col. Scudder formed his staff, Maj. Jorden became the brigade plans and training officer and Maj. Lyles V. Hardin took over the censorship duties.

Maj. Lyles V. Hardin came from Rockhill, SC. He had attended Wafford College before coming out to the islands. Maj. Hardin was six feet, rotund and had a wonderful sense of humor. His personality radiated to all who were around him. We never thought of him as captain or Maj. Hardin, but he was affectionately known to all as Tiny. His happy-go-lucky smile would cheer the bluest of us. Tiny was a captain during most of the war, but after the invasion, he took over the command of the newly formed MP regiment and did a wonderful job in the guerrilla warfare. That is where he earned his rank of major. Tiny surrendered with Gen. Chynoweth and went to Davao Penal Colony. On Feb. 24, 1944, Maj. Hardin went to Lasang as one of Col. Rogers' barracks leaders. On Sept. 8, 1944, he was killed aboard the prison ship when the boat was torpedoed.

Lt. Col. Marcus Boulware was still in charge of special supplies on the Island of Cebu although he was not the brigade officer.

Capt. William R. English came from North Carolina. I believe the town was Spartanburg. Bill had been married only a short time before he came over and was quite disgusted that the war had come when it did. As I recall Bill was the brigade S-4 and it was through him that I went to get my supplies. He didn't surrender on the Island of Cebu when it fell. At that particular time, he was on a special mission for Gen. Chynoweth. When the surrender order came through he surrendered with the American officers on that island. Later he was brought to Cebu as a prisoner, kept in our prison a few hours and shipped on south to Davao. Bill endured the hardships of Davao and in June 1944 was one of the group moved to Cabanatuan, Luzon. He stayed in Luzon, spending some time in Bilibad prison until Dec. 13, 1944, when as part of the *Oryoku Maru* detail, he was shipped to Japan. He survived the bombings of December 14, 15 and 16 when our ship went down at Olongapo, Luzon. He was then shipped up to Takao in southern Formosa where he survived a second bombing which killed a great many of us. Finally on board the third prison ship of that trip, Jan. 23, 1945, Bill died from dysentery, dehydration, malnutrition and exposure while still en route to Japan. Bill was an exceptionally good friend of mine. One of the most heart-wrenching things that happened to me was to see him beg for water on that trip. Somewhere along the line, during that trip, Bill had acquired an extra canteen from one of his friends who had died toward the last of the trip when we were getting a half-pint of water per man every other day. He had no use for this extra canteen. By this time he was so weak, such a skeleton of bones and so helpless that he was in the hospital area of the ship's hold. I happened to pass by him on my way to the latrine area and he caught hold of my hand. His tongue was so badly swollen from lack of water that he could hardly talk. He pulled me down to his face and in a thick, halting, hoarse whisper, said "Bill, will you take this canteen (fumbling with the canteen) and trade it for two spoonfuls of water for me? Just two spoonfuls, Bill." I replied that I would try. I had no water myself or I would have given it to him. I had no luck in trading his canteen for any amount of water, no matter how small. I can still remember the look in his eyes when I returned his canteen to him saying that nobody had any water to trade. At that late stage in our game, material things had no value except food and clothing.

Capt. Russell Cracraft worked in the censor's office with Maj. Hardin from the time Maj. Hardin took over the duties of censor. They were together clear through the invasion of Cebu by the Japs. Somewhere during the battle they were separated and during the guerrilla activities Capt. Cracraft was with me up in the Salambam forest. Cracraft surrendered at Cebu, went to Mindanao and worked in the Davao Penal Colony until Feb. 24, 1944, when he went on the Lasang detail as assistant barracks leader to Maj. Hardin.

Capt. Cracraft died at the same time Maj. Hardin did due to the torpedoing of their prison ship on Sept. 8, 1944. I don't know much of Capt. Cracraft's life before he came to Cebu, but I have the impression that his home state was West Virginia.

Capt. William English's assistant brigade S-4 was 2nd Lt. George M. Wightman. Lt. Wightman was British. He was another of the British who assumed duties and responsibilities of an officer in the American Army. His commission was pending. Wightman had lived in the islands all his life. He knew the native psychology and their ways. Lt. Wightman surrendered with the Cebu group on May 17, 1942, and went to Davao with the group in October 1942. He stayed at Davao until Feb. 24, 1944, when he became part of the detail sent to Lasang. On Sept. 8, 1944, his prison ship was sunk off Liloy Point just north of Zamboanga, Mindanao. Just what George's fate was during that sinking, I can't say.

Sgt. Doyle R. Armstrong was the chief of Col. Scudder's encoding and decoding center. Sgt. Armstrong had been an enlisted man in the 31st Infantry, if my memory is correct. On Sept. 1, 1941, he went to duty with the Philippine army in southern Negros. While there, he contracted dysentery and was sent to Cebu City for hospitalization. The war broke out while he was still in the hospital. When he was returned to duty he was assigned to Brigade Headquarters. Sgt. Armstrong remained in that capacity until after the invasion when he was commissioned a 1st lieutenant in the Signal Corps. Lt. Armstrong surrendered with the Cebu group and went with it to the Davao Penal Colony. From the Davao Penal Colony, he went to Lasang in February 1944. I don't know what his fate was other than he is missing as a result of the sinking of the Lasang detail prison ship.

These men composed Col. Scudder's Provisional Brigade Staff. There were other American officers with various commands and duties over the island and quite a number of civilians working for the Army who were late commissioned. Those will be mentioned from time to time as I proceed with events.

I won't deal too much with the details of our preparation for invasion. To say the least, we didn't have much in the way of equipment. There were only a few machine guns on the island and as I recall, the entire 5,000 troops, all Filipinos, had only seven 81mm mortars (that may be incorrect). To begin with, those who were armed with rifles had only 10 or 12 rounds of ammunition per rifle and the labor battalions were armed with only bolos. There wasn't much of a defense we could put up when invasion came and we knew it, but we were determined to make that initial invasion as costly as possible for the Japs. It was not until Bataan fell that the Japs really turned their attention to the Southern Islands. Prior to that time, they merely captured key points, which would cut off our shipping lanes of supply. They then bypassed us for bigger game in the South Pacific.

From time to time, the Japanese would send large groups of bombers over Cebu City to bomb shipping and supply dumps. I remember two specific instances when the number of bombers were 18 or 20. Another phase was the sending of Japanese cruisers around the Island of Cebu to shell and terrorize the people. Finally on April 10, their task force arrived off shore and landed early on April 11.

Indiana University, 1941

Christmas, 1945

ROTC, 1936, Bloomington, IN

Before leaving States in 1941

Miner (upper left) with a Marine sergeant teaching Filipinos the operation of a machine gun. (US Army photo, 1941)

October 1945

On the bow of the S.S. Pres. Pierce *(center) somewhere in the Pacific (June 1941) heading to the Philippines.*

August, 1945 Hoten POW Camp
Miner (front, right, wearing hat)
Approximate weight, 60 pounds.

Hoten POW Camp, August 1945

Bill Miner (center)

October 1945

August 1945, Hoten POW Camp, Mukden, Manchuria

Hoten POW Camp, August 1945

Late 1970s

Early 1990s

127

Actual diaries used to record days and events. *(Continued on next page.)*

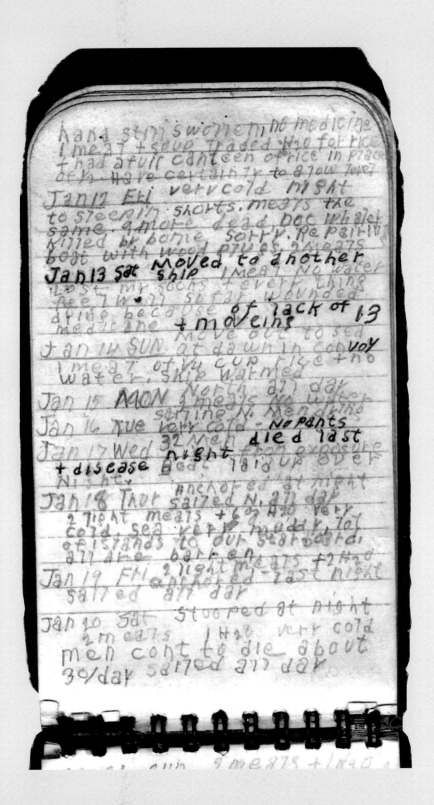

hand still swollen, no medicine
1 meal + soup. Traded H_2O for rice
+ had a full canteen of rice in place
of H. Have certainty to grow Jowet

Jan 12 Fri very cold night
to steering shorts. meals the
same. 4more dead Dec whaler
killed by bomb sorry. Repairing
boat with wood piues 2meals

Jan 13 Sat Moved to another
ship 1meal No water
Lost my socks + everything
feel well so far wounded
dying because of lack of 13
medicine + moveins
Move out to sea

Jan 14 Sun at dawn in convoy
1meal of 1/4 cup rice + no
water. Ship warmed
North all day

Jan 15 Mon 2 meals No water
setting N. No medicine

Jan 16 Tue very cold - no pants

Jan 17 Wed 32 men died last
night from exposure
+ disease Head laid up over
Night. anchored at night

Jan 18 Thur Sailed N. all day
2 light meals + 6oz H_2O very
cold, sea very muddy. Top
of islands to our starboard
all are barren

Jan 19 Fri 2 light meals + 2 H_2O
anchored - Last night
sailed all day

Jan 20 Sat stopped at night
2 meals 1H_2O very cold
men cont to die about
30/day sailed all day

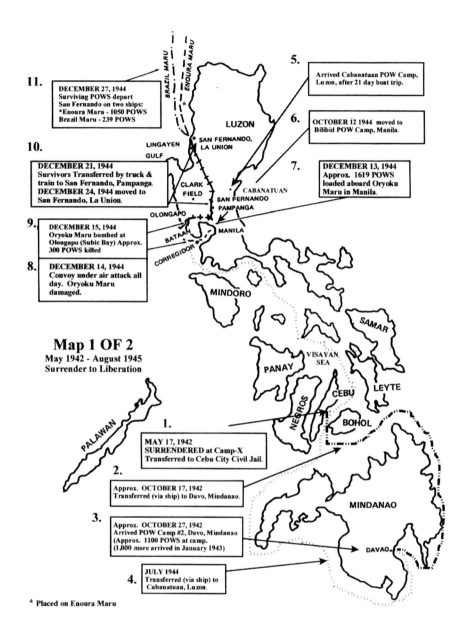

11.
DECEMBER 27, 1944
Surviving POWS depart
San Fernando on two ships:
*Enoura Maru - 1050 POWS
Brazil Maru - 239 POWS

5.
Arrived Cabanatuan POW Camp,
Luzon, after 21 day boat trip.

6.
OCTOBER 12 1944 moved to
Bilibid POW Camp, Manila.

10.
DECEMBER 21, 1944
Survivors Transferred by truck &
train to San Fernando, Pampanga.
DECEMBER 24, 1944 moved to
San Fernando, La Union.

7.
DECEMBER 13, 1944
Approx. 1619 POWS
loaded aboard Oryoku
Maru in Manila.

9.
DECEMBER 15, 1944
Oryoku Maru bombed at
Olongapo (Subic Bay) Approx.
300 POWS killed

8.
DECEMBER 14, 1944
Convoy under air attack all
day. Oryoku Maru
damaged.

LUZON

BRAZIL MARU
ENOURA MARU

LINGAYEN
GULF

SAN FERNANDO,
LA UNION

CLARK
FIELD

CABANATUAN

SAN FERNANDO
PAMPANGA

OLONGAPO

BATAAN

MANILA

CORREGIDOR

MINDORO

SAMAR

Map 1 OF 2
May 1942 - August 1945
Surrender to Liberation

VISAYAN
SEA

PANAY

NEGROS

CEBU

LEYTE

BOHOL

PALAWAN

1.
MAY 17, 1942
SURRENDERED at Camp-X
Transferred to Cebu City Civil Jail.

2.
Approx. OCTOBER 17, 1942
Transferred (via ship) to Davo, Mindanao.

MINDANAO

3.
Approx. OCTOBER 27, 1942
Arrived POW Camp #2, Davo, Mindanao
(Approx. 1100 POWS at camp.
(1,000 more arrived in January 1943)

DAVAO

4.
JULY 1944
Transferred (via ship) to
Cabanatuan, Luzon.

* Placed on Enoura Maru

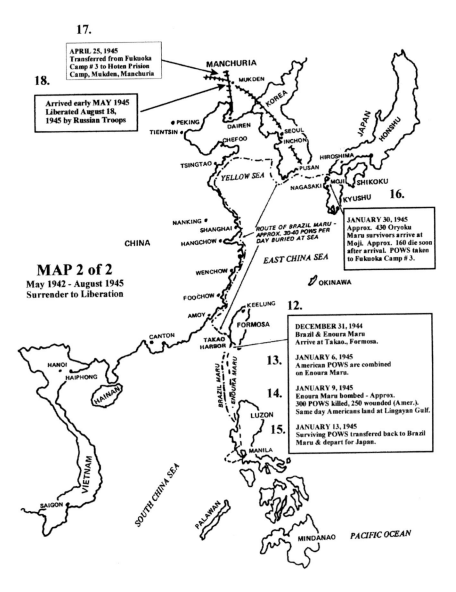

17.

APRIL 25, 1945
Transferred from Fukuoka
Camp # 3 to Hoten Prision
Camp, Mukden, Manchuria

18.

Arrived early MAY 1945
Liberated August 18,
1945 by Russian Troops

MANCHURIA

MUKDEN

● PEKING

TIENTSIN ●

KOREA

DAIREN

SEOUL

CHEFOO

INCHON

JAPAN

HONSHU

TSINGTAO

YELLOW SEA

PUSAN

HIROSHIMA

NANKING ●

SHANGHAI

HANGCHOW ●

CHINA

ROUTE OF BRAZIL MARU -
APPROX. 30-40 POWS PER
DAY BURIED AT SEA

EAST CHINA SEA

NAGASAKI ● MOJI

SHIKOKU

KYUSHU

16.

JANUARY 30, 1945
Approx. 430 Oryoku
Maru survivors arrive at
Moji. Approx. 160 die soon
after arrival. POWS taken
to Fukuoka Camp # 3.

MAP 2 of 2
May 1942 - August 1945
Surrender to Liberation

WENCHOW ●

FOOCHOW ●

OKINAWA

AMOY ●

KEELUNG

FORMOSA

12.

CANTON

TAKAO
HARBOR

DECEMBER 31, 1944
Brazil & Enoura Maru
Arrive at Takao., Formosa.

HANOI

HAIPHONG

HAINAN

BRAZIL MARU

ENOURA MARU

13.

JANUARY 6, 1945
American POWS are combined
on Enoura Maru.

14.

JANUARY 9, 1945
Enoura Maru bombed - Approx.
300 POWS killed, 250 wounded (Amer.).
Same day Americans land at Lingayan Gulf.

LUZON

15.

JANUARY 13, 1945
Surviving POWS transfered back to Brazil
Maru & depart for Japan.

MANILA

VIETNAM

SOUTH CHINA SEA

SAIGON

PALAWAN

MINDANAO

PACIFIC OCEAN

1110 Indiana Ave.
New Castle, Ind.
April 26, 1942

Dear Mrs. Miner:

I was so glad to hear of the radiogram you had received from Bill. Mrs Ingersoll called me a few days later saying that they had also received one.

Since the invasion of Sabu, however, I have thought of Bill so very often and hoped that by some divine act he has been spared injury or capture.

You being his mother, I am sure, feel the thing which I have expressed so poorly. My heart goes out to you, for I can understand the pain and anxiety that you must feel all of the time. I will say to you what I would like to say to him, "Be strong and of good courage."

His friends never get together here that they do not speak of him, and wonder about his safety, so any news you may receive will be appreciated by all of us.

Most sincerely,
Clara Charles

CLEAR CHANNEL · 50,000 WATTS · 890 KILOCYCLES
1230 WASHINGTON BLVD. TELEPHONE-MONROE 9700

Burridge D. Butler PRESIDENT
Glenn Snyder MANAGER

The Prairie Farmer Station

CHICAGO

April 16, 1942

Mr. A. B. Miner
Table Grove,
Illinois

Dear friend:

      I can readily realize your concern over the news from the Philippines. You may rest assured that Ervin Lewis and I will broadcast every available bit of information regarding Cebu. I sincerely hope that you have good news from your son shortly.

Sincerely yours,

Julian Bentley

Julian T. Bentley
News Editor

JTB:EMc

WLS

JULIAN T. BENTLEY
NEWS EDITOR

Aug 10, 1942.

Mrs Anna Miner
Table Grove
Illinois

Dear Friend:
    Please find enclosed a sheet from the Chinese Information Service, relaying a story short-waved from Chungking.
    Erv and I are both glad you were in communication with your son. And I sincerely hope that today's news from the Solomons is the start of an offensive which will eventually bring him home. I noticed in a "Knox Student" that Lee Blessing ('29) was interned at Manila. News from or concerning Cebu is practically non-existent on the wires these days but we'll see that you are informed of anything that is available.

Sincerely yours,

Julian Bentley

WLS jb

CHICAGO
AUG 10
7 PM
1942
ILL.

3 CENTS 3
UNITED STATES POSTAGE

Mrs Anna Miner
Box 663
Table Grove
Illinois

contents sent to
Martha Ellen

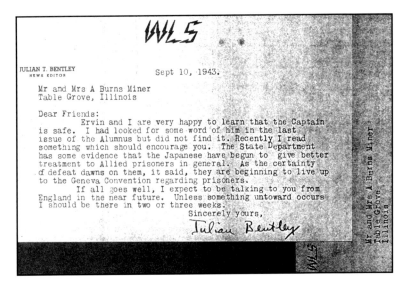

WLS

JULIAN T. BENTLEY
NEWS EDITOR

Sept 10, 1943.

Mr and Mrs A Burns Miner
Table Grove, Illinois

Dear Friends:
    Ervin and I are very happy to learn that the Captain is safe. I had looked for some word of him in the last issue of the Alumnus but did not find it. Recently I read something which should encourage you. The State Department has some evidence that the Japanese have begun to give better treatment to Allied prisoners in general. As the certainty of defeat dawns on them, it said, they are beginning to live up to the Geneva Convention regarding prisoners.
    If all goes well, I expect to be talking to you from England in the near future. Unless something untoward occurs I should be there in two or three weeks.

Sincerely yours,

Julian Bentley

Mr and Mrs A Burns Miner
Table Grove
Illinois

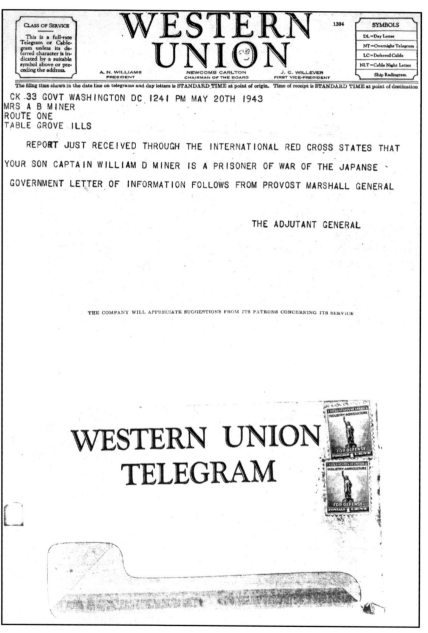

WESTERN UNION

1204

A. N. WILLIAMS
PRESIDENT

NEWCOMB CARLTON
CHAIRMAN OF THE BOARD

J. C. WILLEVER
FIRST VICE-PRESIDENT

The filing time shown in the date line on telegrams and day letters is STANDARD TIME at point of origin. Time of receipt is STANDARD TIME at point of destination

CK 33 GOVT WASHINGTON DC 1241 PM MAY 20TH 1943
MRS A B MINER
ROUTE ONE
TABLE GROVE ILLS

REPORT JUST RECEIVED THROUGH THE INTERNATIONAL RED CROSS STATES THAT

YOUR SON CAPTAIN WILLIAM D MINER IS A PRISONER OF WAR OF THE JAPANSE

GOVERNMENT LETTER OF INFORMATION FOLLOWS FROM PROVOST MARSHALL GENERAL

THE ADJUTANT GENERAL

WESTERN UNION
TELEGRAM

Acknowledgment of POW status came one year after surrender.

WAR DEPARTMENT

ARMY SERVICE FORCES

OFFICE OF THE PROVOST MARSHAL GENERAL

WASHINGTON

May 22, 1943

RE: Captain William D. Miner

Mrs. A. B. Miner,
        Rural Route Number One,
            Table Grove, Illinois.

Dear Mrs. Miner:

The Provost Marshal General directs me
to inform you that by following the inclosed
instructions you may communicate, postage free,
with the above-named prisoner of war.

It is believed that the accompanying
circular #10 contains all information available
at this time.

Rest assured that any and all information received will be promptly forwarded to you.

Sincerely yours,

Howard F. Bresee

Howard F. Bresee,
Colonel, C.M.P.,
Chief, Information Branch.

2 Incls.
Infor. Cirs. Nos. 1 and 10.

24-25544

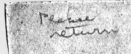

**Sports, Want Ads
and Markets**

LOCAL NEWS

GREETINGS FROM PRISON IN JAPAN

Efforts in Progress to Have Captains Whaley and Miner Exchanged

Word received from Philippine Military Prison Camp No. 2 from Captain Milton Whaley via Imperial Japanese army post card to E. E. Morris indicates that "Doc" seems to be his old congenial self and that he is in excellent health. He indicates under No. 5 to tell his wife to learn to cook rice. He states that he is an experienced RR Tie man at the writing and hopes for a reunion about Christmas.

Mr. Morris is to notify the captain's wife at Petros, Tenn., and regards are sent to Mrs. Morris and daughter, Whipple, Knox college, Mr. Lahr, Punch and love to all in Galesburg.

Prison Camp No. 2 is identified by Mr. Morris as at Davos at the south tip of Mindanao Island and further word received in answer to request to a high officer in the area to release Captains Miner and Whaley is that the job will be accomplished and that it may be accomplished sometime in the not too distant future with the island hopping getting within striking distance with the safety margin.

Captain Miner's home is at Table Grove. He is also a graduate of Knox college.

A Soldier's Creed.

As a soldier in the United States Army let me thank you for your stand against isolationism and isolationists. We realize that the road ahead is still rocky and difficult and that we are fighting a war due mainly to their pigheadedness and disinterest in the national welfare. Many of our comrades have given their lives and unfortunately many more will follow in their hallowed footsteps before we can once again return to a civilian way of life. Yet these same people are still endeavoring to split the nation and set the stage for another world conflict in which we may really be there with "too little and too late."

* * *

I, and most of my buddies, am only out of high school a few years and we realize that it will be our duty to reconstruct the world after the war. We all want to go back home with the knowledge that we have done a complete and final job. But we want to come back to a country united in a defined peace. We don't want to fight another war in 20 years or have our children fight it for us. We all love this nation and its ideals more than words can express. We're doing our job and are willing to give our all for it. You've got to see to it that the people back home—all the people —are willing to do the same. If politics can mean more to a man than America, then America has little need for his "contribution" to democracy. Believe me, there were no atheists on Bataan and I assure you there were no isolationists either.

PVT. M. B. MILLER.
Camp Ellis, Ill.

Table Grove Man Is Prisoner Of Japs

Mr. and Mrs. A. B. Miner of Table Grove received a message Thursday from the U. S. government stating that their son, Captain William Miner, is held prisoner by the Japanese. He was reported missing in action following the fall of the Philippines a year ago.

The last word that has been received from him was last year on Easter Sunday when his parents received a cablegram from him.

Captain Miner is a graduate of Knox college and was a student at the Indiana state university when he was called into active service.

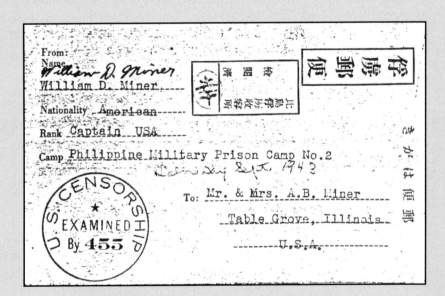

IMPERIAL JAPANESE ARMY

1. I am interned at _Phil. Mil. Prison Camp No. 2_

2. My health is — _excellent;_ good; fair; poor.

3. I am—_uninjured;_ sick in hospital; under treatment; not under treatment.

4. I am — improving; not improving; better; _well._

5. Please see that _hunderd dollar per month allotment ends_ _May Forty Four. Invest Most of it_ is taken care of.

6. (Re: Family); _Love to Grand mother, Aunt Bessie and_ food. Love to Martha. _You all. Received Welcome Br. and Can. REd Cross_

7. Please give my best regards to _Herbert Heller, New Castle_ Ind.

From:
Name _William D. Miner_
Nationality _American_
Rank _Captain USA_
Camp _Philippine Military Prison Camp No. 2_

To: _Mr. & Mrs. A.B. Miner_
Table Grove, Illinois
_U.S.A._

U.S. CENSORSHIP
★
EXAMINED
By 455

THE VICE PRESIDENT OF THE PHILIPPINES

1617 MASSACHUSETTS AVENUE, N. W.

WASHINGTON, D. C.

January 5, 1944.

Mr. A. B. Miner,
P. O. Box 663,
Table Grove, Ill.

Dear Mr. Miner:

I acknowledge receipt of your letter of
January 2, 1944. I am pleased and share with
you the relief for hearing good news from your
son, Captain William D. Miner.

My understanding is that Camp No. 2 is
within a few miles to the North of the town of
Davao, the capital of the Province of Davao,
Mindanao, where the Davao Penal Colony used
to be during the pre-war time. I was also
informed that there are quite a few United
States Officers in that camp but the number
is not known.

Information received recently with regard
to Mr. Camilo Osias was that he was in good
health and living in Manila together with his
family.

If I could be of further service to you,
please let me know.

Sincerely yours,

S. OSMEÑA.

Mr. A. B. Miner,
P. O. Box # 663,
Table Grove, Ill.

From:
Name __William D. Miner__

Nationality __American__

Rank __Captain__

Comp __Philippine Military Prison Camp No. 2__

To: __Mr. & Mrs. A. Miner__

__Table Grove__

__Illinois, USA__

U.S. CENSORSHIP EXAMINED By 585

IMPERIAL JAPANESE ARMY

1. I am interned at __Philippine Military Prison Camp No. 2__

2. My health is — __excellent;__ good; fair; poor.

3. I am — injured; sick in hospital; under treatment; __not under treatment.__

4. I am — improving; not improving; better; __well.__

5. Please see that __Inform Indiana University authorities that I plan to complete graduate work on return__

6. (Re: Family): __Inform Mrs. Rufus H. Rogers, Del Rio, Texas, is taken care of. her husband Col. Rogers is fine. Plan to buy farm in Texas__

7. Please give my best regards to __Love, Martha, you all & friends__

POW Card

miss Ruth mines
5772 Dorchester
Chicago 37, Illinois
A.F.A. Vermont, Ill

140

15 June 1945

RE: Captain William D. Miner
United States Prisoner of War
Fukuoka Prison Camp
Island of Honshu, Japan
Via: New York, New York

Mrs. A. B. Miner
Box 107
Vermont, Illinois

Dear Mrs. Miner:

The Provost Marshal General has directed me
to inform you of the transfer of the above-named
prisoner of war to the camp indicated.

You may communicate with him by following the
inclosed mailing instructions.

Further information will be forwarded as soon
as it is received.

Sincerely yours,

Howard F. Bresee

Howard F. Bresee,
Colonel, C.M.P.,
Assistant Director, Prisoners of War Division.

1 Incl.
Mailing Circular.

24-63094ABCD

IMPERIAL JAPANESE ARMY

1. I am interned at Philippine Military Prison Camp #2

2. My health is — excellent; good; fair; poor.

3. I am—uninjured; sick in hospital; under treatment; not under treatment.

4. I am — improving; not improving; better; well.

5. Please see that Again thank your aunt Sally for the bountiful farewell dinner she gave us. is taken care of.

6. (Re: Family) My love to you.Hello Wanda,tell Ibanez I saw the four horsemen he described to me when I left home. Hello to B.J.

7. Please give my best regards to My folks and yours,best of luck

---

From:
Name William D. Miner

Nationality American

Rank Captain

Camp Philippine Military
Prison Camp #2

To: Miss Martha Bales

Shelbyville, Indiana,

U.S.A.

11390
U.S. CENSOR

From:
Name William D. Miner

Nationality American

Rank Captain

Camp Philippine Military
Prison Camp # 2.

To: Mr & Mrs. A. B. Miner

Table Grove,

Illinois

USA

U.S. CENSOR 11002

IMPERIAL JAPANESE ARMY

1. I am interned at Philippine Military Prison Camp # 2.

2. My health is — excellent; good; fair; poor.

3. I am — injured; sick in hospital; under treatment; not under treatment.

4. I am — improving; not improving; better; well.

5. Please see that last pay drawn included Nov, 1941. Wish you to consider farm in Texas with me is taken care of.

6. (Re: Family); inform uncle Charley that Knox college Buddy, Doc Whaler is here with me and is doing fine

7. Please give my best regards to love to Martha, you all & friends.

SERVICE des PRISONNIERS de GUERRE

Received Feb, 15, 1945

俘虜郵便

NAME William D. Miner

NATIONALITY American

RANK Captain - Army

PHILIPPINE MILITARY PRISON CAMP NO. 1

比島俘虜収容所 検閲済

To: Mr & Mrs A. B. Miner

Table Grove,

Illinois,

11014 U.S. CENSOR

U. S. A.

IMPERIAL JAPANESE ARMY

1. I am interned at—Philippine Military Prison Camp No. 1

2. My health is—excellent; good; fair; poor.

3. Message (50 words limit)

Plan to buy small farm in Texas. on return and hope you can farm it while I finish education and teach in college.

Irmann in Chicago, Love Martha.

July 10, 1944

William D. Miner
Signature

143

Copy of letter from William
Written at Hoten Prisoner of War Camp
Mukden, Manchuria. Sunday, August 19, 1945.
(Retype and edited)

Dear Dad and Mother:

The age of miracles is not yet over- the war has come to an armistice - it is seems unbelievable!! Now that I have a chance to send you a letter I don't know what to say. I am stumped - I have even forgotten how to spell and write. For the last 39 months I, with many other Am, Br, Dutch, Indian and Australian prisoners have existed in many and various camps. We are all Rip Van Winkles, and we have no idea what has gone on out in the world.

It has been the policy of the Japanese to keep us concentrated in camps without any kind of contact from the outside. For months they let our mail lie around in their warehouses, giving it to us in small batches as it suited them. Their attitude has been - "you are a prisoner of war therefore you do not deserve anything. You are indebted to the Imperial Japanese for being permitted to live and you should be grateful to them for that favor no matter how much they maltreat, torture or starve us."

As a POW I received about a total of 66 letters and practically no Red Cross. Fortunately by the grace of God, a background of clean living and help of friends I am coming out of this war in good shape. The educational value of this experience is beyond power of description, but I wouldn't go thru it again for anything - it's indescribable and if I ever describe some events to the fullness of their reality most people will not believe me. At the present I shall waste no more time in that line.

I am looking forward to the future - if I have good fortune I'll be home shortly after this arrives - the diplomats will have to argue and it may cause dely... I am bursting to get some news of things outside.

During the war prior to the surrender out here I was a Special Staff Officer for General Bradford G. Chynoweth in Cebu. I helped in the surrender arrangements there. General Chynoweth is here in camp with me now. We have quite a liking for each other. Without present knowledge I am the only officer left of all his command except for his Chief of Staff who is a full Colonel and has been with him all thru his imprisonment. There may be others, but all that we have any knowledge of died on the Oryoka Maru bombing when we were shipped to Japan last Dec.

That was a fearful trip- it is indescribable. I was slightly wounded in each bombing, but nothing to speak of. The conditions of that trip were unspeakable so I won't speak of it here. Just know we are waiting for our planes to come in, bring food, medicine, and clothing. Soon we can have more communication so I will stop now.

Love,
Wm.

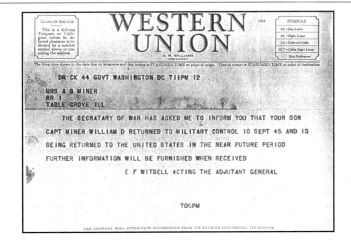

Two Released From Japanese Prison Camps

Sgt. Leo Harmon of Bardolph and Capt. Wm. D. Minerf of Table Grove, prisoners of the Japs for more than three years, have been released from Jap prison camps, according to messages received by their parents, Mrs. Mary Harmon of Jacksonville, and Mr. and Mrs. A. B. Miner of Vermont.

Both were taken prisoner following the fall of the Philippines in the spring of 1942.

The government message to Mrs. Harmon which she received last night was the first word that she has had concerning the safety of Sgt. Harmon since victory over Japan was announced.

By coincidence, a letter which he had written October 7, 1944, was also delivered to Mrs. Harmon yesterday. The letter was written in a Jap prison camp. It is believed it was written about the time he was being transferred from the Philippines to Osaka.

Sgt. Harmon was the third man from the Macomb area to be reported missing in action following the fall of Corregidor. He was not reported officially as a prisoner until May, 1943.

The government message which Mrs. Harmon received was as follows:

"The secretary of war has asked me to inform you that your son, Sgt. Leo Harmon, returned to military control Sept. 11 and is being returned to the United States within the near future and will be given an opportunity to communicate with you upon arrival."

Mr. and Mrs. A. B. Miner, former residents of Table Grove, learned that their son, Capt. Miner is on his way home. The message stated that he was fine but gave no other details.

Earlier in the week the Miners received a letter from Capt. Miner, dated August 19, in which he stated that the men were awaiting planes to bring them food, medicine and other supplies. On the back of the letter he wrote, "Hello to all my friends and relatives in and around Table Grove."

Their last previous message from him was a card dated July 10, 1944, when he was a prisoner on Luzon. About two weeks following victory over Japan, the Miners were informed by the government that their son's name had appeared on a list of prisoners at Camp Hoten, Mukden, Manchuria, and it is from this camp that they presume he was released.

WITH THE U. S.

Miners Hear From Imprisoned Son

Mr. and Mrs. A. B. Miner of Table Grove have received two post cards this week from their son, Capt. William D. Miner, who is interned in the Philippine Islands prison camp No. 2.

He stated that he was well and uninjured and had received welcome food from the British and Canadian Red Cross. He would like to be remembered to relatives and friends. He reported that his Knox college friend, Capt. Milton (Doc) Whaley, is safe.

Mr. and Mrs. Miner had last heard from their son on Easter Sunday, 1942.

—God Bless America—

FIRST NEWS FROM CAPT. WM. MINER SINCE APRIL 5, 1942

Mr. and Mrs. Burns Miner received two cards Monday afternoon from their son William. This is the first news they have received from him since April 5, 1942.

On the cards, which were typewritten, but bearing his signature was the following: "Love to relatives Hello to Hazel Green neighborhood. Am uninjured and well. Received welcome food from British and Canadian Red Cross."

Capt. Miner is in Military Prison Camp No. 2, Philippines.

Words cannot express how joyous Mr. and Mrs. Miner are over receiving the news.

From:
Name

William D. Miner

Nationality American

Rank Captain

Camp Philippine Military
Prison Camp No. 2

U.S. CENSORSHIP
★ EXAMINED
By 538

To: Mr. & Mrs. A. Miner

Table Grove

Illinois, USA

伜勝郵便

比軍伊收容所檢閲濟

きがは便郵

IMPERIAL JAPANESE ARMY

1. I am interned at Philippine Military Prison Camp No. 2

2. My health is — excellent; good; fair; poor.

3. I am — injured; sick in hospital; under treatment; not under treatment.

4. I am — improving; not improving; better; well.

5. Please see that Inform Indiana University authorities that I plan to complete graduate work on return
     _____ is taken care of.

6. (Re: Family): Inform Mrs. Rufus H. Rogers, Del Rio, Texas, her husband Col. Rogers is fine. Plan to buy farm in Texas

7. Please give my best regards to Love, Martha, you all & friends

146

Area lost a proud American this week

I'm so glad that Charleston's Red, White and Blue Days Committee honored World War II veterans in 1994 and 1995.

And I'm equally glad that the Times-Courier and Journal Gazette produced a 70–page section on the 50th anniversary of the end of WWII in September 1995.

Because we are running out of time to hear from those men and women who experienced the worldwide catastrophe that continues to shape our world.

We lost another veteran this week when Bill Miner died at the Odd Fellow-Rebekah Home at the age of 83.

Writing in our WWII section, Harry Read said it best about Bill Miner:

Bill Lair

Lair is managing editor of the Times-Courier and Journal Gazette.

Bill Miner's odyssey in hell began on May 17, 1942, when he was taken by the Japanese on Cebu Island (Philippines), and ended, officially, 39 months later when he was liberated by soldiers of the Russian Army at a POW camp in Manchuria.

"Officially," because Dr. William D. Miner, professor emeritus of history, Eastern Illinois University, probably will never be freed from the physical and emotional ordeal of those 39 months. This gentlemanly, soft-spoken and frail man suffered more than most persons can envision in their most demonic nightmares.

Gentlemanly and soft-spoken is how I remember Bill Miner. We were neighbors on a west side Charleston street.

On balmy spring and summer nights, he and his wife, Mary Ellen, liked to sit in front of their garage, in the driveway, and watch the traffic and people go by. They always spoke to Cheryl and me on our walks.

I knew Bill Miner had been a Japanese prisoner during World War II. But it was Harry Read's story in our commemorative section that described it so graphically.

Miner had been in the ROTC program at Knox College in Galesburg and was a reserve officer until 1941, when he reported for duty in the Philippines.

Bill Miner spent 3 years in captivity during WWII.

He spent most of the war in the capture of the Japanese, and barely survived.

From his diary, Dec. 25, 1944: "This is the lowest Christmas I ever had; we are without hope almost. Waiting to be put on ship again to sail to Japan. 2 meals, total one cup of rice."

And Jan. 1, 1945: "Still on ship in harbor, flies horrible, men dying. No water. Not a nice new year's beginning."

After his freedom:

"I have lost every close friend I had out here — I have been through filth, destruction, near death many times, and lived under conditions that warp men's souls. I haven't come through unscathed in the latter.

"I go home to a land of memories and hope, leaving behind a land of memories — memories of love, hate, fear, heroism, sacrifice, atrocities, destruction, torture, death, and of living friends.

"When I boil it all down, all I want out of life is 'quiet happiness.' All the glory, riches, power, pomp and splendor I have ever had or ever seen I would throw away for happiness and a healthy physical body. Such is life — it's a pretty empty affair at times."

Bill Miner always considered himself fortunate to have survived his ordeal.

"I am lucky. People fell beside me and people were blown apart beside me. Anywhere I went as a prisoner (Miner was in six POW camps) I tried to be aware of the situation and use it the best I could so that I could survive.

"Despite the controversy in recent years over President Truman's decision to authorize dropping A-Bombs on Hiroshima and Nagasaki, I believe it should have been done. I believe it for the tens of thousands of young Americans who would have died on the Japanese homeland. I also believe it for me. Had the war lasted only a few weeks more I could not have survived. My weight was down to 60-some pounds and I could barely stand."

And Bill Miner again said "I am lucky."

During his missions behind enemy lines, Miner earned the Silver Star for valor and the Purple Heart. Other decorations included the American Defense Ribbon with Battle Star, Philippine Liberation Ribbon with Battle Star, Philippine Liberation Ribbon with Battle Star, and a Presidential Unit Citation with two Oak Leaf Clusters).

Bill Miner was one of the WWII veterans who was featured in the July 4, 1995, parade and selected to ring the Liberty Bell.

"I've enjoyed it," he said of the festivities.

But mostly, Bill Miner told our reporter, "I'm proud to be an American."

Personnel on Cebu

Before I go into the events of the Japanese invasion of Cebu and the battle that followed, I am gong to list all of the civilian and military personnel who were actively engaged in the defense of Cebu. The people that I deal with here are those who turned in as prisoners of war or who were killed in action. From time to time, Navy men will be mentioned and if you would wonder how there were Navy personnel in Cebu, it can be easily explained in this manner.

About Feb. 1, 1942, some Navy personnel, newspaper correspondents and civilians sent to the Southern Islands, took a boat to Capiz in northern Panay; buses from Capiz southward across Panay to Iloilo and took the ferry across the straits to Bacoled, Negros. They continued by bus around Negros until they reached San Carlos on the eastcoast and then took the ferry across to Toledo, Cebu. From Toledo, buses brought them over the mountain ranges to Cebu City. Shortly after their arrival, a small cargo ship from Australia came into Cebu with supplies. The civilians and newspaper correspondents went out on this ship while the Navy personnel had to remain behind because of orders to report to the Army for assignment.

As to the personnel on Cebu mentioned here afterward, I shall refer to them at their highest rank.

The first on my list is a Naval commander, Thomas F. O'Brian, who came from Boston. He was single and made his home with his two sisters. Cmdr. O'Brian was not in very good health due to his war background in Luzon. He worked in the Censor's Office under Maj. Hardin. The commander was a jolly fellow and made friends with everyone.

The second was Lt. Cmdr. A.E. Grove. Cmdr. Grove worked in the Quartermaster's Office in Cebu City under Col. John D. Cook. Cmdr. Grove surrendered May 17 with the rest of the Cebu prisoners and went to Davao Penal Colony with the group. He was with the section that went to Luzon and on Oct. 12, 1944, he was put on a Japanese prison ship, which started for Japan. The boat had to dodge subs all through the China Sea and just outside Takao, Formosa, the boat was torpedoed and there were only five survivors.

The British 1st Lt. Lawrie-Smith also worked in the Censor's Office under Maj. Hardin.

Capt. Orville Fossum has already been mentioned as the American commander of the Toledo Garrison. Capt. Fossum held the command until some time in March, I believe, when he volunteered for the special mission of officer in charge of the inter-island ship *Regulas*. This ship was loaded with gasoline and food supplies for Bataan and Corregidor. He got the ship up along the coast of Mindanao some place when it was spotted by some Jap bombers. They bombed and strafed the ship until it caught on fire and had to be abandoned. Capt. Fossum was able to get ashore at Mindanao and finally made his way on to Corregidor by the way of a banca, a small native sailboat. Before going on this journey, Capt. Fossum had talked with Lt. Col. Paul S. Beard, a force finance officer about getting partial payment of his own salary which was due him. He told the colonel that he needed some money as a security factor on this special mission. He was told by the colonel that he didn't need any money and that the Army furnished him everything. I saw Capt. Fossum a few minutes before he boarded the ship and he told me that Col. Scudder had gotten him about 100 pesos. He said the rest of the boys, like himself, were broke and he couldn't borrow any more. It took most of Capt. Fossum's money to pay for the native bancas that got him up to Corregidor. I saw Capt. Fossum a few days before he died in Davao Prison and he said that he couldn't get paid at Corregidor because he didn't belong to the outfit. He told me that after the surrender came, up to the time he ran out of money, he was able to get enough food to keep him going. After his money ran out and he couldn't buy extra rice while in prison, he almost starved to death. He became run down, caught malaria and contracted dysentery.

When the Japs sent a detail of American prisoners from Luzon to Davao in October 1942, Fossum volunteered for the detail. When he arrived at Davao, I was already there. He was in very bad shape. Most of the Luzon men improved on their arrival at Davao, because at first there was plenty of rice and work was not too difficult for the ration we received. However, Capt. Fossum was so drained of physical resources that he did not respond to the increased diet and treatment at Davao Prison Hospital. I talked with him often while he was in the hospital and he repeatedly said that if he could have drawn more of his rightful back pay when he started on this special mission he could have gotten food enough that his health would not have broken from starvation. He said he had several thousand dollars of backpay and it wasn't worth a damn. In January 1943, Capt. Fossum died from malnutrition, dysentery and beriberi in the Davao Prison Hospital. The last two days he was in a coma and did not suffer much.

Capt. Fossum had quite a number of friends in the Cebu group and his ward in the hospital was often a meeting place for the Cebu group of an evening after a day's work. Every man present would have stolen something from the Nips during the day; at the risk of a severe personal beating, smuggled the tidbit into camp and brought it over to Capt. Fossum. These contributions were never much, but a couple of small bananas, a raw bitter sweet potato, a few pieces of coconut meat or a piece of ginger root all helped out. In spite of the attention of his friends, his body gave out, though the spirit was willing.

Lt. Col. Rufus R. Rogers was left in Cebu as finance officer when Gen. Sharp went to Mindanao. I have already related elsewhere the episode of how Col. Rogers became finance officer. Rogers was a husky, young Texan from Del Rio. He was a farmer's son and a graduate of Texas A&M. He had later taught animal husbandry in the Del Rio High School. He had a wonderful sense of humor and common sense stuck out all over him. No situation was so tough that it ever got him down and when things got going the hardest his big bass voice would suddenly roll out to the strains of "Beautiful Texas." Rogers remained in the Finance Office until toward the last of March when Gen. Chynoweth assumed command of the Visayan Force and placed Col. Rogers in command of the 33rd Infantry Regiment located in the mountains northwest of Cebu. Col. Rogers was one of the American emissaries at the surrender of the American Forces on Cebu in May 1942. Of those experiences and events that concerned him later in the various prisons, I shall relate another time.

Lt. Col. A.B. Carlton, QMC was one of the men who came down to Cebu from Corregidor after the war started. He worked in the Quartermaster Office of Cebu under Col. John D. Cook. Carlton had been in the last war and later lived in Chicago. He had been on active duty with the Army as an officer several years before coming to the Philippines. He worked with Col. Cook's office along with Lt. Cmdr. Grove and others until the invasion of Cebu. After the invasion, he still remained on duty under Col. Cook, the quartermaster. He surrendered May 17 with the rest of the Americans on the Island of Cebu. He got along during imprisonment fairly well but none too well with his fellow men. When going got hard, they nicknamed him "Old Lady Carlton." Carlton worked on some of the details at Davao and went north to Luzon in June 1944. He was put on board a ship going to Japan and died en route. He was aboard either the ship sailing October 12 or the *Oryoku Maru*, which sailed Dec. 13, 1944. I have the impression he was of the latter and as to the details of his death, I don't know.

There was a Maj. McClenahan on the Island of Cebu who was assistant provost marshal under Lt. Col. Howard Edmunds. McClenahan had been a school teacher back in Kansas or Nebraska. During the war in Cebu, he was quite a gay bird and after the surrender, just what happened to him, I can't say at the moment.

I have mentioned 2nd Lt. Al Fienstein who ran the radio station in Cebu. He continued to do this until the Nips took the city of Cebu, when he came and joined Gen. Chynoweth as a combatant. He later was one of the guerrillas.

Another of the Navy ensigns, Jimmy Mullins was one of the personnel who came down from Corregidor during the war, February I believe. During the war, his duties on Cebu consisted of an outpost commander along the shore of the island. We would make reconnaissance and keep watch for Jap ships going around the island. With the surrender of the Cebu Forces he became a prisoner of war and proceeded, once we were settled in prison, to become a member of the kitchen force which prepared the prisoner's meals. This was always a choice detail. Mullins then proceeded to get around the Japs enough to learn their language. He became quite fluent in his ability to speak it and to read it. When we moved to Davao, he became a detail leader there for awhile and went north to Luzon with the larger group in June 1944. In December 1944, he was put aboard the *Oryoku Maru* and survived the fearful trip north. From Japan, he was taken to Manchuria where he remained to the end of the war. He made the journey back to the States safely.

Capt. Floyd A. Hawkes, MC, had been in the U.S. Public Health Service before the war began. Capt. Hawkes had his office in the Customs Building in Cebu and his duty was port medical inspector for all foreign ships that entered the harbor of Cebu. I am not certain but I believe Capt. Hawkes was a graduate of Indiana University Medical School. His home was Whiting, IN. When the war started Capt. Hawkes went into the Medical Service and was stationed in Cebu. He was an excellent surgeon as well as doctor. When the island was invaded by the Japs, Capt. Hawkes stood by his wounded patients in the hospital and was captured early in the battle for Cebu. His hospital was located high in the mountains on the east slope of the Talisay-Toledo road. The Japanese captured the road shortly after they invaded the islands. The hospital staff had warning that the Japs were coming down the road so the American doctors told all the Filipino Army nurses to run up the mountain and get away before the Japs came. Lt. Col. Dwight M. Deter and Capt. Hawkes stayed by their patients and were captured by the Japs. Col. Deter, being in command, the Japs took him with them and left Capt. Hawkes at the hospital to take care of the patients. This he did for several days before the Japs came and moved him and the patients down to the City Hospital of Cebu. During the few days, after their capture in the field hospital, several Japanese patrols came through. Each patrol looted among the food and supplies. Each time the Japs found the clothes left behind by the Filipino Army nurses, they beat Capt. Hawkes because he didn't have any of the nurses around and couldn't tell them where the nurses were. When the first patrol came through, Capt. Hawkes had a supply of canned food hidden. He had to hide essential food stuffs in the high cogan grass on the mountain in order to be sure of having food for himself and patients. After he was moved to Cebu, he worked in the city hospital, which had been taken over by the Japs for a number of days. There the flies and filth were terrific and most of the patients died, including Jap soldiers. After several days of this, he was moved to a cell in the Cebu Provincial jail and that is where he remained until the American prisoners were brought in to occupy the entire jail. Capt. Hawkes went to Davao and was on duty with the hospital staff there all during the life of the Penal Colony as a POW camp. He was one of the few who was not sent to the field to plant rice. He was with the group that went to Luzon June 1944. Once we reached the camp in Luzon, he was on the medical staff for awhile for the Davao group at Cabanatuan. On Dec. 13, 1944, he was part of the group of POWs aboard the *Oryoku Maru*. He survived the first bombings and was a wonderful help with the treatment of the wounded on the boat, although he was not a member of the official medical staff which had charge of the sick and wounded during this trip. I wish to say here that Capt. Hawkes was one of the greatest credits to the medical profession aboard the ship. He gave his services as they were needed wherever he could. He died of exposure and starvation late in January 1945 while still aboard ship en route to Japan.

Lt. Cmdr. Mauricett Spriggs was one of the Naval personnel who came down to Cebu after the war started. The commander's health was not good, although he lived through most of the years of imprisonment. He surrendered in Cebu and went to Davao where he spent most of his days on the old man's hat detail which consisted of the old, sick, and lame of the Davao Camp who usually sat in the shade weaving hats under the direction of a Jap guard. (A practiced weaver could weave one hat in a day and we figured that the lieutenant colonel, who could weave one hat a day, made a mighty expensive piece of head-gear on Uncle Sam's payroll, provided he lived).

Cmdr. Spriggs was in the group moved to Luzon in June 1944. He was a member of the October 10 detail to Japan whose ship was torpedoed in the China Sea one-half day out of Takao, Formosa. Cmdr. Spriggs was not listed among the five survivors.

Lt. Col. Marcus Boulware, I have already mentioned as connected with the supplies of the Brigade. Since I have mentioned him elsewhere, I shall not go into the details of his work on the Island of Cebu now.

Lt. Col. Arthur J. Grimes came to Bohol around the middle of October 1941. There he replaced Capt. Paul D. Wood at the Tubigon Cadre School in Bohol. There Col. Grimes was in charge of the island defenses until around the middle or the first of March 1942 when he and his battalion were moved over to the Island of Cebu to augment its defenses.

Lt. Col. Bud Coyle, field artillery, had been sent down to Cebu to the Southern Islands from Gen. MacArthur's headquarters to reorganize an air warning system. Col. Coyle was out to see me several times in regard to this and all his plans were based on receiving equipment from Australia. This equipment never got there.

Capt. Frank E. Merchant was one of the men who went to work for the Army as a civilian and was commissioned on the field of battle during the fighting on Cebu. Capt. Merchant was just a young fellow and I believe an oil engineer. He was employed by the Philippine Development Co. as one of a group of engineers who were drilling for oil at the northern and southern end of the Island of Cebu. Indications were that they found what they were looking for because the oil wells and all of their equipment had to be suddenly destroyed along with all the tests they had made.

After the beginning of the war, the oil drilling was naturally stopped. Capt. Merchant then went to work for me in the censor's office where he worked for quite some time before being transferred to the MP Regiment. There his assignment was somewhat indefinite until the invasion. When the Japs came into Cebu, Capt. Merchant's assignment was no longer indefinite. Because of his experience in handling explosives he was one of the men in charge of the demolition crews who blew up the military installations before the Japs captured them. The Japanese tried very hard after they had captured us all to find out the names of the men who had blown up the military installations and indirectly caused the burning of the city of Cebu. Nobody squealed so Capt. Merchant was never found out by the Japs. Later in the summer, when the Japanese took all the technicians from our group and sent them to Japan around October 1942, Capt. Merchant was one of that detail. I understand he got safely to Japan, but died of dysentery and malnutrition shortly after he got there.

Lt. Cmdr. Chase G. Lade was one of the Navy men who came from Corregidor to Cebu and was assigned to help the Army. I don't recall what his assignment was but I have the impression he was associated with the QMC under Col. John D. Cook. Cmdr. Lade surrendered on the Island of Cebu and went to Davao with the group. He remained with the large group of POWs and went to Luzon June 1944. He was on the last detail to be sent to Japan, which was aboard the *Oryoku Maru*. He survived the first bombing, but when we were bombed in Takao, Formosa, Jan. 9, 1945, he perished.

Capt. Marion G. Sharp was one of the battalion commanders on Cebu Island. He had come from Bohol with Col. Grimes. I don't know much about Capt. Sharp's home or where he came from. I do know that one time during the war while talking with him, he made the remark, "Trouble, you call this war trouble? Brother you don't know what trouble is. I don't care if I never go home. This is sort of a peaceful place out here."

During the battle of Cebu, Capt. Sharp had the misfortune to be killed.

Capt. Frank L. Dixon, Medical Corps Administrative, came down to Cebu from Luzon during the war to set up a medical supply depot. This he did and operated it until the surrender of Cebu. Capt. Dixon spent the usual time at Davao and was moved to Luzon with the Davao detail in the summer of 1944. He was part of the *Oryoku Maru* and survived the trip to Japan. When the remnants of this group was divided into two components, he went with the one that was sent to Korea. Capt. Dixon was rescued in Korea at the end of the war.

C.M. Hunter, USN, CMM, was on the Island of Cebu after the latter part of March. He was part of the PT boat crews and was wounded during an engagement with some Japanese planes. His arm had been broken, and was useless. A bullet had shattered the bone, the flesh wound had healed, but the bone in the forearm had separated, therefore, he had to carry the arm in a splint to keep it from flopping around. Hunter surrendered with the Cebu group and subsequently went to Davao. On June 28, 1944 he was left at Bilibid Hospital because of his injured arm while the rest of the detail went on to Japan and Cabanatuan.

Second Lt. Walter Smith came from the Island of Bohol with Col. Grimes about the last of March 1942. I first knew Smith as a corporal back in the days of the Philippine Army training when he was on the Island of Bohol. Smith had come down from the 31st Infantry of Manila to help Capt. William F. Conner, who has been mentioned several times before. Smith surrendered at Cebu, went to Davao and finally to Lasang. His detail was aboard the ship, which was torpedoed and sunk Sept. 8, 1944.

Second Lt. Geo. T. Holmes, QMC, has been mentioned at length before. Lt. Holmes is the same George T. Holmes, then a sergeant, who helped me place the machine guns on the *Don Estaban* when I came down from Manila to Cebu City just after the war started. Lt. Holmes was captured in Cebu after having been bombed and sunk aboard the *Don Estaban*. They were taking a load of supplies to the hard-pressed Bataan and Corregidor when some Nip reconnaissance found them off the coast of Mendora. The planes attacked at once, bombing and strafing with the result that the *Don Estaban* was lost. Holmes was among the crew members, American and Filipinos, who got ashore on the Mendora coast, from there by banca, bus and Army vehicle, they got from island to island until they arrived at Cebu City. Holmes was never very well after he got into prison. He went to Davao, Luzon, Bilibid and finally was put on board the *Oryoku Maru*. The trip was too much for him in respect to malnutrition, exposure and dehydration. He died en route to Japan and was buried at sea.

Second Lt. Bargvig W. Bardson was another Norwegian who was a survivor of the sunken Norwegian freighter previously mentioned. Bardson was an exceedingly intelligent, fine-looking young Norwegian who like Lt. Jensen had a chance to get to Australia but choose to stay and fight with the Americans. He was given a commission on the field of battle, which has been confirmed by the U.S. government and became a Japanese prisoner of war as an officer in the American Army. He too was determined, even in her hour of defeat, to become a citizen of the U.S. Bardson was sent to Japan as a technician about August 1942. He was rescued in Japan at the end of the war.

Maj. Thomas N. Powell Jr., CE, was a member of the Cebu headquarters at the time of the surrender. His is quite a story, which will be mentioned later.

Perey M. Cotton, lieutenant junior grade, USN, was one of the Naval men who was sent to Cebu during the war. Prior to going on duty in the Navy Reserve, Cotton had been in the Merchant Marines. What his assignment with the Army was, I do not know. The Japanese, after the surrender, classified him as a technician and sent him to Japan about August 1942. He was rescued at the end of the war.

Walter A. Shapertine, carpenter USN, was one of the personnel who came down from Luzon about February 1942. He is another whose assignment in the Army I have no knowledge of. The Japanese classified him as a technician and sent him to Japan August 1942. He was rescued at the end of the war.

Capt. H. D. Weidman was a mining engineer who came from Wisconsin and had been working on the Island of Masbate before the war. After the Japs took the Island of Masbate, he escaped by banca to join the American Forces at Cebu where he was captured. He was sent to Japan as a technician.

Capt. F.A. Bowen was one of the civilians who went to work for the Army at the beginning of the war. Capt. Bowen was attached to the quartermaster service where he worked all during the war. He surrendered with the Cebu group and was taken to Mindanao. There in the Davao Penal Colony he served on some of the lighter details and went with the group to Luzon in June 1944. On Dec. 13, 1944, Capt. Bowen was left in Bilibid Hospital when the rest of the group was placed aboard the *Oryoku Maru* to be sent to Japan.

WO Joseph A. Allen came down to Cebu from Luzon about the same time the rest of the Naval group arrived. He was attached to Capt. Dixon to work in the Medical Supply Depot in the port area of Cebu City. He surrendered with the Cebu group. He went through the various events concerning the group as far as Bilibid Prison Hospital where he remained when the last of the Davao group was placed aboard the *Oryoku Maru*.

SN Albert P. Ross was a member of one of Lt. John D. Bulkeley's PT boat crews who I met in Cebu along with Lt. Bulkeley. His PT boat later sank a Japanese cruiser off the southern end of the coast of Cebu.

Capt. William F. O'Connor has been mentioned before and will be mentioned again. His assignment at this time on Cebu was S-1 for Col. Scudder's Cebu Brigade.

Cpl. Fred R. Schurmm had been a retired corporal at the beginning of the war. When the war broke he was living on the Island of Cebu with his Filipino wife and little girl. He left them to again join the Army and was attached to Col. Edmond's MP unit. He surrendered May 17. When the colonel and technicians were sent north to Japan, Cpl. Schurmm was sent along as an orderly. When the group reached Manila, he was side tracked and sent to Cabanatuan. On Dec. 13, 1944, he was left in Cabanatuan Hospital and shortly thereafter rescued by American troops.

Second Lt. Henry Talmadge had been a civilian at the beginning of the war. He worked for the Army during the war as a well driller for Army installations. At the time of the invasion, he was drilling a well at Camp X and got caught with American Forces between converging Japanese lines. He was given charge of supplies during the fighting and commissioned a second lieutenant in the field. Lt. Talmadge was one of the American officers who carried on guerrilla activities under Gen. Chynoweth. He surrendered with the Cebu group and was subsequently sent to the Davao Penal Colony. On Feb. 24, 1944 he was sent to Lasang to work on the airfield. His detail was sunk Sept. 8, 1944.

Lt. J.G. Otis A. Carmichael was one of the Navy personnel sent to Cebu and attached to the Army. What his assignment was on the island of Cebu before the war ended, I don't recall, but I believe that he was attached to the Quartermaster Corps under Col. Cook. Carmichael surrendered with the Cebu group May 1942 and subsequently went to Davao. For some reason or another, Carmichael was never satisfied with prison life. He always thought he wanted to escape. He would sit by the hour and talk about going over the wall at Cebu, make a dash for the airport, capture a plane and take off for Australia. While he was sitting around talking about escaping and growling about the chow, he grew a long red beard. Being an Irishman, he liked to talk and the time came when he would sit and mumble in his beard. He talked so much that we all got to figuring that his category was all talk and no action. When we were moved to Davao and we had to get out and work, he sort of snapped out of it and became more normal. He went with the group to Luzon June 1944 and spent three months in Cabanatuan. A little later he was moved to Bilibid Prison. He was a member of the prison detail placed aboard the

Oryoku Maru, which sailed out of Manila harbor late in the afternoon of Dec. 13, 1944. When the ill-fated boat sank December 15, Carmichael was one of those who had to swim for it. He was last seen in a boat with 20 Japs after the bombing. What happened to him after that, I do not know.

Capt. Victor R. Browne has been mentioned before as a civilian whom I met socially in Cebu one weekend, when I was visiting in the Morrison home while stationed on the Island of Bohol. Because of his great knowledge of chemistry and science, Capt. Browne assisted, by WO Leroy L. Hoyt, USN, began the manufacture of hand grenades in February 1942, when the Army detailed him to this assignment. Before the end of the war, he had perfected a fairly reliable hand grenade which the Army was beginning to manufacture in large quantities. However, the war ended before they could be put into production.

Second Lt. Curtis L. Sizemore had come from Bohol as an enlisted man with Col. Grimes. Because of the great need for American officers at the time, he was commissioned as second lieutenant and placed in command of a company of Philippine Army troops. Lt. Sizemore has been mentioned before as my corporal at Calape, Bohol. Lt. Sizemore surrendered with the Cebu group and was a member of the ill-fated Lasang group, which was sunk off Mindanao Sept. 8, 1944.

Lt. Wilson, QMC was assigned to the Port Quartermaster after his boat, the *Don Esteban* was sunk and he made his way ashore to finally reach Cebu. Lt. Wilson was the Sgt. Wilson I mentioned as being one of the enlisted men aboard the *Don Estaban* when I made my eventful voyage from Manila to Cebu the first week of the war. Lt. Wilson had been in WWI and been listed as missing in action or killed. After the war was over he returned to the States and was discharged. When he got home, he found his wife married to another man, so he left the situation as it was. He returned to the Army and came out to the Philippines where he remained in the Army. He married a Filipino woman of central Luzon and decided to remain in the Philippines the rest of his life. When the surrender came, Lt. Wilson decided to remain out with the guerrillas. Deciding that the Island of Cebu was much too small for such activities, he went to the Island of Negros. Within a very few hours before I broke camp to join the general in surrendering to the Japs, he came into our camp desiring transportation to the Island of Negros. I still had courier contact with Negros, so I sent him on his way by the way of a banca. That is the last that I ever heard of him.

Capt. L. Howell was another civilian who was commissioned into the Army. He had been an oil driller prior to the war and was drilling on the Island of Cebu at that time that the war began. The first I knew of Capt. Howell, he was working in the kitchen as a cook in one of the Army camps after the invasion of Cebu. He surrendered with the Cebu group and in a few months was sent to Japan as a technician. I believe he endured the imprisonment and was rescued at the end of the war.

WO C.E. Wilson was another of the Navy personnel who came to Cebu in February from Luzon. Shortly after his arrival, he was assigned to me at Camp X as an assistant in communications work. He remained at Camp X on that detail until after the invasion and the headquarters installations were captured. When the headquarters installations were captured by the Nips, he was a member of our forces that retreated to the jungle-infested mountains where we carried on our guerrilla activities. He surrendered with the Cebu group May 1942 and was subsequently take to Davao. In June 1944, he was taken to Luzon and in August 1944, he was a member of a detail headed for Japan. To my knowledge, his detail reached Japan safety.

Capt. Donald C. Gregg, prior to the war, had been a mining engineer working for the Mindanao Mother Lode Gold Mine Co. As soon as the war started, he was one of a group of mining engineers Gen. Sharp sent to work on various defense installations on the Island of Cebu. When Sharp went to Mindanao, Gregg was left behind on Cebu. He was assigned to me at Camp X where be came my post engineer. While on this assignment, he collaborated with Capt. V.R. Browne in perfecting the hand grenade that I mentioned before. Due to various reassignments by the general, I lost sight of Capt. Gregg during the fighting on the Island of Cebu. When we surrendered, Gregg was among the group and because he was a mining engineer, the Japs classified him as a technician. He was sent north to Japan August 1942 where he remained until rescued at the end of the war.

Capt. Edward L. Short, QMC, was in charge of the Quartermaster Motor Pool for Col. John D. Cook, the port quartermaster. In civilian life, Capt. Short had for a number of years been the B.F. Goodrich representative in the southern Philippines with his office at Cebu City. As soon as the war started, Capt. Short along with 1st Lt. David C. Afflick volunteered his services to the U.S. Army in the field of supply. Capt. Short had married a Spanish girl and between the Spanish contacts and business Filipino contacts, his knowledge of supply sources in the Southern Islands was quite broad. Capt. Short held his post as head of the Port Quartermaster Motor Pool until the invasion of the islands when he and his men did an excellent job of sabotaging their own installations. Capt. Short surrendered with the Cebu group and in August 1942 was sent north to Japan as a technician. I later saw him when we were in prison in Luzon and he told me that he took dysentery while on board the prison ship. For that reason, he was left in Bilibid Hospital instead of being sent on to Japan. After a number of months in the hospital, he was sent to Cabanatuan where he stayed until the last of October 1942. By the time Capt. Short reached Cabanatuan, the underground system of communication and supply between the American POWs and friends in Manila had been well established. Over this underground supply line Capt. Sharp received several thousand pesos, a little food and a little clothing such as a pair of shoes. He shared the money he received and like most men with a good heart, when hard times came for him personally, he found himself without a reserve because he had given it away to others less fortunate than himself. By the time I arrived, he was broke with several thousand pesos loaned out, yet he could have bought food from various sources had he had the money. I was in such hard shape that he slipped me a couple of pieces of cornbread one day for old times' sake. Capt. Sharp was a member of the *Oryoku Maru* detail and he survived the first bombing to die of malnutrition and dysentery in January 1945 while still aboard the ship. He was another man who spread sunshine through the prison camp by a cheery word and a generous heart.

First Lt. David C. Afflick had been one of the executives in the Proctor and Gamble offices of Cebu City. Because he was one of the copra buyers in the southern Islands, he, like Capt. Short had a lot of contacts in the southern Philippines and Dave became one of Col. Cook's assistants. I believe he helped with the administration of general supplies. Dave was one of the more fortunate civilians in that his wife and child had been sent back to the States along with Capt. Hawk's when the pressure of the war became evident. Afflick and Hawk continued to live in Afflick's home during the war up to the invasion, when they stuck to their units during the jungle fighting. Afflick surrendered with the Cebu group and went to Mindanao in October 1942 where he worked in the rice fields with the rest of the POWs. Dave was sent to Lasang as part of the Lasang detail in February 1944. To my knowledge, Dave went down with the Lasang detail prison ship on Sept. 8, 1944.

Lt. Col. Dwight M. Deter, MC, came over from Panay around March when the Visayan Force of the Visayan Islands was created out the Visayan and Mindanao Force. Col. Deter then became the force surgeon. He went to Davao with the Cebu group and was later taken to Luzon. He became part of the October 10 detail of 1,800 POWs whose boat was sunk just outside Takao, Formosa. To my knowledge there are five men who survived that torpedoing.

Col. John D. Cook, QMC, PI was the port quartermaster of Cebu City. Col. Cook had been in the islands a long time before the war began. About 10 to 14 days before Pearl Harbor, he arrived in Cebu and took over his assignment. This assignment he held until the surrender. A few weeks after the surrender, he was sent north to Japan with the rest of the colonels and the generals. Years later, Col. Cook was with the group of colonels and generals whom the Japanese brought to Mukden, Manchuria, where I was sent a prisoner. He was rescued at the end of the war in Mukden.

Col. Irvine C. Scudder arrived in Cebu just before the war started. Shortly after the war began he was given command of the Cebu Brigade. Col. Scudder fought the war in Cebu until surrender as commanding officer of the brigade. Col. Scudder was sent north to Japan at the same time that Col. Cook was and he was likewise rescued at Mukden at the end of the war.

There were other Army and Navy personnel whom I but vaguely remember that did not surrender with the fall of the Philippines. What happened to them, what adventures they went through, where they were captured, if they escaped, or what their fate was I do not know and have no way of finding out. For instance there was a Navy man by the name of Leroy who was a radio technician that worked for me at Camp X. He disappeared the night that our headquarters was captured by the Nips and no trace of him was ever found. I was the last man to see him and he had definite instructions as how to reach our new headquarters back in the jungle. He was still talking to me when the machine guns opened up. He disappeared into the night, as the bullets flew over our heads, and is still gone as far as I could ever find out. There was a Navy ensign by the name of Carson who decided to go to Negros. From all that I could ever find out he is still on his way. There was a young American civilian by the name of Kincaid who worked for the Army in the Quartermaster Camp of Maj. Don Sawtell. There was a rumor that Kincaid and several Naval personnel were captured aboard a banca in the Mindanao Sea.

Maj. Don Sawtell, had charge of the Quartermaster Supply Depot about four miles down the valley from my camp. This was his detail during most of the war until the surrender. At the time of the surrender, he became separated from the rest of our forces and took to the hills. Several months after the surrender he was picked up by a Nip patrol boat at the southwest coast of Negros. The only reason that the Nips caught him at that time was that someone betrayed his presence to the Nip patrol. He had the choice of surrendering or being machine gunned in his nepa hut. He chose to surrender. From there he was taken to Dumaguete on the southeast coast of Negros where he was kept in the provincial jail for several days. From there he was moved to the American POW camp not far from Bacoled on the central west coast of Negros. His group of American prisoners was subsequently taken to Davao. Maj. Sawtell was among the Davao group which was taken to Luzon June 1944. After his arrival there I lost track of him.

There were several other groups of Americans who had tentative plans to escape to Australia. Most of these were Naval men, but some were British. These men seemed to have faded away during the conflict or the invasion of the Island of Cebu and how many reached the mainland of Australia I have no way of knowing. If they failed to make Australia, they were evidently lost during the voyage. It is hard to say just what is truth and what is fiction in the rumors that flowed up to our headquarters about men attempting to sail to Australia in bancas and small motor boats. There is one tale concerning an ocean going tug boat called the Sunmaid or the Sunkissed or The Sun which was fully fueled and supplied and hidden in a cove of the Surigao Peninsula on northern Mindanao. Reports from native runners said that after the invasion of Cebu, several Naval men appeared in a banca and discovering the boat hidden in the cove boarded the tug, tossed the Filipino caretaker overboard and sailed out into the Pacific.

Before I mention the events of the war in Cebu, perhaps I had better mention what was happening outside in the rest of the Orient and Southwest Pacific and tell a little of what was known of the Japanese plans.

As I had mentioned before, when I arrived in San Francisco, I began to sense things. In Hawaii, the manger of the Alexander Young Hotel personally told me that they would be lucky if Honolulu were not blown off the map. In Manila most of the civilians I talked with expected war before another year was over, and that was what the ordinary businessman in Manila expected.

When I arrived in Manila in June 1941, the Japanese merchants were glad to have customers enter their stores and buy their merchandise. By

December, their attitude had changed to where they did not care whether customers purchased their goods or not. In June when a customer entered their stores, they hurried to serve him with politeness. By December when a customer entered they would often ignore him and continue to jabber among themselves. If he went up and interrupted them, they would reluctantly wait on him or arrogantly tell him "we do not have." They knew what was in the wind and that the time would come when they would be the masters.

Months, in some cases, years, before Pearl Harbor Day, Japan had closed the Mandated Islands of the Pacific to foreign shipping. Why had they closed these island ports unless they were fortifying them? The last Filipino fishing boat I heard of, which was in Palau before the war, came back with its crew saying that there were three of the islands fortified with artillery and that any two of the three could fire on the third. Of Truk, we knew practically nothing except that it was not open to any but Japanese ships. Other scraps of information came from here and there. One of our commercial airliners ran into a whole flock of Japanese pursuit ships and bombers lying south of the Marianas Islands toward Truk.

The Japanese established a commercial airline from Japan to Portuguese Timor via Truk and the Marianas. The same crew never made the same trip twice. Although they were in civilian dress, they bore the mark of military personnel. The commercial airline to Timor didn't pay. What then was its justification? There were similar instances of other things. For example, we knew approximately how many ships of various kinds that Japan had from checking on the world ports. By a few weeks before Pearl Harbor Day, I understand there were hardly any Japanese ships in foreign ports. Almost all Japanese shipping had disappeared from the seas into the home waters. What was the reason for this unless Japan was going to make a hostile move in the Pacific?

The information we had at our disposal came from all types of sources. Some reliable Filipino or Chinese merchant might go up to Shanghai on business and bring back information that we desired. I know that the British merchants in the Philippines had instructions to send to the British Intelligence Office, by the way of a designated Philippine merchant, anything of military interest they could pick up. There is every reason to think that our commercial agents had the same instructions. Of course, we had the information that came from diplomatic channels through the consuls and vice-consuls, plenipotentiaries, ministers and ambassadors. Attached to the embassies were the usual military attaches and language students whose primary duty for our government was to gain military and Naval information. Often these agents would never get the whole picture. Some agent in Manchuria would report that a large body of troops had moved out of Mukden by rail. Some weeks later some agent in Amoy would report the arrival of a unit of troops. He would observe that some of them were veteran troops and others were recruits. He would estimate the size of the unit and assign it an arbitrary number for identification purposes. For example, he might designate the new unit as 1119th Division, knowing that the Japanese didn't have one-tenth that many divisions. A few days later down at Shanghai, an agent there would report the arrival of a new unit of troops, some of which were veterans and some of which were recruits. He would make some arbitrary designation of this new unit and send the report into our headquarters. After all of these reports reached our headquarters by devious ways and means and our intelligence would sift it, they would come to the following conclusion. The umpty-umph division had left Mukden, Manchuria on a certain date by train and it had just enough time to arrive at Amoy picking up recruits on the way where part of it was left and the remainder proceeding to Shanghai. Then it was logical to assume that the old divisions in Mukden had been divided into two new divisions with recruits being added to bring these divisions up to full strength. These division were located in Amoy and Shanghai respectively. Briefly, that is the way we gained our information.

The Japanese were rapidly expanding their army forces. It was rumored that she expanded her divisions from about 50 to slightly over 100 by the time the war broke out. All her shipping was in her home waters for what purpose we could only guess. When in December 1941 a large convoy of 100 or so Japanese transports appeared from Japanese waters and headed toward Saigon, it was plain to see that the Jap was on the move. If the Japanese went into Saigon, the British Malay States would be in great danger and naturally the British would have to take counter steps for their defense. It was obvious where the Japs were going to strike when the show began.

With the event at Pearl Harbor the show was on. The Japs struck at Pearl Harbor, made landings in the Philippines and Hong Kong and set her island forces in Saigon in motion against the British almost simultaneously.

The Japs landed four places in the Philippines: Aparri, Lingayen and Legaspi in Luzon and lastly at Davao, Mindanao. As soon as the Japs saw that they were winning on the mainland and in the Philippines, they sent invasion forces to occupy the Dutch East Indies, New Guinea and the Solomon Islands. With the fortification of the port of Rabaul on the north end of New Britan, the Japanese were ready to invade Australia. There was only one thorn in their side at this stage of the game that was the thorn of Bataan and the southern Philippine Islands. It was true that there were other locations, which they would have to mop up, but until the American forces in the Philippines had been annihilated, the Japanese could not attack Australia with secure supply lines. That meant that the Philippines must fall before they could move south with safety.

THE WAR ON CEBU

When General Sharp moved to Mindanao he left Col. Irvine C. Scudder (the brigade defender) in charge of the Island of Cebu. Col. Scudder had two Provisional Regiments under his command plus an MP Battalion, which was later enlarged into an MP Regiment. The whole unit of defense was designated the Cebu Brigade.

The 82nd Infantry under the command of the Filipino Lt. Col. David had the defense of the south half of the island. The defenses of the northern half of the island rested with another Filipino, Lt. Col. Bourbon commanding the 83rd Infantry. Lt. Col. Howard E. Edmonds, American, was in command of the defenses of the city of Cebu. His MP Battalion was increased to a regiment. Some of these troops were used as labor battalions and were armed with only bolos. The Cebu Brigade totaled about 5,500 men just before the invasion. In charge of these troops were 12 to 15 American regular Army and Reserve officers. From time to time civilians were commissioned for definite jobs. At the surrender there were 43 Americans ranking from the general to a corporal. Hardly more than half to two-thirds of the troops had rifles. The rifles they had were old obsolete Enfields. The bolts of these old rifles were bad and the ejector mechanism would break. That meant a man had to carry around a ramrod to punch the empty cartridge out each time he fired it.

There was not much time for training the soldiers and when the invasion came, they went into battle without ever having fired their rifles in target practice. There were only eight to 10 rounds of ammunition per rifle and we did not dare waste a single round in practice. Shortly before the invasion a couple of supply boats arrived from Australia, but it was too late then to train the men.

The only machine guns on the island were those which belonged to the regimental companies. Our heavy artillery consisted of seven old, semi-obsolete 81mm mortars the US Army had given to the Philippine Army. With all this high-class equipment and highly trained Army we were bound to make a showing when the Japs came in. We knew it! Ha! Ha!

In the beginning the Japs did not pay too much attention to Cebu City. On December 15, the day I arrived in Cebu City from Manila, there was a small air raid on Shell Island and Opon where there were oil and gasoline storage tanks. Not much damage was done at this time because the bombs hit in the water.

Early in January I awoke one morning about 10:00 a.m. to the air raid siren. Since I had gone to bed at 7:00 a.m. that morning, I was dead on my feet from exhaustion. At the sound of that siren I knew I had about 20 minutes before the planes would arrive. (Being censor at the time, I knew all the details about the workings of the air warning system as it functioned off of messages it received over my telegraph wires.) I turned over and went to sleep. To hell with the Nips and their air raid. I became dead to the world again.

Suddenly I was awakened by a gust of hot air passing over me in three waves. The impact of this hot air was fully equal to the impact of a stream of water from an ordinary hose. I was instantly awake from these three blows and a second or two later my ears registered three earsplitting explosions Wumf! Wumf! Wumf! The curtains on my windows were flying horizontally from their rods almost against the ceiling. I knew then what was happening, the Nips were here and had dropped some of their bombs nearby. The waves of concussion had passed through my room from the window to the corridor where my door was standing open. It was a good thing the windows in the Philippine tropics seldom have glass in them. My windows were the shutter-type of shell panels which swung inside the room. They were standing open at the time of the explosions so they were not wrecked nor was I covered with glass. I thought the building was going to fall apart.

I scrambled out of bed and into some clothes. From there I went up to the trap door on the top floor and onto the roof where I could get a good view of the surrounding areas. The Nips were bombing the oil tanks again. There were only three bombers and they were swinging back to try to hit their objective. Two came toward Shell Island, and one swung wide over the harbor. What was the single plane going for? The sergeant was climbing onto the roof near me.

"Sergeant, what is that lone plane after?"

"I don't know captain, but it just now dropped a bomb. I'll watch the bomb fall."

"We'll soon know then if the bomb's on the way."

Seconds passed, seconds that seemed like an eternity before suddenly I saw a pout of water and wreckage.

"It hit a ship in the harbor captain. I heard Maj. Jordan say yesterday the inter-island ship *Basilian* was in the port. I'll bet that's what it was after, yes sir, it was a ship. See that black smoke beginning to rise, that's from off the ship," said the sergeant.

Wumf! Wumf! The other two planes had dropped their bombs and one had hit Shell Island.

"Looks like they hit an oil tank on the island. See that flame bursting from the oil tank on the left. Now see the black smoke beginning to rise?"

The sergeant said, "They really hit that didn't they!"

We watched the flames steadily mount and the black smoke begin to climb high into the sky.

The three Nip planes seemed to have dumped all their bombs and now turned to strafing the airport concentrating on the hangers and trees around the edge for any installations they might be concealing. One plane would swoop low while the other two circled high. The low swooping plane would climb back to the level of the other two. About half way up to the height it would level off, the sound of its machine guns would reach us. The guns had been fired while the ship was going down but because of the time lag we heard the guns as the ship was climbing. After each bomber had strafed the airport several times they took off.

I went down to the street when the attack was over and drove down to the waterfront. There I could plainly see the burning oil tank and the damaged ship. The oil tank had not been hit directly. One bomb had burst in the nearby sea and fragments had gone through the seaside of the tank. The white heat of the fragments had ignited the gasoline as pressure forced the gasoline out of the tank. Long streams of fire were pouring out of that leaking tank in several places. Jimmy Cushing, who later became a lieutenant colonel in the guerrillas, did some dangerous work helping to get the fire under control.

The ship *Basilian* sank right where she was until her bottom rested on the seabed. This left about a quarter of the ship's body and all the super structure above the water. That ship lay right there until the Nips floated her after we surrendered. From the air it looked like a good ship in the harbor and thereafter whenever the Nips bombed Cebu they were sure to drop several bombs on the sunken *Basilian*. That got to be quite a joke with us.

Shortly after this attack I moved out to Camp X to take charge of Gen. Sharp's Force Communications Station. In three or four days the Nip planes were back again. This time they concentrated on the airfields. I happened to be on duty near a telephone. I called Gen. Sharp's headquarters in Camp X to report the attack.

The general was not there but I got Capt. Cosper, the assistant G-2.

"There's three planes down here bombing and strafing. Guess you want to know it."

"We sure do! The old man wants to know of any attacks so we can lay low up here. I am out on the side of a mountain at an observation post. I'll call you back as soon as I inform the general."

"Okay, I'll hold the phone free for your call."

I hung up and went to the window to watch the low flying planes taking the phone with me. In about three minutes Cosper called back.

"What are they working on now? I just got through telling Gen. Sharp they were over the city. He said to keep him informed!"

"They dropped another bomb near the Basilian again but missed it. Right now they are taking turns strafing the airfield. One is diving low over the field right now. In a few seconds I'll hear the rattle of his guns, there it is."

"I see them, the three are out over the harbor, it looks like they are coming this way, now they are circling back, one is leaving the formation now, he is diving."

"I see him! He is diving on the airfield from the south paralleling the mountains. He is really coming low this time, it looks like he is almost touching the roofs, he has disappeared, now he is climbing again and I hear his gun. He really gave the airfield a long burst. I hope he didn't catch any of our boys out there. If he did he really played hell with them that time."

"The other two are circling back and they seem to be diving, I can't tell yet what they are going to do," observed Capt. Cosper.

"I see them, they are both coming into the airfield wide apart from the south, both are diving now, it looks like their flight will cross about the time they hit the airfield on the south side, they must have located a special target. They are really diving low, I hope they hit each other! Up they come, both of them. From the sound they must have used all their ammunition, that burst must have lasted 30 seconds or more. The lone plane is diving again on the same spot as the other two. Our lads are really catching hell out there."

"I see the two again, they are still climbing. The third is climbing to join them, he is going fast, all three seem to be flying north, they are leaving from the looks. Thanks for all the dope."

"You are quite welcome. I'll phone the boys at the airport and tell them the Nips seem to be leaving. Take it easy."

I called the airport three times before I could get anybody to answer the phone. Finally a scared Filipino voice came shrinkingly over the wire.

"Laburg Airport, Pvt. Gonzoles speaking."

"Tell the captain the Nips have left."

"Oh sir! (gasp) That is very good sir, I will run sir." Bang went the receiver.

Later I learned that we had partially concealed a dummy plane on the edge of the field and the Nips had strafed it severely.

Many months later in prison at Davao, I mentioned this raid to Cosper.

"Yes, I remember that very well. The general told me to keep him informed and then he listened in on our whole conversation. The next time he saw me he bawled the hell out of me for gossiping over the telephone. Now what would you do in a case like that?"

"How would I know, I have never been a general."

When I moved to Camp X, I took charge of the Force Communication Station that Gen. Sharp was leaving on the Island of Cebu. Gen. Sharp left and Col. Scudder made Cebu City his headquarters. That left me the only a.m. officer in Camp X. There were a few civilians working on some of the installation.

Camp X was a mud home if I ever saw one. A large number of tunnels had been excavated and blasted out of the sides of the mountain wall in the valley where the camp was located. The work was still going on and every wheelbarrow of mud and rock wheeled out of the tunnels was dumped so as to shelter some of the buildings. Rain in these high peaks made this mud worse. Since it was being dumped around the installations the mud was naturally traced all over everything and got quite deep in some places. The buildings and installations were housed in nepa shacks, which were blacked out for the use of lights at night. Everything had been hastily "sandbagged" by filling sugar sacks with the mud and rock out of the tunnels. Because of the dampness the sugar sacks soon rotted and the bags had to be replaced. The staff worked and lived in the tunnels while it was there.

When I found myself left with this mess on my hands, I immediately set about organizing the place to fit my need and to cleaning up the mess in general. After I had been out there a month Col. Scudder stopped by one day as he was inspecting other installations. He was very complimentary when he saw how shipshape the camp had been cleaned up. That month had been a nightmare though.

"Hell, Miner, just dropped in to say hello on my way over to Toledo."

"Glad to see you sir. Won't you have the noon meal with me. It gets lonesome up here."

"I'll stop long enough for a cup of coffee. I am out looking over this Talisay-Toledo road. The more I think about it, the more certain I am that this camp will be my field headquarters and last defense area when the Nips come in. If I send supplies up here would you help me out seeing that they were properly stored away?" (I was still one of the assistants on Gen. Sharp's staff and was outside of his command).

"I will Sir."

The colonel left soon afterward.

Before going any farther I should explain the location of Camp X. The Island of Cebu is around 100 miles long and only about 30 miles wide at its broadest point. There are two roads across the island from east to west. One, the Talisay-Toledo Road cuts the island right in half at its broadest part. The Carcar road divides the southern half of the island into almost equal fourths. In this broad part that the Talisay-Toledo Road passed were the highest and most rugged mountains, some of which were heavily forested. Camp X was up in the top of these mountains set down in a valley between two high mountain ridges running length wise of the island. There was a hogback that ran from one mountain to the other forming a right angle with each. This hogback was the watershed divide between the east side canyon and the west side canyon. Any camp located in the forest on the hogback would be protected by high mountains on the east and west sides with deep canyon approaches from the north and south. By using the road from either side of the island, the forces from either side could fall back to these more easily defended areas. The plan looked good but the hitch was that we had no equipment to defend the canyons with. Rifles alone would not do it and we knew it, yet the old bolt action Enfield rifle in the hands of a half-trained native who had never fired a rifle was to be our only weapon of defense.

The defense of the Island of Cebu was planned around Camp X. What few supplies we had were stored out in the regimental defense areas. About the middle of February and the first of March, two cargo ships slipped through the Japanese blockage. The *Anhuai* and *Donna Nati* brought in a lot of food from Australia and quite a bit of ammunition. From that time on we were not short of rifles and machine gun ammunition. There were also some artillery shells, but we had no guns to use them in and by that time it was impossible to get a ship up to Bataan or Corregidor. Those shells were unloaded and stored. When the Nips came in they were set off. All the supplies off these ships were stored in the mountains. No sooner was it stored than Gen. Sharp ordered a lot of it sent down to Mindanao. It had to be trucked back down to the piers and sent in small boats to Mindanao, such a mess.

In general, the defenses of Cebu Island were nil.

Camp X was made the hub around which the island defenses were built. Cebu City was used as a temporary headquarters prior to the invasion when Camp X would be the center of things.

In any war, communications are one of the most vital needs. Here too, we had to improvise. The telephone lines running out of Camp X were few to what we needed and built of anything. Imagine how efficient a telephone line made of bailing wire and Coke bottles would be for ordinary commercial use in your home. This was war, our lines had to run through steep mountains and endure tropical storm. Some were built of bailing wire hung on coke bottles which were in turn wired to bamboo poles stuck in the rocky earth. On a mountainside so steep you could hardly walk, some farmer's caribou would find the pole while grazing and knock it down while trying to rub his back on it. Then we would have to send a repair crew out to trace the wire and repair it. This crew had to carry with it the extra poles and wire for the repair.

How those Filipinos ever climbed up and down those slopes with those heavy loads I'll never know. I could barely climb over them with absolutely no load.

Other lines were covered electrical wire which was laid on the ground. All the farmers would burn the cogan grass off the slopes before they plowed them. Wire that happened to be laid in these areas had the covering burned off so it had to be replaced. There was unceasing repair to be done day and night.

One of the hardest things to do was to get materials to repair with. All the standard radio tubes had been sent to Gen. Sharp in Mindanao. If we burned out a tube, my technician had to tear the radio down, take out the tube socket and solder a special socket into the radio in order that an off brand, odd-sized, tube could replace the burned-out tube.

Toward the last we were running out of these odd tubes for replacement. Then the set was no good. That was our communication equipment to fight a war with—old tubes, bailing wire and coke bottles.

For the equipment to be used we had to have operators. There weren't any! All the good ones had been taken to Mindanao by Gen. Sharp. We had to train new ones from young Filipino students. They made mistakes galore, often because they hardly understood the English language. Because of their lack of knowledge in English they would often fall back to using their native dialects. The messages then were so undeveloped that they could be used for generalities only but not for specific details. This caused more confusion. The frustrations were enough to drive an insane man to saneness.

Small units stationed on outpost duty had only one radio, which was their only contact with their headquarters. Because of the rough handling the sets received they often would not work. For hours at a time we had no contact with these units.

Supplies for these units often had to be carried to their base by cagadores. The work was slow and straining.

While the fortification of the island was going on we were subject to various types of raids from the Nips. For several days following the bombing and strafing of the airport things were quiet. Then one beautiful sunny morning I went down to Cebu City and got caught in another air raid. Eighteen heavy bombers came floating over the city of Cebu from the direction of Pelas Island. Their first flight over, they designated their targets by dropping bombs on the ships in the harbor and the oil tanks and installations. The poor sunken *Basilian* was again bombed. The oil storage tanks on Shell Island and Opon had some very close calls. I had been in the Brigade headquarters when the bombing started so I left the offices and went to the top of the building which was quite tall and overlooked most of the city and harbor. Capt. English went with me while Maj. Jordan stayed down below. We got on the roof in time to see the first bombs land.

"Look at those babies splash, Ouch." Capt. English was interrupted by the sound of the explosions, wunf, wu-wu-wunf, followed by blasts of concussion. "Where the hell is my cap? It's blown off my head."

I looked around. English stood upright, bareheaded and holding his ears. Three feet behind him on the roof lay his overseas cap.

"Horsefeathers, that concussion blast was not that strong. You just knocked it off your head when you tried to cover your ears. You ole Wunf— an invisible blow struck me in the face to be followed by others, all of which were strong enough to shake me, but not strong enough to blow my hat off my head. "Bill did you count those explosions? There were 32 in that series. See where the water is still churning around from their falling in the harbor? I'll bet the Filipinos have fish for supper tonight!"

"The group is splitting up into two bunches and is turning. I wonder, one group is turning toward Opon and the other is going south."

"They are doing a damned poor job. They must have dropped 50 bombs and haven't really hit anything yet. Most of them fell in the sea and the half dozen that hit on land didn't hit anything to speak of. That second group is turning now, its headed toward Shell Island.

"The first group is coming in lower over Opon. They can't be over a mile high now, they must have been 8,000 or 9,000 feet the first time they came over. They dropped some bombs, I saw them leave the bays, it won't be long now."

"This second group is also way lower, I hope they don't keep coming this way much longer, they are on direct bombing line with us now, at least they are turning toward the sea again. I'm sure glad to see that."

"Me too," said Capt. English.

A series of explosions again shook the air over the city. Most of these bombs again landed in the water along the shore of Opon. The oil tanks were lined up in a row along the water for convenience of the tankers when they docked. They presented a very narrow target to the planes. Shortly thereafter the second series of explosions took place by bombs falling to the sea around Shell Island. Neither of us could see that much damage had been done there.

"Those babies are certainly coming down low this time. They can't be over 2,000 to 3,000 feet in height."

We watched the two groups slowly float over the harbor again. This time they dropped only a few bombs.

"That must be their last load of bombs and they certainly are rotten shots. They haven't really hurt anything." I said.

"I hope so."

After the raid by the 18 heavy bombers, things were quiet for awhile. Then came the day we got news of a large Japanese Task Force coming south through the China Sea. The report was that it was passing Luzon and headed toward the Southern Islands. We really sweated out that event. The task force went right on past the Philippines into the Dutch East Indies. It was headed toward Java. This task force got as far as the Straits of Macassar where it was struck by our combined sea and air forces. The report on that action was that the task force was well destroyed. The Macassar Straits lie between Borneo and the Celefes Islands. Our forces caught the convoy in these narrow confines where it could not maneuver and get away. I don't know the particulars of the action, but there were rumors and radio broadcasts that reached us which said the Japanese lost at least 100,000 men due to the sinking of their ships. One airman told us, after we were prisoners, that he took part in the action and a member of his crew counted over 100 Japanese ships either sunk or on fire and there were beached Japanese craft on both sides of the straits in the area that he flew over. The way he talked, the Japs took a hell of a beating in that battle. Be the facts of this battle true or false, it had a great moral effect on our troops in Cebu at the time it happened and on us in prison camp when our fellow prisoner told us his account of this action he had taken part in.

A few days after the first raid by 18 heavy bombers, a single small Nip plane started flying daily over the Island of Cebu about 10 or 11 o'clock in the morning. It always came from the direction of the city of Iloilo on the Island of Panay, flying over Bacoled, the provincial capital of Negros and over Cebu City. At Cebu City it would circle around the harbor a couple of times, fly over the airfield and after awhile it got to flying out over the valley where my camp was supposed to be hidden. One of the boys got a pair of field glasses and told us it looked like he was taking pictures. Since he always came at the same time of day we would arrange our schedules for a siesta or quiet period when "Photo Joe" was due. This was just a single, slow, antiquated Nip plane and we used to get so mad that we didn't even have a gun with which we could fire at him. He came absolutely when he pleased, as he pleased and did what he wanted to. We had not one plane or one gun with which to chase him out of the sky.

The second raid by 18 bombers also caught me in Cebu City but this time I was on the way back to Camp X. It came without warning while I was still in the main port of the city. I wasn't surprised because we always expected the Nips in at anytime. The first flight over I took shelter in the gutter of the street I was traveling. My Filipino chauffeur, Frederico Cortes did likewise. There were no bombs that fell near us, although the explosions were quite loud. The Nips were again bombing the oil and harbor installations and I was a good half-mile away from the nearest of these. However, when you are looking at planes 8,000 or 9,000 feet up in the sky it is pretty hard to judge just where their bombs will fall, especially when there is a heavy breeze blowing from them to you. As the planes passed over us and receded in the distance to circle around and come back, my chauffeur and I got in the car and raced toward the outskirts of the city. As the planes again approached our location we pulled up under a couple of coconut trees in the street and stopped again. Again my chauffeur and I "hit the dirt" of the street just in case. We were far enough away from the car to be out of range of breaking glass unless the car was directly hit. This time we saw the bombs drop out of the planes and knew that we were not in the line with the falling missiles. When the planes had passed far enough over us that we would not be in any danger we ran to the car and again took off down the street. By the time the planes had swung around for their flight across our installation, we were near a coconut grove on the edge of the city. I directed my chauffeur to drive the car into it. With our car hidden under a coconut tree, the chauffeur and I got out and walked back to the edge of the grove where watched the big Japanese bombers float back and forth unmolested over the city of Cebu. They had complete air superiority. When the planes had dropped the last of their bombs they went back toward the east. Then my chauffeur and I got the car out of the coconut grove and headed back toward the city to see the damages of the raid.

After the second raid by 18 bombers, we had an uneventful time for a few days. Then excitement again! This time it wasn't an air raid but a Jap cruiser sailing through the straits around Cebu. It would shell a nepa village on the shore with a salvo or two and then take off and repeat the process in some other location. At the north end of the Island of Cebu, near the town of Medellin, we had established an observation post under the command of one of the Naval officers sent down to Cebu from Corregidor. This commander was on the shore when the cruiser approached. I believe it was the first salvo (it might have been the second) the cruiser fired in which one of the shells struck the commander and severed his head from his body. As I recall the report said the shell hit him in the neck and caused his decapitation. The cruiser didn't make a landing there although it may have sent a small boat ashore to see if it could capture a native or two. The rest of our outpost retreated from the shore as soon as the commander was killed.

The cruiser left the north end of the island and steamed south down the east coast creating panic among the Filipinos along the shore. When it arrived at Mactan Island, which shelters the harbor of Cebu City, it slowed down and finally stopped at the south end of the harbor. From there it started shelling the city of Cebu but it didn't venture inside the harbor. Two or three shells struck my old quarters, Fort San Pedro de Cebu and left holes in its massive, thick stone walls. Other shells landed out in the city. One landed in a garage, managed by a man named Burbinggame, where considerable repair work for the Army was done. Another landed in the palatial home of one of the Spanish families. After half or three quarters of an hour the cruiser ceased and sailed on south past the south end of the Island of Cebu.

Time was growing shorter for the Americans. The Japanese were growing bolder day by day. We couldn't stop them. All we could do was await their pleasure.

As I peviously mentioned, about the first of March a U.S. cargo ship from Australia arrived with ammunition and food supplies. The first one, that arrived in mid-February, had hardly been unloaded and put to sea before a second one arrived. The *Donna Nati* and the *Anhuai* both came in a space of about two weeks. I don't remember which came first. Under Col. John D. Cook, the port quartermaster, facilities worked night and day to unload these ships so that they would not be caught in the harbor by an air raid or by a cruiser roaming around the waters surrounding the island. One of the boats took 16 days to come about 1,500 miles. It had to make so many changes of its course that it could barely make more than 100 miles a day. One morning at dawn, after a night's sailing, it found itself almost within sight of one of the Japanese mandated islands. The captain knew it couldn't sail by the island unobserved in the daylight so he turned around and sailed back away from the island for 50 miles or so and then "lay low" until nightfall hoping that none of the Nip patrol planes would discover the ship. No planes came and with the fall of night the ship sailed past the island undetected by the Japs.

There were several civilians and newspaper corespondents who had been sent from Corregidor to Cebu City to see if they could be sent on to Australia. Among the last was *Life* magazine's photographer Jacobi and his wife. I talked with them briefly at the service club one day. These people were put on the first boat when it sailed and they arrived safely in Australia. Later we heard that Jacobi had been killed in an airplane crash in Australia.

The first boat had hardly left before the second one came. The second one didn't have navigation charts of Philippine waters, I guess, because it ran aground on a sandbar between Cebu and Bohol about an hour out of Cebu harbor. That ship laid out there in plain sight for several days until its load was lightened by barges and it could be towed off the bar. It also had food and ammunition on it. In addition there were several P-40 planes in a dismantled state. Finally the ship was towed off the bar and came into he harbor to finish unloading. It too set out for Australia as soon as it could. The waters of Cebu were much too warm to be healthy for any allied ship.

The food and supplies, that were to remain on Cebu from these tow ships, were taken back into the hills and mountains just as rapidly as it was possible. We knew that the more we got back the more we would have to live on when the going got tough. Invasion was eminent and we all knew it.

First word of the approach of the Japanese reached us on the afternoon of April 9. It was reported that three Japanese cruisers and eleven transports were steaming for Cebu from the south. That night further news was received that the Japanese force had split in two, one sailing along the west coast, the other along the east. By daylight the enemy vessels were near the island, with the larger of the convoys reported to be close to the island's capital, Cebu City, midway up the east coast. Shortly after dawn the Japanese in this convoy landed at Cebu City; at about the same time the men in the other convoy came ashore in the vicinity of Toledo.

On April 11, the Nip's attacked in great strength before dawn. They made quick work of us and our position on the Talisay-Toledo Road was untenable, and we were forced to pull back. Being the force communications officer, I refused to abandon my post. With the Jap's less than 50 yards away, and under constant fire, I remained to destroy the communications installation at Camp X and deny hostile use of the vital equipment.

With the enemy in possession of the cross-island highway, the fight for Cebu was over in a matter of hours. Nothing more could be accomplished in central Cebu. Gen. Chynoweth, with about 200 men, started north to his retreat in the mountains. From there he hoped to organize the few units still remaining on the island into an efficient guerrilla force. The Japanese did not claim the complete subjugation of the island until April 19, but Gen. Wainwright had already acknowledged the loss of Cebu three days earlier when he ordered Gen. Sharp to re-establish the Visayan-Mindanao Force and take command of the remaining garrisons in the Visayan's.

THE SURRENDER

The silence rested uneasily on Sudlon Forest as I descended the jungle-covered trail on the side of Balanban Mountain early in May 1942. It lay heavy and oppressive, broken now and then by the subdued chatter of a monkey or a forest bird. As I moved cautiously down the trail, I reviewed the events of the last few weeks. Bataan had fallen, Corregidor was about to surrender. The few American forces on Cebu had been decimated by the troops of Yamashita, the "Tiger of Malay," and our guerrilla action had been limited on the island, due to the lack of effective weapons with which to fight. I was now on my way to Gen. Chynoweth's headquarters.

Upon arrival, I was received by Lt. Col. Marcus Boulware who informed me that Corregidor had surrendered and that Gen. Wainwright had broadcast a surrender order to all American forces in the Philippine Islands. He also stated that Gen. Chynoweth wished to continue to fight by moving our command to the Island of Leyte where we would operate as guerrillas on the larger, less populated island. However, there was some question about his having authority to refuse to surrender.

Late in the afternoon, I was instructed to go back to my outpost and return with my men the next day. Darkness caught me toiling and stumbling through inky blackness up the steep canyon on the side of Balanban Mountain. Fortunately, I knew the trail well and still had a flashlight. Otherwise, I would have had to spend the night on the canyon side.

The next morning Lt. Henry Talmadge, Capt. Russell Cracraft, Maj. Ernest Jordan and I, accompanied by some Filipinos, made our way back down the mountainside and after hours of travel through the oppressive heat of the jungle, arrived at the general's headquarters.

After reporting to Lt. Col. Boulware and learning that we were to surrender, we sought out Gen. Chynoweth.

We found him sitting on a log looking at the jungle-covered canyon wall. He looked around as we approached and we saluted. "Well, boys," he said, "the news is bad."

"General, do we have to surrender?" I asked.

"The orders from headquarters specifically state that all troops will surrender and anyone who fails to surrender will be charged with refusal to obey orders. Officially, I have tried my best to be authorized to continue the fight in Leyte."

We were struck by the sadness and bitterness in his voice. Here was a young man who had spent all his life preparing to defend his country. Now he was forbidden to do so and was ordered to surrender.

I finally broke the silence.

"General," I said, "Maj. Jordan, Capt. Cracraft, Lt. Talmadge and I have already laid plans against the time when we could not operate here. We have acquired a sea-going banca (out-rigger canoe), stocked it with canned goods and coconuts and we have secured a Filipino navigator. Will you give us a mission to Leyte or some other island that will permit us to set sail for Australia?"

Gen. Chynoweth looked at us sharply. "Have you had any experience in navigation and do you have a compass?"

I shook my head and replied, "We do not have a compass, but our navigator assures us he can sail by the stars."

The general looked thoughtful and after a long study said, "I'm sorry boys, but I cannot consent to it. You will have to go on your own."

Cracraft, Talmadge, Jordan and I looked at each other. I finally said, "General, if you are gong to surrender, I will stay with you." The others did the same and we left.

It was a heavy blow to face the idea of imprisonment when we could escape. I left the encampment and walked alone along the stream. The afternoon became hotter and more oppressive and when I came to a large pool of water below a small waterfall, I stripped and went swimming. The cool water seemed to soothe my tormented mind and body. I perched on a ledge in the water at the foot of the falls and rested. Suddenly, I became aware of a Filipino officer standing on the opposite edge of the pool beside my pile of clothes on which my rifle lay. My first thought was what an ignoble way to meet my end. Then I recognized him. It was 1st Lt. Gavina Lapura, one of my officers from camp.

"Lapura," I exclaimed, "I thought you were gone," and plunged for the shore to dress.

"No, captain," he replied, "I have come through the Japanese lines to join you. I want you to come with me and I will take you through the Japanese lines to the south end of the Island of Cebu. From there we will take a banca to my home Island of Bohol where I will hide you until the Americans return. You must not surrender to the Japanese."

This was one of my hardest personal decisions and I thought a long time before I finally said, "No, Lapura, I think I had better surrender. However, this is my suggestion to you. Take my rifle and go back to Bohol until the Americans return." (He became a captain in the Bohol guerrillas and aided the returning American Forces).

The next morning our little band of hungry, weary Americans left our camp in the valley and traveled all day in a southerly direction over mountains and valleys. As darkness fell, we made torches by binding grass and wood together. Late that night we arrived at the edge of the forest where we camped on a high ridge above a large grass covered valley.

The next morning Col. Irvine C. Scudder, Gen. Chynoweth's chief of staff, directed Cracraft and me to lead an advance party to Camp X and prepare it for the arrival of our few forces. Our party of 10 descended 1,000 feet into the valley and climbed the near vertical opposite side, always traveling in a southerly direction. Late in the afternoon, we descended a long ridge and as we approached the highway in the vicinity of Camp X, we affixed a white flag of truce to a bamboo pole. This precaution proved unnecessary as the area was deserted.

At last we entered the forested area of our old headquarters. There, under the trees of the valley floor, scenes of shambles and destruction met our eyes. Cracraft and I were stunned by how little was left of what had once been an orderly camp. Finally, we sat down and viewed the scene with heavy hearts. This was the end of our efforts. It was the end of the American forces in the Philippines. We were the lost men of a lost cause and we could see only imprisonment and an unknown fate before us.

Later as we crossed the road, a car came swiftly around a nearby curve and skidded to a halt when its driver saw us. Out stepped a Filipino mestizo.

"What are you doing here?" he inquired.

"We have come ahead of our forces to plan for the camping of the American Forces which will surrender here day after tomorrow," Cracraft replied.

"Good," he replied. "I will report this to the Japanese commander at Toledo." With that he stepped back into his car and sped down the road.

The next morning we heard a motor and a shout from the road. Cracraft and I decided we had better investigate and when we reached the road it was the Filipino mestizo, accompanied by an armed Japanese soldier.

"You are to come at once to Toledo where the Japanese commander will question you," said the mestizo. There was little else we could do. We entered an American car and were taken to the Japanese headquarters at Toledo, which was located in a schoolhouse. Cracraft and I grew very uneasy as we stood in the schoolyard surrounded by vicious looking armed guards. Finally, we were led into the building where we entered a large room with four Japanese officers seated in a semi-circle. There were four guards with rifles in the room, one in each corner. The rifles were cocked and the bayonets were fixed. In front of the seated officers were two tables littered with maps.

Our guide, who could speak English, shoved us into the open part of the circle facing the four officers. He then walked around to stand behind one of the officers who proved to be the senior. Finally, after a period of at least two minutes of searching scrutiny, the senior officer let out a shout. Cracraft and I must have batted our eyes because the youngest officer smiled an instant and then recovered his gravity. The English speaking Japanese soldier behind the senior officer then spoke to us.

"What are your names and rank?" I answered and gave my rank. Cracraft did the same.

"What were you doing on the highway in the mountains?"

"We are the advance party of Gen. Chynoweth's forces on their way to surrender to the Japanese at Camp X," I replied bitterly.

"When do you plan to surrender?" was the next question.

"Tomorrow," Cracraft answered.

"What units of your forces are coming to Camp X and how many men are in the units?" was the next question.

Cracraft and I shifted uneasily and looked at one another. Out of the 5,500 troops on the Island of Cebu, we expected only a few dozen to surrender. We realized we were in a tight spot and the air became charged as we were silent.

The Japanese officer spoke again sharply and the interpreter said, "Answer the question."

"To be honest with you," I said, "we do not know exactly how many to expect."

The interpreter spoke in Japanese. The Japanese officer roared in anger at my answer and after a full minute of verbosity, he ceased and the interpreter spoke. "It is very foolish for an American officer who is on a general's staff to lie and say he does not know how many men his general has. The major says he is tempted to strike off your head with his ancestral sword. For your own safety you must answer him."

I made my decision, deciding to tell the truth and resort to flattery. "The Filipinos reported that there was a Japanese general with a large Army here in Toledo and another at Cebu City. All our communications have been disrupted and I do not know how many troops we have. There never has been anything in the history of the U.S. Army like the astounding defeats, which your forces have inflicted upon us in these last few days. So complete has been annihilation of our forces that I would guess the only Americans left alive are at our headquarters. I am sorry if my answer does not please the Japanese commander, but if he doubts my word he has no idea how effective his troops have been."

The interpreter relayed my message and after much conversation, the interpreter turned and asked, "Will 15 large trucks be enough to transport your headquarters to prison?"

"His estimate is very sound," I replied in relief, realizing that he had accepted my statement.

"We are going to continue to treat you as official emissaries for the American forces and we will return you to camp. Tomorrow morning at 11 a.m. our forces will enter that area and formally receive your surrender."

The Japanese then treated us to a cup of hot tea and after a few minutes of informal conversation, sent us back to camp.

The next morning, May 17, a few minutes before 11, 43 Americans and approximately 100 Filipinos gathered in the little open area along the side of the road running through our camp. We were a compact, silent group as Japanese trucks filled with troops rolled into the area. A Japanese officer ordered his troops out of the trucks and motioned for them to surround us. He then requested Gen. Chynoweth; our chief of staff, Col. Scudder and the two emissaries (Cracraft and myself) to come forward.

"Do you have all your men ready to surrender?" he asked.

"Yes," replied Gen. Chynoweth.

"Show my men where your arms are," the Japanese officer instructed.

"Scudder, you and Cracraft show them," the general said.

I remained near the general and slightly behind him as the other two moved off, accompanied by several Japanese soldiers. I watched the general square his shoulders and look at the sky. His look was one of bitter disillusionment and I realized that he was taking the surrender with far more feeling that he had shown. This was a personal defeat for him as well as a most disgraceful way to end a career in the defense of his country. We stood in the sun waiting, surrounded by Japanese. The green forest near us beckoned longingly.

Col. Scudder and Cracraft sweating profusely returned with a Japanese soldier who talked excitedly to the Japanese officer who in turn angrily demanded of us, "Where are your swords? Are there no swords with your arms? Have you destroyed or hidden them? We must have them!"

"American officers do not wear swords," he was informed. "They carry pistols."

"This is preposterous," he replied. "All officers have swords. Even sergeants have swords," he said, pointing to a Japanese soldier. After much conversation, the officer accepted the fact that there were no American swords to be captured.

The interpreter turned to us and told the general to prepare to surrender his troops. Gen. Chynoweth relayed the information to our troop commander and our little group came to attention. The Japanese officer barked an order, spoke a minute or so in Japanese and then turned on his heel. His detail commanders in turn barked orders and the Japanese soldiers surrounded us. I was shoved into the ranks. Shortly, the Japanese soldiers were among us searching each man. They took our few remaining personal belongings such as pocketknives, watches, pens and pencil, family pictures, rings, billfolds, anything that caught their fancy. Lt. Byron Lee Johnson stooped and started to pick up his empty billfold after a Jap soldier tossed it at his feet. The Jap instantly kneed him in the groin and he fell in a heap. There were other incidents of similar violence.

After the plundering of our personal items, we were ordered to climb into waiting trucks. With dragging footsteps our little band approached the vehicles and climbed the best we could into the truck beds amid the sound of rifle butts striking human flesh.

The American Forces on the Island of Cebu had surrendered to the Japanese.

As the trucks started down the canyon road, we were on our way, to march as Roman captives in a triumphant Japanese parade through the City of Cebu, to 39 months of torture, shipwreck and death before our release in faraway Muken, Manchuria.

POW

After the surrender on May 17, 1942, I was confined in the Cebu civil jail. I remained here about five months until October 17, 1942. At that time I was moved to the Philippine POW Camp #2, Davao Mindanao. It was at that time Lt. Junsaburo Toshino and Mr. Shunosuke Wada, a civilian interpreter, first appeared. Mr. Wada was the first to appear and he arrived in camp sometime around December 1942 or January 1943. His designation at camp was the official Japanese interpreter who spoke English for that camp. His job was to act as liaison officer between the Japanese army officials in charge of the camp and the American prisoners of war. From the very beginning, Mr. Wada was inclined to look upon the Americans as criminals to be punished, beaten about and made to suffer. He held the attitude that, instead of being honorable soldiers overcome by superior forces, we had committed an unpardonable crime because we had dared to oppose the imperial forces of the Japanese Emperor. At every opportunity, Mr. Wada would do his utmost to discredit the American POWs with the Japanese camp officials. Under the policy of the Japanese camp commander, Maj. Mieda, all the personnel in the camp were required to work regardless of age and rank. There were exceptions in respect to internal officers of the camp and some of the real sick. Mr. Wada, once or twice a week, would go through the sick barracks of the camp with the American camp commander examining the sick people. He would point to some man, who perhaps had malaria within 24 or 48 hours and who was just beginning a short course of quinine and ask, "Why is this man not out at work. He is not sick, he does not even look sick. The Japanese soldiers are always on duty even though they pretend to be sick." All explanation given in respect to such cases would only infuriate Mr. Wada and he would leave camp very angry. During such occasions the American camp commander would be as diplomatic as possible and do his best to give the sick man a chance to recuperate. Very often, after such occasions, the camp would be shorted a sack or two of rice. When our camp commander asked Mr. Wada why we were shorted in our ration (which consisted mostly of rice and wheat soup and was far inferior to what the Japanese soldiers were eating), Mr. Wada answered, "But you do not need food because you have so many sick. The sick do not work and we cannot feed people who do not work." The result of all this was that our rations were shorted for a day or two.

Mr. Wada often came out to the fields where the men were working. One incident occurred in the sweet potato field. Mr. Wada personally walked out among the potato planters and found Capt. Milton Whaley, who had gotten a little too much dirt covering some of his sweet potato slips. Without any warning Mr. Wada proceeded to use his stick, which he was carrying, to beat Capt. Whaley. As a result, Capt. Whaley was put in the sick barracks for two days. Capt. Whaley was doing a decent job and his sweet potato plants were as efficiently planted as any of the others. By Mr. Wada's manner, it was easy to see that he was looking for something to make an issue of. After beating Capt. Whaley, Mr. Wada lectured the whole detail of about 150 to 200 men on doing a very bad job of planting sweet potatoes. As a result, the whole detail had to stay out on the job for an extra hour with no rest periods during the later three-quarters of the day. Also, after Mr. Wada talked to the guards, they became very vicious and before the day was over two or three other Americans were beaten or clubbed.

Often our little hospital would run out of medical supplies and we would have to ask a Japanese doctor for new supplies. Officially this had to be done through Mr. Wada. At such time Mr. Wada would say he would see to it and our camp commander would hear nothing more about medical supplies. Finally the Japanese doctor would make an inspection and inquire as to why there were so many more people in the hospital and Lt. Col. Dwight M. Deter, the American hospital commander, would immediately tell the Japanese doctor that we had run of out of quinine, anesthetics, bandages and etc. He would also very pointedly tell the Japanese doctor that we had asked for supplies and that they had been promised to us but they had never arrived. Often, very shortly after that, a portion of the quantity of supplies asked for would be brought into camp by a guard. Mr. Wada, after such occasions, would be extremely harsh and revengeful in his contact with all Americans. During such periods he usually beat Americans and would go out on inspection details and by ingenious ways make the detail almost unbearable. For example, in cutting weed greens and bringing them into camp the American detail would carry these greens in big baskets swung on a pole and borne by two men. He would force us to load our own baskets far beyond the weight that we could ably carry. This over-taxed our strength to the point that some of the men would grow so weak that they would fall beneath the weight of their load. On such occasions the guards would beat them for failure to do the work. The only thing we could do was to leave a basket on the way and double up with the weakened detail members. As a result, the camp was again shorted of food.

On the logging detail, several times Mr. Wada would come out and complain that the men were carrying just sticks instead of good firewood logs out of the jungle. We were beaten until we carried out logs of a size that he desired and we would be kept over-time until dark when they were afraid that we would escape. As a specific example, I was one of two men who had to carry a 10-foot log, which we estimated to weigh 200 pounds, through the edge of the jungle for about a half a mile. This task would have been a large one for healthy men on good rations. We were barefoot and naked to the waist. As a result of this we were badly bruised, both in the feet and the shoulders, and so exhausted that we could hardly move when we reached the railroad car which we were loading. There were many other details who performed feats which were equal to or similar to this. I give this just as an example.

In respect to the need of our camp and specifically when our camp commander would protest the beatings of Americans by the Japanese, Mr. Wada was the official go-between the American camp commander and the Japanese officials. On all such occasions Mr. Wada would become very angry and often tell our camp commander and his staff that they were lying. The Japanese officers were unable to understand English to any extent and Mr. Wada in translating what our camp officials were saying to the Japanese camp officials would take three or four times as long to translate to the Japanese officers what our camp officials said. For a specific example in regard to food, Lt. Col. Kenneth S. Olsen asked Maj. Mieda for more food, the conversation went something like this:

Lt. Col. Olsen speaking, "Major we need more food, all of our men are losing weight, we cannot work and maintain our health on the rations that you are giving us." Mr. Wada took the bigger part of seven or eight minutes, in my estimation, to translate these two or three simple statements. As he talked, Mr. Wada would become increasingly vehement. After he was finished Maj. Mieda spoke a few words and Mr. Wada again talked angrily for several minutes. At this point Lt. Col. Olsen made a simple statement, "We need more food." Mr. Wada then turned back to Maj. Mieda and talked for at least five minutes. The end of the conversation was a statement from Wada to this effect, "Maj. Mieda will see if he can get you more food, but all Americans must work harder, they have been lagging on their details."

It was very plain to see that Mr. Wada was coloring the situation with his personal animosity far beyond the statements made by our camp commander.

This was the background and attitude of Mr. Wada at the Davao Penal Colony. This camp lasted for 21 months and was broken up in June 1944 at which time there were 1,200 men left at Davao with a detail at Lasang under Lt. Col. Rufus H. Rogers, which was working on an airstrip. The approximate number of American prisoners in the Lasang detail was 750.

When they moved out 1,200 from Davao to the prison ship at Lasang, we were taken in trucks from camp. Each truck, which was a 1-1/2 ton, contained 40 men in the truck bed. We were placed standing five abreast with our hands tied behind us and ropes tied around the waist of each of us running from one person to another and the men at one end or the other of the rows were tied to the row behind. The result was that every man in the truck had his hands tied behind him and was tied at the waist to his neighbor. Sitting on top of the cab was a Japanese guard with a long pole in his hand. Our instructions were to keep our head bowed and look at the floor of the truck during the entire trip. The guards used the pole on anybody who happened to look up. This trip lasted about six hours and it became extremely torturous to all the American POWs. Some of the men almost went mad from pain and it was nothing to hear them moan or cry out. Mr. Wada was interpreter during this trip and he frequently made the ropes unduly harsh as we were tied.

When we were placed on the ship, there was insufficient room for us to lie down. Lt. Col. Olsen protested to Mr. Wada concerning our crowded conditions and Mr. Wada was able to do nothing for us, so he said, because the captain of the ship had no more room. The 1,200 American prisoners were placed in one hold and deck on the bow of the ship, there was not room enough for the men to lie side by side their bodies touching. The best we could do was have four men to sit with their knees drawn up against their chest in the space that one man's body would normally take. This trip lasted 21 days as I recall. During this time Mr. Wada was asked to get us disposal cans for our bodily waste, he got us a few, but not near what we called for.

During our time at Cabanatuan or Philippine POW Camp No. 1, Mr. Wada had very little association with us. We did not see him again, with the exception of one or two times, until Dec. 13, 1944, when he and Lt. Toshino were placed in charge of the group of 1,619 American prisoners placed on board the *Oryoku Maru*. Lt. Toshino was the Japanese officer in charge of our group of POWs with Mr. Wada as his assistant and interpreter. Lt. Toshino was also at Davao during the last few months of existence of the Davao camp. As one of the Japanese officers in the Davao camp command, he proved himself very unfriendly to the American prisoners. His conduct was the same harassing style as that of Mr. Wadas.

I desire to make it plain at this point that Mr. Wada was undoubtedly following out the policy laid down or at least condoned by the Japanese prison commander. Lt. Toshino, likewise, followed this policy and used every chance he had to make the Americans uncomfortable. In Davao, Lt. Toshino had used all the ingenious Japanese devices, which have been mentioned as part of Mr. Wada's technique. Lt. Toshino, being an officer, can be held as more responsible than Mr. Wada for the roughness of the policy pursued by the Japanese officials and guards toward the American POWs.

On October 12, 1944 we were moved again to Bilibid Camp, Manila, where we remained until Dec. 13, 1944.

The afternoon of Dec. 13, 1944, 1,619 American prisoners were placed in the hold of the *Oryoku Maru* in such a manner that they did not have even standing room.

The prisoners were marched into the hold at the point of a bayonet. The hold became so filled by men sitting down that it was impossible for any more men to enter. At this point the Japanese guards, under Mr. Wada's direction, made about half of the prisoners stand up. With the prisoners standing up it was possible to force more Americans down into the hold. There were three Japanese guards who directed the placing of the prisoners. Two of these men had bamboo poles about six feet long, the third had a shovel or spade. With these poles and spade they beat the Americans, both standing and sitting, until they were squashed into huddles of solid flesh and bones. Then more Americans would be forced into the hold. With the men that were standing the Japanese held their poles horizontal and shoved against the chests of the men as they stood in mass against the side of the hold. While the two guards with the poles were shoving with all their might against the solid mass of prisoners, the third guard with the spade went up and down the line beating them to make them shrink closer against the wall.

In the course of a few minutes a large group of the prisoners were standing in an oblique position of perhaps a 45-degree angle. This was due to the fact that their feet were broader than the thickness of their chests. The time came when the mass of perhaps 200 prisoners against this wall were actually lying against each other in an up-right position. When the Japanese finished loading Americans into this hold, I estimate that there must have been at least 500 American POWs in the lying-standing position. During this loading operation Mr. Wada and Lt. Toshino were up on the deck forcing the Americans into the hold. The fact that there was not sitting room in the hold and that the POWs were standing in great numbers made no difference to them. Both Toshino and Wada would glance into the hold and then at the remainder of the group of prisoners yet to be loaded and would order more into the hold. After each decision by Toshino, Mr. Wada would lean over the edge of the hatch and cry out "more men, more men down here." When the Americans would protest that there was no more room, Mr. Wada would answer, "It does not make any difference, more men must go down." There was no argument that was effective. As near as I can remember, a general estimate in my section of the hold, the number of prisoners forced into that hold was around 800. This included what little baggage each one was carrying. Since this was December we knew that it would be cold in Japan and we tried to take with us what few clothes we had. When the Japanese finished loading us into the hold it was practically impossible to move, we were wedged in so tightly against each other that we could not move if we tried. In a period of about six hours, we were able to shift ourselves a little and make more room for the standing. As a result, most of the American POWs who had been lying against their fellows in an up-right position were able to stand up-right. As soon as our hold was loaded Toshino ordered the hatch closed and we were left in darkness. There was no attempt made to give us ventilation. Even in December the weather in the Philippines is exceedingly tropical. As soon as the prisoners could arrange themselves so that they could move, they started taking off their clothes in order that they would not perspire so much and to keep from being overcome by heat. Within a few hours practically everybody was stripped to a pair of shorts or "G" string.

The ship pulled out into Manila Bay as soon as the American prisoners were loaded. The American prisoners were not the only passengers on this ship. For a period of about four hours we had waited on the dock while Japanese civilians, a small number of troops and a large number of Japanese women and children were loaded on to the ship. These passengers were placed in the passenger quarters and on the various decks.

The ship appeared to get under way as soon as they had fastened the hatch covers. Within a period of an hour American POWs were beginning to faint from lack of air and from the heat. There was no water available except what each individual had in his canteen or any type of a receptacle in which he could carry water. Within about eight hours, fully half of the 800 POWs had used up their small water supply. Within four hours after the hatches had been closed people were beginning to go out of their minds, thrash and struggle around and to scream. That first night was so nearly a reality of hell that I cannot begin to describe the situation as it really was. Men went stark raving mad, screamed, cursed and beat each other up as if they were mad animals. Several times during the night somebody would scream out "he is killing me, he is killing me, get him off of me." All during this time the hold was pitch dark and it was impossible to tell what was going on or who was going mad or who was killing who. In the morning a little light penetrated through the canvas that covered the hatch and we could dimly see the men lying upon one another. There were several men dead, perhaps 15 or 20 this first night. It was impossible to make an accurate count. Some of those dead showed marks of violence with gashes on their throats and wrists. There is no doubt in my mind that some people had gone entirely crazy and reverted to an animal status. Teeth marks would indicate that there had been attempts to suck blood from these victims.

Shortly after sunup, Cmdr. Bridgett, who was the American in charge of our hold, quieted talk in the hold with the following information. "The time is at hand to show ourselves true Americans and not to lose our head, our convoy is under air attack." I won't go into detail concerning the air attacks. Mr. Wada and Lt. Toshino appeared once during the day, looked into the hold and went away. That day we got one meal that consisted of a handful of rice per man, the volume of this rice in my ration was equal to perhaps a teacup. We received no water and there were some who received no food. All during this time no provision had been made for our bodily waste. Quite a number of the men were sick with dysentery and with weak kidneys our hold was fast becoming wet and filthy from these bodily wastes. Wada and Toshino were told of this the one time that they looked into the hold.

As the air attack continued during the day, the hatch covers were taken off of the holds in order that the Japanese guards could see what the prisoners were doing. The men who were directly below the open hatch could see our planes in air attack. We estimated that our ship was under actual dive bombing 12 or 15 times that day. It was hit several times and partially wrecked. Some of the Navy men said that the ship's rudder had been destroyed from the way she handled. During this first day's bombing, the ship was very near the old location of our Naval Base at Olongapo. During the night the ship limped up to shore and discharged the Japanese soldiers, civilians, women and children. In the morning she moved offshore slightly and anchored just offshore from the tennis court at Olongapo. The American prisoners and some of the Japanese guards remained on board the ship. Mr. Wada and Lt. Toshino were nowhere about. The second night was far worse than the first night in respect to American POWs going stark raving mad. In the morning our dive-bombers were back attacking the remainder of the convoy. By 10 a.m. we had undergone a series of dive bomb attacks. At approximately 10 a.m. we underwent a dive bomb attack during which a bomb lit in the hold where I was and blew the side out of the ship. This bomb lit between 20 to 30 feet away from me among a group of about 115 field officers. There were only eight or nine survivors of this group of approximately 115 men. One of the survivors is Lt. Col. John Curtis.

The result of this bomb landing in the hold of the ship was chaos. There was wreckage of all types from the ship and pieces of bodies all over the place. There were wounded men unable to move, others, pinned down by wreckage, who were unable to get free. When the wreckage quit falling, the American POWs began to stir around and some started toward the stairway to the deck, which was still standing. Immediately the Japanese guards, who were uninjured and still at their positions up on deck, tossed hand grenades down into the hold, started firing their rifles and some used their pistols upon the American prisoners who were attempting to climb out of the wreckage. A man about two feet away from me sat up out of the wreckage, got to his knees and placed both hands on the stairway to the deck. He was immediately shot in the chest, very near the heart. He took two full breaths and flopped back into the wreckage dead. While I was watching him die, there were other shots from the deck through the hold. I heard some prisoners say that Lt. Toshino was present and fired his pistol into the hold. I saw a Japanese, who might have been Toshino, but due to the confusion I did not pay particular attention to him and I could not swear that Toshino was the man with the pistol. After a few minutes of this type of treatment, the Japanese guards left their posts and the American prisoners started climbing out of the hold on to the deck of the wrecked ship. Some jumped into the sea going through a hole in the side of the ship. I went up the ladder and on to the deck where I saw several dead Americans who had been shot and a few dead Japanese. Finding a life preserver among the dead, I put it on and jumped overboard. Once in the sea I started swimming to the nearest point of the shore. During this time there were still Japanese guards on the boat and they were firing at American soldiers who were swimming in the water. Several men were killed by those shots. Those of us who went as direct as possible from the ship to the shore were not very often fired at. Those Americans also attempted to swim to more distant points of the shore were often shot as they swam. There were a few who undoubtedly got to shore. After the majority of the survivors of the boat had been recaptured, Japanese details went along the shore searching for escaped prisoners. For several hours after I reached the shore I heard firing in the region of the wrecked ship. The Japanese were undoubtedly mopping up any Americans whom they found alive and attempting to escape.

When we left the ship, it was burning and although the American POWs themselves attempted to remove wreckage from the wounded and helpless, we were so weakened that we were unable to save many. The Japanese made no attempt to rescue any of the wounded. These poor devils were left to burn with the ship. Due to suffocation the first two nights, we estimated that between 50 and 75 Americans died in the hold and it is estimated that 230 some men were killed in the actual bombing or left on the burning ship.

When the Japanese recaptured the majority of the survivors we were herded into a tennis court. Once in the tennis court and settled, we found that there was just room enough to lie down by lying alternately. By this I mean that every second individual had his feet lying near the head of the individual on each side of him. There was no food given us on this day, December 15.

DIARY EXCERPTS

This is the meager diary of the most fantastic and horrible ship trip I ever took, and one of the most horrible voyages of WWII.

Tuesday, December 12, The camp commander of Bilibid Prison was informed late in the afternoon that 1,619 American POWs were to leave in the morning.

Wednesday, December 13, we were placed on board the Oryoku Maru.

Thursday, December 14, we were bombed all day and received one meal.

Friday, December 15, we underwent several bombing attacks and around 10:00 in the morning a bomb exploded inside the hold of the ship blowing the side out and setting in on fire. No food.

Saturday, December 16, the American prisoners who were able to get ashore, approximately 1,333 of 1,619, were confined to the tennis court with water, but no food, torrid sun. I was wounded slightly on both hands and right cheek by flying bomb fuse during raid by our bombers.

Sunday, December 17, the group of POWs were still on the tennis court. There were four deaths and we received our first food since December 14. This food ration consisted of 2-1/2 mess kit spoonfuls of dry uncooked rice. There was no way to cook this rice, consequently it did us very little good. To boil it down, we had one sack of rice for 1,333 men.

Monday, December 18, this day is a repeat of the 17th and our food ration was three mess kit spoons of raw dry rice.

Tuesday, December 19, men can hardly walk, heat stroke by day and freezing by night. Four mess kit spoons of dry rice.

Wednesday, December 20, four and half days on the tennis court with 13-1/2 mess kit spoons of raw dry rice for our total ration. By this time Mr. Wada and Lt. Toshino had made arrangements to take us out of the tennis court. Just as they moved us they brought in some worn out salvaged tropical Japanese uniforms which were nothing but rags. I received two pairs of shorts. By wearing both pairs at the same time I was still unable to cover myself up. During these days on the tennis court we had plenty of water, no food except a few spoonfuls of rice. No sanitation, except a trench just outside the gate of the court and absolutely no medical attention. Many of the men were wounded. In one case a man had his leg amputated on the floor of the tennis court under the tropical sun. Naturally he died after, but it was the best that could be done. Between the damp cold of the night and the fierce rays of the sun by day, men were failing rapidly and beginning to die.

Thursday and Friday, December 21-22, the group was moved from Olongapo to San Fernando Pampanga where we were lodged in the provincial jail and a cockpit. During the days that we were there the flies were terrible. They crawled all over us as though we had been covered with honey. One reason for this attraction was the fact that the Japanese had given us no opportunity for bathing and we were unspeakably filthy with our own filth.

Saturday, December 23, received an estimate of 300 grains of cooked rice, one death occurred this day.

Sunday, December 24, moved to San Fernando La Union by the way of small box cars on the Luzon railroad. The Japanese placed 180 Americans standing in the particular car that I was in. There were also, sick American POWs placed on the top of the prison cars. We were in these cars from about 10 a.m. until 3 a.m. the next morning. During this time we received no food, no water. The hardship of the journey packed in these cars, which were exposed to the tropical sun, caused many men to faint.

Monday, Christmas Day 1944, the group was in a school yard, received two meals and a little water. The amount of rice is estimated as one canteen cup and the water ration is estimated as half a canteen cup. This is the lowest Christmas I ever had; we are without hope almost.

Tuesday, December 26, the group was moved to some sand dunes not far from the San Fernando pier waiting to be placed on board another ship. The day was terribly hot sitting and lying on the sand exposed to the direct rays of the sun. Our ration was five mess kit spoons of water and a half-cup of rice.

I want to make it very plain that on both of these days there were wells very near our location and plenty of water could have been given us had Lt. Toshino and Mr. Wada so directed. No amount of pleading with them would do any good. They refused us water. By this time it was very apparent that the more inhumane they could be, the better they liked it.

Wednesday, December 27, we were placed on board a large empty freighter, *Enoura Maru*, at dawn and got underway. One meal of a third cup of rice and half-pint of tea; one soldier, an officer I believe named D.C. Brown, was shot when he attempted to jump overboard and escape.

Thursday, December 28, half-cup of rice, a little piece of fish and third cup of water for our days food and water ration. As the ship went north, the atmosphere became cool and the men did not suffer so much from the heat. The ship that we were placed on was a large freighter that had just brought a cavalry unit down to Luzon. No attempts had been made to clean the place. As a result, we were forced to sit and lie in horse manure and urine. We just had enough room to sit down if we curled up. This hold was filled with flies, millions of them, which persisted in swarming over us making us more miserable than we were. Again, there was no sanitation.

Friday, December 29, one meal of half-cup of rice and no water.

Saturday, December 30, half-cup of rice, five mess kit spoons of soup and half-pint of water.

Sunday, December 31, one and half meals today, arrived in the Port of Takao on Formosa.

Monday, Jan. 1, 1945, ship lying in the harbor of Formosa, men were dying, received two meals and no water.

Tuesday, January 2, still on board the ship, more dead, usual ration of rice which was half canteen cup, also received one cup of soup to be divided among six. men. We received half a cup of water.

Wednesday, January 3, we received three spoons of dry rice, half-cup cooked rice, quarter cup of soup and one pint of water.

Thursday, January 4, one meal plus a little soup, received one water ration of half-pint. Thirty-four dead since leaving Olongapo, no medicine or dressings of any type. Dysentery is bad. Since boarding this ship, Mr. Wada had appeared almost daily, asked him for more food and water. Lt. Toshino appeared once or twice, all of our requests were either refused or ignored.

Friday, January 5, one meal no soup and one water ration received. Six men were dead. Making a total of 40 since leaving Olongapo. The estimate, 1,293 survivors to date, out of 1,619 that started on the *Oryoku Maru* Dec. 13, 1944.

Saturday, January 6, Japanese were all day loading supplies on board the ship, part of our detail which had been on board another ship was brought on board. We received two meals with soup each time and a short ration of water, which means less than half-pint, four more dead.

Sunday, January 7, recheck on number, 1,619 left Bilibid, 279 lost on the *Oryoku Maru* or 1,340 arrived on the tennis court. Fifteen of the most seriously wounded were sent back to Bilibid, 1,309 got on board the boat at Linguian Gulf, 1262 alive this morning. Two meals and water today. Fifty died since arriving on tennis court.

Monday, January 8, still in Takao Harbor clearing up the ship's mess, we received one meal and one water ration, group was divided into two holds, sitting room only, sitting much worse than before.

Tuesday, January 9, it is about noon and we have just been hit by five bombs in an air raid by our planes, we are still in the harbor of Takao. Ten days now, many are dead. Japanese not doing anything for us.

Wednesday, January 10, many dead in the other hold, estimate about 236, about 40 dead in this hold, many are wounded, myself included.

Thursday, January 11, Japanese cleaned the dead out of the holds, one case of diphtheria today. One meal with soup, very cold at night.

Friday, January 12, night very cold, sleep in shorts, meals the same, nine more dead from wounds, Dr. Whaley killed by bomb. Repairing boat by placing wooden plugs in the small holes, two meals.

Saturday, January 13, moved to another ship, *Brazil Maru*, one meal and no water, wounded are dying for lack of medicine and moving. In reference to the bombing these figures are as near accurate as I could get at the time. There were many who were seriously wounded that we had to move to another ship, about a dozen and half died while they were being moved. We were bombed on the ninth and it was not until the 11th or 12th that the Japanese made any attempt to give us any medical care. I believe it was on the 11th when the Japanese took the carcasses off the ship that they gave us this farcical medical treatment. The treatment consisted of everybody who was able to walk, who had a wound, forming in a line and having a

Japanese first-aid man paint his wound with some red disinfectant and perhaps receiving a bandage. The most beneficial effects of this visit was the fact that some of the wounded received some bandages. We had no bandages with us and what little care we ourselves gave the wounded was done by donation of clothes from our own backs. The Japanese made no effort to give us bandages, disinfectant or any kind of care. The attention they did give us is did not come until the odor pile of dead directly under the hatch became so strong that it must have been unpleasant on the deck. It was terrible down where we were.

Sunday, January 14, moved out to sea at dawn in convoy, one meal of quarter cup of rice and no water.

Monday, January 15, ship sailed north all day, we had two meals and no water.

Tuesday, January 16, ship still sailing north, men dying, very cold and we have no clothes.

Wednesday, January 17, 32 men died last night from exposure and disease, boat stopped and anchored overnight.

Thursday, January 18, the boat anchored at night and sailed north all day, two light meals and quarter canteen cup of water, the weather was very cold.

Friday, January 19, we had two light meals and two rations of water, the ship anchored last night and sailed all day.

Saturday, January 20, ship stopped at night, had two meals and one water ration. It is very cold and the men continue to die at the rate of about 30 a day, the boat sailed all day.

Sunday, January 21, two meals and one water ration, the ship was sailing north. The usual number of men are dying. At this point I wish to make clear that the ship was sailing north every day and each day the weather got colder. We were still naked at this stage of the trip as we had been when we started out from Linguian Gulf. As the men died, which they did at the rate of 30 to 50 a day, the Japanese continued to decrease our ration accordingly so that in spite of the vast numbers dying, those remaining alive received no additional food. Mr. Wada and Lt. Toshino would come around and demand to know exactly how many had died each day. They decreased the food that they were giving us accordingly. A time or two there was a discrepancy between the figures that we gave and the count of the Japanese. On each occasion Mr. Wada would refuse to give us food until they could agree on the figures.

All during this time the Japanese had straw mats and life preservers aboard the ship which they could have given us for covering ourselves as protection against the cold. This they refused to do. I am absolutely certain that these mats were available because I was one of the first in his hold and I saw them lying on the floor. The hold had been used for the transportation of Japanese troops and there were dozens and dozens of mats and life preservers left scattered around by these Japanese troops. We started gathering these mats and life preservers up for our use and the Japanese ordered us to turn them in to a designated place in which they were stored. I afterwards traded a fountain pen for one of these mats. There is no doubt in my mind that receiving this mat through trading with a Japanese guard was what saved my life. Not only did it save my life but it saved the life of Lt. Col. Robert Lawlor and Maj. F.L. Berry. The three of us huddled together covered by this mat. All during this trip there was an open hatch in the center of the deck above our hold. The Japanese refused to entirely cover this and there was always an open hatchway in the deck above. Through these openings rain, snow and sleet often fell. The wind always blew down through the openings over our exposed bodies. Most of us had to lie upon the bare steel floor of the hold or upon the bare boards of the upper tier. No amount of pleading with the Japanese would get them to give us more food and water, give us the unused mats they had taken from us, stop the openings on the deck above and to close a ventilator which blew from another part of the ship throughout the hold. Under these conditions, men were physically numb most of the time. We never knew from one hour to the next who would be alive and who would be dead. After we started this last leg of the journey on the 14th, we had between 30 and 50 deaths daily. Everyday the cadaver detail, composed of the strongest POWs in the group, would go through the bays and pull out the dead which were piled up in the little open space in the center of the hold. Sometime during the day the Japanese guards would have our detail drag the bodies up on deck and leave them there. Then, the Japanese ran every American POW down below and closed the hatch for half an hour. During this half hour the American guard, who happened to be stationed at the bottom of the stairway to the upper deck, often peaked out through a crack and reported that the Japanese were knocking the gold and silver fillings out of the teeth of the cadavers before throwing them overboard.

All during this time the sanitation in the hold of this ship was unspeakable. We only had eight or 10 buckets as catch-all for the bodily waste of this large body of men which numbered around 1,000 when we started out on this ship. The Japanese took no special pains to see that we had an opportunity to empty these buckets. There were times when we could go out on deck to a latrine, this was only during daylight hours. Most of the men were sick with dysentery and diarrhea by this time and of course they had to attend to bodily needs during the hours of darkness. The Japanese refused to let us go on deck. As a result, these eight or 10 wooden buckets were very far from adequate for our sanitary needs. As a result, with so many men sick, the buckets ran over nearly every day. In the area of the hold where these buckets were, the human filth was at least two inches deep in some places. It ran out into the bays where men were lying and lived, slept, ate and died in it. No amount of requesting the Japanese for adequate facilities brought relief.

Monday, January 22, very cold, two meals and one water ration. Some of the men are going down into a lower hold and getting sugar to eat. The Japanese had forbidden our stealing sugar under the pain of death.

Tuesday, January 23, snowed all day and the snow blew down over our exposed bodies.

Wednesday, Wednesday, January 24, snowed all day and seemed unusually cold. We got two meals and one water ration that day.

Thursday, January 25, we received two meals and one water ration, about 30 were dead. As the ship drew nearer to the mainland of Japan it would anchor for hours at a time. On many days we would hardly sail for four hours of the 24.

Friday, January 26, Anchored four hours at night. Sailing between large islands. Pine trees on shore. Two meals and no water.

Saturday, January 27, we received one meal and one water ration, men continue to die at the rate of 30 to 50 a day.

Sunday, January 28, received two meals, the ship sailed a little while during daylight hours and the men continued to die.

Monday, January 29, the ship underwent another submarine attack in the dark hours just before dawn. Submarine attacks have not been mentioned previously because they were merely minor incidents on the trip. From information I could secure, I estimate that we underwent from 10 to 12 separate submarine attacks. At one point the ship following us was damaged by a submarine and our ship was towing it. This was one of the reasons for the slowness of the trip. We reached our destination about four or five hours after this last submarine attack.

The ship pulled into the harbor of Moji shortly after daylight. During the morning the boat was inspected by some high ranking Japanese officers. Mr. Wada and Lt. Toshino were not in evidence that I saw, however, some of the men say Lt. Toshino was standing in the background as the Japanese inspection party stood at the top of the hatch and looked down upon us. Shortly after this inspection party boarded the ship, the Japanese demanded a roll call of all survivors of the trip, this was made. Later one of the doctors told me that the Japanese had forced him to sign a statement that all the men lost on the trip had been due to American forces bombing Japanese prison ships. Of the 1,619 Americans that started out on board this ship there were less than 500 who got off the boat alive. The survivors of this trip continued to die in the camps that we were taken to for a almost a month after we were taken off the ship. The last estimate that Col. Ovid O. Wilson and I made indicated that there were 303 survivors left out of the 1,619.

Tuesday, January 30, the Japanese took us off the boat, marched us a mile through the town of Moji, put us on trains and sent us to various camps on the island. I went to Fukuoka Camp No. 3. Once inside this camp, where there were numerous Dutch, American and Japanese POWs, we had a chance to survive. I desire to say at this time that the major in charge of Camp Fukuoka No. 3, personally was as liberal and as good to us as any individual Japanese that I saw. I think possibly he would have been kinder to us had the policy of the Japanese army permitted it.

January 31, 1945, I am alive 31 days longer than I ever expected to be I think we will make the grade through the war now. Everybody grand to us. 80 lbs.

Thursday, February 1. Have the dysentery. Had beef soup and a 1/4 lb. fresh fish tonight. Am very cold here.

Friday, February 2. Sleep when I can, not too cold. Runs bad. Soup and rice chill before we can eat it.

Saturday, February 3. Coldest day here. Enlisted men moved out last night so we have whole barracks.

Sunday, February 4. Diarrhea better, appetite no good, so cold I can't get warm in bed.

Monday, February 5. Cold as heck, 25 degrees in hospital. Three meals a day.

Tuesday, February 6. Js won't let us lend each other our money. We now have to share Red Cross with camp.

Wednesday, February 7. Received half chocolate bar from Red Cross. Very cold, many men going to hospital with runs and exhaustion.

Thursday, February 8. One man died so suddenly nobody in the barracks knew he was dead. Snowy and very cold. Js very wrought up.

Friday, February 9. Very cold. Got put on intravenous beriberi shots today, more men dying.

Saturday, February 10. Snow, cold, runs still continue. Very miserable.

Sunday, February 11. Pudding issued again, corned beef in rice and four tangerines. Warmer.

Monday, February 12. Usual day, sunny. Butter issued today; a little salmon in night's soup.

Tuesday, February 13. Fish at night. A little warmer today.

Wednesday, February 14. Another died today. Our 100 is now reduced to 90. My diarrhea grows better gradually. Coffee with cream in it tonight.

Thursday, February 15. Cheese and jam issued today. Weather is warmer.

Friday, February 16. Wrote a 40 word radiogram to folks. "Safe in Japan. Plan our homecoming to take place immediately after my return. Answer this radiogram in all letters. Bob and Marion say hello to E.P. Lawlor, Columbus, OH and Mrs. Adda Bates, Louisville, KY. Love, Bill."

Saturday, February 17. More Red Cross. Three squares of chocolate and one tangerine bloated me like a balloon last night. Rumors that one of our task forces bombed Tokyo with carrier planes.

Sunday, February 18. Nothing new, no news. Fish on the side for supper tonight.

Monday, February 19. Another day, issue of coffee and sugar (four men to a coffee can), nothing new.

Tuesday, February 20. Feel better. Runs receding so I feel better.

February 21-28. More Red Cross items issued. Small countries climbing on bandwagon.

Wednesday, March 1. Am just beginning to feel better, like I am gaining in strength. I think we lived on our reserve for two weeks after we arrived. February 27 we were officially made members of this camp. Eighteen of us have died since our arrival, most of them seem to relax and give up, some pneumonia, etc.

Saturday, March 31. Since the night of March 1 four more have died, 22 now. I feel a lot better, am doing light garden work 8:00 to 11:30 and 1:00 to 4:30. We have had a dozen air raids the last of the month, mostly at night, the boys are active all around. Tinko is at 5:00 a.m., 7:00 a.m., 12:00 and 8:00 p.m., have had more numerous inspections, etc. Chow is the same; Red Cross food is now eight men to a box. Bob Lawlor and I still are together sleeping in the same bed.

Sunday, April 1, Easter. Big shakedown by the Js this morning, all officers are in disgrace because two men stole some potatoes slated for the kitchen.

Wednesday, April 25. Transferred from Fukuoka Camp #3 to Hoten Prison Camp, Mukden, Manchuria.

RESCUE FROM THE JAPANESE IN MUKDEN, MANCHURIA

Monday, Aug. 13, 1945. The factory men of T.K.K. and M.K.K. were left in camp. The day before there were many rumors from Chinese and Koreans that the war had about ended. We hardly believed the rumors yet the good sources claimed them reliable.

Tuesday, Aug. 14, 1945. Half M.K.K. men went to work, total 198 remained in camp and 202 went to work, all T.K.K. went to work (36 men). There were many rumors that the war was over. Many of the men thought they would not go to work. Rumors reported Russians had taken Harbin through the junction of three Russians columns. Russians border reported penetrated in several other places. Three main columns approached from east, north and west and all reported advancing down railroads. Rumor also said seven landings on mainland of Japan.

Wednesday, Aug. 15, 1945. About 9:30 a.m. the air alert signal blew. Men from M.K.K. and T.K.K. came rushing in at noon and the Nips were very downcast. The branch camps were beginning to come in. Hot rumors that the war was over and Russians were advancing fast in north Manchuria. No air raid materialized. From the Japanese attitude we knew something was up in the way of bad news for them.

Thursday, Aug. 16, 1945. Men did not go to work. About 10:30 or 11:00 a.m. six men dropped, via parachute, out of a stange (not Nip) large plane. The chutes were varicolored, red, green, white, etc. About 4:30 p.m. six strange men were brought over to Nip headquarters. They were reported variously as American, Chinese and Russian. The Nips smiled and shook hands with them it was rumored. The Americans gave our workers the okay "high sign." Excitement ran high that night in camp as we recognized by their colored parachutes, these men as the six who had dropped out of the strange plane. Rumor was hot that the war was over and many bets were made. Many officers stayed up all night playing poker, reading and talking. The Nip guards failed to fix their bayonets in some cases, they did not order us to bed as they usually did and they did not beat us for smoking after hours and out of reach of ashtrays.

Friday, Aug. 17, 1945. About 8:00 a.m. Gen. Parker, Air Vice Marshall Maltby (British) and the Dutch general were called to Nip headquarters for a conference. Shortly afterward these leaders came back and told us an armistice had been called between the US, Great Britain allies and Japan. We were instructed to remain quietly in camp. Later Maj. Hennesy, leader of the six men came into camp and visited with us. He brought with him via chute a radio and medical supplies. American planes were supposed to precede him here dropping leaflets. These two planes failed to arrive, so the major and his five men soon found themselves surrounded by a Nip battalion of bayonets. The American born Japanese interpreter had to talk pretty fast to save their lives as the Nip troops did not know the war was officially over. Finally they persuaded the Nips of the reality of the armistice and they were brought to this camp where all the Nip colonel promised to do was not to shoot them. By the morning of the 18th the Nip colonel had the news as to what was what and he didn't refuse Maj. Hennesy anything he wanted. It seems the American headquarters in Chungking under Gen. Weidmeyer jumped to the gun at the knowledge in order to forestall anything happening to the American POW at Camp Hoten.

The Nip guards failed to patrol through camp after this announcement. We were given an issue of Nip cigarettes and some of the remainder of the Red Cross food stored in the canteen was issued. Again people stayed up most of the night as Hennesy's party had told us a little news of the States and the outside world. Coffee jags also had a lot to do with the general sleeplessness of the camp.

Saturday, Aug. 18, 1945. Maj. Hennesy had the Nips bring the 14 airmen into camp from the annex 300 yards away. These men had been shot down in raids last December. The British, Dutch and American units began to organize their men in their various organizations. These 14 men under Capt. Campbell had a lot of news about war conditions in the States which all new to us. Americans assumed interior camp guard. Weight down to 60 lbs. If the war had not ended when it did, I would have perished in a few weeks.

Sunday, Aug. 19, 1945. I was asked by Gen. Frank to help distribute the remainder of the Red Cross. I am now working in the canteen with Lt. William Don Thompson. The portable radio of Maj. Hennesy's brings us world news several times a day now. We sent out via radio for food, medicine, clothing, guitar strings, etc. As soon as diplomatic arrangements can be made with the Russians these supplies will be flown in.

Monday, Aug. 20, 1945. Put out the remainder of Red Cross by early p.m. Men are still exclaiming in slight about being free men. The camp organized a jam session for 7:00 p.m. In the p.m. around 4:30 a large American plane few over camp dipping its wings. The men of camp cheered wildly. With the exception of the 14 flyers none of us had ever seen such a large plane. Personally I knew the war was over because I saw an American plane and it didn't bomb or shoot at me.

At 7:00 p.m. the men gathered for the jam session and started singing. The session was interrupted by a call for the senior officers of the three nations in camp to meet the Russian representative at the headquarters. The Russian was a captain, 31 years of age, who had been in Vienna, Austria, Prague, Berlin capitulation's and had had contact with the American 9th Army fighting in Germany. The POWs gathered around him where he stood on the hospital steps where he made the following dramatic speech, quote:

"Liberty, on the very day when our units have occupied the City of Mukdeil we visited the Mukden camp for American and British war prisoners. Small, bowing, commander of the camp Col. Vsiaki came to meet us.

In the inner yard of the camp the war prisoners have formed. When we came into the yard their ranks were immediately broken, the men rushed toward us shouting their greetings in the various tongues.

My God! At last you came! We knew soon you would come! With tears in his eyes said Russian-American from the state of Washington, Michailov. He wanted to be our interpreter.

The representative of the Soviet Military Government ascended an improvised speaker's stand and began to speak.

"This morning our units have occupied the City of Mukden. I am empowered to inform you that from this hour all American, British and other allied war prisoners in this camp are free!"

It is hard to describe the emotion of the liberated men. Up went their military hats, handkerchiefs, the men kissed each other and shed the tears of happiness. The word "liberty" was repeated over and over again. Hundreds of British and the Americans inhumanely shouted it in the Russian language; Liberty, Liberty, Liberty!

"In the name of the Soviet Military Government," continued the officer of the Red army, "I congratulate you with victory of the allied troops over the Japanese imperialism!" And again the storm of applause swept the assemblage.

Oh! Russian youth, the voices shouted, the Russians are so strong! "We are your friends." The meeting goes on. To the porch ran up Alexander Biby. He halfway spoke in English. "The Russian troops have brought us the liberty. Three and a half years we have suffered in the Japanese prison. Thousands of us have died of hunger and thirst. In that time only four were able to escape from this camp and they were recaptured by the Japanese and done to death. The words cannot describe the cruel deeds of the Japanese to the war prisoners. My Russian buddies, it is to you that I address myself, with words of burning thankfulness and love. Not a one of us will ever forget this day. For life you're our faithful friends and this friendship we will bequest to our kin."

We saw the faces of the people who heard Alexander Biby and we realized that he spoke for the multitude.

The Soviet officer announced that the Japanese camp guard will, at once, be disarmed and those guilty of cruel and inhuman treatment to the war prisoners will be arrested.

Temporarily, before the arrival of the Soviet troops, the administration of the camp will be conducted by the American and British generals.

This announcement was met with the unanimous approval of the liberated war prisoners. We are becoming acquainted with the generals. We are being introduced to Gen. Parker, who is the ranking and the oldest general in the Mudken Camp. He is tall, lean, very pale. He has a face of a man of knowledge, a face of parchment with narrow bluish streaks. He asks interpreter Michailov to tell us that he is overjoyed to see the Russians and that he is amazed at the miraculously rapid advance of the Red army. Gen. Parker was asked to take temporary command of the camp.

Gen. Parker thanks our officers for their trust in him and assumes the command. At once it is seen that he is the man who commanded troops all his life and is able to accomplish everything brilliantly.

Also, are introduced vice air-marshal of the Great Britain Maltby. Came generals Jones, Sharp, Chynoweth, all commanding Corps; generals Brougher, Pierce, Funk, Drake, Stevens, Lough, Beebe, division commanders.

We are getting acquainted with the widely known Dutch journalist Joel, who became prisoner three years ago. He says; "I will write about you Russians, the senders of light into our darkness."

Within 30 minutes of our arrival all Japanese form in front of the war prisoners and lay down their arms. Here with the exceptionally fine organization the Americans and the British take up the Japanese arms and post their own sentinels instead of the Japanese.

Gen. Parker occupies the office of the Japanese camp commander. There, for the conference went all other generals.

The men would not let us leave. Each man wants to shake our hands and to receive our autographs. They ask us of the Red army of her battles with the Japanese and all in unison say, "Russians can fight! We are surprised at them! We will mention them at home!" Somebody from the Russian speaking war prisoners says aloud: "Now we will go home soon! Home to our families and children!" and this feeling spreads through the camp. The peoples' faces change and no words could describe their feelings. Now these men are free, the peace and quiet not far away.

And so today the liberty has come to camp. It was brought to them by the Red army fighting and marching over the trackless swamps and desert and the Great Hinken. *Translated from Russian newspaper by Sgt. Hurley, 31st Infantry.*

After his speech the men carried him on their shoulders around in a circle. The jam session continued until we were told to get inside the barracks while the Nips camp guard were disarmed on the compound parade ground. Not many people went inside, just lined up in front of the barracks. The Nips, officers and men marched out onto the field formed up and laid their arms in a pile and formed again. The Russian officer then called for some American prisoners to form a guard, take up the surrendered Nip arms and form a guard on the dejected Nips. The Russian officer then had our guard march the captured Nips around in front of us and away to the guard house. The Nip officers were allowed to keep their swords. There was a mighty cheer from the spectators as we saw the Nips who had kicked, beaten, starved and humiliated us, march away under our guards. This was a new experience for them.

After this the Russian officer answered some questions about his trip here, 1,000 kilometers in 10 days. When he left we all went back to our groups or barracks, had more coffee and spent another sleepless night!

Tuesday, Aug. 21, 1945. Today the Americans had the pleasure of seeing the Nips go out to the fields, digging potatoes, lugging dirty wet sacks of vegetables and stepping to the tune of a bayonet. Last night some of the men got into the Nip storerooms and rifled them of food, writing materials, etc. Things were quiet around camp except the repatriated units are trying to organize themselves and they overlap in claiming men. It's an awful mess trying to proportion out cigarettes, etc.

Wednesday, Aug. 22, 1945. Another plane came in today. Col. Hillsman's son, a captain in the airborne infantry. He says we will likely fly all the way over the Pacific to San Francisco. (Dramatic meeting between Col. Hillsman and his son).

Thursday, Aug. 23, 1945. Worked around in the QM and camp supply. The work keeps me busy and I am not stewing around about conditions in camp. Many enlisted men are going over the fence and coming back with all types of loot, guns, liquor, Nip silks, temple pieces, merchandise, swords, pistols, etc.

Friday, Aug. 24, 1945. Worked around the QM most of the day. About 4 p.m. went with Capt. Grow on a truck out to a Nip food dump the Russki's had taken over. The dump had an area of about 20 square kilometers which contained every conceivable type of food essentials, tobacco and small equipment facilities. On the way back the Russki's gave Grow and myself some Nip arms. Personally I got a Nip non-combat saber, an American .45 pistol and a German-Mauser pistol. I hope to take the first and latter home. Among some other things the Russki's told us we could have were some Japanese kimonos of which I took three, one for my mother and my two sisters. I also got a carved lacquer table which I hope to take home.

Mukden was very deserted looking. The only vehicles moving were American-made Russian equipment and a lot of captured Nip motors in the hands of the Chinese, Russkis and interns. The Russians were bringing Nip prisoners into town in large numbers. What they were doing with them I don't know and I don't care.

The Nip prisoners are scared stiff three ways: scared of the Americans they have had prisoners, scared of the Russians and scared of the Chinese they have lorded it over for 12 or 13 years. Most of the Nip prisoners I have heard quoted doubt if they will ever get back to Japan and well might they doubt such has been their actions in the past.

The Nips never have been able to understand American psychology, they never could break our spirit. As one Nip interpreter here in camp said, when the guardhouse sentence of some men was over and the men were released, as he overheard the Americans uncomplimentary remarks about their treatment quote "I can't understand your attitude, I can't understand why you are not humble and downcast, we punish you by giving you little food so you are very hungry, we make you stand at attention all day until you faint from exhaustion, you have no blankets or mosquito bars so your nights are cold and miserable, we strip you of all your clothes in the sub-arctic cold winter and pour cold water on you and when we let you out of the guardhouse you do not say "Thank You." All you say as you walk away is a contemptuous "— 'em!!!" unquote. They killed many Americans, trying to break our spirit, but they had no luck in general. We knew that America was going to win, kill us though they might. Today the vanquished Nip has no future even if he does live, the Americans always had a future if he lived.

This morning Maj. Jacobs of Chicago left on the first plane carrying sick prisoner patients out of camp. With him he took a radiogram to the folks and as listed below:

- one to folks
- one to Bob Irman
- one to H.G. Ingersoll
- one to Herb Heller

These letters will likely be home before I ever get out of here.

Saturday, Aug. 25, 1945. Worked around QM today, more milk and canned meat were brought in. Am dead on my feet, I have been working too hard.

Sunday, Aug. 26, 1945. Nothing new except a lot of supplies came in from off of a couple of planes.

Monday, Aug. 27, 1945. Gen. Wainwright was in camp a few minutes this morning. Giving the major general's 30 minutes notice, he flew out with them and his aids. I believe he is to go to the Tokyo show. I am still dead on my feet.

Tuesday, Aug. 28, 1945. Work around camp, etc. nothing much new or doing.

Wednesday, Aug. 29, 1945. I went to town in one of the official cars. All I did was to ride around as a passenger wherever it happened to go. Met a Col. Leath of Los Angeles who is one of the six men who parachuted in to get us out.

On return to camp I found the "processing detail" of 19 men had arrived on the plane in the p.m. Among them is a Bud Pearson of Toulon (about 30 miles out of Galesburg, IL). This was like meeting an old neighbor. Needless to say we had quite a visit.

Just at 6:00 p.m. three B-29s came over and dropped food, candy and clothes via parachute. Many of the chutes didn't open so the food cans were smashed. The falling cases knocked out our power lines, fell in the swamp, foxholes and were stolen by swift appearing crowds of Chinese.

Thursday, Aug. 30, 1945. Yet more B-29s dropped more supplies. Supply rooms are a mess of broken crates, mud and smashed supplies.

We now have up-to-date newspapers in camp, magazines, radio and movies.

Several men after seeing the movie remarked they couldn't get enthused about seeing an American girl again, they would rather have seen a steak and chop dinner; show was *To Have and Not to Have* with Humphrey Bogart and a girl called Slim.

Friday, Aug. 31, 1945. Another delay was the day. It's been over two weeks since we were first contacted, a plane a minute goes in and out of Chungking, we are still here, Uncle Sam isn't the "fast, on the ball" man I thought he was.

I understand the censorship of the US is full of bunk like the Nips. All I can freely say is, "Dear Mama and Papa, I am well, How are you? Love, etc."

Seven more planes dropped food. Met a processing man from Macomb. Movie again (Duane Coshill).

Sept. 1-6, 1945 (inclusive). Have been working in the QM all this time. Made several trips outside the gates on missions. Brought a group of Belgium Fathers (Priests) out to get clothes and shoes. A Russian enlisted man, a sentry at an old schoolhouse, gave me an officer's sword (Japanese). I was scheduled to fly out the 7th but the plane goes on another mission so I wait to go until day after or the 8th, if I go by plane, I hope I do.

I have met some fliers who are ferrying food in and men out, Maj. R.B. Young, Mitchell, SD, Phone 2087; Capt. W.A. Thompson, 1301 North Oregon, El Paso, TX or Rancho Patrillo, Palma, NM. Maj. Young took a letter out to send air mail to folks telling them I am on the way home. I like flying and I hope to be able to do some at home.

Sept. 7, 1945. Stood by all day for the plane out. Rested some.

Sept. 8, 1945. Flew from Mudken, Manchuria to Hsian, China about 950 miles. Tomorrow we fly on to Kumming just north of the Himalayan Mountains. Hope to go on to India from there. Today we flew over the Gulf of Korea and then up the Yellow River of China, it sure looked yellow, brown and red from the plane. Our altitude was 7,000 to 7,500 all the way. Passed over several mountain ranges, saw the Great Wall of China where it began at the sea and ran inland.

The erosion of China is tremendous, great gullies hundreds of feet through nice farm land. There are no forests or trees on the mountains. None of the mountains I saw today were over 7,500 feet high.

Sept. 9, 1945. Hsian to Kumming, China. The most used airport in the world here, a plane in or out each minute of the 24 hours. There are always four to seven planes in the air. Once at Kumming we were taken to the base hospital and fed. Everybody treated us grand, brought us ice cream, Red Cross had a little bag of toilet articles on our bed. We were given part of a complete physical examination. For the first time since May 1942 I saw an American woman. The Army nurses are quite a jolly crowd. They are dressed in fine striped (white and tan) smocks for a uniform, slacks, GI trousers and leather jackets, leather boots, field shoes, women's shoes, anything that's adaptable to comfort and activity. They sure looked good. Every American I have met has acquired a broadness of adaptability and tolerance foreign to our race. Everything new and foreign they take in their stride. I am proud to be an American.

Monday, Sept. 10, 1945. Finished the physical examination. Am okay for travel! Left the hospital and moved downtown to a hostel (converted hotel). Sight seeing tour around Kumming.

Tuesday, Sept. 11, 1945. Slept late. Looked around the town of Kumming. Went through town Club of Red Cross, saw its set up, saw a show etc. At 10:30 left for airport to catch plane for Manila. Took a C-54, left Kumming 11:30 and arrived Manila around 7:00 a.m.

Wednesday, Sept. 12, 1945. Arrived Nichols Field, Manila around 7:00 a.m. or 7:30 a.m. Immediately sent me to 29th Replacement Depot.

Rec. Per. Sec.

(688 Co. Tent D-3)

APO 501

c/o Postmaster

San Francisco

Found many of the people here who left Mukden prior to me. Nobody knows when we leave. Sent Red Cross message to home folks.

Thursday, Sept. 13, 1945. Rested, got my physical examination this p.m. Registered for mail with Red Cross. Sent message home to folks in a.m. Meeting more friends. Got uniforms, etc. yesterday and today. Wrote letter to President Osmena and Dr. Francisco Benitez in Manila.

Friday, Sept. 14, 1945. Got my first radio from folks. Everybody okay. It gave me a great feeling of relief to know they were okay. Was processed this p.m. and got an my records up to date. My major's promotion "will likely be retroactive and I will end up a lieutenant colonel." Meeting more friends.

Saturday, Sept. 15, 1945. Checked up on more copies of my promotion order to be made. Rested around camp.

Sunday, Sept. 16, 1945. Chester Richards took me into Manila to see a Spanish girl named Pilar Terrem who was the fiancee of Capt. Harold Bishop. I had the unpleasant job of telling her of Bishop's death.

Also met Betty and Marian Wright. Mrs. Wright, Mrs. Terrem and Don Devon, brother of Mrs. Wright. It is a miracle any of them are alive because in the siege of Manila the Nips raped and pillaged. The Nips sent out personnel destruction squads who shot down anybody and everybody.

Sept. 17-23, 1945. Have been hanging around for an entire week now. Tomorrow the third boat since I have been here goes out and I am not on it. My papers got mixed up and General Headquarters didn't know I existed. I tracked this down three days ago. Ever since, I have gone in every day to check on the things. Majors Earl Short, Charlie Underwood and Bill Nealson, all left today. I stay in town at Wrights' and last night because it was so rainy and...

Sept. 24, 1945. Stayed around camp this p.m. after going into Manila and getting my orders finally. Went to bed early. No word from home, I should have included all address in my messages I guess.

Tuesday, Sept. 25, 1945. Am to finally get on a boat for home. Cleared myself at camp and came into Manila before noon. Left my baggage at Capt. Paul Coker's office in the P. Sanmanilla Bldg., had dinner with him. After eating we went and picked up Betty Wright with whom he had a date and went and had a second meal!! at Rizal Stadium. Rode around the city, ate ice cream, visited Pelie Terren at her job and found her scraping the paint off her fingernails. She couldn't leave to go for a swim at Covite with us so Paul and Betty took me down to the pier (15) to check on the sailing of my ship the *Stormking*. Supposed to be on by 8:00 p.m.

After this we went back and got Pelie, went for something to drink at the Bacombo Nite Club (this was 4:30 p.m. so the club wasn't open but we knew the manager and got fixed up). After this we returned to the girls' home for dinner.

Paul had promised to have a jeep pick me up in front of St. Mesa church at 7:15 p.m. It never came so I hitchhiked down to the motor pool, without saying good-bye to my friends, got a staff car, took my baggage to the ship, checked it in, found I could stay out until 11:00 p.m. and took off for Wrights to pick up my musette bag and say good-bye. Arrived about 9:00 p.m.

Pelie was waiting for me and all were guessing I had hitchhiked to the boat and left my bag. Said farewell to the older folks, took Pelie, Capt. Fred Garrett and Marian Wright and went to a new night club, the El Cairo, for an hour. Said farewell to Mrs. Wright and Betty there and the four of us left for Pier 15 at 10:40 p.m. On arriving at the pier the ship was still loading troops so the girls and Fred waited with me in the car until almost midnight when the operation was through. The girls had to work the next day so I said good-bye to the three of them, started them home in the staff car and boarded the ship. Once on board I met some men who came over on the *P. Pierce* in June 1941. Most of us are gone.

This is another trip I am not expecting to enjoy even though it is the road home. I have lost every close friend I had out here. I have been through filth, destruction, near death many times and lived under conditions that warp men's souls. I haven't come through unscathed in the latter. Now that I return I dread the coming days of inactivity, under good food and rest my mind is beginning to become active again. I go home to a land of memories and hope leaving behind me a land of memories, memories of love, hate, fear, heroism, sacrifice, atrocities, destruction, torture, death and of living friends. There is only one answer to this state of mind, work and physical activity.

Looking back on these last 53 months in which I have lived more than half a dozen people ordinarily do in their entire lives put together. I wonder of what avail are all these events. When I boil it all down all I want out of life is "quiet happiness." All the glory, riches, power, pomp and splendor, I have ever had or ever seen I would throw away for happiness and a healthy physical body. Such is life, it's a pretty empty affair at times.

All through the boat there is no hilarity among the POWs, mostly a feeling of sadness, weariness and boredom!

Sept. 26, 1945. Terribly hot on the boat. I am in a room about water level with 30 other officers from the rank of major on down. Spent the day sleeping and sweating. I slept through the fun last night. Our ship, about midnight near the west end of San Bernadino Straits struck a 60 foot Filipino fishing boat cutting it in half. The ship stopped and the searchlights picked up swimming Filipinos and wreckage. A life boat rescued more than half a dozen from a floating half just as it went down. Out of 17 Filipinos one was lost. They brought the Filipinos on board. Later they sighted another Filipino craft and put the survivors on it.

Thursday, Sept. 27, 1945. They passed out of the San Bernadino Straits before noon. Saw the last of Sanmor about 11:00, more land for two weeks now. This morning I got up about 6:00 a.m. and watched Mayon Volcano pass by in the distance. It has the reputation of being the world's most perfect volcanic cone. A grayish white smoke was drifting in a stream for miles across the sky from its cone. It was quite an impressive sight.

Friday, Sept. 28, 1945. Another day. I slept some, read some, wrote a letter to James A. Wright telling him of my trip after I left him. Now about 1,100 miles out of Manila. Running into a storm tonight, sea very rough.

Saturday, Sept. 29, 1945. Another day on the road home. Spent the day getting my citation and promotion papers ready to send to MacArthur. Wrote letters to Dr. Francisco Bernitez, c/o Bureau of Education, Malocanan Palace, Manila; Mr. and Mrs. K.L. Morrison of Loh Cebu City; Bob Irrmann and Helen DeVault, c/o I.U. At 9:00 p.m. we passed the island of Ulithi of the Mariana group. It is about 150 miles northeast of Yap.

Sunday, Sept. 30-Oct. 7, 1945. One momentous day follows another. I sleep as much as I can. Today sixth at 7:35 we crossed the International Dateline back into the western hemisphere. I am back in the Occident after 52 months in the Orient. We have two Saturdays or two October 6s.

Monday, Oct. 8, 1945. Arrived Honolulu at 3:00 p.m. Got shore leave, hitchhiked with Lt. Meis down to telephone control and called folks at home. Cost $56.00 for 15 minutes. Camp Ellis has taken the farm and the folks now live in Vermont. Ruth gave me the address of a Wave Marjory Fulton at Kaneohe Naval Air Base to look up. Took two hours to call her.

Oct. 10, 1945. Got up at 6:00 a.m., left ship at 7:00 a.m. for Kaneohe, arrived around 9:00 a.m. Visited Marjory for about 50 minutes and got back to ship by noon. About 1:00 p.m. a big liner anchored just ahead of us, it looked familiar. Bands came to serenade it. Tommy Harrison and I sneaked down the gangplank and over long side. Sure enough, some of the men who left Manila two days before us were on it, Charlie Underwood, Earl Short and Bill Nealson.

October 11-14, 1945. More monotonous days, read and wrote letters. Practice debarkation runs.

Monday, Oct. 15, 1945. Debarked about 2:00 p.m. and taken to Letterman General Hospital and quartered in Ward 15. Got about 19 or 20 letters at the pier. One from Florence Smith said Mary Pickering was in Frisco. Called her up about 8:00 p.m. and she told me to come on out. We talked until almost midnight at the Drake-Milkshire Hotel. Took her back to her room at the Federal Hotel in the 10 hundred block on Market Street, room 705, phone Underwood 4946. Mary works for TWA, 441 Post Street, Phone Export 3701.

Tuesday, Oct. 16, 1945. Buying clothes and chased around all day. Met Mary at TWA and went to the sky room at hotel Mark Hopkins about 20? stories up. Went across the street to another large hotel, had dinner in the Birch Room (hotel ?) and danced in the circle room.

Wednesday, Oct. 17, 1945. More Army red tape. Brought Mary out to hospital for dinner, showed her my pictures and we went to the night club Bal Tabarin where there was a floor show, but didn't dance. Back early.

Oct. 18, 1945. Cleared from Letterman today, got authority to take my own transportation. Mary is fixing things up so I can fly to Chicago via Los Angeles so I can visit K.L. and Buster Morrison. Frisco to Chicago via Los Angeles on TWA costs $98.27. Went to a show called *Orders From Tokyo* showing authentic Technicolor pictures of the destruction of Manila with Mary, home early.

Friday, Oct. 19, 1945. Went in to TWA at 11:00 a.m. to speculate on a trip to Los Angeles and took out for the airport at 11:30 a.m. All thanks to Mary. Arrived K.L. Morrison's around 9:00 p.m.

Saturday, Oct. 20, 1945. Visited around Whittier with Morrisons. They are well.

End of Diary.

REMEMBERING

This entire account has been reconstructed largely from memory with the help of a few notes I made on a few scraps of paper, mostly Japanese toilet paper that I happened to have in my pocket. Many of the few notes are not readable at this time or the account would be more specific and definite. All of these notes were processed by the 19-man processing crew who came into our prison camp a day or two after the Japanese surrender. This processing crew was sent from Gen. Wedemier's headquarters at Chungking, China. The camp they went to was the Hoten Prison Camp at Mukden, Manchuria, which was the camp I was in when I was liberated. Lt. Col. Ovid O. Wilson assisted by Lt. Col. Thomas Trapley and various other senior officers of our surviving group, wrote up a complete history of this boat trip which I have just described. This history was written at the direction and under the supervision of this 19-man processing group who processed everybody before they left the camp. All of the information I have placed in this account should be found in a more detailed account in Col. Wilson's history of the trip.

Later I saw a newspaper clipping stating the Mr. Wada and Lt. Toshino were on trial in connection with this trip. There is no doubt that their inhumane treatment was a cold deliberate policy of murder in respect to the American prisoners that they had charge of. They could have gotten clothes for us and given us enough food to live on had they desired. There was absolutely no reason that the sanitation on the ship could not have been adequate for the occasion.

To the best of my belief and knowledge there is no material in this account which has not been included in previous reports made at Muken, Manchuria. These facts were common knowledge to all the survivors.

Epilogue

by Charles, Georgia and Lewis Miner

During Dad's tour of duty in the Pacific, he was involved in battles and campaigns for the liberation of China, bombardment of Japan, Philippine Defense Campaign, Philippine Liberation, Mindanao, Cebu and Luzon. He also received the following decorations and citations: Silver Star, Purple Heart, Asiatic Pacific Ribbon w/4 Bronze Stars, American Defense Ribbon w/Bronze Battle Star, Philippine Liberation Ribbon w/Bronze Star, Presidential Unit Citation w/2 OLCs, Philippine Defense Ribbon w/Bronze Battle Star, Victory Medal, seven Overseas Bars, Atlantic-Pacific Campaign Medal, and POW Medal.

After dad's return to the States from the Pacific in 1945, he married Clara Charles in 1946. He continued his interrupted (due to the war) education at Indiana University where he received his master's degree and doctorate. In 1950 he accepted a position at Eastern Illinois State College (now Eastern Illinois University) in Charleston, IL. He and his wife Clara adopted three children: Charles, Georgia Ann and Lewis. Dad was a faculty member at the university until he retired in 1980 and continued to live in the Charleston area until his passing in 1998 at the age of 83.

Of our father . . .

Despite all of the inhumane treatment that dad suffered as a prisoner of war (POW) he was one of the most "human" of people we have ever met. He did not let his POW experience over run his life. Instead he lifted himself up and proceeded on, utilizing the experience to his benefit. Once we asked him why so many continued to suffer after the war and why he seemed to take it in stride. He replied, "When I saw all of those returning POWs and the various conditions that they were in I decided right then, that there was nothing wrong with me and that I had a future." Dad was a man of strength, discipline and courage. He was also a man of deep emotions and concern. We never saw him quit or get openly discouraged. He was the type of person who did what he said and followed through on things.

Dad talked about his experiences as a POW and he could hold you spell bound with his stories. Despite our best efforts to really understand the pain and suffering that he and others endured, at the hand of the Japanese, it was difficult to fully comprehend such atrocities; people being treated worse than the lowest form of creature. That might be one reason Dad did not go into a lot of detail of the brutality. "It was unbelievable." At the time of liberation, "I weighed approximately 60 pounds and on the verge of death. If you did not have the desire to eat what was given to you each day, you would die. If the war had not ended when it did, I would have died." There is no question in our minds that the starvation, sickness, disease, dozens of beatings, physical torture (and witnessing physical torture of others) psychological torture and long-term stress he suffered during the 39 months of captivity, took its toll on him every year. He suffered from nightmares for many years and did seem to wake up in a daze at times not knowing where he was. Dad did not have any vices and took care of himself physically and kept himself mentally sharp. He did suffer from back and vision problems as well as an irregular heartbeat and edema. At the age of 65 he developed diabetes. He might have had other conditions, but dad was not one to openly discuss these things with you. He was an individual with great common sense and vision. He truly understood the meaning of sacrifice, duty, honor and country. We never met anyone who did not admire and respect our father.

One of the main themes that dad had was that if you are not willing or able to maintain a strong national defense, which involves the commitment of it leaders and citizens, then someone will come and take away your freedoms ...

Dad passed away peacefully on May 8, 1998. Chaplain Robert E. Holmes expressed the following: "The march of our comrade is over and he lieth down in the house appointed for all the living ... Our comrade is in the hands of our heavenly Father and God giveth His beloved sleep." He will be laid to rest, but let us cherish his virtues and learn to imitate them.

ABOUT THE AUTHOR

1994, at age 80

William Miner, a native of Table Grove, IL, received a bachelor of arts degree and ROTC, 2nd lieutenant commission in 1936 from Knox College.

On May 22, 1941 Miner was ordered to active duty and immediately sent to the Philippine Islands and assigned to the 31st Infantry. Beginning in September 1941 he was made commander of the Philippine Army camp in Calape, Bohol. As hostilities developed he was designated force communication officer on the special staff of Gen. B.G. Chynoweth, commanding general of the Visayan Forces in defense of the Visayan Islands. During part of the defense of the Visayans, Miner operated behind Japanese lines and was awarded the Silver Star for this dangerous duty.

After the forces, under Gen. Chynoweth, surrendered on May 17, 1942 the Visayan POWs were sent to the Davao Penal Colony where he served 21 months as a slave laborer in the rice paddies. All told he was in six different POW camps and on six Japanese "Hell Ships," including the notorious "*Oryoku Maru*." Miner was rescued while in Hoten POW Camp at Mukden, Manchuria by the Russian forces Aug. 18, 1945.

Upon returning home, William Miner finished his PhD in history at Indiana University and as a lieutenant colonel was active in USAR units in Bloomington, IN and commanding officer of the Charleston/Mattoon, IL USAR unit.

William Miner was professor of history, assistant dean of students and director of Veterans Services at Eastern Illinois University at Charleston, IL. He also devoted much of his time to community service.